Additional Gleim *CPA Review* books and other accounting study manuals are available directly from

Gleim Publications, Inc.
P.O. Box 12848
University Station
Gainesville, Florida 32604

(800) 87-GLEIM or (800) 874-5346
(352) 375-0772
FAX: (352) 375-6940

E-mail: admin@gleim.com
Internet: www.gleim.com

CPA Review: Auditing	$29.95
CPA Review: Business Law	29.95
CPA Review: Financial	29.95
CPA Review: TAX-MAN-GOV	29.95

CPA Test Prep software ($39.95 per section for diskette version) and *CPA Review* audiotapes ($79.95 per section) are also available to complement your study.

CIA Review, Part I: Internal Audit Process	$22.95
CIA Review, Part II: Internal Audit Skills	22.95
CIA Review, Part III: Management Control and Information Technology	22.95
CIA Review, Part IV: The Audit Environment	22.95
CMA/CFM Review: Part 1, Economics, Finance, and Management	22.95
CFM Review: Part 2CFM, Corporate Financial Management	22.95
CMA Review: Part 2CMA, Financial Accounting and Reporting	22.95
CMA/CFM Review: Part 3, Mgmt. Reporting, Analysis, and Behavioral Issues	22.95
CMA/CFM Review: Part 4, Decision Analysis and Information Systems	22.95

CIA Test Prep and *CMA/CFM Test Prep* software ($35 per section for diskette version) are also available to complement your study. *CMA/CFM Audio Review* is available at $60.00 per section.

Order forms for these and all of our other publications are provided at the back of this book.

Groundwood Paper and Highlighters -- This book is printed on high quality groundwood paper. It is lightweight and easy-to-recycle. We recommend that you purchase a highlighter specifically designed to be non-bleed-through (e.g., Avery *Glidestick*™) at your local office supply store.

REVIEWERS AND CONTRIBUTORS

Eric Hall, M.Acc., J.D. Candidate, University of Florida, provided extensive technical and editorial assistance throughout the project.

Sandra Frankenberger Ogle, M.Acc., University of Florida, provided extensive technical and editorial assistance throughout the project.

Karen A. Hom, B.A., University of Florida, is our book production coordinator. Ms. Hom coordinated the production staff, reviewed the manuscript, and provided production assistance throughout the project.

Grady M. Irwin, J.D., is a graduate of the University of Florida College of Law, and he has taught in the University of Florida College of Business. Mr. Irwin provided substantial editorial assistance throughout the project.

Travis A. Moore, M.B.A., University of Florida, provided technical and editorial assistance, reviewed the final manuscript, and prepared the page layout.

Nancy Y. Raughley, B.A., Tift College, is our editor. Ms. Raughley reviewed the entire manuscript and revised it for readability.

John F. Rebstock is a graduate of the Fisher School of Accounting at the University of Florida and has passed the CIA and CPA exams. Mr. Rebstock reviewed portions of the manuscript.

Greg Zacharias, M.Acc., University of Florida, provided extensive technical and editorial assistance throughout the project.

A PERSONAL THANKS

This manual would not have been possible without the extraordinary effort and dedication of Jim Collis and Terry Hall, who typed the entire manuscript and all revisions as well as prepared the camera-ready pages.

The authors also appreciate the production and editorial assistance of Matt Danner, Svetlana Dzyubenko, Erin Foster, Jose Martinez, Jessica Medina, and Jan Strickland.

The authors also appreciate the critical reading assistance of Walter Mansfield.

Finally, we appreciate the encouragement and tolerance of our families throughout the project.

1999-2000 EDITION

CPA REVIEW

BUSINESS LAW

by
Irvin N. Gleim, Ph.D., CPA, CIA, CMA, CFM
and
Jordan B. Ray, J.D.

ABOUT THE AUTHORS

Irvin N. Gleim is Professor Emeritus in the Fisher School of Accounting at the University of Florida and is a member of the American Accounting Association, Academy of Legal Studies in Business, American Institute of Certified Public Accountants, Association of Government Accountants, Florida Institute of Certified Public Accountants, The Institute of Internal Auditors, and the Institute of Management Accountants. He has had articles published in the *Journal of Accountancy, The Accounting Review,* and *The American Business Law Journal* and is author/ coauthor of numerous accounting and aviation books and CPE courses.

Jordan B. Ray, professor and former Chairman of the Department of Management and Legal Studies at the University of Florida, is a member and past president of the Academy of Legal Studies in Business and the Southeast Regional Academy of Legal Studies in Business. He is the author of a number of business law articles and has served as editor of Notes, Comments, and Case Digests for the *American Business Law Journal*. He has taught proprietary and university CPA Review and CLU courses and has served as the legal consultant to the Florida Real Estate Commission.

Gleim Publications, Inc.
P.O. Box 12848
University Station
Gainesville, Florida 32604
(352) 375-0772
(800) 87-GLEIM or (800) 874-5346
FAX: (888) 375-6940 (toll free)
E-mail: admin@gleim.com
Internet: www.gleim.com

ISSN: 1086-6957

ISBN 1-58194-055-6   *CPA Review: Auditing*
ISBN 1-58194-056-4   *CPA Review: Business Law*
ISBN 1-58194-057-2   *CPA Review: Financial*
ISBN 1-58194-058-0   *CPA Review: TAX-MAN-GOV*
ISBN 1-58194-060-2   *CPA Review*, 4-Book Set

This is the first printing of the seventh edition of *CPA Review: Business Law*. Please e-mail update@gleim.com with CPA LAW 7-1 included in the subject or text. You will receive our current update as a reply.

EXAMPLE:

To: update@gleim.com
From: your e-mail address
Subject: CPA LAW 7-1

ACKNOWLEDGMENTS

Material from *Uniform Certified Public Accountant Examination Questions and Unofficial Answers*, Copyright © 1975-1998 by the American Institute of Certified Public Accountants, Inc., is reprinted and/or adapted with permission. Visit the AICPA web page at www.aicpa.org or call (212) 596-6200 for more information.

This publication is designed to provide accurate and authoritative information with regard to the subject matter covered. It is sold with the understanding that the publisher is not engaged in rendering legal, accounting, or other professional service.

If legal advice or other expert assistance is required, the services of a competent professional person should be sought.

(From a declaration of principles jointly adopted by a Committee of the American Bar Association and a Committee of Publishers.)

Visit our Internet site (www.gleim.com/updates.html) for updates and information on all of our products.

TABLE OF CONTENTS

This is the First Printing to reflect information that will be tested on the November 1999 and May 2000 CPA exams. Updates are available free of charge for the November 1999 and May 2000 CPA exams. See page iv.

PREFACE FOR CPA CANDIDATES

This is the 1999-2000 Edition of *CPA Review*. It reflects relevant authoritative ethics pronouncements (see Study Unit 1) through May 1999.

The purpose of this Gleim *CPA Review* study book is to help YOU prepare to pass the Business Law and Professional Responsibilities section of the November 1999 and May 2000 CPA examinations. The overriding consideration is an inexpensive, effective, and easy-to-use study program. This book

1. Explains how to optimize your grade by focusing on the Business Law section of the CPA exam.

2. Defines the subject matter tested on the Business Law section of the CPA exam.

3. Outlines all of the subject matter tested on the Business Law section in 20 easy-to-use study units.

4. Presents multiple-choice questions from recent CPA examinations to prepare you for business law questions in future CPA exams. Our answer explanations are presented to the immediate right of each question for your convenience. Two bookmarks are provided at the back of this book. Use a bookmark to cover our answer explanations as you study the questions.

5. Provides selected OOF (other objective format) questions on which you can practice your question answering technique. Although you should rely on multiple-choice questions to test your knowledge and help you study, you should practice answering business law OOF questions to perfect your question answering technique.

6. Includes selected essay questions for you to practice answering. Like OOF questions, essay questions are less efficient for studying and knowledge testing than multiple-choice questions. However, you must practice answering selected essay questions until you have perfected your question answering technique as it applies to business law essay questions.

The outline format, spacing, and the question and answer formats in this book are designed to facilitate readability, learning, and understanding. Even though this study book constitutes a complete self-study program for the Business Law section of the CPA exam, you may wish to enroll in a group study CPA review program. Check our website for live courses we recommend. This book and the Gleim *CPA Test Prep* software are compatible with all other CPA review materials and courses that follow the 1999 AICPA Content Specification Outlines.

To maximize the efficiency and effectiveness of your CPA review program, begin by **studying** (not merely reading) *CPA Review: A System for Success*, Chapters 1 through 8. They have been carefully organized and written to provide you with important information to assist you in passing the CPA examination.

Thank you for your interest in the new Gleim *CPA Review* study books and the *CPA Test Prep* software. We deeply appreciate the thousands of letters and suggestions received from CIA, CMA, and CPA candidates during the last 24 years. Please send your suggestions, comments, and corrections concerning this study book. The last page has been designed to help you note corrections and suggestions during your study process. Please tear it out and mail it to us with your comments immediately after you take the CPA exam. We will respond to each letter on an individual basis.

Good Luck on the Exam,

Irvin N. Gleim

Jordan B. Ray

June 1999

OPTIMIZING YOUR BUSINESS LAW SCORE

This introduction is an 18-page summary of Gleim's FREE *CPA Review: A System for Success*, a 112-page booklet containing detailed discussion of the steps to exam success. It is a necessity for all CPA candidates. It should be studied at least twice: at the start of a candidate's study program and 1 or 2 weeks before taking the CPA exam. It is a separate booklet so you do not have to carry it with you when you use this book, *CPA Review: Business Law*.

Business Law is the first and shortest (3 hours) section of the CPA exam.

AICPA title: Business Law & Professional Responsibilities
AICPA acronym: LPR
Gleim title: Business Law
Time: 9:00 to 12:00 Wednesday morning
Question format:
Multiple-choice	50-60%	
Other Objective Format (OOF)	20-30%	
Essay	20-30%	

> Expect 60+6 multiple-choice, 2 OOF, and 2 essay/computational questions, and make adjustments for any changes.

Areas covered:
- I. (15%) Professional and Legal Responsibilities
- II. (20%) Business Organizations
- III. (10%) Contracts
- IV. (10%) Debtor-Creditor Relationships
- V. (15%) Government Regulation of Business
- VI. (20%) Uniform Commercial Code
- VII. (10%) Property

Grading: Multiple-choice and OOF: From optically scanned answer sheets

Essay: Number of correct grading concepts for technical responses, holistic grading method for writing skills

A Possible Allocation Scenario:

Multiple-choice	60%	for 60+6 items*
OOF	20%	for 2 questions, each with multiple items
Essay:		
Technical	15%	for 2 essay questions
Writing skills	5%	
	100%	

*Expect a few extra multiple-choice questions because the AICPA "tests" new questions on candidates. These new questions, which you cannot identify, are not used to compute your grade.

AICPA Description

"The business law & professional responsibilities section tests candidates' knowledge of a CPA's professional responsibilities and of the legal implications of business transactions, particularly as they relate to accounting and auditing. Content covered in this section includes a CPA's professional responsibilities, business organizations, contracts, debtor-creditor relationships, government regulation of business, the Uniform Commercial Code, and property. Candidates will be required to

- Recognize relevant legal issues
- Recognize the legal implications of certain business situations
- Apply the underlying principles of law to accounting and auditing situations"

The AICPA *Code of Professional Conduct* should be sources of answers to ethics and professional responsibility questions rather than individual state board of accountancy ethics rules. Similarly, federal and widely adopted uniform state laws are the basis for business law questions. The study outlines and CPA questions/answer explanations in each of the 20 business law study units in this book (Study Unit 1 covers the AICPA *Code of Professional Conduct*) reflect the majority rule on which the AICPA tests and bases its answers.

The AICPA suggests that the following publications will be sources of questions. Our outlines and answer explanations are based on these publications as revised through June 1, 1999.

1. AICPA *Code of Professional Conduct*

2. AICPA Statements on Auditing Standards dealing explicitly with proficiency, independence, and due care

3. AICPA Statement on Standards for Consulting Services

4. AICPA Statements on Responsibilities in Personal Financial Planning Practice

5. Books covering business law, auditing, and accounting

AICPA CONTENT SPECIFICATION OUTLINES (CSOs)

The AICPA has indicated that the content specification outlines have several purposes including

1. *Ensure consistent coverage of subject matter from one examination to the next.*

2. *Provide guidance to those who are responsible for preparing the examination in order to ensure a balanced examination.*

3. *Assist candidates in preparing for the examination by indicating subjects that may be covered by the examination.*

4. *Alert accounting educators about the subject matter considered necessary to prepare for the examination.*

AICPA CSOs have three levels: areas, groups, and topics. Percentage weights are given for each area but not for groups or topics:

I. Areas . . . .
    A. Groups
      1. Topics

AICPA CSO

EXAMPLE: Area II from LPR

II. Business organizations (20%)
    A. Agency
      1. Formation and termination
      2. Duties of agents and principals
      3. Liabilities and authority of agents and principals
    B. Partnership, joint ventures, and other unincorporated associations
      1. Formation, operation, and termination
      2. Liabilities and authority of partners and owners
    C. Corporations
      1. Formation and operation
      2. Stockholders, directors, and officers
      3. Financial structure, capital, and distributions
      4. Reorganization and dissolution
    D. Estates and trusts
      1. Formation, operation, and termination
      2. Allocation between principal and income
      3. Fiduciary responsibilities
      4. Distributions

Frequently, questions cover more than one area, group, and/or topic. For example, an essay question or an OOF question could test both CPA liability and securities regulations, secured transactions and bankruptcy, or contracts and property.

Business Law

I. Professional and legal responsibilities (15%)
- A. Code of Professional Conduct
- B. Proficiency, independence, and due care
- C. Responsibilities in other professional services
- D. Disciplinary systems imposed by the profession and state regulatory bodies
- E. Common law liability to clients and third parties
- F. Federal statutory liability
- G. Privileged communications and confidentiality
- H. Responsibilities of CPAs in business and industry, and in the public sector

II. Business organizations (20%)
- A. Agency
  1. Formation and termination
  2. Duties of agents and principals
  3. Liabilities and authority of agents and principals
- B. Partnership, joint ventures, and other unincorporated associations
  1. Formation, operation, and termination
  2. Liabilities and authority of partners and owners
- C. Corporations
  1. Formation and operation
  2. Stockholders, directors, and officers
  3. Financial structure, capital, and distributions
  4. Reorganization and dissolution
- D. Estates and trusts
  1. Formation, operation, and termination
  2. Allocation between principal and income
  3. Fiduciary responsibilities
  4. Distributions

III. Contracts (10%)
- A. Formation
- B. Performance
- C. Third-party assignments
- D. Discharge, breach, and remedies

IV. Debtor-creditor relationships (10%)
- A. Rights, duties, and liabilities of debtors and creditors
- B. Rights, duties, and liabilities of guarantors
- C. Bankruptcy

V. Government regulation of business (15%)
- A. Federal securities acts
- B. Employment regulation
- C. Environmental regulation

VI. Uniform Commercial Code (20%)
- A. Negotiable instruments
- B. Sales
- C. Secured transactions
- D. Documents of title

VII. Property (10%)
- A. Real property including insurance
- B. Personal property including bailments and computer technology rights

I. ETHICS/LIABILITY
1. AICPA Ethics
2. CPAs and the Law

II. BUSINESS ORGANIZATIONS
3. Agency
4. Partnerships
5. Corporations
6. Estates and Trusts

III. CONTRACTS
7. Contract Formation
8. Contract Performance

IV. DEBTOR/CREDITOR
9. Rights and Duties
10. Guarantors
11. Bankruptcy

V. GOV'T REGULATION
12. Securities
13. Employment
14. Environmental Reg.

VI. UCC
15. Negotiable Instruments and Bank Transactions
16. Sales
17. Secured Transactions
18. Documents of Title

VII. PROPERTY
19. Real Property and Insurance
20. Personal Property, Bailments, and Computers

A SYSTEM FOR SUCCESS

To assure your success on the Business Law section of the CPA examination, you should focus on the following steps:

1. **Understand the exam, including coverage, content, format, administration, and grading.**

   a. The better you understand the examination process from beginning to end, the better you will be able to perform.

   b. Study Chapters 1 through 8 in Gleim's *CPA Review: A System for Success*. Please be sure you have a current copy of this useful, free booklet.

2. **Learn and understand the subject matter tested.** The previous page contains the AICPA's CSOs for the Business Law section. These CSOs, along with the questions that have appeared in recent CPA examinations and the suggestions from recent CPA candidates*, are the basis for the study outlines which are presented in each of the 20 business law study units that make up Chapters I through VII of this book. You will also learn and understand the business law material tested on the CPA exam by answering numerous multiple-choice questions from recent CPA exams. Multiple-choice questions with the answer explanations to the immediate right of each question are a major component of each business law study unit.

3. **Practice answering recent exam questions to perfect your question answering techniques.** Answering recent exam questions helps you understand the standards to which you will be held. This motivates you to learn and understand while studying (rather than reading) the outlines in each of the 20 business law study units.

   a. Question answering techniques are suggested for multiple-choice, OOF, and essay questions beginning on page 8.

   b. Use *CPA Test Prep* software by Gleim. There is a diskette for each section of the exam containing over 1,200 recent CPA or similar multiple-choice questions. The questions are organized into the same 20 study units used in this book.

      CPA Test Prep is interactive, state-of-the-art software. Each diskette contains hundreds of questions not included in the corresponding Gleim *CPA Review* book. An important key to exam success is answering many multiple-choice questions.

4. **Plan and practice exam execution.** Anticipate the exam environment and prepare yourself with a plan: When to arrive? How to dress? What exam supplies to bring? How many questions and what format? Which order of answering questions? How much time to spend on each question?

   a. Expect the unexpected and adjust! Remember that your sole objective when taking an examination is to maximize your score. CPA exam grading is curved, and you must outperform your peers.

5. **Be in control.** Develop confidence and assure success with a controlled preparation program followed by confident execution during the examination.

---

*Please complete the form on pages 681 and 682 IMMEDIATELY after you take the CPA exam so we can adapt to changes in the exam. The approach has been approved by the AICPA.

HOW TO STUDY A STUDY UNIT (books only)

1. Gain an overview of the study unit -- familiarity with the topic, number of pages of outline, number of multiple-choice questions -- and estimate the time you will invest.

2. Answer five to ten multiple-choice questions. Choose one or two questions from each subunit.

    The purpose of answering multiple-choice questions before working through the study outline is to understand the standards to which you will be held. This will motivate you to concentrate on the study outline.

3. Work through the study outline. Learn and understand the concepts. Remember, you are aiming toward the analysis, synthesis, and evaluation levels of knowledge, not rote memorization. Study the outlines with the objective of being able to explain the subject matter to third parties (including AICPA graders).

4. After you are comfortable with the study outlines, apply your multiple-choice question answering technique (see page 8) to answer all of the multiple-choice questions by marking the correct answer in your book with a pen or pencil before consulting the answer and answer explanation. It is essential to mark your answer choice before looking at the answer. Use the bookmark at the back of each Gleim *CPA Review* book.

5. Develop a 75%+ proficiency level within each study unit. You will achieve this proficiency level by studying the outlines and answering multiple-choice questions.

    Learning from questions you answer incorrectly is very important. Each question you answer incorrectly is an <u>opportunity</u> to avoid missing actual test questions on your CPA exam. Thus, you should carefully study the answer explanations provided until you understand why the original answer you chose is wrong, as well as why the correct answer indicated is correct. This study technique is clearly the difference between passing and failing for many CPA candidates.

    Also, you **must** determine why you answered questions incorrectly and learn how to avoid the same error in the future. Reasons for missing questions include

    a. Misreading the requirement (stem)
    b. Not understanding what is required
    c. Making a math error
    d. Applying the wrong rule or concept
    e. Being distracted by one or more of the answers
    f. Incorrectly eliminating answers from consideration
    g. Not having any knowledge of the topic tested
    h. Employing bad intuition (Why?) when guessing

6. You should perfect your question answering technique for OOF, essay, and computational questions. See Chapters 5 and 6 in *CPA Review: A System for Success*.

    a. Save the OOF, essay, and computational questions (computational questions appear only in Financial) for review until you complete several study units. Plan special practice sessions for practicing your OOF, essay, and computational question answering technique. Move systematically from study unit to study unit, answering OOF, essay, and computational questions.

    b. After you complete each question, critique your performance. This is relatively easy to do with OOF, but more difficult with essay and computational questions. Grade your essay/computational answers by turning to the AICPA answer and circling the grading concepts that you believe the AICPA used. Next, grade your answer by circling the grading concepts in your answer. Compute the ratio of the number of your grading concepts to the number of AICPA grading concepts.

7. Gleim *CPA Test Prep* software will significantly benefit your study efforts, especially when using the 20-question test routine suggested on the next page.

ADDING *CPA TEST PREP* SOFTWARE

Using *CPA Test Prep* really works! The software forces you to commit to your answer choice before looking at answer explanations. It also keeps track of your time and the results of your effort. Each study session and each test session are kept in the performance history and are viewable in either a table or a graphical format.

Each Test Prep disk covers a different part of the CPA exam, includes over 1,200 questions, and contains both a Windows and a DOS version of the program. All questions have been updated to reflect current tax law, authoritative pronouncements, etc., and the subject matter to be tested on the November 1999 and May 2000 exams.

Read and study the six steps regarding how to use the books. Simplify the process of using *CPA Test Prep* software by using the following six steps. DO NOT omit the step in which you diagnose the reasons for answering questions incorrectly; i.e., learn from your mistakes while studying so you avoid making mistakes on the CPA exam.

1 In test mode, answer a 20-question test from each study unit before studying the study unit.

2 Study the knowledge transfer outline for that study unit in your Gleim book.

3 Take two or three 20-question tests in test mode after studying knowledge transfer outlines.

4 After EACH test session, immediately switch to study mode and select questions "missed on last session" so you can reanswer these questions AND analyze why you answered each question incorrectly.

5 Continue the process until you approach a 75% proficiency level.

6 Modify the process to suit your individual learning process.

It is imperative that you complete at least one or two study units a week so you can review your progress and realize how attainable comprehensive CPA exam preparation is when using Gleim books and software. Remember to get ahead of your schedule to give yourself confidence.

After you complete each 20-question test, ALWAYS do a study session of questions you missed. FOCUS on why you selected the incorrect answer, NOT just the correct answer. You want to learn from your mistakes during study so you avoid mistakes on the exam.

GLEIM AUDIOTAPE LECTURES

Gleim *CPA Review* audiotapes provide a 15- to 40-minute introductory lecture for each study unit. Each lecture provides a comprehensive overview of the outline in the *CPA Review* book. The purpose is to get candidates "started" so they can relate to the questions they will answer before reading the study outlines in each study unit. Audios are also excellent for review.

The audiotape lectures are short and to the point as is the entire Gleim System for Success. We are working to get you through the CPA exam with the minimum time, cost, and frustration. A free CPA introductory audiotape is available upon request from Gleim Publications, Inc. by calling (800) 87-GLEIM or by sending e-mail to admin@gleim.com.

MULTIPLE-CHOICE QUESTION ANSWERING TECHNIQUE

Expect 60+6 multiple-choice questions on the Business Law section with a 90-100 minute time allocation. Business law multiple-choice questions are generally conceptual. See Chapter 4 in *CPA Review: A System for Success* for a detailed discussion of how to maximize your score on multiple-choice questions.

1. **Budget your time**. We make this point with emphasis. Just as you would fill up your gas tank prior to reaching empty, so too would you finish your exam before time expires.

   a. Calculate the time allowed for each multiple-choice question after you have allocated time to the other questions (OOF, essays) on the exam; e.g., if there are 66 individual multiple-choice items and you are allocated 90-100 minutes, you should spend 1.5 minutes or less per item (always budget extra time for transferring answers to answer sheets, interruptions, etc.).

   b. Before beginning a series of multiple-choice questions, write the starting time on the exam near the first question.

   c. As you work through the individual questions, check your time. Assuming an allocation of 90-100 minutes for 66 questions, if you have worked five questions in 7 minutes, you are fine, but if you spent 10 minutes on five questions, you need to speed up. Remember that your goal is to answer all questions within the allotted time and achieve the maximum score possible.

2. **Answer the questions in numerical order**.

   a. Do **not** agonize over any one item. Stay within your time budget.

   b. Mark any questions you are unsure of with a big "?" and return to them later if time allows.

   c. Never leave a multiple-choice question unanswered on the objective answer sheet. Remember that your score is based on the number of correct responses. In other words, you will not be penalized for guessing.

3. **For each multiple-choice question**, use the following steps:

   a. **Cover up the answer choices** with your hand or a piece of scratch paper. Do not allow the answer choices to affect your reading of the question.

      1) If four answer choices are presented, three of them are incorrect. They are called **distractors** for good reason.

   b. **Read the stem carefully** (the part of the question that precedes the answer choices) to determine the precise requirement.

      1) You may wish to underline or circle key language or data used in the stem.

      2) Focusing on what is required enables you to ignore extraneous information and to proceed directly to determining the correct answer.

         a) Be especially careful to note when the requirement is an **exception**; e.g., "Which of the following is **not** valid acceptance of an offer?"

   c. **Determine the correct answer** before looking at the answer choices.

      1) By adhering to the steps above, you know what is required and which are the relevant facts.

2)   However, some multiple-choice questions are structured so that the answer cannot be determined from the stem alone.

d.   **Read the answer choices** carefully.

1)   Even if answer (A) appears to be the correct choice, do **not** skip the remaining answer choices. Answer (B), (C), or (D) may be even better.

2)   Treat each answer choice as a true-false question. Consider marking a "T" or "F" next to each answer choice as you analyze it.

e.   **Select the best answer.** Circle the most likely or best answer choice on the test paper. If you are uncertain, guess intelligently by eliminating less likely answers. Improve on the 25% chance of getting the correct answer.

1)   For many of the multiple-choice questions, two answer choices can be eliminated with minimal effort. This can reduce the risk of random guessing and increase your chances of success.

4.   After you have answered all the items in an overall question, **transfer your answers to the objective answer sheet**, which will probably be the back cover of the exam question and answer booklet.

a.   Make sure you are within your time budget so you will be able to perform this vital step in an unhurried manner.

b.   Do not wait to transfer answers until the very end of the exam session because you may run out of time.

c.   Double-check that you have transferred the answers correctly, e.g., recheck every fifth or tenth answer from your test paper to your answer sheet to ensure that you have not fallen out of sequence.

d.   Be very careful when transferring your answers. The numbers are arranged in different formats on the AICPA answer sheets. For more discussion and examples, see Chapter 4 of *CPA Review: A System for Success*.

RECENT BUSINESS LAW OOF QUESTIONS

We expect two OOF questions on the Business Law section. They should be similar to the four OOF questions that appeared on recent CPA exams (two per exam). Each of these OOF questions consisted of a fact pattern scenario followed by 10 to 15 items requiring a true/false or matching-type response, as described below.

One CPA question contained parts A and B, each with six items. Part A concerns the formation and operation of a partnership. Each item has two statements and the candidate is required to select which statement is correct. Part B concerns the formation of a corporation and the rights and duties of its stockholders, directors, and officers. Each item contains three choices and the candidate is required to identify the true statement.

Another CPA question also contained parts A and B, each with six items. Part A contained a fact pattern concerning a contract for the sale of goods whereby the goods were damaged beyond repair during shipment. Each item contains three statements, and the true statement must be identified. Part B contained a fact pattern concerning a secured transaction. As with Part A, each item requires the identification of the true statement.

The AICPA answer sheet for this CPA question was similar to the following:

a. Item	Select one		
73	(A)	(B)	(C)
74	(A)	(B)	(C)
75	(A)	(B)	(C)
76	(A)	(B)	(C)
77	(A)	(B)	(C)
78	(A)	(B)	(C)

b. Item	Select one		
79	(A)	(B)	(C)
80	(A)	(B)	(C)
81	(A)	(B)	(C)
82	(A)	(B)	(C)
83	(A)	(B)	(C)
84	(A)	(B)	(C)

One CPA question contained parts A and B, each with five items. Part A concerns principles of agency law while Part B tests the area of trust law. Each part contains a fact pattern followed by five items with two statements. For each item, it must be determined whether one of the statements is correct, both are correct, or neither is correct.

Another CPA question consisted of parts A and B, each with five items. Part A concerns involuntary bankruptcy. Part B concerns an exempt offering under Regulation D, Rule 506, of the Securities Act of 1933. Each item contains two statements and the candidate is required to determine whether one of the statements is correct, both are correct or neither is correct.

The AICPA answer sheets for the preceding CPA questions were similar to the following:

a. Item	Select one			
61	(A)	(B)	(C)	(D)
62	(A)	(B)	(C)	(D)
63	(A)	(B)	(C)	(D)
64	(A)	(B)	(C)	(D)
65	(A)	(B)	(C)	(D)

b. Item	Select one			
66	(A)	(B)	(C)	(D)
67	(A)	(B)	(C)	(D)
68	(A)	(B)	(C)	(D)
69	(A)	(B)	(C)	(D)
70	(A)	(B)	(C)	(D)

OOF QUESTION ANSWERING TECHNIQUE

1. Write the time you start each OOF question on top of the question in the question booklet.

2. Determine the nature of the OOF.

    a. Are there subparts with different numbers of items and/or requirements?
    b. How many answers should be given per item (e.g., two points on a graph)?
    c. What type of matching?

3. Treat a matching question as a variation of a multiple-choice question, noting

    a. The number of stems having the same answer choices
    b. The number of answer choices, which may vary from 2 to 15 or more

        1) Two answer choices are usually true/false or yes/no.
        2) Three answer choices are usually true/false/not enough information.

    c.   Most matching questions will permit answers to be used once, more than once, or not at all. This makes each stem independent, so answer each stem as if it were a separate multiple-choice question.

    d.   Review the steps of the multiple-choice question answering technique beginning on page 8.

4.   If matching questions require you to use each answer only once, work through all of the stems, selecting the best answer for each stem even if you realize you are selecting one answer more than once.

    a.   After you have completed answering all the stems, note any answers you have used more than once.

        1)   Note the answers you have not used.

    b.   Reevaluate the stems for which you have used the same answer more than once, keeping in mind the answers that you have not used.

    c.   If the answer(s) you did not use do(es) not fit with one of the stems for which you used an answer more than once, you may have to evaluate the answer(s) not used against each of the stems.

        1)   This may result in your changing a number of answers.

    d.   However, most often, the matching sections allow answers to be used more than once or not at all.

5.   Watch your time! Move on to the next question before you get frustrated and lose your composure.

6.   After you complete each OOF, transfer the answers to the objective answer sheet.

    a.   Do not wait until the end of the exam to transfer your answers because you may run out of time.

    b.   Check to make sure there are no transfer errors.

RECENT BUSINESS LAW ESSAY QUESTIONS

    To help you focus on how to answer business law essay questions, we have reproduced the requirements verbatim and have presented excerpts from the fact patterns of the four essay questions that appeared on recent exams. The objective is to familiarize you with the types of requirements to which you will be asked to respond.

Essay Questions

CPA, adapted (updated fact pattern excerpt)

    On October 30, 1999, Dover, CPA, was engaged to audit the financial records of Crane Corp., a tractor manufacturer. During the review of notes receivable, Dover reviewed a promissory note given to Crane by Jones Corp., one of its customers, in payment for a tractor. The note appears below.

    Dover also reviewed a security agreement signed by Harper, a customer, given to Crane to finance Harper's purchase of a tractor for use in Harper's farming business.

Required *(verbatim)*

As the auditor on this engagement, write a memo to the partner-in-charge identifying, explaining, and stating your conclusions about the legal issues pertaining to the note and the security interest.

The memo should address the following:

- Whether Crane is a holder in due course
- Whether Oval will be required to pay the note
- Whether Jones is liable to pay the note
- When Crane's security interest was perfected and whether it had priority over Acron's security interest

CPA, adapted (updated fact pattern excerpt)

During 1999, World Corp. made a $4,000,000 offering of its stock. The offering was sold to 50 nonaccredited investors and 150 accredited investors. There was a general advertising of the offering. All purchasers were provided with material information concerning World Corp. The offering was completely sold by the end of 1999. The SEC was notified 30 days after the first sale of the offering.

World did not register the offering and contends that the offering and any subsequent resale of the securities are completely exempt from registration under Regulation D, Rule 505, of the Securities Act of 1933.

Unity Corp. has 750 equity stockholders and assets in excess of $100,000,000. Unity's stock is traded on a national stock exchange. Unity contends that it is not a covered corporation and is not required to comply with the reporting provisions of the Securities Exchange Act of 1934.

Required *(verbatim)*

a. 1. State whether World is correct in its contention that the offering is exempt from registration under Regulation D, Rule 505, of the Securities Act of 1933. Give the reason(s) for your conclusion.

2. State whether World is correct in its contention that on subsequent resale the securities are completely exempt from registration. Give the reason(s) for your conclusion.

b. 1. State whether Unity is correct in its contention that it is not a covered corporation and is not required to comply with the reporting requirements of the Securities Exchange Act of 1934 and give the reason(s) for your conclusion.

2. Identify and describe two principal reports a covered corporation must file with the SEC.

CPA, adapted (updated fact pattern synopsis)

The fact pattern consists of four two-sentence paragraphs concerning Korn's written offer to clear Wilson's parking lot whenever it snowed through December 31, 1999.

Required *(verbatim)*

a. State and explain the points of law that Korn would argue to show that there was no valid contract.

b. State and explain the points of law that Wilson would argue to show that there was a valid contract.

c. Assuming that a valid contract existed:

1. Determine whether Korn breached the contract and the nature of the breach and

2. State the common law remedies available to Wilson.

CPA, adapted (fact pattern excerpt)

Verge Associates, CPAs, were retained to perform a consulting service engagement by Stone Corp. Verge prepared the software programs in a manner that allowed some of Stone's accounts receivable to be erroneously deleted from Stone's records. As a result, Stone's expense to collect these accounts was increased greatly.

Verge also intentionally recommended, and Stone purchased, a more expensive and less efficient computer which was to become obsolete within a year. Verge received a commission from the computer company for inducing Stone to purchase that computer.

Stone sued Verge for negligence and common-law fraud.

Required *(verbatim)*

a. State whether Stone will be successful in its negligence suit against Verge and describe the elements of negligence shown in the above situation that Stone should argue.

b. State whether Stone will be successful in its fraud suit against Verge and describe the elements of fraud shown in the above situation that Stone should argue.

WRITING SKILLS

Writing skills will constitute 5% of the points available to candidates on the Business Law, Auditing, and Financial sections. At least two questions (or parts of questions) on each section will be selected to be graded for writing skills. The same graders who grade the conceptual and technical content of your answers will also assign a point value (0 to 5) to your writing skills. This approach is known as the holistic grading method.

AICPA Position on Writing Skills

Selected essay answers in the Business Law & Professional Responsibilities, Auditing, and Financial Accounting & Reporting sections are used to assess candidates' writing skills. Five percent of the total points available on each of these sections will be allocated to writing skills. Effective writing can be characterized by the following six elements:

1. *Coherent organization.* The writer arranges ideas in a smooth, logical flow, enabling the reader to easily follow the train of thought. The writer develops each main idea in a separate paragraph and places the idea in the first sentence of the paragraph. Sentences that follow describe, define, clarify, illustrate, or explain the principal idea. Connectives or transition words link sentences and paragraphs.

2. *Conciseness.* The writer conveys points in as few words as possible without scrimping on important detail or substance. Short sentences and simple wording contribute to concise writing.

3. *Clarity.* A clearly written response expresses the writer's meaning or reasoning to the intended reader. Well-constructed sentences and carefully chosen words, including proper technical terms, contribute to clarity.

4. *Use of standard English.* Effective responses use standard English, which is defined in *The Business Writer's Handbook* as follows:

   > There are two broad varieties of written English: standard and nonstandard. These varieties are determined through usage by those who write in the English language. Standard English . . . is used to carry on the daily business of the nation. It is the language of business, industry, government, education, and the professions. Standard English is characterized by exacting standards of punctuation and capitalization, by accurate spelling, by exact diction, by an expressive vocabulary, and by knowledgeable usage choices.[1]

5. *Responsiveness to the requirements of the question.* The writer should address the requirements of the question and demonstrate awareness of the purpose of the writing task. Responses should not be broad expositions on the general subject but should focus on specific aspects presented in the question. However, answers should not be so narrowly focused that they omit key elements of the requirements.

6. *Appropriateness for the reader.* Writing that is appropriate for the reader takes into account the reader's background, knowledge of the subject, interests, and concerns. Some essay questions may require candidates to prepare a written document for a specific reader, such as memorandum to a CPA's client. In such cases, technical terms may have to be defined for the specific reader. When the requirements do not identify a specific reader, the candidate should assume the intended reader is a knowledgeable CPA.

---

[1]Charles T. Brusaw, Gerald J. Alred, and Walter E. Oliu, *The Business Writer's Handbook*, 4th ed. (New York: St. Martin's Press, 1993), p. 227.

The holistic grading method is based on the whole rather than a sum of the parts. Thus, the grader will make an overall assessment based on his/her assessment of your writing ability relative to other papers (s)he is grading.

Each AICPA grader has been trained to be sensitive to six writing attributes, which are discussed in the "AICPA Position on Writing Skills" listed in the box on page 13. The graders do not assign grades on any one of the attributes. Rather, they assign a single grade based on their overall evaluation of the six attributes.

Finally, be aware that if you choose not to answer a question or part of a question which is being graded for writing skills, you will lose the conceptual and technical points as well as the writing skills points. Also be cautious of the parts of computational questions requiring explanation, as they also may be graded for writing skills.

HOW TO MAXIMIZE YOUR WRITING SKILLS GRADE

Understand the process and standards. The process refers to your test preparation, its administration, your performance, and grading. The standards are those listed on the previous page. Review the AICPA's six characteristics and rank-order them; ranking them will help you visualize interrelationships between the six characteristics.

Practice writing and critiquing. As you practice your question answering technique on essay questions, you will be practicing your writing skills. Practice makes perfect! Critiquing your own and other candidates' solutions, as well as AICPA solutions, to essay questions will give you insight into improving your writing skills. Focus on eliminating your weaknesses and faults! Constructive criticism develops a positive frame of mind. It's fun to be positive!

ESSAY QUESTION ANSWERING TECHNIQUE

To institute **control** over your essay questions, we suggest the following steps:

1. **Question overview**. Scan the question to get an overview of the topic covered. Do not pay too much attention to the details of the question.

2. **Understand the requirements**. This includes a mental outline of the grader's expected answer. Then picture how your answer should look. Make sure it conforms to the question requirements. There may be several requirements within a question. When answering the question, make sure you do not miss any part of the requirements. For example, if the requirement is to "list and explain," make sure to include an explanation!

3. **Mentally prepare a "to do" list.** Before you begin, you need to know what, where, when, and how in order to be in control.

4. **Focus your knowledge on the question.** Review core concepts, principles, rules, and exceptions that apply to the topic of the question and its requirements. Do this review prior to reading the question in more detail to avoid having your knowledge of the subject confused by the details of fact patterns.

5. **Read the entire question slowly and carefully**. Pause after each factual statement, and evaluate its significance to the requirements. Make notes in the margin. Circle, highlight, and underline words as appropriate.

6. **Write an abbreviation** for each gradable concept that can be developed in your answer.

7. **Reorganize your gradable concepts** for consistency with the question requirements. Reread the requirements to assure you are providing what the grader expects. Do not rewrite the concepts, but organize them with alphanumeric labels, e.g., 1, 2, 3a, 3b, etc.

8. **Write your answer** using short, clear, uncomplicated sentences and paragraphs. Label your paragraphs so they are consistent with the labels used in the examination. Do **not** write your answer in outline form. Write on every other line, or leave 1/4 of the page blank at the bottom for any additional discussions or insertions when editing your answer. If you are asked to give examples or list advantages of . . . , always give more than required if you can (i.e., if asked to give three examples, give five). This will increase the chance that you have given what the examiners want.

9. **Read the requirements again** to make sure that your answers are consistent with the requirements and that you have not missed any possible gradable concepts for each of the requirements. You should maximize the number of gradable concepts for each requirement in each question. Focusing your effort on only a few parts you know well will not allow you to obtain extra points. There will be only a given amount of points for each part. Thus, you usually cannot compensate for lost points in other areas.

10. **Edit and reread** to assure a well-presented answer. Remember, your writing skill will be graded.

11. See Chapter 6 in *CPA Review: A System for Success* for a discussion of the AICPA's recommendations regarding writing skills.

BUSINESS LAW EXAM EXECUTION

1. Go to the session committed to do your very best so you will not have to return to a future exam.

2. Understand what to expect based on Chapters 2 through 8 in *CPA Review: A System for Success*. Also talk with CPA candidates who sat at the same exam site for the previous exam to get pertinent information.

3. After you sit down and get situated, you will be given an examination question and answer booklet containing a question booklet and an essay ruled paper booklet. The front cover will be your attendance record and the back cover will be your objective question answer sheet.

4. On your question booklet, complete your candidate ID number and your state name on the front cover. Make sure the booklet number (with barcoding) on the front of your question and answer booklet is the same as the number on the front of your examination booklet, your answer sheet, and your essay ruled paper.

5. Write your candidate ID number on each page of the essay ruled paper booklet and on your objective answer sheet.

6. Complete your attendance record with respect to name, address, and candidate number. Write and bubble in your candidate number on your objective answer sheet.

7. Do **not** open your exam question booklet until you are told to open it. Do **not** write anything (other than name, candidate number, etc.) on your exam booklets until the exam begins.

8. Look at the front cover of your question booklet to note any differences from 60 multiple-choice, two OOF, and two essay questions (make adjustments for deviations). Analyze the point value and estimated minutes on the front cover of your exam question booklet. Determine how the point values deviate from 60-10-10-10-10. Confirm that the time allocated to OOF is less than the time allocated to essay questions.

9. As soon as the exam begins, confirm the question formats and do a quick inventory of the OOF questions. What format is used (e.g., matching, computational)? What subject matter do they test? Similarly, take an inventory of the two essay questions.

10. Make a final determination of your question answering sequence. You should make a preliminary plan as you did when preparing for the exam.

11. Be in control of your time. You know how much time is permitted for each question and you should keep yourself on or ahead of schedule during the exam. When you begin answering each question (multiple-choice and OOF), write your starting time on your question booklet next to the first item.

12. Implement your question answering technique on individual questions.

13. Remember to use your question booklet margins for all notes and computations so you know where they are.

14. Do not let anything distract you. View possible distractions as distractions and remain focused on doing your best on the exam. That is all that should matter to you. Tell the proctors to take care of the problem(s).

    a. If someone or something is bugging you, e.g., a table mate shaking the table, a heating or cooling vent making you uncomfortable, ask the proctors to move you.

    b. If proctors are talking amongst themselves or with candidates, tell them to "shhhhh."

    c. If someone is trying to look at your papers, tell them to stop.

    d. Always cover up your papers in such a way so as not to invite others to look at them, both while you are seated at your table and when you leave for the rest room.

15. Transfer your answers to the objective answer sheet as soon as you finish the 60 multiple-choice items or complete an OOF question. Answer all items within each question and transfer all answers (even best-guess answers). Mark all questions you are unsure of with a question mark in your question booklet. You can return to them later, time permitting. If you change an answer, immediately make the change on your objective answer sheet.

CONTROL: HOW TO

Remember, you must be in control to be successful during exam preparation and execution. Perhaps more importantly, control can also contribute greatly to your personal and other professional goals. Control is the process whereby you

1. Develop expectations, standards, budgets, and plans.
2. Undertake activity, production, study, and learning.
3. Measure the activity, production, output, and knowledge.
4. Compare actual activity with what was expected or budgeted.
5. Modify the activity to better achieve the expected or desired outcome.
6. Revise expectations and standards in light of actual experience.
7. Continue the process.

Exercising control will ultimately develop the confidence you need to outperform 2 out of 3 CPA candidates and PASS the CPA exam! Obtain our FREE *CPA Review: A System for Success* booklet for a more detailed discussion of control and other exam tactics.

GLEIM BUSINESS LAW STUDY UNIT LISTING

		Number of Outline Pages	Number of Questions			First Page No.
			MC	OOF	Essay	
1.	AICPA Ethics	22	33	1	1	19
2.	CPAs and the Law	14	40	2	1	54
3.	Agency	12	33	2	1	85
4.	Partnerships	14	39	2	1	111
5.	Corporations	20	30	2	1	143
6.	Estates and Trusts	14	41	1	1	175
7.	Contract Formation	21	45	2	1	205
8.	Contract Performance	13	44	1	3	248
9.	Rights and Duties	11	23	1	1	281
10.	Guarantors	6	25	1	1	302
11.	Bankruptcy	14	50	2	2	320
12.	Securities	18	47	2	1	357
13.	Employment	15	60	1	1	396
14.	Environmental Regulation	9	21	1	1	434
15.	Negotiable Instruments and Bank Transactions	23	49	1	1	453
16.	Sales	21	52	2	1	498
17.	Secured Transactions	19	33	2	1	542
18.	Documents of Title	3	11	0	0	577
19.	Real Property and Insurance	21	57	4	2	585
20.	Personal Property, Bailments, and Computers	16	37	0	2	635

Also see the Business Law Review Checklist presented on pages 666 and 667 and the AICPA's Content Specification Outlines on page 4.

GLEIM'S TECHNICAL SUPPORT VIA FAX

If you FAX us inquiries about errors, omissions, etc., before 1:00 p.m. eastern time, we will respond by FAX the following business day or as soon as possible. If we have trouble FAXing our response, it will be mailed.

Please use the FAX Technical Support Request form that appears on page 668. It must be completed as requested so we can address your issues and questions. If you are outside the United States and seeking technical support, you MUST include your e-mail address or we will not be able to respond to your request. Wait until after you take the CPA exam to send us the separate evaluation form provided on pages 681 and 682. Please do NOT duplicate items via FAX that you will be sending to us on the evaluation form.

CHAPTER I
PROFESSIONAL RESPONSIBILITIES

STUDY UNIT 1: AICPA ETHICS

22 pages of outline
33 multiple-choice questions
1 OOF and 1 essay

A. *Code of Professional Conduct*
B. *Interpretations and Rulings*
C. *Consulting Services*
D. *Personal Financial Planning*
E. *Disciplinary Systems within the Profession*

The Business Law and Professional Responsibilities section of the CPA exam tests the *Code of Professional Conduct* and other ethics pronouncements, not those of individual state boards of accountancy. Professional responsibilities encompass the two topics covered in Study Units 1 and 2. Together they constitute 15% of this section of the exam.

Study Unit 1 covers the AICPA's *Code of Professional Conduct*, Statements on Standards for Consulting Services, and the disciplinary systems within the accounting profession. This study unit has four subunits. The first subunit is a condensed but comprehensive summary of the AICPA Code of Conduct. The second subunit contains summaries of AICPA Ethics Interpretations and Professional Ethics Rulings under the 11 Rules of Conduct. The last three concern consulting services, personal financial planning, and disciplinary systems. In accordance with the AICPA Content Specification Outlines, Statements on Responsibilities in Tax Practice are covered in *CPA Review: TAX-MAN-GOV*.

A. **Code of Professional Conduct**

1. It consists of two sections: **Principles and Rules**. The 6 Principles, which provide the framework for the rules, are goal-oriented and aspirational but nonbinding. The 11 Rules are mandatory. Candidates should learn the Rules but need not know them by rule number.

   The 6 Principles

   I. Responsibilities
   II. The Public Interest
   III. Integrity
   IV. Objectivity and Independence
   V. Due Care
   VI. Scope and Nature of Services

   The 11 Rules of Conduct

   1. Rule 101 -- Independence
   2. *Rule 102 -- Integrity and Objectivity
   3. *Rule 201 -- General Standards
   4. *Rule 202 -- Compliance with Standards
   5. *Rule 203 -- Accounting Principles
   6. Rule 301 -- Confidential Client Information
   7. Rule 302 -- Contingent Fees
   8. *Rule 501 -- Acts Discreditable
   9. Rule 502 -- Advertising and Other Forms of Solicitation
   10. **Rule 503 -- Commissions and Referral Fees
   11. *Rule 505 -- Form of Organization and Name

   a. Of the Principles, Scope and Nature of Services and Independence apply only to members in public practice. The rest apply to all members. Of the Rules of Conduct, the six marked with single asterisks (*) apply to all members. Conduct Rule 503 (**) applies in part (Referrals) to all members and in part (Commissions) only to members in public practice. The remainder of the Rules apply only to members in public practice.

2. **Interpretations** provide guidelines for the scope and application of the Rules.

3. **Ethics Rulings** apply the Rules of Conduct and the Interpretations to specific facts to determine whether a violation of the ethical standards exists.

4. The second subunit, Interpretations and Rulings, contains outlines of the Interpretations followed by brief summaries of the Rulings.

5. **Synopses of the Six Principles**

    I.   **Responsibilities**. Members should exercise sensitive professional and moral judgments when carrying out their professional responsibilities.

    II. **The Public Interest**. Members should act to benefit the public interest, honor the public trust, and demonstrate commitment to professionalism.

         a. The AICPA adopted the ethical standards because a distinguishing mark of a profession is an acceptance of responsibility to the public.

    III. **Integrity**. Members should perform all professional responsibilities with the highest sense of integrity to maintain public confidence.

    IV. **Objectivity and Independence**. A member should maintain objectivity and be free of conflicts of interest. A member in public practice should be independent in fact and appearance when providing attestation services.

    V.   **Due Care**. A member should follow the profession's technical and ethical standards, strive for improved competence and quality services, and discharge professional responsibility to the best of the member's ability.

         a. Members must adequately plan and supervise any activity for which they are responsible.

    VI. **Scope and Nature of Services**. A member in public practice should follow the Principles of the *Code of Professional Conduct* in determining the nature and scope of services.

6. **Synopses of the 11 Rules**

    a. Rule 101 -- *Independence*. A member in public practice should be independent when performing professional services as required by standards-setting bodies.

        1) In this context, the relevant standards-setting bodies are the

            a) Auditing Standards Board (ASB)
            b) Accounting and Review Services Committee
            c) Management Consulting Services Executive Committee

        2) The foregoing bodies are all authorized to promulgate attestation standards.

        3) The ASB issues Statements on Auditing Standards.

            a) The second generally accepted auditing standard requires auditors to maintain "an independence in mental attitude."

        4) The fourth general attestation standard likewise requires practitioners to maintain "an independence in mental attitude" when performing attest engagements.

        5) Under Statements on Standards for Accounting and Review Services, an accountant may not report on a review of the financial statements of a nonpublic entity if (s)he is not independent.

        6) An accountant must also be independent to examine or apply agreed-upon procedures to prospective financial statements (Source: Statement on Standards for Attestation Engagements No. 1).

7) The AICPA's special committee on assurance services has issued a report defining these services as "independent professional services that improve the quality of information, or its context, for decision makers." These services constitute a new expansion of CPAs' traditional role into such areas as elder care, electronic commerce, performance measurement, health care delivery, risk information for internal decision making, and information system design and operation.

8) A notable development is the joint creation of the Independence Standards Board (ISB) by the AICPA and the SEC. The ISB creates, codifies, amends, and preserves independence standards for auditors of public companies. It is an independent part of the SEC Practice Section of the AICPA Division for CPA Firms. The ISB is a response to the need to maintain the independence of the audit function at a time when CPAs are providing a widening array of new services and forming more complex business relationships.

     a) ISB Standard 1, *Independence Discussions with Audit Committees*, requires an auditor who wishes to be deemed independent within the meaning of the securities acts to make an annual written disclosure to the audit committee of all relationships between the auditor and its related entities and the company and its related entities that may reasonably bear on independence. The auditor must confirm its independence in the letter and must discuss its independence with the audit committee.

b. Rule 102 -- *Integrity and Objectivity*. A member shall maintain objectivity and integrity, be free of conflicts of interest, not knowingly misrepresent facts, and not subordinate his/her judgment to others when performing professional services.

c. Rule 201 -- *General Standards*. A member shall comply with the following:

1) Undertake only those services that the member can reasonably expect to complete with professional competence.

2) Exercise due professional care when performing professional services.

     a) Generally accepted auditing standards (see the third general standard) require that due care be exercised in performing the audit and preparing the report. Due care requires critical review at every level of supervision of the work done and the judgment exercised by those assisting in the audit.

3) Adequately plan and supervise performance of professional services.

4) Obtain sufficient relevant data to provide a reasonable basis for conclusions in relation to any professional service.

d. Rule 202 -- *Compliance with Standards*. A member who performs professional services must comply with promulgated standards.

e. Rule 203 -- *Accounting Principles*. A member shall not express an opinion or make an affirmative statement about conformity with GAAP or state that (s)he is not aware of any material modifications that should be made to achieve conformity with GAAP, given any departure from a promulgated accounting principle that has a material effect on the financial statements or data taken as a whole. However, if the member can demonstrate that, due to unusual circumstances, the financial statements or data would have been misleading without a departure from GAAP, the member can comply with the rule by describing the departure, its approximate effects, if practicable, and the reasons compliance with the principle would be misleading.

f. Rule 301 -- *Confidential Client Information*. A member in public practice cannot disclose confidential client information without the client's consent. However, this Rule does not affect a CPA's obligations

1) To comply with a validly issued and enforceable subpoena or summons or with applicable laws and regulations

2) To discharge his/her professional obligations properly under Conduct Rules 202, *Compliance with Standards*, and 203, *Accounting Principles*

3) To cooperate in a review of the CPA's professional practice under AICPA or state CPA society or board of accountancy authorization

4) To initiate a complaint with or respond to any inquiry made by the professional ethics division, trial board of the AICPA, or an investigative or disciplinary body of a state society or board of accountancy

g. Rule 302 -- *Contingent Fees*. A contingent fee is established as part of an agreement under which the amount of the fee is dependent upon the finding or result.

1) The receipt of contingent fees by a member is prohibited when the member performs an audit, a review, a compilation when the report will be used by third parties and the report does not disclose the CPA's lack of independence, or an examination of prospective financial information.

2) A contingent fee is not permitted for preparing an original or amended tax return or claim.

3) Fees are not deemed to be contingent if fixed by courts or other public authorities, or in tax matters, if they are based on the results of judicial proceedings or the findings of governmental agencies.

h. Rule 501 -- *Acts Discreditable*. A member shall not commit an act that is discreditable to the profession.

i. Rule 502 -- *Advertising and Other Forms of Solicitation*. A member in public practice shall not seek to obtain clients by advertising or other forms of solicitation done in a false, misleading, or deceptive manner. Solicitation through coercion, overreaching, or harassing conduct is prohibited.

j. Rule 503 -- *Commissions and Referral Fees*. A member in public practice shall not accept a commission for recommending or referring to a client any product or service, or for recommending or referring any product or service to be supplied by a client, if the member performs for that client an audit, a review, a compilation when a third party will use the financial statement and the report does not disclose the CPA's lack of independence, or an examination of prospective financial information.

1) Permitted commissions must be disclosed to any person or entity to whom the member recommends a product or service.

2) A member who accepts a referral fee for recommending services of a CPA or who pays a referral fee to obtain a client must disclose the arrangement to the client. A referral fee is compensation for recommending or referring any service of a CPA to any person. Referral fees are not considered commissions.

k. Rule 505 -- *Form of Organization and Name*. A member may practice public accounting only in a form of organization allowed by state law that conforms with resolutions of the AICPA Council.

1) The firm name must not be misleading.

2) Names of past owners may be included in the name of the successor organization.

3) A firm cannot designate itself as "members of the AICPA" unless all owners are members.

7. Stop and review! You have completed the outline for this subunit. Study multiple-choice questions 1 through 6 beginning on page 41.

B.   **Interpretations and Rulings** are presented for each of the 11 Rules. The Interpretations are in outline format followed by brief summaries of the Rulings.

    1.   Rule 101 -- *Independence*. Interpretations.

        a.   Independence is impaired by the following transactions, interests, and relationships. However, this list is not all-inclusive.

            1)   Independence is impaired if, during the engagement or at the time of expressing an opinion, a member or his/her firm

                a)   Had a direct financial interest or a material indirect financial interest in the client

                b)   Was a trustee of any trust or executor of any estate that had a direct or material indirect financial interest in the client

                c)   Had any joint, closely held business investment with the client or any officer, director, or principal shareholder that was material in relation to the member's net worth or the member's firm's net worth

                d)   Had a loan to or from a client or any officer, director, or principal shareholder except as permitted in other interpretations

            2)   Independence is impaired if, during the period covered by the financial statements, during the engagement, or when an opinion is expressed, a member or his/her firm

                a)   Was connected with the client as an officer, director, promoter, underwriter, or voting trustee, or in any other position equivalent to a member of management or an employee

                b)   Was a trustee for any pension or profit-sharing trust of the client

            3)   The period of a professional engagement starts when the member begins to perform any professional services requiring independence. This period continues for the entire professional relationship and does not end with the issuance of a report and start again with the next year's engagement.

        b.   "A member or a member's firm" does not include former practitioners provided that

            1)   A written agreement exists whereby the payments due to the former practitioner are not material to the firm, and the payment formula is fixed during the payout period. Retirement may also be adjusted for inflation.

            2)   The former practitioner does not participate in the firm's business or activities, regardless of whether (s)he has been compensated, except for consultations during the transition period.

            3)   The former practitioner does not appear to participate in the firm's activities.

                a)   The appearance of participation results from including the former practitioner's name in membership lists or in the firm's internal directory without listing him/her as retired.

                b)   The former practitioner is not considered to be participating in firm activities solely because (s)he has an office and a secretary in the firm's suite unless (s)he has significant influence with a client.

            4)   A former practitioner having significant influence with a client is not provided with an office.

        c.   Before a member performs other nonattest services for an attest client, (s)he must evaluate the effect on independence. Performing management functions or making management decisions will impair independence.

1) Thus, the member should reach an understanding about the objectives and limitations of the engagement, the services to be performed, and management's and the member's responsibilities. This understanding preferably should be documented in an engagement letter indicating the member will not perform management functions or make management decisions.

2) The member also should be satisfied that the client has an informed judgment about the results of the other services and understand its responsibility to designate a manager(s) to oversee the services; to evaluate the adequacy of the services and any findings; to make management decisions, including accepting responsibility for the results; and to establish and maintain internal controls.

3) General activities that impair a member's independence include

   a) Exercise of authority over transactions or otherwise on behalf of a client
   b) Preparing source documents or originating data evidencing transactions
   c) Custody of assets
   d) Supervision of client employees in normal activities
   e) Determining recommendations to be implemented
   f) Reporting to the board on behalf of management
   g) Service as a stock transfer or escrow agent, registrar, or general counsel

4) The balance of this Interpretation consists of a table in which activities that do and do not impair independence are listed for a selection of other nonattest services (bookkeeping; payroll; benefits administration; investment advisory and management service; corporate finance consulting or advisory services; appraisal, valuation, and actuarial services; employee or executive search; business risk consulting; and information systems design, installation, and integration).

   Authors' Note: For purposes of practice before the SEC, a CPA or public accountant who provides bookkeeping services to an audit client is not deemed to be independent with respect to that client. The AICPA position is that providing certain bookkeeping services (e.g., data processing) does not impair independence.

d. A member in an honorary position will not impair independence if (s)he is associated with the financial statements of a not-for-profit organization that (s)he allows to use his/her name on letterheads and circulated materials to lend prestige to the organization. However, the member should not be able to vote or participate in board or management decisions and should be identified as an honorary director or trustee.

e. Loans from financial institution clients

1) Independence is not impaired by grandfathered loans that were obtained from a financial institution under its normal lending procedures, terms, and requirements, and that

   a) Existed as of January 1, 1992,

   b) Were obtained from a financial institution before it became a client requiring independence,

   c) Were obtained from a client not requiring independence and were sold to a client requiring independence, or

   d) Were obtained from a client requiring independence by a borrower before (s)he became a member with respect to the client.

2)   For purposes of a grandfathered loan, the date a loan commitment or line of credit is granted must be used rather than the date a transaction closes or funds are obtained. Grandfathered loans must be current as to all terms at all times. They include

    a)   Home mortgages

    b)   Secured loans for which the collateral equals or exceeds the remaining balance of the loan during the term of the loan. If the loan exceeds the value of collateral, this excess must not be material to the member's net worth.

    c)   Unsecured loans not material to the member's net worth

3)   A loan is not grandfathered if, after the latest date in e.1) on the previous page, the terms of the loan change in a way not described in the original loan agreement.

4)   In the case of a limited partnership in which members have a combined interest exceeding 50% or a general partnership in which members control the partnership, the loan is ascribed to each partner based on his/her legal liability as a limited or general partner. Even if this amount is zero, renegotiating the loan or entering into a new loan after the latest date in e.1) on the previous page is deemed to impair independence.

5)   Certain loans are permitted even if the financial institution client is one for which independence is required, provided that normal lending procedures, etc., are followed:

    a)   Automobile loans and leases collateralized by the automobile

    b)   Loans fully collateralized by the cash surrender value of insurance

    c)   Loans fully collateralized by cash deposits

    d)   Credit cards and cash advances with an aggregate outstanding balance of $5,000 or less by the payment due date

f.   Effect of actual or threatened litigation

    1)   Litigation between client and member

        a)   Independence is impaired when litigation is begun by

            i)   The present management alleging deficiencies in audit work
            ii)   The member alleging management fraud or deceit

        b)   An expressed intention by the management to litigate against the member for alleged deficiencies in audit work will impair independence if it is probable that the claim will be filed.

        c)   Independence is not impaired when the threatened or actual litigation is not related to the audit and the amount is not material. Examples include disputes over billings for services and results of tax advice.

    2)   Litigation by security holders (primary litigation)

        a)   Shareholders may bring a class action against the client company or its management without impairing independence. Often the member and the client are both defendants, but if cross-claims are filed, adverse interests may arise and independence may be impaired.

        b)   Cross-claims filed by the client to protect a right to legal redress in the event of a future adverse decision do not impair independence in the absence of a significant risk of a material settlement.

        c)   Cross-claims against the member by an underwriter do not impair independence if no similar claims are made by the client.

d) Cross-claims filed against the member by persons who are also officers or directors of other clients do not usually impair independence with respect to the other clients.

3) Other third-party litigation

a) Litigation may be commenced against the member by a creditor or insurer that alleges reliance on financial statements of the client. This litigation does not affect independence if the client is not the plaintiff or is a nominal plaintiff. Independence may be impaired if the third party (e.g., an insurance company) is also a client of the member and there is a significant risk of a material settlement.

4) If a reasonable person would conclude that litigation poses an unacceptable risk of impairment of independence, the member should disengage or disclaim an opinion for lack of independence.

g. Financial interests in nonclients having investor or investee relationships with the client

1) Independence is impaired when

a) A member has a direct or material indirect financial interest in the nonclient if the investee is material to the investor.

b) A member has a material interest in a nonclient who is an immaterial investee of the client investor.

c) A member can exercise significant influence over a nonclient investor who has an immaterial interest in the client investee.

2) Independence is not impaired if a member did not know about the financial interests described above.

h. Family relationships and positions that impair independence

1) "A member or a member's firm" includes

a) The firm and its proprietors, shareholders, or partners

b) All individuals (all employees and contractors except specialists) participating in the engagement except those with routine clerical jobs (e.g., typing and photocopying)

c) All individuals with managerial positions in an office participating in a significant portion of the engagement

d) Any entity whose operating or accounting policies can be controlled by one or more people described in a) through c)

2) The "member" definition includes spouses and dependent persons (i.e., children). A member's independence is impaired if his/her spouse works for a client and is in a job with significant influence or is in an audit-sensitive job (such as cashier, internal auditor, or purchasing agent).

3) The "member" definition excludes nondependent close relatives (i.e., non-dependent children, grandchildren, stepchildren, brothers, sisters, grandparents, parents, parents-in-law, and their spouses). Close relatives do not include the brothers and sisters of the member's spouse.

a) But independence is impaired if

i) An individual participating in the engagement is aware that a close relative has a material interest in the audit client.

ii) An individual participating in the engagement has a close relative with significant influence over the client or is in an audit-sensitive position.

iii)   A partner, proprietor, or shareholder located in an office that is participating in a significant part of the engagement has a close relative who could have significant influence over the client.

i.   Effect on independence of relationships with entities included in governmental financial statements

1)   A financial reporting entity's general purpose financial statements include the primary government; its fund types, funds, account groups, and blended component units; financial statements or disclosures of discretely presented component units; and notes. Disclosures should be made in the notes about related organizations, joint ventures, jointly governed organizations, component units of another government with characteristics of a joint venture or jointly governed organization, etc.

2)   An auditor of the general purpose financial statements (GPFS) of the entity must be independent of it. (S)he need not be independent of a related organization if the entity is not financially accountable for it and the required disclosure does not include financial information.

3)   An auditor of the statements of a material fund type, fund, etc., should be independent with respect to those statements and those of the primary government. (S)he need not be independent of other fund types, funds, etc., provided they are not financially accountable for or to the auditee or cannot significantly influence it.

4)   An auditor of the statements of a fund type, fund, etc., that alone or in the aggregate are immaterial to the GPFS should be independent of those statements and should not be associated with the primary government in any capacity described in Interpretation 101-1-B. If the member is auditing immaterial fund types, funds, etc., that, when aggregated, are material to the financial reporting entity, the member should be independent of those statements and the primary government.

j.   Independence and attest engagements

1)   This Interpretation applies only to engagements covered by SSAEs and by AU 622, *Engagements to Apply Agreed Upon Procedures to Specified Elements, Accounts, or Items of a Financial Statement*, when the report is restricted. It does not apply to such engagements if the report is not restricted. It also does not apply to engagements requiring independence under other standards.

2)   Independence is impaired if, during the engagement or at the time the written communication is issued,

a)   An individual on the engagement team or his/her spouse, dependent, or firm has a relationship with the responsible party prohibited by Interpretation 101-1.

b)   An individual on the engagement team has a nondependent close relative who has a position of significant influence with or a material interest in the responsible party.

c)   An owner, partner, or shareholder (or a spouse or dependent thereof) located in an office significantly participating in the engagement has such an influence or interest.

d)   Any of the individuals or entities mentioned above contributes to the development of the subject matter of the engagement or stands to gain financially directly from the outcome.

e)   An individual on the team could reasonably be expected to know that an owner, partner, or shareholder located in other offices of the firm had any of the characteristics prohibited in b), c), and d) above.

k.   Independence and cooperative arrangements with clients

   1)   Independence is impaired if, during the engagement or at the time of expressing an opinion, a member's firm had any material cooperative arrangement with the client.

      a)   A cooperative arrangement means joint participation in a business activity.

l.   Extended audit services

   1)   Extended audit services include assistance in internal audit activities or an extension of audit service beyond the requirements of GAAS. They do not impair independence if the member does not act or appear to act as a member of management or as an employee.

   2)   The responsibilities of the client and the member should preferably be documented in an engagement letter.

   3)   A member should be satisfied that the client understands its responsibility for internal control and the internal audit function.

   4)   Independence is not impaired by performing separate evaluations of internal control, including separate evaluations of the client's monitoring activities.

   5)   The member should be satisfied that the board or audit committee is informed about the responsibilities of management and the member with respect to the engagement.

   6)   The member is responsible for the audit procedures in accordance with the terms of the engagement.

      a)   The report should include information that allows the internal audit director to evaluate the adequacy of the procedures and the findings, including recommendations for improvements.

      b)   The member may assist the director in performing preliminary risk assessments, preparing audit plans, and recommending priorities, but the member should not undertake responsibilities of the director.

   7)   Procedures that are extensions of the audit scope, such as confirming receivables and analyzing account balances, do not impair independence.

   8)   Activities performed as part of extended audit services that impair independence include

      a)   Performing ongoing monitoring or control activities that affect transactions and routine activities in connection with operations or production and that are equivalent to a compliance or quality control function

      b)   Choosing which recommendations for improving internal control are implemented

      c)   Reporting to the board or audit committee on behalf of management or the internal audit director

      d)   Exercising transactional or other authority on behalf of the client

      e)   Preparing source documents

      f)   Having custody of assets

      g)   Approving or being responsible for the overall internal audit work plan

m.   Effect of APSs on independence rules

   1)   The independence rules for an alternative practice structure (APS) apply to all structures in which "the 'traditional firm' engaged in attest services is closely aligned with another organization, public or private, that performs other

professional services." For example, a CPA firm may be sold to another entity having subsidiaries or divisions such as a bank, an insurance company, a broker-dealer, and entities providing nonattest services (tax, management consulting, etc.). The owners and employees of the CPA firm become employees of one of the parent's subsidiaries or divisions and may offer nonattest services. Moreover, the owners of the acquired CPA firm create a new CPA firm to offer attest services. The majority ownership of the new firm must be held by CPAs, but it leases employees, offices, and equipment from the parent, which may also provide advertising and perform back office functions. The owners of the new CPA firm pay a negotiated amount for such services.

2) The term "member or member's firm" is defined in B.1.h.1). In the example in B.1.m.1), this term includes the new CPA firm (the firm) and any leased or employed person or entity.

3) When two or more new CPA firms are "closely aligned" with another organization, issues arise as to whether owners of one perform services or have significant economic interests in another. Thus, if an owner of one performs services for another, (s)he is deemed to be an owner of both. Similar issues arise regarding managers (leased or otherwise).

4) In an APS, persons and entities included in Member are closely aligned with other persons and entities. The latter include direct superiors who can directly control the activities of an owner or manager. A direct superior is an immediate superior who can direct the activities of an owner or manager so as to be able to directly or indirectly derive a benefit. Direct superiors are subject to the same independence rules as persons Included In Member.

5) An indirect superior (defined to include a spouse, cohabitant, or dependents of an indirect superior) is one or more levels above a direct superior and does not have a direct reporting relationship with the new CPA firm's owners and managers. Less restrictive standards apply to indirect superiors and to other entities in the consolidated group.

   a) These parties may not have a relationship covered in B.1.a.1) with an attest client of the new CPA firm that is material.

   b) These parties also should not exercise significant influence over the attest client.

   c) Other entities in the consolidated group and their employees may not be promoters, underwriters, directors, officers, or voting trustees of an attest client. However, with the foregoing exceptions, indirect superiors and other consolidated entities may provide services to an attest client that a Member could not without impairing independence.

6) The new CPA firm may not perform a service requiring independence for any entity in the consolidated group.

7) Independence is impaired with regard to an attest client who exercises significant influence over, or has a material investment in, the parent.

8) Referrals within the consolidated group are subject to the provisions regarding conflicts of interest.

2. Ethics Rulings on Independence -- Rule 101.

Independence Not Impaired

1. Membership in a client trade association provided the member is not an officer or a director, or in a position equivalent to management.

2. The member's spouse is an accountant of a client and performs bookkeeping services, but the spouse does not make management decisions.

3. The member provides advisory services for a client.

4. A member is designated to serve as an executor of an individual's estate that owns the majority of the stock of a corporation. Independence with respect to the corporation is not impaired unless the member serves as executor.

5. A CPA is a director of a federated fund-raising org-anization, e.g., United Way, and audits local charities receiving funds. Independence with respect to the charities is not impaired unless the organization exercises managerial control over them.

6. A CPA has a pro rata share of securities in a social club, unless (s)he is on the governing board or takes part in management.

7. A member serves on a citizens' committee advising a county and on another committee advising the state where the county is located.

8. A CPA's ownership of shares in a mutual fund that holds some of a client's shares. Independence becomes impaired if the indirect interest becomes material or the CPA has significant influence over the mutual fund.

9. A member and a client bank serve in a co-fiduciary capacity with respect to an estate, provided the estate assets are not material.

10. A member's retirement plan is managed by an insurance company (an audit client) in a pooled separate account, not part of the general assets.

11. A CPA performing appraisal, valuation, or actuarial services if the client determines or approves all significant judgments.

12. A CPA implementing an information system for a client may also train personnel provided no significant management decisions are made.

13. A CPA audits an employee benefit plan unless the CPA has significant influence over the employer(s).

14. The mere servicing of a member's loan by a client financial institution.

15. When a member has a checking or savings account, certificate of deposit, or money market account in a client financial institution, provided the amounts are fully insured by the government. Uninsured amounts do not impair independence if they are immaterial.

16. Membership in a client credit union if all the following are met:
    a. Each member qualifies to join the credit union without regard to the professional services.
    b. The member's vote must not have significant influence over policies.
    c. Loans must be limited to grandfathered and other permitted loans made under normal procedures, terms, and requirements.
    d. Any deposits with the credit union must meet the conditions in number 15.

17. A member's service as treasurer of a mayoral campaign organization. Independence is impaired with respect to the organization itself, but not the political party of the candidate or the city.

18. If a member leases property to or from a client under an operating lease with terms comparable to those of similar leases, and all amounts are paid in accordance with the lease. If, however, the lease is a capital lease, independence would be impaired unless the lease is tantamount to a permitted loan.

19. Inclusion of a clause in an engagement letter providing for member indemnification by the client.

20. A predispute agreement with a client to use alternative dispute resolution (ADR) techniques.

21. Commencement of an ADR proceeding. However, Interpretation 101-6 applies, and independence may be impaired if the proceeding is sufficiently similar to litigation because the parties have material adverse interests, e.g., in binding arbitration.

22. Performing extended audit services regarding reporting on internal control if management assumes responsibility for control, and management does not rely on the member's work as the primary basis for its assertion.

23. Providing operational auditing services if the member does not appear to act as a client employee or manager.

24. Frequent performance of extended audit services within the limits of the related Interpretation, provided the procedures performed constitute separate evaluations of ongoing monitoring and control activities.

Independence Impaired

1. Acceptance of more than a token gift from a client.

2. The member has the ability to sign or cosign a client's checks.

3. The member performs payroll preparation services for a client.

4. The member enters into a contract with a client to supervise personnel and approve disbursements (management functions).

5. The member signs or cosigns checks or purchase orders or exercises general supervision to ensure compliance as a representative of a creditors' committee in control of a debtor corporation.

6. The member serves as an elected legislator in a municipal body at the same time as (s)he is performing an audit of that body.

7. With respect to a foundation and an estate if the member is a trustee of the foundation that is the beneficiary of the estate.

8. A CPA serves on the board of directors of a client nonprofit social club.

9. A CPA is on a client's committee that administers the deferred compensation program.

10. A CPA is a director of a company and an auditor of the profit sharing and retirement trust.

11. A CPA owns an immaterial amount of bonds in a municipal authority (considered a loan).

12. With respect to a common interest realty association (CIRA) as a result of owning or leasing realty. But no impairment occurs if the CIRA has governmental functions, the CPA's annual assessment is immaterial, sale of the CIRA or common assets does not result in a distribution to the member, CIRA creditors have no recourse to the member, and the CPA is not a manager or employee of the CIRA.

13. A CPA owns an investment club that holds a client's shares (a direct financial interest).

14. A CPA serves as an officially appointed client stock transfer agent.

15. A member of a university's faculty audits the student senate fund (the member will audit functions performed by the university, which is his/her employer).

16. A member who is an attorney serving as general counsel for a client (acting as management).

17. If billed or unbilled fees, or a note arising from the fees, for client services rendered more than 1 year before the current year's report date remain unpaid. Not applicable if the client is in bankruptcy.

18. When a CPA recruits and hires a controller and a cost accountant for a client. Independence is not im-paired if a CPA recommends a position description and candidate specifications, searches for and initial-ly screens candidates, and recommends candidates.

19. When a CPA is on the board of directors of a fund-raising organization, unless the position is honorary.

20. If a member's retirement or savings plan has a direct or material indirect financial interest in a client.

21. A direct financial interest in a client whether or not the interest is placed in a blind trust.

22. For both partnerships, when two limited partnerships have the same general partner and a member has a material interest in one of the partnerships.

23. The use of partners, shareholders, and professional employees from another firm that is not independent of the client. Their work can be used in the same manner as that of internal auditors.

24. A CPA's service on a client's advisory board unless it

    a. Is in fact advisory.

    b. Has no authority to make management decisions, and

    c. Is distinct from the board of directors with few common members.

25. A CPA may not express an audit opinion or issue a review report, but (s)he may issue a compilation report disclosing the lack of independence.

26. A member who is a general partner in a partnership that invests in a client. If the member is a limited partner, independence would not be impaired unless the interest in the client is material.

27. A joint closely held business investment is a business investment that is subject to control by the member, the client, its officers, directors, or principal shareholders, individually or in any combination.

28. If a member is a limited partner in a limited partnership (LP) and the client is a general partner, the member lacks independence with respect to the LP, the client if the client has a material interest in the LP, and a subsidiary of the LP if the member's interest is material.

29. A member's joint interest in a vacation home with a principal shareholder of a client will be considered a "joint closely held business investment" (even if it is only intended for personal use) if the interest is material.

30. Unless a loan from a nonclient subsidiary of a client parent is "grandfathered" or "permitted" under Interpretation 101-5, it impairs independence with respect to the parent. However, a loan from a nonclient parent does not impair independence with respect to a client subsidiary if the subsidiary is not material to the parent.

31. If a report was issued when a member was independent, (s)he may reissue it or consent to its use when his/her independence is impaired provided (s)he did not do any post-audit work (not including reading subsequent statements or inquiries of subsequent auditors) while not independent.

32. Agreeing to indemnify a client for losses arising from lawsuits, etc., that relate directly or indirectly to client acts impairs independence.

33. When a member has significant influence over an entity with significant influence over a client.

34. With respect to the client and the plan if a member participates in a client's health and welfare plan. But, if participation arises from permitted employment of a spouse or cohabitant, no impairment occurs provided the plan is offered to all employees in equivalent positions.

35. With respect to a sponsoring client or an investee client if the member or spouse participates in a retirement, savings, or similar plan that is sponsored by a client or invests in a client. But the same exception applies as in 34. if the spouse selects an investment option that is not in a client; no other option is available, a right of possession exists, and the investment is promptly disposed; and, if no right of possession exists, the spouse's plan investment in a client is an indirect interest and not material.

36. When investment contributions by a member are invested or managed by a nonclient firm that offers financial services products (FSPs) that allow the member to direct his/her investment, independence is impaired if the FSP is invested in that client, whether or not the member directs the investment (a direct interest). If the member does not have authority to direct the investment, and the FSP invests in the client, an indirect interest results. If it is material to the member, independence is impaired. If the FSP invests only in the member's clients, the interest is direct, and independence is impaired.

37. See Ethics Ruling 7 under Rule 102.

3. **Rule 102 --** *Integrity and Objectivity*. **Interpretations.**

   a. Knowing misrepresentations of facts include knowingly making materially false and misleading entries in financial statements or records, failing to make corrections in materially false or misleading statements or records when the member has such authority, or signing a document with materially false and misleading information.

   b. If a conflict of interest arises that could impair objectivity when a member performs a professional service, Rule 102 will not prohibit the service if disclosure is made to and permission is obtained from the appropriate parties. However, an independence objection cannot be overcome by disclosure and consent. The following are examples of situations in which objectivity may be impaired:

      1) Performing litigation services for the plaintiff when the defendant is a client

      2) Providing tax or personal financial planning (PFP) services to both parties to a divorce

      3) Suggesting that a PFP client invest in a business in which the member has an interest

      4) Providing tax or PFP services to family members with conflicting interests

5)   Performing consulting services for a client that is a major competitor of a company in which the member has a significant financial interest, occupies a management position, or exercises influence

6)   Serving on a board of tax appeals that hears matters involving clients

7)   Providing services in connection with a real estate purchase from a client

8)   Referring a tax or PFP client to a service provider that refers clients to the member under an exclusive arrangement

9)   Referring a client to a service bureau in which the member or a partner in the member's firm has a material interest

c.   In dealings with an employer's external accountant, a member must be candid and not knowingly misrepresent facts or fail to disclose material facts.

d.   If a member and his/her supervisor have a dispute about statement preparation or recording of transactions, the member should do nothing if the supervisor's position is an acceptable alternative and does not materially misrepresent the facts.

1)   If the member concludes that a material misstatement would result, (s)he should consult the appropriate higher level(s) of management and should consider documenting relevant matters.

2)   If, after such discussions, the member concludes that action was not taken, (s)he should consider the continuing relationship with the employer, the obligation to communicate with third parties, and the desirability of consulting legal counsel.

e.   Educational services, e.g., teaching and research, are professional services subject to Rule 102.

f.   Professional services involving client advocacy are governed by the Code, e.g., Rules 201, 202, 203, and 102. If independence is required for a service, Rule 101 also applies.

1)   If the service stretches the bounds of performance standards, exceeds sound and reasonable professional practice, or compromises credibility, and therefore poses an unacceptable risk of injury to the member's or the firm's reputation, the propriety of accepting the engagement should be considered.

4.   Ethics Rulings on Integrity and Objectivity -- Rule 102.

1.   A member in public practice should not ordinarily serve as a director of a bank if it engages in significant transactions with his/her clients. The rules on confidential client information and conflict of interest may be violated.

2.   The use of the CPA designation by a member not in public practice if it implies the member is independent of his/her employer is an intentional misrepresentation. The member should clearly indicate the employment title in any transmittal in which (s)he uses the CPA designation. If the member states that a financial statement conforms with GAAP, Rule 203 applies.

3.   If during an engagement a member is offered employment with a client the member should remove himself or herself from the engagement until the offer is rejected or employment is no longer being sought. If employment was being considered during an engagement, reperformance may be necessary.

4.   A member is a director of a federated fund-raising organization from which local charities that are clients (with significant relationships with the member) receive funds. If the significant relationship is disclosed and consent received from the appropriate parties, performance of services not requiring independence is allowed.

5.   A company approaches a member to provide PFP or tax services for its executives, who consent to the arrangement and are aware of any relationship the member has with the company. The result of the services could be recommendations adverse to company interests. Rule 102 and Rule 301 do not prohibit acceptance of the engagement if the member believes (s)he can perform objectively. The member should consider informing all parties of possible results. The member should also consider responsibilities to the company and to the executives under Rule 301.

6.   Service as an expert witness does not constitute client advocacy.

7.   If a member is an officer, director, or principal shareholder of an entity having a loan to or from a client, independence is impaired with respect to that client if the member controls the entity, unless the loan is specifically permitted (see B.1.e.). If the member does not control the entity, the guidance in B.3.b. should be considered. Disclosure and consent may therefore overcome the conflict-of-interest objection and permit the performance of the professional service for the client, provided the member believes it can be done with objectivity.

5.   Rule 201 -- *General Standards*. Interpretations.

    a.   A member should have the competence to complete professional services according to professional standards and with reasonable care and diligence, but without assuming responsibility for infallibility.

        1)   Competence involves technical qualifications and the ability to supervise and evaluate the work. It relates to knowledge of standards, techniques, and technical subject matter and to the ability to exercise sound judgment.

        2)   In some cases, additional research and consultation is a normal part of performing services. However, if a member cannot gain sufficient competence, (s)he should suggest the engagement of someone competent.

6.   Rule 202 -- *Compliance with Standards*. No interpretations.

7.   Rule 203 -- *Accounting Principles*. Interpretations.

    a.   Professional judgment should be used in determining what constitutes unusual circumstances requiring a departure from established principles to prevent the financial statements or data from being misleading. Events that may justify such departures are new legislation or evolution of a new form of business transaction. An unusual degree of materiality or conflicting industry practices ordinarily do not justify departures.

    b.   The body designated to establish accounting principles is the FASB.

        1)   Unsuperseded SFASs, ARBs, and APB Opinions are accounting principles within the meaning of Rule 203.

    c.   Rule 203 applies to all members regarding any affirmative statement about GAAP conformity.

        1)   Thus, Rule 203 applies to members who sign client reports to regulatory agencies, creditors, or auditors that contain such representations.

8.   Ethics Rulings on General and Technical Standards -- Rules 201, 202, 203.

1.   The member has a responsibility to make sure that a subcontractor (s)he has selected has the professional qualifications and skills needed.

2.   A member is not required to be able to perform all the services of a newly hired systems analyst. But the member must be qualified to supervise and evaluate the specialist's work.

3.   If a member prepares financial statements in his/her capacity as an officer, shareholder, partner, director, or employee that are transmitted to a third party, the member's relationship to the entity should be clearly indicated. No implication of independence should be made. Rule 203 applies if the transmittal states that the statements conform with GAAP. If the member acts as a public practitioner or transmits the statements on his/her public practitioner's letterhead, (s)he should comply with applicable standards, including disclosure of lack of independence.

4.   Rule 203 applies to members who perform litigation support services.

9.   Rule 301 -- *Confidential Client Information*. Interpretations.

    a.   The rule against disclosure of confidential information does not prohibit the review of a member's professional practice pursuant to a purchase, sale, or merger of the practice. However, appropriate precautions (e.g., a written confidentiality agreement) should be taken so that the prospective buyer does not disclose any confidential client information.

10.   Rule 302 -- *Contingent Fees*. Interpretations.

    a.   An example of circumstances in which a contingent fee is not allowed is the preparation of an amended income tax return for a client claiming a refund of taxes because of an inadvertent omission of a proper deduction.

        1)   Examples of circumstances in which a contingent fee is allowed include

            a)   Representation of a client in an examination by a revenue agent

            b)   Representation of a client who is obtaining a private letter ruling

            c)   Filing an amended tax return claiming a refund based on a tax issue that is the subject of a test case involving a different taxpayer

11. Ethics Rulings on Responsibilities to Clients -- Rules 301 and 302.

1. A member may use an outside service to process tax returns provided (s)he takes all necessary precautions to prevent the release of confidential information.

2. A member may give a client's profit and loss percentages to a trade association provided the member has permission from the client.

3. A member who withdrew from an engagement because of fraud on a client's tax return should suggest that the successor obtain permission from the client to reveal the reasons for leaving.

4. A member may use a records-retention agency to store client records, but the responsibility for confidentiality still lies with the member.

5. A member may work for a municipality in verifying that proper amounts of taxes have been paid by the area businesses. Members are prohibited from releasing any confidential information obtained in their professional capacity.

6. A member may reveal a client's name without permission unless disclosure would constitute release of confidential information.

7. A member performing a consulting service must maintain the confidentiality of nonclient outside sources. If the client does not agree to this arrangement, the member should withdraw.

8. Knowledge and expertise obtained from a prior engagement may be used on behalf of a current client provided that the details of the other engagement are not revealed without permission.

9. A member who prepares a joint tax return should consider both spouses to be clients. After the spouses have divorced, the member will not violate Rule 301 if (s)he releases information to either spouse. But the legal implications should be discussed with an attorney.

10. A contingent fee is considered to be received when the performance of related services is complete and the fee or commission is determined.

11. Rule 301 does not prohibit a member from releasing confidential client information to the member's liability insurance carrier solely to assist the defense against a claim against the member.

12. A member may make disclosures necessary to initiate, pursue, or defend legal or alternative dispute resolution proceedings. Rule 301 does not prohibit compliance with laws or regulations.

13. A member who provides investment advisory services for an attest client for a percentage of the investment portfolio violates Rule 302 unless the fee is a specified percentage of the portfolio, the dollar amount of the portfolio is determined at the beginning of each quarterly (or longer) period and is adjusted only for the client's additions or withdrawals, and the fee arrangement is not renewed more often than quarterly.

12. Rule 501 -- *Acts Discreditable.* Interpretations.

a. Client records must be returned after a client demands them even if fees have not been paid. This ethical standard applies even if the state in which the member practices grants a lien on certain records in his/her possession.

  1) Client records are defined as "any accounting or other records belonging to the client that were provided to the member by or on behalf of the client."

  2) However, if this material does not fall within the narrow definition of client records, the duty to return is not absolute. If the material is not reflected in the client's books and records, and the client's financial information is therefore incomplete, it need not be returned if fees due the member with respect to a completed engagement have not been paid.

  3) Moreover, "a member's workpapers -- including, but not limited to, analyses and schedules prepared by the client at the request of the member -- are the member's property, not client records, and need not be made available."

b. When a court or administrative agency has made a final determination that a member has violated an antidiscrimination law, (s)he is deemed to have committed an act discreditable.

c. In a governmental audit, failure to adhere to applicable audit standards, guides, procedures, statutes, rules, and regulations is an act discreditable to the profession unless the report discloses the failure and the reasons therefor.

d. Negligently making materially false and misleading entries in the financial statements or records, negligently failing to correct materially false and misleading statements when the member has such authority, or negligently signing a document with materially false and misleading information is an act discreditable to the profession.

e. A member must follow GAAS and the reporting requirements of governing bodies, commissions, or regulatory agencies when performing attestation services for clients subject to their jurisdiction. If the requirements are not followed, the member should disclose the reasons in the report.

f.   Solicitation or knowing disclosure of May 1996 or later CPA examination questions or answers is an act discreditable.

g.   Failing to comply with laws regarding timely filing of personal or firm tax returns or the timely remittance of taxes collected on others' behalf is an act discreditable to the profession.

13. Rule 502 -- *Advertising and Other Forms of Solicitation*. Interpretations.

a.   False, misleading, or deceptive acts are prohibited because they are against public interest. These prohibited activities include

1) Creating false expectations of favorable results

2) Implying the ability to influence any court, regulatory agency, or similar body

3) Representing that specific services will be performed for a stated fee when it is likely at the time of the representation that the fees will be substantially increased and the client is not advised of the possibility

4) Other representations that would cause a reasonable person to misunderstand or be deceived

b.   Members are permitted to render services to clients of third parties. If the third party obtained its clients through advertising, the members must ascertain that all promotional efforts were within the Rules of Conduct. Members must not do through others what they are prohibited from doing themselves.

14. Rule 503 -- *Commissions and Referral Fees*. No interpretations.

15. Rule 505 -- *Form of Organization and Name*. Council Resolution and Interpretations.

a.   According to the relevant **AICPA Council Resolution**, a member may practice public accounting only in a firm or organization with the following characteristics:

1) CPAs must own a majority of the firm in terms of financial interests and voting rights.

2) A non-CPA owner, including an investor or commercial enterprise, must be actively engaged in providing services to clients as his/her/its principal occupation.

3) A CPA must have ultimate responsibility for all services provided.

4) A non-CPA owner must have a baccalaureate degree.

5) Non-CPA owners cannot hold themselves out to be CPAs, must abide by the Code, must complete the work-related CPE requirements, and are ineligible for AICPA membership.

6) Owners must own their equity in their own right.

7) Ownership must be transferred to the firm or to other qualified owners if the non-CPA ceases to be actively engaged in the firm.

b.   A member in the practice of public accounting may own an interest in a separate business that performs the types of services for which standards are established by bodies designated by the AICPA Council. If the member, individually or with his/her firm or members thereof, controls that business, all its owners and employees must comply with the Code. The business would therefore be within the definition of "member or member's firm." Absent such control, the member, but not the separate business, its other owners, and its employees, would be subject to the Code.

c.   The overriding focus of the Council Resolution (see above), the Code, and other AICPA requirements is that CPAs remain responsible, financially and otherwise, for the attest work performed to protect the public interest. However, in the context of alternative practice structures (APSs), CPAs may own the majority of financial interests in the attest firm, but substantially all revenues may be paid to another entity in return for services and the lease of employees, equipment, etc. Nevertheless, given the previously mentioned safeguards, if the CPA-owners of the attest firm remain financially responsible under state law, they are deemed to be in compliance with the financial-interests requirement of the Resolution.

16. Ethics Rulings on Other Responsibilities and Practices -- Rules 501-503, and 505.

1. A firm may arrange with a bank to collect notes issued by a client in payment of fees.

2. A CPA employed by a firm with one or more non-CPA practitioners must obey the Rules of Conduct. If the CPA becomes a partner, (s)he is responsible for compliance with the Rules of Conduct by all associated practitioners.

3. A CPA who teaches a course is responsible for determining that promotional efforts are within Rule 502.

4. A member not in public practice who is controller of a bank may use the CPA title on bank stationery and in paid advertisements.

5. A member who is an attorney and a CPA may use a letterhead with both titles on it.

6. A member interviewed by the press should observe the Rules of Conduct and not provide information that the member could not publish.

7. A member may serve as a director of a consumer credit company if (s)he does not audit the company and avoids conflicts of interest.

8. Although members may share an office, have the same employees, etc., they should not use a letterhead with both their names unless a partnership exists.

9. CPA firms that wish to form an association are not allowed to use the title of an association (e.g., Smith, Jones & Associates) because the public may believe a true partnership exists instead of an association. Each firm should use its own letterhead indicating the others as correspondents.

10. A CPA and a non-CPA who dissolve their partnership should sign an audit report, after dissolution, in a way not implying a partnership.

11. The title "nonproprietary partner" should not be used by someone who is not a partner because it is misleading.

12. A member may have his/her own CPA practice and be a partner of a public accounting firm all other members of which are noncertified.

14. A partnership may continue to practice using the managing partner's name as the firm name after (s)he withdraws. "And Company" should be added to the partnership name.

15. If a CPA forms a partnership with a non-CPA, the CPA is responsible for the non-CPA's violation of the Code.

16. A firm may use an established firm name in different states even though the roster of partners differs.

17. When two partnerships merge, they may retain a title that includes a retired or former partner's name.

18. The designation that a firm is a member of the AICPA is not allowed on the letterhead of a partnership unless all its partners or shareholders are members of the AICPA. In a mixed partnership, however, individual members may be designated as such.

20. A newsletter, tax booklet, etc., not prepared by the member or member's firm (member) may be attributed to the member if the member has a reasonable basis to believe the information attributed to the member is not false, misleading, or deceptive.

21. If a CPA in public practice forms a separate business that centralizes billing services for physicians, the CPA must comply with the Rules of Conduct because this service is of a type performed by public accountants.

22. CPA firms that are associated for joint advertising and other purposes should practice under their own names and indicate the association in other ways.

23. A CPA is not required to give the client a prepared tax return if the engagement to prepare the return is terminated prior to completion. Only the records originally provided by the client must be returned.

24. The designation "Personal Financial Specialists" may only be used on a letterhead when all partners or shareholders have the AICPA-awarded designation. However, the individual members holding the designation may use it after their names.

25. See Ethics Ruling 10 under Rule 302 on page 34.

26. A member is permitted to purchase a product and resell it to a client. Any profits collected are not considered a commission because the member had title to the product and assumed the risks of ownership.

27. A member may contract with a computer hardware maintenance servicer to support a client's computer operations and charge a higher fee to the client than the servicer charges the member.

28. A member's spouse may provide services to the member's attest client for a contingent fee or refer products or services for a commission to or from the member's attest client, provided the spouse's activities are separate from the member's practice and the member is not significantly involved. However, a conflict of interest issue may arise.

29. A CPA may not refer for commissions products to clients through distributors and agents when the CPA is performing any of the services described in Rule 503. If the services are not being provided by the CPA, (s)he may refer the products provided (s)he discloses the commissions to the clients.

30. Individuals associated with a client may be involved in an internal dispute, and each may request client records and other information. The CPA is under an obligation to supply certain information specified by Interpretation 501-1. This obligation is satisfied by turning over any required information to the designated client representative.

31. A CPA in partnership with non-CPAs may sign the firm name to a report and below it affix his/her name with the CPA designation. However, it must be clear that the partnership does not consist entirely of CPAs.

32. Unless permitted by contract, if the relationship of a member who is not an owner of a firm is terminated, (s)he may not take or retain originals or copies from the firm's client files or proprietary information without permission.

17. Stop and review! You have completed the outline for this subunit. Study multiple-choice questions 7 through 19 beginning on page 42.

C. Consulting Services

1.   The AICPA issues Statements on Standards for Consulting Services that apply to any AICPA member holding out as a CPA while performing consulting services. Only CS 100, *Consulting Services: Definitions and Standards*, has been issued to date.

  a.   The nature and scope of a consulting service is determined solely by the agreement between the practitioner and the client. The work is usually performed for the sole use and benefit of the client.

  b.   Consulting services employ the practitioner's skill, education, observations, experiences, and knowledge. CS 100 lists the following services:

    1)   Advisory services develop findings, conclusions, and recommendations. They include assistance in strategic planning, operational review and improvement study, analysis of an accounting system, and definition of requirements for an information system.

    2)   Implementation services include computer system installation and support, productivity improvement, and assisting with mergers.

    3)   Staff and support services include facilities management, programming, bankruptcy trusteeship, and controllership activities.

    4)   Consultations to provide counsel in a short time frame include reviewing client-prepared business plans and suggesting computer software.

    5)   Transaction services include preparing information to obtain financing, litigation support, and analysis of mergers and acquisitions.

    6)   Product services to provide the client with a product and associated professional services include sale and delivery of training programs, sale and implementation of software, and sale and installation of systems development methodologies.

  c.   Among the services not included under CS 100 are tax return preparation, personal financial planning, bookkeeping services, and services that are subject to other standards.

  d.   CS 100 states that the consulting process typically involves some combination of activities relating to

    1)   Determination of client objectives
    2)   Fact-finding
    3)   Definition of the problems or opportunities
    4)   Evaluation of alternatives
    5)   Formulation of proposed action
    6)   Communication of results
    7)   Implementation
    8)   Follow-up

  e.   The general standards for consulting services include the general standards for the profession given in the AICPA *Code of Professional Conduct*: professional competence, due professional care, planning and supervision, and sufficient relevant data.

    1)   In addition, CS 100 requires that the consulting services practitioner observe the following general standards for all consulting services:

      a)   Serve the client interest by seeking to accomplish the objectives established by the understanding with the client while maintaining integrity and objectivity.

      b)   Establish with the client a written or oral understanding about the responsibilities of the parties and the nature, scope, and limitations of the services to be performed.

      c)   Inform the client of conflicts of interest, significant reservations concerning the scope or benefits of the engagement, and significant engagement findings or events.

f.   Although a client may limit the gathering of relevant data, the CPA is not required to decline or withdraw from the consulting engagement if the limitation was part of the agreed-upon scope.

g.   Objectivity standards apply to all services provided by a CPA, but independence standards apply only to attestation services. Thus, they do not apply to consulting services.

h.   Performing consulting services does not impair independence for attestation services.

2. Stop and review! You have completed the outline for this subunit. Study multiple-choice questions 20 through 27 beginning on page 47.

D. **Personal Financial Planning.** Statements on Responsibilities in Personal Financial Planning Practice provide guidance but are not enforceable under Conduct Rule 202.

1. PFP 100 addresses engagement functions and responsibilities regarding assisting a client to define and achieve personal financial goals. A PFP engagement entails defining engagement objectives and specific procedures, developing a basis for recommendations, communicating them to the client, and identifying what needs to be done to take action on planning decisions. If undertaken by specific agreement with the client, a PFP engagement may also involve assisting the client in taking action, monitoring the client's progress, and updating recommendations and helping to revise planning decisions.

a.   A PFP engagement is not limited to, for example, compiling personal financial statements or giving tax advice.

b.   The CPA should conform to the relevant sections of the *Code of Professional Conduct* and to other applicable guidance, for example, the standards related to tax practice, consulting services, personal financial statements, and financial forecasts and projections.

c.   A CPA is not responsible for certain other PFP services barring a specific agreement with the client. These services include assisting the client to act on planning decisions, monitoring client progress in achieving goals, and updating recommendations and revising planning decisions.

2. PFP 200 furnishes guidance in a PFP engagement for using the work of other advisers and recommending other advisers.

3. PFP 300 pertains to implementation engagements, that is, to assisting the client to take action on planning decisions made during the PFP engagement, such as choosing investment advisers, budgeting, restructuring debt, or making specific investments.

4. PFP 400 applies to situations in which a CPA is specifically engaged to provide monitoring or updating services. Monitoring entails determining the client's progress in reaching established PFP goals. Updating entails revision of the client's financial plan and financial planning recommendations.

5. PFP 500 furnishes guidance when a CPA is engaged to develop PFP recommendations. Developing a basis for recommendations requires collection of information; analysis of the client's situation; and formulation, evaluation, and recommendation of strategies for achieving the client's goals.

6. Stop and review! You have completed the outline for this subunit. Study multiple-choice questions 28 and 29 on page 49.

E. **Disciplinary Systems within the Profession**

1. The AICPA's disciplinary mechanisms include the Professional Ethics Division and a joint trial board.

a.   The Professional Ethics Division investigates ethics violations. It imposes sanctions in less serious cases. For example, it may require an AICPA member to take additional CPE courses as a remedial measure.

    b.   More serious infractions come before a joint trial board panel, which can acquit, admonish, suspend for a period of not more than 2 years, or expel a member. It may also take such other disciplinary, remedial, or corrective action as it deems to be appropriate. The *CPA Newsletter* publishes information about suspensions and expulsions.

        1)   A decision of a trial board panel may be appealed to the full trial board. The determination of this body is conclusive.

        2)   Upon the member's exhaustion of legal appeals, automatic expulsion without a hearing results when a member has been convicted of, or has received an adverse judgment for,

           a)   Committing a felony
           b)   Willfully failing to file a tax return
           c)   Filing a fraudulent tax return on the member's or a client's behalf
           d)   Aiding in preparing a fraudulent tax return for a client

        3)   Automatic expulsion also occurs when a member's CPA certificate is revoked by action of any governmental agency, e.g., a state board of accountancy.

        4)   Expulsion from the AICPA or a state society does not bar the individual from the practice of public accounting.

           a)   A valid state-issued license is required to practice.

           b)   Thus, violation of a state code of conduct promulgated by a board of accountancy is more serious than expulsion from the AICPA because it may result in revocation of the CPA certificate.

    c.   Joint Ethics Enforcement Program (JEEP)

        1)   The AICPA and most state societies have agreements that permit referral of an ethics complaint either to the AICPA or to a state society.

        2)   The AICPA handles matters of national concern, those involving two or more states, and those in litigation.

           a)   JEEP also promotes formal cooperation between the ethics committees of the AICPA and of the state societies.

2.   The SEC and IRS may also discipline accountants.

    a.   The SEC may seek an injunction from a court to prohibit future violations of the securities laws. Moreover, under its Rule of Practice 2(e), the SEC may conduct administrative proceedings that are quasi-judicial.

        1)   Pursuant to such proceedings, it may suspend or permanently revoke the right to practice before the SEC, including the right to sign any document filed by an SEC registrant, if the accountant

           a)   Does not have the qualifications to represent others

           b)   Lacks character or integrity

           c)   Has engaged in unethical or unprofessional conduct

           d)   Has willfully violated, or willfully aided and abetted the violation of, the federal securities laws or their rules and regulations

        2)   Suspension by the SEC may also result from

           a)   Conviction of a felony, or a misdemeanor involving moral turpitude
           b)   Revocation or suspension of a license to practice
           c)   Being permanently enjoined from violation of the federal securities acts

        3)   Some Rule 2(e) proceedings have prohibited not only individuals but also accounting firms from accepting SEC clients.

4) Under the Securities Law Enforcement Act of 1990, the SEC may impose civil penalties in administrative proceedings of up to $100,000 for a natural person and $500,000 for any other person. Furthermore, the SEC may order a violator to account for and surrender any profits from wrongdoing and may issue cease-and-desist orders for violations.

b. The IRS may prohibit an accountant from practicing before the IRS if the person is incompetent or disreputable or does not comply with tax rules and regulations.

1) The IRS may also impose fines.

3. State boards of accountancy and state CPA societies also have codes of ethics and/or rules of conduct.

a. State boards are governmental agencies that license CPAs to use the designation "Certified Public Accountant" and prohibit non-CPAs from performing the attest function. They can suspend or revoke licensure through administrative process.

1) Like the AICPA, state boards have trial boards to conduct administrative hearings.

b. State societies are voluntary, private organizations that can admonish, suspend, or expel members.

c. CPA exam questions will not test individual state disciplinary systems.

4. Stop and review! You have completed the outline for this subunit. Study multiple-choice questions 30 through 33 on page 50.

MULTIPLE-CHOICE QUESTIONS

A. Code of Professional Conduct

1. Which of the following statements best explains why the CPA profession has found it essential to promulgate ethical standards and to establish means for ensuring their observance?

- A. A distinguishing mark of a profession is its acceptance of responsibility to the public.
- B. A requirement for a profession is to establish ethical standards that stress primarily a responsibility to clients and colleagues.
- C. Ethical standards that emphasize excellence in performance over material rewards establish a reputation for competence and character.
- D. Vigorous enforcement of an established code of ethics is the best way to prevent unscrupulous acts.

The correct answer is (A). *(CPA, adapted)*

REQUIRED: The best reason for promulgation of ethical standards.

DISCUSSION: According to Article II of the Principles section of the AICPA *Code of Professional Conduct*, "Members should accept the obligation to act in a way that will serve the public interest, honor the public trust, and demonstrate commitment to professionalism." According to the accompanying explanation, "A distinguishing mark of a profession is acceptance of its responsibility to the public."

Answer (B) is incorrect because the responsibility of CPAs is to a public that is not limited to clients and colleagues but includes all those who rely on their objectivity and integrity. Answer (C) is incorrect because excellence in performance is but one of the effects of accepting responsibility to the public. Answer (D) is incorrect because vigorous enforcement is significant but secondary to the creation of an environment in the profession that fosters voluntary adherence to ethical principles.

2. Which of the following reports may be issued only by an accountant who is independent of a client?

- A. Standard report on an examination of a financial forecast.
- B. Report on consulting services.
- C. Compilation report on historical financial statements.
- D. Compilation report on a financial projection.

The correct answer is (A). *(CPA, adapted)*

REQUIRED: The report issued only if the accountant is independent.

DISCUSSION: Conduct Rule 101 states, "A member in public practice shall be independent in the performance of professional services as required by standards promulgated by bodies designated by Counsel." Such standards include AT 200, *Financial Forecasts and Projections* (Statement on Standards for Attestation Engagements No. 1). AT 200 requires an accountant to be independent when performing an examination of prospective financial statements (financial forecasts and financial projections).

Answer (B) is incorrect because consulting services engagements do not require independence. Answers (C) and (D) are incorrect because compilations do not require independence.

3. To exercise due professional care, an auditor should

- A. Exercise professional skepticism.
- B. Examine all available corroborating evidence supporting management's assertions.
- C. Design the audit to detect all instances of fraud.
- D. Attain the proper balance of professional experience and formal education.

The correct answer is (A). *(CPA, adapted)*

REQUIRED: The requirement imposed by the due professional care standard.

DISCUSSION: Conduct Rule 201 requires auditors to exercise due professional care. Moreover, GAAS (see the third general standard) require that due professional care be exercised in the planning and performance of the audit and preparation of the report. Exercising due professional care requires professional skepticism. Thus, the auditor should have "an attitude that includes a questioning mind and a critical assessment of audit evidence" (AU 230).

Answer (B) is incorrect because sufficient competent evidence should be examined. Answer (C) is incorrect because the auditor should "plan and perform the audit to obtain reasonable assurance about whether the financial statements are free of material misstatement, whether caused by error or fraud" (AU 316). Answer (D) is incorrect because the proper balance of professional experience and formal education is required by the first general standard, which states that the audit must be performed by persons with adequate technical training and proficiency.

4. A CPA is permitted to disclose confidential client information without the consent of the client to

I. Another CPA firm if the information concerns suspected tax return irregularities

II. A state CPA society voluntary peer review board

    A. I only.

    B. II only.

    C. Both I and II.

    D. Neither I nor II.

The correct answer is (B). *(CPA, adapted)*

    REQUIRED: The event(s) that allow disclosure of confidential client data without the client's consent.

    DISCUSSION: Under Conduct Rule 301, a CPA may reveal confidential information without the client's permission for a state board- or state society-sponsored peer review. Identifying information revealed to the review team is precluded from disclosure. However, a CPA may not disclose information to another CPA firm without the client's permission or unless pursuant to a valid subpoena.

    Answers (A), (C), and (D) are incorrect because a CPA may disclose confidential client information in a state society-sponsored peer review but may not disclose information regarding suspected irregularities without a subpoena or the client's permission.

5. According to the ethical standards of the profession, which of the following acts is generally prohibited?

    A. Purchasing a product from a third party and reselling it to a client.

    B. Writing a financial management newsletter promoted and sold by a publishing company.

    C. Accepting a commission for recommending a product to an audit client.

    D. Accepting engagements obtained through the efforts of third parties.

The correct answer is (C). *(CPA, adapted)*

    REQUIRED: The prohibited act.

    DISCUSSION: Conduct Rule 503 prohibits a member in public practice from recommending any product or service to a client when the firm performs (1) an audit or review of financial statements, (2) a compilation of a financial statement that is reasonably expected to be used by a third party if the report does not disclose the CPA's lack of independence, or (3) an examination of prospective financial information for that client.

    Answer (A) is incorrect because an Ethics Ruling permits resale of products to clients. The profit is not a commission. Answer (B) is incorrect because, if the CPA reasonably concludes that the newsletter does not contain false, misleading, or deceptive information, the arrangement is not an ethics violation. Answer (D) is incorrect because an Interpretation of Rule 502 permits accepting engagements obtained through the efforts of third parties.

6. Which of the following is required for a CPA firm to designate itself as "Members of the American Institute of Certified Public Accountants" on its letterhead?

    A. All owners must be members.

    B. The owners whose names appear in the firm name must be members.

    C. At least one of the owners must be a member.

    D. The firm must be a dues-paying member.

The correct answer is (A). *(CPA, adapted)*

    REQUIRED: The requirement for a CPA firm to use the designation, "Members of the AICPA."

    DISCUSSION: Conduct Rule 505 states that a firm may not use the quoted designation unless all of its owners are members of the AICPA.

    Answer (B) is incorrect because all owners, not just certain owners, must be AICPA members. Answer (C) is incorrect because all owners must be members. Answer (D) is incorrect because the owners, not the firm, must be members of the AICPA.

B. Interpretations and Rulings

7. The concept of materiality would be least important to an auditor when considering the

    A. Adequacy of disclosure of a client's illegal act.

    B. Discovery of weaknesses in a client's internal control.

    C. Effects of a direct financial interest in the client on the CPA's independence.

    D. Decision whether to use positive or negative confirmations of accounts receivable.

The correct answer is (C). *(CPA, adapted)*

    REQUIRED: The item with respect to which materiality is least important.

    DISCUSSION: According to an Interpretation of Conduct Rule 101, independence is impaired if a CPA has any direct financial interest in a client. Whether this direct financial interest is material is irrelevant. The test of materiality is applied, however, if the financial interest is indirect.

    Answer (A) is incorrect because, in considering the effect of an illegal act on the financial statements and its implications for other aspects of the audit, materiality is important. Answer (B) is incorrect because an auditor who is considering internal control in a financial statement audit must make materiality judgments. Answer (D) is incorrect because materiality is one factor considered when deciding between positive or negative confirmations.

8. According to the profession's ethical standards, an auditor would be considered independent in which of the following instances?

A. The auditor is the officially appointed stock transfer agent of a client.

B. The auditor's checking account, which is fully insured by a federal agency, is held at a client financial institution.

C. The client sponsors an employee benefit plan in which the auditor participates.

D. The client is the only tenant in a commercial building owned by the auditor.

The correct answer is (B). *(CPA, adapted)*
REQUIRED: The circumstance in which the CPA would be considered independent.
DISCUSSION: A CPA's independence is not impaired with respect to a financial institution if checking accounts, savings accounts, or certificates of deposit are fully insured by the appropriate deposit insurance agency.
Answer (A) is incorrect because serving as a stock transfer or escrow agent, registrar, general counsel, or its equivalent involves performing management functions or making management decisions for the attest client (Interpretation 101-3). Answer (C) is incorrect because the auditor's independence is impaired with regard to the plan and its sponsor. Answer (D) is incorrect because leasing property to a client results in an indirect financial interest in that client.

9. A violation of the profession's ethical standards most likely would have occurred when a CPA

A. Expressed an unqualified opinion on the current year's financial statements when fees for the prior year's audit were unpaid.

B. Recommended a controller's position description with candidate specifications to an audit client.

C. Purchased a CPA firm's practice of monthly write-ups for a percentage of fees to be received over a 3-year period.

D. Made arrangements with a financial institution to collect notes issued by a client in payment of fees due for the current year's audit.

The correct answer is (A). *(CPA, adapted)*
REQUIRED: The violation of the ethical standards.
DISCUSSION: The AICPA has ruled that audit fees that are long past due take on the characteristics of a loan under Conduct Rule 101. An Ethics Ruling considers independence to be impaired if billed or unbilled fees, or a note arising from the fees, for client services rendered more than 1 year prior to the current year's report date remain unpaid when the current year's report is issued. However, this Ruling does not apply if the client is in bankruptcy. Moreover, long overdue fees do not preclude the CPA from performing services not requiring independence.
Answer (B) is incorrect because a CPA will not impair independence by recommending job position descriptions. However, the CPA will be in violation if (s)he is responsible for the ultimate hiring. Answer (C) is incorrect because no pronouncement prohibits purchase of a bookkeeping firm for a percentage of fees. Answer (D) is incorrect because the AICPA has ruled that this practice does not violate the Code.

10. According to the standards of the profession, which of the following circumstances will prevent a CPA performing audit engagements from being independent?

A. Obtaining a collateralized automobile loan from a financial institution client.

B. Litigation with a client relating to billing for consulting services for which the amount is immaterial.

C. Employment of the CPA's spouse as a client's internal auditor.

D. Acting as an honorary trustee for a not-for-profit organization client.

The correct answer is (C). *(CPA, adapted)*
REQUIRED: The circumstance preventing an auditor from being independent.
DISCUSSION: An accountant in public practice must be independent when conducting audit engagements. Interpretations of Conduct Rule 101, *Independence*, define certain family relationships that impair independence. Employment of the CPA's spouse in a sensitive position, such as internal auditor of the client, would impair the CPA's independence.
Answer (A) is incorrect because collateralized automobile loans are a type of permitted loan and do not impair independence. Answer (B) is incorrect because litigation regarding immaterial amounts, if the litigation is not related to the quality of the auditor's work product, does not impair independence. Answer (D) is incorrect because holding an honorary title such as trustee or director for a not-for-profit client will not affect independence.

11. Which of the following acts by a CPA who is not in public practice would most likely be considered a violation of the ethical standards of the profession?

A. Using the CPA designation without disclosing employment status in connection with financial statements issued for external use by the CPA's employer.

B. A CPA firm indicates on its letterhead that other CPA firms are correspondents rather than members of an association.

C. A member sells a newsletter bearing his/her name.

D. Compiling the CPA's employer's financial statements and making reference to the CPA's lack of independence.

The correct answer is (A). *(CPA, adapted)*

REQUIRED: The action violating ethical standards.

DISCUSSION: According to an Ethics Ruling, a member not in public practice who uses the CPA designation in a manner implying that (s)he is independent of the employer has committed a knowing misrepresentation of fact in violation of Conduct Rule 102.

Answer (B) is incorrect because CPA firms are not allowed to use a firm name indicating an association. The public may believe a partnership exists when it does not. Answer (C) is incorrect because a member may sell a newsletter bearing his/her name if the member writes it and ensures that those promoting it do not make statements about the author or his/her writings that violate the Conduct Rule on advertising and other forms of solicitation. Answer (D) is incorrect because an accountant may compile a nonpublic entity's financial statements if (s)he issues the appropriate report. The lack of independence, but not the reason therefor, should be disclosed (AR 100). If an accountant who is not independent is associated with the financial statements of a public entity (except a compilation report) but has not audited or reviewed them, (s)he must issue a disclaimer of opinion that states his/her lack of independence (AU 504).

12. According to the standards of the profession, which of the following activities may be required in exercising due professional care?

	Consulting with Experts	Obtaining Specialty Accreditation
A.	Yes	Yes
B.	Yes	No
C.	No	Yes
D.	No	No

The correct answer is (B). *(CPA, adapted)*

REQUIRED: The activity(ies) that may be required in exercising due professional care.

DISCUSSION: A CPA should undertake only those services that (s)he reasonably expects to complete with professional competence and should exercise due professional care in performing those services. According to an Interpretation of Conduct Rule 201, additional research or consultation with others may be necessary to gain sufficient competence to complete a service in accordance with professional standards. However, professional standards do not require specialty accreditation, although many CPAs choose to specialize in specific services.

Answers (A), (C), and (D) are incorrect because due professional care may require additional research or consultation with others but not specialty accreditation.

13. According to the profession's ethical standards, which of the following events may justify a departure from a Statement of Financial Accounting Standards?

	New Legislation	Evolution of a New Form of Business Transaction
A.	No	Yes
B.	Yes	No
C.	Yes	Yes
D.	No	No

The correct answer is (C). *(CPA, adapted)*

REQUIRED: The event(s), if any, that may justify departure from an SFAS.

DISCUSSION: In general, strict compliance with accounting principles is required. However, Conduct Rule 203 recognizes that, due to unusual circumstances, adhering to GAAP may cause financial statements to be misleading. An Interpretation under Conduct Rule 203 lists new legislation and the evolution of a new form of business transaction as events that may justify departure from an SFAS.

Answers (A), (B), and (D) are incorrect because new legislation and the evolution of a new form of business transaction may justify departure from an SFAS.

14. AICPA Conduct Rule 301, *Confidential Client Information*, is violated when a member in public practice

- A. Provides client profit and loss percentages to a trade association without the client's consent.
- B. Uses outside computer services to process tax returns.
- C. Performs consulting services for similar clients.
- D. Advises potential consulting services clients about previous problems on similar engagements.

The correct answer is (A). *(Publisher)*
REQUIRED: The activity that violates Rule 301.
DISCUSSION: An Ethics Ruling states that, prior to disclosing confidential client profit and loss percentages to a trade association, the CPA must have specific client consent.

Answer (B) is incorrect because, according to an Ethics Ruling, using outside computer services to process tax returns is permissible as long as client confidentiality is maintained. Answer (C) is incorrect because most CPAs perform consulting services for clients in the same or related industries. Answer (D) is incorrect because, according to an Ethics Ruling, CPAs must make full disclosure about any reservations concerning the usefulness of potential consulting services, especially those based on past experience with similar engagements. However, client confidentiality must be preserved or waived.

15. According to the ethical standards of the profession, which of the following acts is generally prohibited?

- A. Issuing a modified report explaining a failure to follow a governmental regulatory agency's standards when conducting an attest service for a client.
- B. Revealing confidential client information during a peer review of a professional practice by a team from the state CPA society.
- C. Accepting a contingent fee for representing a client in an examination of the client's federal tax return by an IRS agent.
- D. Retaining client records after an engagement is terminated prior to completion and the client has demanded their return.

The correct answer is (D). *(CPA, adapted)*
REQUIRED: The prohibited act.
DISCUSSION: Retention of client records after the client has demanded their return is an act discreditable to the profession and a violation of Conduct Rule 501. Even if the state in which a member practices grants a lien on certain records, this ethical standard is still applicable.

Answer (A) is incorrect because an Interpretation of Rule 501 states, "Failure to substantially follow such requirements is an act discreditable to the profession, unless the member discloses in his or her report that such requirements were not followed and the reasons therefor. Not following such requirements could require the member to modify his or her report." Answer (B) is incorrect because the prohibition does not apply to peer reviews under AICPA, a state CPA society, or state board of accountancy authority. Answer (C) is incorrect because an Interpretation of Rule 302 permits a contingent fee for representing a client in an examination of the client's federal or state income tax return by a revenue agent.

16. Conduct Rule 501 states that a member shall not commit an act discreditable to the profession. Which of the following would not be considered such an act?

- A. After the relationship of a member who is not an owner of the firm is terminated, the member takes copies from the firm's client files without permission.
- B. Retention of a client's records after a demand is made for them in a state that specifically grants the CPA a lien on all client records.
- C. Withholding as a result of nonpayment of fees for a completed engagement certain information about adjusting, closing, and consolidating entries not contained in the client's books.
- D. Failure to provide the client with client records that are part of the working papers.

The correct answer is (C). *(Publisher)*
REQUIRED: The act not considered discreditable to the profession.
DISCUSSION: The member's duty to return client records is absolute. However, the duty to return certain other information not reflected in the client's books and records is not absolute. Although the client's financial information may be incomplete as a result, if fees for a completed engagement have not been paid, such other information may be withheld. Thus, the duty to return is conditional upon payment of fees with respect to information such as adjusting, closing, combining, or consolidating entries and information normally found in books of original entry and general or subsidiary ledgers.

Answer (A) is incorrect because, under an Ethics Ruling, after the relationship of a member who is not an owner of the firm is terminated, the member may not take or retain copies or originals from the firm's client files or proprietary information without permission. However, an exception is made when such action is pursuant to a contractual arrangement. Answer (B) is incorrect because an Interpretation of Rule 501 states that an auditor who retains client records after a demand is made for their return is in violation of the Code even if state law permits the lien. Answer (D) is incorrect because, even though client records are part of the audit working papers, the CPA has an obligation to provide the client with those records.

17. With respect to records in a CPA's possession, the *Code of Professional Conduct* provides that

A. An auditor may retain client records if fees due with respect to a completed engagement have not been paid.

B. Worksheets in lieu of a general ledger belong to the auditor and need not be furnished to the client upon request.

C. Extensive analyses of inventory prepared by the client at the auditor's request are working papers that belong to the auditor and need not be furnished to the client upon request.

D. The auditor who returns client records must comply with any subsequent requests to again provide such information.

The correct answer is (C). *(CPA, adapted)*
REQUIRED: The correct statement regarding records in the CPA's possession.
DISCUSSION: According to an Interpretation of Rule 501, "A member's workpapers -- including, but not limited to, analyses and schedules prepared by the client at the request of the member -- are the member's property, not client records, and need not be made available."
Answer (A) is incorrect because client records must be returned even if fees have not been paid. Answer (B) is incorrect because worksheets in lieu of a general ledger are, in effect, the client's books of original entry and must be returned to the client upon request if the engagement is complete and fees are paid. Answer (D) is incorrect because, once the member has complied with the requirements for the return of client records, (s)he has no further obligation to provide such information.

18. According to Conduct Rule 502, advertising or other forms of solicitation that are false, misleading, or deceptive are not in the public interest, and AICPA members in public practice shall not seek to obtain clients in such a manner. Such activities include all the following except those that

A. Indicate the CPA's educational and professional attainments.

B. Imply the ability to influence a court.

C. Claim to be able to save the taxpayer 20% of a determined tax liability.

D. Create unjustified expectations of favorable results.

The correct answer is (A). *(Publisher)*
REQUIRED: The advertising activity not considered false, misleading, or deceptive.
DISCUSSION: Advertising and solicitation are acceptable as long as they do not involve falsehood or deception.
Answer (B) is incorrect because advertisement of influence over courts, tribunals, regulatory agencies, or a similar body or official is deceptive. Answer (C) is incorrect because a correct amount of tax liability exists and a claim to save a taxpayer part of that amount is deceptive. Answer (D) is incorrect because it is misleading to create false and unjustified expectations of favorable results.

19. The profession's ethical standards most likely are violated when a CPA represents that specific consulting services will be performed for a stated fee and it is apparent at the time of the representation that the

A. Actual fee would be substantially higher.

B. Actual fee would be substantially lower than the fees charged by other CPAs for comparable services.

C. CPA would not be independent.

D. Fee was a competitive bid.

The correct answer is (A). *(CPA, adapted)*
REQUIRED: The action that violates ethical standards regarding fee representation.
DISCUSSION: An Interpretation of Rule 502 prohibits forms of solicitation that are false, misleading, or deceptive. A representation that specific services will be performed for a stated fee, when it is likely at the time that the actual fee will be substantially higher, is a prohibited form of solicitation.
Answer (B) is incorrect because a CPA is permitted to charge lower fees than other CPAs. Answer (C) is incorrect because independence is required in an audit, but not for consulting services. Answer (D) is incorrect because competitive bids for consulting services are allowed.

C. Consulting Services

20. Nile, CPA, on completing an audit, was asked by the client to provide technical assistance in implementing a new computer system. The set of pronouncements designed to guide Nile in this engagement is the Statement(s) on

A.   Quality Control Standards.

B.   Auditing Standards.

C.   Standards for Accountants' Computer Services.

D.   Standards for Consulting Services.

The correct answer is (D). *(CPA, adapted)*
   REQUIRED: The authoritative pronouncements that guide CPAs in consulting engagements.
   DISCUSSION: The AICPA Management Consulting Services Executive Committee issues Statements on Standards for Consulting Services. These standards cover the following types of services: consultations, advisory services, implementation services, transaction services, staff and other support services, and product services.
   Answer (A) is incorrect because Statements on Quality Control Standards, which are issued by the Quality Control Standards Committee, concern quality control for the CPA firm as a whole. Answer (B) is incorrect because Statements on Auditing Standards, which are issued by the Auditing Standards Board, concern the attest function. Answer (C) is incorrect because Standards for Accountants' Computer Services do not exist. This activity is covered by Standards for Consulting Services.

21. Statements on Standards for Consulting Services are issued by the AICPA Management Consulting Services Executive Committee in connection with consulting services. Which of the following statements concerning consulting services is false?

A.   Consulting services differ fundamentally from the CPA's function of attesting to the assertions of other parties.

B.   Consulting services ordinarily involve external reporting.

C.   Most practitioners, including those who provide audit and tax services, also provide consulting services to their clients.

D.   The performance of consulting services for attest clients does not, in and of itself, impair independence.

The correct answer is (B). *(Publisher)*
   REQUIRED: The false statement about consulting services.
   DISCUSSION: The nature and scope of a consulting service is determined solely by the agreement between the practitioner and the client. The work is usually performed for the sole use and benefit of the client.
   Answer (A) is incorrect because, in an attest service, the practitioner expresses a conclusion about the reliability of a written assertion that is the responsibility of another party. Answer (C) is incorrect because consulting services have evolved from accounting-related matters to a broad array of services involving many technical disciplines, industry knowledge, and consulting skills. Answer (D) is incorrect because the CPA can maintain independence in fact and appearance for attestation clients while performing consulting services.

22. According to the profession's standards, which of the following are considered consulting services?

	Advisory Services	Implementation Services	Product Services
A.	Yes	Yes	Yes
B.	Yes	Yes	No
C.	Yes	No	Yes
D.	No	Yes	Yes

The correct answer is (A). *(CPA, adapted)*
   REQUIRED: The services that are considered to be consulting services.
   DISCUSSION: CS 100 specifically includes advisory services, implementation services, and product services as applicable consulting services. Other consulting services include consultations, transaction services, and staff and other support services.
   Answers (B), (C), and (D) are incorrect because advisory services, implementation services, and product services are all consulting services.

23. According to the standards of the profession, which of the following activities would most likely not impair a CPA's independence?

- A. Providing extensive advisory services for a client.

- B. Contracting with a client to supervise the client's office personnel.

- C. Signing a client's checks in emergency situations.

- D. Accepting a luxurious gift from a client.

The correct answer is (A). *(CPA, adapted)*
REQUIRED: The activity not impairing independence.
DISCUSSION: Performance of consulting services does not, in and of itself, impair the independence required for attest services (CS 100).
Answers (B) and (C) are incorrect because performing management functions impairs independence. Answer (D) is incorrect because acceptance of more than a token gift impairs independence.

24. Which of the following services may a CPA perform in carrying out a consulting service for a client?

I. Analysis of the client's accounting system
II. Review of the client's prepared business plan
III. Preparation of information for obtaining financing

- A. I and II only.

- B. I and III only.

- C. II and III only.

- D. I, II, and III.

The correct answer is (D). *(CPA, adapted)*
REQUIRED: The services that can be performed by a CPA carrying out consulting services.
DISCUSSION: Each of the three services may be performed as a consulting service. CS 100 describes analysis of an accounting system as an advisory service, review of a client's prepared business plan as a consultation, and preparation of information for obtaining financing as a transaction service. Other possible services are implementation services, staff and other support services, and product services.
Answer (A) is incorrect because preparation of information for obtaining financing is a transaction service. Answer (B) is incorrect because review of a client's prepared business plan is a consultation service. Answer (C) is incorrect because analysis of an client's accounting system is a consulting advisory service.

25. A pervasive characteristic of a CPA's role in a consulting services engagement is that of being a(n)

- A. Objective advisor.

- B. Independent practitioner.

- C. Computer specialist.

- D. Confidential reviewer.

The correct answer is (A). *(CPA, adapted)*
REQUIRED: The pervasive characteristic of a CPA's role in a consulting services engagement.
DISCUSSION: A consulting services practitioner should serve the client's interest by seeking to accomplish the objectives established by the understanding with the client while maintaining integrity and objectivity.
Answer (B) is incorrect because independence is not a requirement for consulting services. Answer (C) is incorrect because a consultant need not be a computer specialist to develop findings and provide recommendations to clients. Answer (D) is incorrect because a review is an attestation service.

26. Under the Statements on Standards for Consulting Services, which of the following statements best reflects a CPA's responsibility when undertaking a consulting services engagement? The CPA must

- A. Not seek to modify any agreement made with the client.

- B. Not perform any attest services for the client.

- C. Inform the client of significant reservations concerning the benefits of the engagement.

- D. Obtain a written understanding with the client concerning the time for completion of the engagement.

The correct answer is (C). *(CPA, adapted)*
REQUIRED: The CPA's responsibility in consulting services.
DISCUSSION: CS 100 establishes general standards applicable to all consulting services. Regarding communication with the client, CS 100 states that the client should be informed of significant reservations concerning the scope or benefits of the engagement.
Answer (A) is incorrect because CS 100 states that the understanding should be modified if circumstances require a significant change during the engagement. Answer (B) is incorrect because the performance of consulting services does not, in and of itself, impair independence. Answer (D) is incorrect because the understanding with the client may be oral.

27. According to the standards of the profession, which of the following events would require a CPA performing a consulting services engagement for a nonaudit client to withdraw from the engagement?

I. The CPA has a conflict of interest that is disclosed to the client, and the client consents to the CPA's continuing the engagement.

II. The CPA fails to obtain a written understanding from the client concerning the scope of the engagement.

    A. I only.

    B. II only.

    C. Both I and II.

    D. Neither I nor II.

The correct answer is (D). *(CPA, adapted)*
REQUIRED: The event(s) that would force a CPA to withdraw from a consulting engagement for a nonaudit client.
DISCUSSION: The additional general standards for consulting services require serving the client interest with integrity and objectivity. If a conflict of interest is disclosed and consented to, objectivity is not deemed to be impaired, and the professional service may be performed. In addition, an accountant may establish either a written or an oral understanding with the client regarding the scope of the engagement. Thus, an accountant need not withdraw from an engagement when the understanding of the scope of the engagement is not in writing.
Answers (A), (B), and (C) are incorrect because neither a disclosed and consented to conflict of interest nor a lack of a written agreement concerning the scope of the engagement forces a CPA to withdraw from a consulting engagement for a nonaudit client.

D. Personal Financial Planning

28. Personal financial planning services include those that are limited to

    A. Projecting future taxes.

    B. Compiling personal financial statements.

    C. Assisting the client to act on personal financial planning decisions.

    D. Preparing tax returns.

The correct answer is (C). *(Publisher)*
REQUIRED: The service that, by itself, does not constitute personal financial planning.
DISCUSSION: "Personal financial planning engagements are only those that involve developing strategies and making recommendations to assist a client in defining and achieving personal financial goals" (PFP 100). However, "other personal financial planning services," undertaken only by specific agreement with the client, include such services as assisting the client to act on personal financial planning decisions, monitoring progress in achieving goals, and updating recommendations and revising planning decisions.
Answers (A), (B), and (D) are incorrect because projecting future taxes, compiling personal financial statements, preparing tax returns, and tax advice are among the services specifically mentioned in PFP 100 as not, by themselves, constituting personal financial planning.

29. The guidance least likely to be applicable to personal financial planning (PFP) engagements is

    A. Conduct Rule 301, *Confidential Client Information*.

    B. Conduct Rule 101, *Independence*.

    C. Statement on Standards for Consulting Services.

    D. Statement on Standards for Attestation Engagements, Financial Forecasts, and Projections.

The correct answer is (B). *(Publisher)*
REQUIRED: The guidance least likely to be applicable to PFP engagements.
DISCUSSION: Personal financial planning is not a professional service that requires a CPA to be independent of the client. However, the CPA must follow the other pertinent Conduct Rules, including Rule 102, *Integrity and Objectivity*; Rule 201, *General Standards*; Rule 301, *Confidential Client Information*; and Rule 302, *Contingent Fees*.
Answer (A) is incorrect because PFP engagements require the CPA not to disclose confidential client information without the client's specific consent. Answer (C) is incorrect because the Statement on Standards for Consulting Services is relevant when a CPA values a business as part of a PFP engagement. Answer (D) is incorrect because a PFP engagement may entail preparation of personal financial statements or financial projections.

E. Disciplinary Systems within the Profession

30. Which entity has the authority to prohibit an individual from practicing public accounting?

- A. The Division for CPA Firms.
- B. A state board of accountancy.
- C. A state CPA society.
- D. A joint trial board of the AICPA.

The correct answer is (B). *(Publisher)*
REQUIRED: The entity with the authority to prohibit an individual from practicing public accounting.
DISCUSSION: A license issued by a state board of accountancy (a governmental agency) is a prerequisite to the practice of public accounting. Thus, suspension or revocation of that license precludes the practice of public accounting.
Answers (A), (C), and (D) are incorrect because the AICPA, state societies, and their subunits are not governmental bodies and have no authority to license public accountants.

31. If an ethics complaint is filed against a CPA, the matter

- A. Must be handled by the professional ethics division of the AICPA.
- B. Must be handled by a state CPA society.
- C. Must be handled by a joint trial board of the AICPA.
- D. May be handled, in most cases, by either the AICPA or a state CPA society.

The correct answer is (D). *(Publisher)*
REQUIRED: The body(ies) that handle(s) ethics complaints against CPAs.
DISCUSSION: Under the Joint Ethics Enforcement Program (JEEP), the AICPA and most state societies have agreements that permit referral of an ethics complaint either to the AICPA or to a state society. However, the AICPA handles matters of national concern, those involving two or more states, and those in litigation.
Answers (A), (B), and (C) are incorrect because JEEP permits referral of many cases either to the AICPA or to a state society.

32. A CPA may be automatically expelled from membership in the AICPA for

	Conviction of a Felony	Revocation of CPA License	Willful Failure to File a Tax Return
A.	Yes	Yes	Yes
B.	Yes	Yes	No
C.	Yes	No	Yes
D.	No	Yes	No

The correct answer is (A). *(Publisher)*
REQUIRED: The grounds for automatic expulsion from the AICPA.
DISCUSSION: Automatic expulsion without a hearing results when a member has been convicted of, or has received an adverse judgment for, committing a felony, willfully failing to file a tax return, filing a fraudulent tax return on the member's or a client's behalf, or aiding in preparing a fraudulent tax return for a client. Automatic expulsion also occurs when a member's CPA license is revoked by action of any governmental agency.
Answers (B), (C), and (D) are incorrect because willful failure to file a tax return, revocation of the CPA's license to practice, and conviction of a felony are all bases for expulsion from the AICPA.

33. The SEC can suspend or revoke the right of an accountant to sign any document filed by an SEC registrant if the accountant

	Lacks Integrity	Engages in Unethical Conduct
A.	No	No
B.	No	Yes
C.	Yes	No
D.	Yes	Yes

The correct answer is (D). *(Publisher)*
REQUIRED: The basis for discipline by the SEC.
DISCUSSION: Under its Rule of Practice 2(e), the SEC may conduct quasi-judicial proceedings. Pursuant to such proceedings, it may suspend or permanently revoke the right to practice before the SEC, including the right to sign any document filed by an SEC registrant, if the accountant does not have the qualifications to represent others, lacks character or integrity, has engaged in unethical or unprofessional conduct, or has willfully violated the federal securities laws or their rules and regulations.
Answers (A), (B), and (C) are incorrect because unethical conduct and lack of character or integrity are bases for SEC discipline.

Use Gleim's *CPA Test Prep* for interactive testing with over 2,000 additional multiple-choice questions!

OOF QUESTION *(Publisher)* 20-25 minutes

The AICPA's *Code of Professional Conduct* consists of 11 Rules listed as A through K. The AICPA also issues Interpretations of the Rules and Ethics Rulings on specific fact situations.

Required

For the following 12 cases based on AICPA Ethics Interpretations or Rulings, indicate which Conduct Rule (A through K) most clearly applies. Each answer may be used once, more than once, or not at all. Also indicate whether each case illustrates an ethics violation (V) or no ethics violation (N).

1. A CPA is not competent to perform the tasks of a newly hired systems analyst. However, the CPA is qualified to supervise and evaluate this specialist's work.

2. A member in public practice serves as a director of a bank when the member's clients are bank customers and engage in significant transactions with the bank. The member's fiduciary obligations to the bank may interfere with the member's ability to serve his/her clients.

3. A member's spouse provides services to a member's attest clients for a contingent fee. The spouse's activities are separate from the member's and the member is not significantly involved.

4. A member who specializes in bankruptcy reveals his/her clients' names.

5. A member represents that specific services will be performed for a stated fee when it is likely at the time of representation that the fees will be substantially increased and the client was not told of the possibility.

6. A CPA firm has both partners who are CPAs and partners who are not CPAs.

7. A member has a $9,500 aggregate outstanding balance of credit cards and cash advances from a client financial institution.

8. A CPA knowingly recommends a tax position to a client that (s)he feels does not have a realistic possibility of being sustained if challenged.

9. A CPA expresses an unqualified audit opinion on financial statements containing a justified departure from established accounting principles based upon evolution of a new form of business transaction.

10. A member who provides extended audit services to a client accepts an attestation engagement to report on the client's assertion about the effectiveness of internal control over financial reporting.

11. A member leases property from a client under an operating lease made under normal procedures.

12. A member undertakes a professional service but a conflict of interest arises that may impair objectivity. The conflict is disclosed to the client who consents to the performance of the service.

A. Rule 101 -- Independence

B. Rule 102 -- Integrity and Objectivity

C. Rule 201 -- General Standards

D. Rule 202 -- Compliance with Standards

E. Rule 203 -- Accounting Principles

F. Rule 301 -- Confidential Client Information

G. Rule 302 -- Contingent Fees

H. Rule 501 -- Acts Discreditable

I. Rule 502 -- Advertising and Other Forms of Solicitation

J. Rule 503 -- Commissions and Referral Fees

K. Rule 505 -- Form of Organization and Name

Knowledge Tested

1. AICPA Conduct Rules
2. AICPA Ethics Interpretations
3. AICPA Ethics Rulings

Authors' Comments

This question requires a matching of the 11 AICPA Rules (discussed on pages 20 through 36) with 12 fact situations. You must also indicate whether a *Code of Professional Conduct* violation occurred. The answer sheet will appear as follows:

1.	Ⓐ Ⓑ Ⓒ Ⓓ Ⓔ Ⓕ Ⓖ Ⓗ Ⓘ Ⓙ Ⓚ	Ⓝ Ⓥ
2.	Ⓐ Ⓑ Ⓒ Ⓓ Ⓔ Ⓕ Ⓖ Ⓗ Ⓘ Ⓙ Ⓚ	Ⓝ Ⓥ
3.	Ⓐ Ⓑ Ⓒ Ⓓ Ⓔ Ⓕ Ⓖ Ⓗ Ⓘ Ⓙ Ⓚ	Ⓝ Ⓥ

There are 24 items, and your score will be computed as the number of correct responses divided by 24, times the points available on this question. On OOF questions in this *CPA Review* book, you should write the correct answer(s) next to each item number, as you will on your actual CPA exam. Plan to transfer your answers to the AICPA optically scannable answer sheet when you have answered all items in a question.

Even if you do not feel knowledgeable as you begin to answer this and other OOF or essay questions, force yourself to persevere and answer them to the best of your ability. This effort is required on the CPA exam -- practice makes perfect.

1. The correct answer is (C, N).

DISCUSSION: Rule 201, *General Standards*, requires members to undertake only those services in which they are competent. CPAs must have knowledge of the profession's standards, techniques, and technical subject matter involved in an engagement and the ability to use sound judgment when applying such knowledge. A CPA may be able to supervise and evaluate a specialist's work without having the specialist's skills.

2. The correct answer is (B, F, V).

DISCUSSION: Rule 301, *Confidential Client Information*, precludes a member in public practice from disclosing confidential client information without the client's consent. A member serving as a bank director cannot violate the confidentiality of client information. These circumstances may also indicate a conflict of interest in violation of Rule 102. It is usually not desirable for a member in public practice to serve as a bank director when clients are likely to have significant transactions with the bank. The CPA's fiduciary responsibilities to the bank may interfere with the CPA's responsibility to serve his/her clients.

3. The correct answer is (G, N).

DISCUSSION: Rule 302, *Contingent Fees*, prohibits contingent fees for audits, reviews, or compilations when the report will be used by third parties and the report does not disclose the lack of independence, examinations of prospective financial information, and preparation of original or amended tax returns or claims for refund. An Ethics Ruling permits a spouse to provide contingent fee services to a member's attest clients if the spouse's activities are separate from the member's and the member is not significantly involved.

4. The correct answer is (F, V).

DISCUSSION: Rule 301, *Confidential Client Information*, precludes a member in public practice from disclosing confidential client information without the client's consent. A member who specializes in bankruptcy who reveals his/her clients' names may be disclosing confidential information indicating that those clients are in financial difficulty.

5. The correct answer is (I, V).

DISCUSSION: Rule 502, *Advertising and Other Forms of Solicitation*, precludes obtaining clients by advertising in a false, misleading, or deceptive manner. This prohibition extends to representing that specific services will be performed for a stated fee when it is likely that the fees will have substantially increased at the time of the representation and the client is not told of the possibility.

6. The correct answer is (K, N).

DISCUSSION: Under Rule 505, *Form of Organization and Name*, the AICPA does not prohibit non-CPA partners as long as the member is practicing in a form of organization permitted by state law or regulation that conforms with the application Council Resolution (see B.15.a.).

7. The correct answer is (A, V).

DISCUSSION: Rule 101, *Independence*, requires members to be and appear independent when performing attestation services. Although certain restrictions are placed on loans, credit card debts and cash advances are permitted if the aggregate outstanding balance on the current statement is $5,000 or less by the payment due date. The size of the balance therefore indicates a violation of the Code.

8. The correct answer is (D, V).

DISCUSSION: Rule 202, *Compliance with Standards*, requires a member performing auditing, review, compilation, management consulting, tax, or other services to comply with the standards developed by the relevant standard-setting bodies. A CPA who recommends a tax position to a client that (s)he believes will not have a realistic possibility of being sustained violates TX 112, *Tax Return Positions*.

9. The correct answer is (E, N).

DISCUSSION: Rule 203, *Accounting Principles*, requires that members not express an opinion that financial statements are in conformity with GAAP if the statements contain departures from accounting principles that have a material effect on the statements taken as a whole, unless the departures are covered by unusual circumstances or are based upon unusual events such as new legislation or evolution of a new form of business transaction. In this case, the departure from GAAP is justified by the evolution of a new form of business transaction and there is no violation of the Code.

10. The correct answer is (A, N).

DISCUSSION: Independence is not impaired if management assumes responsibility for establishing and maintaining internal control, management does not rely on the member's work as the primary basis for the assertion, and the member complies with Interpretation 101-13, Extended Audit Services.

11. The correct answer is (A, N).

DISCUSSION: Rule 101, *Independence*, requires members to be independent when performing attestation services. An Ethics Ruling specifically permits a CPA to lease property from a client under an operating lease entered into in accordance with normal procedures, terms, and requirements. In contrast, a capital lease impairs independence because it involves a loan. No violation exists because the lease is an operating lease.

12. The correct answer is (B, N).

DISCUSSION: Rule 102, *Integrity and Objectivity*, requires CPAs to be free of conflicts of interest and not knowingly misrepresent facts or judgments when performing professional services. However, if the conflict is disclosed to the appropriate parties and their consent is obtained, Rule 102 is not violated.

ESSAY QUESTION *(Publisher)* 15-20 minutes

Each of the following cases involves a member of the AICPA in the practice of public accounting whose spouse is employed by the client.

1. The spouse of the member is an accountant for the client. The member provides bookkeeping services to the client.
2. The spouse of the member is a purchasing agent for the client but does not exercise significant influence over the client's operating policies. The member participates in an engagement to audit the client's financial statements.
3. The spouse is employed by the client in a position that neither permits significant influence over client policies nor is audit sensitive. However, the spouse participates in the client's employee stock ownership plan.

Required

Explain in each case whether the member's independence has been impaired.

Knowledge Tested

1. AICPA Conduct Rule 101
2. AICPA Interpretations Under Rule 101

Authors' Comments

This essay question requires specific knowledge of Conduct Rule 101, which concerns the independence of AICPA members in the practice of public accounting. A member in public practice must maintain independence, in fact and in appearance, when performing certain services (e.g., attestation engagements). This question also requires specific knowledge of the AICPA's Interpretations of this rule. For example, independence is impaired when a member has a direct financial interest in a client.

1. This case involves two issues: (a) whether providing bookkeeping services impairs independence and (b) whether a spouse's employment by the client impairs independence. The first issue is addressed by Interpretation 101-3, *Performance of Other Services*. Before a member performs other nonattest services for an attest client, (s)he must evaluate the effect on independence. Performing management functions or making management decisions will impair independence. Thus, the member should reach an understanding about the objectives and limitations of the engagement, the services to be performed, and management's and the member's responsibilities. This understanding preferably should be documented in an engagement letter indicating the member will not perform management functions or make management decisions. The member also should be satisfied that the client has an informed judgment about the results of the other services and understand its responsibility to designate a manager(s) to oversee the services; to evaluate the adequacy of the services and any findings; to make management decisions, including accepting responsibility for the results; and to establish and maintain internal controls. For example, when providing bookkeeping services, independence would not be impaired if the member records transactions for which management has approved the account classifications, posts coded transactions to the general ledger, prepares financial statements based on the trial balance, posts client-approved entries to the trial balance, proposes entries or other changes in the financial statements, or provides data processing services. However, determining or changing entries, account codings, or classifications for transactions, and other accounting records without client approval; authorizing or approving transactions; preparing source documents or originating data; and making changes in source documents without client approval are activities that would impair independence.

The second issue must be considered under Interpretation 101-9, *The Meaning of Certain Independence Terminology and the Effect of Family Relationships on Independence*. Under that Interpretation, independence of the member is not normally impaired by a spouse's employment by the client unless (a) the spouse has significant influence over the client's operating, financial, or accounting policies or (b) the spouse has an audit-sensitive position.

2. Under an Interpretation of Rule 101, independence is considered to be impaired if a spouse or dependent of an individual participating in the engagement exercises significant influence over the client's operating, financial, or accounting policies or occupies an audit-sensitive position. Activities are audit-sensitive if they are normally subject to significant internal accounting controls. Examples of audit-sensitive positions are cashier, internal auditor, and purchasing agent.

3. Any financial interest of the spouse in the stock of the client, e.g., through an ESOP, is ascribed to the member. If the spouse has a right of possession of stock in the client, the financial interest is direct. Any direct financial interest impairs independence if it is held during the period of the engagement or at the time of expressing an opinion. If the right of possession has not yet accrued to the spouse, the financial interest is indirect. It impairs the member's independence only if it is material to the member's net worth.

STUDY UNIT 2: CPAs AND THE LAW

14 pages of outline
40 multiple-choice questions
2 OOFs and 1 essay

A. *Common-Law Liability to Clients and Third Parties*
B. *Federal Statutory Liability*
C. *Privileged Communication and Confidentiality*

This study unit encompasses an accountant's responsibility to clients and third parties under common law and federal statutes. The focus is to whom and for what accountants have responsibility (liability). Also covered are ownership and confidentiality of working papers, tax return preparation responsibility, and accountants' privileged communications.

A. **Common-Law Liability to Clients and Third Parties**. Certified public accountants may be liable to clients and third parties based on the common-law doctrines of breach of contract, negligence, or fraud.

   1. **Contractual Liability**. The accountant-client contract is a personal service contract.

      a. All of the elements of a contract must exist: offer, acceptance, consideration, competent parties, and legal purpose.

      b. The accountant-client contractual agreement should be documented in an engagement letter.

         1) An engagement letter sets forth the contract between the accountant and the client. It is not absolutely required, but its use is common business practice.

      c. The accountant is implicitly bound by the contract to perform the engagement in compliance with the standards of the profession.

      d. An engagement letter may provide for services or procedures beyond those required by generally accepted auditing standards (GAAS) or generally accepted accounting principles (GAAP).

         1) EXAMPLE: Provision for positive confirmation of all accounts receivable might be made.

      e. The accountant is usually an independent contractor, not an agent or employee, of the client.

         1) The accountant may not delegate responsibility for the engagement to another without the client's permission.

         2) The accountant may hire another as an employee to assist in performing the engagement.

         3) The accountant may perform services for the client's competitors.

      f. Accountants are liable for breach of contract both to clients and to those third parties who are intended beneficiaries of the contract.

         1) Intended beneficiaries and clients are in privity of contract with the CPA.

         2) **Privity** means a direct contractual relationship. It confers standing to sue.

      g. Damages for breach of contract depend on the nature of the breach.

         1) Recovery for breach of contract is ordinarily limited to compensatory damages; punitive damages are rarely allowed.

         2) If the breach is material, expectancy damages may be recovered. Expectancy damages are the value of the benefit expected from the contract.

    3) If the breach is minor, i.e., if the accountant substantially performs all contractual duties, the accountant is entitled to the agreed-upon fee minus losses suffered.

 2. **Liability for Negligence**. An accountant may be liable in tort to a client for losses caused by the accountant's negligence.

   a. A client suing an accountant for negligence must establish the following:

    1) The accountant owed the client a duty.
    2) The accountant breached this duty.
    3) The accountant's breach proximately caused the client's injury.
    4) The client suffered damages.

   b. The accountant's duty is to exercise reasonable care and diligence. The accountant should have the degree of skill commonly possessed by other accountants. Thus, (s)he should have the judgment, skill, competence, and knowledge of an ordinarily prudent accountant in the same or similar circumstances.

   c. Negligence (failure to exercise reasonable care and diligence) may be an act or an omission. An omission is a failure to act given a duty to act, e.g., not counting inventory during an audit.

   d. Courts have held that auditors are not guarantors and therefore do not have a general duty to discover fraud or embezzlement.

    1) Nevertheless, an auditor is held liable for failure to discover fraud or embezzlement when the auditor's negligence prevented discovery.

     a) EXAMPLE: An auditor who fails to follow GAAS and does not discover embezzlement will probably be liable if compliance with GAAS would have revealed the embezzlement.

     b) GAAS now require an auditor to plan and perform the audit to provide reasonable assurance about whether the financial statements are free of material misstatement, whether caused by error or fraud.

   e. Accountants may be liable for failure to communicate to the client findings or circumstances that indicate

    1) The possibility of misstatements in the accounting records, or
    2) The commission of fraud.

   f. The CPA's duty extends to correcting his/her report if (s)he subsequently discovers it is erroneous.

    1) The CPA should ordinarily disclose the new information to any user relying on the previous report. An attorney should be consulted.

   g. A lesser standard applies to an engagement to prepare unaudited financial statements.

    1) The accountant must still adhere to standards of loyalty and honesty.
    2) A client may still recover for losses resulting from negligence.

 3. **Liability for Fraud**. An accountant is liable for losses that result from his/her common-law fraud.

   a. A finding of fraud requires proof of the following:

    1) The accountant made a misstatement.
    2) The misstatement was made with scienter, that is, knowingly.

     a) EXAMPLE: An accountant is engaged to audit a company's financial statements. To increase profits from the engagement, the accountant planned to, and did, omit necessary audit procedures. The accountant committed fraud.

        3)   The misstatement was of a material fact.
        4)   The misstatement induced reliance.
        5)   Another person justifiably relied on the misstatement.
        6)   The other person suffered a loss.

    b.   The element of intent, with regard to fraud, may be satisfied by proof of a reckless disregard for the truth.

        1)   Reckless disregard for the truth is synonymous with gross negligence.

            a)   Either is considered constructive fraud.

    c.   Liability is to all foreseeable users of the work product.

        1)   Privity is not required. Privity, in this context, means that the accountant and the plaintiff were parties to the contract that resulted in the loss.

        2)   The status of foreseeable user provides the standing to sue.

4.   Compliance with professional standards may be raised in defense to malpractice lawsuits.

    a.   GAAS prescribe rules and procedures for conducting audits.

        1)   **Audits** are examinations made to determine whether recorded financial information fairly reflects the economic events that occurred during a given period.

    b.   GAAP prescribe rules for presentation of financial information.

    c.   Failure to comply with GAAS or GAAP is prima facie evidence of malpractice.

    d.   Courts have occasionally insisted on higher standards than the professional standards.

5.   **Disclaimers**. An accountant's effort to disclaim liability by including an exculpatory clause in a contract is usually not favored by the courts.

    a.   A court will consider the relative bargaining positions of the parties.
    b.   Properly worded disclaimers might succeed.
    c.   Unclear disclaimers are construed against the accountant.

NOTE: Disclaimers are often invalidated because they violate public policy. For purposes of the CPA exam, assume that disclaimers are usually ineffective.

6.   **Contractual Defenses**. Typical defenses to breach of contract include the following:

    a.   Failure of consideration
    b.   Alleged obligation not within scope of contract
    c.   Full or substantial performance rendered
    d.   Illegal purpose
    e.   Suspension or termination of performance justified because of client's breach
    f.   Failure of a condition precedent

7.   **Defenses to Negligence**. Typical defenses to negligence include the following:

    a.   The alleged duty was not owed.

    b.   The accountant did not breach the duty.

        1)   The accountant exercised reasonable care.

        2)   Compliance with the relevant professional standards is evidence of, but not necessarily sufficient proof of, the accountant's exercising the diligence due under the circumstances.

      c.   The plaintiff did not suffer a loss.

      d.   The accountant's behavior was not the cause of the party's loss; e.g., it was caused by the party's own negligence/fault or by a third party.

      e.   The plaintiff's loss was not reasonably foreseeable (or the plaintiff was neither a party nor a primary beneficiary of a contract with defendant).

      f.   The person alleging harm assumed the risk, e.g., by accepting a contract containing an effective disclaimer.

8.   An accountant must comply with law and is responsible for exercising independent professional judgment.

      a.   An accountant might not incur liability for refusing to sign a tax return in which the client insists on taking a position contrary to established law.

9.   **Defenses to Fraud**. A plaintiff has the burden to prove each element of fraud, usually by clear and convincing evidence. Credible evidence that the accountant can introduce to disprove one of those elements tends to negate liability.

10.   **Liability to Third Parties**

      a.   Liability for fraud extends to all foreseeable users of the accountant's work product.

      b.   The traditional view is that an accountant is liable for negligence only to a plaintiff that was in privity of contract with the accountant or a primary beneficiary of the engagement. (This was the holding of the *Ultramares* case.) Typically, a third party is considered to be a **primary beneficiary** if the following apply:

          1)   The accountant is retained principally to benefit the third party.

          2)   The third party is identified.

          3)   The benefit pertains to a specific transaction; that is, the accountant knows the particular purpose for which the third party will use the work.

              a)   EXAMPLE: Smith, CPA, was engaged by Client, Inc. to audit Client's annual financial statements. Client told Smith that the audited financial statements were required by Bank in connection with a loan application. Bank is a primary beneficiary and may recover damages caused by the CPA's negligence.

          4)   A primary beneficiary is the same as an intended third-party beneficiary in general contract law.

      c.   The primary beneficiary test for negligence liability has been abandoned by many states. Other approaches include the following:

          1)   One approach imposes liability if the accountant knows

              a)   The financial statements are for a third party's benefit, and
              b)   The third party is identified.

                 i)   EXAMPLE: Smith, CPA, was engaged by Client, Inc. to audit its annual financial statements. Client told Smith that the statements would be distributed to Client's three primary suppliers. Smith will be liable to the identified suppliers for negligence if they suffer losses by relying on the statements in extending credit to Client.

2)   The Restatement of Torts, Second, extends the accountant's liability to foreseen third parties (foreseen users and users within a foreseen class of users). This approach appears to be the majority rule.

   a)   **Foreseen third parties** are those the accountant knows will use the information.

      i)   They also include persons who use the information in a way the accountant knows it will be used.

   b)   The accountant's liability is limited to losses that foreseeably result from his/her negligence.

   c)   EXAMPLE: Smith, CPA, was engaged by Client, Inc. to audit its annual financial statements. Client's president told Smith that the financial statements would be distributed to South Bank in connection with a loan application. Smith was negligent in performing the audit. Subsequently, the financial statements were given to West Bank as well. West Bank lent Client $50,000 in reliance on the financial statements. West Bank suffered a loss on the loan. Smith is liable to West Bank because it is within a foreseen class of users, and the loan is a transaction similar to that for which the financial statements were audited.

3)   Some courts adopt a broader approach based on ordinary principles of negligence law.

   a)   The accountant is liable to all reasonably foreseeable third parties.

   b)   **Reasonably foreseeable third parties** are all members of the class of persons whose reliance on the financial statements the accountant may reasonably anticipate.

      i)   EXAMPLE: Smith, CPA, is engaged to audit the annual financial statements of Client. Smith is not informed of the intended use of the financial statements. However, Smith knows that Client's financial statements are routinely distributed to lessors, suppliers, trade creditors, and lending institutions. Client uses the financial statements, which were negligently prepared, to obtain a lease from XYZ Leasing, Inc., a foreseeable party. Smith will be liable to XYZ because XYZ is a member of a class of reasonably foreseeable third parties.

11.   Stop and review! You have completed the outline for this subunit. Study multiple-choice questions 1 through 12 beginning on page 67.

B.   **Federal Statutory Liability**. Especially significant is an accountant's exposure to liability under the federal securities laws, which are explained in Study Unit 12, Securities.

   1.   **Civil Liability under the Securities Act of 1933**

      a.   An accountant who prepares and certifies the financial statements included in a registration statement or prospectus is civilly liable under Section 11 if both of the following conditions apply:

         1)   The statements

            a)   Include a misstatement of a material fact or

            b)   Omit a material fact which was required by the act or was necessary to prevent the statements from being misleading.

         2)   Loss (damages) was incurred by a person who purchased the securities.

b. Liability extends to acquirers of a security described in the registration statement or the prospectus. Privity of contract is not required.

1) EXAMPLE: Public Corp. engages Accountant to review events subsequent to the date of a certified balance sheet to ascertain whether any material change has occurred that should be disclosed to prevent the balance sheet figures from being misleading with regard to the registration statement required for a bond issue. Accountant does not report a material uninsured loss. Astute purchases some of the bonds. Public files for protection from creditors under the Bankruptcy Act. It defaults in payment of interest on the bonds. No contract exists between Astute and Accountant. Nevertheless, Accountant is liable to Astute for damages incurred as a result of the failure to report the material fact.

c. The accountant is prima facie liable for such misstatements or omissions. The plaintiff need not prove reliance, negligence, or fraud.

d. The act requires the accountant to exercise due diligence in preparing the financial statements.

1) Due diligence means the accountant reasonably believed, at the time the registration statement became effective, that the financial statements were true and did not suffer from an omission or misstatement of a material fact.

a) The belief must be based on a reasonable investigation.

b) The standard of reasonableness is that of a prudent person engaged in the management of his/her own property.

c) The essence of due diligence is that the misstatements or omissions were not caused by the accountant's negligence.

2) Failure to comply with GAAP or GAAS is significant evidence of, but may or may not be sufficient to prove, failure to exercise due diligence.

e. **Defenses** to accountant liability under Section 11 include the following:

1) No misstatement or omission occurred.
2) The misstatements or omissions did not concern material facts.
3) The plaintiff knew of the misstatements or omissions.
4) The accountant exercised due diligence.
5) Plaintiff's loss was not caused by accountant's omission or misstatement.
6) The statute of limitations has expired.

f. A purchaser's damages under Section 11 are measured as the difference between the price paid for the security and one of the following:

1) The market value of the security at the time of suit, if the security was not sold

2) The sales price, if the security was sold before suit

3) The sales price, if the security was disposed of after suit and the sales price exceeded the market value of the security at the time the suit was brought

a) EXAMPLE: Reni successfully sued CPA under Section 11. Reni paid $50 per share for the stock that was the basis for the suit. The suit was brought on June 1. The market value of the stock on June 1 was $45. Reni sold the stock for $47 on June 5 before the jury reached a verdict. Reni's damages are $3 per share ($50 – $47). If Reni had not sold the stock, damages would be $5 per share ($50 – $45). If Reni had sold the stock on June 5 for $40, damages would be $5 per share ($50 – $45).

g. **Statute of limitations**. A legal action under Section 11 must be commenced before the earlier of

   1) Three years after the security was offered to the public, or
   2) One year after the misstatement was or should have been discovered.

h. An accountant may be civilly liable for aiding and abetting securities fraud in new issues under Section 17. Section 17 prohibits the use of any untrue or misleading statement in the offer or sale of any security.

2. **Criminal Liability under the Securities Act of 1933**. An accountant is subject to criminal penalties under Section 24 of the 1933 act. Liability is based on willful violations of the act in the sale of securities.

   a. Willful violations are essentially fraud.
   b. The maximum penalty is 5 years' incarceration and a $10,000 fine.

3. **Civil Liability under the Securities Exchange Act of 1934**. Accountants may incur civil liability to third parties under Section 18 and Section 10B of the 1934 act.

   a. Section 18 imposes liability for making or causing false or misleading statements of a material fact in any report, application, document, or registration statement filed with the SEC under the act.

      1) Liability applies to both purchasers and sellers of securities.

      2) A plaintiff must prove the following to establish a prima facie case:

         a) A false statement about, or omission of, a material fact
         b) Reliance on the misstatement in buying or selling the security
         c) Damages (loss)

      3) Proof that the price of the security was affected by the misstatement (fraud-on-the-market theory) may substitute for proof of reliance.

      4) Justifiable reliance is negated if the plaintiff was aware of the misstatement.

      5) The plaintiff's establishment of a prima facie case shifts the burden of proof to the accountant. An accountant's defense to a suit based on Section 18 is to prove that (s)he acted in good faith and had no knowledge that the statement was false or misleading.

   b. **Section 10(b)** is the antifraud provision of the 1934 act. **Rule 10b-5** was adopted by the SEC pursuant to that section.

      1) **Rule 10b-5** states that it is illegal for any person, directly or indirectly, to use the mails or any instrumentality of interstate commerce or a national securities exchange to defraud anyone in connection with the purchase or sale of any security.

         a) Instrumentalities of interstate commerce include telephones, telegraphs, and facsimile machines.

      2) Rule 10b-5 applies to all securities, including those exempt from registration.

      3) Rule 10b-5 prohibits any person, in connection with the purchase or sale of any security, from

         a) Employing any device, scheme, or artifice to defraud;

         b) Making any untrue statement of a material fact or omitting to state a material fact necessary to make the statements made, in the light of the circumstances under which they were made, not misleading; or

    c) Engaging in any act, practice, or course of business that operates, or would operate, as a fraud or deceit upon any person.

4) Liability applies to actual purchasers or sellers.

5) A plaintiff must prove each of the following:

    a) A misstatement or omission of a material fact or other fraud
    b) Its connection with the purchase or sale of securities
    c) The accountant's intent to deceive or defraud

        i) This intent is the scienter element of fraud. It may be satisfied by proof of gross negligence or reckless disregard for the truth.

    d) Reliance on the misstatement

        i) If the plaintiff is the SEC rather than a private investor, reliance is not required.

        ii) A private plaintiff ordinarily is not required to prove reliance in omission cases. Reliance is presumed.

        iii) A private plaintiff's reliance may be presumed based on the fraud-on-the-market theory. The plaintiff might never have seen the misstatement, but material misrepresentations to the public affect market price, which is usually assumed to reflect available information.

          • This presumption may be rebutted by showing the investor knew of the incorrect market price.

    e) Loss caused by the reliance

        i) EXAMPLE: Spectre, Inc. employed Will-do CPAs to provide audited financial statements for a filing under the Securities Exchange Act of 1934. Accordingly, Will-do performed an audit and expressed an unqualified opinion. However, Will-do's audit procedures were so inadequate to comply with GAAS that they constituted gross negligence. Plaintiff observed an increasing quoted price and purchased stock. Spectre was declared insolvent after a massive fraud was uncovered. Plaintiff brought a civil suit against Will-do for damages. Will-do's defense was that Plaintiff never read the registration statements or any materials prepared by, or based on materials prepared by, Will-do. But reliance could be presumed from the underlying material misstatements and omissions that affected quoted market prices.

6) An accountant may be liable for misrepresentations contained in unaudited financial statements if (s)he knew or should have known of the errors.

    a) The accountant has a duty to perform a minimal investigation.
    b) The accountant has a duty not to ignore suspicious circumstances.

7) An accountant may be liable for aiding and abetting violations of the act. An accountant aids and abets when (s)he

    a) Is generally aware of his/her participation in an activity that, as a whole, is improper, and

    b) Knowingly aids the activity. Silence may constitute aiding.

        i)   EXAMPLE: In the example above, Will-do CPAs may be liable under the act for aiding and abetting Spectre insofar as they knew or should have known of material misrepresentations inherent in statements upon which investors would be likely to rely.

c.   **Statute of limitations**. A plaintiff must bring a suit under Section 18 or Section 10 before the earlier of

    1)   One year after discovering the facts on which the suit is based, or

    2)   Three years after the time the cause of action arose.

d.   **The Private Securities Litigation Reform Act of 1995** amends the 1933 and 1934 acts. Among its provisions are a prohibition on solicitation or acceptance of referral fees from an attorney by brokers, dealers, and associated persons for obtaining the representation of a customer in any implied private action; a prohibition on the payment of legal fees to private parties seeking funds disgorged solely as the result of an action brought by the SEC; modification of class action guidelines; a statute of limitations for private rights of action; and safe harbor rules for forward-looking statements. Of special interest to accountants are the act's provisions concerning audit requirements for fraud detection and disclosure and proportionate liability.

    1)   Audits should provide reasonable assurance of detecting illegal acts having a direct and material effect on financial statement amounts, be designed to identify material related party transactions, and include an evaluation as to whether there is a substantial doubt about the issuer's ability to continue as a going concern.

        a)   Accountants must report illegal acts to the appropriate level of management and the audit committee unless they are clearly inconsequential.

        b)   If senior management and the board fail to take action on reported material illegal acts, and this failure will result in a departure from a standard report or resignation from the audit, the accountants should report their conclusions to the board immediately. The board must then, within 1 business day, notify the SEC.

        c)   If the accountants do not receive a copy of the notice within the 1-day period, they must furnish the SEC with a copy of their report within 1 business day.

    2)   Joint and several liability is imposed only for a knowing violation of the securities laws. Otherwise, liability is proportionate to the defendant's percentage of responsibility for the total damages.

        a)   However, if a share of the judgment is uncollectible, each defendant is jointly and severally liable to an individual plaintiff who suffered damages exceeding 10% of his/her net worth if such plaintiff has a net worth less than $200,000.

        b)   With respect to other plaintiffs, the defendant is liable for the uncollectible share in proportion to his/her percentage of responsibility, but the defendant's liability in this regard is limited to 50% of his/her proportionate share of the total damages.

4. **Criminal Liability under the Securities Exchange Act of 1934**. The 1934 act imposes criminal penalties for willfully and knowingly making false or misleading statements.

    a. The maximum penalty is a fine of $100,000 and 5 years' incarceration.

    b. A common defense to criminal charges is the accountant's lack of intent to commit the crime.

        1) EXAMPLE: In the example on page 61, Will-do's accountant proprietor is subject to criminal prosecution under the 1934 act. If the prosecutor can introduce evidence sufficient to remove reasonable doubts from a jury that the accountant deliberately closed his eyes to facts plainly to be seen, or recklessly stated as facts things of which he was without knowledge, the accountant might be found to have willfully conspired with Spectre to defraud investors in the sale of securities.

    c. Compliance with GAAP and GAAS is not an absolute defense.

5. **Tax Return Preparer Liability**. The Internal Revenue Code (IRC or tax code) imposes penalties on return preparers.

    a. A tax return preparer is a person who prepares for compensation, or who hires a person to prepare for compensation, a substantial portion of an income tax return or a claim for a refund.

    b. Taking a position which has no realistic possibility of being sustained on its merits subjects a preparer to a $250 penalty if a substantial understatement of the client's liability results.

        1) The position must have a one-in-three possibility of being sustained by a court.

        2) Whether a position has a realistic possibility of success on the merits is a conclusion as to whether substantial authority supporting the position outweighs authority contrary to it.

            a) A frivolous position (patently without merit) fails the test.

        3) The realistic possibility is based not only on what the preparer knew, but also on what a competent practitioner should have known.

        4) The penalty does not apply if the preparer proves both of the following:

            a) (S)he acted in good faith.
            b) There is reasonable cause for the understatement.

        5) Disclosure of a position may shield a preparer from liability for a nonfrivolous position with a less than 1-in-3 chance of success.

    c. Understatement of liability that is willful, or is caused by intentional disregard of IRS rules and regulations, is subject to a $1,000 penalty ($10,000 for a corporation).

    d. Aiding or assisting in preparation of any document is subject to a $1,000 penalty ($10,000 for a corporation) if using the document would result in an understatement of tax liability.

    e. Any income tax return preparer who endorses or otherwise negotiates any income tax refund check issued to a taxpayer is liable for a $500 penalty (for each check), unless the check is deposited into the taxpayer's account.

    f. Violations of tax preparer rules may result in disciplinary action by the Director of Practice of the IRS; ability to represent clients in matters with the IRS may be jeopardized.

g.   Other provisions of the tax code and general laws impose liability on CPAs. Three examples follow:

   1)   Each of the following will subject a preparer to a $50 penalty:

      a)   Failure to provide the taxpayer with a copy of the tax return

      b)   Failure to include an identifying number on the return

      c)   Failure to keep copies or lists of returns prepared

      d)   Failure to retain and make available a list of return preparers employed

   2)   A person who promotes an abusive tax shelter is subject to a penalty equal to the lesser of $1,000 or 20% of the income derived or to be derived from the activity. The IRS may also seek to enjoin the promoter from engaging in further acts subject to the penalty.

   3)   Any act constituting a willful attempt to evade tax liability (even of another) is subject to criminal penalty, including imprisonment.

h.   A CPA exam question might be based on any matter of general tax law; e.g., a question tested the following:

   1)   Additional tax may generally not be assessed until 90 days after an official 90-day letter has been sent to the taxpayer. Unless the taxpayer has settled with the Internal Revenue Service (IRS) or filed a petition in the Tax Court before then, the IRS may assess the deficiency and may initiate collection proceedings not less than 10 days thereafter (if not paid). More than a 30-day letter is required.

6.   An accountant's defenses to statutory liability, e.g., a fine, include the following:

a.   Anything negating a statutory element or condition upon which liability is based

   1)   EXAMPLE: Securities fraud liability under Rule 10b-5 requires proof of intent to deceive. If a client concealed information that the accountant relied upon in preparing a financial statement, and that the accountant is unlikely to have discovered, proving that the accountant intended to deceive anyone in certifying a financial statement may be impossible.

b.   Any defense provided for by statute

   1)   EXAMPLE: A tax preparer may not be liable for the penalty for a substantial understatement of tax liability if the preparer disclosed the position taken.

7.   In 1970, Congress passed the Organized Crime Control Act. This act contained the **Racketeer Influenced and Corrupt Organization Act (RICO)**.

a.   RICO was enacted primarily to combat organized crime's control of legitimate businesses, but it is also applied in cases involving unethical practices by legitimate businesses that have no connection with organized crime.

b.   Criminal RICO defines the following as federal crimes:

   1)   Using income derived from a **pattern of racketeering activity** to acquire an interest in an enterprise

   2)   Acquiring or maintaining an interest in an enterprise through a pattern of racketeering activity

   3)   Conducting or participating, directly or indirectly, in the conduct of an enterprise's affairs through a pattern of racketeering activity

                a)   This language has been interpreted by the Supreme Court to mean that the defendant must participate in the operation or management of the enterprise, an interpretation favorable to CPA firm defendants.

            4)   Conspiring to do any of the foregoing acts

    c.   An enterprise is a partnership, corporation, association, other legal entity, union, or group of individuals associated in fact although not a legal entity.

    d.   A pattern of racketeering activity includes at least two instances of specified federal and state crimes (predicate offenses) committed within a 10-year period. The predicate offenses should be related and amount to, or constitute a threat of, continuing racketeering activity.

            1)   The predicate offenses in civil cases are usually securities violations, wire fraud, mail fraud, and bribery. Accordingly, most forms of business fraud may be predicate offenses.

    e.   Criminal sanctions include fines of up to $25,000, imprisonment for up to 20 years, and forfeiture of the gains from illegal acts.

    f.   Civil sanctions include divestiture of the defendant's interest in the enterprise, dissolution or reorganization of the enterprise, and injunctions against future predicate offenses.

            1)   Moreover, a plaintiff whose business or property has been injured may receive treble damages, attorney's fees, and court costs.

            2)   Civil defendants in RICO cases often include insurance companies, brokers, banks, employment agencies, and accountants.

            3)   The Supreme Court has ruled that criminal conviction of the predicate offenses is not necessary to sustain a civil RICO claim. Given the lower burden of proof in a civil suit (preponderance of the evidence) than in a criminal prosecution (beyond a reasonable doubt), a civil claimant has an obvious advantage.

                a)   However, under the Private Securities Litigation Reform Act of 1995, securities fraud is not a predicate offense unless the defendant has been criminally convicted in connection with the fraud.

            4)   The Supreme Court has also ruled that a "distinct racketeering injury" need not be proven in a civil case.

    8.   Stop and review! You have completed the outline for this subunit. Study multiple-choice questions 13 through 34 beginning on page 71.

C. Privileged Communication and Confidentiality

    1.   **Accountant-Client Privilege**

        a.   Federal law does not recognize a broad privilege for accountant-client communications. However, the **Internal Revenue Service Restructuring and Reform Act of 1998** extends a confidentiality privilege to most tax advice provided to a current or prospective client by any individual (CPA, attorney, enrolled agent, or enrolled actuary) qualified under federal law to practice before the IRS. The federal law does not extend to criminal tax matters, private civil matters, disclosures to other federal regulatory bodies, or state and local tax matters. The privilege is available only in matters brought before the IRS or in proceedings in federal court in which the U.S. is a party. The privilege applies only to advice on legal issues.

    b.   A majority of the states do not recognize a privilege for accountant-client communications.

    c.   A minority of the states have statutes that grant the privilege.

        1)   EXAMPLE: State law provides for an accountant-client privilege. The IRS, in conducting a proper investigation, requests Accounting Firm to provide it with records on Client. Accounting Firm complies. Client sues Firm in state court. Firm asserts that federal law does not recognize the privilege and preempts state law. State court determines that, because the disclosure was without notice to the client and was made in the absence of service of legal process compelling disclosure, it is not inconsistent with federal law to hold Firm liable for the voluntary disclosure.

    d.   If the privilege exists, it belongs to the client.

    e.   If any part of the privileged communication is disclosed by either the client or his/her accountant, the privilege is lost completely.

        1)   EXAMPLE: Continuing the above example, disclosure by Firm to a third party (the IRS) negates the privilege with respect to the information. The information is no longer recognized as protected confidential communication(s) under the law of State.

    f.   Client communications with accountants retained by attorneys to aid in litigation are protected by the attorney-client privilege.

        1)   The accountant is considered the attorney's agent.

2.   **Working papers** are privileged and confidential records made by an accountant while performing an engagement. Working papers may include each of the following:

    a.   Plans for the engagement
    b.   Documentation of the client's accounting system
    c.   Results of tests performed
    d.   Written representations from the client or the client's legal counsel
    e.   Explanations
    f.   Reconciliations

3.   Working papers belong to the accountant, but the client has the right to access them. Working papers are deemed to be the property of the accountant because they are prepared by the accountant and because they provide the best evidence of the accountant's efforts in the event of a lawsuit.

    a.   Generally, working papers may be subpoenaed by a third party for use in litigation.

        1)   A few states, by statute, grant a privilege to accountant-client communications. These states generally do not allow compulsory production of working papers without the client's consent.

    b.   Absent a court order or client consent, third parties are not allowed access to working papers.

        1)   The accountant may be liable for malpractice if (s)he allows a third party unauthorized access to working papers.

2) However, the AICPA *Code of Professional Conduct* does allow for disclosure without client consent under certain circumstances, e.g., to government agencies in compliance with applicable laws or regulations.

   c. At a minimum, the accountant should retain working papers until the statute of limitations on litigation that might arise has lapsed. The limitations period varies according to the type of claim. See B.3.c. on page 62.

     1) Retention of working papers ensures that the accountant will have the evidence necessary to defend against claims in a lawsuit.

4. **Professional Standards**. The AICPA *Code of Professional Conduct* (Rule 301) states that a member shall not disclose any confidential client information except with the specific consent of the client. For the exceptions, see A.6.f. in Study Unit 1.

   a. If confidential accountant-client communications are privileged under state law, disclosure is not permitted except in limited circumstances, for example,

     1) When an exception is provided for by the statute to a state peer review board

     2) When federal law preempts the state law

5. Stop and review! You have completed the outline for this subunit. Study multiple-choice questions 35 through 40 beginning on page 78.

MULTIPLE-CHOICE QUESTIONS

A. Common-Law Liability to Clients and Third Parties

1. Sun Corp. approved a merger plan with Cord Corp. One of the determining factors in approving the merger was the financial statements of Cord that were audited by Frank & Co., CPAs. Sun had engaged Frank to audit Cord's financial statements. While performing the audit, Frank failed to discover certain irregularities that later caused Sun to suffer substantial losses. For Frank to be liable under common-law negligence, Sun at a minimum must prove that Frank

  A. Knew of the irregularities.

  B. Failed to exercise due care.

  C. Was grossly negligent.

  D. Acted with scienter.

The correct answer is (B). *(CPA, adapted)*
  REQUIRED: The plaintiff's burden of proof under common-law negligence.
  DISCUSSION: An accountant has a duty to exercise the skill and care that an ordinarily prudent accountant would in the same circumstances. An accountant who fails to exercise due care is negligent.
  Answer (A) is incorrect because, if the accountant knew of the irregularities, (s)he would be negligent (and possibly fraudulent) for failure to investigate further or to notify Sun of the irregularities. Answer (C) is incorrect because all that is needed to establish common-law negligence is proof that the accountant failed to exercise due care. Answer (D) is incorrect because proving scienter is necessary to establish fraud but not negligence.

2. If a CPA recklessly departs from the standards of due care when conducting an audit, the CPA will be liable to third parties who are unknown to the CPA based on

  A. Negligence.

  B. Gross negligence.

  C. Strict liability.

  D. Criminal deceit.

The correct answer is (B). *(CPA, adapted)*
  REQUIRED: The basis of liability of a CPA to unknown third parties.
  DISCUSSION: In some states, if the accountant has not contracted to perform for the third party, (s)he is not liable to that third party for negligence. Lack of privity is a defense. However, reckless departure from the standards of due care is treated as a form of constructive fraud and results in liability to foreseeable third parties that may be unknown to the CPA.
  Answer (A) is incorrect because the CPA's liability for negligence may be limited to parties in privity and intended third-party beneficiaries. Answer (C) is incorrect because a CPA departing from the common-law requirement of due care is not strictly liable. Answer (D) is incorrect because reckless disregard of the standards of due care does not result in criminal liability.

3. Which of the following statements is generally correct regarding the liability of a CPA who negligently expresses an opinion on an audit of a client's financial statements?

- A. The CPA is liable only to those third parties who are in privity of contract with the CPA.

- B. The CPA is liable only to the client.

- C. The CPA is liable to anyone in a class of third parties who the CPA knows will rely on the opinion.

- D. The CPA is liable to all possible foreseeable users of the CPA's opinion.

The correct answer is (C). *(CPA, adapted)*
REQUIRED: The liability of a CPA to third parties for negligence in auditing a client's financial statements.
DISCUSSION: Until recently, nearly all American courts followed the landmark case of *Ultramares v. Touche.* The *Ultramares* rule limits a CPA's liability to persons in privity of contract with the accountant. Currently, most courts extend a CPA's liability to anyone in a class of third parties who the CPA knows will rely on the audit without regard to privity.
Answer (A) is incorrect because lack of privity is not an effective defense against foreseen users that a CPA knows will rely on his/her opinion. Answer (B) is incorrect because a CPA incurs liability to certain third parties that are foreseen. Answer (D) is incorrect because, while a few courts have adopted the broader view of holding the negligent CPA liable to reasonably foreseeable third-party users, none have adopted a rule of liability for all possible users of the CPA's opinion.

4. Under common law, which of the following statements most accurately reflects the liability of a CPA who fraudulently gives an opinion on an audit of a client's financial statements?

- A. The CPA is liable only to third parties in privity of contract with the CPA.

- B. The CPA is liable only to known users of the financial statements.

- C. The CPA probably is liable to any person who suffered a loss as a result of the fraud.

- D. The CPA probably is liable to the client even if the client was aware of the fraud and did not rely on the opinion.

The correct answer is (C). *(CPA, adapted)*
REQUIRED: The liability of a CPA for a fraudulent opinion.
DISCUSSION: Because fraud entails moral turpitude, the courts permit all foreseeable users of an accountant's work product to bring suit for damages proximately caused by the fraud. The distinctive feature of fraud is scienter, that is, intentional misrepresentation or reckless disregard for the truth (sometimes found in gross negligence).
Answers (A) and (B) are incorrect because accountant liability can extend to all persons who incur loss resulting from the accountant's fraud regardless of privity. Answer (D) is incorrect because an element of a fraud action is that the plaintiff relied justifiably on the material misstatement.

5. The best description of whether a CPA has met the required standard of care in conducting an audit of a client's financial statements is

- A. The client's expectations with regard to the accuracy of audited financial statements.

- B. The accuracy of the financial statements and whether the statements conform to generally accepted accounting principles.

- C. Whether the CPA conducted the audit with the same skill and care expected of an ordinarily prudent CPA under the circumstances.

- D. Whether the audit was conducted to investigate and discover all acts of fraud.

The correct answer is (C). *(CPA, adapted)*
REQUIRED: The statement that best describes whether a CPA has met the required standard of care.
DISCUSSION: An accountant owes a general duty to exercise the skill and care of the ordinarily prudent accountant in the same circumstances. The purpose of an independent external audit of financial statements is the expression of an opinion on whether they are fairly presented in conformity with GAAP. To achieve this objective, the CPA must follow GAAS. The auditor provides only reasonable assurance that the statements are free of material misstatements, whether caused by errors or fraud.
Answer (A) is incorrect because the standard is the conduct of an ordinarily prudent accountant under the circumstances. Answer (B) is incorrect because management is responsible for the financial statements. Answer (D) is incorrect because an accountant does not undertake detection of all material errors or acts of fraud.

6. When performing an audit, a CPA will most likely be considered negligent when the CPA fails to

   A. Detect all of a client's fraudulent activities.

   B. Include a negligence disclaimer in the client engagement letter.

   C. Warn a client of known internal control weaknesses.

   D. Warn a client's customers of embezzlement by the client's employees.

The correct answer is (C). *(CPA, adapted)*
   REQUIRED: The most likely reason an auditor will be deemed to be negligent.
   DISCUSSION: Failure to comply with professional standards is prima facie evidence of malpractice. Under AU 325, an auditor is required to communicate to the client's audit committee significant deficiencies in the design or operation of internal control.
   Answer (A) is incorrect because an auditor who exercises due care does not undertake to detect all fraud. Answer (B) is incorrect because a disclaimer is usually ineffective. Answer (D) is incorrect because the auditor must notify the client, not the client's customers.

7. Which of the following facts must be proven for a plaintiff to prevail in a common-law negligent misrepresentation action?

   A. The defendant made the misrepresentations with a reckless disregard for the truth.

   B. The plaintiff justifiably relied on the misrepresentations.

   C. The misrepresentations were in writing.

   D. The misrepresentations concerned opinion.

The correct answer is (B). *(CPA, adapted)*
   REQUIRED: The fact that must be proven to have a valid negligence action.
   DISCUSSION: Misrepresentation occurs when the defendant makes a false representation of a material fact not known to be false but intended to induce reliance. In order to establish negligence, the plaintiff must reasonably rely on the plaintiff's misrepresentation, resulting in damages.
   Answer (A) is incorrect because reckless disregard of the truth is an element in proving fraud or gross negligence, not ordinary negligence. Answer (C) is incorrect because, under the negligence theory, the statements relied upon may be oral or written. A written misstatement is not necessary to prove negligent misrepresentation. Answer (D) is incorrect because facts, not opinions, form the bases of a negligent misrepresentation case.

8. Krim, president and CEO of United Co., engaged Smith, CPA, to audit United's financial statements so that United could secure a loan from First Bank. Smith issued an unqualified opinion on May 20, but the loan was delayed. On August 5, on inquiry to Smith by First Bank, Smith, relying on Krim's representation, made assurances that there was no material change in United's financial status. Krim's representation was untrue because of a material change which took place after May 20. First relied on Smith's assurances of no change. Shortly thereafter, United became insolvent. If First sues Smith for negligent misrepresentation, Smith will be found

   A. Not liable, because Krim misled Smith, and a CPA is not responsible for a client's untrue representations.

   B. Liable, because Smith should have undertaken sufficient auditing procedures to verify the status of United.

   C. Not liable, because Smith's opinion only covers the period up to May 20.

   D. Liable, because Smith should have contacted the chief financial officer rather than the chief executive officer.

The correct answer is (B). *(CPA, adapted)*
   REQUIRED: The auditor's liability for assurances given about events subsequent to the report.
   DISCUSSION: AU 333, *Client Representations*, states that written representations corroborate information received orally from management, but they do not substitute for the procedures necessary to afford a reasonable basis for the assurances given. Moreover, the auditor ordinarily has no responsibility for events after the end of field work or the date of the report, if later. If the auditor decides to assume such responsibility, (s)he must comply with GAAS, including AU 333. Accordingly, the auditor will be liable for failure to exercise due care.
   Answer (A) is incorrect because a CPA should make an independent investigation. Answer (C) is incorrect because Smith made assurances to the bank that covered the period subsequent to May 20 and therefore assumed responsibility for the additional period. Answer (D) is incorrect because Smith should have performed additional audit procedures and not have relied solely on management's representations, including those of the chief financial officer.

9. Ford & Co., CPAs, expressed an unqualified opinion on Owens Corp.'s financial statements. Relying on these financial statements, Century Bank lent Owens $750,000. Ford was unaware that Century would receive a copy of the financial statements or that Owens would use them to obtain a loan. Owens defaulted on the loan. To succeed in a common-law fraud action against Ford, Century must prove, in addition to other elements, that Century was

- A. Free from contributory negligence.
- B. In privity of contract with Ford.
- C. Justified in relying on the financial statements.
- D. In privity of contract with Owens.

The correct answer is (C). *(CPA, adapted)*
REQUIRED: The element of a prima facie case of common-law fraud.
DISCUSSION: The tort of intentional misrepresentation (fraud, deceit) consists of a material misrepresentation made with scienter and an intent to induce reliance. The misstatement must also have proximately caused damage to a defendant who justifiably relied upon it. Scienter exists when the defendant makes a false representation with knowledge of its falsity or with reckless disregard as to its truth.
Answer (A) is incorrect because contributory negligence is a defense to negligence, not fraud. Answers (B) and (D) are incorrect because Century will have standing to bring an action based on fraud because it was a foreseeable third party.

10. Which of the following elements, if present, would support a finding of constructive fraud on the part of a CPA?

- A. Gross negligence in applying generally accepted auditing standards.
- B. Ordinary negligence in applying generally accepted accounting principles.
- C. Identified third-party users.
- D. Scienter.

The correct answer is (A). *(CPA, adapted)*
REQUIRED: The element supporting a finding of constructive fraud on the part of a CPA.
DISCUSSION: Scienter is a prerequisite to liability for fraud. Scienter exists when the defendant makes a false representation with knowledge of its falsity or with reckless disregard as to its truth. For constructive fraud, the scienter requirement is met by proof of gross negligence (reckless disregard for the truth).
Answer (B) is incorrect because failure to apply GAAS in good faith is evidence of negligence. To prove fraud, more is required. Answer (C) is incorrect because, for fraud, a CPA may be liable to all foreseeable users of his/her work. Answer (D) is incorrect because scienter is a necessary element of fraud. For constructive fraud, the scienter element is proved by evidence of gross negligence. Thus, (A) is the better answer.

11. Cable Corp. orally engaged Drake & Co., CPAs, to audit its financial statements. Cable's management informed Drake that it suspected the accounts receivable were materially overstated. Though the financial statements Drake audited included a materially overstated accounts receivable balance, Drake expressed an unqualified opinion. Cable used the financial statements to obtain a loan to expand its operations. Cable defaulted on the loan and incurred a substantial loss.

If Cable sues Drake for negligence in failing to discover the overstatement, Drake's best defense would be that Drake did not

- A. Have privity of contract with Cable.
- B. Sign an engagement letter.
- C. Perform the audit recklessly or with an intent to deceive.
- D. Violate generally accepted auditing standards in performing the audit.

The correct answer is (D). *(CPA, adapted)*
REQUIRED: The best defense of auditors who failed to discover an overstated accounts receivable balance.
DISCUSSION: The purpose of an independent external audit of financial statements is the expression of an opinion on whether they are fairly presented in conformity with GAAP. To achieve this objective, the CPA must follow GAAS. The auditor provides only reasonable assurance that the statements are free of material misstatements, whether caused by errors or fraud. Thus, their best defense will be to prove that they performed the audit in accordance with GAAS. Although following GAAS does not eliminate the possibility of negligence, it is strong evidence of adherence to the due care standard.
Answer (A) is incorrect because a client is always in privity of contract with the auditors. Answer (B) is incorrect because an engagement letter is not required to form a contract between auditors and their client. The oral agreement therefore required the auditors to perform the audit in a nonnegligent manner. Answer (C) is incorrect because absence of recklessness or an intent to deceive would be a defense to fraud, but not to negligence.

12. Hark, CPA, failed to follow generally accepted auditing standards in auditing Long Corp.'s financial statements. Long's management had told Hark that the audited statements would be submitted to several banks to obtain financing. Relying on the statements, Third Bank gave Long a loan. Long defaulted on the loan. In a jurisdiction applying the *Ultramares* decision, if Third sues Hark, Hark will

A. Win because there was no privity of contract between Hark and Third.

B. Lose because Hark knew that banks would be relying on the financial statements.

C. Win because Third was contributorily negligent in granting the loan.

D. Lose because Hark was negligent in performing the audit.

The correct answer is (A). *(CPA, adapted)*
REQUIRED: The liability of a CPA to a third party under the *Ultramares* decision.
DISCUSSION: An accountant is not liable to all persons who are damaged by his/her negligence. Lack of privity is still a defense in some states. For example, under the holding in the *Ultramares* case, an accountant is liable for negligence only if the plaintiff was in privity of contract with the accountant or a primary beneficiary of the engagement. Under the primary benefit test, the accountant must have been aware that (s)he was hired to produce a work product to be used and relied upon by a particular third party.
Answer (B) is incorrect because *Ultramares* required that the accountant be engaged principally to benefit the third party and that the third party be identified. Answer (C) is incorrect because, although contributory negligence is a complete or partial limit on liability in certain circumstances, under *Ultramares*, Hark is not liable to Third. Answer (D) is incorrect because Hark had not contracted to perform for Third, and Third was not a primary beneficiary of Hark's contract with Long.

B. Federal Statutory Liability

13. How does the Securities Act of 1933, which imposes civil liability on auditors for misrepresentations or omissions of material facts in a registration statement, expand auditors' liability to purchasers of securities beyond that of common law?

A. Purchasers only have to prove loss caused by reliance on audited financial statements.

B. Privity with purchasers is not a necessary element of proof.

C. Purchasers have to prove either fraud or gross negligence as a basis for recovery.

D. Auditors are held to a standard of care described as "professional skepticism."

The correct answer is (B). *(CPA, adapted)*
REQUIRED: The factor that results in expanded liability of a CPA under the Securities Act of 1933.
DISCUSSION: Under the Securities Act of 1933, a purchaser need only prove damages resulting from the purchase of securities covered by a registration statement containing a false statement or omission of a material fact in a section audited or prepared by the auditor. The auditor must then prove that (s)he was not negligent (or fraudulent), usually by showing that (s)he acted with "due diligence."
To recover damages at common law based on contract or negligence, privity between the plaintiff and accountant may be required. To recover under the Securities Act of 1933, however, a purchaser of securities need not prove privity of contract with a CPA.
Answer (A) is incorrect because more must be proved under the 1933 act, e.g., material misstatement or omission. Answer (C) is incorrect because purchasers need not even prove negligence under the 1933 act. Answer (D) is incorrect because such a standard does not apply at common law or under the 1933 act.

14. Quincy bought Teal Corp. common stock in an offering registered under the Securities Act of 1933. Worth & Co., CPAs, gave an unqualified opinion on Teal's financial statements that were included in the registration statement filed with the SEC. Quincy sued Worth under the provisions of the 1933 act that deal with omission of facts required to be in the registration statement. Quincy must prove that

A. There was fraudulent activity by Worth.

B. There was a material misstatement in the financial statements.

C. Quincy relied on Worth's opinion.

D. Quincy was in privity with Worth.

The correct answer is (B). *(CPA, adapted)*
REQUIRED: The element a plaintiff must prove to recover losses from a CPA under the Securities Act of 1933.
DISCUSSION: Section 11 is the most frequently invoked basis for suit under the Securities Act of 1933. Under Section 11, the investor need only prove that (s)he suffered losses in a transaction involving the particular securities covered by the registration statement, and that the registration statement contained a false statement or an omission of a material fact for which the CPAs were responsible, e.g., in the audited financial statements.
Answer (A) is incorrect because the plaintiff need not prove fraud to prevail under Section 11. Answer (C) is incorrect because the plaintiff need not prove reliance, but the defendant can plead the plaintiff's knowledge of the misstatement or omission as a defense. Answer (D) is incorrect because plaintiff and defendant need not have been in privity of contract under Section 11.

Questions 15 and 16 are based on the following information. Under the liability provisions of Section 11 of the Securities Act of 1933, a CPA may be liable to any purchaser of a security for certifying materially misstated financial statements that are included in the security's registration statement.

15. Under Section 11, a CPA usually will not be liable to the purchaser

A. If the purchaser is contributorily negligent.

B. If the CPA can prove due diligence.

C. Unless the purchaser can prove privity with the CPA.

D. Unless the purchaser can prove scienter on the part of the CPA.

The correct answer is (B). *(CPA, adapted)*
REQUIRED: The defense to liability under Section 11.
DISCUSSION: A CPA is prima facie liable to investors under Section 11 but will not be liable if (s)he can prove due diligence. Due diligence is absence of negligence. This defense requires proof that a reasonable investigation was conducted and that the CPA reasonably believed that the financial statements were accurate on the effective date of the registration statement.
Answer (A) is incorrect because the investor need not have read or even seen the financial statements. Hence, contributory negligence is irrelevant. Answer (C) is incorrect because privity is not required under Section 11. Any person who purchased a security pursuant to a defective registration statement may sue. Answer (D) is incorrect because scienter is required to hold a CPA liable under Rule 10b-5, not Section 11.

16. Under Section 11, which of the following must be proven by a purchaser of the security?

	Reliance on the Financial Statements	Fraud by the CPA
A.	Yes	Yes
B.	Yes	No
C.	No	Yes
D.	No	No

The correct answer is (D). *(CPA, adapted)*
REQUIRED: The element(s), if any, to be proved under Section 11.
DISCUSSION: Under Section 11 of the Securities Act of 1933, a purchaser must prove only that the accountant prepared and certified the financial statements, the statements contained a misstatement or omission of material fact, and (s)he incurred a loss. A purchaser does not need to prove fraud or reliance. Criminal liability under Section 24 of the 1933 act and civil liability under Sections 18 and 10B of the 1934 act require proof of fraud.
Answers (A), (B), and (C) are incorrect because neither proof of reliance nor proof of fraud is required.

17. Petty Corp. made a public offering subject to the Securities Act of 1933. In connection with the offering, Ward & Co., CPAs, rendered an unqualified opinion on Petty's financial statements included in the SEC registration statement. Huff purchased 500 of the offered shares. Huff has brought an action against Ward under Section 11 of the Securities Act of 1933 for losses resulting from misstatements of facts in the financial statements included in the registration statement. Ward's weakest defense would be that

A. Huff knew of the misstatements when Huff purchased the stock.

B. Huff's losses were not caused by the misstatements.

C. Ward was not in privity of contract with Huff.

D. Ward conducted the audit in accordance with GAAS.

The correct answer is (C). *(CPA, adapted)*
REQUIRED: The defense least helpful to an accountant sued under the Securities Act of 1933.
DISCUSSION: Under Section 11, the plaintiff-purchaser of securities issued under a registration statement containing a misstatement or omission of a material fact need not prove either reliance or privity.
Answer (A) is incorrect because the plaintiff's knowledge at the time of purchase of the material misstatement or omission will defeat the claim. Answer (B) is incorrect because other possible defenses are that the plaintiff's losses were the result of another's misstatements or omissions or of a widespread stock market decline. Answer (D) is incorrect because proof of adherence to GAAS and GAAP is the usual basis for a due diligence defense, i.e., that the accountant was not negligent.

Questions 18 and 19 are based on the following information. Dart Corp. engaged Jay Associates, CPAs, to assist in a public stock offering. Jay audited Dart's financial statements and gave an unqualified opinion, despite knowing that the financial statements contained misstatements. Jay's opinion was included in Dart's registration statement. Larson purchased shares in the offering and suffered a loss when the stock declined in value after the misstatements became known.

18. In a suit against Jay and Dart under the Section 11 liability provisions of the Securities Act of 1933, Larson must prove that

A. Jay knew of the misstatements.

B. Jay was negligent.

C. The misstatements contained in Dart's financial statements were material.

D. The unqualified opinion contained in the registration statement was relied on by Larson.

The correct answer is (C). *(CPA, adapted)*
REQUIRED: The investor's burden of proof to recover losses from a CPA under Section 11 of the 1933 act.
DISCUSSION: Under Section 11, the investor need only prove that (s)he suffered losses in a transaction involving the particular securities covered by the registration statement and that the registration statement contained a false statement or an omission of a material fact for which the CPAs were responsible, e.g., in the audited financial statements.
Answer (A) is incorrect because scienter is not an element of a case brought under Section 11. Answer (B) is incorrect because the plaintiff need not show negligence, but the defendant may prevail by proving that it exercised due diligence. Answer (D) is incorrect because the plaintiff need not prove reliance, but the defendant can plead the plaintiff's knowledge of the misstatement or omission as a defense.

19. If Larson succeeds in the Section 11 suit against Dart, Larson would be entitled to

A. Damages of three times the original public offering price.

B. Rescission of the transaction.

C. Monetary damages only.

D. Damages, but only if the shares were resold before the suit was started.

The correct answer is (C). *(CPA, adapted)*
REQUIRED: The remedies of an investor under Section 11 of the Securities Act of 1933.
DISCUSSION: In a civil suit under Section 11 of the 1933 act, a purchaser's remedy is a suit for monetary damages. The damages are measured as the difference between the price paid for the securities and (1) the sales price, if the security was sold before suit; (2) the market value of the security at the time of the suit, if the security was not sold; or (3) the sales price, if the security was disposed of after suit and the sales price exceeded the market value of the security at the time the suit was brought.
Answer (A) is incorrect because the damages, generally, are a measure of the investor's loss. Answer (B) is incorrect because Section 11 does not provide for rescission as a remedy. Answer (D) is incorrect because resale before suit is not prerequisite to recovery under Section 11.

20. Holly Corp. engaged Yost & Co., CPAs, to audit the financial statements to be included in a registration statement Holly was required to file under the provisions of the Securities Act of 1933. Yost failed to exercise due diligence and did not discover the omission of a fact material to the statements. A purchaser of Holly's securities may recover from Yost under Section 11 of the Securities Act of 1933 only if the purchaser

A. Brings a civil action within 1 year of the discovery of the omission and within 3 years of the offering date.

B. Proves that the registration statement was relied on to make the purchase.

C. Proves that Yost was negligent.

D. Establishes privity of contract with Yost.

The correct answer is (A). *(CPA, adapted)*
REQUIRED: The requirement to recover, under the 1933 act, for a CPA's failure to discover a material fact.
DISCUSSION: The statute of limitations on an action by a purchaser of securities relying on the Securities Act of 1933 is 1 year after the false statements or omissions of material fact were discovered or should have been discovered. The latest the suit may be brought is within 3 years after the security was first offered to the public.
Answer (B) is incorrect because the plaintiff need not prove reliance, but the defendant can plead the plaintiff's knowledge of the misstatement or omission as a defense. Answer (C) is incorrect because the plaintiff need not show negligence. Answer (D) is incorrect because privity of contract is not required under Section 11 of the Securities Act of 1933.

21. Under Section 11 of the Securities Act of 1933, which of the following standards may a CPA use as a defense?

	Generally Accepted Accounting Principles	Generally Accepted Fraud Detection Standards
A.	Yes	Yes
B.	Yes	No
C.	No	Yes
D.	No	No

The correct answer is (B). *(CPA, adapted)*
REQUIRED: The standards a CPA may use as a defense under Section 11.
DISCUSSION: A CPA is strictly liable to investors under Section 11 but will not be liable if (s)he can prove due diligence. This defense requires proof that a reasonable investigation was conducted and that the CPA reasonably believed that the financial statements were accurate on the effective date of the registration statement. Proof of adherence to GAAP and GAAS is the usual basis for such a due diligence defense.
Answers (A), (C), and (D) are incorrect because adherence to GAAP and GAAS is a defense, but generally accepted fraud detection standards do not exist.

22. Ocean and Associates, CPAs, audited the financial statements of Drain Corporation. As a result of Ocean's negligence in conducting the audit, the financial statements included material misstatements. Ocean was unaware of this fact. The financial statements and Ocean's unqualified opinion were included in a registration statement and prospectus for an original public offering of stock by Drain. Sharp purchased shares in the offering. Sharp received a copy of the prospectus prior to the purchase but did not read it. The shares declined in value as a result of the misstatements in Drain's financial statements becoming known. Under which of the following acts is Sharp most likely to prevail in a lawsuit against Ocean?

	Securities Exchange Act of 1934, Section 10(b), Rule 10b-5	Securities Act of 1933, Section 11
A.	Yes	Yes
B.	Yes	No
C.	No	Yes
D.	No	No

The correct answer is (C). *(CPA, adapted)*
REQUIRED: The basis for recovery under securities law in a suit against negligent accountants.
DISCUSSION: Section 11 is the most frequently invoked basis for suit under the Securities Act of 1933. Under Section 11, the investor need prove only that (s)he suffered losses in a transaction involving the particular securities covered by the registration statement and that the registration statement contained a false statement or an omission of a material fact for which the CPAs were responsible, e.g., in the audited financial statements. Thus, under Section 11, Sharp need not prove reliance or negligence and will prevail if Ocean fails to prove due diligence. Sharp is unlikely to prevail under the antifraud provisions of the Securities Exchange Act of 1934 because of the absence of scienter.
Answers (A), (B), and (D) are incorrect because Sharp would most likely prevail under the 1933 act but not the 1934 act.

23. Under the provisions of Section 10(b) and Rule 10b-5 of the Securities Exchange Act of 1934, which of the following activities must be proven by a stock purchaser in a suit against a CPA?

I. Intentional conduct by the CPA designed to deceive investors

II. Negligence by the CPA

A. I only.

B. II only.

C. Both I and II.

D. Neither I nor II.

The correct answer is (A). *(CPA, adapted)*
REQUIRED: The elements, if any, a plaintiff must prove under Rule 10b-5 to recover damages from a CPA.
DISCUSSION: Under Rule 10b-5, a plaintiff must prove a misstatement or omission of a material fact or other fraud, its connection with purchase or sale of securities, an intent to deceive or defraud, reliance on the misstatement, and loss caused by the reliance. Thus, intentional misconduct, not negligence, must be proven.
Answer (B) is incorrect because the plaintiff must prove more than negligence. (S)he must prove the accountant intended to deceive, manipulate, or defraud. Answer (C) is incorrect because only a showing of intentional conduct to deceive is required. Furthermore, intentional misconduct is inconsistent with negligence. Answer (D) is incorrect because a plaintiff must prove intentional conduct to deceive.

Questions 24 and 25 are based on the following information. Dart Corp. engaged Jay Associates, CPAs, to assist in a public stock offering. Jay audited Dart's financial statements and gave an unqualified opinion, despite knowing that the financial statements contained misstatements. Jay's opinion was included in Dart's registration statement. Larson purchased shares in the offering and suffered a loss when the stock declined in value after the misstatements became known.

24. In a suit against Jay under the anti-fraud provisions of Section 10(b) and Rule 10b-5 of the Securities Exchange Act of 1934, Larson must prove all of the following except

A. Larson was an intended user of the false registration statement.

B. Larson relied on the false registration statement.

C. The transaction involved some form of interstate commerce.

D. Jay acted with intentional disregard of the truth.

The correct answer is (A). *(CPA, adapted)*
REQUIRED: The element an investor need not prove under Rule 10b-5 to recover damages from a CPA.
DISCUSSION: A CPA can be held liable for a misstatement or omission of a material fact relied upon by a purchaser or seller of a security, provided the misconduct involves interstate commerce, the mails, or a national securities exchange. The intent to deceive, manipulate, or defraud (called scienter) must be shown in a private action under Rule 10b-5, and the wrongful act must have caused the plaintiff's damages. Liability runs to any actual purchaser or seller who incurs a loss resulting from the reliance.
Answers (B) and (C) are incorrect because the purchaser or seller must prove each to recover. Answer (D) is incorrect because, although more than gross negligence is required under Section 10(b), intentional disregard of the truth would satisfy the scienter element.

25. If Larson succeeds in the Section 10(b) and Rule 10b-5 suit, Larson would be entitled to

A. Recovery of the original public offering price only.

B. Rescission of the transaction only.

C. The amount of any loss caused by the fraud.

D. Punitive damages.

The correct answer is (C). *(CPA, adapted)*
REQUIRED: The remedy or remedies available to a private plaintiff under Section 10(b) of the 1934 act.
DISCUSSION: Section 10(b) and Rule 10b-5 do not expressly provide for a private right of action, but courts have implied such a right. Remedies for violations include rescission of the securities contract, damages, and injunctions. Courts are divided over the measure of damages recoverable from a CPA. The amount of loss caused by the fraud, however, is recoverable.
Answers (A) and (B) are incorrect because other remedies are available under Section 10(b). Answer (D) is incorrect because Section 10(b) does not provide for punitive damages.

26. Burt, CPA, issued an unqualified opinion on the financial statements of Midwest Corp. These financial statements were included in Midwest's annual report, and Form 10-K was filed with the SEC. As a result of Burt's reckless disregard for GAAS, material misstatements in the financial statements were not detected. Subsequently, Davis purchased stock in Midwest in the secondary market without ever seeing Midwest's annual report or Form 10-K. Shortly thereafter, Midwest became insolvent, and the price of the stock declined drastically. Davis sued Burt for damages based on Section 10(b) and Rule 10b-5 of the Securities Exchange Act of 1934. Burt's best defense is that

A. There has been no subsequent sale for which a loss can be computed.

B. Davis did not purchase the stock as part of an initial offering.

C. Davis did not rely on the financial statements or Form 10-K.

D. Davis was not in privity with Burt.

The correct answer is (C). *(CPA, adapted)*
REQUIRED: The best defense of a grossly negligent accountant sued under Rule 10b-5.
DISCUSSION: The plaintiff must have relied on the misstatement or omission of a material fact with regard to the purchase or sale of a security if (s)he is to recover under Rule 10b-5. In the case of an omission, reliance is implied by materiality. Davis did not see the relevant annual report or Form 10-K and will therefore have difficulty in proving reliance.
Answer (A) is incorrect because damages may be proven without a subsequent sale. Answer (B) is incorrect because Rule 10b-5 applies to a misstatement or an omission of a material fact in connection with any purchase or sale of a security if the wrongful act involved interstate commerce, the U.S. mail, or a national securities exchange. Answer (D) is incorrect because privity is not required.

27. Under the antifraud provisions of Section 10(b) of the Securities Exchange Act of 1934, a CPA may be liable if the CPA acted

    A. Negligently.

    B. With independence.

    C. Without due diligence.

    D. Without good faith.

The correct answer is (D). *(CPA, adapted)*
    REQUIRED: The basis for a CPA's liability under Section 10(b).
    DISCUSSION: The distinguishing element of fraud is scienter, which is the intent to deceive or defraud. Acting in good faith indicates lack of scienter. Hence, a CPA who acted without good faith cannot assert the good faith defense.
    Answer (A) is incorrect because fraud entails an intent to deceive or defraud, not mere negligence. Answer (B) is incorrect because a CPA who performs attest services must be independent. Answer (C) is incorrect because lack of due diligence, per se, does not signify the existence of scienter.

28. Accounting Firm is among several defendants found liable in a private civil action brought by an individual plaintiff under the Securities Exchange Act of 1934. Plaintiff, who has a net worth of $500,000, received a judgment for damages of $1 million. The jury determined that Accounting Firm did not commit a knowing violation of the securities laws but that it was responsible for 10% of the total damages. If Accounting Firm is the only defendant from which plaintiff can recover, it will be liable for

    A. $50,000

    B. $100,000

    C. $150,000

    D. $1,000,000

The correct answer is (C). *(Publisher)*
    REQUIRED: The liability of a defendant when a share of the judgment is uncollectible.
    DISCUSSION: Under the Private Securities Litigation Reform Act of 1995, joint and several liability is imposed only for a knowing violation of the securities laws. Otherwise, liability is proportionate to the defendant's percentage of responsibility for the total damages. However, if a share of the judgment is uncollectible, each defendant is jointly and severally liable to an individual plaintiff who suffered damages exceeding 10% of his/her net worth if such plaintiff has a net worth less than $200,000. Thus, Firm is not jointly and severally liable. The violation was not knowing, and the individual plaintiff's net worth exceeded the ceiling amount. Firm's liability for the uncollectible share is its 10% percentage of responsibility limited to 50% of its proportionate share of the total damages. Given that the uncollectible share is $900,000 [$1,000,000 total − (10% × $1,000,000) proportionate share of Firm], Firm's maximum potential additional liability is $90,000 (10% × $900,000), but this amount exceeds 50% of its 10% share of the total damages (50% × $100,000 = $50,000). Accordingly, the total amount for which Firm is liable is $150,000 ($100,000 proportionate share + $50,000 liability for uncollectible share).
    Answer (A) is incorrect because $50,000 is the liability for the uncollectible share. Answer (B) is incorrect because $100,000 is the proportionate share of the total damages. Answer (D) is incorrect because $1,000,000 equals the total damages.

29. A CPA who prepares clients' federal income tax returns for a fee must

    A. File certain required notices and powers of attorney with the IRS before preparing any returns.

    B. Keep a completed copy of each return for a specified period of time.

    C. Receive client documentation supporting all travel and entertainment expenses deducted on the return.

    D. Indicate the CPA's federal identification number on a tax return only if the return reflects tax due from the taxpayer.

The correct answer is (B). *(CPA, adapted)*
    REQUIRED: The duty of a tax return preparer.
    DISCUSSION: A CPA who prepares clients' federal income tax returns for a fee meets the definition in the federal tax code of an income tax return preparer. An income tax return preparer is subject to penalties for certain types of failures. For example, for each failure to retain a copy of a prepared return, the penalty is $50. The copy must be retained for 3 years.
    Answer (A) is incorrect because the IRC does not require such filing. Answer (C) is incorrect because the preparer is not required to examine documents to verify independently information provided by the taxpayer. But (s)he must make reasonable inquiry, if the information appears to be incorrect or incomplete, or determine the existence of required facts and circumstances incident to a deduction. Answer (D) is incorrect because the preparer is required to indicate his/her federal identification number on each return filed.

30. Kopel was engaged to prepare Raff's 1999 federal income tax return. During the tax preparation interview, Raff told Kopel that he paid $3,000 in property taxes in 1999. Actually, Raff's property taxes amounted to only $600. Based on Raff's word, Kopel deducted the $3,000 on Raff's return, resulting in an understatement of Raff's tax liability. Kopel had no reason to believe that the information was incorrect. Kopel did not request underlying documentation and was reasonably satisfied by Raff's representation that Raff had adequate records to support the deduction. Which of the following statements is correct?

A. To avoid the preparer penalty for willful understatement of tax liability, Kopel was obligated to examine the underlying documentation for the deduction.

B. To avoid the preparer penalty for willful understatement of tax liability, Kopel would be required to obtain Raff's representation in writing.

C. Kopel is not subject to the preparer penalty for willful understatement of tax liability because the deduction that was claimed was more than 25% of the actual amount that should have been deducted.

D. Kopel is not subject to the preparer penalty for willful understatement of tax liability because Kopel was justified in relying on Raff's representation.

The correct answer is (D). *(CPA, adapted)*
REQUIRED: The correct statement concerning tax return preparer liability.
DISCUSSION: A tax return preparer may rely, without verification, on information provided by the client when the preparer is reasonably justified in relying upon the client's representations. However, a preparer must make a reasonable inquiry if the information appears to be incorrect or incomplete.
Answer (A) is incorrect because the preparer is not subject to preparer penalties for willful understatement because (s)he is justified in relying on the data furnished by the taxpayer. The preparer is not a guarantor of the accuracy of the return. Answer (B) is incorrect because a preparer is not required to obtain a written representation from the client prior to preparing a client's return. Answer (C) is incorrect because preparer penalties are assessed only when the preparer has recommended a position that does not have a realistic possibility of success.

31. Which of the following acts by a CPA will not result in a CPA's incurring an IRS penalty?

A. Failing, without reasonable cause, to provide the client with a copy of an income tax return.

B. Failing, without reasonable cause, to sign a client's tax return as preparer.

C. Understating a client's tax liability as a result of an error In calculation.

D. Negotiating a client's tax refund check when the CPA prepared the tax return.

The correct answer is (C). *(CPA, adapted)*
REQUIRED: The act that will not result in a CPA's incurring an IRS penalty.
DISCUSSION: Understating a client's tax liability as a result of an error in calculation will not result in an IRS penalty to a CPA unless it is the result of gross negligence or a willful attempt to avoid tax liability.
Answer (A) is incorrect because a CPA is required to provide his/her client with a copy of the tax return. Answer (B) is incorrect because a tax preparer is required to sign the return. Answer (D) is incorrect because any tax return preparer who endorses or otherwise negotiates a refund check issued to a taxpayer is liable for a $500 penalty.

32. In general, the provisions of the Racketeer Influenced and Corrupt Organizations Act (RICO) prohibit

A. Specific acts of racketeering, such as murder or trafficking in stolen property.

B. Organized crime from operating legitimate businesses.

C. Organized crime from operating illegitimate businesses.

D. Operation of any business with funds obtained through a pattern of racketeering acts.

The correct answer is (D). *(R. Welton)*
REQUIRED: The correct statement about the scope of RICO.
DISCUSSION: RICO prohibits (1) using income derived from a pattern of racketeering activity to acquire an interest in an enterprise, (2) acquiring or maintaining an interest in an enterprise through a pattern of racketeering activity, (3) conducting or participating, directly or indirectly, in the conduct of an enterprise's affairs through a pattern of racketeering activity, or conspiring to do any of the foregoing acts.
Answer (A) is incorrect because RICO does not prohibit acts of racketeering per se. Answers (B) and (C) are incorrect because RICO does not prohibit the mere ownership or operation of a business by organized crime.

33. The Racketeer Influenced and Corrupt Organizations Act (RICO) concerns, among other things, connections between organized crime and business. The act

- A. Is invoked only in prosecutions of organized crime figures.
- B. Applies only to illegitimate business activities.
- C. Permits the confiscation of legitimate businesses.
- D. Creates accounting requirements for businesses that report to the SEC.

The correct answer is (C). *(Publisher)*
    REQUIRED: The correct statement about the RICO Act.
    DISCUSSION: Under RICO, profits from "racketeering" activities may be forfeited. The statute not only makes racketeering a federal offense, it also permits tracing of the proceeds to legitimate enterprises. These businesses can now be seized, thus reducing the effect of organized crime on legal business activities.
    Answer (A) is incorrect because the civil provisions of the act have been applied to activities of persons not related to organized crime. Answer (B) is incorrect because RICO allows the seizure of legal businesses purchased with funds obtained through illegal activities. Answer (D) is incorrect because the Foreign Corrupt Practices Act created these requirements.

34. Under the Racketeer Influenced and Corrupt Organizations Act (RICO), an injured party who is not a governmental entity

- A. Cannot bring suit.
- B. May bring suit for treble damages.
- C. May bring suit for punitive damages.
- D. May bring suit to recover only the amount of the actual injury plus any court costs.

The correct answer is (B). *(R. Welton)*
    REQUIRED: The correct statement about RICO actions by private parties.
    DISCUSSION: An injured party who is not a governmental entity may bring suit under the civil provisions of RICO for treble damages (three times the actual loss). In addition, the party may also recover court costs and reasonable attorney's fees.
    Answer (A) is incorrect because RICO permits a civil remedy. Answer (C) is incorrect because the plaintiff may not recover punitive damages in addition to treble damages, which are themselves intended as a penalty. Answer (D) is incorrect because the plaintiff may recover attorney's fees, court costs, and treble damages.

C. Privileged Communication and Confidentiality

35. Which of the following statements is correct with respect to ownership, possession, or access to a CPA firm's audit working papers?

- A. Working papers may never be obtained by third parties unless the client consents.
- B. Working papers are not transferable to a purchaser of a CPA practice unless the client consents.
- C. Working papers are subject to the privileged communication rule, which, in most jurisdictions, prevents any third-party access to the working papers.
- D. Working papers are the client's exclusive property.

The correct answer is (B). *(CPA, adapted)*
    REQUIRED: The true statement about a CPA firm's working papers.
    DISCUSSION: Transferring working papers to a purchaser of a practice constitutes communication of the information they contain and violates the AICPA's Conduct Rule 301, *Confidential Client Information*. However, this rule does not prohibit review of the CPA's practice, including a review in conjunction with the purchase, sale, or merger of the practice.
    Answer (A) is incorrect because a third party may obtain working papers without client consent when they are lawfully subpoenaed. Answer (C) is incorrect because the privileged communication rule does not exist at common law but has been provided for by statute in a minority of states. Answer (D) is incorrect because the working papers are the property of the CPA unless agreed otherwise. However, a CPA must not only return client records upon request but must also make available information in the working papers not reflected in the client's books and records, without which the client's financial information would be incomplete.

36. Which of the following statements is correct regarding a CPA's working papers? The working papers must be

- A. Transferred to another accountant purchasing the CPA's practice even if the client has not given permission.
- B. Transferred permanently to the client if demanded.
- C. Turned over to any government agency that requests them.
- D. Turned over pursuant to a valid federal court subpoena.

The correct answer is (D). *(CPA, adapted)*
    REQUIRED: The true statement about working papers.
    DISCUSSION: The AICPA's Conduct Rule 301, *Confidential Client Information*, does not affect a CPA's obligation to comply with a validly issued and enforceable subpoena. Because no federal accountant-client privilege exists, a federal court may subpoena working papers.
    Answer (A) is incorrect because a CPA is required to obtain the client's permission before transferring his/her working papers to another CPA. This is true even if the other accountant is purchasing the CPA's firm. Answer (B) is incorrect because working papers are the property of the CPA and ordinarily need not be transferred to the client upon request. Answer (C) is incorrect because, unless a summons or subpoena is issued, a governmental request need not be honored. Moreover, some states have provided for an accountant-client privilege.

37. Which of the following statements concerning an accountant's disclosure of confidential client data is generally correct?

- A. Disclosure may be made to any state agency without subpoena.
- B. Disclosure may be made to any party with the consent of the client.
- C. Disclosure may be made to comply with an IRS audit request.
- D. Disclosure may be made to comply with generally accepted accounting principles.

The correct answer is (B). *(CPA, adapted)*
    REQUIRED: The condition allowing disclosure of confidential client data.
    DISCUSSION: Under Conduct Rule 301, an accountant may disclose any confidential client information with the specific consent of the client.
    Answer (A) is incorrect because disclosure may be made to a state agency only pursuant to a subpoena or summons or with the client's consent. Answer (C) is incorrect because, without a client's consent, an accountant may disclose confidential information to the IRS only pursuant to a subpoena or summons. Answer (D) is incorrect because compliance with GAAP is a responsibility of clients who issue financial statements, not the accountants who report on them.

38. To which of the following parties may a CPA partnership provide its working papers, without being lawfully subpoenaed or without the client's consent?

- A. The IRS.
- B. The FASB.
- C. Any surviving partner(s) on the death of a partner.
- D. A CPA before purchasing a partnership interest in the firm.

The correct answer is (C). *(CPA, adapted)*
    REQUIRED: The party to whom working papers can be provided by a CPA without a subpoena or client consent.
    DISCUSSION: Working papers may be disclosed to another partner of the accounting firm without the client's consent because such information has not been communicated to outsiders. A partner of the accountant has a fiduciary obligation to the client not to disclose confidential information without consent.
    Answer (A) is incorrect because the partnership may not provide the IRS with confidential client information without client permission, a subpoena, or a summons. Answer (B) is incorrect because the CPA or his/her firm may not disclose confidential information to the FASB without client consent. Answer (D) is incorrect because a CPA may not provide working papers to a prospective purchaser. However, an exception to the rule against disclosure of confidential client information is made for a review of a professional practice in conjunction with a prospective purchase, sale, or merger.

39. Thorp, CPA, was engaged to audit Ivor Co.'s financial statements. During the audit, Thorp discovered that Ivor's inventory contained stolen goods. Ivor was indicted and Thorp was subpoenaed to testify at the criminal trial. Ivor claimed accountant-client privilege to prevent Thorp from testifying. Which of the following statements is correct regarding Ivor's claim?

    A. Ivor can claim an accountant-client privilege only in states that have enacted a statute creating such a privilege.

    B. Ivor can claim an accountant-client privilege only in federal courts.

    C. The accountant-client privilege can be claimed only in civil suits.

    D. The accountant-client privilege can be claimed only to limit testimony to audit subject matter.

The correct answer is (A). *(CPA, adapted)*
REQUIRED: The true statement concerning accountant-client privilege.
DISCUSSION: Although communication between lawyers and clients is privileged, no common-law concept extends this privilege to the accountant-client relationship. A minority of states have enacted statutes recognizing as privileged the confidential communication between an accountant and a client.

Answer (B) is incorrect because federal law recognizes a limited privilege for accountant-client communications in certain civil tax matters before the IRS or in proceedings in federal court in which the U.S. is a party. Answer (C) is incorrect because, in states where the privilege exists, it also applies to criminal actions. Answer (D) is incorrect because, in states where the privilege exists, it is not limited to audit matters.

40. A CPA is permitted to disclose confidential client information without the consent of the client to

  I. Another CPA who has purchased the CPA's tax practice

  II. A successor CPA firm if the information concerns suspected tax return irregularities

  III. A voluntary peer review board

    A. I and III only.

    B. II and III only.

    C. II only.

    D. III only.

The correct answer is (D). *(CPA, adapted)*
REQUIRED: The accountant's permitted disclosure(s) without the client's consent.
DISCUSSION: The AICPA *Code of Professional Conduct* (Rule 301) states that a member shall not disclose any confidential client information except with the specific consent of the client. But this rule should not be understood to preclude a CPA from responding to an inquiry made by an investigative body of a state CPA society, the trial board of the AICPA, or an AICPA or state peer review body, or pursuant to a validly issued and enforceable subpoena.

Answer (A) is incorrect because no exception to Rule 301 permits disclosure to a successor CPA. Answers (B) and (C) are incorrect because, in the case of tax irregularities, the AICPA has ruled that the predecessor auditor may, if contacted by the successor, suggest that the successor ask the client for consent to discuss all matters freely with the predecessor. The AICPA also recommends that the predecessor seek legal advice. However, this Ethics Ruling stops short of permitting unconsented-to disclosure.

Use Gleim's **CPA Test Prep** for interactive testing with over 2,000 additional multiple-choice questions!

OOF QUESTION 1 *(CPA, adapted)* 5-10 minutes

Items 1 through 6 are based on the following information. Under Section 11 of the Securities Act of 1933 and Section 10(b), Rule 10b-5, of the Securities Exchange Act of 1934, a CPA may be sued by a purchaser of registered securities.

Required

Items 1 through 6 relate to what a plaintiff who purchased securities must prove in a civil liability suit against a CPA. For each item, determine whether the statement must be proven under Section 11 of the Securities Act of 1933; under Section 10(b), Rule 10b-5, of the Securities Exchange Act of 1934; under both acts; or under neither act. If the item must be proven only under Section 11 of the Securities Act of 1933, choose answer (A). If the item must be proven only under Section 10(b), Rule 10b-5, of the Securities Exchange Act of 1934, choose answer (B). If the item must be proven under both acts, choose answer (C). If the item must be proven under neither of the acts, choose (D).

The plaintiff security purchaser must allege or prove

1. Material misstatements were included in a filed document.

2. A monetary loss occurred.

3. The CPA demonstrated a lack of due diligence.

4. Privity with the CPA existed.

5. The document was relied upon.

6. The CPA had scienter.

Knowledge Tested

The elements and defenses to liability for misstatements under

1. Section 11 of the Securities Act of 1933

2. Section 10(b) of the Securities Exchange Act of 1934

Authors' Comments

This question covers liability for misstatements. It requires you to distinguish elements of, and defenses to, liability under Section 11 and Rule 10b-5.

1. The correct answer is (C).
DISCUSSION: Under both Section 11 and Section 10(b), the plaintiff must prove a material misstatement. However, under Section 10b-5, a material misstatement need not have been included in a filed document. Nevertheless, since a CPA acting in that capacity would not usually make such a misstatement other than in a filed writing, the examiner is probably looking for answer (C).

2. The correct answer is (C).
DISCUSSION: To recover under either Section 11 or Section 10(b), the plaintiff is required to prove that (s)he incurred a monetary loss.

3. The correct answer is (D).
DISCUSSION: To recover under Section 11, an investor must prove that (1) the investor acquired a security subject to registration, (2) the registration statement contained a material misstatement or omission, and (3) the investor incurred a loss. Exercising due diligence is a defense to liability. As a defense, it need not be proved by the plaintiff. Under Section 10(b), the plaintiff (purchaser or seller) must prove (1) a misstatement or omission, (2) that is material, (3) made with scienter (intent to deceive), and (4) relied upon, (5) in connection with the purchase or sale of a security. Due diligence is no defense.

4. The correct answer is (D).
DISCUSSION: To recover under Section 11, intent to deceive, reliance, privity, or value given by the plaintiff need not be shown. Under Section 10(b), any buyer or any seller of any security who suffers a monetary loss may sue for recovery. Proof of privity is not required.

5. The correct answer is (B).
DISCUSSION: To recover under Section 11, intent to deceive, reliance, privity, or value given by the plaintiff need not be shown. However, recovery under Rule 10b-5 is generally conditioned upon reliance by the plaintiff. Note, however, that the fraud-on-the-market theory can sometimes represent constructive reliance.

6. The correct answer is (B).
DISCUSSION: To recover under Section 11, intent to deceive, reliance, privity, or value given by the plaintiff need not be shown. One of the requirements for recovery under Section 10(b) and Rule 10b-5 is that the defendant made the material misstatement with scienter (intent to deceive).

OOF QUESTION 2 *(CPA, adapted)* 15-20 minutes

Sleek Corp. is a public corporation whose stock is traded on a national securities exchange. Sleek hired Garson Associates, CPAs, to audit Sleek's financial statements. Sleek needed the audit to obtain bank loans and to make a public stock offering so Sleek could undertake a business expansion program.

Before the engagement, Fred Hedge, Sleek's president, told Garson's managing partner that the audited financial statements would be submitted to Sleek's banks to obtain the necessary loans.

During the course of the audit, Garson's managing partner found that Hedge and other Sleek officers had embezzled substantial amounts of money from the corporation. These embezzlements threatened Sleek's financial stability. When these findings were brought to Hedge's attention, Hedge promised that the money would be repaid and begged that the audit not disclose the embezzlements.

Hedge also told Garson's managing partner that several friends and relatives of Sleek's officers had been advised about the projected business expansion and proposed stock offering, and had purchased significant amounts of Sleek's stock based on this information.

Garson submitted an unqualified opinion on Sleek's financial statements, which did not include adjustments for or disclosures about the embezzlements and insider stock transactions. The financial statements and audit report were submitted to Sleek's regular banks including Knox Bank. Knox, relying on the financial statements and Garson's report, gave Sleek a $2 million loan.

Sleek's audited financial statements were also incorporated in a registration statement prepared under the provisions of the Securities Act of 1933. The registration statement was filed with the SEC in conjunction with Sleek's public offering of 100,000 shares of its common stock at $100 per share.

An SEC investigation of Sleek Corp. disclosed the embezzlements and the insider trading. Trading in Sleek's stock was suspended, and Sleek defaulted on the Knox loan.

Required

The following causes of action, elements, and defenses are alleged by plaintiffs against accountants or raised by defendant accountants.

1. Negligence
2. Common-law fraud
3. Constructive fraud
4. Privity
5. Scienter
6. Due diligence
7. Breach of contract
8. Reliance

Select the best description for each of these eight items from the following. Each description may be used only once.

A. Accountant's failure to perform as agreed, which resulted in a loss

B. Gross negligence or reckless disregard for the truth substituting for intentional misstatement

C. The plaintiff's reasonable response (argument or defense) to the accountant's work product

D. Intent or mental state element of fraud claim

E. Breach of the duty to exercise reasonable care

F. The accountant acting in good faith and following professional standards in SEC registration

G. Intentional misstatement of a material fact, which was made with intent to induce reliance and was justifiably and detrimentally relied upon

H. Both the plaintiff and the defendant being parties to the contract on which the claim was based

For items 9-13, mark (A) if the statement is correct with respect to recovery from Garson under the antifraud provisions of Rule 10b-5 of the Securities Exchange Act of 1934. Mark (B) if it is incorrect.

9. Knox could recover, even though it lacks privity of contract with Garson.

10. A purchaser of the stock who had no contractual relationship with Garson or Sleek could recover.

11. Reliance must generally be proved.

12. Reliance will not be presumed.

13. Gross negligence is sufficient to show scienter.

Knowledge Tested

Elements of and defenses to

1. Negligence
2. Common-law fraud
3. Statutory fraud under Rule 10b-5

Authors' Comments

Items 1-8 are a traditional matching question; i.e., each answer is used only once, and the number of answers equals the number of items. This approach is not used frequently on the CPA exam, but you must be experienced with it. The subject matter is legal terms used in the area of accountant's legal liability.

Items 9-13 are true-false questions about the fact pattern. This type of question is easy to construct and has appeared frequently.

1. The correct answer is (E).

DISCUSSION: The accountant's duty is to exercise the care and competence an ordinarily prudent accountant would under the circumstances.

2. The correct answer is (G).

DISCUSSION: Common-law fraud is an intentional misstatement of a material fact, which induced justifiable reliance and resulted in a loss to the plaintiff.

3. The correct answer is (B).

DISCUSSION: Scienter is an element of fraud. Scienter is the mental state of intentionally misstating a material fact while knowing that it will be relied upon. However, if reckless disregard for the truth or gross negligence results in material misstatement or omission, the scienter element of constructive fraud is present even if the CPA is unaware of the misstatement.

4. The correct answer is (H).

DISCUSSION: For a negligence claim, there must be a relationship between the defendant's breach of duty and the plaintiff's loss (proximate causation). Causation is proximate if there is privity of contract, i.e., if the accountant's work product was provided pursuant to a contract with the defendant.

5. The correct answer is (D).

DISCUSSION: Scienter is an element of a fraud claim. A plaintiff must prove that the defendant acted with a particular mental state: intending a misstatement and intending that it induce reliance.

6. The correct answer is (F).

DISCUSSION: If part of a registration statement for which a CPA was responsible contains a false statement or omission of a material fact, the CPA is liable to an acquirer of securities subject to the registration under Section II of the Securities Act of 1933. However, the CPA is not liable if (s)he exercised due diligence. Compliance with GAAS and GAAP is evidence that the CPA exercised due diligence.

7. The correct answer is (A).

DISCUSSION: Parties to an enforceable contract are legally obligated to perform as promised. Breach of contract is unexcused failure to perform an unconditional contractual obligation as promised. For a party to be liable for damages, the breach must have resulted in a loss.

8. The correct answer is (C).

DISCUSSION: To recover for fraud, a plaintiff must generally show that (s)he suffered a loss as a result of justifiably relying on the CPA's intentional material misstatement of fact.

9. The correct answer is (B).

DISCUSSION: Under Rule 10b-5, liability is to purchasers and sellers of stock of Sleek.

10. The correct answer is (A).

DISCUSSION: Under Rule 10b-5, liability is to purchasers and sellers of stock of Sleek. Privity with Garson or Sleek is not required for recovery from Garson.

11. The correct answer is (A).

DISCUSSION: To recover under Rule 10b-5, the plaintiff must generally show reliance on Garson's intentional misstatement or omission of a material fact.

12. The correct answer is (B).

DISCUSSION: When omission of material facts renders the work product misleading, reliance is presumed. This shifts the responsibility of proving lack of reliance to the accountant. Furthermore, actual reliance on Garson's work product need not be shown when the fraud-on-the-market theory is applied.

13. The correct answer is (A).

DISCUSSION: The intent to misstate a material fact is a required element of fraud. If a purchaser proves that material misstatement resulted from Garson's gross negligence or reckless disregard for the truth, however, the scienter element is also satisfied. This is known as constructive fraud.

ESSAY QUESTION 1 *(CPA, adapted)* 15 to 25 minutes

Dredge Corp. engaged Crew, a CPA licensed by a state board of accountancy, to perform an audit of Dredge's financial statements so that Dredge could obtain a large capital improvement loan. During the audit, Bold, Dredge's CFO, asked Crew to accept a consulting engagement to assist Dredge with the installation of a new computerized accounting system. Crew accepted the consulting engagement and performed it simultaneously with the audit.

While performing the audit, Crew discovered material misstatements in Dredge's financial statements resulting from management fraud committed by Bold. Crew notified Bold of the discovery and was told to disregard it or Crew would lose the consulting engagement. Believing that the consulting engagement would be lost, Crew intentionally did not notify Dredge's audit committee of the fraud and expressed an unqualified opinion on Dredge's financial statements.

Dredge submitted to Ocean Bank the materially misstated financial statements together with Crew's auditor's report. Ocean relied on the opinion in agreeing to finance Dredge's capital improvement.

While performing the consulting engagement, Crew failed to discover that Dredge's new computerized accounting system had insufficient control procedures because Crew omitted steps in order to complete the engagement on time. The insufficient control procedures had allowed and were allowing employees to steal from the corporation.

As a result of Bold's fraud, Dredge defaulted on the Ocean loan and was petitioned into bankruptcy under Chapter 11 of the Federal Bankruptcy Code.

The following events resulted from the above situation:

* Dredge Corp. reported Crew's actions to the state board of accountancy that licensed Crew.

* Dredge Corp. sued Crew for negligence in performing the consulting engagement.

* Ocean Bank sued Crew for common-law fraud for expressing an unqualified opinion on Dredge's financial statements.

Required

1. State the outcome of Dredge Corp.'s suit against Crew for negligence in performing the consulting engagement, and give the reasons for your conclusion.

2. State the outcome of Ocean Bank's suit against Crew for common-law fraud for giving an unqualified opinion on Dredge's financial statements, and give the reasons for your conclusion.

Knowledge Tested

1. A CPA's common-law liability to clients and third parties for negligence and fraud
2. Requirements of negligence
3. Requirements of fraud
4. Performing consulting services simultaneously with an audit engagement

Authors' Comments

The common-law liability of a CPA to clients and third parties should be anticipated on each exam. Be prepared to state the requirements of negligence and fraud and to organize and order the facts that relate to the allegations. Make sure you understand the standards for consulting services engagements. The liability of a CPA for fraud is broad, but liability for negligence is limited to clients and certain third parties. Be very clear on these matters.

AICPA Unofficial Answer

1. Dredge Corp. will be successful in its negligence suit against Crew. Crew owed a duty of care to Dredge to perform the consulting engagement according to the standards of the profession. Crew breached that duty by failing to discover that there were insufficient control procedures in Dredge's new computerized accounting system. Dredge was damaged by Crew's breach of duty because the insufficient control procedures had allowed and were continuing to allow employees to steal.

2. Ocean Bank will be successful in its common-law fraud suit against Crew. Crew intentionally expressed an unqualified opinion on Dredge's materially misstated financial statements. The financial statements and Crew's accountant's report were submitted to Ocean. Ocean justifiably relied on Crew's unqualified opinion in agreeing to finance Dredge's capital improvement. Ocean was damaged as a result of Dredge's default on the loan, which was caused by the fraud.

CHAPTER II
BUSINESS ORGANIZATIONS

These four study units will constitute approximately 20% of the Business Law section.

STUDY UNIT 3: AGENCY

12 pages of outline
33 multiple-choice questions
2 OOFs and 1 essay

A. *Formation and Termination*
B. *Principal's Liabilities*
C. *Disclosed and Nondisclosed Principals*
D. *Agent's Authority and Liabilities*

Agency is a relationship formed when two parties expressly or implicitly consent that one, the agent, will represent the other, the principal, in dealing with third parties. The relationship does not require a contract. The law of agency provides the rights and liabilities of the principal, the agent, and third parties. The major focus of the exam has been on the formation and termination of the agency relationship, the fiduciary duty of the agent, the contract and tort liability of both the principal and the agent, the agent's authority, and the importance of disclosure.

A. Formation and Termination

1. **Formation.** Agency is an express or implied consensual relationship formed when two parties agree that one, the agent, will represent the other, the principal, in dealing with third parties. The agent has authority to act on behalf of the principal and is subject to his/her control. An employer-employee relationship is an example of an agency relationship.

    a. The **principal** must represent that the agent may act on the principal's behalf. The test is objective, i.e., intent as measured by the "reasonable person."

        1) EXAMPLE: Bud overheard Harold say, "I wish I had a boat." Bud went to Boatworld and told them that, acting as Harold's agent, he wanted to buy a boat. An agency was not formed.

    b. An agency may be implied in law without intent to form the relationship. Thus, a person may be held liable as a principal for the act of another even though (s)he did not know (s)he granted any authority.

        1) For example, an **agency by estoppel** may arise if a person holds him/herself out as an agent, the alleged principal knows (or should know) of the representation and fails to adequately deny it, and a third party detrimentally relies on the existence of an agency.

    c. The **agent** must agree to act on the principal's behalf.

    d. Some acts are personal, and may not be delegated, e.g., voting in a public election, executing a will.

    e. An agency relationship need not be contractual. But if the agency arises by contract, each element of a contract must be present (e.g., consideration, mutual assent, etc.).

f.   The agency must have a legal purpose.

g.   Oral agreement is sufficient to form an agency. But if the object of the agency is subject to the statute of frauds, e.g., the sale of land, a writing is required.

h.   The principal must have the legal capacity to perform the act authorized.

1)   A contract entered into by an agent with a party on behalf of an incompetent principal, e.g., a minor, is generally voidable by the principal.

i.   An incompetent agent can bind a competent principal. The agent's act is deemed the act of the principal.

1)   But incapacity of the agent to perform the act authorized may suspend or terminate the agency.

j.   An agency may be formed by ratifying another's acts.

k.   A **power of attorney** is a formal written appointment of an agent. The agent need not be an attorney at law; attorney means agent or spokesperson.

1)   A general power of attorney authorizes the agent to do anything that may be necessary to transact the principal's legal affairs.

2)   A special power of attorney grants authority for only specifically enumerated acts.

2.   **Types of Agents**

a.   **General agents** are authorized to perform a range of acts. They are authorized to perform all acts relevant to the purpose for which they are engaged.

1)   The term universal agent is sometimes used to refer to a person who is authorized to conduct all of the principal's business that the principal may legally delegate.

b.   **Special agents** are engaged for a particular transaction and are authorized to perform specific activities subject to specific instructions.

c.   Uncompensated agents are known as **gratuitous agents**.

d.   A **del credere agent** guarantees the obligations of the third party to the principal.

1)   EXAMPLE: Distributor and Seth contract that Seth will be paid a 10% commission on sales agreements entered into with retailers by Seth as sales agent of Distributor, providing that Seth guarantees the retail customers' credit accounts. Thus, as a condition of formation of the agency, Seth is obligated to pay if a customer does not. Seth is a del credere agent.

3.   **Termination by Act of the Parties.** Because the agency relationship is based on the mutual consent of the parties, the relationship may be terminated by either party, or both of them, even if the termination breaches a contract between principal and agent.

a.   A principal may revoke a grant of authority at any time. Revocation may be implicit or explicit.

b.   An agent may renounce the grant of authority by giving notice to the principal.

c.   If termination breaches a contract, the nonbreaching party has remedies provided by contract law.

d.   An agency relationship terminates when its purpose is fulfilled.

e.   A grant of authority for a specified period of time terminates when the period lapses.

4. **Termination by Operation of Law**. An agency may be terminated by operation of law.

    a. A principal's act of filing a petition in **bankruptcy** terminates an existing agency.

    b. **Insanity** of the principal or the agent terminates the agency.

        1) The agency may merely be suspended during temporary mental incapacity.

            a) Contracts entered into during temporary mental incapacity may be merely voidable by the principal, **not** void.

        2) **Durable agency** or power of attorney continues beyond legal incompetence of the principal if the agency power was conferred in a writing which expressly provided for the agency to exist subsequent to incompetence of the principal.

            a) The durable agency does not extend beyond death of the principal.

    c. **Death** of either the principal or the agent terminates the agency.

    d. **Destruction of the subject matter** of the agency makes fulfilling the purpose of the agency impossible and terminates the agency.

    e. The agent's **violation of his/her fiduciary duty** terminates the agency.

        1) An agent's actual authority may be terminated if the agent obtains an interest in the subject matter of the agency (the object with regard to which the authority is to be exercised). This circumstance breaches the agent's duty of loyalty when that interest is both

            a) Adverse to the principal's own interest in it, and

            b) Obtained without the knowledge and consent of the principal.

    f. A **change of law** that makes an authorized act illegal terminates the agency.

    g. Agency may be terminated by a **change in circumstances** that the agent should realize would cause the principal not to want the agent to act any longer.

        1) A serious change in the value of property or in the business climate may be a basis for such a termination.

            a) EXAMPLE: Chris authorized Sue to sell some platinum when its market value was $100,000. Two weeks later, the market price dropped to $50,000. Sue sold it for $50,000, although she knew the market was volatile and prices would probably revert to $100,000 in another week. The authority might have terminated or been suspended by operation of law when Sue learned of the substantial change in market price.

        2) The agency might be revived upon a recovery or return to the initial circumstances.

        3) If the agent knows that the principal knows of the change and the principal does not give new directions, the agency may not terminate.

        4) If the agent has reasonable doubts as to how or whether the principal would want the agent to act, the agent may act reasonably. That is, the agency would not be terminated.

    h. **War** between the principal's and the agent's countries terminates the agency because there is no way to enforce the relationship.

5. **Agency Coupled with an Interest**. An agency coupled with an interest is one in which the agent has a specific, present, beneficial interest in property which is the subject matter of the agency. (The interest is in the object itself over which the agent's authority is to be exercised.) This form of agency is irrevocable.

   a. EXAMPLE: Dan borrowed $100,000 from Bank, giving Bank security in the form of a grant of authority to sell Dan's farm in case of default.

   b. In themselves, agreements such as the following do not represent agencies coupled with an interest:

      1) Attorney contingent fee contract
      2) Real estate management contract
      3) Real estate exclusive listing agreement

   c. An agency coupled with an interest may be terminated

      1) According to the terms of the agreement whereby it is granted,
      2) By surrender of the authority by the beneficiary of the agency, or
      3) Upon destruction of the subject matter of the agency.

   d. But an agency coupled with an interest is generally not terminated by

      1) Revocation by the principal,
      2) Death of the principal, or
      3) Loss of legal capacity of the principal.

   e. Although an agency coupled with an interest is in form an agency, in theory it is not because it is formed to principally benefit the agent rather than the principal.

6. **Effect of Termination on Authority**. **Actual authority** of the agent to act for, and on behalf of, the principal ceases to exist upon termination, whether by act of the parties or by operation of law.

   a. **Apparent authority** of the agent continues to exist until the third party receives notice of the termination, if the termination is by an act of the parties.

      1) **Actual notice** to the third party is required if the third party has already dealt with the agent.

      2) **Constructive notice**, e.g., in a trade journal, is generally sufficient for other third parties.

   b. If the authorization of the agent was written, the revocation of authorization must be written (equal dignities rule).

   c. Apparent authority ceases to exist upon termination of the agency by operation of law. Notice to third parties is not required.

7. Stop and review! You have completed the outline for this subunit. Study multiple-choice questions 1 through 13 beginning on page 96.

B. Principal's Liabilities

1. **Duties to the Agent**. Most agency relationships are governed by contract. Thus, duties are expressed or implied in the agency agreement. Some of the implied duties of the principal follow:

   a. The principal has a duty to compensate the agent for his/her services unless the agent agrees to act gratuitously. If the duty or if the rate or amount is not expressed, the reasonable value of the agent's services will be implied.

b. The principal has a duty to indemnify (reimburse) the agent for authorized payments made or expenses incurred by the agent on behalf of the principal.

   1) Authorization may be implied from the customs of the business or the course of dealings between the principal and the agent.

c. The principal has a duty to indemnify the agent for losses suffered or expenses incurred while the agent acted as instructed in a legal transaction or in a transaction that the agent did not know to be wrongful.

d. The principal has a duty not to act to impair the agent's performance.

e. The principal is not relieved of the general duty of care (that of a reasonable person under the circumstances) owed by one person to another because a principal-agent relationship exists. Thus, a principal may be liable for negligence to the agent.

f. The principal has a duty to disclose known risks involved in the task for which the agent was engaged if the principal knows the agent is unaware of the risks.

   1) The duty applies if the principal should know of the risk.

   2) The duty applies if the principal should know the agent is unaware of the risk.

g. The principal has a duty to provide an agent who is an employee with reasonably safe working conditions.

   1) The principal has a duty to inspect the premises and warn the agent of unsafe conditions.

2. **Agent's Remedies for Principal's Breach**. Tort and contract remedies are available, such as damages and injunctive relief. The agent may also terminate the agency relationship and/or counterclaim if the principal sues.

3. **Contractual Liability to Third Parties**. If the agent has authority, either actual or apparent, the principal will be liable on contracts entered into with a third party by the agent.

4. **Tort Liability**. A principal may be liable in tort from either his/her personal or his/her agent's wrongful act that results in harm to a third party.

   a. **Direct liability** results from the principal's own negligent or reckless action or failure to act in conducting business through agents if the principal

      1) Negligently selects an agent,

         a) EXAMPLE: Principal hires a person (s)he knows to be a convicted embezzler for a position of trust. The principal is liable for so doing.

      2) Fails to give proper orders or make proper regulations,
      3) Fails to employ the proper person or machinery and there is risk of harm,
      4) Fails to supervise the activity, and/or
      5) Allows wrongful conduct by others on or with his/her property.

b. Except in the case of a gratuitous or noncontractual relationship, an agent is either an employee or an independent contractor. The distinction has significant legal effect. A principal/employer has actual right of control over the physical efforts of an employee. In contrast, an independent contractor is responsible only for the finished product of his/her labor. The degree of control a principal exerts, and whether it results in the agent's having employee or independent contractor status is a factual determination based on considerations such as

1) What the parties agreed would be the degree of control to be exercised by the principal

2) The amount of control and direction the principal actually exerts over the agent's work

3) Whether the agent provides services exclusively for the principal

4) The relationship between the nature of the principal's business and the occupation and work of the agent

5) The specialization required for the task

6) How the agent is compensated, e.g., upon completed work compared to periodically per unit of time

7) Which party provides the agent's place of work, tools, and supplies, and who otherwise pays the agent's overhead expenses

8) The duration of the relationship

c. **Vicarious liability** results from acts of the agent attributed to the principal.

1) The principal is liable if (s)he authorizes the agent's wrongful act that results in damage to another.

2) The principal is liable for the agent's unauthorized wrongful acts if the agent is an employee and if the act was done within the scope and during the course of employment. This is the doctrine of *respondeat superior*, or let the superior respond.

a) With respect to the employer, *respondeat superior* is a form of strict liability (not based on any negligence of the employer).

3) Conduct of an employee is within the scope of employment if

a) Such conduct is of the kind (s)he is employed to perform.

b) It occurs substantially within the authorized time and space limits.

c) It is actuated in part by a purpose or intent to serve the employer.

d) Force is used intentionally by the employee against a third party, and the use of force was reasonably foreseeable and not unexpected by the employer.

4) Whether an employee's departure from the authorized or most direct manner of performance of the employer's business removes the employee's activity from the scope of employment and vicarious liability is determined by the degree of deviation. Slight deviations are within the scope of employment; however, material or gross deviations are outside the scope, and the employer is not vicariously liable under *respondeat superior*.

5) Courts often use the terms **detour** and **frolic** to determine the relative departure and the principal's liability.

    a) An employee that is doing his/her employer's business and serving a purpose of his/her own, or is doing the employer's business in an unauthorized manner, is usually deemed to be engaged in a mere detour and remains within his/her scope of employment.

    b) A frolic denotes that the employee has permanently or temporarily abandoned his employer's business.

        i) The principal is not vicariously liable to third parties for torts within such time and space limits.

6) The principal is liable for torts involving misrepresentation, regardless of whether the agent is an employee or an independent contractor. The agent's act must be within the scope of actual or apparent authority.

    a) EXAMPLE: Mary Lou engaged John, a real estate broker, to market her home. John told Michelle that the home was only 5 years old. The home was actually 15 years old. Michelle bought the home. Both Mary Lou and John are liable for any harm suffered by Michelle as a result of the misrepresentation. (Mary Lou is entitled to indemnification from John.)

d. **Independent contractors**. The principal is generally not liable for the tortious acts of the independent contractor. Exceptions whereby a principal has liability in tort for acts of an independent contractor are based on the principal's own negligence or strict liability. This liability of a principal is not vicarious.

1) Some duties may not be delegated as a matter of law or public policy, e.g., a duty of an employer to provide employees with a safe workplace.

    a) The employer does not avoid liability by engaging an independent contractor to ensure a safe workplace.

2) Ultrahazardous activity is usually the subject of strict liability. Contracting out ultrahazardous activity or a project that involves such activity is not a shield to liability. Examples include using explosives (blasting), using poisonous gas, and transporting hazardous substances such as volatile chemicals.

3) A principal who negligently selects an independent contractor to perform an activity that causes injury is liable for his/her own negligence.

    a) If the principal knows of tortious conduct of the independent contractor and ignores it, the principal may be liable for injury caused by the conduct.

4) The principal is liable for representations made on behalf of the principal that are authorized (or ratified) by the principal.

5. **Criminal Liability**. A principal is liable for his/her own criminal conduct.

  a. A principal is generally not liable for a crime committed by his/her agent.
  b. A principal may be held criminally liable for a crime of his/her agent if

    1) The principal approves or directs the crime,
    2) The principal participates or assists in the crime, or
    3) Violation of a regulatory statute constituted the crime.

6. Stop and review! You have completed the outline for this subunit. Study multiple-choice questions 14 through 19 beginning on page 100.

C. Disclosed and Nondisclosed Principals

1. **Disclosed Principal**. The principal is known to exist by the third party. The third party knows the agent is acting for the principal and knows who the principal is.

2. **Partially Disclosed Principal**. The principal is known to exist by the third party. The third party knows the agent is acting for the principal, but the third party does not know the principal's identity.

3. **Nondisclosed Principal**. The principal is not known to the third party. The third party, in dealing with the agent for the nondisclosed principal, believes that (s)he is dealing with the principal party and not an agent.

    a. Under general contract law principles, the third party can sue the agent of the nondisclosed principal personally, and vice versa, because the third party intended to deal only with the agent and the agent is a party to the contract.

    b. When an agent contracts for a partially disclosed or a nondisclosed principal, both the principal and the agent are liable to the third party.

    c. The nondisclosed principal can generally sue on the contract made on his/her behalf, except when it would be unfair or unjust to the other party. The nondisclosed principal may not be able to enforce a contract that involves

        1) Credit extended by the third party
        2) Unique personal services of the agent
        3) Nondelegable duties
        4) A contract that is a negotiable instrument

        NOTE: A nondisclosed principal does not escape vicarious liability for an agent's tort just because (s)he conceals his/her identity.

        NOTE: If the identity of a principal becomes known to the third party, and the third party has thereafter consented to the principal's performing the contract involving personal services or credit, then the principal may enforce it.

    d. Once the principal is discovered, the third party must elect whether to hold the principal or the agent liable for performance.

    e. If the agent acts outside the scope of actual authority, the nondisclosed principal is generally not liable to the third party.

    f. The nondisclosed principal may ratify a contract formed beyond the scope of the agent's actual authority by accepting the benefits of the contract or other affirmative conduct.

4. **Nonexistent principal** refers to a person representing to a third party that (s)he is acting as an agent when the purported principal has not, in fact, established the purported agency relationship.

    a. EXAMPLE: Purporting to be an agent of a to-be-formed corporation.

    b. A nonexistent principal may ratify or adopt most contracts. Generally, this operates as if the agent assigned a contract to which the agent was a party.

    c. An agent who lacks authority (or exceeds his/her authority) is liable to the third party for breach of an implied warranty of authority.

5. Stop and review! You have completed the outline for this subunit. Study multiple-choice questions 20 through 26 beginning on page 102.

D. **Agent's Authority and Liabilities**

1. **Authority of Agent**. An agency relationship involves mutual understanding that the agent will act on behalf of the principal under the principal's direction and control. The agent can legally bind the principal only when the agent has authority to do so. The Restatement (second) of Agency defines authority as the agent's ability to affect the principal's relations with third parties.

   a. **Actual authority** is conveyed by the principal's manifestation to the agent. It grants the agent the right and power to bind the principal to third parties.

      1) **Express actual authority** results from written or spoken words communicated by the principal to the agent.

      2) **Implied actual authority** is incidental authority inferred from words or conduct manifested by the principal to the agent. It is authority necessary to carry out the purposes for which the agency was established.

         a) It may also be inferred from custom and usage of the business or the agent's position relative to the purposes for which the agency is formed.

         b) Express authority to achieve a result necessarily carries the implied authority to use reasonable means to accomplish the expressly authorized action.

            i) EXAMPLE: Prince hired Aggie to manage a marine fuel dock. Authority to purchase fuel for resale may be implied.

   b. **Apparent authority** or ostensible authority (authority by estoppel) is granted by words or conduct of the principal manifested to a third party that reasonably induce the third party to rely on the agent's authority. Apparent authority gives the agent the power but not necessarily the right to bind the principal to third parties.

      1) EXAMPLE: Prince authorizes Gas Depot to fill Aggie's truck when she uses it for business. After several months, Aggie fills up on Friday. Aggie has apparent authority to get gas on Prince's account, but not the legal right to do so for personal use.

      2) Apparent authority is not based on the words or actions of the agent, nor can it exist if the principal is nondisclosed. It is based on justifiable reliance on conduct of the principal.

      3) The third party does not know the agent lacks actual authority.

         a) If the third party knows the agent lacks actual authority, (s)he cannot justify reliance on the principal's manifestation.

      4) Apparent authority may continue after termination of the agency relationship until the third party receives notice.

2. **Subagents**. Generally, an agent does not have the power to delegate authority or to appoint a subagent unless the principal intends to grant it.

   a. Evidence that the principal intends that the agent be permitted to delegate authority may include any of the following:

      1) An express authorization
      2) The character of the business
      3) Usage of trade
      4) Prior conduct of the principal and agent

    b.   If the agent lacks authority to appoint a subagent but does so anyway, the subagent cannot bind the principal.

    c.   If the agent is authorized to appoint a subagent, the subagent

        1)   Is an agent of both the principal and the agent,
        2)   Binds the principal as if (s)he is the agent, and
        3)   Owes a fiduciary duty to both the principal and the agent.

3.   **Duties to the Principal.** The majority of agency relationships are formed by contract; the parties must perform according to the terms of the agreement. The law of agency supplements an agent's contractual obligations with five duties owed to the principal. They arise by operation of law whether or not they are expressed in the agency agreement. Generally, parties may modify or eliminate, by agreement, one or all of the duties to each other.

    a.   **Fiduciary duty.** The agent must

        1)   Act with utmost loyalty and good faith solely in the principal's interest
        2)   Not compete with the principal
        3)   Not buy from him/herself for the principal without permission
        4)   Not make secret profits on transactions entered into for the principal
        5)   Not represent the principal if (s)he has a conflict of interest

            a)   The principal may consent to representation with full knowledge of all material facts.

                i)   EXAMPLE: Agent representing both Buyer and Seller.

    b.   **Duty of obedience.** The agent must follow lawful explicit instructions of the principal.

        1)   If the instructions are not clear, the agent must act in good faith and in a reasonable manner considering the circumstances.

        2)   If an emergency arises and the agent cannot reach the principal, the agent may deviate from instructions, to the extent warranted.

    c.   **Duty of care and diligence.** The agent must use

        1)   The care and skill of a reasonable person in like circumstances, and
        2)   Special skills or knowledge (s)he has.

    d.   **Duty of notification.** The agent must use reasonable efforts to notify his/her principal of all information (s)he possesses that is relevant to the subject matter of the agency and that (s)he knows or should know will be imputed to the principal.

        1)   EXAMPLE: A 20% change in market price.

    e.   **Duty to account.** The agent must

        1)   Account for money or property received or expended on behalf of the principal

        2)   Not commingle his/her own money or property with that of the principal

4.   **Agent's Breach of Duty.** The agent is liable to the principal for losses resulting from the agent's breach of a duty.

    a.   Transactions between the principal and the agent may be voidable by the principal.

b. A constructive trust in favor of the principal is imposed on profits obtained by the agent as a result of breaching his/her fiduciary duty. The agent in effect holds the profits in trust for the benefit of the principal. The principal recovers the profits by suing the agent.

c. If the principal is sued for the agent's negligence, or the agent ignores the principal's instructions, the principal has a right to indemnification from the agent.

5. **Contractual Liability to Third Parties**. When an agent acts within the scope of actual or apparent authority and contracts with a third party on behalf of a disclosed principal, the agent is generally not liable on the contract to the third party.

   a. Only the principal is liable to the third party.

   b. But if the agent is acting for a nondisclosed or partially disclosed principal, the agent is contractually liable to the third party.

   c. The agent may assume liability on any contract by

      1) Making the contract in his/her own name,
      2) Co-making the contract with his/her principal, or
      3) Guaranteeing the principal's performance.

   d. **Implied warranty of authority**. An agent, by purporting to represent a principal, implicitly warrants to the third party that (s)he has actual authority for his/her conduct.

      1) By the warranty, the agent also warrants that the principal exists and is competent (legally), but not that the principal is capable of performing, or will perform, a contract.

6. **Agent's Tort Liability**. The agent is liable for his/her torts. Acting as an agent does not reduce tort liability.

7. **Criminal Liability**. An agent is personally liable for his/her own criminal conduct.

8. **Ratification**. In the law of agency, ratification is a voluntary election to treat an act purportedly done on one's behalf as if it were originally authorized. It allows the principal to authorize the previously unauthorized act after the act is done.

   a. The principal must be aware of all material facts when manifesting acquiescence in the agent's act.

   b. Ratification may be either express or implied. It may be inferred from the principal's words or conduct that reasonably indicates intent to ratify.

      1) EXAMPLE: Tony contracted to purchase 500 pounds of fish from Greg on behalf of Philly's Restaurant. Philly did not know Tony or Greg. When the fish arrived, Philly accepted the shipment. Her ratification may be inferred.

   c. Ratification is all-or-nothing; the principal may not ratify part of a transaction.

   d. Ratification is irrevocable.

   e. Ratification relates back to the time of the act. The act is treated as if it were authorized at the time it was performed.

   f. An agent has no liability to the third party after ratification. If a principal does not ratify, the agent is also liable to the third party for breach of the implied warranty of authority.

   g. A nondisclosed principal may not be able to ratify certain contracts involving personal services, credit extended by the third party, or nondelegable duties.

1)   A nonexistent principal may ratify the contract if it could have been authorized by that principal when the agent entered into it.

2)   If the agent's unauthorized act is purportedly for an identified principal, only that identified person may ratify it; i.e., the agent cannot find another principal if the identified principal does not ratify it.

9.   Stop and review! You have completed the outline for this subunit. Study multiple-choice questions 27 through 33 beginning on page 104.

MULTIPLE-CHOICE QUESTIONS

A. Formation and Termination

1. Forming an agency relationship requires that

A.   The agreement between the principal and agent be supported by consideration.

B.   The principal and agent not be minors.

C.   Both the principal and agent consent to the agency.

D.   The agent's authority be limited to the express grant of authority in the agency agreement.

The correct answer is (C). *(CPA, adapted)*
REQUIRED: The requirement to form an agency relationship.
DISCUSSION: Agency is an express or implied consensual relationship. Both the principal and agent must manifest consent to the grant of authority. The purpose and subject matter of the agency must be legal. The principal must have legal capacity to perform the act authorized.
Answer (A) is incorrect because consideration is not required to form an agency relationship. Answer (B) is incorrect because an agent need not have legal capacity to enter into a contract to be able to bind a principal on the contract. Answer (D) is incorrect because an agent's authority can extend to more than acts specifically expressed in the agreement. For example, a universal agent is authorized to conduct all business that the principal may legally delegate.

2. A principal and agent relationship requires a

A.   Meeting of the minds and consent to act.

B.   Specified consideration.

C.   Written agreement.

D.   Power of attorney.

The correct answer is (A). *(CPA, adapted)*
REQUIRED: The requirement of a principal/agent relationship.
DISCUSSION: The requirements to form an agency relationship are an agreement between principal and agent on the relationship and subject matter, legality of the subject matter, and capacity of the principal.
Answer (B) is incorrect because formation of the agency relationship does not require consideration. Answer (C) is incorrect because most agency relationships do not require a written agreement. Answer (D) is incorrect because a power of attorney is a specific type of agency.

3. The key characteristic of a servant (employee) is that

A.   His physical conduct is controlled or subject to the right of control by the employer.

B.   He is paid at an hourly rate as contrasted with the payment of a salary.

C.   He is precluded from making contracts for and on behalf of his employer.

D.   He lacks apparent authority to bind his employer.

The correct answer is (A). *(CPA, adapted)*
REQUIRED: The key characteristic of an employee.
DISCUSSION: Master-servant is old terminology (which you may still run across) for employer-employee. A servant is a type of employee whose actions are entirely subject to control by the employer during the relationship. The servant/employee is employed to do physical acts and perform services for the employer, rather than act as a business representative. Other employees may qualify as agents and be subject to lesser physical control.
Answer (B) is incorrect because servants may be paid either at an hourly rate or by salary. Answer (C) is incorrect because a servant may make contracts for and on behalf of his/her employer as long as the servant has authority. Answer (D) is incorrect because a servant may have apparent authority to bind his/her employer, depending on what the servant is doing.

4. Jay White, an engineer, entered into a contract with Sky, Inc., agreeing to provide Sky with certain specified consulting services. After performing the services, White was paid pursuant to the contract, but Social Security taxes were not withheld from his check since Sky considered White an independent contractor. The IRS has asserted that White was an employee and claims that a deficiency exists because of Sky's failure to withhold and pay Social Security taxes. Which of the following factors is most likely to support the IRS's position that White is an employee?

    A. White was paid in one lump sum after all the services were performed.

    B. White provided his own office and supplies.

    C. Sky supervised and controlled the manner in which White performed the services.

    D. Sky reserved the right to inspect White's work.

The correct answer is (C). *(CPA, adapted)*
    REQUIRED: The factor supporting the view that a person is an employee.
    DISCUSSION: An employee's actions are entirely subject to control by the employer during the relationship. An independent contractor is generally hired to achieve certain results without much control over his/her performance. Other factors to be considered are the mode of payment, whether the contracting parties are in distinct businesses or occupations, whether the work is supervised and performed with the employer's tools and supplies, the length of the employment, and the degree of skill involved.
    Answers (A) and (B) are incorrect because they state facts typical of independent contractor status. Answer (D) is incorrect because actual control is the strongest argument in favor of employee status.

5. Which of the following actions requires an agent for a corporation to have a written agency agreement?

    A. Purchasing office supplies for the principal's business.

    B. Purchasing an interest in undeveloped land for the principal.

    C. Hiring an independent general contractor to renovate the principal's office building.

    D. Retaining an attorney to collect a business debt owed the principal.

The correct answer is (B). *(CPA, adapted)*
    REQUIRED: The action requiring a written agency agreement.
    DISCUSSION: Oral agreement usually suffices to form an agency, but purchase of land is subject to the statute of frauds. Under the equal dignities rule, an agency relationship must be in writing if the object of the agency is subject to the statute of frauds.
    Answer (A) is incorrect because purchasing office supplies does not require any formality and is not subject to the requirement of a writing. Answer (C) is incorrect because an independent contractor may be an agent, but the object of the agency, office renovations, is not subject to the formality of a writing. Answer (D) is incorrect because a written agreement is not required. The object of the agency, collecting a debt, does not require a writing.

6. Trent was retained, in writing, to act as Post's agent for the sale of Post's memorabilia collection. Which of the following statements is correct?

   I. To be an agent, Trent must be at least 21 years of age.

  II. Post would be liable to Trent if the collection was destroyed before Trent found a purchaser.

    A. I only.

    B. II only.

    C. Both I and II.

    D. Neither I nor II.

The correct answer is (D). *(CPA, adapted)*
    REQUIRED: The correct statement(s) concerning an agency relationship.
    DISCUSSION: Neither statement is correct because an agent's acts are deemed to be the acts of the principal. Therefore, whether Trent lacks capacity to enter into a contract because he is under 21 years old is irrelevant. In addition, the age of majority in most states is 18 years of age. Further, Post is not liable to Trent if the collection is destroyed because the principal is not required to compensate the agent unless the collection is sold. The agency relationship was terminated by operation of law when the subject matter of the agency relationship was destroyed.
    Answers (A), (B), and (C) are incorrect because Trent's capacity to enter into a contract does not affect the agency relationship because the agent's acts are deemed to be the acts of the principal. In addition, the principal is not liable to the agent because the agency terminated by operation of law when the object of the agency was destroyed.

7. Generally, an agency relationship is terminated by operation of law in all of the following situations except the

- A. Principal's death.
- B. Principal's incapacity.
- C. Agent's renunciation of the agency.
- D. Agent's failure to acquire a necessary business license.

The correct answer is (C). *(CPA, adapted)*
    REQUIRED: The event that terminates an agency relationship but not by operation of law.
    DISCUSSION: An agency is based on the consent of both principal and agent and may be terminated by an act of either party. Thus, it may be terminated by the agent's giving notice of renunciation to the principal. This intentional form of termination is in contrast to the automatic termination by operation of law that results from the occurrence of certain events.
    Answers (A), (B), and (D) are incorrect because death, incapacity, and illegality result in termination by operation of law.

8. Thorp was a purchasing agent for Ogden, a sole proprietor, and had the express authority to place purchase orders with Ogden's suppliers. Thorp placed an order with Datz, Inc. on Ogden's behalf after Ogden was declared incompetent in a judicial proceeding. Thorp was aware of Ogden's incapacity. Which of the following statements is correct concerning Ogden's liability to Datz?

- A. Ogden will be liable because Datz was not informed of Ogden's incapacity.
- B. Ogden will be liable because Thorp acted with express authority.
- C. Ogden will not be liable because Thorp's agency ended when Ogden was declared incompetent.
- D. Ogden will not be liable because Ogden was a nondisclosed principal.

The correct answer is (C). *(CPA, adapted)*
    REQUIRED: The correct statement regarding a principal's liability after being declared incompetent.
    DISCUSSION: An agency relationship is terminated by operation of law when the principal is declared incompetent in a judicial proceeding. Therefore, the principal will not be bound by the contract for supplies entered into by his agent after the principal is declared incompetent.
    Answer (A) is incorrect because notice to third parties is not required when an agency terminates by operation of law. Answer (B) is incorrect because actual authority ceases when an agency is terminated either by operation of law or by action of the parties. Answer (D) is incorrect because the principal's liability for contracts entered into by his agent ended because he was declared incompetent and the agency was terminated, not because he was a nondisclosed principal.

9. Noll gives Carr a written power of attorney. Which of the following statements is correct regarding this power of attorney?

- A. It must be signed by both Noll and Carr.
- B. It must be for a definite period of time.
- C. It may continue in existence after Noll's death.
- D. It may limit Carr's authority to specific transactions.

The correct answer is (D). *(CPA, adapted)*
    REQUIRED: The correct statement regarding a power of attorney.
    DISCUSSION: A power of attorney is a written authorization for the agent to act on behalf of the principal. It can be general, or it can grant the agent restricted authority.
    Answer (A) is incorrect because a power of attorney is a delegation of authority and need only be signed by the principal. Answer (B) is incorrect because, to be effective, a written power of attorney need not be for a definite period of time. Note that the statute of frauds may render an oral power of attorney unenforceable. Answer (C) is incorrect because, in the absence of a special statute, the death of a principal terminates an agency relationship.

10. The apparent authority of a general agent for a disclosed principal will terminate without notice to third parties when the

- A. Principal dismisses the agent.
- B. Principal or agent dies.
- C. Purpose of the agency relationship has been fulfilled.
- D. Time period set forth in the agency agreement has expired.

The correct answer is (B). *(CPA, adapted)*
    REQUIRED: The occurrence automatically terminating a general agent's apparent authority.
    DISCUSSION: In the absence of a special rule, an agency and the agent's power to bind the principal terminate instantly upon the death of the principal because the principal must exist at the time the agent acts.
    Answer (A) is incorrect because, when an agent is dismissed, existing customers must be given actual notice. Other persons must be given constructive notice to terminate apparent authority. Answers (C) and (D) are incorrect because neither fulfillment of the purpose of the agency nor expiration of the agreed period terminates apparent authority.

11. Pell is the principal and Astor is the agent in an agency coupled with an interest. In the absence of a contractual provision relating to the duration of the agency, who has the right to terminate the agency before the interest has expired?

	Pell	Astor
A.	Yes	Yes
B.	No	Yes
C.	No	No
D.	Yes	No

The correct answer is (B). *(CPA, adapted)*
REQUIRED: The person with the right to terminate an agency coupled with an interest.
DISCUSSION: An agency coupled with an interest is one in which the agent has a specific, present, beneficial interest in property which is the subject matter of the agency. A principal does not have the right or power to terminate an agency coupled with an interest. In any agency relationship, the agent may terminate at any time without liability if no specific period for the agency has been established.
Answers (A), (C), and (D) are incorrect because the agent has the right to terminate an agency coupled with an interest, but the principal does not.

12. Young was a purchasing agent for Wilson, a sole proprietor. Young had the express authority to place purchase orders with Wilson's suppliers. Young conducted business through the mail and had little contact with Wilson. Young placed an order with Vanguard, Inc. on Wilson's behalf after Wilson was declared incompetent in a judicial proceeding. Young was aware of Wilson's incapacity. With regard to the contract with Vanguard, Wilson (or Wilson's legal representative) will

A. Not be liable because Vanguard dealt only with Young.

B. Not be liable because Young did not have authority to enter into the contract.

C. Be liable because Vanguard was unaware of Wilson's incapacity.

D. Be liable because Young acted with express authority.

The correct answer is (B). *(CPA, adapted)*
REQUIRED: The effect of the principal's legal incompetence on an agent's authority.
DISCUSSION: An agency relationship is terminated by operation of law if the principal becomes legally incompetent. (Some exceptions apply. See durable agency or power of attorney on pages 86 and 87.) Apparent authority ceases upon termination that occurs by operation of law.
Answers (A) and (C) are incorrect because notice to third parties is not required for apparent authority to cease when an agency terminates by operation of law. Answer (D) is incorrect because actual authority ceases when an agency terminates, whether by act of the parties or by operation of law.

13. Bolt Corp. dismissed Ace as its general sales agent and notified all of Ace's known customers by letter. Young Corp., a retail outlet located outside of Ace's previously assigned sales territory, had never dealt with Ace. Young knew of Ace as a result of various business contacts. After his dismissal, Ace sold Young goods, to be delivered by Bolt, and received from Young a cash deposit for 20% of the purchase price. It was not unusual for an agent in Ace's previous position to receive cash deposits. In an action by Young against Bolt on the sales contract, Young will

A. Lose, because Ace lacked any implied authority to make the contract.

B. Lose, because Ace lacked any express authority to make the contract.

C. Win, because Bolt's notice was inadequate to terminate Ace's apparent authority.

D. Win, because a principal is an insurer of an agent's acts.

The correct answer is (C). *(CPA, adapted)*
REQUIRED: The outcome of a suit by a third party against a principal whose agent had no actual authority.
DISCUSSION: When a principal discharges an agent, (s)he must give actual notice of the discharge to those the agent had previously dealt with and constructive notice to others who might have known of the agency. Ace continued to have apparent authority because of Bolt's failure to give constructive notice by publication in a newspaper of general circulation in the place where the agency activities occurred. Publication in trade journals of the termination would have provided such notice and effectively terminated Ace's apparent authority.
Answers (A) and (B) are incorrect because Young will win. Ace had apparent although not actual (express or implied) authority. Answer (D) is incorrect because a principal is not an insurer of an agent's acts. A principal is only liable when an agent acts with authority, actual or apparent.

B. Principal's Liabilities

14. In an agency relationship, the principal owes a duty to the agent to

- A. Follow lawful explicit instructions of the agent.
- B. Disclose known risks involved in the agency if the agent is known to be unaware of them.
- C. Account for monies received or expended on behalf of the agent.
- D. Use any special skills or knowledge (s)he possesses.

The correct answer is (B). *(Publisher)*
REQUIRED: The duty owed by a principal to an agent.
DISCUSSION: The principal has a duty to disclose known risks involved in the task for which the agent was engaged if the principal knows the agent is unaware of the risks. The duty applies if the principal should know of the risk and if the principal should know the agent is unaware of the risk.
Answer (A) is incorrect because the agent should follow lawful explicit instructions of the principal. Answer (C) is incorrect because the agent should account for monies received or expended on behalf of the principal. Answer (D) is incorrect because the agent should use any special skills or knowledge (s)he possesses.

15. Which of the following statements represent(s) a principal's duty to an agent who works on a commission basis?

I. The principal is required to maintain pertinent records, account to the agent, and pay the agent according to the terms of their agreement.

II. The principal is required to reimburse the agent for all authorized expenses incurred unless the agreement calls for the agent to pay expenses out of the commission.

- A. I only.
- B. II only.
- C. Both I and II.
- D. Neither I nor II.

The correct answer is (C). *(CPA, adapted)*
REQUIRED: The duty owed by a principal to an agent who works on commission.
DISCUSSION: Most agency relationships are governed by contract, and thus fundamental duties are set forth in the agreement. The fundamental duties set forth in the agency agreement may be expressed or implied. Two implied fundamental duties of a principal to an agent are to compensate the agent for his/her services and to indemnify or reimburse the agent for authorized expenses incurred on behalf of the principal. Any renunciation of these duties would require an express agreement.
Answers (A), (B), and (D) are incorrect because the principal has a duty to compensate and reimburse in accordance with the express or implied terms of the employment agreement.

16. Alice Able, on behalf of Pix Corp., entered into a contract with Sky Corp. by which Sky agreed to sell computer equipment to Pix. Able disclosed to Sky that she was acting on behalf of Pix. However, Able had exceeded her actual authority by entering into the contract with Sky. If Pix does not want to honor the contract, it will nonetheless be held liable if Sky can prove that

- A. Able had apparent authority to bind Pix.
- B. Able believed she was acting within the scope of her authority.
- C. Able was an employee of Pix and not an independent contractor.
- D. The agency relationship between Pix and Able was formalized in a signed writing.

The correct answer is (A). *(CPA, adapted)*
REQUIRED: The important factor in determining if a principal is liable for unauthorized acts of an agent.
DISCUSSION: Apparent authority is what third parties believe an agent possesses because of the actions of the principal or the outward appearances of the agency relationship. It is a form of estoppel. Express limitations do limit an agent's actual authority. But if they are not known by third parties, they do not affect apparent authority.
Answer (B) is incorrect because what Sky believed is important, not what Able believed. Answer (C) is incorrect because employees and independent contractors can both be agents. Answer (D) is incorrect because the signed writing does not affect apparent authority with respect to third parties. The signed writing primarily affects the parties involved.

17. Neal, an employee of Jordan, was delivering merchandise to a customer. On the way, Neal's negligence caused a traffic accident that resulted in damages to a third party's automobile. Who is liable to the third party?

	Neal	Jordan
A.	No	No
B.	Yes	Yes
C.	Yes	No
D.	No	Yes

The correct answer is (B). *(CPA, adapted)*
REQUIRED: The liability of the employer and employee for the employee's negligence.
DISCUSSION: A principal is strictly liable for a tort committed by an agent within the scope and during the course of the agent's employment (vicarious liability). This liability is without regard to fault of the principal. Vicarious liability does not apply when the agent performs as an independent contractor. A person is liable for his/her own negligent acts, even if performed as an agent of another.
Answer (A) is incorrect because agent status is not a shield to liability for one's own negligence, and an employer is vicariously liable for his/her employee's acts. Answer (C) is incorrect because an employer is vicariously liable for his/her employee's acts. This is also referred to as *respondeat superior*. Answer (D) is incorrect because agent status is not a shield to liability for one's own negligence.

18. Generally, a disclosed principal will be liable to third parties for its agent's unauthorized misrepresentations if the agent is an

	Employee	Independent Contractor
A.	Yes	Yes
B.	Yes	No
C.	No	Yes
D.	No	No

The correct answer is (B). *(CPA, adapted)*
REQUIRED: The type(s) of agent for whose unauthorized misrepresentations the principal is liable.
DISCUSSION: A principal is liable to third parties for all acts of its employees committed within the course and scope of their employment (even if the employee was instructed not to do the act). A principal is generally not liable for the acts of an independent contractor because an independent contractor is not subject to the control of the employer. There are exceptions, e.g., if the principal authorizes fraud.
Answers (A) and (D) are incorrect because a principal is generally not liable for the acts of an independent contractor because an independent contractor is not subject to the control of the employer. Answer (C) is incorrect because a principal is liable to third parties for all acts of its employees committed within the course and scope of their employment.

19. A principal will not be liable to a third party for a tort committed by an agent

A. Unless the principal instructed the agent to commit the tort.

B. Unless the tort was committed within the scope of the agency relationship.

C. If the agency agreement limits the principal's liability for the agent's tort.

D. If the tort is also regarded as a criminal act.

The correct answer is (B). *(CPA, adapted)*
REQUIRED: The liability of a principal to a third party for a tort committed by the agent.
DISCUSSION: A principal is strictly liable for the torts of an agent committed within the course and scope of the agency agreement, that is, in furtherance of the purpose of the agency. The principal's liability to the third party would be for acts of the agent within the scope of the agent's actual or apparent authority.
Answer (A) is incorrect because a principal is liable for the torts of his/her agent within the scope of employment even if the agent acted without the principal's instruction. Answer (C) is incorrect because an exculpatory clause (a clause relieving a party of a duty or liability) has no effect on a third party not privy to the agreement between the principal and agent. Answer (D) is incorrect because a principal may be liable for torts of his/her agent whether or not the tort is also regarded as a criminal act.

C. Disclosed and Nondisclosed Principals

20. Easy Corp. is a real estate developer and regularly engages real estate brokers to act on its behalf in acquiring parcels of land. The brokers are authorized to enter into such contracts, but are instructed to do so in their own names without disclosing Easy's identity or relationship to the transaction. If a broker enters into a contract with a seller on Easy's behalf,

    A. The broker will have the same actual authority as if Easy's identity had been disclosed.

    B. Easy will be bound by the contract because of the broker's apparent authority.

    C. Easy will not be liable for any negligent acts committed by the broker while acting on Easy's behalf.

    D. The broker will not be personally bound by the contract because the broker has express authority to act.

The correct answer is (A). *(CPA, adapted)*
    REQUIRED: The authority of an agent acting for a nondisclosed principal.
    DISCUSSION: Actual authority is conveyed by the principal's manifestation of consent to the agent to bind the principal to third parties. Actual authority is not affected by failure to disclose the principal.
    Answer (B) is incorrect because an agent of a nondisclosed principal, by definition, has no apparent authority. Answer (C) is incorrect because Easy may be bound by the actions of its agent. Once the third party discovers the nondisclosed principal, the third party may hold Easy liable for the actions of its agent. Answer (D) is incorrect because third parties may hold the agent for a nondisclosed principal personally liable. They entered into agreements intending to deal with the broker only.

21. An agent will usually be liable under a contract made with a third party when the agent is acting on behalf of a

	Disclosed Principal	Nondisclosed Principal
A.	Yes	Yes
B.	Yes	No
C.	No	Yes
D.	No	No

The correct answer is (C). *(CPA, adapted)*
    REQUIRED: The liability of an agent to a third party when the principal is disclosed and nondisclosed.
    DISCUSSION: When a principal is nondisclosed, the third party believes (s)he is dealing directly with the agent. Thus, under general contract law, an agent is liable to the third party because the third party intended to deal only with the agent. An agent who discloses the principal and acts within actual or apparent authority ordinarily binds only the principal.
    Answers (A), (B), and (D) are incorrect because an agent is usually not liable to a third party under a contract when the principal is disclosed. An agent acting for a nondisclosed principal is usually liable.

22. Parc contracted with Furn Brothers Corp. to buy hotel furniture on behalf of Global Motor House, a motel chain. Global instructed Parc to use Parc's own name and not to disclose to Furn that Parc was acting on Global's behalf. Who is liable to Furn on this contract?

	Parc	Global
A.	Yes	No
B.	No	Yes
C.	Yes	Yes
D.	No	No

The correct answer is (C). *(CPA, adapted)*
    REQUIRED: The contract liability of a nondisclosed principal and an agent to a third party.
    DISCUSSION: The third party can look to either the agent or the nondisclosed principal for performance of the contract.
    Answers (A) and (D) are incorrect because the nondisclosed principal is bound by the contract when the third party discovers the arrangement and elects to hold the principal liable. Answer (B) is incorrect because an agent is liable to a third party with whom (s)he has entered into a contract on behalf of a nondisclosed principal.

23. Which of the following rights will a third party be entitled to after validly contracting with an agent representing a nondisclosed principal?

- A. Disclosure of the principal by the agent.
- B. Ratification of the contract by the principal.
- C. Performance of the contract by the agent.
- D. Election to void the contract after disclosure of the principal.

The correct answer is (C). *(CPA, adapted)*
REQUIRED: The right of a third party contracting with an agent representing a nondisclosed principal.
DISCUSSION: The third party is entitled to enforce a contract against the agent of a nondisclosed principal and against the nondisclosed principal when the third party discovers the principal and elects to hold him/her liable.

Answer (A) is incorrect because business may be conducted by a principal without disclosing the agency relationship. The third party does not have a legal right to disclosure of the relationship. Answer (B) is incorrect because a nondisclosed principal may ratify a contract beyond the scope of the agent's actual authority. The third party does not, however, have a legal right to it. Answer (D) is incorrect because the third party has no right to void an otherwise valid contract based on disclosure of a nondisclosed principal.

24. When a valid contract is entered into by an agent on the principal's behalf, in a nondisclosed principal situation, which of the following statements concerning the principal's liability is correct?

	The Principal May Be Held Liable Once Disclosed	The Principal Must Ratify the Contract to Be Held Liable
A.	Yes	Yes
B.	Yes	No
C.	No	Yes
D.	No	No

The correct answer is (B). *(CPA, adapted)*
REQUIRED: The event(s) that would cause a nondisclosed principal to be held liable.
DISCUSSION: A third party may elect to hold a nondisclosed principal liable once the principal is disclosed. A principal, whether nondisclosed or not, can always be held liable for a valid contract entered into by an agent acting within the scope of actual authority, regardless of whether the principal ratifies the contract.

Answers (A), (C), and (D) are incorrect because a principal is liable to a third party once the principal is disclosed, and a principal is liable under a contract entered into by an agent regardless of whether the principal ratifies the contract.

25. When an agent acts for a nondisclosed principal, the principal will not be liable to third parties if the

- A. Principal ratifies a contract entered into by the agent.
- B. Agent acts within an implied grant of authority.
- C. Agent acts outside the grant of actual authority.
- D. Principal seeks to conceal the agency relationship.

The correct answer is (C). *(CPA, adapted)*
REQUIRED: The nondisclosed principal's liability.
DISCUSSION: A nondisclosed principal is generally not liable for acts of the agent beyond the scope of actual authority.

Answer (A) is incorrect because the nondisclosed principal is fully liable following ratification. Answer (B) is incorrect because implied authority is authority to do what is reasonably necessary to perform what is expressly authorized. Whether the principal is disclosed does not affect its scope. Implied authority is actual authority. Answer (D) is incorrect because this is common business practice. It is not per se fraudulent. A nondisclosed (concealed) principal does have duties to third parties.

26. Able, as agent for Baker, a nondisclosed principal, contracted with Safe to purchase an antique car. In payment, Able issued his personal check to Safe. Able could not cover the check but expected Baker to give him cash to deposit before the check was presented for payment. Baker did not do so, and the check was dishonored. Baker's identity became known to Safe. Safe may not recover from

A. Baker individually on the contract.

B. Able individually on the contract.

C. Baker individually on the check.

D. Able individually on the check.

The correct answer is (C). *(CPA, adapted)*
   REQUIRED: The liability of agent and nondisclosed principal when the agent issued a personal check.
   DISCUSSION: The third party may recover for breach of contract from the agent of a nondisclosed principal and from the nondisclosed principal when the third party discovers the principal and elects to hold him/her liable. The drawer (Able) is individually liable on his/her check because the check is commercial paper which has been negotiated. Safe has no recourse on the check against a person who has not endorsed it.
   Answer (A) is incorrect because the third party who discovers the nondisclosed principal may elect to hold him/her liable on the contract. Answer (B) is incorrect because the agent of a nondisclosed principal is liable on contracts. Answer (D) is incorrect because a person is liable for payment on a check (s)he has endorsed, without regard to underlying contracts.

D. Agent's Authority and Liabilities

27. Kent Corp. hired Blue as a sales representative for 9 months at a salary of $2,000 per month plus 2% of sales. Under the circumstances,

A. Kent does not have the power to dismiss Blue during the 9-month period without cause.

B. The agreement between Kent and Blue is not enforceable unless it is in writing and signed by Blue.

C. The agreement between Kent and Blue formed an agency coupled with an interest.

D. Blue is obligated to act solely in Kent's interest in matters concerning Kent's business.

The correct answer is (D). *(CPA, adapted)*
   REQUIRED: The correct statement about an employment relationship.
   DISCUSSION: As a sales representative, Blue is an agent for Kent Corp. As an agent, Blue owes a fiduciary duty to the principal. An agent must act solely in the interest of the principal, and not in his/her own interest or the interest of a third party.
   Answer (A) is incorrect because Kent can dismiss Blue for any reason but may be liable for damages if the termination is wrongful. Answer (B) is incorrect because employment and agency contracts may be oral (but not if they cannot be performed within 1 year of their making). Answer (C) is incorrect because the agent must have a beneficial interest in an agency coupled with an interest. The commission arrangement does not constitute a beneficial interest.

28. Ace engages Butler to manage Ace's retail business. Butler has the implied authority to do all of the following, except

A. Purchase inventory for Ace's business.

B. Sell Ace's business fixtures.

C. Pay Ace's business debts.

D. Hire or discharge Ace's business employees.

The correct answer is (B). *(CPA, adapted)*
   REQUIRED: The agent's implied authority.
   DISCUSSION: An agent's actual authority is conveyed by communication to the agent from the principal. It is not practical to expressly state each act authorized to perform the agent's purpose. So the law recognizes an agent to have both expressed and implied actual authority. Implied actual authority is for acts reasonably necessary to execute express authority. Selling the business fixtures is not necessary to manage a retail business.
   Answers (A), (C), and (D) are incorrect because each is an act necessary to execute the express authorization to manage the store.

29. Frost's accountant and business manager has the authority to

A. Mortgage Frost's business property.

B. Obtain bank loans for Frost.

C. Insure Frost's property against fire loss.

D. Sell Frost's business.

The correct answer is (C). *(CPA, adapted)*
REQUIRED: The authorized act of an agent.
DISCUSSION: An agent has express and implied actual authority, which is conveyed by manifestations of the principal to the agent. Implied authority is to do what is reasonably necessary to accomplish that which was expressly authorized. Obtaining insurance against fire loss would be implied.

Answers (A), (B), and (D) are incorrect because apparent authority depends on reasonable reliance on manifestations of the principal to the third party. It is unlikely that a third party would reasonably rely on nonspecific communications that the principal intended to authorize such acts of an accountant and business manager.

30. Ted Simmons, an agent for Jensen, has the express authority to sell Jensen's goods. Simmons also has the express authority to grant discounts of up to 5% of list price. Simmons sold Hemple goods with a list price of $1,000 and granted Hemple a 10% discount. Hemple had not previously dealt with either Simmons or Jensen. Which of the following courses of action may Jensen properly take?

A. Seek to void the sale to Hemple only.

B. Seek recovery of $50 from Hemple only.

C. Seek recovery of $50 from Simmons only.

D. Seek recovery of $50 from either Hemple or Simmons.

The correct answer is (C). *(CPA, adapted)*
REQUIRED: The right of a principal to collect from an agent after the agent gave an unauthorized discount.
DISCUSSION: Simmons had apparent authority to grant a 10% discount to Hemple because Jensen would reasonably rely on the express authority as implicit authority to give the discount. Simmons, however, had actual authority to grant only a 5% discount. Simmons has violated his actual authority and is liable to the principal for any loss [(10% – 5%) of $1,000] sustained as a result of his actions.

Answer (A) is incorrect because Simmons had apparent authority, and the principal therefore cannot void the contract by denying the existence of actual authority. Answers (B) and (D) are incorrect because Hemple is not liable to Jensen.

31. North, Inc. hired Sutter as a purchasing agent. North gave Sutter written authorization to purchase, without limit, electronic appliances. Later, Sutter was told not to purchase more than 300 of each appliance. Sutter contracted with Orr Corp. to purchase 500 tape recorders. Orr had been shown Sutter's written authorization. Which of the following statements is correct?

A. Sutter will be liable to Orr because Sutter's actual authority was exceeded.

B. Sutter will not be liable to reimburse North if North is liable to Orr.

C. North will be liable to Orr because of Sutter's actual and apparent authority.

D. North will not be liable to Orr because Sutter's actual authority was exceeded.

The correct answer is (C). *(CPA, adapted)*
REQUIRED: The correct statement regarding liability for a contract beyond the agent's actual authority.
DISCUSSION: A principal is liable on contracts made by the agent with actual or apparent authority. Sutter had apparent authority to make the contract because of the principal's communication (letter) manifested to the third party. The third party's rights are not limited by the secret limits placed on actual authority. Sutter had actual authority for up to 300 units and apparent authority for the balance.

Answer (A) is incorrect because the agent is not liable to the third party for acting as an agent with apparent authority. Answer (B) is incorrect because the agent is liable to the principal for acting beyond actual authority. Answer (D) is incorrect because the principal is liable for acts of the agent within actual or apparent authority.

32. Able exceeded her actual authority when she concluded an agreement with Sky Corp. on behalf of Pix Corp. If Pix wishes to ratify the contract with Sky, which of the following statements is correct?

- A. Pix must notify Sky that Pix intends to ratify the contract.
- B. Able must have acted reasonably and in Pix's best interest.
- C. Able must be a general agent of Pix.
- D. Pix must have knowledge of all material facts relating to the contract at the time it is ratified.

The correct answer is (D). *(CPA, adapted)*
REQUIRED: The requirement to ratify an unauthorized act.
DISCUSSION: The person who ratifies becomes legally bound on a contract that was entered into by another who, without authority, purported to act as the principal's agent. To ratify a contract, the principal must have full knowledge of the material facts.
Answer (A) is incorrect because a principal does not need to notify a third party to make a ratification effective. Answer (B) is incorrect because whether the agent acted reasonably and in the principal's best interest is irrelevant if the principal has the power to ratify and knows all material facts. Answer (C) is incorrect because whether the agency was general does not affect the power to ratify.

33. H&M, Inc. owns and operates a fast food restaurant under a franchise agreement with Foodco, Inc., a large national franchisor. Eighty percent of all Foodco Restaurants are owned by franchisees. The Foodco restaurants uniformly use the same name, building design, colors, signs, advertising, promotions, employee work apparel, menus, and prices. The strategy stated in the franchise materials is that the public must believe that Foodco is "a chain that sells a product across the nation." Foodco requires H&M to follow standardized methods of operation, deal exclusively with the franchisor for supplies, and pay a stated percentage of sales for the franchise license. A customer injured on the premises through H&M's negligence discovered that H&M is behind in its debts and carries inadequate liability insurance. Which of the following statements is correct concerning Foodco's possible liability to the injured customer?

- A. Foodco, as the franchisor, is not liable in the absence of an actual agency relationship between it and H&M, the franchisee.
- B. A franchise agreement usually creates a principal-agency relationship making the franchisor liable for torts of the franchisee that occur in the course of business.
- C. The theory of agency by estoppel, rather than express agency, is a plausible basis for finding an agency relationship resulting in liability of the franchisor for the actions of the franchisee.
- D. If an express, implied, or apparent agency relationship exists between the franchisee and the franchisor, the principal franchisor has a duty to indemnify the agent franchisee for tort liability incurred within the course and scope of the relationship.

The correct answer is (C). *(Publisher)*
REQUIRED: The basis for finding a franchisor liable for injuries to its franchisee's customer.
DISCUSSION: Two relationships must be established for the customer to recover from Foodco. First, a principal-agency relationship between Foodco and H&M must have existed at the time the customer was injured. Second, the negligent act that injured the customer must have occurred within the scope and during the course of H&M's franchise agreement with and employment by Foodco. The most likely agency relationship that may be established here is agency by estoppel rather than actual or express agency. Foodco caused the public (including the injured customer) to hold a reasonable belief that each restaurant was part of a chain operated by Foodco, Inc., which is a basis for finding agency by estoppel. Foodco's actions created an appearance of agency that in fact did not exist. Thus, because of its actions, Foodco is estopped (prevented) from denying the existence of an agency relationship. If an agency relationship is established, Foodco, as principal, is liable for any harm caused to a third party by its agent, H&M, within the course and scope of employment.
Answer (A) is incorrect because an agency relationship can be express, implied, or apparent (i.e., through estoppel), and in each case the principal incurs liability. Answer (B) is incorrect because a franchise agreement is usually not a principal-agency relationship due to the lack of control or right to control. A franchisor may control a franchisee to the extent that an actual agency relationship is established. Answer (D) is incorrect because agents are not entitled to indemnification by their employers for torts unless the tort is the fault of the principal. Agents are directly liable to third parties for their own negligence or other misconduct. Furthermore, agents may be required to indemnify their principals for liabilities imputed to the principals because of the agents' wrongdoings.

Use Gleim's ***CPA Test Prep*** for interactive testing with over 2,000 additional multiple-choice questions!

OOF QUESTION 1 *(CPA, adapted)* 15 minutes

Exotic Pets, Inc. hired Peterson to be the manager of one of its stores. Exotic sells a wide variety of animals. Peterson was given considerable authority by Exotic to operate the store, including the right to buy inventory. Peterson was told that any inventory purchase exceeding $3,000 required the approval of Exotic's general manager.

On June 1, 1999, Peterson contracted with Creatures Corp. to buy birds for $5,000. Peterson had regularly done business with Creatures on Exotic's behalf in the past, and on several occasions had bought $2,000 to $2,750 worth of birds from Creatures. Creatures was unaware of the limitation on Peterson's authority to buy inventory.

Peterson occasionally would buy, for Exotic, a certain breed of dog from Premier Breeders, Inc., which was owned by Peterson's friend. Whenever Exotic bought dogs from Premier, Premier paid Peterson 5% of the purchase price as an incentive to do more business with Premier. Exotic's management was unaware of these payments to Peterson.

On June 20, 1999, Mathews went to the Exotic store managed by Peterson to buy a ferret. Peterson allowed Mathews to handle one of the ferrets. Peterson knew that this particular ferret had previously bitten one of the store's clerks. Mathews was bitten by the ferret and seriously injured.

On July 23, 1999, Peterson bought paint and brushes for $30 from Handy Hardware. Peterson charged the purchase to Exotic's account at Handy. Peterson intended to use the paint and brushes to repaint the pet showroom. Exotic's management had never specifically discussed with Peterson whether Peterson had the authority to charge purchases at Handy.

Required

For questions 1 through 15, answer (A) if the better answer is yes and answer (B) if the better answer is no.

Items 1 through 6 relate to the following: On August 1, 1999, Exotic's president learned of the Creatures contract and advised Creatures that Exotic would neither accept delivery of the birds nor pay for them because Peterson did not have the authority to enter into the contract.

1. Did Peterson agree to buy the birds for $5,000 with actual authority?
2. Did Peterson have apparent authority to make a $5,000 bird purchase?
3. Was Creatures bound by the limitation on the amount of inventory Peterson could buy?
4. Is Exotic liable for the full amount of Creatures' damages?
5. Is Peterson liable to Creatures for the amount of Creatures' damages?
6. Is Peterson liable to Exotic for the amount of Creatures' damages?

Items 7 through 9 relate to the following: Exotic's president has learned about the incentive payments Premier made to Peterson.

7. Did Peterson breach a duty to Exotic?
8. Is Premier liable to Exotic for the 5% amounts paid to Peterson?
9. Is Peterson liable to Exotic for the incentive payments?

Items 10 through 13 relate to the following: Mathews has sued both Peterson and Exotic for the injuries sustained from the ferret bite.

10. Could Exotic be sued for negligence?
11. Is Exotic liable for Peterson's negligence?
12. Is Peterson liable for Peterson's negligence?
13. Could Exotic recover from Peterson any amount which it pays Mathews?

Items 14 and 15 relate to the following: Exotic paid the Handy bill, but Exotic's president believes that Peterson is obligated to reimburse Exotic for the charges.

14. Did Peterson have the authority to charge the purchases at Handy?
15. Is Peterson obligated to reimburse Exotic?

Knowledge Tested

1. Scope of agent's authority
2. Agent's fiduciary duty to principal
3. Liability of principal to third party
4. Liability of agent to third party
5. Liability of agent to principal
6. Liability of third party to principal

Authors' Comments

This question distinguishes express, implied, and actual authority of an agent, and the liability of the principal, agent, and third party which results from the agent's acts. Both contractual and tort liability are presented. Remember that the third party is generally not contractually liable beyond his/her agreement. Success on this type of question requires you to keep the parties and the issues straight.

1. The correct answer is (B).

DISCUSSION: Actual authority is either express or implied. Express authority is by written or spoken words to the agent. Authority may be implied from the principal's words or conduct manifested to the agent. Implied authority is incidental, but not contrary, to express authority. Peterson was authorized to make inventory purchases of only $3,000 and thus did not have actual authority to make a $5,000 purchase.

2. The correct answer is (A).

DISCUSSION: Apparent authority arises by words or conduct of the principal manifested to a third party which induces the third party to rely on the agent's authority. From Creatures' perspective, Peterson, as a store manager whose previous contracts had been performed, appeared to have authority.

3. The correct answer is (B).

DISCUSSION: The limitation was to actual authority which would negate apparent authority only if Creatures were aware of it. Creatures was not aware of the $3,000 limit and thus was not bound by the $3,000 limitation.

4. The correct answer is (A).

DISCUSSION: A disclosed principal is liable on contracts entered into with a third party by an agent with actual or apparent authority. Thus, Exotic is liable for the full amount of Creatures' damages.

5. The correct answer is (B).

DISCUSSION: An agent acting within the scope of actual or apparent authority who contracts with a third party on behalf of a disclosed principal is generally not liable on the contract to the third party. The principal, Exotic, is liable to Creatures for the amount of its damages.

6. The correct answer is (A).

DISCUSSION: The agent is liable to the principal for losses resulting from the agent's breach of duty (contractual or otherwise) to the principal. Even if the agent has the power to act beyond express or implied actual authority, the agent does not have the right to do so. Therefore, Peterson is liable to Exotic for its damages.

7. The correct answer is (A).

DISCUSSION: Peterson, as agent, may not make secret profits or otherwise benefit directly or indirectly from the agency relationship to the principal's detriment. Thus, he has breached his implied fiduciary duty of loyalty to the principal in retaining the 5% commissions.

8. The correct answer is (B).

DISCUSSION: Premier's contractual liability to Exotic is limited to the obligations it agreed to perform with respect to Exotic in the agreement Premier entered into with Peterson acting as agent on behalf of Exotic as principal. Thus, Premier is not liable to Exotic for the amounts paid to Peterson.

9. The correct answer is (A).

DISCUSSION: Peterson, as agent, must pay to the principal any profits received from the agency relationship without the principal's consent. A constructive trust is implied by law on the profits for the principal's benefit.

10. The correct answer is (A).

DISCUSSION: A party is liable for his/her own negligence. Exotic is liable for its own negligence, if any, e.g., if it continued to employ Peterson knowing Peterson allowed customers to handle animals that had previously bitten customers.

11. The correct answer is (A).

DISCUSSION: An employer has vicarious liability, that is, the employer is strictly liable for the torts of its employees if the tort occurs within the scope and course of employment. An employee is one whose physical efforts are subject to the employer's control. The conduct occurred on the job, during working hours, and with the intention of benefiting Exotic. Therefore, Exotic is liable for Peterson's negligence.

12. The correct answer is (A).

DISCUSSION: All persons are liable for their own negligence.

13. The correct answer is (A).

DISCUSSION: Mathews can recover for losses from either Exotic or Peterson. If Exotic pays Mathews, Exotic is entitled to indemnification from Peterson. Peterson is liable for Exotic's losses which result from Peterson's breach of any duty to Exotic.

14. The correct answer is (A).

DISCUSSION: Peterson had actual authority. It was not express. Implied authority is inferred from words or conduct of the principal to the agent. It is incidental authority to do that which is necessary to exercise actual authority. As store manager, Peterson would have actual implied authority to purchase supplies to improve the store.

15. The correct answer is (B).

DISCUSSION: As an agent acting within the scope of actual authority, Peterson is not liable on a contract entered into with a third party on behalf of the principal and is not obligated to reimburse Exotic.

OOF QUESTION 2 *(CPA, adapted)* 10-15 minutes

Lace Computer Sales Corp. orally contracted with Banks, an independent consultant, for Banks to work part-time as Lace's agent to perform Lace's customer service calls. Banks, a computer programmer and software designer, was authorized to customize Lace's software to the customers' needs on a commission basis but was specifically told not to sell Lace's computers.

On September 15, Banks made a service call on Clear Co. to repair Clear's computer. Banks had previously called on Clear, customized Lace's software for Clear, and collected cash payments for the work performed. During the call, Banks convinced Clear to buy an upgraded Lace computer for a price much lower than Lace would normally charge. Clear had previously purchased computers from other Lace agents and had made substantial cash down payments to the agents. Clear had no knowledge that the price was lower than normal. Banks received a $1,000 cash down payment and promised to deliver the computer the next week. Banks never turned in the down payment and left town. When Clear called the following week to have the computer delivered, Lace refused to honor Clear's order.

Required

Items 1 through 5 relate to the relationship between the parties. For each item, select A. if only statement I is correct, select B. if only statement II is correct, select C. if both statements are correct, or select D. if neither statement is correct.

A. I only.
B. II only.
C. Both I and II.
D. Neither I nor II.

1. I. Lace's agreement with Banks had to be in writing for it to be a valid agency agreement.

   II. Lace's agreement with Banks empowered Banks to act as Lace's agent.

2. I. Clear was entitled to rely on Banks's implied authority to customize Lace's software.

   II. Clear was entitled to rely on Banks's express authority when buying the computer.

3. I. Lace's agreement with Banks was automatically terminated by Banks's sale of the computer.

   II. Lace must notify Clear before Banks's apparent authority to bind Lace will cease.

4. I. Lace is not bound by the agreement made by Banks with Clear.

   II. Lace may unilaterally amend the agreement made by Banks to prevent a loss on the sale of the computer to Clear.

5. I. Lace, as a disclosed principal, is solely contractually liable to Clear.

   II. Both Lace and Banks are contractually liable to Clear.

Knowledge Tested

1. Agency: formation; actual, implied, and apparent authority; liabilities of the parties; and termination

Authors' Comments

Agency is an express or implied consensual relationship formed when two parties agree that one, the agent, will represent the other, the principal, in dealing with third parties.

1. The correct answer is (B).
   DISCUSSION: This agreement calls for Banks to represent Lace on all customer service calls and, therefore, forms an agency relationship. Unless the object of the agency is subject to the statute of frauds (e.g., the agent is to buy or sell land) or a power of attorney, an oral agreement suffices to form an agency relationship.

2. The correct answer is (A).
   DISCUSSION: Banks, as agent for Lace, was expressly authorized to provide computer services including customizing software to Lace's customers. He was specifically told not to sell Lace's computers. A principal is bound on contracts with third parties if the agent had actual apparent authority at the time the contract was formed. Actual authority includes both express and implied authority. Clear Co., a customer of Lace, was entitled to rely on Banks's implied authority to customize the software. Clear Co. was not entitled to rely on Banks's express authority when buying the computer because it did not exist.

3. The correct answer is (B).
   DISCUSSION: Agency relationships are terminated by an act of the parties or by operation of law. Agency relationships are terminated automatically by operation of law upon the death or insanity of either party, bankruptcy of the principal, destruction of the subject, and war. Other terminations are by an act of the parties and are not automatic. An agent's disregard for the express limitation of his/her authority would be cause for termination by the principal, but termination would not occur automatically. A terminated agent continues to have apparent authority to bind the principal until actual notice is given to parties such as Clear Co. that have done business with the agent. Others who may know of the agency relationship are entitled to constructive notice by publication. Notice is not required when the termination is by operation of law.

4. The correct answer is (D).
   DISCUSSION: Banks lacked actual authority to sell Clear Co. a computer, but based on previous purchases made from other agents and not objected to by Lace's management (including large cash down payments), Banks had apparent authority to make computer sales and receive cash deposits. Lace is bound by the agreement made by Banks with Clear Co. and may not impose changes in the contract without Clear's consent.

5. The correct answer is (A).
   DISCUSSION: A disclosed principal is solely liable on contracts with third parties by an agent with actual or apparent authority. An agent who acts within actual or apparent authority is not liable on the contract to the third party. An agent who disobeys instructions as Banks did is liable to his/her principal for the amount of any damages.

ESSAY QUESTION (CPA, adapted) 15-20 minutes

Prime Cars, Inc. buys and sells used automobiles. Occasionally Prime has its salespeople purchase used cars from third parties without disclosing that the salesperson is in fact buying for Prime's used car inventory. Prime's management believes better prices can be negotiated using this procedure. One of Prime's salespeople, Peterson, entered into a contract with Hallow in accordance with instructions from Prime's sales manager. The car was to be delivered 1 week later. After entering into the contract with Hallow, and while driving back to Prime's place of business, Peterson was involved in an automobile accident with another vehicle. Peterson's negligence, and the resulting collision, injured Mathews, the driver of the other car involved in the accident.

Prime terminated Peterson's employment because of the accident. Following Prime's general business practices, Prime published an advertisement in several trade journals that gave notice that Peterson was no longer employed by Prime. Shortly thereafter, Peterson approached one of Prime's competitors, Bagley Autos, Inc., and contracted to sell Bagley several used cars in Prime's inventory. Bagley's sales manager, who frequently purchased cars out of Prime's inventory from Peterson, paid 25% of the total price to Peterson, with the balance to be paid 10 days later when the cars were to be delivered. Bagley's sales manager was unaware of Peterson's termination. Prime refused to deliver the cars to Bagley or to repay Bagley's down payment, which Prime never received from Peterson.

Prime also refused to go through with the contract entered into by Peterson with Hallow. Mathews sued both Peterson and Prime for the injuries sustained in the automobile accident. Bagley sued Prime for failing to deliver the cars or return the down payment paid to Peterson.

Required

Answer each of the following questions, setting forth the reasons for your conclusions.

a. What rights does Hallow have against Prime or Peterson?

b. Will Mathews prevail in the lawsuit against Prime and Peterson?

c. Will Bagley prevail in its lawsuit against Prime?

Knowledge Tested

1. Liability of principal and agent for contracts
2. Negligence by agent
3. Effect of nondisclosure of principal
4. Termination of actual and apparent authority

Authors' Comments

In Part a., a third party who is unaware of the agency relationship may enforce the contract against the agent as well as against the principal after its identity is known. Agents may exercise apparent authority only after the third party learns of the agency relationship. Third parties may recover only their actual damages from the principal and/or the agent. Note: Liability of the principal **or** the agent was questioned, but discussion of liability of **each** was required.

In Part b., an employer's vicarious liability is strict liability for an employee's acts within the scope and course of employment. Agents are also liable for their own torts.

In Part c., apparent authority can continue after express termination. Actual notice is necessary to third parties who dealt with the agent before termination. Constructive notice is effective for others.

Note: If you wish to work additional essay material, see Parts a. and b. of the essay question in Study Unit 10.

AICPA Unofficial Answer

a. Peterson was acting for a nondisclosed principal (Prime) with regard to the contract with Hallow. Peterson was acting with actual authority; therefore, Prime is liable to Hallow. Peterson is also liable to Hallow because agents acting on behalf of nondisclosed principals are liable to the third parties on the contracts they enter into with such third parties on behalf of the principal. Hallow, however, cannot collect damages from both Peterson and Prime and must make an election between them.

b. At the time of the accident, Peterson was acting within the scope of employment because the conduct engaged in (that is, entering into a contract with Hallow) was authorized by Prime. Prime, therefore, will be liable to Mathews because the accident occurred within the scope of Peterson's employment.

Peterson will also be liable to Mathews because all persons are liable for their own negligence.

c. Peterson's actual authority to enter into contracts on Prime's behalf ceased on termination of employment by Prime. Peterson, however, continued to have apparent authority to bind Prime because

- Peterson was acting ostensibly within the scope of authority as evidenced by past transactions with Bagley.
- Bagley was unaware of Peterson's termination.

The trade journal announcement was not effective notice to terminate Peterson's apparent authority in relation to Bagley because

- Prime was obligated to give actual notice to Bagley that Peterson was no longer employed.
- Actual notice is required because of Bagley's past contact with Peterson while Peterson was employed by Prime.

STUDY UNIT 4: PARTNERSHIPS

14 pages of outline
39 multiple-choice questions
2 OOFs and 1 essay

A. *Formation and Existence*
B. *Authority and Liabilities*
C. *Allocation of Profit or Loss*
D. *Transfer of Interest*
E. *Dissolution and Termination*

A partnership is an association of two or more persons carrying on a business as co-owners for profit. In some ways a partnership is treated as an entity distinct from its members but is usually treated as a form of agency between the individual partners. The relationship can be created without formality, and intent to form a partnership is not required.

A limited partnership is formed by two or more persons in accordance with the requirements of a state statute. A limited partnership has one or more general partners who assume unlimited liability and one or more limited partners. Other variations of the traditional partnership include limited liability partnerships and limited liability companies. Examination questions usually relate to the characteristics of partnerships, limited liability companies, and joint ventures, rules of formation, allocation of profit and losses, transfer and termination, and the rights and liabilities of partners to each other and to third parties.

A. **Formation and Existence**. Partnership law is codified in the Uniform Partnership Act (UPA). The UPA has been adopted by all states except Louisiana.

1. **Definition.** A **partnership** is an association of two or more persons, conducting a business, which they co-own, for profit.

2. The UPA defines **business** as every trade, occupation, or profession.

3. Partners must intend that their business make a profit, even if no profit is earned.

   a. Intent is tested objectively. Whether the parties intend to become, or do not think they are becoming, partners is immaterial. Thus, parties may be estopped from denying a partnership was formed.

4. Partnerships can be formed without any formality.

5. There must be an agreement among persons to associate. The agreement may be written, oral, or implied from conduct.

   a. Any person who has the legal capacity to enter into a contract may enter into a partnership agreement. Persons include individuals, partnerships, corporations, and other associations.

   b. If the partnership is to exist for a definite period exceeding one year, the statute of frauds requires the partnership agreement to be in writing.

6. Each of the parties must be a co-owner; i.e., they share profits and losses of the venture and management authority (unless they agree otherwise). But more than mere co-ownership of property is required.

   a. A person who receives a share of the profits of a business is generally presumed a partner, but not if the receipt is merely as payment of or for any of the following:

      1) Debt
      2) Wages to an employee
      3) Rent to a landlord
      4) An annuity to the widow or a representative of a deceased partner
      5) Purchase of goodwill of either a business or a property

7. In some ways, a partnership is treated as an entity distinct from its members.

   a. The assets of a partnership are treated as those of the business unit.
   b. Title to real property may be acquired in the partnership name.
   c. Each partner is considered a fiduciary of the partnership.
   d. Each partner is considered an agent of the partnership.

8. In other ways, a partnership is treated as an aggregate of the individual partners.

   a. A partnership lacks continuity of existence.
   b. No person can become a partner without consent of all the partners.
   c. Debts of a partnership are ultimately the debts of the individual partners.
   d. A partnership is not subject to regular federal income tax.
   e. A partnership can generally neither sue nor be sued in the firm name.

   NOTE: Statute or procedural rules permit such suits in many states.

9. A **trading partnership** is in the business of buying and selling property. A nontrading partnership only provides services, e.g., accounting.

10. **Partnership for a Term**. The partners specify the duration of the partnership for a specific term or until the completion of a specific project.

11. **Partnership at Will**. No fixed duration of partnership existence is specified. The partnership can rightfully be dissolved at any time by any partner.

12. A **general partnership** is one in which all partners have unlimited liability for partnership debts and activities. A general partnership agreement must be in writing if the partnership agreement is for a definite period in excess of one year.

13. A **limited partnership** is a partnership formed by two or more persons under a state statute. These statutes are based on the Uniform Limited Partnership Act (ULPA). A limited partnership has one or more general partners and one or more limited partners.

    a. **Person** includes natural person, partnership, limited partnership, trust, estate, association, or corporation.

    b. A **general partner** assumes management of the partnership and has full personal liability for debts of the partnership.

       1) A general partner may be another partnership or a corporation if its articles of incorporation as amended permit.

    c. A **limited partner** is an investor who makes a contribution of cash or other property to the partnership in exchange for an interest in the partnership and is

       1) Not personally liable for partnership debts
       2) Not active in management of the partnership

       NOTE: The limited partner's exposure for partnership liabilities is limited to his/her contributions to the partnership.

    d. A person can be both a general partner and a limited partner.

    e. The Revised Uniform Limited Partnership Act (RULPA) requires that a written **certificate of limited partnership** be filed as a public record with the secretary of state of the state in which it is organized. The certificate gives potential creditors notice of the limited liability of the limited partners. If a certificate is not filed, the organization is treated as an ordinary business partnership.

1) Under RULPA, the certificate must contain the following:

   a) Name of the limited partnership
   b) Address of the office of its agent for service of process
   c) Name and address of its agent for service of process
   d) Name and business address of each general partner
   e) Latest date upon which the limited partnership is to dissolve
   f) Other matters the general partners include in the certificate

2) The certificate must be signed by all general partners.
3) Amendments must also be filed.

  f. To do business in any other state, registration as a foreign limited partnership with the secretary of state of that state is required.

14. A **limited liability partnership (LLP)** is a favorable form of organization for professionals who have not incorporated. In many states, this form is restricted to use by professionals. All partners are limited partners, and no one is personally liable for partnership obligations except to the extent of the LLP's assets. However, a partner remains personally liable for his/her own professional malpractice. An LLP must file a form with the secretary of state and maintain professional liability insurance.

15. A **joint venture** is an association to accomplish a specific business purpose or objective. It is commonly organized solely for a single transaction.

  a. A joint venture does not meet the partnership definitional requirement that the partners carry on a business as opposed to an isolated transaction.

  b. Otherwise, joint ventures are formed similarly to partnerships.

  c. The rules governing partnerships generally apply to joint ventures.

16. **Limited Liability Company (LLC).** An LLC is a statutory entity combining aspects of corporations, partnerships, and limited partnerships. Investors are allowed limited liability and special tax treatment. For example, losses pass through to investors who may be able to use them to offset other taxable income. However, an LLC's life may not exceed a specified time, e.g., 30 years.

  a. Typically, two or more persons may form an LLC by filing **articles of organization** with the appropriate secretary of state. The LLC may be managed by its members or an elected group of managers. This arrangement must be disclosed to the secretary of state upon filing the articles. Also, the total value of all cash and property contributed by the members must be disclosed and becomes a matter of public record.

  b. An LLC is taxed as a partnership if it has no more than four of the following traits: associates, an objective to carry on a business and divide the gains, limited liability, centralized management, continuity of life, and free transferability of interests.

17. Stop and review! You have completed the outline for this subunit. Study multiple-choice questions 1 through 8 beginning on page 125.

B. Authority and Liabilities

1. **Partnership Capital and Property.** A partnership may begin with no capital. The total assets contributed for permanent use is partnership capital.

a. **Partnership capital** is usually a fixed amount altered only by amending the Articles of Partnership (the partnership agreement), which state the rights of the partners and their duties to each other and to the partnership.

b. A person can become a **services partner** without a capital contribution. (S)he receives no return of capital at the time of dissolution.

c. **Partnership property** is all property, including contributed capital, brought into or acquired by a partnership. Under the UPA, it consists of all of the following:

   1) Real and personal property contributed by the partners
   2) Real and personal property acquired with partnership funds
   3) Property produced or manufactured by the partnership
   4) Profits earned by the partnership

d. Title to real property acquired in the partnership name can be conveyed only in the partnership name.

   1) Any partner can convey title to real property by a conveyance signed on behalf of a partnership if title is in the name of the partnership.

   2) If a partner conveys property titled in the partnership name without proper authority, the partnership can recover it. But if it is reconveyed for value to a subsequent purchaser without knowledge or notice that the partner exceeded his/her authority by the prior conveyance, the partnership cannot recover it.

e. Title to partnership real property held in the name of each of the partners individually can be conveyed if each of the partners signs the conveyance.

f. If title to property is in the name of one or more of the partners, a partner in whose name the title stands can convey title.

g. No partner owns any specific partnership property directly or individually. The property is owned by the partnership. Partnership property is for partnership use exclusively. An individual partner is merely a tenant in partnership in the property with his/her co-partners. Absent consent of all other partners, a partner has no right to personally use, control, or sell partnership property.

   1) Individual partners have an insurable interest in partnership property.

h. A partner who conveys partnership property without authority is liable for resulting losses.

i. Creditors of an individual partner have no right to specific partnership property.

j. Specific partnership property is not part of a deceased partner's estate and is not subject to claim by a spouse or other beneficiary.

2. **Partner's Interest in the Partnership**. It includes his/her share of partnership profits and surplus (the value of all its assets, including goodwill, net of liabilities).

   a. In order for a creditor to reach a partner's individual interest in the partnership, e.g., to enforce payment of a personal debt, the creditor must secure a charging order from a proper court.

   b. The order allows a creditor to petition the court to appoint a receiver to collect and turn over to the creditor all partnership profits due to the debtor partner.

   c. A creditor may also foreclose under a charging order, causing the debtor's interest in the partnership to be sold at judicial sale.

      1) At any time before the judicial sale, the debtor partner, his co-partners, or the partnership itself may purchase the debtor partner's partnership interest by paying the debt.

3. **Classification of Partners**

    a. A **general partner** has unlimited liability for partnership liabilities, has full management powers, and shares in both profits and losses.

    b. A **limited partner** is liable for partnership liabilities only to the extent of his/her capital contribution.

    c. A **silent partner** has no voice in management and takes no active part in partnership business.

    d. A **secret partner**'s membership in the partnership is not disclosed to the public.

    e. A **dormant partner** is a partner who is both silent and secret.

    f. An **ostensible partner** has consented to being held out to be a partner. An ostensible partner is more commonly known as a **partner by estoppel**.

        1) A partner by estoppel, although not an actual partner, is liable to those who in good faith have extended credit to such person or his/her apparent partner on the reasonable assumption that (s)he was a partner.

    g. A **subpartner** is not a partner at all, but has a contractual arrangement with a partner which entitles him/her to a share of the profits realized by the partner.

    NOTE: Only a limited partner enjoys limited liability.

4. **Rights among Partners.** The rights, duties, and powers between and among partners are largely defined by the rules of law applicable to agents. Partners may agree (in writing or orally) to limit rights to which individual partners may otherwise be entitled by law. But neither the partners nor the partnership can (between themselves alone) diminish or otherwise modify obligations imposed by law to third parties.

    a. Unless otherwise agreed (as is often the case), each partner is entitled to equal participation in management of the partnership.

        1) The general rule for ordinary matters is majority rule.

        2) Issues not ordinarily connected with day-to-day partnership business (such as amending a partnership agreement or admitting a new partner) require a unanimous decision. If unanimity is impossible, any partner may bring suit to dissolve the partnership.

        3) Different classes of partners may be formed with different management rights.

    b. Each partner has the right to share in distributions, i.e, a transfer of partnership property from the partnership to the partner. The distribution may be in the form of

        1) A share of profits
        2) A return of capital contributions
        3) Repayment of a loan
        4) An advance (sometimes called a draw)
        5) Compensation for services rendered to the partnership

    c. Each partner has the right to inspect and copy the partnership books at all times.

    d. Unless otherwise agreed, each partner is presumed to have an equal share in partnership profits.

    e. Each partner is entitled to the return of his/her capital contribution upon termination of the partnership.

f.   The UPA provides that a partner is entitled to remuneration for conducting partnership business. But this compensation for services is no more than that partner's share of the profits, even if (s)he performs a disproportionate share of the work.

1)   A partnership agreement can provide for additional compensation.

g.   If a partner makes an advance (loan) to the partnership, over and above his/her capital contribution, (s)he is entitled to the return of the advance plus interest.

h.   A partner who expends personal funds, above and beyond capital contributions, in furtherance of partnership business is entitled to indemnification (repayment) with interest from the partnership assets.

i.   The right to choose associates. No person can become a member of a partnership without the consent of all the partners.

j.   A partner is entitled to an accounting, which is an equitable proceeding to provide a comprehensive and effective settlement of all partnership affairs, including the specific claims of each partner. An accounting is the exclusive remedy. No other suit between partners or between the partnership and a partner is permitted. A partner may invoke an accounting when

1)   (S)he is wrongfully excluded from the partnership business or possession of its property by his/her co-partners.

2)   The partnership agreement so provides.

3)   A partner profits in violation of his/her fiduciary duty.

4)   Other circumstances render an accounting just and reasonable.

5.   **Duties among Partners**. A partner who violates a duty to other partners is individually liable for the loss.

a.   **Fiduciary duty**. A partnership is a fiduciary relationship among the partners. It is breached if a partner attempts to secure an advantage over the other partners in or by internal or external dealings.

1)   Each partner owes a duty of absolute and utmost good faith and continuous undivided loyalty to each other. A partner must not

a)   Profit from the partnership except by any agreed-to compensation
b)   Compete with the partnership

2)   Each partner must account to the partnership for any benefit and hold as trustee for it any profits derived by the partner in connection with any transaction not authorized by the partners.

3)   A partner may not prefer him/herself over the firm nor may (s)he deal at arm's length with his/her partners.

4)   A partner cannot acquire a partnership asset for him/herself without the consent of all the partners.

5)   Each partner owes the highest duty of honesty and fair dealing to the other partners, including the duty to disclose fully and accurately all material facts.

6) A partner cannot engage in any other business within the scope of partnership business without the consent of his/her partners.

   a) Any profit acquired from an illicit transaction must be disgorged by the disloyal partner. Additionally, the partner must compensate the partnership for any damage suffered by the partnership as a result of an illicit transaction.

7) A partner may enter into any business not in competition with or within the scope of the partnership's business.

b. **Duty of obedience.** Each partner owes his/her partners a duty to act in accordance with the partnership agreement and with any business decisions properly made by the partnership. Each partner undertakes to

1) Serve the partnership according to the terms of the agreement
2) Discharge fiduciary duties owed to his/her co-partners
3) Share in the losses of the partnership

6. **Powers among Partners.** Every partner is a principal. Every partner is also an agent of the partnership and of each partner. The authority granted each partner is governed by the UPA (except in Louisiana) and by the specific terms of the partnership agreement.

a. Certain acts usually require the consent of all the partners:

1) Assigning partnership property for the benefit of creditors
2) Consenting to the entry of a court judgment against the partnership
3) Submitting a partnership claim or liability to arbitration
4) Disposing of partnership goodwill
5) Acting in any way that makes ordinary partnership business impossible

b. **Apparent authority.** A partner's status grants authority to act as an agent of the partnership in any legal transaction within the usual course of partnership business. Express permission from other partners is not needed.

1) If a partner acts without authority on a matter not within the apparent scope of partnership business, neither the partnership nor the other partners are bound by the act, unless the other partners ratify the transaction.

c. **Actual authority.** A partner's actual authority may be broader or narrower than his/her apparent authority.

1) **Express authority** is stated orally or in writing.
2) **Implied authority** is incidental and necessary to exercise express authority.

7. **Contractual Liability.** Because a partner acts concurrently as a principal and an agent, (s)he may obligate the partnership and each co-partner by contract when

a. Actually authorized to do so by the partnership agreement
b. Apparently carrying on the business of the partnership in the usual manner
c. Acting with the actual or implicit consent of the other partners

1) The apparent authority of a partner in a trading partnership is broader than the apparent authority of a partner in a nontrading partnership.

NOTE: When the partners agree among themselves to limit the authority of a partner to act on behalf of the partnership, a third party who has no notice of the limitation of authority is not bound by it. The partners are joint obligors. Suit must be brought against all the partners by name. Contracts are enforceable first against partnership assets and then against personal assets of partners.

8. **Tort Liability**. A partnership is liable for loss or injury caused by wrongdoing of any partner while acting within the scope of partnership business. Note that a partnership may be liable for torts committed by an employee of the partnership. Each general partner has unlimited personal liability for the partnership obligation.

   a. An activity within the scope of partnership business is one that relates to or seeks to further the interests of the partnership.

   b. Partner liability is joint and several.

9. A statement or representation by any partner concerning partnership affairs, within the scope of his/her authority, may be used as evidence against the partnership.

10. Information. Under principles of agency law, knowledge of a partner is imputed to all other partners. This creates a duty for a partner to share all pertinent knowledge with his/her partners.

11. **Limited Partnership**. A general partner in a limited partnership has the same rights and powers and is subject to the same liabilities as a partner in a general partnership. Note that a general partner may also be a limited partner.

    a. A limited partner has no right to participate in control of the business.

       1) Control refers to participation in the day-to-day management decisions of the partnership.

    b. A limited partner does have the right to

       1) Propose and vote on partnership affairs which do not directly control partnership operations, e.g., admission of a new general partner

       2) Withdraw from the partnership upon 6 months' notice or according to the partnership agreement

       3) Do business with the partnership, e.g., make a loan to it

       4) Inspect and copy the partnership records, including tax returns

       5) Receive other partnership information (if just and reasonable)

       6) Institute a derivative action on behalf of the partnership

       7) Assign his/her partnership interest

       8) Apply for dissolution of the partnership

       9) Obtain an accounting

    c. Typically, the financial risk of a limited partner is limited to his/her investment in the partnership. But a limited partner may incur personal liability for the firm debts if

       1) No limited partnership certificate was filed.

       2) (S)he knowingly permits his/her surname to be used as part of the partnership name.

       3) His/her participation in control is substantially the same as that of a general partner. Then (s)he is personally liable to the same extent as a general partner to persons who reasonably believed (s)he was a general partner.

    d.   But the RULPA provides that a limited partner does not lose limited liability on the basis of any of the following:

        1)   Disapproving amendments to the partnership agreement

        2)   Voting on certain fundamental changes, such as removal of a general partner

        3)   Advising or counseling a general partner regarding the partnership

        4)   Acting as a surety for the partnership

        5)   Serving as agent, employee, or contractor of the partnership or a general partner

        6)   Other activity that a court determines does not require it to hold the limited partner personally responsible for partnership liabilities

12. **Joint Venturers**. Courts commonly hold that the rights and duties of joint venturers are governed by the UPA.

    a.   A joint venturer, like a partner, is entitled to an accounting in equity.

    b.   Joint venturers owe each other the same fiduciary duties.

    c.   The most significant difference between joint venturers and partners is that joint venturers are typically held to have less implied and apparent authority due to the limited scope of the joint venture.

    d.   Each joint venturer is personally liable for debts of the venture.

    e.   Each joint venturer is liable for negligence of another acting within the scope and course of the business of the venture.

    f.   Joint ventures are treated as partnerships for federal income tax purposes.

13. A **limited liability company** is typically managed by its members or an elected group of managers.

    a.   The LLC enjoys many powers accorded corporations. It can

        1)   Be governed by internal bylaws
        2)   Sue or be sued in its own name
        3)   Acquire and dispose of both real and personal property
        4)   Hold title in its own name
        5)   Make donations for charitable, scientific, or educational purposes
        6)   Be a general or a limited partner in a partnership
        7)   Appoint agents

    b.   If the articles vest management of the LLC in elected managers, any one manager may have the statutory authority to contractually bind the LLC.

    c.   If the articles vest management in its members, it may be possible, depending on statute, for any one member to incur indebtedness or otherwise contractually bind the company.

    d.   Persons who conduct business as an LLC when statutory requirements for its formation have not been complied with are jointly and severally liable as partners.

14. Stop and review! You have completed the outline for this subunit. Study multiple-choice questions 9 through 21 beginning on page 127.

C. Allocation of Profit or Loss

1. **General Partnerships.** Unless otherwise agreed, each partner is presumed to have an equal share in partnership profits, notwithstanding any difference in the amount or character of contributions.

    a. Conversely, unless otherwise agreed, each partner is liable for losses in the same proportion as (s)he is entitled to share in profits.

2. **Limited Partnership.** A limited partner has the right and obligation to share in profits and losses, distributions, and surplus on termination in proportion to the relative value of his/her contributions to capital (less prior withdrawals) or as otherwise agreed.

3. **Joint Venturers.** General partnership rules apply.

4. **Limited Liability Company.** Profits of an LLC are typically shared among members based on the articles or bylaws (generally in proportion to the capital contributions).

5. Stop and review! You have completed the outline for this subunit. Study multiple-choice questions 22 through 25 beginning on page 131.

D. Transfer of Interest. Each partner's interest in the partnership consists, basically, of his/her share of the value of all its assets, including goodwill, net of liabilities. It includes his/her share of partnership profits and surplus.

1. A partner may sell or otherwise dispose of his/her partnership interest to the partnership, another partner, or a third party.

    a. Consent of the other partners is not required.

    NOTE: If consent is required by the partnership agreement, a partner may assign his/her interest but is liable to the other partners for violating the agreement.

    b. The assignee does not become a partner in the firm, unless and until all the other partners agree to accept the assignee as a new partner.

    c. The above also applies to interests in a limited partnership.

    d. The assignee is not entitled to participate in management. (S)he is entitled only to receive the profits (and surplus upon liquidation) allocable to the interest (s)he has acquired.

2. **Inheritance.** If a partner dies, his/her interest in the partnership is part of the estate.

    a. A partnership interest is considered personal property and may be inherited according to the provisions of the deceased partner's will. If there is no valid will, the applicable laws of intestacy govern.

    b. The heir of the partnership interest is an assignee, not a partner.

    c. Many partnership agreements provide that the surviving partners or the partnership itself will have a right of first refusal to purchase the interest.

        1) A partnership agreement may incorporate a provision to fund the purchase of the interest using life insurance proceeds.

3. A new partner has unlimited liability for partnership obligations arising subsequent to his/her admission as partner.

    a. Satisfaction of any partnership liability incurred before his/her admission may come only from partnership property unless agreed otherwise. This means that the new partner's liability for antecedent debts and other obligations of the partnership is limited to his/her capital contribution. However, incoming partners may assume personal liability for existing partnership debts.

4. Stop and review! You have completed the outline for this subunit. Study multiple-choice questions 26 through 30 beginning on page 133.

E.   Dissolution and Termination. A partnership ends by a three-step process: dissolution, winding up, and termination.

1.   **Dissolution** is the change in relations of the partners caused by any partner's ceasing to be associated in carrying on the business. Dissolution is not itself termination of the partnership or the rights and powers of the partners.

    a.   **Act of the partners**. Because a partnership is a consensual relationship, a partner always has the power to dissolve the partnership. A partner who withdraws in violation of the partnership agreement (i.e., without right) is liable to the remaining partners for damages resulting from wrongful dissolution. A partnership may be rightfully dissolved by any of the following:

        1)   The period the partners fixed for the partnership to last expires.
        2)   The purpose for which the partnership was formed is accomplished.
        3)   The partners expressly agree to dissolve the partnership.
        4)   A partner withdraws from a partnership at will.
        5)   A partner withdraws without violating the partnership agreement.
        6)   A partner is expelled in accordance with the partnership agreement.

    b.   **Operation of law**. Partnership is dissolved by operation of law upon

        1)   Death of a partner

        2)   Bankruptcy of a partner or the partnership

        3)   Subsequent illegality of the partnership, including any event that makes it unlawful for the business to be carried on

    c.   **Court order**. Upon application by a partner, a court will order a dissolution if it finds that one of the following reasons applies:

        1)   A partner is incompetent or suffers from incapacity that prevents him/her from functioning as a partner.

        2)   A partner has engaged in misconduct prejudicial to the partnership or has willfully and consistently breached the partnership agreement.

        3)   Continuance of the partnership business will result in financial loss.

        4)   Other circumstances exist that justify dissolution by court order.

2.   **Effect on Authority**. Dissolution ends normal working relationships of the partners, but the partnership continues until the winding up of partnership affairs is complete.

    a.   Upon dissolution, the actual authority of a partner terminates except as necessary to wind up partnership affairs. Actual authority to wind up includes authority to

        1)   Complete existing contracts
        2)   Convert partnership assets into cash
        3)   Pay partnership obligations

    b.   Apparent authority may continue during winding up.

        1)   A third party who extends credit to the partnership prior to dissolution may hold the partnership liable for any transaction that would bind the partnership if dissolution had not taken place, unless the third party has knowledge or actual notice of the dissolution. **Actual notice** requires

            a)   A verbal statement to the third party, or
            b)   Actual delivery of a written statement.

2) A third party who knew of the existence of the partnership but had not extended credit to it before its dissolution can hold the partnership liable for the extension of credit during dissolution unless the creditor has knowledge, actual notice, or constructive notice of the dissolution.

   a) **Constructive notice** is provided by publishing a notice of dissolution, usually in a local newspaper of general circulation in the geographic areas in which partnership business was regularly conducted.

3) After dissolution, notice is not required to preclude apparent authority with respect to third parties who did not know of the partnership's existence prior to its dissolution or if the dissolution resulted from operation of law.

3. **Winding up** is the administrative process of settling partnership affairs.

   a. Winding up involves

      1) Completing unfinished partnership business
      2) Collecting debts
      3) Identifying inventory
      4) Converting assets to cash
      5) Auditing the partnership books
      6) Paying creditors
      7) Distributing the remaining assets to the partners

   b. During this period, the fiduciary duties of the partners remain in effect.

   c. All partners have the right to participate in the winding-up process. They typically agree that one or more of them shall act as **liquidating partners**.

      1) If the partners do not agree on who will conduct the winding up, a court will appoint a receiver to take charge of it.

      2) A partner who has wrongfully withdrawn or whose bankruptcy caused the dissolution may not conduct winding up.

   d. Winding up is a normal partnership function, but a partner who conducts it is entitled to compensation for that activity.

   e. The liquidating partner(s) must take all action necessary to preserve the partnership's assets; any perishable assets must be carefully protected, and all assets should be adequately insured.

   f. A liquidating partner is a sole agent for the partnership. (S)he has the authority necessary for final settlement of partnership affairs but has no authority to take on new business.

      1) Agreement by the partners, judicial decree, or statutory requirements may alter this general rule.

      2) Third parties have the right to performance of uncompleted contracts entered into by the partnership.

      3) Completion of existing contracts and payments to employees may make it necessary to borrow money in the partnership name. The partnership and its members are liable for such debts.

      4) The partnership and the partners are liable for any tort committed by a winding-up partner.

g. The person who conducts the winding-up process must exert best efforts to collect all debts due the partnership.

    1) If necessary, (s)he may collect a compromise amount.
    2) Partnership funds may be used for collection (e.g., legal fees, court costs).

h. The person winding up prepares an accounting, which shows

    1) All transactions that were involved in the winding-up process

    2) Assets, debts, and equity of the firm at the date of the dissolution and at the conclusion of the winding-up process

i. The liabilities of a dissolved partnership are paid in the following order of priority:

    1) Debts owed to partnership creditors other than the partners themselves
    2) Debts owed to partners for loans or advances made to the partnership
    3) Repayments of partners' capital contributions
    4) Payment of surplus (profits), if any, to partners

    NOTE: The partners may by agreement change the order of payment of items 2), 3), and 4), but not the preferred position of third parties [item 1)].

j. In the absence of any contrary agreement, each partner shares equally in any surplus remaining after all liabilities are satisfied.

k. Moreover, each partner must contribute toward losses sustained by the partnership. Absent agreement, contributions toward losses are borne in the proportion in which profits are shared.

    1) If there are insufficient assets to satisfy all creditors and to return each partner's capital contribution, each partner is obligated to contribute sufficient cash to satisfy the outstanding obligations in the same proportion in which profits were shared.

    2) The partners are jointly and severally liable for the obligations of a dissolved partnership. If one or more of the partners are insolvent, bankrupt, or out of the jurisdiction, and refuse to contribute, the other partners must contribute the additional amount necessary to pay the liabilities.

4. **Continuing Partnership Business.** Dissolution and winding up involve elements of a forced sale.

a. To protect innocent partners against loss of going-concern value, the partnership business may be continued without winding up after

    1) Agreement among the partners to continue business
    2) The admission of a new partner
    3) Wrongful withdrawal of a partner
    4) Expulsion of a partner
    5) Retirement or death of a partner
    6) Dissolution in contravention of the partnership agreement

b. If a partnership is to be continued, an accounting is made. The value of each partner's interest is determined as of the date of the accounting.

    1) However, if a dissolution and winding up occur, the value of each partner's interest is determined at the end of the winding-up process.

c. The partner who carries on the business does so as a sole proprietorship or, if more than one of the partners of the dissolved partnership continue the business, as a new partnership.

d. Unless the partners agree otherwise, the rights and duties of the partners generally remain the same as they were under the prior partnership agreement.

e. Rights of creditors of the dissolved partnership are enforceable against the partnership continuing the business.

5. **Limited Partnership**. A limited partnership also goes through dissolution and winding up before it is terminated.

    a. A limited partnership can be dissolved upon any of the following events:

        1) The time or event specified in the limited partnership agreement occurs.

        2) All the partners agree, in writing, to dissolve.

        3) A general partner dies or withdraws from the partnership, unless one of two exceptions applies.

            a) The written terms of the agreement provide that the business may be carried on by the remaining general partners (if any).

            b) If there is no remaining general partner, the limited partners agree in writing within 90 days to continue the business and appoint one or more new general partners.

        4) The limited partnership is dissolved by court order.

    b. After dissolution, winding up is by a general partner who has not caused the dissolution. If there is no general partner to conduct the winding up, it may be performed by the limited partners or by some person designated by a court.

    c. Remaining assets, if any, are distributed as follows:

        1) To creditors, including creditors who are partners

        2) To present partners and former partners for distributions previously due to them and unpaid, except as otherwise provided in the limited partnership agreement

        3) To the partners as a return of their contributions, except as otherwise provided in the limited partnership agreement

        4) To the partners according to the terms of the limited partnership agreement (to the extent of any remaining assets)

    d. The Revised Uniform Limited Partnership Act requires notice of dissolution to every party affected.

    e. The final distribution terminates the limited partnership.

6. **Joint Venture**. General partnership rules apply to joint ventures with respect to dissolution.

7. **Limited Liability Company**. Generally, subject to the LLC's solvency, a member is entitled to a return of his/her capital contribution upon dissolution or other specified event. An LLC will be dissolved upon

    a. Expiration of a specified time period

    b. Unanimous written consent of all members

    c. Death, retirement, resignation, expulsion, bankruptcy, or dissolution of a member, or upon the occurrence of any other event that terminates the LLC under the articles or by unanimous consent of remaining members

8. Stop and review! You have completed the outline for this subunit. Study multiple-choice questions 31 through 39 beginning on page 134.

MULTIPLE-CHOICE QUESTIONS

A. Formation and Existence

1. A general partnership must

A. Pay federal income tax.

B. Have two or more partners.

C. Have written articles of partnership.

D. Provide for apportionment of liability for partnership debts.

The correct answer is (B). *(CPA, adapted)*
REQUIRED: The essential element of a general partnership.
DISCUSSION: A partnership is an association of two or more persons conducting a business which they co-own for profit. Absent association by agreement of at least two persons as partners, there is no partnership.
Answer (A) is incorrect because a partnership is not subject to regular federal income tax. Answer (C) is incorrect because a general partnership may be formed orally. Answer (D) is incorrect because a general partnership agreement need not provide for apportionment of liability for partnership debts. General partners have joint and several liability for partnership debts.

2. Generally, under the Uniform Partnership Act, a partnership has which of the following characteristics?

	Unlimited Duration	Obligation for Payment of Federal Income Tax
A.	Yes	Yes
B.	Yes	No
C.	No	Yes
D.	No	No

The correct answer is (D). *(CPA, adapted)*
REQUIRED: The characteristics of a partnership.
DISCUSSION: A partnership is an association of two or more persons to carry on a business as co-owners for profit. For federal income tax purposes, it is a flow-through entity. Thus, partnership income (loss) is reported on the owners' tax returns, but the partnership itself does not pay taxes. Moreover, one of the distinguishing characteristics of the partnership form of business is its lack of continuity of life.
Answers (A), (B), and (C) are incorrect because a partnership is not an entity that pays federal income tax, but it generally has a limited life.

3. When parties intend to create a partnership that will be recognized under the Uniform Partnership Act, they must agree to

	Conduct a Business for Profit	Share Gross Receipts From a Business
A.	Yes	Yes
B.	Yes	No
C.	No	Yes
D.	No	No

The correct answer is (B). *(CPA, adapted)*
REQUIRED: The item(s), if any, that must be agreed to when parties intend to create a partnership that will be recognized under the Uniform Partnership Act.
DISCUSSION: Partnership law is codified in the Uniform Partnership Act (UPA). A partnership is an association of two or more persons conducting a business, which they co-own, for profit. Thus, partners must intend that their business make a profit, even if no profit is earned. Each of the parties must be a co-owner; i.e., they share profits and losses of the venture and management authority (unless they agree otherwise).
Answer (A) is incorrect because the partnership agreement may specify that gross receipts are not shared. Answer (C) is incorrect because partners must intend that their business make a profit, but partners do not have to agree to share gross receipts. Answer (D) is incorrect because partners must intend that their business make a profit.

4. Which of the following is not necessary to create an express partnership?

A. Execution of a written partnership agreement.

B. Agreement to share ownership of the partnership.

C. Intention to conduct a business for profit.

D. Intention to create a relationship recognized as a partnership.

The correct answer is (A). *(CPA, adapted)*
REQUIRED: The item unnecessary to formation of an express partnership.
DISCUSSION: Partnership formation requires agreement to associate. The agreement may be expressed orally or in writing, or it may be implied from conduct. Thus, execution of a written partnership agreement is generally not required.
Answer (B) is incorrect because a partnership requires co-ownership. Answer (C) is incorrect because intent to conduct a business for profit is required to form a partnership, even if profit is not actually earned. Answer (D) is incorrect because intent that an agreed-to association be recognized as a partnership is one element of an express partnership. But existence of a partnership may be implied without regard to such intent if other requisite elements are present.

5. Which of the following statements about the form of a general partnership agreement is correct?

- A. It must be in writing if the partnership is to last for longer than 1 year.
- B. It must be in writing if partnership profits would not be equally divided.
- C. It must be in writing if any partner contributes more than $500 in capital.
- D. It could not be oral if the partnership would deal in real estate.

The correct answer is (A). *(CPA, adapted)*
REQUIRED: The true statement regarding whether a general partnership agreement must be in writing.
DISCUSSION: Most oral agreements to enter into a partnership are valid. If the partnership agreement is for a definite period in excess of 1 year, however, the majority of states require that the partnership agreement be in writing to be enforceable. If the statute of frauds is not complied with, a partnership at will results.
Answer (B) is incorrect because a choice by the partners to divide profits unequally has no impact on whether the partnership agreement must be written. Answer (C) is incorrect because there is no threshold on contributions beyond which a written agreement is required. Answer (D) is incorrect because a partnership agreement to enter into the real estate business does not involve the transfer of real estate and therefore does not need to be in writing.

6. A general partnership, a limited partnership, and a joint venture differ in all the following ways except

- A. In the method of formation.
- B. In the liability of its principals.
- C. In the authority of its management.
- D. In that each should have a carefully drafted agreement detailing the rights and liabilities of its partners.

The correct answer is (D). *(Publisher)*
REQUIRED: The factor common to a general partnership, a limited partnership, and a joint venture.
DISCUSSION: In each type of organization, an express or implied agreement is reached and should be in writing. This memorial of the rights and obligations of the parties is desirable but not legally required. It should address in sufficient detail as many questions as can be anticipated. When legal issues arise, courts look primarily to written agreements, except to determine the rights of third parties. The Limited Partnership Act requires the filing of a certificate of limited partnership to give notice of the limited liability of the limited partners. The certificate is not a detailed partnership agreement, but it is similar in content to a corporate charter.
Answer (A) is incorrect because the formation of a limited partnership requires a validating statute, the filing of a certificate, and the payment of fees, but general partnerships and joint ventures do not have such requirements. Answer (B) is incorrect because the liability of limited partners for claims of third parties is limited to their investment in the partnership, but general partners in a limited partnership, every partner in a general partnership, and the partners in a joint venture have unlimited liability to third parties. Answer (C) is incorrect because, unless agreed otherwise, a general partner in a general or limited partnership and a joint venturer are required to take part in management of the firm. Limited partners, however, may not participate in the general management of a partnership without losing their limited liability.

7. A joint venture is

- A. An association limited to no more than two persons in business for profit.
- B. An enterprise of numerous co-owners in a nonprofit undertaking.
- C. A corporate enterprise for a single undertaking of limited duration.
- D. An association of persons engaged as co-owners in a single undertaking for profit.

The correct answer is (D). *(CPA, adapted)*
REQUIRED: The definition of a joint venture.
DISCUSSION: A joint venture is similar to a partnership, but it does not carry on a business. The joint venture is an association of persons to undertake a specific business project for profit.
Answer (A) is incorrect because the association is not limited to two persons, and the venture involves only a specific project, not a business. Answer (B) is incorrect because a joint venture is undertaken for profit. Answer (C) is incorrect because a corporation formed for a single undertaking is governed by corporate, not partnership, law.

8. A relatively new form of business organization is the limited liability company (LLC). An LLC

- A. Has an indefinite existence.
- B. Has a tax status similar to that of a partnership.
- C. Permits limited liability provided the members do not participate in management.
- D. Allows members to conceal the amount of their investment.

The correct answer is (B). *(Publisher)*
REQUIRED: The true statement about an LLC.
DISCUSSION: Many states have statutorily provided for organization of this entity. The LLC combines some aspects of corporations, partnerships, and limited partnerships. Investors in an LLC are allowed limited liability and special tax treatment; e.g., losses pass through to investors who may be able to use them to offset other taxable income (like a partnership).
Answer (A) is incorrect because the LLC's life may not exceed a statutorily specified time, e.g., 30 years. Answer (C) is incorrect because members may manage or exert control without loss of their limited liability. Answer (D) is incorrect because the total value of all cash and property contributed by the members must be disclosed and becomes a matter of public record.

B. Authority and Liabilities

9. A partner's interest in specific partnership property is

	Assignable to the Partner's Individual Creditors	Subject to Attachment by the Partner's Individual Creditors
A.	Yes	Yes
B.	Yes	No
C.	No	Yes
D.	No	No

The correct answer is (D). *(CPA, adapted)*
REQUIRED: The nature of a partner's interest in specific partnership property.
DISCUSSION: Partnership property is held by the partners as tenants in partnership. A partner may assign his/her interest in the partnership but is not allowed to assign rights in specific partnership property. A partner's individual creditors may not attach partnership property but may charge a partner's interest in the partnership. Only a claim against the entire partnership allows specific partnership property to be attached.
Answers (A), (B), and (C) are incorrect because a partner's interest in specific partnership property cannot be assigned or attached by a partner's individual creditors.

10. In a general partnership, a partner's interest in specific partnership property is

- A. Transferable to a partner's individual creditors.
- B. Subject to a partner's liability for alimony.
- C. Transferable to a partner's estate upon death.
- D. Subject to a surviving partner's right of survivorship.

The correct answer is (D). *(CPA, adapted)*
REQUIRED: The rights of a general partner in specific partnership property.
DISCUSSION: The partnership owns specific partnership property. Each partner's legal interest is a tenancy in partnership: the partner owns no specific partnership property but co-owns all partnership property with all other partners. Nevertheless, specific partnership property is subject to a right of survivorship in the surviving partners.
Answers (A), (B), and (C) are incorrect because the partner's interest in the partnership and the partner's tenancy in partnership, not his/her interest in specific partnership property, are transferable to a partner's individual creditors or estate and are subject to a claim for alimony from the partner.

11. In a general partnership, the authorization of all partners is required for an individual partner to bind the partnership in a business transaction to

A. Purchase inventory.

B. Hire employees.

C. Sell goodwill.

D. Sign advertising contracts.

The correct answer is (C). *(CPA, adapted)*
REQUIRED: The partner's act that must be actually authorized by all partners.
DISCUSSION: Each partner, as agent of a general partnership, has apparent authority legally to obligate the partnership in any transaction within the usual course of partnership business. Unauthorized acts not within the apparent scope of partnership business obligate neither the partnership nor the other partners (unless they ratify it). Disposing of partnership goodwill is one of the acts that requires consent of all partners.
Answers (A), (B), and (D) are incorrect because a partner may purchase inventory, hire employees, or sign advertising contracts within the usual course of partnership business. Each partner has apparent authority regarding such acts.

12. Cass is a general partner in Omega Company, a general partnership. Which of the following unauthorized acts by Cass will bind Omega?

A. Submitting a claim against Omega to arbitration.

B. Confessing a judgment against Omega.

C. Selling Omega's goodwill.

D. Leasing office space for Omega.

The correct answer is (D). *(CPA, adapted)*
REQUIRED: The partner's unauthorized act that binds the partnership.
DISCUSSION: Because a general partner is an agent of the business, (s)he has apparent authority to bind the partnership to contracts with third parties formed while carrying on the partnership business in the usual way. Thus, a partner ordinarily need not be explicitly authorized to make an agreement to lease office space.
Answers (A), (B), and (C) are incorrect because authorization by all partners is required to submit a partnership claim to arbitration, to confess a legal judgment against the partnership, or to dispose of the goodwill of the partnership.

13. Locke and Vorst were general partners in a kitchen equipment business. On behalf of the partnership, Locke contracted to purchase 15 stoves from Gage. Unknown to Gage, Locke was not authorized by the partnership agreement to make such contracts. Vorst refused to allow the partnership to accept delivery of the stoves, and Gage sought to enforce the contract. Gage will

A. Lose, because Locke's action was not authorized by the partnership agreement.

B. Lose, because Locke was not an agent of the partnership.

C. Win, because Locke had express authority to bind the partnership.

D. Win, because Locke had apparent authority to bind the partnership.

The correct answer is (D). *(CPA, adapted)*
REQUIRED: The effect of a general partner's acting without actual authority.
DISCUSSION: A general partner is an agent of the partnership. Agents may have express, implied, and apparent authority. Apparent authority is authority that a reasonable third person believes the agent to have. Contracting for delivery of stoves is within the scope of ordinary business of a partnership in a kitchen equipment business. It is therefore within the scope of the general partner's apparent authority. Limitations imposed on an agent by the principal are ineffective as to third persons who have relied on the agent's apparent authority.
Answer (A) is incorrect because, even though Gage was not aware of Locke's lack of actual authority, (s)he can enforce contracts entered into by Locke with apparent authority. Answer (B) is incorrect because a general partner is an agent of the partnership. Answer (C) is incorrect because Locke did not have written or spoken authority from Vorst.

14. The apparent authority of a partner to bind the partnership in dealing with third parties

- A. Will be effectively limited by a formal resolution of the partners of which third parties are aware.
- B. Will be effectively limited by a formal resolution of the partners of which third parties are unaware.
- C. Would permit a partner to submit a claim against the partnership to arbitration.
- D. Must be derived from the express powers and purposes contained in the partnership agreement.

The correct answer is (A). *(CPA, adapted)*
REQUIRED: The true statement concerning apparent authority of a partner.
DISCUSSION: Each partner in a general partnership is an agent of the partnership. The partners may not limit partnership liability to third parties by agreement between the partners alone. But apparent authority would effectively be limited to the extent a third party knows of limitations imposed on a partner's authority.

Answer (B) is incorrect because the scope of apparent authority is limited by communications of the principal (the partnership) manifested to the third party. Answer (C) is incorrect because the scope of apparent authority is limited to conducting usual partnership business. The UPA provides that actual authority is required to bind the partnership to arbitration. Answer (D) is incorrect because apparent authority is based on communications manifested to third parties to the agency relationship.

15. Eller, Fort, and Owens do business as Venture Associates, a general partnership. Trent Corp. brought a breach of contract suit against Venture and Eller individually. Trent won the suit and filed a judgment against both Venture and Eller. Trent will generally be able to collect the judgment from

- A. Partnership assets only.
- B. The personal assets of Eller, Fort, and Owens only.
- C. Eller's personal assets only after partnership assets are exhausted.
- D. Eller's personal assets only.

The correct answer is (C). *(CPA, adapted)*
REQUIRED: The assets from which a judgment against a partnership and a specific partner may be collected.
DISCUSSION: Partners are jointly liable on a partnership contract. All partners must be named in a lawsuit to enforce it. A judgment can be enforced against the personal assets of any partner, but only after partnership assets are exhausted.

Answers (A), (B), and (D) are incorrect because a general partnership's contractual obligation is enforceable against partnership assets and then the personal assets of each partner.

16. Which of the following statements is(are) usually correct regarding general partners' liability?

I. All general partners are jointly and severally liable for partnership torts.

II. All general partners are liable only for those partnership obligations they actually authorized.

- A. I only.
- B. II only.
- C. Both I and II.
- D. Neither I nor II.

The correct answer is (A). *(CPA, adapted)*
REQUIRED: The true statement(s), if any, about general partners' liability.
DISCUSSION: Partners are jointly and severally liable for the torts committed by another partner who acted within the ordinary course of the partnership business or with the authorization of the other partners. Joint and several liability means that all of the partners are liable, but a third party may hold any partner liable for the entire amount. Because a general partner is an agent of the business, (s)he has apparent authority to bind the partnership to contracts with third parties formed while carrying on the partnership business in the usual way.

Answers (B), (C), and (D) are incorrect because all general partners are jointly and severally liable for all partnership torts.

17. Which of the following statements is correct regarding the apparent authority of a partner to bind the partnership in dealings with third parties? The apparent authority

A. Must be derived from the express powers and purposes contained in the partnership agreement.

B. Will be effectively limited by a formal resolution of the partners of which third parties are unaware.

C. May allow a partner to bind the partnership to representations made in connection with the sale of goods.

D. Would permit a partner to submit a claim against the partnership to arbitration.

The correct answer is (C). *(CPA, adapted)*
REQUIRED: The liability of a partnership based on a partner's apparent authority.
DISCUSSION: The UPA provides that the act of a partner for the apparent purpose of carrying on the partnership business or business of the kind carried on by the partnership binds the partnership unless the person with whom (s)he is dealing knows the acting partner lacks actual authority. Courts interpret this language as establishing the apparent authority of partners to take actions that are usual for partnerships. These actions include buying and selling goods and making representations in connection with the sale. The apparent authority of a general partner is substantial.
Answer (A) is incorrect because apparent authority is not derived from the partnership agreement. Answer (B) is incorrect because apparent authority is not effectively limited by a resolution of the partners of which third parties are unaware. Answer (D) is incorrect because the UPA requires that submitting a claim or liability to arbitration and certain other acts require the consent of all partners.

18. Under the Uniform Partnership Act (UPA), which of the following statements concerning the powers and duties of partners in a general partnership is(are) correct?

I. Each partner is an agent of every other partner and acts as both a principal and an agent in any business transaction within the scope of the partnership agreement.

II. Each partner is subject to joint liability on partnership debts and contracts.

A. I only.

B. II only.

C. Both I and II.

D. Neither I nor II.

The correct answer is (C). *(CPA, adapted)*
REQUIRED: The true statement(s), if any, about the powers and duties of general partners.
DISCUSSION: Under the UPA, a general partnership is primarily an agency relationship. Each partner is an agent of every other partner and acts as both a principal and an agent in any business transaction within the actual or apparent scope of the partnership. Application of this principle of agency law results in joint liability of the partners for the partnerships debts and contracts. (NOTE: Under the UPA, a partner's liability for partnership torts is joint and several. Joint liability requires that all partners be sued; joint and several liability provides a third party the option of suing one or more partners separately. The Revised UPA provides that all partners are jointly and severally liable for all obligations of the partnership unless agreed otherwise by the claimant or provided by state law).
Answers (A), (B), and (D) are incorrect because a general partner acts as an agent and principal with respect to the other partners and therefore subjects them to joint liability for partnership debts and contracts.

19. Which of the following statements regarding a limited partner is(are) usually correct?

I. The limited partner is subject to personal liability for partnership debts.

II. The limited partner has the right to take part in the control of the partnership.

A. I and II.

B. I only.

C. II only.

D. Neither I nor II.

The correct answer is (D). *(CPA, adapted)*
REQUIRED: The true statement(s), if any, about a limited partner.
DISCUSSION: A limited partner's liability for partnership obligations is limited to his/her capital contribution to the business, whereas a general partner has unlimited personal liability for partnership debts. The limited partner is also restricted in the right to control the partnership; (s)he is not allowed to participate in the day-to-day management of the partnership business.
Answers (A) and (B) are incorrect because a limited partner is not personally liable for partnership obligations. Answer (C) is incorrect because a limited partner's right to control partnership business is restricted.

20. Which of the following statements is correct with respect to a limited partnership?

- A. A limited partner may not be an unsecured creditor of the limited partnership.

- B. A general partner may not also be a limited partner at the same time.

- C. A general partner may be a secured creditor of the limited partnership.

- D. A limited partnership can be formed with limited liability for all partners.

The correct answer is (C). *(CPA, adapted)*
   REQUIRED: The characteristics of a limited partnership.
   DISCUSSION: A limited partner's liability is limited to his/her contributions to partnership capital. But a limited partnership must have at least one general partner with unlimited liability. A general partner may be another partnership, a corporation, or another entity. A general partner may also be a limited partner. A limited partner and the partnership may engage in transactions such as extending secured credit or property sales.
   Answer (A) is incorrect because a limited partner and the partnership may engage in such a transaction. Answer (B) is incorrect because one person may be a general and a limited partner. Answer (D) is incorrect because every limited partnership must have at least one partner with unlimited liability for obligations of the partnership.

21. In general, which of the following statements is correct with respect to a limited partnership?

- A. A limited partner has the right to obtain from the general partner(s) financial information and tax returns of the limited partnership.

- B. A limited partnership can be formed with limited liability for all partners.

- C. A limited partner may not also be a general partner at the same time.

- D. A limited partner may hire employees on behalf of the partnership.

The correct answer is (A). *(CPA, adapted)*
   REQUIRED: The true statement about a limited partnership.
   DISCUSSION: Both general and limited partners have the right to inspect and copy the books of the partnership at any time. Thus, they can obtain financial information and tax returns of the limited partnership.
   Answer (B) is incorrect because a limited partnership must have at least one general partner with unlimited liability. Answer (C) is incorrect because it is possible for a person to be both a general and a limited partner in the same partnership. Answer (D) is incorrect because a limited partner is not an agent of the partnership and is not allowed to participate in day-to-day management.

C. Allocation of Profit or Loss

22. Gillie, Taft, and Dall are partners in an architectural firm. The partnership agreement is silent about the payment of salaries and the division of profits and losses. Gillie works full-time in the firm, and Taft and Dall each work half-time. Taft invested $120,000 in the firm, and Gillie and Dall invested $60,000 each. Dall is responsible for bringing in 50% of the business, and Gillie and Taft 25% each. How should profits of $120,000 for the year be divided?

	Gillie	Taft	Dall
A.	$60,000	$30,000	$30,000
B.	$40,000	$40,000	$40,000
C.	$30,000	$60,000	$30,000
D.	$30,000	$30,000	$60,000

The correct answer is (B). *(CPA, adapted)*
   REQUIRED: The division of partnership profits when the partnership agreement is silent about salaries and the division of profits and losses.
   DISCUSSION: Partners are not entitled to compensation for their actions, skill, and time applied on behalf of the partnership, except when such an arrangement is explicitly provided for in the partnership agreement. The partnership agreement is silent on this point, so salaries are not paid to the partners. Profits and losses may be divided among the partners according to any formula stipulated in the partnership agreement. In the absence of such a stipulation, partners share equally in the profits. Thus, each partner will receive $40,000.
   Answers (A), (C), and (D) are incorrect because an equal share is required absent a contrary agreement.

23. Which of the following statements is correct regarding the division of profits in a general partnership when the written partnership agreement provides only that losses be divided equally among the partners? Profits are to be divided

- A. Based on the partners' ratio of contribution to the partnership.
- B. Based on the partners' participation in day-to-day management.
- C. Equally among the partners.
- D. Proportionately among the partners.

The correct answer is (C). *(CPA, adapted)*
   REQUIRED: The division of profits when the partnership agreement provides only for division of losses.
   DISCUSSION: The partnership agreement, to the extent it allocates partnership profits and losses among partners, governs. Absent agreement, each partner is entitled to an equal share of profits and must contribute toward losses in the same proportion (s)he is entitled to share in profits.
   Answers (A), (B), and (D) are incorrect because profits are shared equally when there is no agreement to divide them otherwise.

24. The partnership agreement for Owen Associates, a general partnership, provided that profits be paid to the partners in the ratio of their financial contribution to the partnership. Moore contributed $10,000, Noon contributed $30,000, and Kale contributed $50,000. For the year ended December 31, 1999, Owen had losses of $180,000. What amount of the losses should be allocated to Kale?

- A. $20,000
- B. $60,000
- C. $90,000
- D. $100,000

The correct answer is (D). *(CPA, adapted)*
   REQUIRED: The partner's share of partnership loss.
   DISCUSSION: The partnership agreement specifies that profits are to be allocated based on financial contributions. The Uniform Partnership Act provides that, unless otherwise agreed, losses are allocated in the same manner as profits. Hence, Kale will be allocated losses of $100,000 {$180,000 x [$50,000 ÷ ($10,000 + $30,000 + $50,000)]}.
   Answer (A) is incorrect because $20,000 equals Moore's share of the losses. Answer (B) is incorrect because $60,000 is Noon's share of the losses. Answer (C) is incorrect because $90,000 is the sum of the contributions.

25. D, E, F, and G formed a general partnership. Their written partnership agreement provides that the profits will be divided so that D will receive 40%; E, 30%; F, 20%; and G, 10%. There is no provision for allocating losses. At the end of its first year, the partnership has losses of $200,000. Before allocating losses, the partners' capital account balances are D, $120,000; E, $100,000; F, $75,000; and G, $11,000. G refuses to make any further contributions to the partnership. Ignore the effects of federal partnership tax law. What is G's share of the partnership losses?

- A. $9,000
- B. $20,000
- C. $39,000
- D. $50,000

The correct answer is (B). *(CPA, adapted)*
   REQUIRED: The partner's share of loss.
   DISCUSSION: The partnership agreement, to the extent it allocates partnership losses among partners, governs. Absent agreement (as here), a partner shares losses in the same proportion (s)he shares profits. The partnership agreement, to the extent it allocates partnership profits among partners, governs. Thus, G's share of the losses is 10% of $200,000.
   Answers (A) and (C) are incorrect because G's refusal does not affect the rule for allocating losses among the partners. A third party might seek to enforce more or less of a claim against any partners, who might then seek to enforce their agreement against each other. Answer (D) is incorrect because, when the partnership agreement allocates either profits or losses, the default rule of equal shares does not apply.

D. Transfer of Interest

26. Cobb, Inc., a partner in TLC Partnership, assigns its partnership interest to Bean, who is not made a partner. After the assignment, Bean asserts the rights to

I. Participation in the management of TLC
II. Cobb's share of TLC's partnership profits

Bean is correct as to which of these rights?

A. I only.

B. II only.

C. I and II.

D. Neither I nor II.

The correct answer is (B). *(CPA, adapted)*
REQUIRED: The rights of an assignee of a partnership interest.
DISCUSSION: The UPA allows the assignment of partnership rights without the dissolution of the partnership. The assignee is entitled only to the profits the assignor would normally receive. The assignee does not automatically become a partner and would not have the right to participate in managing the business or to inspect the books and records of the partnership.
Answers (A), (C), and (D) are incorrect because an assignee is entitled to receive the assignor's share of profits, but not to participate in management.

27. Which of the following statements best describes the effect of the assignment of an interest in a general partnership?

A. The assignee becomes a partner.

B. The assignee is responsible for a proportionate share of past and future partnership debts.

C. The assignment automatically dissolves the partnership.

D. The assignment transfers the assignor's interest in partnership profits and surplus.

The correct answer is (D). *(CPA, adapted)*
REQUIRED: The effect of assignment of an interest in a partnership.
DISCUSSION: The UPA allows the assignment of partnership rights without the dissolution of the partnership. The assignee is entitled to receive only those profits the assignor would normally receive. The assignee does not automatically become a partner and would not have the right to participate in managing the business or to inspect the books and records of the partnership.
Answer (A) is incorrect because admission as a partner requires approval by the other partners. Answer (B) is incorrect because the assignee has no liability for partnership debts unless (s)he becomes a partner. Answer (C) is incorrect because an assignment does not dissolve the partnership.

28. Laura Lark, a partner in DSJ, a general partnership, wishes to withdraw from the partnership and sell Lark's interest to Ward. All of the other partners in DSJ have agreed to admit Ward as a partner and to hold Lark harmless for the past, present, and future liabilities of DSJ. As a result of Lark's withdrawal and Ward's admission to the partnership, Ward

A. Acquired only the right to receive Ward's share of DSJ profits.

B. Has the right to participate in DSJ's management.

C. Is personally liable for partnership liabilities arising before and after being admitted as a partner.

D. Must contribute cash or property to DSJ to be admitted with the same rights as the other partners.

The correct answer is (B). *(CPA, adapted)*
REQUIRED: The rights and obligations of a newly admitted partner.
DISCUSSION: The other partners agreed to admit Ward as a partner. Accordingly, Ward is vested with all partnership rights, duties, and powers, including the right to participate in management.
Answer (A) is incorrect because Lark's assignment of her interest to Ward was approved by the other partners, and Ward was admitted as a partner. Ward succeeds fully to Lark's interest in the partnership, not just the right to share in profits. Answer (C) is incorrect because, when a new partner is admitted, (s)he is usually subject to any partnership liabilities arising before admission. However, satisfaction of such liability is limited to the investment in the partnership. Answer (D) is incorrect because a partner may be admitted to a partnership without a contribution of cash or property.

29. Unless the partnership agreement prohibits it, a partner in a general partnership may validly assign rights to

	Partnership Property	Partnership Distributions
A.	Yes	Yes
B.	Yes	No
C.	No	Yes
D.	No	No

The correct answer is (C). *(CPA, adapted)*
REQUIRED: The assignability of a partner's right to specific partnership property and/or distributions.
DISCUSSION: Partnership property is held by the partners as tenants in partnership. Each partner co-owns all partnership property with the other partners but has no right to possess that property without their consent. A partner may assign his/her interest in the partnership but is not allowed to assign rights in specific partnership property. However, unless the partnership agreement prohibits it, a partner in a general partnership may validly assign rights to his/her share of partnership distributions.
Answers (A) and (B) are incorrect because a partner's interest in specific partnership property cannot be assigned. Answer (D) is incorrect because, unless the partnership agreement prohibits it, a partner in a general partnership may validly assign rights to his/her share of partnership distributions.

30. Dawn was properly admitted as a partner in the ABC Partnership after purchasing Jim's partnership interest. Jim immediately withdrew from the partnership. The partnership agreement states that the partnership will continue on the withdrawal or admission of a partner. Unless the partners otherwise agree,

A. Dawn's personal liability for existing partnership debts will be limited to Dawn's interest in partnership property.

B. Jim will automatically be released from personal liability for partnership debts incurred before Dawn's admission.

C. Jim will be permitted to recover from the other partners the full amount that Jim paid on account of partnership debts incurred before Dawn's admission.

D. Dawn will be subjected to unlimited personal liability for partnership debts incurred before being admitted.

The correct answer is (A). *(CPA, adapted)*
REQUIRED: The effect of admitting a new partner on partnership liabilities.
DISCUSSION: As a new partner, Dawn's liability for previously existing partnership debts is limited to the amount of her capital contribution, which is Dawn's interest in partnership property.
Answer (B) is incorrect because, absent a novation, a withdrawing partner remains liable for debts incurred prior to withdrawal. Answer (C) is incorrect because Jim is liable for his share of debts incurred while he was a partner and would only be permitted to recover amounts he paid in excess of his share. Answer (D) is incorrect because Dawn's liability is limited to her capital contribution.

E. Dissolution and Termination

31. The partners of College Assoc., a general partnership, decided to dissolve the partnership and agreed that none of the partners would continue to use the partnership name. Under the Uniform Partnership Act, which of the following events will occur on dissolution of the partnership?

	Each Partner's Existing Liability Would Be Discharged	Each Partner's Apparent Authority Would Continue
A.	Yes	Yes
B.	Yes	No
C.	No	Yes
D.	No	No

The correct answer is (C). *(CPA, adapted)*
REQUIRED: The liability and authority of partners upon dissolution.
DISCUSSION: Dissolution can occur by an agreement of the partners to end the partnership. Although actual authority to act on behalf of the partnership ceases at dissolution, apparent authority to conduct business in the usual way continues until notice is given to third parties or the partnership business winds up. A partner's liability for the existing obligations of the partnership does not cease when the partnership is terminated. The unilateral act of the partners cannot discharge obligations to third parties.
Answers (A), (B), and (D) are incorrect because existing liabilities are not discharged, but apparent authority continues.

32. Park and Graham entered into a written partnership agreement to operate a retail store. Their agreement was silent as to the duration of the partnership. Which of the following statements is correct?

   A. Park may dissolve the partnership at any time.

   B. Unless Graham consents to a dissolution, Park must apply to a court and obtain a decree ordering the dissolution.

   C. Park may not dissolve the partnership unless Graham consents.

   D. Park may dissolve the partnership only after notice of the proposed dissolution is given to all partnership creditors.

The correct answer is (A). *(CPA, adapted)*
REQUIRED: The extent of a partner's right to dissolve a partnership.
DISCUSSION: Partners always have the power to dissolve a partnership, although they do not always have the right to do so. Dissolution in violation of a partnership agreement is wrongful and carries with it exposure to liability for damages. When the partnership agreement does not specify a duration or objective, the partnership is at will and may be rightfully dissolved at any time.

Answers (B) and (C) are incorrect because a partner desiring to dissolve a partnership need not obtain a court decree or the consent of the other partner(s). Answer (D) is incorrect because notice is not required for dissolution, but it is necessary to rescind apparent authority.

33. On dissolution of a general partnership, distributions will be made on account of

I. Partners' capital accounts

II. Amounts owed partners with respect to profits

III. Amounts owed partners for loans to the partnership

in the following order:

   A. III, I, II.

   B. I, II, III.

   C. II, III, I.

   D. III, II, I.

The correct answer is (A). *(CPA, adapted)*
REQUIRED: The priority of distributions in winding up a partnership.
DISCUSSION: In winding up, partnership assets must be applied in the following order:

1) Claims of outside creditors
2) Claims of partners as creditors
3) Claims of partners for capital
4) Claims of partners for profits

Answer (B) is incorrect because partner claims as creditors are superior to those for capital and profits. Answers (C) and (D) are incorrect because partner claims for capital are superior to those for profits.

34. D, E, F, and G formed a general partnership. Their written partnership agreement provides that the profits will be divided so that D will receive 40%; E, 30%; F, 20%; and G, 10%. There is no provision for allocating losses. At the end of its first year, the partnership has losses of $200,000. Before allocating losses, the partners' capital account balances are D, $120,000; E, $100,000; F, $75,000; and G, $11,000. G refuses to make any further contributions to the partnership. Ignore the effects of federal partnership tax law. After losses are allocated to the partners' capital accounts and all liabilities are paid, the partnership's sole asset is $106,000 in cash. How much will E receive on dissolution of the partnership?

   A. $29,500

   B. $35,333

   C. $37,000

   D. $40,000

The correct answer is (C). *(CPA, adapted)*
REQUIRED: The share of assets received by a partner on dissolution.
DISCUSSION: Absent agreement, the loss is allocated in the same proportion as profits (D, $80,000; E, $60,000; F, $40,000; G, $20,000). G's excess over his/her capital account balance ($9,000) must be allocated to the other partners in the same ratio as that for sharing profits (4:3:2). Thus, $4,000 is allocated to D, $3,000 to E, and $2,000 to F. The $106,000 is allocated in full to the balance of partnership capital accounts (D, $36,000; E, $37,000; F, $33,000).

Answer (A) is incorrect because partners' claims to return of capital are superior to those for surplus. Answer (B) is incorrect because partners' claims to return of capital are superior to those for surplus. No excess over the partners' capital account balances is available for distribution. If there were, it would be allocated according to the partnership agreement. Answer (D) is incorrect because the excess of G's share of the loss over his/her capital account balance is allocated to the other partners in the same ratio as that for sharing profits (4:3:2).

35. X, Y, and Z have capital balances of $30,000, $15,000, and $5,000, respectively, in the XYZ Partnership. The general partnership agreement is silent as to the manner in which partnership losses are to be allocated but does provide that partnership profits are to be allocated as follows: 40% to X, 25% to Y, and 35% to Z. The partners have decided to dissolve and liquidate the partnership. After paying all creditors, the amount available for distribution will be $20,000. X, Y, and Z are individually solvent. Z will

A. Receive $7,000.

B. Receive $12,000.

C. Personally have to contribute an additional $5,500.

D. Personally have to contribute an additional $5,000.

The correct answer is (C). *(CPA, adapted)*
REQUIRED: The distribution of partnership assets after dissolution and liquidation.
DISCUSSION: Upon termination, a partnership must first pay all creditors and then distribute the remaining assets to the partners. In this case, $20,000 is available for distribution. However, the total of capital contributions is $50,000, and a $30,000 loss must be allocated among the partners. When the partnership agreement does not specify otherwise, losses are allocated in the same ratio as profits. Thus, Z is properly allocated 35% of the loss, or $10,500 (35% x $30,000). Z's capital contribution of $5,000 is less than Z's share of the loss. Hence, Z must contribute an additional $5,500 to the partnership.
Answers (A) and (B) are incorrect because partner rights to return of capital contribution are superior to those for profits. If partnership assets are insufficient to return any partner's capital contribution, each partner is obligated to contribute cash to enable it. Answer (D) is incorrect because the obligation to contribute cash to permit return of capital is allocated to partners in the same proportion as is a partnership loss.

Questions 36 and 37 are based on the following information. Downs, Frey, and Vick formed the DFV General Partnership to act as manufacturers' representatives. The partners agreed Downs would receive 40% of any partnership profits and Frey and Vick would each receive 30% of such profits. It was also agreed that the partnership would not terminate for 5 years. After the fourth year, the partners agreed to terminate the partnership. At that time, the partners' capital accounts were as follows: Downs, $20,000; Frey, $15,000; and Vick, $10,000. There also were undistributed losses of $30,000.

---

36. Vick's share of the undistributed losses will be

A. $0

B. $1,000

C. $9,000

D. $10,000

The correct answer is (C). *(CPA, adapted)*
REQUIRED: The partner's share of losses when the partnership agreement is silent.
DISCUSSION: If the partnership agreement does not specifically allocate losses, they are shared in the same proportion as profits. Vick's share of the losses is $9,000 ($30,000 x 30%).
Answers (A), (B), and (D) are incorrect because, absent agreement, losses are shared in the same proportion as profits.

37. If Frey died before the partnership terminated,

A. Downs and Vick, as a majority of the partners, would have been able to continue the partnership.

B. The partnership would have continued until the 5-year term expired.

C. The partnership would automatically dissolve.

D. Downs and Vick would have Frey's interest in the partnership.

The correct answer is (C). *(CPA, adapted)*
REQUIRED: The effect on a partnership of a partner's death.
DISCUSSION: The death of a partner automatically dissolves a partnership by operation of law. Bankruptcy of a partner or partnership or subsequent illegality of a partnership also causes dissolution by operation of law.
Answer (A) is incorrect because the death of any partner automatically dissolves the partnership. The partners may have an agreement to continue the business by forming a new partnership, thereby obviating the need for winding up the partnership's affairs. Answers (B) and (D) are incorrect because the death of any partner automatically dissolves a general partnership.

38. On February 1, Addison, Bradley, and Carter, physicians, formed ABC Medical Partnership. Dr. Bradley was placed in charge of the partnership's financial books and records. On April 1, Dr. Addison joined the City Hospital Medical Partnership, retaining the partnership interest in ABC. On May 1, ABC received a writ of attachment from the court attaching Dr. Carter's interest in ABC. The writ resulted from Dr. Carter's failure to pay a credit card bill. On June 1, Dr. Addison was adjudicated bankrupt. On July 1, Dr. Bradley was sued by the other partners of ABC for an accounting of ABC's revenues and expenses. Under the Uniform Partnership Act, which of the preceding events resulted in the dissolution of the ABC Medical Partnership?

- A. Dr. Addison's joining the City Hospital Medical Partnership.

- B. Dr. Carter's interest in the partnership being attached by the court.

- C. Dr. Addison's being adjudicated bankrupt.

- D. Dr. Bradley's being sued for an accounting by the other partners of ABC.

The correct answer is (C). *(CPA, adapted)*
REQUIRED: The event resulting in the dissolution of a partnership.
DISCUSSION: The Uniform Partnership Act defines dissolution as the change in the relation of the partners caused by any partner's ceasing to be associated in the carrying on of the business. A dissolution may be brought about by (1) an act of the partners, (2) an operation of law, or (3) a court order. Whether a partner has the right to dissolve a partnership is determined by the partnership agreement. The bankruptcy of a partner or the partnership is an example of a dissolution by operation of law. Other examples are death of a partner and subsequent illegality of the partnership's purpose.
Answer (A) is incorrect because a partner becoming a member or partner in a competing organization is a breach of duty but does not result in dissolution without further action by another partner to expel or seek a court order of dissolution. Answers (B) and (D) are incorrect because an attachment of a partner's interest and a partner's legal efforts to obtain an accounting do not trigger a dissolution under the Uniform Partnership Act.

39. Unless otherwise provided in a general partnership agreement, which of the following statements is correct when a partner dies?

	The Deceased Partner's Executor Would Automatically Become a Partner	The Deceased Partner's Estate Would Be Free from Any Partnership Liabilities	The Partnership Would Be Dissolved Automatically
A.	Yes	Yes	Yes
B.	Yes	No	No
C.	No	Yes	No
D.	No	No	Yes

The correct answer is (D). *(CPA, adapted)*
REQUIRED: The effect of a partner's death.
DISCUSSION: Under the Uniform Partnership Act, the partnership is dissolved by operation of law upon the death of a partner. The partnership interest becomes part of the deceased partner's estate. However, neither the executor nor the successor to the partnership interest automatically becomes a partner unless the other partners agree. The estate is responsible for the partner's allocated share of any partnership liabilities.
Answers (A), (B), and (C) are incorrect because the executor does not become a partner automatically, the estate assumes the decedent's liabilities, and the partnership is automatically dissolved.

Use Gleim's *CPA Test Prep* for interactive testing with over 2,000 additional multiple-choice questions!

OOF QUESTION 1 *(CPA, adapted)* 15-20 minutes

Gennie, Gerry, and Lem formed Sterling Properties Limited Partnership to engage in the business of buying, selling, and managing real estate. Gennie and Gerry were general partners. Lem was a limited partner entitled to 50% of all profits. Gennie, Gerry, and Lem agreed that Gerry's personal liability be limited to 25% of each partnership liability.

Within a few months of Sterling's formation, it became apparent to Lem that Gennie and Gerry's inexperience was likely to result in financial disaster for the partnership. Therefore, Lem became more involved in day-to-day management decisions. Lem met with prospective buyers and sellers of properties, assisted in negotiating partnership loans with its various lenders, and took an active role in dealing with personnel problems. Things continued to deteriorate for Sterling, and the partners began blaming each other for the partnership's problems.

Finally, Gennie could no longer deal with the situation and withdrew from the partnership. Gerry reminded Gennie that the Sterling partnership agreement specifically prohibited withdrawal by a general partner without the consent of all the other partners. Gennie advised Gerry and Lem that she would take no part in any further partnership undertaking and would not be responsible for partnership debts incurred after this withdrawal.

With Sterling on the verge of collapse, the following situations have occurred:

- Lem demanded the right to inspect and copy the partnership's books and records, and Gerry refused to allow Lem to do so, claiming that Lem's status as a limited partner precludes that right.

- Anchor Bank, which made a loan to the partnership prior to Gennie's withdrawal, is suing Sterling and each partner individually, including Gennie, because the loan is in default. Lem denied any liability based on his limited partner status. Gennie denies liability based on her withdrawal.

- Gerry sued Gennie for withdrawing from the partnership and is uncertain about the effect of her withdrawal on the partnership.

- Lem assigned his partnership interest to Larry, who wants to become a substitute limited partner. Lem is uncertain about his right to assign this interest to Larry and, further, the right of Larry to become a substitute limited partner. The Sterling partnership agreement and certificate are silent in this regard.

- Gerry, after all the above occurs, assigns his partnership interest to Garth. Larry consents to Garth's admission as a new partner, and Garth and Larry release Gerry from all prior or future partnership obligations.

The following list represents possible levels of liability for an obligation of Sterling Properties:

(A) No liability

(B) A share of partnership capital

(C) Partnership capital

(D) A share of partnership profits

(E) The partner's partnership interest

(F) 25% of the obligation

(G) The amount of the obligation

(H) Partnership property

(I) The net assets of the partnership

(J) The partner's net personal assets

For items 1 through 6 below, select the level of liability, from (A) through (J) above, which best describes the named person's liability for the Anchor Bank loan. Each answer may be used once, more than once, or not at all.

1. Sterling Properties

2. Gennie

3. Gerry

4. Garth

5. Lem

6. Larry

For items 7 through 13, mark (A) if the statement is correct. Mark (B) if it is incorrect.

7. Lem had the right to inspect Sterling's books.

8. Lem's assignment dissolved the partnership.

9. Larry has the right to inspect Sterling's books.

10. Gennie's withdrawal is void.

11. Gennie's withdrawal may dissolve Sterling.

12. Gerry has a claim against Gennie.

13. Notice is required to terminate authority upon Sterling's bankruptcy.

Knowledge Tested

1. Liability for partnership obligations
2. Rights of partners
3. Authority of partners
4. Liability between partners
5. Assignment of partner's interest
6. Withdrawal of a partner
7. Admission of a new partner
8. Termination of a partnership

Authors' Comments

Essay questions tend to test several elements of a few specific topics. The objective format can reach diverse topics of a broad area of law. Fundamental principles (e.g., a partnership has at least two partners) and unique rules (e.g., extent of liability after assignment) can be woven together. This question illustrates that the "best" answer is not always clear. You must use judgment. You should always expect agency law to be tested in a partnership setting.

1. The correct answer is (I).

DISCUSSION: A partnership is liable for the full amount of its obligations. Partnership property is all property brought into, produced, or otherwise acquired by the partnership.

2. The correct answer is (J).

DISCUSSION: A general partner has unlimited liability for partnership liabilities. Thus, a creditor of the partnership has a claim against the general partner's personal assets for the partnership obligation. Withdrawal from the partnership does not relieve from liability for partnership obligations incurred prior to withdrawal.

3. The correct answer is (J).

DISCUSSION: An agreement between partners limiting or allocating partnership liabilities does not limit the amount of each partner's liability to the partnership's creditors. Assignment of the general partnership interest does not relieve the general partner from liability to a creditor for partnership obligations incurred before the assignment.

4. The correct answer is (D).

DISCUSSION: Satisfaction of any partnership liability incurred before admission of a new partner may be from partnership property but not the new partner's personal assets. However, upon Lem's assignment, the partnership terminated because a partnership definitionally requires two partners. Neither Gerry nor Lem was admitted as a partner in Sterling Partnership such that they might admit Garth as a partner.

5. The correct answer is (J).

DISCUSSION: The limited partner's liability to a partnership creditor is generally limited to the value of his/her interest in the partnership. However, Lem has taken part in the control of the business. Thus, he will be treated as a general partner with unlimited liability.

6. The correct answer is (D).

DISCUSSION: A new partner's personal assets are not subject to the claims of a creditor for a partnership obligation incurred before admission. Partnership property, which includes both contributed capital and other property acquired by the partnership and which represents the value of the partnership interests, is subject to the creditor's claim. However, Larry was a mere assignee of Lem's interest.

7. The correct answer is (A).

DISCUSSION: A limited partner has the right to have the partnership books kept at the principal place of business of the partnership and to inspect them at any reasonable time.

8. The correct answer is (B).

DISCUSSION: A limited partnership agreement is assignable, subject to limitations in the partnership agreement or certificate. The assignment does not dissolve the limited partnership.

9. The correct answer is (B).

DISCUSSION: The assignee does not become a limited partner without the consent of the remaining partner. The assignee has the right to receive distributions to which the assignor would have been entitled, but not to exercise rights of a partner such as inspecting the partnership books.

10. The correct answer is (B).

DISCUSSION: A partnership is fundamentally consensual. A general partner's withdrawal is effective even without consent of other partners, notwithstanding the prohibition in the partnership agreement.

11. The correct answer is (A).

DISCUSSION: Withdrawal of a general partner dissolves the partnership unless the remaining general partners continue the business of the partnership under a right to do so provided for in the limited partnership certificate or unless all partners consent.

12. The correct answer is (A).

DISCUSSION: Gennie's withdrawal was a breach of an enforceable partnership agreement. Thus, Gennie is liable to Gerry for damages resulting from her withdrawal.

13. The correct answer is (D).

DISCUSSION: Termination upon bankruptcy of the partnership is by operation of law. Thus, no notice is required to terminate authority.

OOF QUESTION 2 (CPA, adapted) 10-15 minutes

In 1997, Anchor, Chain, and Hook created ACH Associates, a general partnership. The partners orally agreed that they would work full time for the partnership and would distribute profits based on their capital contributions. Anchor contributed $5,000; Chain, $10,000; and Hook, $15,000.

For the year ended December 31, 1998, ACH Associates had profits of $60,000 that were distributed to the partners. During 1999, ACH Associates was operating at a loss. In September 1999, the partnership dissolved.

In October 1999, Hook contracted in writing with Ace Automobile Co. to purchase a car for the partnership. Hook had previously purchased cars from Ace Automobile Co. for use by ACH Associates partners. ACH Associates did not honor the contract with Ace Automobile Co., and Ace Automobile Co. sued the partnership and the individual partners.

Required

For items 1 through 6, determine whether (A) or (B) is correct.

1. A. The ACH Associates' oral partnership agreement was valid.

    B. The ACH Associates' oral partnership agreement was invalid because the partnership lasted for more than one year.

2. A. Anchor, Chain, and Hook jointly owning and conducting a business for profit establishes a partnership relationship.

    B. Anchor, Chain, and Hook jointly owning income-producing property establishes a partnership relationship.

3. A. Anchor's share of ACH Associates' 1998 profits was $20,000.

    B. Hook's share of ACH Associates' 1998 profits was $30,000.

4. A. Anchor's capital account would be reduced by 1/3 of any 1999 losses.

    B. Hook's capital account would be reduced by 1/2 of any 1999 losses.

5. A. Ace Automobile Co. would lose a suit brought against ACH Associates because Hook, as a general partner, has no authority to bind the partnership.

    B. Ace Automobile Co. would win a suit brought against ACH Associates because Hook's authority continues during dissolution.

6. A. ACH Associates and Hook would be the only parties liable to pay any judgment recovered by Ace Automobile Co.

    B. Anchor, Chain, and Hook would be jointly and severally liable to pay any judgment recovered by Ace Automobile Co.

Knowledge Tested

1. Characteristics of partnerships
2. Formation of partnerships
3. Application of statute of frauds
4. Authority of partners
5. Notice of dissolution
6. Joint liability of partners
7. Formation of corporations
8. Election of officers and directors
9. Voting agreements

Authors' Comments

A question from each of the major areas of general partnerships is included. As expected, agency law applied in the partnership setting is included. A distinction is made between liability of partners for partnership debts and their liability as judgment debtors.

1. The correct answer is (A).

DISCUSSION: A valid partnership agreement may be written, oral, or implied from conduct. When no fixed duration is specified, the result is a partnership at will which is not within the statute of frauds. If the partnership agreement is for a period in excess of one year, the statute of frauds requires the agreement to be in writing. However, even if the partnership lasts longer than one year, this agreement does not automatically become subject to the statute of frauds. It must specifically state that the partnership is to exist for a definite period in excess of one year. If the requirements of the statute of frauds are not met, a partnership at will is formed.

2. The correct answer is (A).

DISCUSSION: A partnership is defined as an association of two or more persons carrying on a business as co-owners with the intent to make a profit. Each partner must be a co-owner of the partnership business, which entails sharing of profits and participation in management. Joint ownership of income-producing property does not establish a partnership because no business (trade, occupation, or profession) is being carried on other than the management of the property.

3. The correct answer is (B).

DISCUSSION: Partnership profits and losses are divided equally unless otherwise stated in the partnership agreement. ACH agreed to allocate profits and losses in accordance with each partner's capital contribution. Total contributed capital is $30,000; Anchor contributed $5,000 (16.67%), and Hook contributed $15,000 (50%). Since the 1998 partnership profits were $60,000, Anchor's share of the profits was $10,000 ($60,000 x 16.67%), and Hook's share of the profits was $30,000 ($60,000 x 50%).

4. The correct answer is (B).

DISCUSSION: Partnership profits and losses are divided equally unless otherwise stated in the partnership agreement. ACH agreed to allocate profits and losses in accordance with each partner's capital contribution. Total contributed capital is $30,000; Anchor contributed $5,000 (16.67%), and Hook contributed $15,000 (50%). Losses incurred by ACH would be allocated among the partners according to these percentages. Hook's capital account would be reduced by one-half of the 1999 losses.

5. The correct answer is (B).

DISCUSSION: A general partner usually has the actual and apparent authority to act as an agent of the partnership in any legal transaction within the usual course of partnership business. The apparent authority of a partner may continue during dissolution until the third party receives actual or constructive notice of the dissolution of the partnership. Ace Automobile requires actual notice of the dissolution because, in nearly identical transactions, Ace has previously extended credit to ACH through Hook prior to its dissolution.

6. The correct answer is (B).

DISCUSSION: Under the Uniform Partnership Act, all general partners have joint liability for the debts incurred by the partnership and joint and several liability for torts. Joint liability required Ace to name each partner as a defendant (which Ace did). If successful in the suit, Ace will have a judgment against Anchor, Chain, and Hook individually. Joint judgment debtors are jointly and severally liable. Thus, Ace can collect the entire judgment from Anchor, Hook, or Chain.

ESSAY QUESTION *(CPA, adapted)* 15-25 minutes

Best Associates is a general partnership engaged in buying, selling, and servicing used planes. Best's original partners were Martin and Kent. They formed the partnership on January 1, 1997 under an oral partnership agreement which provided that the partners would share profits equally. There was no agreement as to how the partners would share losses. When the partnership was formed, Martin contributed $320,000 and Kent contributed $80,000.

On December 1, 1998, Best hired Baker to be a salesperson and to assist in purchasing used aircraft for Best's inventory. On December 15, 1998, Martin instructed Baker to negotiate the purchase of a used airplane from Jackson without disclosing that Baker was acting on Best's behalf. Martin thought a better price could be negotiated by Baker if Jackson was not aware that the aircraft was being acquired for Best. Baker contracted with Jackson without disclosing that the airplane was being purchased for Best. The agreement provided that Jackson would deliver the airplane to Baker on January 2, 1999, at which time the purchase price was to be paid. On January 2, 1999, Jackson attempted to deliver the used airplane. Baker, acting on Martin's instructions, refused to accept delivery or pay the purchase price.

On December 20, 1998, Kent assigned Kent's partnership interest in Best to Green. On December 31, 1998, Kent advised Martin of the assignment to Green. On January 11, 1999, Green contacted Martin and demanded to inspect the partnership books and to participate in the management of partnership affairs, including voting on partnership decisions.

On January 13, 1999, it was determined that Best had incurred an operating loss of $160,000 in 1998. Martin demanded that Kent contribute $80,000 to the partnership to account for Kent's share of the loss. Kent refused to contribute.

On January 28, 1999, Laco Supplies, Inc., a creditor of Best, sued Best and Martin for unpaid bills totaling $92,000. Best had not paid the bills because of a cash shortfall caused by the 1998 operating loss.

Jackson has taken the following position:

- Baker is responsible for any damages incurred by Jackson as a result of Best's refusal to accept delivery or pay the purchase price.

Martin has taken the following positions:

- Green is not entitled to inspect partnership books or participate in management of the partnership.

- Only the partnership is liable for amounts owed to Laco, or, in the alternative, Martin's personal liability is limited to 50% of the total of the unpaid bills.

Kent has taken the following positions:

- Only Martin is liable for the 1998 operating loss because of the assignment to Green of Kent's partnership interest.

- Any personal liability of the partners for the 1998 operating loss should be allocated between them on the basis of their original capital contributions.

Required

a. Determine whether Jackson's position is correct and state the reasons for your conclusions.

b. Determine whether Martin's positions are correct and state the reasons for your conclusions.

c. Determine whether Kent's positions are correct and state the reasons for your conclusions.

Knowledge Tested

1. Liability of principal and agent for contracts
2. Effect of nondisclosure of principal
3. Rights of assignee of partnership interest
4. Liability of partners for partnership liability
5. Allocation of partnership losses

Authors' Comments

This essay illustrates the applicability of agency law in the partnership context. Note that oral agreement was sufficient to form the partnership. The problem requires application of general law (the Uniform Partnership Act) when the agreement is silent.

AICPA Unofficial Answer

a. Jackson is correct. Baker, as an agent acting on behalf of an undisclosed principal (Best), is personally liable for any contracts entered into in that capacity.

b. Martin's first position that Green is not entitled to inspect the partnership books or participate in partnership management is correct. Green, as an assignee of Kent's partnership interest, is entitled to receive Kent's share of partnership profits only. Green is not entitled, as an assignee of Kent's partnership interest, to inspect the partnership records or to participate in the management of the partnership.

Martin's second position that only the partnership is responsible for the debt owed Laco is incorrect. Although the partnership is primarily liable for the unpaid bills, both Martin and Kent, as Best's partners, are personally liable for the unpaid amount of the debt. Laco will be entitled to seek recovery against Martin or Kent for the full amount owed.

c. Kent's first position that only Martin is liable for the 1997 operating loss because of the assignment of Kent's partnership interest to Green is incorrect. A partner's assignment of a partnership interest does not terminate that partner's liability for the partnership's losses and debts.

Kent's second position that any personal liability of the partners for the 1998 operating loss should be allocated on the basis of their original capital contributions is incorrect. The 1998 loss will be allocated in the same way that profits were to be allocated between the parties, that is, equally, because Martin and Kent had not agreed on the method for allocating losses between themselves.

STUDY UNIT 5: CORPORATIONS

20 pages of outline
30 multiple-choice questions
2 OOFs and 1 essay

A. Formation, Purposes, and Powers
B. Shareholders, Directors, and Officers
C. Financial Structure, Capital, and Distributions
D. Merger, Consolidation, and Dissolution

A corporation is a legal entity created under authority of a statute to carry out the purposes permitted by its statute and corporate charter. The corporation is treated as a legal person separate from its shareholders.

Corporations are governed by shareholders electing a board of directors and approving fundamental changes in the corporate structure. Directors establish corporate policies and elect or appoint corporate officers who carry out the policies in the day-to-day management of the organization. The exam focuses particular attention upon the power and general characteristics of corporations; comparisons with other forms of business organizations; problems arising during formation (e.g., stock subscriptions and promotion activities); the financing structure of a corporation (especially dividends); the rights and liabilities of shareholders, directors, and officers; and matters concerning dissolution or other significant changes in the corporation.

A. **Formation, Purposes, and Powers**. A corporation is formed under a state statute when persons, called incorporators, file articles of incorporation and receive a charter from the state.

1. **Classification**. A **corporation** is a form of business organization recognized as a legal entity with rights and liabilities separate and distinct from those of the persons who own and manage it. Corporations are classified in a variety of ways.

   a. A **private corporation** is organized to earn profits for its owners (for-profit corporation) or for charitable purposes (nonprofit corporation).

      1) A **close** (or closely held) **corporation** is distinguished by four primary features:

         a) It is owned by a relatively small number of shareholders.
         b) It does not sell its stock to the public.
         c) Its officers and directors own all the stock.
         d) Shareholders are active in management and control.

      2) A **publicly held corporation**'s stock is sold to the public at large, generally on a nationally recognized stock exchange. Its share price quotations are regularly published.

   b. **Quasi-public corporations** owe a duty to the public because they enjoy a favored status granted by the state; e.g., a utility may enjoy monopoly status and a limited power of eminent domain. They are highly regulated.

   c. A **public corporation** is organized for public purposes related to the administration of government, e.g., an incorporated municipality. It is formed by specific legislation that defines its purpose and powers. It may be funded by local taxes.

   d. A corporation is classified as domestic in the state in which it is organized, i.e., where its articles of incorporation are filed.

   e. A corporation is foreign in every other state. A certificate required to do business within the borders of another state is obtained by

      1) Filing appropriate documents with the secretary of state
      2) Paying required fees
      3) Designating a resident agent

   f. A corporation organized in another country is classified as alien. It must obtain a certificate to do business from each host state.

g. The **S corporation** is a close corporation that has made an IRS election to be taxed similarly to a partnership. An S corporation does not usually pay income tax. The shareholders are taxed on the corporation's current earnings, whether distributed or not, and may personally benefit from corporate losses. Eligibility requirements for S status include the following:

1) The corporation may have only one class of stock.

2) The number of shareholders is limited to 75 (35 for tax years beginning before 1997).

3) The corporation must be incorporated in the U.S.

4) The corporation must not be a financial institution or a member of an affiliated group.

5) An S corporation should not have excessive net passive investment income.

6) Shareholders are limited to individuals, estates, and qualified trusts.

7) Nonresident aliens may not own shares.

h. **Professional corporations** (professional service associations). State statutes may allow accountants, lawyers, and other professionals to incorporate. The statutes typically restrict stock ownership to specific professionals licensed within that state. See page 35 for restrictions on the form of organization in which accountants may practice.

i. See Study Unit 4, Partnerships, for coverage of the limited liability company, a hybrid form of organization.

2. **Characteristics of a Corporation**. A business is organized in corporate form to avail the investors of characteristics of that form.

a. **Limited liability**. A shareholder owns a property interest in the underlying net assets of the corporation and is entitled to share in its profits, but his/her personal assets are not subject to corporate liabilities. The shareholder's exposure is limited to the investment in the corporation.

b. **Separation of ownership from management**. Shareholders have no inherent right to participate directly in management. They elect a board that sets corporate policy and appoints officers to conduct operations. A shareholder may be an officer or a director.

c. **Free transferability of interest**. Absent contractual restriction, shares in a corporation may be freely transferred, e.g., by sale, gift, pledge, or inheritance.

1) A shareholder has no interest in specific corporate property. (S)he owns a proportional, intangible property interest in the entire corporation.

2) The shareholder's ownership interest is often represented by a stock certificate. The interest is usually transferred by endorsing the certificate.

d. **Perpetual life**. A corporation has perpetual existence unless the articles provide for a shorter life or it is dissolved by the state. Death, withdrawal, or addition of a shareholder, director, or officer does not end its existence.

e. **Ease of raising capital**. A corporation raises capital (to start or expand the business) by selling stock or issuing bonds. The sale of stock may be governed by state "blue sky" laws and federal securities laws.

3. **Disadvantages**. Adopting corporate status may result in

a. Reduced individual control of the business
b. Income taxed to both corporation and shareholder (unless S corporation)
c. Costs of meeting requirements of corporate form

4. **Powers of a Corporation**. Authority for corporate action derives from the state incorporation statute or the articles of organization. The Model Business Corporation Act (MBCA) has been adopted to some degree by every state.

    a. A corporation has rights and powers to

        1) Be treated as a separate entity or person
        2) Sue and be sued
        3) Acquire and dispose of real or personal property
        4) Hold, acquire, and dispose of shares of stock
        5) Lend money and guarantee obligations of others
        6) Enter into contracts
        7) Mortgage corporate property
        8) Compensate employees
        9) Become a partner in a partnership
        10) Pursue a nonprofit objective
        11) Donate for charitable, scientific, educational, or public purposes
        12) Establish incentives for officers, directors, and employees

    b. These powers and rights are referred to as **inherent** and/or **statutory powers**.

    c. **Express powers** are specifically granted to a particular corporation by its charter, i.e., the articles of organization. It describes ownership, control, and overall operational structure.

    d. **Implied powers** are necessary and appropriate to carry out express powers.

    e. Acts beyond the corporation's express or implied powers are said to be *ultra vires*.

        1) Generally, if a corporation acts *ultra vires*, shareholders (or the state's attorney general) can institute a legal proceeding to enjoin (prohibit) the act.

        2) The corporation (or the shareholders on its behalf) can sue the directors or officers responsible for the act for damages.

        3) Articles of organization authorizing any lawful business transaction are now common.

5. **Preincorporation Contracts**. A promoter is one who arranges for formation of the corporation. The promoter provides for the capital structure and financing of the corporation and for compliance with any relevant securities law. The promoter may also arrange for procurement of necessary personnel, services, assets, licenses, equipment, leases, etc.

    a. Prior to incorporation, the promoter enters into ordinary and necessary contracts required for initial operation of the business. If the contracts are executed in the promoter's name and there is no further action, the promoter is personally liable on them. The corporation is not liable. Because a promoter cannot be an agent of a not-yet-existing corporation,

        1) A preincorporation contract made by promoters in the name of a corporation and on its behalf does not bind the corporation, except if so provided by statute, and

        2) A corporation is unable to ratify preincorporation contracts.

    b. However, the corporation may adopt contracts formed by a promoter. This is acceptance of assignment of rights and delegation of duties.

        1) Adoption may be implied from accepting the benefits of a contract.

        2) The contract, by its terms, may provide that the promoter is released from liability upon adoption of the contract by the corporation.

c. A promoter may avoid liability by acquiring an option (assignable to the corporation) to bind the third party to a contract.

d. If the promoter has no liability by the terms of an agreement, and the agreement is not an option, it may be treated as a continuing offer until revoked or accepted by the corporation.

e. If the promoter, the third party, and the corporation enter into a novation substituting the corporation for the promoter, only the corporation is liable and the promoter is released.

f. Promoters owe a fiduciary duty to each other, to the corporation, and to subscribers and shareholders. This fiduciary duty requires good faith, fair dealing, and full disclosure of all material facts concerning transactions on behalf of the soon-to-be-formed corporation.

    1) Promoters have a duty to account for any secret profits earned when dealing with the corporation, e.g., by a sale of their own property to the corporation.

g. The promoter secures potential investors using stock subscription agreements whereby a subscriber agrees to purchase a certain amount of stock at a specified price, payable at an agreed future time.

    1) Technically, the subscriber is an offeror; (s)he offers to enter into a contract to purchase the stock.

    2) The MBCA provides that a preincorporation subscription agreement is irrevocable for 6 months, unless otherwise provided for in the subscription agreement or unless all of the subscribers consent to the revocation.

6. **Incorporation**. Each state requires that **articles of incorporation** (also referred to as articles of organization) be filed with the secretary of state or another designated official. (A corporation may incorporate in one state but have its principal place of business or conduct its business operations in another state or states.)

    a. **Incorporators** are the persons who sign the articles. Typically, an incorporator may not be a minor. Modern statutes require only one incorporator and permit it to be a corporation.

    b. The Revised MBCA requires that the articles of incorporation include the

        1) Corporation's name
        2) Number of authorized shares of stock
        3) Street address of the corporation's initial registered office
        4) Name of the registered agent at that office
        5) Name and address of each incorporator

    c. Generally, a corporation becomes an artificial legal entity when the articles are filed. Filing is a technical term, generally meaning state approval of the documents by

        1) Affixing an official stamp to the documents
        2) Issuing a formal charter
        3) Issuing a dated receipt of filing fee

        NOTE: Actual delivery by the state of a formal charter or certificate of incorporation is not necessarily required for formation in every state.

    d. After filing, the incorporators elect the members of the initial board of directors, if the board has not been named in the articles of organization. The incorporators then resign.

e. The board of directors holds an organizational meeting. It

1) Adopts bylaws that govern internal management of the corporation, consistent with state laws and the articles of organization, but which are not binding on persons outside the corporation

a) The power to alter, amend, or repeal bylaws is vested in the board unless specifically reserved to the shareholders in the charter.

2) Elects officers, typically a president, a treasurer, and a secretary (who may not be the president)

3) Takes other steps to complete the organizational structure for carrying on the business purpose of the corporation

a) EXAMPLE: The board might adopt stock subscription agreements.

7. **Defective Incorporation**. A corporation incorporated in strict compliance with statute is a *de jure* corporation.

a. A *de facto* corporation is recognized if there was a(n)

1) Statute under which the business could have incorporated
2) Good-faith attempt (unsuccessful) to comply with it
3) Actual or attempted exercise of corporate powers

NOTE: The legal existence of a *de facto* corporation can be challenged only by the state (in a *quo warranto* proceeding), not by a creditor of the corporation.

b. An organization that is neither a *de jure* nor a *de facto* corporation may be estopped (prohibited) from denying it is a corporation if

1) The organization has represented itself as a corporation,

2) The representation is followed by reasonable reliance and material alteration of position by a third party based on that representation,

3) The party asserting the estoppel argument demonstrates fair and equitable conduct, and

4) Injustice can be avoided only by treating the business as a corporation.

NOTE: The organization, although not a corporation, is treated as if it were.

c. Many state corporation statutes establish a conclusive presumption that, when a certificate of incorporation has been issued, the corporation exists even if the filing was defective.

8. **Piercing the Corporate Veil**. Courts disregard the separate corporate entity when the corporate form is used merely to commit wrongdoing, shield its shareholders from liability for fraud, or otherwise circumvent the law. If so, shareholder(s) are personally liable for corporate acts (as is a general partner in a partnership). A court might disregard a corporate entity if it finds

a. The corporation is merely the *alter ego* of a shareholder, for example, if assets of the corporation and the shareholder(s) are commingled, corporate formalities are ignored, and the corporation was established for a sham purpose.

b. Two or more business enterprises are related corporations (such as parent-subsidiary or brother-sister corporations) and in practice do not maintain sufficiently independent existence.

c. A corporation is inadequately capitalized to carry on its intended business.

9. **Jurisdiction of State**. A state may exercise jurisdiction (authority) over a foreign corporation, e.g., to require registration or to effect service of process in another state, only if the corporation has at least minimum contacts with the state.

    a. Minimum contacts might consist of activity that is not isolated and that

        1) Is purposefully directed towards the state, e.g., advertising on radio stations heard within the state and intended to generate product demand in the state, or

        2) Places a product in the stream of interstate commerce with an expectation or intent that it will ultimately be used in the state.

    b. Thus, a state long-arm statute may authorize general jurisdiction over a foreign corporation based on an active business office or substantial activity in the state, e.g., maintaining inventory and records.

    c. However, mere solicitation of offers to be accepted out of state, to be delivered by interstate carrier from out of state, and to be paid for by mail, is not doing business sufficient to constitute minimum contacts.

    d. State long-arm statutes also authorize jurisdiction over foreign corporations that perform isolated or single acts in the state or whose conduct directly affects the state, but only for causes of action arising from those acts.

10. Stop and review! You have completed the outline for this subunit. Study multiple-choice questions 1 through 11 beginning on page 163.

B. Shareholders, Directors, and Officers

1. **Shareholder Rights**. Shareholders (stockholders) participate indirectly in corporate policy and management by meeting annually and electing directors. In addition, shareholders must approve fundamental changes: amendments to the articles of incorporation; all actions of merger or consolidation; and any proposal by directors to sell, lease, or exchange all or substantially all of the corporation's assets.

    a. **Voting rights**. The articles may provide for more or less than one vote per share.

        1) Usually, each shareholder is entitled to one vote for each share owned for each new director to be elected, i.e., straight voting. Shareholders also have the right to remove directors by vote.

        2) **Cumulative voting** is mandatory in almost one-half of the states that permit it.

            a) Cumulative voting entitles each shareholder who has one vote per share owned per director to accumulate votes and either give one candidate as many votes as the number of directors to be elected multiplied by the number of shares owned or distribute that number of votes among as many candidates as (s)he wishes.

            b) *Number of directors to be elected × Number of shares of the shareholder = Number of votes the shareholder may allocate to any one or more candidates*

            NOTE: Cumulative voting allows a minority shareholder or group of them to obtain representation on the board, if they own a certain minimum number of shares. It can preclude the holders of more than 50% of the voting stock from electing the entire board of directors.

        3) The MBCA permits different voting rights for different classes of shares. Thus, each class may have the right to elect one director. This results in **class voting**.

        4) The MBCA specifically permits a **voting agreement**, whereby shareholders contract how they will vote their shares. It may be perpetual and secret.

5) **Voting trusts**. Shareholders transfer their shares to one or more voting trustees in exchange for voting trust certificates. The trustees elect directors based on instructions from the shareholders.

    a) The term of voting trusts is initially limited to 10 years.

        i) Shareholders can agree to continue it beyond 10 years.

    b) A voting trust indenture (document) must be made public, and copies must be available for inspection at the corporate offices.

6) A **proxy** is an authorization by a shareholder for someone else to vote on his/her behalf. Typically, a proxy must be in writing and is revocable at any time.

    a) A proxy is effective for no more than 11 months, unless another time period is otherwise permitted by statute and specifically included in the writing or unless the proxy is coupled with an interest; e.g., the shares are collateral for a loan, a buy/sell agreement, or a voting agreement. The proxy coupled with an interest may be irrevocable.

    b) An otherwise irrevocable proxy is revocable by a bona fide purchaser of the shares who has no notice of the proxy.

    c) A general proxy permits a holder to vote on all corporate proposals other than fundamental corporate changes. A limited proxy permits a holder to vote only on matters specified in the proxy.

b. **Preemptive rights** give a shareholder an option to subscribe to a new issuance of shares in proportion to the shareholder's current interest in the corporation. They limit dilution of shareholders' equity in the corporation.

1) All states except New Hampshire recognize preemptive rights. However, in most states, preemptive rights may not exist unless they are specifically reserved in the articles of incorporation.

2) There are substantial limitations on preemptive rights. For example, under the RMBCA, preemptive rights do not apply to stock issued

    a) As an incentive to officers, directors, or employees
    b) In satisfaction of conversion or option rights

3) Publicly traded corporations sometimes issue options to purchase stock at a specified (usually below market) price. These securities are frequently given to executives as a form of incentive. Moreover, options to purchase (call options) or to sell (put options) may be created by parties other than the issuer of the underlying stock.

    a) Rights are short-term options. They are issued to current shareholders, most often in connection with a preemptive right.

    b) Warrants are longer-term options evidenced by certificates that are usually attached to other securities, for example, bonds or preferred stock.

    c) The foregoing securities may be transferable and traded on stock exchanges.

c. Shareholders have a fundamental right to inspect the corporation's books and records.

1) Inspection must generally be at the corporation's home office during usual business hours, subsequent to 5 days' written notice of demand.

2) Inspection must be in good faith and for a proper purpose, e.g., to determine

        a) Corporate financial condition
        b) The propriety of dividends
        c) Mismanagement of the corporation
        d) The names and addresses of other shareholders

3) Improper purpose includes an ulterior motive to

        a) Harass management
        b) Discover trade secrets
        c) Gain a competitive advantage
        d) Develop a mailing list for sale or for similar use

4) Courts have permitted a shareholder to obtain a copy of a shareholder list, even when the only purpose was to engage in a takeover battle.

d. **Meetings**. Generally, shareholders can act only at a meeting.

1) Annual shareholders' meetings are required and must be held at a time fixed in the bylaws. The purpose is to elect new directors and to conduct other necessary business. Lack of or defective notice voids action taken at the meeting.

2) Special shareholder meetings, e.g., to approve a merger, may be called by the board of directors, the owner(s) of at least 10% of the issued and outstanding common stock, or any other persons authorized in the articles of incorporation. Special meetings require written notice.

3) A quorum must be represented in person or by proxy to conduct business at a shareholders' meeting. The MBCA defines a quorum as a majority of shares outstanding. Most state statutes permit the articles to establish a greater percentage (supermajority).

4) The MBCA permits shareholders to act without a meeting if all shareholders entitled to vote consent in writing to the action.

e. **Shareholder suits**. An individual shareholder may sue a corporation to preclude *ultra vires* acts and enforce preemptive, inspection, or other rights of shareholders created by statute, the charter, the bylaws, or common law.

1) Shareholders may sue directly on their own behalf either individually or as members of a class. In a class action, the plaintiffs represent not only themselves but "all others similarly situated."

2) A shareholder may also file a **shareholder derivative suit** to recover for wrong done to the corporation. The action is for the benefit of the corporation, and any recovery belongs to it, not to the shareholder. The corporation is the real plaintiff.

    a) A shareholder must first demand that the corporation bring suit unless it is obvious demand would be futile; i.e., the action is against corporate officers or directors.

    b) Most states require that the shareholder show the following:

        i) (S)he owned shares at the time of wrongdoing.
        ii) Demand was made.
        iii) The directors refused to sue.
        iv) The refusal was in bad faith.

    c) The business judgment rule applies to the board's decision not to pursue a corporate legal claim.

    d) A shareholder can generally recover reasonable litigation expenses from the corporation but no compensation for his/her time.

2. **Shareholder Liability**. A shareholder's liability is limited to his/her capital contribution except in certain instances, for example, if the corporate veil is pierced.

    a. **Stock subscription agreements**. The subscriber remains liable to the corporation for any unpaid installment balance, even if the corporation becomes insolvent or declares bankruptcy. If the subscriber dies, his/her estate may be liable for any balance due.

    b. If authorized stock is issued with a stated par value and is originally issued (sold) for less, the purchasing shareholder is and remains liable (to the corporation) for the deficiency.

        1) A person who subsequently purchases the stock is subject to liability if (s)he knows the stock was issued for less than par value.

        2) The MBCA and RMBCA have eliminated the concept of par value.

    c. If stock is issued in exchange for overvalued property (watered stock) and the facts indicate fraud or bad faith by the shareholders, they (and probably the directors) will be personally liable for any amount underpaid.

    d. Some states permit a corporation to recover damages from shareholders who receive a dividend or other corporate distribution when the shareholder knows that the distribution is wrong.

        1) A shareholder may be held liable for unpaid debts of the corporation up to the amount received as an illegal dividend or distribution.

    e. A seller of a controlling block of stock may be liable to nonselling minority shareholders if the seller has or should have had a reasonable suspicion that the purchaser would mismanage or loot the corporation, unless investigation shows no basis for it.

    f. If a purchaser wishes to buy the corporation's assets and the controlling shareholder proposes that the purchaser buy his/her stock instead, the controlling shareholder may be liable for usurping a corporate opportunity.

    g. A breach of the fiduciary duty owed by the majority to the minority (in a closely held corporation) of utmost good faith, loyalty, and impartiality gives rise to liability. Controlling shareholders must

        1) Not cause the corporation to purchase their shares at a price unavailable to the minority

        2) Act in good faith regarding payment of salaries and dividends

3. **Board of Directors**. A minimum of one director is required. Some states require three, but if there are fewer than three shareholders, the number of directors may be equal to the number of shareholders. A corporation with 50 or fewer shareholders may dispense with an authorized board. Inside directors are also officers of the corporation. An outside director is not an officer of that corporation.

    a. The initial board named in the articles of incorporation serves until the first meeting of shareholders.

    b. Generally, a director serves a 1-year term. The charter or bylaws may provide for a longer term. Generally, directors on a board of nine or more may be classified. This permits staggering of terms by creating separate classes of directors. The members of one class will then be elected at each annual meeting.

    c. Power authorizing the board to increase its size without shareholder approval can be reserved in the articles or bylaws.

d.   Normally, a director is elected by a plurality (rather than a majority) of shareholder votes.

    1)   EXAMPLE: Candidates A, B, and C receive 150, 100, and 100, respectively, of 350 possible votes. Candidate A has received a plurality of votes.

    2)   Cumulative voting may be permitted or mandatory.

e.   Typically, if a director dies or resigns, the board of directors can elect a director to fill the vacancy.

f.   In most states, shareholders may by a majority vote remove, with or without cause, any director or the entire board.

g.   Statutes usually permit the board to remove a director who has been declared insane or convicted of a felony. Rarely would a board be permitted to remove a director for any other reason.

h.   The RMBCA authorizes a court to issue an order to remove a director in a proceeding brought by the corporation or by shareholders who own at least 10% of the outstanding shares of any class of stock if the court finds

    1)   The director engaged in fraudulent or dishonest conduct, or
    2)   The director abused his/her authority, and
    3)   Removal is in the best interest of the corporation.

4.   **Board Authority and Actions**. While the directors formulate overall corporate policy, they are neither trustees nor agents of the corporation. A director cannot act individually to bind the corporation. But directors are fiduciaries who must perform their duties in good faith, with due care, and in the best interests of the corporation.

a.   The board establishes and implements corporate policy including

    1)   Selection and removal of officers
    2)   Determination of capital structure
    3)   Adding, amending, or repealing bylaws
    4)   Initiation of fundamental changes
    5)   Declaration of dividends
    6)   Setting of management compensation

b.   Because directors owe a fiduciary duty to the shareholders and to the corporation, express agreement is necessary to authorize compensation. It is now common to compensate outside directors.

c.   Directors have power to bind the corporation only when acting as a board.

d.   The board may act only at a formal meeting of directors or by duly executed written consent, if authorized by statute, unless contrary to the charter or bylaws.

e.   Many statutes, charters, and bylaws permit boards to act

    1)   By simultaneous telephone conference call
    2)   By video conference
    3)   Without a meeting by unanimous written consent

f.   Formal meetings are held at fixed intervals established in the bylaws.

g.   Special meetings can be held after proper notice has been given to all directors.

    1)   A director's attendance at any meeting is a waiver of notice, unless the director attends for the express purpose of objecting to the transaction on the ground that the meeting is not lawfully convened.

h.   Unless required by statute or bylaws, the board need not meet at the corporate offices or even in the state of incorporation. Most modern statutes allow meetings outside the U.S.

i. Actions taken by a board are expressed in formal resolutions adopted by a majority of the board during a meeting at which a quorum is present. Generally, a quorum consists of a majority of board members. A director is not allowed to vote by proxy.

j. If a formal dissent (by entry in the minutes) is not communicated, concurrence with the majority decision is presumed.

   1) Written dissent may be sent by registered mail to the secretary of the corporation immediately after adjournment of the meeting.

k. A board may form committees composed of its members or corporate officers. Committee members usually have a specific skill or extensive experience in an area of concern.

   1) The RMBCA requires that a committee formation and an appointment of members be approved by the greater of

      a) A majority of all the directors in office when the action is taken, or

      b) The number of directors required by the charter or bylaws to take action.

   2) The committees can exercise broad powers consistent with the limits of the resolutions by which they were established but may not initiate extraordinary transactions, e.g., issuance of stock.

   3) New York Stock Exchange rules require every listed corporation to have an audit committee consisting of outside directors.

l. Directors have the right to inspect corporate books and records so they can perform their duties.

5. **Directors' Duty of Care**. Directors have a fiduciary relationship to the corporation and its shareholders. They can be held personally liable for failure to be informed of matters internal and external to, but also relevant to, the corporation. A director's conduct is tested objectively.

   a. The RMBCA requires that a director discharge his/her duties

      1) In good faith
      2) With reasonable care
      3) In a manner believed to be in the best interests of the corporation

   b. Reasonable care is the care an ordinarily prudent person in a similar position would exercise under similar circumstances.

      1) Thus, a director must not be negligent.

   c. In exercising reasonable care, a director can rely on information, reports, opinions, and statements prepared or presented by officers or employees whom the director reasonably believes to be competent in the matters presented.

   d. A director can also rely on the specialized knowledge of lawyers, accountants, investment bankers, and board committees.

   e. Directors are expected to be informed and conversant with pertinent corporate information when rendering advice to the board. A director has not exercised the required care if (s)he does not

      1) Attend meetings of the board
      2) Analyze corporate financial statements
      3) Review pertinent legal opinions
      4) Become conversant with the available relevant information

6. **Directors' Duty of Loyalty**. Directors of a corporation owe a duty of loyalty to the corporation and its shareholders.

    a. To protect the corporation against self-dealing, a director is required to make full disclosure of any financial interest (s)he may have in any transaction to which both the director and the corporation may be a party.

        1) Unanimous approval of a self-dealing transaction by disinterested, informed shareholders may release an interested director from liability for self-dealing, even if the transaction is unfair to the corporation.

    b. Under the MBCA, a transaction is not voidable merely on the grounds of a director's conflict of interest if the transaction is fair to the corporation or has been approved by a majority of informed, disinterested directors or shareholders.

        1) A transaction is fair if reasonable persons, bargaining at arm's-length (independently) would have entered into the transaction if they had been in the same circumstances as the corporation.

        2) A contract between a director and the corporation that is neither fair nor approved by disinterested directors or shareholders may be rescinded or upheld by the corporation, and the director may be required to pay damages.

    c. The MBCA does not permit a corporation to lend money to its directors without authorization by its shareholders. The RMBCA does permit specific loans if approved by

        1) A majority of disinterested shareholders, or
        2) The board of directors after determining it is beneficial to the corporation.

    d. Directors may not usurp any corporate opportunity. A director must give the corporation the right of first refusal.

        1) A corporate opportunity is one in which the corporation has a right, property interest, or expectancy.

        2) A corporate opportunity arises when

            a) A director becomes aware of the opportunity in his/her corporate capacity,

            b) The opportunity is within the scope of corporate activity, or

            c) Corporate capital, equipment, personnel, or facilities were used to develop the opportunity.

        3) Generally, a corporate opportunity does not exist if

            a) Action by the corporation would be *ultra vires*,

            b) The corporation cannot obtain necessary financing or capital to take advantage of the opportunity, or

            c) The opportunity is rejected by a majority vote of disinterested directors.

7. **Business Judgment Rule**. Courts avoid substituting their business judgment for that of the corporation's officers or directors.

    a. The rule protects a director from personal liability if (s)he

        1) Acted in good faith
        2) Was not motivated by fraud, conflict of interest, or illegality
        3) Was not guilty of gross negligence

    b.   To avoid personal liability, directors and officers must

        1)   Make informed decisions (educate themselves about the issues)
        2)   Be free from conflicts of interest
        3)   Have a rational basis to support their position

    c.   Some recent decisions concern incumbent management's opposition to **tender offers**, i.e., offers to shareholders made by a third party to buy the shareholders' stock at a price above the market price. Directors may be liable to shareholders; i.e., the business judgment rule may not apply if

        1)   The directors make a decision to oppose a tender offer before they have carefully studied it, or

        2)   The directors' actions indicate that they are opposing the tender offer in order to preserve their jobs.

    d.   Most states do permit corporations to indemnify directors for expenses of litigation concerning business judgment.

8.   **Officers** are elected or appointed by the board. They generally serve at the will of the board, which may remove any officer at any time. However, the board may not remove without cause an officer elected or employed by the shareholders.

    a.   Typically, state statutes set a minimum number of officers, but not a maximum. One officer must be delegated responsibility for

        1)   Preparing the minutes of directors' meetings
        2)   Authenticating records of the corporation

    b.   Officers typically appointed are president, vice president, secretary, and treasurer. One person may hold more than one office. Many states require that the same person not hold the offices of president and secretary simultaneously.

    c.   The officers are agents of the corporation. They have **express authority** conferred by the bylaws or the board. They have **implied authority** to do things that are reasonably necessary to accomplish their express duties. Courts have held that official titles confer limited **inherent authority** on officers.

        1)   **President**. (S)he supervises and controls all the business and affairs of the corporation, subject to the discretion of the board.

            a)   (S)he presides at board and shareholders' meetings.

            b)   Traditionally, the president had no inherent authority. However, the trend is that (s)he can bind the corporation in the ordinary course of its business, e.g., by signing on behalf of the corporation deeds, mortgages, bonds, contracts, or any instrument subject to board approval.

        2)   **General manager or chief executive officer**. The title grants broad implied authority to conduct the corporation's business.

        3)   **Vice president**. (S)he traditionally performs the duties of the president if the president is unable to.

            a)   A vice president has no inherent authority. But a person named vice president of a specific department, e.g., finance, has authority to transact business within the scope of that department.

4)   **Secretary**. (S)he is the custodian of the corporate seal and records.

a)   The secretary notifies participants of shareholders' and board meetings and maintains the minutes (records).

b)   The secretary maintains the stock transfer ledgers and, along with the president, signs for the issuance of stock certificates.

c)   The secretary certifies the authenticity of the president's signature and corporate records when necessary.

5)   **Treasurer**. (S)he maintains the financial accounts and records. Typically, the treasurer signs all checks and gives receipts for, and deposits money due and payable to, the corporation.

d.   Officers, like directors, owe fiduciary duties to the corporation.

1)   As an agent, an officer has a duty to act within authority granted by the articles, the bylaws, and the board.

2)   Officers are subject to the same duties of care and loyalty to the corporation as are directors.

3)   Likewise, absent bad faith, fraud, or breach of a fiduciary duty, the business judgment rule applies to officers. Like a director, the officer is insulated by the business judgment rule if the management decision is informed, conflict-free, and rational.

a)   Officers may be indemnified to the extent, consistent with public policy, provided by the articles of incorporation, bylaws, actions of the board, or contract.

9.   Stop and review! You have completed the outline for this subunit. Study multiple-choice questions 12 through 17 beginning on page 166.

C. Financial Structure, Capital, and Distributions

1.   **Debt Securities**. Two basic ways to initially finance a corporation include issuing equity securities and issuing debt securities.

a.   Short-term debt financing may consist of securing short-term bank credit, assigning accounts receivable, pledging some or all of the corporation's properties, and issuing short-term promissory notes.

b.   A corporation accomplishes long-term debt financing through issuing debt securities, i.e., the sale of bonds. Debt securities represent, not an ownership interest in the corporation, but a debtor-creditor relationship between the corporation and the security holder.

c.   A **bond** is a negotiable security expressing the corporation's promise to pay

1)   The amount of the bond at a future date (generally principal), and
2)   Interest (typically semiannually at a fixed rate).

d.   The board of directors may issue bonds without shareholder authorization.

e.   **Secured bonds**. The creditor's claim is enforceable against the general assets of the corporation pursuant to a lien upon specific corporate property.

f.   **Unsecured bonds** (debentures) are backed only by the general obligation of the corporation. No property is pledged as security.

1)   Debenture holders are unsecured creditors and rank equally with other general creditors.

g. Most corporate bonds are registered. In this context, the term "registered" means a bond issued to an owner whose name is stated on the face of the bond. The owner is registered in the records of the issuing corporation.

h. **Callable bonds** are subject to a redemption privilege which permits the corporation to redeem or pay off all or part of the issue before maturity.

i. **Convertible bonds** are convertible into a share or shares of stock of the issuing corporation based on a formula stated on the face of the bond.

j. Debt securities do not include voting rights.

k. On liquidation of a corporation, the holders of debt securities receive no more than the amount of their claims.

l. Interest on debt is a tax deductible expense.

2. **Equity Securities**. Shareholders have an ownership interest in the corporation. But a share of stock does not confer title to any specific property owned by the corporation.

    a. In the event of bankruptcy or liquidation, creditors including bondholders have first claim on corporate assets. Any surplus is distributed to the shareholders.

    b. Most state incorporation statutes require that the articles specify the number of authorized shares and the classes of stock.

        1) Authorized capital stock cannot be increased or decreased without amending the articles.

    c. The board can choose to issue all, part, or none of the authorized stock.

    d. Subject to state and federal securities regulation, stock can be issued for cash, property (tangible or intangible), or past services rendered. The RMBCA, but not most state statutes, permits stock to be issued for promissory notes and future services.

    e. Until shares of stock have been issued, they are "authorized but unissued" shares. Afterward they are "issued and outstanding" shares.

    f. Any issuance of stock in violation of state corporate law is voidable (not void) at the option of the recipient shareholder.

    g. Par value, if set by the promoters or the board, is a dollar amount below which the shares may not be initially sold without future assessment.

    h. All states do (and the articles may) authorize issuance of no-par stock. No-par stock is sold by the issuing corporation at whatever price the board of directors determines is reasonable, which is upheld in the absence of fraud or self-dealing.

    i. **Treasury stock** is stock issued and later reacquired by the corporation. Under the MBCA, repurchased shares are restored to unissued status. The shares may be held indefinitely, resold, or retired.

        1) The corporation may not vote or receive dividends on treasury stock.

    j. **Common stock**. Common shareholders are entitled to receive distributions only after all other claims have been satisfied, including those of preferred shareholders.

        1) State statutes typically permit different classes of common stock with different rights or privileges, e.g., class A common with voting rights and class B common with no voting rights.

        2) If only one class of stock is issued, it is treated as common, and each shareholder must be treated equally.

        3) Common shareholders elect directors to the board.

k. **Preferred stock**. The shareholders have the right to receive dividends at a specified rate stated on the face of the shares (before common shareholders may receive any) and the right to receive distributions before common shareholders upon liquidation or bankruptcy.

    1)   The articles must designate which shares are preferred.

    2)   If a board issues preferred stock, it may establish different classes or series, assigning to each independent rights, dividend rates, and redemption prices.

l. **Cumulative preferred stock** gives the holder the right to receive the stated dividend in full each year. If payment is not made in any year, the unpaid cumulative preferred dividends accumulate and must be paid in full before any dividends are paid to common shareholders.

    1)   If the nature of preferred stock is unclear, most courts have ruled that preferred stock is impliedly cumulative.

m. **Participating preferred stock**. In addition to being entitled to the stated dividend before any dividend can be paid to common shareholders, the holders participate with the common shareholders in any remaining funds allocated for dividend payments.

n. **Convertible preferred stock**. Shareholders have the option to convert the stock into shares of another class (at a predetermined ratio set forth in the charter or bylaws).

o. **Redeemable preferred stock** is issued with the condition that it may be redeemed (repurchased) by the issuing corporation at a stated price and time. Issuing corporations may establish a sinking fund for redemption purposes.

3. **Distributions**. The board has discretion to determine the time and amount of dividends.

  a. All states impose the equity insolvency test. Payment of a dividend is prohibited when the corporation is insolvent or when the payment would render it so.

  b. The majority of states require that dividends be paid out of earned surplus and not stated capital.

  c. A nimble dividend is permitted by the Delaware corporation statute. A dividend may be paid out of current earnings if sufficient capital exists to pay the liquidation preference of all shares, even if the corporation has a negative surplus.

  d. Directors who approve a dividend declared in violation of the applicable state test have abused their discretion. They are jointly and severally liable to the corporation for the amount. Shareholders who know a dividend is illegal must repay it. Those who do not know must repay it only if the corporation is insolvent or made insolvent by it.

  e. The **declaration date** is the date the board of directors by vote approves a resolution to declare a dividend. The vote is irrevocable. Once declared, payment of the dividend is a legal obligation of the corporation.

  f. The directors fix a **record date**. The registered holder on the record date is sent the payment on the payment date.

    1)   If the record holder receives payment but has transferred the stock, the corporation is not liable to the transferee provided it was unaware of the transfer. The transferee must sue the transferor (not the corporation) for the amount.

2) Absent an agreement with the transferee to the contrary, the transferor is entitled to all dividends declared prior to the transfer.

3) However, stock of a company traded on an organized exchange (listed stock) and purchased during the settlement period, i.e., the 5 business days prior to the record date, is ex dividend (without dividend) to the buyer.

4) If a record date is not set, the declaration date is treated as the record date.

g. The **payment date** is the date that the corporation will actually tender payment of the dividend to the shareholders of record.

h. **Dividends** are usually paid in cash or property (a dividend in kind).

i. A **stock dividend** is payable in the stock of the dividend-paying corporation.

1) The corporation generally issues new stock for this purpose.

2) Stock dividends do not increase the equity of each shareholder because they are in proportion to the shares already owned.

3) When a stock dividend is declared, the corporation transfers the value of the new stock from earned surplus (profits) to the stated capital account.

4) The dividend shares are typically of the same class as the shares entitled to the dividend and are distributed in a fixed ratio.

5) Dividend shares may be of another class or series if authorized by the articles or a majority of outstanding shares of the same class as the proposed dividend.

j. A **stock split** is an issuance of shares for the purpose of reducing the unit value of each share. Accordingly, the par or stated value is also reduced. The ratio at which shares are exchanged is arbitrary. Shares may be split one-and-a half to one, two-to-one, or in any other way.

1) Unlike a stock dividend, a stock split must be authorized by an amendment to the articles of incorporation.

2) A stock split does not increase a shareholder's proportionate ownership.

3) A stock split does not require that a corporation possess retained earnings or meet any statutory dividend requirements.

4) In a reverse stock split, the number of shares owned is reduced in reverse proportion.

4. Stop and review! You have completed the outline for this subunit. Study multiple-choice questions 18 through 25 beginning on page 168.

D. Merger, Consolidation, and Dissolution

1. **Appraisal Rights.** Shareholders who disagree with fundamental corporate changes may have dissenters' or appraisal rights. The corporation must pay dissenting shareholders the fair value of their stock in cash within 60 days.

    a. Under the MBCA, fair value is the value immediately before the corporation acts on the proposed fundamental change, excluding any increase or decrease due to any anticipated effects of the fundamental change.

    b. The MBCA requires that a shareholder demanding appraisal

        1) Have the right to vote on the action to which (s)he objects

        2) Not vote in favor of the transaction

        3) Make written demand before the vote that the corporation purchase his/her stock if the action is approved

    c. Under the MBCA, the right of appraisal covers

        1) Amendments to the articles of incorporation that materially and adversely affect shareholder rights

        2) Sales of all or substantially all corporate assets

        3) Mergers and consolidations

    d. Most state statutes exclude shares traded on a nationally recognized exchange from appraisal rights.

2. **Charter Amendments.** Modern corporation statutes permit the articles of incorporation to be freely amended.

    a. Generally, the board adopts a resolution setting forth, in writing, the proposed amendment. The resolution must be approved by a majority of the shareholders entitled to vote.

        1) Some statutes require a two-thirds shareholder vote.
        2) A class of shareholders may be entitled to vote as "a class."

    b. Shareholders may amend the articles by unanimous written consent without prior adoption of a resolution by the board.

    c. After shareholder approval, articles of amendment are filed with the secretary of state. Amendment is effective when a certificate of amendment is issued.

    d. The RMBCA permits the board to adopt certain *de minimis* amendments, e.g., changing the corporation's registered agent, without shareholder action, unless the articles of incorporation provide otherwise.

3. **Sale or Lease of Corporate Assets.** If a sale or lease of all or substantially all corporate assets is not in the usual and regular course of business, approval of the board and a majority of shareholders is required.

    a. In most states, dissenting shareholders have appraisal rights.

    b. A mortgage or pledge of any or all of the property and assets of a corporation, whether or not in the usual course of business, requires director, but not shareholder, approval (absent a contrary provision in the articles).

4. **Merger**. A merger is the combination of all the assets of two or more corporations. In a merger, one corporation is absorbed by another corporation and ceases to exist, e.g., A + B = A. State statutes set forth specific procedures for mergers.

    a. The shareholders of a merged corporation may receive stock or other securities issued by the surviving corporation.

    b. Stock of the merged (acquired) corporation is canceled.

    c. A merger requires the approval of each board and of a majority of shareholders entitled to vote for each corporation.

        1) Shareholders of each corporation must be provided a copy of the merger plan to enable informed voting.

    d. The surviving corporation succeeds to the rights, duties, liabilities, and title to all of the assets of the merged corporation.

    e. Dissenting shareholders of each corporation have an appraisal remedy.

    f. No shareholder approval is required in a short-form merger. A corporation that owns at least 90% of the issued and outstanding shares of a subsidiary merges the subsidiary into itself.

        1) Dissenting shareholders of the subsidiary have appraisal rights.

5. **Consolidations**. A new corporation is formed and the two or more consolidating corporations cease operating as separate entities, e.g., A + B = C.

    a. A consolidation requires approval by vote of the boards and a majority of shareholders of each consolidating corporation.

    b. The shareholders receive stock or other securities issued by the new corporation.

6. **Tender Offers**. A merger, consolidation, or purchase of substantially all of a corporation's assets requires approval of the board of directors of the corporation whose shares or assets are acquired. An acquiring corporation may bypass board approval by extending a tender offer directly to shareholders to purchase a certain number of the outstanding shares.

    a. After obtaining control of the target corporation, the tender offeror can cause a merger or consolidation.

    b. Management of target corporations has implemented diverse strategies to counter hostile tender offers. Courts apply the business judgment rule when such strategies are challenged. They have generally upheld the strategies. Examples of antitakeover strategies follow:

        1) **Persuasion**. Management of the target persuades target shareholders to reject an offer.

        2) **Poison pill**. A target corporation's charter, bylaws, or contracts include provisions that reduce the value of the target to potential tender offerors. For example, a valuable contract may terminate by its terms upon a specified form of change of ownership of the target.

        3) **Flip-over rights**. The charter of a target corporation provides for its shareholders to acquire in exchange for their stock a greater interest (e.g., twice the shares of stock of equivalent value) in an acquiring entity.

        4) **Flip-in rights**. Acquisition of more than a specified ownership interest (e.g., 25%) in the target corporation by a raider triggers additional rights in the stock not acquired by the raider; e.g., each share becomes entitled to two votes.

5)   **Issuing stock**. The target corporation significantly increases the amount of outstanding stock.

6)   **Reverse tender**. The target corporation makes a tender offer to acquire control of the tender offeror.

7)   **Self-tender**. The target borrows money to tender an offer to repurchase shares of itself.

8)   **ESOP**. An employee stock ownership plan is likely to result in a vote of the shares allocated to it against a raider who is likely to destabilize the target corporation's current structure.

9)   **White knight merger**. Target management arranges an alternative tender offer with a different acquirer that will be more favorable to incumbent management and shareholders.

10)   **Crown jewel transfer**. The target corporation sells or otherwise disposes of one or more assets that made it a desirable target.

11)   **Legal action**. A target corporation may challenge one or more aspects of a tender offer. A resulting delay increases costs to the raider and enables further defensive action.

12)   **Scorched earth**. A target firm sells off the assets or divisions that the offeror finds most attractive or acquires substantial amounts of debt that would come due if the firm was acquired by a takeover. Either scenario renders the target firm less desirable to the offeror.

c.   States regulate tender offers by statutes or administrative regulations to protect interests other than those of a would-be raider.

d.   The Williams Act of 1968 extended reporting and disclosure requirements of federal securities regulation to tender offers.

7.   **Dissolution**. The MBCA permits voluntary dissolution of a corporation that has not commenced business or issued stock by a majority vote of its incorporators or directors.

a.   A corporation that has issued stock and commenced business may be voluntarily dissolved upon one of the following occurrences:

1)   Unanimous written consent of all shareholders

2)   Majority shareholder vote at a special meeting called for the purpose, if the directors have adopted a resolution of dissolution

b.   The corporation files articles of dissolution with the secretary of state petitioning the state to dissolve the corporation. A dissolution is effective when filed.

c.   The secretary of state may proceed administratively to dissolve involuntarily a corporation that fails to file its annual report, pay its franchise tax, or appoint or maintain a resident agent.

1)   Typically, the secretary of state gives written notice to the corporation to correct the default or demonstrate that none exists.

d.   Under the MBCA, any shareholder may seek judicial dissolution when there is a deadlock of the board that is harmful to the corporation or when the director's actions are contrary to the best interests of the corporation.

e.   The secretary of state may petition a court to order voluntary dissolution of a corporation if it is proved that a corporation obtained its articles of incorporation by fraud or that it exceeded or abused its legal authority.

8.   Stop and review! You have completed the outline for this subunit. Study multiple-choice questions 26 through 30 beginning on page 170.

MULTIPLE-CHOICE QUESTIONS

A. Formation, Purposes, and Powers

1. Which of the following statements is correct with respect to the differences and similarities between a corporation and a limited partnership?

   A. Directors owe fiduciary duties to the corporation, and limited partners owe such duties to the partnership.

   B. A corporation and a limited partnership may be created only under a state statute, and each must file a copy of its organizational document with the proper governmental body.

   C. Shareholders may be entitled to vote on corporate matters, but limited partners are prohibited from voting on any partnership matters.

   D. Stock of a corporation may be subject to registration under federal securities laws, but limited partnership interests are automatically exempt from such requirements.

The correct answer is (B). *(CPA, adapted)*
   REQUIRED: The true statement of a difference or similarity between a corporation and a limited partnership.
   DISCUSSION: Common law is not a basis for formation of either a corporation or a limited partnership. Each is formed and exists only under the authority of a statute. Filing organizational documents (articles of incorporation or certificates of limited partnership) with appropriate state authorities is required for both.
   Answer (A) is incorrect because limited partners are investors, not fiduciaries, and owe no such duty to the partnership. Answer (C) is incorrect because, although not allowed to participate in management, limited partners may still vote on such matters as dissolution of the partnership or the removal of a general partner. Answer (D) is incorrect because limited partnership interests are securities and are subject to registration and reporting requirements under federal securities laws.

2. Unless prohibited by the organization documents, a shareholder in a publicly held corporation and the owner of a limited partnership interest both have the right to

   A. Own the business's assets.

   B. Control management of the business.

   C. Assign their interest in the business.

   D. Invest in a business that has perpetual life.

The correct answer is (C). *(CPA, adapted)*
   REQUIRED: The right common to owners of a corporation and a limited partnership.
   DISCUSSION: Both a limited partner and a shareholder in a corporation may assign an ownership interest. Each owns an intangible property right in an undivided share of all the assets of the business. Neither has an interest in specific property of the business.
   Answer (A) is incorrect because neither owns the business assets. Answer (B) is incorrect because neither has the right to manage the business. Each participates by voting on fundamental matters, such as selection of directors or removal of a general partner. Answer (D) is incorrect because statutes authorizing corporations provide for their perpetual existence, whereas those providing for limited partnerships do not.

3. Which of the following statements best describes an advantage of the corporate form of doing business?

   A. Day-to-day management is strictly the responsibility of the directors.

   B. Ownership is contractually restricted and is not transferable.

   C. The operation of the business may continue indefinitely.

   D. The business is free from state regulation.

The correct answer is (C). *(CPA, adapted)*
   REQUIRED: The advantage of the corporate form.
   DISCUSSION: A corporation has perpetual existence unless it is given a shorter life under the articles of incorporation or is dissolved by the state. Death, withdrawal, or addition of a shareholder, director, or officer does not terminate its existence.
   Answer (A) is incorrect because officers run day-to-day operations. Answer (B) is incorrect because, absent a specific contractual restriction, shares are freely transferable, e.g., by gift, sale, pledge, or inheritance. Answer (D) is incorrect because a corporation can be created only under state law.

4. Assuming all other requirements are met, a corporation may elect to be treated as an S corporation under the Internal Revenue Code if it has

A. Both common and preferred shareholders.

B. A partnership as a shareholder.

C. Seventy-five or fewer shareholders.

D. The consent of a majority of the shareholders.

The correct answer is (C). *(CPA, adapted)*
REQUIRED: The requirement for S corporation status.
DISCUSSION: An S corporation meets specific requirements, such as having no more than 75 shareholders, and makes an election under subchapter S of the Internal Revenue Code. The corporation is generally not subject to federal tax on its income. Its shareholders are taxed on the corporate earnings, even if not distributed, and may deduct corporate losses.
Answer (A) is incorrect because an S corporation may have only one class of (common) stock. Answer (B) is incorrect because a corporation is ineligible for S status if it has a partnership as a shareholder. Answer (D) is incorrect because all shareholders must consent to the election.

5. Under the Revised Model Business Corporation Act, which of the following must be contained in a corporation's articles of incorporation?

A. Quorum voting requirements.

B. Names of shareholders.

C. Provisions for issuance of par and no-par shares.

D. The number of shares the corporation is authorized to issue.

The correct answer is (D). *(CPA, adapted)*
REQUIRED: The information required in the articles of incorporation.
DISCUSSION: Under the Revised Model Business Corporation Act, the number of shares the corporation is authorized to issue must be contained in the articles of incorporation.
Answers (A), (B), and (C) are incorrect because inclusion in the articles of incorporation of voting requirements, names of shareholders, and provisions for issuance of par and no-par shares is not mandatory. However, including such information is permissible.

6. Under the Revised Model Business Corporation Act, which of the following statements regarding a corporation's bylaws is(are) correct?

I. A corporation's initial bylaws shall be adopted by either the incorporators or the board of directors.

II. A corporation's bylaws are contained in the articles of incorporation.

A. I only.

B. II only.

C. Both I and II.

D. Neither I nor II.

The correct answer is (A). *(CPA, adapted)*
REQUIRED: The true statement(s), if any, regarding a corporation's bylaws.
DISCUSSION: The bylaws of a corporation are the rules and regulations that govern its internal management. The adoption of the bylaws is one of the first items of business at the organizational meeting. Under the Revised Model Business Corporation Act, either the incorporators or the board of directors may adopt the bylaws. Bylaws are independent of the articles of incorporation and do not have to be publicly filed. The articles are filed with the appropriate public official. They include the name of the corporation, the names of the incorporators, the name of the registered agent, the address of the initial registered office, and the number of authorized shares.
Answers (B), (C), and (D) are incorrect because the bylaws may be adopted by the incorporators or the board of directors and are not contained in the articles of incorporation.

7. A challenge to the limited liability of a shareholder of a closely held corporation will most likely be successful if the shareholder

A. Sold property or lent money to the corporation.

B. Was a corporate officer, director, or employee.

C. Undercapitalized the corporation when it was formed.

D. Formed the corporation solely to limit personal liability.

The correct answer is (C). *(CPA, adapted)*
REQUIRED: The factor most likely a basis for disregarding the form of a close corporation.
DISCUSSION: A closely held corporation is owned by a few shareholders. Statutes permit closely held corporations to be managed as if they were partnerships. But if the shareholders do not treat the corporation as a separate entity, a corporate creditor may persuade a court to ignore the corporate form and hold the shareholders personally liable. Undercapitalization is evidence of possible fraud on creditors.
Answer (A) is incorrect because a corporation may buy or borrow from a shareholder if the objective is not to defraud other creditors. Answer (B) is incorrect because shareholders of close corporations do serve in these positions. Answer (D) is incorrect because limited liability is a major incentive for incorporation.

8. The corporate veil is most likely to be pierced and the shareholders held personally liable if

A. The corporation has elected S corporation status under the Internal Revenue Code.

B. The shareholders have commingled their personal funds with those of the corporation.

C. An *ultra vires* act has been committed.

D. A partnership incorporates its business solely to limit the liability of its partners.

The correct answer is (B). *(CPA, adapted)*
REQUIRED: The factor most likely a basis for piercing the corporate veil.
DISCUSSION: A closely held corporation is owned by a few shareholders. Statutes permit closely held corporations to be managed as if they were partnerships. But if the shareholders do not treat the corporation as a separate entity, e.g., by disregarding formalities, a corporate creditor may persuade a court to ignore the corporate form and hold the shareholders personally liable. Commingling of shareholders' personal funds with those of the corporation is evidence that the corporation is merely the alter ego of the shareholders and that the corporate form is a sham.
Answer (A) is incorrect because the law expressly allows a corporation to elect S status. Answer (C) is incorrect because, to the degree an act is recognized as *ultra vires*, the existence of the corporation is recognized. Answer (D) is incorrect because limited liability is a major incentive for incorporation.

9. The close corporation furnishes not only the usual advantages of the corporate form but also various advantages of partnerships, such as active participation in the business by owners, security of control, and choice of current and future associates. Disadvantages of the close corporation include all but which of the following?

A. Difficulties in raising equity capital when shares are not traded publicly.

B. Potential deadlocks concerning vital corporate activities when a minority interest has veto power.

C. Problems encountered by owners who wish to withdraw their capital.

D. Inability to enter into contracts in its own name.

The correct answer is (D). *(Publisher)*
REQUIRED: The item not a disadvantage of a close corporation.
DISCUSSION: A close corporation has relatively few shareholders, the shares are not publicly traded, and the owners are usually involved in management. Many state statutes are not drafted to allow the flexibility and simplicity needed by organizers of a close corporation. However, the close corporation is a separate legal entity: it may sue and be sued, own property, make contracts, and exercise a wide range of rights in its own name.
Answer (A) is incorrect because the capital must generally come from the existing shareholders or loans guaranteed by them. Answer (B) is incorrect because minority shareholders often insist upon voting provisions giving them a veto over corporate actions. The result may be an impasse in which no corporate action may be taken. Answer (C) is incorrect because, absent a market for the stock, shareholders may have difficulty in liquidating their investments.

10. Lobo Manufacturing, Inc. is incorporated under the laws of New Mexico. Its principal place of business is in California, and it has permanent sales offices in several other states. Under the circumstances, which of the following is correct?

A. California may validly demand that Lobo incorporate under the laws of the state of California.

B. Lobo must obtain a certificate of authority to transact business in California and the other states in which it does business.

C. Lobo is a foreign corporation in California, but not in the other states.

D. California may prevent Lobo from operating as a corporation if the laws of California differ regarding organization and conduct of the corporation's internal affairs.

The correct answer is (B). *(CPA, adapted)*
REQUIRED: The correct statement regarding operations outside the state of incorporation.
DISCUSSION: Because Lobo has its principal place of business in California, it has sufficient contact with the state to qualify as "doing business" there. A corporation doing business but not incorporated in that state is considered a foreign corporation and must obtain a certificate of authority to transact business there.
Answer (A) is incorrect because no state may require an existing corporation to incorporate under its laws simply because it is doing business within the state. Answer (C) is incorrect because Lobo is a foreign corporation in all states in which it is not incorporated. Answer (D) is incorrect because, under the Full Faith and Credit Clause of the U.S. Constitution, a corporation validly formed in one state must be recognized as a corporate entity in all other states.

11. Boyle, as a promoter of Delaney Corp., signed a 9-month contract with Austin, a CPA. Prior to the incorporation, Austin rendered accounting services pursuant to the contract. After rendering accounting services for an additional period of 6 months pursuant to the contract, Austin was discharged without cause by the board of directors of Delaney. Absent agreements to the contrary, who will be liable to Austin for breach of contract?

A. Both Boyle and Delaney.

B. Boyle only.

C. Delaney only.

D. Neither Boyle nor Delaney.

The correct answer is (A). *(CPA, adapted)*
REQUIRED: The liability of a corporation and a promoter on a preincorporation agreement.
DISCUSSION: A promoter who contracts for a nonexistent corporation is personally liable on such contracts. Delaney is also liable because it impliedly adopted the contract by accepting Austin's performance.
Answer (B) is incorrect because the corporation impliedly ratified the contract by accepting its benefits. Answer (C) is incorrect because a promoter is generally liable on preincorporation contracts. Answer (D) is incorrect because Boyle was not released nor was there a novation. Delaney ratified the contract by implication.

B. Shareholders, Directors, and Officers

12. A shareholder's right to inspect books and records of a corporation will be properly denied if the shareholder

A. Wants to use corporate shareholder records for a personal business.

B. Employs an agent to inspect the books and records.

C. Intends to commence a shareholder's derivative suit.

D. Is investigating management misconduct.

The correct answer is (A). *(CPA, adapted)*
REQUIRED: The basis for denying a shareholder the right to inspect books and records.
DISCUSSION: A shareholder has a right to inspect corporate books and records. But the right must be exercised for a proper purpose and in a proper manner. Use of corporate shareholder records for a personal business is not a proper purpose because it does not concern the shareholder's interest in the corporation.
Answer (B) is incorrect because an agent may exercise the right on the shareholder's behalf. Answer (C) is incorrect because a shareholder's derivative suit is a proper purpose, except if instituted in bad faith. Answer (D) is incorrect because investigating management misconduct is a proper purpose.

13. A corporate shareholder is entitled to which of the following rights?

A. Elect officers.

B. Receive annual dividends.

C. Approve dissolution.

D. Prevent corporate borrowing.

The correct answer is (C). *(CPA, adapted)*
REQUIRED: The right of a shareholder.
DISCUSSION: Shareholders do not have the right to manage the corporation or its business. Participation in policy and management is through exercising the right to elect directors.
Answer (A) is incorrect because the board elects officers. Answer (B) is incorrect because a shareholder does not have a general right to receive dividends. The board determines dividend policy. Answer (D) is incorrect because determining capital structure and whether the corporation should borrow are policy and management determinations to be made according to the board's business judgment.

14. For what purpose will a shareholder of a publicly held corporation be permitted to file a shareholders' derivative suit in the name of the corporation?

A. To compel payment of a properly declared dividend.

B. To enforce a right to inspect corporate records.

C. To compel dissolution of the corporation.

D. To recover damages from corporate management for an *ultra vires* management act.

The correct answer is (D). *(CPA, adapted)*

REQUIRED: The basis for a shareholder's derivative suit.

DISCUSSION: A derivative suit is a cause of action brought by one or more shareholders on behalf of the corporation to enforce a right belonging to the corporation. Shareholders may bring such an action when the board of directors refuses to act on the corporation's behalf. Generally, the shareholder must show (1) (s)he owned stock at the time of the wrongdoing, (2) (s)he made a demand to the corporation to bring suit or take other appropriate action, and (3) a bad faith refusal of the board of directors to pursue the corporation's interest. The recovery, if any, belongs to the corporation. An action to recover damages from corporate management for an *ultra vires* act is an example of a derivative suit. An *ultra vires* act is one beyond the limits of the corporate purposes defined in the articles of incorporation.

Answers (A), (B), and (C) are incorrect because shareholders must sue directly on their own behalf to compel payment of a properly declared dividend, to enforce a right to inspect corporate records, or to compel dissolution of the corporation.

15. Absent a specific provision in its articles of incorporation, a corporation's board of directors has the power to do all of the following, except

A. Repeal the bylaws.

B. Declare dividends.

C. Fix compensation of directors.

D. Amend the articles of incorporation.

The correct answer is (D). *(CPA, adapted)*

REQUIRED: The limit on the board's authority.

DISCUSSION: Authority to formulate and implement corporate policy is vested in the board, including selecting officers, determining capital structure, proposing fundamental changes, declaring dividends, and setting management compensation. Amending the corporate charter, however, is a power reserved to the shareholders.

Answer (A) is incorrect because the board has authority to add, amend, or repeal bylaws to govern the corporation's internal structure and operation. Answer (B) is incorrect because the board has discretion to formulate and implement dividend policy. Answer (C) is incorrect because director compensation is fixed by the board.

16. Knox, president of Quick Corp., contracted with Tine Office Supplies, Inc. to supply Quick's stationery on customary terms and at a cost less than that charged by any other supplier. Knox later informed Quick's board of directors that Knox was a majority shareholder in Tine. Quick's contract with Tine is

A. Void because of Knox's self-dealing.

B. Void because the disclosure was made after execution of the contract.

C. Valid because of Knox's full disclosure.

D. Valid because the contract is fair to Quick.

The correct answer is (D). *(CPA, adapted)*

REQUIRED: The enforceability of a contract entered into by a corporate officer with an interest in the contract.

DISCUSSION: An officer, like a director, owes fiduciary duties of care and loyalty to the corporation and its share-holders. Knox was required to disclose fully the financial interest in the transaction to which the corporation was a party. But a transaction that is approved by a majority of informed, disinterested directors or shareholders, or that is fair to the corporation, is valid notwithstanding a conflict of interest.

Answers (A) and (B) are incorrect because self-dealing and nondisclosure do not render a transaction voidable if it is fair to the corporation. Answer (C) is incorrect because full disclosure merely forms a basis for approval by a majority of informed, disinterested directors or shareholders.

17. Under the Revised Model Business Corporation Act, which of the following statements is correct regarding corporate officers of a public corporation?

- A. An officer may not simultaneously serve as a director.

- B. A corporation may be authorized to indemnify its officers for liability incurred in a suit by shareholders.

- C. Shareholders always have the right to elect a corporation's officers.

- D. An officer of a corporation is required to own at least one share of the corporation's share.

The correct answer is (B). *(CPA, adapted)*
    REQUIRED: The true statement regarding corporate officers of a public corporation.
    DISCUSSION: According to the RMBCA, corporations may indemnify their officers for liability incurred in a suit by shareholders, except when inconsistent with public policy, to the extent provided by the articles of incorporation, bylaws, actions of the board, or contract.
    Answer (A) is incorrect because an individual may serve as both a director and an officer. Answer (C) is incorrect because a corporation's officers are appointed by the board of directors, not by shareholders. Answer (D) is incorrect because an officer of a corporation need not be a shareholder.

C. Financial Structure, Capital, and Distributions

18. Which of the following securities are corporate debt securities?

	Convertible Bonds	Debenture Bonds	Warrants
A.	Yes	Yes	Yes
B.	Yes	No	Yes
C.	Yes	Yes	No
D.	No	Yes	Yes

The correct answer is (C). *(CPA, adapted)*
    REQUIRED: The securities classified as corporate debt.
    DISCUSSION: A corporation may be financed by issuing equity and debt securities. Debt securities represent a debtor-creditor relationship between the corporation and the security holder, whereas equity securities reflect an ownership interest. A bond is a negotiable security that embodies the corporation's promise to pay a specified amount at a future date (plus interest). A convertible bond is convertible into a share or shares of stock. A debenture is an unsecured bond, backed only by the general obligation of the corporation to pay.
    Answers (A), (B), and (D) are incorrect because a stock warrant is a certificate evidencing a right to purchase shares of stock at a specified price within a specified period. Thus, it is an equity security. Warrants are usually attached to other securities.

19. An owner of common stock will not have any liability beyond actual investment if the owner

- A. Paid less than par value for stock purchased in connection with an original issue of shares.

- B. Agreed to perform future services for the corporation in exchange for original issue par value shares.

- C. Purchased treasury shares for less than par value.

- D. Failed to pay the full amount owed on a subscription contract for no-par shares.

The correct answer is (C). *(CPA, adapted)*
    REQUIRED: The liability of a shareholder for the shares.
    DISCUSSION: Consideration for issuance of shares may be in the form of cash, property, or past services rendered. If stated par value exceeds the amount a shareholder paid for shares at issuance, the shareholder remains liable for the difference. A purchaser of treasury shares is not liable for any such excess.
    Answer (A) is incorrect because a shareholder who paid less than par value for stock remains liable for the difference. Answer (B) is incorrect because neither promissory notes nor future services are valid consideration for the issuance of shares. The acquirer remains liable for not less than their par value. Answer (D) is incorrect because a subscriber who has failed to perform the subscription contract is liable for the unpaid balance.

20. In general, which of the following statements concerning treasury stock is correct?

- A. A corporation may not reacquire its own stock unless specifically authorized by its articles of incorporation.

- B. On issuance of new stock, a corporation has preemptive rights with regard to its treasury stock.

- C. Treasury stock may be distributed as a stock dividend.

- D. A corporation is entitled to receive cash dividends on its treasury stock.

The correct answer is (C). *(CPA, adapted)*
    REQUIRED: The characteristic of treasury stock.
    DISCUSSION: Shares may be issued pro rata and without consideration to the shareholders by an action of the directors. Treasury shares have the status of authorized but unissued shares, which may be used for stock dividends.
    Answer (A) is incorrect because a corporation may acquire its own shares provided it remains solvent. Answers (B) and (D) are incorrect because a corporation has no dividend or preemptive rights regarding treasury stock.

21. When no-par shares are issued in a corporation, the value that must be allocated to capital surplus as distinct from stated capital is

- A. The book value of the shares.
- B. The fair market value of the shares.
- C. The entire amount of the consideration received.
- D. Any portion of the proceeds so directed by the board of directors.

The correct answer is (D). *(Publisher)*
    REQUIRED: The amount that must be allocated to capital surplus for no-par shares.
    DISCUSSION: If the state statute requires that the corporation maintain a stated or legal capital account, and if no-par shares are issued, the entire consideration received for the shares must be allocated to the stated capital of the corporation except to the extent that the directors in their discretion allocate (within 60 days) any part of the proceeds to capital surplus.
    Answers (A), (B), and (C) are incorrect because the allocation is in the directors' discretion.

22. Carr Corp. declared a 7% stock dividend on its common stock. The dividend

- A. Must be registered with the SEC pursuant to the Securities Act of 1933.
- B. Is includable in the gross income of the recipient taxpayers in the year of receipt.
- C. Has no effect on Carr's earnings and profits for federal income tax purposes.
- D. Requires a vote of Carr's shareholders.

The correct answer is (C). *(CPA, adapted)*
    REQUIRED: The nature and effect of a stock dividend.
    DISCUSSION: A stock dividend is a distribution of additional shares of the corporation's stock in proportion to current holdings. Total shareholders' equity is not changed. The value is transferred from earned or capital surplus to stated capital. Earnings and profits is a tax account that is not changed by a stock dividend because it does not affect the corporation's economic ability to pay a cash or property dividend.
    Answer (A) is incorrect because the Securities Act of 1933 does not require registration of stock issued to shareholders who hold previously issued stock. Answer (B) is incorrect because stock dividends are usually not treated as gross income for federal tax purposes. Answer (D) is incorrect because dividend policy is within the discretion of the board.

23. All of the following distributions to shareholders are considered asset or capital distributions, except

- A. Liquidating dividends.
- B. Stock splits.
- C. Property distributions.
- D. Cash dividends.

The correct answer is (B). *(CPA, adapted)*
    REQUIRED: The distribution not from corporate capital or other assets.
    DISCUSSION: A stock split is not a distribution from assets or capital. The amount of earned or capital surplus or stated capital does not change. Instead, each share of a class of stock is divided into multiple units. The effect is to reduce the value of each share, not the size of the equity interest or a shareholder's proportionate ownership.
    Answer (A) is incorrect because a dividend distributed on liquidation of the corporation is from asset surplus. Answer (C) is incorrect because a distribution to shareholders of noncash property might constitute a dividend or a return of capital. Answer (D) is incorrect because dividends are usually distributed in the form of money or property from corporate assets.

24. Price owns 2,000 shares of Universal Corp.'s $10 cumulative preferred stock. During its first year of operations, cash dividends of $5 per share were declared on the preferred stock but were never paid. In the second year, dividends on the preferred stock were neither declared nor paid. If Universal is dissolved, which of the following statements is correct?

- A. Universal will be liable to Price as an unsecured creditor for $10,000.
- B. Universal will be liable to Price as a secured creditor for $20,000.
- C. Price will have priority over the claims of Universal's bond owners.
- D. Price will have priority over the claims of Universal's unsecured judgment creditors.

The correct answer is (A). *(CPA, adapted)*
    REQUIRED: The entitlement to and priority of dividends on cumulative preferred stock.
    DISCUSSION: A preferred shareholder has the right to a dividend of a fixed amount before a common shareholder may receive any dividends. But a dividend on any kind of stock is only a legal obligation (debt) of a corporation after it has been declared. Thus, the corporation's liability is limited to the $5 per share declared but unpaid.
    Answer (B) is incorrect because the liability is unsecured. Moreover, the amount is limited to the declared dividend. Answers (C) and (D) are incorrect because bondholders are creditors who have priority over all shareholders on dissolution.

25. Johns owns 400 shares of Abco Corp. cumulative preferred stock. In the absence of any specific contrary provisions in Abco's articles of incorporation, which of the following statements is correct?

- A. Johns is entitled to convert the 400 shares of preferred stock to a like number of shares of common stock.

- B. If Abco declares a cash dividend on its preferred stock, Johns becomes an unsecured creditor of Abco.

- C. If Abco declares a dividend on its common stock, Johns will be entitled to participate with the common shareholders in any dividend distribution made after preferred dividends are paid.

- D. Johns will be entitled to vote if dividend payments are in arrears.

The correct answer is (B). *(CPA, adapted)*
REQUIRED: The rights of a holder of cumulative preferred stock.
DISCUSSION: The holder of preferred stock must be paid the stated dividend before a common shareholder may receive any dividends. If payment of the stated dividend is not made to a cumulative preferred shareholder in any year(s), the dividends accumulate and must be paid in full prior to payment of any dividends to common shareholders. But a dividend on any stock does not become a payment obligation (debt) of the corporation until it has been declared.
Answers (A), (C), and (D) are incorrect because cumulative preferred stock is not inherently convertible, participating, or endowed with voting rights.

D. Merger, Consolidation, and Dissolution

26. Which of the following statements is a general requirement for the merger of two corporations?

- A. The merger plan must be approved unanimously by the shareholders of both corporations.

- B. The merger plan must be approved unanimously by the boards of both corporations.

- C. The absorbed corporation must amend its articles of incorporation.

- D. The shareholders of both corporations must be given due notice of a special meeting, including a copy or summary of the merger plan.

The correct answer is (D). *(CPA, adapted)*
REQUIRED: The prerequisite to a merger.
DISCUSSION: A corporation is merged into another when shareholders of the target corporation receive cash or shares of the surviving corporation in exchange for their shares. The target shares are canceled, and the target corporation ceases to exist. State law usually requires approval by a majority of the board and a majority of the shareholders of each corporation. A special shareholder meeting notice (stating the purpose) and a copy of the merger plan must be provided to shareholders of each corporation to permit informed voting.
Answers (A) and (B) are incorrect because, unless state statute or the charter imposes a supermajority requirement, majority approval is usually required. Answer (C) is incorrect because the absorbed corporation ceases to exist.

27. Which of the following actions may be taken by a corporation's board of directors without shareholder approval?

- A. Purchasing substantially all of the assets of another corporation.

- B. Selling substantially all of the corporation's assets.

- C. Dissolving the corporation.

- D. Amending the articles of incorporation.

The correct answer is (A). *(CPA, adapted)*
REQUIRED: The action by a corporation's board of directors not requiring shareholder approval.
DISCUSSION: The board of directors directly controls a corporation by establishing overall corporate policy and overseeing its implementation. In exercising their powers, board members must maintain high standards of care and loyalty but need not obtain shareholder approval except for fundamental corporate changes. Purchasing substantially all of the assets (or stock) of another corporation is a policy decision properly made by the board of directors, not a fundamental change. It does not require shareholder approval in the absence of a bylaw or special provision in the articles of incorporation.
Answers (B), (C), and (D) are incorrect because selling substantially all of the corporation's assets, dissolving the corporation, and amending the articles of incorporation are considered fundamental changes and therefore must be voted on and approved by the shareholders. Fundamental changes are usually initiated by resolution of the board of directors urging the shareholders to approve the change.

28. Which of the following actions may a corporation take without its shareholders' consent?

    A. Consolidate with one or more corporations.

    B. Merge with one or more corporations.

    C. Dissolve voluntarily.

    D. Purchase 55% of another corporation's stock.

The correct answer is (D). *(CPA, adapted)*

    REQUIRED: The corporate act not requiring shareholders' consent.

    DISCUSSION: Certain actions affect the corporation and its shareholders so fundamentally that they are beyond the exclusive authority of the board and require voted approval of (usually a majority of) shareholders. Purchase of stock in another corporation does not usually require approval by shareholders of each corporation.

    Answers (A), (B), and (C) are incorrect because consent of the shareholders of each corporation consolidating, merged or surviving, or voluntarily dissolved is ordinarily required under state law.

29. Under the Revised Model Business Corporation Act, a merger of two public corporations usually requires all of the following except

    A. A formal plan of merger.

    B. An affirmative vote by the holders of a majority of each corporation's voting shares.

    C. Receipt of voting stock by all shareholders of the original corporations.

    D. Approval by the board of directors of each corporation.

The correct answer is (C). *(CPA, adapted)*

    REQUIRED: The item not required for merger of two public corporations.

    DISCUSSION: A corporation is merged into another when shareholders of the target corporation receive cash or shares of the surviving corporation in exchange for their shares. State law usually requires approval of the board and a majority of shareholders of each corporation, and a copy of the merger plan must be provided to the shareholders of each corporation prior to voting.

    Answers (A), (B), and (D) are incorrect because a formal plan of merger and approval of the directors and shareholders of both corporations are required.

30. Under the Revised Model Business Corporation Act (RMBCA), which of the following actions by a corporation would entitle a shareholder to dissent from the action and obtain payment of the fair value of his/her shares?

I. An amendment to the articles of incorporation that materially and adversely affects rights in respect of a dissenter's shares because it alters or abolishes a preferential right of the shares

II. Consummation of a plan of share exchange to which the corporation is a party as the corporation whose shares will be acquired, if the shareholder is entitled to vote on the plan

    A. I only.

    B. II only.

    C. Both I and II.

    D. Neither I nor II.

The correct answer is (C). *(CPA, adapted)*

    REQUIRED: The corporate action(s), if any, permitting a shareholder to exercise the appraisal right.

    DISCUSSION: Shareholders who disagree with fundamental corporate changes may have dissenters' or appraisal rights. The corporation must pay dissenting shareholders the fair value of their stock in cash. Under the RMBCA, an existing right of appraisal may be invoked only when a shareholder has a right to vote on a fundamental change, does not vote in favor, and gives written notice of a demand for payment. Fundamental changes include an amendment to the articles that materially and adversely affects rights in respect of a dissenter's shares because it alters or abolishes a preferential right. Appraisal rights may also derive from a merger required to be voted on by the shareholders, the merger of the corporation into its parent, the sale or exchange of substantially all of the property of the corporation in a transaction not in the ordinary course of business, and consummation of a plan of share exchange to which the corporation is a party as the corporation whose shares will be acquired.

    Answers (A), (B), and (D) are incorrect because fundamental corporate changes that result in appraisal rights include an amendment to the articles that alters or abolishes a preferential right and a share exchange when the corporation's shares are to be acquired.

OOF QUESTION 1 (CPA, adapted) 10-15 minutes

Drain Corp. has two classes of stock: 100,000 shares of authorized, issued, and outstanding voting common stock; and 10,000 shares of authorized, issued, and outstanding nonvoting 5% cumulative, nonparticipating preferred stock with a face value of $100 per share. In 1998, Drain's officers and directors intentionally allowed pollutants to be discharged by Drain's processing plant. These actions resulted in Drain's having to pay penalties. Solely as a result of the penalties, no dividends were declared for the years ended December 31, 1998 and December 31, 1999. The total amount Drain paid in penalties was $1 million. In 1999, Drain was able to recover the full amount of the penalties from an insurance company that had issued Drain a business liability policy. Drain's directors refused to use this money to declare a dividend and decided to hold the $1 million in a special fund to pay future bonuses to officers and directors.

Required

For each item, select the correct answer that completes the statement. An answer may be selected once, more than once, or not at all.

1. The actions by Drain's officers and directors in allowing pollutants to be discharged generally would be considered a violation of the _____.

2. A shareholder's derivative suit, if successful, probably would result in the officers and directors being _____.

3. A shareholder's derivative suit, if successful, probably would result in the $1 million being considered _____.

4. If the $1 million had been distributed to the shareholders in 1999, the distribution would be characterized as a _____.

5. If the $1 million had been distributed in 1999, each share of 5% cumulative preferred stock would receive _____.

6. If the $1 million had been distributed in 1999, each share of voting common stock would receive _____.

A. Available for distribution as a dividend
B. Fiduciary duty to prevent losses
C. Cash dividend
D. Fiduciary duty of care
E. Fiduciary duty of loyalty
F. Illegal dividend
G. Immune from liability
H. Liable for abuse of discretion
I. Liable to the corporation for $1 million
J. Property dividend
K. Stock dividend
L. Surplus or earnings held for expansion
M. $5.00
N. $9.00
O. $10.00
P. $18.00

Knowledge Tested

Officers and directors of a corporation

1. Fiduciary duties of care and loyalty
2. Business judgment rule

Authors' Comments

This question specifically covers the responsibilities of officers and directors of a corporation. Officers and directors are subject to duties of care and loyalty to the corporation. The duty of care is fulfilled if the officers and directors discharge their duties in good faith, with reasonable care, and in a manner believed to be in the best interests of the corporation. The duty of loyalty includes granting the corporation the right of first refusal in regards to any corporate opportunity. Officers' and directors' conduct is tested objectively, and they can be held personally liable for failure to fulfill the fiduciary duties.

The business judgment rule may protect directors and officers from personal liability if they acted in good faith; were not motivated by fraud, conflict of interests, or illegality; and were not guilty of gross negligence.

1. The correct answer is (D).
   DISCUSSION: The officers and directors have a fiduciary duty of care to the corporation. By intentionally incurring these liabilities, they are breaching this duty. Their actions were not protected by the business judgment rule because they acted in bad faith and were motivated by illegality.

2. The correct answer is (H).
   DISCUSSION: The officers and directors have a duty to use their discretion in making business decisions. The action described here is grossly unfair and an abuse of discretion.

3. The correct answer is (A).
   DISCUSSION: The $1 million should have been used as a cash dividend in the first place.

4. The correct answer is (C).
   DISCUSSION: Cash distributions to shareholders are classified as cash dividends.

5. The correct answer is (O).
   DISCUSSION: $5.00 per share must be paid for both 1997 and 1998 because the shares are cumulative.

6. The correct answer is (N).
   DISCUSSION: After the preferred dividends are issued, $900,000 is left for distribution ($900,000 ÷ 100,000 shares = $9.00 per share).

OOF QUESTION 2 *(CPA, adapted)* 10-15 minutes

In 1995, Amber Corp., a closely held corporation, was formed by Adams, Frank, and Berg as incorporators and shareholders. Adams, Frank, and Berg executed a written voting agreement providing that they would vote for each other as directors and officers. In 1999, stock in the corporation was offered to the public. This resulted in an additional 300 shareholders. After the offering, Adams holds 25%, Frank holds 15%, and Berg holds 15% of all issued and outstanding stock. Adams, Frank, and Berg have been directors and officers of the corporation since its formation. Regular meetings of the board of directors and annual shareholders meetings have been held.

Required

Items 1 through 6 refer to the formation of Amber Corp. and the rights and duties of its shareholders, directors, and officers. For each item, determine whether (A), (B), or (C) is correct.

1. A. Amber Corp. must be formed under a state's general corporation statute.

    B. Amber Corp.'s articles of incorporation must include the names of all shareholders.

    C. Amber Corp. must include its corporate bylaws in the incorporation documents filed with the state.

2. Amber Corp.'s initial bylaws ordinarily would be adopted by its

    A. Shareholders.
    B. Officers.
    C. Directors.

3. Amber Corp.'s directors are elected by its

    A. Officers.
    B. Outgoing directors.
    C. Shareholders.

4. Amber Corp.'s officers ordinarily would be elected by its

    A. Shareholders.
    B. Directors.
    C. Outgoing officers.

5. Amber Corp.'s day-to-day business ordinarily would be operated by its

    A. Directors.
    B. Shareholders.
    C. Officers.

6. A. Adams, Frank, and Berg must be elected as directors because they own 55% of the issued and outstanding stock.

    B. Adams, Frank, and Berg must always be elected as officers because they own 55% of the issued and outstanding stock.

    C. Adams, Frank, and Berg must always vote for each other as directors because they have a voting agreement.

Knowledge Tested

1. Formation of corporations
2. Election of officers and directors
3. Voting agreements

Authors' Comments

This question contains a set of basic, straightforward questions on corporations. The hierarchy of authority within a corporation and methods of controlling elections are emphasized.

1. The correct answer is (A).
DISCUSSION: Corporations are legal entities that must be formally created pursuant to a state's general corporation statute. They cannot be formed under common-law principles without a statute. The articles of incorporation must include the names and addresses of the incorporators but not the shareholders. The bylaws are adopted after the company is already incorporated and are not filed.

2. The correct answer is (C).
DISCUSSION: The board of directors holds an organizational meeting to adopt the bylaws that govern the internal management of the corporation. The power to alter, amend, or repeal the bylaws is vested in the board of directors unless this power is specifically reserved to the shareholders in the charter.

3. The correct answer is (C).
DISCUSSION: Shareholders participate indirectly in corporate policy by electing all directors and approving all fundamental corporate changes. However, the initial board of directors is usually elected by the incorporators and serves until the first meeting of shareholders.

4. The correct answer is (B).
DISCUSSION: The board of directors establishes and implements overall corporate policy and is responsible for electing or appointing the corporate officers.

5. The correct answer is (C).
DISCUSSION: The corporate officers are charged with the day-to-day operations of the business. Typically, officers elected include president, treasurer, and secretary, although there is no limit on the number of officers. Each officer is an agent of the corporation and has the express and implied authority to perform the duties of the office.

6. The correct answer is (C).
DISCUSSION: A voting agreement in which shareholders contract as to how they will vote their shares is specifically allowable by the MBCA and is enforceable. Absent an enforceable voting agreement or voting trust, the majority interest shareholders are not required to be elected to the board of directors or as officers by the total body of shareholders.

ESSAY QUESTION *(CPA, adapted)* 15-25 minutes

Edwards, a director and a 10% shareholder in National Corp., is dissatisfied with the way National's officers, particularly Olsen, the president, have been operating the corporation. Edwards has made many suggestions, which the board of directors has rejected. Edwards has also made several unsuccessful attempts to have Olsen removed as president.

National and Grand Corp. have been negotiating a merger that Edwards has adamantly opposed. Edwards has blamed Olsen for initiating the negotiation and has urged the board to fire Olsen. National's board refused to fire Olsen. In an attempt to defeat the merger, Edwards approached Jenkins, the president of Queen Corp., and contracted for Queen to purchase several of National's assets. Jenkins knew Edwards was a National director but had never done business with National. When National learned of the contract, it notified Queen that the contract was invalid.

Edwards filed an objection to the merger before the shareholders' meeting called to consider the merger proposal was held. At the meeting, Edwards voted against the merger proposal.

Despite Edwards's efforts, the merger was approved by both corporations. Edwards then orally demanded that National purchase Edwards's stock, citing the dissenters rights provision of the corporation's bylaws, which reflects the Model Business Corporation Act.

National's board has claimed National does not have to purchase Edwards's stock.

As a result

- Edwards initiated a minority shareholder's action to have Olsen removed as president and to force National to purchase Edwards's stock.

- Queen sued National to enforce the contract and/or collect damages.

- Queen sued Edwards to collect damages.

Required

Answer the following questions and give the reasons for your answers.

a. Will Edwards be successful in a lawsuit to have Olsen removed as president?

b. Will Edwards be successful in a lawsuit to have National purchase the stock?

c. 1. Will Queen be successful in a lawsuit against National?

2. Will Queen be successful in a lawsuit against Edwards?

Knowledge Tested

1. Shareholders' and directors' roles in corporate action

2. Appraisal rights

3. Authority to contract for the corporation

Authors' Comments

Shareholders vote to elect directors and to make fundamental changes. The board sets corporate policy and elects officers who serve at the board's discretion.

Dissenters' appraisal rights must be exercised by satisfying specific requirements.

A director has no implied or apparent authority merely because of his/her status as a member of the board of directors. Apparent authority as an agent would have required communication by the principal (corporation) to the third person (Queen).

Agency law does not shield a person from liability for acting as agent without authority.

AICPA Unofficial Answer

a. Edwards will not win the suit to have Olsen removed as president. The right to hire and fire officers is held by the board of directors. Individual shareholders, regardless of the size of their holding, have no vote in the selection of officers. Individual shareholders may exert influence in this area by voting for directors at the annual shareholders' meeting.

b. Edwards will lose the suit to have National purchase the stock. A shareholder who dissents from a merger may require the corporation to purchase his/her shares if the statutory requirements are met, and (s)he would be entitled to the fair value of the stock (appraisal remedy). To compel the purchase, Edwards would have had to file an objection to the merger before the shareholders meeting at which the merger proposal was considered, vote against the merger proposal, and make a written demand that the corporation purchase the stock at an appraised price. Edwards will lose because the first two requirements were met but Edwards failed to make a written demand that the corporation purchase the stock.

c. 1. Queen will lose its suit against National to enforce the contract even though Edwards was a National director. Jenkins may have assumed that Edwards was acting as National's agent, but Edwards had no authority to contract with Queen. A director has a fiduciary duty to the shareholders of a corporation but, unless expressly authorized by the board of directors or the officers of the corporation, has no authority to contract on behalf of the corporation. Hence, a director has no implied agency authority.

2. Queen will win its suit against Edwards because Edwards had no authority to act for National. Edwards will be personally liable for Queen's damages.

STUDY UNIT 6: ESTATES AND TRUSTS

14 pages of outline
41 multiple-choice questions
1 OOF and 1 essay

A. Formation and Purposes
B. Allocation between Principal and Income
C. Fiduciary Responsibilities
D. Distributions and Termination

This study unit reviews the administration of a decedent's estate and the creation, administration, and termination of trusts. An estate is an artificial entity that is established under probate law following a person's death to succeed to the decedent's property, pay his/her debts, and distribute the remaining property as specified by the decedent's will or the state's intestacy statute. A personal representative of the estate must be appointed by a probate court to administer the functions of the estate. Questions on the CPA examination typically concern the identification of an estate as testate (decedent had a will) or intestate (no will), the appointment of the administrator, and the administrator's responsibilities.

A trust is created when a grantor or settlor transfers legal title to property to a trustee for the use and benefit of another person called a beneficiary. The trustee is a fiduciary charged with exercising great care in performing the responsibilities of managing the trust property. The CPA examination contains questions concerning formation and termination of a trust, rights of beneficiaries, and duties of the trustee, with heavy emphasis on allocations between income and principal as directed by the trust instrument or the Uniform Principal and Income Act.

A. Formation and Purposes

1. **Estates.** An estate is an artificial legal entity that arises by operation of law when a person dies. It succeeds to his/her property. It is liable to pay all his/her obligations. It is administered by a personal representative who, according to law, accounts for the property and transfers it. If the decedent died testate (with a valid will), the property passes according to directions in the will; otherwise it passes under state law of descent and distribution.

   a. The **probate estate** holds all the person's property subject to the jurisdiction of the probate court, i.e., property that will pass by will or applicable intestacy law rather than by contract, by right of survivorship, or by being held in trust.

   b. The **taxable estate** may differ from the probate estate.

2. **Wills.** A will is an expression of a person's direction for distribution of his/her estate. Such issues as whether and how a court will give effect to a will, whether a will was revoked, and what the order of distribution is under state intestate succession laws are generally addressed by attorneys.

a. Fundamental definitions

1) **Testator** -- a person who makes a will

2) **Decedent** -- a person who has died

3) **Testate** -- the estate of a person who died leaving a valid will

4) **Intestate** -- the estate of a person who died without leaving a valid will

5) **Executor** -- personal representative named by testator to carry out the provisions of the will

6) **Administrator** -- court-appointed personal representative when there is no will or the will does not nominate an executor

7) **Bequest** -- a gift of personal property under a will

8) **Devise** -- a gift of real property under a will

9) **Formal will** -- one prepared and executed in compliance with the state's law of wills

10) **Invalid will** -- one failing to meet statutory requirements. The estate passes by intestate succession.

11) **Holographic will** -- one written entirely in the testator's handwriting and signed by the testator but not witnessed by attesting witnesses. A holographic will is given effect in some states.

12) **Nuncupative will** -- oral will. Some states permit oral (nuncupative) wills under limited circumstances. Typically, they must have been recited during the decedent's last illness and can be effective to dispose of personal property only. Some states recognize oral wills only for members of the armed forces.

13) **Codicil** -- a testamentary instrument that alters, amends, or modifies a previously executed will. It must be executed with the same formalities as a will.

b. The **Uniform Probate Code (UPC)** addresses preparation of legally enforceable wills, administration of estates, and resolution of related controversies. Most of its provisions have been adopted by about one-third of the states. Some other states have adopted parts of it. Thus, statutory requirements vary from state to state. Typical requirements of a valid will follow.

c. A person 18 years of age or older on the date of execution can make a will.

d. **Testamentary capacity** (not the same as contractual capacity) is, at the time of execution, the ability to understand the nature and extent of property involved, the persons who are the natural objects of transfer, and the disposition, i.e., a general understanding of the practical effect of the will as executed.

1) Testamentary capacity is presumed. A person who is old, frail, physically incapacitated, or ill, or who has a failing memory, is a habitual drinker, is addicted to drugs, has been adjudicated insane, or has had a guardian or conservator appointed does not necessarily lack testamentary capacity.

e. The will must be signed by the testator (or by another person at the testator's direction and in his/her presence) in the presence of the witnesses.

1) Two attesting witnesses must sign in the testator's and each other's presence.

a) In some states, no minimum age is required to witness a will.

b) Witnesses are competent if they have the ability to observe the testator affix his/her signature to the will and the ability to comprehend the nature of this act.

2) Some states require that the testator publish the will, i.e., communicate to the witnesses that they are signing a will as opposed to some other legal document.

3) **Self-proving wills**. Notarization of the signatures on the will itself or an affidavit sworn before a notary public attached to the will can render a will self-proving in some states. The signatures on the will are then presumed valid, and the will may be admitted to probate without testimony by one of the attesting witnesses or other evidence that it was validly executed by the testator(s).

f. The testator and the witnesses sign and attest only on the last page of the will. Occasionally, a page in the will is missing at the time of execution. If an integration issue is raised, the proponent must demonstrate that the pages were present when the will was executed and were intended by the testator to become a part of the will. Intent and presence are presumed from the physical connection of the pages, e.g., by staple, or from the internal coherence of provisions running from one page to the next.

g. An extrinsic document (not present at the time the will was executed) may be incorporated into the will by reference if it exists when the will is executed, is sufficiently described in the will, and is proved to be the one described in the will.

h. A will may dispose of property by reference to acts and events that have independent legal significance from their effect on the disposition made by the will.

1) EXAMPLE: Testator's will provides a bequest of "$3,000 to each person who is in my employ at the time of my death." Thereafter, Testator hires 10 new employees and fires two longtime employees. Employment has legal significance independent of Testator's will. The bequests are valid.

2) The doctrine of independent legal significance permits identification of property that is to be the subject matter of the bequest.

a) EXAMPLE: Testator's will bequeaths "my house and its contents to my cousin, Faith." Thereafter, Testator purchases new furniture. The bequest is valid and includes all items of furniture in Testator's house at death. The bequest does not include intangible personal property that may be stored in the house, e.g., stock certificates.

i. When the execution of a will or the inclusion of a particular gift is the result of fraud, the will or the particular gift is void. An innocent misrepresentation does not constitute fraud.

j. A mistake relating to the nature of the instrument affects whether the testator had the requisite testamentary intent. A mistake relating to the contents of the instrument is difficult to correct, especially a patent ambiguity (the uncertainty appears on the face of the will).

k. Undue influence such that a will or a term in a will is invalid is actual influence exerted on the testator that overpowered his/her judgment, resulting in a disposition of property that would not otherwise have been made. Nagging is not enough. A presumption of undue influence arises if a person

    1) Occupies a confidential relationship with the testator
    2) Is active in procuring the will
    3) Is a substantial beneficiary under the will

l. A **joint will** is a single instrument executed by two or more persons that provides for testamentary disposition of property owned by each. **Mutual wills** are two or more separate wills (of different persons) with reciprocal provisions. A contract is often implied between the parties to a joint will or mutual wills, based on the nature of the wills, not to revoke them after the first of the parties dies.

m. A person with testamentary capacity may completely or partially revoke a will at any time prior to death.

    1) A will or any part thereof may be revoked or altered by a subsequent written will, codicil, or any other writing executed with the same formalities required of a will.

    2) If a testator executes a second instrument that does not specifically state that the first is revoked, the second instrument is deemed a codicil that revokes only the inconsistent provisions of the first will.

    3) A will or codicil can be revoked by a physical act with the intent to revoke, e.g., burning or canceling.

    4) Depending on the applicable state law, a valid will may be partially or wholly revoked by operation of law in the event of subsequent marriage, divorce, or birth or adoption of a child or children.

        a) The majority view provides that marriage following the execution of a will has no effect on a preexisting will even though it makes no provisions for the new spouse. However, the surviving spouse receives a share of the estate as determined by the intestacy statutes.

        b) Furthermore, divorce following execution usually revokes all gifts in favor of the former spouse. The balance of the will remains in force.

        c) Under the UPC, a child born or adopted after execution of the will or unintentionally left out of the will takes under the intestacy statutes.

3. **Trusts**. A trust is formed when a **settlor** or grantor delivers the property (called trust res or trust corpus) to a trustee, intending to transfer legal title to the trustee to hold, manage, and administer it for the benefit of beneficiaries. The beneficiaries receive equitable title to trust property. The essence of a trust is the separation of legal and equitable title to the trust property. Statutes governing trusts vary from state to state.

    a. No special words are required to form a trust. Use of the word "trust" or "trustee" is not necessary. The expression of intent must be sufficiently definite that a court can enforce it, particularly the description of the trust property, the beneficiaries, and their interests.

        1) A writing is not required to form a trust, but a writing is required to make an effective transfer of an interest in land.

        2) The terms of the trust must be legal.

b. The trust property must be existing property, tangible or intangible.

   1) The settlor must have a recognizable and assignable interest.

   2) Property that the settlor expects to own in the future but has no present right to transfer cannot be the subject matter of a present trust.

   3) Trust property must be adequately and specifically described.

c. The settlor, with intent to form a trust and with legal capacity (e.g., legal age and sound mind), owns property (s)he transfers into trust.

   1) The settlor can also be a trustee and a beneficiary.

d. The beneficiaries of a trust hold equitable title to the trust res.

   1) A trust may be formed without notice to the beneficiaries.

   2) There may be more than one beneficiary.

   3) A trustee named by the settlor can also be a beneficiary.

   4) However, the settlor cannot be the only trustee and the only beneficiary. Then legal and equitable title to the trust property merges in the same person, and the trust terminates.

e. An *inter vivos* **trust** is one formed and effective during the settlor's lifetime.

f. A **testamentary trust** is one provided for in the settlor's will to become effective upon that person's death.

g. In most states, a trust is irrevocable and cannot be amended by the settlor unless power to revoke or amend is expressly retained in the trust instrument.

h. An **express trust** is formed when a settlor clearly intends to, and does, transfer property to a trustee for the benefit of beneficiaries.

i. A **resulting trust** arises by operation of law when an express trust fails or when the disposition of property by the settlor is not complete and effective.

j. A **constructive trust** arises by operation of law as a remedy to prevent unjust enrichment. A transfer of property must be induced by a promise made in the context of a confidential or fiduciary relationship, and the transfer must result in unjust enrichment of the transferee.

k. A **spendthrift trust** prohibits beneficiaries from voluntarily assigning or transferring their trust assets or interests.

   1) Creditors of the beneficiaries cannot reach the trust assets in the hands of the trustee.

   2) A spendthrift trust cannot be established by the settlor for personal benefit.

l. A **charitable trust** is a trust established for charitable purposes only. It is usually categorized as for relief of poverty, aid to education, advancement of religion, advancement of a governmental purpose, or the general benefit of the community.

   1) Beneficiaries of a charitable trust must be indefinite. Those of a private express trust must be definite and ascertainable.

   2) The doctrine of *cy pres* preserves a charitable trust by allowing the property to be used for a different charitable purpose. *Cy pres* applies only if

      a) There was a valid charitable trust.
      b) The settlor possessed a general charitable intent.
      c) The trust's purpose became impossible, impractical, or illegal.

3)   A charitable trust is not subject to the rule against perpetuities.

m.   A **Totten trust** is a savings account for which the depositor executes a document declaring that (s)he is the trustee of the account for the benefit of another. A Totten trust is revocable by the settlor/trustee merely by withdrawing the funds.

n.   A **real estate investment trust (REIT)** is a trust that owns real estate or loans secured by real property and is managed for beneficiaries. A REIT has at least 100 beneficiaries who own transferable shares. An initial offering of interests in a REIT must be registered under the Securities Act of 1933.

o.   An **honorary trust** is a trust, not set up for charitable purposes, having no private individuals as beneficiaries. Examples are trusts formed for maintenance of a cemetery plot or pets.

4.   Stop and review! You have completed the outline for this subunit. Study multiple-choice questions 1 through 10 beginning on page 189.

B.   Allocation between Principal and Income

1.   **Rules to Apply**. Receipts and disbursements of a trust or estate must be allocated by the trustee between principal and income accounts.

a.   State law defines what is principal and what is income. Many states have adopted the Revised Uniform Principal and Income Act, some with modifications.

b.   The act provides that trust instrument designations of principal and income control, and it provides designations that control to the extent a trust is silent.

c.   Frequently a trust instrument provides for trust income to be distributed to one or more income beneficiaries and for principal to be distributed to others.

1)   Income beneficiaries are often referred to as life estates, and beneficiaries entitled to trust property after expiration of the prior interest are called remaindermen.

2.   **Principal Receipts**. Principal is property transferred gratuitously to the trust and any changes in the form of existing trust property. Principal is property held to be delivered eventually to the remaindermen (unless the terms of the trust specify otherwise). The Uniform Act generally allocates the following receipts to principal:

a.   Consideration for principal, including gain
b.   Replacement property acquired with principal
c.   Insurance proceeds for loss of principal
d.   Stock received in a stock split
e.   Nontaxable stock dividends
f.   Stock rights in a corporation distributing them
g.   Gain attributable to acquiring bonded debt at discount

3.   **Disbursements from Principal**. Extraordinary expenses (not ordinary and current) are allocated to principal, e.g., costs to set up the trust, purchase and sell investments, or improve trust property. The act, generally, allocates the following to principal:

a.   Capital costs, e.g., local assessments for improvements
b.   Payments on debt principal
c.   Tax on principal items, e.g., capital gain
d.   Fiduciary fees
e.   Amortization of investment that trustee purchased at a premium
f.   Distribution to principal beneficiary

4.   **Income Receipts**. Income is the return (in money or property) on or for the use of principal. Income of a trust or estate is narrower than income for financial or individual income tax purposes. Receipts charged to income under the act include the following:

   a.   Business income
   b.   Rents, including prepaid rent
   c.   Insurance proceeds for lost profits
   d.   Interest
   e.   Discount gain on redemption of treasury bills
   f.   Taxable dividends of cash or property
   g.   Taxable stock dividends
   h.   Extraordinary dividends
   i.   Royalties

5.   **Disbursements against Income**. Ordinary and current operating and administrative expense is charged against income. The act, generally, attributes the following costs to income:

   a.   Business expense, ordinary and necessary, e.g., interest
   b.   Production of income costs, e.g., rent collection fee
   c.   Insurance premiums
   d.   Maintenance and repair of trust property
   e.   Tax on fiduciary income
   f.   Trustee insurance bond premiums
   g.   Ordinary loss passed through from a partnership

6.   **Specific Items**

   a.   The act provides that **depreciation** is a required charge against income unless the trust instrument provides otherwise. Many state statutes grant the trustee discretion to determine whether to recognize it at all.

      1)   Depreciation charged against income preserves principal.

   b.   **Stock**. Undistributed earnings of a corporation are not income.

   c.   **Annuity**. The proceeds are partly allocable to principal and partly to income (interest).

   d.   **Bonds**. The act does not require that bond discount or premium be amortized or specially allocated. Stated interest is allocated to income. Gain/loss attributable to discount is allocated to principal, unless on a treasury bill.

7.   Stop and review! You have completed the outline for this subunit. Study multiple-choice questions 11 through 20 beginning on page 192.

C.   Fiduciary Responsibilities

1.   **Estate Administration**. The estate is administered by the decedent's personal representative in accordance with the statutorily prescribed probate process.

   a.   Administration of an estate involves collection of the decedent's property, payment of his/her debts and taxes, and distribution of remaining assets.

   b.   The **probate process** is the process by which the will of a testate decedent or entitlement to the property of an intestate is proved.

      1)   The probate process is opened by filing the will, if any, with a court of competent jurisdiction, typically the probate court of the state and county where the decedent was domiciled.

2)   A proffered document is proved by showing it was executed by a competent testator as required by law as his/her last will. Mental competency is presumed.

c.   The probate court may award a family allowance for the maintenance of the spouse and minor children.

d.   A will may designate a personal representative. If the will does not, or there is no will, the probate court will appoint one.

e.   The personal representative must cause notice to creditors of the decedent to be published in a newspaper of general circulation in the jurisdiction where the estate is probated. It notifies all creditors when and where to file claims against the estate.

f.   The personal representative develops an inventory of the assets in the estate and assigns a value to them.

g.   The personal representative pays the decedent's debts. If the estate is not sufficient (not solvent) priority of payment is determined by state statute, typically as follows:

1)   Administration expenses
2)   Reasonable funeral expense not to exceed $3,000
3)   Federal debts and taxes
4)   Reasonable last illness expenses
5)   Family allowance
6)   Debts acquired after death
7)   All other claims

h.   The personal representative then submits a final accounting to the court. It discloses the assets accumulated and the debts paid.

i.   The probate court holds a hearing to approve or reject the accounting.

j.   Remaining assets, if any, are then distributed to beneficiaries in accordance with the will, if there is one, or otherwise as prescribed by state intestacy laws.

k.   **Summary administration** is an expedited process available when the value of the entire estate does not exceed a relatively small amount, e.g., $25,000, or the decedent has been dead for more than 3 years.

1)   A will must be proved. A hearing is held. The court may enter an order of summary administration and permit distribution.

l.   **Family administration** is available if the estate is relatively small, e.g., less than $60,000, and the entire estate consists of personal property (or, if there is real property, formal administration has proceeded to the point that the estate is not indebted or all claims have been barred).

1)   Family administration typically permits collection of small bank accounts, wage claims, and transfer of title to automobiles.

m.   **Ancillary administration** is necessary if a nonresident dies leaving assets in a state other than the state of domicile. One may have more than one residence, but only one domicile. Ancillary administration applies only to assets located in the nondomiciliary state.

1)   Two of the objectives of ancillary administration are to prove title in the situs state (the state where the property is located) and to protect local creditors by subjecting the property to that state's probate process.

2. **The Personal Representative**. The personal representative is a fiduciary whose function is limited to winding up the estate. (S)he is responsible for administering the estate in accordance with instructions in the will, if applicable, and state law. (S)he must usually post bond to assure that the wishes of the decedent are carried out.

   a. Typically, a person is qualified to act as a personal representative if (s)he

      1) Is over 18 years of age
      2) Has never been convicted of a felony
      3) Has the appropriate mental capacity
      4) Is a resident of the state of administration

   b. The personal representative has powers and duties to

      1) Exercise the degree of care that prudent persons exercise in managing their personal affairs

      2) Exercise the degree of skill (s)he has claimed to possess

      3) Not delegate responsibilities of administration

      4) Secure assets and preserve the estate

      5) Not commingle assets

      6) File an inventory and employ an appraiser

      7) Act impartially with respect to beneficiaries

      8) Promptly and efficiently settle the estate and distribute assets

      9) Sell real property pursuant to statutory authority

      10) Operate the decedent's business according to statutory authority, if any

         a) Otherwise, the representative may liquidate the business.

      11) Perform other actions authorized by will if not contrary to law

   c. A personal representative is liable for any breach of duty or improper exercise of power.

   d. Generally, a personal representative is not personally liable on contracts entered into by the estate, e.g., regarding funeral expenses.

   e. A personal representative is not liable for loss due to reasonable reliance on the advice of professionals, e.g., an investment advisor.

   f. A personal representative is liable for torts committed during the course of his/her administration of the estate.

   g. A personal representative is entitled to reasonable compensation for the time and labor required to administer the estate.

3. **Trustees**. The trustee (appointed by the settlor) is a fiduciary who holds legal title to, manages, and administers the trust property for the benefit of the beneficiaries.

   a. A trustee has both express and implied powers.

      1) Express -- granted by terms of the trust or by the law of the state where the trust is formed

      2) Implied -- reasonably needed to carry out the express powers and the purpose of the trust

   b. A trustee may be either an individual or a corporation. There may be more than one trustee, and if the settlor fails to appoint one, a court will.

c.   The trustee has the following duties:

1)   Show reasonable prudent care
2)   Maintain undivided loyalty to the beneficiaries
3)   Earmark and segregate the trust res
4)   Preserve and protect the trust res
5)   Demonstrate impartiality toward beneficiaries and remaindermen
6)   Maintain accurate records
7)   Refrain from delegating trust powers

d.   As a fiduciary, the trustee owes a duty of undivided loyalty to the trust and its beneficiaries. The trustee must hold, manage, and administer trust property in the interests of the beneficiaries. Self-dealing by the trustee constitutes a breach of this fiduciary duty of loyalty.

e.   It is normally a *per se* breach of trust for a trustee to engage in a transaction with the trust in his/her individual capacity or as a trustee of another trust. Exceptions include transactions

1)   Approved by a court
2)   Provided for by the trust instrument
3)   Consented to by all beneficiaries

f.   The beneficiary of a trust has a personal claim against the trustee for breach of trust.

g.   A trustee is personally liable on contracts entered into on behalf of the trust, unless the contract states otherwise.

h.   The trustee has a right of exoneration, whereby contract or tort liability incurred by the trustee in performing his/her trust duties is payable out of trust property.

i.   The trustee's creditors cannot reach the trust property to settle their claims.

j.   If the trustee declares bankruptcy or wrongfully disposes of the trust property, the beneficiary can recover the property, but not from a bona fide purchaser for value.

k.   The beneficiary can impose a trust on property purchased by the trustee with the proceeds from a wrongful sale of trust property.

4.   Stop and review! You have completed the outline for this subunit. Study multiple-choice questions 21 through 30 beginning on page 195.

D.   Distributions and Termination

1.   **Testamentary Disposition**. The personal representative, to the extent of the probate estate and consistent with law, pays claims against the estate and then distributes remaining assets as directed by the terms of a valid will. Following are some rules that might vary otherwise proper testamentary disposition.

a.   A will disposes of probate assets only.

b.   Three primary categories of nonprobate assets are

1)   Property passing by contract, e.g., life insurance proceeds
2)   Property passing by right of survivorship, e.g., joint tenancy
3)   Property held in trust

c.   If a will names a beneficiary who died before the will was executed, the attempted gift is void.

d.   If a beneficiary under a will dies before the testator does, the gift lapses.

1)   Anti-lapse statutes (enacted in nearly all states) save the gift if the predeceasing beneficiary held a specified degree of relationship to the testator and left descendants who survived the testator. The beneficiary's descendants take by substitution.

2)   Anti-lapse statutes apply unless a contrary intention is expressed in the will.

e.   The Uniform Simultaneous Death Act, adopted by many states, provides that, if there is no sufficient evidence of survival, property passes as though the beneficiary or heir predeceased the other decedent.

1)   The act prevents double administration and double taxation of the same assets in rapid succession.

2)   The act applies to distributions of property by any method, e.g., life insurance contract, right of survivorship, will, intestacy.

3)   The dispositive document may direct that the act does not apply.

4)   It is common for a will to make gifts contingent on the beneficiary's surviving the testator by a stated period of time.

f.   If a will makes a gift to a class (e.g., children or brothers and sisters) a member of which dies before the testator, surviving members take the entire gift (absent contrary provision in the will).

g.   A **specific bequest** is a gift of personal property particularly designated and is satisfied only by the receipt of the particular property.

1)   **Ademption.** When specifically bequeathed property is not in the testator's estate at death (e.g., it was lost, destroyed, sold, or given away), it is adeemed, and the attempted gift fails.

2)   **Partial ademption** applies to a portion of property not in the estate, e.g., a tract of land sold by the testator. The remaining portion passes under the will.

h.   A **demonstrative bequest** of a general amount identifies a particular asset as the primary source. Ademption does not apply.

1)   EXAMPLE: "I bequeath $1 million to my brother Craig, to be paid out of proceeds of my W Corp. stock." No stock is in the probate estate. The $1 million must be allocated from assets in the estate.

i.   A **general bequest** is of an amount payable out of the general assets of the estate without a claim on any particular source. Ademption does not apply.

j.   **Satisfaction of legacies.** A testamentary gift is satisfied in whole or in part by a transfer during life subsequent to execution of the will if the testator intends the transfer to have that effect.

k.   Many states provide an **elective share** to both husbands and wives and no longer recognize dower or curtesy.

1)   Typically, the elective share is 30% of the net estate, paid in cash or in kind. The net estate is the probate estate minus all

a)   Claims against the estate
b)   Security interests in assets in the probate estate

2)   Usually, only real property located within the state and personal property wherever located is subject to inclusion in the elective share, unless the parties provide otherwise in an agreement to include more.

3)   In some states, certain property transferred *inter vivos* is subject to inclusion in the elective share. In others, such property is excluded unless the effect would be to disinherit the surviving spouse totally.

4)   The right to an elective share can be waived before or after marriage.

5)   The elective share, if claimed, is in lieu of the provision in the decedent's will, the distribution under the intestacy statutes, or the effect of pretermission (becoming a spouse after the will was executed).

6)   Generally, the surviving spouse must file notice of the election within a statutorily prescribed period, e.g., 3 months after first publication of notice of administration. The election, once made, is irrevocable.

l.   In some states, the homestead (e.g., a statutorily specified acreage and all improvements thereon) is not subject to devise if the owner is survived by spouse or minor child, and, if it is held by husband and wife as tenants by the entirety, it passes by right of survivorship in all cases.

m.   A majority of states authorize a family allowance (from the probate estate) for support of a surviving spouse and dependent lineal heirs during probate administration. The spouse or lineal heir must petition for the allowance.

n.   Most states permit the heirs to receive or set aside certain items of personal property, exempt from all claims against the estate except perfected security interests, typically

1)   Furniture and household furnishings up to a statutory amount
2)   All personal automobiles held in the decedent's name

NOTE: Property specifically bequeathed is not subject to exemption.

2.   **Intestate Succession**. Each state provides by a descent and distribution statute for disposition of an intestate decedent's estate. Typical rules follow. An heir is a person who succeeds to probate assets under an intestacy statute, and a lineal heir can be an ascendant or descendant, e.g., grandparent, father, mother, child, or grandchild.

a.   Real property descends according to the laws of the state in which it is located; personal property according to the laws of the state in which the decedent was domiciled.

b.   If only the spouse survived the decedent, (s)he takes the entire estate.

c.   If the decedent was survived by a spouse and lineal descendants (children, grandchildren, etc.), the surviving spouse takes a lump sum of money and a portion of the remaining estate (e.g., one half). The rest passes to the descendants, *per capita* or *per stirpes*, depending on the statute.

d.   An ex-spouse, but not a legally separated spouse, takes nothing.

e.   If an intestate's children survive the intestate individual, they divide equally any net estate (after any spousal share).

f. ***Per stirpes***. If a predeceased person would have been an heir if (s)he had survived the intestate, surviving heirs of that person represent the person and take the share (s)he would have succeeded to. That share is then divided among those surviving heirs.

    1) EXAMPLE: D had three children: X, Y, and Z. Spouse, Y, and Z survive D, as do X's two children, xa and xb. Spouse succeeds to $20,000 and 1/2 of the remaining net estate. Y and Z each succeed to 1/3 of the other 1/2 (i.e., 1/6). Also, xa and xb take the other 1/3 of 1/2 and divide it between themselves (i.e., 1/12 each).

g. ***Per capita*** means that all persons with the same degree of relationship to the intestate share equally, without regard to representation.

    1) EXAMPLE: Q survived both Spouse and Q's only two children: X and Y. Grandchildren xa, xb, ya, yb, and yc survive Q. Each grandchild takes 1/5.

h. Residue that does not pass to a surviving spouse passes to the first of the following in which a person in a named category survives.

    1) **Lineal descendants** -- *per capita* or *per stirpes*

    2) The **decedent's mother and father** -- equal shares. If only one survives, (s)he takes all.

    3) The **decedent's brothers and sisters** and their descendants -- *per capita* or *per stirpes*

    4) The paternal and maternal **grandparents** -- half to each. If only one side survives, all of the residue passes to that side.

    5) The maternal and paternal **kindred** -- possibly

    6) Kindred of the last deceased spouse -- possibly

    7) The state -- The residue escheats to the state.

i. An **adopted child** is treated as a natural child of the adoptive parents.

    1) An adopted child can inherit from and through his/her adoptive parents.

    2) Adoptive parents can inherit from and through the adopted child.

    3) The adopted child and his/her adoptive kin, spouse, and children have no inheritance rights from or through his/her natural parents, and the natural parents and their kin have no inheritance rights from or through the natural child.

    4) However, adoption of a child by the spouse of the child's natural parent does not affect inheritance rights between the child and the natural parent or his/her family.

j. **Stepchildren** have no inheritance rights with respect to the stepparent.

k. A child born out of wedlock is a lineal descendant of the mother and is one of the natural kindred of all members of the mother's family. The child inherits from the father and the father's family only if one of the following events occurs:

    1) The parents participate in a marriage ceremony (even if it is void).
    2) Paternity is established by adjudication.
    3) The father acknowledges paternity in writing.

l.   **Advancements**. The common law presumed that an intestate desired to treat all his/her children equally. A substantial *inter vivos* gift to one child and not to others was treated as an advance payment of that child's intestate share. In order for that child to take a share of the estate as an heir, the value of the gift (as of the date of the gift) is brought back into the estate.

   1)   The doctrine has been extended to any next of kin.

   NOTE: After payment of claims, filing an accounting, a court hearing, and distribution under the will or the descent and distribution statute, the personal representative is discharged and the estate is closed (terminated).

3.   **Trust Distributions and Termination**. The trustor grants to the trustee authority to distribute trust property according to specific instructions or the trustee's discretion.

   a.   Generally, trust income is distributed or held for the designated income beneficiaries, and principal is distributed to the remaindermen when the trust is terminated.

   b.   The trustee's duty is to comply with legal terms of the trust agreement, which may grant broad discretion to the trustee as to amounts, conditions warranting, and time of distributions.

   1)   Unless specifically authorized by the trust instrument, a trustee may not accumulate income without the consent of the beneficiaries or court approval.

   c.   **Modification**. If changes in circumstances not anticipated by the settlor occur, the trustee, the settlor, or the beneficiary may petition a court to modify the terms of (or possibly terminate) a trust.

   1)   This modification is plausible only when compliance with the trust's current administrative provisions would defeat or substantially impair a material purpose of the trust.

   d.   A settlor who reserves the power of revocation may terminate the trust at any time.

   1)   An irrevocable trust can be terminated by the settlor if all the beneficiaries consent.

   e.   All the beneficiaries may join in a suit to terminate a trust if termination would not defeat a material purpose of the trust.

   f.   However, spendthrift trusts cannot be terminated except by their terms because to do so would defeat the material purpose of the trust.

   g.   A trust terminates automatically upon expiration of the time specified in the instrument.

   h.   The trust instrument may provide that the trust will exist for the life of a named individual. When the named individual dies, the trust terminates.

   i.   Ownership of both equitable title and legal title by the same person is a merger and terminates a trust.

4.   Stop and review! You have completed the outline for this subunit. Study multiple-choice questions 31 through 41 beginning on page 199.

MULTIPLE-CHOICE QUESTIONS

A. Formation and Purposes

1. Generally, an estate is liable for which debts owed by the decedent at the time of death?

    A. All of the decedent's debts.

    B. Only debts secured by the decedent's property.

    C. Only debts covered by the statute of frauds.

    D. None of the decedent's debts.

The correct answer is (A). *(CPA, adapted)*

REQUIRED: The scope of an estate's liability for decedent's debts.

DISCUSSION: An estate is an artificial legal entity that arises by operation of law when a person dies and immediately succeeds to his/her property. The estate is liable for all of his/her debts. The personal representative administering the estate has a duty to ascertain those liabilities and to cause them to be satisfied to the extent of probate assets.

Answer (B) is incorrect because security interests affect, not the estate's liability, but priority and rights of the creditor. Answer (C) is incorrect because the estate is also liable for debts not subject to the statute of frauds. Answer (D) is incorrect because, by operation of law, the estate is liable for any and all debts of a person who dies.

2. To form a valid *inter vivos* trust to hold personal property, the trust must be

    A. In writing and signed by the settlor (creator).

    B. Specific concerning the property to be held in trust.

    C. Irrevocable.

    D. In writing and signed by the trustee.

The correct answer is (B). *(CPA, adapted)*

REQUIRED: The characteristic of an *inter vivos* trust.

DISCUSSION: A trust is formed when one party transfers property to another to hold for the benefit of a third. All beneficiaries and trustees must be identified, the property must be sufficiently described so that legal title can pass to the trustee, and the settlor must deliver the property with intent to transfer title.

Answers (A) and (D) are incorrect because a trust may be established and funded orally if it involves only personal property. Answer (C) is incorrect because a trust is revocable in most states if the transferor reserves the right to revoke. It is generally presumed irrevocable unless the trust states it is not.

3. To establish an enforceable *inter vivos* spendthrift trust, funded with an office building and having a life income beneficiary and a residuary beneficiary, the grantor must

    A. Execute a written trust instrument.

    B. Deed the property to the trustee.

    C. Provide for payment of fees to the trustee.

    D. Designate an alternate trust beneficiary.

The correct answer is (B). *(CPA, adapted)*

REQUIRED: The element necessary to form a spendthrift *inter vivos* trust funded with an office building.

DISCUSSION: An *inter vivos* trust is one formed and effective during the settlor's or grantor's life. A spendthrift trust prohibits beneficiaries from voluntarily transferring their interests in trust assets. The settlor, having legal capacity, with intent to form a trust, must have a present and assignable ownership interest in property, to which (s)he transfers legal title to one or more trustees to hold, manage, and administer for the benefit of one or more beneficiaries. The usual method of transfer of real estate is by deed. The property may be real or personal, tangible or intangible.

Answer (A) is incorrect because the expression of intent to form a trust, the property transfer and description, and the designation of trustee and beneficiaries may all be oral. A written instrument is required to transfer real property to the trustee involved, to satisfy the statute of frauds. Answer (C) is incorrect because trustee entitlement to reasonable fees out of trust funds is generally implied if no provision is made for it. But such provision is not necessary to trust formation. Answer (D) is incorrect because an alternate trust beneficiary is not required for trust formation.

4. To which of the personal creditors of a life income beneficiary of an enforceable spendthrift trust may the trustee pay that beneficiary's share of trust income?

- A. Bank holding a home mortgage note deficiency judgment.
- B. Judgment creditor as a result of an automobile accident.
- C. Both A and B.
- D. None.

The correct answer is (D). *(CPA, adapted)*
REQUIRED: The creditor entitled to receive income from a spendthrift trust.
DISCUSSION: Creditors of beneficiaries of a spendthrift trust cannot reach the trust assets in the hands of a trustee. However, creditors of the beneficiary who have provided necessaries may petition a court to order payment. Once trust property is distributed to a beneficiary, it is subject to valid claims of others.
Answers (A), (B), and (C) are incorrect because neither creditor may reach trust assets in the hands of a trustee.

5. Which of the following is not necessary to create an express trust?

- A. A successor trustee.
- B. A trust corpus.
- C. A beneficiary.
- D. A valid trust purpose.

The correct answer is (A). *(CPA, adapted)*
REQUIRED: The element unnecessary to express trust formation.
DISCUSSION: An express trust is formed when a settlor, with intent to form a trust, transfers legal title to at least one trustee for the benefit of at least one beneficiary. Absent a complete and effective disposition of the settlor's property to the trust, a resulting but not an express trust might be formed. The property is referred to as trust property, the *res*, trust corpus, or trust principal.
Answer (B) is incorrect because the settlor must transfer to a trustee a recognizable and assignable interest in real or personal, tangible or intangible, property that (s)he owns. Answer (C) is incorrect because formation of an express private trust requires specific designation and description of at least one beneficiary and his/her interest. Answer (D) is incorrect because a trust must have a legal purpose.

6. Which of the following situations would cause a resulting trust to be created?

I. Failure of an express trust
II. Application of the *cy pres* doctrine
III. Fulfillment of the trust purpose

- A. I and II.
- B. I and III.
- C. II and III.
- D. I, II, and III.

The correct answer is (B). *(CPA, adapted)*
REQUIRED: The situations in which a resulting trust arises.
DISCUSSION: A resulting trust is one which arises by operation of law. It is generally an implied trust when the beneficial interest has not passed to a beneficiary other than the trustee. A resulting trust may be implied by law (1) when an express or charitable trust fails, (2) when the trust purpose has been performed but some trust property remains, and (3) when a buyer makes installment payments to the seller while title to the purchased property is held by a third person. The law presumes that the settlor [(1) and (2)] or the buyer [(3)] has the remaining beneficial interest in the property.
Answers (A), (C), and (D) are incorrect because the *cy pres* doctrine operates to preserve an otherwise valid existing charitable trust when its purpose becomes impossible, impractical, or illegal. The settlor's general charitable intent is transferred to a different charitable purpose.

7. Wyman is planning to create a trust. If she follows through, which of the following statements is correct?

    A.   The trustee may not delegate trust powers.

    B.   The trust instrument or deed must be in writing and witnessed by two disinterested persons.

    C.   The trust is usually presumed to be revocable.

    D.   Any spendthrift provision in the trust is primarily intended to protect the settlor, Wyman.

The correct answer is (A). *(Publisher)*
    REQUIRED: The correct statement concerning formation and administration of a trust.
    DISCUSSION: A trust is formed when a settlor transfers title to property to a trustee to manage for the benefit of beneficiaries. A trustee is a fiduciary selected to administer a trust in accordance with either the express or implied powers granted by the settlor in establishing the trust or the powers granted by trust law. A trustee may hire others to assist in the performance of ministerial duties, but a trustee may not delegate the trust powers without liability for breach of trust.
    Answer (B) is incorrect because neither a writing nor witnesses are required to form a trust. Answer (C) is incorrect because a trust is usually presumed irrevocable unless the power to revoke is reserved by the settlor or state law. Answer (D) is incorrect because a spendthrift clause restricts beneficiaries from anticipating income or transferring their trust interest and limits the ability of creditors to reach assets of the trust prior to distribution. A spendthrift trust provision established by the settlor for personal benefit would be against public policy.

8. Cord's will created a trust to take effect on Cord's death. The will named Cord's spouse as both the trustee and personal representative (executor) of the estate. The will provided that all of Cord's securities were to be transferred to the trust and named Cord's child as the beneficiary of the trust. Under the circumstances,

    A.   Cord has created an *inter vivos* trust.

    B.   Cord has created a testamentary trust.

    C.   The trust is invalid because it will not become effective until Cord's death.

    D.   Cord's spouse may not serve as both the trustee and personal representative because of the inherent conflict of interest.

The correct answer is (B). *(CPA, adapted)*
    REQUIRED: The correct statement about the trust formed.
    DISCUSSION: At Cord's death, upon determination that his will is valid, a trust will be created. This is a testamentary trust because it is provided for in Cord's will and becomes effective upon his death.
    Answer (A) is incorrect because an *inter vivos* trust is created and effective during the life of the settlor. Answer (C) is incorrect because a trust may be created by a valid will upon the testator's death. Answer (D) is incorrect because a settlor's spouse (or other competent party) may serve as both the per-sonal representative of the settlor's estate and the trustee of a testamentary trust. Estates and trusts are separate entities and may be administered by the same person.

9. To which of the following trusts would the rule against perpetuities not apply?

    A.   Charitable.

    B.   Spendthrift.

    C.   Totten.

    D.   Constructive.

The correct answer is (A). *(CPA, adapted)*
    REQUIRED: The trust not subject to the rule against perpetuities.
    DISCUSSION: A charitable trust is not subject to the rule against perpetuities. Property interests granted by the trust agreement must conform to the rule against perpetuities. That is, a purported future interest is invalid unless it vests or fails to vest within some life in being plus 21 years.
    Answers (B), (C), and (D) are incorrect because the rule against perpetuities restricts attempts to convey future interests in property by way of such a trust.

10. Which of the following parties is necessary to create an express trust?

	A Remainderman	A Successor Trustee
A.	Yes	Yes
B.	Yes	No
C.	No	Yes
D.	No	No

The correct answer is (D). *(CPA, adapted)*

REQUIRED: The parties necessary to create an express trust.

DISCUSSION: An express trust is formed when a settlor or trustor, with intent to form a trust, transfers legal title of property to at least one trustee for the benefit of at least one beneficiary. Courts will not permit a trust to fail for lack of a trustee and will make appointments of trustees as necessary to preserve the trust. A remainderman is a person designated in the trust as successor beneficiary after the interest of another beneficiary terminates. For example, the First Bank in trust for the benefit of my son Tom Brown, for his life, and remainder to Tom's children. Remaindermen are optional and are not necessary to form an express trust.

Answers (A), (B), and (C) are incorrect because neither successor beneficiaries or trustees are legal requirements to form an express trust.

B. Allocation between Principal and Income

11. Receipts and disbursements of a trust or estate must be allocated by the trustee between principal and income. Under the Revised Uniform Principal and Income Act, which of the following is allocated to income?

A. Amortization of an investment purchased by the trustee at a premium.

B. Depreciation even though the trust instrument provides otherwise.

C. Insurance proceeds for lost profits.

D. Rights to buy stock in the distributing corporation.

The correct answer is (C). *(Publisher)*

REQUIRED: The item allocated to income under the RUPIA.

DISCUSSION: State law defines what is trust principal and what is income. Many states have adopted the Revised Uniform Principal and Income Act to make the allocation. Income is the return (in money or property) on or for the use of principal. Income of a trust or estate is narrower than income for financial or individual income tax purposes. Receipts charged to income under the act include business income, rents, including prepaid rent, insurance proceeds for lost profits, interest, discount gain on redemption of treasury bills, taxable dividends of cash or property, taxable stock dividends, extraordinary dividends, and royalties.

Answers (A) and (D) are incorrect because amortization of an investment purchased by the trustee at a premium and rights to buy stock in the distributing corporation are allocated to principal. Answer (B) is incorrect because the trust instrument controls.

12. Frost's will created a testamentary trust naming Hill as life income beneficiary, with the principal going to Brown when Hill dies. The trust was silent on allocation of principal and income. The trust's sole asset was a commercial office building originally valued at $100,000 and having a current market value of $200,000. If the building was sold, which of the following statements would be correct concerning the allocation of the proceeds?

A. The entire proceeds would be allocated to principal and retained.

B. The entire proceeds would be allocated to income and distributed to Hill.

C. One-half of the proceeds would be allocated to principal and one-half to income.

D. One-half of the proceeds would be allocated to principal and one-half distributed to Brown.

The correct answer is (A). *(CPA, adapted)*

REQUIRED: The allocation of the sale proceeds of the trust's sole asset.

DISCUSSION: Receipts and disbursements of a trust or an estate must be allocated between principal and income accounts. State law defines what is principal and what is income. The rules of the Revised Uniform Principal and Income Act control when the trust instrument is silent. Principal remains principal even if its form changes from a building to cash. An income beneficiary is not entitled to trust principal, including any gain from its sale. The remainderman interest is entitled to the entire proceeds.

Answers (B), (C), and (D) are incorrect because none of the proceeds from the sale of the building by the trustee are allocated to the income account. An income beneficiary is entitled to receive only the income derived from trust principal, regardless of its form.

13. A trust agreement is silent on allocation of the following trust receipts between principal and income:

Cash dividends on investments in common stock	$1,000
Royalties from property subject to depletion	$2,000

What is the total amount of the trust receipts that should be allocated to trust income?

A. $0

B. $1,000

C. $2,000

D. $3,000

The correct answer is (D). *(CPA, adapted)*
REQUIRED: The allocation of cash dividends and royalties if the trust agreement is silent.
DISCUSSION: The rules of the Uniform Principal and Income Act apply, except when the terms of the trust specify otherwise. Under the act, income is the return in money or property from the use of the trust principal, such as common stock or depletable property (mineral deposits and the like). Cash dividends and royalties are both allocated to trust income.
Answers (A), (B), and (C) are incorrect because both the royalties and cash dividends (assuming they do not represent return of capital) are allocated to income under the act.

14. Jay properly created an *inter vivos* trust. The trust's sole asset is a fully rented office building. Rental receipts exceed expenditures. The trust instrument is silent about allocation of items between principal and income. Among items to be allocated during the year are insurance proceeds received as a result of fire damage to the building and mortgage interest payments made during the year. Properly allocable to principal are

	Insurance Proceeds on Building	Current Mortgage Interest Payments
A.	No	No
B.	No	Yes
C.	Yes	No
D.	Yes	Yes

The correct answer is (C). *(CPA, adapted)*
REQUIRED: The allocation of insurance proceeds for damage to trust property and of mortgage interest payments between principal and income of a trust.
DISCUSSION: Generally, receipts representing change in form or return of principal and extraordinary disbursements are allocated to trust principal. The trust instrument may designate an item as chargeable to trust principal or income. Otherwise, designations provided in the Uniform Principal and Income Act control. Insurance proceeds upon damage to or loss of trust property are principal. Interest paid on a debt owed by the trust is charged against Income.
Answers (A), (B), and (D) are incorrect because, although recovery on loss of or damage to trust principal is principal, the trust's interest obligation on investment property is a charge against income under the act.

15. An enforceable spendthrift trust was formed with a life income beneficiary and a residuary beneficiary. The trust's sole asset was an office building. Which of the following will be allocated to trust principal?

	Annual Property Tax	Monthly Mortgage Principal Payment
A.	Yes	Yes
B.	Yes	No
C.	No	Yes
D.	No	No

The correct answer is (C). *(CPA, adapted)*
REQUIRED: The proper allocation of property tax and monthly mortgage principal payments between principal and income.
DISCUSSION: Generally, ordinary operating expenses are chargeable to trust income, whereas extraordinary expenses and principal payments on indebtedness are chargeable to trust principal. Therefore, regularly recurring property taxes are not allocated to trust principal, while monthly mortgage principal payments are.
Answers (A), (B), and (D) are incorrect because property taxes are ordinary and recurring, so they are allocated to trust income. Monthly mortgage principal payments qualify as principal payments on indebtedness and are allocated to trust principal.

16. Which of the following expenditures resulting from a trust's ownership of commercial real estate should be allocated to the trust's principal?

A. Building management fees.

B. Insurance premiums.

C. Sidewalk assessments.

D. Depreciation.

The correct answer is (C). *(CPA, adapted)*
REQUIRED: The expenditure allocated to trust principal.
DISCUSSION: Unless the trust instrument specifically allocates an item to principal or income, designation by the Uniform Principal and Income Act applies. Expenditures which are not current and ordinary to the administration and operation of the trust are generally allocable to principal. Extraordinary costs for capital improvements are charges against principal. An assessment for roads, sidewalks, etc., is a capital improvement that materially enhances the value of the property and is charged against principal.
Answers (A), (B), and (D) are incorrect because, under the rules of the Uniform Act, each of these expenditures is allocated to income.

17. Which of the following would ordinarily be distributed to a trust income beneficiary?

I. Royalties

II. Stock received in a stock split

III. Cash dividends

IV. Settlements of claims for damages to trust property

A. I and II.

B. I and III.

C. II and III.

D. II and IV.

The correct answer is (B). *(CPA, adapted)*
REQUIRED: The items distributable to the income beneficiary of a trust.
DISCUSSION: Trust income is return on or for the use of trust principal (*res*). Trust income is held for distribution to an income beneficiary of the trust. Unless the trust instrument specifies otherwise, royalties and taxable dividends are allocated to trust income. Note that undistributed corporate earnings are not considered income, and corporate distributions representing return of capital are principal.
Answer (A) is incorrect because stock received in a stock split (and any proceeds on its sale) is principal unless the trust instrument specifies otherwise. An income beneficiary is not entitled to trust principal. Answers (C) and (D) are incorrect because stock received in a stock split is treated as a change in the form of principal, as is recovery for damage to trust property. The remainderman, not the income beneficiary, has the beneficial interest in trust principal.

18. Harper transferred assets into a trust under which Drake is entitled to receive the income for life. Upon Drake's death, the remaining assets are to be paid to Neal. In 1999, the trust received rent of $1,000, royalties of $3,000, cash dividends of $5,000, and proceeds of $7,000 from the sale of stock previously received by the trust as a stock dividend. Both Drake and Neal are still alive. How much of the receipts should be distributed to Drake?

A. $4,000

B. $8,000

C. $9,000

D. $16,000

The correct answer is (C). *(CPA, adapted)*
REQUIRED: The allocation between principal and income.
DISCUSSION: Rent, royalties, and cash dividends are all properly allocated to trust income under the Uniform Principal and Income Act. Stock dividends are allocated entirely to principal, as are the proceeds of the subsequent sale of such dividends. The $9,000 income ($1,000 rent + $3,000 royalties + $5,000 cash dividends) should be distributed to the income beneficiary under the terms of the trust.
Answer (A) is incorrect because taxable dividends are allocated to trust income. Answer (B) is incorrect because rent is a return for use of principal and is allocated to trust income unless the trust instrument specifies otherwise. Answer (D) is incorrect because a dividend of stock issued by the distributing corporation is allocated to principal, unless any distributee may choose to receive money or other property instead or the dividend is otherwise taxable. Proceeds received from the sale of principal are also principal.

19. On January 1, 1999, Dix transferred certain assets into a trust. The assets consisted of Lux Corp. bonds with a face amount of $500,000 and an interest rate of 12%, payable semiannually on May 1 and November 1. Dix had purchased the bonds at their face amount. As of January 1, 1999, the bonds had a fair market value of $600,000. The accounting period selected for the trust is a calendar year. Assuming the trust is valid, how should the amount of interest received in 1999 be allocated between principal and income if the trust instrument is otherwise silent?

	Principal	Income
A.	$0	$60,000
B.	$0	$72,000
C.	$10,000	$50,000
D.	$12,000	$60,000

The correct answer is (C). *(CPA, adapted)*
REQUIRED: The allocation between trust principal and income of interest on and proceeds from the sale of bonds.
DISCUSSION: Unless the trust instrument specifically otherwise allocates a receipt or disbursement to principal or income, default designations provided in the Uniform Principal and Income Act generally control. Interest is allocated to income. But interest accrued but not yet payable when an asset is delivered to the trustee is principal. Proceeds on sale of principal, including gain or loss, is generally allocated to principal, even if partially attributable to an interest feature.
Answers (A) and (B) are incorrect because interest received by the trust but attributable to the period before the asset was conveyed to the trustee is allocated to principal. Bond interest is computed on the face amount. Answer (D) is incorrect because bond interest is computed on the face amount.

20. Cox transferred assets into a trust under which Smart is entitled to receive the income for life. After Smart's death, the remaining assets are to be given to Mix. In 1999, the trust received rent of $1,000, stock dividends of $6,000, interest on certificates of deposit of $3,000, municipal bond interest of $4,000, and proceeds of $7,000 from the sale of bonds. Both Smart and Mix are still alive. What amount of the 1999 receipts should be allocated to trust principal?

A. $7,000
B. $8,000
C. $13,000
D. $15,000

The correct answer is (C). *(CPA, adapted)*
REQUIRED: The allocation between trust principal and income.
DISCUSSION: Trust principal is property gratuitously acquired and any changes in its form, held for eventual delivery to remaindermen. Trust income is return for use of principal, held for or distributed to the income beneficiary. Unless the trust instrument specifically otherwise allocates a receipt or expense to principal or income, default designations in the Uniform Principal and Income Act control. Rent and interest (even if tax exempt) are allocated to income. Nontaxable stock dividends are allocated to principal, as are proceeds from the sale of principal. Gain on the sale of property which constitutes principal, even if partially attributable to an interest feature, is generally principal.
Answer (A) is incorrect because nontaxable dividends of stock issued by the distributee are allocated to principal. Answer (B) is incorrect because rent is income (return on principal), but nontaxable dividends of stock issued by the distributee are principal. Answer (D) is incorrect because tax-exempt and taxable interest and rent are allocated income. A stock dividend is principal. Consideration received for trust principal is also principal.

C. Fiduciary Responsibilities

21. A personal representative of an estate would breach fiduciary duties if the personal representative

A. Combined personal funds with funds of the estate so that both could purchase treasury bills.

B. Represented the estate in a lawsuit brought against it by a disgruntled relative of the decedent.

C. Distributed property in satisfaction of the decedent's debts.

D. Engaged a non-CPA to prepare the records for the estate's final accounting.

The correct answer is (A). *(CPA, adapted)*
REQUIRED: The breach of the personal representative's fiduciary duty.
DISCUSSION: The personal representative is responsible to administer the estate according to legal directions. (S)he is a fiduciary with respect to the estate and must act primarily for the benefit of the estate. (S)he is accountable for the estate assets. One fiduciary duty is to keep the estate's property separate from his/her own.
Answer (B) is incorrect because representing the estate in a lawsuit is a proper duty of a fiduciary. Answer (C) is incorrect because the estate is liable for all of the decedent's debts. Settling those debts is a duty of the personal representative. Answer (D) is incorrect because the final accounting of the estate need not be performed by an independent public accountant.

22. Rusk properly created an *inter vivos* trust naming Gold as the trustee. The sole asset of the trust is an office building that is fully rented. Which of the following statements is correct concerning Gold's responsibility as trustee?

A. Gold's duty of loyalty will be breached by Gold's purchasing assets from the trust despite a provision in the trust agreement permitting such a purchase.

B. Gold owes a duty of loyalty to the trust but not to the beneficiaries.

C. Gold must exercise reasonable care and skill while performing the duties of a trustee.

D. Gold will be free from personal liability with regard to all contracts entered into by Gold on behalf of the trust absent fraud by Gold.

The correct answer is (C). *(CPA, adapted)*

REQUIRED: The duty, breach, or liability of a trustee.

DISCUSSION: A trustee is a fiduciary owing duties of care and loyalty. (S)he must exercise the same degree of care and skill in holding, managing, and administering trust property as would reasonably prudent persons in managing their personal affairs.

Answer (A) is incorrect because it is a *per se* breach of a trustee's duty of loyalty to engage in a transaction with the trust in his/her individual capacity unless the trust agreement expressly provides for the transaction. Answer (B) is incorrect because the trustee's duties of care and loyalty are to both the trust and its beneficiaries. Answer (D) is incorrect because a trustee incurs personal liability for a transaction entered into on behalf of the trust in breach of his/her fiduciary duties of care and loyalty. Thus, (s)he has liability for fraud and for other conduct which falls below the required standard of care or loyalty.

23. When a trust instrument is silent regarding a trustee's powers, which of the following implied powers does a trustee generally have?

	The Power to Make Distributions of Principal to Income Beneficiaries	The Power to Lease Trust Property to Third Parties
A.	Yes	Yes
B.	Yes	No
C.	No	Yes
D.	No	No

The correct answer is (C). *(CPA, adapted)*

REQUIRED: The implied powers of a trustee.

DISCUSSION: A trustee is a fiduciary appointed by a settlor to hold, manage, and administer trust property for the benefit of the beneficiaries. When not acting contrary to express provisions in the trust agreement or law, the trustee has the implied power to do anything reasonably necessary to perform these functions. A trustee has the implied power to sell or lease trust property to third parties. Absent specific or discretionary powers in the trust instrument, a trustee may not make distributions of principal to income beneficiaries.

Answers (A), (B), and (D) are incorrect because when a trust instrument is silent regarding a trustees' powers, the trustee has the implied power to lease trust property to third parties, but may not make distributions of principal to income beneficiaries.

24. Which of the following fiduciary duties may be violated by the trustee if the trustee, without express direction in the trust instrument, invests trust assets in unsecured loans to a co-trustee?

I. Duty to invest prudently
II. Duty of loyalty to the trust

A. I only.

B. II only.

C. Both I and II.

D. Neither I nor II.

The correct answer is (C). *(CPA, adapted)*

REQUIRED: The duty(ies) violated by a trustee when trust assets are lent to a co-trustee.

DISCUSSION: The trustee violated the duty to invest prudently and the duty of loyalty by investing trust assets in an unsecured loan to a co-trustee. An unsecured loan to a fellow trustee breaches the duty of loyalty because the loan was to a person with whom the trustee is familiar and was not an arm's-length transaction. A trustee also has a duty to invest trust property in a prudent, safe manner. The trustee breached the duty to invest prudently because the loan is not secured by any property and is probably not a bargained-for, arm's-length transaction.

Answers (A), (B), and (D) are incorrect because a trustee owes both a duty of loyalty to the trust and a duty to invest the trust assets prudently.

25. Dix transferred L Corp. into a trust on January 1, 1999 when the FMV of the bonds was $600,000. The bonds had a face amount of $500,000 and an interest rate of 12%. The trust instrument named Dix as trustee, Dix's child as life beneficiary, and Dix's grandchild as remainderman. Dix had purchased the bonds at their face amount. The trust instrument is silent as to whether Dix may revoke the trust. Which of the following statements is correct?

A. Dix is not a fiduciary because Dix is also the creator (settlor).

B. The trust is invalid under the merger doctrine because Dix is both the creator and the trustee.

C. A duty is owed by Dix to administer the trust.

D. Dix has the implied right to revoke the trust without the court's permission.

The correct answer is (C). *(CPA, adapted)*
REQUIRED: The correct statement concerning the settlor as trustee.
DISCUSSION: A trustee is a fiduciary of the trust and the beneficiaries, even if (s)he is the trustor and reserved a right to revoke the trust. The trustee owes a fiduciary duty of continuing undivided loyalty. (S)he is obligated to hold, manage, and administer the trust property for the sole benefit of the beneficiaries.
Answer (A) is incorrect because, although the settlor may be a trustee, Dix has a fiduciary duty, in the capacity of trustee, to the trust and its beneficiaries. Answer (B) is incorrect because the settlor may be the sole trustee if (s)he is not also the sole beneficiary. If legal title (held by the trustee) and equitable title (in the beneficiaries) merge completely, the trust terminates. Answer (D) is incorrect because in most states a trust is irrevocable unless the trustor expressly retains the right to revoke it.

26. A trustee's fiduciary duty will probably be violated if the trustee

A. Invests trust property in government bonds.

B. Performs accounting services for the trust.

C. Sells unproductive trust property.

D. Borrows money from the trust.

The correct answer is (D). *(CPA, adapted)*
REQUIRED: The trustee's breach of fiduciary duty.
DISCUSSION: A trustee, as fiduciary, owes duties of reasonable care and undivided loyalty to the trust and its beneficiaries. It is generally an automatic violation of trust to engage in self-dealing, i.e., in a transaction with the trust (such as a sale or a loan) in a capacity other than as trustee for the trust. Exceptions which allow for such transactions (e.g., court approval) are not presented in the facts.
Answer (A) is incorrect because the trustee's duty of care is to manage trust assets with the care a reasonably prudent person would in conducting his/her own affairs. Such a person might invest personal assets in government bonds. Answer (B) is incorrect because, in itself, this is not a breach of duty. But a reasonably prudent person would assure that accounting for his/her personal affairs be performed by a competent person. Answer (C) is incorrect because, as would a reasonably prudent person in managing his/her personal assets, a trustee might sell unproductive property after weighing anticipated returns and risks.

27. Which of the following investments generally will be a violation of a trustee's fiduciary duty to the trust?

A. Secured first mortgages on land.

B. High-interest unsecured loans.

C. Tax-exempt municipal bonds.

D. Guaranteed savings certificates.

The correct answer is (B). *(CPA, adapted)*
REQUIRED: The investment that generally violates a trustee's fiduciary duty.
DISCUSSION: A trustee of a trust must exercise the same degree of care and skill in holding, managing, and administering trust property as would reasonably prudent persons managing their personal affairs. Investment of trust funds in first mortgages on real estate, municipal bonds, or guaranteed savings certificates meets the test of prudent investment. Only in very unusual circumstances would a trustee be warranted in making unsecured loans of trust assets. This investment is usually a violation of a trustee's fiduciary duty because the unsecured loan is not secured by any property and probably is not bargained for in an arm's-length transaction.
Answers (A), (C), and (D) are incorrect because they each meet the test of prudent investment of trust property.

28. Which of the following fiduciary duties will a trustee violate by borrowing money from the trust?

- A. Duty of loyalty.
- B. Duty to properly account.
- C. Duty to safeguard the trust res.
- D. Duty to properly manage the trust.

The correct answer is (A). *(CPA, adapted)*

REQUIRED: The fiduciary duty violated when a trustee borrows money from the trust.

DISCUSSION: A trustee, as fiduciary, owes duties of reasonable care and undivided loyalty to the trust and its beneficiaries. It is generally an automatic violation of the duty of loyalty to the trust to engage in self-dealing in a capacity other than as trustee. A trustee's borrowing from the trust presents a conflict of interest that is a *per se* breach of the trustee's duty of undivided loyalty.

Answers (B), (C), and (D) are incorrect because, while each constitutes a duty of a trustee, borrowing money from the trust is a breach of the fiduciary duty of undivided loyalty.

29. If not expressly granted, which of the following implied powers would a trustee have?

I. Power to sell trust property
II. Power to borrow from the trust
III. Power to pay trust expenses

- A. I and II.
- B. I and III.
- C. II and III.
- D. I, II, and III.

The correct answer is (B). *(CPA, adapted)*

REQUIRED: The trustee's implied powers.

DISCUSSION: A trustee is a fiduciary appointed by a settlor to hold, manage, and administer trust property for the sole benefit of the beneficiaries. To the extent not contrary to express provisions in the trust agreement or law, the trustor has implied power to do that which is reasonably necessary to perform those functions. Provided that a trustee does so in accordance with any pertinent instructions expressed in the instrument and his/her duties of reasonable care and undivided loyalty, (s)he may sell trust property and pay trust expenses.

Answers (A), (C), and (D) are incorrect because a trustee borrowing from the trust presents a conflict of interests which is a *per se* breach of the trustee's duty of undivided loyalty whereby (s)he must hold, manage, and administer trust property in the interests of the beneficiaries unless (1) a court approves the transaction, (2) the trust instrument provides for it, or (3) all beneficiaries consent to it.

30. Colt's will created a testamentary trust for the benefit of Colt's spouse. Colt's sister and Colt's spouse were named as co-trustees of the trust. The trust provided for discretionary principal distributions to Colt's spouse. It also provided that, on the death of Colt's spouse, any remaining trust property was to be distributed to Colt's children. Part of the trust property consisted of a very valuable baseball card collection. After Colt's death, which of the following statements would be correct?

- A. The co-trustees must use the same degree of skill, judgment, and care in managing the trust assets as reasonably prudent persons would exercise in managing their own affairs.
- B. The co-trustees must employ an investment advisor to manage the trust assets.
- C. Colt's sister may delegate her duties as co-trustee to the spouse and thereby not be liable for the administration of the trust.
- D. Under no circumstances could the spouse purchase the baseball card collection from the trust without breaching fiduciary duties owed to the trust and Colt's children.

The correct answer is (A). *(CPA, adapted)*

REQUIRED: The effect of appointing a beneficiary as co-trustee.

DISCUSSION: A trustee is expected to use the degree of care and skill that an ordinarily prudent person would employ in the conduct of his/her own affairs. A trustee is expected to act with due care, and is subject to removal (upon the beneficiaries' petition to court) if (s)he does not. This duty applies to each co-trustee.

Answer (B) is incorrect because there is no such requirement and a trustee may not delegate his/her trust powers. A trustee normally makes investment decisions in his/her own discretion subject to reasonable care and local fiduciary administration statutes. Answer (C) is incorrect because a trustee may not delegate his/her trust powers. Answer (D) is incorrect because, while a trustee normally may not enter into a transaction between him/herself and the trust, there are some exceptions, e.g., court approval of the transaction or a provision in the trust instrument permitting the transaction.

D. Distributions and Termination

31. A decedent's will provided that the estate was to be divided among the decedent's issue, *per capita* and not *per stirpes*. If there are two surviving children and three grandchildren who are children of a predeceased child at the time the will is probated, how will the estate be divided?

A. 1/2 to each surviving child.

B. 1/3 to each surviving child and 1/9 to each grandchild.

C. 1/4 to each surviving child and 1/6 to each grandchild.

D. 1/5 to each surviving child and grandchild.

The correct answer is (D). *(CPA, adapted)*
REQUIRED: The result when a will directs *per capita* division.
DISCUSSION: Distribution of the probate estate, net of claims against the estate and security interests in probate assets, is according to intent expressed in a valid will, if there is one. *Per capita* means that all persons within the stated degree of relationship to the decedent take equally, without regard to representation.
Answer (A) is incorrect because the will did not express a grant only to surviving children, but rather to the decedent's issue *per capita*. The descendants of the predeceased child take *per capita*, i.e., equally and not by representation, with the two surviving children. Answer (B) is incorrect because it describes *per stirpes* division, whereby the grandchildren take by representation of the predeceased child. Between them, they divide the share the child would have been entitled to if (s)he had not predeceased the testator. Answer (C) is incorrect because, by directing *per capita* distribution in a valid will, the testator gave an equal share to each person within the same degree of relationship to the testator.

32. Generally, which of the following parties would have the first priority to receive the estate of a person who dies without a will?

A. The state.

B. A child of the deceased.

C. A parent of the deceased.

D. A sibling of the deceased.

The correct answer is (B). *(CPA, adapted)*
REQUIRED: The priority of parties under intestacy statutes.
DISCUSSION: When a person dies intestate (without a will), their property passes under a statutory will called an intestacy statute. Each state has an intestacy statute. Some variations exist but priority is invariably given to surviving spouses and children of the decedent.
Answer (A) is incorrect because the property of an intestate decedent escheat to the state only if no living relatives are found. Answers (C) and (D) are incorrect because parents and siblings of the deceased have lower priority in intestacy statutes than children and spouses.

33. Which of the following assets generally will be distributed outside of the probate estate and regardless of intestacy laws, provided the estate is not the named beneficiary?

	Totten Trusts	Proceeds from Insurance Policies
A.	Yes	Yes
B.	Yes	No
C.	No	Yes
D.	No	No

The correct answer is (A). *(CPA, adapted)*
REQUIRED: The assets that will be distributed outside the decedent's estate.
DISCUSSION: A probate estate is defined as all property of a decedent that pass under the terms of his/her will or the intestacy statute of the state wherein decedent resided. Any other property the decedent had an interest in passes outside the probate estate. A Totten Trust is a deposit of money in a financial institution in the name of the depositor as trustee for a named beneficiary. The depositor may revoke the trust but if it is revoked at death the funds belong to the beneficiary without passing through the depositor's estate. Many insurance policies are contracts with third-party beneficiaries. If the event insured against occurs, the insurance company is obligated to pay the beneficiary directly. Hence, insurance proceeds payable to third parties are outside the decedent's probate estate.
Answers (B), (C), and (D) are incorrect because both Totten Trusts and proceeds from insurance policies (where the estate is not the named beneficiary) pass outside the probate estate.

34. A trust will be terminated if

   A.   A beneficiary becomes incompetent.

   B.   The trustee dies.

   C.   The grantor dies.

   D.   The trust term expires.

The correct answer is (D). *(CPA, adapted)*

   REQUIRED: The trust terminating event.

   DISCUSSION: A trust is set up for a particular purpose and terminates when that purpose is accomplished or becomes impossible or illegal. If the trust instrument expresses a condition upon which, or a period after which, the trust terminates, it terminates by those terms of the trust.

   Answer (A) is incorrect because providing support after such a possibility might be a purpose of a valid trust. Answer (B) is incorrect because the trust instrument may provide for a successor trustee. Otherwise, a court will appoint one. Answer (C) is incorrect because testamentary trusts take effect only upon a settlor's death.

35. Absent specific directions, which of the following parties will ordinarily receive the assets of a terminated trust?

   A.   Income beneficiaries.

   B.   Remaindermen.

   C.   Grantor.

   D.   Trustee.

The correct answer is (B). *(CPA, adapted)*

   REQUIRED: The parties that will receive the assets of a terminated trust.

   DISCUSSION: A trust is formed for the benefit of its beneficiaries. Beneficiaries are usually classified as either income beneficiaries or remaindermen. The income beneficiaries receive the income from the trust property for a predetermined duration. Upon termination of the trust, the remaindermen receive the trust assets.

   Answer (A) is incorrect because income beneficiaries receive only distributions of income until the trust is terminated. Answer (C) is incorrect because a grantor will generally create a trust for the benefit of other parties. Therefore, while a trust may revert back to the settlor (if the settlor holds the reversionary interest), the trust property generally passes to third-party remaindermen. Answer (D) is incorrect because the trustee holds legal title to the trust assets and administers the trust property for the benefit of the beneficiaries. When the trust is terminated, title to the trust property passes to the remaindermen.

36. An irrevocable testamentary trust was created by Park, with Gordon named as trustee. The trust provided that the income will be paid to Hardy for life with the principal then reverting to Park's estate to be paid to King. The trust will automatically end on the death of

   A.   Park.

   B.   Gordon.

   C.   Hardy.

   D.   King.

The correct answer is (C). *(CPA, adapted)*

   REQUIRED: The event that will automatically terminate an irrevocable testamentary trust.

   DISCUSSION: A trust will terminate on a specific date, upon the occurrence of a specific event, or with the impossibility or illegality of carrying out the trust purpose. In this case, termination will occur upon the death of the income beneficiary because the trust purpose will have been completed.

   Answer (A) is incorrect because this is a testamentary trust created by Park. Park is dead at the time the trust is created. Answer (B) is incorrect because the death of the trustee will not cause termination of the trust because a replacement trustee will be appointed by a court. Answer (D) is incorrect because, since King is not a beneficiary of the trust, his death is irrelevant to the trust.

37. Which of the following events will terminate an irrevocable spendthrift trust established for a period of 5 years?

- A. Grantor dies.
- B. Income beneficiaries die.
- C. Grantor decides to terminate the trust.
- D. Income beneficiaries agree to the trust's termination.

The correct answer is (B). *(CPA, adapted)*
REQUIRED: The event terminating a spendthrift trust.
DISCUSSION: A spendthrift trust restricts the beneficiaries from transferring their interest in the trust. Creditors of the beneficiaries cannot reach trust assets in the hands of the trustee. The spendthrift trust is intended to provide protection for the beneficiaries. If they die, the purpose of the trust cannot be accomplished and would therefore terminate.
Answer (A) is incorrect because the death of the grantor under an irrevocable trust does not have the effect of terminating the trust. Answer (C) is incorrect because a grantor may revoke or amend a trust when such right is not reserved only if all beneficiaries consent. Answer (D) is incorrect because a spendthrift trust does not terminate by their consent.

38. On the death of the grantor, which of the following testamentary trusts would fail?

- A. A trust created to promote the public welfare.
- B. A trust created to provide for a spouse's health care.
- C. A trust created to benefit a charity.
- D. A trust created to benefit a childless person's grandchildren.

The correct answer is (D). *(CPA, adapted)*
REQUIRED: The event that would cause a testamentary trust to fail.
DISCUSSION: A trust fails when there are no specifically designated beneficiaries or it is otherwise impossible to carry out the purpose of the trust. Because the grantor had no children, there can be no grandchildren and, therefore, no beneficiaries to the trust. When a testamentary trust fails, the trust property (corpus) is distributed as specified in the residuary clause of the will or through intestate succession if no will was created.
Answers (A), (B), and (C) are incorrect because these trusts, which come into existence upon the death of the grantor, appear to have sufficiently definite beneficiaries and valid trust purposes. Funds from the decedent's estate will pour over into the testamentary trust to be administered by the trustee for the designated beneficiaries.

39. A trust was created in 1988 to provide funds for sending the settlor's child through medical school. The trust agreement specified that the trust was to terminate in 1999. The child entered medical school in 1995, took a leave of absence in 1996, and died in 1998. This trust terminated in

- A. 1995
- B. 1996
- C. 1998
- D. 1999

The correct answer is (C). *(CPA, adapted)*
REQUIRED: The termination date of an express trust.
DISCUSSION: A trust may terminate by expiration of a specific period, occurrence of a specific event, or impossibility or illegality of carrying out the trust purpose. In this case, termination occurred when death of the child made the trust unnecessary. Trust purpose is more important than a specified termination date, which may have been set merely to satisfy the rule against perpetuities.
Answer (A) is incorrect because the trust was intended to provide funds to the child for medical school. Answer (B) is incorrect because the child's leave of absence did not make the trust's purpose unattainable. Answer (D) is incorrect because death of the child terminated the trust when the trust purpose became impossible.

40. An irrevocable trust that contains no provision for change or termination can be changed or terminated only by the

- A. Courts.
- B. Income beneficiaries.
- C. Remaindermen.
- D. Grantor.

The correct answer is (A). *(CPA, adapted)*
REQUIRED: The parties that can successfully change an irrevocable trust.
DISCUSSION: Most states follow the rule that a trust is irrevocable unless expressly made revocable. Therefore, an irrevocable trust may be modified or revoked only if the grantor, trustee, or beneficiary successfully petitions a court to change or terminate the trust.

Answers (B), (C), and (D) are incorrect because only the courts may change or terminate an irrevocable trust. Other interested parties are limited to filing a petition. Unanimous consent of the settlor and all beneficiaries may terminate an irrevocable trust in some jurisdictions.

41. In a written trust containing no specific powers, the trustee will have all of the following implied powers except

- A. Sell trust property.
- B. Pay management expenses.
- C. Accumulate income.
- D. Employ a CPA to prepare trust tax returns.

The correct answer is (C). *(CPA, adapted)*
REQUIRED: The implied power that a trustee lacks.
DISCUSSION: A trustee is appointed by the settlor as a fiduciary who holds legal title to, manages, and administers the trust property, including its income, in the interests of the beneficiaries. Absent specific powers in the trust instrument, the trustee may not accumulate income without the consent of the beneficiaries or approval by a court.

Answers (A), (B), and (D) are incorrect because a trustee has the implied power to sell trust property and pay reasonable trust expenses.

Use Gleim's ***CPA Test Prep*** for interactive testing with over 2,000 additional multiple-choice questions!

OOF QUESTION (CPA, adapted) 10-15 minutes

Under the provisions of Glenn's testamentary trust, after payment of all administrative expenses and taxes, the entire residuary estate was to be paid to Strong and Lake as trustees. The trustees were authorized to invest the trust assets and directed to distribute income annually to Glenn's children for their lives, then distribute the principal to Glenn's grandchildren, *per capita*. The trustees were also authorized to make such principal payments to the income beneficiaries that the trustees determined to be reasonable for the beneficiaries' welfare. Glenn died in 1996. On Glenn's death there were two surviving children, aged 21 and 30, and one 2-year-old grandchild.

On June 15, 1999, the trustees made the following distributions from the trust:

- Paid the 1996, 1997, and 1998 trust income to Glenn's children. This amount included the proceeds from the sale of stock received by the trust as a stock dividend.
- Made a $10,000 principal payment for medical school tuition to one of Glenn's children.
- Made a $5,000 principal payment to Glenn's grandchild.

Required

Items 1 through 5 relate to the above facts. For each item, select (A) if only statement I is correct, select (B) if only statement II is correct, select (C) if both statements are correct, or select (D) if neither statement is correct.

A. I only.
B. II only.
C. Both I and II.
D. Neither I nor II.

1. I. Glenn's trust was valid because it did not violate the rule against perpetuities.
   II. Glenn's trust was valid even though it permitted the trustees to make principal payments to income beneficiaries.

2. I. Glenn's trust would be terminated if both of Glenn's children were to die.
   II. Glenn's trust would be terminated because of the acts of the trustees.

3. I. Strong and Lake violated their fiduciary duties by making any distributions of principal.
   II. Strong and Lake violated their fiduciary duties by failing to distribute the trust income annually.

4. I. Generally, stock dividends are considered income and should be distributed.
   II. Generally, stock dividends should be allocated to principal and remain as part of the trust.

5. I. The $10,000 principal payment was an abuse of the trustees' authority.
   II. The $5,000 principal payment was valid because of its payment to a non-income beneficiary.

Knowledge Tested

1. Agency: formation; actual, implied, and apparent authority; liabilities of the parties; and termination
2. Rule against perpetuities
3. Trusts: trustee's duties; and allocations to and distributions of income and principal.

1. The correct answer is (C).
   DISCUSSION: The rule against perpetuities requires that an interest in property vest within a period measured by the life of a person in being plus 21 years. Glenn's trust provides for the income to be paid to Glenn's children for life (income beneficiaries). The trust principal is then to vest in Glenn's grandchildren in equal shares (remaindermen). Glenn's trust does not violate the perpetuities rule. The testamentary trust is properly formed, and its validity is not affected by the discretion granted to the trustee in the trust instrument to make distributions of principal to the income beneficiaries. The powers of a trustee are primarily derived from the trust instrument.

2. The correct answer is (A).
   DISCUSSION: The terms of the trust provide that it will continue until the death of the last of the income beneficiaries (Glenn's children). The assets will then be distributed to the residual beneficiaries. A trust terminates upon completion of its purpose or by court order. A trust will not terminate because of unauthorized actions by the trustees. The trustees are liable for damages resulting from a breach of their fiduciary duty and are subject to removal by court order.

3. The correct answer is (B).
   DISCUSSION: A trustee is appointed to carry out the terms of a trust and to act as a fiduciary to the beneficiaries. A fiduciary is charged with exercising the utmost care, loyalty, and concern for the welfare of the parties to whom (s)he owes the duty. Failure to distribute the annual income to the beneficiaries as directed was a breach of a fiduciary duty, but exercising the discretion with respect to distribution of principal to the income beneficiaries was not a breach if done in good faith after careful consideration of its effect. The duty of the trustees was to distribute the principal and income of the trust as directed in the trust instrument.

4. The correct answer is (B).
   DISCUSSION: A stock dividend is payable in the stock of the dividend-paying corporation. It does not increase the equity of a shareholder because stock dividends are distributed in proportion to the shares already owned. Ordinarily, stock dividends are not income and should be allocated to principal and remain as trust assets unless, as here, the trustees are granted the discretion to distribute from principal.

5. The correct answer is (D).
   DISCUSSION: The trust provisions allowed the trustees to make discretionary distributions from principal when they determined such activities to be in the best interest of the beneficiaries' welfare. It appears that the settlor's intent was to limit distributions from principal to income beneficiaries, and he did not make provisions for distribution to the residual beneficiaries. Thus, the $5,000 payment to the grandchild was not authorized. The $10,000 payment to Glenn's child was authorized and does not appear to be an abuse of the trustees' discretion.

ESSAY QUESTION *(CPA, adapted)* 15-25 minutes

On January 1, 1999, Stone prepared an *inter vivos* spendthrift trust. Stone wanted to provide financial security for several close relatives during their lives, with the remainder payable to several charities. Stone funded the trust by transferring stocks, bonds, and a commercial building to the trust. Queen Bank was named as trustee. The trust was to use the calendar year as its accounting period. The trust instrument contained no provision for the allocation of receipts and disbursements to principal and income.

The following transactions involving trust property occurred in 1999:

- The trust sold stock it owned for $50,000. The cost basis of the stock was $10,000. $40,000 was allocated to income and $10,000 to principal.

- The trust received a stock dividend of 500 shares of $10 par value common stock selling, at the time, for $50 per share. $20,000 was allocated to income and $5,000 to principal.

- The trust received bond interest of $18,000, which was allocated to income. The interest was paid and received semiannually on May 1 and November 1.

- The trust made mortgage amortization payments of $40,000 on the mortgage on the commercial building. The entire amount was allocated to principal.

On December 31, 1999, all the income beneficiaries and the charities joined in a petition to have the court allow the trust to be terminated and all trust funds distributed.

Required

a. State the requirements to establish a valid *inter vivos* spendthrift trust, and determine whether the Stone trust meets those requirements.

b. State whether the allocations made in the four transactions were correct and, if not, state the proper allocation to be made under the majority rule. Disregard any tax effect of each transaction.

c. State whether the trust will be terminated by the court, and give the reasons for your conclusion.

Knowledge Tested

1. Requirements to establish an *inter vivos* spendthrift trust

2. Allocation of trust receipts and disbursements to principal and income

3. Requirements for trust termination

Authors' Comments

This essay requires an understanding of all the major subdivisions of trust law: formation, administration, and termination of private and charitable trusts. Most of the knowledge tested consists of general principles except for the allocations between principal and income.

AICPA Unofficial Answer

a. The requirements to establish a valid *inter vivos* spendthrift trust are as follows:

- Grantor
- Trust res
- Intent to create a trust
- Lawful purpose
- Trustee and separate beneficiaries

Stone created a valid spendthrift trust. As grantor, Stone transferred stocks, bonds, and real estate (res) to the trust with a present intent to create the trust for the express lawful purpose of providing income for life to close relatives with the remainder left to charity. Stone designated Queen Bank as trustee.

b.
- Incorrect. The entire proceeds from the sale of the stock should be allocated to principal.

- Incorrect. The entire amount of the stock dividend should be allocated to principal.

- Incorrect. One-third of the semiannual payment of bond interest received on May 1 had already accrued when the trust was created on January 1, 1999. Thus, it could not have been income of the trust. Accordingly, $3,000 should be allocated to principal and $15,000 to income.

- Correct/Incorrect. All mortgage payments representing a repayment of a mortgage debt should be allocated to principal. However, if any portion of the payment includes interest on the mortgage, that amount should be allocated to income.

c. The petition to have the trust terminated and distributed will fail. Even though all beneficiaries and remaindermen joined in the petition, termination of the trust, while any of the income beneficiaries are alive, would defeat the intent of the grantor in establishing a spendthrift trust.

CHAPTER III
CONTRACTS

These two study units will constitute approximately 10% of the Business Law section.

STUDY UNIT 7: CONTRACT FORMATION

21 pages of outline
45 multiple-choice questions
2 OOFs and 1 essay

A. Offer and Acceptance
B. Consideration
C. Statute of Frauds
D. Capacity and Legality
E. Mutual Assent
F. Interpreting a Contract

This is the first of two study units on contracts. Contracts is a core area of business law and business transactions and, as such, will be of considerable interest to you as an accountant, auditor, and business person. Preparation for the examination requires a thorough understanding of the rules of formation reviewed in this study unit. When reviewing Offer and Acceptance, pay particular attention to options, firm offers, the effects of counteroffers, rejections, and revocations on the duration of an offer and the effective date of acceptance. Other significant topics include consideration, parol evidence, and the statute of frauds.

NOTE: Article 2 of the Uniform Commercial Code (UCC) contains some changes to contract common law with respect to goods (i.e., tangible personal property). Thus, there are occasional references to the UCC rules for tangible personal property in this study unit. These differences will be explained in Study Unit 16, Sales.

1. Contracts require each of the following:

   a. Offer and acceptance
   b. Mutual assent (meeting of the minds)
   c. Consideration (bargained-for exchange)
   d. Legality (legal purpose)
   e. Capacity of parties (legal ability)

2. A **contract** is a promise or a set of promises for the breach of which the law gives a remedy or the performance of which the law in some way recognizes as a duty. The following are definitions of types of contracts:

   a. A **promise** is a manifestation of intent to perform or refrain from an act.

   b. An **agreement** is manifestation of mutual assent by two or more persons.

   c. An **express contract's** terms are stated in writing or orally.

   d. An **implied contract's** terms are wholly or partially inferred from conduct and circumstances.

   e. A **unilateral contract** is one in which only one party makes a promise. The promisor expects the promisee to accept the offer merely by performance, not by making a return promise.

      1) EXAMPLE: Mary tells John, "I'll pay you $10 to polish my car."

f.   A **bilateral contract** is one in which both parties make promises. Each party has both an obligation to perform and an expectation that the other party will perform.

  1)   EXAMPLE: Mary tells John, "I'll provide you lodging if you agree to pay me $55."

g.   A contract is **executory** if any duty remains to be performed.

h.   An **executed contract** has been fully performed by all parties.

i.   An **enforceable contract** is one for the breach of which the law provides a remedy.

j.   An **unenforceable contract** is composed of all fundamental contract elements except compliance with the statute of frauds.

k.   A **voidable contract** is one which a party may either enforce or avoid.

l.   A **purported contract** which is void as a contract is a legal nullity.

  1)   It cannot be ratified and made enforceable by the parties.

m.   A **valid contract** is legally binding on both parties and is enforceable in a court of law.

n.   A **formal contract** is given special effect under the law because of its form, e.g., a formal contract includes

  1)   Contract under seal
  2)   Negotiable instrument
  3)   Letter of credit

o.   **Informal contracts** are those for which the law does not require a particular set of formalities or special language. They are often referred to as simple contracts. They may be written, oral, or implied.

p.   A **quasi-contract** is not a contract; it is a remedy to prevent unjust enrichment of one party at another party's expense. It is an equitable remedy available when there is no adequate remedy at law.

A.   Offer and Acceptance. A contract is formed when an offeree accepts an offer.

1.   An **offer** is a statement or other communication by which the offeror confers upon the offeree the power of acceptance (to form an agreement).

a.   An offer need not take any particular form, but it must

  1)   Be communicated to an offeree
  2)   Manifest, objectively, an intent to enter into a contract
  3)   Be sufficiently definite and certain

b.   An offer may be communicated by words or conduct.

  1)   An offer may be made to the public at large. However, no person can accept such an offer unless and until (s)he has knowledge that the offer exists.

    a)   EXAMPLE: Sid advertises a reward for return of his dog.

c.   To have legal effect, an offer must manifest an intent to enter into a contract.

  1)   Whether an offer has been made is determined by an objective standard. The test is whether a reasonable person would assume that the power of acceptance had been conferred. Subjective intent is not important.

2) To constitute an offer, a proposal must be made with serious intent, not in anger or in jest.

3) Invitations to negotiate and preliminary negotiations do not constitute an offer. Distinguish language of commitment from phrases such as

   a) "Are you interested in . . . ?"
   b) "I'll probably take . . . ."

4) Advertisements, circulars, and catalogs are usually not offers but are invitations to submit offers.

   a) Catalogs, e.g., L.L. Bean, merely solicit offers. The mail-order catalog house may accept or reject the offer (order) based on such criteria as a quantity limitation or creditworthiness of the offeror.

   b) Many states have enacted statutes that require retail sellers to stock a sufficient supply of advertised goods to meet a reasonably expected demand for them or to issue rain checks.

   c) An advertisement can constitute an offer if it uses clear, definite, and explicit language leaving nothing open for negotiation.

      i) EXAMPLE: "To the first five customers on May 5th, we will sell a Model Z boat for $7,000 cash." The advertisement identifies offerees and contains language of commitment.

5) A price tag in a store is considered a quotation or an invitation, not an offer.

6) Notices of reward are treated as offers.

7) **Auctions**. If with reserve, the auctioneer may accept or reject all bids. If without reserve, the auctioneer is an offeror, and the bidders have the power of acceptance.

   a) Unless expressly advertised as without reserve, an auction is with reserve.

d. Generally, a contract must be reasonably definite as to all material terms and must set forth clearly all rights and duties of the parties.

   1) Essential terms generally include

      a) The names of the parties
      b) The subject matter involved
      c) The price and quantity
      d) The time and place of performance

   2) If a term is missing, it can be implied by the court (with the exception of a quantity term, which must be supplied by the parties). The presumption is that the parties intended to include a reasonable term.

   3) An agreement to agree does not fix an enforceable obligation.

      a) EXAMPLE: Richard leased a tractor for 1 year at $200 per month. The lease included an option to extend at monthly payments to be agreed upon. Lack of definiteness of a material term renders the renewal option unenforceable.

   4) If a contract does not specify the time of performance, courts will generally imply that performance within a reasonable time was intended.

5) **Price**. The common law has traditionally required a very specific degree of definiteness in contracts. A court will not imply the price of real estate.

    a) In contrast, the Uniform Commercial Code (UCC) permits a contract for the sale of goods to be made "in any manner sufficient to show agreement." Nearly every term of a sales contract can be implied, including price.

6) An agreement by a buyer to purchase the entire output of a seller's product for a specified period, or an agreement by a seller to supply a buyer with all of the buyer's requirements of specified goods, is enforceable under both the UCC and the Restatement of Contracts.

    a) The **Restatement of Contracts** is a scholarly treatise frequently referred to by courts as persuasive authority.

    b) The courts apply an objective standard based upon good faith by both parties; e.g., a buyer cannot expand his/her operations extraordinarily and demand that the seller supply all of his/her requirements.

7) A buyer and a seller may agree to an exclusive dealing in goods. Such an agreement imposes an obligation on the seller to use best efforts to supply the goods, and on the buyer to promote their sale.

2. **Termination of Offer**. An offer does not remain effective forever. Events which terminate an offer are discussed below. After termination, the power to accept the offer no longer exists.

    a. **Lapse of time**. An offer may be worded so as to terminate after a specified period or on a specified date. Unless otherwise terminated, the offer remains open for the specified time.

        1) If no time is stated in the offer, the offer will terminate after a reasonable period of time. What is reasonable depends on facts and circumstances, such as

            a) Previous dealings between the parties
            b) Custom in the industry
            c) The subject matter of the contract
            d) The means of communication

                i) EXAMPLE: An oral offer made in face-to-face conversation typically expires when the conversation ends.

    b. **Rejection** terminates the offer. It is a manifestation of intent not to accept the offer. It may be express or implied by words or conduct.

        1) Rejection is effective when received by the offeror.

            a) EXAMPLE: Lisa receives an offer from Dwight and mails a letter of rejection. Lisa changes her mind. Lisa could telephone Dwight and accept the offer before he receives the rejection.

        2) A **counteroffer** is both a proposal from the offeree and a rejection. It indicates a willingness to contract but with variation in one or more terms of the offer.

        3) In contrast, a mere inquiry about terms is tentative and does not indicate intent to reject the offer. It requests information while the offer is being considered.

            a) EXAMPLE: "Would you consider taking payments?"

4) A conditional acceptance purports to accept the offer but expressly makes acceptance conditional upon the offeror's assent to additional or different terms. Conditional acceptance is a counteroffer.

5) At common law, a counteroffer is a rejection and a new offer. An acceptance response had to match the offer exactly (the mirror image rule).

6) The UCC sets forth specific rules to follow with respect to the sale of goods between merchants.

c. **Revocation**. The offeror has the power to revoke (withdraw/cancel) an offer at any time prior to acceptance.

1) Revocation must be communicated to the offeree prior to acceptance.

2) Notice may be communicated by any means, directly or indirectly.

3) Revocation is effective when it is received by the offeree.

4) An offer stating it will remain open, e.g., for 30 days, may be terminated by giving the offeree notice that it is withdrawn.

a) EXAMPLE: Jen offers to sell her stereo to Ken. She tells him that he has 5 days to accept. Two days later, Quick tells Ken that he purchased it. The next day Ken mails an acceptance. There is no contract. The offer was effectively revoked when Ken learned of Jen's inability to sell the stereo.

5) An option contract gives rise to an irrevocable offer. In an option, the offeree exchanges something of value (consideration) for the offeror's promise to hold the offer open for a specified period of time. The offeror is precluded from revoking the offer during the stated option period. The option contract represents an

a) Offer that does not become a contract unless accepted
b) Option, which is a contract to hold the offer open for a specified time

6) **Firm offer rule**. A merchant who gives assurance in a signed writing that an offer to buy or sell goods will be held open is bound to keep the offer open for the stated period.

7) Certain offers are irrevocable under state statutes, such as

a) Bids made to a state, municipality, or other governmental organization

b) Preincorporation stock subscription agreements (may be irrevocable for 6 months)

8) An offer for a unilateral contract is accepted by the offeree completing the requested act.

d. **Death or incompetency** of either the offeror or the offeree generally terminates the power of acceptance, whether or not either party is aware of it.

1) Incompetence refers to a lack of legally required qualifications or fitness to discharge a required duty.

2) It does not terminate an offer contained in a valid option. The personal representative would have the right to exercise the option.

e. **Destruction** or loss of the specific subject matter of an offer terminates it.

f. **Illegality**. If a proposed contract or performance becomes illegal, the offer is terminated.

3.   **Acceptance** of an offer forms a contract.

  a.   The power of acceptance rests exclusively in the offeree, even if the offer does not require personal performance by the offeree.

  b.   An acceptance must relate to the terms of the offer and must be positive, unequivocal, and unconditional. It may not change, subtract from, add to, or qualify in any way the terms of the offer. This is known as the mirror image rule.

    1)   The common-law mirror image rule has been relaxed by the UCC for the sale of goods.

  c.   Acceptance is the manifestation of the offeree's assent to the offer. It must be communicated to the offeror. Communication of any combination of words and actions will be effective provided that a reasonable person would understand that an acceptance has been made. The test is objective. The offeree's subjective (personal) understanding does not control.

    1)   Taking possession of or exercising dominion over something may constitute acceptance.

      a)   EXAMPLE: Sal has a stack of firewood. Sal tells Mike, "If it's worth $100 to you, take it away." Mike hauls it away. The offeree who objectively manifests an intent to accept is not permitted to testify that his subjective intent was otherwise.

    2)   Silence is generally not acceptance. But silence accompanied by the appropriate circumstances from which assent can reasonably be inferred may constitute acceptance. Thus, silence coupled with inaction may constitute acceptance in context of the following:

      a)   Acceptance by the offeree of the benefit of offered services with reasonable opportunity to reject them and with reason to know that the offeror expects payment

      b)   Previous dealings (e.g., Book-of-the-Month Club)

      c)   Trade custom (e.g., failure to respond to an offer in a particular trade in which silence is considered acceptance)

  d.   A unilateral contract is accepted by performance.

    1)   The offeree need not notify the offeror of acceptance of a unilateral contract. The offeree need only begin to perform.

    2)   Courts have held that, if complete performance of a unilateral offer is necessary to accept, the offeree's making a substantial beginning of performance gives rise to an option contract, enabling the offeree to complete performance and thereby accept the offer.

  e.   If an offer for a bilateral contract requires acceptance to be communicated in a particular manner, such as in writing, the acceptance must be communicated in the manner specified or it will not be effective.

  f.   If the offer states nothing regarding the medium of acceptance, the offeree is implicitly authorized to accept by any reasonable medium, i.e., one that is

    1)   Used by the offeror

    2)   Customary in similar transactions

    3)   Appropriate under the particular circumstances, considering the prior dealings between offeror and offeree or the usage of trade

g. If the offer specifies a time for acceptance, the acceptance must be communicated within that time.

NOTE: A requirement in an offer that it must be accepted immediately or at once requires that acceptance be communicated within a reasonably short time, not instantaneously.

h. Under the deposited acceptance or mailbox rule, acceptance is effective at the moment of dispatch if the offeree has used an authorized medium of acceptance and the offer is still open.

   1) EXAMPLE: An offer is sent by mail. It does not specify a particular medium for acceptance. A letter of acceptance is dispatched (deposited in the mail). If it was properly addressed and had proper postage affixed, the acceptance is effective even if it never reaches the offeror.

   2) Generally, acceptance by an unauthorized mode is effective only upon receipt by the offeror (provided that the offer is still open).

   3) Under the mailbox rule,

      a) Once acceptance has been dispatched, it is effective, and the offer cannot be revoked.

      b) When an acceptance is dispatched following prior dispatch of a rejection, the acceptance is effective only if (and when) received by the offeror before receipt of the rejection.

         i) The first communication received by the offeror is effective.

      c) If the offeror expressly provides for a different result, acceptance is not effective upon dispatch.

         i) EXAMPLE: "Any acceptance is effective only when received in my office."

   4) After an offer terminates (expires), it cannot be validly accepted. A late or defective acceptance may constitute a new offer.

i. An offer, a revocation, a rejection, or a counteroffer is effective when it is received. But an acceptance is generally effective on dispatch.

j. Compliance with particular terms of an offer with respect to manner of acceptance may be waived by the offeror.

k. Generally, the validity of a contract is governed by the law of the state where the contract was formed.

   1) When the parties live in different states, the contract is enforceable in the state in which the acceptance becomes effective.

l. A contract is formed when an agreement is reached or when the agreement is put into writing and signed. If the parties did not make clear their intentions, a court will attempt to determine their intentions from all of the surrounding facts and circumstances, e.g.,

   1) Prior dealings between the parties
   2) The amount of money involved
   3) The number and complexity of the details
   4) The amount of time required for performance

4. Stop and review! You have completed the outline for this subunit. Study multiple-choice questions 1 through 10 beginning on page 226.

B.   Consideration. A basic requirement of an enforceable contract is legally sufficient consideration or a substitute for it. A promise unsupported by consideration is not enforceable.

1.   Consideration is something of value given in a bargained-for exchange, when the parties intend an exchange. Two elements must be present to satisfy the consideration requirement: legal sufficiency and bargained-for exchange.

2.   There is legally sufficient consideration to render a promise enforceable if the promisee incurs a legal detriment or the promisor receives a legal benefit.

   a.   The promisor makes the promise to the promisee.

   b.   To incur a legal detriment, the promisee must act in one of the ways specified below:

      1)   Do (or promise to do) something (s)he is not legally obligated to do

      2)   Refrain from doing (or promise to refrain from doing) something (s)he is legally privileged to do

   c.   By a promisee's legal detriment, the promisor gains a legal benefit.

      1)   EXAMPLE: Kid drives negligently and injures Sue. Kid says, "I'll pay you $5,000 not to sue me." Sue accepts. Sue gives up a legal right; she incurs a legal detriment, thereby giving Kid consideration that makes his promise enforceable by her. Kid receives a legal benefit: the right not to be sued by Sue.

   d.   Generally, any legal detriment, no matter how economically inadequate, is legally sufficient. Extreme inadequacy or inequality of consideration may be evidence of fraud, mistake, unconscionability, or a gift.

   e.   An agreement stating that a promise was made in consideration of an amount, e.g., $5, which was neither bargained for by the promisor nor paid by the promisee may be viewed as a sham without sufficient consideration.

   f.   Nominal (token) consideration, something almost devoid of value, e.g., $1, will generally not be sufficient.

   g.   An illusory promise (its literal terms impose no obligation on the promisor) is not sufficient.

      1)   EXAMPLE: Tex offers to sell to Bev as many barrels of oil as Bev might order at $28 a barrel. Bev accepts. Bev is not obligated to purchase any oil. Her promise is illusory.

      2)   An unrestricted right to cancel an agreement renders a promise illusory.

   h.   A promise to buy as much as needed in a business is not illusory. It is called a requirements contract. There is an objective standard for determining some minimum amount of purchase.

   i.   Distinguish motives. Love and affection may be motives for making a promise, but they do not represent the act of bargaining.

3.   **Bargained-for Exchange**. Consideration must be bargained for and given in exchange for the promise. The legal detriment is incurred by a party in exchange for the promise or performance by the other.

   a.   Purely social or gratuitous promises are not enforceable.

b. **Mutuality of obligation**. In a bilateral contract, each promise acts as the consideration for the other. The parties must be mutually obligated to perform their respective promises. Otherwise, the agreement lacks consideration and is not a valid contract.

c. **Past consideration** is not given in exchange for a promise to induce the promise. It is not consideration.

    1) EXAMPLE: Father said to Daughter, "Because you graduated, I promise to pay you $10,000 at the end of next month."

    2) The common law generally requires that an enforceable modification of a contract must be supported by new bargained-for consideration.

d. **Moral consideration**. Promises made out of a sense of honor or moral obligation are not enforceable if they lack the bargain element.

    1) EXAMPLE: An object falls. Quick pushes Slow out of its path, but it strikes Quick. Slow promises to pay Quick $500 a month for life.

4. **Preexisting Legal Duty**. Consideration does not exist if an existing duty was imposed by law or a person is already under a contractual obligation to render a specified performance but demands more or insists on doing less than originally promised.

a. EXAMPLE 1: Lee stole Bob's yacht. Snap, the county sheriff, witnessed the theft. Bob tells Snap, "I'll pay you $100 to arrest Lee." Snap arrests Lee. Snap suffered no new legal detriment.

b. EXAMPLE 2: A contractor tells a homeowner that unless she pays him an extra $500 he will leave her roof half repaired. The contractor has a preexisting duty to repair the entire roof.

c. Some courts and the Restatement of Contracts recognize an exception to the preexisting duty rule: Parties may modify an executory contract if the modification is fair and equitable in light of surrounding facts which were not anticipated by either party when the contract was entered into.

d. Part payment of a liquidated debt is not consideration for a promise by the creditor to accept the part payment as payment in full.

    1) An obligation is liquidated when there is no dispute about its existence or amount. The debt is undisputed if the debtor made an express promise to pay a specific sum of money or the obligation can (by computation) be reduced to a sum certain in money.

    2) Courts tend to find consideration if the debtor has done anything at all which might constitute new or additional consideration, e.g., promising to pay part before due.

    3) A disputed (unliquidated) debt is an obligation which is contested as to existence or amount. Thus, payment of less than the disputed amount (but not less than any amount that is not disputed) can constitute sufficient consideration.

    NOTE: Most courts have held that a creditor may cash a check marked "payment in full" and later seek the balance still owed, by writing the words "under protest" or "without prejudice" on the check.

        a) Under the UCC, accepting a check generally operates to discharge the debt to the extent of the amount of the check (on condition the check is honored).

5.   **Substitutes for Consideration.** An agreement may lack consideration but be enforceable on the basis of promissory estoppel, quasi-contract, public policy, or contracts under seal.

  a. **Promissory estoppel** means that a party is estopped to deny (prevented from denying) (s)he has an obligation. It always involves a gratuitous promise. There is no bargained-for consideration. The first and second Restatements of Contracts sets forth three requirements for promissory estoppel:

    1) A promise is given that the promisor should reasonably expect to induce action or forbearance by the promisee.

    2) The promise induces the action or forbearance.

    3) Injustice can be avoided only by enforcing the promise.

      a) EXAMPLE: Jim pledges to donate $5 million to the University of Georgia. The university begins construction of a new building. Jim retracts the pledge.

  b. The parties to a quasi-contract make no promises and reach no agreement. However, one of the parties is substantially benefited at the expense of the other party. And there is no adequate legal remedy.

    1) EXAMPLE: A doctor came upon an unconscious person on the sidewalk and rendered medical treatment. To avoid unjust enrichment, the patient must pay the doctor a reasonable fee even though the aid was unsolicited and no actual contract was entered into.

  c. Sometimes courts cite public policy to support enforcement of a promise despite lack of bargained-for consideration.

    1) If a debtor promises to pay a debt when collection is barred by the statute of limitations, courts hold the promise to pay enforceable without consideration.

      a) An enforceable promise to pay an entire debt is inferred from any partial payment accompanied by an acknowledgement of the larger debt.

      b) If the debtor does not make a partial payment, the mere promise to pay must generally be in writing and signed by the debtor to be enforceable.

    2) **Debts barred by a bankruptcy proceeding.** Promises to repay debts made by a debtor to a creditor during bankruptcy proceedings but prior to discharge may be enforceable without consideration.

      a) The bankruptcy court must first hold a hearing and explain that the debtor need not promise to repay the debt.

      b) Promises to pay a debt previously discharged in bankruptcy are unenforceable.

  d. **Contracts under seal.** At common law, a seal is a substitute for consideration. The requirements of a sealed promise are a writing, the seal, and delivery. Moreover, it must appear that the parties to the agreement intended it to be a sealed instrument.

    1) Statutes of many states have abolished any distinction between sealed and unsealed contracts.

NOTE: Modern trends permit the word "seal" or the letters "L.S." (*locus sigilli*) to constitute a valid seal. Many attorneys incorporate a recital of a common phrase to substitute for a seal; e.g., "In witness whereof I have hereunto set my hand and seal."

6. Stop and review! You have completed the outline for this subunit. Study multiple-choice questions 11 through 17 beginning on page 229.

C. Statute of Frauds

1. **The Required Writing**. An oral contract is usually enforceable. However, the statute of frauds requires that some contracts be in writing to be enforceable. They are within the statute and must therefore comply with its requirements.

    a. Generally, a written memorandum complies with the statute if it contains

        1) A reasonably certain description of the parties
        2) A reasonably certain description of the subject matter
        3) The terms and conditions of the contract
        4) A recitation of the consideration
        5) The signature of the party to be charged

    b. No particular form is required. The writing may be in the form of a letter, a receipt, an invoice, a check, or an entry in a diary.

    c. The agreement may consist of several writings if one is signed and the facts and circumstances clearly indicate that they all relate to the same transaction.

    d. The signature may consist of any symbol or mark made with an intention to authenticate the writing as that of the signatory, e.g., initials, stamp, etc.

        1) Signatures need not appear at any particular place on the memorandum unless the statute provides otherwise.

    e. Most state statutes expressly allow the memorandum to be signed by an authorized agent. Oral authorization is generally sufficient.

    f. There is no requirement that the memorandum be completed at the time that the contract is made.

    g. An oral agreement to rescind an executory written contract is generally valid, even if the contract is one required by the statute of frauds to be in writing.

2. **Contracts within the Statute**. The signed writing requirement applies only if a contract is within the statute. Contracts within the statute are described below.

    a. **Agreements for sale of an interest in land**. "An interest" is broad: sales, long-term leases (more than 1 year), mortgages, easements, and options.

        1) Improvements and new structures are part of the land.

        2) Courts generally agree that growing crops, e.g., corn, are personal property, whereas items that grow spontaneously, e.g., grass and timber, are an integral part of the land and are real property.

            a) After grass or timber has been cut, it is treated as personal property.

            UCC NOTE: Under the UCC, contracts for the sale of growing crops and timber are considered contracts for the sale of personal property.

        3) A contract to construct a building is not an interest in land.

        4) A contract whereby a broker is engaged to market real property (a real estate listing contract) is not a contract for the sale of an interest in land.

b. **Agreements not performable within 1 year**. They cannot be fully performed within 1 year of the making of the contract. Mere possibility that they may be performed within 1 year removes them from the statute.

  1) The day the contract is made is excluded, and the 1-year period expires at the close of the contract's express termination date.

  2) EXAMPLE: John orally contracts to maintain Mary's truck for as long as she owns it. The contract may be enforceable. If John contracted to maintain her vehicle for the next 4 years, the contract is unenforceable unless evidenced by a writing.

c. **Agreements for sale of goods over $500**. The UCC provides that a contract for the sale of goods for the price of $500 or more is not enforceable unless there is some writing sufficient to indicate that a contract for sale has been made between the parties.

  1) Goods are defined as movable personal property.

  2) The basic rule has many exceptions which are covered in Study Unit 16, Sales.

d. **Agreements to answer for the debt of another**. Under the suretyship provision of the statute of frauds, the promise of one to answer for the debt of another must be in writing.

  1) **Exception**. Under the main purpose or leading object rule, no writing is required if the main purpose is to obtain a substantial benefit for the promisor, as opposed to guaranteeing a third party's debt.

  2) A primary promise is one to pay or perform one's own obligation. A secondary promise is one to answer for the debt of another.

  a) The secondary, not the primary, promise must be in a signed writing.

  3) Thus, a promise made by the surety to the debtor (as opposed to the promise made by the surety to the creditor) is not within the statute.

e. **Agreements of an executor or an administrator**. A promise of an executor of an estate (or an administrator if there is no will) to pay a debt of the decedent out of the executor's (or administrator's) own funds, must be evidenced by a signed writing.

f. **Agreements made in contemplation of marriage**. A promise to marry is made in consideration for some promise other than a reciprocal promise to marry. But mutual promises to marry are not within the statute.

3. **Alternatives to the Writing Requirement**. The purpose of the statute of frauds is to prevent fraud and perjury by requiring evidence more reliable than memories of oral conversation. Courts and legislatures apply alternatives to the writing requirement to prevent injustice.

a. Full performance by both sides to an oral contract removes the contract from within the statute.

b. When only one party has fully performed, the majority view is that lack of written evidence of the agreement does not preclude enforcement. The party who fully performed may bring suit.

  1) Under the minority view, contract damages or specific performance is typically not available. The plaintiff might recover in quasi-contract for the reasonable value of the benefit conferred on the nonperforming party.

    c.   Under the doctrine of equitable estoppel, if one party to a contract has misrepresented (or concealed) a material fact and the other party has relied on the misrepresentation to his/her detriment, the party who made the misrepresentation is estopped from relying on the statute as a defense. This doctrine is also called detrimental reliance.

        1)   EXAMPLE: Bill tells Snap, "I typed and signed a memorandum of our oral agreement and mailed you a copy," when he has not. Bill may be estopped from denying a contract was formed.

    d.   Under the doctrine of part performance, an oral contract for the sale of land may be enforced when the contract has been partially performed, if the purchaser takes action which is "unequivocally referable to the oral agreement" and has reasonably relied on the agreement to his/her substantial detriment.

        1)   Typically, one must show that the purchaser

            a)   Paid money or rendered services, and either
            b)   Took possession of the land, or
            c)   Made valuable improvements on the land.

        2)   If part performance is established, a court may grant specific performance because it may be considered a quasi-contract.

    e.   Under the UCC, a writing is only one of several ways to evidence a contract for the sale of goods. Other ways include

        1)   Part performance of an oral contract
        2)   Admission in court that the contract exists
        3)   Prior dealings between merchants
        4)   A written confirmation after formation

4.   Stop and review! You have completed the outline for this subunit. Study multiple-choice questions 18 through 25 beginning on page 231.

D. Capacity and Legality

1.   **Minors** can make contracts. However, a minor's contract is voidable (not void) by the minor. The minor may repudiate it. Until repudiation, (s)he is liable. The other party is bound to the agreement (unless (s)he also lacks legal capacity).

    a.   In most states, a natural person under the age of 18 is a minor. How old (s)he looks or how experienced (s)he is, is irrelevant to the power to repudiate.

    b.   Power to repudiate continues until a reasonable time after reaching majority.

        1)   Any unequivocal act that indicates an intent to repudiate is sufficient.

        2)   When the contract has been partially or wholly executed, the minor must, if possible, return any consideration received from the other party. But, if the consideration has been used up, lost, or destroyed, most courts do not require the minor to pay the other party.

    c.   Public policy supports enforcement of certain contracts entered into by minors, e.g., military enlistment and auto insurance contracts. Some jurisdictions do not allow repudiation of a real estate transaction until the minor reaches the age of majority.

d. A minor who enters into a contract for necessaries may repudiate. To prevent unjust enrichment, quasi-contract renders the minor liable.

  1) Food, lodging, medical services, and education are typically necessaries.

  2) Liability under quasi-contract theory is based on

  a) Necessaries actually furnished (not contract expectations)
  b) Reasonable value (not the contract price)

  3) If a parent or guardian is furnishing the minor's reasonable needs, quasi-contract is not applied.

e. **Third parties**. If a minor sells goods to an adult, the adult obtains voidable title to the goods. The minor can repudiate and recover possession from the adult buyer.

  1) One who subsequently purchased the property from the adult could not retain it.

  a) The UCC modified this rule such that a person with voidable title to goods has the "power to transfer a good title to a good-faith purchaser for value."

  b) The common-law rule still applies to sales of real property by minors. The minor must return all remaining consideration. And the adult is liable on the deed to the good-faith purchaser.

f. A contract entered into by a minor may be ratified by the minor after (s)he has reached the age of majority.

  1) Ratification may be either explicit or implied. The "minor" affirms the contract and loses the right to repudiate based on minority.

  2) Ratification is all or nothing. Thus, ratification is of all the terms of the contract.

  3) A contract is ratified if the minor retains the consideration for an unreasonable time after (s)he reaches majority.

  4) Ratification may result from accepting benefits incidental to ownership, such as rents, dividends, or interest.

  5) Selling the property constitutes ratification by the minor.

2. **Mental Incompetence**. An incompetent person is one whose mental capacity is such that (s)he is unable to understand the nature and consequences of his/her acts. A mental disease does not necessarily render a person incompetent.

a. If a person was adjudicated insane or otherwise incompetent before the contract was entered into, the contract is void and cannot be ratified (even after the person is later adjudged competent).

b. If a person is adjudged to have been insane or otherwise incompetent at the actual time the contract was entered into, but there was no adjudication of incompetence prior to that time, the contract is voidable (later ratification is possible).

c. Courts permit repudiation of executory contracts only if the other party may be restored to the position (s)he occupied prior to the contract.

d. Incompetents are generally liable for contracts involving necessaries to the same extent as are minors.

3. **Intoxication**. If mental capacity is lacking, even if the intoxication is voluntary, the contract is voidable at the option of the intoxicated person.

    a. It must be shown that the intoxicated person's reason and judgment were impaired to such an extent that (s)he did not understand the legal consequences of his/her actions. Otherwise, (s)he may not avoid the contract.

4. **Legal Purpose**. Requisite to an enforceable contract is legality of purpose. Contracts are illegal if they are inconsistent with the Constitution, violate a statute or other rule of law, or are against public policy as declared by the courts.

    a. A promise to commit a tort or to induce the commission of a tort is void on grounds of public policy.

    b. Likewise, agreements to commit a crime are void.

    c. EXAMPLE: An employer promises not to press criminal charges. The promise is not enforceable. The state prosecutes violations of criminal statutes. It is public policy to protect the interests of society.

5. **Statutory Violation**. An agreement that cannot be performed without violating a statute is void.

    a. The fact that some illegal act is committed during the performance of a contract does not render the contract itself illegal. If the formation of the contract violated no law and the contract could be performed without violating any law, the contract is enforceable.

    b. A party who agrees to supply goods or services, unaware that the thing supplied will be used for an unlawful purpose, can enforce the agreement. However, a person who intends to accomplish an unlawful purpose may not enforce a contract made for the purpose of enabling him/her to accomplish the unlawful purpose.

    c. Most states have adopted statutes that prohibit gambling agreements. But many states now permit specific types of regulated gambling.

    d. Some states have blue laws that forbid certain business transactions on Sunday.

6. **Usury laws** specify the highest rate at which interest may be charged for the use of money. Under some state statutes, a usurious contract is absolutely void, and the lender can recover neither principal nor interest. Other states permit recovery of principal and interest up to the legally permitted rate only.

7. **Licensing statutes** require a person to obtain a license to carry on a designated trade or business, subject to fine, imprisonment, or both.

    a. The statute itself may provide that an unlicensed person is not entitled to recover for services rendered.

    b. Even if a statute, regulatory in nature, does not so provide, a person cannot recover for services unless (s)he holds the required license.

        1) A regulatory statute is one enacted for the protection of the public against unqualified or incompetent persons.

        2) Distinguish a licensing statute from a revenue collection statute enacted merely to collect revenue, e.g., vendor's license. Recovery may be possible even if the service provider did not have the license required by the statute.

8. **Effects of Illegality**. As a general rule, courts will not assist either party to an illegal agreement. The court will leave the parties as it finds them.

   a. The general rule is that an illegal term taints the whole agreement, rendering it void.

   b. If an agreement is divisible, most courts will enforce the legal portion.

   c. If an agreement containing an illegal portion has been partially performed and the illegal portion has not yet been performed, the party who has rendered performance can withdraw from the bargain and recover the performance or its value.

   d. If one of the parties is less at fault than the other, (s)he may be allowed to recover payments made or property transferred. This might occur if one party is induced by another to enter into an illegal bargain by fraud, duress, or undue influence.

   e. An agreement which appears to be legal on its face may, nonetheless, be illegal due to facts and circumstances of which one party is unaware.

      1) EXAMPLE: Mutual promises to marry when, unknown to the man, the woman is already married. Performance would constitute the crime of bigamy.

      2) Most courts ignore the underlying illegality and allow the ignorant (innocent) party to sue the other for damages.

9. **Contracts in restraint of trade** restrict competition or otherwise interfere with the normal flow of goods or services.

   a. An agreement to refrain from a particular trade, profession, or business may be valid if

      1) The purpose of the restraint is to protect an ancillary property interest of the promisee, and

      2) The restraint is no more extensive in scope and duration than is reasonably necessary to protect that property interest.

   b. The reasonableness of restraint is a question of fact determined from all the circumstances. The restraint may cover territory, time, scope of activities, or all of these, but it must be reasonable.

   c. The buyer of a business may bargain with the seller for his/her promise not to compete with the buyer, as part of the contract for the sale of the business, to ensure recovery of his/her investment in goodwill.

      1) Courts will not enforce a restraint that is more than necessary to recapture the investment.

   d. An employment contract may include an agreement not to compete, during or after the period of employment, prohibiting the employee from

      1) Setting up a business in competition with the (former) employer
      2) Entering the employment of a competitor
      3) Revealing the (former) employer's trade secrets (nondisclosure agreement)

   e. To determine whether the duration, territory, and scope are reasonable, a court considers the

      1) Degree of hardship imposed on the employee
      2) Harm to the public resulting from the reduced competition
      3) Validity of the employer's need to prevent the competition

      NOTE: Courts have the power to rewrite the duration, territory, and scope of activities provisions to make them reasonable.

f.   A court order enjoining the former employee from competing in the described territory for the stated period of time is the typical method for enforcement.

10. Exculpatory clauses are contractual terms that excuse one party from liability for injury or damage caused by his/her own acts. They are frequently challenged as violating public policy.

a.   Generally, courts will not enforce an exculpatory clause that excuses a party from his/her own criminal conduct, intentional torts, or gross negligence.

b.   If one party has a decidedly weaker bargaining position, a contract that relieves the dominant party of liability for negligence may be held invalid as contrary to public policy. But, if both parties have approximately equal bargaining power, the courts are more likely to uphold an exculpatory clause.

c.   A contract of adhesion is one formed between parties with so great a disparity of bargaining power that the weaker party's only choice is to accept the terms imposed by the stronger party or to forgo the transaction.

1)   Most such contracts are upheld. They are considered a necessary evil in complex business.

2)   However, courts have invalidated entire contracts or clauses in contracts by holding that such a contract or clause is contrary to public policy.

11. **Unconscionability.** A court may scrutinize any contract to determine whether, given all the facts and circumstances, the effect is unconscionable. By most accepted definitions, unconscionability relates to unscrupulous or unreasonable activity.

a.   If a contract or a term thereof is unconscionable at the time the contract is made, a court may refuse to enforce the contract, may enforce the remainder of the contract without the unconscionable term, or may so limit the application of any unconscionable term as to avoid any unconscionable result.

12. Stop and review! You have completed the outline for this subunit. Study multiple-choice questions 26 through 31 beginning on page 234.

E.   **Mutual Assent.** When there has been, objectively, manifestation of mutual assent, a party to the contract may have the right to rescind if the assent was not genuine.

1.   **Fraud.** A contract induced by fraud is voidable.

a.   **Fraud in the execution** occurs when the signature of a party is obtained by a fraudulent misrepresentation that directly relates to the signing of the document. The purported contract is void.

b.   **Fraud in the inducement.** The defrauded party is aware of entering into a contract, and intends to do so, but is deceived about some aspect of the contract. The underlying consideration is misrepresented, i.e., the nature or quality of the goods or services. The contract is voidable.

c.   The elements of actionable fraud vary from state to state. However, proof of the following elements is generally required:

1)   A false representation (or concealment) of a material fact
2)   Intent to misrepresent (scienter)
3)   Intent to induce reliance
4)   Reliance by the innocent party on the false statement or concealment
5)   Justifiable reliance by the innocent party
6)   Damage (loss) suffered by the innocent party

d.   Fraud requires an actual or implied misrepresentation of a fact. Misrepresentation may be expressly spoken or written words; it can be implied from conduct.

1)   A statement of opinion is not usually subject to a claim of fraud. A fact is objective and verifiable; an opinion is generally subject to debate.

a)   EXAMPLE: "This car will last forever." Sellers are given latitude in puffing their wares.

2)   When a purchaser relies on a so-called expert's opinion, the innocent party may be entitled to rescission or reformation of the contract.

3)   Misrepresentations of future events are not fraud. Statements of probabilities and predictions of future business results do not usually give rise to fraud.

a)   EXAMPLE: Mechanic estimates tune-up will increase gas mileage by 25%.

4)   Misrepresentations of law generally do not entitle a party to be relieved of a contract. Everyone is presumed to know the law and to have equal means of obtaining knowledge of the law.

e.   Usually neither party to a contract has a duty to come forth and disclose facts. The parties to a contract are required to exercise ordinary business sense in their dealings. However, in at least the following three situations, there is an affirmative duty to disclose; failure to do so constitutes actionable fraud.

1)   A fiduciary relationship exists between the parties. (A fiduciary has a legal duty to act primarily for the benefit of another in matters of his/her undertaking. It is a position of trust.)

2)   A material fact is known by one party, and the other could not reasonably discover it. Had the unknowing party known the fact, there would have been no agreement.

3)   A person misstates an important fact. (S)he must correct the statement when negotiations are renewed or as soon as (s)he learns of the misstatement.

f.   The misrepresentation must be material, i.e., a factor important in inducing the party to enter into the contract.

g.   **Scienter** refers to knowledge of the falsity, or utter disregard for the truth, when making a statement.

h.   The deceived party must have a justifiable reason for relying on the misrepresentation.

i.   For a tort claim based on fraud, injury must have been caused by the misrepresentation.

j.   The injured party may ask for damages or for rescission of the entire contract. The injured party can seek monetary damages.

1)   Rescission seeks to return the parties to the positions they would have occupied if the contract had not been made.

2.   **Innocent Misrepresentation**. The elements of fraud, other than scienter, are present. There was a false representation of a material fact, intended to be relied upon, and reasonably relied upon. It can be oral, written, or implied from conduct.

a.   Rescission is the only remedy available.

3.   **Mistake** is an unintended act, omission, or error that arises in the formation of a contract.

    a.   Only mistakes of fact have legal significance. Distinguish them from mistakes in judgment of value or quality.

    b.   A mutual mistake occurs when both parties to a contract are mistaken about the same material fact.

        1)   A material fact is one that is important and central to the contract. It is a basis of the bargain.

        2)   EXAMPLE: Cal has two dogs. Curt wants to buy one. Cal agrees to sell one for $100. Cal believes he agreed to sell the brown dog. Curt believes he has just purchased the black one.

        3)   Mutual mistake of material fact is grounds for rescission or is a sufficient defense for failure to perform the contract.

    c.   If only one party to a contract acts on the basis of a mistaken belief or assumption, it is a unilateral mistake. That party is generally not relieved from contractual obligation. But limited circumstances in which a unilateral mistake of a material fact may justify rescission include

        1)   The other party knew or should have known of the mistake. The mistake is obvious; a reasonable person would suspect a mistake was made.

        2)   Enforcement would result in extreme hardship such that injustice would occur (provided the parties can be returned to the positions they held prior to the contract).

        3)   The error was due to mathematical mistake or omission of items in computing the cost of the contract (provided the error was inadvertent and without gross negligence).

4.   **Duress** occurs when one party, by means of threats or actions, instills fear or apprehension in the other party so as to deny that party's exercise of free will.

    a.   The Restatement (second) of Contracts (a scholarly treatise frequently referred to by courts) describes two forms of duress:

        1)   "If conduct that appears to be a manifestation of assent by a party who does not intend to engage in that conduct is physically compelled by duress, the conduct is not effective as a manifestation of assent."

           a)   Threats of violence render the contract voidable.

        2)   "If a party's manifestation of assent is induced by an improper threat by the other party that leaves the victim no reasonable alternative, the contract is voidable by the victim."

    b.   Sales pressure or hard selling is not duress.

    c.   However, the threat need not be of violence, an illegal act, a tort, or a breach of contract. If made in bad faith and with an ulterior motive, a threat based on a legal right may be improper, e.g., a threat to foreclose on a mortgage.

    d.   **Economic duress.** Courts recognize that, if one party exerts extreme economic pressure that leaves the threatened party with no real alternative but to comply, it may constitute duress.

        1)   Such duress arises from threats of economic harm if the buyer does not accept the seller's terms.

        2)   Merely taking advantage of another's financial difficulty, however, is not duress. Rather, the person alleging financial difficulty must allege that it was contributed to or caused by the one accused of coercion.

5. **Undue Influence**. If one party to a contract so dominates the other party as to deprive the latter of free will, the contract may be voidable as a result of undue influence.

    a.   A fiduciary relationship, such as between a trusted lawyer, doctor, or guardian and a weaker party, most often gives rise to such a claim.

        1)   When the dominant party is the beneficiary of a contract with the weaker, it is presumed that the contract was the result of undue influence. The burden of proof is on the dominant party to prove otherwise.

    b.   A fiduciary relationship is not essential to a claim of undue influence. Although difficult to prove, a case may arise in the context of emotionally or romantically involved parties.

6. Stop and review! You have completed the outline for this subunit. Study multiple-choice questions 32 through 40 beginning on page 236.

F.   **Interpreting a Contract**. To resolve disputes, courts apply general rules of construction to interpret the language of a contract and determine its effect.

1. A contract is interpreted as a whole.

    a.   All writings that are part of the same transaction are interpreted together.

    b.   Specific clauses are subordinated to the contract's general intent.

    c.   But if specific clauses directly contradict general clauses, weight is given to specifics.

    d.   If terms and clauses appear inconsistent, written or typed provisions take priority over printed form provisions.

    e.   If words conflict with figures or numerals, the words prevail.

2. Words used in a contract are given their plain meaning.

    a.   Technical terms are given their technical meaning when used in a technical transaction.

3. Words and other conduct are interpreted in light of all surrounding circumstances. Wherever possible, courts give weight to any relevant dealings between parties with respect to

    a.   Course of performance (under the contract at issue)
    b.   Course of dealing (prior contracts between same parties)
    c.   Usage of trade (trade custom and practice)

4. An interpretation that gives an agreement full force and effect is preferred over one that renders all or part of it unreasonable, unlawful, or void.

    a.   Courts can supply a term to save an agreement (there must first be a valid agreement) but not to make an agreement for the parties.

    b.   When a contract is ambiguous and two reasonable interpretations are possible, the contract is interpreted more strictly against the party who drafted it and such that neither party gains unreasonable advantage over the other.

    c.   An interpretation that favors a public interest is preferred over one that favors a private interest.

5. Generally, and unless it specifically states otherwise, a contract is governed by the law of the state having the most significant contracts with the transaction.

6. **Parol evidence rule** is a rule of substantive contract law, not a rule of evidence. The rule renders evidence of a prior or contemporaneous understanding of the parties (whether expressed in writing or orally) inadmissible if offered to contradict or modify the terms of a written agreement.

    a. A **completely integrated agreement** is one stated by the parties to be an exhaustive and exclusive statement of all the terms of the agreement.

        1) An integration clause states that the parties intend that the writing constitutes the entire and final agreement and that all prior negotiations and agreements are merged in the writing.

        2) A completely integrated agreement may not be contradicted or supplemented by evidence of prior written or oral negotiations or agreements, or contemporaneous oral agreements.

    b. A **partially integrated agreement** states something less than the complete understanding of the parties.

        1) A partially integrated agreement may not be contradicted but may be supplemented with consistent additional terms of prior negotiations or agreements, whether written or oral.

7. **Exceptions.** Parol evidence is admissible to show or explain

    a. A circumstance under which the written agreement is void, voidable, or unenforceable, e.g., based on capacity, fraud, duress, undue influence, mistake, or illegality of purpose

    b. The existence or nonexistence of a condition precedent, i.e., that performance is dependent on occurrence of an event

    c. Ambiguous terms in the contract, but not to contradict or vary the terms of the contract

    d. Typographical or obvious drafting errors which clearly do not represent the intention of the parties

    e. Custom and usage not inconsistent with the agreement

        1) Custom refers to custom within the industry.

        2) Usage refers to a method of dealing regularly observed and followed among members of a vocation or trade in a particular place.

8. Parol evidence may be used to prove the existence of any prior or contemporaneous separate agreement.

    a. If it is reasonable to assume that the parties' intent was a collateral agreement to be separate as opposed to included in the same contract, then parol evidence is admissible to prove the existence and terms of the separate agreement.

9. The parol evidence rule does not apply to statements after the written contract was signed.

    a. Extrinsic evidence is admissible to prove modification, rescission, etc.
    b. A term common in contracts requires that any modification be in writing.

10. Note that, theoretically, the parol evidence rule does not apply to a contract if the parties do not intend the writing to be the entire agreement, but a court may view what has been reduced to writing as the complete agreement.

11. Stop and review! You have completed the outline for this subunit. Study multiple-choice questions 41 through 45 beginning on page 239.

MULTIPLE-CHOICE QUESTIONS

A. Offer and Acceptance

1. On September 10, Harris, Inc., a new car dealer, placed a newspaper advertisement stating that Harris would sell 10 cars at its showroom for a special discount only on September 12, 13, and 14. On September 12, King called Harris and expressed an interest in buying one of the advertised cars. King was told that five of the cars had been sold and that King should come to the showroom as soon as possible. On September 13, Harris made a televised announcement that the sale would end at 10:00 p.m. that night. King went to Harris's showroom on September 14 and demanded the right to buy a car at the special discount. Harris had sold the 10 cars and refused King's demand. King sued Harris for breach of contract. Harris's best defense to King's suit would be that Harris's

A. Offer was unenforceable.

B. Advertisement was not an offer.

C. Television announcement revoked the offer.

D. Offer had not been accepted.

The correct answer is (B). *(CPA, adapted)*

REQUIRED: The legal effect of a newspaper advertisement quoting sales prices.

DISCUSSION: Newspaper advertisements that merely cite prices on items in stock are invitations to negotiate, not offers. In rare instances, an advertisement may be so definite and manifest such clear intent that it constitutes an offer and not a solicitation of offers, e.g., a promise to give one mink stole for $1 to the first person requesting it on April 5.

Answers (A), (C), and (D) are incorrect because the advertisement was only an invitation seeking offers.

2. Ann Mayer wrote Tom Jackson and offered to sell Jackson a building for $200,000. The offer stated it would expire 30 days from July 1. Mayer changed her mind and does not wish to be bound by the offer. If a legal dispute arises between the parties regarding whether there has been a valid acceptance of the offer, which of the following is correct?

A. The offer cannot be legally withdrawn for the stated period of time.

B. The offer will not expire prior to the 30 days even if Mayer sells the property to a third person and notifies Jackson.

C. If Jackson phoned Mayer on August 1 and unequivocally accepted the offer, a contract would be formed, provided Jackson had no notice of withdrawal of the offer.

D. If Jackson categorically rejects the offer on July 10th, Jackson cannot validly accept within the remaining stated period of time.

The correct answer is (D). *(CPA, adapted)*

REQUIRED: The correct statement as to termination of an offer.

DISCUSSION: Rejection of an offer terminates it. An offeree cannot accept an offer after rejection is effective. An attempted acceptance after rejection is a new offer.

Answer (A) is incorrect because the offer may be legally withdrawn at any time prior to acceptance even though it states it will be held open for a specified period. It is not a firm offer under the UCC because it is not for a sale of goods. Answer (B) is incorrect because notice to the offeree of sale of the property to a third person has the effect of terminating the offer. Answer (C) is incorrect because acceptance on August 1st would be ineffective. The time provided for acceptance expires on July 31.

3. Which of the following statements concerning the effectiveness of an offeree's rejection and an offeror's revocation of an offer are ordinarily correct?

	An Offeree's Rejection Is Effective When	An Offeror's Revocation Is Effective When
A.	Received by offeror	Sent by offeror
B.	Sent by offeree	Received by offeree
C.	Sent by offeree	Sent by offeror
D.	Received by offeror	Received by offeree

The correct answer is (D). *(CPA, adapted)*

REQUIRED: The true statements about the effectiveness of an offeree's rejection and an offeror's revocation of an offer.

DISCUSSION: The general rule is that a revocation of an offer is effective when received by the offeree. Receipt occurs when the revocation comes into possession of the offeree or his/her agent, or when it is delivered to his/her office. Similarly, a rejection must actually be received to be effective. Only an acceptance can be effective upon dispatch.

Answers (A), (B), and (C) are incorrect because a rejection, like a revocation, becomes effective upon receipt.

4. On July 1, Silk, Inc. sent Blue a telegram offering to sell Blue a building for $80,000. In the telegram, Silk stated that it would give Blue 30 days to accept the offer. On July 15, Blue sent Silk a telegram that included the following statement: "The price for your building seems too high. Would you consider taking $75,000?" This telegram was received by Silk on July 16. On July 19, Tint made an offer to Silk to purchase the building for $82,000. Upon learning of Tint's offer, Blue, on July 27, sent Silk a signed letter agreeing to purchase the building for $80,000. This letter was received by Silk on July 29. However, Silk now refuses to sell Blue the building. If Blue commences an action against Silk for breach of contract, Blue will

- A. Win, because Blue effectively accepted Silk's offer of July 1.

- B. Win, because Silk was obligated to keep the offer open for the 30-day period.

- C. Lose, because Blue sent the July 15 telegram.

- D. Lose, because Blue used an unauthorized means of communication.

The correct answer is (A). *(CPA, adapted)*

REQUIRED: The outcome when the offeree has made both an inquiry about terms and an acceptance.

DISCUSSION: An attempt by the offeree to vary an offer operates as a rejection that terminates the offer and a counteroffer. But it is reasonable to construe Blue's telegram as a mere inquiry about terms because the telegram is tentative and does not indicate intent to reject the offer. Blue was still considering the offer. Also, Blue's knowledge of Tint's offer did not revoke the offer. Termination of the offer prior to acceptance, e.g., by a sale to Tint communicated to Blue, would have revoked the offer. Blue should prevail because it validly accepted an offer that had not terminated by lapse of time, rejection, or revocation.

Answer (B) is incorrect because Silk received no consideration to keep the offer open. Answer (C) is incorrect because, if the telegram was an inquiry rather than a counteroffer, it did not terminate the offer. Answer (D) is incorrect because a reasonable means of acceptance may be used if a particular method is not stipulated by the offeror.

5. On June 15, Peters orally offered to sell a used lawn mower to Mason for $125. Peters specified that Mason had until June 20 to accept the offer. On June 16, Peters received an offer to purchase the lawn mower for $150 from Bronson, Mason's neighbor. Peters accepted Bronson's offer. On June 17, Mason saw Bronson using the lawn mower and was told the mower had been sold to Bronson. Mason immediately wrote to Peters to accept the June 15 offer. Which of the following statements is correct?

- A. Mason's acceptance would be effective when received by Peters.

- B. Mason's acceptance would be effective when mailed.

- C. Peters' offer had been revoked and Mason's acceptance was ineffective.

- D. Peters was obligated to keep the June 15 offer open until June 20.

The correct answer is (C). *(CPA, adapted)*

REQUIRED: The result when the offeree communicates acceptance after the subject matter was sold.

DISCUSSION: An offeror has the power to revoke (cancel) an offer at any time prior to acceptance. Exceptions arise when there is an option contract or a merchant of goods makes a written commitment to keep an offer open. To be effective, revocation must be communicated to the offeree prior to acceptance. Notice of revocation may be indirectly communicated. Sale of the subject matter was an exercise of the power of revocation. It was effective when the offeree received communication of it, i.e., when the offeree was told it had been sold.

Answers (A) and (B) are incorrect because, having received notice of revocation prior to dispatch of acceptance, Mason could by no means effect acceptance. Answer (D) is incorrect because no consideration was provided to keep the offer open. Furthermore, the UCC firm offer rule applies only to a written offer made by a merchant.

6. Opal offered, in writing, to sell Larkin a parcel of land for $300,000. If Opal dies, the offer will

- A. Terminate prior to Larkin's acceptance only if Larkin received notice of Opal's death.

- B. Remain open for a reasonable period of time after Opal's death.

- C. Automatically terminate despite Larkin's prior acceptance.

- D. Automatically terminate prior to Larkin's acceptance.

The correct answer is (D). *(CPA, adapted)*

REQUIRED: The effect of the death of the offeror.

DISCUSSION: Prior to effective acceptance, an offeror may revoke the offer by words or conduct. An offer is also terminated by operation of law under certain circumstances. Death or incompetence of either the offeror or the offeree generally terminates the power of acceptance. But it does not terminate an offer contained in a valid option contract.

Answer (A) is incorrect because an offer terminates by operation of law upon the death of the offeror or the offeree, whether or not either party is aware of it. Answer (B) is incorrect because a power of acceptance does not extend beyond the death of the offeror or the offeree, unless it is in an option contract. Answer (C) is incorrect because a contract is formed upon acceptance. A contract, generally, is not terminated upon the death of a party to it.

7. Kay, an art collector, promised Hammer, an art student, that if Hammer could obtain certain rare artifacts within 2 weeks, Kay would pay for Hammer's postgraduate education. At considerable effort and expense, Hammer obtained the specified artifacts within the 2-week period. When Hammer requested payment, Kay refused. Kay claimed that there was no consideration for the promise. Hammer would prevail against Kay based on

A. Unilateral contract.

B. Unjust enrichment.

C. Public policy.

D. Quasi-contract.

The correct answer is (A). *(CPA, adapted)*
REQUIRED: The basis for enforcing a promise conditioned on performance only.
DISCUSSION: Kay's promise is an offer to form a unilateral contract. Acceptance is expected and can only be by performance. Once accepted, there is a contract enforceable against the unilateral offeror. The consideration supporting enforcement of Kay's promise is Hammer's performance.
Answers (B) and (D) are incorrect because, when there is no adequate remedy at law, equity will impose an obligation on a party unjustly enriched at the expense of another. This remedy is referred to as quasi-contract. Damages for breach of a unilateral contract is a remedy at law. Answer (C) is incorrect because, in context, public policy refers to a basis for enforcing a promise when an element necessary to formation of a valid contract is lacking, e.g., a minor's insurance contract. But there is a basis in contract law to enforce Kay's promise.

8. On February 12, Harris sent Fresno a written offer to purchase Fresno's land. The offer included the following provision: "Acceptance of this offer must be by registered or certified mail, received by Harris no later than February 18 by 5:00 p.m. CST." On February 18, Fresno sent Harris a letter accepting the offer by private overnight delivery service. Harris received the letter on February 19. Which of the following statements is correct?

A. A contract was formed on February 19.

B. Fresno's letter constituted a counteroffer.

C. Fresno's use of the overnight delivery service was an effective form of acceptance.

D. A contract was formed on February 18 regardless of when Harris actually received Fresno's letter.

The correct answer is (B). *(CPA, adapted)*
REQUIRED: The result of acceptance by a means other than that required in an offer.
DISCUSSION: The offeror is the master of the offer. To the extent (s)he expressly limits what constitutes effective acceptance, it is limited under both common law and the UCC. The mailbox rule operates only to the extent the offeror does not expressly provide for a different result.
Answer (A) is incorrect because a contract could not have been formed because effective acceptance was expressly limited by the terms of the offer. Answer (C) is incorrect because the offer expressly limited effective acceptance to another, specified mode. Answer (D) is incorrect because the mailbox rule did not apply in that the offer expressed a specific mode for acceptance.

9. In response to an inquiry from Chris, Indira sent Chris a letter offering to sell certain described goods for $2,750. The offer stated that, unless Indira heard from Chris by return mail, she would interpret the silence as an acceptance. Which of the following statements is correct concerning acceptance of an offer by silence?

A. If Chris intends to accept and makes no reply, an agreement is formed.

B. If Chris replies, expressly accepting the offer, no agreement will have been formed.

C. An agreement will automatically result from Indira's offer and Chris's silence if they have had similar prior dealings.

D. Chris must reply if she does not wish to accept.

The correct answer is (A). *(Publisher)*
REQUIRED: The effect of an offer specifying silence as acceptance.
DISCUSSION: When an offer states that silence is an acceptance, the offeree may accept by remaining silent if the offeree intends the silence to be acceptance. Thus, if Chris makes no reply but intends to accept, the silence will be an acceptance, and an agreement will be formed.
Answer (B) is incorrect because the offer did not indicate that silence was the exclusive method of acceptance. Hence, any reasonable means of acceptance will be effective. Answer (C) is incorrect because an offeree may always reject an offer in a timely manner even if silence has been considered acceptance in prior dealings. Answer (D) is incorrect because an offeree is not required to respond to an offer unless a course of prior dealings has established silence as acceptance.

10. On April 1, Fine Corp. faxed Moss an offer to purchase Moss's warehouse for $500,000. The offer stated that it would remain open only until April 4 and that acceptance must be received to be effective. Moss sent an acceptance on April 4 by overnight mail and Fine received it on April 5. Which of the following statements is correct?

    A. No contract was formed because Moss sent the acceptance by an unauthorized method.

    B. No contract was formed because Fine received Moss's acceptance after April 4.

    C. A contract was formed when Moss sent the acceptance.

    D. A contract was formed when Fine received Moss's acceptance.

The correct answer is (B). *(CPA, adapted)*
    REQUIRED: The result when an offer stipulates that acceptance is effective only when received.
    DISCUSSION: Unless an offer expresses otherwise, an acceptance by the same means used to transmit the offer is effective upon dispatch. Communication by another mode effects acceptance, if at all, upon receipt by the offeror. If the offer specifies a time for its termination, it terminates at that time. Thereafter, it cannot be effectively accepted.
    Answer (A) is incorrect because acceptance by an unauthorized method is effective upon receipt, unless the offer expressly rendered the method ineffective. Answer (C) is incorrect because it was transmitted by a mode different from that used to transmit the offer, and the offer did not expressly authorize the mode. Answer (D) is incorrect because a terminated offer cannot be effectively accepted.

B. Consideration

11. In determining whether the consideration requirement to form a contract has been satisfied, the consideration exchanged by the parties to the contract must be

    A. Of approximately equal value.

    B. Legally sufficient.

    C. Exchanged simultaneously by the parties.

    D. Fair and reasonable under the circumstances.

The correct answer is (B). *(CPA, adapted)*
    REQUIRED: The requirement of consideration for an enforceable contract to be formed.
    DISCUSSION: Consideration must be legally sufficient and intended as a bargained-for exchange. A promisee has provided legally sufficient consideration if (s)he incurs a legal detriment or if the promisor receives a legal benefit.
    Answer (A) is incorrect because legally sufficient consideration exchanged may be disparate in value. Answer (C) is incorrect because, as long as a genuine bargained-for exchange is intended, the consideration need not be simultaneously exchanged. Answer (D) is incorrect because the amount of consideration is set in the market, not the courts. But extreme disparity of value may evidence fraud, unconscionability, a gift, etc.

12. For there to be consideration for a contract, there must be

    A. A bargained-for detriment to the promisor(ee) or a benefit to the promisee(or).

    B. A manifestation of mutual assent.

    C. Genuineness of assent.

    D. Substantially equal economic benefits to both parties.

The correct answer is (A). *(CPA, adapted)*
    REQUIRED: The element which is necessary for there to be consideration.
    DISCUSSION: The consideration provided by one party (the promisee) to support the enforceability of the other party's (the promisor's) promise may be a bargained-for legal detriment to the promisee or a legal benefit to the promisor. Consideration is always in the form of a promise, act, or forbearance.
    Answers (B) and (C) are incorrect because mutual genuine assent is an element of a contract distinct from consideration. Answer (D) is incorrect because courts rarely question adequacy or equality of consideration.

13. Dye sent Hill a written offer to sell a tract of land for $60,000. They were engaged in a separate dispute. The offer stated that it would be irrevocable for 60 days if Hill would promise to refrain from suing Dye during this time. Hill promptly delivered a promise not to sue during the term of the offer. Dye subsequently decided that the possible suit by Hill was groundless. Dye then phoned Hill and revoked the offer. Hill mailed an acceptance. Dye did not reply. Under the circumstances,

- A.   Dye's offer was supported by consideration and was not revocable when accepted.

- B.   Dye's written offer would be irrevocable even without consideration.

- C.   Dye's silence was an acceptance of Hill's promise.

- D.   Dye's revocation, not being in writing, was invalid.

The correct answer is (A). *(CPA, adapted)*
   REQUIRED: The effect of a promise to keep an offer open if the offeree promised to forgo a lawsuit.
   DISCUSSION: Hill's promise not to sue during the term of the offer formed an option contract. That is, Hill's promise to forgo a legal right was consideration for Dye's promise not to revoke the offer for 60 days. Consequently, Dye's attempted revocation was ineffective, and Hill's acceptance within the 60-day period resulted in a contract.
   Answer (B) is incorrect because an offer to sell realty is not irrevocable solely because it is in writing. Answer (C) is incorrect because Dye's silence was legally irrelevant because Hill's actions were sufficient to establish a contract. Answer (D) is incorrect because a written revocation would likewise have been invalid.

14. Which of the following requires consideration to be binding on the parties?

- A.   Material modification of a contract involving the sale of real estate.

- B.   Ratification of a contract by a person after reaching the age of majority.

- C.   A written promise signed by a merchant to keep an offer to sell goods open for 10 days.

- D.   Material modification of a sale of goods contract under the UCC.

The correct answer is (A). *(CPA, adapted)*
   REQUIRED: The transaction which must be supported by consideration to be enforceable.
   DISCUSSION: Common law requires that a material modification to a contract be supported by new bargained-for consideration.
   Answer (B) is incorrect because a minor's contract is ratified after majority by mere express or implied affirmation, e.g., using or retaining the subject matter. Answer (C) is incorrect because, under the UCC, such a promise is enforceable without consideration. Answer (D) is incorrect because the UCC does not require consideration as a condition to enforcement of a good-faith oral modification of a contract for the sale of goods.

15. In which of the following situations does the first promise serve as valid consideration for the second promise?

- A.   A police officer's promise to catch a thief for a victim's promise to pay a reward.

- B.   A builder's promise to complete a contract for a purchaser's promise to extend the time for completion.

- C.   A debtor's promise to pay $500 for a creditor's promise to forgive the balance of a $600 liquidated debt.

- D.   A debtor's promise to pay $500 for a creditor's promise to forgive the balance of a $600 disputed debt.

The correct answer is (D). *(CPA, adapted)*
   REQUIRED: The promise which serves as valid consideration.
   DISCUSSION: A promise unsupported by consideration is unenforceable. Consideration must be legally sufficient and provided in a bargained-for exchange. Legal sufficiency is found in the promisee's incurring a legal detriment or the promisor's receiving a legal benefit. The debtor's promise to pay part of a disputed liability incorporates legally sufficient consideration: the legal detriment of forgoing the dispute.
   Answer (A) is incorrect because a preexisting legal duty does not constitute consideration. Answer (B) is incorrect because the builder's promise was consideration for a past contract. (S)he already had a contractual liability to perform it. Answer (C) is incorrect because the debtor's promise to pay a liquidated (undisputed) debt was to perform a preexisting obligation.

16. Grove is seeking to avoid performing a promise to pay Brook $1,500. Grove is relying on lack of consideration on Brook's part. Grove will prevail if he can establish that

A. Prior to Grove's promise, Brook had already performed the requested act.

B. Brook's only claim of consideration was the relinquishment of a legal right.

C. Brook's asserted consideration is worth only $400.

D. The consideration to be performed by Brook will be performed by a third party.

The correct answer is (A). *(CPA, adapted)*

REQUIRED: The event preventing the contract from being valid and enforceable.

DISCUSSION: A contract is not valid and enforceable unless there has been legally sufficient consideration for the exchange of promises or acts between the parties. Since Brook has already performed the act, he does not incur any legal detriment in the exchange between himself and Grove. Past consideration is treated the same as no consideration, and Grove is not required to pay Brook.

Answer (B) is incorrect because, by relinquishing a legal right, Brook would have incurred a legal detriment because he had given up a prior right (forbearance). This is a form of valid consideration. Answer (C) is incorrect because the actual value of the services is irrelevant. Since the parties determined in a bargained-for exchange that the value of Brook's performance was $1,500, Grove is required to pay that amount upon Brook's performance. Answer (D) is incorrect because the important issue is not who performs the duty, but that the duty is performed. Brook is responsible for the performance of the duty, but he may contract with a third party to complete the task.

17. Which of the following will be legally binding despite lack of consideration?

A. An employer's promise to make a cash payment to a deceased employee's family in recognition of the employee's many years of service.

B. A promise to donate money to a charity on which the charity relied in incurring large expenditures.

C. A modification of a signed contract to purchase a parcel of land.

D. A merchant's oral promise to keep an offer open for 60 days.

The correct answer is (B). *(CPA, adapted)*

REQUIRED: The promise enforceable absent consideration.

DISCUSSION: A requirement for enforceability of an agreement is legally sufficient consideration, or a substitute for it. One substitute is promissory estoppel: a promise that induces action or forbearance, which the promisor should reasonably have expected, is enforceable absent consideration if it is the only way to avoid injustice. The doctrine has been applied to promises to charitable organizations.

Answers (A) and (C) are incorrect because the common law allows no applicable substitute for consideration required to render the new promise enforceable. Answer (D) is incorrect because the merchant's firm offer rule under the UCC applies to a written commitment.

C. Statute of Frauds

18. King sent Foster, a real estate developer, a signed offer to sell a specified parcel of land to Foster for $200,000. On the same day that King's letter was received, Foster telephoned King and accepted the offer. Which of the following statements is correct under the statute of frauds?

A. No contract was formed because Foster did not sign the offer.

B. No contract was formed because King is not a merchant and therefore King's letter is not binding on Foster.

C. A contract was formed, although it would be enforceable only against King.

D. A contract was formed and would be enforceable against both King and Foster because Foster is a merchant.

The correct answer is (C). *(CPA, adapted)*

REQUIRED: The correct statement regarding oral acceptance of a written offer to sell real property.

DISCUSSION: An agreement to sell real property is within the statute of frauds. The agreement is enforceable only against a party who signs a written memorandum of the offer. Foster's oral acceptance bound King to the offer.

Answer (A) is incorrect because a promisee need not sign a written offer to legally enforce a promise under the statute of frauds. Answer (B) is incorrect because the UCC contains rules which apply specifically to merchants. But real property does not constitute goods such that its sale is subject to the UCC. Answer (D) is incorrect because real property sales are not subject to the UCC. UCC rules do not apply. An agreement to sell real property, within the statute of frauds, is generally not enforceable at law by a party who does not sign the required writing.

19. Which of the following statements is true with regard to the statute of frauds?

A. All contracts involving consideration of more than $500 must be in writing.

B. The written contract must be signed by all parties.

C. The statute of frauds applies to contracts that can be fully performed within 1 year from the date they are made.

D. The contract terms may be stated in more than one document.

The correct answer is (D). *(CPA, adapted)*

REQUIRED: The correct statement with regard to the statute of frauds.

DISCUSSION: If a contract is within the statute of frauds, it is not enforceable at law unless requirements of the statute are satisfied. There must be a sufficient written memorandum of the contract. It may be stated in more than one document if evidence shows they are all related. One of them must be signed by the party against whom enforcement is sought.

Answer (A) is incorrect because, under the UCC, such contracts for the sale of goods must be in writing. Not all other such agreements are within the general statute of frauds. Answer (B) is incorrect because a party who signs a sufficient writing may be bound to performance, even if the other parties do not sign. Answer (C) is incorrect because it applies to a contract which cannot be performed within a year of its making.

20. Bond and Spear orally agreed that Bond would buy a car from Spear for $475. Bond paid Spear a $100 deposit. The next day, Spear received an offer of $575, the car's fair market value. Spear immediately notified Bond that Spear would not sell the car to Bond and returned Bond's $100. If Bond sues Spear and Spear defends on the basis of the statute of frauds, Bond will probably

A. Lose, because the agreement was for less than the fair market value of the car.

B. Win, because the agreement was for less than $500.

C. Lose, because the agreement was not in writing and signed by Spear.

D. Win, because Bond paid a deposit.

The correct answer is (B). *(CPA, adapted)*

REQUIRED: The result of repudiation of an oral agreement to sell a car for $475.

DISCUSSION: A car constitutes goods under the UCC. A contract for the sale of goods for $500 or more is enforceable at law only against a party who signed a writing sufficient to show the contract was made.

Answer (A) is incorrect because the statute of frauds does not relate to adequacy of consideration. Answer (C) is incorrect because an agreement for the sale of goods at under $500 is not within the statute of frauds. A writing is not required to enforce it at law. Answer (D) is incorrect because a deposit does not render an agreement enforceable. The doctrine of part performance is an exception to the writing requirement of the statute of frauds relating to real property. It requires substantial detrimental reliance exceeding partial payment.

21. Carson agreed orally to repair Ives's rare book for $450. Before the work was started, Ives asked Carson to perform additional repairs to the book and agreed to increase the contract price to $650. After Carson completed the work, Ives refused to pay and Carson sued. Ives's defense was based on the statute of frauds. What total amount will Carson recover?

A. $0

B. $200

C. $450

D. $650

The correct answer is (D). *(CPA, adapted)*

REQUIRED: The amount of recovery at law for breach of oral contract for services.

DISCUSSION: Oral contracts are enforceable. But if a contract is within the statute of frauds, it cannot be enforced at law against a party who did not sign a writing which sufficiently evidences the contract. But a services contract is not subject to the statute unless it cannot be performed within a year of its making. (The oral modification is enforceable because new consideration was given.)

Answers (A), (B), and (C) are incorrect because the contract is not subject to the statute of frauds. Thus, doctrines such as equitable estoppel and quasi-contract need not be applied. Note that the UCC is inapplicable to a services contract.

22. Able hired Carr to restore Able's antique car for $800. The terms of their oral agreement provided that Carr was to complete the work within 18 months. Actually, the work could be completed within 1 year. The agreement is

A. Unenforceable because it covers services with a value in excess of $500.

B. Unenforceable because it covers a time period in excess of 1 year.

C. Enforceable because personal service contracts are exempt from the statute of frauds.

D. Enforceable because the work could be completed within 1 year.

The correct answer is (D). *(CPA, adapted)*
REQUIRED: The enforceability of an oral services contract.
DISCUSSION: Oral contracts are generally enforceable. But the statute of frauds conditions enforcement at law of certain contracts on a signed writing which contains essential contract terms. A services contract is within the statute of frauds unless it can be completed within a year of entering into the contract.
Answer (A) is incorrect because applicability of the statute of frauds does not depend on the price for services, as it does on the price of goods. Answer (B) is incorrect because the stated time for completion is not determinative. If it is possible that performance could be rendered during the year following contract formation, the contract is not within the statute of frauds. Answer (C) is incorrect because a services contract is within the statute of frauds if execution within a year of its formation is impossible.

23. On June 1, 1999, Decker orally guaranteed the payment of a $5,000 note Decker's cousin owed Baker. Decker's agreement with Baker provided that Decker's guaranty would terminate in 18 months. On June 3, 1999, Baker wrote Decker confirming Decker's guaranty. Decker did not object to the confirmation. On August 23, 1999, Decker's cousin defaulted on the note and Baker demanded that Decker honor the guaranty. Decker refused. Which of the following statements is correct?

A. Decker is liable under the oral guaranty because Decker did not object to Baker's June 3 letter.

B. Decker is not liable under the oral guaranty because it expired more than 1 year after June 1.

C. Decker is liable under the oral guaranty because Baker demanded payment within 1 year of the date the guaranty was given.

D. Decker is not liable under the oral guaranty because Decker's promise was not in writing.

The correct answer is (D). *(CPA, adapted)*
REQUIRED: The correct statement concerning an oral guarantee confirmed by the person to whom it was made.
DISCUSSION: A contract within the statute of frauds is unenforceable against a party who did not sign a writing expressing its essential terms. An agreement to answer for the debt of another is within the statute, as is one which cannot be performed within a year of contract formation. The guarantee agreement might have been fully performed by May 31, 2000.
Answer (A) is incorrect because failure to act does not bind a person to contractual performance, except in certain instances under the UCC. Answers (B) and (C) are incorrect because the guarantee agreement could have been fully executed within a year of its making, so the 1-year rule of the statute of frauds does not apply.

24. Nolan agreed orally with Train to sell Train a house for $100,000. Train sent Nolan a signed agreement and a down payment of $10,000. Nolan did not sign the agreement but allowed Train to move into the house. Before closing, Nolan refused to go through with the sale. Train sued Nolan to compel specific performance. Under the provisions of the statute of frauds,

A. Train will win because Train signed the agreement and Nolan did not object.

B. Train will win because Train made a down payment and took possession.

C. Nolan will win because Nolan did not sign the agreement.

D. Nolan will win because the house was worth more than $500.

The correct answer is (B). *(CPA, adapted)*
REQUIRED: The enforceability of a partly performed oral real property contract of sale.
DISCUSSION: An agreement for the sale of land is within the statute of frauds and is not enforceable against a party who did not sign a written memorandum containing the essential terms. But specific performance may be granted the purchaser if (s)he paid part of the consideration and either took possession of the property or made valuable improvements to the land. This is known as the part performance doctrine.
Answer (A) is incorrect because the party to be charged must have signed the agreement. Answer (C) is incorrect because partial performance is sufficient such that specific performance may be decreed. Answer (D) is incorrect because only if an agreement is for the sale of goods is a threshold amount of $500 significant to a signed writing requirement.

25. Sand orally promised Frost a $10,000 bonus, in addition to a monthly salary, if Frost would work 2 years for Sand. If Frost works for the 2 years, will the statute of frauds prevent Frost from collecting the bonus?

A. No, because Frost fully performed.

B. No, because the contract did not involve an interest in real estate.

C. Yes, because the contract could not be performed within 1 year.

D. Yes, because the monthly salary was the consideration for the contract.

The correct answer is (A). *(CPA, adapted)*
REQUIRED: The enforceability of a contract which cannot be performed within a year.
DISCUSSION: Under the statute of frauds, if it is not possible to complete performance of a contract within a year of formation, the contract is not enforceable at law. A fully executed contract, however, is enforceable notwithstanding the statute of frauds. Also enforceable in most states is a contract fully performed by one party.
Answer (B) is incorrect because many contracts other than those involving real property are within the statute of frauds. Answer (C) is incorrect because, in most states, a contract fully performed by one of the parties is enforceable at law by the other. Answer (D) is incorrect because the promise of a bonus constitutes consideration.

D. Capacity and Legality

26. Rail, who was 16 years old, purchased an $800 computer from Elco Electronics. Rail and Elco are located in a state where the age of majority is 18. On several occasions, Rail returned the computer to Elco for repairs. Rail was very unhappy with the computer. Two days after reaching the age of 18, Rail was still frustrated with the computer's reliability. He returned it to Elco, demanding an $800 refund. Elco refused, claiming that Rail no longer had a right to disaffirm the contract. Elco's refusal is

A. Correct, because Rail's multiple requests for service acted as a ratification of the contract.

B. Correct, because Rail could have transferred good title to a good-faith purchaser for value.

C. Incorrect, because Rail disaffirmed the contract within a reasonable period of time after reaching the age of 18.

D. Incorrect, because Rail could disaffirm the contract at any time.

The correct answer is (C). *(CPA, adapted)*
REQUIRED: The enforceability of a contract made with a minor.
DISCUSSION: The UCC adopts the common-law rule that, until a reasonable time after reaching the age of majority, a person may repudiate (disaffirm) a contract (s)he entered into as a minor. Repudiation is by any unequivocal act that indicates intent to do so. Rail returned consideration received to the extent possible and is entitled to receive the full amount of consideration given.
Answer (A) is incorrect because ratification cannot occur until the minor reaches majority. Answer (B) is incorrect because, even though a person with voidable title to goods can transfer title to a good-faith purchaser for value, the minor's contract is voidable. Answer (D) is incorrect because the power to disaffirm continues only until a reasonable time after the minor reaches majority.

27. All of the following are effective methods of ratifying a contract entered into by a minor except

A. Expressly ratifying the contract after reaching the age of majority.

B. Failing to disaffirm the contract within a reasonable time after reaching the age of majority.

C. Ratifying the contract before reaching the age of majority.

D. Impliedly ratifying the contract after reaching the age of majority.

The correct answer is (C). *(CPA, adapted)*
REQUIRED: The method ineffective to ratify a contract entered into by a minor.
DISCUSSION: Contracts of minors are usually voidable at the option of the minor. Upon attainment of the age of majority, however, the minor can ratify the contract. After ratification, (s)he will be bound from the inception of the contract. An attempt to ratify while still a minor is not effective. One who lacks contractual capacity clearly lacks the capacity to ratify. Note that ratification is all or nothing. That is, all the terms of the contract are ratified or none are.
Answer (A) is incorrect because express ratification of a contract formed in minority, after reaching the age of majority, renders the contract binding on the minor. Answer (B) is incorrect because failing to disaffirm a contract within a reasonable period of time after reaching majority operates as ratification. Answer (D) is incorrect because ratification may be either expressed or implied.

28. Payne entered into a written agreement to sell a parcel of land to Stevens. At the time the agreement was executed, Payne had consumed alcoholic beverages. Payne's ability to understand the nature and terms of the contract was not impaired. Stevens did not believe that Payne was intoxicated. The contract is

A. Void as a matter of law.

B. Legally binding on both parties.

C. Voidable at Payne's option.

D. Voidable at Stevens's option.

The correct answer is (B). *(CPA, adapted)*
REQUIRED: The capacity to contract when intoxicated.
DISCUSSION: A contract entered into by a person when intoxicated is not void. It is voidable by that person only if his/her reason and judgment were impaired to the extent that (s)he did not understand the legal consequences of his/her actions. If so, (s)he may disaffirm the contract even if the intoxication was voluntary and unknown to the other party.

Answer (A) is incorrect because intoxication of one or more of the parties does not void contract formation. Answer (C) is incorrect because Payne understood the nature and terms of the contract. Answer (D) is incorrect because Stevens was bound by the contract. Awareness of Payne's intoxication is irrelevant.

29. West, an Indiana real estate broker, misrepresented to Zimmer that West was licensed in Kansas under the Kansas statute that regulates real estate brokers and requires all brokers to be licensed. Zimmer signed a contract agreeing to pay West a 5% commission for selling Zimmer's home in Kansas. West did not sign the contract. West sold Zimmer's home. If West sued Zimmer for nonpayment of commission, Zimmer would be

A. Liable to West only for the value of services rendered.

B. Liable to West for the full commission.

C. Not liable to West for any amount because West did not sign the contract.

D. Not liable to West for any amount because West violated the Kansas licensing requirements.

The correct answer is (D). *(CPA, adapted)*
REQUIRED: The recovery for services rendered in violation of a regulatory statute.
DISCUSSION: A person who performs services without obtaining a statutorily required license may recover only if the statute is solely a revenue measure. If the legislative intent was to protect the public from incompetent work by unqualified persons, the statute is regulatory and the contract is unenforceable even if the defendant was benefited and the work performed was satisfactory.

Answer (A) is incorrect because a court will not give any remedy to a party who violates a regulatory statute. West will not recover in quasi-contract although Zimmer was unjustly enriched. Answer (B) is incorrect because a violator of a regulatory statute is not permitted any recovery. Answer (C) is incorrect because the contract is not subject to the statute of frauds. (It is not a contract to sell real property.) If it were, failure of West to sign would not relieve Zimmer of liability.

30. Which of the following would be unenforceable because the subject matter is illegal?

A. A contingent fee charged by an attorney to represent a plaintiff in a negligence action.

B. An arbitration clause in a supply contract.

C. A restrictive covenant in an employment contract prohibiting a former employee from using the employer's trade secrets.

D. An employer's promise not to press embezzlement charges against an employee who agrees to make restitution.

The correct answer is (D). *(CPA, adapted)*
REQUIRED: The contract unenforceable as illegal.
DISCUSSION: Legal purpose is requisite to enforceability of a contract. An agreement that cannot be performed without violating a statute is void, as are other agreements which violate public policy. The state, not a private citizen, prosecutes violations of criminal statutes. The interest protected is that of society. Thus, an employer's promise not to press criminal charges is not an enforceable contract.

Answers (A), (B), and (C) are incorrect because such agreements are legal and common, and have been determined to further public policy.

31. Parr is the vice president of research of Lynx, Inc. When hired, Parr signed an employment contract prohibiting Parr from competing with Lynx during and after employment. While employed, Parr acquired knowledge of many of Lynx's trade secrets. If Parr wishes to compete with Lynx and Lynx refuses to give Parr permission, which of the following statements is correct?

- A. Parr has the right to compete with Lynx upon resigning from Lynx.

- B. Parr has the right to compete with Lynx only if fired from Lynx.

- C. In determining whether Parr may compete with Lynx, the court should not consider Parr's ability to obtain other employment.

- D. In determining whether Parr may compete with Lynx, the court should consider, among other factors, whether the agreement is necessary to protect Lynx's legitimate business interests.

The correct answer is (D). *(CPA, adapted)*
REQUIRED: The rights under a covenant not to compete.
DISCUSSION: A covenant not to compete may violate the public policy to preserve and promote competition. Such an agreement must be ancillary to an otherwise enforceable agreement (not the sole object of the contract). It should state reasonable time, geographic area, and scope restrictions. Moreover, the covenant should not unduly burden the public interest or the party who is prevented from competing. The hardship factor is especially important if the covenant is part of an employment contract. Hence, restrictions on future employment tend to be more strictly scrutinized than covenants found in agreements to sell a business. If the restraint is unreasonable, a court may void the provision or reformulate it in an acceptable form.
Answers (A) and (B) are incorrect because whether Parr resigns or is fired is irrelevant to the enforceability of the covenant. Answer (C) is incorrect because the ability to find other employment is a factor in determining how heavily the covenant will weigh upon the employee.

E. Mutual Assent

32. The intent, or scienter, element necessary to establish a cause of action for fraud will be met if the plaintiff can show that the

- A. Defendant made a misrepresentation with a reckless disregard for the truth.

- B. Defendant made a false representation of fact.

- C. Plaintiff actually relied on the defendant's misrepresentation.

- D. Plaintiff justifiably relied on the defendant's misrepresentation.

The correct answer is (A). *(CPA, adapted)*
REQUIRED: The proof of intent to defraud.
DISCUSSION: The essence of fraud is that one party intentionally deceives to take advantage of another. The scienter, or intent, element of a fraud action is satisfied if the defendant knew of the falsity of a representation or (s)he made it with reckless disregard for whether it was true. The defendant must have intended that the other party rely on the representation.
Answers (B), (C), and (D) are incorrect because, although they are necessary elements of fraud, they do not constitute intent to misrepresent.

33. To prevail in a common-law action for fraud in the inducement, a plaintiff must prove that the

- A. Defendant was an expert with regard to the misrepresentations.

- B. Defendant made the misrepresentations with knowledge of their falsity and with an intention to deceive.

- C. Misrepresentations were in writing.

- D. Plaintiff was in a fiduciary relationship with the defendant.

The correct answer is (B). *(CPA, adapted)*
REQUIRED: The element(s) of a *prima facie* case of fraud in the inducement.
DISCUSSION: Elements of fraud are a false representation of a material fact, scienter (knowledge of the falsehood or reckless disregard for its truth), intent to deceive, and reliance on the false representation that is both justifiable and detrimental. Fraud in the inducement occurs when the underlying consideration is misrepresented, i.e., the nature or quality of the goods or services. Such an agreement is voidable.
Answers (A), (C), and (D) are incorrect because none is an element of fraud.

34. Which of the following, if intentionally misstated by a seller to a buyer, would be considered a fraudulent inducement to make a contract?

- A. Nonexpert opinion.
- B. Appraised value.
- C. Prediction.
- D. Immaterial fact.

The correct answer is (B). *(CPA, adapted)*
REQUIRED: The false statement which is a sufficient basis for a fraud action.
DISCUSSION: An element of actionable fraud is a false representation or the concealment of a material fact. A material fact is a fact which forms a basis of the bargain. Stating a false amount to be the appraised value of the subject matter is actionable as fraud, if the other elements are alleged.
Answer (A) is incorrect because facts, not opinions, may form a basis for fraud. Furthermore, a reasonable person would not be justified in relying on nonexpert opinion. Answer (C) is incorrect because statements of future events, predictions, or probabilities are not a basis for fraud. Answer (D) is incorrect because false statement of a fact may support a finding of fraud, but only if the fact was material (i.e., formed a basis of the bargain).

35. Steele, Inc. wanted to purchase Kalp's distribution business. On March 15, 1999, Kalp provided Steele with copies of audited financial statements for the period ended December 31, 1998. The financial statements reflected inventory in the amount of $1.2 million. On March 29, 1999, Kalp discovered that the December 31 inventory was overstated by at least $400,000. On April 3, 1999, Steele, relying on the financial statements, purchased all of Kalp's business. On April 29, 1999, Steele discovered the inventory overstatement. Steele sued Kalp for fraud. Which of the following statements is correct?

- A. Steele will lose because it should not have relied on the inventory valuation in the financial statements.
- B. Steele will lose because Kalp was unaware that the inventory valuation was incorrect at the time the financial statements were provided to Steele.
- C. Steele will prevail because Kalp had a duty to disclose the fact that the inventory value was overstated.
- D. Steele will prevail but will not be able to sue for damages.

The correct answer is (C). *(CPA, adapted)*
REQUIRED: The correct statement about failure to disclose a known error.
DISCUSSION: Neither party to a contract has a duty to disclose facts. Each is responsible to exercise ordinary business sense in his/her dealings. But a fraud action might be based on failure to disclose material facts when (1) there is a fiduciary relationship between the parties, (2) one party could not reasonably discover a fact known to the other, or (3) a person who misstates an important fact subsequently learns of it. Kalp had an affirmative duty to disclose the overstated inventory to Steele.
Answer (A) is incorrect because reliance on audited financial statements is both common and reasonable. Answer (B) is incorrect because Kalp, having provided the statements, effected a representation. When (s)he learned that it was false, (s)he incurred an affirmative duty to disclose that it was a misstatement. Answer (D) is incorrect because, when one party induces a contract by fraud, the other party may elect to rescind or to sue for damages.

Note: For additional questions on liability for fraud under common law, refer to Study Unit 2, which addresses liability of accountants. For questions on statutory fraud liability, refer to Study Unit 2, and Study Unit 12, which addresses federal regulation of securities.

36. Miller negotiated the sale of Miller's liquor store to Jackson. Jackson asked to see the prior year's financial statements. Using the store's checkbook, Miller prepared a balance sheet and profit and loss statement as well as he could. Miller told Jackson to have an accountant examine Miller's records because Miller was not an accountant. Jackson failed to do so and purchased the store in reliance on Miller's financial statements. Jackson later learned that the financial statements included several errors that resulted in a material overstatement of assets and net income. Miller was not aware that the errors existed. Jackson sued Miller, claiming that Miller misrepresented the store's financial condition and that Jackson relied on the financial statements in making the decision to acquire the store. Which of the following statements is correct?

- A. Jackson will prevail if the errors in the financial statements were material.
- B. Jackson will not prevail because Jackson's reliance on the financial statements was not reasonable.
- C. Receiving money damages is the only remedy available to Jackson if, in fact, Miller has committed a misrepresentation.
- D. Jackson would be entitled to rescind the purchase even if the errors in the financial statements were not material.

The correct answer is (B). *(CPA, adapted)*
REQUIRED: The result when a contract was induced by misrepresentation.
DISCUSSION: Innocent misrepresentation is, basically, a false representation not known to be false. To prevail in a contract suit based on innocent misrepresentation, the plaintiff must prove (1) a representation (2) of a fact that was (3) material and (4) false, (5) intended to induce reliance, and (6) that induced reliance which was (7) reasonable and (8) detrimental. A reasonable person would have suspected that the statements could contain inaccuracy, especially after Miller's caution. Reliance by Jackson under the circumstances was not justifiable.
Answer (A) is incorrect because the fact misstated must be a basis for the bargain, but another element necessary to an innocent misrepresentation claim is missing. Answer (C) is incorrect because rescission is generally the only remedy for innocent misrepresentation. The contract is canceled, and the parties are restored to their original positions. If Miller knew of the errors or was grossly negligent, Jackson might have proved fraud and recovered contract damages. Answer (D) is incorrect because the fact at issue must be material (a basis of the bargain), whether the theory of the claim is fraud, innocent misrepresentation, mutual mistake, or unilateral mistake.

37. On April 6, Apple entered into a signed contract with Bean, by which Apple was to sell Bean an antique automobile, having a fair market value of $150,000, for $75,000. Apple believed the auto was worth only $75,000. Unknown to either party, the auto had been destroyed by fire on April 4. If Bean sues Apple for breach of contract, Apple's best defense is

- A. Unconscionability.
- B. Risk of loss borne by Bean.
- C. Lack of adequate consideration.
- D. Mutual mistake.

The correct answer is (D). *(CPA, adapted)*
REQUIRED: The result when the parties do not know that the subject matter has been destroyed.
DISCUSSION: A mistake of material fact made by both parties is grounds for rescission or is a sufficient defense in an action on the contract. Existence of the subject matter of the contract is a material fact. The parties generally are assumed to accept the risks concerning future events. Thus, a mistake about future facts is ordinarily not a basis for relief.
Answer (A) is incorrect because an agreement is unconscionable if it is so unfair as to be oppressive, but the facts do not suggest that Bean took unfair advantage of Apple. Answer (B) is incorrect because the seller initially has the risk of loss. No event occurred that transferred the risk to Bean. Answer (C) is incorrect because courts seldom inquire into the adequacy or value of consideration.

38. A building subcontractor submitted a bid for construction of a portion of a high-rise office building. The bid contained material computational errors. The general contractor accepted the bid with knowledge of the errors. Which of the following statements best represents the subcontractor's liability?

- A. Not liable because the contractor knew of the errors.
- B. Not liable because the errors were a result of gross negligence.
- C. Liable because the errors were unilateral.
- D. Liable because the errors were material.

The correct answer is (A). *(CPA, adapted)*
REQUIRED: The effect of a material unilateral mistake.
DISCUSSION: Generally, a unilateral mistake in fact does not invalidate a contract except in limited circumstances. In this case, the subcontractor is not liable because the mistake was an obvious mathematical error and the general contractor was aware of the mistake and was not acting in good faith. The contract is voidable at the subcontractor's option.
Answer (B) is incorrect because the subcontractor would be liable under the contract if the error was the result of gross negligence. Answer (C) is incorrect because it states the general rule. In this case, however, the other contracting party knew of the mistake and was acting unfairly. Answer (D) is incorrect because only if the unilateral mistake was material to formation would it be voidable by the mistaken party in limited circumstances.

39. Jordan leased an apartment from Olsen. Shortly before the lease expired, Olsen threatened Jordan with eviction and physical harm if Jordan did not sign a new lease for twice the old rent. Jordan, unable to afford the expense to fight eviction, and in fear of physical harm, signed the new lease. Three months later, Jordan moved and sued to void the lease claiming duress. The lease will be held

A. Void because of the unreasonable increase in rent.

B. Voidable because of Olsen's threat to bring eviction proceedings.

C. Void because of Jordan's financial condition.

D. Voidable because of Olsen's threat of physical harm.

The correct answer is (D). *(CPA, adapted)*
REQUIRED: The nature and effect of duress.
DISCUSSION: Duress is a threat (words or acts which instill fear or apprehension) which coerces a person to enter a contract (s)he did not intend to enter. The threat of physical violence is sufficient to render the contract voidable on grounds of duress.
Answer (A) is incorrect because inadequacy of consideration neither voids a contract nor is it an element of duress. It might be evidence that Jordan did not intend to contract. Answer (B) is incorrect because, if it was made in bad faith and for an ulterior motive, the threat might be a basis for duress. But Olsen had the right to evict absent renewal. It was probably mere hard bargaining. Answer (C) is incorrect because merely taking advantage of another's financial condition is not duress. Duress renders a contract voidable, not void.

40. Maco, Inc. and Kent contracted for Kent to provide Maco certain consulting services at an hourly rate of $20. Kent's normal hourly rate was $90 per hour, the fair market value of the services. Kent agreed to the $20 rate because Kent was having serious financial problems. At the time the agreement was negotiated, Maco was aware of Kent's financial condition and refused to pay more than $20 per hour for Kent's services. Kent has now sued to rescind the contract with Maco, claiming duress by Maco during the negotiations. Under the circumstances, Kent will

A. Win, because Maco refused to pay the fair market value of Kent's services.

B. Win, because Maco was aware of Kent's serious financial problems.

C. Lose, because Maco's actions did not constitute duress.

D. Lose, because Maco cannot prove that Kent, at the time, had no other offers to provide consulting services.

The correct answer is (C). *(CPA, adapted)*
REQUIRED: The circumstances under which duress is a defense to a contract for services at 2/9 of their value.
DISCUSSION: Duress sufficient to render a contract voidable is a threat which is so coercive that the victim has no reasonable alternative but to make the contract. Duress may result from extreme economic pressure. Taking advantage of another's financial difficulty is not enough. Kent will lose because Maco made no improper threat; it did not exert extreme economic pressure on Kent. Even if Kent was coerced by threat, on those facts, Maco was not the source.
Answer (A) is incorrect because legal sufficiency of consideration does not depend on its relative value. Duress is not a function of the adequacy of consideration. Answer (B) is incorrect because coercive threat, not awareness of financial problems, is the basis for duress. Answer (D) is incorrect because Kent has the burden to prove the defense. Although Kent may have felt pressured to enter the contract, Maco did not exert the coercive pressure.

F. Interpreting a Contract

41. Two individuals signed a written contract that was intended to be their entire agreement. The parol evidence rule will prevent the admission of evidence that is offered to

A. Prove the existence of a contemporaneous oral agreement that modifies the contract.

B. Prove the existence of a subsequent oral agreement that modifies the contract.

C. Explain the meaning of an ambiguity in the written contract.

D. Establish that fraud had been committed in formation of the contract.

The correct answer is (A). *(CPA, adapted)*
REQUIRED: The applicability of the parol evidence rule.
DISCUSSION: The parol evidence rule excludes prior or contemporaneous oral or written agreements that would tend to add to, vary, or contradict the terms of a written agreement intended to be complete. If the parties meant their written agreement to be entire, only terms incorporated directly or by reference are part of the contract as it existed at the time it was set forth in writing and signed.
Answer (B) is incorrect because evidence of a later agreement does not modify the contract as it existed at the time it was made. Answers (C) and (D) are incorrect because evidence to clarify an ambiguity or to prove fraud, duress, undue influence, mutual mistake, illegality, innocent misrepresentation, or another invalidating condition is admissible.

42. Dunne and Cook signed a contract requiring Cook to rebind 500 of Dunne's books at 80¢ per book. Later, Dunne requested, in good faith, that the price be reduced to 70¢ per book. Cook agreed orally to reduce the price to 70¢. Under the circumstances, the oral agreement is

- A. Enforceable, but proof of it is inadmissible into evidence.

- B. Enforceable, and proof of it is admissible into evidence.

- C. Unenforceable, because Dunne failed to give consideration, but proof of it is otherwise admissible into evidence.

- D. Unenforceable, due to the statute of frauds, and proof of it is inadmissible into evidence.

The correct answer is (C). *(CPA, adapted)*

REQUIRED: The enforceability of an oral modification and admissibility of evidence of it.

DISCUSSION: The parol evidence rule restricts admission, as evidence, of oral statements made prior to or contemporaneous with formation of a written contract to contradict terms of the contract. The consideration requirement of an enforceable contract also applies to an agreement to modify a contract. Dunne provided no new consideration bargained for in exchange for the modification.

Answer (A) is incorrect because the modification was not supported by consideration. Answer (B) is incorrect because no consideration supported the modification, and the oral statements were made subsequent to contract formation and contemporaneous with an oral modification. Answer (D) is incorrect because the underlying contract was not subject to the statute, nor was the contract as modified. The oral statements were made subsequent to contract formation and contemporaneous with an oral modification.

43. Rogers and Lennon entered into a written computer consulting agreement that required Lennon to provide certain weekly reports to Rogers. The agreement also stated that Lennon would provide the computer equipment necessary to perform the services, and that Rogers's computer would not be used. As the parties were executing the agreement, they orally agreed that Lennon could use Rogers's computer. After executing the agreement, Rogers and Lennon orally agreed that Lennon would report on a monthly, rather than a weekly, basis. The parties now disagree on Lennon's right to use Rogers's computer and how often Lennon must report to Rogers. In the event of a lawsuit between the parties, the parol evidence rule will

- A. Not apply to any of the parties' agreements because the consulting agreement did not have to be in writing.

- B. Not prevent Lennon from proving the parties' oral agreement that Lennon could use Rogers's computer.

- C. Not prevent the admission into evidence of testimony regarding Lennon's right to report on a monthly basis.

- D. Not apply to the parties' agreement to allow Lennon to use Rogers's computer because it was contemporaneous with the written agreement.

The correct answer is (C). *(CPA, adapted)*

REQUIRED: The applicability and/or effect of the parol evidence rule.

DISCUSSION: When parties integrate an agreement in a writing, they intend that all negotiations and agreed-to understandings be merged into the writing. The writing constitutes the entire final agreement. The parol evidence rule is a rule of substantive contract law. It prohibits admission of extrinsic evidence of prior or contemporaneous expressions, written or oral, which tend to contradict or otherwise vary the integrated written agreement. It does not exclude evidence which tends to prove the contract is void or voidable. Neither does it exclude evidence of expressions after the integrated writing was executed. Monthly reporting was agreed to after execution of the writing. Evidence tending to prove the modification is admissible.

Answer (A) is incorrect because the parol evidence rule applies to all written contracts, whether or not the statute of frauds requires them to be in writing. Answer (B) is incorrect because this oral agreement was expressed contemporaneously with execution of the written agreement. Answer (D) is incorrect because the parol evidence rule renders inadmissible extrinsic evidence of contemporaneous expressions of understanding which vary terms of the writing.

44. When parties have entered into a written contract intended as the final expression of their agreement, which of the following agreements will be admitted into evidence because they are not prohibited by the parol evidence rule?

	Subsequent Oral Agreements	Prior Written Agreements
A.	Yes	Yes
B.	Yes	No
C.	No	Yes
D.	No	No

The correct answer is (B). *(CPA, adapted)*
    REQUIRED: The agreement(s) admissible under the parol evidence rule.
    DISCUSSION: When parties integrate an agreement in a writing, they intend that all negotiations and agreed-to understandings be merged into the writing. The writing constitutes the entire final agreement. It prohibits admission of extrinsic evidence of prior or contemporaneous expressions, written or oral, which tend to contradict or otherwise vary the integrated written agreement. It does not exclude evidence which tends to prove the contract is void or voidable. Neither does it exclude evidence of expressions, written or oral, after the integrated writing was executed.
    Answers (A), (C), and (D) are incorrect because subsequent agreements that interpret or modify the terms of the contract are allowable. In addition, prior agreements are not allowable when the writing constitutes the entire agreement.

45. In negotiations with Andrews for the lease of Kemp's warehouse, Kemp orally agreed to pay one-half of the cost of the utilities. The written lease, later prepared by Kemp's attorney, provided that Andrews pay all of the utilities. Andrews failed to read the lease carefully and signed it. When Kemp demanded that Andrews pay all of the utilities, Andrews refused, claiming that the lease did not accurately reflect the oral agreement. Andrews also learned that Kemp intentionally misrepresented the condition of the structure of the warehouse during the negotiations between the parties. Andrews sued to rescind the lease and intends to introduce evidence of the parties' oral agreement about sharing the utilities and the fraudulent statements made by Kemp. The parol evidence rule will prevent the admission of evidence concerning the

	Oral Agreement Regarding Who Pays the Utilities	Fraudulent Statements by Kemp
A.	Yes	Yes
B.	No	Yes
C.	Yes	No
D.	No	No

The correct answer is (C). *(CPA, adapted)*
    REQUIRED: The evidence inadmissible under the parol evidence rule.
    DISCUSSION: Extrinsic evidence inadmissible under the parol evidence rule is of written or other expressions (1) made prior to or contemporaneous with an integrated written contract and (2) offered to contradict or vary the terms of the written contract. The evidence may not supplement the terms if the writing was intended as a complete integration. But typographical or obvious errors in drafting which clearly do not represent the intention of the parties may be proved. Also, parol evidence which is offered to prove the contract as written is void or voidable is admissible, e.g., based on lack of genuine mutual assent due to fraud, mistake, etc. Finally, parol evidence may be offered to prove an ambiguous term in the written contract, provided it does not vary or contradict the writing. Statements made after the writing is executed are not parol evidence.
    Answer (A) is incorrect because proof of fraud affects validity of the contract. Answer (B) is incorrect because the agreement contradicts the written contract and was made prior to it. And if fraud is proved, the contract is voidable. Answer (D) is incorrect because the agreement contradicts the written contract and was made prior to it.

OOF QUESTION 1 *(CPA, adapted)* 10-15 minutes

On December 15, Blake Corp. telephoned Reach Consultants, Inc. and offered to hire Reach to design a security system for Blake's research department. The work would require 2 years to complete. Blake offered to pay a fee of $100,000 but stated that the offer must be accepted in writing, and the acceptance must be received by Blake no later than December 20.

On December 20, Reach faxed a written acceptance to Blake. Blake's offices were closed on December 20, and Reach's fax was not seen until December 21.

Reach's acceptance contained the following language:

"We accept your $1,000,000 offer. Weaver has been assigned $5,000 of the fee as payment for sums owed Weaver by Reach. Payment of this amount should be made directly to Weaver."

On December 22, Blake sent a signed memo to Reach rejecting Reach's December 20 fax but offering to hire Reach for a $75,000 fee. Reach telephoned Blake on December 23 and orally accepted Blake's December 22 offer.

Required

a. Items 1 through 7 relate to whether a contractual relationship exists between Blake and Reach. For each item, determine whether the statement is true (T) or false (F).

1. Blake's December 15 offer had to be in writing to be a legitimate offer.
2. Reach's December 20 fax was an improper method of acceptance.
3. Reach's December 20 fax was effective when sent.
4. Reach's acceptance was invalid because it was received after December 20.
5. Blake's receipt of Reach's acceptance created a voidable contract.
6. Reach's agreement to a $1,000,000 fee prevented the formation of a contract.
7. Reach's December 20 fax was a counteroffer.

b. Items 8 through 12 relate to the attempted assignment of part of the fee to Weaver. Assume that a valid contract exists between Blake and Reach. For each item, determine whether the statement is true (T) or false (F).

8. Reach is prohibited from making an assignment of any contract right or duty.
9. Reach may validly assign part of the fee to Weaver.
10. Under the terms of Reach's acceptance, Weaver would be considered a third-party creditor beneficiary.
11. In a breach of contract suit by Weaver, against Blake, Weaver would not collect any punitive damages.
12. In a breach of contract suit by Weaver, against Reach, Weaver would be able to collect punitive damages.

c. Items 13 through 15 relate to Blake's December 22 signed memo. For each item, determine whether the statement is true (T) or false (F).

13. Reach's oral acceptance of Blake's December 22 memo may be enforced by Blake against Reach.
14. Blake's memo is a valid offer even though it contains no date for acceptance.
15. Blake's memo may be enforced against Blake by Reach.

Knowledge Tested

1. Contract law
   a. Offer and acceptance
   b. Statute of frauds
   c. Assignment
   d. Third-party beneficiaries
   e. Punitive damages

Authors' Comments

This question raises a variety of issues regarding the common law of offer and acceptance, including the offeror's control over the time and manner of acceptance, the mirror image rule, and whether receipt of the acceptance requires knowledge of receipt. The question also concerns what rights are assignable and what terms of contracts are enforceable by third parties. Another issue is what contracts must be written in order to be enforceable.

1. The correct answer is (F).

DISCUSSION: The statute of frauds applies to certain types of contracts, not to offers. If an oral offer is made to enter into a contract that is within the statute, the parties will be protected after an acceptance by the requirement that a writing be signed by the party to be bound. This contract must be in writing. An agreement not performable within a year is covered by the statute.

2. The correct answer is (F).

DISCUSSION: The fax complied with the method of acceptance specified by Blake. A signed fax is a valid writing that, in this case, meets the deadline.

3. The correct answer is (F).

DISCUSSION: The purported acceptance was not effective when sent or received. It was a counteroffer under the mirror image rule because it changed terms of the offer.

4. The correct answer is (F).

DISCUSSION: Reach's purported acceptance was timely because it met the condition of delivery to Blake's office by December 20.

5. The correct answer is (F).

DISCUSSION: Blake's receipt of Reach's fax did not create any type of contract. The fax did not mirror the terms of Blake's offer. It was a rejection and a counteroffer.

6. The correct answer is (T*).

DISCUSSION: Reach's reply purporting to accept Blake's proposal for a $100,000 fee made a counteroffer of $1,000,000 and did not form a contract. * Both answers received credit on the exam. The F answer is apparently based on the reasoning that Reach made an obvious clerical mistake and intended to accept the $100,000 fee proposal.

7. The correct answer is (T).

DISCUSSION: Reach's fax was not an acceptance. Under the mirror image rule, it constituted a rejection and a counteroffer.

8. The correct answer is (F).

DISCUSSION: Public policy favors the assignment of contract rights unless expressly or implicitly prohibited by the contract. However, the assignment of the right to receive money cannot be prohibited. To the extent the agreement is a personal services contract, it is not assignable, but the mere right to receive a fee is assignable.

9. The correct answer is (T).

DISCUSSION: Future rights under an existing contract are assignable unless prohibited by contract or statute, except that a contract cannot prevent assignment of money. The assignor may assign clearly defined portions to different assignees and retain any balance.

10. The correct answer is (T).

DISCUSSION: Weaver is a creditor beneficiary of the contract between Blake and Reach because Weaver was intended to benefit from the formation and performance of the contract.

11. The correct answer is (T).

DISCUSSION: Courts rarely award punitive damages in a suit for breach of contract. Proof of malice is required. Weaver may sue Blake for breach of contract but will likely be limited to compensatory damages.

12. The correct answer is (F).

DISCUSSION: Courts rarely award punitive damages in a suit for breach of contract. Proof of malice is required. Weaver may sue Reach for breach of contract but will likely be limited to compensatory damages.

13. The correct answer is (F).

DISCUSSION: Blake's memo implicitly incorporated the earlier terms of a 2-year contract period and the requirement of a written acceptance. Thus, Blake does not have any writing signed by Reach to enforce. An oral acceptance was therefore ineffective to bind Blake.

14. The correct answer is (T).

DISCUSSION: Blake's memo to Reach satisfies the requirements of a valid offer (intent, communication, and reasonable definiteness). A time of acceptance is not required for definiteness. When an offer does not specify a deadline, a reasonable time under the circumstances is implied.

15. The correct answer is (T).

DISCUSSION: Blake's written memo is an offer to enter a contract that is within the statute of frauds. It empowers the offeree to form a contract by making a valid acceptance. Reach's oral acceptance of Blake's written offer was effective to form a contract that is enforceable against Blake. Blake, the party to be bound, has signed a writing sufficient to satisfy the statute of frauds.

OOF QUESTION 2 *(CPA, adapted)* 15-20 minutes

On April 1, Sam Stieb signed and mailed to Bold Corp. an offer to sell Bold a parcel of land for $175,000. On April 5, Bold called Stieb and requested that Stieb keep the offer open until June 1, by which time Bold would be able to determine whether financing for the purchase was available. That same day, Stieb signed and mailed a letter indicating that he would hold the offer open until June 1 if Bold mailed Stieb $100 by April 20.

On April 17, Stieb sent Bold a signed letter revoking his offers dated April 1 and April 5. Bold received that letter on April 19. However, Bold had already mailed on April 18 its acceptance of Stieb's offer of April 5 along with a check for $100. Stieb received the check and letter of acceptance on April 20.

On May 15, Bold wrote Stieb stating that the $175,000 purchase price was too high but that it would be willing to purchase the land for $160,000. Upon receipt, Stieb immediately sent a telegram to Bold indicating that he had already revoked his offer and that, even if his revocation was not effective, he considered Bold's offer a counteroffer which he would not accept. Otherwise, Stieb did nothing as a result of Bold's May 15 letter.

On May 25, Bold executed and delivered the original contract of April 1 to Stieb without any variation of the original terms.

Stieb does not wish to sell the land to Bold because he has received another offer for $200,000.

Required

Items 1 through 15 are statements based on the facts to the left. Mark (A) if the statement is correct. Mark (B) if the statement is incorrect.

1. When Stieb accepted Bold's request to keep the offer open until June 1, an option contract was formed.

2. Stieb's revocation was effective on April 17.

3. Bold's purported acceptance mailed on April 18 was by an authorized means.

4. Even if Stieb's letter of April 5 was an offer, acceptance would be futile because the $100 was not adequate consideration.

5. An unsigned acceptance is ineffective to form a contract to sell real property.

6. Bold's acceptance mailed on April 18 was effective before Stieb knew of it.

7. Bold could simply have bound Stieb to a contract to sell on April 5 by accepting Stieb's offer of April 1 subject to obtaining financing within 30 days (provided Bold made a good-faith effort to obtain it).

8. If Bold had called Stieb on April 4 and inquired whether Stieb would consider going lower on the price, and if Stieb had said no, there would have been a rejection, a counteroffer, and a rejection of the counteroffer.

9. An option contract was formed on April 18.

10. An option contract was formed on April 20.

11. Assuming an option contract was formed on April 18, the revocation terminated the option contract on April 19.

12. Even if Stieb's revocation was not effective, Bold's letter of May 15 was a counteroffer which automatically terminated Bold's right to accept Stieb's offer of April 1.

13. Stieb entered into a contract to sell the land on May 25.

14. Stieb's acceptance of the other offer to purchase the land for $200,000 would have been a breach of contract.

15. Bold's remedy for Stieb's breach would be monetary damages of $25,000.

Knowledge Tested

1. Effect of inquiries, revocation, conditions, acceptance, and rejection
2. Statute of frauds
3. Option contracts

Authors' Comments

This set of questions requires that you relate the basic rules for offer and acceptance to each other. Notice the effect of the option contract. The performance obligation results in irrevocability of the underlying offer. Item 15 illustrates that contract law favors efficiency: breach is permitted at a cost.

1. The correct answer is (B).

DISCUSSION: Bold's request was a solicitation of an offer. Stieb's letter on April 1 was an offer to sell land. Stieb's letter on April 5 was an offer to form a contract to keep the April 1 offer open.

2. The correct answer is (B).

DISCUSSION: A revocation is effective upon receipt by the offeree.

3. The correct answer is (A).

DISCUSSION: Unless the terms of an offer require acceptance by a specified means, the offeree is implicitly authorized to accept by any reasonable means, including the one used by the offeror.

4. The correct answer is (B).

DISCUSSION: If consideration provided in a bargained-for exchange is legally sufficient, its value need not be comparable to that of consideration received. The $100 was legally sufficient because, by paying it, Bold incurred a legal detriment (gave up a legal right to the $100).

5. The correct answer is (B).

DISCUSSION: An agreement within the statute of frauds is unenforceable absent a sufficient written memorandum of the agreement. The writing need only have been signed by the party against whom enforcement is sought.

6. The correct answer is (A).

DISCUSSION: Since Bold had not yet received the revocation, Bold still had the power of acceptance on April 18. Acceptance by an authorized means is effective on dispatch.

7. The correct answer is (B).

DISCUSSION: Conditional acceptance is rejection of the offer. Rejection is effective when received, and it terminates the offer. Conditional acceptance is also a counteroffer effective upon receipt.

8. The correct answer is (B).

DISCUSSION: Attempting acceptance which varies from the offer operates both as a rejection which terminates the power of acceptance and as a counteroffer. However, Bold's call was a mere tentative inquiry which did not indicate intent to reject the offer.

9. The correct answer is (A).

DISCUSSION: Stieb's letters revoking his offers would have been effective when received by Bold on April 19. However, Bold's acceptance operated as an exercise of the power of acceptance, forming a contract, when it was dispatched on April 18. Revocation of an offer cannot be effective after the power of acceptance the offer conferred has been exercised.

10. The correct answer is (B).

DISCUSSION: Bold's acceptance was effective, forming a contract, when it was dispatched on April 18. A revocation cannot be effective after acceptance.

11. The correct answer is (B).

DISCUSSION: If supported by consideration, an acceptance of an offer to keep another offer open binds the offeror to keep the offer open. The binding offer to keep an offer open results in an option contract.

12. The correct answer is (B).

DISCUSSION: In general, the power of acceptance under an option contract is not terminated by a rejection or a counteroffer made by the offeree, unless the requirements are met for the discharge of a contractual duty or the offeror changes its position to its detriment in reliance on such rejection or counteroffer.

13. The correct answer is (A).

DISCUSSION: When Bold exercised the power of acceptance under the option contract, Stieb's offer of April 1 ripened into a contract.

14. The correct answer is (B).

DISCUSSION: Failure to perform the contract to sell to Bold is what would have constituted breach of contract. If the other offeree accepted, Stieb could not have performed both contracts. Thus, Stieb would eventually breach one or both.

15. The correct answer is (B).

DISCUSSION: If Stieb breached, Bold might seek a court order of specific performance. If Bold instead sought monetary damages, they would be measured by Bold's expectation or reliance interest in the May 25 contract.

ESSAY QUESTION *(CPA, adapted)* 15-25 minutes

West Corp. is involved in the following disputes:

- On September 16, West's president orally offered to hire Dodd Consultants, Inc. to do computer consulting for West. The offer provided for a 3-year contract at $5,000 per month. West agreed that Dodd could have until September 30 to decide whether to accept the offer. If Dodd chose to accept the offer, its acceptance would have to be received by September 30.

  On September 27, Dodd sent West a letter accepting the offer. West received the letter on October 2. On September 28, West's president decided that West's accounting staff could handle West's computer problems and notified Dodd by telephone that the offer was withdrawn. Dodd argued that West had no right to revoke its offer and that Dodd had already accepted the offer by mail.

  Dodd claims that it has a binding contract with West because

  - West's offer could not be revoked before September 30.

  - Dodd's acceptance was effective on September 27, when the letter accepting the offer was mailed.

  West's president claims that if an agreement exists, that agreement would not be enforceable against West because of the statute of frauds requirement that the contract be in writing.

- On March 1, West signed a lease with Abco Real Estate, Inc. for warehouse space. The lease required that West repair and maintain the warehouse. On April 14, West orally asked Abco to paint the warehouse. Despite the lease provision requiring West to repair and maintain the warehouse, Abco agreed to do so by April 30. On April 29, Abco advised West that Abco had decided not to paint the warehouse. West demanded that Abco paint the warehouse under the April 14 agreement. Abco refused and has taken the following positions:

  - Abco's April 14 agreement to paint the warehouse is not binding on Abco because it was a modification of an existing contract.

  - Because the April 14 agreement was oral and the March 1 lease was in writing, West would not be allowed to introduce evidence in any litigation relating to the April 14 oral agreement.

Required

a. State whether Dodd's claims are correct and give the reasons for your conclusions.

b. State whether West's president's claim is correct and give the reasons for your conclusion.

c. State whether Abco's positions are correct and give the reasons for your conclusions.

Knowledge Tested

1. Offer, revocation, and acceptance
2. Statute of frauds
3. Contract modification
4. Parol evidence rule

Authors' Comments

Fundamental common-law contract rules must be applied to facts. Briefly, the rules are

1. Offers are revocable, absent consideration.

2. Acceptance is effective upon dispatch, unless the offer stipulates otherwise. A revocation is effective upon receipt prior to acceptance.

3. Consideration may be by mutual promises.

4. A promise that cannot be performed within a year is unenforceable absent a signed writing.

5. Modification of a contract requires consideration.

6. Prior or contemporaneous statements are inadmissable to contradict an integrated written contract.

Note: If you wish to work additional essay material, see Part b. of the first essay in Study Unit 8.

AICPA Unofficial Answer

a. Dodd's claim, that West's offer could not be revoked before September 30, is incorrect. Offers can be revoked at any time before acceptance unless the offeror receives consideration to keep the offer open. West did not receive any consideration from Dodd in exchange for its promise to keep the offer open until September 30. Therefore, West effectively revoked its offer during the September 28 telephone conversation.

Dodd's claim, that the September 27 letter accepting West's offer was effective when mailed to West, is incorrect. The general rule is that an acceptance is effective when dispatched if the acceptance is made using a reasonable mode of communication. In this case, the offer required that the acceptance be received by West to be effective. Therefore, Dodd's acceptance could not have been effective until after the offer expired because it was received after September 30.

b. West's claim, that any agreement that existed between West and Dodd would not be enforceable against West because of the statute of frauds, is correct. The term of the agreement was for 3 years. The statute of frauds requires that contracts that cannot be performed within 1 year from the date made be in writing. Because this was an oral contract for a period of 3 years, it would not be enforceable under the statute of frauds. Dodd's attempted acceptance of the offer would not be such a writing because it was not signed by West and could not be enforceable against West.

c. Abco's first position, that the oral April 14 agreement regarding the painting of the warehouse is not binding, is correct. This agreement was intended to modify the existing lease between the parties. Under common law, agreements modifying existing contracts require consideration to be binding. Abco did not receive any consideration in exchange for its promise to paint the warehouse; therefore, the agreement is not enforceable against Abco.

Abco's second position, that evidence of the April 14 oral agreement could not be admitted into evidence, is incorrect. The parol evidence rule allows the admission of proof of a later oral agreement that modifies an existing written contract.

STUDY UNIT 8: CONTRACT PERFORMANCE

13 pages of outline
44 multiple-choice questions
1 OOF and 3 essays

A. *Duties of Parties to Contract*
B. *Contract Beneficiaries and Assignees*
C. *Types of Discharges and Contract Remedies*

This study unit reviews contract problems arising after formation. The CPA exam places less emphasis on this material than the rules reviewed in Study Unit 7. However, the examination requires knowledge of the duties of parties to enforceable contracts, recognition of the distinction between performance and breach, the point at which a contract is discharged, and the type of remedy(ies) available under various breaches and under quasi-contract. Also tested is the ability to recognize the rights of third-party beneficiaries and the rights and duties of the parties to an assignment and delegation.

A. Duties of Parties to Contract

1. **Performance**. Contracts are formed with the expectation that the promises made, unless conditional or excused, will be fulfilled by performance.

2. **Conditions**. A condition is an act, an event, or a set of facts that (unless excused) triggers, limits, or extinguishes an absolute contractual duty to perform. A condition can be either the happening or the nonhappening of an event. A contractual breach subjects the promisor to liability, but failure of a condition in itself subjects neither party to liability.

    a. A **condition precedent** is an event that must occur before contractual performance is due. Until the condition is fulfilled, there is no absolute duty of performance.

        1) EXAMPLE: Buyer promises to purchase Seller's property provided Buyer can obtain a 3-year loan from City Bank at 10% (or less) rate of interest.

    b. **Concurrent conditions** are conditions whereby duties of parties to a contract mature simultaneously.

        1) EXAMPLE: Rose contracts to sell Harry a boat for $5,000 with delivery to take place upon payment of the total price. The proposed and reciprocally agreed-to performances are to take place simultaneously. The conditions are concurrent.

    c. A **condition subsequent** is an event which operates to terminate an existing duty and a right to compensation for a breach of contract.

        1) EXAMPLE: A clause in a fire insurance policy specifies that coverage lapses if the house is unoccupied for 6 consecutive months.

    d. An **express condition** is explicitly set forth in language, usually preceded by such terms as "provided that," "on condition that," "after," "while," "upon," "as soon as," or "subject to." Failure to properly perform an express condition may result in loss of the right to receive payment or performance of a return promise.

        1) To resolve disputes about an express condition that performance by one party be to the personal satisfaction of the other, courts apply an objective standard if the dispute involves mechanical fitness, marketability, or utility. If the average person would be satisfied, the party must pay.

        2) Courts apply a subjective standard in matters of personal taste, opinion, or judgment. But dissatisfaction must be genuine: honest and in good faith. Refusal to pay based on mere dissatisfaction with the bargain (e.g., cost) is in bad faith. Then the condition is excused. Testimony of experts can be used as circumstantial evidence of bad faith.

e.   An **implied condition** (a **constructive condition**) is one not expressly stated in the contract.

f.   **Implied-in-fact conditions** are not stated in express language but are understood by both parties to be part of the agreement. They are necessarily inferred from promises contained in the contract.

    1)   EXAMPLE: Snap contracts to paint Donna's house for $1,000. It is necessarily implied that Donna will inform Snap of the desired color.

g.   An **implied-in-law condition** is imposed by law to serve justice and promote fairness.

    1)   EXAMPLE: Alan contracts to sell a certain tract of land to Larry for $850,000. The contract is silent as to time for delivery of the deed and payment of the purchase price. The law implies that the respective performances are mutually dependent. Alan must deliver the deed, and Larry must tender the $850,000.

    NOTE: For an express condition, strict performance is required. Substantial performance is sufficient for an implied condition. But if time is of the essence of the contract, a party who fails to tender performance on or before the date stated is in breach.

3.   **Strict Performance**. A party to a contract discharges his/her contractual obligations by performing according to the terms of the contract.

a.   **Part performance** is generally insufficient to discharge from contractual duties.

    1)   But the parties may agree to accept less than full performance.

b.   If a contract does not specify a time for performance, it is due within a reasonable time after the contract is made.

c.   Exceptions to the general rule of strict performance follow in 4. through 9. beginning below.

4.   **Tender** is an offer by one party, having the present ability to perform, to the other party to perform an obligation according to the terms of the contract.

a.   In a bilateral contract, a party who tenders performance which is refused or rejected by the other may treat the contract as repudiated. The repudiation excuses or discharges the tendering party from further duty under the contract. (S)he may sue for damages.

b.   A tender of payment requires that there be a bona fide, unconditional offer of payment of the amount of money due, coupled with an actual production of money or its equivalent.

    1)   A tender of payment by check is not valid tender when a party objects and demands cash.

    UCC NOTE: Unless otherwise provided, tender of payment by the buyer is a condition to the seller's duty to deliver the goods. Unless the seller demands payment in legal tender, the buyer may pay by check.

5.   **Substantial Performance**. To mitigate the harshness of requiring strict performance, courts have developed a somewhat lesser standard of performance for application when duties are difficult to perform without some deviation from perfection (e.g., construction contracts, agricultural contracts, and some personal or professional services.

a. A builder or other party who in good faith completes the job in substantial compliance with the contract has discharged his/her duties and can enforce the contract and collect the contract price. Perfection is not required, but the performance must not vary greatly from the promise in the contract. Any damages that result from noncompliance can be collected by the buyer or deducted from the contract price.

b. The doctrine is not applied if the builder has intentionally substituted inferior materials or used other production shortcuts.

c. The doctrine does not apply if the builder or other party has only partially, rather than substantially, performed. Whether substantial performance has been rendered is determined from facts such as the following:

　　1) To what extent has the injured party received benefits?
　　2) Can the injured party be adequately compensated?
　　3) Is the breaching party close to complete performance?
　　4) Will the breaching party face great hardship if termination is permitted?
　　5) How willful is the breach?
　　6) How great is the certainty of completion?

6. **Divisible Contracts**. A contract is divisible if performance by each party is divided into two or more parts and performance of each part by one party is the agreed exchange for the corresponding part by the other party.

a. Parties may specify whether a contract is divisible or not. Some contracts are obviously divisible.

b. A contract is not divisible merely because it is to be performed in installments, e.g., tenant signs a 2-year lease with rent of $24,000 payable in monthly installments of $1,000.

c. Rights and duties of one of the severable parts of a divisible contract are not dependent on rights and duties of another.

7. **Impossibility** is an exception to the general rule of strict performance. Circumstances must have changed so radically since the contract was formed that the parties could not reasonably have contemplated and expressly provided for the change.

a. Performance will be excused, and the contract terminated, if

　　1) An essential party to the contract dies.
　　2) An essential item or commodity has been destroyed.
　　3) An intervening change of law has rendered performance illegal.

b. The impossibility must be objective, i.e., no one could perform the duty or duties.

　　1) A promise to supply a commodity is not impossible to perform when an alternative supply is available.

c. The impossibility must arise after the contract was made.
d. If performance is partially impossible, discharge is partial.
e. Temporary impossibility merely suspends contractual duties.

8. **Commercial Impracticability**. A less rigid doctrine than impossibility, commercial impracticability requires unreasonable difficulty and/or expense.

a. The unreasonable difficulty and/or expense must be caused by some unforeseeable event.

b. This standard is very difficult for seasoned business persons.

9. **Frustration of Purpose**. The doctrine permits discharge from obligations to perform, even if it is still possible to perform, if the purpose of the contract becomes valueless. Performance is excused when a supervening act or event completely (or almost) destroys the purpose of the contract if

   a. Such event could not reasonably have been foreseen when the parties contracted.
   b. The parties clearly realized the purpose when the contract was made.

10. **Good faith** is expected of the parties in performing contractual promises.

    a. A party has a duty to act in good faith to fulfill a condition to the extent to which (s)he has power, e.g., to obtain financing.

    b. A duty of good faith in performance is implied in output and requirements contracts; e.g., to double the output of the preceding month might constitute a breach.

    c. Lack of good faith is a bar to certain defenses and remedies, e.g., to specific performance.

11. Stop and review! You have completed the outline for this subunit. Study multiple-choice questions 1 through 6 beginning on page 261.

B. Contract Beneficiaries and Assignees

1. **Third-Party Beneficiaries**. A party to a contract, an assignee, and an intended beneficiary have legal rights to performance of the contract.

   a. A **third-party beneficiary contract** is one in which at least one of the performances is intended for the direct benefit of a person other than the parties who actually made the contract.

   b. An **intended beneficiary** is a person, not a party to the contract, whom the parties intended to directly benefit from the contract. (S)he is a creditor or donee beneficiary.

   c. If a promisee's main purpose in making a contract with the promisor is to discharge a debt (s)he owes to a third party, the third party is **a creditor beneficiary**.

   d. If a promisee's main purpose in entering into a contract with the promisor is to confer a benefit on a third party as a gift, the third party is a **donee beneficiary**.

   e. An **incidental beneficiary** is a person, not a party to a contract, who might derive a benefit if the contract is performed, but whom the parties did not intend to benefit directly. (S)he is not an intended beneficiary and has no standing to sue on the contract.

      1) EXAMPLE: Sid and Manuel are the only parties to a contract to build a roller skating rink. The owner of a nearby restaurant might benefit incidentally from completion of the contract.

   f. An intended beneficiary can sue the promisor directly for breach of a contract made for the beneficiary's benefit but only when his/her rights have vested. They vest when they are fixed, accrued, or absolute, not contingent.

      1) EXAMPLE: Larry owes Reni $450. Larry contracts to overhaul an engine for Rick in exchange for Rick's promise to pay Reni $450. If Rick does not pay, Reni may sue Rick or she may sue Larry on the underlying debt.

      2) A donee beneficiary generally has no contract rights against the donor.

      3) Until the rights vest, the original parties to the contract can modify, rescind, or novate the contract without consent of the third party.

g. Under the Restatement, there are three alternatives. An intended beneficiary's rights vest when (s)he

    1) Learns of the contract and detrimentally changes position in reliance on it;

    2) Commences an action against the promisor for any failure to perform the contract; or

    3) Consents, in response to a request by the promisor or promisee, to receive performance of the promisor.

NOTE: Any question on the CPA exam should be sufficiently specific that you can apply a particular rule or rules in selecting the best answer.

    a) EXAMPLE: Debtor promises Creditor to obtain coverage from Insurer and to name Creditor as beneficiary. Debtor does not. Creditor sues Insurer as an intended beneficiary. Creditor can have no vested rights in a contract before its formation.

h. A third party's rights are derivative, i.e., the same as the promisee's. The promisor may assert any defense against the beneficiary that the promisor could have asserted against the promisee if the promisee had sought to enforce the contract. Examples are fraud, duress, mistake, incapacity, lack of consideration, illegality, or statute of frauds.

2. **Assignment of Rights**. A party to a contract may transfer his/her rights under the contract to a third person. The party making the assignment is the **assignor**, and the person to whom the assignment is made is the **assignee**.

a. Any act or statement, written or oral, which indicates an intention to make a present transfer of a right effects assignment. The assignor must manifest a present intent to extinguish all right, title, and interest in the subject matter in him/herself and to transfer the same immediately and exclusively to the assignee.

b. The assignor must clearly identify the subject matter and the assignee and must take all steps necessary to transfer interest in the subject matter of the contract to the assignee.

c. When rights under a contract are assigned unconditionally, the rights of the assignor are extinguished.

d. Generally, no writing is required, but some assignments must be in writing:

    1) Wage assignments
    2) Interests in land
    3) Assignments involving the sale of goods over $500
    4) Assignments intended to act as security interests under Article 9 of the UCC

e. The assignor may assign a clearly defined portion of the subject matter to an assignee and retain a portion.

f. The assignor may assign the right to receive clearly defined portions of the subject matter to different assignees.

g. Contract rights are generally assignable, but an attempted assignment of a contract right is not effective if the contract expressly states that it is not assignable. The following are exceptions:

    1) A right to receive money

    2) Negotiable instruments

    3) In a contract for the sale of goods, the right to receive damages for breach of contract or for payment of an account owed

NOTE: A common clause is that contract rights are not assignable without consent of the obligor. Consent is then required to effect assignment.

h. A right cannot be assigned if the assignment would result in a material increase or alteration of the duties or risks of the obligor.

    1) EXAMPLE: Able owns a building which is insured against loss due to fire by Insurance Co. Able sells the building to Seth. Able may not assign his rights under the policy to Seth without the consent of Insurance Co.

i. A contract entered into in reliance by one party on the character or creditworthiness of the other party cannot be assigned without consent.

j. When assignment would result in the obligor's being required to perform personal services to someone other than the original obligee, the attempted assignment may be invalid. This typically occurs when the nature of personal services is unique as opposed to routine.

    1) But payments of money under a personal services contract may be assigned.

k. Rights under output and requirements contracts are not assignable.

    1) An **output contract** is one whereby a supplier agrees to deliver its entire output (e.g., production) to another who agrees to accept it.

    2) A **requirements contract** is one whereby one of the parties agrees to purchase all its requirements of a particular product or commodity from the other.

l. Future rights in a not-yet-existing future contract may not be assigned.

m. A contract cannot be assigned if a state statute expressly forbids assignment.

3. **Notice of Assignment**. Between assignor and assignee, assignment is effective when made, even if no notice of assignment has been communicated to the obligor.

    a. The assignee should notify the obligor of the assignment.

    b. Payment or other performance that the obligor renders to the assignor prior to receiving notification discharges the original contract obligation to the extent of the payment or performance.

    c. If proper notice is not given by the assignee, (s)he cannot sue the obligor and force a repeat performance, but would instead have to sue the assignor.

4. **Revocability of Assignments**. An assignment given for consideration is irrevocable.

    a. A gratuitous assignment is usually revocable by the assignor. Revocation is by

        1) Notice of revocation communicated by assignor to assignee or obligor
        2) Assignor's taking performance directly from obligor
        3) Assignor's subsequently assigning the same right to another assignee
        4) Bankruptcy of assignor
        5) Death of assignor

    b. A gratuitous assignment is irrevocable when

        1) The obligor has already performed.
        2) Some symbol of the rights has been delivered, e.g., stock certificates.
        3) The assignment is of an intangible and in writing.
        4) Detrimental reliance by the assignee, reasonably foreseeable, occurs.

5. **Assignor's Warranties**. If assignment is for value, the assignor makes three implied warranties:

   a. (S)he will do nothing to affect or impair the value of the assignment and has no knowledge of any fact which would.

   b. The right assigned exists and is subject to no limitations or defenses good against the assignor, except any that are stated or apparent.

   c. Any writing given or shown to the assignee as evidence of the right is genuine and is what it purports to be.

6. **Assignee's Rights**. The assignee of a contract acquires all the rights possessed by the assignor, and no more.

   a. The assignee stands in the shoes of the assignor.

   b. Any defenses or counterclaims the obligor might have asserted against the assignor can be asserted against the assignee.

     1) But the obligor can assert only those that arose before the assignee notified the obligor of the assignment.

     NOTE: An agreement by a buyer or lessee of personal property under a consumer contract that waives defenses or claims against the seller or lessor is generally enforceable by an assignee only if taken for value, in good faith, and without notice of any defenses or claims.

   c. An assignor might wrongfully assign the same right to two assignees. If the first assignment was gratuitous, it is revoked by the second. Otherwise courts apply one of the following rules:

     1) The first assignee's rights have priority, or
     2) The first assignee to notify the obligor prevails.

7. **Delegation of Duties**. A contract involves rights and duties. Rights are assigned. Duties are delegated. Delegation means that a person under a duty of performance authorizes another person to render the required performance.

   a. **Terminology**. Able and Baker have a contract. Able delegates his duties to Carr. Able is the **delegator**. Carr is the **delegatee**. Baker is the **obligee**.

   b. The delegator's expressed intention to make the delegation effects the delegation. No special formalities are required.

     1) The delegator need not use the word delegate.

     2) Both the Restatement and the UCC recognize that general language such as "I hereby assign my contract" effects an assignment of the rights and a delegation of the duties thereunder.

   c. A delegator may delegate performance of his/her duties under a contract to a delegatee provided the delegatee's performance would be substantially similar to the performance by the delegator. Duties that may be delegated include the duty to

     1) Pay money
     2) Manufacture ordinary goods
     3) Build according to a set of plans and specifications
     4) Deliver standard merchandise

d. Duties may not be delegated if

1) Performance by the delegatee would materially change the expectations of the obligee, e.g., under an output contract.

2) They involve a special trust, e.g., attorney and client.

3) They involve personal judgment and skill, e.g., custom artwork.

e. Duties which generally may not be delegated include the duty to

1) Provide professional services
2) Represent another as an exclusive agent
3) Render personal services to an employer
4) Manufacture or special order a distinct class of high-quality goods

8. **Liability after Delegation**. Delegation of duties does not relieve the delegator of obligations under the contract.

a. If the delegatee makes a promise of performance that will directly benefit the obligee and that promise is supported by consideration, there is an assumption of duty.

b. Breach of this duty makes the delegatee liable to the obligee.

c. The general rule is that the obligee can sue both the delegatee and the obligor.

d. If an assignee releases the obligor, the assignor is also released.

e. A **novation** will release the delegator. A novation is a contract to discharge an existing contract by substituting a new contract, which usually substitutes a new obligor.

9. Stop and review! You have completed the outline for this subunit. Study multiple-choice questions 7 through 25 beginning on page 263.

C. Types of Discharges and Contract Remedies

1. **Performance**. Liability for contract obligations is discharged by strict performance according to the terms of the contract or by substantial performance in certain circumstances. A duty discharged is no longer enforceable.

a. Performance might be excused by impossibility, impracticability, or frustration of purposes.

2. **Breach of contract** is a failure of a party to perform a duty imposed by a contract. A promisor who does not perform an absolute duty, not yet discharged, according to the contract terms, is in breach.

a. A **material breach** is unjustified failure to perform substantially obligations arising from promises in a contract, such that one party is deprived of what (s)he bargained for.

b. A material breach discharges the other party from any obligation to perform under the contract and entitles that party to seek damages or other appropriate relief as a remedy for the breach.

1) The modern trend allows the injured party to suspend his/her performance while the breaching party uses any time remaining under the contract to cure defective performance. If the breaching party does not cure, the injured party's performance is discharged when the time for performance expires.

      c.   A **nonmaterial breach** does not deprive the nonbreaching party of the benefit of the bargain and does not discharge that party.

          1)   The nonbreaching party may sue for damages.

      d.   **Anticipatory breach** occurs when one party indicates that (s)he has no intention to perform the contract prior to the time set for performance. Most courts allow the aggrieved party to

          1)   Suspend his/her own performance, and

          2)   Respond with one of the following actions:

              a)   Await a change of mind by the breaching party
              b)   Act to find a substitute performance
              c)   Immediately sue for damages

          NOTE: A party's repudiation of a contract must be absolute and clear. It may be expressed or implied, but it must be unequivocal. Most courts have held that anticipatory breach does not apply to promises to pay money.

3.   **Discharge by Agreement**. The parties to a contract may by agreement end it without performance or alter their performance obligations.

      a.   **Mutual rescission**. The parties to an executory bilateral contract agree to cancel it. They are restored to their original positions.

          1)   The agreement to rescind is itself a contract. The mutual surrender of rights constitutes the consideration necessary for, and the performance of, the contract of rescission.

      b.   **Accord and satisfaction**. Parties to a contract may make a new contract whereby both the prior and the new contracts are to be discharged by performance of the new.

          1)   The new agreement made after maturity or breach of the original contract is called an accord. The performance is called a satisfaction.

              a)   EXAMPLE: Dwight owes Lisa $10,000. Repayment is past due. Dwight offers Lisa a truck worth about $10,000 in lieu of the debt. Lisa accepts. This new consideration is sufficient to form a valid accord. It suspends the right to enforce. Performance of the accord discharges both the original contract and the accord.

          2)   The new agreement, if made before maturity or breach of the original, is sometimes called a substitute contract.

          3)   When a debt is not genuinely disputed, accepting an offer of part payment "in full satisfaction" does not bar entitlement to the balance.

              a)   But accepting an offer in full satisfaction of a liquidated debt earlier than due discharges the obligation in full.

    c.   A **novation** is an agreement among all parties that cancels an existing contract and, simultaneously, replaces it with a new contract, usually substituting a party to the prior contract with another who was not a party to it.

        1)   A novation completely releases the replaced party.

        2)   Consent of the remaining party may be express or implied.

        3)   Novation often involves discharge of an original debtor by substitution of a new debtor.

        4)   EXAMPLE: Bob has a contract with Barbie, but Barbie is unable to perform it. Bob agrees with Barbie and Jim that Jim will perform Barbie's duties under the original contract. Barbie will be freed from any further liability to Bob. The resulting contract is a novation under which Barbie is discharged from her duties under the original agreement.

    d.   A **release** refers to one party relieving another of a performance obligation without restoration to original positions. Releases are commonly used if there is a contingent or disputed liability.

        1)   In some states, a written release is effective without consideration.

    e.   A **waiver** is an intentional and voluntary giving up, relinquishment, or surrender of a known right. Waivers may result from an express agreement or be inferred from the circumstances.

        1)   EXAMPLE: Landlord says that, notwithstanding the fact that payment is due the 1st day of every month, it may be made by the 10th. This is a waiver of the right to insist on payment by the first.

4.   **Discharge by Operation of Law**. Some contractual obligations are discharged by law, regardless of the will of the parties.

    a.   A contract is said to be merged, and thereby discharged, when its terms are embodied by the parties in another contract of a higher legal standing.

        1)   EXAMPLE: By an integration clause, all prior negotiations are merged into a final complete document.

    b.   Provided requirements of the Bankruptcy Act are met, certain obligations are discharged in bankruptcy. Some are not, e.g., alimony.

    c.   **Statutes of limitations** designate a period after which litigation may not be commenced. The period of limitations varies from state to state and by the type of action, e.g., for breach of contract.

        1)   Expiration of the period bars judicial remedy.

        2)   The duties to perform are not discharged. If a party agrees to a new contract after the period has run, there is no need for new consideration.

        3)   The statute period begins from the later of the date of the breach or the date when it should reasonably have been discovered.

        4)   The period is tolled (temporarily stops running) under certain circumstances, e.g., a party out of the jurisdiction.

    d.   When one party to a contract obtains a judgment against the other for breach, the duty to perform is merged in the judgment and thereby discharged.

        1)   The judgment debtor is obligated under the terms of the judgment for any new performance, e.g., payment.

5. **Remedies**. Legal remedies for a party's breach of contract are primarily to compensate the other party in money for any effect of the breach or interest in the contract.

    a. **Expectation interest** is the expected benefit of the bargain. It is protected by awarding damages to put the nonbreaching party in as good a position as (s)he would have been in had the contract been performed. The nonbreaching party is given the benefit of the bargain made.

    b. **Reliance interest** arises from action (or forgoing action) in reliance on the other party's duty to perform the contract. It is protected by restoring the nonbreaching party to the position (s)he would have been in had the contract not been entered into.

    c. **Restitution interest**. A party has an interest in recovering the value of the benefit that his/her performance conferred on the other party even if a valid contract was not formed. Restitution is available to prevent unjust enrichment, to correct an erroneous payment, and to permit an aggrieved party to recover deposits advanced on a contract.

6. **Damages**. A judgment awarding an amount of money to compensate for damages is the most common judicial remedy for breach of contract.

    a. **Nominal damages** are awarded when a breach is proven but the nonbreaching party cannot prove any actual damages (loss). The usual amount is $1.00.

    b. **Compensatory damages** are those that flow from the wrongful conduct of the breaching party. The usual measure of compensatory damages is the amount of money necessary to compensate the nonbreaching party for the breach. It depends upon the interest for which the law is attempting to compensate, i.e., expectation, reliance, or restitution.

        1) Damages are intended to place the injured party in as good a position as if the breaching party had not breached and had performed the contract as the plaintiff reasonably expected.

        2) The plaintiff must be able to prove the amount of damages with reasonable certainty.

            a) Damages for lost profits and mental stress are difficult to prove adequately.

    c. **Consequential (special) damages** are foreseeable (results of a breach to a reasonable person at the time the contract was entered into). They might result from specific needs of the injured party of which the breaching party knew or should have known.

        1) Consequential damages are in addition to compensatory damages.

        2) EXAMPLE: Hadley contracts with a common carrier to deliver a broken part for a flour mill to a foundry as a model to forge a new one. The carrier promises delivery in 2 days, but it takes 7. Court finds the carrier not liable for Hadley's lost profits caused by the delay because the carrier had no notice the mill was stopped. The court limits damages for breach to those which flow naturally from the breach and those which the defendant had reason to foresee as a probable result of the breach.

d. **Punitive damages** are intended to punish a wrongdoer and to set an example for others.

1) The traditional view is that a party to a contract may perform or compensate the other party for his/her expectation interest. (This tends to favor efficient allocation of resources.)

2) Thus, it is rare for a court to award punitive damages in a contract suit. It might if a breach is malicious, willful, or physically injurious to the nonbreaching party, e.g., willful and malicious refusal to pay valid medical claims of an insured.

NOTE: For purposes of the CPA exam, assume that punitive damages are not awarded for a breach of contract, unless a question is worded in such a way as to indicate that the best answer requires otherwise.

e. By a **liquidated damages** clause, the parties to a contract agree in advance to the damages to be paid in the event of a breach. A liquidated damages clause is enforceable if all of the following apply:

1) It is not intended as a penalty.
2) It reasonably forecasts the probable loss due to the breach.
3) The loss is difficult to calculate.

NOTE: If a contract provides that an aggrieved party may choose liquidated damages or actual damages, the liquidated damages clause is probably unenforceable.

f. **Mitigation.** If a breach of contract occurs, the injured party is required to take reasonable steps to mitigate (reduce or lessen) damages (s)he may sustain. The injured party may not recover damages for loss that (s)he could have avoided without undue risk, burden, or humiliation. Thus, the nonbreaching party must

1) Refrain from piling up losses after notice of breach

2) Not incur further costs or expenditures

3) Make reasonable efforts to limit losses by obtaining a substitute at a reasonable price

7. **Specific Performance.** A nonbreaching party may seek an injunction: a court order restraining or compelling action.

a. It is an equitable remedy; that is, it is granted only under the following conditions:

1) There is no adequate remedy at law.

a) Monetary damages are not available or would not be an adequate remedy.

b) The subject matter of the contract is unique, e.g., a rare painting, land.

i) EXAMPLE: A court might order a seller to specifically perform a contract for the sale of land.

2) Irreparable injury will result if it is not granted.

b. Specific performance of a personal service contract is not granted.

8. **Rescission** cancels a contract and returns the parties to the positions they would have occupied if the contract had not been made. Rescission may be brought about by a mutual consent, conduct of the parties, or an equitable decree by a court. Rescission is an appropriate remedy in the following situations:

    a. A material breach, e.g., an unjustified failure to perform
    b. Innocent misrepresentation (Rescission is the only remedy.)
    c. A mutual mistake in contract formation
    d. A unilateral mistake in contract formation, and one of the following:

        1) The mistake was due to fraud, duress, or undue influence.

        2) The other party knew or should have known of the mistake. The mistake is so obvious that a reasonable person must suspect that a mistake was made.

        3) Enforcement of the contract would result in such extreme hardship to the mistaken party that an injustice would occur (provided the parties can be returned to the positions they held prior to the contract).

        4) The error was due to a mathematical mistake or omission of certain items in the computation of the cost of the contract (provided the error was inadvertent and without gross negligence).

    NOTE: A party who substantially violates the contract him/herself cannot seek rescission. A fully executed contract cannot be rescinded.

9. **Reformation**. When parties to a contract have imperfectly expressed their understanding in a written agreement, reformation allows the contract to be rewritten to reflect the parties' true intention.

    a. Reformation is generally ordered by a court only upon a clear and convincing demonstration of mutual mistake.

    b. If only one party was mistaken, reformation will not be decreed unless the mistake on one side was caused by the other party's fraud.

10. **Quasi-contract** is not a contract but an equitable remedy whereby obligations are imposed by law to prevent unjust enrichment of one party at another's expense.

    a. To recover based on quasi-contract the plaintiff must prove the following:

        1) The plaintiff conferred a benefit on the defendant.
        2) The plaintiff reasonably expected to be paid (not a gift).
        3) The plaintiff did not force unwanted services on the defendant.
        4) There is no adequate remedy at law.
        5) Unjust enrichment would result unless the defendant paid.

    b. The amount of recovery is the reasonable value of services rendered or property delivered (not a contract price).

11. Stop and review! You have completed the outline for this subunit. Study multiple-choice questions 26 through 44 beginning on page 269.

MULTIPLE-CHOICE QUESTIONS

A. Duties of Parties to Contract

1. Which of the following types of conditions affecting performance may validly be present in contracts?

	Conditions Precedent	Conditions Subsequent	Concurrent Conditions
A.	Yes	Yes	Yes
B.	Yes	Yes	No
C.	Yes	No	Yes
D.	No	Yes	Yes

The correct answer is (A). *(CPA, adapted)*
   REQUIRED: The conditions permitted.
   DISCUSSION: Parties to a contract may validly protect themselves from assuming an absolute contractual duty to perform by the use of conditions. A condition is an act, an event, or a set of facts that activates, limits, or extinguishes an absolute contractual duty to perform. A condition subsequent is an event that will delay or terminate a contract duty without being in breach of contract. A condition precedent is an event that must occur before contractual performance is binding. Concurrent conditions are provisions requiring the parties to perform certain duties simultaneously.
   Answers (B), (C), and (D) are incorrect because a contract may have any of these types of conditions.

2. On June 15, 1998, Alpha, Inc. contracted with Delta Manufacturing, Inc. to buy a vacant parcel of land Delta owned. Alpha intended to build a distribution warehouse on the land because of its location near a major highway. The contract stated: "Alpha's obligations hereunder are subject to the vacant parcel being rezoned to a commercial zoning classification by July 31, 1999." Which of the following statements is correct?

A.   If the parcel is not rezoned by July 31, and Alpha refuses to purchase it, Alpha would not be in breach of contract.

B.   If the parcel is rezoned by July 31, and Alpha refuses to purchase it, Delta would be able to successfully sue Alpha for specific performance.

C.   The contract is not binding on either party because Alpha's performance is conditional.

D.   If the parcel is rezoned by July 31, and Delta refuses to sell it, Delta's breach would not discharge Alpha's obligation to tender payment.

The correct answer is (A). *(CPA, adapted)*
   REQUIRED: The effects of condition precedent.
   DISCUSSION: An express condition precedent must occur to trigger an absolute contractual duty to perform. Absent a present duty, there can be no breach.
   Answer (B) is incorrect because specific performance of a contract to sell land is based on its uniqueness and inadequacy of a legal remedy. The purchaser's consideration is not unique on these facts. Answer (C) is incorrect because conditional performance does not render a contract nonbinding. Note also that, when there is a condition over which a party has some power, (s)he is required to act in good faith to fulfill it. Answer (D) is incorrect because occurrence of the contingency renders performance obligations absolute. Delta's breach would constitute a repudiation, discharging Alpha and giving rise to a cause of action.

3. On May 25, 1999, Smith contracted with Jackson to repair Smith's cabin cruiser. The work was to begin on May 31, 1999. On May 26, 1999, the boat, while docked at Smith's pier, was destroyed by arson. Which of the following statements is correct with regard to the contract?

A.   Smith would not be liable to Jackson because of mutual mistake.

B.   Smith would be liable to Jackson for the profit Jackson would have made under the contract.

C.   Jackson would not be liable to Smith because performance by the parties would be impossible.

D.   Jackson would be liable to repair another boat owned by Smith.

The correct answer is (C). *(CPA, adapted)*
   REQUIRED: The parties' liability when the subject matter of a contract is destroyed.
   DISCUSSION: Nonperformance is excused when circumstances change so radically that performance is objectively impossible; i.e., nobody could perform the duty. Impossibility occurs when the subject matter of, or an item or commodity essential to, the contract is destroyed. The impossibility must arise after, and could not have been reasonably contemplated at, contract formation.
   Answer (A) is incorrect because mutual mistake is present at, not after, contract formation. It would apply if, unbeknownst to the parties, the boat was destroyed before formation. Answer (B) is incorrect because, to the extent the doctrine of impossibility applies, performance by both parties is excused and the contract is canceled. Answer (D) is incorrect because, under the doctrine of impossibility, duties are discharged, not substituted. But performance of a promise to supply a commodity is not impossible when an alternative supply is available.

4. Ames Construction Co. contracted to build a warehouse for White Corp. The construction specifications required Ames to use Ace lighting fixtures. Inadvertently, Ames installed Perfection lighting fixtures, which are of slightly lesser quality than Ace fixtures but in all other respects meet White's needs. Which of the following statements is correct?

   A.   White's recovery will be limited to monetary damages because Ames's breach of the construction contract was not material.

   B.   White will not be able to recover any damages from Ames because the breach was inadvertent.

   C.   Ames did not breach the construction contract because the Perfection fixtures were substantially as good as the Ace fixtures.

   D.   Ames must install Ace fixtures or White will not be obligated to accept the warehouse.

The correct answer is (A). *(CPA, adapted)*
   REQUIRED: The correct statement regarding failure to strictly perform a construction contract.
   DISCUSSION: If performance is only marginally deficient and the obligor acts in good faith, (s)he has substantially performed and is entitled to receive damages or the contract price minus the cost of correction. If the cost of correction is excessive, the obligor is entitled to receive the contract price minus the diminished value. The doctrine does not apply when the substantially performing party has not acted in good faith.
   Answer (B) is incorrect because damages are recoverable for any breach of contract. Answer (C) is incorrect because the terms of the contract were breached. The substantial performance doctrine affects the remedy. Answer (D) is incorrect because, when the cost of correction is excessive, a party who substantially performs a construction contract is liable for damages.

5. Maco contracted to sell 500 bushels of potatoes to LBC Chips. The contract did not refer to any specific supply source for the potatoes. Maco intended to deliver potatoes grown on its farms. An insect infestation ruined Maco's crop but not the crops of other growers in the area. Maco failed to deliver the potatoes to LBC. LBC sued Maco for breach of contract. Under the circumstances, Maco will

   A.   Lose, because it could have purchased potatoes from other growers to deliver to LBC.

   B.   Lose, unless it can show that the purchase of substitute potatoes for delivery to LBC would make the contract unprofitable.

   C.   Win, because the infestation was an act of nature that could not have been anticipated by Maco.

   D.   Win, because both Maco and LBC are assumed to accept the risk of a crop failure.

The correct answer is (A). *(CPA, adapted)*
   REQUIRED: The seller's liability when the subject matter of the contract is destroyed.
   DISCUSSION: Impossibility, to excuse contract performance, must be objective; i.e., performance was impossible for anyone. A substitute supply means performance was possible.
   Answer (B) is incorrect because unprofitability does not discharge liability for performance. Impracticability is inapplicable because crop failure is reasonably foreseeable, and the cost to render performance is neither extreme nor unreasonable. Answer (C) is incorrect because crop failure is an event foreseeable to a farmer. Impracticability might provide excuse only if extremely unreasonable hardship is required to obtain a substitute. Answer (D) is incorrect because crop production risk is attributed to the farmer.

6. In September 1999, Cobb Company contracted with Thrifty Oil Company for the delivery of 100,000 gallons of heating oil at the price of $.75 per gallon at regular specified intervals during the forthcoming winter. Due to an unseasonably warm winter, Cobb took delivery on only 70,000 gallons. In a suit against Cobb for breach of contract, Thrifty will

   A.   Lose, because Cobb acted in good faith.

   B.   Lose, because both parties are merchants and the UCC recognizes commercial impracticability.

   C.   Win, because this is a requirements contract.

   D.   Win, because the change of circumstances could have been contemplated by the parties.

The correct answer is (D). *(CPA, adapted)*
   REQUIRED: The liability when a contract to purchase a commodity is partly performed due to reduced demand.
   DISCUSSION: Performance was not conditioned on customer usage or demand. The doctrines of impossibility, impracticability, and frustration of purpose excuse performance only if a supervening circumstance was not reasonably contemplated or foreseeable when the contract was made. Unseasonably warm weather is not such a circumstance; it is an ordinary business risk.
   Answer (A) is incorrect because lack of good faith is a bar to certain legal defenses and remedies, but good faith is expected of parties in performing contractual promises. The reward is return performance, not excuse. Answer (B) is incorrect because commercial impracticability excuses nonperformance only when the nonoccurrence of the contingency was a basic assumption on which the contract was made. Answer (C) is incorrect because, in a requirements contract, the buyer agrees to purchase all the product or service needed, not a stipulated quantity.

B. Contract Beneficiaries and Assignees

7. Jones owned an insurance policy on her life, on which she paid all the premiums. Smith was named the beneficiary. Jones died and the insurance company refused to pay the insurance proceeds to Smith. An action by Smith against the insurance company for the insurance proceeds will be

- A. Successful because Smith is a third-party donee beneficiary.

- B. Successful because Smith is a proper assignee of Jones's rights under the insurance policy.

- C. Unsuccessful because Smith was not the owner of the policy.

- D. Unsuccessful because Smith did not pay any of the premiums.

The correct answer is (A). *(CPA, adapted)*
REQUIRED: The outcome of a suit by a beneficiary against an insurer and the reason.
DISCUSSION: A contract entered into by primary parties that is intended to directly benefit a third person is a third-party beneficiary contract. If the intent is to make a gift of the promised performance to the third party, (s)he is a donee beneficiary. The beneficiary of a life insurance policy is commonly such a donee. The intent is to provide benefits to a named party at the death of the insured. Smith's rights vested at the death of Jones if not before.
Answer (B) is incorrect because no rights held by Jones were transferred (assigned) to Smith, such as the right to borrow against the cash surrender value or change the beneficiary. Answers (C) and (D) are incorrect because Smith prevails as the party intended to be benefited by the contract.

8. Ferco, Inc. claims to be a creditor beneficiary of a contract between Bell and Allied Industries, Inc. Allied is indebted to Ferco. The contract between Bell and Allied provides that Bell is to purchase certain goods from Allied and pay the purchase price directly to Ferco until Allied's obligation is satisfied. Without justification, Bell failed to pay Ferco and Ferco sued Bell. Ferco will

- A. Not prevail, because Ferco lacked privity of contract with either Bell or Allied.

- B. Not prevail, because Ferco did not give any consideration to Bell.

- C. Prevail, because Ferco was an intended beneficiary of the contract between Allied and Bell.

- D. Prevail, provided Ferco was aware of the contract between Bell and Allied at the time the contract was entered into.

The correct answer is (C). *(CPA, adapted)*
REQUIRED: The rights of a creditor who is also a third party to, and a payee under, a contract with the debtor.
DISCUSSION: A creditor beneficiary has standing to enforce a contract to which (s)he is a third party. Since the intent of the promisee (Allied) in entering into the contract with Bell was specifically to have return performance (payment) to discharge the debt to a third party (Ferco), the third party is a creditor beneficiary.
Answer (A) is incorrect because Ferco was an intended beneficiary of the contract. Answer (B) is incorrect because an intended beneficiary may enforce a contract enforceable between the parties. A prerequisite element of the contract was consideration, but not from Ferco. Answer (D) is incorrect because creditor awareness is not sufficient. The parties to the contract must have intended direct benefit to the third party.

9. Union Bank lent $200,000 to Wagner. Union required Wagner to obtain a life insurance policy naming Union as beneficiary. While the loan was outstanding, Wagner stopped paying the premiums on the policy. Union paid the premiums, adding the amounts paid to Wagner's loan. Wagner died and the insurance company refused to pay the policy proceeds to Union. Union may

- A. Recover the policy proceeds because it is a creditor beneficiary.

- B. Recover the policy proceeds because it is a donee beneficiary.

- C. Not recover the policy proceeds because it is not in privity of contract with the insurance company.

- D. Not recover the policy proceeds because it is only an incidental beneficiary.

The correct answer is (A). *(CPA, adapted)*
REQUIRED: The rights of a creditor named the beneficiary of a life insurance policy on the debtor.
DISCUSSION: Life insurance policies, especially decreasing term, designating a creditor as beneficiary are common. The parties to the contract (insured and insurer) intend it to benefit the third party directly by discharging a liability if the insured dies. The intended creditor beneficiary is entitled to the proceeds.
Answer (B) is incorrect because the purpose of the insurance contract was not to confer a gift on the creditor. Answer (C) is incorrect because an assignee or a third-party beneficiary may be entitled to performance of a contract. Answer (D) is incorrect because the contract was intended to confer a benefit directly on the creditor.

10. Egan contracted with Barton to buy Barton's business. The contract provided that Egan would pay the business debts Barton owed Ness and that the balance of the purchase price would be paid to Barton over a 10-year period. The contract also required Egan to take out a decreasing term life insurance policy naming Barton and Ness as beneficiaries to ensure that the amounts owed Barton and Ness would be paid if Egan died. Which of the following would describe Ness's status under the contract and insurance policy?

	Contract	Insurance Policy
A.	Donee beneficiary	Donee beneficiary
B.	Donee beneficiary	Creditor beneficiary
C.	Creditor beneficiary	Donee beneficiary
D.	Creditor beneficiary	Creditor beneficiary

The correct answer is (D). *(CPA, adapted)*
REQUIRED: The status of a seller's creditor regarding the business sale contract and credit life insurance policy.
DISCUSSION: Ness is a beneficiary although a third party to both contracts. When the contracting parties entered into the sale contract (Egan and Barton) and the insurance contract (Egan and insurer), they specifically intended that the contracts directly benefit a third party by providing for discharge of debt to the third party. Ness is a creditor beneficiary of both contracts.
Answers (A), (B), and (C) are incorrect because, although the contracting parties intended that Ness receive direct benefit, they never intended to confer it as a gift.

11. Rice contracted with Locke to build an oil refinery for Locke. The contract provided that Rice was to use United pipe fittings. Rice did not do so. United learned of the contract and, anticipating the order, manufactured additional fittings. United sued Locke and Rice. United is

A. Entitled to recover only from Rice because Rice breached the contract.

B. Entitled to recover from either Locke or Rice because it detrimentally relied on the contract.

C. Not entitled to recover because it is a donee beneficiary.

D. Not entitled to recover because it is an incidental beneficiary.

The correct answer is (D). *(CPA, adapted)*
REQUIRED: The status of a manufacturer regarding a construction contract stipulating the use of its product.
DISCUSSION: A person who is neither a primary contracting party nor an intended third-party beneficiary has no standing to sue on a contract. United is a mere incidental beneficiary, a person who may have been indirectly affected by the agreement but was not intended to be directly benefited.
Answers (A) and (B) are incorrect because United was not an intended beneficiary and has no standing to sue. Answer (C) is incorrect because a person is a donee beneficiary if the promisor's performance was intended as a gift to that person.

12. Graham contracted with the City of Harris to train and employ high school dropouts residing in Harris. Graham breached the contract. Long, a resident of Harris and a high school dropout, sued Graham for damages. Under the circumstances, Long will

A. Win, because Long is a third-party beneficiary entitled to enforce the contract.

B. Win, because the intent of the contract was to confer a benefit on all high school dropouts residing in Harris.

C. Lose, because Long is merely an incidental beneficiary of the contract.

D. Lose, because Harris did not assign its contract rights to Long.

The correct answer is (C). *(CPA, adapted)*
REQUIRED: The rights of a third party when breach resulted in nonreceipt of the anticipated benefit.
DISCUSSION: Long was neither a party to the contract nor an assignee of rights under it. The right to enforce the contract is denied to Long, a mere incidental beneficiary. The contract was not intended to inure primarily to the benefit of Long but rather to the city.
Answer (A) is incorrect because Long is not an intended beneficiary, i.e., one the parties intended to directly and personally benefit from the contract. Answer (B) is incorrect because the primary intent of the contract was not to confer benefit on any particular person within the class, although one might incidentally receive personal benefit. Answer (D) is incorrect because Long would have standing to sue if (s)he were a donee or creditor beneficiary.

13. Ordinarily, which of the following transfers will be valid without consent of the other parties?

- A. Assignment by the lessee of a lease contract if rent is a percentage of sales.
- B. Assignment by a purchaser of goods of the right to buy on credit without giving security.
- C. Assignment by an architect of a contract to design a building.
- D. Assignment by a patent holder of the right to receive royalties.

The correct answer is (D). *(CPA, adapted)*
REQUIRED: The transfer valid without the consent of the other parties.
DISCUSSION: Unless agreed otherwise, most contract rights can be assigned. If exercising the rights calls for personal skill or judgment, they may not be assigned. Also, assignment which materially changes a duty, increases risk, or reduces opportunity for repeat performance is ineffective. Assignments may be against public policy; e.g., statute regulates assignment of future wages. Assignment of a right to receive money or goods, however, is usually valid. The right to receive royalties is therefore assignable.
Answer (A) is incorrect because the lessor's risk is materially changed. Answer (B) is incorrect because the assignee may not be as creditworthy as the assignor, and the seller's bad debt risk could increase. Answer (C) is incorrect because personal service contracts generally cannot be assigned.

14. Yost contracted with Egan for Yost to buy certain real property. If the contract is otherwise silent, Yost's rights under the contract are

- A. Assignable only with Egan's consent.
- B. Nonassignable because they are personal to Yost.
- C. Nonassignable as a matter of law.
- D. Generally assignable.

The correct answer is (D). *(CPA, adapted)*
REQUIRED: The assignability of rights in a contract to buy real property.
DISCUSSION: Rights in a contract to buy real property, as in other contracts, are generally assignable. The other party's duties or risks must not be materially increased. When real property rights are transferred, the statute of frauds requires a writing.
Answer (A) is incorrect because, generally, unless the contract so requires, consent of a party is not required for assignment. Answer (B) is incorrect because, if the contract involved unique personal services, assignment without consent would be ineffective. This is not the case. Answer (C) is incorrect because, since an exception to the general rule, e.g., by statute, does not apply, the contract rights are assignable.

15. Moss entered into a contract to purchase certain real property from Shinn. Which of the following statements is not correct?

- A. If Shinn fails to perform the contract, Moss can obtain specific performance.
- B. The contract is nonassignable as a matter of law.
- C. The statute of frauds applies to the contract.
- D. Any amendment to the contract must be agreed to by both Moss and Shinn.

The correct answer is (B). *(CPA, adapted)*
REQUIRED: The legal effect and assignability of a valid real estate contract.
DISCUSSION: Contracts are generally assignable. Assignment is ineffective if a risk or duty of a party to the contract is materially increased, or an exception otherwise applies.
Answer (A) is incorrect because, since each parcel of real property is considered unique, monetary damages are deemed an inadequate remedy for the buyer. (S)he may seek specific performance. Answer (C) is incorrect because a contract for the purchase and sale of real property is within the statute of frauds. Answer (D) is incorrect because, to be enforceable, contract amendments must be agreed to by both parties.

16. One of the criteria for a valid assignment of a sales contract to a third party is that the assignment must

A. Be supported by adequate consideration from the assignee.

B. Be in writing and signed by the assignor.

C. Not materially increase the other party's risk or duty.

D. Not be revocable by the assignor.

The correct answer is (C). *(CPA, adapted)*
REQUIRED: The requirement for a valid assignment of a sales contract.
DISCUSSION: Unless agreed otherwise, most contract rights can be assigned. However, a contract right cannot be assigned if it would materially increase the risk or duty of the other party. If an assignment would materially increase the risk or duty sustained by the other party, the assignment is invalid.
Answer (A) is incorrect because adequate consideration is not a required element of a valid assignment. Gratuitous assignments are permissible. Answer (B) is incorrect because, generally, no writing is required for an assignment of contract rights to be valid. However, the statute of frauds requires a writing in certain situations. Answer (D) is incorrect because a gratuitous assignment is generally revocable by the assignor.

17. Generally, which of the following contract rights are assignable?

	Option Contract Rights	Malpractice Insurance Policy Rights
A.	Yes	Yes
B.	Yes	No
C.	No	Yes
D.	No	No

The correct answer is (B). *(CPA, adapted)*
REQUIRED: The assignable contract rights.
DISCUSSION: A party to a contract may generally transfer its rights under the contract to a third party. An option contract may be assigned. However, certain types of personal contracts cannot be assigned. A malpractice insurance contract may not be assigned if the contract prohibits the assignment or if the assignment would be against public policy because it may materially increase the risk of the obligor (insurance company).
Answers (A), (C), and (D) are incorrect because option contract rights may be assigned, but malpractice insurance policy rights may not be assigned.

18. On April 1, Neptune Fisheries contracted in writing with West Markets to deliver to West 3,000 pounds of lobsters at $4.00 a pound. Delivery of the lobsters was due May 1 with payment due June 1. On April 4, Neptune entered into a contract with Deep Sea Farms which provided: "Neptune Fisheries assigns all the rights under the contract with West Markets dated April 1 to Deep Sea Farms." The April 4 contract was

A. Only an assignment of rights by Neptune.

B. Only a delegation of duties by Neptune.

C. An assignment of rights and a delegation of duties by Neptune.

D. An unenforceable third-party beneficiary contract.

The correct answer is (C). *(CPA, adapted)*
REQUIRED: The legal effect of a general assignment.
DISCUSSION: The UCC, like the common law, recognizes that general language such as "I hereby assign my contract" effects both an assignment of the rights and a delegation of the duties.
Answer (A) is incorrect because such general language also effects a delegation of the duties under the contract. Answer (B) is incorrect because the expressed intention is effective to assign the rights. Answer (D) is incorrect because the beneficiary is not a party to such a contract. One might have characterized Deep Sea as an incidental beneficiary of the April 1, not the April 4, contract.

19. Pix borrowed $80,000 from Null Bank. Pix gave Null a promissory note and mortgage. Subsequently, Null assigned the note and mortgage to Reed. Reed failed to record the assignment or notify Pix of the assignment. If Pix pays Null pursuant to the note, Pix will

A. Be primarily liable to Reed for the payments made to Null.

B. Be secondarily liable to Reed for the payments made to Null.

C. Not be liable to Reed for the payments made to Null because Reed failed to record the assignment.

D. Not be liable to Reed for the payments made to Null because Reed failed to give Pix notice of the assignment.

The correct answer is (D). *(CPA, adapted)*

REQUIRED: The liability of an obligor without notice of assignment.

DISCUSSION: Valid assignment of rights is effective between assignor and assignee even if the obligor is without notice. But an obligor is discharged to the extent of performance rendered to the assignor before receiving notice of assignment.

Answers (A) and (B) are incorrect because an obligor is discharged to the extent of performance rendered to the assignor before receiving notice of assignment. Answer (C) is incorrect because an obligor does not have an implied duty to monitor public records to determine whether assignment has occurred. Furthermore, had Pix received actual notice, failure to record would not have effected liability relief.

20. Wilcox Co. contracted with Ace Painters, Inc. for Ace to paint Wilcox's warehouse. Ace, without advising Wilcox, assigned the contract to Pure Painting Corp. Pure failed to paint Wilcox's warehouse in accordance with the contract specifications. The contract between Ace and Wilcox was silent with regard to a party's right to assign it. Which of the following statements is correct?

A. Ace remained liable to Wilcox despite the fact that Ace assigned the contract to Pure.

B. Ace would not be liable to Wilcox if Ace had notified Wilcox of the assignment.

C. Ace's duty to paint Wilcox's warehouse was nondelegable.

D. Ace's delegation of the duty to paint Wilcox's warehouse was a breach of the contract.

The correct answer is (A). *(CPA, adapted)*

REQUIRED: The delegability of a contractual duty to paint a warehouse, and the liability after delegation.

DISCUSSION: A general indication of contract assignment effects assignment of rights and delegation of duties, unless an exception applies. Painting a warehouse, generally, is not so personal that performance by a delegatee in itself would materially change the expectations of the obligee. Because the contract did not prohibit assignment, delegation was valid and not a breach. But the delegator remains liable on the contract to the obligee.

Answer (B) is incorrect because notice of delegation to an obligee does not relieve the delegator of liability (unless the contract so provided). Answer (C) is incorrect because the contract did not prohibit delegation, and painting a warehouse is not a unique skill. Nor did the duty involve special trust. Painting of a warehouse by a delegatee would normally be substantially similar to that of the delegator, such that material expectations of the obligee would not change by delegation. Answer (D) is incorrect because delegation itself would constitute breach only if a valid contract term prohibited it.

21. Baxter, Inc. and Globe entered into a contract. After receiving valuable consideration from Clay, Baxter assigned its rights under the contract to Clay. In which of the following circumstances would Baxter not be liable to Clay?

A. Clay released Globe.

B. Globe paid Baxter.

C. Baxter released Globe.

D. Baxter breached the contract.

The correct answer is (A). *(CPA, adapted)*

REQUIRED: The assignor's liability to the assignee.

DISCUSSION: When Baxter unconditionally assigned its rights to Clay, Baxter no longer had rights in the contract. But Clay has rights, as assignee, against Baxter (1) if the assignor's warranties are breached (in that the rights were transferred for value) and (2) if Baxter accepts performance of the contract. But if Clay releases Globe from obligation to perform the contract, there is no basis for holding liable the assignor of the right to receive performance. Keep the parties straight.

Answer (B) is incorrect because, if Globe without notice of the assignment paid the assignor, the assignee has recourse against the assignor. Answer (C) is incorrect because Baxter, by impairing the value of the assignment, would breach the assignor's implied warranty. Answer (D) is incorrect because Baxter would be liable for breach of the assignor's implied warranty because a breach of contract would impair the value of the contract or subject it to defense.

22. On February 1, Burns contracted in writing with Nagel to sell Nagel a used car. The contract provided that Burns was to deliver the car on February 15 and Nagel was to pay the $800 purchase price not later than March 15. On February 21, Burns assigned the contract to Ross for $600. Nagel was not notified of the assignment. Which of the following statements is correct?

- A. By making the assignment, Burns implicitly warranted Nagel would pay the full purchase price.

- B. The assignment to Ross is invalid because Nagel was not notified.

- C. Ross will not be subject to any contract defenses Nagel could have raised against Burns.

- D. By making the assignment, Burns implicitly warranted a lack of knowledge of any fact impairing the value of the assignment.

The correct answer is (D). *(CPA, adapted)*
REQUIRED: The correct statement concerning contract assignment.
DISCUSSION: When an assignment is made for value, the Restatement of Contracts states that the assignor makes three implied warranties to the assignee: (1) The assignor will do nothing to affect or impair the value of the assignment, and (s)he has no knowledge of any fact which would do so; (2) the right, as assigned, actually exists and is subject to no limitations or defenses good against the assignor, except those stated or apparent; and (3) any writing given or shown to the assignee as evidence of the right is genuine and is what it purports to be.
Answer (A) is incorrect because the assignor makes no implied warranty that the debtor is solvent or will pay. Answer (B) is incorrect because an assignment can be effective absent notice to the obligor (Nagel). Answer (C) is incorrect because any defenses that the obligor might have asserted against the assignor can also be asserted against the assignee.

23. Omega Corp. owned a factory that was encumbered by a mortgage securing Omega's note to Eagle Bank. Omega sold the factory to Spear, Inc., which assumed the mortgage note. Later, Spear defaulted on the note, which had an outstanding balance of $15,000. To recover the outstanding balance, Eagle

- A. May sue Spear only after suing Omega.

- B. May sue either Spear or Omega.

- C. Must sue both Spear and Omega.

- D. Must sue Spear first and then proceed against Omega for any deficiency.

The correct answer is (B). *(CPA, adapted)*
REQUIRED: The recourse against delegator and delegatee.
DISCUSSION: Delegation did not relieve Omega of its payment obligation under the note. The delegatee assumes the performance duty when (s)he receives consideration for the promise to perform which directly benefits the obligee. The obligee is a creditor beneficiary of the assumption contract. The obligee may sue for breach of either contract.
Answer (A) is incorrect because the right of the creditor beneficiary of the assumption contract to enforce it is not conditioned on first suing on the contract assumed. Answer (C) is incorrect because an obligee has no implied obligation to sue a delegatee as a condition to enforcing contract rights. Answer (D) is incorrect because an obligee has no implied obligation to sue a delegatee as a condition precedent to enforcing contract rights.

24. Which of the following statements, if any, is(are) correct regarding a valid assignment?

I. An assignment of an interest in a sum of money must be in writing and must be supported by legally sufficient consideration.

II. An assignment of an insurance policy must be made to another party having an insurable interest in the property.

- A. I only.

- B. II only.

- C. Both I and II.

- D. Neither I nor II.

The correct answer is (D). *(CPA, adapted)*
REQUIRED: The statement(s), if any, describing a valid assignment.
DISCUSSION: Contract rights are property and may be transferred by gift, by will or descent, or by sale. A person entitled to payment of money may assign his/her rights orally and without consideration. Promises to assign without consideration ordinarily are unenforceable. A valid assignment of an insurance policy on property does not require that the assignee have an insurable interest at the time of assignment, but the insurable interest must exist at the time of loss. Consent of the insurer is required.
Answers (A), (B), and (C) are incorrect because consideration for assignment of an interest in money is not required, and an assignee of property insurance must have an insurable interest only at the time of the loss.

25. Buyer contracted with Sally to buy Sally's business. The contract provided that Buyer would pay the business debts Sally owed Ness and that the balance of the purchase price would be paid to Sally over a 10-year period. The contract also required Buyer to take out a decreasing term life insurance policy naming Sally and Ness as beneficiaries to ensure that the amounts owed Sally and Ness would be paid if Buyer died. Sally's contract rights were assigned to Vim, and Buyer was notified of the assignment. Despite the assignment, Buyer continued making payments to Sally. Buyer died before completing payment, and Vim sued Sally for the insurance proceeds and the other payments on the purchase price received by Sally after the assignment. To which of the following is Vim entitled?

	Payments on Purchase Price	Insurance Proceeds
A.	No	Yes
B.	No	No
C.	Yes	Yes
D.	Yes	No

The correct answer is (C). *(CPA, adapted)*
REQUIRED: The assignee's rights when notice was given to obligee.
DISCUSSION: This problem requires distilling the transaction from the verbiage. Diagram it. Vim as assignee has a right to the payments and the insurance proceeds.
Answers (A) and (B) are incorrect because, in that Buyer was notified, the payment obligation was not discharged by rendering it to the assignor. Answer (D) is incorrect because the rights as intended beneficiary of the insurance contract were also assigned.

C. Types of Discharges and Contract Remedies

26. Dell owed Stark $9,000. As the result of an unrelated transaction, Stark owed Ball that same amount. The three parties signed an agreement that Dell would pay Ball instead of Stark, and Stark would be discharged from all liability. The agreement among the parties is

A. A novation.

B. An executed accord and satisfaction.

C. Voidable at Ball's option.

D. Unenforceable for lack of consideration.

The correct answer is (A). *(CPA, adapted)*
REQUIRED: The true statement about an agreement to discharge a debtor from liability.
DISCUSSION: A novation is a contract to discharge an existing contract by substituting a new contract or new debtor. Substitution of a new promisor (Dell) for the old (Stark) is a novation.
Answer (B) is incorrect because by an accord a promisee agrees to accept a substituted performance by the promisor. Performance of the accord is the satisfaction. Answer (C) is incorrect because no basis for voidability is apparent. Answer (D) is incorrect because the promise by Dell to pay Stark's debt is consideration for Ball's discharge of Stark.

27. Wren purchased a factory from First Federal Realty. Wren paid 20% at the closing and gave a note for the balance secured by a 20-year mortgage. Five years later, Wren defaulted. First Federal threatened to accelerate the loan and foreclose. First Federal told Wren to make payment or obtain an acceptable third party to assume the obligation. Wren offered the land to Moss, Inc. for $10,000 less than Wren's equity in the property. This was acceptable to First Federal. At closing, Moss paid the arrearage, assumed the mortgage and note, and had title transferred to its name. First Federal released Wren. The transaction in question is a(n)

A. Purchase of land subject to a mortgage.

B. Assignment and delegation.

C. Third-party beneficiary contract.

D. Novation.

The correct answer is (D). *(CPA, adapted)*
REQUIRED: The classification of the contract.
DISCUSSION: A novation is an agreement between all parties that cancels an existing contract and replaces it with a new contract in which one party to the canceled contract is usually replaced by another who was not a party to it. The novation releases the replaced party from obligations to perform under the prior contract.
Answer (A) is incorrect because Moss assumed the mortgage and note, and Wren was released from liability to perform contractual obligations. Answer (B) is incorrect because a new contract was formed between First Federal and Moss, and Wren's liability to perform was discharged. Answer (C) is incorrect because Moss had no rights under the first contract, and First Federal was a party to (not a creditor beneficiary of) the new contract.

28. Castle borrowed $5,000 from Nelson and executed and delivered to Nelson a promissory note for $5,000 due on April 30. On April 1, Castle offered, and Nelson accepted, $4,000 in full satisfaction of the note. On May 15, Nelson demanded that Castle pay the $1,000 balance on the note. Castle refused. If Nelson sued for the $1,000 balance, Castle would

- A. Win, because the acceptance by Nelson of the $4,000 constituted an accord and satisfaction.
- B. Win, because the debt was unliquidated.
- C. Lose, because the amount of the note was not in dispute.
- D. Lose, because no consideration was given to Nelson in exchange for accepting only $4,000.

29. Which of the following actions will result in the discharge of a party to a contract?

	Prevention of Performance	Accord and Satisfaction
A.	Yes	Yes
B.	Yes	No
C.	No	Yes
D.	No	No

30. Under a personal services contract, which of the following circumstances will cause the discharge of a party's duties?

- A. Death of the party who is to receive the services.
- B. A substantial increase in the cost of performing the services.
- C. Bankruptcy of the party who is to receive the services.
- D. Illegality of the services to be performed.

The correct answer is (A). *(CPA, adapted)*
REQUIRED: The right to the balance of an undisputed debt when tender of less is accepted in full satisfaction.
DISCUSSION: A new contract between the same parties whereby both prior and new contracts are to be discharged by performance of the obligation in the new is an accord. Performance is the satisfaction.
Answer (B) is incorrect because a debt is unliquidated if there is a genuine controversy as to its amount. Answer (C) is incorrect because a creditor who accepts tender of less than the full amount of an undisputed debt "in full satisfaction" generally has the right to claim the balance. But when, as here, the accepted offer was to pay a lesser amount earlier than was required, acceptance discharges the entire debt. Answer (D) is incorrect because payment before it was due was a legal detriment which constituted legally sufficient consideration.

The correct answer is (A). *(CPA, adapted)*
REQUIRED: The action(s) that discharge a party from a contract.
DISCUSSION: After formation of a contract, a party may be discharged by either prevention of performance or accord and satisfaction. When a party is prevented from performance by objective impossibility (e.g., death or incapacity, destruction of subject of contract, a change in law, or commercial impracticability), the duty of performance is discharged by operation of law. Parties may discharge each other by entering into an accord and satisfaction. An accord and satisfaction requires the parties to make a new contract in which both the new and prior contracts are discharged by performance of the new contract.
Answers (B), (C), and (D) are incorrect because either prevention of performance or accord and satisfaction will discharge a party from performance under a contract.

The correct answer is (D). *(CPA, adapted)*
REQUIRED: The event that will discharge a party from performance under a personal services contract.
DISCUSSION: The nonperformance of a contractual duty may be excused if, after formation, the contract becomes objectively impossible to perform. A change in the law that renders the performance called for in the contract as illegal will discharge the party who is to perform the services.
Answer (A) is incorrect because it is the death or incapacity of the party promising to perform the services, not contracting to receive them, that will discharge the duty due to impossibility. Answer (B) is incorrect because commercial impracticability will excuse performance only when an extreme or unexpected expense occurs. Rising costs are not abnormal and do not cause the discharge of the performing party's duties. Answer (C) is incorrect because the bankruptcy of the receiving party does not necessarily interfere with the personal service contract. The ability of the performing party to complete the services is not hindered; therefore, his/her obligations under the contract are not discharged.

31. On May 1, 1984, CPA entered into an oral contract with Dell to provide certain accounting services to Dell. The contract was fully performed by both parties on March 31, 1985. On April 25, 1999, Dell commenced a breach of contract action against CPA claiming that CPA had improperly performed the services. CPA's best defense to the action would likely be the

- A. Parol evidence rule.

- B. Statute of limitations.

- C. Statute of frauds.

- D. Lack of consideration.

The correct answer is (B). *(CPA, adapted)*
REQUIRED: The best defense to a contract action that was not timely filed.
DISCUSSION: Over time, evidence may be lost, witnesses may become unavailable, and memories may dim. It is unfair for exposure to litigation to continue indefinitely. Thus, statutes stipulate a reasonable but limited time within which legal action can be brought. The statute of limitations may be pleaded as a complete defense, defeating a claim irrespective of its merits.
Answers (A), (C), and (D) are incorrect because, even if it applied, the claim would be barred by the statute of limitations.

32. The statute of limitations for an alleged breach of contract

- A. Does not apply if the contract was oral.

- B. Requires that a lawsuit be commenced and a judgment rendered within a prescribed period of time.

- C. Is determined on a case-by-case basis.

- D. Generally commences on the date of the breach.

The correct answer is (D). *(CPA, adapted)*
REQUIRED: The characteristic of the statute of limitations for a breach of contract claim.
DISCUSSION: Statutes of limitations bar initiating a lawsuit after a specified period has passed. The period varies in different states and for different types of claims. It generally commences on the date of the breach.
Answer (A) is incorrect because statutes of limitations apply to all contracts, expressed and implied, written and oral. Answer (B) is incorrect because statutes of limitations do not require that judgment be rendered within a prescribed period of time. Answer (C) is incorrect because the applicable period does vary with the nature and basis of a claim. But those variables are statutorily defined and not based on case law.

33. In 1962, Dart bought an office building from Graco under a written contract signed only by Dart. In 1999, Dart discovered that Graco made certain false representations during their negotiations concerning the building's foundation. Dart could have reasonably discovered the foundation problems by 1973. Dart sued Graco claiming fraud in the formation of the contract. Which of the following statements is correct?

- A. The parol evidence rule will prevent the admission into evidence of proof concerning Dart's allegations.

- B. Dart will be able to rescind the contract because both parties did not sign it.

- C. Dart must prove that the alleged misrepresentations were part of the written contract because the contract involved real estate.

- D. The statute of limitations would likely prevent Dart from prevailing because of the length of time that has passed.

The correct answer is (D). *(CPA, adapted)*
REQUIRED: The defense to a breach of contract claim based on misrepresentation.
DISCUSSION: Even if the misrepresentations were intentional, fraud in the inducement would have resulted in a voidable, not a void, contract. Statutes of limitations vary from state to state. The actionable period usually begins when a contract is breached, but not later than when the alleged breach could reasonably have been discovered. Although the period is sometimes longer for a claim based on fraud, it is improbable that it would exceed 26 years. A claim is barred when a statute of limitations period has expired even if the basis of the claim is otherwise sufficient.
Answer (A) is incorrect because, although the rule does not prevent admission of evidence of fraud, the claim is barred by the statute of limitations, even if there was fraud. Answer (B) is incorrect because compliance with the statute of frauds requires the signature of the party charged with liability, not of both parties. Answer (C) is incorrect because, although the statute of frauds is not intended to be used as a shield for fraud, the claim (even if meritorious) is barred by the statute of limitations.

34. Teller brought a lawsuit against Kerr 10 years after an oral contract was made and 8 years after it was breached. Kerr raised the statute of limitations as a defense. Which of the following allegations would be most important to Kerr's defense?

    A.   The contract was oral.

    B.   The contract could not be performed within 1 year from the date made.

    C.   The action was not timely brought because the contract was entered into 10 years prior to the commencement of the lawsuit.

    D.   The action was not timely brought because the contract was allegedly breached 8 years prior to the commencement of the lawsuit.

The correct answer is (D). *(CPA, adapted)*
    REQUIRED: The most important allegation to a defense based on the statute of limitations.
    DISCUSSION: The statute of limitations may be pleaded as a complete defense to a claim if the period for bringing an action has expired. The statute operates to defeat the claim irrespective of the merits of the case. The statute begins to run when a cause of action arises, which is usually the time at which suit may be brought. For contracts, that moment is usually the date of breach.
    Answer (A) is incorrect because the statute of limitations is the applicable defense. Absence of a writing would generally be an independent defense based on the statute of frauds. Answer (B) is incorrect because this allegation would support a defense based on the statute of frauds. Answer (C) is incorrect because the statute of limitations period generally begins to run when the contract is breached.

35. Which of the following statements correctly applies to a typical statute of limitations?

    A.   The statute requires that a legal action for breach of contract be commenced within a certain period of time after the breach occurs.

    B.   The statute provides that only the party against whom enforcement of a contract is sought must have signed the contract.

    C.   The statute limits the right of a party to recover damages for misrepresentation unless the false statements were intentionally made.

    D.   The statute prohibits the admission into evidence of proof of oral statements about the meaning of a written contract.

The correct answer is (A). *(CPA, adapted)*
    REQUIRED: The correct statement about the statute of limitations.
    DISCUSSION: Each state has statutes of limitations which designate a period after which litigation may not be commenced. Thus, the running (expiration) of the statute of limitations bars judicial remedy. The statute begins to run from the time of the breach of contract. Note that the duties to perform are not discharged. There is no need for new consideration to form a new contract after the period has run.
    Answer (B) is incorrect because this is a feature of the statute of frauds. Answer (C) is incorrect because this describes an exculpatory clause. Answer (D) is incorrect because this is a feature relevant to the parol evidence rule.

36. Ordinarily, in an action for breach of a construction contract, the statute of limitations time period would be computed from the date the

    A.   Contract is negotiated.

    B.   Contract is breached.

    C.   Construction is begun.

    D.   Contract is signed.

The correct answer is (B). *(CPA, adapted)*
    REQUIRED: The action that begins the statute of limitations period.
    DISCUSSION: The statute of limitations is a time period during which a party may commence litigation against another party. The statute of limitations period for breach of contract commences on the later of the date when the contract is breached or the date when the breach should have been discovered. Statutes of limitations vary from state to state, but the common limitation for bringing a contract action is either 4 or 5 years.
    Answers (A), (C), and (D) are incorrect because the statute of limitations period for breach of contract commences when the breach occurs or should be discovered.

37. In general, a clause in a real estate contract entitling the seller to retain the purchaser's down payment as liquidated damages if the purchaser fails to close the transaction, is enforceable

A. In all cases, when the parties have a signed contract.

B. If the amount of the down payment bears a reasonable relationship to the probable loss.

C. As a penalty, if the purchaser intentionally defaults.

D. Only when the seller cannot compel specific performance.

The correct answer is (B). *(CPA, adapted)*
REQUIRED: The enforceability of a liquidated damages clause.
DISCUSSION: By a liquidated damages clause, the parties agree in advance to the damages to be paid in the event of a breach. The clause must reasonably forecast the probable loss due to a breach, the loss must be difficult to calculate, and the clause must not be intended as a penalty.
Answer (A) is incorrect because a clause that provides for liquidated damages without a reasonable relationship to the probable loss is not enforceable. Answer (C) is incorrect because the courts will not enforce a liquidated damages clause intended to punish default. Answer (D) is incorrect because liquidated damages might reasonably compensate for loss even when a seller obtains specific performance.

38. Master Mfg., Inc. contracted with Accur Computer Repair Corp. to maintain Master's computer system. Master's manufacturing process depends on its computer system operating properly at all times. A liquidated damages clause in the contract provided that Accur pay $1,000 to Master for each day that Accur was late responding to a service request. On January 12, Accur was notified that Master's computer system failed. Accur did not respond to Master's service request until January 15. If Master sues Accur under the liquidated damages provision of the contract, Master will

A. Win, unless the liquidated damages provision is determined to be a penalty.

B. Win, because under all circumstances liquidated damages provisions are enforceable.

C. Lose, because Accur's breach was not material.

D. Lose, because liquidated damages provisions violate public policy.

The correct answer is (A). *(CPA, adapted)*
REQUIRED: The effect of a liquidated damages clause.
DISCUSSION: The parties to a sales contract may stipulate an amount in the contract that the parties agree to be a reasonable estimation of the damages owing to one in the event of a breach by the other. To be enforceable, the liquidated damages amount must constitute a reasonable forecast of the damages likely to result from the breach. The amount must have a reasonable relationship to the loss expected to result from the breach. If the liquidated damages provision was motivated by a desire to deter a breach as opposed to a good faith effort to estimate probable damages, the provision will be deemed to be a penalty and will be declared void.
Answer (B) is incorrect because liquidated damages provisions are enforceable only if they reasonably forecast the damages likely to result from a breach. Answer (C) is incorrect because reasonable liquidated damages are definitively material. Answer (D) is incorrect because contracting parties are encouraged to fashion their own reasonable remedies. Public policy favors reasonable liquidated damages clauses.

39. K contracted to sell H a building for $310,000. The contract required H to pay the entire amount at closing. K refused to close the sale. H sued K. To what relief is H entitled?

A. Punitive damages and compensatory damages.

B. Specific performance and compensatory damages.

C. Consequential damages or punitive damages.

D. Compensatory damages or specific performance.

The correct answer is (D). *(CPA, adapted)*
REQUIRED: The relief available for breach of a contract to sell realty.
DISCUSSION: The equitable remedy of specific performance is available only when damages are inadequate to remedy a breach of contract, usually when the subject matter is unique. Land is usually considered not interchangeable; it is unique. But a plaintiff may accept compensatory damages in lieu of specific performance.
Answers (A) and (C) are incorrect because punitive damages are seldom awarded in contracts cases. Answer (B) is incorrect because the common law election of remedies doctrine requires the plaintiff to choose one of alternative remedies. Note that remedies are cumulative under Article 2 of the UCC.

40. Jones, CPA, entered into a signed contract with Foster Corp. to perform accounting and review services. If Jones repudiates the contract prior to the date performance is due to begin, which of the following is not correct?

- A. Foster could successfully maintain an action for breach of contract after the date performance was due to begin.

- B. Foster can obtain a judgment ordering Jones to perform.

- C. Foster could successfully maintain an action for breach of contract prior to the date performance is due to begin.

- D. Foster can obtain a judgment for the monetary damages it incurred as a result of the repudiation.

The correct answer is (B). *(CPA, adapted)*
REQUIRED: The legal recourse not available to the nonbreaching party after anticipatory repudiation.
DISCUSSION: Repudiation before the time of performance is an anticipatory breach. Anticipatory breach occurs when a party indicates that (s)he will not perform. This indication may be expressed or implied by express statement, selling property, going out of business, or not meeting an installment due. The injured party may treat the contract as breached and immediately file suit, or as continuing and hold the breaching party accountable when performance is due. But a contract for personal services is not specifically enforced. Damages might be inadequate when the subject matter is unique. But forced performance may not be satisfactory and could be construed as involuntary servitude.

Answers (A) and (C) are incorrect because anticipatory repudiation gives ground for immediate suit. Answer (D) is incorrect because Foster can recover compensatory damages.

41. To cancel a contract and to restore the parties to their original positions before the contract, the parties should execute a

- A. Novation.
- B. Release.
- C. Rescission.
- D. Revocation.

The correct answer is (C). *(CPA, adapted)*
REQUIRED: The means to cancel a contract and restore the parties to their original positions.
DISCUSSION: Mutual rescission is a new contract whereby parties agree to discharge their obligations under a prior contract and are restored to their original positions.

Answer (A) is incorrect because a novation is a contract which replaces a prior one. Usually a new party substitutes for a party to the prior one. Answer (B) is incorrect because by a release one party relieves another of a performance obligation without restoration to original positions. Answer (D) is incorrect because revocation is voiding of a prior act, e.g., an offer.

42. Paco Corp., a building contractor, offered to sell Preston used construction equipment. Preston was in the business of buying and selling equipment. In the written offer, Paco's secretary typed the price as $10,900 rather than $109,000. Preston, on receipt of the offer, immediately accepted it. Paco refused to deliver the equipment to Preston unless Preston agreed to pay $109,000. Which of the following statements is correct?

- A. Paco will not be liable because there has been a mutual mistake of fact.

- B. Paco will be able to rescind the contract because Preston should have known that the price was erroneous.

- C. Preston will prevail because Paco is a merchant.

- D. The contract between Paco and Preston is void because the price set forth in the offer is substantially less than the equipment's fair market value.

The correct answer is (B). *(CPA, adapted)*
REQUIRED: The result when an offer with a clerical error is accepted.
DISCUSSION: The offer contained a unilateral mistake of fact. A contract is formed. But rescission is available under certain circumstances; e.g., (1) the other party knew or should have known of the mistake, and (2) the error was clerical/mathematical and not grossly negligent.

Answer (A) is incorrect because this is a unilateral mistake. Answer (C) is incorrect because a sales contract under the UCC is a contract. Basic contract principles apply if not modified by the UCC. Answer (D) is incorrect because a unilateral mistake of fact results in a contract. Mistake in judgment or opinion (e.g., FMV) is no basis for rescission.

43. Which of the following is a correct statement about remedies for breach of contract?

    A.   A party injured by breach of contract may recover from the breaching party all the general and special damages suffered as a result of the breach.

    B.   If the payment of money is an adequate substitute for performance by the breaching party, the nonbreaching party must seek damages in an action at law and may not pursue the equitable remedy of specific performance.

    C.   The mitigation of damages rule requires the nonbreaching party to do everything possible to avoid all damages caused by the breach.

    D.   To obtain a remedy, the injured party must establish that the breach is material.

The correct answer is (B). *(Publisher)*

REQUIRED: The correct statement concerning remedies for breach of contract.

DISCUSSION: The primary remedy at law for breach of contract is monetary damages in amounts sufficient to place the injured party in as good a position as if the contract had been performed in the manner the nonbreaching party reasonably expected. Equitable remedies such as specific performance are permitted in breach of contract cases only when the nonbreaching party persuades the court that monetary damages are not an adequate remedy and irreparable injury will result if the equitable remedy is withheld. Specific performance is usually granted when the subject of the breached contract is land or other unique property.

Answer (A) is incorrect because recovery of special damages requires a plaintiff to prove the breaching party knew or should have known of the special circumstances at the time the contract was formed. Answer (C) is incorrect because the mitigation of damages rule requires the nonbreaching party to take reasonable steps to avoid or limit the consequences of the breach. Answer (D) is incorrect because a party is entitled to recover the general and special damages resulting from any breach of contract, whether material or immaterial.

44. Which of the following statements is correct regarding the effect of the expiration of the period of the statute of limitations on a contract?

    A.   Once the period of the statute of limitations has expired, the contract is void.

    B.   The expiration of the period of the statute of limitations extinguishes the contract's underlying obligation.

    C.   A cause of action barred by the statute of limitations may not be revived.

    D.   The running of the statute of limitations bars access to judicial remedies.

The correct answer is (D). *(CPA, adapted)*

REQUIRED: The true statement about the effect of the lapse of the statute of limitations on a contract.

DISCUSSION: A statute of limitations declares that an action for breach of contract or other legal duty must be filed in an appropriate court prior to the expiration of a definite period of time measured in years. Failure to meet the time limitations for a particular case bars access to judicial remedies and renders the contract unenforceable.

Answers (A) and (B) are incorrect because expiration of the statute bars access to judicial remedies but does not void or extinguish the underlying contract. Answer (C) is incorrect because the cause of action can be revived by an express or implied agreement of the party benefited by the statute.

Use Gleim's *CPA Test Prep* for interactive testing with over 2,000 additional multiple-choice questions!

OOF QUESTION *(CPA, adapted)*

On January 15, East Corp. orally offered to hire Bean, CPA, to perform management consulting services for East and its subsidiaries. The offer provided for a 3-year contract at $10,000 per month. On January 20, East sent Bean a signed memorandum stating the terms of the offer. The memorandum also included a payment clause that had not been discussed and the provision that Bean's acceptance of the offer would not be effective unless it was received by East on or before January 25. Bean received the memorandum on January 21, signed it, and mailed it back to East the same day. East received it on January 24. On January 23, East wrote to Bean revoking the offer. Bean received the revocation on January 25.

On March 1, East Corp. orally engaged Snow Consultants to install a corporate local area network (LAN) system for East's financial operations. The engagement was to last until the following February 15, and East would pay Snow $5,000 twice a month. On March 15, East offered Snow $1,000 per month to assist in the design of East's Internet home page. Snow accepted East's offer. On April 1, citing excess work, Snow advised East that Snow would not assist with the design of the home page. On April 5, East accepted Snow's withdrawal from the Internet home page design project. On April 15, Snow notified East that Snow had assigned the fees due Snow on the LAN installation engagement to Band Computer Consultants. On April 30, East notified Snow that the LAN installation agreement was canceled.

Required

Items 1 through 5 are based on the transaction between East Corp. and Bean. For each item, select the best answer from List I. An answer may be selected once, more than once, or not at all.

1. What was the effect of the event(s) that took place on January 20?
2. What was the effect of the event(s) that took place on January 21?
3. What was the effect of the event(s) that took place on January 23?
4. What was the effect of the event(s) that took place on January 24?
5. What was the effect of the event(s) that took place on January 25?

Items 6 through 10 are based on the transaction between East Corp. and Snow Consultants. For each item, select the best answer from List II. An answer may be selected once, more than once, or not at all.

6. What was the effect of the event(s) that took place on March 1?
7. What was the effect of the event(s) that took place on March 15?
8. What was the effect of the event(s) that took place on April 5?
9. What was the effect of the event(s) that took place on April 15?
10. What was the effect of the event(s) that took place on April 30?

List I

A. Acceptance of a counteroffer.
B. Acceptance of an offer governed by the mailbox rule.
C. Attempted acceptance of an offer.
D. Attempted revocation of an offer.
E. Formation of an enforceable contract.
F. Formation of a contract enforceable only against East.
G. Invalid revocation because of prior acceptance of an offer.
H. Offer revoked by sending a revocation letter.
I. Submission of a counteroffer.
J. Submission of a written offer.

List II

A. Breach of contract.
B. Discharge from performance.
C. Enforceable oral contract modification.
D. Formation of a voidable contract.
E. Formation of an enforceable contract.
F. Formation of a contract unenforceable under the statute of frauds.
G. Invalid assignment.
H. Mutual rescission.
I. Novation.
J. Unilateral offer.
K. Valid assignment of rights.
L. Valid assignment of duties.
M. Valid assignment of rights and duties.

Knowledge Tested

Contract law

1. Offer, acceptance, and revocation
2. Statute of frauds
3. Breach
4. Rescission
5. Assignment

Authors' Comments

This question covers the three major areas of Article Z: formation, performance, and enforcement of contracts for the sale of goods. Fundamental common-law contract rules must be applied to facts. Briefly, the rules are

1. Offers are revocable, absent consideration.

2. Acceptance is effective upon dispatch, unless the offer stipulates otherwise. A revocation is effective upon receipt prior to acceptance.

3. Consideration may be by mutual promises.

4. A promise that cannot be performed within a year is unenforceable absent a signed writing.

5. Modification of a contract requires consideration.

6. Prior or contemporaneous statements are inadmissable to contradict an integrated written contract.

7. Contracts may be discharged by performance, legal excuses for nonperformance, mutual rescission, novation, release, waiver, and operation of law.

1. The correct answer is (J).
DISCUSSION: The memorandum that East sent Bean was a submission of a written offer. The oral offer from East Corp. to Bean was not enforceable because an agreement that cannot be performed within 1 year must be in writing to be enforceable according to the statute of frauds.

2. The correct answer is (C).
DISCUSSION: Bean attempted an acceptance of the offer on January 21 by signing and mailing the memorandum. This action did not form an enforceable contract because the terms of the offer stated that acceptance would not be effective until received by East on or before January 25.

3. The correct answer is (D).
DISCUSSION: East attempted to revoke the offer on January 23. Revocation is effective when it is received by the offeree prior to acceptance. By January 25, a valid acceptance had already occurred.

4. The correct answer is (E).
DISCUSSION: An enforceable contract was formed on January 24 according to the stated terms of the offer made by East in the memorandum. The offeror received the valid acceptance 1 day before the offeree received the attempted revocation.

5. The correct answer is (G).
DISCUSSION: The revocation required on January 25 was ineffective because an enforceable contract had already been formed the day before.

6. The correct answer is (E).
DISCUSSION: Oral contracts are usually enforceable unless they are within the statute of frauds. A services contract is not within the statute of frauds if it can be completed within a year of entering into the contract. The oral contract between East and Snow is enforceable because it was entered into on March 1 and will be completed by February 15 of the following year.

7. The correct answer is (E).
DISCUSSION: The contract entered into on March 15 by East and Snow is enforceable because it had all of the following requirements of a contract: offer and acceptance, mutual assent, consideration, legality, and capacity of parties.

8. The correct answer is (H).
DISCUSSION: The parties to a contract may by agreement end it without performance or alter their performance obligations. Mutual rescission occurs when the parties to an executory bilateral contract agree to cancel it. They are restored to their original positions. The agreement to rescind is itself a contract. The mutual surrender of rights constitutes the consideration necessary for, and the performance of, the contract of rescission.

9. The correct answer is (K).
DISCUSSION: Contract rights are generally assignable, but an attempted assignment of a contract right is not effective if the contract expressly states that it is not assignable. The following are exceptions: a right to receive money; negotiable instruments; and, in a sale of goods, the right to receive damages for breach or for payment of an amount owed.

10. The correct answer is (A).
DISCUSSION: East and Show had an enforceable contract for the LAN installation. East's failure to perform a duty imposed by the contract, i.e., to pay Snow, was a breach of contract.

ESSAY QUESTION 1 *(CPA, adapted)* 15-25 minutes

Suburban Properties, Inc. owns and manages several shopping centers. On May 4, 1999, Suburban received from Bridge Hardware, Inc., one of its tenants, a signed letter proposing that the existing lease between Suburban and Bridge be modified to provide that certain utility costs be equally shared by Bridge and Suburban, effective June 1, 1999. Under the terms of the original lease, Bridge was obligated to pay all utility costs. On May 5, 1999, Suburban sent Bridge a signed letter agreeing to share the utility costs as proposed. Suburban later changed its opinion and refused to share in the utility costs.

On June 4, 1999, Suburban received from Dart Associates, Inc. a signed offer to purchase one of the shopping centers owned by Suburban. The offer provided as follows: The offer stipulated a price of $9,250,000; the offer would not be withdrawn before July 1, 1999; and an acceptance would have to be received by Dart to be effective. On June 9, 1999, Suburban mailed Dart a signed acceptance. On June 10, before Dart had received Suburban's acceptance, Dart telephoned Suburban and withdrew its offer. Suburban's acceptance was received by Dart on June 12, 1999.

On June 22, 1999, one of Suburban's shopping centers was damaged by a fire, which started when the center was struck by lightning. As a result of the fire, one of the tenants in the shopping center, World Popcorn Corp., was forced to close its business and will be unable to reopen until the damage is repaired. World sued Suburban claiming that Suburban is liable for World's losses resulting from the fire. The lease between Suburban and World is silent in this regard.

Suburban has taken the following positions:

a. Suburban's May 5, 1999 agreement to share equally the utility costs with Bridge is not binding on Suburban.

b. Dart could not properly revoke its June 4 offer and must purchase the shopping center.

c. Suburban is not liable to World for World's losses resulting from the fire.

Required

In separate paragraphs, determine whether Suburban's positions are correct and state the reasons for your conclusions.

Knowledge Tested

1. Modification of a lease
2. Statute of frauds
3. Offer and acceptance or revocation
4. Remedies for breach of contract
5. Rights and duties of landlord and tenant

Authors' Comments

This essay problem tests knowledge of contract formation fundamentals. Although the statute of frauds is not a real issue, the facts suggest that it might be. Thus, it should be briefly discussed. Note the continuing potential impact of tort law in landlord-tenant relationships.

AICPA Unofficial Answer

a. Suburban is correct concerning the agreement to share utility costs with Bridge. A modification of a contract requires consideration to be binding on the parties. Suburban is not bound by the lease modification because Suburban did not receive any consideration in exchange for its agreement to share the cost of utilities with Bridge.

b. Suburban is not correct with regard to the Dart offer. An offer can be revoked at any time prior to acceptance. This is true despite the fact that the offer provides that it will not be withdrawn prior to a stated time. If no consideration is given in exchange for this promise not to withdraw the offer, the promise is not binding on the offeror. The offer provided that Suburban's acceptance would not be effective until received. Dart's June 10 revocation terminated Dart's offer. Thus, Suburban's June 9 acceptance was not effective.

c. Suburban is correct with regard to World's claim. The general rule is that destruction of, or damage to, the subject matter of a contract without the fault of either party terminates the contract. In this case, Suburban is not liable to World because Suburban is discharged from its contractual duties as a result of the fire, which made performance by it under the lease objectively impossible.

ESSAY QUESTION 2 *(CPA, adapted)* 15-25 minutes

On July 5, 1999, Korn sent Wilson a written offer to clear Wilson's parking lot whenever it snowed through December 31, 1999. Korn's offer stated that Wilson had until October 1 to accept.

On September 28, 1999, Wilson mailed Korn an acceptance with a request that the agreement continue through March 2000. Wilson's acceptance was delayed and did not reach Korn until October 3.

On September 29, 1999, Korn saw weather reports indicating the snowfall for the season would be much heavier than normal. This would substantially increase Korn's costs to perform under the offer.

On September 30, 1999, Korn phoned Wilson to insist that the terms of the agreement be changed. When Wilson refused, Korn orally withdrew the offer and stated that Korn would not perform.

Required

a. State and explain the points of law that Korn would argue to show that there was no valid contract.

b. State and explain the points of law that Wilson would argue to show that there was a valid contract.

c. Assuming that a valid contract existed,

1. Determine whether Korn breached the contract and the nature of the breach, and

2. State the common-law remedies available to Wilson.

Knowledge Tested

1. Contract formation
   a. Offer and acceptance
2. Anticipatory breach
3. Remedies

Authors' Comments

This question requires the lawyerly skill of being able to argue both sides of a case. Basic to Korn's position are the principles that the offeror is master of the offer, that an offer unsupported by consideration is revocable at any time, and that an acceptance must be the mirror image of the offer. Basic to Wilson's position is the principle that acceptance is effective upon dispatch if the offer is still open and an authorized medium is used (the mailbox rule). Wilson also relies on the principle that a valid contract is formed even when the acceptance contains a mere inquiry about terms. Such an inquiry does not indicate an intent to reject the offer.

AICPA Unofficial Answer

a. Korn would argue two points of law to show there was no valid contract. Korn would argue that the July 5 offer was not accepted by Wilson before it was withdrawn on September 30. An offer can be withdrawn at any time before it is accepted even if it states that it will remain open for a definite period of time.

Korn would also argue that Wilson's response of September 28 was not a valid acceptance because Wilson included additional terms and Wilson's attempt to change the term of the contract was a rejection and a counteroffer.

b. Wilson would argue two points of law to show there was a valid contract. Wilson would argue that the mailing of the acceptance on September 28 was an effective acceptance under the mailbox rule. There is a valid contract because there was a valid acceptance before the offer was withdrawn.

Wilson would also argue that the attempt to extend the contract was not a condition of acceptance but a requested immaterial modification that did not negate the acceptance.

c. If a valid contract existed, Korn's September 30 telephone call resulted in Korn's anticipatory breach of the contract because Wilson could no longer rely on Korn's performing.

Under common law, Wilson could either cancel the contract or sue to collect compensatory damages for the additional amount it would cost to obtain the services.

ESSAY QUESTION 3 *(CPA, adapted)* 15-20 minutes

In a signed letter dated March 2, 1999, Stake offered to sell Packer a specific vacant parcel of land for $100,000. Stake had inherited the land, along with several apartment buildings in the immediate vicinity. Packer received the offer on March 4. The offer required acceptance by March 10 and required Packer to have the property surveyed by a licensed surveyor so that the exact legal description of the property could be determined.

On March 6, Packer sent Stake a counteroffer of $75,000. All other terms and conditions of the offer were unchanged. Stake received Packer's counteroffer on March 8, and, on that day, telephoned Packer and accepted it. On learning that a survey of the vacant parcel would cost about $1,000, Packer telephoned Stake on March 11 requesting that they share the survey cost equally. During this conversation, Stake agreed to Packer's proposal.

During the course of the negotiations leading up to the March communications between Stake and Packer, Stake expressed concern to Packer that a buyer of the land might build apartment units that would compete with those owned by Stake in the immediate vicinity. Packer assured Stake that Packer intended to use the land for a small shopping center. Because of these assurances, Stake was willing to sell the land to Packer. Contrary to what Packer told Stake, Packer had already contracted conditionally with Rolf for Rolf to build a 48-unit apartment development on the vacant land to be purchased from Stake.

During the last week of March, Stake learned that the land to be sold to Packer had a fair market value of $200,000. Also, Stake learned that Packer intended to build apartments on the land. Because of this information, Stake sued Packer to rescind the real estate contract, alleging the following:

- Packer committed fraud in the formation of the contract, thereby entitling Stake to rescind the contract.

- Stake's innocent mistakes as to the fair market value of the land entitles Stake to rescind the contract.

- The contract was not enforceable against Stake because Stake did not sign Packer's March 6 counteroffer.

Required

State whether Stake's allegations are correct and give the reasons for your conclusions.

Knowledge Tested

1. Availability of rescission
2. Sufficiency of consideration
3. Statute of frauds

Authors' Comments

Key words in an extensive fact pattern can indicate the subject matter being tested is narrow. "Stake sued Packer to **rescind** . . . ." Rescission requires that a contract was formed! However, one of the parties entered this contract based on misinformation. Review the outline for when rescission is available under such circumstances. Rescission may be based on fraud. Recite the elements (see Study Unit 2). If consideration was sufficient for contract formation, its sufficiency does not form a basis for rescission.

The unilateral mistake was not mathematical or clerical. Disparity in the value of consideration exchanged is not considered unjust such that extreme hardship to a party would provide a basis for rescission.

The third allegation addresses when a signed writing is required for formation of an enforceable contract.

AICPA Unofficial Answer

Stake's first allegation, that Packer committed fraud in the formation of the contract, is correct and Stake may rescind the contract. Packer assured Stake that the vacant parcel would be used for a shopping center when, in fact, Packer intended to use the land to construct apartment units that would be in direct competition with those owned by Stake. Stake would not have sold the land to Packer had Packer's real intentions been known. Therefore, the elements of fraud are present:

- A false representation of a material fact
- Packer's knowledge of the falsity
- Intention to deceive
- Justifiable reliance on the misrepresentation

Stake's second allegation, that the mistake as to the fair market value of the land entitles Stake to rescind the contract, is incorrect. Generally, mistakes as to adequacy of consideration or fairness of a bargain are insufficient grounds to entitle the aggrieved party to rescind a contract.

Stake's third allegation, that the contract was not enforceable against Stake because Stake did not sign the counteroffer, is correct. The contract between Stake and Packer involves real estate and, therefore, the statute of frauds requirements must be satisfied. The statute of frauds requires that a writing be signed by the party against whom enforcement is sought. The counteroffer is unenforceable against Stake because Stake did not sign it. As a result, Stake is not obligated to sell the land to Packer under the terms of the counteroffer.

CHAPTER IV
DEBTOR-CREDITOR
RELATIONSHIPS

These three study units will constitute approximately 10% of the Business Law section.

STUDY UNIT 9: RIGHTS AND DUTIES

11 pages of outline
23 multiple-choice questions
1 OOF and 1 essay

A. Contract Rights and Duties
B. Liens
C. Consumer Credit Protection
D. Remedies upon Default

This study unit reviews the rights and duties of debtors and creditors under general contract law and under the variety of consumer protection statutes that have been enacted in recent years to provide oversight of liens and credit transactions. Past exams have focused on suretyship and bankruptcy questions. However, the recently revised Content Specification Outline indicates that future exams will contain questions on the material reviewed in this study unit.

A. **Contract Rights and Duties**. A debtor-creditor relationship is primarily a contract between the debtor and the creditor.

1. **Contract law** generally governs validity and performance of a contract. Contract rights and remedies presented in Study Units 7 and 8 generally apply.

2. Specific to debtors and creditors, common law and federal and state statutory law provide an additional regulatory layer that limits freedom of contract to assure fairer treatment of debtors.

a. EXAMPLE: State usury laws prohibit lenders from charging interest in excess of a designated amount to consumers and small businesses. The federal Truth-in-Lending Act requires disclosure of the interest charges, and states regulate the terms of mortgages extensively.

3. Stop and review! You have completed the outline for this subunit. Study multiple-choice question 1 on page 292.

B. **Liens**. A lien is a legal claim or charge on property, either real or personal, as security for payment or performance of a debt or obligation. Liens protect the interests of those who provide skills, materials, or services to property owners.

1. A **common-law lien** arises when a party, through labor, skills, or materials, adds value to another party's personal property by agreement. A common-law lien is the right of one person to retain possession of the property of another until the owner pays for the goods or services.

2. A **statutory lien** secures payment, but only if the creditor complies with statutory requirements.

a. Many states, through enactment of statutes, have codified some of the common-law liens and added new lienholder remedies, such as sale of the property.

3. The common-law and statutory liens described in this study unit differ from those arising under Article 9 of the UCC, which is covered in Study Unit 17, Secured Transactions.

    a. Article 9 governs statutory security interests (liens) in such items as consumer goods, inventory, equipment, fixtures, farm products, and certain intangibles, e.g., accounts, investment securities, documents, and chattel paper. However, it does not govern the common-law and statutory liens discussed in this study unit.

4. An accountant does not acquire a common-law lien on a client's books and materials.

    a. (S)he may acquire a statutory lien on such books and records.

    b. A CPA who fails to register and be licensed as required by state statute may be denied the right to recover against the lien.

5. An **artisan's lien** arises in favor of a repairer or improver of personal property who retains possession of the property until paid.

    a. The repair or improvement need not increase the value of the property.

    b. The work or improvement must be performed subject to an express or implied agreement for cash payment, as opposed to credit.

        1) EXAMPLE: Mechanic agreed to repair a flat on Customer's car and wait 2 weeks for payment. Mechanic repaired the tire. An artisan's lien did not arise because Mechanic agreed to extend credit.

    c. The lien does not attach unless the owner relinquishes possession.

    d. The artisan's lien terminates when payment is tendered or when the repairer or improver relinquishes possession of the property.

    e. If the lienholder temporarily relinquishes the property subject to an agreement that it will be returned to his/her possession, the lien does not terminate.

        1) However, if a third party obtains rights to the property before it is returned, the lien terminates.

        2) Modern statutes may provide that the lienholder may protect the lien by recording notice of the lien in the public records.

    f. Modern statutes may allow the lienholder to judicially foreclose the lien and sell the property if the owner does not pay the debt.

        1) The lienholder has this right only if the statutes grant it.

        2) The lienholder must give notice to the owner prior to foreclosure and sale.

        3) Sale proceeds are used to pay the costs of foreclosure and sale and to satisfy the debt. Any remaining proceeds are paid to the former owner.

6. **Mechanic's and materialman's liens** are statutory liens against real property. The liens secure unpaid debts that arise from contracts for labor, materials, or services to improve real property.

7. A **mortgage** is a voluntary lien on real property given by contract to secure a debt, e.g., the initial contract of purchase or a subsequent loan against equity.

    a. The rule "first in time, first in right" generally applies to mortgages.

    b. Most liens or other interests that subsequently attach to mortgaged property are subordinate or secondary to the mortgage.

    c. The priority among mortgage liens may be modified by legislation.

    d. Foreclosure on mortgage liens is regulated extensively for the protection of mortgagors (debtors).

8. A **hotelkeeper's lien** arises when a guest fails to pay the agreed-upon hotel charges. The lien attaches to the guest's baggage.

    a. If the charges are not expressly agreed upon in advance, the charges that must be paid are reasonable charges for the accommodations.

    b. The hotelkeeper's lien terminates when payment is tendered, when the hotelkeeper relinquishes possession of the baggage, or when conversion of the baggage by the hotelkeeper occurs.

    c. If the hotelkeeper temporarily relinquishes possession of the baggage to the guest subject to an agreement that the baggage will be returned to the hotelkeeper, the lien does not terminate.

    d. Conversion occurs when the hotelkeeper appropriates the property to his own beneficial use or enjoyment.

    e. Statutes often provide for conversion by public sale after a prescribed period of time lapses, or pursuant to court order. The trend is for the guest to receive an impartial judicial hearing prior to conversion.

9. In the absence of statutory regulation, the common law establishes the **relative priority** of liens in the order of their acquisition: the first in time is the first in right.

    a. A common-law lien is based directly on possession. Such a lien arises only when possession is obtained, and exists only as long as it is retained.

    b. **Concurrent liens**. Simultaneously arising liens have equal rank in distribution of a fund.

    c. **Subordination**. Parties may agree that an otherwise junior lien be given priority over an otherwise superior lien.

        1) A subordination agreement is one whereby a lienholder agrees that claims of other lienholders must be fully paid before there is any payment to him/herself, the subordinate lienholder.

    d. **Statutory provisions**. The legislature has the power to fix the priorities of liens.

        1) The legislature has the power to give a statutory lien (e.g., a tax lien) priority over other liens.

            a) States may also exempt certain property from collection by creditors.

                i)   EXAMPLE: State homestead exemption acts may shield a debtor's equity in his/her home from most liens. Mortgage liens and tax liens would not be exempted.

        2) In the absence of a statute giving precedence to a statutory lien, its relative priority or rank is determined under the general principle of first in time, first in right.

    e. Artisan's and mechanic's liens have priority over all other security interests in property, unless a statute expressly provides otherwise.

        1) EXAMPLE: Owner is in default on a loan from Creditco, which has a perfected security interest in a '65 Chevy. Owner, wishing to be able to sell the Chevy at a higher price and discharge the Creditco debt, contracts for, and then fails to pay for, a custom paint job from Artco. Artco retains possession of the Chevy. On (foreclosure) sale of the Chevy to discharge the liens, Artco's artisan's lien has priority over Creditco's previously perfected security interest. If proceeds are insufficient to satisfy both, Creditco will receive any balance only after Artco has been paid in full.

        2) This **superpriority** is confirmed by the UCC with respect to goods (UCC 310).

10. **Enforcement**. A lien is enforceable only as to lienable items.

    a. Because a common-law lienholder is merely given the right to retain possession of certain property until the claim is satisfied, there is no right of sale of the property, unless such a right is conferred by statute.

        1) A personal action to recover the amount of the debt may be maintained independently of a right of action to foreclose a lien, and both remedies may be pursued concurrently.

        2) The manner of enforcing common-law liens is usually prescribed by statute.

        3) A lienholder must usually enforce his/her lien in an appropriate proceeding.

            a) Such action, according to the nature of the lien, or the statutory provision by which the lien is provided for, may be

                i) An action at law
                ii) A bill in equity

            b) Either action may be a proceeding *in rem* (against the property).

            c) Any proceeding must satisfy the requirements of due process.

    b. The method for enforcing statutory liens is generally provided by the statutes that provide for the liens. The statutory remedy is generally regarded as exclusive.

        1) If the statutory remedy is pursued, all statutory requirements must be strictly complied with.

        2) When a statute that provides for a lien does not provide a method for its enforcement, it may be enforced by an ordinary action at law for the collection of the debt.

11. A **judicial lien** is a legally enforceable interest in property that secures performance of an obligation, such as payment of a debt, and that is acquired by a judgment, by a levy, or by another legal or equitable process.

    a. A court, after a civil proceeding, may issue a monetary judgment for one of the parties, e.g., the plaintiff. That party is a **judgment creditor**.

    b. Should the other party fail to voluntarily pay (satisfy the judgment), the judgment creditor may, typically, petition the court to issue a writ of execution.

    c. The **writ of execution** generally operates to authorize the sheriff to seize and to sell personal (nonexempt) property of the judgment debtor to satisfy the judgment.

        1) When the claimant persuades the court that the risk of improper transfer or concealment of defendant's property is high, the court may grant a prejudgment remedy.

        2) A prejudgment remedy establishes a lien on a debtor's property before issuance of the court's final judgment and writ of execution.

        3) Prejudgment remedies include the writ of attachment, the writ of garnishment, and replevin.

            a) Attachment is the process of seizing a defendant's property pursuant to judicial authorization and placing it in the custody of the court. Attachment is intended to secure satisfaction of a pending judgment.

            b) Garnishment is a prejudgment or postjudgment remedy directed toward a third party (a garnishee) who is a debtor, or holds property, of the defendant-debtor, for example, an employer who is holding wages.

        c)   Replevin may be used by a creditor to obtain possession of specific property when (s)he has a lien or a right of repossession.

    d.   If the writ of execution is returned unsatisfied to the court, e.g., because the value of personal property seized and sold was less than the judgment amount, the judgment ordinarily becomes a lien on any real property owned by the judgment debtor and located within the jurisdiction of the court.

    e.   Some states require that the judgment creditor file the judgment with a specified county official in order to either establish or perfect the judgment lien.

    f.   Real property located in the jurisdiction and acquired by the judgment debtor subsequent to the beginning of the civil proceeding, but prior to satisfaction of the judgment, becomes subject to the judgment. That is, the judgment creditor has a lien on any newly acquired real property.

    g.   The judgment creditor may be entitled to foreclose on the lien and have the judgment satisfied from proceeds of a judicial sale.

    h.   The judgment debtor would, nonetheless, generally not be able to transfer marketable title to the property prior to satisfaction of the judgment.

        1)   A transferee might, however, take the property subject to the lien.

    i.   A trustee in bankruptcy has the rights of a judicial lienholder in property of the estate (i.e., property of the petitioner on the date of the petition).

        1)   The rights of the trustee are the same as those of a creditor with a judicial lien upon return of a writ of execution that remains unsatisfied.

        2)   Thus the interest of the trustee has priority over all but already secured interests in property of the estate.

        3)   Any other (than a trustee in bankruptcy) judgment lienholder's interest in property may have priority over all other interests not yet secured and perfected at the time of return of the writ or filing.

12. **Termination of Lien**. The right to retain an existing lien until the debt secured thereby is paid is a substantive property right which may not be taken from a rightful lienholder. A lien is effective until it is satisfied, terminated, or extinguished.

    a.   **Surrender of possession**. Generally, a lien dependent on possession is lost if the lienholder voluntarily and unconditionally parts with possession or control of the underlying property.

        1)   However, between the parties a lien is not necessarily terminated by parting with possession if there is an intention to preserve the lien and the lienholder only conditionally parts with the underlying property, e.g., by allowing the owner to take possession of the property expressly without prejudice to the lien.

            a)   However, such a surrender may destroy the lien as to third parties.

        2)   A lien cannot be destroyed by a removal of property from the possession of the lienholder without his/her consent.

    b.   A lien may be terminated by waiver or estoppel.

        1)   A **waiver** is a voluntary relinquishment of a right, which may be expressed or implied from conduct that is inconsistent with the existence of the lien.

        2)   **Estoppel** assumes that the lienholder, by his/her acts and conduct, e.g., not registering a lien, has precluded him/herself from asserting his/her liens.

    c.   If a lienholder fails to assert a lien against property (s)he retains possession of, when that possession is retained for some other reason, the lien is waived.

        1)   However, one does not waive one's right to a lien by failing to ask for recognition of the lien unless and until there is some necessity for having it recognized.

        2)   A party who has two liens on the same property and forecloses one of the liens but claims no right under the other at the same time, waives the right to subsequently claim that (s)he retained the other lien.

    d.   **Destruction of property**. A lien remains effective only as long as the property subject to the lien continues in existence.

    e.   **Payment or tender**. A lien is discharged by a proper and sufficient payment of the debt it secures.

        1)   A lienholder may be held criminally liable for failure to discharge a lien after receiving payment.

        2)   A proper and sufficient tender of payment operates to discharge a lien.

            a)   A tender does not discharge the underlying debt.

            b)   The tender relieves the debtor from liability for further interest or damages, such as legal fees.

    f.   **Satisfaction or release**. A lienholder has the duty to prepare, execute, and deliver to the debtor a valid release of his/her lien upon tender of the amount due.

        1)   Some statutes provide sanctions for failure to enter a satisfaction of the lien in the appropriate register if there has been payment or tender.

13.   Stop and review! You have completed the outline for this subunit. Study multiple-choice questions 2 through 8 beginning on page 292.

C.   **Consumer Credit Protection**. In 1968, Congress passed the **Consumer Credit Protection Act (CCPA)**, regulating extensions of credit for personal, family, household, or agricultural purposes.

    1.   The Consumer Credit Protection Act is made up of the following:

        a.   The Truth-in-Lending Act
        b.   The Fair Credit Reporting Act
        c.   The Equal Credit Opportunity Act
        d.   The Fair Debt Collection Practices Act

    2.   Basically, consumer credit protection provides for the following:

        a.   Access to the consumer credit market by both creditors and consumers
        b.   Full disclosure of information to the consumer
        c.   Regulation of contract terms
        d.   Fair reporting of credit information concerning consumers
        e.   Creditors' remedies

    3.   **Truth-in-Lending Act (TILA)**. Title I of the CCPA is commonly known as the Truth-in-Lending Act. It requires disclosure by creditors of the terms and conditions of consumer credit before extending credit to consumer-debtors.

a. The TILA applies to all transactions in which

1) The lender is in the business of extending credit in connection with a loan of money, a sale of property, or even the furnishing of services.

2) The debtor is a natural person (not a corporation or other business association).

3) A finance charge may be imposed.

4) The credit is obtained primarily for personal, family, household, or agricultural purposes.

5) The amount financed is $25,000 or less.

a) The $25,000 maximum does not apply when the creditor takes a security interest in the debtor's real property or in personal property used as the debtor's principal dwelling (e.g., a mobile home).

NOTE: The extension of credit need not be the creditor's primary business. Retail stores and automobile dealerships are creditors if they regularly arrange or extend financing.

b. For a business organization to qualify as a creditor, either it must impose a finance charge or the loan must be evidenced by some written agreement requiring payment in more than four installments.

1) Thus, disclosure is necessary whenever a buyer pays in installments.

c. Precisely what must be disclosed depends on whether the transaction is for closed-end or open-end credit.

1) **Closed-end credit** is extended for a specific time period, and the total amount financed, number of payments, and due dates are all agreed on at the time of the transaction.

a) It includes automobile loans and consumer loans from finance companies.

2) **Open-end credit** arrangements, such as VISA or MasterCard or a revolving charge account, involve a plan that permits the consumer to enter into a series of transactions and allows the consumer the option of paying in variable installments or in full.

d. Disclosure required before completion of a closed-end transaction includes

1) The total amount financed
2) The total number of payments
3) The amount of each payment
4) The due date of each payment
5) The annual interest rate
6) The total finance charge
7) The total dollar value of all payments
8) Any and all late charges assessable for past-due payments
9) Any security interest taken by the creditor and the collateral

e. Under open-end credit arrangements, it is not always possible to disclose the total amount financed, the total number of payments, the amount of each payment, etc.

f. The finance charge and annual percentage rate (APR) are made known to borrowers by use of a **financing statement**, which must be given to the borrower before credit is extended.

g.   The TILA also prevents a creditor from baiting customers by advertising credit terms that it does not generally make available.

h.   The TILA serves as a federal credit card fraud act by limiting a credit cardholder's liability for unauthorized use of the card to a maximum of $50.

   1)   Unauthorized use is use by a person other than the cardholder without actual, implied, or apparent authority for such use.

   2)   A credit cardholder that loses his/her card will avoid all liability for any unauthorized charges if notice is given to the issuer before any charges are made.

   3)   Under TILA, an addressee that is sent an unsolicited credit card has no liability to the issuer for charges made prior to receipt and acceptance of the card.

   4)   A consumer who has a problem with goods or services purchased with a credit card may notify the issuer, require its intervention, and withhold payment until the problem is resolved.

i.   There are both civil and criminal penalties for violation of the TILA.

   1)   The civil liability provisions make creditors liable to debtors for an amount equal to twice the finance charge but not less than $100 or more than $1,000. The costs of filing suit plus attorney's fees are also recoverable.

   2)   The Department of Justice may institute criminal actions against those who willfully and knowingly violate the act.

4.   The **Fair Credit Reporting Act (FCRA)** of 1970 requires consumer credit reporting agencies to adopt reasonable procedures to maintain the confidentiality, accuracy, and relevancy of their records while meeting the needs of lenders.

a.   Under the FCRA, a reporting agency must adopt reasonable procedures to assure consumer creditors that its reports will be furnished only to parties designated or qualified under the FCRA.

b.   The FCRA imposes a duty on users of credit reports to disclose to the individual affected that the report has been requested and that the report may contain information on the individual's character, reputation, personal traits, and/or mode of living.

c.   The user of a credit report incurs a duty of disclosure to the individual affected whenever such user

   1)   Rejects an applicant for consumer credit, insurance, or employment
   2)   Charges a higher rate for credit or insurance

   NOTE: The user must maintain reasonable procedures for advising the affected individual that it relied on the credit report in making its decision. The user must also supply the individual with the name and address of the consumer reporting agency that supplied the report.

d.   Typically, the consumer reporting agency must, if contacted, disclose to the affected individual the

   1)   Nature and substance of all its information about the individual (except medical information)

   2)   Source of all information

   3)   Names of any users of the report who have received the consumer's file in the last 6 months (in the last 2 years if used for employment evaluation)

e. The consumer has a right to correct information in his/her file.

  1) The consumer does not have the right to adjust the file him/herself, but (s)he may request that items be changed.

  2) The reporting agency must investigate any alleged error and must assume that the correction is not frivolous or irrelevant.

  3) Upon request, the reporting agency must notify any users of the report of the disputed information.

  4) If a requested change is refused, the consumer may file an additional report that must be kept in the file.

f. The FCRA subjects to criminal penalties

  1) Persons who knowingly and willfully obtain consumer information from a credit bureau under false pretenses

  2) Credit bureau officers or employees who knowingly or willfully provide information to unauthorized persons

g. Civil liability is also provided for if there is a willful violation of the FCRA by either the reporting agency or the user.

5. The **Equal Credit Opportunity Act (ECOA)** prohibits discrimination based on sex, marital status, race, color, age, religion, national origin, or receipt of welfare in any aspect of a consumer credit transaction.

a. A creditor may not ask for information about race, age, sex, religion, or national origin.

b. The ECOA prohibits any request for information concerning marital status, former spouses, alimony, child support, use of birth control pills, and receipt of welfare.

  1) If other sources of income are disclosed, the creditor may take them into account.

  2) However, the creditor is required to inform the applicant that (s)he need not disclose these sources unless (s)he is relying on them to obtain the credit.

c. The ECOA requires that a creditor give an applicant notification of action it has taken on his/her completed application for credit within 30 days of receipt.

d. The ECOA applies to all businesses and individuals that regularly extend credit, including financial institutions, retail stores, and credit card services.

  1) ECOA also affects automobile dealers, real estate brokers, and others who steer consumers to lenders.

e. The Federal Trade Commission (FTC), as well as individuals, may sue to enforce the ECOA.

  1) An injured person may recover both actual and punitive damages.

6. The **Fair Debt Collection Practices Act (FDCPA)** contains a number of restrictions on collection practices. It was enacted to prevent abusive, deceptive, and unfair debt collection practices of some debt collectors.

a. The FDCPA is directed at agencies that are collecting debts for others but not at banks and businesses that are trying to collect their own accounts.

b. The debts must involve money, property, insurance, or services obtained by a consumer and used for personal, family, or household purposes.

c.   Under the FDCPA, a collector, generally, may not

1)   Use harassing or intimidating practices

2)   Use abusive language

3)   Use false or misleading tactics

4)   Contact the consumer at work if the employer objects

5)   Contact the consumer at unusual or inconvenient times

6)   Contact the consumer at all if the debtor is represented by an attorney

7)   Unless specifically authorized by a court, contact third parties other than a spouse, parent, or financial advisor expressly about the account

NOTE: A debtor need only make written request to the collection agency for it to refrain from contacting him/her or informing neighbors and coworkers of the debts. The collection agency is then required to stop all further contact, and its sole remedy is to sue the debtor.

d.   The collector may not contact the consumer-debtor about the account after receiving a written refusal to pay, except to notify the consumer of possible ramifications of nonpayment. Moreover, a debt collector may not deposit a postdated check prior to its effective date.

e.   The FTC is the principal enforcement agency for the FDCPA.

1)   The FDCPA also permits civil actions and class actions by the affected debtor or debtors.

2)   A debt collector can be liable for up to $1,000 without proof of damages for violation of the act.

7.   Stop and review! You have completed the outline for this subunit. Study multiple-choice questions 9 through 13 beginning on page 294.

D. **Remedies upon Default**. Solutions to tension between debtor relief and creditor protection include both formal (bankruptcy) and informal solutions. Bankruptcy is discussed in Study Unit 11.

1.   A debtor can enter into a composition or extension agreement with his/her creditors.

a.   A **composition** with creditors is a contract whereby the debtor arranges to pay the creditors some fraction of the amount the debtor owes in full satisfaction of the creditors' claims.

1)   A nonconsenting creditor may choose to pursue typical debt collection processes and proceed against the debtor's assets.

2)   Under general contract law, the original debts are not discharged until the debtor has performed the new obligations.

b.   In an **extension agreement**, the debtor agrees to pay the full amount of all debts (with or without interest), but the creditors agree to allow the debtor to pay over a longer time than originally agreed to.

1)   Nonconsenting creditors are not bound by an extension agreement and may pursue usual collection processes as to the amounts owed them.

2)   An extension agreement is one form of composition agreement.

c.   **Liquidation** of an unliquidated claim means that a debtor and a creditor agree on the amount of a previously disputed claim.

2.   A **general assignment for the benefit of creditors** is a voluntary transfer by the debtor of all of his/her assets to a third party (the assignee or trustee).

     a.   The trustee named by the debtor receives the debtor's property, converts the property into cash, and distributes the cash to the creditors in exchange for their promises to release the debtor from further liability.

     b.   The trustee is often one of the creditors.

     c.   Assignment is similar to a composition agreement: it usually allows creditors to receive more than they would in a bankruptcy proceeding. However, distinctions include

        1)   Assent of creditors is not required. The right to make an assignment is an incident of property ownership.

        2)   An assignment for the benefit of creditors is a sufficient ground for a dissatisfied creditor to institute proceedings for the debtor's involuntary bankruptcy.

     d.   An assignment for the benefit of creditors places the debtor's property out of the reach of his/her creditors because legal title passes to the assignee.

        1)   A basic requirement for a valid assignment for creditors is that the debtor act in good faith.

        2)   An assignment that reserves to the assignor any interest in, or benefit or advantage of, the property conveyed to the injury of creditors is probably a fraudulent conveyance.

        3)   Some jurisdictions treat a partial assignment for the benefit of creditors as a fraudulent conveyance.

     e.   The creditors are presumed to have consented to the assignment. If otherwise valid, the assignment will take effect unless a majority of the creditors object.

     f.   The debtor cannot revoke an assignment for creditors. (S)he has no further interest in the assigned property.

        1)   Because the debtor has no interest in the assigned property, creditors cannot levy or garnish the property.

           a)   A **levy** consists of obtaining money by legally seizing and selling property.

           b)   **Garnishment** is a legal procedure by which a creditor acquires money or other property of a debtor when the property is rightfully in the hands of a third party, such as a bank (bank account) or employer (wages).

              i)   Property includes a debt owed by a third party to the debtor, such as wages due from his/her employer.

     g.   An assignment for the benefit of creditors discharges only those debts that are paid in full by the trustee.

        1)   The debtor can emerge with some or all of his/her debts not fully paid.

        2)   Assignments for creditors are used primarily by corporations. Even if all of a corporation's property has been assigned, the corporation continues to exist. But, unless it acquires more assets, its remaining debts are uncollectible.

3.   Stop and review! You have completed the outline for this subunit. Study multiple-choice questions 14 through 23 beginning on page 296.

MULTIPLE-CHOICE QUESTIONS

A. Contract Rights and Duties

1. Which of the following statements is correct concerning usury laws?

   A. Usury laws generally apply to businesses or large transactions but not to ordinary consumer transactions.

   B. Most usury laws have been held to be a violation of an individual's right to contract.

   C. Usury laws are intended to prevent the charging of an excessive interest rate.

   D. Usury laws can be avoided by using a lease rather than a bill of sale.

The correct answer is (C). *(Publisher)*

REQUIRED: The correct statement concerning usury laws.

DISCUSSION: Usury laws prevent the charging of interest rates in excess of a legal amount established by state statute. They are intended to prevent the charging of an excessive interest rate to small businesses and consumers.

Answer (A) is incorrect because usury laws generally apply to ordinary consumer transactions. In some states business transactions are exempt, and in most states large transactions are exempt. Answer (B) is incorrect because usury laws have been upheld for a long time and are not considered a violation of an individual's right to contract. Answer (D) is incorrect because usury laws cannot be avoided by use of a lease. The substance of a transaction will control rather than the form.

B. Liens

2. On April 14, Jack Jackson, CPA, watched as his copy machine malfunctioned. Jackson delivered the copier to Copy, Inc. for repair. Jackson agreed to pay $150 under terms of 2/10, n/30 for parts and labor if Copy would fix the copier by 8 a.m. on April 15. Jackson arrived at 8 a.m. on April 15 to pick up the copier but refused to pay for the repairs at that time. Copy is entitled to

   A. An artisan's lien.

   B. A mechanic's lien.

   C. A materialman's lien.

   D. Payment in 30 days.

The correct answer is (D). *(Publisher)*

REQUIRED: The right to payment or a lien for services performed on personal property.

DISCUSSION: An artisan's lien is a common-law possessory lien that arises in favor of a repairer or other improver of personal property as a result of a specific debt. The holder of an artisan's lien ordinarily must have agreed expressly or implicitly to perform the services on a cash basis. Payment terms of 2/10, n/30 are a common extension of credit. Because Copy agreed to bill Jackson for the repairs, the work was done on a credit basis, and Copy is not entitled to an artisan's lien. Copy must await performance under the contract.

Answer (A) is incorrect because Copy agreed to extend credit to Jackson. Answers (B) and (C) are incorrect because mechanic's and materialman's liens attach to real property, and a copy machine is personal property.

3. Which of the following liens generally require(s) the lienholder to give notice of legal action before selling the debtor's property to satisfy the debt?

	Mechanic's Lien	Artisan's Lien
A.	Yes	Yes
B.	Yes	No
C.	No	Yes
D.	No	No

The correct answer is (A). *(CPA, adapted)*

REQUIRED: The lien(s), if any, requiring notice before sale of the debtor's property.

DISCUSSION: A mechanic's lien is a statutory lien against realty that secures an unpaid debt arising from a contract for labor, materials, or services to improve the property. An artisan's lien arises in favor of a repairer or improver of personal property who retains possession of the property until paid. Failure to pay the debt permits the lienholder to foreclose on the property and sell it. Statutes require notice to the owner prior to foreclosure and sale.

Answers (B), (C), and (D) are incorrect because both liens require notice of foreclosure and sale.

4. One night Chris Lee was driving to a client's office when her car collided with another vehicle. Both headlights on Lee's car were smashed in the collision. A police officer quickly arrived on the scene accompanied by a tow truck from XYZ Towing Co. As Lee signed a traffic citation, XYZ towed Lee's car to its lot at the direction of the police officer. The next day Lee went to XYZ to get the car. XYZ charged Lee $100 for two new headlights that had been installed. Lee refused to pay for the headlights. Is XYZ entitled to a common-law lien for the value of the headlights?

- A. Yes, XYZ is entitled to an artisan's lien for the value of the headlights.

- B. No, XYZ is not entitled to a common-law possessory lien for the value of the headlights.

- C. Yes, XYZ is entitled to a common carrier's lien for the value of the headlights.

- D. No, but XYZ is entitled to a mechanic's lien for the value of the headlights.

The correct answer is (B). *(Publisher)*
REQUIRED: The entitlement of a repairer to a common-law lien when the owner did not consent to the work.
DISCUSSION: Common-law possessory liens (e.g., artisan's, hotelkeeper's) require the owner's consent to performance of the work or service that benefited the property. Lee did not consent to XYZ's installation of new headlights, so XYZ is not entitled to a common-law possessory lien.
Answer (A) is incorrect because an artisan's lien is a common-law possessory lien and requires consent of the owner to the work. Answer (C) is incorrect because a common carrier's lien typically arises from freight charges for transportation of goods. Answer (D) is incorrect because mechanic's liens attach to real property.

5. Art owns a mobile automobile repair business. Ann's car would not start so she called Art. Art went to Ann's home and replaced the distributor cap on Ann's car. Ann was unable to pay for the repair. Art is not entitled to an artisan's lien because

- A. Ann did not relinquish possession of the car.

- B. Artisan's liens attach only to improvements to real property.

- C. Automobile repairers are essentially mechanics and therefore are entitled to mechanic's liens rather than artisan's liens.

- D. The distributor cap did not appreciably increase the value of the car.

The correct answer is (A). *(Publisher)*
REQUIRED: The reason the improver is not entitled to an artisan's lien.
DISCUSSION: An artisan's lien is a possessory lien. If possession of the personal property is not relinquished by the owner and retained by the improver, the lien cannot exist. Because Art repaired the car at Ann's home, Ann retained possession.
Answers (B) and (C) are incorrect because artisan's liens attach to personal property, and mechanic's liens attach to real property. Answer (D) is incorrect because an increase in the value of the personal property is not a necessary condition of an artisan's lien. The lien arises for labor done or value added.

6. Which of the following is a true statement about foreclosure by the holder of a lien?

- A. The holder of an artisan's lien must foreclose within a prescribed period or lose the lien.

- B. The sales proceeds resulting from statutorily permitted foreclosure and sale are awarded to the holder of an artisan's lien regardless of the size of the debt secured by the lien.

- C. State statutes permitting a foreclosure and sale require a lienholder to give notice to the property owner.

- D. The holder of an artisan's lien may foreclose on the real property subject to the lien.

The correct answer is (C). *(Publisher)*
REQUIRED: The correct statement concerning foreclosure by a lienholder.
DISCUSSION: An artisan's lien is a common-law possessory lien. The holder may retain possession of the secured property and may sue for payment of the debt. But unless a statute grants it, the artisan does not have the right to foreclose and sell the property. State statutes which provide for foreclosure and sale also require prior notice to the property owner.
Answer (A) is incorrect because, unless a statute grants it, the artisan does not have the right to foreclose and sell the property. Answer (B) is incorrect because the lienholder is entitled only to satisfaction of the debt secured by the lien. Answer (D) is incorrect because an artisan's lien does not attach to real property.

7. A homestead exemption ordinarily could exempt a debtor's equity in certain property from post-judgment collection by a creditor. To which of the following creditors will this exemption apply?

	Valid Home Mortgage Lien	Valid IRS Tax Lien
A.	Yes	Yes
B.	Yes	No
C.	No	Yes
D.	No	No

The correct answer is (D). *(CPA, adapted)*
REQUIRED: The creditors that are affected by a homestead exemption.
DISCUSSION: State homestead exemption acts ordinarily exempt a debtor's equity in his/her home from post-judgment collections by a creditor. However, these acts generally do not apply to a holder of a valid mortgage against the home or a valid IRS tax lien.
Answers (A), (B), and (C) are incorrect because a home mortgage and an IRS tax lien have priority over a homestead exemption under state law.

8. Which of the following statements is(are) correct regarding debtors' rights?

I. State exemption statutes prevent all of a debtor's personal property from being sold to pay a federal tax lien.

II. Federal Social Security benefits received by a debtor are exempt from garnishment by creditors.

A. I only.

B. II only.

C. Both I and II.

D. Neither I nor II.

The correct answer is (B). *(CPA, adapted)*
REQUIRED: The true statement(s), if any, about debtors' rights.
DISCUSSION: Federal statutes, not state statutes, exempt debtor assets from federal tax liens. Social Security benefits, however, are exempt from garnishment.
Answers (A) and (C) are incorrect because federal exemption statutes, not state statutes, exempt debtors' assets. Answer (D) is incorrect because Social Security benefits are exempt from garnishment.

C. Consumer Credit Protection

9. The Consumer Credit Protection Act was enacted due to unfair and predatory practices by creditors in their extension of credit to consumers. Which of the following was not enacted as a part of, or as an amendment to, the Consumer Credit Protection Act?

A. Truth in lending.

B. Fair credit reporting.

C. Uniform Consumer Credit Code.

D. Credit card liability limitations.

The correct answer is (C). *(Publisher)*
REQUIRED: The provisions not enacted as part of the Consumer Credit Protection Act.
DISCUSSION: The Uniform Consumer Credit Code is a model act similar to the Uniform Commercial Code, Model Business Corporation Act, and Uniform Partnership Act. It contains many provisions similar to the Consumer Protection Act; however, it has been enacted by only a few states and is not expected to be a significant uniform statute.
Answers (A), (B), and (D) are incorrect because each is a part of the Consumer Credit Protection Act.

10. The federal Credit Card Fraud Act protects a credit cardholder from loss by

A. Restricting the interest rate charged by the credit card company.

B. Limiting the cardholder's liability for unauthorized use.

C. Requiring credit card companies to issue cards to qualified persons.

D. Allowing the cardholder to defer payment of the balance due on the card.

The correct answer is (B). *(CPA, adapted)*
REQUIRED: The protection provided by federal law to a credit cardholder.
DISCUSSION: The Consumer Credit Protection Act (CCPA) regulates the extension of credit for personal, household, or agricultural purposes. Title 1 of CCPA is known as the Truth-in-Lending Act (TILA). It requires disclosure by creditors before credit is extended. The TILA, as amended, regulates credit cards and serves as an antifraud act by limiting the holder's liability for unauthorized use of the card to $50 or the amount of money, property, labor, or services obtained by unauthorized use before the card issuer is notified, whichever is lower.
Answer (A) is incorrect because state usury law, not federal law, regulates interest charges. Answers (C) and (D) are incorrect because federal law pertaining to credit card fraud does not require card companies to issue cards or to allow a cardholder to defer payment of the balance due on a card. However, federal law does prohibit certain types of discrimination in consumer credit transactions.

11. The Equal Credit Opportunity Act was enacted to prevent discrimination in credit extension. Which of the following is not prohibited by the act?

  A. Discrimination based on receipt of welfare.

  B. Denial of a married woman from opening a credit account separate from her husband's.

  C. Asking if the credit applicant is married.

  D. Denial of credit based on lack of assets.

The correct answer is (D). *(Publisher)*
  REQUIRED: The item not prohibited by the Equal Credit Opportunity Act.
  DISCUSSION: The act prohibits discrimination based on race, sex, marital status, etc. However, it does not prevent a denial of credit based on a lack of assets. Lack of assets and lack of income are allowable and logical reasons for denying credit.
  Answer (A) is incorrect because a lender may not discriminate based on receipt of welfare, since the source of a person's income is generally not to be taken into account. Answer (B) is incorrect because a married woman may not be denied the opening of a credit account separate from her husband's. Answer (C) is incorrect because asking if a credit applicant is married is also prohibited. Marital status is not to be taken into account.

12. Tom Debtor incurred substantial debts. Much of this debt was turned over to a collection agency. Employees of this agency called Debtor repeatedly at home during the middle of the night. They also made collect telephone calls to Debtor from distant places and confronted him in the presence of his neighbors and coworkers.

  A. Debtor can prevent this harassment with a written note to the collection agency.

  B. Debtor can end this harassment only by filing a lawsuit against the collection agency.

  C. Debtor can prevent the disparaging remarks in front of neighbors and coworkers, but telephone calls are not subject to restrictions.

  D. In order to have any recourse against the collection agency, Debtor must be able to prove damages.

The correct answer is (A). *(Publisher)*
  REQUIRED: The correct statement concerning a debtor who is harassed by a collection agency.
  DISCUSSION: A debtor need only notify the collection agency in writing of his/her wish that the agency refrain from contacting him/her or informing the neighbors and coworkers of the debts. The collection agency is then required by the federal Fair Debt Collection Practices Act to stop all further contact, and its sole remedy is to sue Debtor.
  Answer (B) is incorrect because Debtor can write a letter; he does not have to file a lawsuit. Answer (C) is incorrect because telephone calls by debt collectors are prohibited before 8 a.m. and after 9 p.m., and collect calls are prohibited. Answer (D) is incorrect because a debt collector can be liable for up to $1,000 without proof of damages for violation of the act.

13. Under the federal Fair Debt Collection Practices Act, to which of the following would a collection service using improper debt collection practices be subject?

  A. Abolishment of the debt.

  B. Reduction of the debt.

  C. Civil lawsuit for damages for violating the act.

  D. Criminal prosecution for violating the act.

The correct answer is (C). *(CPA, adapted)*
  REQUIRED: The remedy available to a debtor under the Fair Debt Collection Practices Act.
  DISCUSSION: The FDCPA permits aggrieved debtors to pursue civil actions, including class action suits, against collection agencies that engage in abusive, deceptive, and unfair debt collection practices.
  Answers (A) and (B) are incorrect because the FDCPA was enacted to prevent abusive, deceptive, and unfair debt collection practices. The act does not provide for the reduction or extinguishment of the debt itself. Answer (D) is incorrect because the FDCPA does not provide for criminal penalties.

D. Remedies upon Default

14. A client has joined other creditors of the Martin Construction Company in a composition agreement seeking to avoid the necessity of a bankruptcy proceeding against Martin. Which statement describes the composition agreement?

- A. It provides a temporary delay, not to exceed 6 months, insofar as the debtor's obligation to repay the debts included in the composition.

- B. It does not discharge any of the debts included until performance by the debtor has taken place.

- C. It provides for the appointment of a receiver to take over and operate the debtor's business.

- D. It must be approved by all creditors.

The correct answer is (B). *(CPA, adapted)*
REQUIRED: The correct statement describing a composition among creditors.
DISCUSSION: A composition with creditors is a common-law contractual undertaking between the debtor and the creditors. The participating creditors agree to extend time for payment, take lesser sums in satisfaction of the debts owed, or accept some other plan of financial adjustment. Under general contract law, the original debts will not be discharged until the debtor has performed the new obligations.
Answer (A) is incorrect because, although a composition may involve an extension of time, it is not limited to 6 months. Furthermore, the more common composition is to take lesser sums in satisfaction. Answer (C) is incorrect because it describes the appointment of a receiver. A composition agreement is a contractual agreement not involving judicial intervention. Answer (D) is incorrect because a composition agreement need not be approved by all creditors but is binding only upon those participating.

15. Which of the following actions between a debtor and its creditors will generally cause the debtor's release from its debts?

	Composition of Creditors	Assignment for the Benefit of Creditors
A.	Yes	Yes
B.	Yes	No
C.	No	Yes
D.	No	No

The correct answer is (B). *(CPA, adapted)*
REQUIRED: The action(s), if any, that will release a debtor.
DISCUSSION: Both compositions and assignments are alternatives to bankruptcy. However, only a composition will ordinarily result in a debtor's release. An assignment for the benefit of creditors allows for the discharge of debts only to the extent that actual payments are made to creditors by the trustee. It does not act as a full release of the debt. A composition of creditors is a contractual agreement in which creditors agree to accept less than the total amount of debt owed in full satisfaction of the debt.
Answers (A), (C), and (D) are incorrect because a composition of creditors, not an assignment for the benefit of creditors, usually results in the release of a debtor.

16. Which of the following will enable a creditor to collect money from a debtor's wages?

- A. An order of receivership.

- B. An order of garnishment.

- C. A writ of execution.

- D. A writ of attachment.

The correct answer is (B). *(CPA, adapted)*
REQUIRED: The legal proceeding that will allow a creditor to collect from a debtor's wages.
DISCUSSION: Garnishment is the legal action by which a creditor acquires money (or other property) of a debtor when the property is rightfully in the hands of a third party such as an employer (wages) or a financial institution (money in a bank account). Garnishment is limited by state and federal law especially when used as a prejudgment remedy.
Answer (A) is incorrect because an order of receivership empowers an impartial third party, not a creditor, to obtain control of the debtor's assets. Answer (C) is incorrect because execution is a postjudgment remedy similar to attachment. Answer (D) is incorrect because attachment is a prejudgment remedy. It instructs the sheriff to take control of the debtor's property pending the outcome of the litigation.

17. FGC, Inc. is in serious financial trouble. Trade accounts payable total $1 million. FGC has not paid its vendors in over 120 days. Although the vendors are anxious for payments, they agree that everyone will benefit if FGC avoids bankruptcy. FGC and all the vendors agree to a plan calling for FGC to make monthly payments on the overdue accounts for 24 months. All vendors will be paid in full. This plan is best described as a(n)

A. Composition with creditors.

B. Liquidation of unliquidated claims.

C. Extension agreement.

D. Assignment for the benefit of creditors.

The correct answer is (C). *(Publisher)*
    REQUIRED: The best description of an agreement by a debtor and its creditors to delay payment.
    DISCUSSION: An extension agreement is a variation of the composition with creditors. Rather than agree to the reduced but immediate payment of debts, the creditors and debtor agree that payments will be made over an extended period. The key characteristic of an extension agreement is the extended payment period.
    Answer (A) is incorrect because a composition involves satisfaction of debts by reduced payments. Answer (B) is incorrect because liquidation of unliquidated claims is merely agreement between the debtor and creditors on the amount of previously disputed claims. Answer (D) is incorrect because an assignment for the benefit of creditors involves the transfer of the debtor's assets to a trustee. It does not involve an agreement for an extended payment period.

18. Dexter had assets of $80,000 and liabilities of $100,000, all unsecured. He owed $25,000 to each of the following: Petrie, Dey, Mabley, and Norris. Petrie, Dey, and Mabley agreed with each other and with Dexter to accept 70 cents on the dollar in immediate satisfaction of their debts. Under these circumstances,

A. The agreement is void for lack of consideration.

B. The agreement is a composition with creditors.

C. Norris would be bound by the agreement.

D. The agreement described is an assignment for the benefit of creditors.

The correct answer is (B). *(CPA, adapted)*
    REQUIRED: The correct statement concerning an agreement by a debtor with three of four creditors to accept reduced payment.
    DISCUSSION: The agreement is a common-law composition with creditors. Under general contract law, Dexter's old debts of $25,000 to each of the three will not be discharged until he performs the new obligation of paying 70%. The problem with this arrangement is that Norris can still petition Dexter into involuntary bankruptcy and void the composition.
    Answer (A) is incorrect because consideration is found in the mutual promises made among the creditors to accept a lesser payment or is excused by the courts on the basis that public policy requires that informal settlement of debts should be encouraged. Answer (C) is incorrect because Norris is a nonparticipant and under general contract principles would not be bound. Answer (D) is incorrect because an assignment for the benefit of creditors occurs when the debtor places his/her assets in the hands of a trustee who distributes the property to the creditors on a proportional basis as the intended beneficiaries.

19. Hance, doing business as Hance Fashions, is hopelessly insolvent. As a means of staving off his aggressive creditors and avoiding bankruptcy, Hance has decided to make a general assignment for the benefit of his creditors. Consequently, he transferred all his nonexempt property to a trustee for equitable distribution to his creditors. What are the legal consequences of Hance's actions?

A. A debtor may not make an assignment for the benefit of creditors if he has been adjudicated a bankrupt and discharged within the preceding 6 years.

B. All his creditors must participate in the assignment and distribution of property if a majority in number and amount participate.

C. Upon distribution of all his assigned property to the participating creditors, he is discharged from all liability.

D. He may be petitioned into bankruptcy by his creditors.

The correct answer is (D). *(CPA, adapted)*
    REQUIRED: The legal consequences of an assignment for the benefit of creditors.
    DISCUSSION: An involuntary petition by the creditors will be upheld even if contested by the debtor if the debtor is not paying his/her debts as they come due or if, during the preceding 120 days before the filing of the petition, a custodian (trustee, receiver, etc.) was appointed or permitted to take possession of the debtor's property. For this reason, Hance may not be able to avoid bankruptcy.
    Answer (A) is incorrect because an assignment for the benefit of creditors under state law is not an official proceeding and is not subject to federal bankruptcy rules. Answer (B) is incorrect because all creditors need not participate in the assignment, and distribution would not discharge any nonassenting creditors' claims. Answer (C) is incorrect because distribution of assigned property to the participating creditors does not discharge the debtor from liability to the nonparticipants.

20. One advantage of an assignment for the benefit of creditors over a composition with creditors is that the assignment

    A. Prevents attachment of the debtor's assets.

    B. Discharges the debtor's obligations.

    C. Involves the transfer of assets directly to creditors.

    D. Requires the consent of creditors.

The correct answer is (A). *(Publisher)*
    REQUIRED: The correct statement about the advantage of an assignment for the benefit of creditors.
    DISCUSSION: An assignment for the benefit of creditors requires the transfer of legal title to the assets from the debtor to a trustee. Creditors cannot attach the transferred assets because the debtor does not own them. Creditors can attach the debtor's assets prior to the execution of a composition agreement.
    Answer (B) is incorrect because an assignment for the benefit of creditors does not discharge the debtor's obligations. Answer (C) is incorrect because an assignment for the benefit of creditors requires the debtor to transfer assets to a trustee. Answer (D) is incorrect because an assignment for the benefit of creditors does not require the creditors' consent.

21. Which of the following prejudgment remedies would be available to a creditor when a debtor owns no real property?

	Writ of Attachment	Garnishment
A.	Yes	Yes
B.	Yes	No
C.	No	Yes
D.	No	No

The correct answer is (A). *(CPA, adapted)*
    REQUIRED: The prejudgment remedy(ies), if any, available to a creditor when a debtor owns no realty.
    DISCUSSION: A writ of attachment is a prejudgment remedy allowing for the seizure of property, real or personal, in the debtor's possession while a lawsuit is proceeding. A garnishment procedure is a prejudgment remedy that allows the creditor to acquire real or personal property of the debtor that is rightfully in the hands of a third party.
    Answers (B), (C), and (D) are incorrect because garnishment is a prejudgment as well as a postjudgment remedy, and attachment is the major prejudgment remedy available to a creditor.

22. Which of the following methods will allow a creditor to collect money from a debtor's wages?

    A. Arrest.

    B. Mechanic's lien.

    C. Order of receivership.

    D. Writ of garnishment.

The correct answer is (D). *(CPA, adapted)*
    REQUIRED: The method which will allow a creditor to collect from a debtor's wages.
    DISCUSSION: Garnishment is the legal procedure by which a creditor acquires money or other property of a debtor when the property is rightfully in the hands of a third party such as an employer.
    Answers (A), (B), and (C) are incorrect because neither arrest, which is a criminal law term, a mechanic's lien, which is a lien against real property, or an order of receivership, which is a form of trust, are effective ways for a creditor to collect money from a debtor's wages.

23. A debtor may attempt to conceal or transfer property to prevent a creditor from satisfying a judgment. Which of the following actions will be considered an indication of fraudulent conveyance?

	Debtor Remaining in Possession after Conveyance	Secret Conveyance	Debtor Retains an Equitable Benefit in the Property Conveyed
A.	Yes	Yes	Yes
B.	No	Yes	Yes
C.	Yes	Yes	No
D.	Yes	No	Yes

The correct answer is (A). *(CPA, adapted)*
    REQUIRED: The actions that will be considered indications of fraudulent conveyance.
    DISCUSSION: Any transfer of property that is made with the purpose and intent to delay, hinder, or defraud creditors is voidable by the transferor's creditors. Courts have developed various criteria that will be considered an indication of fraudulent conveyances. These criteria are known as badges of fraud and include the debtor remaining in possession after conveyance, the transfer being made in secret, and the debtor retaining an equitable benefit in the property conveyed. These criteria are currently embodied in the Uniform Fraudulent Transfer Act of 1984.
    Answers (B), (C), and (D) are incorrect because each is a "badge" or an indication of a fraudulent conveyance.

OOF QUESTION *(Publisher)* 15 minutes

Each of items 1 through 14 is a statement related to debtor-creditor rights and duties. If the statement is correct, mark (A). If it is incorrect, mark (B).

1. The Truth-in-Lending Act limits liability for use of a credit card to $50.

2. The debtor-creditor relationship is fundamentally fiduciary in nature.

3. A writ of execution authorizes sale of property.

4. The Equal Credit Opportunity Act requires that the creditor respond to a completed application within 90 days.

5. The Equal Credit Opportunity Act notice requirements apply only if the applicant is a woman or a minority.

6. An assignment for benefit of creditors entitles the creditors to take possession of the debtor's property.

7. Under the Fair Credit Reporting Act, the user of a credit report incurs a duty of disclosure when (s)he charges a higher rate for credit or insurance.

8. A composition is an agreement between creditors to accept less than the amount which the debtor owes in full satisfaction of their claims.

9. A hotelkeeper's lien terminates whenever the lienholder returns the baggage to the guest.

10. The Fair Debt Collection Practices Act does not apply to a retailer using harassing tactics to collect an account receivable it accrued when it sold a consumer item to the debtor.

11. For professional services rendered, a CPA acquires a common-law lien analogous to an artisan's lien on any books and materials of the client which are in the CPA's possession.

12. If personal property which is the subject matter of an artisan's lien is destroyed, subsequently acquired property of the debtor located in the same county becomes subject to the lien.

13. A bankruptcy trustee has the rights of a judicial lienholder in the property in which petitioner had an interest when the petition was filed.

14. The Truth-in-Lending Act applies to a consumer transaction if the creditor is in the business of extending credit, the debtor is a natural person, the transaction is for a consumer item for which the down payment is $1,000, and another $1,000 plus a finance charge is to be paid on the first day of the following month.

Knowledge Tested

1. Contract law applicability
2. Common-law liens
3. Remedies other than bankruptcy
4. Consumer protection statutes

Authors' Comments

Debtor-creditor rights and duties arise from contract and statute. Liens provide some assurance of repayment to creditors. The nature of particular alternatives to bankruptcy, e.g., a composition, is frequently tested. Remember which ones bind which creditors. Consumer protection statutes have not previously been tested but might be, in that the topic of debtor-creditor rights and duties has been specified as a discrete testing area starting in 1994.

1. The correct answer is (B).
DISCUSSION: The TILA $50 limit applies only to unauthorized use, that is, use by a person other than the cardholder without actual, implied, or apparent authority for the use.

2. The correct answer is (B).
DISCUSSION: A debtor-creditor relationship is, primarily, a contract between the debtor and the creditor. Contract law generally applies to formation, performance, and remedies.

3. The correct answer is (A).
DISCUSSION: A court may award a monetary judgment in a breach of contract suit. If the judgment debtor does not pay, the court may issue a writ of execution authorizing the sheriff to seize and sell nonexempt personal property of the debtor to satisfy the judgment.

4. The correct answer is (B).
DISCUSSION: The ECOA requires that a creditor give an applicant notification of action it has taken on his/her completed application for credit within 30 days.

5. The correct answer is (B).
DISCUSSION: The ECOA requires that notice be provided to any credit applicant provided it is a consumer credit transaction.

6. The correct answer is (B).
DISCUSSION: A general assignment for benefit of creditors is a voluntary transfer by the debtor of all of his/her assets to a third party. Legal title passes to the assignee/trustee. This places the property out of the reach of the creditors.

7. The correct answer is (A).
DISCUSSION: Disclosure under FRCA is also required whenever the user rejects an applicant for consumer credit, insurance, or even employment.

8. The correct answer is (B).
DISCUSSION: A composition is a contract between the debtor and one or more consenting creditors.

9. The correct answer is (B).
DISCUSSION: Like an artisan's lien, the common-law hotelkeeper's lien generally requires that the lienholder have the personal property in his/her possession. However, the lien does not terminate if the lienholder temporarily relinquishes possession of the property to the owner subject to an agreement that the property will be returned to the lienholder.

10. The correct answer is (A).
DISCUSSION: The FDCPA is directed at agencies that are collecting debts for others, but not to banks and businesses that are trying to collect their own accounts.

11. The correct answer is (B).
DISCUSSION: A statutory lien on such books and records may be provided for by the state but is not recognized by the common law.

12. The correct answer is (B).
DISCUSSION: The common-law artisan's lien terminates if and when the property subject to the lien is destroyed.

13. The correct answer is (A).
DISCUSSION: The rights of the trustee are the same as those of a creditor with a judicial lien upon return of a writ of execution which remains unsatisfied.

14. The correct answer is (B).
DISCUSSION: TILA disclosure requirements do not apply when the buyer pays in less than four installments.

ESSAY QUESTION *(Publisher)* 15 minutes

Tom, CPA, decided to sell his 1975 Camaro. Shine, Inc. agreed to paint and detail the car for $500 cash. When Tom took the car in to Shine, Inc.'s shop on Monday, Meg Mechanic said they could also tune it up for an extra $75. Tom suggested the next month would be better, when he would have more cash. Shine's manager told Tom he could pay the $75 next month if Tom would let them do the tune-up now. Tom gave them the go-ahead.

Shine's manager called Friday to say the car was red and ready. When Tom explained that he would have the $500 the following Friday, the manager said they would keep the car until then to protect Shine's rights to payment. Upon Tom's request, the manager said he could take the car for a few hours Saturday to park it at a show if Tom would place a card on the dash declaring, "Renewed by Shine, Inc.," and on condition that he return the car by evening.

At the show, Tom sold the car to Larry. Shine, Inc.'s manager called Tom Monday to demand the car back. Tom told him that the car was sold and that he would not pay. Tom said the car had sold for no more than it would have before Shine, Inc. worked on it.

Shine, Inc. gave Larry notice that it intended to foreclose liens it had on the Camaro with respect to the paint job and the tune-up and to sell the car unless Larry paid the $575. Larry answered that Shine, Inc. had no mechanic's liens on his Camaro.

Required

Discuss whether Shine, Inc. may enforce the liens it asserts.

Knowledge Tested

1. Artisan's lien requirements
2. Termination of the lien

Authors' Comments

The topic of debtor-creditor rights and duties has been specified as a discrete area for testing on the CPA exam since 1994. We have prepared this sample essay question for you to practice.

Suggested Answer

Shine, Inc. is asserting common-law artisan's liens. Mechanic's liens are analogous but apply to real property. The artisan's lien arises in favor of the repairer or improver of personal property. The property's value need not be increased by the work. The lien does not arise when payment on credit is agreed to. Thus, there is no common-law artisan's lien to secure payment for the tune-up. The lien only attaches if the owner relinquishes possession to the artisan, and it terminates if the artisan relinquishes that possession. However, when Shine, Inc. relinquished possession, the lien did not terminate because Shine gave up possession only temporarily, subject to an agreement that the car would be returned to its possession. Recording is generally not necessary to protect the common-law lien. However, a state statute might provide for it. When Larry, a third party, obtained rights to the car before it was to be returned, Shine, Inc.'s lien terminated. Shine's recourse is against Tom for damages for breach of contract.

STUDY UNIT 10: GUARANTORS

6 pages of outline
25 multiple-choice questions
1 OOF and 1 essay

A. Definitions
B. Formation of Suretyship Contract
C. Creditor's Duty to Disclose
D. Liability of a Surety
E. Defenses of a Surety
F. Rights of a Surety
G. Discharge of a Surety

Guaranty or suretyship is a relationship arising out of a contract in which a person is liable for the debt or default of another person. The purpose of suretyship is to provide security to a creditor. A surety or guarantor promises to pay the creditor if the debtor becomes insolvent, incapacitated, or unwilling to pay. Exam questions should be expected on formation and enforceability of surety relationships, especially the statute of frauds, and the rights and duties of the debtor, creditor, and surety, with an emphasis on defenses, subrogation rights, and contribution among cosureties.

A. **Definitions**. A **surety** is a person who by contract is liable for the debt or default of another. The surety promises to answer for the payment of a debt or the performance of a duty if the debtor or obligor fails to make payment or otherwise perform the obligation. Thus, suretyship provides security for the creditor by way of a third party's promise to be responsible for the debtor's obligation if the debtor defaults.

1. The suretyship relationship involves at least three parties: the debtor, the creditor, and the surety.

2. The person who actually receives the money or the credit is referred to as the **debtor**, **principal**, **principal debtor**, or **obligor**.

3. The **creditor (obligee)** is the person who has permitted another party (usually the debtor) to receive goods, services, money, or other value without having fully paid the price.

4. When more than one person is obligated to pay the same debt if the principal debtor defaults, they are **cosureties**.

    a. Generally, a cosurety's liability is determined by agreement.

    b. Cosureties need not be liable in the same amounts, give equivalent (or any) security interests, sign the same agreement, or even be aware of each other.

    c. Cosurety liability is joint and several. A creditor may sue any or all, alone or jointly, for up to the cosureties' maximum liability. But the creditor may recover no more than the principal debt. Suit against one does not release the others.

5. Sureties who are not paid are called gratuitous, voluntary, or accommodation sureties.

6. **Compensated sureties** undertake a surety obligation for consideration. The promise of a compensated surety is often referred to as a **bond**. Types of surety bonds include bail bond, bid bond, completion bond, fidelity bond, fiduciary bond, and license or permit bond.

7. Under modern legal theory, a guarantor is substantially the same as a surety. Some states, however, recognize the following technical distinctions.

    a. A **surety** is primarily liable for the debtor's obligation. The creditor need not first proceed against the principal to collect the debt upon default but may proceed immediately and directly against the surety. The term **absolute surety** applies to a surety with primary liability.

    b. A **guarantor** is secondarily liable. The creditor must first proceed against the principal and obtain a judgment that is returned unsatisfied. Only then may the creditor proceed against the guarantor.

8. Stop and review! You have completed the outline for this subunit. There are no multiple-choice questions for this section.

B. **Formation of Suretyship Contract**. Generally, a suretyship arises by express contract at the request of either the debtor or the creditor.

1. A contract for suretyship requires acceptance.

2. A contract for suretyship must be supported by sufficient consideration. For example, if a buyer directs the seller to deliver goods to a third party and agrees to pay $300 for them, the promise is original, and the promisor is not undertaking to answer for the debt of another.

   a. EXAMPLE: Mom is engaged as surety to a note signed by Son. The surety contract is between Mom and Lender (not Son). A gratuitous suretyship arises. The legally sufficient consideration received by Mom is the legal benefit of the Lender's promise to continue dealing with Son. Mom is bound to performance of the suretyship contract with Lender, provided the credit is extended to Son. The actual benefit is the consideration received by Son.

3. The contract for suretyship (or the guaranty) must be in writing. The statute of frauds requires that a contract to answer for the debt of another be in writing.

   a. The purpose of the writing requirement is to provide reliable evidence of what was promised and to protect the surety from fraudulent claims.

   b. This section of the statute of frauds requires a writing to enforce a **collateral promise** to pay a debt or perform a contract only if the principal debtor fails to pay. Collateral promises create secondary liability. They are conditional promises that are ancillary or secondary to the primary contract between a debtor and a creditor.

      1) The **main purpose doctrine** states an exception to the writing requirement. If the main purpose of the surety's promise to answer for the debt of another is to obtain some new economic benefit for him/herself, the promise is not within the statute of frauds and may be enforced even though it is oral.

      2) Furthermore, an **original promise** is also outside the statute of frauds.

      NOTE: Other sections of the statute of frauds may be applicable.

4. An enforceable contract for suretyship must be signed by the surety.

5. A **delegator** remains responsible as a surety for the performance of duties if the delegatee fails to perform, unless the obligee (the person to whom the duty is owed) releases the delegator (or grants a novation).

6. The law of the place where a contract of suretyship is made and performed generally governs, unless it is shown that the parties intended to contract with reference to the law of another jurisdiction.

7. **Indemnification Contracts**. A contract by which one party agrees to protect an obligor (debtor) from loss creates a right of indemnification. Contrast this to the contract of a surety who promises to protect a creditor from loss.

   a. Liability insurance is an example of an indemnity contract.

8. Stop and review! You have completed the outline for this subunit. Study multiple-choice questions 1 through 4 beginning on page 307.

C. **Creditor's Duty to Disclose**. A creditor must communicate to the surety, prior to formation of the contract, information concerning significant risk to the surety, i.e., specific facts which make the risk of default materially greater than the surety intends to assume.

   1. The duty exists only if the creditor has reason to believe that the surety does not know the facts and the creditor has reasonable opportunity to communicate them to the surety.

   2. Consistent with conservative lending practices, the creditor should disclose what (s)he knows about the debtor if the surety inquires.

   3. A surety may not avoid the surety contract on the basis of misconduct of the debtor that induced the surety to enter into the surety agreement. The surety contract is between the surety and the creditor, not the debtor.

   4. Stop and review! You have completed the outline for this subunit. There are no multiple-choice questions for this section.

D. **Liability of a Surety**. An absolute surety becomes liable immediately after the debtor defaults. Notice of default is not required to hold the surety liable. However, the potential liability and timing thereof are usually defined in the surety agreement. It is ordinarily no greater than that of the debtor.

   1. Stop and review! You have completed the outline for this subunit. Study multiple-choice question 5 on page 308.

E. **Defenses of a Surety**. A surety has three kinds of defense: the surety's own contractual defenses, some of the debtor's contractual defenses, and special suretyship defenses.

   1. **Suretyship Contract**. A person has no suretyship liability if

      a. A valid contract of suretyship never arose.

      b. A valid contract did arise but the surety exercises a right to avoid it, e.g., for failure to comply with the statute of frauds.

      c. The creditor procured the surety's promise by means of fraud or duress. Fraud might be based on breach of the creditor's duty to disclose.

         1) EXAMPLE: Quickbank seeks a fidelity bond to protect it from loss due to embezzlement. Quickbank knows but does not reveal to the surety that three of the bank's employees have been convicted of embezzlement.

      d. The surety performs the suretyship contract by performing the debtor's promise.

      e. The surety tenders performance of the suretyship contract.

      f. An intended cosurety does not sign the suretyship contract.

   2. **Debtor's Contract**. The surety may assert against the creditor defenses that the debtor could have asserted had there been only the contract between debtor and creditor.

      a. Personal defenses of a debtor are available only to the debtor. They include

         1) The debtor's **incapacity** due to infancy or mental incompetence
         2) Discharge of the debtor's obligation in **bankruptcy**
         3) A debtor's claim against the creditor for set-off

            a) **Set-off** is a counterclaim that arises from an independent cause of action and diminishes the creditor's potential recovery.

            b) EXAMPLE: Debtor defaults on loan to Obligee. Obligee sues for payment from Surety. Surety will not be successful in claiming a reduction in the amount to be paid, a set-off on the principal debt, by the value of a separate liability of Obligee to pay tort damages to Debtor.

    b.   Defenses available to the debtor and surety include the following:

        1)   The debtor's signature forged on an instrument
        2)   Fraudulent or material alteration of the contractual document by the creditor
        3)   No valid creditor-debtor contract
        4)   Illegality or impossibility of performance of the creditor-debtor agreement
        5)   Performance by the debtor
        6)   Creditor's refusal to accept tender of performance by debtor or surety

3.   **Surety's Special Defenses**. Those defenses that only the surety may assert are personal defenses of the surety. They include defenses to the surety-creditor contract and special surety defenses. The latter include

    a.   Creditor's **release** of debtor, unless the creditor reserves his/her rights against the surety

    b.   **Modification** of the debtor-creditor contract, absent consent by the surety

    c.   Creditor's impairment of **collateral**

    NOTE: A surety may set off the amount of his/her liability as a surety with the amount of any claim (s)he has against the creditor if the creditor is insolvent.

4.   Stop and review! You have completed the outline for this subunit. Study multiple-choice questions 6 through 10 beginning on page 309.

F.   **Rights of a Surety**. If required to perform, the surety possesses rights of reimbursement, subrogation, and exoneration against the principal debtor.

1.   **Reimbursement**. A surety, whether compensated or not, has a right to sue the debtor for reimbursement of amounts (s)he actually paid to the creditor.

    a.   The surety, to be reimbursed, may enforce a security interest the creditor acquired in collateral.

    b.   **Exception**. The surety is not entitled to reimbursement of amounts paid after receiving notice of a valid defense of the principal debtor to the payment.

2.   **Subrogation**. The surety as subrogee is entitled to enforce the debt against the debtor.

    a.   After payment, the surety automatically acquires whatever legal rights the creditor had, including any

        1)   Rights in collateral provided by the principal debtor
        2)   Rights against other parties indebted in the same obligation
        3)   Rights against cosureties
        4)   Priority in bankruptcy

    b.   If the debtor has received a discharge in bankruptcy as to the creditor's claim, the surety's claim for reimbursement is barred.

3.   **Exoneration** is the right of a surety to request that a court of equity compel a capable but reluctant debtor to pay the debt before the creditor collects the debt from the surety.

4.   **Cosurety's Right of Contribution**. A cosurety who pays more than the share (s)he agreed to pay is entitled to contribution from the cosureties.

    a.   Each cosurety is liable for the agreed-to proportionate part of a loss.

    b.   A cosurety's contributive share is computed by the following formula:

        1)

$$\frac{\text{Maximum liability of the cosurety}}{\text{Sum of maximum liability of each cosurety}} \times \text{Default amount}$$

        2)   EXAMPLE 1: PD borrowed $100,000 from C. CS1 agreed to act as surety for up to $100,000. CS2 agreed to act as surety for up to $50,000. PD defaulted when the principal owed was $90,000. C recovered the full $90,000 from CS1. The cosureties' contributive shares are computed as follows:

CS1: $100,000 ÷ ($100,000 + $50,000) = 2/3 × $90,000 = $60,000
CS2: $50,000 ÷ ($100,000 + $50,000) = 1/3 × $90,000 = $30,000

CS1 has a right to a $30,000 contribution from CS2.

    c.   Cosureties, like sureties, have rights of subrogation and exoneration.

    d.   A cosurety's relative interest in collateral is in the proportion used to compute his/her contributive share.

  5.   Stop and review! You have completed the outline for this subunit. Study multiple-choice questions 11 through 17 beginning on page 310.

G. **Discharge of a Surety**. Typically, the discharge (termination) of a surety's liability is governed by provisions of the suretyship contract.

  1.   A surety is discharged by **performance** of the obligations for which (s)he was bound (i.e., those of the principal debtor). It does not matter who renders the performance.

    a.   Partial payment discharges a surety to the extent of the payment.

    b.   If a note, bond, or draft is accepted as payment, the surety is discharged.

    c.   Refusal by the creditor to accept tender by the principal debtor or a surety discharges the surety.

    d.   Death of a surety does not necessarily terminate liability, particularly if terms of the surety agreement bind the surety's heirs and representatives.

  2.   If the principal contract or the contract of suretyship is **materially altered** without the surety's knowledge or consent, the surety is discharged from liability.

    a.   A gratuitous surety is discharged by a modification, even if it does not materially alter the surety's risk.

  3.   An agreement between the creditor and the principal **extending time** of payment discharges a surety, even if oral, unless the surety consents. Consent may be implied.

    a.   An agreement to extend time does not discharge the surety unless it is supported by consideration.

    b.   If time for performance was not fixed, extension does not discharge the surety.

    c.   Merely changing the form or the evidence of indebtedness, or taking additional security, does not discharge the surety. The creditor does not extend the time of payment so as to discharge the surety by taking new security maturing after the debt comes due.

    d.   If, in the original instrument of indebtedness, the creditor or obligee reserves the right, extension does not discharge the surety. The reservation must be express, clear, and definite.

4. **Rescission** or **revocation** of the principal contract releases the surety from any further liability, but not from liability already incurred.

5. **Release** by the creditor of a cosurety releases the other cosurety to the extent (s)he cannot obtain contribution from the first cosurety.

   a. If one cosurety is released, the total liability of the remaining cosureties is the total liabilities of all cosureties prior to the release reduced by the portion for which the released cosurety would have been responsible.

      1) The remaining cosureties are not released if they consent to the underlying release or if the creditor expressly reserves rights against them.

      2) EXAMPLE 2: If, in Example 1 on the previous page, C released CS1 without consent of CS2 and without reserving rights against CS2, CS2 can no longer obtain the contribution of $60,000 from CS1, and CS2 is released to that extent. Thus CS2's liability to C is limited to $30,000.

6. Stop and review! You have completed the outline for this subunit. Study multiple-choice questions 18 through 25 beginning on page 313.

MULTIPLE-CHOICE QUESTIONS

B. Formation of Suretyship Contract

1. Payne borrowed $500 from Onest Bank. At the time the loan was made to Payne, Gem orally agreed with Onest that Gem would repay the loan if Payne failed to do so. Gem received no personal benefit as a result of the loan to Payne. Under the circumstances,

A. Gem is secondarily liable to repay the loan.

B. Both Gem and Payne are primarily liable to repay the loan.

C. Gem is free from liability concerning the loan.

D. Gem is primarily liable to repay the loan.

The correct answer is (C). *(CPA, adapted)*
REQUIRED: The liability for an oral promise to pay the debt of another.
DISCUSSION: A surety contract is an agreement to answer for the debt or default of another. It is required to be in writing by the statute of frauds, whatever its amount. If the contract is not in writing, it is not enforceable.
Answer (A) is incorrect because the surety would have been primarily liable if the agreement had been written. Answers (B) and (D) are incorrect because an oral promise to incur surety liability is not enforceable.

2. A party contracts to guarantee the collection of the debts of another. As a result of the guaranty, which of the following statements is correct?

A. The creditor may proceed against the guarantor without attempting to collect from the debtor.

B. The guaranty must be in writing.

C. The guarantor may use any defenses available to the debtor.

D. The creditor must be notified of the debtor's default by the guarantor.

The correct answer is (B). *(CPA, adapted)*
REQUIRED: The correct statement concerning a guaranty of collection.
DISCUSSION: A person who guarantees the payment of a debt of another without qualification is required to pay the debt upon default. The guarantor of collection is a person who guarantees the debt upon condition that the creditor first make use of ordinary legal means to collect from the debtor. Surety and guaranty arrangements that constitute collateral promises are within the statute of frauds and are required to be in writing.
Answer (A) is incorrect because a guarantor of collection is not liable until the creditor exercises due diligence in enforcing its remedies against the debtor. Answer (C) is incorrect because a guarantor may not use defenses that are personal to the debtor, e.g., infancy. Answer (D) is incorrect because the creditor should notify the guarantor of the debtor's default.

3. Anthony is a surety on a debt owed by Victor to Day. Which of the following is correct?

- A. Day must satisfy the Uniform Commercial Code's filing requirements in order to perfect his security interest.
- B. The surety undertaking need not be in writing if the surety is obtained by Victor at Day's request.
- C. The extension of credit by Day to Victor, contingent upon Anthony's agreeing to act as a surety, provides the consideration for Anthony's promise.
- D. Upon default, Anthony would be allowed to deduct a personal claim that he has against Victor from his required payment to Day.

The correct answer is (C). *(CPA, adapted)*
  REQUIRED: The correct statement regarding a surety arrangement.
  DISCUSSION: A contract for suretyship must be supported by adequate consideration. The extension of credit by the creditor to the debtor, contingent upon the surety's agreeing to act as a surety, supports the promises of both the debtor and the surety. Thus, separate consideration is not required.
  Answer (A) is incorrect because surety arrangements are not security interests and are not governed by the UCC. Answer (B) is incorrect because surety arrangements are required by the statute of frauds to be in writing to be enforceable. Answer (D) is incorrect because, when the debt is in default, the surety must pay it in full without set-off by any amount owed by the debtor to the surety. A surety could use as a set-off amounts owed by the creditor to either the surety or the debtor.

4. When the debtor has defaulted on its obligation, the creditor is entitled to recover from the surety unless which of the following is present?

- A. The surety is in the process of exercising its right of exoneration against the debtor.
- B. The debtor died or became insolvent.
- C. The creditor can collect the entire debt from the debtor's collateral in its possession.
- D. The surety is a guarantor of collection and the creditor failed to exercise due diligence in enforcing its remedies against the debtor.

The correct answer is (D). *(CPA, adapted)*
  REQUIRED: The situation that will prevent a creditor from recovering from a surety.
  DISCUSSION: The general rule is that a surety is liable to the creditor immediately upon the debtor's default without the necessity of notice or demand. When the surety has conditioned the obligation to pay by requiring the creditor to first proceed against the debtor, the surety is described as a guarantor of collection and is not liable until the creditor exercises due diligence in enforcing its remedies against the debtor.
  Answer (A) is incorrect because the surety's right to exoneration from the debtor (compelling the debtor to pay) does not suspend the creditor's right to recover from the surety. Answer (B) is incorrect because the death or insolvency of the debtor does not release the surety. Answer (C) is incorrect because a creditor can proceed directly against the surety without first exercising any rights against collateral in the creditor's possession.

D. Liability of a Surety

5. Sorus and Ace have agreed, in writing, to act as guarantors of collection on a debt owed by Pepper to Towns, Inc. The debt is evidenced by a promissory note. If Pepper defaults, Towns will be entitled to recover from Sorus and Ace unless

- A. Sorus and Ace are in the process of exercising their rights against Pepper.
- B. Sorus and Ace prove that Pepper was insolvent at the time the note was signed.
- C. Pepper dies before the note is due.
- D. Towns has not attempted to enforce the promissory note against Pepper.

The correct answer is (D). *(CPA, adapted)*
  REQUIRED: The guarantor's defense against the creditor.
  DISCUSSION: A surety is primarily liable for the debtor's obligation. A creditor may proceed directly against the surety immediately upon default by the debtor. Some states still distinguish a guarantor as having only secondary liability; the creditor must first proceed against the principal debtor. Only when a judgment is returned unsatisfied may (s)he proceed against the guarantor.
  Answer (A) is incorrect because the creditor's rights do not depend on sureties' rights of exoneration and subrogation. Answer (B) is incorrect because the surety-creditor contract may be enforced even if an insolvent debtor induced them into it. This is not so if the contract was induced by fraud of the creditor. Answer (C) is incorrect because that might be the very reason for a lender to enter into a surety contract. Note that death of a surety does not of itself terminate a surety contract.

E. Defenses of a Surety

6. Ford was unable to repay a loan to City Bank when due. City refused to renew the loan unless an acceptable surety could be provided. Ford asked Owens, a friend, to act as surety on the loan. To induce Owens to agree to become a surety, Ford made fraudulent representations about Ford's financial condition and promised Owens discounts on merchandise sold at Ford's store. Owens agreed to act as surety, and the loan to Ford was renewed. Subsequently, Ford's obligation to City was discharged in Ford's bankruptcy, and City wishes to hold Owens liable. Owens may avoid liability

- A. Because the arrangement was void at the inception.

- B. If Owens was an uncompensated surety.

- C. If Owens can show that City Bank was aware of the fraudulent representations.

- D. Because the discharge in bankruptcy will prevent Owens from having a right of reimbursement.

The correct answer is (C). *(CPA, adapted)*
REQUIRED: The defense of a surety if the principal debtor has committed fraud.
DISCUSSION: A principal debtor's fraudulent misrepresentation is a material fact that the creditor has a duty to disclose to the surety. Because the surety arrangement is between the surety and the creditor, concealment or nondisclosure is a form of fraud against the surety by the creditor and is a personal defense of the surety. However, the principal debtor's fraud is not a defense against an innocent creditor.
Answer (A) is incorrect because the arrangement was voidable, not void. Answer (B) is incorrect because the loan renewal agreement and the suretyship contract were formed at the same time, so no separate consideration was required to bind the surety. Answer (D) is incorrect because a surety may not exercise certain defenses of the principal debtor, including discharge in bankruptcy, expiration of the statute of limitations, and the principal debtor's lack of capacity. Discharge in bankruptcy is not a permissible defense because protection from the debtor's nonperformance is the essence of suretyship.

7. Green was unable to repay a loan from State Bank when due. State refused to renew the loan unless Green provided an acceptable surety. Green asked Royal, a friend, to act as surety on the loan. To induce Royal to agree to become a surety, Green fraudulently represented Green's financial condition and promised Royal discounts on merchandise sold at Green's store. Royal agreed to act as surety, and the loan was renewed. Later, Green's obligation to State was discharged in Green's bankruptcy. State wants to hold Royal liable. Royal may avoid liability

- A. If Royal can show that State was aware of the fraudulent representations.

- B. If Royal was an uncompensated surety.

- C. Because the discharge in bankruptcy will prevent Royal from having a right of reimbursement.

- D. Because the arrangement was void at the inception.

The correct answer is (A). *(CPA, adapted)*
REQUIRED: The event that releases a surety.
DISCUSSION: A debtor's fraudulent misrepresentation of his/her financial condition at the time of contract is a material fact that the creditor has a duty to disclose to the surety. If State knew of Green's fraud and did not inform Royal, the nondisclosure is a form of fraud against the surety by the creditor. If State had been unaware of the fraud, Royal would be required to repay the loan.
Answer (B) is incorrect because, when a loan renewal agreement and the surety contract are formed at the same time, no separate consideration is required to bind the surety. Royal is compensated for acting as a surety with discounts on merchandise. Answer (C) is incorrect because Royal, as a surety, may not assert the defense of Green's discharge in bankruptcy because the essence of a suretyship is that the creditor may turn to the surety for the principal debtor's nonperformance. Answer (D) is incorrect because the arrangement between Royal and Green was voidable, not void, because of Green's fraud.

8. Which of the following defenses may a surety assert against a creditor to avoid liability after the debtor's default?

- A. Lack of notice of the debtor's default.

- B. Lack of consideration for the surety agreement.

- C. Insolvency of the debtor at the time the surety agreement was made.

- D. Misrepresentation on financial statements provided by the debtor to the surety.

The correct answer is (B). *(Publisher)*
REQUIRED: The effective defense of the surety to avoid liability.
DISCUSSION: The contract of a surety must be supported by consideration or a legal substitute. If the surety enters into the agreement when the obligation is assumed by the debtor, the consideration given by the creditor to the debtor extends to the surety as well. If the surety's promise is given later, separate consideration is required.
Answer (A) is incorrect because, unless agreed otherwise, a surety is liable immediately upon the debtor's default, without notice. Answer (C) is incorrect because the insolvency of the debtor is not a valid defense of a surety to liability. Answer (D) is incorrect because fraud committed by the debtor upon the surety has no effect on the surety's liability to the creditor, unless the creditor knew of the fraud.

9. Which of the following defenses would a surety be able to assert successfully to limit the surety's liability to a creditor?

- A. A discharge in bankruptcy of the principal debtor.
- B. A personal defense the principal debtor has against the creditor.
- C. The incapacity of the surety.
- D. The incapacity of the principal debtor.

The correct answer is (C). *(CPA, adapted)*
REQUIRED: The defense a surety could assert to limit his/her liability to a creditor.
DISCUSSION: The surety may assert a defense personal to the surety to limit his/her liability to a creditor. The surety may use the defense of incapacity of the surety to avoid liability to the principal debtor's creditor.
Answer (A) is incorrect because a surety may not assert a principal debtor's discharge in bankruptcy as a defense. Bankruptcy is a common reason for a debtor to use a surety. Answer (B) is incorrect because a surety may assert only a limited number of contractual defenses of the principal debtor. A surety may not ordinarily assert a defense personal to the principal debtor. Answer (D) is incorrect because a surety may not assert the incapacity of the principal debtor as a defense. A debtor's incapacity is a common reason to use a surety.

10. Dustin is a very cautious lender. When approached by Lanier regarding a $2,000 loan, he demanded not only an acceptable surety but also collateral equal to 50% of the loan. Lanier obtained King Surety Company as his surety and pledged rare coins worth $1,000 with Dustin. Dustin was assured by Lanier one week before the due date of the loan that he would have no difficulty in making payment. He persuaded Dustin to return the coins since they had increased in value and he had a prospective buyer. What is the legal effect of the release of the collateral upon King Surety?

- A. It totally releases King Surety.
- B. It does not release King Surety if the collateral was obtained after its promise.
- C. It releases King Surety to the extent of the value of the security.
- D. It does not release King Surety unless the collateral was given to Dustin with the express understanding that it was for the benefit of King Surety as well as Dustin.

The correct answer is (C). *(CPA, adapted)*
REQUIRED: The legal effect on the surety of the release of the collateral by the creditor.
DISCUSSION: When a debtor has put up security or collateral, the surety (after payment) succeeds to it if the creditor has not sold it to satisfy the debt. Hence, a creditor who releases collateral interferes with the subrogation rights of the surety to the collateral. This interference releases the surety. Therefore, when Dustin released the $1,000 coin collection, he also released King Surety to that extent.
Answer (A) is incorrect because release of security by the creditor only releases the surety to the extent of its value. Answer (B) is incorrect because a surety has subrogation rights to the collateral no matter when pledged. Therefore, its release prejudices the surety, and (s)he is released. Answer (D) is incorrect because the surety has subrogation rights to the collateral automatically under law.

F. Rights of a Surety

11. Which of the following rights does a surety have?

	Right to Compel the Creditor to Collect from the Principal Debtor	Right to Compel the Creditor to Proceed against the Principal Debtor's Collateral
A.	Yes	Yes
B.	Yes	No
C.	No	Yes
D.	No	No

The correct answer is (D). *(CPA, adapted)*
REQUIRED: The right(s), if any, of a surety.
DISCUSSION: A surety is primarily liable for the debtor's obligation. A creditor may proceed directly against the surety upon the default of the debtor. The rights of the surety are against the principal debtor, not the creditor. Consequently, a surety has the right neither to compel the creditor to collect from the principal debtor nor to compel the creditor to proceed against the principal debtor's collateral.
Answers (A), (B), and (C) are incorrect because a surety may not compel the creditor to collect from the principal debtor or to proceed against the principal debtor's collateral.

12. When a principal debtor defaults and a surety pays the creditor the entire obligation, which of the following remedies gives the surety the best method of collecting from the debtor?

- A. Exoneration.
- B. Contribution.
- C. Subrogation.
- D. Attachment.

The correct answer is (C). *(CPA, adapted)*
REQUIRED: The surety's right after (s)he satisfies the principal debtor's obligation.
DISCUSSION: Subrogation is the right of a surety, after paying the obligation of a debtor who has defaulted, to succeed to the legal rights of the creditor against the principal debtor, cosureties, or any collateral.
Answer (A) is incorrect because exoneration is the right to request a decree from a court compelling performance by the principal debtor. Answer (B) is incorrect because contribution is the right of a cosurety who has paid more than his/her proportionate or agreed-to share to proceed against the other cosureties to recover their share. Answer (D) is incorrect because attachment is the judicial process of taking property.

13. Burns borrowed $240,000 from Dollar Bank as additional working capital for his business. Dollar required that the loan be collateralized to the extent of 20% and that an acceptable surety for the entire amount be obtained. Surety Co. agreed to act as surety on the loan, and Burns pledged $48,000 of negotiable bearer bonds. Burns defaulted. Which of the following statements is correct?

- A. Dollar must first liquidate the collateral before it can proceed against Surety.
- B. Surety is liable in full immediately upon default by Burns but will be entitled to the collateral upon satisfaction of the debt.
- C. Dollar must first proceed against Burns and obtain a judgment before it can proceed against the collateral.
- D. Surety may proceed against Burns for the full amount of the loan even if Surety settles with Dollar for a lower amount.

The correct answer is (B). *(CPA, adapted)*
REQUIRED: The rights of a surety after default on a partially collateralized debt.
DISCUSSION: Subrogation is the right of a surety, after paying the obligation of a debtor who has defaulted, to succeed to the legal rights of the creditor against the principal debtor, cosureties, or any collateral. This includes rights in the collateral provided by the principal debtor, a priority in bankruptcy, rights against other parties indebted on the same obligation, and rights against cosureties. Surety is therefore subrogated to Dollar's rights against the bonds.
Answer (A) is incorrect because, unless otherwise agreed, Dollar may proceed directly against Surety after default. Answer (C) is incorrect because only if the surety is a conditional guarantor of collection must the creditor exhaust legal remedies against the principal debtor before proceeding to collect from the surety. Answer (D) is incorrect because the surety's right of reimbursement is limited to amounts paid to the creditor.

14. If a debtor defaults and the debtor's surety satisfies the obligation, the surety acquires the right of

- A. Subrogation.
- B. Primary lien.
- C. Indemnification.
- D. Satisfaction.

The correct answer is (A). *(CPA, adapted)*
REQUIRED: The surety's right after (s)he satisfies the principal debtor's obligation.
DISCUSSION: Subrogation is the right of a surety, after paying the obligation of a debtor who has defaulted, to succeed to the legal rights of the creditor against the principal debtor, cosureties, or any collateral.
Answer (B) is incorrect because the surety stands in the shoes of the creditor, who may or may not have had a senior security interest or a priority in bankruptcy. Answer (C) is incorrect because a right of indemnification arises from a contract by which one party agrees to hold another party harmless. Indemnity (e.g., insurance) protects a debtor from loss. A suretyship contract protects a creditor. Answer (D) is incorrect because satisfaction is the creditor's acceptance of a performance stipulated in an accord, which is an agreement to accept some performance by the debtor that is different from, and usually less than, what was originally agreed.

15. A distinction between a surety and a cosurety is that only a cosurety is entitled to

A.   Reimbursement (indemnification).

B.   Subrogation.

C.   Contribution.

D.   Exoneration.

The correct answer is (C). *(CPA, adapted)*
REQUIRED: The right unique to a cosurety.
DISCUSSION: Contribution is the right of a cosurety who has paid more than his/her proportionate or agreed-to share to proceed against the other cosureties to recover their share.

Answer (A) is incorrect because reimbursement is the right of a surety who has paid the debt to be paid by the principal debtor. Indemnification arises from an agreement by one party to protect an obligor (debtor), not an obligee (creditor), from loss. Answer (B) is incorrect because subrogation is the right of a surety who has paid the principal debtor's obligation to exercise rights the creditor had against or through the principal debtor. Answer (D) is incorrect because exoneration is the right to request a decree from a court compelling performance by the principal debtor.

16. Sklar borrowed $360,000 from Rich Bank. At Rich's request, Sklar entered into an agreement with Aker, Burke, and Cey to act as cosureties on the loan. The agreement between Sklar and the cosureties provided that the maximum liability of each cosurety was Aker, $72,000; Burke, $108,000; and Cey, $180,000. After making several payments, Sklar defaulted on the loan. The balance was $240,000. If Cey pays $180,000 and Sklar subsequently pays $60,000, what amounts may Cey recover from Aker and Burke?

A. $0 from Aker and $0 from Burke.

B. $60,000 from Aker and $60,000 from Burke.

C. $48,000 from Aker and $72,000 from Burke.

D. $36,000 from Aker and $54,000 from Burke.

The correct answer is (D). *(CPA, adapted)*
REQUIRED: The amounts recoverable from cosureties.
DISCUSSION: A cosurety who has paid more than his/her proportionate or agreed share of the debt has a right to proceed against the other cosureties for their proportionate or agreed share. A cosurety's contributive share is determined by dividing the maximum liability of that cosurety by the sum for all the cosureties and then multiplying by the amount of the default:

Aker $ 72 ÷ ($72 + $108 + $180) = 1/5 × $180 = $36
Burke $108 ÷ ($72 + $108 + $180) = 3/10 × $180 = $54
Cey $180 ÷ ($72 + $108 + $180) = 1/2 × $180 = $90

Hence, Cey should receive contributions of $36,000 and $54,000 from Aker and Burke, respectively.

Answers (A), (B), and (C) are incorrect because contributive shares are determined by dividing the maximum liability of each surety by the sum for all the cosureties and then multiplying by the amount of the default.

17. Lane promised to lend Turner $240,000 if Turner obtained sureties to secure the loan. Turner agreed with Rivers, Clark, and Zane for them to act as cosureties on the loan from Lane. The agreement between Turner and the cosureties provided that compensation be paid to each of the cosureties. It further indicated that the maximum liability of each cosurety would be as follows: Rivers, $240,000; Clark, $80,000; and Zane, $160,000. Lane accepted the commitments of the sureties and made the loan to Turner. After paying 10 installments totaling $100,000, Turner defaulted. Clark's debts, including the surety obligation to Lane on the Turner loan, were discharged in bankruptcy. Later, Rivers properly paid the entire outstanding debt of $140,000. What amount may Rivers recover from Zane?

A. $0

B. $46,667

C. $56,000

D. $96,000

The correct answer is (C). *(CPA, adapted)*
REQUIRED: The contribution recoverable from a cosurety when third cosurety's obligation was discharged in bankruptcy.
DISCUSSION: A cosurety who pays more than his/her share has a right of contribution, i.e., to proceed against the other cosureties to recover his/her proportionate or agreed-to share. A cosurety's contributive share is determined by dividing the maximum liability of each surety by the sum for all cosureties and multiplying the result by the amount of the default. But contribution cannot be obtained from the cosurety whose obligation was discharged in bankruptcy. Rivers may recover from Zane [$160,000 ÷ ($160,000 + $240,000)] x $140,000 = $56,000.

Answer (A) is incorrect because a cosurety who pays more than his/her share is entitled to contribution from the other cosureties. Answer (B) is incorrect because Clark's cosurety obligation was discharged in bankruptcy. Answer (D) is incorrect because contribution is based on the amount of the default, not the original loan amount.

G. Discharge of a Surety

18. Which of the following events will release a noncompensated surety from liability?

A. Release of the principal debtor's obligation by the creditor but with the reservation of the creditor's rights against the surety.

B. Modification by the principal debtor and the creditor of their contract that materially increases the surety's risk of loss.

C. Filing of an involuntary petition in bankruptcy against the principal debtor.

D. Insanity of the principal debtor at the time the contract was entered into with the creditor.

The correct answer is (B). *(CPA, adapted)*
REQUIRED: The event which releases a surety.
DISCUSSION: Modification by the principal debtor and the creditor of their contract that materially increases the surety's risk of loss operates to release from liability a compensated or gratuitous surety unless the surety consents to the modification. A gratuitous surety is released even if the modification is not material.

Answer (A) is incorrect because, by reserving rights, the release is treated as a covenant not to sue the principal. It does not operate to release the surety. Answer (C) is incorrect because this is one of the reasons a creditor enters into a surety contract. Answer (D) is incorrect because this is a personal defense of the debtor, who is not a party to the surety contract.

19. Mane Bank lent Eller $120,000 and received securities valued at $30,000 as collateral. At Mane's request, Salem and Rey agreed to act as uncompensated cosureties on the loan. The agreement provided that Salem's and Rey's maximum liability would be $120,000 each. Mane released Rey without Salem's consent. Eller later defaulted when the collateral held by Mane was worthless and the loan balance was $90,000. Salem's maximum liability is

A. $30,000

B. $45,000

C. $60,000

D. $90,000

The correct answer is (B). *(CPA, adapted)*
REQUIRED: The effect of releasing a cosurety without the consent of the other cosurety.
DISCUSSION: When a creditor releases a cosurety without the consent of, or without reserving rights against, the other cosurety, the other cosurety is released to the extent (s)he cannot obtain contribution from the released cosurety. The share of each cosurety would have been half of the unpaid amount, or $45,000.

Answers (A) and (C) are incorrect because collateral to the debtor-creditor loan does not affect surety liability unless it is impaired by the creditor. Answer (D) is incorrect because Salem is released to the extent Salem cannot obtain contribution from the released cosurety.

20. Ott and Bane agreed to act as cosureties on an $80,000 loan that Cread Bank made to Dash. Ott and Bane are each liable for the entire $80,000 loan. Subsequently, Cread released Ott from liability without Bane's consent and without reserving its rights against Bane. If Dash subsequently defaults, Cread will be entitled to collect a maximum of

A. $0 from Bane.

B. $0 from Dash.

C. $40,000 from Bane.

D. $40,000 from Dash.

The correct answer is (C). *(CPA, adapted)*
REQUIRED: The liability of a cosurety after the creditor releases the other cosurety.
DISCUSSION: The unconsented-to release of Ott by Cread without reservation of rights against Bane is regarded as a true release. Consequently, Bane will also be released to the extent that Bane cannot obtain contribution from Ott. Because both cosureties agreed to be liable for the entire loan, Ott's pro rata contributive share was $40,000. Hence, Bane's potential liability to Cread will be reduced from $80,000 to $40,000.

Answer (A) is incorrect because Bane is released only to the extent that Bane cannot obtain contribution from the other cosurety. Answers (B) and (D) are incorrect because release of a surety does not discharge the principal debtor.

21. Ingot Corp. lent Flange $50,000. At Ingot's request, Flange entered into an agreement with Quill and West for them to act as compensated cosureties on the loan in the amount of $100,000 each. Ingot released West without Quill's or Flange's consent, and Flange later defaulted on the loan. Which of the following statements is correct?

A.   Quill will be liable for 50% of the loan balance.

B.   Quill will be liable for the entire loan balance.

C.   Ingot's release of West will have no effect on Flange's and Quill's liability to Ingot.

D.   Flange will be released for 50% of the loan balance.

The correct answer is (A). *(CPA, adapted)*
REQUIRED: The liability of a cosurety after the creditor releases the other cosurety.
DISCUSSION: Release of a cosurety by a creditor without the consent or the reservation of rights against the other cosurety releases the remaining surety to the extent (s)he cannot obtain contribution from the released surety. Thus, Quill remains liable for 50% of the loan balance.
Answer (B) is incorrect because Quill is not liable for the entire loan balance upon Flange's default. The remaining cosurety is liable only for the agreed-upon share of the loan balance. Answer (C) is incorrect because Ingot's release of West will affect Quill's liability. Quill is now primarily liable for 50% of the loan balance. Answer (D) is incorrect because the release of a cosurety does not affect the debtor.

22. Which of the following rights does one cosurety generally have against another cosurety?

A.   Exoneration.

B.   Subrogation.

C.   Reimbursement.

D.   Contribution.

The correct answer is (D). *(CPA, adapted)*
REQUIRED: The right of one cosurety against another.
DISCUSSION: Contribution is the right of a cosurety who has paid more than his/her proportionate or agreed-to share to proceed against the other cosureties.
Answer (A) is incorrect because exoneration is the right to request a decree from a court compelling performance by the principal debtor. Answer (B) is incorrect because subrogation is the right of a surety who has paid the principal debtor's obligation to exercise rights the creditor had against or through the principal debtor. Answer (C) is incorrect because reimbursement is the right of a surety who has paid the debt to be paid by the principal debtor.

23. Nash, Owen, and Polk are cosureties with maximum liabilities of $40,000, $60,000, and $80,000, respectively. The amount of the loan on which they have agreed to act as cosureties is $180,000. The debtor defaulted at a time when the loan balance was $180,000. Nash paid the lender $36,000 in full settlement of all claims against Nash, Owen, and Polk. The total amount that Nash may recover from Owen and Polk is

A. $0

B. $24,000

C. $28,000

D. $140,000

The correct answer is (C). *(CPA, adapted)*
REQUIRED: The amount recoverable from cosureties by one who has paid the full amount.
DISCUSSION: A cosurety who has paid more than his/her proportionate or agreed share has a right to contributions from the other cosureties. A cosurety's contributive share is determined by dividing the maximum liability of that cosurety by the sum for all the cosureties and then multiplying by the amount of the default. In this case, Nash negotiated a settlement of $36,000 with the lender.

Nash $40 ÷ ($40 + $60 + $80) = 2/9 × $36,000 = $8,000
Owen $60 ÷ ($40 + $60 + $80) = 1/3 × $36,000 = $12,000
Polk $80 ÷ ($40 + $60 + $80) = 4/9 × $36,000 = $16,000

Hence, Nash should receive a total of $28,000 from Owen and Polk.
Answer (A) is incorrect because a cosurety who has paid more than his/her proportionate or agreed share has a right to contributions from the other cosureties. Answer (B) is incorrect because contributive shares are determined by dividing the maximum liability of each surety by the sum for all the cosureties and then multiplying by the amount of the default. Answer (D) is incorrect because contribution is based on the amount of the obligation, which became $36,000 under the composition agreement.

24. Which of the following acts always will result in the total release of a compensated surety?

- A. The creditor changes the manner of the principal debtor's payment.

- B. The creditor extends the principal debtor's time to pay.

- C. The principal debtor's obligation is partially released.

- D. The principal debtor's performance is tendered.

The correct answer is (D). *(CPA, adapted)*
REQUIRED: The event resulting in total release of a compensated surety.
DISCUSSION: A surety is released to the extent that the principal debtor's obligations under the debtor-creditor contract have been performed or have been tendered. It does not matter who tenders the performance.

Answers (A) and (B) are incorrect because modification of the principal debtor-creditor contract operates to release a compensated surety only if it is material, and only if the surety does not consent to it. Answer (C) is incorrect because release of the surety is at most to the extent the principal was released.

25. Wright cosigned King's loan from Ace Bank. Which of the following events would release Wright from the obligation to pay the loan?

- A. Ace seeks payment of the loan only from Wright.

- B. King is granted a discharge in bankruptcy.

- C. Ace is paid in full by King's spouse.

- D. King is adjudicated mentally incompetent.

The correct answer is (C). *(CPA, adapted)*
REQUIRED: The event that releases a surety.
DISCUSSION: The surety, Wright, is released from his/her obligation to repay King's debt to the extent the loan is repaid. It does not matter who made the performance. When King's spouse repaid the loan in full, Wright's obligation as a surety was terminated.

Answer (A) is incorrect because Ace may look to King as principal debtor to repay the loan. Wright, as surety, remains liable until the debt is repaid or the surety is released. Answer (B) is incorrect because the surety contract is between Wright and Ace. Wright may not assert a defense personal to the principal debtor, King. Ace may look to Wright for repayment because the debtor's bankruptcy does not discharge the surety. The purpose of a surety contract is that the creditor may turn to the surety for repayment if the debtor defaults. Answer (D) is incorrect because the defense of incapacity may be asserted only by King, who is not a party to the surety contract.

Use Gleim's **CPA Test Prep** for interactive testing with over 2,000 additional multiple-choice questions!

OOF QUESTION *(CPA, adapted)* 15-20 minutes

Items 1 through 7 below are descriptive words, phrases, and statements related to surety law. Select the term from the list A through G below which best matches the phrase or statement in each of items 1 through 7. Each answer may be used only once.

A. Exoneration
B. Surety
C. Set-off
D. Guarantor
E. Indemnification
F. Unenforceable
G. Accommodation surety

1. Sued after a judgment is returned unsatisfied

2. Protects obligor from loss

3. Oral guaranty

4. Compelling debtor to pay before surety

5. Primarily liable even though never paid

6. Diminishes creditor's recovery only if asserted by debtor

7. Liable to pay debt of person not sued by creditor

Items 8 through 14 are based on the following fact pattern, which appeared as part of an essay question on the 1983 CPA exam.

Mars Finance Company was approached by Grant, the president of Hoover Corp., for a loan of $25,000 for Hoover. After careful evaluation of Hoover's financial condition, Mars decided it would not make the loan unless the loan was collateralized or guaranteed by one or more sureties for a total of $30,000. Hoover agreed to provide collateral in the form of a security interest in Hoover's equipment. The initial valuation of the equipment was $20,000, and Hoover obtained Victory Surety Company as a surety for the additional $10,000. Prior to the granting of the loan, the final valuation on the equipment was set at $15,000, and Mars insisted on additional surety protection of $5,000. Grant personally assumed this additional surety obligation. Hoover defaulted, and Mars first proceeded against the collateral, which was sold for $17,000. It then proceeded against Victory for the balance. Victory paid the $8,000 and now seeks a $4,000 contribution from Grant.

Required

Items 8 through 14 are statements about or conclusions from the above facts. Mark (A) if the statement is correct. Mark (B) if it is incorrect.

8. Mars may have had a duty to Victory before a contract between them even existed.

9. Grant is not liable because Mars elected to proceed against the collateral.

10. Grant is not liable because Mars's election to sue Victory released him.

11. Grant is not a cosurety because Victory did not know of his existence until after default.

12. Grant is not a cosurety because his surety obligation was not assumed at the same time as Victory's and it was not equal in amount to that of Victory's.

13. Mars may exercise its right of subrogation against Grant.

14. Grant is not liable for the full $4,000 sought by Victory.

Knowledge Tested

1. Types of sureties
2. Primary vs. secondary liability
3. Defenses of a surety
4. Rights of a surety
5. Cosurety liability

Authors' Comments

Definitions in the outline provide the basis for several answers. Note that oral suretyship is unenforceable. Build your understanding of the point at which the creditor may sue sureties, surety defenses, and rights and liabilities of cosureties.

1. The correct answer is (D).

DISCUSSION: A guarantor is secondarily liable for the principal debtor's obligation. The creditor may proceed against the guarantor only after the debtor has defaulted and the creditor has sued the principal debtor and obtained a judgment that is returned unsatisfied.

Author's Note: The AICPA has specified "Guarantors" as a CPA exam testing area. Surety, however, is a more general term describing one person's obligation to pay the debt of another. A guarantor is one type of surety. The law of some states no longer distinguishes between a surety and a guarantor.

2. The correct answer is (E).

DISCUSSION: A right of indemnification arises from a contract whereby one party agrees to protect a debtor (obligor) from loss. A surety contract protects a creditor from loss.

3. The correct answer is (F).

DISCUSSION: Under the statute of frauds, a contract to answer for the debt of another must be in a writing signed by the party to be charged. Thus, an oral suretyship agreement is unenforceable.

4. The correct answer is (A).

DISCUSSION: Exoneration occurs when a court of equity compels an able but reluctant debtor to pay the debt before the creditor collects the debt from the surety.

5. The correct answer is (G).

DISCUSSION: An accommodation (or gratuitous or voluntary) surety is one who is not paid. Consideration to support enforceability of the contract of the accommodation surety is found in the legal detriment to the creditor (and the benefit to the debtor).

6. The correct answer is (C).

DISCUSSION: Set-off diminishes the creditor's recovery by the amount of an obligation of the creditor to the debtor. Set-off is a personal defense of the debtor. It may not be asserted by the surety. Nonpersonal defenses of the debtor may be asserted by the surety.

7. The correct answer is (B).

DISCUSSION: A surety has primary liability for the principal debtor's obligation. The creditor is not required to sue the principal debtor before proceeding against the surety.

8. The correct answer is (A).

DISCUSSION: Prior to formation of the surety contract, the creditor has a duty to disclose to the proposed surety facts which make the risk of default materially greater than the surety intends to assume, e.g., that Hoover previously defaulted on a loan from Mars.

9. The correct answer is (B).

DISCUSSION: A creditor has the right to proceed against any available collateral. Resorting to collateral does not affect the creditor's right to proceed against a surety for the balance.

10. The correct answer is (B).

DISCUSSION: The liability of cosureties is joint and several. A creditor may choose to sue one or more of the sureties without impairing his/her rights against those not sued. Suing one surety does not release any surety or affect rights of contribution.

11. The correct answer is (B).

DISCUSSION: The parties to the cosurety's contract were the creditor and Grant. What a party to another contract of suretyship knew is not a valid defense.

12. The correct answer is (B).

DISCUSSION: For a cosurety's contract to be enforceable, there is no requirement that it be entered into simultaneously with the contracts of the other cosureties or that the cosureties be obligated for equal amounts.

13. The correct answer is (B).

DISCUSSION: The surety has a right of subrogation after (s)he actually pays the debt. The surety acquires whatever legal rights the creditor had, e.g., to collateral, to sue the principal debtor, against cosureties.

14. The correct answer is (A).

DISCUSSION: A cosurety's liability is generally determined by the agreement. Grant's surety agreement was for one-third of the combined surety undertakings. Thus, Grant's liability is limited to $2,667.

ESSAY QUESTION *(CPA, adapted)* 15-20 minutes

Part a. Hardaway Lending, Inc. had a 4-year $800,000 callable loan to Superior Metals, Inc. outstanding. The loan was callable at the end of each year upon Hardaway's giving 60 days' written notice. Two and one-half years remained of the 4 years. Hardaway reviewed the loan and decided that Superior Metals was no longer a prime lending risk, and it therefore decided to call the loan. The required written notice was sent to, and received by, Superior 60 days prior to the expiration of the second year. Merriweather, Superior's chief executive officer and principal shareholder, requested that Hardaway continue the loan at least for another year. Hardaway agreed, provided that an acceptable commercial surety would guarantee $400,000 of the loan and Merriweather would personally guarantee repayment in full. These conditions were satisfied, and the loan was permitted to continue.

The following year, the loan was called, and Superior defaulted. Hardaway released the commercial surety but retained its rights against Merriweather and demanded that Merriweather pay the full amount of the loan. Merriweather refused, asserting the following:

- There was no consideration for his promise. The loan was already outstanding, and he personally received nothing.

- Hardaway must first proceed against Superior before it can collect from Merriweather.

- Hardaway had released the commercial surety, thereby releasing Merriweather.

Required

Discuss the validity of each of Merriweather's assertions, setting forth reasons for any conclusions stated.

Part b. In connection with the audit of One-Up, Inc., a question has arisen regarding the validity of a $10,000 purchase money security interest in certain machinery sold to Essex Company on March 2. Essex was petitioned into bankruptcy on May 1 by its creditors. The trustee is seeking to avoid One-Up's security interest on the grounds that it is a preferential transfer, hence voidable. The machinery in question was sold to Essex on the following terms: $1,000 down and the balance plus interest at 9% to be paid over a 3-year period. One-up obtained a signed security agreement which created a security interest in the property on March 2, the date of the sale. A financing statement was filed on March 10.

Required

Answer the following, setting forth reasons for any conclusions stated.

1. Would One-Up's security interest in the machinery be a voidable preference?

2. In general, what are the requirements necessary to permit the trustee to assert a preferential transfer successfully and thereby set aside a creditor's security interest?

Knowledge Tested

1. Consideration requirement for suretyship contract
2. Primary liability of cosurety
3. Effect of release of cosurety
4. Voidable preferences in bankruptcy

Authors' Comments

Part a. of this question tests the topic of sureties. A surety's obligation is based on a legally enforceable contract. The consideration element may be satisfied by any legal detriment incurred by the obligee (legal benefit may be to the principal debtor). A surety has primary liability, unless the contract of suretyship or state law limits liability to a guaranty. Release of a cosurety effects discharge of other cosureties. The portion the released cosurety would have been responsible for is discharged. Absent agreement, the ratio of the maximum obligation of each cosurety determines his/her obligation.

Part b. of the question addresses voidable preferences under bankruptcy law, which is discussed in the next study unit. Note how the CPA examiners tacked into an essay question a topic which is not directly related to the subject matter of the rest of the essay, but which is relatively self-contained and brief.

At some point in your review, however, it would be prudent to look at and compare the relationships among materials presented in different study units on priority among creditors and on primary and secondary liability. Developing understanding of these materials by reviewing and comparing them in a cohesive manner will increase your confidence of success.

Note: Part b. of this question relates to voidable preferences under bankruptcy law, which are discussed in Study Unit 11.

AICPA Unofficial Answer

Part a.

The first two defenses asserted by Merriweather are invalid. The third defense is partially valid.

Consideration on Hardaway's part consisted of forgoing the right to call the Superior Metals loan. The fact that the loan was already outstanding is irrelevant. By permitting the loan to remain outstanding for an additional year instead of calling it, Hardaway relinquished a legal right, which is adequate consideration for Merriweather's surety promise. Consideration need not pass to the surety; in fact, it usually primarily benefits the principal debtor.

There is no requirement that the creditor first proceed against the debtor before it can proceed against the surety, unless the surety undertaking expressly provides such a condition. Basic to the usual surety undertaking is the right of the creditor to proceed immediately against the surety. Essentially, that is the reason for the surety.

Hardaway's release of the commercial surety from its $400,000 surety undertaking partially released Merriweather. The release had the legal effect of impairing Merriweather's right of contribution against its cosurety (the commercial surety). Thus, Merriweather is released to the extent of 1/3 [$400,000 (commercial surety's guarantee)/$1,200,000 (the aggregate of the cosureties' guarantees)] of the principal amount ($800,000), or $266,667.

Part b.

1. No. The Bankruptcy Reform Act of 1978 has not only modified the requirements for establishing a voidable preference, but has also specified transactions that do not constitute preferences. One such transaction is the creditor's taking a security interest in property acquired by the debtor as a contemporaneous exchange for new value given to the debtor to enable him to acquire such property (a purchase money security interest). The security interest must be perfected (filed) within 10 days after attachment. The act is in harmony with the secured transactions provisions of the Uniform Commercial Code. Thus, One-Up has a valid security interest in the machinery it sold to Essex.

2. The Bankruptcy Reform Act of 1978 does not require that the creditor have knowledge or reasonable cause to believe the debtor is insolvent in the bankruptcy sense. Instead, under the act, if such insolvency exists on or within 90 days before the filing of the petition, knowledge of insolvency by the transferee need not be established. The act also assumes that the debtor's insolvency is presumed if the transfer alleged to be preferential is made within 90 days. Finally, the time period in which transfers may be set aside is 90 days unless the transferee is an "Insider." If the transfer is to an insider, the trustee may avoid transfers made within 1 year prior to the filing of the petition. Thus, the trustee may avoid as preferential any transfer of property of the debtor that is

- To or for the benefit of a creditor
- For or on account of an antecedent debt owed by the debtor before such transfer was made
- Made while the debtor is insolvent in the bankruptcy sense (However, if the transfer is made within 90 days, the debtor's insolvency is presumed.)
- Made on or within 90 days of the filing of the petition (Or if made after the 90 days but within one year prior to the date of the filing of the petition, and the transfer was to an "insider," it may be set aside if the transferee had reasonable cause to believe the debtor was insolvent at the time of the transfer.)
- Such that it enables the creditor to receive more than (s)he would if it were a straight liquidation proceeding

The bankruptcy act contains a lengthy definition of the term "insider" that includes common relationships that the transferee has to the debtor, which, in case of an individual debtor, could be certain relatives, a partnership in which (s)he is a general partner, his/her fellow general partners, or a corporation controlled by him/her.

STUDY UNIT 11: BANKRUPTCY

A. Voluntary and Involuntary Bankruptcy
B. Effects of Bankruptcy on Debtors and Creditors
C. Reorganizations and Adjustments

14 pages of outline
50 multiple-choice questions
2 OOFs and 2 essays

This study unit reviews federal bankruptcy law. To prepare for the exam, a student should understand the two purposes of bankruptcy and the division of bankruptcy proceedings into liquidations, reorganizations, and adjustment plans. The emphasis is on liquidation or straight bankruptcy. However, rules of reorganization are tested frequently. Some specific topics to be prepared for are the filing requirements of a voluntary or involuntary petition, the effects of an automatic stay and order of relief, the definition of the bankruptcy estate including property exempted for the debtor's benefit and property subject to a security interest, the power of a trustee to enlarge the estate by setting aside prior transactions, the various priorities among creditors, and the eligibility of a debtor for discharge.

A. **Voluntary and Involuntary Bankruptcy.** Bankruptcy proceedings, always administered in Federal Bankruptcy Court, represent a formal alternative means to resolving tension between creditor rights and debtor relief. The debtor, the creditor(s), the trustee, and the creditors' committee are all parties in interest.

1. Chapters 7, 9, 11, 12, and 13 of the Bankruptcy Code provide for five different types of proceedings:

   Chapter 7 Liquidation
   Chapter 9 Adjustment of Debts of a Municipality
   Chapter 11 Reorganization
   Chapter 12 Adjustment of Debts of a Family Farmer with Regular Income
   Chapter 13 Adjustments of Debts of an Individual with Regular Income

2. Primary **purposes** of a bankruptcy proceeding are twofold:

   a. To assure debtor assets are equitably distributed to creditors
   b. To permit the debtor a fresh start by granting a discharge (release)

3. A **debtor** is an individual or business organization, or even a municipality, that owes payment to a creditor.

4. Under the Bankruptcy Code, a **creditor** is an individual or an entity that has a claim against the debtor that arose before the order for relief.

   a. A **claim** consists of a right to payment, whether or not reduced to judgment, liquidated, unliquidated, fixed, contingent, matured, unmatured, disputed, legal, equitable, secured, or unsecured.

5. The **trustee** in bankruptcy represents the debtor's estate.

   a. A trustee is required in Chapter 7 and Chapter 13 cases. A trustee is not required in a Chapter 11 case, although the court may for cause order the appointment of a trustee who may then be elected by the creditors.

   b. In Chapter 7 proceedings, the trustee is typically elected by the creditors. Under all other chapters, the trustee, if any, is appointed by the bankruptcy judge.

   c. The trustee is usually a private citizen, not a government employee.

6. **Creditor committees** are either required or permitted. They serve to ease communication between the debtor, the trustee, and the creditors.

   a. In a Chapter 7 case, the creditors may, but do not have a legal duty to, elect a committee of between three and 11 unsecured creditors to consult with and make recommendations to the trustee. Election (if done) must be within a reasonable time after the order for relief.

7. **Administration of a Bankruptcy Proceeding**. Each federal judicial district has its own bankruptcy court. A bankruptcy case is heard by a bankruptcy judge. The jurisdiction of the bankruptcy court is invoked by the filing of a petition with the bankruptcy court, specifying the specific chapter under which relief is requested. The filing of the petition gives rise to an estate, which generally consists of the property of the debtor at the time of filing that becomes subject to the bankruptcy proceeding. The estate is treated as a separate legal entity, distinct from the debtor.

    a. The filing of any bankruptcy petition operates as an automatic stay of all civil actions against the debtor or his/her property until the court takes further action.

8. **Insolvency** is not a prerequisite to filing a petition under the Bankruptcy Act.

    a. Insolvency is a financial condition in which

        1) One is unable or is failing to meet one's financial obligations as they mature in the ordinary course of business, or

        2) One's liabilities exceed one's assets.

9. The majority of petitions are filed voluntarily. Any person eligible to be a debtor under a given bankruptcy proceeding may file a voluntary petition under a specific chapter (7, 11, 12, 13). Thus, debtor-initiated cases are referred to as voluntary. No minimum debt is required. A voluntary petition must include the following:

    a. List of all creditors (both secured and unsecured)
    b. List of all property owned by the debtor
    c. List of property claimed by the debtor to be exempt
    d. Statement of the debtor's affairs

10. An involuntary bankruptcy proceeding can be commenced only under Chapter 7 or Chapter 11 against an eligible debtor.

    a. An involuntary petition cannot be filed against the following:

        1) Farmers

        2) Charitable organizations

        3) Persons who owe less than $10,775 ($10,000 for cases filed before April 1, 1998)

    b. If the debtor has 12 or more different creditors, any three or more creditors who together hold unsecured claims of at least $10,775 ($10,000 for cases filed before April 1, 1998) can file an involuntary petition.

    c. If there are fewer than 12 creditors, any one or more creditors who alone or together have unsecured claims of at least $10,775 ($10,000 for cases filed before April 1, 1998) (over and above any security interests) can file an involuntary petition.

        1) In determining whether there are fewer than 12 creditors, those creditors who are the debtor's employees or are insiders, e.g., officers or directors of a corporation, relatives, or a partner, are not counted.

    d. The debtor can oppose the involuntary petition for bankruptcy by filing an answer.

        1) If no answer is filed, the court will enter an order for relief.

        2) If the debtor opposes the petition by filing an answer, the court must hold a hearing to determine whether either of two statutory grounds for involuntary bankruptcy exists. The two grounds are

            a) The debtor is generally not paying his/her undisputed debts as they become due.

            b) Within 120 days before the filing of the petition, a custodian or receiver took possession of all or most of the debtor's property to enforce a lien against the property.

3) If neither ground for involuntary bankruptcy exists, the court can order the petitioning creditors to pay the debtor for legal expenses and reasonable attorney's fees.

a) The court may also require a petitioner who has acted in bad faith to pay compensatory damages and punitive damages.

11. The petition requests that the bankruptcy judge grant an order for relief with respect to the particular debtor alleged to be insolvent. An order for relief is a court-issued stay suspending collection activities.

12. The debtor can continue to use, acquire, and dispose of his/her property until the bankruptcy court orders otherwise.

a. If necessary, the court can appoint a temporary trustee to preserve the debtor's assets.

13. In addition to performing all other duties outlined in the Bankruptcy Code, a debtor must

a. Attend and submit to all court-scheduled examinations

b. Testify if called as a witness in a hearing

c. Inform the trustee in writing of the location of all real property in which the debtor has an interest

d. Inform the trustee in writing of the name and address of every person holding money or property subject to the debtor's withdrawal or order if a schedule of property has not yet been filed

e. Cooperate with the trustee in the preparation of an inventory, examination of proofs of a claim, and administration of the estate

f. Inform the court of any change in the debtor's address

g. Attend any hearings held with respect to discharge

14. Upon entry of the order for relief, the bankruptcy judge generally appoints an interim trustee to investigate the financial affairs of the debtor. The interim trustee

a. Takes control of the debtor's estate
b. Notifies creditors of the bankruptcy proceeding
c. Collects and distributes the debtor's nonexempt property

15. Within a reasonable time after entry of the order for relief, the bankruptcy judge convenes the first meeting of creditors.

a. The creditors may elect a permanent trustee.

b. If they fail to do so, the interim trustee continues as a permanent trustee.

c. The debtor must attend the creditors' meeting and submit to examination under oath.

d. The judge is not permitted to attend the meeting.

16. **Trustee Powers.** Broad powers are granted the trustee to perform his/her duties. They include the power/duty to do the following:

a. Collect property and convert it to money

b. Account for all property received

c. Investigate the financial affairs of the debtor

d. Affirm or disaffirm contracts of the debtor which are yet to be performed

e. Sue or be sued

f.   Set aside (disregard) fraudulent conveyances by the debtor

  1)   Fraudulent conveyances or transfers include any transfers of property interests and any debts incurred by the debtor within 1 year of filing the bankruptcy petition if such transfers were intended to delay or defraud creditors.

g.   Void certain transfers of property by the debtor to creditors which prefer some creditors over others

h.   Set aside statutory liens (e.g., a mechanic's lien) or a judgment lien on the debtor's property which would take effect upon the beginning of the bankruptcy proceedings (referred to as a strong-arm clause)

i.   Operate the debtor's business in certain circumstances

j.   Hire attorneys, accountants, and other professionals as needed

  1)   If (s)he has appropriate qualifications, the trustee may hire him/herself to perform a professional service, but only with court approval.

k.   Examine proof of claims and object to allowance of any improper claim

l.   If appropriate, oppose the discharge of the debtor

m.   Furnish information to a party in interest

n.   File reports and summaries with the court and taxing authorities

o.   Close up the estate as expeditiously as possible

p.   Prepare a final report and file a final accounting of the administration of the estate with the court

17.   **Core proceedings** are those conducted and decided by the bankruptcy court (judge). They resolve issues most directly determinative of reorganization or discharge, such as allowing creditor claims, determining the relative priority of creditor claims, confirming a plan of reorganization, and granting a discharge.

  a.   **Noncore proceedings** are resolved in state or other federal courts but may affect rights of the creditors or debtor. Noncore proceedings could involve property rights claims (e.g., royalties), personal injury claims, divorce, etc.

18.   Stop and review! You have completed the outline for this subunit. Study multiple-choice questions 1 through 12 beginning on page 334.

B.   **Effects of Bankruptcy on Debtors and Creditors**. The petition requests that the bankruptcy judge grant an order for relief with respect to a particular debtor.

1.   An **order for relief** is a court-issued stay, suspending virtually all legal action and collection activity until the bankruptcy case is completed or the bankruptcy court vacates (terminates) the stay. For example,

  a.   All actions by creditors to begin or continue to pursue claims against the debtor, to enforce existing judgments, or to create or enforce liens including a security interest are stopped until a further court order.

  NOTE: A secured creditor can petition the court to recognize the priority of the existing security interest and to grant relief from the automatic stay, thus permitting foreclosure.

2.   The order for relief does not stay all activity, e.g.,

  a.   Alimony and child support collection
  b.   Criminal proceedings
  c.   Issuance of a notice of tax deficiency

3. **Chapter 7 Liquidations**. Chapter 7 uses a liquidation approach by converting a debtor's nonexempt assets into cash. The cash is distributed as dictated by the Bankruptcy Code. An honest debtor is then discharged from most of the remaining debts.

4. **Eligible Parties**. Proceedings under Chapter 7 apply to all debtors (persons), including individuals, partnerships, and corporations, but not to

    a. Municipalities
    b. Railroads
    c. Insurance companies
    d. Banks
    e. Savings and loan associations
    f. Credit unions

5. A husband and wife may file a joint petition.

6. Upon commencement of a Chapter 7 proceeding, an estate in property is formed. The estate consists of all the debtor's legal and equitable interests in property. It includes each of the following:

    a. All property presently held (wherever located)
    b. Community property
    c. Property the trustee recovers from third parties
    d. Proceeds and profits from the property of the estate
    e. Certain after-acquired property

        1) Interests in property, such as gifts, inheritances, property settlements (divorce), or life insurance proceeds, to which the debtor becomes entitled within 180 days after filing may also become part of the estate.

        2) Earnings after commencement of a Chapter 7 proceeding are not included in the bankruptcy estate.

7. **Exempt assets** are considered basic necessities for a fresh start. Precisely what is exempt (from claims of creditors) depends on state law.

    a. Only individual debtors, and not corporations, are eligible for exemptions.

    b. States are permitted to opt out of the exemptions provided for debtors in the federal act and require their citizens to accept the exemptions of property permitted under state law. If a state has made such an election, the debtor is limited to the exemptions of property allowed by the state in which (s)he resides.

        1) If the state has not rejected the federal list, the debtor has the choice of either the state or the federal list.

        2) More than 30 states have opted out.

    c. The Bankruptcy Code exempts the following property:

        1) Up to $16,150 ($15,000 for cases filed before April 1, 1998) in equity in the debtor's residence and burial plot

        2) An interest in a motor vehicle, up to a value of $2,575 ($2,400 for cases filed before April 1, 1998)

        3) An interest, up to a value of $425 ($400 for cases filed before April 1, 1998), in any particular item of household goods and furnishings, wearing apparel, appliances, books, animals, crops, or musical instruments

            a) The aggregate total of all these items is limited to $8,625 ($8,000 for cases filed before April 1, 1998)

4) An interest in jewelry, up to a value of $1,075 ($1,000 for cases filed before April 1, 1998)

5) Any other property worth up to $850 ($800 for cases filed before April 1, 1998), plus any unused part of the $16,150 homestead exemption up to an amount of $8,075 ($7,500 for cases filed before April 1, 1998)

6) An interest in any tools of the debtor's trade, up to a value of $1,625 ($1,500 for cases filed before April 1, 1998) in the aggregate

7) Any unmatured life insurance contract owned by the debtor

8) Certain interests in accrued dividends or interest under life insurance contracts owned by the debtor

9) Professionally prescribed health aids

10) The right to receive Social Security, certain welfare benefits, disability benefits, alimony and support, and certain pension benefits

11) The right to receive certain personal injury and other awards up to $16,150 ($15,000 for cases filed before April 1, 1998)

8. **Voidable Preferences**. The trustee has power to avoid preferential transfers. The property would not otherwise be in the bankruptcy estate.

   a. A voidable preferential transfer is one made

      1) For the benefit of a creditor,

      2) For or on account of an antecedent debt,

      3) During the debtor's insolvency,

      4) Within 90 days prior to filing the petition, and

      5) For the purpose of entitling the creditor to receive a larger portion of its claim than otherwise would be received under a distribution in bankruptcy.

      NOTE: A debtor is presumed insolvent during the 90 days prior to filing for purposes of preferential transfers.

   b. Property purchased by an innocent third party from a preferential transferee cannot be recovered. That transfer is not voidable.

      1) The preferential transferor may be liable for its value.

   c. Other transfers not voidable by the trustee include

      1) Payments of accounts payable in the ordinary course of the debtor's business

      2) Payment of less than $600 on a consumer debt within 90 days preceding the filing of the petition

      3) Asset transfers for current consideration (such as new materials delivered in exchange for cash)

      4) Bona fide transfers for alimony, maintenance, or support to a former spouse, spouse, or child of the debtor.

   d. The trustee has the power to avoid preferential liens. Similar to preferential transfers, they are liens granted when the debtor grants a security interest in property

      1) For an antecedent debt,

      2) Within 90 days preceding filing the petition, and

      3) For the purpose of entitling the creditor to more than it would otherwise receive on bankruptcy distribution.

e. **Exception**. A security interest given by the debtor to acquire property that is perfected within 20 days after the debtor takes possession of the property is not a voidable preference because new value is received. (This arrangement is an enabling security interest.)

f. **Insiders**. The trustee may avoid preferential transfers and grants of security interests to insiders if made within 1 year before the filing of the petition.

   1) The debtor must have been insolvent at the time of the transfer or grant.
   2) Insiders are related parties, including

      a) Relatives
      b) Partners and partnerships
      c) Corporate directors and officers
      d) Controlling shareholders

9. The trustee has power to avoid **fraudulent transfers**.

   a. Proof that a property transfer within 1 year prior to filing was with intent to hinder, delay, or defraud creditors renders it voidable.

   b. When a fraudulent transfer to a bona fide purchaser in good faith is avoided, the consideration paid is restored.

   c. The trustee also has power to avoid transfers fraudulent under state law.

      1) State statutes of limitations usually exceed the 1-year window for voidable transfers in the Bankruptcy Act.

10. **Leases**. If the estate includes an unexpired lease, the trustee representing the lessee's estate has one of the following options:

    a. Assume and perform it
    b. Assume and assign it
    c. Reject it

       1) The lease is treated as rejected unless the trustee acts to assume it within 60 days after the order for relief.

11. **Set-off**. Any right of a creditor to offset a debt it owes to the debtor against a claim it has against the debtor is generally unaffected by a bankruptcy proceeding, if both the debt and claim arose before the petition was filed.

12. The distribution process commences with creditors' filing of documents called proofs of claim.

    a. Generally, a **proof of claim** must be filed not more than 90 days after the first meeting of creditors.

    b. Only unsecured creditors are required to file proofs of claim.

    c. A secured creditor whose claim exceeds the value of the collateral is an unsecured creditor as to the deficiency. A proof of claim must be filed to recover any of the deficiency.

    d. Upon filing a proof of claim, the claim is deemed valid and allowable.

       1) But if an interested party such as a creditor or the trustee objects, the bankruptcy court must decide whether to allow the claim.

       2) If a debtor has a defense to an alleged debt (e.g., fraud, failure of consideration), the claim will not be allowed.

13. Three kinds of creditors may be involved in the distribution of the debtor's estate. They are secured creditors, priority creditors (unsecured), and general creditors (other unsecured creditors).

    a. **Secured creditors' rights**. Secured creditors have property rights that are not affected by the trustee.

        1) They are paid in full if the collateral is sufficient.

        2) If the collateral is insufficient, the secured creditor is a general creditor as to the deficiency.

    b. **Priority creditors** are unsecured creditors next in line for payment. The Bankruptcy Code gives them priority over the claims of the general creditors.

        1) Members of a higher class of priority creditors are paid in full before members of a lower class receive anything. If the assets are insufficient to pay all claims in a given class, the claimants share pro rata.

        2) The classes of priority claims listed in order of rank are as follows:

            a) Claims for administrative expenses and expenses incurred in preserving and collecting the estate

                i) These include fees of the trustee and persons hired by the trustee.

            b) Claims of tradespeople who extend unsecured credit in the ordinary course of business after the filing of an involuntary petition but before the appointment of a trustee

            c) Certain wages owed to the debtor's employees earned within the 90 days preceding the earlier of bankruptcy or cessation of the debtor's business

                i) A maximum of $4,300 ($4,000 for cases filed before April 1, 1998) of an employee's wage claim can be classified as a priority claim. The balance is a general claim.

            d) Certain contributions owed to the debtor's employee benefit plans

            e) Claims of grain producers and fishermen for up to $4,300 ($4,000 for cases filed before April 1, 1998) each for grain or fish deposited with the debtor but not paid for or returned

            f) Claims of consumers for the return of up to $1,950 ($1,800 for cases filed before April 1, 1998) each in pre-bankruptcy deposits paid to the debtor for services not rendered, or for the purchase or rental of property not delivered, if the services or property were for personal, family, or household use

            g) Claims for alimony, maintenance, and child support.

            h) Claims for federal, state, and local taxes

    c.   Finally, if any money remains, the **general creditors** are paid.

        1)   General creditors are unsecured creditors that are not priority creditors.

        2)   Higher-ranking claims are paid in full before lower-ranking claims receive anything.

        3)   The rankings under this final set of priorities are as follows:

            a)   Allowed unsecured claims for which creditors filed proofs of claim in time, or had acceptable excuses for filing late

            b)   Allowed unsecured claims for which proofs of claim were filed late and without acceptable excuse

            c)   Interest on claims already paid, for the period between the filing of the petition and the date of payment of the claims

14.   The debtor is entitled to any funds remaining after all the previously mentioned claims have been paid.

15.   **Discharge**. Individual debtors under Chapter 7 may receive a discharge from most debts that remain unpaid after distribution of the debtor's estate.

    a.   A discharge in a bankruptcy case means the debtor is free from further liability on certain debts.

    b.   The Bankruptcy Code requires a discharge hearing before a debtor receives a discharge.

    c.   The court will generally grant a discharge in a Chapter 7 proceeding.

    d.   Corporations and partnerships are precluded from Chapter 7 discharge.

    e.   Most debtors are eligible for a discharge only once every 6 years.

16.   Grounds for denying a general discharge include the following:

    a.   Fraudulently transferring or concealing property (within 1 year preceding the filing of the bankruptcy petition)

    b.   Unjustifiably concealing or destroying business records or failing to keep adequate business records

    c.   Making a false oath, a fraudulent account, or a false claim in connection with the bankruptcy case

    d.   Failing to explain satisfactorily any loss or deficiency of assets

    e.   Refusal of the debtor to obey lawful orders of the court

17.   Certain debts are not covered by a Chapter 7 discharge. They remain binding on the debtor. They do not preclude a general discharge. **Nondischargeable debts** include the following:

    a.   Federal tax liability

        1)   Accrued within 3 years prior to bankruptcy (or loans to pay taxes)
        2)   Stemming from tax fraud
        3)   Arising from failure to file returns

    b.   Debts incurred on the basis of materially false financial statements if issued with the intent to deceive and the creditor reasonably relied on them

    c.   Debts not scheduled by the debtor or others in time to permit a creditor without notice of the case to make a timely filing of a proof of claim

    d.   Debts resulting from embezzlement, larceny, or violation of a fiduciary duty

    e.   Debts arising from alimony, maintenance, or child support awards

    f.   Debts arising from willful and malicious injury to an entity or conversion of its property

    g.   Debts arising from certain educational loans made, funded, or guaranteed by a governmental unit

    h.   Governmental fines and penalties, except those relating to dischargeable taxes

    i.   Debts arising from liability for operating a motor vehicle while legally intoxicated

18.   Under the 1984 Amendments to the Bankruptcy Act, certain debts are presumed nondischargeable:

    a.   Consumer debts greater than $1,075 ($1,000 for cases filed before April 1, 1998) owed to a single creditor by an individual debtor for luxury goods or services, incurred on or within 60 days prior to the order for relief

    b.   Cash advances aggregating more than $1,075 ($1,000 for cases filed before April 1, 1998) under an open-end credit plan obtained by an individual debtor on or within 60 days prior to the order for relief

19.   **Reaffirmation**. A debtor may enter into a reaffirmation agreement to perform an unsatisfied obligation to be discharged in bankruptcy.

    a.   To be legally enforceable, such an agreement must

        1)   Be entered into prior to the discharge (in bankruptcy)
        2)   Be in writing and filed with the court

    b.   In addition, a reaffirmation agreement must be either

        1)   Accompanied by an affidavit filed by the debtor's attorney stating that the debtor voluntarily and knowingly (fully informed of consequences) entered into the agreement and that it causes no undue hardship, or

        2)   Approved by the court, if the debtor is not represented by an attorney.

            a)   The court will require that the agreement be in the best interest of, and not impose undue hardship on, the debtor.

    c.   The reaffirmation agreement must conspicuously state the debtor's right of rescission.

        1)   The debtor has the right to rescind the reaffirmation until the later of the discharge or 60 days after the agreement is filed with the court.

        2)   A reaffirmation made after the bankruptcy proceeding is not enforceable.

20.   A discharge previously granted may be revoked on the request of the trustee or a creditor, upon proof that the discharge was obtained through fraud, or that the debtor knowingly and fraudulently retained property belonging to the estate or failed to obey a court order.

21.   Stop and review! You have completed the outline for this subunit. Study multiple-choice questions 13 through 42 beginning on page 338.

C. Reorganizations and Adjustments

1. **Chapter 11 Reorganizations.** A debtor qualified for relief under Chapter 7 liquidation is also eligible for relief under Chapter 11 reorganization. A Chapter 11 reorganization allows for a distressed debtor (including a business enterprise) to restructure its finances, the business to continue, and the creditors to be paid.

   a. A case under Chapter 11 is commenced by filing a petition requesting an order for relief.

      1) Petitions may be voluntary or involuntary. The petition may be filed by the debtor or the creditors.

      2) A petition will result in a stay or suspension of creditors' actions against the debtor.

      3) An involuntary petition must meet the same tests as in a Chapter 7 liquidation, e.g., required number of creditors, nonpayment of debts, or establishment of custodian, etc.

      4) Insolvency is not a condition precedent to a voluntary petition.

   b. An individual or company seeking protection under Chapter 11 is generally permitted to operate its own business as a **debtor-in-possession**.

      1) A debtor-in-possession has basically the same rights and duties as a trustee but does not receive special compensation.

      2) The court may order the appointment of a trustee for cause, i.e., upon a sufficient showing by any interested party of dishonesty or incompetence of the debtor or management. Under the 1994 amendments to the Bankruptcy Act, the creditors may elect the trustee in these circumstances. The duties of a trustee are identical to those in a Chapter 7 liquidation.

      3) A court that does not order the appointment of a trustee may appoint an examiner to investigate any allegations of fraud, misconduct, or mismanagement if all of the following apply:

         a) Appointment is requested by a party in interest.
         b) It is in the interests of creditors or equity security holders.
         c) The debtor's fixed, liquidated, unsecured debts exceed $5 million.

   c. A **committee of unsecured creditors** is appointed by the court as soon as practicable after an order for relief has been granted. The committee generally consists of persons who hold the seven largest unsecured claims against the debtor.

      1) The committee may

         a) Consult with the debtor-in-possession or the trustee
         b) Request appointment of a trustee
         c) Independently investigate the debtor's affairs
         d) Participate in formulating the plan of reorganization

      2) The committee may employ attorneys, accountants, and other professionals to perform services or to represent it.

      3) The court may order the appointment of additional committees to assure adequate representation.

   d. A **plan of reorganization** is prepared and filed.

      1) The debtor has the exclusive right to file a plan during the 120 days after the order for relief (unless a trustee has been appointed) and may file a plan at any time. The debtor has 180 days to gain the creditors' approval of the plan. A trustee can file a plan at any time.

e.   A Chapter 11 reorganization plan must divide creditors' claims and shareholders' interests into classes. Claims in each class must be treated equally.

f.   The plan must specify which classes of creditors are impaired creditors and how they will be treated. A claim of a creditor or an interest of an owner is impaired if the plan

1)   Alters legal, equitable, or contractual rights of its holder,

2)   Fails to cure a pre-petition default, or

3)   Fails to provide for payment of the allowed amount of a claim or an interest on the effective date of the plan.

g.   To become effective, the plan must be confirmed (approved and put into operation) by the bankruptcy court. Confirmation makes the plan binding on the debtor, on creditors, on equity security holders, and others.

h.   **Confirmation** occurs by acceptance or by cramdown.

i.   **Acceptance**

1)   Before acceptance, the impaired classes of claims and interests can vote to accept or reject the plan.

2)   Acceptance by a class of claims requires half of the voters representing two-thirds of the dollar totals to approve the plan. A class of equity interests accepts the plan if two-thirds of the voting interests approve.

3)   The plan must provide for payment of all administrative expenses associated with the reorganization.

j.   Confirmation over the objection of one or more classes of creditors is a **cramdown**. A bankruptcy court may force an impaired class of creditors to participate in, and the court may confirm, a plan that is fair and equitable to the impaired class. The plan is treated as fair and equitable if the impaired class consists of

1)   **Secured creditors** that are allowed to

a)   Retain their security interests in the collateral, even if that collateral is transferred to a third party;

b)   Acquire security interests in proceeds of a sale of the collateral; or

c)   Receive indisputable equivalents to the security interests, e.g., in different property.

2)   **Unsecured creditors** if one of the following qualifications applies:

a)   They are paid an amount in cash or in property the value of which is equal to the present value of the debts.

b)   No class of creditors with lower-priority claims receives anything (absolute priority rule).

3)   **Equity holders** if one of the following applies:

a)   They are paid the greater of the present value of their equity interest or any fixed liquidation or redemption preference.

b)   No class of equity holders with lower-priority claims receives anything.

i)   EXAMPLE: A Chapter 11 plan proposes to allow all secured creditors to retain their current liens. All equity holders and unsecured creditors are impaired. The equity owners will receive nothing. The unsecured creditors are a single class and will receive 25% of their claims. The plan is deemed fair and equitable to the unsecured creditors in that no class with lower-priority claims receives anything. The same applies to the equity holders.

k.   Confirmation does not discharge a debtor from debts that are not dischargeable. All other claims not provided for by the plan are discharged.

l.   Persons entitled to participate in the plan have not less than 5 years from the date of the final decree to exchange securities in the old business organization for securities in the new business organization.

m.   Under the 1994 amendments, streamlined reorganization procedures are allowed for a **small business** (total liquidated, noncontingent debt not greater than $2 million). Such an entity may proceed without a creditors' committee and adopt simpler procedures for disclosing, and seeking votes for, a proposed plan.

2.   **Chapter 13 Plans**. Chapter 13, *Adjustment of Debts of Individuals*, provides for adjustment of debts of an individual with regular income who owes unsecured debts of less than $269,250 and secured debts of less than $807,750 ($250,000 and $750,000, respectively, for cases filed on or before April 1, 1998). Sole proprietorships are also eligible if the debt limitations are met. The debts must be owing and unpaid at the time the debtor files the petition.

a.   A Chapter 13 proceeding may be initiated only by filing a voluntary petition.

b.   The debtor must file the plan with the bankruptcy court within the 15 days after filing the petition. The debtor may modify the plan at any time before confirmation.

c.   A trustee is required under Chapter 13.

d.   The plan must meet three requirements of the Bankruptcy Code. The plan must provide for

1)   The debtor to submit all or any portion of future earnings, as is necessary for the execution of the plan, to the trustee

2)   Full payment on a deferred basis to all priority creditors, unless they agree to different treatment of their claims

3)   The same treatment for each claim in the same class, if the plan classifies the claims

NOTE: Repayment must generally occur over a period of not more than 3 years, although the court can approve a period as long as 5 years for cause.

e.   Typically, the debtor will propose either a composition or an extension plan. (A composition plan allows the debtor to pay less than 100% of claims, on a pro rata basis for each class of claims. In an extension plan, the debtor pays the full amount, but over a longer period than originally agreed to.)

f.   Chapter 13 plan confirmation requirements include the following:

1)   The plan complies with law and is proposed in good faith.

2)   The value of the property to be distributed to unsecured creditors is no less than would be paid to them under Chapter 7.

3)   Secured creditors accept the plan or the plan provides for the debtor to surrender the collateral to the secured creditors.

a)   Alternatively, the plan must permit any nonconsenting secured creditors to retain their security interests and provide that they will receive the value of their claims.

4)   The debtor is able to make all payments and comply with the plan.

5)   If the trustee or holder of an unsecured claim objects to the confirmation of a plan, the plan provides for full payment of that claim or for all the debtor's disposable income for 3 years being applied to payments under the plan.

a)   Disposable income is income not reasonably necessary for maintenance or support of the debtor and his/her dependents or for continuance of a business.

g. The court must hold a confirmation hearing.

h. For the protection of creditors, the court may dismiss the proceeding or convert it into a Chapter 7 proceeding after a request by a party in interest, including the debtor.

i. After a debtor completes all or substantially all payments under the plan, the court will grant a discharge of all debts, except for

1) Alimony and child support
2) Student loans
3) Debts from unlawfully driving while impaired
4) Criminal restitution requirements and fines
5) Long-term debts requiring payment over a period longer than that of the plan

j. The Chapter 13 discharge upon completion of the plan bars another discharge for 6 years unless payments equaled at least 100% of unsecured claims or the following apply:

1) The debtor has made at least 70% of the payments.
2) The plan was proposed in good faith.
3) The plan was the best effort of the debtor.

k. A hardship discharge is available if the debtor's failure is due to circumstances for which (s)he is not justly accountable, creditors have received what they would have paid under Chapter 7, and modification of the plan is not feasible.

3. **Chapter 12 for Family Farmers**. Chapter 12, *Adjustments of Debts of a Family Farmer with Regular Annual Income*, provides for the adjustment of debts of a family farmer with regular annual income.

a. A family farmer is an individual or individual and spouse who are engaged in farming and receive 50% or more of their gross income from farming.

1) Aggregate debts may not exceed $1.5 million.
2) At least 80% of debts must arise out of the farming operation.

b. A corporation or partnership may also qualify as a family farmer.

1) Its aggregate debts may not exceed $1.5 million.
2) At least 80% of its debts must arise out of farming.
3) More than 80% of its assets must be related to the farming operation.
4) At least 50% of the stock or equity must be held by one family.

c. Generally, the farmer-debtor remains in possession of property in the estate.

1) After notice and a hearing, the court may remove a debtor-in-possession for cause, e.g., for fraud, dishonesty, incompetence, or gross mismanagement.

d. The farmer-debtor is required to file a plan within 90 days of the order for relief (unless the court grants an extension).

1) Only the debtor may file a plan (voluntary only).
2) The debtor may modify the plan at any time before confirmation.

4. Stop and review! You have completed the outline for this subunit. Study multiple-choice questions 43 through 50 beginning on page 349.

MULTIPLE-CHOICE QUESTIONS

A. Voluntary and Involuntary Bankruptcy

1. Which of the following statements is correct concerning the voluntary filing of a petition in bankruptcy?

    A. The debtor must be insolvent.

    B. The petition may be filed by husband and wife jointly.

    C. If the debtor has 12 or more creditors, the debtor's unsecured claims must total at least $10,775.

    D. If the debtor has fewer than 12 creditors, the debtor's unsecured claims must total at least $10,775.

The correct answer is (B). *(CPA, adapted)*

REQUIRED: The correct statement concerning the voluntary filing of a petition in bankruptcy.

DISCUSSION: A bankruptcy case may be commenced voluntarily or involuntarily. In a voluntary case, the debtor files the petition with the bankruptcy court. Debtors can include individuals, partnerships, corporations, and couples, if the husband and wife file together.

Answer (A) is incorrect because insolvency is not a prerequisite for filing a voluntary petition. Answers (C) and (D) are incorrect because the 12-creditor threshold is applicable only to involuntary petitions.

2. Which of the following conditions, if any, must a debtor meet to file a voluntary bankruptcy petition under Chapter 7 of the Federal Bankruptcy Code?

	Insolvency	Three or More Creditors
A.	Yes	Yes
B.	Yes	No
C.	No	Yes
D.	No	No

The correct answer is (D). *(CPA, adapted)*

REQUIRED: The requirement to file a voluntary petition under Chapter 7 of the Bankruptcy Code.

DISCUSSION: A debtor need not be insolvent to file for protection under Chapter 7 of the Bankruptcy Code. The debtor need merely state (s)he has a debt, and (s)he must be an eligible type of person.

Answers (A), (B), and (C) are incorrect because a debtor need not be insolvent to file for protection under Chapter 7 of the Bankruptcy Code, and number-of-creditor thresholds apply only to involuntary petitions.

3. To file for bankruptcy under Chapter 7 of the Federal Bankruptcy Code, an individual must

    A. Have debts of any amount.

    B. Be insolvent.

    C. Be indebted to more than three creditors.

    D. Have debts in excess of $10,775.

The correct answer is (A). *(CPA, adapted)*

REQUIRED: The requirement to file for protection under Chapter 7 of the Bankruptcy Code.

DISCUSSION: Under Chapter 7, generally, a debtor's nonexempt assets are converted into cash, the cash is distributed among creditors, and the debtor is discharged from most remaining obligations. Any person with a debt, if (s)he is a type of entity eligible under Chapter 7, may file a petition for protection.

Answer (B) is incorrect because insolvency is not required to file a voluntary petition. It is only necessary that the person have a legal obligation. Answers (C) and (D) are incorrect because amount-of-debt and number-of-creditors thresholds apply only to involuntary petitions filed by creditors.

4. Which of the following statements is correct with respect to a voluntary bankruptcy proceeding under the liquidation provisions of the Bankruptcy Code?

    A.   The debtor must be insolvent.

    B.   The liabilities of the debtor must total $10,775 or more.

    C.   It may be properly commenced and maintained by any person who is insolvent.

    D.   The filing of the bankruptcy petition constitutes an order for relief.

The correct answer is (D). *(CPA, adapted)*
    REQUIRED: The correct statement with respect to a voluntary bankruptcy proceeding.
    DISCUSSION: The voluntary bankruptcy petition is a formal request by the debtor to the court for an order for relief. Under the liquidation provisions of the Bankruptcy Code, an order for relief is automatically given to the debtor upon the filing of the petition.
    Answer (A) is incorrect because insolvency is not required. A statement that the debtor has debts is all that is needed. Answer (B) is incorrect because, in a voluntary bankruptcy proceeding, there is no minimum amount of debtor liabilities. Answer (C) is incorrect because the courts have discretion not to grant relief that would constitute a substantial abuse of the bankruptcy laws. Also, certain entities, e.g., banks, are not eligible for voluntary bankruptcy.

5. A voluntary petition filed under the liquidation provisions of Chapter 7 of the Federal Bankruptcy Code

    A.   Is not available to a corporation unless it has previously filed a petition under the reorganization provisions of Chapter 11 of the Federal Bankruptcy Code.

    B.   Automatically stays collection actions against the debtor except by secured creditors.

    C.   Will be dismissed unless the debtor has 12 or more unsecured creditors whose claims total at least $10,775.

    D.   Does not require the debtor to show that the debtor's liabilities exceed the fair market value of assets.

The correct answer is (D). *(CPA, adapted)*
    REQUIRED: The correct statement concerning a voluntary petition under Chapter 7 of the Bankruptcy Code.
    DISCUSSION: A debtor need not be insolvent to file for protection of Chapter 7 of the Bankruptcy Code. The debtor need merely state (s)he has a debt, and (s)he must be an eligible type of person.
    Answer (A) is incorrect because a corporation is eligible to file a voluntary petition. It need not previously have filed under Chapter 11. Answer (B) is incorrect because the stay operates against a secured creditor. Only if the court grants a petition to vacate the stay might the secured party proceed to repossess the collateral or take other action. Answer (C) is incorrect because number-of-creditors and amount-of-debt thresholds apply only to involuntary petitions.

6. Green owes unsecured creditors: Rice, $3,000; Vick, $4,500; Young, $12,000; and Zinc, $3,500. Green has not paid any creditor since January 1, 1999. On March 15, 1999, Green's sole asset, a cabin cruiser, was seized by Xeno Marine Co., the holder of a perfected security interest in the boat. On July 1, 1999, Rice, Vick, and Zinc involuntarily petitioned Green into bankruptcy under Chapter 7 of the Federal Bankruptcy Code. If Green opposes the involuntary petition, the petition will be

    A.   Upheld, because the three filing creditors are owed more than $10,775.

    B.   Upheld, because one creditor is owed more than $10,775.

    C.   Dismissed, because there are fewer than 12 creditors.

    D.   Dismissed, because the boat was seized more than 90 days before the filing.

The correct answer is (A). *(CPA, adapted)*
    REQUIRED: The status of involuntary petition under Chapter 7 by creditors.
    DISCUSSION: For cases filed on or after April 1, 1998, if the debtor has fewer than 12 creditors, any one or more creditors who alone or together have unsecured claims of $10,775 or more can file an involuntary petition. If there are 12 or more creditors, any three or more who together hold unsecured claims of at least $10,775 can file an involuntary petition.
    Answer (B) is incorrect because Young did not join in filing the petition. Answer (C) is incorrect because, when there are fewer than 12 creditors, a debtor may be involuntarily petitioned into bankruptcy by one or more creditors who alone or together are owed more than $10,775. Answer (D) is incorrect because a challenged involuntary petition is not dismissed if the debtor is generally not paying his/her bills as they become due or, within 120 days before filing, a custodian or receiver took possession of all or most of the debtor's property to enforce a lien against the property.

7. A contested involuntary petition in bankruptcy will be dismissed if the debtor

- A. Owes unsecured obligations exceeding $10,775 to less than three creditors.
- B. Had all its property taken to enforce a lien within 120 days of filing.
- C. Is failing to pay undisputed debts as they become due.
- D. Is an individual engaged in the business of farming.

The correct answer is (D). *(CPA, adapted)*
REQUIRED: The basis for dismissal of an involuntary petition in bankruptcy.
DISCUSSION: Creditors may petition a debtor involuntarily into bankruptcy proceedings under Chapters 7 and 11 of the Bankruptcy Code. The debtor must be a person eligible for protection under the particular chapter. But an individual engaged in the business of farming may not be involuntarily petitioned into bankruptcy.
Answer (A) is incorrect because, if there are fewer than 12 different creditors, any one creditor who has an unsecured claim of at least $10,775 can file an involuntary petition. Answer (B) is incorrect because an involuntary petition will not be dismissed if, within 120 days before filing, a custodian or receiver took possession of all or most of the debtor's property to enforce a lien against the property. Answer (C) is incorrect because an involuntary petition will not be dismissed if the debtor is generally not paying his/her bills as they become due in the ordinary course of business.

8. If a debtor opposes an involuntary bankruptcy petition filed under Chapter 7 of the Federal Bankruptcy Code, the court will determine that statutory grounds for involuntary bankruptcy exist

- A. If the debtor has not been paying its bona fide debts as they become due.
- B. Only if the debtor has at least 12 creditors.
- C. If at least one secured creditor joins in the petition.
- D. Only if a receiver took possession of the debtor's property within the preceding 120 days.

The correct answer is (A). *(Publisher)*
REQUIRED: The basis for granting an involuntary bankruptcy petition.
DISCUSSION: The petition will be granted, even if it is contested, if the creditor(s) can prove either that the debtor owes $10,775 or more and is not paying his/her debts as they become due or that, during the 120 days preceding the filing of the petition, a custodian took possession of the debtor's property.
Answer (B) is incorrect because as few as one creditor may file. Answer (C) is incorrect because a secured creditor is not required to join in filing the petition. Answer (D) is incorrect because not paying debts as they become due is also grounds for involuntary bankruptcy.

9. Wilk owes a total of $50,000 to eight unsecured creditors and one fully secured creditor. Rusk is one of the unsecured creditors and is owed $17,000. Rusk has filed a petition against Wilk under the liquidation provisions of the Bankruptcy Code. Wilk has been unable to pay her debts as they become due, and Wilk's liabilities exceed her assets. Wilk has filed the papers that are required to oppose the bankruptcy petition. Which of the following statements is correct?

- A. The petition will be granted because Wilk is unable to pay her debts as they become due.
- B. The petition will be granted because Wilk's liabilities exceed her assets.
- C. The petition will be dismissed because three unsecured creditors must join in the filing of the petition.
- D. The petition will be dismissed because the secured creditor failed to join in the filing of the petition.

The correct answer is (A). *(CPA, adapted)*
REQUIRED: The correct statement concerning the entry of an order for relief in an involuntary bankruptcy case.
DISCUSSION: In an involuntary bankruptcy case, a single creditor may file a petition for relief if (s)he is owed $10,775 or more and there are fewer than 12 creditors. The petition will be granted, even if it is contested, if the creditor can prove either that the debtor is not paying his/her debts as they become due or that, during the 120 days preceding the filing of the petition, a custodian took possession of the debtor's property. In this case, Rusk has met the conditions to file the petition and has proved that Wilk is unable to pay her debts as they become due. Thus, even though the petition was contested, it will still be granted.
Answer (B) is incorrect because having liabilities in excess of assets is not a criterion for automatic granting of a petition for relief. Answer (C) is incorrect because three unsecured creditors must join in filing the petition only if there are 12 or more creditors. Answer (D) is incorrect because a secured creditor is not required to join in filing the petition.

10. A party involuntarily petitioned into bankruptcy under Chapter 7 of the Federal Bankruptcy Code who succeeds in having the petition dismissed could recover

	Court Costs and Attorney's Fees	Compensatory Damages	Punitive Damages
A.	Yes	Yes	Yes
B.	Yes	Yes	No
C.	No	Yes	Yes
D.	Yes	No	No

The correct answer is (A). *(CPA, adapted)*
REQUIRED: The recovery allowed a debtor whose involuntary bankruptcy was dismissed.
DISCUSSION: A debtor who successfully controverts an involuntary bankruptcy petition could recover his/her costs, including reasonable attorney's fees. The court may require the petitioner to pay damages if (s)he is found to have acted in bad faith. A petitioner whose conduct is malicious or otherwise egregious may also be required to pay punitive damages.
Answers (B), (C), and (D) are incorrect because costs, compensatory damages, and punitive damages might each be awarded in appropriate circumstances.

11. Flax, a sole proprietor, has been petitioned involuntarily into bankruptcy under the Federal Bankruptcy Code's liquidation provisions. Simon & Co., CPAs, has been appointed trustee of the bankruptcy estate. If Simon also wishes to act as the tax return preparer for the estate, which of the following statements is correct?

A. Simon is prohibited from serving as both trustee and preparer under any circumstances because serving in that dual capacity would be a conflict of interest.

B. Although Simon may serve as both trustee and preparer, it is entitled to receive a fee only for the services rendered as a preparer.

C. Simon may employ itself to prepare tax returns if authorized by the court and may receive a separate fee for services rendered in each capacity.

D. Although Simon may serve as both trustee and preparer, its fee for services rendered in each capacity will be determined solely by the size of the estate.

The correct answer is (C). *(CPA, adapted)*
REQUIRED: The authority and compensation of a trustee in bankruptcy.
DISCUSSION: The trustee in bankruptcy is either appointed by the judge or elected by the creditors to administer most of the bankruptcy proceeding. Primary duties include collecting estate property and liquidating it. The trustee has authority, with court approval, to employ professionals such as attorneys or accountants to perform services requiring expertise. If (s)he has appropriate qualifications, the trustee may employ him/herself to perform a professional service, with court approval. Professionals employed by the trustee are entitled to reasonable compensation for their services out of the bankruptcy estate.
Answer (A) is incorrect because the trustee may also provide services for hire in a professional capacity, but only with approval of the court. Answer (B) is incorrect because the trustee is also entitled to compensation for professional services rendered with court approval. Answer (D) is incorrect because, although the estate is the source of payment, the amount is based on the value of the services rendered.

12. Deft, CPA, is an unsecured creditor of Golf Co. for $15,000. Golf has a total of 10 creditors, all of whom are unsecured. Golf has not paid any of the creditors for 3 months. Under Chapter 11 of the Federal Bankruptcy Code, which of the following statements is correct?

A. Golf may not be petitioned involuntarily into bankruptcy because there are fewer than 12 unsecured creditors.

B. Golf may not be petitioned involuntarily into bankruptcy under the provisions of Chapter 11.

C. Three unsecured creditors must join in the involuntary petition in bankruptcy.

D. Deft may file an involuntary petition in bankruptcy against Golf.

The correct answer is (D). *(CPA, adapted)*
REQUIRED: The requirement for filing an involuntary bankruptcy petition under Chapter 11.
DISCUSSION: Deft may file an involuntary petition for bankruptcy against Golf under Chapter 11. A single creditor may file an involuntary petition for relief if (s)he has at least $10,775 of unsecured claims and if the debtor has fewer than 12 creditors.
Answer (A) is incorrect because one creditor may file an involuntary petition if (s)he has unsecured claims of $10,775 or more. Answer (B) is incorrect because a proceeding under Chapter 11 may be initiated by a voluntary or involuntary petition. Answer (C) is incorrect because the debtor has 10 creditors, which allows a single unsecured creditor to file an involuntary petition if (s)he is owed at least $10,775. When a debtor has 12 or more creditors, at least three unsecured creditors with claims totaling $10,775 or more must join to file an involuntary petition.

B. Effects of Bankruptcy on Debtors and Creditors

13. The filing of an involuntary bankruptcy petition under the Federal Bankruptcy Code

- A. Terminates liens on exempt property.
- B. Terminates all security interests in property in the bankruptcy estate.
- C. Stops the debtor from incurring new debts.
- D. Stops the enforcement of judgment liens against property in the bankruptcy estate.

The correct answer is (D). *(CPA, adapted)*
REQUIRED: The effect of filing an involuntary petition in bankruptcy.
DISCUSSION: The automatic stay resulting from filing the petition operates to postpone certain actions against the debtor and his/her property whether the filing is voluntary or involuntary. All acts, with certain exceptions, to establish, enforce, or perfect any lien against estate property are stayed when a petition in bankruptcy is filed. The stay also applies to judgment liens.
Answer (A) is incorrect because the automatic stay does not affect the existence of liens on exempt property but postpones efforts to foreclose the liens. Answer (B) is incorrect because the automatic stay does not affect the existence of all security interests in estate property. Answer (C) is incorrect because the debtor may incur new debts.

14. Filing a valid petition in bankruptcy acts as an automatic stay of actions to

	Garnish the Debtor's Wages	Collect Alimony from the Debtor
A.	Yes	Yes
B.	Yes	No
C.	No	Yes
D.	No	No

The correct answer is (B). *(CPA, adapted)*
REQUIRED: The actions affected by the automatic stay.
DISCUSSION: The filing of a valid petition in bankruptcy automatically postpones certain actions and proceedings that involve the debtor or his/her property. This automatic stay operates to give the debtor protection from creditors. Actions and proceedings not covered by the automatic stay include criminal prosecution of the debtor, collection of child support, and collection of alimony.
Answer (A) is incorrect because the automatic stay does not operate to prohibit collecting alimony. Answer (C) is incorrect because the automatic stay does not operate to prohibit collecting alimony, but it does prohibit garnishing the debtor's wages. Answer (D) is incorrect because the automatic stay does prohibit garnishing the debtor's wages.

15. Chapter 7 of the Federal Bankruptcy Code will deny a debtor a discharge when the debtor

- A. Made a preferential transfer to a creditor.
- B. Accidentally destroyed information relevant to the bankruptcy proceeding.
- C. Obtained a Chapter 7 discharge 10 years previously.
- D. Is a corporation or a partnership.

The correct answer is (D). *(CPA, adapted)*
REQUIRED: The basis for denying a discharge to a debtor under Chapter 7 of the Bankruptcy Code.
DISCUSSION: A general discharge of most debts is provided a person under Chapter 7. But certain types of entities are not eligible. They include railroads, insurance companies, banks, credit unions, and savings and loan associations. Partnerships and corporations do not receive a general discharge under Chapter 7. They are merely liquidated.
Answer (A) is incorrect because a preferential transfer may be set aside by the trustee, but it does not prevent discharge. Answer (B) is incorrect because destroying information can result in denial of general discharge. But if it is justified, e.g., accidental and not an attempt to defraud creditors, it may not result in denial of discharge. Answer (C) is incorrect because discharge is barred if there was a Chapter 7 discharge within 6 years of filing the petition.

16. On February 28, 1999, Master, Inc. had total assets with a fair market value of $1.2 million and total liabilities of $990,000. On June 15, 1999, Master voluntarily filed a petition in bankruptcy under the liquidation provisions of Chapter 7 of the Federal Bankruptcy Code. If a creditor challenged Master's right to file, the petition would be dismissed

A. If Master had fewer than 12 creditors at the time of filing.

B. Unless Master can show that a reorganization under Chapter 11 of the Federal Bankruptcy Code would have been unsuccessful.

C. Unless Master can show that it is unable to pay its debts in the ordinary course of business or as they come due.

D. If Master is an insurance company.

The correct answer is (D). *(CPA, adapted)*
REQUIRED: The prerequisite to filing a voluntary petition under Chapter 7's liquidation provisions.
DISCUSSION: A debtor may voluntarily file a petition for protection from creditors under Chapter 7's liquidation provisions. The debtor, if an eligible person, need only state that it has debts. Persons ineligible to file under Chapter 7 include insurance companies, banks, and others.
Answer (A) is incorrect because the number of creditors is relevant to creditor eligibility to file an involuntary petition. Answer (B) is incorrect because liquidation and discharge under Chapter 7 is not restricted to cases in which Chapter 11 reorganization would not be successful. Answer (C) is incorrect because insolvency is not a condition for Chapter 7 discharge.

17. The Bankruptcy Code provides that a debtor is entitled to claim as exempt property the right to receive

	Social Security Benefits	Disability Benefits
A.	No	No
B.	Yes	No
C.	Yes	Yes
D.	No	Yes

The correct answer is (C). *(CPA, adapted)*
REQUIRED: The benefit a debtor is entitled to claim as exempt property.
DISCUSSION: The filing of a petition under Chapter 7 gives rise to an estate in property. The estate is a legal entity separate from the debtor. The estate consists of all the legal and equitable interests in property, wherever located, on the date of filing. Community property is included. Proceeds and profits from the property are also included, as is certain other property acquired after filing. Certain estate assets, considered essential to a fresh start, are exempt from claims of creditors, such as rights to receive Social Security, disability benefits, alimony, child support, and certain pension benefits.
Answers (A), (B), and (D) are incorrect because both Social Security and disability benefits are listed in the Bankruptcy Code as assets exempt from claims of creditors.

18. Which of the following assets would be included in a debtor's bankruptcy estate in a liquidation proceeding?

A. Proceeds from a life insurance policy received 90 days after the petition was filed.

B. An inheritance received 270 days after the petition was filed.

C. Property from a divorce settlement received 365 days after the petition was filed.

D. Wages earned by the debtor after the petition was filed.

The correct answer is (A). *(CPA, adapted)*
REQUIRED: The correct statement about the assets that would be included in a debtor's bankruptcy estate.
DISCUSSION: Any asset in which the debtor has a legal or equitable interest at the date the proceedings began is included in the estate. Other property may be added to the estate. For example, it includes property acquired by the debtor (1) within 180 days of filing the petition if the property was acquired by inheritance, (2) as proceeds of a life insurance policy, or (3) from a property settlement in a divorce case.
Answers (B) and (C) are incorrect because the property was acquired more than 180 days after filing. Answer (D) is incorrect because wages earned by the debtor after the petition for relief was filed are not included in the estate.

19. A person who voluntarily filed bankruptcy and received a discharge in bankruptcy under the provisions of Chapter 7 of the Federal Bankruptcy Code

- A. May obtain another voluntary discharge in bankruptcy under Chapter 7 after 5 years have elapsed from the date of the prior filing.

- B. Will receive a discharge of any and all debts owed.

- C. Is precluded from owning or operating a similar business for 2 years.

- D. Must surrender for distribution to the creditors any amount received as an inheritance if received within 180 days after filing the petition.

The correct answer is (D). *(CPA, adapted)*
REQUIRED: The correct statement concerning a discharge under Chapter 7.
DISCUSSION: The bankruptcy estate available for distribution to creditors includes all the debtor's nonexempt legal and equitable interests in property on the date of filing. It includes proceeds and profits from that estate. Certain property acquired by the debtor after filing is also brought into the estate: gifts, inheritances, property settlements (divorce), and life insurance proceeds to which the debtor becomes entitled within 180 days after filing.
Answer (A) is incorrect because discharge is barred if there was a Chapter 7 discharge within the 6 years preceding filing the petition. Answer (B) is incorrect because certain debts are nondischargeable. Answer (C) is incorrect because there is no such requirement.

20. Under the liquidation provisions of Chapter 7 of the Federal Bankruptcy Code, which of the following statements applies to a person who has voluntarily filed for and received a discharge in bankruptcy?

- A. The person will be discharged from all debts.

- B. The person can obtain another voluntary discharge in bankruptcy under Chapter 7 after 3 years have elapsed from the date of the prior filing.

- C. The person must surrender for distribution to the creditors amounts received as an inheritance, if the receipt occurs within 180 days after filing the bankruptcy petition.

- D. The person is precluded from owning or operating a similar business for 2 years.

The correct answer is (C). *(CPA, adapted)*
REQUIRED: The correct statement about a debtor who voluntarily filed for and received a Chapter 7 discharge.
DISCUSSION: The bankruptcy estate consists of all the debtor's legal and equitable interests in property, including gifts, insurance proceeds, property settlements, and inheritances received within 180 days of the commencement of bankruptcy proceedings.
Answer (A) is incorrect because certain debts are not dischargeable. Answer (B) is incorrect because a person ordinarily is eligible for Chapter 7 bankruptcy relief once every 6 years. Answer (D) is incorrect because a person who obtains relief under Chapter 7 is not restricted from operating a similar business. Bankruptcy proceedings are intended to provide the debtor with a fresh start.

21. Under the liquidation provisions of Chapter 7 of the Federal Bankruptcy Code, a debtor will be denied a discharge in bankruptcy if the debtor

- A. Fails to list a creditor.

- B. Owes alimony and support payments.

- C. Cannot pay administration expenses.

- D. Refuses to explain satisfactorily a loss of assets.

The correct answer is (D). *(CPA, adapted)*
REQUIRED: The act resulting in a denial of discharge in bankruptcy.
DISCUSSION: In a Chapter 7 proceeding, the debtor's nonexempt assets are liquidated; creditors are paid pro rata according to the priority of their claims; and the debtor, if an individual, is discharged from unsatisfied obligations except certain nondischargable debts listed in the Bankruptcy Act. The purpose of Chapter 7 is to assure a fair distribution of assets among the creditors and provide an honest individual with a fresh start. Refusal or failure of a debtor to explain satisfactorily the loss or disappearance of assets will result in a denial of discharge.
Answer (A) is incorrect because not listing a creditor on a schedule required to be filed with the court will not result in denial of a discharge, but the debtor will remain liable for the unlisted claim. Answer (B) is incorrect because alimony and support payments are never discharged through a bankruptcy proceeding. Answer (C) is incorrect because individuals unable to pay administrative expenses are not denied a discharge of their debts through bankruptcy.

Questions 22 and 23 are based on the following information. On February 28, 1999, Master, Inc. had total assets with a fair market value of $1.2 million and total liabilities of $990,000. On January 15, 1999, Master made a monthly installment note payment to Acme Distributors Corp., a creditor holding a properly perfected security interest in equipment having a fair market value greater than the balance due on the note. On June 15, 1999, Master voluntarily filed a petition in bankruptcy under the liquidation provisions of Chapter 7 of the Federal Bankruptcy Code. One year later, the equipment was sold for less than the balance due on the note to Acme.

22. If Master's voluntary petition is filed properly,

- A. Master will be entitled to conduct its business as a debtor-in-possession unless the court appoints a trustee.

- B. A trustee must be appointed by the creditors.

- C. Lawsuits by Master's creditors will be stayed by the Federal Bankruptcy Code.

- D. The unsecured creditors must elect a creditors' committee of three to 11 members to consult with the trustee.

The correct answer is (C). *(CPA, adapted)*
REQUIRED: The effect of properly filing a petition under Chapter 7 of the Bankruptcy Act.
DISCUSSION: If a voluntary petition has been properly completed, sworn to, and signed by the debtor, it functions as an automatic order for relief. One effect is to stay most legal proceedings and other activities of creditors seeking to collect from the debtor. Secured creditors' actions are also stayed. The court may decide a creditor is entitled to relief from the automatic stay on the grounds that it does afford the creditor adequate protection.
Answer (A) is incorrect because the court appoints an interim trustee. But, with court approval, the debtor may file a bond and reacquire property under the trustee's control. Answer (B) is incorrect because, under Chapter 7, the court appoints an interim trustee. The creditors may then elect a permanent trustee. Otherwise, the interim trustee continues as trustee. Answer (D) is incorrect because the creditors may, but do not have a legal duty to, elect such a committee.

23. Which of the following statements correctly describes Acme's distribution from Master's bankruptcy estate?

- A. Acme will receive the total amount it is owed, even if the proceeds from the sale of the collateral were less than the balance owed by Master.

- B. Acme will have the same priority as unsecured general creditors to the extent that the proceeds from the sale of its collateral are insufficient to satisfy the amount owed by Master.

- C. The total proceeds from the sale of the collateral will be paid to Acme even if they are less than the balance owed by Master, provided there is sufficient cash to pay all administrative costs associated with the bankruptcy.

- D. Acme will receive only the proceeds from the sale of the collateral in full satisfaction of the debt owed by Master.

The correct answer is (B). *(CPA, adapted)*
REQUIRED: The portion of a bankruptcy estate distributable to a secured creditor.
DISCUSSION: Under the Bankruptcy Code, to the extent a creditor's claim is secured, it must be satisfied in full before distribution is made on any other claims. But the secured creditor is treated the same as a general unsecured creditor to the extent its claim exceeds the value of the collateral. Note that the collateral is part of the estate. The secured creditor's priority right is to the amount of the security interest as opposed to the property itself.
Answer (A) is incorrect because Acme is treated as a general unsecured creditor with respect to any portion of its claim which exceeds the value of the collateral. Answer (C) is incorrect because the security interest has a higher priority than claims for administrative costs. Answer (D) is incorrect because Acme may receive an amount in addition to the proceeds of the collateral, but only in an unsecured creditor capacity.

Questions 24 through 26 are based on the following information. On August 1, 1999, Hall filed a voluntary petition under Chapter 7 of the Federal Bankruptcy Code. Hall's assets are sufficient to pay general creditors 40% of their claims. The following transactions occurred before the filing:

- On May 15, 1999, Hall gave a mortgage on Hall's home to National Bank to secure payment of a loan National had given Hall 2 years earlier. When the loan was made, Hall's twin was a National employee.
- On June 1, 1999, Hall purchased a boat from Olsen for $10,000 cash.
- On July 1, 1999, Hall paid off an outstanding credit card balance of $500. The original debt had been $2,500.

24. The National mortgage was

- A. Preferential, because National would be considered an insider.
- B. Preferential, because the mortgage was given to secure an antecedent debt.
- C. Not preferential, because Hall is presumed insolvent when the mortgage was given.
- D. Not preferential, because the mortgage was a security interest.

The correct answer is (B). *(CPA, adapted)*

REQUIRED: The reason for the status of a transfer as preferential or nonpreferential.

DISCUSSION: The trustee has legal authority to set aside a preferential transfer. A preferential transfer is one made for the benefit of a creditor, within 90 days prior to filing the petition, on account of an antecedent debt. The transfer must have been effected when the debtor was insolvent, and it must result in the creditor's receiving a larger portion of its claim than it otherwise would have received as a distribution in the bankruptcy proceeding.

Answer (A) is incorrect because, although an otherwise preferential transfer is preferential if made to an insider between 1 year and 90 days prior to filing, National is not related to the debtor such as to be classified as an insider. Answer (C) is incorrect because a debtor is presumed insolvent during the 90 days prior to filing for purposes of preferential transfers. The transfer is preferential because the insolvency and other definitional requirements were met. Answer (D) is incorrect because transfer of a security interest can, and does here, meet the requirements to be classified as preferential.

25. The payment to Olsen was

- A. Preferential, because the payment was made within 90 days of the filing of the petition.
- B. Preferential, because the payment enabled Olsen to receive more than the other general creditors.
- C. Not preferential, because Hall is presumed insolvent when the payment was made.
- D. Not preferential, because the payment was a contemporaneous exchange for new value.

The correct answer is (D). *(CPA, adapted)*

REQUIRED: The reason for the status of a transfer as preferential or nonpreferential.

DISCUSSION: A preference voidable by the trustee is a transfer (1) of the debtor's property, (2) on an antecedent debt, (3) made within 90 days before filing, (4) made while the debtor was insolvent, and (5) enabling the creditor to receive more than (s)he would have in the bankruptcy proceeding. One important exception is a contemporaneous exchange in which the debtor receives new value, even if from a creditor.

Answers (A) and (B) are incorrect because, although a general requirement for classifying the transfer as preferential is stated, the transfer was in a contemporaneous exchange between the debtor and another (even a creditor) for new value. Answer (C) is incorrect because, for purposes of preferential status of a transfer, the debtor is presumed insolvent during the 90 days preceding the filing of the petition, and insolvency at the time of transfer is a requirement for voidable preferential status.

26. The credit card payment was

- A. Preferential, because the payment was made within 90 days of the filing of the petition.
- B. Preferential, because the payment was on account of an antecedent debt.
- C. Not preferential, because the payment was for a consumer debt of less than $600.
- D. Not preferential, because the payment was less than 40% of the original debt.

The correct answer is (C). *(CPA, adapted)*
REQUIRED: The reason for the status of a transfer as preferential or nonpreferential.
DISCUSSION: A preference voidable by a trustee is a transfer (1) of the debtor's property to or for the benefit of a creditor, (2) on an antecedent debt, (3) made within 90 days before filing, (4) made while the debtor was insolvent, and (5) enabling the creditor to receive more than (s)he would have in the bankruptcy proceeding. One exception is payment of up to $600 on a consumer debt within the 90-day period.
Answers (A) and (B) are incorrect because, although a general requirement for status of the transfer as a voidable preference is stated, the transfer was a remittance of not more than $600 on a consumer debt. Answer (D) is incorrect because the percentage of the original debt remitted is not determinative of whether the exception to voidability of the preference applies. The otherwise voidable transfer may not be set aside by the trustee if it is not more than $600 and on a consumer debt.

27. Which of the following transfers by a debtor, within 90 days of filing for bankruptcy, could be set aside as a preferential payment?

- A. Making a gift to charity.
- B. Paying a business utility bill.
- C. Borrowing money from a bank secured by giving a mortgage on business property.
- D. Prepaying an installment loan on inventory.

The correct answer is (D). *(CPA, adapted)*
REQUIRED: The reason for the status of a transfer as preferential or nonpreferential.
DISCUSSION: A preferential transfer is one made for the benefit of a creditor, within 90 days prior to filing the petition, on account of an antecedent debt. The transfer must have been effected when the debtor was insolvent, and it must result in the creditor receiving a larger portion of its claim than it otherwise would have received as a distribution in the bankruptcy proceeding. A prepayment is on account of an existing debt and an avoidable preference.
Answer (A) is incorrect because a gift to a charity is not on account of an antecedent debt. Answer (B) is incorrect because remittance of accounts payable in the ordinary course of the debtor's business is not a voidable preference. Answer (C) is incorrect because a contemporaneous exchange between the debtor and another, even a creditor, for new value, may not be set aside. Also, this is a transfer of a security interest which enables the debtor to acquire the new property.

28. Which of the following types of claims would be paid first in the distribution of a bankruptcy estate under the liquidation provisions of Chapter 7 of the Federal Bankruptcy Code if the petition was filed July 15, 1999?

- A. A secured debt properly perfected on March 20, 1999.
- B. Inventory purchased and delivered August 1, 1999.
- C. Employee wages due April 30, 1999.
- D. Federal tax lien filed June 30, 1999.

The correct answer is (A). *(CPA, adapted)*
REQUIRED: The claim that will be paid first.
DISCUSSION: The Bankruptcy Reform Act of 1978 classifies creditors into several categories according to the priority of their claims against the debtor. It also states that secured creditors' claims will be satisfied in full up to the extent of the value of the security before unsecured creditors' claims will be considered. To the extent the security is insufficient, the secured creditor becomes an unsecured creditor. The tax lien, even if a security interest, would have lower priority than the secured debt perfected earlier.
Answers (B) and (C) are incorrect because secured claims are satisfied before unsecured claims are satisfied. Answer (D) is incorrect because, even if it is a secured claim, the first perfected of two security interests has priority.

29. In a voluntary bankruptcy proceeding under Chapter 7 of the Federal Bankruptcy Code, which of the following claims incurred within 90 days prior to filing will be paid first?

- A. Unsecured federal taxes.

- B. Utility bills up to $1,000.

- C. Voluntary contributions to employee benefit plans.

- D. Employee vacation and sick pay up to $4,300 per employee.

The correct answer is (D). *(CPA, adapted)*
REQUIRED: The correct statement about the relative priorities of claims in a bankruptcy liquidation distribution.
DISCUSSION: The Bankruptcy Code sets priorities for claims. All of the claims at a higher-priority level must be satisfied in full before any lower-priority claims. Secured claims must be satisfied in full before any unsecured claims may be paid. The list of priorities among unsecured claims is as follows: administrative expenses, unsecured claims arising in the ordinary course of business after the petition was filed but before the order for relief was granted, unsecured claims up to $4,300 for wages earned by an individual within 90 days before filing, unsecured claims for contributions to employee benefit plans, unsecured claims of grain producers and fishermen, unsecured claims of depositors of money for the purchase of undelivered consumer goods, and unsecured tax claims of governmental units. Employee vacation and sick pay are a form of compensation (wages).
Answers (A), (B), and (C) are incorrect because all of these debts have a lower relative priority in bankruptcy liquidation distribution.

30. Peters Co. repairs computers. On February 9, 1999, Stark Electronics Corp. sold Peters a circuit tester on credit. Peters executed an installment note for the purchase price, a security agreement covering the tester, and a financing statement that Stark filed on February 11, 1999. On April 13, 1999, creditors other than Stark filed an involuntary petition in bankruptcy against Peters. What is Stark's status in Peters's bankruptcy?

- A. Stark will be treated as an unsecured creditor because Stark did not join in the filing against Peters.

- B. Stark's security interest constitutes a voidable preference because the financing statement was not filed until February 11.

- C. Stark's security interest constitutes a voidable preference because the financing statement was filed within 90 days before the bankruptcy proceeding was filed.

- D. Stark is a secured creditor and can assert a claim to the circuit tester that will be superior to the claims of Peters's other creditors.

The correct answer is (D). *(CPA, adapted)*
REQUIRED: The status in bankruptcy of a seller with a perfected security interest.
DISCUSSION: Stark obtained a purchase-money security interest in equipment which was perfected because Stark filed a financing statement within 10 days. Thus, Stark has a valid security interest that cannot be avoided by the trustee, and Stark may assert a claim to the machine.
Answer (A) is incorrect because a secured creditor does not forfeit priority by not joining in filing an involuntary petition in bankruptcy. Answers (B) and (C) are incorrect because Stark's security interest is not a voidable preference even though the transaction occurred within 90 days of bankruptcy. The transaction constituted the giving of new value (the machine) for the debt and security interest, and was not on account of an antecedent debt.

31. Eagle Corp. is a general creditor of Dodd. Dodd filed a petition in bankruptcy under the liquidation provisions of the Bankruptcy Code. Eagle wishes to have the bankruptcy court either deny Dodd a general discharge or not have its debt discharged. The discharge will be granted, and it will include Eagle's debt even if

- A. Dodd filed and received a previous discharge in bankruptcy under the liquidation provisions within 5 years of the filing of the present petition.

- B. Eagle's debt is unscheduled.

- C. Eagle was a secured creditor not fully satisfied from the proceeds obtained on disposition of the collateral.

- D. Dodd unjustifiably failed to preserve the records from which Dodd's financial condition might be ascertained.

The correct answer is (C). *(CPA, adapted)*
   REQUIRED: The circumstance that will allow discharge of a general creditor's debt.
   DISCUSSION: Chapter 7 contains the liquidation provisions of the Bankruptcy Code. The nature of the debt or debtor or the debtor's conduct may prevent discharge of all or specific debts. However, secured creditor status does not guarantee full satisfaction of a debt. If the secured claim is not fully satisfied by the proceeds resulting from the sale of collateral, the unsatisfied portion of the debt may still be discharged.
   Answer (A) is incorrect because discharge will not be granted if an objection is made and the debtor was granted a discharge under Chapter 7 in a case commenced within 6 years of the petition in the current case. Answer (B) is incorrect because unscheduled debts are not discharged. Answer (D) is incorrect because the debtor's unjustifiable failure to preserve the debtor's financial records is reason to deny discharge of all indebtedness.

32. Rolf, an individual, filed a voluntary petition in bankruptcy. A general discharge in bankruptcy will be denied if Rolf

- A. Negligently made preferential transfers to certain creditors within 90 days of filing the petition.

- B. Unjustifiably failed to preserve his books and records.

- C. Filed a fraudulent federal income tax return 2 years prior to filing the petition.

- D. Obtained a loan by using financial statements that he knew were false.

The correct answer is (B). *(CPA, adapted)*
   REQUIRED: The action that is grounds for denying a general discharge in bankruptcy.
   DISCUSSION: Discharge will be denied if the debtor conceals or destroys property with the intent to hinder, delay, or defraud a creditor, or fails to adequately explain the loss of assets. Similarly, unjustifiable or fraudulent concealment or destruction of the debtor's financial records is a basis for denying discharge of indebtedness.
   Answer (A) is incorrect because preferential transfers resulting from the debtor's negligence will result only in avoidance of the transfers. Answers (C) and (D) are incorrect because the debtor's fraudulent actions may result in denial of discharge of the specific debts but will not affect the general discharge.

33. Which of the following acts by a debtor could result in a bankruptcy court's revoking the debtor's discharge?

I. Failure to list one creditor

II. Failure to answer correctly material questions on the bankruptcy petition

- A. I only.

- B. II only.

- C. Both I and II.

- D. Neither I nor II.

The correct answer is (B). *(CPA, adapted)*
   REQUIRED: The true statement about a discharge in bankruptcy.
   DISCUSSION: Fraud or dishonesty committed by the debtor during the bankruptcy proceedings is the basis for revocation of discharge by the bankruptcy court. Revocation may occur after a request by either the trustee or a creditor, notice, and a hearing. The time limit is 1 year. A debt to a creditor omitted from the list of creditors is not discharged, but proof of dishonesty or fraud is required to revoke the general discharge.
   Answers (A), (C), and (D) are incorrect because the general discharge may be revoked on account of debtor misconduct. However, more than failure to list one creditor, especially if inadvertent, is generally required.

34. Which of the following claims will not be discharged in bankruptcy?

- A. A claim that arises from alimony or maintenance.

- B. A claim that arises out of the debtor's breach of a contract.

- C. A claim brought by a secured creditor that remains unsatisfied after the sale of the collateral.

- D. A claim brought by a judgment creditor whose judgment resulted from the debtor's negligent operation of a motor vehicle.

The correct answer is (A). *(CPA, adapted)*
REQUIRED: The claim not dischargeable in bankruptcy.
DISCUSSION: Certain claims cannot be discharged in bankruptcy. Among these claims are debts arising from alimony, maintenance, or child support.

Answer (B) is incorrect because a claim arising from a debtor's breach of contract may be discharged in bankruptcy. Only specific debts are nondischargeable. Answer (C) is incorrect because unsatisfied claims of secured creditors will be discharged. A bankruptcy discharge includes all debts except those specified as nondischargeable. Answer (D) is incorrect because debts arising from operating a motor vehicle are dischargeable unless the operator was under the influence of alcohol.

35. In general, which of the following debts will be discharged under the voluntary liquidation provisions of the Bankruptcy Code?

- A. A debt incurred more than 90 days before the filing of the bankruptcy petition and not disclosed in the petition.

- B. Income taxes due as the result of filing a fraudulent return 7 years prior to the filing of the bankruptcy petition.

- C. A debt arising before the filing of the bankruptcy petition caused by the debtor's negligence.

- D. Alimony payments owed to the debtor's spouse under a separation agreement entered into prior to the filing of the bankruptcy petition.

The correct answer is (C). *(CPA, adapted)*
REQUIRED: The debt that will be discharged under the voluntary liquidation provisions.
DISCUSSION: Discharge in a voluntary liquidation proceeding may be denied based on certain acts or circumstances of the debtor or the nature of particular debts if a trustee or creditor objects to the discharge. Examples of debts that will be statutorily denied a discharge include penalties imposed by government entities, unpaid taxes, and unpaid child support. A debt that was the result of negligence, e.g., from a malpractice claim, in contrast to willful or malicious activity, is dischargeable.

Answer (A) is incorrect because debts not disclosed in the petition are not discharged unless the creditor had knowledge of the petition. Answer (B) is incorrect because ordinarily, the only tax debts that will not be discharged are income taxes due from the filing of a tax return within the last 3 years. However, any debt that was incurred by fraudulent means will not be discharged regardless of the time the return was filed. Answer (D) is incorrect because the Code specifically denies a discharge for any unpaid alimony or child support.

Questions 36 through 41 are based on the following information. On May 1, 1999, Dart Inc., a closely held corporation, was petitioned involuntarily into bankruptcy under the liquidation provisions of Chapter 7 of the Federal Bankruptcy Code. Dart contested the petition.

Dart has not been paying its business debts as they become due, has defaulted on its mortgage loan payments, and owes back taxes to the IRS. The total cash value of Dart's bankruptcy estate after the sale of all assets and payment of administration expenses is $100,000.

A listing of Dart's creditors is presented in the next column.

- Fracon Bank is owed $75,000 principal and accrued interest on a mortgage loan secured by Dart's real property. The property was valued at and sold, in bankruptcy, for $70,000.
- The IRS has a $12,000 recorded judgment for unpaid corporate income tax.
- JOG Office Supplies has an unsecured claim of $3,000 that was timely filed.
- Nanstar Electric Co. has an unsecured claim of $1,200 that was not timely filed.
- Decoy Publications has a claim of $14,000, of which $2,000 is secured by Dart's inventory that was valued and sold, in bankruptcy, for $2,000. The claim was timely filed.

36. Which of the following creditors must join in the filing of the involuntary petition?

I. JOG Office Supplies
II. Nanstar Electric Co.
III. Decoy Publications

    A. I, II, and III.

    B. II and III.

    C. I and II.

    D. III only.

The correct answer is (D). *(CPA, adapted)*
REQUIRED: The creditor(s) required to join in the filing of an involuntary petition.
DISCUSSION: Under Chapter 7, an involuntary bankruptcy petition may be filed by a single creditor if (s)he has $10,775 or more of unsecured claims and there are fewer than 12 creditors. Only Decoy must file to meet the statutory requirement.
Answers (A), (B), and (C) are incorrect because only Decoy is required to file an involuntary petition in bankruptcy. JOG and Nanstar may also file, but they must join with Decoy to meet the $10,775 minimum unsecured debt requirement.

37. Which of the following statements would correctly describe the result of Dart's opposing the petition?

    A. Dart will win because the petition should have been filed under Chapter 11.

    B. Dart will win because there are not more than 12 creditors.

    C. Dart will lose because it is not paying its debts as they become due.

    D. Dart will lose because of its debt to the IRS.

The correct answer is (C). *(CPA, adapted)*
REQUIRED: The result of the debtor's opposing the petition.
DISCUSSION: There are two grounds for filing an involuntary petition for bankruptcy under Chapter 7. Either the debtor is not paying its bills on time or a receiver took possession of all or most of the debtor's property in order to enforce a lien against the property within 120 days of the filing of the petition. Because Dart was not paying its bills when they became due, Dart will lose.
Answer (A) is incorrect because the involuntary petition could have been filed under Chapters 7 or 11 because Dart is not paying its bills on time. Answer (B) is incorrect because a debtor having 12 or fewer creditors and unsecured claims of at least $10,775 may be petitioned into bankruptcy. Answer (D) is incorrect because IRS claims against Dart will not cause Dart to lose in its opposition to being placed into involuntary bankruptcy, even though the IRS claims against Dart cannot be discharged.

38. Which of the following events will follow the filing of the Chapter 7 involuntary petition?

	A Trustee Will Be Appointed	A Stay against Creditor Collection Proceedings Will Go into Effect
A.	Yes	Yes
B.	Yes	No
C.	No	Yes
D.	No	No

The correct answer is (A). *(CPA, adapted)*
REQUIRED: The event(s) following the filing of an involuntary petition.
DISCUSSION: When an involuntary petition in bankruptcy is filed, the court issues an order of relief, which suspends almost all legal action and collection activities against the debtor. An interim trustee is also appointed by the bankruptcy judge to manage the bankruptcy estate assets. The interim trustee serves until replaced by a permanent trustee elected by the creditors.
Answers (B), (C), and (D) are incorrect because, upon the filing of an involuntary petition under Chapter 7, a stay of all collection proceedings occurs and a trustee is appointed.

Questions 39 through 41 are based on the
information preceding question 36 on page 347.

39. Assuming the bankruptcy estate was distributed, what dollar amount would Nanstar Electric Co. receive?

A. $0

B. $800

C. $1,000

D. $1,200

The correct answer is (A). *(CPA, adapted)*

REQUIRED: The amount distributed to an unsecured creditor who did not file a timely claim.

DISCUSSION: Nanstar will not receive any money when the bankruptcy estate is distributed because all the other parties either have claims secured by collateral or filed their claims in a timely manner. Because Nanstar did not properly file its claim in bankruptcy, it is placed behind all other creditors. Nanstar will receive no payment because the other claims against the bankruptcy estate exceed the estate's cash value.

Answers (B), (C), and (D) are incorrect because there will not be any money left in the bankruptcy estate to pay an unsecured general creditor. Since Nanstar did not preserve its right to repayment by filing a timely claim, it is considered a second-tier general creditor and is in the last class of creditors to be paid.

40. Assuming the bankruptcy estate was distributed, what total dollar amount would Fracon Bank receive on its secured and unsecured claims?

A. $70,000

B. $72,000

C. $74,000

D. $75,000

The correct answer is (C). *(CPA, adapted)*

REQUIRED: The amount distributed to a creditor with secured and unsecured claims.

DISCUSSION: Fracon would receive a total of $74,000 because $5,000 of its $75,000 claim against Dart was not recovered when the real estate was sold for $70,000. Therefore, Fracon had a secured claim of $70,000, which will be fully paid, and an unsecured claim of $5,000. Since there was not enough money in the bankruptcy estate to pay the general unsecured claims in full, each creditor received a pro rata share of the remaining proceeds. Since Fracon held one-fourth of the valid claims ($5,000 ÷ $20,000), it received one-fourth of the remaining proceeds of $16,000, or $4,000, to settle its unsecured claim.

Answers (A), (B), and (D) are incorrect because Fracon receives a pro rata share of the remaining proceeds for its unsecured claim. The second claim is paid in full.

41. Assuming the bankruptcy estate was distributed, what dollar amount would the IRS receive?

A. $0

B. $8,000

C. $10,000

D. $12,000

The correct answer is (D). *(CPA, adapted)*

REQUIRED: The amount distributed to the IRS by the bankruptcy estate.

DISCUSSION: The IRS would receive the full amount owed to it. Taxes are a priority claim that is paid in full before any general unsecured creditors are paid. Therefore, the proceeds from the sale of Dart's assets would go to the IRS after satisfying the secured claims and any other unsecured claims having a higher priority than unpaid taxes.

Answer (A) is incorrect because debts owed to the IRS for unpaid income taxes have priority over general unsecured creditors. Answers (B) and (C) are incorrect because the unpaid portion of the income taxes owed to the IRS is a priority unsecured claim. After secured claims, the taxes will be paid in full before payment on any general unsecured claims.

42. By signing a reaffirmation agreement on April 15, 1999, a debtor agreed to pay certain debts that would be discharged in bankruptcy. On June 20, 1999, the debtor's attorney filed the reaffirmation agreement and an affidavit with the court indicating that the debtor understood the consequences of the reaffirmation agreement. The debtor obtained a discharge on August 25, 1999. The reaffirmation agreement would be enforceable only if it was

A. Made after discharge.

B. Approved by the bankruptcy court.

C. Not for a household purpose debt.

D. Not rescinded before discharge.

The correct answer is (D). *(CPA, adapted)*
   REQUIRED: The enforceable reaffirmation of debt.
   DISCUSSION: To be enforceable, a reaffirmation agreement must conspicuously state the debtor's right of rescission. The debtor has the right to rescind the reaffirmation until the later of the discharge or 60 days after the agreement is filed with the court.
   Answer (A) is incorrect because, to be legally enforceable, the reaffirmation agreement must be entered into prior to the general discharge in bankruptcy. Answer (B) is incorrect because, in the alternative, the reaffirmation may be accompanied by an affidavit filed by the debtor's attorney that the debtor voluntarily and knowingly entered into the agreement and it caused no undue hardship. Answer (C) is incorrect because almost any debt, including one incurred for household purposes, may be reaffirmed.

C. Reorganizations and Adjustments

43. Under Chapter 11 of the Federal Bankruptcy Code, which of the following would not be eligible for reorganization?

A. Retail sole proprietorship.

B. Advertising partnership.

C. CPA professional corporation.

D. Savings and loan corporation.

The correct answer is (D). *(CPA, adapted)*
   REQUIRED: The entity ineligible for Chapter 11 reorganization.
   DISCUSSION: Reorganization under Chapter 11 of the Bankruptcy Code is available only for eligible debtors. These include partnerships and corporations, railroads, and any person that may be a debtor under Chapter 7 (but not stock or commodity brokers). Ineligible debtors under Chapter 7 include municipalities, insurance companies, banks, credit unions, and savings and loan associations.
   Answers (A), (B), and (C) are incorrect because individuals, partnerships, and corporations are generally eligible for Chapter 11 reorganization.

44. A reorganization under Chapter 11 of the Federal Bankruptcy Code requires all of the following except the

A. Liquidation of the debtor.

B. The filing of a reorganization plan.

C. Confirmation of the reorganization plan by the court.

D. Opportunity for each class of claims to accept the reorganization plan.

The correct answer is (A). *(CPA, adapted)*
   REQUIRED: The item not required for reorganization under the Bankruptcy Code.
   DISCUSSION: A reorganization proceeding under Chapter 11 of the Bankruptcy Code provides for payment of creditors and restructuring of the debtor's finances. It permits his/her business to be continued. Chapter 11 enables restructuring instead of liquidation.
   Answer (B) is incorrect because a reorganization plan is required for a Chapter 11 restructuring. Answer (C) is incorrect because the plan must be confirmed by the bankruptcy court. Answer (D) is incorrect because a plan which the bankruptcy judge finds is fair and equitable may be confirmed without approval of all classes of creditors (a cram-down plan).

45. Which of the following statements is correct with respect to the reorganization provisions of Chapter 11 of the Federal Bankruptcy Code?

   A.   A trustee must always be appointed.

   B.   The debtor must be insolvent if the bankruptcy petition was filed voluntarily.

   C.   A reorganization plan may be filed by a creditor anytime after the petition date.

   D.   The commencement of a bankruptcy case may be voluntary or involuntary.

The correct answer is (D). *(CPA, adapted)*
   REQUIRED: The correct statement concerning reorganization under Chapter 11.
   DISCUSSION: A reorganization proceeding under Chapter 11 of the Bankruptcy Code provides for payment of creditors and restructuring of the debtor's finances, but permits his/her business to be continued. The commencement of a proceeding may be voluntary or involuntary.
   Answer (A) is incorrect because the debtor is usually permitted to operate the business during a Chapter 11 proceeding. A trustee would be appointed only for cause, including dishonesty or incompetence. Answer (B) is incorrect because insolvency is not a condition precedent to a voluntary Chapter 11 petition. Answer (C) is incorrect because the debtor has the exclusive right to file a plan during the 120 days after the order for relief. A trustee, but not a creditor, may file a plan at any time.

46. Robin Corp. incurred substantial operating losses for the past 3 years. Unable to meet its current obligations, Robin filed a petition for reorganization under Chapter 11 of the Federal Bankruptcy Code. Which of the following statements is correct?

   A.   The creditors' committee must select a trustee to manage Robin's affairs.

   B.   The reorganization plan may be filed only by Robin.

   C.   A creditors' committee, if appointed, will consist of unsecured creditors.

   D.   Robin may continue in business only with the approval of a trustee.

The correct answer is (C). *(CPA, adapted)*
   REQUIRED: The correct statement concerning a Chapter 11 reorganization.
   DISCUSSION: Under Chapter 11, the debtor may operate its own business as debtor-in-possession. A trustee would be appointed only for cause shown, such as dishonesty or mismanagement. Chapter 11 requires that, as soon as practicable after an order for relief has been granted, the court appoint a committee of unsecured creditors. It may participate in formulating the plan of reorganization.
   Answer (A) is incorrect because the committee may request, for cause, that the court appoint a trustee. Appointment of a trustee is within the court's discretion. Answer (B) is incorrect because a trustee, if one has been appointed, may file a plan at any time. Answer (D) is incorrect because the debtor continues to operate the business unless, for good cause shown, the court appoints a trustee.

47. Under Chapter 11 of the Federal Bankruptcy Code, which of the following actions is necessary before the court may confirm a reorganization plan?

   A.   Provision for full payment of administration expenses.

   B.   Acceptance of the plan by all classes of claimants.

   C.   Preparation of a contingent plan of liquidation.

   D.   Appointment of a trustee.

The correct answer is (A). *(CPA, adapted)*
   REQUIRED: The prerequisite to court confirmation of a reorganization plan.
   DISCUSSION: The debtor generally has the exclusive right to file a reorganization plan during the 120 days after the order of relief. To be effective, the plan must be confirmed by the bankruptcy court. The plan must provide for full payment of administration expenses.
   Answer (B) is incorrect because a plan which is fair and equitable may be confirmed without approval of all classes of creditors (a cram-down plan). Answer (C) is incorrect because Chapter 11 enables restructuring instead of liquidation. A contingent plan of liquidation is not required. Answer (D) is incorrect because the court has discretion to appoint a trustee when there is evidence of dishonesty or mismanagement. But normally the debtor remains in possession of his/her assets and continues to operate the business.

48. Under the reorganization provisions of Chapter 11 of the Federal Bankruptcy Code, after a reorganization plan is confirmed and a final decree closing the proceedings entered, which of the following events usually occurs?

- A. A reorganized corporate debtor will be liquidated.

- B. A reorganized corporate debtor will be discharged from all debts except as otherwise provided in the plan and applicable law.

- C. A trustee will continue to operate the debtor's business.

- D. A reorganized individual debtor will not be allowed to continue in the same business.

The correct answer is (B). *(CPA, adapted)*
   REQUIRED: The status of a debtor after completing a Chapter 11 reorganization.
   DISCUSSION: At the conclusion of Chapter 11 proceedings, a corporate debtor is discharged from most debts of the business. Exceptions include debts that are provided for in the plan of reorganization approved by the creditors and certain nondischargeable debts.
   Answer (A) is incorrect because a Chapter 11 reorganization allows the debtor's finances to be restructured, not liquidated. Answer (C) is incorrect because a trustee is usually not appointed to run the debtor's business. The creditors' committee may, however, request the court to appoint a trustee. Appointment of a trustee is within the court's discretion. Answer (D) is incorrect because a reorganized individual debtor may continue in the same business without any restrictions.

Questions 49 and 50 are based on the following information. Strong Corp. filed a voluntary petition in bankruptcy under the reorganization provisions of Chapter 11 of the Federal Bankruptcy Code. A reorganization plan was filed and agreed to by all necessary parties. The court confirmed the plan and a final decree was entered.

---

49. Which of the following parties ordinarily must confirm the plan?

	One-half of the Secured Creditors	Two-thirds of the Shareholders
A.	Yes	Yes
B.	Yes	No
C.	No	Yes
D.	No	No

The correct answer is (D). *(CPA, adapted)*
   REQUIRED: The party(ies) that must confirm a reorganization plan.
   DISCUSSION: Creditors and shareholders accept, not confirm, plans of reorganization under Chapter 11. Confirmation is performed by the bankruptcy court. In voting to accept or reject a plan, only one-half of any class of creditors that votes is needed to accept provided the voting creditors represent two-thirds of the dollar amount of the claims that actually voted. A class of shareholders accepts the plan if two-thirds of the interests that actually voted approve the plan.
   Answers (A), (B), and (C) are incorrect because in no event is one-half of a class of secured creditors or two-thirds of the shareholders required to accept the plan. Rather, the above percentages apply to the creditors and shareholders that actually voted.

50. Which of the following statements best describes the effect of the entry of the court's final decree?

- A. Strong Corp. will be discharged from all its debts and liabilities.

- B. Strong Corp. will be discharged only from the debts owed creditors who agreed to the reorganization plan.

- C. Strong Corp. will be discharged from all its debts and liabilities that arose before the date of confirmation of the plan.

- D. Strong Corp. will be discharged from all its debts and liabilities that arose before the confirmation of the plan, except as otherwise provided in the plan, the order of confirmation, or the Bankruptcy Code.

The correct answer is (D). *(CPA, adapted)*
   REQUIRED: The correct statement concerning the bankruptcy court's final decree.
   DISCUSSION: Under a Chapter 11 reorganization, generally, an entity that is granted Chapter 11 status will be discharged from its debts and liabilities that occurred prior to the confirmation of the plan, except as provided for in the plan of reorganization, the order of confirmation, or the Bankruptcy Code. The effect of confirmation is to make the plan binding on all parties and to grant the debtor a discharge from claims not protected by the plan.
   Answer (A) is incorrect because the debtor will not be discharged from all its debts because a Chapter 11 bankruptcy proceeding allows a business to continue to operate after it has been reorganized and has restructured its debts and finances. Answer (B) is incorrect because the confirmation of a reorganization plan binds all parties in interest. Creditors may be forced to accept a reorganization plan approved by the court. Answer (C) is incorrect because, under a reorganization plan, the debtor may not be discharged from certain debts prior to the confirmation of the plan if the court finds it is inequitable to discharge those debts or if a discharge of debts is prohibited by the Code.

OOF QUESTION 1 *(CPA, adapted)* 15-25 minutes

On April 15, 1999, Wren Corp., an appliance whole-saler, was petitioned involuntarily into bankruptcy under the liquidation provisions of Chapter 7 of the Federal Bankruptcy Code. When the petition was filed, Wren's creditors included

Secured Creditors	Amount Owed
Fifth Bank -- 1st mortgage on ware-house owned by Wren	$50,000
Hard Manufacturing Corp. -- perfected purchase money security interest in inventory	30,000
TVN Computers, Inc. -- perfected security interest in office computers	15,000

Unsecured Creditors	Amount Owed
IRS -- 1997 federal income taxes	$20,000
Acme Office Cleaners -- services for January, February, and March 1999	750
Ted Smith (employee) -- February and March 1999 wages	2,400
Joan Sims (employee) -- March 1999 commissions	1,500
Power Electric Co. -- electricity charges for January, February, and March 1999	600
Soft Office Supplies -- supplies purchased in 1998	2,000

The following transactions occurred before the bankruptcy petition was filed:

- On December 31, 1998, Wren paid off a $5,000 loan from Mary Lake, the sister of one of Wren's directors.

- On January 30, 1999, Wren donated $2,000 to Universal Charities.

- On February 1, 1999, Wren gave Young Finance Co. a security agreement covering Wren's office fixtures to secure a loan previously made by Young.

- On March 1, 1999, Wren made the final $1,000 monthly payment to Integral Appliance Corp. on a 2-year note.

- On April 1, 1999, Wren purchased from Safety Co. a new burglar alarm system for its factory, for $5,000 cash.

All of Wren's assets were liquidated. The warehouse was sold for $75,000, the computers were sold for $12,000, and the inventory was sold for $25,000. After paying the bankruptcy administration expenses of $8,000, secured creditors, and priority general creditors, there was enough cash to pay each nonpriority general creditor $0.50 on the dollar.

Required

a. Items 1 through 5 represent the transactions that occurred before the filing of the bankruptcy petition. For each transaction, determine if the transaction would be set aside as a preferential transfer by the bankruptcy court. Indicate (A) if the transaction would be set aside or (B) if the transaction would not be set aside.

1. Payment to Mary Lake
2. Donation to Universal Charities
3. Security agreement to Young Finance Co.
4. Payment to Integral Appliance Corp.
5. Purchase from Safety Co.

b. Items 6 through 10 represent creditor claims against the bankruptcy estate. Select from List I each creditor's order of payment in relation to the other creditors named in items 6 through 10. Each answer may be used only once.

		List I
6.	Bankruptcy administration expense	A. First
7.	Acme Office Cleaners	B. Second
8.	Fifth Bank	C. Third
9.	IRS	D. Fourth
10.	Joan Sims	E. Fifth

c. Items 11 through 15 also represent creditor claims against the bankruptcy estate. For each of the creditors listed in items 11 through 15, select from List II the amount that creditor will receive. Each answer may be used once, more than once, or not at all.

		List II
11.	TVN Computers, Inc.	A. $ 0
12.	Hard Manufacturing Corp.	B. $ 300
13.	Ted Smith	C. $ 600
14.	Power Electric Co.	D. $ 1,000
15.	Soft Office Supplies	E. $ 1,200
		F. $ 2,000
		G. $ 2,200
		H. $ 2,400
		I. $12,000
		J. $13,500
		K. $15,000
		L. $25,000
		M. $27,500
		N. $30,000

Knowledge Tested

1. Identifying voidable preferences
2. Priority between claims
3. Amounts payable on competing claims

Authors' Comments

Carefully apply the facts to the outline definition of a voidable preference and exceptions, remembering that Wren must have assets in addition to the receipts from sale of the warehouse, computers, and inventory. Part b. simply requires you to place each claim in the priority hierarchy of the Bankruptcy Code. Part c. superimposes that higher-priority claims are paid in full before lower-priority claims receive anything and that payment is pro rata to claims of equal priority.

1. The correct answer is (A).
    DISCUSSION: The payment to Mary Lake is a preferential transfer since she is considered an insider. A trustee may set aside preferential transfers and grants of security interests to insiders within 1 year before the petition, provided the debtor was insolvent at the time of the transfer or grant.

2. The correct answer is (B).
    DISCUSSION: The donation to Universal Charities would not be a preferential transfer because it was not for, or on account of, an antecedent debt.

3. The correct answer is (A).
    DISCUSSION: The security agreement to Young Finance Co. is a preferential transfer because it was for the benefit of Young, it was given when Wren was insolvent, and it was given within the 90 days prior to filing the bankruptcy petition to secure an antecedent debt.

4. The correct answer is (B).
    DISCUSSION: The payment to Integral Appliance Corp. is not a preferential transfer because it is a payment in the ordinary course of business to a supplier.

5. The correct answer is (B).
    DISCUSSION: The purchase from Safety Co. is not a preferential transfer because asset transfers for current consideration are not voidable by the trustee.

6. The correct answer is (B).
    DISCUSSION: The bankruptcy administration expense has first priority among the priority creditors. Therefore, once the secured creditors have been paid, the bankruptcy administration expense is paid off. Hence, for this example, they rank second in priority.

7. The correct answer is (E).
    DISCUSSION: The debt owed to Acme Office Cleaners ranks last (fifth) in priority since Acme is a general (nonpriority unsecured) creditor.

8. The correct answer is (A).
    DISCUSSION: Fifth Bank has first priority since it is a secured creditor.

9. The correct answer is (D).
    DISCUSSION: The IRS ranks next to last (fourth) since it is a priority creditor. It ranks ahead of Acme because Acme is a general creditor, and after bankruptcy administration expenses and Joan Sims because claims of federal, state, and local taxes rank last among priority creditors.

10. The correct answer is (C).
    DISCUSSION: Joan Sims ranks third because she is a priority creditor. Employees' wages of up to $4,300 earned within the 90 days preceding bankruptcy qualify as a priority claim. Her claim ranks lower than bankruptcy administrative expenses among the priority creditors.

11. The correct answer is (J).
    DISCUSSION: TVN Computers is a secured creditor and is therefore paid in full to the extent that the underlying collateral (office computers) is sufficient. TVN is then a general creditor as to the deficiency. Therefore, TVN will receive $12,000 and $0.50 on the dollar for the $3,000 deficiency, or $13,500 [$12,000 + ($3,000 x $0.50)].

12. The correct answer is (M).
    DISCUSSION: Hard Manufacturing is also a secured creditor and will therefore receive $25,000 and $0.50 on the dollar for the $5,000 deficiency, or $27,500 [$25,000 + ($5,000 x $0.50)].

13. The correct answer is (H).
    DISCUSSION: Ted Smith is a priority creditor on wages up to $4,300. He is paid a total of $2,400.

14. The correct answer is (B).
    DISCUSSION: The Power Electric Company is a general creditor and will receive only $0.50 on the dollar for its $600 claim, or $300 ($600 x $0.50).

15. The correct answer is (D).
    DISCUSSION: Soft Office Supplies is a general creditor and will receive only $0.50 on the dollar for its $2,000 claim, or $1,000 ($2,000 x $0.50).

OOF QUESTION 2 *(CPA, adapted)* 10-15 minutes

a. On June 1, 1999, Rusk Corp. was petitioned involuntarily into bankruptcy. At the time of the filing, Rusk had the following creditors:

- Safe Bank, for the balance due on the secured note and mortgage on Rusk's warehouse
- Employee salary claims
- 1998 federal income taxes due
- Accountant's fees outstanding
- Utility bills outstanding

Prior to the bankruptcy filing, but while insolvent, Rusk engaged in the following transactions:

- On February 1, 1999, Rusk repaid all corporate directors' loans made to the corporation.

- On May 1, 1999, Rusk purchased raw materials for use in its manufacturing business and paid cash to the supplier.

Required

Items 1 through 5 relate to Rusk's creditors and the February 1 and May 1 transactions. For each item, select (A) if only statement I is correct, select (B) if only statement II is correct, select (C) if both statements I and II are correct, or select (D) if neither statement I nor II is correct.

A. I only.
B. II only.
C. Both I and II.
D. Neither I nor II.

1. I. Safe Bank's claim will be the first paid of the listed claims because Safe is a secured creditor.
    II. Safe Bank will receive the entire amount of the balance of the mortgage due as a secured creditor regardless of the amount received from the sale of the warehouse.

2. I. The employee salary claims will be paid in full after the payment of any secured party.
    II. The employee salary claims up to $4,300 per claimant will be paid before payment of any general creditors' claims.

3. I. The claim for 1998 federal income taxes due will be paid as a secured creditor claim.
    II. The claim for 1998 federal income taxes due will be paid prior to the general creditor claims.

4. I. The February 1 repayments of the directors' loans were preferential transfers even though the payments were made more than 90 days before the filing of the petition.
    II. The February 1 repayments of the directors' loans were preferential transfers because the payments were made to insiders.

5. I. The May 1 purchase and payment was not a preferential transfer because it was a transaction in the ordinary course of business.
    II. The May 1 purchase and payment was a preferential transfer because it occurred within 90 days of the filing of the petition.

Knowledge Tested

Bankruptcy: priority of claims and voidable transfers

Authors' Comments

The rules of bankruptcy proceedings are tested frequently. This question tests your knowledge of voidable transfers and priorities of claims. These rules should be committed to memory.

1. The correct answer is (A).
DISCUSSION: The priority among classes of creditors in bankruptcy is as follows: secured creditors, priority creditors, and general creditors. Secured creditors have property rights in collateral pledged by the debtor that are not affected by the bankruptcy proceedings.

2. The correct answer is (B).
DISCUSSION: The classes of priority claims listed in order of rank are as follows: administrative expenses; claims of unsecured tradespeople extending credit in the ordinary course of business in the gap between filing of the petition and appointment of the trustee; wages of employees of the debtor earned within 90 days preceding the earlier of filing or cessation of the debtor's business; certain contributions owed to employee benefit plans; claims of unpaid grain producers and fishermen up to $4,300; consumer claims of $1,950 for services or goods not delivered; and claims for federal, state, and local taxes.

The employee wage claims are limited by the priority rules to $4,300, and any unpaid balances are treated as general claims.

3. The correct answer is (B).
DISCUSSION: Federal income taxes are a priority claim under the Bankruptcy Code and are not a secured creditor claim. Priority claims are paid after secured claims and prior to payment of any general creditor claims.

4. The correct answer is (C).
DISCUSSION: A trustee in bankruptcy may void and recall a transfer of property by the debtor while the debtor is insolvent, if it results in a creditor's receiving a larger portion of an antecedent debt than (s)he would have received under a distribution in bankruptcy. Only transfers made within 90 days of the filing of the petition are voidable unless the transfer is to an insider. Transfers to insiders are preferential if made within 1 year prior to filing of the petition. The act presumes insolvency (liabilities exceed assets) for the 90 days prior to the date of filing. To void an insider transaction occurring more than 90 days before filing, the trustee must prove insolvency at the time of the transfer.

5. The correct answer is (A).
DISCUSSION: Nonpreferential transfers include payment of a debt in the ordinary course of the debtor's business, payment up to $600 on a consumer debt within 90 days of filing, and a contemporaneous exchange of property for new value.

ESSAY QUESTION 1 *(CPA, adapted)* 15-20 minutes

Techno, Inc. is a computer equipment dealer. On March 3, 1999, Techno was 4 months behind in its payments to Allied Building Maintenance, Cleen Janitorial Services, Inc., and Jones and Associates, CPAs, all of whom provide monthly services to Techno. In an attempt to settle with these three creditors, Techno offered each of them a reduced lump-sum payment for the past-due obligations and full payment for future services. These creditors rejected Techno's offer, and on May 9, 1999, Allied, Cleen, and Jones filed an involuntary petition in bankruptcy against Techno under the provisions of Chapter 7 of the Federal Bankruptcy Code. At the time of the filing, Techno's liability to the three creditors was $11,500, all of which was unsecured.

Techno, at the time of the filing, had liabilities of $229,000 (owed to 23 creditors) and assets with a fair market value of $191,000. During the entire year before the bankruptcy filing, Techno's liabilities exceeded the fair market value of its assets.

Included in Techno's liabilities was an installment loan payable to Dollar Finance Co., properly secured by cash registers and other equipment.

The bankruptcy court approved the involuntary petition.

On May 21, 1999, Dollar filed a motion for relief from automatic stay in bankruptcy court claiming it was entitled to take possession of the cash registers and other equipment securing its loan. Dollar plans to sell these assets immediately and apply the proceeds to the loan balance. The fair market value of the collateral is less than the loan balance, and Dollar claims to lack adequate protection. Also, Dollar claims it is entitled to receive a priority distribution, before distribution to unsecured creditors, for the amount Techno owes Dollar less the proceeds from the sale of the collateral.

During the course of the bankruptcy proceeding, the following transactions were disclosed:

- On November 6, 1998, Techno paid its president $9,900 as repayment of an unsecured loan made to the corporation on October 18, 1996.

- On March 19, 1999, Techno paid $1,150 to Alexis Computers, Inc. for eight color computer monitors. These monitors were delivered to Techno on March 9, 1999, and placed in inventory.

- On February 12, 1999, Techno bought a new delivery truck from Maple Motors for $7,900 cash. On the date of the bankruptcy filing, the truck was worth $7,000.

Required

Answer the following questions and give the reasons for your conclusions.

a. What circumstances had to exist to allow Allied, Cleen, and Jones to file an involuntary bankruptcy petition against Techno?

b. 1. Will Dollar's motion for relief be granted?
2. Will Dollar's claim for priority be approved by the bankruptcy court?

c. Are the payments to Techno's president, Alexis, and Maple preferential transfers?

Knowledge Tested

1. Requirements of an involuntary petition
2. Secured creditor's rights to
   a. Order for relief
   b. Priority
3. Identification of preferential transfers

Authors' Comments

You should mechanically apply rules in the outline to respond to this essay question. When a debtor has 12 or more creditors, any three or more of them with unsecured claims of $10,775 in the aggregate can file an involuntary petition. Collection activity is automatically stayed on filing. However, an order for relief from the stay will be issued to the extent of a security interest when the debt equals or exceeds the value of the collateral. (The secured creditor is entitled to the security anyway.) The secured creditor is treated as a general creditor to the extent of debt which exceeds the collateral's value. Voidable preferences have been consistently tested. What constitutes a preferential transfer and who is an insider must simply be memorized from the outline and applied. Note that a corporation does not receive a general discharge under Chapter 7. Instead, its assets are merely liquidated.

Note: If you wish to work additional essay material, see part b. of the essay question in Study Unit 10.

AICPA Unofficial Answer

a. An involuntary bankruptcy petition may be filed against a debtor having 12 or more creditors by at least three creditors having unsecured claims of at least $10,775, provided the debtor is not paying its undisputed debts as they become due.

b. 1. Dollar's motion for relief will be granted. Dollar's claim that it is entitled to take possession of the collateral securing its loan is correct. Generally, a secured creditor is allowed to take possession of its collateral if there is no equity in it (that is, the debt balance exceeds the collateral's fair value). Dollar would then be entitled to sell the collateral and apply the proceeds to the loan balance.

2. Dollar's claim that it is entitled to a priority distribution to the extent that the proceeds from the sale of its collateral are less than the loan balance will not be approved by the bankruptcy court. Dollar is entitled to the value of its collateral. As to any deficiency, Dollar will be treated as an unsecured creditor.

c. The payment to Techno's president would be regarded as a preferential transfer. Because the president is an "insider," any payments made on the unsecured loan during the year preceding the bankruptcy filing would be considered a preferential transfer.

The payment to Alexis was not a preferential transfer because it was made in the ordinary course of business and under ordinary business terms.

The $7,900 payment to Maple for the truck was not a preferential transfer because it was not made on account of an antecedent debt but as a contemporaneous exchange for new value.

ESSAY QUESTION 2 *(CPA, adapted)* 10-15 minutes

On May 1, 1999, Fender was petitioned involuntarily into bankruptcy under the liquidation provisions of Chapter 7 of the Federal Bankruptcy Code.

At the time of the filing, Fender listed the following unsecured claims:

Judgment creditor	$4,000
Alimony and maintenance due under divorce decree	1,200
IRS assessment for 1997 taxes	500
1998 state income tax due	750
Unsecured personal loan from Ranch Bank	7,000
Rent on residence	2,000
Electricity charges on residence	200
Ace Finance Co.	1,000

The Ace Finance Company claim is listed because, in 1997, Fender agreed to guarantee payment of a $1,000 loan by Ace Finance Co. to Fender's cousin. The cousin defaulted on the loan and Ace is attempting to collect from Fender.

Fender had not been paying bills and obligations as they became due.

Required

a. State and name the fewest number of creditors that would have had to join in filing the petition against Fender and give the reasons for your decision.

b. State which two creditor claims would be satisfied first from the bankruptcy estate and give the reasons for your decision.

c. State which claim(s) would not be discharged if unpaid and give the reasons for your decision.

d. State whether Fender's guarantee of payment would be discharged and give the reasons for your decision.

Knowledge Tested

1. Requirements of an involuntary petition
2. Priority among claims
3. Debts which are discharged
4. Effect of guarantor's discharge

Authors' Comments

This question illustrates the usual pattern of bankruptcy problems in requiring a determination of the requirements in number of creditors and amounts necessary to file an involuntary petition, identification of priority creditors and amounts, and recognition of which debts are not discharged. These rules should be committed to memory. The effect of a guarantor's discharge, voidable preferences, and questions on orders of relief should be anticipated frequently.

AICPA Unofficial Answer

a. Ranch Bank and the judgment creditor would have had to join in the involuntary bankruptcy petition. Fender had fewer than 12 unsecured creditors. Under the liquidation provisions of Chapter 7 of the Federal Bankruptcy Code, when there are fewer than 12 creditors, one or more creditors having unsecured claims in the aggregate of $10,775 must join in the petition.

b. The IRS assessment for 1997 taxes and the 1998 state income taxes due would be paid first.

Taxes due and owing within 3 years of the bankruptcy, unless evidenced by liens or otherwise secured, are considered to be general creditor claims but are accorded a higher priority than the other general creditor claims.

c. The alimony and maintenance claim and the tax claims would not be discharged if unpaid because these are two of the ten types of debts specifically excepted from discharge under the Federal Bankruptcy Code.

d. Fender's discharge in bankruptcy would discharge the guarantee of payment given to Ace. Bankruptcy of the guarantor is an absolute defense to payment, and any claim by Ace would be included in the bankruptcy proceeding and would be discharged.

CHAPTER V
GOVERNMENT REGULATION OF BUSINESS

These three study units will constitute approximately 15% of the Business Law section.

STUDY UNIT 12: SECURITIES

18 pages of outline
47 multiple-choice questions
2 OOFs and 1 essay

A. *Federal Securities Regulation*
B. *Securities Registration*
C. *Reporting Requirements*
D. *Exemptions*
E. *Resale of Restricted Securities*

Two major federal securities acts provide the foundation of the law of securities: the 1933 Securities Act and the 1934 Securities Exchange Act. In addition, state securities laws are important. The purpose of the 1933 Securities Act is to regulate the initial offering of securities by requiring the filing of a registration statement with the SEC prior to sale or offer to sell. The 1934 Securities Exchange Act governs dealings in securities subsequent to their initial issue. The examination questions emphasize the purposes of the various securities laws, the registration process, the securities and transactions which are exempt from registration, the all-inclusive antifraud provisions, and the accountant's role and liability in securities transactions.

A. **Federal Securities Regulation** requires full disclosure of all material facts relevant to the issuance of securities and a continuous reporting of information pertaining to the issuer in order to maintain an informed investing public.

1. The foundation of federal securities law consists primarily of two major federal securities acts:

    a. The **Securities Act of 1933**
    b. The **Securities Exchange Act of 1934**

2. The 1933 act has two fundamental objectives. Both pertain to the initial offering of securities for sale to the public:

    a. Disclosure to potential investors of all material information
    b. Prevention of fraud

3. The 1934 act deals primarily with secondary distribution (resale) of securities. The fundamental provisions of the 1934 act involve the following:

    a. Registration of all regulated public companies with the Securities and Exchange Commission (the SEC)

    b. Periodic reporting, which requires providing up-to-date statements of all business operations and matters potentially affecting the value of securities

    c. Sweeping antifraud provisions

    d. Imposing liability on insiders for short-swing profits

4. **State Law**. Each state has adopted its own securities laws (blue-sky laws).

    a. Federal securities laws do not preempt the existence of blue-sky laws.

    b. Both federal and state securities laws must generally be complied with.

        1) State statutes may require more detailed disclosure than federal statutes.

    c. A Uniform Securities Act was proposed in 1956. Many states have utilized it as a model for their blue-sky laws.

5. The **Securities and Exchange Commission (SEC)** is an administrative agency provided for by the Securities Exchange Act of 1934. It is an independent quasi-judicial agency charged with responsibility to enforce and administer the federal securities laws.

    a. The SEC has broad power to investigate violations of federal securities laws, to hold formal hearings, to subpoena witnesses, to require the production of documents, and to issue orders, e.g., suspending or expelling broker-dealers.

        1) A final order of the SEC may be appealed to the United States circuit courts for judicial review.

    b. The SEC may bring an action in federal court to enjoin violations.

        1) A person or firm that violates an injunction may be held in contempt of court and may be fined, imprisoned, or both.

        2) The SEC may also request that the court appoint independent directors or a special agent to ensure full cooperation.

    c. The SEC has no power to prosecute criminal violations. The SEC informs the Department of Justice of suspected criminal activity. The latter handles any criminal prosecution.

6. **Definition of a Security**. The term security encompasses almost any offering that constitutes an investment:

    > *Note, stock, treasury stock, bond, debenture, evidence of indebtedness, certificate of interest or participation in any profit-sharing agreement, collateral-trust certificate, preorganization certificate or subscription, transferrable share, investment contract, voting-trust certificate, certificate of deposit for a security, fractional undivided interest in oil, gas, or other mineral rights, any put, call, straddle, option or privilege on any security or, in general, any interest or instrument commonly known as a "security," or any certificate of interest or participation in, temporary or interim certificate for receipt for, guarantee of, or warrant or right to subscribe to or purchase, any of the foregoing.* (1933 act)

    a. The U.S. Supreme Court held (in the *Howey* case) that the fundamental test of whether something is a security requires analysis of whether

        1) A person invests in a common enterprise,

        2) With a reasonable expectation of profits,

        3) To be derived solely from the efforts of a promoter or third party but not from the investors themselves.

    b. Recently the courts have held an investment to be a security even though the investor provided some of his/her own effort.

7. **Securities markets** may have a physical location, such as the New York Stock Exchange (NYSE) or no physical location, such as the over-the-counter (OTC) market.

    a. The Securities Exchange Act of 1934 defines the term exchange as "any organization, association, or group of persons, whether incorporated or unincorporated, which constitutes, maintains, or provides a marketplace or facilities for bringing together purchasers and sellers of securities."

    b. In an NYSE transaction, a buyer or seller goes to an investment firm, which acts as a broker (a retailer). (Neither the 1933 act nor the SEC Rules promulgated thereunder define "broker.") The broker transmits the customer's order to the exchange floor. Only a registered specialist (a wholesaler) may buy or sell as a dealer in the security. The broker's firm charges the client a commission on the transaction.

    c. In an OTC transaction, anyone can act as a dealer. The OTC market has no physical facilities and no registered specialists. Most transactions are accomplished via computer network and telephone. Brokers in the OTC generally specialize in a specific type of security or they deal in most, if not all, the securities of a specific locale, e.g., Boston Stock Exchange. If a client orders a specific stock on the OTC market and the dealer does not deal in the specific stock, the dealer will act as broker and obtain the security from another dealer.

    d. The 1934 act states that it is unlawful for anyone, including a broker/dealer, to use the mails or any other instrumentality of interstate commerce, e.g., telephone, to consummate a security transaction using the facilities of an exchange unless the exchange is registered with the SEC as a "national securities exchange."

8. **Parties to an Issuance**. Every person involved in the initial offering and sale of securities is governed by the 1933 act. These persons might be classified as issuers, underwriters, or dealers.

    a. An **issuer** is the individual or the business organization offering a security for sale to the public (generally, to raise money).

        1) **Control person**. An issuer may also include one who directly or indirectly controls or is under common control with the issuer. A control person has power to influence the policies or management, by stock ownership, position, contract, or otherwise; e.g., an officer who owns 10% (or less) of the stock could be a control person.

    b. An **underwriter** is any person who participates in the original offering of securities from the issuer with a view to distributing these securities.

        1) Corporate officers and directors who participate in the distribution of securities may be considered underwriters if they receive commissions or payments in addition to their usual salaries.

        2) A person is an underwriter if (s)he purchases securities from a control person with the intention of offering, selling, or distributing such securities.

        3) Merrill Lynch is an example of a company that serves as an underwriter.

    c. A **broker** buys from an underwriter to effect business transactions for the accounts of others.

    d. A **dealer** buys from an underwriter to resell to the general public for his/her own account.

        1) A dealer is any person who is engaged in the business of offering, selling, dealing, or otherwise trading in securities issued by another.

9. Stop and review! You have completed the outline for this subunit. Study multiple-choice questions 1 through 4 beginning on page 375.

B.   Securities Registration. The 1933 act is essentially a disclosure statute. The act prohibits the offer or sale through the use of the mails or any means of interstate commerce of any security unless a registration statement for that security is in effect or an exemption from registration is applicable. Thus, any offer or sale of a security to the public requires registration unless a specific exemption applies.

1.   To comply with the 1933 act, an issuer of securities must prepare and file both a registration statement (Form S-1) and a prospectus.

2.   A **registration statement** is a complete disclosure to the SEC of all material information with respect to the issuance of the specific securities.

3.   The purpose of registration is to provide adequate and accurate disclosure of financial and other pertinent information with which potential investors may evaluate the merits of the securities. Generally, registration calls for

    a.   A description of

        1)   The registrant's business and property

        2)   The significant provisions of the security to be offered for sale and its relationship to registrant's other capital securities

        3)   Management

    b.   The most recent audited financial statements

    NOTE: The principal purposes for which the offering's proceeds will be used are included in the disclosure.

4.   The SEC does not make any judgment on the financial health of an investment nor guarantee the accuracy of the information contained in the registration statement.

    a.   Registration does not insure investors against loss.

    b.   The SEC has approved new rules to protect investors in low-cost, high-risk penny stocks.

        1)   Brokers that sell penny stocks must provide potential investors with documents which explain the (high) risks of the investments.

        2)   The broker must inform the investor of the

            a)   Commission structure
            b)   Current price of any stock
            c)   Value of the investor's holdings once each month

    c.   In response to the Emerging Company Marketplace initiative of the American Stock Exchange (Amex), the SEC has proposed rules to simplify the process for small businesses to register securities.

        1)   Simpler financial reporting forms are being devised to reduce registration costs.

        2)   The rules would facilitate active auction-type trading of stock of emerging companies on a branch of the Amex. This could provide greater access to capital than the OTC markets did.

5.   There are three distinct periods during the registration process:

    a.   The **prefiling period**, during which time the issuer may engage in preliminary negotiations and agreements with underwriters. Offers to buy or sell securities are prohibited during this period.

    b.   The **waiting period** begins when the registration statement is filed. During this time, it is still illegal to sell a security; however, it is not illegal to make an oral offer to buy or sell a security.

1) To condition the market for later purchases, **tombstone ads** may be published. Such an ad is not to be construed as an offer to sell or a solicitation to buy. It merely contains the

   a) Name and the business of the issuer

   b) Amount of securities being offered and the price if known

   c) Approximate date when the offering will be made

   d) Person by whom the orders will be executed and from whom a prospectus may be obtained

2) Dealers may make offers to buy from underwriters subject to later acceptance.

3) There are no restrictions on oral offers made during the waiting period.

4) A **preliminary (red herring) prospectus** is another common type of offering material that may be issued during the waiting period. It contains much of the same basic information about the issuer as the final prospectus.

   a) The outside front cover page of the preliminary prospectus must bear, in red ink and printed in large type, the title "preliminary prospectus," the date of issuance, and a required legend.

   b) The legend states, among other things, that a registration statement has been filed, it has not yet become effective, the securities may not be sold and offers to buy may not be accepted prior to the time the registration statement becomes effective, and the prospectus shall not constitute an offer to sell or the solicitation of an offer to buy.

5) The SEC uses the 20-day waiting period to review the registration statement. If the registration statement substantially complies with the statutory requirements, the SEC will issue detailed comments as to how the statement can be brought into conformity. Any amendments to the registration statement have the effect of starting the 20-day waiting period anew.

c. The **post-effective period**. Once a registration statement becomes effective, the underlying securities may be sold.

   1) A registration becomes effective 20 days (the waiting period) after it is filed, unless the SEC accelerates the effective date or issues a "bedbug" letter.

   2) In a bedbug letter, the SEC has determined that the registration statement is poorly prepared or fails to adequately disclose information.

   3) An issuer who receives a bedbug letter must either redraft the registration statement or cancel the public offering.

   4) If the registration is not rewritten, the SEC will issue a stop order preventing registration.

6. A **prospectus** must be furnished to any interested investor. Its purpose is to supply sufficient facts to make an informed investment decision.

   a. The prospectus contains material information (financial and otherwise) with respect to the offering and the issuer.

   b. An issuer can amend a prospectus by filing 10 copies of the modified document with the SEC.

c.   The 1933 act requires that any prospectus that is still in use more than 9 months after its effective date must be updated so that the information contained in the prospectus is not more than 16 months old.

    1)   Developments after the effective date which would render the existing prospectus misleading give rise to an obligation to update the prospectus without regard to the 9-month period.

        a)   EXAMPLE: A pending lawsuit, if successful, would result in a liability equal to 25% of the corporation's current net asset value. If there is a legal and factual basis for the claim, Issuer must update the prospectus disclosing the contingent liability without regard to the 9-month period.

d.   A disclaimer must be printed on the outside front cover of the prospectus in boldface type. It must state that the securities have not been approved or disapproved by the SEC nor has the SEC passed upon the accuracy or adequacy of this prospectus. The disclaimer also must state that any representation to the contrary is a criminal offense.

7.   Generally, the entire allotment of securities is made available for purchase on the effective date of the registration statement. An exception is a shelf registration of securities.

a.   In a **shelf registration**, the registration statement is filed, but the securities are put "on the shelf" until the most opportune time for offering is determined.

    1)   Shelf registrations allow issuers to respond rapidly to volatile market conditions.

b.   A shelf registration is available only to the most established issuers.

c.   The information in the original registration (shelf registration) must be continuously updated to be accurate and current.

8.   **Civil Liability**. The 1933 act imposes a number of sanctions for noncompliance with the act's requirements with respect to submission of a registration statement.

a.   Under the 1933 act, any person who acquires a security issued pursuant to a misstatement or omission of a material fact may sue

    1)   The issuer

    2)   Every person who signed the registration statement

    3)   Every director of the corporation or partner in the partnership issuing the security

    4)   Experts who participated in preparation of the registration statement, e.g., accountants, engineers, lawyers

    5)   Every underwriter

b.   To recover under Section 11, an investor must prove

    1)   The investor acquired a security subject to registration.
    2)   The registration statement contained a material misstatement or omission.
    3)   The investor incurred a loss.

NOTE: That there was an intent to deceive, reliance, or privity or that the plaintiff gave value need not be shown. The term material has been interpreted by the courts to mean "a fact which if it had been correctly stated or disclosed would have deterred or tended to deter the average prudent investor from purchasing the securities in question."

c. Exercising due diligence with respect to the material information contained in the registration statement is a defense to liability.

    1) Due diligence is the standard of care exercised by a prudent person in the management of his/her own affairs.

    2) Due diligence is no defense for an issuer.

d. Liability under Section 11 is for the amount paid for the security minus either its value at the time of suit or the price for which it was sold.

e. Additionally, the 1933 act imposes civil liability if the required registration was not made, if a registered security was sold but a prospectus was not delivered or was not current, or if an offer to sell was made before a required registration.

    1) Liability is absolute. The acquirer of an unregistered security has the right to tender it back to the seller and recover the purchase price. If the original purchaser no longer owns the security, (s)he may recover monetary damages from the seller.

    2) Exemptions from liability apply for short-term commercial paper and small or limited offerings.

    3) Certain transactions involving issuers, dealers, and private offerings are also exempted.

9. **Antifraud Provisions**. The 1933 act contains sweeping antifraud provisions applying to all securities, registered and exempt.

a. Liability is imposed on any person who offers or sells a security by means of a prospectus or oral communication that contains a material misstatement or omission.

    1) The seller's liability extends only to the immediate purchaser.

    2) The offeror or seller may avoid liability by proving that (s)he did not know and, in the exercise of reasonable care, should not have known of the misstatement or omission.

    3) If the seller is liable, the purchaser may recover the net amount paid for the security. The purchaser must, however, tender the security.

        a) If the purchaser no longer owns the security, (s)he may recover monetary damages from the seller.

b. Liability is imposed on any person who participates in a fraudulent interstate securities transaction (registered or exempt). An offeror or seller will be liable if, when using any means of transportation or communication in interstate commerce or the mails, it does any one of the following acts:

    1) Employs any device, scheme, or artifice to defraud

    2) Obtains money or property by means of any untrue statement of a material fact or any omission of a material fact

    3) Engages in any transaction, practice, or course of business that operates or would operate as a fraud or deceit on the purchaser

c. Criminal sanctions are imposed on any person who willfully violates any of the provisions of the 1933 act or the rules and regulations promulgated by the SEC pursuant to the 1933 act. Conviction carries a penalty of a fine of not more than $10,000, up to 5 years of imprisonment, or both.

10. Stop and review! You have completed the outline for this subunit. Study multiple-choice questions 5 through 15 beginning on page 376.

C.   Reporting Requirements. The Securities Exchange Act of 1934 governs dealings in securities subsequent to their initial issue (resales). The 1934 act established the SEC to ensure fair trading practices for investors.

1.   The 1934 act has the following purposes:

   a.   To regulate the securities exchanges and markets
   b.   To make available information about issuers to investors
   c.   To prevent fraud in the marketplace
   d.   To regulate proxy solicitations and tender offers

2.   The SEC is authorized by the 1934 act to impose sanctions to enforce its provisions. The SEC may deny, suspend, or revoke registration, or it may order a suspension of trading in the securities. These sanctions are in addition to civil and criminal liability imposed by the federal securities laws.

3.   The 1934 act requires all regulated publicly held companies to register with the SEC. Registration is required of all companies (covered corporations) that

   a.   List shares on a national securities exchange or on NASDAQ, or

   b.   Have at least 500 shareholders of equity securities and total gross assets of at least $10 million.

4.   Also required to report under the 1934 act are

   a.   An issuer that has registered securities under the 1933 act
   b.   National securities exchanges

5.   Registration and reporting requirements under the 1934 act are in addition to, not a substitute for, those under the 1933 act.

6.   These registrations are one-time registrations that apply to an entire class of securities.

7.   Registration requires disclosure of the following:

   a.   Corporate organization
   b.   Financial structure
   c.   Description of all securities
   d.   Names of officers, directors, underwriters, and all 10% security holders
   e.   Description of the nature of the business
   f.   Financial statements
   g.   A description of bonus and profit-sharing arrangements

8.   Following registration, an issuer must file with the SEC specific up-to-date and accurate reports, including

   a.   **Annual reports** filed on **Form 10-K**, which must be certified by an independent public accountant. The report must be filed within 90 days after the end of the reporting company's current fiscal year.

      1)   The 10-K report contains information about the entity's business activities, securities, management-related parties, disagreement concerning accounting and disclosure, audited financial statements, etc. For example, it would list newly appointed officers.

   b.   **Quarterly reports** filed on **Form 10-Q** for each of the first three fiscal quarters of each fiscal year of the reporting company. These must be filed within 45 days of the end of the appropriate quarter. They need not be certified.

       c.   **Current reports** filed on **Form 8-K** describing material events such as changes in control of the reporting company or the acquisition or disposition of a significant amount of assets other than in the ordinary course of business. Form 8-K must be filed within the first 10 days of the month after certain material events occur.

9.   Any director, officer, or owner of more than 10% of any class of equity securities of a covered corporation must file an individual report with the SEC disclosing his/her holdings.

10. **Proxy Solicitation.** The 1934 act makes it unlawful for any person to solicit any proxy with respect to any registered security in contravention of SEC rules and regulations.

       a.   A **proxy** is a power of attorney given by a shareholder to a third party authorizing the party to exercise the voting rights of the shares.

       b.   Solicitation includes any request for a proxy or any request to revoke a proxy.

       c.   Proxies are generally utilized in either of two instances:

            1)   Management seeks proxies from its shareholders to defeat a proposal placed before the board.

            2)   Proxies are given by shareholders for the purpose of electing new directors or preventing a takeover of a company.

       d.   Ten days prior to mailing a proxy statement to shareholders, the issuing company must file a copy with the SEC.

       e.   SEC rules require the solicitor of proxies to furnish shareholders with

            1)   All material information concerning the matter subject to vote
            2)   A form to indicate their agreement or disagreement

       f.   Proxies solicited for the purpose of voting for directors must be accompanied by an annual report.

       g.   Any issuer that supplies a proxy that is misleading may be civilly liable to any person who relies on it in the purchase or sale of registered securities.

            1)   A court may enjoin a shareholder meeting or any action(s) taken at a meeting if it finds a violation of the proxy filing or disclosure requirements.

            2)   Other remedies may include rescission and attorney fees.

       h.   If an eligible shareholder requests that a certain proposal be placed on the agenda at an annual meeting, management must include the proposal in its proxy statement.

            1)   An eligible shareholder owns no less than the lesser of 1% or $1,000 in market value of the security for at least 1 year prior to submitting the proposal.

            2)   SEC rules allow management to exclude shareholder proposals for any of the following reasons:

                a)   The issue relates to ordinary business operations.

                b)   The issue is not significantly related to the issuing company's business.

                c)   Under state law, the subject is not a proper one for shareholder consideration.

                d)   The issue would violate state or federal law if included in a proxy proposal passed by the board.

11. **Tender Offers**. In 1968, Congress enacted the **Williams Act**. It amended the 1934 act to extend reporting and disclosure requirements to tender offers and other block acquisitions.

    a.   A **tender offer** is a general invitation by an individual or a corporation to all shareholders of another corporation to tender their shares for a specified price.

    b.   Any person or group that acquires more than 5% of a class of registered securities is required, within 10 days of the tender offer, to file a statement with both of the following:

        1)   The SEC

        2)   The issuing company

    c.   If the tender offer is a hostile (unsolicited) tender offer, the target corporation must also file a statement with the SEC.

        1)   The target has 10 days in which to respond to the bidder's tender offer.

        2)   A bidder's tender offer must be kept open for at least 20 business days.

    d.   It is a criminal offense for any person to misstate or omit a material fact or to engage in fraudulent or deceptive practices in connection with a tender offer.

    e.   Courts have upheld various strategies implemented by corporate management to counter hostile tender offers, e.g., flip-in rights.

12. **Insiders** are directors, officers, and any person owning 10% or more of the stock of a corporation listed on a national stock exchange or registered with the SEC.

    a.   Officers who merely run day-to-day operations but who do not perform policy-making functions are not insiders.

    b.   With respect to the securities, these insiders are required to report to the SEC their

        1)   Holdings

        2)   Transactions (promptly)

        3)   Purchases and sales made within 6 months before or after becoming an insider

    c.   **Short-swing trading** occurs when any insider sells such stock within 6 months from the date of its purchase or purchases such stock within 6 months from the date of sale of the stock.

        1)   The corporation is entitled to recover any and all profits realized by the insider from short-swing trading.

        2)   Profits are calculated by matching the highest sales price against the lowest purchase price within 6 months of each other.

        3)   Losses cannot be offset against profits.

13. **Antifraud Provisions**. Section 10(b) of the 1934 act and SEC Rule 10b-5 make it unlawful for any person to employ, in connection with the purchase or sale of any security, any manipulative or deceptive device or any contrivance in contravention of SEC rules and regulations.

    a.   **Section 10(b)** of the 1934 act is a catchall provision dealing with securities fraud.

    b.   **Rule 10b-5** states

> *It shall be unlawful for any person directly or indirectly, by use of any means or instrumentality of interstate commerce, or the mails, or of any facility of any national securities exchange,*
>
>   *(1) To employ any device, scheme, or artifice to defraud,*
>
>   *(2) To make any [oral or written] untrue statement of a material fact or to omit to state a material fact necessary in order to make the statements made, in light of the circumstances under which they were made, not misleading, or*
>
>   *(3) To engage in any act, practice, or course of business which operates or would operate as a fraud or deceit upon any person in connection with the purchase or sale of any security.*

    c.   Rule 10b-5 applies to the purchase or sale of any security,

        1)   Whether or not the security is registered

        2)   Whether the issue is publicly traded or closely held

        3)   Whether the purchase or sale is part of an initial issuance or a secondary distribution

       NOTE: There are no exemptions.

    d.   Any buyer or seller of any security who suffers a monetary loss may sue

        1)   To rescind the transaction
        2)   To receive monetary damages

       NOTE: Most courts hold that punitive damages are not recoverable in civil actions for violations of the securities laws.

    e.   The plaintiff purchaser or seller must prove a misstatement or an omission, or misleading conduct, that

        1)   Is material
        2)   Is made with scienter (intent to deceive)
        3)   Is relied upon in connection with the purchase or sale of a security

    f.   Rule 10b-5 is read very broadly by the courts. Any person who violates the antifraud provisions of Rule 10b-5, whether or not (s)he actively participated in the purchase or sale of the security, may be sued.

        1)   The rule has been applied to hold underwriters, dealers, accountants, and lawyers accountable.

        2)   All that is required is that the party's activity be connected with the purchase or sale of the security.

    g.   **Materiality** under the 1934 act is the same as materiality under the 1933 act; i.e., "a fact which if it had been correctly stated would have deterred or tended to deter the average prudent investor from purchasing the security in question."

    h.   Rule 10b-5 has been most frequently applied to insider trading, corporate misstatements, and corporate mismanagement.

i.   **Insider trading** is the purchase or sale of securities by individuals who have access to nonpublic information and have a fiduciary obligation to shareholders and potential investors. Insiders may include not only officers and directors but also consultants, lawyers, engineers, auditors, bankers, reporters, public relations advisors, and personnel in government agencies who are entrusted with confidential corporate information for corporate purposes.

   1)   Insider trading can represent a form of fraud. A person with nonpublic, confidential, inside information may not use that information to trade with a person who does not possess the information. (S)he must either disclose the information before trading or refrain from trading.

   2)   EXAMPLE: An insider makes a public statement concerning loss of a source of supply critical to its manufacturing process. The market responds with a reduced price for the company's stock. Insider purchases stock at the reduced price. Insider knew at the time of the announcement or purchase that a contract was being negotiated which would secure an alternative source of the critical supply.

   3)   A person who receives nonpublic material information from an insider is a **tippee**. The **tipper** is liable for profits made by the tippee. If the tippee tips others, the original tipper (insider) and the tippee (now a tipper) are liable.

   4)   Under the **Insider Trading Sanctions Act of 1984**, the SEC may bring a civil action against anyone violating the 1934 act by "purchasing or selling a security while in possession of material nonpublic information." Civil penalties sought by the SEC for insider trading may not exceed three times the profit gained or loss avoided. For a **controlling person**, the maximum is the greater of $1 million or three times the profit gained or loss avoided. A bounty of up to 10% of recovered penalties may be paid to an informant.

   5)   A private suit for damages may be brought by a contemporaneous purchaser or seller of shares of the same class.

j.   **Fraud on the Market Theory**. Courts follow a presumption that the selling price of a security reflects market response (or lack of response) to statements. This presumption of reliance might be rebutted by evidence that at the time of sale the "market" or the purchaser was actually informed of the statement.

k.   **Corporate misstatement**. Claims by buyers or sellers of securities claiming reliance and damages under Section 10b often arise in connection with releases of information by corporations through reports, speeches, or public announcements or press releases concerning mergers, research developments, rumors, or other matters of material importance. The **Private Securities Litigation Reform Act of 1995** provides a **safe harbor** from liability for companies that make such statements if they are accompanied by meaningful cautionary statements that identify risk factors that could cause actual results to differ from those in the statement.

14. **Criminal Liability**. The 1934 act provides for criminal sanctions for willful violations of its provisions or rules adopted under it.

a.   Officers, directors, and even advisors have been found guilty of crimes, e.g., for failure to disclose important facts to shareholder-investors.

b.   Liability is imposed for false material statements in applications, reports, documents, registration statements, and press releases.

    c.   For an individual, the penalty is a fine not to exceed $1 million or 10 years in prison, or both. An individual who proves (s)he had no knowledge of the rule or regulation will not be imprisoned. If the person is not a natural person (e.g., a corporation), the maximum fine is $2.5 million.

15.   The **Foreign Corrupt Practices Act (FCPA)** was enacted in 1977 as an amendment to the Securities Exchange Act of 1934. The FCPA is designed to prevent secret payments of corporate funds for purposes that Congress has determined to be contrary to public policy.

    a.   The act prohibits a domestic concern, including any person acting on its behalf, whether or not doing business overseas and whether or not registered with the SEC, from offering or authorizing corrupt payments to any

        1)   Foreign official
        2)   Foreign political party or official thereof
        3)   Candidate for political office in a foreign country

        NOTE: Only political payments to foreign officials are prohibited. Payments paid to foreign business owners or corporate officers are not addressed by the FCPA.

    b.   **Corrupt payments** are payments the purpose of which is to induce the recipient to act or refrain from acting so that the domestic concern might obtain or retain business.

        1)   The FCPA prohibits a mere offer or promise of a bribe, even if it is not consummated.

        2)   The FCPA prohibits payment of anything of value. *De minimis* gifts and tokens of hospitality are excepted.

        3)   Payments are prohibited if the person making them knew or should have known that some or all of them would be used to influence a governmental official.

    c.   Foreign officials do not include clerical or ministerial employees.

        1)   EXAMPLE: Payments made to a clerk in order to speed up the processing of goods through customs may not be prohibited by the act.

        2)   Such payments are not prohibited so long as the recipient has no discretion in carrying out a governmental function.

    d.   To deter violations, the FCPA imposes record-keeping and internal control requirements on firms that are subject to the reporting provisions of the Securities Exchange Act, i.e., public nonexempt companies.

    e.   The SEC can bring only civil actions to enforce the FCPA. The Department of Justice has authority to proceed civilly and criminally. Substantial penalties may be imposed.

        1)   Officers, directors, and employees or agents may be liable for fines of up to $100,000 or imprisonment of up to 5 years, or both. Corporations are subject to a fine of up to $2 million.

16.   Stop and review! You have completed the outline for this subunit. Study multiple-choice questions 16 through 28 beginning on page 380.

D.   Exemptions. The 1933 act exempts a number of specific securities from its registration requirements.

1.   The 1933 act generally exempts transactions by any person other than an issuer, an underwriter, or a dealer.

   a.   This rule applies to securities transactions involving ordinary investors selling on their own account.

   b.   A controlling person is treated as an issuer.

   c.   The exemption does not apply to restricted securities.

2.   The 1933 act exempts the following types of securities from registration:

   a.   Securities of domestic governments used for a governmental purpose

   b.   Securities of not-for-profit organizations

   c.   Securities of domestic banks and savings and loan associations

   d.   Securities of issuers that are federally regulated common carriers

   e.   Securities issued by a receiver or trustee in bankruptcy with prior court approval

   f.   Insurance policies and annuity contracts issued by state-regulated insurance companies

   g.   Securities issued with respect to a corporate reorganization

   h.   Securities issued solely for exchange with the issuer's existing security holders if no commission is paid.

      1)   Thus, stock dividends and stock splits are generally exempt.

      2)   Also, securities issued in mergers and other reorganizations are exempt if no cash is involved and the securities are given solely for other securities.

3.   **Short-Term Commercial Paper**. The 1933 act exempts from registration any note, draft or banker's acceptance, issued to acquire working capital, that has a maturity of not more than 9 months when issued.

   a.   The exemption is not available if the proceeds are to be used for permanent purposes, such as acquisition of a manufacturing plant, or if the paper is of a type not ordinarily purchased by the general public.

4.   **Intrastate Offerings**. The 1933 act exempts from registration any security of an issuance offered and sold only to persons residing within a single state if the issuer is primarily doing business in that state and is organized or incorporated there.

   a.   The intrastate offering exemption is intended to apply to local financing by local industries through local investment.

   b.   The courts and the SEC interpret the intrastate offering exemption strictly.

   c.   **Rule 147**, promulgated by the SEC, provides a safe harbor for qualifying for the intrastate exemption. Rule 147 requires that

      1)   The issuer be incorporated or organized in the state in which the securities are issued

      2)   All of the offerees (who need not be purchasers) and purchasers be residents of the state in which the securities are issued

      3)   The issuer derive at least 80% of its annual gross revenue from the state in which the securities are issued

          4)   At least 80% of the issuer's assets be located within the state in which the securities are issued

          5)   At least 80% of the net proceeds from the issuance be used in that state

          6)   No resales be made to nonresidents during the 12-month sale period and for 9 months after the last sale.

          7)   Safeguards against interstate distributions be taken, such as

             a)   Placing a legend on the certificate stating that the securities are unregistered and resales are limited to residents only

             b)   Obtaining a written statement of residence from each purchaser

    d.   State **blue-sky laws** may require registration before the intrastate offering can be made.

5.   **Regulation A** permits an issuer that is not an investment company or subject to the reporting requirements of the 1934 act to offer up to $5 million of securities in any 12-month period without registering them. It imposes no limitations on the number and nature of investors, and resale is not restricted.

    a.   The SEC integrates all registrations and exempted offerings; e.g., three registrations of $2 million each would not qualify for exemption under Regulation A if issued within one 12-month period. Each would qualify if issued over 3 years.

          1)   The SEC adopted a rule whereby it does not integrate an offering unless it is made within 6 months before or after another offering.

          2)   EXAMPLE: Cap Corp. issues $4.5 million in cumulative 6% preferred stock on March 1, 1999. Regulation A exemption is unavailable for any further issue of more than $500,000 until September 1, 1999.

    b.   Regulation A filings are less detailed, time consuming, and costly than full registration statements.

          1)   A formal registration statement and prospectus are not required.

          2)   An offering statement must be filed with the SEC's regional office. An offering circular must also be provided to offerees and purchasers of the underlying securities. Sales may be made after the SEC has approved the filing.

          3)   An issuer under Rule 254 of Regulation A may "test the waters" prior to filing by advertisements to determine whether there is interest in the offering.

    c.   In addition to being available to issuer companies, Regulation A is available on a limited basis (up to $1.5 million) to shareholders who desire to make resales of their securities but cannot find another exemption from registration.

6.   **Regulation D** integrates certain exemptions related to small issues and small issuers.

    a.   Regulation D establishes three separate exemptions (Rules 504, 505, and 506).

    b.   Three procedural rules must generally be complied with to qualify for a Regulation D exemption.

          1)   No general solicitation or advertising is permitted (but Rule 504 is an exception).

          2)   The issuer must exercise reasonable care to ensure that the purchasers of the securities are not underwriters and that such purchasers are purchasing strictly for their own investment purposes.

          3)   The SEC must be notified within 15 days of the first offering.

      c.   The rules provide exemption only for the transactions in which securities are offered or sold by the issuer, not for the securities themselves.

          1)   The securities are **restricted securities**. Resale must be after registration or under some exemption (but Rule 504 is an exception).

          2)   Immediate rollover of the securities is precluded.

7.   **Rule 504**. In 1992, the SEC adopted the Small Business Initiatives (SBI) to allow greater access to capital markets. SBI expanded Rule 504 beyond the general requirements under Regulation D. Qualified issuers may sell up to $1 million of securities during a 12-month period to any number of purchasers without registration or specific financial information being provided, if other applicable conditions are met.

      a.   No more than $500,000 of the securities may be offered or sold without registration under state blue-sky laws.

      b.   Sales of stock to directors, officers, and employees are not counted in the $1 million limitation.

      c.   Unlike the other Regulation D exemptions, a Rule 504 offering can use general solicitation and advertising.

      d.   Nonaccredited and accredited investors may purchase the securities.

      e.   The securities issued are not restricted and can be freely traded.

      f.   The issuer cannot be an SEC-reporting company or an investment company.

8.   **Rule 505** provides exemption from registration to all issuers other than investment companies for sales of securities up to $5 million in any 12-month period.

      a.   The issue may be purchased by an unlimited number of accredited investors. Under Regulation D, an **accredited investor** is defined to include

          1)   Banks, insurance companies, registered investment companies, business development companies, and certain employee benefit plans within the meaning of Title I of the Employee Retirement Income Security Act with total assets in excess of $5 million

          2)   Private placement development companies

          3)   Charitable organizations with assets in excess of $5 million

          4)   Directors, executive officers, and general partners of the issuer who purchase at least $150,000 of securities being offered so long as the total purchase price does not exceed 20% of the purchaser's net worth

          5)   Any person who had an income over $200,000 in each of the last 2 years and who reasonably expects an income in excess of $200,000 in the current year

          6)   Any person with a net worth of at least $1 million

      b.   The issuer must reasonably believe that there are no more than 35 nonaccredited investors/offerees.

          1)   If the offering is to any nonaccredited investors, prior to the sale they must be furnished with material information about the issuer, its business, and the securities being offered.

9. Section 4(2) of the 1933 act provides an exemption from registration for "transactions by an issuer not involving any public offering." **Rule 506** under Regulation D implements this exemption. Rule 506, unlike Rules 504 and 505, has no ceiling on the amount that may be raised.

    a. Rule 506 provides a safe harbor for a private placement, but noncompliance with Rule 506 does not necessarily mean that the exemption cannot be claimed.

    b. The offering may be purchased by an unlimited number of accredited investors.

    c. The issuer must reasonably believe that there are no more than 35 nonaccredited investors/offerees.

        1) If the offering involves any nonaccredited investors, prior to the sale they must be furnished with material information about the issuer, its business, and the securities being offered.

        2) Each nonaccredited person (either alone or with his/her purchaser representative) must demonstrate to the issuer the knowledge and experience in financial and business matters needed to evaluate the merits and risks of the prospective investment. (This requirement is usually met by using a purchaser questionnaire.)

    d. Generally, the issuer requires the purchaser to sign an investment letter stating that (s)he is purchasing for investment only and not for resale.

        1) For this reason, shares issued pursuant to Rule 506 are commonly referred to as lettered stock.

10. In 1980, **Section 4(6)** was added to the Securities Act of 1933 to exempt up to $5 million of offers and sales if made only to accredited investors. The number of such investors may be unlimited, and no information is required to be given to them, but general advertising and solicitation are not permitted. Moreover, the SEC must be informed of sales under the exemption, resale is restricted, and precautions must be taken to prevent nonexempt or unregistered resales.

11. Stop and review! You have completed the outline for this subunit. Study multiple-choice questions 29 through 43 beginning on page 383.

E. **Resale of Restricted Securities**. Although private offerings may be exempt from registration, that exemption does not apply to a public resale of such securities by the purchaser.

    1. Restricted securities bear a legend that the shares of stock are restricted securities, purchased for personal investment.

        a. Restricted securities are those acquired directly or indirectly from an issuer or from a person in a control relationship with an issuer (an affiliate) in a transaction not involving a public offering.

        b. The legend limits the securities' marketability.

    2. **Rule 144**, promulgated by the SEC, provides an exception to the registration requirement by providing an exemption from registration. Rule 144 permits the resale of restricted securities provided that

        a. Adequate public information is available about the issuer.

        b. The reseller has owned and fully paid for the securities for a period not less than 2 years prior to resale.

    c.   The amount of securities sold during any subsequent 3-month period generally does not exceed any of the following limitations:

        1)   1% of the stock outstanding

        2)   The average weekly reported volume of trading on all national securities exchanges for the preceding 4 weeks

        3)   The average weekly volume of trading of securities reported through the consolidated transactions reporting system (NASDAQ)

    d.   Notice of resale is provided to the SEC if the amount of securities sold in reliance on Rule 144 in any 3-month period exceeds 500 shares or if they have an aggregate sales price in excess of $10,000.

    e.   Persons who are not affiliates and have owned the securities for at least 3 years are not subject to requirements a. through d. However, state securities laws may impose different requirements and must be complied with before a purchase.

3.   **Rule 144A** allows qualified institutional investors (those owning and investing at least $100 million of securities) to purchase unregistered securities without regard to the holding periods specified in Rule 144. The securities must not belong to a class listed on an exchange or traded through an automated quotation system.

4.   **Regulation A** also provides an exemption to facilitate resales of restricted securities by nonissuers of up to $1.5 million in any 12-month period.

    a.   Use of this exemption requires compliance with all the conditions imposed upon issuers under Regulation A.

5.   Stop and review! You have completed the outline for this subunit. Study multiple-choice questions 44 through 47 beginning on page 389.

MULTIPLE-CHOICE QUESTIONS

A. Federal Securities Regulation

1. The principal purpose of the federal securities laws is to

A. Prevent public offerings of securities in which management fraud or unethical conduct is suspected.

B. Provide the SEC with the information necessary to determine the accuracy of the facts presented in the financial statements.

C. Assure that investors have adequate information upon which to base investment decisions.

D. Provide the SEC with the information necessary to evaluate the financial merits of the securities being offered.

The correct answer is (C). *(CPA, adapted)*
REQUIRED: The basic purpose of the securities laws of the United States.
DISCUSSION: The basic purpose of the federal securities laws is to provide disclosure of adequate information so that investors can evaluate investments. This is accomplished through complex registration and reporting requirements concerning the issuance and subsequent trading of securities.
Answer (A) is incorrect because, except to the extent that the disclosure rules and the penalties for violations serve as a deterrent, the securities laws are not designed to prevent unethical conduct. Answer (B) is incorrect because the SEC does not have the means to verify the facts in financial statements. Also, the disclosures required are not limited to financial statement data. The SEC reviews information for completeness and statements fraudulent on their face but not for accuracy. Answer (D) is incorrect because the SEC does not evaluate the merit or value of securities.

2. The registration of a security under the Securities Act of 1933 provides an investor with

A. A guarantee by the SEC that the facts contained in the registration statement are accurate.

B. An assurance against loss resulting from purchasing the security.

C. Information on the principal purposes for which the offering's proceeds will be used.

D. Information on the issuing corporation's trade secrets.

The correct answer is (C). *(CPA, adapted)*
REQUIRED: The benefit available to an investor under the Securities Act of 1933.
DISCUSSION: The Securities Act of 1933 requires registration of securities, including disclosure of material information. This provides potential purchasers with information to evaluate investments. Material information includes the issuer's most recent certified financial statements, the significant provisions of the securities to be offered, and the principal purposes for which the offering's proceeds will be used.
Answer (A) is incorrect because the SEC does not guarantee the accuracy of information in the registration statement. Answer (B) is incorrect because the SEC does not give assurance of the financial health of the issuer nor does it insure against loss. Answer (D) is incorrect because the disclosures required do not encompass the issuing corporation's trade secrets.

3. Which of the following is least likely to be considered a security under the Securities Act of 1933?

A. General partnership interests.

B. Limited partnership interests.

C. Stock options.

D. Warrants.

The correct answer is (A). *(CPA, adapted)*
REQUIRED: The investment least likely to be considered a security under the Securities Act of 1933.
DISCUSSION: The term security is defined very broadly by the Securities Act of 1933, as interpreted by the U.S. Supreme Court. In general, a security is an investment through which one reasonably anticipates a financial return through the efforts of others. A general partner is entitled to participate directly in the management of the business. Thus, return on the investment in the partnership might be attributed to his/her own efforts.
Answers (B), (C), and (D) are incorrect because the owner of such an interest might reasonably anticipate a return on the investment through the efforts of others.

4. Under the Securities Exchange Act of 1934, which of the following types of instruments is excluded from the definition of "securities"?

    A. Investment contracts.

    B. Convertible debentures.

    C. Nonconvertible debentures.

    D. Certificates of deposit.

The correct answer is (D). *(CPA, adapted)*

    REQUIRED: The instrument excluded from the definition of a security under the Securities Exchange Act of 1934.

    DISCUSSION: The term security is defined very broadly by the Securities Act of 1933 and the Securities Exchange Act of 1934 as interpreted by the U.S. Supreme Court. In general, a security is an investment through which one reasonably anticipates a financial return through the efforts of others. Examples of securities would include investment contracts, convertible debentures, and nonconvertible debentures. A certificate of deposit would not normally be interpreted to be a security.

    Answers (A), (B), and (C) are incorrect because each is an example of a security. Securities issued by banks, S&Ls, and similar organizations are exempted from the act because they are subject to supervision by other government agencies.

B. Securities Registration

5. Universal Corp. intends to sell its common stock to the public in an interstate offering that will be registered under the Securities Act of 1933. Under the act,

    A. Universal can make offers to sell its stock before filing a registration statement, provided that it does not actually issue stock certificates until after the registration is effective.

    B. Universal's registration statement becomes effective at the time it is filed, assuming the SEC does not object within 20 days thereafter.

    C. A prospectus must be delivered to each purchaser of Universal's common stock unless the purchaser qualifies as an accredited investor.

    D. Universal's filing of a registration statement with the SEC does not automatically result in compliance with the "blue-sky" laws of the states in which the offering will be made.

The correct answer is (D). *(CPA, adapted)*

    REQUIRED: The correct statement concerning an interstate offering that will be registered under the Securities Act of 1933.

    DISCUSSION: Any issuer of a security is required by the Securities Act of 1933 to file a registration statement, unless a specific exemption applies. Each state has adopted its own securities laws, which may require more detailed disclosure than federal securities laws. Both federal and state securities laws must generally be complied with.

    Answer (A) is incorrect because an issuer may not offer to sell its stock prior to filing the required registration statement. Answer (B) is incorrect because registration is effective 20 days after the filing, unless the SEC accelerates or defers it. Answer (C) is incorrect because, if registration is required, a prospectus must be furnished to any interested investor.

6. Under the Securities Act of 1933, an initial offering of securities must be registered with the SEC, unless

    A. The offering is made through a broker-dealer licensed in the states in which the securities are to be sold.

    B. The offering prospectus makes a fair and full disclosure of all risks associated with purchasing the securities.

    C. The issuer's financial condition meets certain standards established by the SEC.

    D. The type of security or the offering involved is exempt from registration.

The correct answer is (D). *(CPA, adapted)*

    REQUIRED: The initial offering of securities which does not need to be registered with the SEC.

    DISCUSSION: In general, any offer to sell securities in interstate commerce must be registered with the SEC unless the securities or the transaction is specifically exempt.

    Answer (A) is incorrect because licensure of a broker-dealer in the states in which the securities are to be sold does not exempt a security or a transaction from registration requirements. Answer (B) is incorrect because an offering prospectus must be provided to a potential investor in a security required to be registered. The prospectus discloses information which is material but does not disclose all associated risks. Answer (C) is incorrect because the SEC regulates disclosure but does not set financial condition standards for issuers of securities.

7. When a common stock offering requires registration under the Securities Act of 1933,

A. The registration statement is automatically effective when filed with the SEC.

B. The issuer would act unlawfully if it were to sell the common stock without providing the investor with a prospectus.

C. The SEC will determine the investment value of the common stock before approving the offering.

D. The issuer may make sales 10 days after filing the registration statement.

The correct answer is (B). *(CPA, adapted)*
REQUIRED: The correct statement about an offering which must be registered under the Securities Act of 1933.
DISCUSSION: If an issue is required to be registered under the Securities Act of 1933, a registration statement and a prospectus must be prepared and filed with the SEC. The prospectus contains material financial and other information about the issuer and the offering. A prospectus must be provided to any person interested in investing in the security offered.
Answer (A) is incorrect because a registration statement generally becomes effective 20 days after filing. Answer (C) is incorrect because the SEC does not determine the investment value of the security. Answer (D) is incorrect because the issuer may not sell the security until registration is effective. Registration generally becomes effective no sooner than the end of a 20-day waiting period.

8. Which of the following disclosures must be contained in a securities registration statement filed under the Securities Act of 1933?

A. A list of all existing shareholders.

B. The principal purposes for which the offering proceeds will be used.

C. A copy of the corporation's latest proxy solicitation statement.

D. The names of all prospective accredited investors.

The correct answer is (B). *(CPA, adapted)*
REQUIRED: The disclosure required in a registration statement filed under the 1933 act.
DISCUSSION: The purpose of registration is to provide adequate and accurate disclosure of financial and other pertinent information with which potential investors may evaluate the merits of the securities. Generally, registration calls for disclosure of a description of the registrant's business and property; a description of management; a description of the significant provisions of the security to be offered for sale, its relationship to registrant's other capital securities, and the use of the proceeds of the issuance; and the most recent certified financial statements.
Answers (A), (C), and (D) are incorrect because disclosure of this information is not required in a registration statement filed under the 1933 act.

9. Under the Securities Act of 1933, which of the following statements most accurately reflects how securities registration affects an investor?

A. The investor is provided with information on the shareholders of the offering corporation.

B. The investor is provided with information on the principal purposes for which the offering's proceeds will be used.

C. The investor is guaranteed by the SEC that the facts contained in the registration statement are accurate.

D. The investor is assured by the SEC against loss resulting from purchasing the security.

The correct answer is (B). *(CPA, adapted)*
REQUIRED: The benefit to an investor of registration under the Securities Act of 1933.
DISCUSSION: The 1933 act states that prospective investors must be provided with a prospectus disclosing pertinent financial and other types of information. The principal purposes for which the offering's proceeds will be used are disclosed.
Answer (A) is incorrect because the investor is not provided with the names of the corporation's shareholders. This information is not pertinent to an informed decision regarding the purchase of a security. Answer (C) is incorrect because the SEC is not a guarantor of the information provided in the registration statement. Answer (D) is incorrect because the investor is not assured against loss by the SEC. However, the 1933 act does impose sanctions against those involved with the registration of the security for failure to comply with the act's requirements.

10. A tombstone advertisement

A. May be substituted for the prospectus under certain circumstances.

B. May contain an offer to sell securities.

C. Notifies prospective investors that a previously offered security has been withdrawn from the market and is therefore effectively "dead."

D. Makes known the availability of a prospectus.

The correct answer is (D). *(CPA, adapted)*
REQUIRED: The correct statement concerning a tombstone advertisement.
DISCUSSION: There is a 20-day waiting period following the filing of a registration statement before sales may occur. Under SEC rules, it is permissible to make announcements during the waiting period in advertisements called tombstone ads. These ads give the approximate date when the offering will be made, the person by whom the orders will be executed, and the person from whom a prospectus may be obtained.
Answer (A) is incorrect because a tombstone advertisement is never a substitute for the prospectus. Answer (B) is incorrect because offers to sell securities are not included in a tombstone advertisement. The purpose of tombstone ads is to condition the market for later purchases. Answer (C) is incorrect because the advertisement announces that a security is to be issued.

11. A preliminary prospectus, permitted under SEC Regulations, is known as the

A. Unaudited prospectus.

B. Qualified prospectus.

C. "Blue-sky" prospectus.

D. "Red-herring" prospectus.

The correct answer is (D). *(CPA, adapted)*
REQUIRED: The name a preliminary prospectus is known by.
DISCUSSION: In order to comply with the 1933 act, an issuer of securities must prepare a registration statement and a prospectus. A preliminary prospectus is called a red-herring prospectus because of the required red legend identifying it as preliminary; it contains most of the information to be contained in the final prospectus. It can be distributed to potential purchasers during the 20-day waiting period.
Answers (A), (B), and (C) are incorrect because a preliminary prospectus is known as a red-herring prospectus.

12. One of the elements necessary to recover damages if there has been a material misstatement in a registration statement filed under the Securities Act of 1933 is that the

A. Issuer and plaintiff were in privity of contract with each other.

B. Issuer failed to exercise due care in connection with the sale of the securities.

C. Plaintiff gave value for the security.

D. Plaintiff suffered a loss.

The correct answer is (D). *(CPA, adapted)*
REQUIRED: The element necessary to recover damages under the 1933 act.
DISCUSSION: Under Section 11, the plaintiff must prove that (s)he was an acquirer of a security covered by a registration statement, (s)he suffered a loss, and the statement misstated or omitted a material fact.
Answer (A) is incorrect because plaintiff may have obtained the security from a party other than defendant. Answer (B) is incorrect because neither negligence nor fraud need be proven by the plaintiff. However, any defendant except an issuer may employ the due diligence defense by proving that (s)he was not negligent and that (s)he reasonably investigated the statement and reasonably believed it to be free of material falsehoods or omissions. Answer (C) is incorrect because that plaintiff gave value need not be shown.

13. To be successful in a civil action under Section 11 of the Securities Act of 1933 concerning liability for a misleading registration statement, the plaintiff must prove the

	Defendant's Intent to Deceive	Plaintiff's Reliance on the Registration Statement
A.	Yes	Yes
B.	Yes	No
C.	No	Yes
D.	No	No

The correct answer is (D). *(CPA, adapted)*
   REQUIRED: The element(s) of a plaintiff's case under Section 11.
   DISCUSSION: Under the 1933 act, the issuer, its chief executive and directors, its chief finance and accounting officers, other signers, the underwriters, and experts who prepared or attested to the statement are liable for misstatements or omissions of material fact. In a private action, a plaintiff establishes a prima facie case pursuant to Section 11 by proving that (s)he suffered damages and was an acquirer of a security issued under a registration statement that misstated or omitted a material fact. Exercise of due diligence in determining the accuracy of the statement is a defense. An issuer, however, cannot assert the due diligence defense, but any defendant may show that the plaintiff knew of the misstatement or omission at the time of acquisition.
   Answer (A) is incorrect because intent to deceive and reliance need not be shown. Answer (B) is incorrect because intent to deceive need not be shown. Answer (C) is incorrect because reliance need not be shown.

14. Which of the following statements concerning the prospectus required by the Securities Act of 1933 is correct?

   A. The prospectus is a part of the registration statement.

   B. The prospectus should enable the SEC to pass on the merits of the securities.

   C. The prospectus must be filed after an offer to sell.

   D. The prospectus is prohibited from being distributed to the public until the SEC approves the accuracy of facts embodied therein.

The correct answer is (A). *(CPA, adapted)*
   REQUIRED: The correct statement concerning the prospectus required by the 1933 Securities Act.
   DISCUSSION: A prospectus is prepared as part of the registration statement. A prospectus is a written document proposing a sale of securities to potential investors. The prospectus contains most of the information in the registration statement. It must be furnished to each potential investor prior to the time of delivery of the securities.
   Answers (B) and (D) are incorrect because the SEC does not pass on the merits of any security registered under the 1933 act. Answer (C) is incorrect because, as part of the registration statement, it must be filed prior to the time that offers to sell are made.

15. Which of the following requirements must be met by an issuer of securities who wants to make an offering by using shelf registration?

	Original Registration Statement Must Be Kept Updated	The Offeror Must Be a First-Time Issuer of Securities
A.	Yes	Yes
B.	Yes	No
C.	No	Yes
D.	No	No

The correct answer is (B). *(CPA, adapted)*
   REQUIRED: The requirements for a shelf registration.
   DISCUSSION: SEC Rule 415 permits shelf registration of securities. Under a shelf registration, issuers may file the registration statement prior to the actual sale. This type of registration allows issuers to leave the securities on the shelf until market conditions are favorable. Only the most established issuers are eligible for the use of shelf registration. However, issuers are required to update the registration statement frequently to avoid stale information.
   Answers (A), (C), and (D) are incorrect because the original registration statement must be kept updated, and first-time issuers of securities are ineligible.

C. Reporting Requirements

16. Integral Corp., with assets in excess of $4 million, has issued common and preferred stock and has 350 shareholders. Its stock is sold on the New York Stock Exchange. Under the Securities Exchange Act of 1934, Integral must be registered with the SEC because

- A. It issues both common and preferred stock.
- B. Its shares are listed on a national stock exchange.
- C. It has more than 300 shareholders.
- D. Its shares are traded in interstate commerce.

The correct answer is (B). *(CPA, adapted)*
REQUIRED: The basis for required registration under the Securities Exchange Act of 1934.
DISCUSSION: The Securities Exchange Act of 1934 requires all regulated publicly held corporations to register with the SEC. Covered corporations either (1) list shares on a national securities exchange or (2) have at least 500 shareholders of equity securities and total gross assets of at least $10 million.
Answer (A) is incorrect because issuing preferred stock is not a sufficient condition for registering or reporting under the 1934 act. Answer (C) is incorrect because the threshold is 500 shareholders and total gross assets of $10 million or more. Answer (D) is incorrect because shares trading in interstate commerce are insufficient to trigger registration requirements under the 1934 act.

17. Which of the following factors, by itself, requires a corporation to comply with the reporting requirements of the Securities Exchange Act of 1934?

- A. Six hundred employees.
- B. Shares listed on a national securities exchange.
- C. Total assets of $2 million.
- D. Four hundred holders of equity securities.

The correct answer is (B). *(CPA, adapted)*
REQUIRED: The factor by itself which requires a corporation to comply with the 1934 act.
DISCUSSION: The 1934 act requires all regulated, publicly held companies to register with the SEC if their shares are listed on a national securities exchange, or they have at least 500 equity holders and total assets of at least $5 million.
Answers (A), (C), and (D) are incorrect because none of these factors, by itself, requires reporting under the 1934 act.

18. The registration provisions of the Securities Exchange Act of 1934 require disclosure of all of the following information except the

- A. Names of owners of at least 5% of any class of nonexempt equity security.
- B. Bonus and profit-sharing arrangements.
- C. Financial structure and nature of the business.
- D. Names of officers and directors.

The correct answer is (A). *(CPA, adapted)*
REQUIRED: The information which need not be disclosed under the registration provisions of the 1934 act.
DISCUSSION: Registration under the 1934 act requires disclosure of (1) corporate organization; (2) financial structure; (3) description of all securities; (4) names of officers, directors, and underwriters; (5) names of all owners of at least 10% of any class of nonexempt equity security; (6) description of the nature of the business; (7) financial statements; and (8) bonus and profit-sharing arrangements.
Answers (B), (C), and (D) are incorrect because the information must be disclosed.

19. Under the Securities Exchange Act of 1934, a corporation whose common stock is listed on a national stock exchange

- A. Is prohibited from making private placement offerings.
- B. Must submit Form 10-K to the SEC except in those years in which the corporation has made a public offering.
- C. Must distribute copies of Form 10-K to its shareholders.
- D. Is subject to having the registration of its securities suspended or revoked.

The correct answer is (D). *(CPA, adapted)*
REQUIRED: The effect of the 1934 act on a corporation whose common stock is listed on a national stock exchange.
DISCUSSION: The SEC is authorized by the 1934 act to impose sanctions to enforce its provisions. The SEC may deny, suspend, or revoke registration, or it may order a suspension of trading the securities. These sanctions are in addition to civil and criminal liability imposed by the federal securities laws.
Answer (A) is incorrect because registration required, and exemption therefrom, under the 1933 act is independent of the 1934 act. The 1934 act contains no such prohibition. Answer (B) is incorrect because reporting requirements under the 1934 act do not substitute for those under the 1933 act. Answer (C) is incorrect because a covered corporation under the 1934 act is not required to provide copies of Forms 10-K, 10-Q, or 8-K to its shareholders. However, the annual report required to be sent to shareholders is comparable to the Form 10-K.

20. The reporting requirements of the Securities Exchange Act of 1934 and its rules

- A. Apply only to issuers, underwriters, and dealers.
- B. Apply to a corporation that registered under the Securities Act of 1933 but that did not register under the Securities Exchange Act of 1934.
- C. Require all corporations engaged in interstate commerce to file an annual report.
- D. Require all corporations engaged in interstate commerce to file quarterly audited financial statements.

The correct answer is (B). *(CPA, adapted)*
REQUIRED: The persons and entities required to report under the 1934 act.
DISCUSSION: The following must file periodic reports under the 1934 act: national securities exchanges, an issuer with more than $10 million in assets and 500 or more shareholders of a class of equity securities traded in interstate commerce, an issuer whose securities are traded on a national exchange, and an issuer that has registered under the 1933 act. These issuers must file annual (10-K), quarterly (10-Q), and material events (8-K) reports and send similar reports to shareholders. However, an issuer that must report solely on the basis of registration under the 1933 act need not transmit an annual report to its shareholders.
Answer (A) is incorrect because national exchanges must also report. Answers (C) and (D) are incorrect because doing business in interstate commerce is not a sufficient condition for registering or reporting. Also, statements included in quarterly reports need not be audited.

21. Which of the following statements is correct concerning corporations subject to the reporting requirements of the Securities Exchange Act of 1934?

- A. The annual report (Form 10-K) need not include audited financial statements.
- B. The annual report (Form 10-K) must be filed with the SEC within 20 days of the end of the corporation's fiscal year.
- C. A quarterly report (Form 10-Q) need only be filed with the SEC by those corporations that are also subject to the registration requirements of the Securities Act of 1933.
- D. A report (Form 8-K) must be filed with the SEC after a material important event occurs.

The correct answer is (D). *(CPA, adapted)*
REQUIRED: The reporting required under the Securities Exchange Act of 1934.
DISCUSSION: Form 8-K is the report that must be filed after certain specified material events occur. These events include changes in control of the issuer; a significant revaluation, acquisition, or disposition of assets; default on an issuance of securities; a change in the amount of securities; and "any material important event." The latter may include resignation of a director or a change of independent accountants.
Answer (A) is incorrect because Form 10-K must include audited financial statements: balance sheets for the current and 2 prior fiscal year-ends and statements of income, cash flows, and changes in shareholders' equity for the current and preceding 2 years. Answer (B) is incorrect because Form 10-K is due 90 days after the entity's fiscal year-end, but some schedules may be filed 120 days after year-end. Answer (C) is incorrect because an entity required to file Form 10-K must also file Form 10-Q for each of the first three quarters.

22. Which of the following events must be reported to the SEC under the reporting provisions of the Securities Exchange Act of 1934?

	Tender Offers	Insider Trading	Soliciting Proxies
A.	Yes	Yes	Yes
B.	Yes	Yes	No
C.	Yes	No	Yes
D.	No	Yes	Yes

The correct answer is (A). *(CPA, adapted)*
REQUIRED: The events which must be reported to the SEC under the Securities Exchange Act of 1934.
DISCUSSION: The Securities Exchange Act of 1934 governs dealings in securities subsequent to their initial issuance. The act requires all regulated publicly held companies to register with the SEC. The act requires disclosure of matters concerning tender offers, insider trading, and the solicitation of proxies.
Answers (B), (C), and (D) are incorrect because each event must be reported under the 1934 act.

23. Integral Corp. is subject to the reporting provisions of the Securities Exchange Act of 1934. For its 1999 fiscal year, Integral filed the following with the SEC: quarterly reports, an annual report, and a periodic report listing newly appointed officers of the corporation. Integral did not notify the SEC of shareholder "short-swing" profits, report that a competitor made a tender offer to Integral's shareholders, and report changes in the price of its stock as sold on the New York Stock Exchange. Under the SEC reporting requirements, which of the following was Integral required to do?

A. Report the tender offer to the SEC.

B. Notify the SEC of shareholder "short-swing" profits.

C. File the periodic report listing newly appointed officers.

D. Report the changes in the market price of its stock.

The correct answer is (C). *(CPA, adapted)*
REQUIRED: The reporting required of a covered corporation under the 1934 act.
DISCUSSION: A covered corporation is required to file annual (10-K), quarterly (10-Q), and material events (8-K) reports with the SEC. Similar reports are sent to shareholders. The 10-K report contains information about the entity's business activities, securities, management, related parties, disagreements concerning accounting and disclosure, audited financial statements, etc. It is intended to bring the information in the registration statement up to date. Thus, newly appointed officers will be listed.
Answer (A) is incorrect because the target need only file a statement with the SEC if the tender offer is hostile (unsolicited). Answer (B) is incorrect because insiders are liable to the corporation for short-swing profits. Insiders include directors, officers, and owners of more than 10% of the corporation's stock. Answer (D) is incorrect because, although the annual report (Form 10-K) requires disclosure of the market price of the common stock of the registrant, including the high and low sales prices, for each quarter of the last 2 fiscal years and any subsequent interim periods, not every change in the market price of its stock need be reported.

24. Link Corporation is subject to the reporting provisions of the Securities Exchange Act of 1934. Which of the following documents must Link file with the SEC?

	Quarterly Reports (Form 10-Q)	Proxy Statements
A.	Yes	Yes
B.	Yes	No
C.	No	Yes
D.	No	No

The correct answer is (A). *(CPA, adapted)*
REQUIRED: The reporting requirements of a company whose securities are registered under the 1934 act.
DISCUSSION: Following registration, a company subject to the reporting requirements of the 1934 act must file specific reports with the SEC on a regular basis. These reports include the 10-K (annual report), the 10-Q (quarterly report), and a proxy statement. In addition, the 8-K (current report) must be filed to disclose material events within 15 days of occurrence.
Answers (B), (C), and (D) are incorrect because a 10-Q (quarterly report) and a proxy statement must be filed with the SEC.

25. Wool, Inc. is a reporting company under the Securities Exchange Act of 1934. The only security it has issued is its voting common stock. Which of the following statements is correct?

A. It is unnecessary for the required annual report (Form 10-K) to include audited financial statements.

B. Any person who owns more than 5% of Wool's common stock must file a report with the SEC.

C. Because Wool is a reporting company, it is not required to file a registration statement under the Securities Act of 1933 for any future offerings of its common stock.

D. Wool need not file its proxy statements with the SEC because it has only one class of stock outstanding.

The correct answer is (B). *(CPA, adapted)*
REQUIRED: The correct statement concerning a reporting company under the Securities Exchange Act of 1934.
DISCUSSION: Any person who owns more than 5% of any class of the securities of a covered corporation must file an individual report with the SEC disclosing his/her holdings.
Answer (A) is incorrect because Form 10-K must include audited financial statements: balance sheets for the current and 2 prior fiscal year-ends and statements of income, cash flows, and changes in shareholders' equity for the current and preceding 2 years. Answer (C) is incorrect because a reporting company is not exempt from registration requirements of the Securities Act of 1933. Answer (D) is incorrect because a corporation with only one class of stock must comply with the proxy filing and distribution requirements of the 1934 act.

26. Which of the following persons is not an insider of a corporation subject to the Securities Exchange Act of 1934 registration and reporting requirements?

- A. An attorney for the corporation.
- B. An owner of 5% of the corporation's outstanding debentures.
- C. A member of the board of directors.
- D. A shareholder who owns 10% of the outstanding common stock.

The correct answers are (A) and (B). *(CPA, adapted)*
    REQUIRED: The person not subject to the insider reporting provisions of the 1934 act.
    DISCUSSION: Statutory insiders are subject to reporting provisions under the 1934 act. These insiders include officers, directors, and owners of 10% or more of a class of registered equity securities. An attorney or a creditor is not deemed to be an insider for registration and reporting purposes. However, insider trading rules may apply if they are in possession of confidential corporate information.
    Answers (C) and (D) are incorrect because each is a Section 16 statutory insider.

27. Corporations that are exempt from registration under the Securities Exchange Act of 1934 are subject to the act's

- A. Provisions dealing with the filing of annual reports.
- B. Provisions imposing periodic audits.
- C. Antifraud provisions.
- D. Proxy solicitation provisions.

The correct answer is (C). *(CPA, adapted)*
    REQUIRED: The provisions of the 1934 act to which a corporation not required to register under the act is subject.
    DISCUSSION: A corporation required to register under the 1934 act must comply with its reporting requirements. The antifraud provisions of the act apply to any person who performs a prohibited act in connection with the purchase or sale of any security, whether or not the security is registered.
    Answers (A), (B), and (D) are incorrect because only a corporation required to register (a covered corporation) by the 1934 act is subject to these provisions.

28. The antifraud provisions of Rule 10b-5 of the Securities Exchange Act of 1934

- A. Apply only if the securities involved were registered under the Securities Act of 1933 or the Securities Exchange Act of 1934.
- B. Require that the plaintiff show negligence on the part of the defendant in misstating facts.
- C. Require that the wrongful act be accomplished through the mail, any other use of interstate commerce, or through a national securities exchange.
- D. Apply only if the defendant acted with intent to defraud.

The correct answer is (C). *(CPA, adapted)*
    REQUIRED: The element of a violation of the antifraud provisions of Rule 10b-5.
    DISCUSSION: The scope of Rule 10b-5 is broad, but not absolute. Rule 10b-5 renders it unlawful for any person to directly or indirectly perform fraudulent (deceptive) acts, by use of any means or instrumentality of interstate commerce, the mails, or any facility of any national securities exchange, in connection with the purchase or sale of any security.
    Answer (A) is incorrect because Rule 10b-5 also applies to unregistered securities. Answer (B) is incorrect because it is sufficient that the defendant omitted to state a material fact necessary to make the statements not misleading. Also, intent must be proved. Answer (D) is incorrect because any act which would operate as a deceit is sufficient.

Note: Refer to Study Unit 2, subunit B, Federal Statutory Liability, for additional questions on federal securities law and on Rule 10b-5 in particular.

D. Exemptions

29. The Securities Act of 1933 provides an exemption from registration for

	Bonds Issued by a Municipality for Governmental Purposes	Securities Issued by a Not-for-Profit Charitable Organization
A.	Yes	Yes
B.	Yes	No
C.	No	Yes
D.	No	No

The correct answer is (A). *(CPA, adapted)*
    REQUIRED: The securities exempt from registration under the 1933 act.
    DISCUSSION: The 1933 act specifically exempts certain types of securities from registration. Types exempt include securities of domestic governments issued for governmental purposes, securities of nonprofit charitable organizations, and others. The 1933 act also provides exemptions for certain transactions and limited offerings.
    Answers (B), (C), and (D) are incorrect because both bonds issued by a municipality for government purposes and securities issued by a nonprofit charitable organization are exempt under Section 3 of the 1933 act.

30. Which of the following facts will result in an offering of securities being exempt from registration under the Securities Act of 1933?

    A.   The securities are nonvoting preferred stock.

    B.   The issuing corporation was closely held prior to the offering.

    C.   The sale or offer to sell the securities is made by a person other than an issuer, underwriter, or dealer.

    D.   The securities are AAA-rated debentures that are collateralized by first mortgages on property that has a market value of 200% of the offering price.

The correct answer is (C). *(CPA, adapted)*

    REQUIRED: The exemption from registration under the 1933 act.

    DISCUSSION: Under Section 4(1) of the 1933 act, an initial offering of securities is exempt from registration if the sale is made by an ordinary investor, that is, a person who is not an issuer, an underwriter, or a dealer.

    Answer (A) is incorrect because the type of stock offered by the issuer is irrelevant to the SEC reporting requirement. Answer (B) is incorrect because an initial public issuance is not exempt. Answer (D) is incorrect because secured debt is not exempt.

31. Which of the following securities is exempt from registration under the Securities Act of 1933?

    A.   A class of stock given in exchange for another class by the issuer to its existing shareholders without the issuer paying a commission.

    B.   Limited partnership interests sold for the purpose of acquiring funds to invest in bonds issued by the United States.

    C.   Corporate debentures that were previously subject to an effective registration statement, provided they are convertible into shares of common stock.

    D.   Shares of nonvoting common stock, provided their par value is less than $1.00.

The correct answer is (A). *(CPA, adapted)*

    REQUIRED: The securities exempt from registration under the Securities Act of 1933.

    DISCUSSION: If securities are transferred between the issuer and its existing shareholders without payment of commissions or other consideration, the transaction is exempt from registration. Hence, stock dividends and stock splits are exempt. Securities issued in mergers and reorganizations are also exempt if no cash is involved and the securities are given solely for other securities.

    Answers (B), (C), and (D) are incorrect because each states no basis for exemption. The purpose for which funds will be used, prior registration, par value, and whether stock has voting rights are irrelevant in the circumstances described.

32. Which of the following securities would be regulated by the provisions of the Securities Act of 1933?

    A.   Securities issued by not-for-profit, charitable organizations.

    B.   Securities guaranteed by domestic governmental organizations.

    C.   Securities issued by savings and loan associations.

    D.   Securities issued by insurance companies.

The correct answer is (D). *(CPA, adapted)*

    REQUIRED: The securities regulated by the 1933 act.

    DISCUSSION: The 1933 act exempts certain types of securities from the registration requirements. These include securities issued by not-for-profit organizations, domestic governments, banks, savings and loans associations, companies in reorganization, parties regulated by the ICC, receivers or trustees in bankruptcy, and companies in exchange for existing securities if no commission is paid. Intrastate offerings, short-term commercial paper, and securities sold under Regulation A are also exempt. Insurance policies and annuity contracts are regulated by the states, not by the federal government. However, other securities issued by insurance companies are regulated by the 1933 act.

    Answers (A), (B), and (C) are incorrect because securities issued by not-for-profit organizations, domestic governments, and savings and loan associations are exempt from the 1933 act.

33. Which of the following statements concerning an initial intrastate securities offering made by an issuer residing in and doing business in that state is correct?

- A. The offering would be exempt from the registration requirements of the Securities Act of 1933.

- B. The offering would be subject to the registration requirements of the Securities Exchange Act of 1934.

- C. The offering would be regulated by the SEC.

- D. The shares of the offering could not be resold to investors outside the state for at least 1 year.

The correct answer is (A). *(CPA, adapted)*
  REQUIRED: The true statement about an initial intrastate securities offering.
  DISCUSSION: The intrastate offering exemption is available to an issuer that is incorporated or organized in the state in which the offering is made. All offerees and purchasers must be residents of the state. Furthermore, the issuer must derive 80% or more of its gross revenue from the state, have at least 80% of its assets located in the state, and use at least 80% of the proceeds from the issuance in the state.
  Answer (B) is incorrect because the 1934 act applies to the resale of securities in an interstate market. Answer (C) is incorrect because the offering will be exempt. Answer (D) is incorrect because securities issued under the intrastate exemption may not be resold to nonresidents during the 12-month sale period and for 9 months afterward.

34. Which of the following are exempt from the registration requirements of the Securities Act of 1933?

- A. All industrial development bonds issued by municipalities.

- B. Stock of a corporation offered and sold only to residents of the state in which the issuer was incorporated and doing all of its business.

- C. Bankers' acceptances with maturities at the time of issue ranging from 1 to 2 years.

- D. Participation interests in a money market fund that consists wholly of short-term commercial paper.

The correct answer is (B). *(CPA, adapted)*
  REQUIRED: The securities exempt from registration under the 1933 act.
  DISCUSSION: One exemption from registration under the Securities Act of 1933 is an intrastate issue of securities. Under SEC Rule 147, an issue qualifies as intrastate if the issuer is incorporated in the state in which the issue is made, 80% of the proceeds are to be used in that state, 80% of its assets are located in the state of incorporation, the issuer does at least 80% of its business (gross revenues) within that state, all the purchasers and offerees are residents of the state, no resales to nonresidents occur for at least 9 months after the last sale, and steps are taken to prevent interstate distribution.
  Answer (A) is incorrect because bonds of a municipality not used for a governmental purpose are not exempt. Answer (C) is incorrect because the maturity limit is 9 months. Answer (D) is incorrect because sales of short-term commercial paper, not interests in a money market fund, are exempt if certain conditions are met.

35. An offering made under the provisions of Regulation A of the Securities Act of 1933 requires that the issuer

- A. File an offering circular with the SEC.

- B. Sell only to accredited investors.

- C. Provide investors with the prior 4 years' audited financial statements.

- D. Provide investors with a proxy registration statement.

The correct answer is (A). *(CPA, adapted)*
  REQUIRED: The requirement for a stock offering made under Regulation A.
  DISCUSSION: Under Regulation A, a small public issue of securities is exempt from full registration with the SEC if certain requirements are met. Regulation A applies to issuances not exceeding $5 million if the issuer files an offering circular with the SEC, provides it to each offeree and purchaser, and observes the 10-day waiting period.
  Answer (B) is incorrect because Regulation A does not restrict resale, have an investor sophistication requirement, or limit the number of buyers. Also, no disclosure is necessary if the offering is $100,000 or less. Answer (C) is incorrect because Regulation A even provides an exemption from the otherwise required filing of a registration statement and prospectus. Answer (D) is incorrect because filing proxy statements is required under the 1934 act. Regulation A provides exemption from filing requirements of the 1933 act.

36. For an offering to be exempt under Regulation D of the Securities Act of 1933, Rules 505 and 506 each require that

- A. The SEC be notified within 10 days of the first sale.
- B. The offering be made without general advertising.
- C. All accredited investors receive the issuer's financial information.
- D. There be a maximum of 35 investors.

The correct answer is (B). *(CPA, adapted)*
REQUIRED: The common provision of Rules 505 and 506.
DISCUSSION: Regulation D of the 1933 act provides an exemption from registration for relatively small offerings. To meet the requirements under Rules 505 and 506, the offering must be made without the benefit of general solicitation or advertising. NOTE: Under Rule 504, the advertising restriction does not apply.
Answer (A) is incorrect because the SEC must be notified by filing Form D within 15 days of the first sale of the securities. Answer (C) is incorrect because, under Rules 505 and 506, if sales are only to accredited investors, no financial disclosure is required. If sales are made to unaccredited investors, all buyers (accredited and unaccredited) must receive financial information about the issuer. A short-form prospectus satisfies this requirement. Answer (D) is incorrect because, although Rules 505 and 506 require that an issuer reasonably believe that no more than 35 unaccredited investors will participate, the maximum number of accredited investors is not limited.

37. Zack Limited Partnership intends to sell $6 million of its limited partnership interests. Zack conducts all of its business activities in the state in which it was organized. Zack intends to use the offering proceeds to acquire municipal bonds. Which of the following statements is correct concerning the offering and the registration exemptions that might be available to Zack under the Securities Act of 1933?

- A. The offering is exempt from registration because of the intended use of the offering proceeds.
- B. Under Rule 147 (regarding intrastate offerings), Zack may make up to five offers to nonresidents without jeopardizing the Rule 147 exemption.
- C. If Zack complies with the requirements of Regulation D, any subsequent resale of a limited partnership interest by a purchaser is automatically exempt from registration.
- D. If Zack complies with the requirements of Regulation D, Zack may make an unlimited number of offers to sell the limited partnership interests.

The correct answer is (D). *(CPA, adapted)*
REQUIRED: The correct statement concerning registration exemptions under the Securities Act of 1933.
DISCUSSION: Rules 504, 505, and 506 of Regulation D represent three exemptions from registration otherwise required by the 1933 act. Rule 506 exempts qualifying transactions without regard to the dollar amount of the offering. Although (as with Rule 505) the issuer must reasonably believe there are no more than 35 unaccredited investors, offers and sales may be made to an unlimited number of accredited investors.
Answer (A) is incorrect because no exemption is based on the intended use of the proceeds alone. Answer (B) is incorrect because the intrastate offering exemption is strictly construed. Rule 147 requires that all offers be made to residents. Answer (C) is incorrect because the resale of securities exempt from registration under Rules 505 and 506 of Regulation D is restricted. Registration is required before resale unless another exemption (e.g., under Regulation A) applies.

38. Pate Corp. is offering $3 million of its securities solely to accredited investors pursuant to Regulation D of the Securities Act of 1933. Under Regulation D, Pate is

- A. Not required to provide any specified information to the accredited investors.

- B. Required to provide the accredited investors with audited financial statements for the 2 most recent fiscal years.

- C. Permitted to make a general solicitation.

- D. Not eligible for an exemption if the securities are debentures.

The correct answer is (A). *(CPA, adapted)*
REQUIRED: The true statement about an offering made solely to accredited investors.
DISCUSSION: Rule 504 of Regulation D does not apply to this offering because it exceeds $1 million and more than $500,000 is unregistered under the state law. But Rules 505 ($5 million limit) and 506 (no dollar limit) may be relevant. Under Rules 505 and 506 of Regulation D, no financial disclosure is necessary if all investors are accredited. But if some are nonaccredited, all investors must receive the information contained in a short-form prospectus.
Answer (B) is incorrect because this disclosure is not necessary if all investors are accredited. Answer (C) is incorrect because Regulation D generally prohibits general solicitation, except in a Rule 504 offering. Answer (D) is incorrect because debentures fall within the broad definition of securities stated in the 1933 act.

39. Lux Limited Partnership intends to offer $300,000 of its limited partnership interests under Rule 504 of Regulation D of the Securities Act of 1933. Which of the following statements is correct?

- A. The resale of the limited partnership interests by a purchaser generally will not be restricted.

- B. The limited partnership interests may be sold only to accredited investors.

- C. The exemption under Rule 504 is not available to an issuer of limited partnership interests.

- D. The limited partnership interests may not be sold to more than 35 investors.

The correct answer is (A). *(CPA, adapted)*
REQUIRED: The correct statement about Rule 504 of Regulation D.
DISCUSSION: Under Rule 504, a limited offer of securities is exempt from registration if the aggregate price is no more than $1 million in a 12-month period. Securities issued under Rule 504 are not restricted and may be resold without registration.
Answers (B) and (D) are incorrect because Rule 504 places no limit on the number or nature of investors, and no disclosure of financial information is required. Answer (C) is incorrect because Regulation D provides for exemption of issuers of securities from registration requirements of the 1933 act. A security is an investment from which a profit is reasonably expected to result from efforts of another.

40. Frey, Inc. intends to make a $2 million common stock offering under Rule 505 of Regulation D of the Securities Act of 1933. Frey

- A. May sell the stock to an unlimited number of investors.

- B. May make the offering through a general advertising.

- C. Must notify the SEC within 15 days after the first sale of the offering.

- D. Must provide all investors with a prospectus.

The correct answer is (C). *(CPA, adapted)*
REQUIRED: The correct statement concerning a securities offering under Rule 505.
DISCUSSION: Rule 505 provides exemption from the requirements of the 1933 act to all issuers other than investment companies for sales of securities up to $5 million in any 12-month period. Under Rule 505, securities may be sold to no more than 35 nonaccredited investors and to an unlimited number of accredited investors. Rule 505 also provides that the issuer must notify the SEC within 15 days after the first offering.
Answer (A) is incorrect because Rule 505 prohibits sale to more than 35 nonaccredited investors. Answer (B) is incorrect because exemption under Regulation D is conditioned on no general solicitation. Answer (D) is incorrect because a prospectus need not be provided. However, all investors must be furnished with material information about the issuer, its business, and the securities being offered.

41. If securities are exempt from the registration provisions of the Securities Act of 1933, any fraud committed in the course of selling such securities can be challenged by

	SEC	Person Defrauded
A.	Yes	Yes
B.	Yes	No
C.	No	Yes
D.	No	No

The correct answer is (A). *(CPA, adapted)*
    REQUIRED: The party/parties that may challenge fraud in the selling of a security exempt from registration.
    DISCUSSION: Both the SEC and the investor defrauded have legal standing to challenge fraud in the sale of securities whether they are exempt from registration or not. Fraud is illegal under the Securities Act, and the SEC is the administrative agency which enforces the act.
    Answers (B), (C), and (D) are incorrect because Rule 10b-5 permits any buyer or seller of a security to sue for fraudulent activity. The SEC may also enforce antifraud provisions of the securities laws.

Questions 42 and 43 are based on the following information. Pix Corp. is making a $6 million stock offering. Pix wants the offering exempt from registration under the Securities Act of 1933.

---

42. Which of the following provisions of the act would Pix have to comply with for the offering to be exempt?

A. Regulation A.

B. Regulation D, Rule 504.

C. Regulation D, Rule 505.

D. Regulation D, Rule 506.

The correct answer is (D). *(CPA, adapted)*
    REQUIRED: The applicable exemption from registration of the stock offering.
    DISCUSSION: Regulation A does not apply to this offering because it exceeds $5 million. Neither would Rule 504 ($1 million limit) or Rule 505 ($5 million limit) apply. The offering may, however, comply with Rule 506 (no dollar limit).
    Answer (A) is incorrect because no more than $5 million of securities may be sold during a 12-month period under Regulation A. Answer (B) is incorrect because no more than $1 million of securities may be sold during a 12-month period under Rule 504. Answer (C) is incorrect because no more than $5 million of securities may be sold during a 12-month period under Rule 505.

43. Which of the following requirements would Pix have to comply with when selling the securities?

A. No more than 35 investors.

B. No more than 35 nonaccredited investors.

C. Accredited investors only.

D. Nonaccredited investors only.

The correct answer is (B). *(CPA, adapted)*
    REQUIRED: The requirements for exemption from registration of the stock offering.
    DISCUSSION: There is no limit to the amount which may be raised under Rule 506 of Regulation D. The offering may be purchased by an unlimited number of accredited investors. However, the issuer must reasonably believe that there are no more than 35 nonaccredited investors.
    Answers (A) and (D) are incorrect because the offering may be purchased by an unlimited number of accredited investors. Answer (C) is incorrect because up to 35 nonaccredited investors may purchase the securities.

E. Resale of Restricted Securities

44. Under the Securities Act of 1933, which of the following statements concerning an offering of securities sold under a transaction exemption is correct?

- A. The offering is exempt from the antifraud provisions of the 1933 act.

- B. The offering is subject to the registration requirements of the 1933 act.

- C. Resales of the offering are exempt from the provisions of the 1933 act.

- D. Resales of the offering must be made under a registration or a different exemption provision of the 1933 act.

45. Taso Limited Partnership intends to offer $400,000 of its limited partnership interests under Rule 504 of Regulation D of the Securities Act of 1933. Which of the following statements is correct?

- A. The exemption under Rule 504 is not available to an issuer of limited partnership interests.

- B. The limited partnership interests may be sold only to accredited investors.

- C. The total number of nonaccredited investors who purchase the limited partnership interests may not exceed 35.

- D. The resale of the limited partnership interests by a purchaser generally will NOT be restricted.

The correct answer is (D). *(CPA, adapted)*
REQUIRED: The true statement about an offering of securities sold under a transaction exemption.
DISCUSSION: Although certain security transactions are exempt from the registration requirements under the 1933 act, public resale of these securities must be made pursuant to another exemption, or a registration must be filed prior to resale. All resales are regulated by the Securities Exchange Act of 1934.
Answer (A) is incorrect because exempt security transactions are subject to the antifraud provisions of the 1933 act. Answer (B) is incorrect because exempt security transactions are not subject to the registration requirements of the 1933 act. Answer (C) is incorrect because public resales are usually not exempt. An exception under SEC Rule 144 is available in specific, limited circumstances when public information about the stock is available and the volume of stock traded and sold is low.

The correct answer is (D). *(CPA, adapted)*
REQUIRED: The correct statement concerning exemption under Regulation D.
DISCUSSION: A purchaser of securities under Rules 505 and 506 of Regulation D may not immediately resell without being considered an underwriter. Thus, the exemption from registration for transactions by a person not an issuer, underwriter, or dealer is inapplicable. Moreover, the issuer must take steps to prevent nonexempt, unregistered resale and must notify the SEC of the sale. After the securities have been held for 2 years, limited resales are allowed under SEC Rule 144 without registration. Unlimited resales by a noninsider purchaser are allowed after 3 years. However, these limits on resale apply to the exemptions under Rules 505 and 506, not Rule 504. Securities issued under Rule 504 are not restricted and may be resold without registration.
Answer (A) is incorrect because Rule 504 applies to issuers of securities, even when the security is a limited partnership interest. Answer (B) is incorrect because Rule 504 allows qualified issuers to sell up to $1 million of securities during a 12-month period to any number of purchasers without registration. Answer (C) is incorrect because Rule 504 allows sales to an unlimited number of investors, without regard to whether they are accredited or nonaccredited.

46. Under Regulation D of the Securities Act of 1933, which of the following conditions apply to private placement offerings? The securities

- A. Cannot be sold for longer than a 6-month period.
- B. Cannot be the subject of an immediate unregistered reoffering to the public.
- C. Must be sold to accredited institutional investors.
- D. Must be sold to fewer than 20 nonaccredited investors.

The correct answer is (B). *(CPA, adapted)*

REQUIRED: The conditions that apply to private placement offerings under Regulation D.

DISCUSSION: Under Rule 506 of Regulation D, securities may be sold under the private placement exemption. Securities sold under this exemption are restricted securities and may be resold only by registration or in a transaction exempt from registration. The securities' certificates bear a legend that the shares of stock are restricted and purchased for personal investment.

Answer (A) is incorrect because, under the private placement exemption, there is no time limitation specified. Answer (C) is incorrect because Rule 506 is not limited to accredited institutional investors but may be sold to accredited and (not more than 35) nonaccredited investors. Answer (D) is incorrect because the limitation is 35 nonaccredited investors. Accredited investors are persons or entities that are considered to be sufficiently sophisticated to assume risk and obtain information without the Securities Act.

47. Dee is the owner of 12% of the shares of common stock of D&M Corporation that she acquired in 1992. She is the treasurer and a director of D&M. The corporation registered its securities in 1993 and made a public offering pursuant to the Securities Act of 1933. If Dee decides to sell part of her holdings in 1999, the shares

- A. Would be exempt from registration because the corporation previously registered them within 3 years.
- B. Must be registered regardless of the amount sold or manner in which they are sold.
- C. Would be exempt from registration because she is not an issuer.
- D. Must be registered if Dee sells 50% of her shares through her broker to the public.

The correct answer is (D). *(CPA, adapted)*

REQUIRED: The true statement as to whether a controlling person's stock sale must be registered.

DISCUSSION: In general, any offer to sell securities in interstate commerce is subject to registration unless the securities or the transaction is exempt. Most transactions are exempt because they involve sales by persons other than issuers, underwriters, or dealers, e.g., transactions by ordinary investors selling on their own account. Dee, however, is considered an issuer because she is a controlling person, that is, one who owns more than 10% of the company's stock and who has the direct or indirect ability to control the company. A sale of 6% of D&M's common stock to the public in the ordinary course of business (e.g., through a broker) would not qualify for an exemption under the Securities Act of 1933 and would be subject to SEC registration.

Answer (A) is incorrect because the previous registration is irrelevant. Answer (B) is incorrect because, under Rule 144, an insider who has held restricted securities for at least 2 years may resell without registration in any 3-month period the greater of 1% of the total shares of that class outstanding or the average weekly volume traded. Rule 144 also requires that notice be given to the SEC and that adequate information about the issuer be publicly available. Also, the sale might be exempt if no public offer is made or if certain other requirements are met. Answer (C) is incorrect because a controlling person is an issuer.

Use Gleim's *CPA Test Prep* for interactive testing with over 2,000 additional multiple-choice questions!

OOF QUESTION 1 *(CPA, adapted)* 10-15 minutes

Coffee Corp., a publicly held corporation, wants to make an $8 million exempt offering of its shares as a private placement offering under Regulation D, Rule 506, of the Securities Act of 1933. Coffee has more than 500 shareholders and assets in excess of $1 billion and has its shares listed on a national securities exchange.

Required

Items 1 through 5 relate to the application of the provisions of the Securities Act of 1933 and the Securities Exchange Act of 1934 to Coffee Corp. and the offering. For each item, select (A) if only statement I is correct, (B) if only statement II is correct, (C) if both statements I and II are correct, or (D) if neither statement I nor II is correct.

A. I only.
B. II only.
C. Both I and II.
D. Neither I nor II.

1. I. Coffee Corp. may make the Regulation D, Rule 506, exempt offering.
   II. Coffee Corp., because it is required to report under the Securities Exchange Act of 1934, may not make an exempt offering.

2. I. Shares sold under a Regulation D, Rule 506, exempt offering may be purchased only by accredited investors.
   II. Shares sold under a Regulation D, Rule 506, exempt offering may be purchased by any number of investors provided there are no more than 35 nonaccredited investors.

3. I. An exempt offering under Regulation D, Rule 506, must not be for more than $10 million.
   II. An exempt offering under Regulation D, Rule 506, has no dollar limit.

4. I. Regulation D, Rule 506, requires that all investors in the exempt offering be notified that, for 9 months after the last sale, no resale may be made to a nonresident.
   II. Regulation D, Rule 506, requires that the issuer exercise reasonable care to assure that purchasers of the exempt offering are buying for investment and are not underwriters.

5. I. The SEC must be notified by Coffee Corp. within 5 days of the first sale of the exempt offering securities.
   II. Coffee Corp. must include an SEC notification of the first sale of the exempt offering securities in Coffee's next filed quarterly report (Form 10-Q).

Knowledge Tested

Securities Act of 1933: Regulation D, Rule 506

Authors' Comments

This question primarily concerns the provisions of Rule 506 of Regulation D of the Securities Act of 1933. Remember that there are two other rules (504 and 505) in Regulation D. We recommend that you memorize the specifics of each rule.

1. The correct answer is (A).
   DISCUSSION: Coffee Corporation, as issuer, is permitted to engage in an exempted private placement under Rule 506 of Regulation D of the 1933 act if it complies with three procedural provisions: (1) No general advertising or solicitation is permitted; (2) an issuer must exercise care to determine that purchasers are not underwriters; and (3) the SEC must be notified within 15 days of the first offering. The Securities Exchange Act of 1934 requires publicly held corporations with more than 500 shareholders and assets exceeding $5 million to register with the SEC and report on a periodic basis. Being a covered corporation under the Securities Exchange Act of 1934 does not affect eligibility for a Regulation D offering.

2. The correct answer is (B).
   DISCUSSION: Shares offered under Regulation D, Rule 506, may be purchased by an unlimited number of accredited investors, but the issuer must reasonably believe that there are no more than 35 nonaccredited investors. All nonaccredited investors must be furnished with material information about the issuer, its business, and the securities being offered prior to the sale. Each nonaccredited purchaser must demonstrate to the issuer the knowledge and experience needed to evaluate the merits and risks of the investment.

3. The correct answer is (B).
   DISCUSSION: An exempt offering under Regulation D, Rule 506, has no dollar limit. Rules 504 and 505 of Regulation D are limited to $1 million and $5 million, respectively, in any 12-month period.

4. The correct answer is (B).
   DISCUSSION: Regulation D requires that issuers exercise reasonable care to assure that purchasers of the exempt offering are buying for their own investment and are not underwriters. Ordinarily, the issuer requires purchasers to sign an investment letter stating that the purchase is for investment only and not for resale. Shares issued pursuant to Rule 506 are referred to as lettered stock and bear a legend that the shares are restricted. After the securities have been held for 2 years, limited resales are allowed without registration. Unlimited resales by a noninsider purchaser are allowed after 3 years. A similar 9-month resale restriction is placed on securities purchased under an intrastate offering exemption.

5. The correct answer is (D).
   DISCUSSION: An issuer of an exempt offering of securities under Regulation D must file a notice on Form D with the SEC within 15 days of the first offering. The issuer may at its discretion include a copy of Form D in the next quarterly report.

OOF QUESTION 2 *(CPA, adapted)* 30-50 minutes

Butler Manufacturing Corp. planned to raise capital for a plant expansion by borrowing from banks and making several stock offerings. Butler engaged Weaver, CPA, to audit its December 31, 1998, financial statements. Butler told Weaver that the financial statements would be given to certain named banks and included in the prospectuses for the stock offerings.

In performing the audit, Weaver did not confirm accounts receivable and, as a result, failed to discover a material overstatement of accounts receivable. Also, Weaver was aware of a pending class action product liability lawsuit that was not disclosed in Butler's financial statements. Despite being advised by Butler's legal counsel that Butler's potential liability under the lawsuit would result in material losses, Weaver issued an unqualified opinion on Butler's financial statements.

In May 1999, Union Bank, one of the named banks, relied on the financial statements and Weaver's opinion in giving Butler a $500,000 loan.

Butler raised an additional $16,450,000 through the following stock offerings, which were sold completely:

- June 1999 -- Butler made a $450,000 unregistered offering of Class B nonvoting common stock under Rule 504 of Regulation D of the Securities Act of 1933. This offering was sold over 2 years to 30 nonaccredited investors and 20 accredited investors by general solicitation. The SEC was notified 8 days after the first sale of this offering.

- September 1999 -- Butler made a $10 million unregistered offering of Class A voting common stock under Rule 506 of Regulation D of the Securities Act of 1933. This offering was sold over 2 years to 200 accredited investors and 30 nonaccredited investors through a private placement. The SEC was notified 14 days after the first sale of this offering.

- November 1999 -- Butler made a $6 million unregistered offering of preferred stock under Rule 505 of Regulation D of the Securities Act of 1933. This offering was sold during a 1-year period to 40 nonaccredited investors by private placement. The SEC was notified 18 days after the first sale of this offering.

Shortly after obtaining the Union loan, Butler began experiencing financial problems but was able to stay in business because of the money raised by the offerings. Butler was found liable in the product liability suit. This resulted in a judgment Butler could not pay. Butler also defaulted on the Union loan and was involuntarily petitioned into bankruptcy. This caused Union to sustain a loss and Butler's shareholders to lose their investments.

As a result,

- The SEC claimed that all three of Butler's offerings were made improperly and were not exempt from registration.

- Union sued Weaver for
  - Negligence
  - Common-law fraud

- The shareholders who purchased Butler's stock through the offerings sued Weaver, alleging fraud under Section 10(b) and Rule 10b-5 of the Securities Exchange Act of 1934.

These transactions took place in a jurisdiction providing for accountant's liability for negligence to known and intended users of financial statements.

Required

a. Items 1 through 5 are questions related to the June 1999 offering made under Rule 504 of Regulation D of the Securities Act of 1933. For each item, indicate (A) if the better answer is Yes and (B) if the better answer is No.

1. Did the offering comply with the dollar limitation of Rule 504?
2. Did the offering comply with the method of sale restrictions?
3. Was the offering sold during the applicable time limit?
4. Was the SEC notified timely of the first sale of the securities?
5. Was the SEC incorrect in claiming that this offering was not exempt from registration?

b. Items 6 through 10 are questions related to the September 1999 offering made under Rule 506 of Regulation D of the Securities Act of 1933. For each item, indicate (A) if the better answer is Yes and (B) if the better answer is No.

6. Did the offering comply with the dollar limitation of Rule 506?
7. Did the offering comply with the method of sale restrictions?
8. Was the offering sold to the correct number of investors?
9. Was the SEC notified timely of the first sale of the securities?
10. Was the SEC correct in claiming that this offering was not exempt from registration?

c. Items 11 through 15 are questions related to the November 1999 offering made under Rule 505 of Regulation D of the Securities Act of 1933. For each item, indicate (A) if the better answer is Yes and (B) if the better answer is No.

11. Did the offering comply with the dollar limitation of Rule 505?
12. Was the offering sold during the applicable time limit?
13. Was the offering sold to the correct number of investors?
14. Was the SEC notified timely of the first sale of the securities?
15. Was the SEC correct in claiming that this offering was not exempt from registration?

Knowledge Tested

1. Requirements to qualify for exemption from registration under Rules 504, 505, and 506 of Regulation D of the Securities Act of 1933

2. Notification requirement of issuer claiming exemption under Regulation D

Authors' Comments

This recital of facts formed the basis for both an essay question and the following objective-type questions. The essay question addressed legal liability of CPAs, and appears after Study Unit 2. You may wish to review it to improve your skill at identifying relevant facts. The objective questions require both understanding of how federal securities laws operate and memorization of the relevant SEC rules which appear in the outline so that you can apply them. The fundamental principle is, if something is a security, the issuer must register unless the security or transaction qualifies for an exemption.

1. The correct answer is (A).
   DISCUSSION: To qualify for Rule 504 exemption, no more than $1 million of securities may be offered. Note that no more than $500,000 of these securities may be sold without registration under a state's blue-sky laws. Consequently, the $450,000 offering in June 1999 complies.

2. The correct answer is (A).
   DISCUSSION: Under Rule 504, general solicitation is a permissible method of sale.

3. The correct answer is (B).
   DISCUSSION: To qualify for Rule 504 exemption, the $1 million of securities must be sold within an applicable time period of 12 months.

4. The correct answer is (A).
   DISCUSSION: The issuer claiming exemption under a Regulation D rule must notify the SEC on Form D within 15 days after the first sale of securities.

5. The correct answer is (B).
   DISCUSSION: General solicitation is permissible under Rule 504, so this offering is exempt from registration.

6. The correct answer is (A).
   DISCUSSION: Sales may qualify for Rule 506 exemption no matter how large the amount of proceeds.

7. The correct answer is (A).
   DISCUSSION: Since the method was private placement, there was no general solicitation of the public.

8. The correct answer is (A).
   DISCUSSION: Under Rule 506, sales may be made to any number of accredited investors. However, sales to more than 35 nonaccredited investors would disqualify from exemption under Rule 506.

9. The correct answer is (A).
   DISCUSSION: The issuer claiming exemption under one of the Regulation D rules is required to notify the SEC within 15 days of the first sale.

10. The correct answer is (B).
   DISCUSSION: The offering was exempt because each of the conditions of Rule 506 was satisfied. Distinguish between requirements for an exemption to apply and compliance with registration requirements.

11. The correct answer is (B).
   DISCUSSION: To qualify for exemption under Rule 505, no more than $5 million of the securities may be sold within the applicable time limit.

12. The correct answer is (A).
   DISCUSSION: Up to $5 million in securities may be sold with the offering qualifying for exemption under Rule 505, but only if they are sold within a period of 12 months.

13. The correct answer is (B).
   DISCUSSION: Under Rule 505, the sales may be to any number of accredited investors, but the issuer must reasonably believe that there are no more than 35 nonaccredited investors.

14. The correct answer is (B).
   DISCUSSION: Under each of Rules 504, 505, and 506 of Regulation D, the issuer must notify the SEC within 15 days of the first sale of the securities.

15. The correct answer is (A).
   DISCUSSION: More than $5 million in sales of the securities was made within the applicable 12-month period. Furthermore, the securities were sold to more than 35 nonaccredited investors. Exemption under Rule 506 is unavailable. It is also not available under Rule 504 ($ limit exceeded) or Rule 505 (sales to more than 35 nonaccredited investors).

ESSAY QUESTION *(CPA, adapted)* 15-25 minutes

Perry, a staff accountant with Orlean Associates, CPAs, reviewed the following transactions engaged in by Orlean's two clients: World Corp. and Unity Corp.

WORLD CORP.

During 1999, World Corp. made a $4 million offering of its stock. The offering was sold to 50 nonaccredited investors and 150 accredited investors. There was a general advertising of the offering. All purchasers were provided with material information concerning World Corp. The offering was completely sold by the end of 1999. The SEC was notified 30 days after the first sale of the offering.

World did not register the offering and contends that the offering and any subsequent resale of the securities are completely exempt from registration under Regulation D, Rule 505, of the Securities Act of 1933.

UNITY CORP.

Unity Corp. has 750 equity shareholders and assets in excess of $100 million. Unity's stock is traded on a national stock exchange. Unity contends that it is not a covered corporation and is not required to comply with the reporting provisions of the Securities Exchange Act of 1934.

Required

a. 1. State whether World is correct in its contention that the offering is exempt from registration under Regulation D, Rule 505, of the Securities Act of 1933. Give the reason(s) for your conclusion.

2. State whether World is correct in its contention that on subsequent resale the securities are completely exempt from registration. Give the reason(s) for your conclusion.

b. 1. State whether Unity is correct in its contention that it is not a covered corporation and is not required to comply with the reporting requirements of the Securities Exchange Act of 1934, and give the reason(s) for your conclusion.

2. Identify and describe two principal reports a covered corporation must file with the SEC.

Knowledge Tested

1. Requirements for a Regulation D, Rule 505 exemption from registration
2. Resale of securities sold under an exemption
3. Reporting requirements for covered corporation

Authors' Comments

It is difficult to imagine an exam that does not test the requirements of registration under the 1933 Securities Act and transactions exempted from its requirements. The 1934 act focuses on continuous reporting, so that affected parties will be reasonably current with respect to financial performance and externalities affecting the issuer.

AICPA Unofficial Answer

a. 1. World Corp.'s position is incorrect. It did not strictly comply with the requirements of obtaining an exemption under Rule 505 of Regulation D and has violated the Securities Act of 1933. The 1933 act prohibits the offer or sale through the mail or other means of interstate commerce of any security unless a registration statement and prospectus for that security is in effect or an exemption from registration is applicable. The offering would have been exempt had World complied with the conditions imposed by Rule 505. Limited offers not exceeding $5 million in sales in any 12-month period exempt issuers from the registration requirements of the 1933 act. World complied with this requirement. Offerings made under this exemption must not be made through any general solicitations or advertising, and the issuer must notify the SEC of the claimed exemption within 15 days of the first offering of the securities. World violated both of these rules. Sales may be made to an unlimited number of accredited investors, but an issuer must limit sales to 35 nonaccredited investors. World violated this condition by selling to 50 nonaccredited investors. If any sales are made to nonaccredited purchasers, all investors must receive material information concerning the issuer and the securities offering. World complied. Because it did not abide by all the required conditions of Rule 505, World Corp. has sold securities in violation of the Securities Act of 1933 and has incurred potential civil liability under Section 12 to each purchaser of the stock and possible criminal sanctions.

2. World Corp.'s contention that resales of the above securities are completely exempt from registration is incorrect. Securities issued under a Regulation D exemption are restricted securities and may not be resold except by registration or through an applicable exemption. Note that Regulation D provides an exemption only for the transaction in which securities are sold by the issuer, not for the securities themselves. World was obligated to inform each purchaser of the resale restriction, to place a boldface legend on the securities warning that restrictions apply, and to take other reasonable steps to determine that all purchasers had investment intent and were not acting as underwriters with intent to make rollover sales. In general, securities issued under Regulation D must be held for a minimum of 2 years and thereafter sold in sufficiently small amounts so as not to overly influence trading in the security.

b. 1. Unity Corp. is incorrect in its claim that it is not a covered corporation and not required to comply with the reporting requirements of the Securities Exchange Act of 1934. The 1934 act requires registration and continuous periodic reporting by all companies that

a) List shares on a national securities exchange, or
b) Have at least 500 shareholders of equity securities and total gross assets of at least $5 million.

Unity is classified as a covered corporation under both of these tests and is subject to the reporting requirements of the Securities Exchange Act of 1934.

2. Two principal reports that a covered corporation under the 1934 act must file with the SEC are the annual and quarterly reports. These disclosures are intended to keep security holders, analysts, and securities markets reasonably current with the registrant's financial performance. Quarterly reports are made on Form 10Q and are less detailed than the annual reports. For example, quarterly reports may contain unaudited financial statements, abbreviated discussions of management, and the company's overall strengths and weaknesses. Quarterly reports are signed by the corporation's officers and must be filed within 45 days of the end of each of the first three quarters. The annual reports on Form 10K include extensive audited financial statements (balance sheet, income statement, cash flow statements, and some comparative past financial information) and extensive analysis of management, executive compensation, the company's securities, securities markets, etc. The 10K must be certified by an independent public accountant and filed within 90 days of the close of the company's fiscal year. Important current matters (e.g., a change in auditors) are reported on Form 8K within 15 days of the event.

STUDY UNIT 13: EMPLOYMENT

15 pages of outline
60 multiple-choice questions
1 OOF and 1 essay

A. Social Security FICA Tax
B. Federal Unemployment Tax Act (FUTA)
C. Workers' Compensation
D. Occupational Safety and Health Act (OSHA)
E. Employment Discrimination
F. Wage and Hour
G. Fringe Benefits

The new AICPA content specification for the CPA exam indicates that employment issues will receive increased coverage on future exams. The material reviewed in this study unit is the various federal and state statutes that supplement employment generally which was reviewed in Study Unit 3, Agency. Candidates should be knowledgeable of the provisions of the Social Security FICA tax, unemployment taxes (FUTA), workers' compensation, and the wage and hour law. You should also be familiar with the issues of safety, discrimination in employment, and fringe benefits.

A. **Social Security FICA Tax**. The **Social Security Act** of 1935 was enacted to provide limited retirement and death benefits to certain employees. Subsequent legislation established programs for disabled employees and families of retired, disabled, and deceased workers.

1. Both employers and employees contribute under this program to help compensate for loss of income upon retirement or disability.

   a. An exemption from FICA taxes is available for both an employer and an employee when they belong to the same recognized religious sect and have filed and had approved identical applications for the exemption.

   b. The following are employees for purposes of the Federal Insurance Contributions Act (FICA):

      1) Parents employed by their children
      2) Officers of a corporation
      3) Professional service providers
      4) Insurance salespeople
      5) Federal employees
      6) State and local employees, unless excepted
      7) Resident aliens who perform services in the U.S.

      NOTE: The determinative variable is employee status.

   c. **Children**. Excluded from employee status for FICA is a child under 18 in his/her parent's employ.

2. Under FICA, employers are required to contribute (pay tax) based on the employee's pay.

3. The FICA tax has been separated into two components, each with its own wage base:

   a. Old-age, survivors, and disability insurance (OASDI)
   b. Hospital insurance (HI) (i.e., Medicare)

4. Under FICA, a combined tax rate of 7.65% is imposed on both the employer and the employee.

   a. 6.20% of the OASDI wage base of $72,600 for 1999
   b. For HI, 1.45% of all wages paid for 1999

5. **Wages** are defined as all remuneration for employment. Some exceptions apply.

   a. Wages include all forms of consideration paid for employment, including cash and the cash value of compensation in any medium other than cash.

b. Wages include each of the following:

1) Wages salary
2) Commissions (including contingent fees)
3) Bonuses
4) Tips
5) Vacation pay
6) Sick pay
7) Severance allowance
8) Fringe benefits
9) Personal use of company car

c. Not included as wages are the following:

1) Payments to the extent it is reasonable to believe a corresponding deduction is allowable for moving expenses

2) Medical care reimbursements under a self-insured plan

a) They are excludable from gross income.

d. **Tips** are treated as wages. An employee is required to report as wages all tips received in a calendar month, if more than a total of $20, to the employer

1) No later than the 10th day of the following month

e. **Domestic service**. An employer is required to pay FICA tax on wages paid to an employee who provides service in a private home if the employee is paid at least $1,000 in any year.

f. **Group term life insurance**. Payments for such insurance for retirees are treated as wages insofar as they

1) Constitute wages gross income, and
2) Are for periods during which the employee status no longer exists.

6. The employer must withhold an equal amount of FICA tax from the employee's wages.

a. The employee's contribution (tax) must be withheld upon each payment of wages, up to the same maximum bases, at the same rates.

7. It is the employer's responsibility to withhold the employee's contribution and to forward the full amount of tax to the Internal Revenue Service. The employer has primary liability for the employee's share.

a. If an employer fails to withhold and pays the employee's share to the IRS, the employer is entitled to reimbursement from the employee.

8. Each employer must withhold the FICA tax, as computed on the previous page, from an employee's wages without considering wages earned from, or FICA tax withheld by, another employer.

9. Contributions made by the employee are not tax deductible by the employee, while those made by the employer are deductible by the employer if they are trade or business expenses.

10. **Self-employed persons** are required to report their own taxable income and pay Social Security tax. This FICA tax liability of a self-employed individual is equal to the combined employer/employee contribution, which is 15.3%.

a. The **self-employment FICA tax** is imposed on net earnings from self-employment.

b. To arrive at net earnings from self-employment, total self-employment income is reduced by one-half of the FICA tax percentage for a self-employed individual.

        1)   EXAMPLE: A self-employed individual earning $100,000 in self-employment income would be taxed on a base amount of $92,350 {$100,000 x [1 − (.5)(.153)]}. This amount represents the net earnings from self-employment.

    c.   If net earnings from self-employment are less than $400, no self-employment tax is imposed.

    d.   Under FICA, a self-employed individual must pay (for 1999)

        1)   12.40% of the OASDI wage base of $72,600 of net earnings from self-employment
        2)   2.90% of all net earnings from self-employment for HI

    e.   An individual is allowed a for-AGI deduction for one-half of self-employment FICA tax paid in computing personal income tax liability.

    f.   Self-employment tax is computed separately for each spouse. If separate returns are filed, each reports his/her own self-employment income.

11.   **Benefits** under FICA vary greatly depending on the status of the beneficiary. A fully insured worker is entitled to the maximum monthly benefit.

    a.   To be **fully insured** an employee must be credited with 40 quarters of coverage (10 years). A quarter of coverage is received for each $370 of earnings in a year up to a maximum of 4 quarters per year.

    b.   A **currently insured** worker is one who has been credited with at least 6 quarters of coverage in the last 3 years. The benefits are somewhat less than those paid to a fully insured worker.

12.   **Retirement benefits** are payable to retired workers who are at least 62 years old, their spouses and divorced spouses who are 62, and dependent children or grandchildren.

    a.   For people (ages 62 through 64) who take the early retirement option, $1 in benefits is lost for each $2 in excess of the statutorily permitted amount ($9,600 in 1999).

        1)   The limit is no longer effective when the retiree reaches age 65.

    b.   For people ages 65 and over, retirement benefits are reduced by $1 for every $3 of annual income from work above $15,500 in 1999 ($17,000 in 2000, $25,000 in 2001, and $30,000 in 2002).

        1)   The limit is no longer effective when the retiree reaches age 70.

    c.   The limit applies to earned income. Compensation from self-employment, e.g., director's fees, may reduce benefits.

        1)   Income derived from investments, e.g., savings, insurance, and private pension plans, does not affect FICA benefits.

    d.   Once a person stops earning above the limit or reaches age 70, checks are increased (delayed retirement credits) to compensate for the lost benefits. However, to obtain delayed retirement credits for lost benefits, a person must forgo his/her entire check for each month worked.

13.   Employees who are unable to engage in gainful employment are eligible for disability benefits if they have been disabled for 5 months and the disability is likely to continue for at least 12 months.

14.   FICA is also used to fund Medicare. For persons over 65 (and certain individuals under 65, such as the disabled), Medicare provides insurance for hospitalization costs and for supplementary medical costs such as doctor's office visits.

15.   Up to 85% of Social Security benefits may be included in the recipient's gross income (subject to income tax) if certain limits are exceeded.

16.   Stop and review! You have completed the outline for this subunit. Study multiple-choice questions 1 through 11 beginning on page 411.

B. **Federal Unemployment Tax Act (FUTA).** The Social Security Act of 1935 also provides for a system of temporary financial assistance for unemployed workers.

1. Under the FUTA, a tax is imposed on employers who

   a. Employ one or more individuals for some portion of a day in each of 20 weeks in the current or preceding calendar year, or

   b. Pay $1,500 or more in wages in any calendar quarter of a current or preceding calendar year.

2. The FUTA tax is 6.2% of the first (up to) $7,000 of wages paid each year to each employee.

   a. The employee does not pay any part of the FUTA tax.
   b. The employer pays the FUTA tax to the IRS.

3. Generally, unemployed workers can receive payments for a maximum of 26 weeks; however, payments are often extended when economic conditions warrant.

4. Benefits are granted on a state plan basis. There are ordinarily three requirements to collect unemployment compensation. The worker

   a. Was employed and was laid off through no fault of the worker
   b. Filed a claim for the benefits
   c. Is able, available, and willing to work but cannot find employment

5. A state may refuse benefits to employees who

   a. Have voluntarily quit work without good cause
   b. Have been discharged for good cause (misconduct)
   c. Refuse to actively seek or accept suitable work

6. FUTA tax is a deductible business expense of the employer.

7. Credit against FUTA tax liability is provided to an employer who pays state unemployment tax.

   a. The credit cannot exceed 5.4% of the first $7,000 of wages.

   b. The amount paid to a state usually depends on the employer's past experience regarding the frequency and amount of unemployment claims.

8. Stop and review! You have completed the outline for this subunit. Study multiple-choice questions 12 through 18 beginning on page 414.

C. **Workers' compensation** laws were passed by all 50 states to reimburse employees for losses sustained because of work-related injury or disease regardless of who, if anyone, was at fault.

1. The coverage of workers' compensation statutes varies from state to state.

   a. Most employers provide workers' compensation by purchasing insurance. Others act as self-insurers.

2. Generally, all employers are covered unless exempted. Exempt employers are usually firms that employ fewer than a stated number of employees.

3. Independent contractors are not covered, nor are casual, agricultural, or domestic employees.

4. Workers' compensation statutes allow the injured employee to recover on the basis of strict liability, thus eliminating the need to prove the employer's negligence.

    a. Employee negligence, including disobeying an employer safety rule, does not prevent recovery of workers' compensation benefits.

    b. The only requirement is that the employee be injured and that the injury arise out of, and in the course of, his/her employment.

        1) Travel to and from work or lunch is generally not within the course and scope of employment because the employer is not in control of the activity.

    c. The typical workers' compensation statute eliminates the employer's traditional defenses of contributory negligence and assumption of the risk.

5. Workers' compensation statutes establish administrative commissions or boards which determine whether an injured employee is entitled to receive compensation and, if so, how much.

6. Generally, the amounts recoverable are fixed by statute according to the type of injury and are less than a court or jury would award. Typical recoveries include

    a. Reasonable medical expenses
    b. A portion of wage-earning capacity (wage-loss)

        1) EXAMPLE: Artisan, a precision tool worker, suffers work-related injury to her thumb. Doctor requires Artisan to keep a restrictive device on her hand for 6 months. It prevents Artisan from performing the usual tasks of her position. Artisan works as a lower-paid inventory clerk during the 6-month period. Her wage impairment disability would be designated temporary partial, and her workers' compensation benefits would be as a portion of diminution of wages.

    c. Specified recoveries for loss of body members, e.g., finger, hand, arm
    d. Survivors' death benefits

NOTE: Medical expenses may include the cost of prosthetic devices. Death benefits include both burial expenses and payments to surviving dependents.

7. Recovery under the statute for applicable injuries is the employee's exclusive remedy against the employer.

8. However, if a third party causes the injury, the employee is not limited to a recovery based on workers' compensation. The injured employee may bring suit in tort against a third-party tort-feasor.

    a. A portion of any recovery is used to reimburse the employer or its insurance carrier for workers' compensation payments.

9. Recovery for injury resulting from some conduct or circumstances may be barred, even if it otherwise arises out of and occurs in the course of employment. Recovery may be unavailable for injury resulting from

    a. Intentional self-infliction
    b. Willful intoxication (alcohol or drugs)
    c. Fighting induced by the injured worker
    d. Preexisting physical conditions

10. Stop and review! You have completed the outline for this subunit. Study multiple-choice questions 19 through 29 beginning on page 417.

D. Occupational Safety and Health Act (OSHA). In 1970 Congress passed the Occupational Safety and Health Act. The purpose of the act was to develop safety standards, prevent injuries, and promote job safety.

   1. OSHA applies to all employees engaged in a business affecting interstate commerce. Exempt are the U.S. government, the states and their political subdivisions, and certain industries regulated by other federal safety legislation.

   2. OSHA is not intended to preempt state regulation of workplace safety.

      a. The act encourages states to develop their own standards, albeit under federal supervision.

   3. The OSHA is administered by the Occupational Safety and Health Administration (OSHA) of the Department of Labor.

      a. OSHA is authorized to develop detailed health and safety standards and to enforce them. It investigates complaints and conducts inspections, and it has developed procedures to encourage compliance.

      b. Employers can insist that OSHA obtain a search warrant prior to inspection. Evidence must provide a reasonable basis for inspection of the workplace.

         1) Employee complaints or a higher-than-usual accident rate may constitute a reasonable basis.

   4. The act requires employers to provide employees with a workplace free from recognized hazards that are likely to cause death or serious physical harm.

   5. Employers are required to comply with specific regulations promulgated by OSHA.

   6. Employers must keep detailed records of job-related injuries, post annual summaries of the records, and report serious accidents to OSHA.

   7. The act prohibits any employer from discharging or discriminating against any employee who exercises his/her rights under the act. If a violation causes a threat of physical harm or imminent danger exists, the employee may

      a. File a written request for an inspection, and
      b. Refuse to work, if in good faith, to avoid exposure.

         1) The employer need not pay the employee.

   8. If an employer is found to be in violation of the act, OSHA inspectors will direct immediate correction of the unsafe condition.

      a. For conditions that are not immediately correctable, OSHA will issue a citation that states the nature of the violation and fixes a date by which it must be corrected.

         1) The citation becomes final after 15 work days following receipt by the employer, unless it is contested.

         2) Contested citations are reviewed by the Occupational Safety and Health Review Commission, a three-member board composed of presidential appointees. Further review by OSHA and federal courts is possible.

   9. OSHA may assess civil penalties of up to $1,000 for each violation, and repeat offenders can be assessed fines as high as $10,000 per violation. Some penalties have totaled several million dollars.

10. Any employer who commits a willful violation resulting in death to an employee may incur a fine, imprisonment, or both. Moreover, the Secretary of Labor may seek injunctive relief when an employment hazard that cannot be corrected immediately presents an imminent danger of death or physical harm.

11. The act also imposes responsibilities on employees to comply with OSHA standards.

    a. Employees who fail to comply with OSHA standards can be discharged.

    NOTE: An injured employee may not use the act as a basis for recovery of civil damages.

12. Stop and review! You have completed the outline for this subunit. Study multiple-choice questions 30 through 34 beginning on page 420.

E. **Employment discrimination** may be defined as employer behavior that penalizes certain individuals because of personal traits that bear no relation to job performance. The most far-reaching federal statute prohibiting job discrimination is **Title VII of the Civil Rights Act of 1964**.

1. Title VII forbids discrimination in employment on the basis of race, color, religion, sex, or national origin.

    a. Job discrimination encompasses more than hiring. Title VII bars employers from discriminating with respect to any term, condition, or privilege of employment, including but not limited to compensation, job assignment, promotion, transfer, or discharge.

2. Title VII applies to all employers of 15 or more employees, whose business affects interstate commerce including

    a. Employment agencies

    b. Labor unions that have 15 or more members or which operate a hiring hall

    c. As amended in 1972 by the **Equal Opportunity Employment Act**, state, federal, and local employees

3. Title VII is enforced through lawsuits by both private individuals and by the Equal Employment Opportunity Commission (EEOC), a federal administrative agency.

    a. The EEOC issues binding regulations and nonbinding guidelines with respect to Title VII issues.

    b. Most EEOC actions are initiated by the filing of a complaint by an individual who believes that (s)he has been discriminated against. However, the EEOC may initiate an investigation on its own volition.

    c. If the EEOC cannot resolve a Title VII case, it issues a right-to-sue letter to the complaining party. This letter enables the plaintiff to file suit.

    d. A successful plaintiff suing under Title VII may obtain back pay, lost wages, and attorney's fees.

        1) In an extreme case, a court might order quotas which afford preferential treatment to individuals of a particular class.

4. Most states and many communities have their own fair-employment-practices law and enforcement agencies. Title VII defers to those agencies when required.

5. **Illegal discrimination** occurs when a plaintiff shows that (s)he has been the victim of disparate treatment. (It is not illegal discrimination to treat employees differently.)

    a. **Disparate treatment** occurs if a person is treated differently from a person not of his/her race, color, religion, sex, national origin, or similar criteria.

        1) The U.S. Supreme Court has held that a prima facie case (a case sufficient on its face) of discrimination exists if both of the following conditions apply:

            a) The plaintiff

                i)   Is within a protected class
                ii) Applied for an open position
                iii) Was qualified for the position
                iv) Was denied the job

            b) The employer continued to interview for the open position.

        2) Once the plaintiff establishes a prima facie case, the burden shifts to the defendant employer to articulate legitimate and nondiscriminatory reasons for the disparate treatment. The discriminating practice is allowable under the conditions discussed below.

            a) The practice serves a compelling business purpose and effectively carries out that purpose.

            b) No reasonable alternative would carry out the purpose at least as well but with less impact on the protected group.

    b. A second theory of illegal discrimination, disparate impact, concerns an employer's adopting "neutral" rules that have an adverse impact on a protected class and which are not justified as being necessary to the business.

        1) Examples of such neutral rules include testing; high school diploma requirements; and height, weight, or strength requirements.

    c. Another common Title VII situation involves allegations that the employer has engaged in a pervasive pattern or practice of discrimination.

        1) Here, evidence of discrimination is primarily statistical.

    d. Finally, an employer sometimes engages in conduct that is neutral on its face (it appears nondiscriminatory) but that perpetuates past (preexisting) discriminatory practices.

        1) Such conduct may violate Title VII.

6. Even if the plaintiff proves a violation of Title VII, there are defenses. The more common are listed below:

    a. A bona fide seniority or merit system
    b. A system based on quality or quantity of production
    c. A professionally developed ability test
    d. A bona fide occupational qualification
    e. National security reasons

7. **Racial Discrimination**. Title VII prohibits all discriminatory employment practices based on race or color that relate to recruiting, hiring, and promotion. Following are examples of practices having disparate impact based on race.

    a. Discriminatory personnel tests with no substantial relation to job qualification

    b. Hiring relatives of current employees when minorities are underrepresented in the workforce

    c.   Not hiring unwed mothers where minorities have a higher rate of illegitimate births than the general working population

NOTE: The U.S. Supreme Court has upheld voluntary employment preferences that favor minorities.

8.   **Sex Discrimination**. Title VII's prohibition of sex discrimination applies to gender-based discrimination against both men and women.

    a.   EEOC guidelines prohibit employers from

       1)   Classifying job positions as either male or female

       2)   Advertising in help-wanted columns that are designated male or female, unless sex is a bona fide job qualification

       3)   Maintaining separate male or female seniority lists

    b.   To find an illegal sexual bias, gender need only be a substantial factor in the discriminatory practice. Following is a three-part test which was used to identify a valid case of discrimination:

       1)   Is the plaintiff a member of the protected class?

       2)   Was (s)he qualified for the job from which (s)he was fired?

       3)   Was the misconduct for which (s)he was discharged nearly identical to that engaged in by an employee outside the protected class whom the employer retained?

    c.   Courts have recognized sexual harassment as sexual discrimination under Title VII. EEOC guidelines define sexual harassment as "unwelcome sexual advances, requests for sexual favors, and other verbal or physical conduct of a sexual nature" that

       1)   Involve submission to some conduct that is either implicitly or explicitly a term or condition of employment

       2)   May require a submission to or rejection of such conduct which serves as the basis for an employment decision

       3)   Have the purpose or effect of substantially interfering with the individual's work performance

       4)   Produce an intimidating, hostile, or offensive work environment

    d.   A theory known as comparable worth maintains that certain jobs, largely held by women, are underpaid relative to their true worth.

       1)   The comparable worth theory concludes that relative values of different jobs to an employer should be measured through a rating or other job evaluation system that is free from any sexual bias.

       2)   The theory was not upheld by the U.S. Supreme Court.

    e.   The **Pregnancy Discrimination Act** amended the Civil Rights Act in 1978.

       1)   This act covers both unmarried and married pregnant women.

       2)   Employers may not discriminate against workers who become pregnant or give birth.

       3)   The employer with health and disability plans must cover pregnancy, childbirth, and related medical conditions in the same manner as other medical conditions are covered.

9. **The Family and Medical Leave Act** was enacted by Congress in 1993 to balance the demands of the workplace with the needs of families.

   a. The act entitles an eligible employee to 12 work weeks of leave

      1) Without pay
      2) Without losing his/her job

   b. The leave is provided for the following:

      1) Birth of a son or daughter

      2) A serious health condition that makes the employee unable to perform his/her job

      3) Care for a spouse, son, daughter, or parent who has a serious health condition

   c. Eligibility requires employment by the employer for at least

      1) 12 months, and
      2) 1,250 hours during the preceding 12 months.

   d. The employee must request the leave.

10. **Age Discrimination**. Neither Title VII nor the EEOC Act forbids discrimination based on age.

   a. The 1967 **Age Discrimination in Employment Act (ADEA)** is intended to prohibit arbitrary age discrimination. Job applicants and employees are to be evaluated on the basis of ability rather than age.

   b. The act protects individuals at least 40 years of age, with no ceiling on age.

   c. Protection is against age discrimination that favors both younger and older individuals, including favored individuals within the protected age group.

   d. The act also prohibits mandatory retirement of most classes of employees under 70 years of age.

   e. Those who must comply with the ADEA include individuals, partnerships, labor organizations (with at least 25 members), corporations, and state and local governments.

      1) Each of these entities must

         a) Be engaged in an industry affecting interstate commerce
         b) Employ at least 20 people

      2) Referrals by an employment agency to a covered employer are within the ADEA's scope, regardless of the agency's size.

   f. A state statute that is broader in scope than the federal statute can be applied concurrently with the ADEA.

   g. The ADEA allows an employer to discharge or otherwise penalize an individual for good cause and to use reasonable factors other than age in making employment decisions. The ADEA also allows

      1) Age criteria in bona fide employee benefit plans
      2) A bona fide seniority system
      3) A bona fide occupational qualification defense

   h. Remedies include unpaid back wages and other benefits related to the discrimination, attorney fees, equitable relief, and perhaps a promotion.

11. **Handicap Discrimination**

    a.   The **Vocational Rehabilitation Act** of 1973 requires employers with federal contracts exceeding $2,500 to take affirmative action to employ and advance qualified handicapped individuals.

        1)   Handicapped persons include ones who meet at least one of the following requirements:

            a)   Have a physical or mental impairment which substantially limits a major life activity

            b)   Have a record of such impairment

            c)   Are regarded as having (deemed to have) such an impairment

        2)   The individual must be qualified, i.e., capable of performing a particular job with reasonable accommodation for his/her handicap.

            a)   Persons whose handicaps prevent them from performing important aspects of their jobs or threaten others' health and safety may not be protected.

        3)   Alcohol or drug dependency is specifically exempted from this statute.

    b.   The **Vietnam-Era Veterans Readjustment Assistance Act** of 1974 requires those employers who are recipients of federal contracts of at least $10,000 to take affirmative action to hire and promote

        1)   Qualified disabled veterans
        2)   Qualified veterans of the Vietnam era

    c.   The **Americans with Disabilities Act** of 1990 expands the Civil Rights Act of 1964 and the Vocational Rehabilitation Act to include protection for disabled persons from employment discrimination with respect to hiring, promotion, and termination.

        1)   The employment provisions of the act are administered by the EEOC.

        2)   Private enforcement actions by a claimant are allowed.

        3)   The act applies to all private businesses with 15 or more employees.

        4)   Three definitions of a disabled person, as defined by this act, are as follows:

            a)   Anyone with physical or mental impairment that substantially limits one or more major life functions (e.g., walking, talking, seeing, working, learning)

            b)   Anyone having a record of such an impairment

            c)   Anyone who is regarded or perceived as having such an impairment

        5)   Employers are required by the ADA to make reasonable accommodation for disabled applicants or employees (e.g., better accessibility, equipment or tool modification, flexibility in work scheduling, or other restructuring).

        6)   Businesses may be exempted from implementing the act by demonstration of an undue burden or hardship (e.g., financial hardship -- probably will be difficult for a large company to demonstrate).

    NOTE: Many rules pertaining to handicap discrimination are enforced by the Department of Labor's Office of Federal Contract Compliance Programs (OFCCP).

12. **Religious and National Origin Discrimination**. Overt discrimination based on the religion or national origin of an employee is prohibited under Title VII.

   a. The term religion includes all aspects of religious observances and practices, as well as belief, unless an employer demonstrates that it is unable to reasonably accommodate an employee's or prospective employee's religious observance or practice without undue hardship on the conduct of the employer's business.

   b. The EEOC's stated position is that almost any set of moral beliefs that are sincerely held are afforded the same protection as traditional religious views.

      1) Title VII forbids religious discrimination against atheists as well.

   c. Overt national origin discrimination includes discrimination based on

      1) The country of one's origin or one's ancestors' origin

      2) Physical, cultural, or linguistic characteristics identified with people of a particular nation

13. Affirmative action addresses policies and practices which present barriers to equal opportunity in employment. Affirmative action programs are twofold. They encourage employers to eliminate present discriminatory practices and conditions, and they indicate affirmative steps to increase female and other minority-group participation in the workforce.

   a. Authority for affirmative action programs is derived primarily from

      1) Executive order 11246 as amended
      2) Title VII of the 1964 Civil Rights Act as amended

   b. Large employers are required to formulate and implement a plan to bring female and minority representation in the workforce up to percentages appropriate to the available labor pool.

      1) They are required to set goals to eliminate discrimination and time tables to achieve these goals.

   c. Certain employers with federal contracts must actively recruit members of minority groups.

14. Stop and review! You have completed the outline for this subunit. Study multiple-choice questions 35 through 46 beginning on page 422.

F. **Wage and Hour**. The **Fair Labor Standards Act** of 1938 **(FLSA)** establishes a federal minimum wage, mandates extra pay for overtime work, and regulates the employment of children.

   1. The FLSA is also known as the Wage and Hour Law.

   2. The FLSA applies to all employers whose business affects interstate commerce.

   3. The FLSA's key provisions entitle an employee covered by the act to

      a. A specified minimum wage (currently $5.15 per hour) subject to amendment
      b. At least the minimum wage per hour for the 40 hours in a work week
      c. 1½ times his/her regular rate for hours worked in excess of 40 per week

      NOTE: In calculating hours worked, employers must include all hours "suffered or permitted to be worked," not merely those formally scheduled.

4.   Certain employees are excluded from some or all of the FLSA minimum wage and overtime provisions. These employees include

    a.   Executive, administrative, and professional personnel
    b.   Outside salespersons
    c.   Certain employees of retail businesses
    d.   Some agricultural workers
    e.   Some commercial fishing workers
    f.   Child actors

5.   Certain employees are excluded from the overtime but not the minimum wage provisions, including

    a.   Air carrier and railroad employees
    b.   Sailors on American vessels
    c.   Taxi drivers
    d.   Certain employees of motor carriers
    e.   Certain local delivery employees

6.   The FLSA also prohibits certain kinds of child labor.

    a.   The basic minimum age for employment is 16, at which age children may be employed in any nonhazardous work.

    b.   Employment of 14- and 15-year-olds is limited to certain occupations such as sales and clerical work. There are limitations on the total hours the children are permitted to work, and they may work only outside regularly scheduled school time.

    c.   Persons under 18 are not permitted to be employed in occupations which are declared hazardous by the Secretary of Labor.

7.   The FLSA is enforced by the Department of Labor.

    a.   Willful violations of the FLSA may be criminally prosecuted.

    b.   Violators may be punished by a fine of up to $10,000 for the first offense. Subsequent offenses may warrant a fine of up to $10,000 or imprisonment for up to 6 months or both.

    c.   Violators of the child-labor provisions can incur a civil penalty: a fine of up to $1,000 for each violation.

        1)   The federal courts may issue injunctions to restrain violators.

8.   The **Equal Pay Act** of 1963 is an amendment to the FLSA of 1938.

    a.   The Equal Pay Act prohibits an employer from discriminating between employees on the basis of sex by paying unequal wages for the same work.

    b.   The act does permit different wages on the basis of seniority, merit, or quality or quantity of work.

    c.   Unlike FLSA, it covers executive, administrative, and professional employees.

    d.   It also reaches state and local government employees.

9.   Stop and review! You have completed the outline for this subunit. Study multiple-choice questions 47 through 55 beginning on page 425.

G. Fringe Benefits. The Internal Revenue Code provides for exclusion from the gross income of an employee certain fringe benefits supplied or paid for by the employer.

  1. An employee's gross income does not include any fringe benefit which qualifies as a

      a. No-additional cost service
      b. Qualified employee discount
      c. Working condition fringe
      d. *De minimis* fringe

  2. A **no-additional cost fringe** is a service or product that the employer offers for sale to customers in the ordinary course of the employer's line of business in which the employee performs substantial services.

      a. The employer must not incur any substantial additional costs in providing the service to the employee.

      b. The fringe benefit must be available to employees on a nondiscriminatory basis.

      c. EXAMPLE: A telephone repairperson is permitted by his/her employer to use company telephone lines to make a long-distance call to his/her parents for free.

  3. An **employee discount** is the difference between the price at which the employer offers property or service to customers and the price at which the employer offers the property or service to the employee.

      a. The product or service must be purchased by the employee for his/her own use.

      b. Qualified property or services are offered in the ordinary course of the employer's line of business in which the employee is performing services.

      c. To be properly excluded, the discounts must be available to employees on a nondiscriminatory basis.

  4. The fair market value of any property or services provided to an employee by an employer as a **working condition fringe** benefit is excludable to the extent that the employer can deduct the costs as an ordinary and necessary business expense.

      a. Property or services provided to an employee qualify as a working condition fringe benefit only if the employee's use of the property or services relates to the employer's trade or business.

      b. EXAMPLE: Corp. provides a car to its sales manager.

  5. The value of any property or service provided to an employee is excludable as a **de minimis fringe** benefit if the property or service has such a minimal value that accounting for it would be unreasonable or impracticable.

      a. EXAMPLE: Occasional use of company copy machines.

      b. An eating facility for employees is treated as a *de minimis* fringe benefit if it is located on or near the business premises of the employer and the revenue derived from the facility normally equals or exceeds its direct operating costs.

6. **Cafeteria Plans**. Employer contributions under a written cafeteria plan are excluded from the participants' gross income. Cafeteria plans are employer-sponsored benefit packages that offer employees a choice between cash and statutory nontaxable benefits. Nontaxable benefits include

    a. Dependent care assistance
    b. Group term life insurance coverage up to $50,000
    c. Disability benefits
    d. Accident and health benefits
    e. Group legal services

    NOTE: To be a cafeteria plan, the plan must allow a participant employee to choose cash rather than one or more of the statutory nontaxable benefits.

7. **Dependent Care Assistance**. The Code provides for limited exclusion from an employee's gross income of the cost of dependent care assistance provided by the employer.

    a. Assistance which qualifies is care for dependents who are under the age of 15 or disabled and which allows the employee to be gainfully employed.

8. **Federal Consolidated Budget Reconciliation Act of 1985 (COBRA)**. The act provides that an employee of a private employer or the employee's spouse or other beneficiaries must be notified and offered the opportunity to continue their group health insurance for 18 months after termination (or loss of coverage due to certain events) at the employee's expense.

9. **Employee Retirement Income Security Act (ERISA)**. The act created guidelines for employers that establish pension plans for their employees. Requirements of the act include the following:

    a. The pension fund manager owes a fiduciary duty to the fund.

    b. A pension plan is not allowed to

        1) Lend money to the employer or its insiders
        2) Invest more than 10% of its assets in the employer's securities

    c. Contributions made by employees must vest immediately.

    d. Contributions made by employers must be

        1) Completely nonvested for up to 5 years and then fully vested thereafter, or
        2) Gradually vested over a maximum of 7 years.

    e. Participation in the Pension Benefit Guaranty Corporation is mandatory and provides for the payment of some benefits when underfunded plans cannot make the payments.

10. Other income types which might be acquired in an employment context may be excluded from gross income. A partial list follows:

    a. Meals and lodging
    b. Accident and health benefits
    c. Death benefits
    d. Group term life insurance premiums paid by an employer
    e. Compensation for injuries and sickness
    f. Scholarship and fellowship grants
    g. Prizes and awards

    NOTE: For further details, refer to *CPA Review: TAX-MAN-GOV*.

11. Stop and review! You have completed the outline for this subunit. Study multiple-choice questions 56 through 60 beginning on page 428.

MULTIPLE-CHOICE QUESTIONS

A. Social Security FICA Tax

1. Syl Corp. does not withhold FICA taxes from its employees' compensation. Syl voluntarily pays the entire FICA tax for its share and the amounts that it could have withheld from the employees. The employees' share of FICA taxes paid by Syl to the IRS is

A. Deductible by Syl as additional compensation that is includable in the employees' taxable income.

B. Not deductible by Syl because it does not meet the deductibility requirement as an ordinary and necessary business expense.

C. A nontaxable gift to each employee, provided that the amount is less than $1,000 annually to each employee.

D. Subject to prescribed penalties imposed on Syl for its failure to withhold required payroll taxes.

The correct answer is (A). *(CPA, adapted)*
REQUIRED: The correct statement concerning an employee's FICA taxes.
DISCUSSION: The employer is required to withhold the employees' share of FICA taxes from its employees' wages. However, on these facts, the employer will be treated as having paid additional compensation to the employees in the amount of the employees' share. This additional compensation is a deductible ordinary and necessary business expense.
Answers (B), (C), and (D) are incorrect because payment of a liability of an employee (e.g., the employee's share of FICA taxes) by the employer is treated as additional compensation.

2. Tower drives a truck for Musgrove Produce, Inc. The truck is owned by Musgrove. Tower is paid on the basis of a formula that takes into consideration the length of the trip, cargo, and fuel consumed. Tower is responsible for repairing or replacing all flat tires. Musgrove is responsible for all other truck maintenance. Tower drives only for Musgrove. If Tower is a common-law employee and not an independent contractor, which of the following statements is correct?

A. All Social Security retirement benefits are fully includable in the determination of Tower's federal taxable income if certain gross income limitations are exceeded.

B. Musgrove remains primarily liable for Tower's share of FICA taxes if it fails to withhold and pay the taxes on Tower's wages.

C. Musgrove would not have to withhold FICA taxes if Tower elected to make FICA contributions as a self-employed person.

D. Bonuses or vacation pay that are paid to Tower by Musgrove are not subject to FICA taxes because they are not regarded as regular compensation.

The correct answer is (B). *(CPA, adapted)*
REQUIRED: The correct statement concerning FICA taxes and benefits.
DISCUSSION: Under the Federal Insurance Contribution Act (FICA), the employer is required to withhold the employee's share of Social Security taxes from the employee's wages and remit that amount, along with the employer's own equal share, to the government. An employer that underwithholds and underpays is liable for the unpaid balance of the employee's share.
Answer (A) is incorrect because only up to one-half of Social Security benefits is taxable. Answer (C) is incorrect because the facts specify that Tower is an employee. Employee status under common law depends on the employer's right to control the employee. There is no election for a person with employee status to make FICA contributions as a self-employed person. Answer (D) is incorrect because almost all types of compensation for employment are subject to FICA tax, including money or other forms of wages, bonuses, commissions, vacation pay, severance pay, and tips.

3. Under the Federal Insurance Contributions Act (FICA), which of the following acts will cause an employer to be liable for penalties?

	Failure to Supply Taxpayer Identification Numbers	Failure to Make Timely FICA Deposits
A.	Yes	Yes
B.	Yes	No
C.	No	Yes
D.	No	No

The correct answer is (A). *(CPA, adapted)*
REQUIRED: The acts for which an employer is liable.
DISCUSSION: An employer subject to FICA taxes must file quarterly returns and deposit appropriate amounts on a monthly or semiweekly basis with an authorized depository institution. For example, a monthly depositor must deposit each month's taxes on or before the 15th day of the following month. Failure to deposit appropriate amounts results in penalties. Penalties are also imposed on persons who file returns and other documents without supplying taxpayer identification numbers.
Answers (B), (C), and (D) are incorrect because an employer is liable for not supplying taxpayer identification numbers and for failure to make timely FICA deposits.

4. Which of the following types of income is subject to taxation under the provisions of the Federal Insurance Contributions Act (FICA)?

A. Interest earned on municipal bonds.

B. Capital gains of $3,000.

C. Car received as a productivity award.

D. Dividends of $2,500.

The correct answer is (C). *(CPA, adapted)*
REQUIRED: The type of income to which Social Security tax applies.
DISCUSSION: The Social Security tax imposed by the FICA applies to virtually all compensation received for employment, including money or other forms of wages, bonuses, commissions, vacation pay, severance allowances, and tips. A car received as a productivity award is a form of compensation for employment which is not excepted from application of FICA tax.
Answers (A), (B), and (D) are incorrect because income derived from an investment, as opposed to compensation for employment, is not subject to FICA tax.

5. An employer who fails to withhold Federal Insurance Contributions Act (FICA) taxes from covered employees' wages, but who pays both the employer and employee shares, would

A. Be entitled to a refund from the IRS for the employees' share.

B. Be allowed no federal tax deduction for any payments.

C. Have a right to be reimbursed by the employees for the employees' share.

D. Owe penalties and interest for failure to collect the tax.

The correct answer is (C). *(CPA, adapted)*
REQUIRED: The correct statement about an employer who pays an employee's share of FICA taxes after failing to withhold it.
DISCUSSION: An employer is primarily liable to pay an employee's share of FICA tax if the employer fails to pay and remit it. The employer then has a right to reimbursement of the amount paid.
Answer (A) is incorrect because the employer's right is to reimbursement from the employee. No IRS refund is payable for satisfying a liability. Answer (B) is incorrect because the employer's share of FICA tax paid is deductible by the employer. Answer (D) is incorrect because failure to remit the employer and employee shares of FICA tax is subject to penalty and interest. Failure to collect it is not.

6. Under the Federal Insurance Contributions Act (FICA), all of the following are considered wages except

A. Contingent fees.

B. Reimbursed travel expenses.

C. Bonuses.

D. Commissions.

The correct answer is (B). *(CPA, adapted)*
REQUIRED: The type of payment not treated as wages for purposes of the Social Security FICA tax.
DISCUSSION: The Social Security tax imposed by the FICA applies to virtually all compensation received for employment, including money or other forms of wages, bonuses, commissions, vacation pay, severance allowances, and tips. Reimbursed travel expenses are not included as wages to the extent a corresponding deduction is allowable.
Answers (A), (C), and (D) are incorrect because each is treated as a form of compensation from employment for purposes of FICA.

7. Which of the following statements is correct with respect to Social Security taxes and benefits?

- A. A self-employed individual with net earnings of $35,000 will pay more tax than an employee with wages of $35,000.

- B. Both employees and self-employed individuals are subject to Social Security taxes based on their respective gross wages or gross earnings from self-employment.

- C. To the extent the amount received as retirement benefits is less than the amount contributed to the Social Security fund by the individual, it will never be included in the individual's adjusted gross income for federal income tax purposes.

- D. An individual whose gross income exceeds certain maximum limitations is required to include the entire amount received as disability benefits in the computation of the individual's adjusted gross income for federal income tax purposes.

The correct answer is (A). *(CPA, adapted)*
REQUIRED: The correct statement about Social Security taxes and benefits.
DISCUSSION: For tax years beginning in 1990, a tax rate of 15.3% applies to an individual's earnings from self-employment. However, a tax deduction is available for half of the tax. The Social Security tax employers and employees each pay is 6.20% of the employee's wages up to $72,600 and 1.45% of all wages paid for 1999. The employee pays less tax than the self-employed individual because the employer must also pay Social Security taxes on the employee's wages.

Answer (B) is incorrect because net earnings from self-employment, not gross earnings, is the Social Security tax base for a self-employed individual. Answer (C) is incorrect because a portion of Social Security benefits received by an individual may be included in the individual's adjusted gross income. Answer (D) is incorrect because only a portion of an individual's disability benefits is included in his/her gross income if certain limitations on gross income are exceeded. The exact amount is computed on the basis of a formula set forth in the Internal Revenue Code.

8. Which of the following forms of income, if in excess of the annual exempt amount, will cause a reduction in a retired person's Social Security benefits?

- A. Annual proceeds from an annuity.

- B. Director's fees.

- C. Pension payments.

- D. Closely held corporation stock dividends.

The correct answer is (B). *(CPA, adapted)*
REQUIRED: The type of income that may reduce a retiree's Social Security benefits.
DISCUSSION: Retired employees are subject to an annual earnings limitation (which changes periodically) that reduces the amount of Social Security benefits when exceeded. Employees ages 62 through 64 will lose $1 in Social Security benefits for each $2 of earnings in excess of the statutorily permitted amount. Employees ages 65 through 69 will lose $1 in Social Security benefits for each $3 of earnings in excess of the statutorily permitted amount. A limitation is no longer effective when the retiree reaches age 70. Compensation from self-employment, such as director's fees, may reduce benefits. However, income derived from investments, such as insurance, savings, and private pension plans, does not affect benefits.

Answers (A), (C), and (D) are incorrect because this income is treated as derived from investments, rather than as earnings which may reduce Social Security benefits.

9. Under the Federal Insurance Contributions Act (FICA) and the Social Security Act (SSA),

- A. Persons who are self-employed are not required to make FICA contributions.

- B. Employees who participate in private retirement plans are not required to make FICA contributions.

- C. Death benefits are payable to an employee's survivors only if the employee dies before reaching the age of retirement.

- D. The receipt of earned income by a person who is also receiving Social Security retirement benefits may result in a reduction of such benefits.

The correct answer is (D). *(CPA, adapted)*
REQUIRED: The correct statement about FICA and the Social Security Act (SSA).
DISCUSSION: Retired employees are subject to an annual earnings limitation (which changes periodically) that reduces the amount of Social Security benefits when exceeded. Employees ages 62 through 64 will lose $1 in Social Security benefits for each $2 of earnings in excess of the statutorily permitted amount. Employees ages 65 through 69 will lose $1 in Social Security benefits for each $3 of earnings in excess of the statutorily permitted amount. A limitation is no longer effective when the retiree reaches age 70.

Answer (A) is incorrect because self-employed persons are subject to FICA tax on net earnings from self-employment. Answer (B) is incorrect because participation by an employee in a private retirement plan affects deductibility of contributions to IRAs, but not liability for FICA tax. Answer (C) is incorrect because there is no such condition upon entitlement to the benefits.

10. After serving as an active director of Lee Corp. for 20 years, Ryan was appointed an honorary director with the obligation to attend directors' meetings with no voting power. In 1999, Ryan received an honorary director's fee of $5,000. This fee is

A.   Reportable by Lee as employee compensation subject to Social Security tax.

B.   Reportable by Ryan as self-employment income subject to Social Security self-employment tax.

C.   Taxable as "other income" by Ryan, not subject to any Social Security tax.

D.   Considered to be a gift not subject to Social Security self-employment or income tax.

The correct answer is (B). *(CPA, adapted)*
REQUIRED: The tax treatment of honorary director's fees.
DISCUSSION: A person is not an employee of a corporation when acting as a director. However, fees for acting as a director are treated as earnings from self-employment, subject to both income tax and Social Security self-employment tax.
Answer (A) is incorrect because a person is not an employee of a corporation when acting as a director. Answers (C) and (D) are incorrect because director's fees are treated as taxable compensation from self-employment. Ryan's attendance at directors' meetings was obligatory.

11. Social Security benefits may include all of the following except

A.   Payments to divorced spouses.

B.   Payments to disabled children.

C.   Medicare payments.

D.   Medicaid payments.

The correct answer is (D). *(CPA, adapted)*
REQUIRED: The payment that is not a Social Security benefit.
DISCUSSION: Benefits provided by the Social Security Act as amended are paid to retired workers over a certain age, to the surviving spouse and children of deceased workers, and to disabled workers and certain of their dependents. Also, health and medical insurance are provided for the elderly under Medicare. Medicaid payments are not funded as a Social Security benefit.
Answers (A), (B), and (C) are incorrect because each type of payment may be made as a Social Security benefit.

B. Federal Unemployment Tax Act (FUTA)

12. Unemployment tax payable under the Federal Unemployment Tax Act (FUTA) is

A.   Payable by all employers.

B.   Deducted from employee wages.

C.   Paid to the Social Security Administration.

D.   A tax-deductible employer's expense.

The correct answer is (D). *(CPA, adapted)*
REQUIRED: The correct statement concerning FUTA tax.
DISCUSSION: The Internal Revenue Code imposes federal unemployment taxes on certain employers. The tax is a deductible business expense of the employer.
Answer (A) is incorrect because certain employers are exempt from FUTA tax liability, e.g., one who pays employees less than $1,500 during any calendar quarter in a year or the preceding year and whose employees work less than a threshold number of hours. Answer (B) is incorrect because employees are not subject to FUTA tax. The tax is not deducted from their wages. Answer (C) is incorrect because FUTA tax is paid to the IRS.

13. For the entire year 1999, Ral Supermarket, Inc. conducted its business operations without any permanent or full-time employees. Ral employed temporary and part-time workers during each of the 52 weeks in the year. Under the provisions of the Federal Unemployment Tax Act (FUTA), which of the following statements is correct regarding Ral's obligation to file a federal unemployment tax return for 1999?

- A. Ral must file a 1999 FUTA return only if aggregate wages exceeded $100,000 during 1999.

- B. Ral must file a 1999 FUTA return because it had at least one employee during at least 20 weeks of 1999.

- C. Ral is obligated to file a 1999 FUTA return only if at least one worker earned $50 or more in any calendar quarter of 1999.

- D. Ral does not have to file a 1999 FUTA return because it had no permanent or full-time employees in 1999.

The correct answer is (B). *(CPA, adapted)*
REQUIRED: The filing requirements of FUTA.
DISCUSSION: Under FUTA, an employer must file a return if it employs at least one person for some portion of the day during at least 20 weeks in the current or preceding calendar year. Although Ral Supermarket did not have any full-time employees, it must file a FUTA return because it employed temporary and part-time workers for more than 20 weeks in 1999.

Answer (A) is incorrect because an employer must file a FUTA return if it paid more than $1,500 in wages during any quarter in the preceding or current calendar year. Answer (C) is incorrect because there is no minimum amount of wages that an employer must pay in order to be subject to FUTA tax. Answer (D) is incorrect because an employer's requirement to pay FUTA taxes is based on the total use of labor, not employment of full-time personnel. Even though the employer had no full-time personnel, it was subject to FUTA tax in 1999 because it employed temporary and part-time workers on a regular basis.

14. Taxes payable under the Federal Unemployment Tax Act (FUTA) are

- A. Calculated as a fixed percentage of all compensation paid to an employee.

- B. Deductible by the employer as a business expense for federal income tax purposes.

- C. Payable by employers for all employees.

- D. Withheld from the wages of all covered employees.

The correct answer is (B). *(CPA, adapted)*
REQUIRED: The correct statement concerning FUTA tax.
DISCUSSION: Federal unemployment tax must be paid by an employer who employs one or more persons covered under the federal Social Security Act or who pays wages of $1,500 or more during any calendar quarter. These payments are deductible as a business expense for tax purposes.

Answer (A) is incorrect because the tax is a fixed percentage of each covered employee's salary up to a stated maximum (6.2% up to $7,000). Answer (C) is incorrect because they are payable only for covered employees. Answer (D) is incorrect because federal unemployment taxes are imposed on the employer only, not the employee.

15. The Federal Unemployment Tax Act (FUTA)

- A. Requires both the employer and employee to pay FUTA taxes, although the amounts to be paid by each are different.

- B. Does not apply to businesses with fewer than 35 employees.

- C. Does not apply to employers that conduct business in only one state and employ only residents of that state.

- D. Allows the employer to take a credit against the FUTA tax if contributions are made to a state unemployment fund.

The correct answer is (D). *(CPA, adapted)*
REQUIRED: The correct statement about the FUTA.
DISCUSSION: FUTA permits an employer who made contributions to a state unemployment fund to take a credit against the federal unemployment tax.

Answer (A) is incorrect because employees are not required to pay any tax under FUTA. Answer (B) is incorrect because the tax is imposed on employers having as few as one employee for a portion of a day in each of 20 weeks in any year, or who have a payroll of at least $1,500 in any calendar quarter. Answer (C) is incorrect because no such exemption to FUTA tax liability is provided.

16. An employer having an experience unemployment tax rate of 3.2% in a state having a standard unemployment tax rate of 5.4% may take a credit against a 6.2% federal unemployment tax rate of

A. 3.0%

B. 3.2%

C. 5.4%

D. 6.2%

The correct answer is (C). *(CPA, adapted)*

REQUIRED: The credit against FUTA tax allowable to an employer who pays state unemployment tax.

DISCUSSION: An employer is allowed a credit against FUTA tax for unemployment tax paid to a state. The credit is the tax paid to the state but is limited to 5.4% of the first $7,000 of wages paid. Because the state in the question taxes 5.4% of wages, that is the amount of the credit.

Answers (A) and (B) are incorrect because, although the amount paid to the state usually depends upon the employer's prior experience regarding the frequency and amount of unemployment claims, the state in question has a standard rate of 5.4%. Answer (D) is incorrect because the credit is limited to 5.4% of the first $7,000 of wages paid each employee.

17. In general, which of the following statements is correct with respect to unemployment compensation?

A. An employee who is unable to work because of a disability is entitled to unemployment compensation.

B. An individual who has been discharged from employment because of work-connected misconduct is ineligible for unemployment compensation.

C. The maximum period during which unemployment compensation may be collected is uniform throughout the United States.

D. The maximum amount of weekly unemployment compensation payments made by a state is determined by federal law.

The correct answer is (B). *(CPA, adapted)*

REQUIRED: The correct statement with respect to unemployment compensation under FUTA.

DISCUSSION: There are ordinarily three conditions to collect unemployment compensation: (1) The worker was employed and laid off through no fault of the worker; (2) the worker filed a claim for the benefits; (3) the worker is able, available, and willing to work but cannot find employment.

Answer (A) is incorrect because to collect unemployment compensation, an individual must be able, available, and willing to work. Answers (C) and (D) are incorrect because, although federal law provides general guidelines, standards, and requirements for the program, the states administer the benefit payments under the program. A state may determine the maximum amount of and period for unemployment compensation.

18. An unemployed CPA generally would receive unemployment compensation benefits if the CPA

A. Was fired as a result of the employer's business reversals.

B. Refused to accept a job as an accountant while receiving extended benefits.

C. Was fired for embezzling from a client.

D. Left work voluntarily without good cause.

The correct answer is (A). *(CPA, adapted)*

REQUIRED: The circumstances in which a person would generally qualify to receive unemployment compensation benefits.

DISCUSSION: There are ordinarily three conditions to collect unemployment compensation: (1) The worker was employed and laid off through no fault of the worker; (2) the worker filed a claim for the benefits; (3) the worker is able, available, and willing to work but cannot find employment. A worker is disqualified if (s)he refuses other suitable work, was discharged for good cause, or quit voluntarily.

Answer (B) is incorrect because the CPA is not required to accept the other job but is not entitled to the unemployment compensation if (s)he refuses the job. Answers (C) and (D) are incorrect because a worker is disqualified if (s)he refuses other suitable work, was discharged for good cause, or quit voluntarily.

C. Workers' Compensation

19. The primary purpose for enacting workers' compensation statutes was to

- A. Eliminate all employer-employee negligence lawsuits.
- B. Enable employees to recover for injuries regardless of negligence.
- C. Prevent employee negligence suits against third parties.
- D. Allow employees to recover additional compensation for employer negligence.

The correct answer is (B). *(CPA, adapted)*
REQUIRED: The primary purpose for enacting workers' compensation statutes.
DISCUSSION: Workers' compensation laws were enacted to provide a sure remedy for injured employees. Under common law, they had to sue the employer, prove negligence, and be subject to various defenses. Workers' compensation is usually the exclusive remedy for an injured employee against the employer.
Answer (A) is incorrect because certain employers are exempt, such as employers with fewer than a certain number of employees. Answer (C) is incorrect because an injured employee may, in addition to recovering workers' compensation benefits, pursue legal action against a third party. Answer (D) is incorrect because workers' compensation is usually the exclusive remedy for an injured employee against the employer.

20. Workers' compensation acts require an employer to

- A. Provide coverage for all eligible employees.
- B. Withhold employee contributions from the wages of eligible employees.
- C. Pay an employee the difference between disability payments and full salary.
- D. Contribute to a federal insurance fund.

The correct answer is (A). *(CPA, adapted)*
REQUIRED: The requirement under workers' compensation laws.
DISCUSSION: All employers are within the scope of workers' compensation law unless exempted. An exemption usually applies to employers with less than a designated number of employees. All employees are covered unless ineligible. Ineligible workers include independent contractors and casual, agricultural, and domestic employees.
Answers (B) and (D) are incorrect because, although an employer may purchase workers' compensation liability insurance, employer liability under workers' compensation law does not depend on it. Thus, funding of awards is neither by withholding nor by contribution to a federal insurance fund. Answer (C) is incorrect because the employee's award typically provides for only a percentage of full salary.

21. Which of the following claims is(are) generally covered under workers' compensation statutes?

	Occupational Disease	Employment-Aggravated Preexisting Disease
A.	Yes	Yes
B.	Yes	No
C.	No	Yes
D.	No	No

The correct answer is (A). *(CPA, adapted)*
REQUIRED: The claim(s), if any, covered by workers' compensation statutes.
DISCUSSION: Workers' compensation is a form of strict liability whereby the employer is liable to an employee for injuries or diseases sustained by the employee that arise out of and in the course of employment.
Answers (B), (C), and (D) are incorrect because workers' compensation generally covers all work-related injuries and diseases.

22. Which of the following payments are deducted from an employee's salary?

	Unemployment Compensation Insurance	Workers' Compensation Insurance
A.	Yes	Yes
B.	Yes	No
C.	No	Yes
D.	No	No

The correct answer is (D). *(CPA, adapted)*
    REQUIRED: The tax(es) paid by an employee.
    DISCUSSION: Neither unemployment compensation insurance nor workers' compensation insurance is deducted from an employee's salary. The employer is required by law to pay these amounts. Under FUTA, an employer pays a specific amount to the IRS to provide temporary financial assistance to workers who become unemployed as a result of being laid off. Workers' compensation insurance is a state program in which employers must insure employees for losses sustained due to work-related injuries, regardless of fault.
    Answers (A), (B), and (C) are incorrect because both unemployment compensation insurance and workers' compensation insurance are paid by the employer and are not deducted from an employee's salary.

23. Which of the following provisions is basic to all workers' compensation systems?

A. The injured employee must prove the employer's negligence.

B. The employer may invoke the traditional defense of contributory negligence.

C. The employer's liability may be ameliorated by a coemployee's negligence under the fellow-servant rule.

D. The injured employee is allowed to recover on strict liability theory.

The correct answer is (D). *(CPA, adapted)*
    REQUIRED: The provision of workers' compensation.
    DISCUSSION: Workers' compensation statutes allow for recovery based on strict liability. A worker need only prove that (s)he suffered an injury that arose out of and occurred in the course of employment.
    Answer (A) is incorrect because the employer is strictly liable. Answer (B) is incorrect because the employer's traditional defenses of contributory negligence and assumption of the risk are not permitted. Answer (C) is incorrect because the fellow-servant rule is not a defense. However, if a third party causes the injury, the employee may sue that party. A portion of any recovery is used to reimburse the employer for any workers' compensation payments.

24. Generally, which of the following statements concerning workers' compensation laws is correct?

A. The amount of damages recoverable is based on comparative negligence.

B. Employers are strictly liable without regard to whether or not they are at fault.

C. Workers' compensation benefits are not available if the employee is negligent.

D. Workers' compensation awards are payable for life.

The correct answer is (B). *(CPA, adapted)*
    REQUIRED: The true statement concerning workers' compensation laws.
    DISCUSSION: Workers' compensation is a form of strict liability whereby the employer is liable to an employee for injuries or diseases sustained by the employee that arise out of and in the course of employment. The employer is liable even if (s)he is not negligent. The employee is generally entitled to workers' compensation benefits without regard to fault.
    Answer (A) is incorrect because the amount of damages the employee will be allowed is as prescribed by state statute, usually a percentage of the injured employee's wages. Answer (C) is incorrect because the employee will receive workers' compensation despite his/her negligence. Answer (D) is incorrect because workers' compensation provides limited remedies.

25. Workers' compensation laws provide for all of the following benefits except

A. Burial expenses.

B. Full pay during disability.

C. The cost of prosthetic devices.

D. Monthly payments to surviving dependent children.

The correct answer is (B). *(CPA, adapted)*
    REQUIRED: The benefit not provided for by workers' compensation laws.
    DISCUSSION: Amounts awarded under typical workers' compensation laws may be for (1) wage loss, (2) medical costs and devices, (3) loss of body members, and (4) death. Only a portion of wage-earning capacity is usually awarded.
    Answers (A) and (D) are incorrect because death benefits under workers' compensation include both burial expenses and payments to surviving dependents. Answer (C) is incorrect because medical expenses covered include the cost of prosthetic devices.

26. Which one of the following statements concerning workers' compensation laws is generally correct?

- A. Employers are strictly liable without regard to whether or not they are at fault.
- B. Workers' compensation benefits are not available if the employee is negligent.
- C. Workers' compensation awards are not reviewable by the courts.
- D. The amount of damages recoverable is based on comparative negligence.

The correct answer is (A). *(CPA, adapted)*

REQUIRED: The true statement concerning workers' compensation laws.

DISCUSSION: Workers' compensation is a form of strict liability whereby the employer is liable to an employee for injuries or diseases sustained by the employee that arise out of and in the course of employment. The employer is liable even if (s)he is not negligent. The employee is generally entitled to workers' compensation benefits without regard to fault.

Answer (B) is incorrect because the employee will receive workers' compensation despite his/her negligence. Answer (C) is incorrect because the outcome of an administrative hearing may be appealed to the courts. Answer (D) is incorrect because the amount of damages the employee will be allowed is not based on comparative fault but on a scheme prescribed by state statute, usually a percentage of the injured employee's wages.

27. If an employee is injured, full workers' compensation benefits are not payable if the employee

- A. Was injured because of failing to abide by written safety procedures.
- B. Was injured because of the acts of fellow employees.
- C. Intentionally caused self-inflicted injury.
- D. Brought a civil suit against a third party who caused the injury.

The correct answer is (C). *(CPA, adapted)*

REQUIRED: The circumstances under which full workers' compensation benefits are not payable.

DISCUSSION: Workers' compensation is generally awarded an employee for injury which arises out of and occurs during the course of employment. But benefits are unavailable for injury resulting from intentional self-infliction, willful intoxication, fighting not induced by the employer, or preexisting physical conditions.

Answer (A) is incorrect because an employee's failure to abide by safety procedures is not a defense to a workers' compensation claim. Answer (B) is incorrect because such a claim is compensable provided it arose out of and in the course of employment. Answer (D) is incorrect because, if a third party causes the injury, the employee may receive workers' compensation and sue the third party.

28. Kroll, an employee of Acorn, Inc., was injured in the course of employment while operating a forklift manufactured and sold to Acorn by Trell Corp. The forklift was defectively designed by Trell. Under the state's mandatory workers' compensation statute, Kroll will be successful in

	Obtaining Workers' Compensation Benefits	A Negligence Action against Acorn
A.	Yes	Yes
B.	Yes	No
C.	No	Yes
D.	No	No

The correct answer is (B). *(CPA, adapted)*

REQUIRED: The correct statement about the rights of an injured employee.

DISCUSSION: The law of workers' compensation permits recovery for a work-related injury (arising out of and in the course of employment), but a negligence suit against the employer is barred. However, when an employee's injuries are caused by a third party, the injured employee may, in addition to recovering workers' compensation benefits, pursue a legal action against the third party. Thus, a strict liability suit against the manufacturer of defective equipment is not barred.

Answers (A) and (C) are incorrect because, if the injury is compensable under the state's mandatory workers' compensation statute, a negligence suit against an employer is barred. Answer (D) is incorrect because Kroll was injured in the scope of employment. This is all that is required for an employee covered by workers' compensation laws to obtain benefits.

29. Bing was employed as a taxi driver by Speedy, Inc. While acting in the scope and course of his employment with Speedy, Bing collided with a van driven by Hart. Hart was an independent contractor making a delivery for Troy Corp. The collision was caused solely by Bing's negligence. As a result of the collision, both Bing and Hart suffered permanent injuries. Speedy and Troy were both in compliance with the state's workers' compensation statute. If Hart commences an action against Bing and Speedy for negligence, which of the following statements is correct?

- A. Hart is entitled to recover damages from Bing or Speedy.

- B. Bing will either be denied workers' compensation benefits or have his benefits reduced because of his negligence.

- C. Hart's action for negligence will be dismissed because Hart is an independent contractor.

- D. Hart is entitled to recover damages from Speedy's workers' compensation carrier to the extent no duplicate payment has been received by Hart.

The correct answer is (A). *(CPA, adapted)*
    REQUIRED: The liability of a principal and an agent for the negligent acts of the agent.
    DISCUSSION: A person is always responsible for his/her negligent acts. Thus, Bing is liable. An employer is liable in tort for acts of employees or agents in the course and scope of employment. Accordingly, Speedy is also liable.
    Answer (B) is incorrect because workers' compensation benefits do not depend on lack of care or fault. Answer (C) is incorrect because Hart's being an independent contractor is irrelevant. (It would, however, be relevant to a workers' compensation claim.) Answer (D) is incorrect because Hart cannot receive workers' compensation benefits from Speedy because Hart is not employed by Speedy.

D. Occupational Safety and Health Act (OSHA)

30. The Occupational Safety and Health Act (OSHA)

- A. Is administered by the Occupational Safety and Health Administration of the Department of Commerce.

- B. Is administered by the National Institute of Occupational Safety and Health of the Department of Health and Human Services.

- C. Applies to all public and private sector employees.

- D. Applies to most employees engaged in a business affecting commerce.

The correct answer is (D). *(Publisher)*
    REQUIRED: The correct statement about OSHA.
    DISCUSSION: The primary legislative purposes of OSHA are to require safe and healthy working conditions in the place of employment and to prevent injuries. OSHA has extremely broad coverage because virtually all private employers engaged in a business affecting interstate commerce are covered. However, the federal government and state and local government entities are exempt.
    Answer (A) is incorrect because OSHA is administered by the Occupational Safety and Health Administration (which is also called OSHA) of the Department of Labor. Answer (B) is incorrect because the institute recommends safety standards, conducts research, and formulates training programs to educate workers about work safety. Answer (C) is incorrect because OSHA does not apply to governments (federal, state, or local).

31. Which of the following statements is correct regarding the scope and provisions of the Occupational Safety and Health Act (OSHA)?

- A. OSHA requires employers to provide employees a workplace free from risk.

- B. OSHA prohibits an employer from discharging an employee for revealing OSHA violations.

- C. OSHA may inspect a workplace at any time regardless of employer objection.

- D. OSHA preempts state regulation of workplace safety.

The correct answer is (B). *(CPA, adapted)*
    REQUIRED: The correct statement about OSHA.
    DISCUSSION: OSHA prohibits an employer from discharging or discriminating against any employee who exercises a right under the act, in particular, if an employee reveals OSHA violations.
    Answer (A) is incorrect because the purpose of OSHA is to assure safe and healthy working conditions in the place of employment and to prevent injuries. The act does not ensure a workplace free from risk. Answer (C) is incorrect because an OSHA inspection is a search within the meaning of the Fourth Amendment, and when an employer objects to such an inspection, the OSHA representatives are required to obtain a search warrant. Answer (D) is incorrect because OSHA does not preempt state regulation of workplace safety. However, state regulation must not conflict with the provisions of OSHA.

32. Which of the following statements is(are) correct regarding the authority of the Occupational Safety and Health Administration (OSHA)?

I. OSHA is authorized to establish standards that protect employees from exposure to substances that maybe harmful to their health.

II. OSHA is authorized to develop safety equipment and require employers to instruct employees in its use.

   A. I only.

   B. II only.

   C. Both I and II.

   D. Neither I nor II.

The correct answer is (A). *(CPA, adapted)*
   REQUIRED: The true statement(s), if any, concerning the authority of OSHA.
   DISCUSSION: The Occupational Safety and Health Administration (OSHA) was established by Congress to develop safety standards, prevent injuries, and promote job safety. OSHA is authorized to develop detailed health and safety standards and to enforce them through fines and other sanctions. The act requires employers to provide employees with a workplace free from recognized hazards and substances that are likely to cause death or serious physical harm.
   Answers (B), (C), and (D) are incorrect because OSHA is authorized to establish safety and health standards but is not authorized to develop safety equipment. However, to accomplish its goal of worker health and safety regulations require employees to be supplied with appropriate safety equipment and trained in its use (e.g., hard hats, safety glasses, steel-toe shoes, masks and other protective gear).

33. Under which of the following conditions is an on-site inspection of a workplace by an investigator from the Occupational Safety and Health Administration (OSHA) permissible?

   A. Only if OSHA obtains a search warrant after showing probable cause.

   B. Only if the inspection is conducted after working hours.

   C. At the request of employees.

   D. After OSHA provides the employer with at least 24 hours notice of the prospective inspection.

The correct answer is (C). *(CPA, adapted)*
   REQUIRED: The requirement for an OSHA inspection.
   DISCUSSION: Employees may request in writing that OSHA investigate for unsafe working conditions within an organization. OSHA is not required to notify the employer prior to inspection in most cases.
   Answer (A) is incorrect because OSHA is required to obtain a search warrant in order to conduct an on-site inspection. However, the search warrant may be issued under a lesser standard than probable cause; e.g., inspection is random. Answer (B) is incorrect because an inspection by OSHA may occur at any time the agency chooses to audit the company in question. Answer (D) is incorrect because OSHA is not required to give an employer 24-hour notice prior to conducting its investigation except in limited circumstances.

34. Tom and Wendy were employed at Poolywhirl. Their job entailed working at great heights in a factory, protected by a safety net. This net had proven inadequate in the past, and when asked to walk on it, they refused for fear of death or great bodily harm. Poolywhirl fired them.

   A. They could not be discharged under the Fair Labor Standards Act.

   B. They must be reinstated and paid double time for the work missed.

   C. They were improperly discharged under the Occupational Safety and Health Act.

   D. They have no recourse against Poolywhirl since they refused a directive of their employer.

The correct answer is (C). *(Publisher)*
   REQUIRED: The correct statement concerning discharging employees for refusing a dangerous task.
   DISCUSSION: OSHA prohibits an employer from discharging or discriminating against any employee who exercises a right under the act. Employees' rights include refusing to work when an employee believes in good faith that (s)he is in risk of death or great bodily harm from the activity. Therefore, the discharge was improper under OSHA.
   Answer (A) is incorrect because the Fair Labor Standards Act does not regulate job safety or discharges for refusal to work. Answer (B) is incorrect because, although they must be reinstated, there is no provision for double pay for the work missed. Answer (D) is incorrect because OSHA does provide recourse when an employee is forced to work in dangerous conditions and refuses.

E. Employment Discrimination

35. Which of the following employee benefits is(are) exempt from the provisions of the National Labor Relations Act?

	Sick Pay	Vacation Pay
A.	Yes	Yes
B.	Yes	No
C.	No	Yes
D.	No	No

The correct answer is (D). *(CPA, adapted)*

REQUIRED: The benefits exempt from the provisions of the NLRA.

DISCUSSION: The NLRA (1935) gave employees the right to organize unions and to bargain collectively. It also defined certain unfair labor practices by employers. Employers are required to negotiate and bargain in good faith with regard to wages, hours, and other terms and conditions of employment. The NLRA does not exempt either sick pay or vacation pay from collective bargaining.

Answers (A), (B), and (C) are incorrect because the NLRA covers all labor practices including employee benefits.

36. Under Title VII of the Civil Rights Act of 1964, a covered entity is prohibited from engaging in employment discrimination on the basis of race, color, religion, national origin, or sex. The practices subject to the act include

A. Any term, condition, or privilege of employment.

B. Hiring and discharge by the employer but not classified advertising by an employment agency.

C. Compensation and fringe benefits but not retirement plans.

D. Job taking, classifications, and assignments but not union discrimination.

The correct answer is (A). *(Publisher)*

REQUIRED: The practices subject to the employment discrimination provisions of Title VII.

DISCUSSION: Covered employers, employment agencies, and unions may not discriminate with regard to the following: classified advertising; receiving, classifying, or referring applicants; job testing and interviewing; hiring or firing; compensation and job classifications or assignments; promotions, transfers, layoffs, or recalls; training; fringe benefits; retirement and disability benefits; and any other term, condition, or privilege of employment.

Answer (B) is incorrect because employment agencies serving an employer with at least 15 employees are covered. Answer (C) is incorrect because retirement plans are covered. Answer (D) is incorrect because unions in industries affecting interstate commerce are covered.

37. Jane Adams applied for a job in a factory, driving a forklift truck. The job requirements included weighing at least 160 pounds to have sufficient strength to pick up the 100-pound boxes which were carried by, but frequently fell off, the forklift. Jane only weighs 150 pounds and was refused the job on this basis. Under these facts,

A. The weight requirement is invalid under the Civil Rights Act.

B. The weight requirement can be justified by the work required.

C. The factory must hire Jane.

D. The weight requirement discriminates against women under the Fair Labor Standards Act.

The correct answer is (A). *(Publisher)*

REQUIRED: The correct statement regarding a minimum weight requirement for a job.

DISCUSSION: The Civil Rights Act prohibits discrimination on the basis of race, color, national origin, religion, or sex. Height and weight requirements are discriminatory if they have the effect of screening out employees on the basis of race, sex, national origin, etc. The employer has the burden of proving that the requirement has a valid business purpose and that no alternate method of selection is less discriminatory.

Answer (B) is incorrect because the weight requirement cannot be justified since a strength test would be less discriminatory. Answer (C) is incorrect because the factory need not hire Jane, but it must give her an opportunity to apply for the job in a nondiscriminatory manner. Answer (D) is incorrect because discrimination in wages, not discrimination in hiring, is covered by the Fair Labor Standards Act.

38. Under Title VII of the 1964 Civil Rights Act, which of the following forms of discrimination is not prohibited?

A. Sex.

B. Age.

C. Race.

D. Religion.

The correct answer is (B). *(CPA, adapted)*

REQUIRED: The type of discrimination not prohibited under Title VII of the 1964 Civil Rights Act.

DISCUSSION: The Civil Rights Act prohibits discrimination on the basis of race, color, national origin, religion, or sex. Title VII does not prohibit discrimination based on age. Some forms of age discrimination are regulated by the Age Discrimination in Employment Act.

Answers (A), (C), and (D) are incorrect because Title VII prohibits discrimination based on sex, race, and religion.

39. Employment discrimination is prohibited by Title VII of the Civil Rights Act of 1964. Which of the following is least likely to be a violation?

- A. Disparate treatment of an individual.

- B. A statistical comparison showing a pervasive pattern or practices of discrimination.

- C. An express policy of discrimination but supported by business necessity.

- D. Disparate impact of a rule neutral on its face.

The correct answer is (C). *(Publisher)*
REQUIRED: The least likely basis of a Title VII violation.
DISCUSSION: A defense to a challenged practice, rule, or policy is that it is justified by business necessity. The practice, etc., is allowable if it serves a compelling business purpose, it effectively carries out this purpose, and no alternative would accomplish the purpose at least as well but with less impact on the protected group.
Answer (A) is incorrect because an isolated instance of discrimination is enough to constitute a violation. Answer (B) is incorrect because a statistical comparison may be sufficient to prove a pattern or practice of discrimination, such as when the percentage of a minority group in the defendant's work force is substantially below that in the relevant population. Answer (D) is incorrect because a work rule, regulation, requirement, or practice may be neutral on its face and yet have an impermissibly disparate impact on a protected class, e.g., height, weight, or lifting requirements.

40. Which of the following acts prohibit(s) an employer from discriminating among employees based on sex?

	Equal Pay Act	Title VII of the Civil Rights Act
A.	Yes	Yes
B.	Yes	No
C.	No	Yes
D.	No	No

The correct answer is (A). *(CPA, adapted)*
REQUIRED: The legislation, if any, prohibiting sex discrimination.
DISCUSSION: The Equal Pay Act amended the Fair Labor Standards Act. It prohibits an employer from discriminating between employees on the basis of sex by paying unequal wages for the same work. Title VII of the Civil Rights Act of 1964 prohibits discrimination on the basis of race, color, national origin, religion, or sex.
Answers (B), (C), and (D) are incorrect because the Equal Pay Act and Title VII of the Civil Rights Act of 1964 prohibit sex discrimination.

41. Airline has three cockpit positions: flight officer, copilot, and pilot. It has a policy of requiring flight officers to advance to the post of pilot or be fired, a progression that takes about 10 to 15 years. The FAA requires retirement at age 60. Applicant is 45 years old and otherwise fully qualified. Airline rejects her application on the basis of its policy of not hiring flight officers over the age of 30. Applicant files suit. At trial, evidence is presented showing that the incidence of aviation accidents decreases as a pilot gains experience and that the best experience for Airline's purposes is acquired by flying in Airline's three cockpit positions. Applicant will most likely

- A. Lose because age is a permissible basis for discrimination.

- B. Lose because Airline has a bona fide occupational qualification (BFOQ) defense.

- C. Win because the BFOQ defense applies only to discrimination based on sex, religion, and national origin.

- D. Win because the Age Discrimination in Employment Act applies to persons who are at least 40 but not yet 65.

The correct answer is (B). *(Publisher)*
REQUIRED: The outcome of an age discrimination suit and its legal basis.
DISCUSSION: Under the Age Discrimination in Employment Act (ADEA), persons who are at least 40 are protected from most forms of age discrimination in employment. However, a defendant may prevail by asserting a bona fide occupational qualification (BFOQ) defense. An employment decision based solely on age may be made when age is a BFOQ reasonably necessary to the normal operation of the particular business. Because the experience of pilots is related to safety, the company does not permit anyone to follow a career solely as a flight officer or copilot. Given that the time required to advance would allow Applicant to serve only briefly as a pilot, it is reasonable to conclude that Airline's hiring policy is based on a BFOQ.
Answer (A) is incorrect because the ADEA protects persons of Applicant's age. Answer (C) is incorrect because the BFOQ may be asserted to justify limited discrimination based on age, sex, religion, or national origin, but not race or color. Answer (D) is incorrect because the upper age limit was eliminated in 1986. (Note, however, that ADEA prohibits mandatory retirement of most employees under 70.) Moreover, Airline most likely has a valid BFOQ defense.

42. Under the Federal Age Discrimination in Employment Act, which of the following practices would be prohibited?

	Compulsory Retirement of Employees below the Age of 65	Termination of Employees between the Ages of 65 and 70 for Cause
A.	Yes	Yes
B.	Yes	No
C.	No	Yes
D.	No	No

The correct answer is (B). *(CPA, adapted)*

REQUIRED: The practice(s), if any, prohibited by the ADEA.

DISCUSSION: Under the ADEA, compulsory retirement of most classes of employees before the age of 70 is prohibited. The ADEA is intended to prevent arbitrary discrimination based on age. However, it allows an employer to discharge an employee for good cause.

Answers (A), (C), and (D) are incorrect because compulsory retirement of most employees below age 70 is prohibited, but an employee may be discharged or otherwise penalized for good cause.

43. Under the federal Age Discrimination in Employment Act, which of the following practices is prohibited?

A. Termination of employees between the ages of 65 and 70 for cause.

B. Mandatory retirement of any employee.

C. Unintentional age discrimination.

D. Termination of employees as part of a rational business decision.

The correct answer is (C). *(CPA, adapted)*

REQUIRED: The practice prohibited by the federal Age Discrimination in Employment Act (ADEA).

DISCUSSION: The ADEA prohibits arbitrary age discrimination and requires job applicants and employees to be evaluated on the basis of ability rather than age. Neither the language of the act nor its case interpretations require proof of intent. The issue in ADEA cases is whether prohibited age discrimination has in fact occurred.

Answer (A) is incorrect because ADEA does not prohibit termination of employment for cause. Answer (B) is incorrect because ADEA does not prohibit mandatory retirement for managerial employees. Nonmanagerial employees are protected from mandatory retirement policies. Answer (D) is incorrect because only arbitrary age discrimination is prohibited by ADEA. Terminations as part of a rational business decision are not prohibited by the act.

44. Under the Age Discrimination in Employment Act, which of the following remedies is(are) available to a covered employee?

	Early Retirement	Back Pay
A.	Yes	Yes
B.	Yes	No
C.	No	Yes
D.	No	No

The correct answer is (C). *(CPA, adapted)*

REQUIRED: The remedy(ies), if any, available under the ADEA.

DISCUSSION: ADEA remedies include unpaid back wages and other benefits arising from the discrimination; an additional equal award for liquidated damages if the employer's conduct was willful; attorneys' fees; and equitable relief, which may include hiring, reinstatement, and promotion. But most courts do not provide awards for punitive damages, pain and suffering, etc.

Answers (A), (B), and (D) are incorrect because back pay, but not early retirement, is a possible remedy under the ADEA.

45. Since the passage of the Civil Rights Act of 1964 and the establishment of the Equal Employment Opportunity Commission in 1972, large firms have been required to establish programs to eliminate discrimination. Federal law requires large firms to

A. Give preference in hiring to women and minority groups.

B. Establish quotas for hiring women and minority groups.

C. Set wage scales so that average wages for women equal average wages for men.

D. Set goals to eliminate discrimination and timetables to achieve these goals.

The correct answer is (D). *(CMA, adapted)*
    REQUIRED: The correct statement about affirmative action.
    DISCUSSION: Large employers are required to create and implement a plan of affirmative action to bring female and minority work forces up to the appropriate percentages as they relate to the available labor pool.
    Answers (A) and (B) are incorrect because, although these goals may involve preferential hiring of women and minorities, such techniques are not required. Answer (C) is incorrect because equality of wages is not based on average wages but on equal pay for equal work, giving consideration to differing skills and abilities.

46. Under the provisions of the Americans with Disabilities Act of 1990, in which of the following areas is a disabled person protected from discrimination?

	Public Transportation	Privately Operated Public Accommodations
A.	Yes	Yes
B.	Yes	No
C.	No	Yes
D.	No	No

The correct answer is (A). *(CPA, adapted)*
    REQUIRED: The area(s) in which disabled persons are protected.
    DISCUSSION: The Americans with Disabilities Act of 1990 prohibits discrimination with respect to employment and access to public accommodations. Employers and those who operate private and public accommodations are required to make reasonable changes to accommodate disabled persons by eliminating discriminatory policies and practices.
    Answers (B), (C), and (D) are incorrect because a disabled person is protected from discrimination in the use of public transportation and privately operated public accommodations and in employment within those areas.

F. Wage and Hour

47. Under the Federal Fair Labor Standards Act, which of the following would be regulated?

	Minimum Wage	Overtime	Number of Hours in the Workweek
A.	Yes	Yes	Yes
B.	Yes	No	Yes
C.	Yes	Yes	No
D.	No	Yes	Yes

The correct answer is (A). *(CPA, adapted)*
    REQUIRED: The activities regulated by the FLSA.
    DISCUSSION: The FLSA establishes a minimum wage, regulates overtime by requiring time and a half pay for overtime hours, and regulates the number of hours in a workweek by requiring overtime pay for all hours worked over 40 hours per week.
    Answers (B), (C), and (D) are incorrect because the FLSA regulates the minimum wage, overtime, and the number of hours in a workweek.

48. Under the Fair Labor Standards Act, which of the following pay bases may be used to pay covered, nonexempt employees who earn, on average, the minimum hourly wage?

	Hourly	Weekly	Monthly
A.	Yes	Yes	Yes
B.	Yes	Yes	No
C.	Yes	No	Yes
D.	No	Yes	Yes

The correct answer is (A). *(CPA, adapted)*
    REQUIRED: The pay bases that may be used to pay covered, nonexempt employees who earn, on average, the minimum hourly wage.
    DISCUSSION: The Fair Labor Standards Act (FLSA) specifies a minimum hourly wage and provides for payment of 150% of a covered, nonexempt worker's regular hourly rate for every hour worked in excess of 40 per week. An employer may utilize an hourly, weekly, or monthly pay base for a covered employee under FLSA provided the minimum hourly rate of pay and overtime pay standards are met. An hourly rate is determined by dividing the employee's pay by the number of hours worked during the period.
    Answers (B), (C), and (D) are incorrect because minimum wage employees may be paid hourly, weekly, or monthly.

49. When verifying a client's compliance with statutes governing employees' wages and hours, an auditor should check the client's personnel records against relevant provisions of which of the following statutes?

- A. National Labor Relations Act.
- B. Fair Labor Standards Act.
- C. Taft-Hartley Act.
- D. Americans with Disabilities Act.

The correct answer is (B). *(CPA, adapted)*
REQUIRED: The statute containing requirements concerning wages and hours.
DISCUSSION: An auditor should verify the client's compliance with wage and hour laws by reviewing the Fair Labor Standards Act (FLSA) to determine if the employer has followed statutory requirements. The FLSA provides for a federal minimum wage, mandates additional pay when an individual works overtime, and regulates the employment of children. The Equal Pay Act, an amendment to the FLSA, requires equal pay for equal work done by male and female employees.
Answer (A) is incorrect because the National Labor Relations Act establishes the right of labor to organize and bargain collectively with management. Answer (C) is incorrect because the Taft-Hartley Act amended the National Labor Relations Act to balance the power between unions and management. Answer (D) is incorrect because the Americans with Disabilities Act seeks to assure that disabled persons have access to both public and private accommodations and employment.

50. Which of the following classes of employees is exempt from both the minimum wage and maximum hours provisions of the federal Fair Labor Standards Act?

- A. Members of a labor union.
- B. Administrative personnel.
- C. Hospital workers.
- D. No class of employees is exempt.

The correct answer is (B). *(CPA, adapted)*
REQUIRED: The class of employees exempt from the minimum wage and maximum hour provisions.
DISCUSSION: The federal Fair Labor Standards Act (FLSA) provides for equal pay, minimum wages, overtime, and prohibition of child labor. Certain employees are partially excluded from coverage of the act, including administrative personnel (managers, not general office workers) who usually receive some minimum guaranteed annual wage and are required by conditions of their employment to work as long as necessary to accomplish their task.
Answer (A) is incorrect because employees who belong to a labor union are not exempt. Answer (C) is incorrect because, although hospital workers are not exempt from minimum wages, they are partially exempt from the overtime provision if they so agree. Hospitals must pay overtime for more than 8 hours daily and for more than 80 hours in 14 days, but not for more than 40 hours in a week. Answer (D) is incorrect because certain classes of employees are excluded, including executives, professionals, administrators, and outside salesmen. Partial exemptions exist for certain others.

51. Which of the following employees are exempt from the overtime provisions of the Fair Labor Standards Act?

- A. Independent contractors.
- B. Railroad and airline employees.
- C. Members of a union recognized as the bargaining agent by the National Labor Relations Board.
- D. Office workers.

The correct answer is (B). *(CPA, adapted)*
REQUIRED: The employees not covered by the overtime provisions of the FLSA.
DISCUSSION: Certain workers are excluded from the overtime but not the minimum wage provisions. Railroad and air carrier employees, taxi drivers, certain employees of motor carriers, sailors on American vessels, and certain local delivery employees are in this category.
Answer (A) is incorrect because an employer cannot escape coverage under the act by designating a person as an independent contractor if the circumstances of the employment relation suggest that (s)he is an employee. Answers (C) and (D) are incorrect because both groups are covered.

52. Fashion Industries, Inc. manufactures dresses which it sells throughout the United States and South America. Among its 5,000 employees in 1999 were 165 youngsters aged 14 and 15 who worked full-time during the day and were paid at a rate less than the minimum wage. Which statement is correct in accordance with the general rules of the Fair Labor Standards Act?

A. Fashion was exempt from regulation because fewer than 5% of its employees were children.

B. Fashion did not violate the law since both male and female youngsters were paid at the same rate and worked only on Saturdays.

C. Fashion violated the law by employing children under 16 years of age.

D. Fashion was exempt from regulation if more than 10% of its sales were in direct competition with foreign goods.

The correct answer is (C). *(CPA, adapted)*
REQUIRED: The correct statement concerning the general rules of child labor.
DISCUSSION: Under the Fair Labor Standards Act (FLSA), child labor is defined as employment of a child under 16. It is prohibited with certain exceptions (14- and 15-year-olds may work at sales and clerical-type jobs for limited hours and outside of school time). The employment of 165 children aged 14 and 15 to work full time is a violation of the law.

Answer (A) is incorrect because there is no exemption from regulation under the FLSA simply because fewer than 5% of one's employees are children. Answer (B) is incorrect because it is not a sufficient defense that male and female youngsters were paid at the same rate and worked only on Saturdays. Answer (D) is incorrect because there is no exemption for direct competition with foreign goods. The general rule is that a U.S. employer must comply with the U.S. laws regulating employment.

53. The Fair Labor Standards Act as amended

A. Applies to all employers whether or not engaged in interstate commerce.

B. Requires that double time be paid to any employee working in excess of 8 hours in a given day.

C. Prohibits discrimination based upon the sex of the employee.

D. Requires all employees doing the same job to receive an equal rate of pay.

The correct answer is (C). *(CPA, adapted)*
REQUIRED: The correct statement concerning the Fair Labor Standards Act (FLSA).
DISCUSSION: The FLSA regulates the relationship between an employer and employees by providing for minimum wages, overtime, and prohibition of child labor. Also, the equal pay provision prohibits discrimination on the basis of sex. It requires equal pay for equal work.

Answer (A) is incorrect because the Fair Labor Standards Act applies only to employers engaged in interstate commerce, since that is the constitutional limit on federal jurisdiction over commerce. Answer (B) is incorrect because the general overtime requirement is to pay at least time-and-one-half the regular rate for all hours worked over 40 per week. Answer (D) is incorrect because the act does not require all employees doing the same job to receive an equal rate of pay but permits differentials on the basis of seniority, merit, quality, or quantity.

54. Which of the following statements is correct under the Federal Fair Labor Standards Act?

A. Some workers may be included within the minimum wage provisions but exempt from the overtime provisions.

B. Some workers may be included within the overtime provisions but exempt from the minimum wage provisions.

C. All workers are required to be included within both the minimum wage provisions and the overtime provisions.

D. Possible exemptions from the minimum wage provisions and the overtime provisions must be determined by the union contract in effect at the time.

The correct answer is (A). *(CPA, adapted)*
REQUIRED: The correct statement about the FLSA.
DISCUSSION: The FLSA, known as the wage and hour law, establishes a minimum wage, mandates extra pay for overtime work, and regulates the employment of children. Certain employees are excluded from some or all of the FLSA minimum wage and overtime provisions, while other employees are excluded from the overtime but not the minimum wage provisions.

Answers (B) and (C) are incorrect because of the reasons stated above. Answer (D) is incorrect because there is no requirement that provisions of the FLSA be determined by a union contract.

55. Under the Fair Labor Standards Act, if a covered, nonexempt employee works consecutive weeks of 45, 42, 38, and 33 hours, how many hours of overtime must be paid to the employee?

- A. 0
- B. 7
- C. 18
- D. 20

The correct answer is (B). *(CPA, adapted)*
REQUIRED: The hours of overtime.
DISCUSSION: The FLSA specifies a minimum hourly wage and provides for payment of 150% of a covered, nonexempt worker's regular hourly rate for every hour worked in excess of 40 per week. Hence, the employee must be paid for 5 overtime hours in the first week and 2 in the second week.
Answers (A), (C), and (D) are incorrect because overtime hours are all hours worked in excess of 40 each week.

G. Fringe Benefits

56. Under the Employee Retirement Income Security Act of 1974 (ERISA), which of the following areas of private employer pension plans is(are) regulated?

	Employee Vesting	Plan Funding
A.	Yes	Yes
B.	Yes	No
C.	No	Yes
D.	No	No

The correct answer is (A). *(CPA, adapted)*
REQUIRED: The area(s), if any, of private employer pension plans regulated by ERISA.
DISCUSSION: ERISA does not require establishment of pension plans or set benefits. Instead, ERISA regulates private pension plans to protect employees' rights to benefit payments. It imposes fiduciary duties on fund managers as well as record-keeping, reporting, and disclosure requirements. In general, the vesting rules require that employee contributions vest immediately and that employer contributions vest after 5 years of employment.
Answers (B), (C), and (D) are incorrect because ERISA regulates both employee vesting and funding of employer pension plans.

57. Under the Federal Consolidated Budget Reconciliation Act of 1985 (COBRA), when an employee voluntarily resigns from a job, the former employee's group health insurance coverage that was in effect during the period of employment with the company

- A. Automatically ceases for the former employee and spouse if the resignation occurred before normal retirement age.

- B. Automatically ceases for the former employee's spouse but continues for the former employee for an 18-month period at the former employer's expense.

- C. May be retained by the former employee at the former employee's expense for at least 18 months after leaving the company but must be terminated for the former employee's spouse.

- D. May be retained for the former employee and spouse at the former employee's expense for at least 18 months after leaving the company.

The correct answer is (D). *(CPA, adapted)*
REQUIRED: The status of a former employee's group health insurance coverage after the employee voluntarily resigns from a job.
DISCUSSION: The Consolidated Budget Reconciliation Act of 1985 (COBRA) provides that an employee of a private employer or the employee's beneficiaries must be offered the opportunity to continue their group health insurance for 18 months after termination or the loss of coverage due to certain qualifying events. The employer must notify the employee and his/her beneficiaries of their rights under the act.
Answer (A) is incorrect because continued coverage must be offered if resignation occurs before normal retirement age. Answer (B) is incorrect because the former employee must pay the premium, and coverage may continue for the spouse. Answer (C) is incorrect because coverage may continue for the spouse.

58. Which of the following statements correctly describes the funding of noncontributory pension plans?

- A. All of the funds are provided by the employees.

- B. All of the funds are provided by the employer.

- C. The employer and employee each provide 50% of the funds.

- D. The employer provides 90% of the funds, and each employee contributes 10%.

The correct answer is (B). *(CPA, adapted)*
   REQUIRED: The funding of a noncontributory pension plan.
   DISCUSSION: Under a noncontributory pension plan, plan assets equal amounts provided by the employer, plus earnings, minus benefits paid. The employees do not make any contributions.
   Answers (A), (C), and (D) are incorrect because, under a noncontributory pension plan, no funds are provided by the employees.

59. Which of the following will be included in the gross income of a highly compensated employee if provided to such employees on a discriminatory basis?

- A. No-additional-cost service.

- B. Working condition fringe.

- C. *De minimis* fringe.

- D. Free parking.

The correct answer is (A). *(Publisher)*
   REQUIRED: The fringe benefit included in income if provided on a discriminatory basis.
   DISCUSSION: Each of the listed fringe benefits is excluded under Sec. 132 of the Internal Revenue Code. However, no-additional-cost services and employee discounts are excludable by an officer, owner, or highly compensated employee only if they are also available at substantially the same terms to the other employees.
   Answers (B), (C), and (D) are incorrect because these fringe benefits may be provided by an employer on a discriminatory basis (except for eating facilities).

60. Under the provisions of the Employee Retirement Income Security Act of 1974 (ERISA), which of the following statements is correct?

- A. Employees are entitled to have an employer established pension plan.

- B. Employers are prevented from unduly delaying an employee's participation in a pension plan.

- C. Employers are prevented from managing retirement plans.

- D. Employees are entitled to make investment decisions.

The correct answer is (B). *(CPA, adapted)*
   REQUIRED: The correct statement about employer pension provisions under ERISA.
   DISCUSSION: Under ERISA, an employer may not unduly delay the vesting of an employee's participation in a pension program. The act requires strict record keeping, disclosure, and other requirements of private employers while establishing a pension plan.
   Answer (A) is incorrect because ERISA does not require employers to establish pension plans for their employees, but it does specify certain procedures that must be followed in the administration of the plan. Answer (C) is incorrect because an employer may manage the investment portfolio once it establishes a pension plan for its employees. Answer (D) is incorrect because employees are not entitled to make decisions regarding the management of their portfolio.

Use Gleim's *CPA Test Prep* for interactive testing with over 2,000 additional multiple-choice questions!

OOF QUESTION *(Publisher)* 20-25 minutes

Items 1 through 15 test your general understanding of employment taxes and benefits.

Required

For items 1 through 12, select the best answer, (A)-(R), from the list below. An answer may be used more than once.

(A)	$0.00	(J)	$1,530.00
(B)	$7.70	(K)	$1,912.50
(C)	$290.00	(L)	$2,700.00
(D)	$378.00	(M)	$3,500.00
(E)	$434.00	(N)	$3,825.00
(F)	$507.50	(O)	$5,951.20
(G)	$637.47	(P)	$7,000.00
(H)	$765.00	(Q)	$7,500.00
(I)	$1,350.00	(R)	$7,650.00

During 1999, Bob's gross pay as an employee of Temp Inc. was $4,167 each month, or $50,000 for the year.

1. What is the amount of Social Security (FICA) tax liability of Temp as Bob's employer for 1999?

2. What is Bob's 1999 FICA tax liability?

3. What is the amount of federal unemployment tax (FUTA) liability of Temp as Bob's employer for 1999?

4. What is Bob's 1999 FUTA tax liability?

5. What is the maximum credit against FUTA tax allowable to Temp for state unemployment tax paid?

6. What is the maximum credit against FUTA tax allowable to Bob for state unemployment tax paid?

For items 7 through 12, assume that during 1999 Bob's gross pay as an employee of Temp Inc. was $8,333 each month, or $100,000 for the year.

7. What is the amount of Social Security (FICA) tax liability of Temp as Bob's employer for 1999?

8. What is the amount of federal unemployment tax (FUTA) liability of Temp as Bob's employer for 1999?

9. If Bob also had $300 of net earnings from self-employment from professional accounting services to his neighbor in April 1999, what is Bob's 1999 FICA tax liability?

10. If Bob's net earnings from self-employment for providing accounting services to his friend were $10,000 during 1999, what is Bob's FICA tax liability arising from this $10,000?

11. Bob's $10,000 net income from self-employment was received as $2,500 during each of the first 4 months of 1999. What amount of FICA tax was Temp required to withhold from Bob's January 1999 wages?

12. Bob's wife Jane was also employed by Temp Inc. Her gross pay was $4,167 each month, or $50,000 for the 1999 tax year. Disregarding any income from self-employment, what is the amount of Jane's FICA tax liability?

For items 13 through 15, select the best answer, (A)-(I), from the list below.

(A)	6	(F)	40
(B)	10	(G)	62
(C)	13	(H)	65
(D)	26	(I)	70
(E)	39		

13. Unless Congress extends the period, for how many weeks can unemployed workers generally receive payments as benefits funded by the Federal Unemployment Tax Act (FUTA)?

14. At least how many quarters of coverage must a worker have been credited to be currently insured for purposes of benefits under the old age, survivors, and disability insurance (OASDI) component of Social Security?

15. Until a person reaches what age will the amount of Social Security retirement benefits be reduced by $1 for every $2 of earnings above the annual limit?

Knowledge Tested

1. Social Security taxes imposed on employers, employees, and self-employed persons

2. Withholding requirements

3. Social Security benefits

Authors' Comments

The computational approach is a method to quickly test knowledge of the basic structure of the Social Security system, its funding, and benefits available.

1. The correct answer is (N).
   DISCUSSION: For 1999, the old-age, survivors, and disability insurance (OASDI) component of FICA tax liability of the employer is 6.20% of wages paid up to $72,600. The hospital insurance (HI) component is 1.45% of all wages. Thus, Temp's liability is $3,825 [(.062 + .0145) x $50,000].

2. The correct answer is (N).
   DISCUSSION: The employee's FICA tax liability is the same as that of the employer.

3. The correct answer is (E).
   DISCUSSION: The FUTA tax liability (before any credit for payments to state unemployment funds) is 6.2% of the first $7,000 of wages paid each year to each employee. Accordingly, Temp's liability is $434 (.062 x $7,000).

4. The correct answer is (A).
   DISCUSSION: The employee does not pay FUTA tax. The tax is imposed on employers only.

5. The correct answer is (D).
   DISCUSSION: A credit against FUTA tax liability is provided for an employer who pays state unemployment tax. The amount of state tax usually varies with the frequency and amount of unemployment claims. However, the credit is limited to 5.4% of wages for state taxes paid. Maximum wages subject to FUTA are $7,000 for each employee. Thus, the maximum credit is $378 (.054 x $7,000).

6. The correct answer is (A).
   DISCUSSION: Because the employee does not pay FUTA tax, there is no tax for which to provide a credit.

7. The correct answer is (O).
   DISCUSSION: The OASDI component (6.2%) is applied to the first $72,600 of wages for 1999. The hospital insurance (HI) component is 1.45% and is applied to all wages. Temp's liability is $5,951.20 [(.062 x $72,600) + (.0145 x $100,000)].

8. The correct answer is (E).
   DISCUSSION: The FUTA tax liability (before any credit for payments to state unemployment funds) is 6.2% of the first $7,000 of wages paid each year to each employee. Accordingly, Temp's liability is $434 (.062 x $7,000).

9. The correct answer is (A).
   DISCUSSION: If net earnings from self-employment are less than $400, no self-employment tax is imposed.

10. The correct answer is (C).
   DISCUSSION: FICA tax liability of a self-employed person is equal to the combined employer/employee contribution. Bob's total income exceeds the OASDI component cap of $72,600; therefore, Bob is only responsible for the HI portion of the FICA tax, or $290 (0.0145 x 2 x $10,000).

11. The correct answer is (G).
   DISCUSSION: An employer must withhold the employee's FICA tax liability from his/her wages. It must be withheld from all wages paid starting from the beginning of the year until the applicable maximums are reached, and this is so without regard to self-employment income. For January, Temp must withhold $637.47 ($8,333 x .0765).

12. The correct answer is (N).
   DISCUSSION: Self-employment tax liability is computed separately for each spouse. There is no combining of incomes for determining whether the maximum of wages subject to the tax has been reached. Jane's liability is $3,825 (.0765 x $50,000).

13. The correct answer is (D).
   DISCUSSION: Unemployed workers can generally receive benefits for a maximum of 26 weeks.

14. The correct answer is (A).
   DISCUSSION: A currently insured worker has been credited with at least 6 quarters of coverage in the past 3 years. To be fully insured, an employee must be credited with at least 40 quarters of coverage.

15. The correct answer is (H).
   DISCUSSION: Reduction of retirement benefits by $1 for every $2 of earnings no longer applies when the retiree reaches age 65.

ESSAY QUESTION (CPA, adapted) 20-25 minutes

Part a. Rapid Delivery Service, Inc. hired Dolson as one of its truck drivers. Dolson was carefully selected and trained by Rapid. He was specifically instructed to obey all traffic and parking rules and regulations. One day while making a local delivery, Dolson double parked and went into a nearby customer's store. In doing so, he prevented a car legally parked at the curb from leaving. The owner of the parked car, Charles, proceeded to blow the horn of the truck repeatedly. Charles was doing this when Dolson returned from his delivery. As a result of a combination of several factors, particularly Charles' telling him to "move it" and that he was "acting very selfishly and in an unreasonable manner," Dolson punched Charles in the nose, severely fracturing it. When Charles sought to restrain him, Dolson punched Charles again, this time fracturing his jaw. Charles has commenced legal action against Rapid.

Required (Part a.)

Answer the following, setting forth reasons for any conclusions stated.

1. Will Charles prevail?
2. What liability, if any, would Dolson have?

Part b. Harold Watts was employed by Superior Sporting Goods as a route salesman. His territory, route, and customers were determined by Superior. He was expected to work from 9:00 a.m. to 5:00 p.m., Monday through Friday. He received a weekly salary plus time and one-half for anything over 40 hours. He also received a small commission on sales which exceeded a stated volume. The customers consisted of sporting goods stores, department stores, athletic clubs, and large companies which had athletic programs or sponsored athletic teams. Watts used his personal car in making calls or, upon occasion, making a delivery when the customer was in a rush and the order was not large. Watts was reimbursed for the use of the car for company purposes. His instructions were to assume the customer is always right and to accommodate the customer when to do so would cost little and would build goodwill for the company and himself.

One afternoon while making a sales call and dropping off a case of softballs at the Valid Clock Company, the personnel director told Watts that he had planned to watch the company's team play a game at a softball field located on the other side of town, but that his car would not start. Watts said, "Don't worry. It will be my pleasure to give you a lift; I would like to take in a few innings myself." Time was short and while on the way to the ballpark, Watts ran a light and collided with another car. The other car required $800 of repairs, and the owner suffered serious bodily injury.

Required (Part b.)

Answer the following, setting forth reasons for any conclusions stated.

1. What is Superior's potential liability, if any, to the owner of the other car?
2. What is Valid's potential liability, if any, to the owner of the other car?

Part c. Eureka Enterprises, Inc. started doing business in July 1977. It manufactures electronic components and currently employs 35 individuals. In anticipation of future financing needs, Eureka has engaged a CPA firm to audit its financial statements. During the course of the examination, the CPA firm discovers that Eureka has no workers' compensation insurance, which is in violation of state law, and so informs the president of Eureka.

Required (Part c.)

Answer the following, setting forth reasons for any conclusions stated.

1. What is the purpose of a state workers' compensation law?
2. What are the legal implications of not having workers' compensation insurance?

Knowledge Tested

1. Liability of agent and principal for torts
2. Nature and purpose of workers' compensation law
3. Effect of no workers' compensation insurance

Authors' Comments

This essay question appeared in the 1978 CPA exam. Only Part c. deals with employment as generally addressed by state statutes and regulations. Parts a. and b. address other issues that frequently arise in the context of employment, but the knowledge tested is of the law of agency (mostly common-law) discussed in Study Unit 3. Some questions on the CPA exam are set up to test your knowledge of more than one area of business law.

Workers' compensation law provides for persons injured at work and for certain dependents. Basic components of the system are

1. Employers compensate for on-the-job injuries.
2. Employee fault does not reduce compensation.
3. Employer fault is not required.
4. Funding is by insurance.
5. Employers must participate.

Entitlements under the system displace common-law rights against the employer. An employer who fails to acquire mandatory insurance is nevertheless strictly liable to compensate and may be subject to penalties.

AICPA Unofficial Answer

Part a.

1. Probably yes. A master is liable for the servant's unauthorized tortious conduct within the scope of employment. This is true despite the fact that the master is in no way personally at fault or has forbidden the type of conduct engaged in by the servant. A servant is normally an employee who renders personal service to his/her employer and whose activities are subject to the control of the employer. A truck driver such as Dolson would clearly fall within such a description. Once this has been established, the question is whether the assaults committed upon Charles by Dolson were within the scope of his employment. When the intentional use of force is involved, the courts have taken an expansive view insofar as imposition of liability upon the employer. If the servant's actions are predictable, there is likelihood that liability will be imposed upon the master. If the servant deals with third persons in carrying out his/her job, the courts ask whether the wrongful act which occurred was likely to arise out of the performance of the job. Additionally, consideration is given to whether any part of his/her motive was the performance of the job or, if not, whether it was a normal reaction to a situation created by the job. The use of force by truck drivers in situations involving parking space or after a collision resulting in a dispute is not uncommon. The courts have usually imposed liability in cases such as this unless the assault was unrelated to the job, was solely personal, or was outrageous.

2. Dolson is liable to Charles for the tortious injury inflicted. The fact that Dolson may have been acting as a servant of Rapid and may impose liability upon his employer does not relieve him from liability.

Part b.

1. Superior Sporting Goods is liable for the negligence of its servant-agent Watts. The requisite control of his activities is apparent from the facts. Furthermore, based upon the instructions Watts received, it would appear that he was acting within the scope of his employment. In fact, one could conclude from the facts that Watts had express authority to make a trip such as the one he made when the accident occurred. He specifically was told to generally accommodate the customer if to do so would cost little and would build goodwill for the company and himself. This appears to be exactly what he did. Superior will undoubtedly attempt to assert the "independent frolic" doctrine and claim that Watts had abandoned his employment in order to pursue his own interests or pleasures. However, the deviation was not great, it took place during normal working hours, and, most importantly, it was at the request of a customer and was a type of conduct Superior specifically encouraged.

2. Valid Clock Company has no liability. Its agent was not at fault, nor can it be reasonably argued that an agency relationship was created between itself and Watts because its personnel director accepted the ride offered by Watts. The requisite control of Watts's physical activities by Valid is not present.

Part c.

1. Workers' compensation laws provide a system of compensation for employees who are injured, disabled, or killed as a result of accidents or occupational diseases in the course of their employment. Benefits also extend to survivors or dependents of these employees.

2. Workers' compensation laws are present in all 50 states to reimburse employees for losses sustained because of work-related injury or disease regardless of who, if anyone, was at fault. Failure of an employer to secure compensation coverage creates a serious problem. The effect of such unwise conduct on the part of the employer is to deny him/her the use of the common-law defenses of fellow-servant, assumption of risk, and contributory negligence. Employer liability under workers' compensation law does not depend on whether (s)he secured compensation coverage. Several states have provided for the payment of workers' compensation by the state to the injured employee of the uninsured employer. The state in turn proceeds against the employer to recover the compensation cost and to impose penalties that include fines and imprisonment. Other jurisdictions provide for a penalty in the form of additional compensation payments over and above the basic amounts, or they require an immediate lump-sum payment.

STUDY UNIT 14: ENVIRONMENTAL REGULATION

9 pages of outline
21 multiple-choice questions
1 OOF and 1 essay

This study unit reviews environmental regulation. The new AICPA Content Specification Outlines indicate coverage of this topic on future CPA exams. Preparation should include familiarity with the coverage of statutes regulating air, water, and hazardous waste, liability provisions, enforcement procedures, and penalties. The Environmental Impact Statement (EIS); Resource Conservation and Recovery Act (RCRA); the Comprehensive Environmental Response, Compensation, and Liability Act (CERCLA); citizen suits; and property owner liability appear to be the areas of major importance that are likely to appear on the exam.

A. **Environmental Regulation: Introduction**. Environmental laws reflect policy choices concerning preservation and enhancement of the environment. They may minimize, prevent, punish, or remedy actions that threaten or harm the environment. Environmental law consists of rules in the form of federal and state constitutions and statutes, local ordinances, regulations promulgated by federal, state, and local agencies, together with decisions interpreting those laws and regulations.

　　1. Environmental law today is primarily statutory and regulatory in nature.

　　　　a. Early environmental protection was attempted by the common-law tort of public or private nuisance.

　　　　b. Nuisance is activity that unreasonably interferes with a person's use and enjoyment of his/her land.

　　　　c. A nuisance can be remedied by an injunction or damages.

　　　　d. Common-law nuisance has proved to be inadequate as the main means to promote protection of the environment.

　　2. Nearly all environmental litigation involves disputes between private parties and government agencies, as opposed to disputes solely between private parties.

　　3. The fundamental issue in early environmental litigation was whether a party had a sufficient interest in the controversy to obtain judicial resolution of the controversy (**standing**).

　　　　a. Under the **Administrative Procedures Act** (the "APA"), a cause of action is recognized only when a plaintiff can satisfactorily demonstrate that both of the following statements apply:

　　　　　　1) The alleged action or inaction by an agency did or will result in an injury in fact.

　　　　　　2) The injury is to an interest arguably within the zone of interests to be protected by the statute in question.

　　　　b. The latest U.S. Supreme Court case addressing "injury in fact" is

　　　　　　1) *Lujan v. National Wildlife Federation*, 110 S.Ct. 3177 (1990), which limited standing to those who allege and prove actual specific injury

　　　　c. In summary, almost anyone who alleges a specific injury can sue the government and most other parties for activity that harms or threatens the environment.

4. **The Environmental Protection Agency (EPA)**. The EPA was formed in 1970 to centralize most of the environmental control functions of the Interior, Agriculture, and other government departments.

    a. The EPA is an administrative agency charged with ensuring compliance with most environmental protection laws.

    b. The EPA has been delegated broad adjudicative powers to hold formal and informal hearings and to render decisions in hearings involving environmental law.

        1) It is the largest federal agency.

    c. Enforcement actions are normally referred by EPA to the Department of Justice.

5. **Enforcement and Liability**. Corporate officers, directors, and managers must be aware of the possibility of criminal prosecutions and imprisonment for negligent violations of environmental statutes and regulations.

    a. Under most federal environmental statutes, states are delegated criminal, civil, and administrative powers to enforce federal environmental programs within their boundaries.

        1) In some instances, state authority is in addition to federal environmental requirements.

    b. Moreover, local and regional entities sometimes institute enforcement actions against violators.

    c. Private citizens can initiate litigation in two broad forms:

        1) Citizen suits
        2) Private enforcement actions

    d. Most environmental statutes permit some form of citizen suits.

        1) Such statutes typically grant citizens the right to participate in or initiate civil enforcement actions.

        2) Usually, citizens must notify both the EPA and the Department of Justice of

            a) The state where the violation occurred
            b) The identity of the alleged violator

        3) Citizen suits are a major contributor to environmental enforcement litigation.

    e. **Private enforcement actions** are also quite numerous.

        1) Private citizens seek damages for personal injuries allegedly caused by violation of environmental statutes.

        2) Significant punitive damages may be awarded if a statute or regulation is proven to have been violated knowingly.

    f. The greatest environmental enforcement effort is by the EPA.

        1) The EPA normally refers both criminal and civil enforcement actions to the Department of Justice.

        2) The EPA does not have the power to bypass the Justice Department and bring enforcement actions to court itself.

g. Virtually every environmental statute now imposes criminal liability for its violation.

1) Congress believes that threat of imprisonment encourages corporate officers and directors to cause their corporations to comply.

2) Generally, conviction for a criminal violation requires proof of an element of conscious wrongdoing or criminal intent.

a) The rule enunciated by the U.S. Supreme Court in the *Park* case is that, if a corporate officer has, by reason of his position in the corporation, responsibility and authority either to prevent in the first instance, or promptly to correct, the violation complained of and fails to do so, (s)he has criminal intent to violate the statute.

b) Thus, liability might be imputed to supervisors of employees who violate environmental statutes.

i) Environmental statutes have been broadly construed such that employees who do not personally participate in or have knowledge of illegal activities might be found to have knowingly violated such a statute merely because they work in a field that is governed by health- and safety-related statutes or are in a management position.

6. Stop and review! You have completed the outline for this subunit. Study multiple-choice questions 1 through 3 on page 443.

B. National Environmental Policy Act (NEPA). NEPA became law on January 1, 1970. It declares a national environmental policy and promotes consideration of environmental issues by all federal agencies.

1. NEPA requires all federal agencies to consider any adverse impact they may have on the environment through their

a. Actions
b. Proposals
c. Legislation
d. Regulations

2. **The Environmental Impact Statement (EIS).** Section 102(2)(c) of NEPA requires that an EIS shall be "included in every recommendation or report on proposals for legislation and other major federal actions significantly affecting the quality of the human environment." An EIS is a written document that is prepared by agencies of the federal government. The purpose of an EIS is to ensure full and fair consideration of any significant environmental impact of proposed federal projects.

a. The first step in deciding whether an EIS must be prepared at all is analysis of whether the proposed action

1) Is federal
2) Is major
3) Has significant environmental impact

b. Federal action includes action undertaken directly by federal agencies. Federal action also includes

1) A federal agency's decision on granting permits or licensing for activities such as construction of highways or nuclear power plants

2) "Actions which may be major and which are potentially subject to Federal control and responsibility" (40 C.F.R. Section 1508.18)

      c.   For a project to be major requires merely a substantial commitment of resources, financial or otherwise.

          1)   It is arguable that any project having a significant environmental impact is major.

      d.   Section 102(2)(c) of NEPA requires that the EIS

          1)   Be a detailed statement

          2)   Be issued only after consultation with other appropriate government agencies

          3)   Address the impact of the proposed action

          4)   Consider all possible adverse environmental effects

          5)   Consider all possible alternatives

          NOTE: Generally, no agency action should occur earlier than 90 days after the draft EIS nor 30 days after the final EIS is made available to the Council on Environmental Quality (CEQ) and the public.

3.   **Finding of No Significant Impact (FONSI)**. If an agency decides not to prepare an EIS, it must make a FONSI available to the public.

      a.   A FONSI is a "document prepared by a federal agency briefly presenting the reasons why an action, not otherwise excluded . . . , will not have a significant effect on the human environment and for which an environmental impact statement therefore will not be prepared." 40 C.F.R. Section 1508.13

      b.   If properly substantiated, a FONSI can substitute for the costly and lengthy EIS process.

4.   **The Pollution Prevention Act of 1990** is viewed by many as a change of policy. It is an effort to shift some pollution regulation from dictated standards (called command and control) and from mandated technology (called end-of-pipe treatment) to encourage industry to prevent the initial creation of pollution.

      a.   The act establishes a new EPA office to administer the act, provides grant funds to promote source reduction, and serves as a clearinghouse for source reduction technology transfer.

      b.   The primary mode of preventing pollution of the environment remains traditional regulatory enforcement; however, various incentive programs have been developed.

5.   Stop and review! You have completed the outline for this subunit. Study multiple-choice questions 4 through 7 beginning on page 444.

C. Clean Water Laws

1.   Congress has long recognized the need for protection of the nation's water. The most comprehensive attempt is the **Clean Water Act (CWA)** as amended. The CWA's stated goal is to "restore and maintain the chemical, physical, and biological integrity of the nation's waters." In 1990, Congress substantially revised Section 311 of the CWA, enacting the **Oil Pollution Act** to protect our nation's water from oil and hazardous substance discharge.

2.   **Scope of CWA**. The CWA has five main elements:

      a.   A national effluent standard for each industry
      b.   Water quality standards
      c.   A discharge permit program
      d.   Special provisions for unique situations such as oil spills
      e.   A construction grant program for publicly owned treatment plants

3. **Liability**. Under Section 309(c) of the CWA, criminal penalties are imposed. Citizen suits against dischargers and/or the EPA to protect water quality are authorized.

4. **The Safe Drinking Water Act (SDWA)**, passed in 1974 and amended in 1986 and 1996, provides national standards for public water systems.

   a. Public water systems are defined as systems having 15 or more service connections or serving 25 or more people for at least 60 days annually.

   b. Private wells are not regulated.

   c. Private persons may sue public water systems in federal court for failure to meet the standards.

5. **The Marine Protection, Research, and Sanctuaries Act of 1972** prohibits dumping of radiological, chemical, and biological waste in the ocean.

   a. Transporting and dumping other material is by permit only.

   b. Violations can result in revocation of permit, civil penalties up to $50,000, incarceration for 1 year, and/or $50,000 fines.

6. Stop and review! You have completed the outline for this subunit. Study multiple-choice questions 8 through 10 beginning on page 445.

D. Clean Air Laws

1. The federal **Clean Air Act (CAA)** was enacted in 1970, extensively amended in 1977, and expanded in 1990.

   a. The act made health protection a priority, forced automotive and other heavy industry to close or meet specific emission standards, largely prevented air pollution problems from getting worse, and authorized the EPA to conduct testing and certification programs to increase compliance with the act and regulations adopted thereunder.

   b. The 1990 amendments, among other things, address the problem of acid rain and power plant emissions, which are suspected to be the primary cause thereof. The amendments also mandate the phaseout of chlorofluorocarbons (CFCs), which are thought to deplete the ozone layer.

   c. The act and the amendments cover five areas including

      1) National ambient air quality standards (NAAQSs),
      2) New source performance standards,
      3) No significant deterioration policy,
      4) Mobile source emission standards, and
      5) Hazardous air toxins standards.

2. **Goals and Objectives**. The primary purpose of the act is to set pollution controls on both stationary and mobile sources of air pollution.

   a. Section 108 of the act requires that the EPA publish and revise periodically a list of pollutants that "may reasonably be anticipated to endanger" public health or welfare and that are emitted from stationary or mobile sources.

   b. Section 112 of the act provides for uniform national emission standards for air pollutants emitted from mobile sources such as

      1) Airplanes
      2) Automobiles

3. **National ambient air quality standards** protect the air quality in an area from pollutants emanated from mobile and stationary sources that have an adverse impact on human health and welfare. Each state determines how to meet these standards.

4. **Stationary Sources, the State Implementation Plan**. The first step in attempting to meet the EPA standards with respect to stationary sources is for a state to prepare a **state implementation plan (SIP)**.

   a. The SIP is the mechanism through which emission controls are imposed by the states on stationary sources in order to meet national standards.

   b. The EPA has divided each state into air quality control regions (AQCRs).

   c. An SIP must include a description of the air quality in each AQCR.

      1) The EPA allows offsets in AQCRs whereby the pollution from a clean factory can be offset against pollution from a dirty factory.

   d. Among other things, the 1990 amendments require that an acceptable SIP contain detailed provisions addressing

      1) Monitoring devices and their operation

      2) A permit program for major stationary sources, including requirements that permit fees be paid

      3) Demonstration by the state of adequate resources and sufficient personnel to enforce the program

5. The **new source performance standards** require industry to use a certain level of technology that may or may not be in use when the standard is promulgated. The states have no control over these standards.

6. **No significant deterioration policy** developed due to the preservation of clean regions that already meet the NAAQSs. Regions are divided into three classes, and depending upon the class, each can have only a certain amount of air deterioration.

7. **Mobile Source Emission Control**. The CAA also regulates mobile sources of pollution, e.g., motor vehicle emissions and fuel, via a certification and registration program. The 1990 amendments require manufacturers of new motor vehicles, engines, and components to establish and maintain records, perform tests, and permit EPA access to the records and the results of the tests, and they authorize the EPA to inspect all files, papers, and processes.

8. **National emission standards for hazardous air pollutants** are included under the act to prevent long- and short-term damage to human health and the environment from toxic or hazardous pollutants and substances.

9. **Liability**. When the EPA finds a violation, it issues a **Notice of Violation** through the appropriate regional office.

   a. The notice is sent to any appropriate state or local agency.

   b. If a violation continues for more than 30 days after the notice is issued, EPA may take the following actions:

      1) Commence a civil suit
      2) Issue an administrative order

   c. The 1990 amendments provide authority for private citizens to sue in federal court to require any state or federal official to perform his/her duties against the source of pollution.

   d. Section 113(c) authorizes criminal penalties for knowing violations of the law.

   e. The EPA also has power to seek a federal court order restraining activity in an appropriate action when air pollution is "presenting an imminent and substantial danger to the health of persons."

10. Stop and review! You have completed the outline for this subunit. Study multiple-choice questions 11 through 15 beginning on page 446.

E.   Management of Hazardous Waste

1.   **Resource Conservation and Recovery Act of 1976 (RCRA).** RCRA is a regulatory statute designed to provide "cradle-to-grave" control of hazardous waste. It imposes management requirements on generators, transporters, and owners of waste as well as on operators of treatment, storage, and disposal (TSD) facilities. Under the **Toxic Substances Control Act of 1976**, the EPA is authorized to regulate toxic substances that endanger health or the environment by labeling, limiting, or prohibiting the use of a substance.

   a.   RCRA applies primarily to operating facilities and does not address abandoned and inactive sites. Refer to CERCLA on page 441.

   b.   Pursuant to RCRA, the EPA must promulgate regulations that identify specific hazardous wastes, either by listing them or identifying the characteristics that render them hazardous.

      1)   All handlers of such waste are required to notify the EPA of their activities.

2.   **Solid and Hazardous Waste.** RCRA applies to virtually any waste regardless of its physical form.

   a.   If a listed commercial chemical product is spilled and if the spilled chemical and any residue, e.g., dirt, are discarded, they are deemed to be hazardous.

   b.   Thus, even businesses that generally do not discard hazardous waste must be prepared to comply with the RCRA hazardous waste regulations in case of an accidental spill.

   c.   EPA has defined the term "solid waste" to include many recycling and reclamation activities.

3.   **Generators of Hazardous Waste.** EPA regulations define the term **generator** as "any person, by site, whose act or process produces hazardous waste identified or listed in Part 261 of this chapter or whose act first causes hazardous waste to become subject to regulation."

   a.   Congress requires all generators to prepare a Uniform Hazardous Waste Manifest, which identifies and accompanies the hazardous waste at all times.

   b.   When hazardous materials are transported to a treatment, storage, and disposal (TSD) facility, a final copy of the manifest must be returned to the generator by the TSD facility. A copy of the final manifest must be retained for at least 3 years.

   c.   Additionally, the EPA and most states require periodic reports describing the "cradle-to-grave" handling of all hazardous and solid waste.

4.   **Transporters of Hazardous Waste.** Any person engaged in the off-site transportation of hazardous waste by air, rail, highway, or water is a **transporter**.

   a.   Persons who move hazardous or solid waste, such as shippers, common carriers, and those who move solid or hazardous waste on their own trucks, are transporters.

   b.   Transporters are subject to strict EPA and Department of Transportation (DOT) regulation with respect to the movement of hazardous or solid waste.

5.   **Treatment, Storage, and Disposal Facilities.** The EPA strictly regulates TSDs. The EPA has promulgated specific design, construction, and operating standards for each type of TSD facility regulated under RCRA, e.g., containers, tanks, storage compounds, landfills, incinerators, waste piles.

   a.   RCRA requires every owner or operator of a TSD facility to obtain a permit.

6.   The **Toxic Substances Control Act (TSCA)** was enacted in 1976 to prevent "unreasonable risk of injury to health or the environment" by toxic chemicals. It requires that notice be given to the EPA before production of a new chemical or a new

use of one already in production. If the data provided in the premanufacturing notice are insufficient for an evaluation of a chemical that may pose an "unreasonable risk," the EPA may in principle prohibit its production or distribution, but this remedy is rarely used. The TSCA also may require testing of such chemicals. Violations of the TSCA may result in civil penalties of up to $20,000 per day and criminal penalties for intentional wrongdoing, of up to $25,000 a day and a year's imprisonment.

7.   Stop and review! You have completed the outline for this subunit. Study multiple-choice questions 16 and 17 on page 448.

F.   **Comprehensive Environmental Response, Compensation, and Liability Act of 1980 (CERCLA)**. While RCRA establishes a cradle-to-grave regulatory program for present hazardous waste activities, CERCLA establishes a comprehensive response program for past hazardous waste activities.

1.   **Purpose**. In 1980, Congress established CERCLA to address the many abandoned hazardous waste sites and sites that the owners were financially incapable of cleaning up. CERCLA is designed as a response program to deal with sites that were established without negligence. Because no one was aware that a cleanup would be required in the future, the cleanup costs were not built into pricing structures.

   a.   CERCLA is known as the **Superfund**. It allots billions of dollars for cleanup of hazardous wastes.

2.   **Goals and Objectives**. CERCLA's objectives are much broader than any other federal environmental statute.

   a.   CERCLA covers all environmental media including air, surface water, groundwater, and soil.

   b.   CERCLA applies to any type of commercial, industrial, or even noncommercial facility, regardless of whether there are specific regulations affecting that type of facility.

   c.   The act requires anyone who releases unauthorized amounts of hazardous substances into the environment to notify the government.

      1)   Whether notified or not, the government has the power to order those responsible to clean up such releases.

      2)   Refusal to obey can lead to a suit for reimbursement for any cleanup monies drawn from the Superfund plus punitive damages of up to triple the cleanup costs.

3.   **Fundamental Prerequisites**. The release or threat of release into the environment of a hazardous substance, pollutant, or contaminant may trigger CERCLA response or liability.

   a.   **Environment** is also broadly defined. It includes all navigable and other surface waters, groundwaters, drinking water supplies, land surface, subsurface strata, and ambient air within the United States.

   b.   Under CERCLA, a **hazardous substance** is any substance that EPA has designated for special consideration under

      1)   The Clean Air Act (CAA)
      2)   The Clean Water Act (CWA)
      3)   The Toxic Substances Control Act (TSCA)
      4)   The Resource Conservation and Recovery Act (RCRA)

      NOTE: Moreover, the EPA must designate additional substances as hazardous that may present substantial danger to health and the environment.

4.   **Liability**. CERCLA imposes liability for site remedial costs.

  a.   These costs may be allocated under CERCLA to any one or all of those listed below:

    1)   Present and past owners including trustees and operators of the site

    2)   Parties who transported wastes to the site

    3)   Parties who arranged for wastes to be disposed of or treated, either directly with an owner/operator or indirectly with a transporter

    4)   Lenders that participate in a borrower's management or can influence hazardous waste policy may also be liable.

  b.   CERCLA imposes liability on those responsible for unauthorized discharges of hazardous wastes without proof of negligence. The liability has the following characteristics:

    1)   It is retroactive.

    2)   It is strict.

    3)   It is joint and several.

    4)   EXAMPLE: A commercial landfill accepted hazardous wastes for disposal from 1970 through 1980, during which time the landfill was owned by Sludge, Inc. During the landfill's operation, companies Abco, Babco, and Cabco were engaged in the hauling business and transported hazardous wastes from manufacturing plants to the landfill. Moreover, during these years, Carco and Truckco were manufacturing businesses that generated hazardous waste as a by-product of their operations. Each company had individually arranged with Abco, Babco, and Cabco to have its waste disposed of at the landfill in question. In 1992, 12 years after the landfill was closed, X Corp. purchased the site and merely held it for 5 more years. In 1998, the EPA determined that a $750 million cleanup was necessary. Pursuant to CERCLA as interpreted by the courts, all parties, i.e., Sludge, Inc., Abco, Babco, Cabco, Carco, Truckco, and X Corp. may be liable for some or all of the $750 million cleanup cost.

  NOTE: It is important to note that liability can be imposed both for damage to natural resources and for cleanup costs.

  c.   The EPA collects more than $1 billion from private parties annually.

  d.   However, the so-called innocent landowner's defense is available under CERCLA. For the exception to apply, the owner must have purchased the land after the placement of the hazardous substances occurred. Moreover, the owner must prove that (s)he did not know or have any reason to know that such substances were on the land. Finally, the owner must show that someone else caused the release or threat of release of the substances and that (s)he exercised reasonable care and took reasonable precautions in preventing the release of such substances.

5.   Stop and review! You have completed the outline for this subunit. Study multiple-choice questions 18 through 21 beginning on page 448.

MULTIPLE-CHOICE QUESTIONS

A. Environmental Regulation: Introduction

1. The most widely used regulatory approach to pollution control in the United States is

A. Pollution charges and fees.

B. Private markets in which pollution rights can be bought and sold.

C. Environmental standards and penalties for noncompliance.

D. Total deregulation of pollution control resulting in state regulation with no federal involvement.

The correct answer is (C). *(CMA, adapted)*
REQUIRED: The most widely used regulatory approach to pollution control in the United States.
DISCUSSION: Congress passed the National Environmental Policy Act and formed the Environmental Protection Agency (EPA) to control the pollution in the United States of air, water, and land. Other legislation, such as the Clean Air Act, Water Pollution Control Act, Noise Control Act, and Solid Waste Disposal Act, has been passed by Congress. Many states have enacted environmental laws that in some instances are more stringent than the federal standards. Violations of federal and state regulations are subject to civil and criminal penalties stated in the written legislation and regulations.
Answer (A) is incorrect because charges and fees are imposed when environmental regulations are violated. Answer (B) is incorrect because the government regulates how much pollution can be in the environment. Answer (D) is incorrect because the environment is subject to federal, state, and municipal regulations.

2. Which of the following remedies is available against a real property owner to enforce the provisions of federal acts regulating air and water pollution?

	Citizen Suits against the EPA to Enforce Compliance with the Laws	State Suits against Violators	Citizen Suits against Violators
A.	Yes	Yes	Yes
B.	Yes	Yes	No
C.	No	Yes	Yes
D.	Yes	No	Yes

The correct answer is (A). *(CPA, adapted)*
REQUIRED: The remedy available against a real property owner to enforce provisions of federal acts regulating air and water pollution.
DISCUSSION: Most environmental statutes permit some form of citizen suit. These statutes grant citizens the right to participate in or initiate civil enforcement actions. The citizens must, however, notify the EPA and Department of Justice. The primary responsibility for enforcing air quality standards lies with the states, but the federal government has the right to step in and enforce the standards if the states fail to.
Answers (B), (C), and (D) are incorrect because any person may institute a citizen suit, and a government agency may be sued to enforce the laws.

3. A federal regulation sets a quantitative limitation on the amount of a certain pollutant that may be emitted from industrial smoke stacks. Your state also has a standard, but the permissible amount is lower. In determining whether the state's standard is applicable, a court's decision will depend upon

A. The way in which the balance of interests (state versus federal) is best served.

B. Whether the state standard tends to interfere with the purposes of the federal regulations.

C. The way in which the balance of interests (health versus economics) is best served.

D. Whether the state standard tends to be more restrictive or more permissive than the federal standard.

The correct answer is (B). *(S. Sibary)*
REQUIRED: The basis for determining whether state regulation is applicable.
DISCUSSION: Federal regulatory schemes preempt state regulations that interfere with the federal purposes, whether the federal regulation is meant to be exclusive (in which case no state regulation will be allowed) or allows parallel state regulation. To decide the case, a court will need to determine whether the effect of the state law is consistent with or interferes with the federal goals.
Answers (A) and (C) are incorrect because the courts do not have authority to favor state interests over federal interests once it has been determined that federal jurisdiction is legitimate. The court must apply the standard for preemption. Answer (D) is incorrect because whether the state standard is more restrictive or more permissive does not answer whether the state standard is consistent with the federal standard.

B. National Environmental Policy Act (NEPA)

4. Which of the following statements about the National Environmental Policy Act (NEPA) is most likely to be incorrect?

A. NEPA requires federal agencies to consider environmental consequences in their decision-making process.

B. NEPA allows the federal government to bring suit against any private person who violates NEPA's provisions.

C. Under NEPA, federal agencies do not have to give environmental considerations priority over other concerns in their decision-making processes.

D. NEPA augments the power of existing agencies with respect to considering environmental consequences of proposed actions.

The correct answer is (B). *(Publisher)*
    REQUIRED: The incorrect statement about NEPA.
    DISCUSSION: The provisions of NEPA focus on federal governmental actions. Federal agencies are specifically directed to incorporate an analysis of environmental consequences in their decision-making processes. Actions of private persons are affected by NEPA only when federal involvement (approval, funding, etc.) is necessary before such persons may act (e.g., federal approval before drilling for oil in ocean waters within U.S. jurisdiction). Otherwise, NEPA does not directly concern activities of private persons.
    Answers (A) and (C) are incorrect because under NEPA, federal agencies must give environmental considerations a weight equal to, but not greater than, that afforded nonenvironmental concerns. Answer (D) is incorrect because NEPA augments the existing powers of federal agencies to deal with these environmental matters.

5. The environmental impact statement (EIS) lies at the heart of the NEPA. Which of the following states a condition that must be present before a federal agency is required to prepare an EIS?

A. There must be a recommendation or report on a proposal for legislation or certain other "major" federal action.

B. If a "major" federal action is involved, all that is needed is a slight chance that a small amount of irreparable environmental damage may result.

C. An embryonic discussion of a legislative proposal is all that is necessary to trigger the requirement for an EIS.

D. Congress must specifically direct a federal agency to begin preparing an EIS.

The correct answer is (A). *(Publisher)*
    REQUIRED: The condition necessary for the preparation of an EIS.
    DISCUSSION: The NEPA directs federal agencies to prepare an EIS for inclusion in every recommendation or report on proposals for legislation and other major federal actions significantly affecting the quality of the human environment.
    Answer (B) is incorrect because more than a small amount of environmental damage is needed. The term "significantly affecting" implies more harm (or potential harm) is necessary. Answer (C) is incorrect because the legislation must at least have been prepared, not be in its earliest stage. Answer (D) is incorrect because, if a federal agency already is empowered to act in a manner that constitutes "major" federal action, the agency is not allowed to wait until it receives a congressional directive to prepare an EIS.

6. Before actually preparing an EIS, a federal agency is required under NEPA to

A. Obtain local approval for its proposed actions through an official referendum presented to the people of the locality that will be affected by the agency's actions.

B. Consult with any federal agency that has special expertise with respect to any environmental impact involved.

C. Disregard any comments made by any federal agency with special expertise because, in effect, NEPA requires that each federal agency become its own expert in any environmental area.

D. Obtain approval for its proposed actions from the highest official in each affected locality.

The correct answer is (B). *(Publisher)*
    REQUIRED: The requirement before a federal agency prepares an EIS.
    DISCUSSION: Prior to preparing an EIS, the federal agency preparing the action must consult with any federal agency that has jurisdiction over the proposal or special expertise with respect to any environmental impact involved. This is consistent with another broad NEPA requirement of a systematic, interdisciplinary approach to decision making.
    Answers (A) and (D) are incorrect because NEPA does not require any formal local approval for an agency's proposed actions. However, the EIS, once prepared, must be open to public comment. Answer (C) is incorrect because agencies with special expertise must be consulted.

7. An EIS need not contain

   A. The environmental impact of the proposed action.

   B. Alternatives to the proposed action.

   C. Any adverse environmental effects that cannot be avoided.

   D. An independent opinion on the proposed action prepared by the Council on Environmental Quality.

The correct answer is (D). *(Publisher)*

   REQUIRED: The item that an EIS need not contain.

   DISCUSSION: An EIS must contain, in detail, the environmental impact of the proposed action, any adverse environmental effects that cannot be avoided should the proposal be implemented, alternatives to the proposed action, the effects on maintaining the long-term productivity of the environment affected by the proposal, and the irreparable commitment of resources as a result of the action. NEPA established the Council on Environmental Quality in the Executive Office of the President. It has an advisory function but has also promulgated regulations. It does not render opinions.

   Answers (A), (B), and (C) are incorrect because an EIS contains each of these items.

C. Clean Water Laws

8. Which of the following statements regarding the Clean Water Act (CWA) is correct?

   A. It allows persons to discharge pollutants into waters subject to its jurisdiction as long as navigation thereon will not be permanently obstructed.

   B. The CWA subjects all bodies of water located in the United States, whether flowing or not, to its protection.

   C. The notion of protecting waters within the jurisdiction of the United States began with the CWA.

   D. The CWA seeks to restore and maintain the physical and biological integrity of the waters of the United States.

The correct answer is (D). *(Publisher)*

   REQUIRED: The correct statement about the CWA.

   DISCUSSION: The CWA (1972) substantially amended the Federal Water Pollution Control Act of 1948. It seeks to restore and maintain the physical and biological integrity of the waters of the United States. Its objectives are to render water suitable for recreation and propagation of fish and other wildlife and to eliminate discharges of pollutants.

   Answer (A) is incorrect because the CWA broadly prohibits any discharges of pollutants into waters, except if in compliance with the act. Impairment of navigation is irrelevant. Answer (B) is incorrect because, to be subject to the CWA, the waters must be "navigable waters." Answer (C) is incorrect because the Rivers and Harbors Act of the late 1800s was used to combat pollutive discharges, although its original purpose was to keep waterways clear from obstructions to navigation.

9. Which of the following situations is not a "discharge of a pollutant" as defined in the CWA?

   A. A construction company's dumping of sand and gravel into the Mississippi River.

   B. A utility company's dumping of pure water that is heated to 200°F into Lake Michigan.

   C. A landowner's dumping of radioactive waste in a small flooded limestone quarry located on his/her private property and totally self-contained.

   D. A state municipality's dumping of garbage into the Ohio River.

The correct answer is (C). *(Publisher)*

   REQUIRED: The situation not within the definition of "discharge of a pollutant."

   DISCUSSION: The CWA defines the term "discharge of a pollutant" as any addition of any pollutant to navigable waters from any point source. A "point source" is any discernable, confined, and discrete conveyance. A "pollutant" is an addition to water that alters its chemical, physical, biological, or radiological integrity. But not all waters located in the United States are included in the act's definition of the term "navigable waters." Having no contact with any other water system, the small flooded limestone quarry is not a body of water of the United States.

   Answer (A) is incorrect because sand and gravel might alter the physical integrity of the body of water. Answer (B) is incorrect because thermal discharges may constitute pollution. Answer (D) is incorrect because garbage is an obvious pollutant.

10. Which of the following activities is(are) regulated under the Federal Water Pollution Control Act (Clean Water Act)?

	Discharge of Heated Water by Nuclear Power Plants	Dredging of Wetlands
A.	Yes	Yes
B.	Yes	No
C.	No	Yes
D.	No	No

The correct answer is (A). *(CPA, adapted)*
   REQUIRED: The activity(ies), if any, regulated by the Clean Water Act.
   DISCUSSION: Under this legislation, standards have been established regulating discharges of pollutants into navigable waters, a term that is interpreted to include wetlands. Thus, dredging or filling in wetlands falls within the statute, as does a discharge by a power plant.
   Answers (B), (C), and (D) are incorrect because dredging of wetlands and discharges by power plants are within the Clean Water Act (Federal Water Pollution Control Act).

D. Clean Air Laws

11. Under the Clean Air Act (CAA), a state must submit a state implementation plan (SIP) after the promulgation of a national ambient air quality standard (NAAQS). The EPA must approve the SIP if all the statutorily prescribed SIP requirements are contained therein. Which of the following is not a general SIP requirement?

A. The SIP must contain a plan for attaining primary NAAQSs as expeditiously as practicable.

B. The SIP must contain a plan for attaining secondary NAAQSs within a reasonable time.

C. The SIP must include an enforcement program regarding emission limitations for modifying, constructing, or operating any stationary source.

D. The SIP must provide for a so-called pollution tax, which the CAA stipulates must be no less than $500 per stationary source.

The correct answer is (D). *(Publisher)*
   REQUIRED: The alternative which is not a general SIP requirement.
   DISCUSSION: Nowhere in the CAA is a SIP required to contain a "pollution tax." However, the CAA does provide for civil and criminal sanctions.
   Answers (A), (B), and (C) are incorrect because they reflect major SIP requirements, but there are many more. The primary standards are public health oriented, whereas the secondary standards are directed toward protection of vegetation, climate, economic values, etc. Also, point sources are defined as stationary (e.g., power plants and factories) and moving (automobiles, etc.), and standards have been promulgated for each category.

12. Under the CAA, a "major stationary source" is

A. A facility whose emissions will cause an air quality control region of a state to exceed the primary NAAQS.

B. One that directly emits 100 tons per year or more of sulphur dioxide.

C. Any stationary facility or source of air pollutants that emits 20 tons per year or more of any air pollutant.

D. Any source of air pollutants that indirectly emits 20 tons per year or more of an air pollutant for which an NAAQS has been promulgated.

The correct answer is (B). *(Publisher)*
   REQUIRED: The definition of a "major stationary source" under the CAA.
   DISCUSSION: A major stationary source is any stationary facility or source of air pollutants that directly emits, or has the potential to emit, 100 tons per year or more of any air pollutant. The NAAQSs cover six pollutant categories: hydrocarbons, carbon monoxide, sulphur dioxide, nitrogen oxides, photochemical oxidants, and particulates.
   Answer (A) is incorrect because it states an erroneous definition of the term. Answer (C) is incorrect because the statutory threshold amount is 100 tons, not 20 tons. Answer (D) is incorrect because 100 tons of any air pollutant satisfies the definition; the pollutant need not be one for which an NAAQS has been promulgated.

13. A so-called Part D SIP is required to be submitted by states that have not attained the NAAQS for any listed pollutant in one or more air quality control regions located within their borders. Which of the following is a provision that a Part D SIP must contain?

A. A system for issuing permits to allow new or modified major stationary sources to emit air pollutants.

B. A mechanism for closing highways located in residential areas where the actual levels of pollution exceed primary and secondary NAAQSs.

C. Provision for the implementation of all reasonably available control measures (RACM) as expeditiously as possible.

D. Before full implementation of RACM, the Part D SIP must require the use of the best available control technology (BACT).

The correct answer is (A). *(Publisher)*

REQUIRED: The correct Part D SIP requirement.

DISCUSSION: The CAA prescribes many requirements for SIP. One is the permit requirement for new or modified major stationary sources.

Answer (B) is incorrect because the CAA does not specifically require that heavily traveled highways be closed. Answer (C) is incorrect because a Part D SIP must also provide for the implementation of all reasonably available control measures (RACM) as expeditiously as practicable, not as possible. Answer (D) is incorrect because, in the interim, the CAA requires reasonably available control technology to be used.

14. A person who desires to build a new major stationary source must first obtain a permit. Which of the following will not be a condition of obtaining such a permit in a state subject to the Part D SIP requirements?

A. The proposed new source must comply with the lowest achievable emission rate.

B. The owner or operator of the proposed new source must demonstrate that all other major stationary sources owned or operated by the person in the state comply (or are on schedule for compliance) with all applicable emissions limitations.

C. The new source will not impede the attainment of reasonable further progress toward NAAQS compliance otherwise required of a state under a Part D SIP.

D. The new source cannot be constructed in a "dirty air area."

The correct answer is (D). *(Publisher)*

REQUIRED: The item not a condition for obtaining a permit to construct a new major stationary source.

DISCUSSION: The Part D SIP requirements established by the 1977 amendments to the CAA departed from the path taken by Congress in the original CAA's SIP requirements. Originally, states were given significant leeway in deciding how to achieve the NAAQSs. Part D of the CAA now imposes specific restrictions on persons who desire to construct new, or modify old, major stationary sources. Under Part D, states are required to impose certain uniform restrictions. One restriction is on construction in "dirty air areas." New sources are permitted if they have the lowest achievable emission rates and if other sources under the operator's control are in compliance with applicable standards.

Answers (A), (B), and (C) are incorrect because each is an important restriction on a person who wishes to build or modify a major stationary source in a state subject to the Part D SIP provisions.

15. Under the Clean Air Act, which of the following statements is(are) correct regarding actions that may be taken against parties who violate emission standards?

I. The federal government may require an automobile manufacturer to recall vehicles that violate emission standards.

II. A citizens' group may sue to force a coal-burning power plant to comply with emission standards.

A. I only.

B. II only.

C. Both I and II.

D. Neither I nor II.

The correct answer is (C). *(CPA, adapted)*

REQUIRED: The action(s), if any, that may be taken to enforce the Clean Air Act (CAA).

DISCUSSION: The CAA regulates mobile as well as stationary sources of pollution; e.g., the 1990 amendments require manufacturers of new motor vehicles, engines, and components to establish and maintain records, perform tests, and permit EPA access to the records and the results of the tests, and they authorize the EPA to inspect all files, papers, and processes. If the emission standards developed for pollutants by the EPA are not met, then, with certain exceptions, the vehicles not conforming cannot be sold in the U.S. One enforcement mechanism provided by the CAA is private litigation. Thus, private citizens may bring civil suits against violators. They may also sue regulators to enjoin them to perform their duties under the CAA.

Answer (A), (B), and (D) are incorrect because vehicles that violate emission standards may not be sold in the U.S., and private enforcement of the CAA is permitted.

E. Management of Hazardous Waste

16. The Resource Conservation and Recovery Act (RCRA) defines hazardous waste broadly. The act generally applies to which of the following?

A. Solid waste.

B. Liquid waste.

C. Corrosive ash buried in an inactive waste site.

D. All of the answers are correct.

The correct answer is (A). *(Publisher)*
REQUIRED: The substance(s) to which the RCRA applies.
DISCUSSION: The policy of RCRA is reduction or elimination of hazardous waste as soon as possible. The act defines hazardous waste as solid waste that may cause or significantly contribute to an increase in mortality or serious illness or pose a hazard to human health or the environment if improperly managed. RCRA applies primarily to operating facilities and to new waste, rather than to abandoned or inactive sites.
Answers (B), (C), and (D) are incorrect because RCRA applies to solid waste newly generated at operating facilities.

17. The Resource Conservation and Recovery Act of 1976 (RCRA) imposes requirements on generators, transporters and owners of waste. A generator can include

A. A person the law recognizes as holding title to waste with high uranium content.

B. A person engaged in off-site transportation by water of hazardous waste.

C. A person whose process produces hazardous waste.

D. All of the answers are correct.

The correct answer is (D). *(Publisher)*
REQUIRED: The person identified as a generator by the RCRA.
DISCUSSION: The RCRA is designed to provide comprehensive control of hazardous waste. A generator must, for example, prepare a Uniform Hazardous Waste Manifest to identify and accompany the hazardous waste at all times. A generator is any person whose act or process produces hazardous waste or causes it to become subject to regulation. An owner or transporter can also be a generator if (s)he also fits the above definition.
Answers (A), (B), and (C) are incorrect because a transporter or an owner can be a generator also. For example, a transporter might generate hazardous waste by allowing two wastes to mix in transit.

F. Comprehensive Environmental Response, Compensation, and Liability Act of 1980 (CERCLA)

18. The Comprehensive Environmental Response, Compensation, and Liability Act (CERCLA), also generically known as the "Superfund," applies to the release of "hazardous substances." Which of the following is statutorily included in the definition of the term "hazardous substance"?

A. Crude oil.

B. Gasoline.

C. Asbestos.

D. Natural gas.

The correct answer is (C). *(Publisher)*
REQUIRED: The item within the definition of "hazardous substances" as defined in CERCLA.
DISCUSSION: Asbestos is a hazardous substance subject to the provisions of CERCLA.
Answers (A), (B), and (D) are incorrect because the definition of the term "hazardous substance" as used in CERCLA does not include petroleum or any derivatives thereof or natural gas.

19. Under CERCLA, proof by a preponderance of the evidence of which of the following is not a defense to liability?

A. Release of hazardous substances was caused solely by a *force majeure*.

B. Release of hazardous substances was caused solely by an act of war.

C. Payment of cleanup costs will result in personal or business financial ruin.

D. The release was caused by acts or omission of an unrelated third party, and the owner or operator exercised reasonable care and took reasonable precautions.

The correct answer is (C). *(Publisher)*
REQUIRED: The item not a defense to liability under CERCLA.
DISCUSSION: The inability to pay damages is not an absolute bar to liability under CERCLA.
Answers (A), (B), and (D) are incorrect because they comprise three exceptions to liability under CERCLA. A fourth, the so-called innocent landowner's defense, is indirectly available through the exception in answer (D).

20. Dan bought a vacation home in the mountains of North Carolina. One day as he was sitting on the porch of his vacation home, Dan saw a stream of gray liquid bubbling up from an opening in his front yard. Dan immediately notified the EPA, which, after extensive examination, informed him that hazardous substances (within the meaning of CERCLA) had been previously buried deep beneath his house and a shift in the rock formation underlying his house caused a barrel to rupture releasing its contents. Under CERCLA, Dan

A. Will be liable for the actions of the previous owner since CERCLA will not provide him with any defense to CERCLA liability.

B. Is released from all liability under CERCLA simply because he immediately notified the EPA of the release.

C. Will not be liable under CERCLA because he did not own the land at the time when the substances were buried.

D. Will not be liable under CERCLA, despite the act's broad liability, if he is able to avail himself of the so-called innocent landowner's defense.

The correct answer is (D). *(Publisher)*
REQUIRED: The potential liability of a homeowner under CERCLA.
DISCUSSION: Liability under CERCLA is broadly applied to all owners or operators of "facilities" where releases of hazardous substances occur. Thus, all owners of land where such releases occur are subject to liability under CERCLA.
    However, the so-called innocent landowner's defense is available under CERCLA. For the exception to apply, the owner must have purchased the land after the placement of the hazardous substances occurred. Moreover, the owner must prove that (s)he did not know or have any reason to know that such substances were on the land. Finally, the owner must show that someone else caused the release or threat of release of the substances and that (s)he exercised reasonable care and took reasonable precautions in preventing the release of such substances. If Dan proves the foregoing, he will not be subject to CERCLA liability.
    Answer (A) is incorrect because CERCLA does provide for defenses, albeit very limited ones. Answer (B) is incorrect because, by itself, immediate notification of a release by an owner or operator of an onshore facility will not absolve such person of CERCLA liability. Answer (C) is incorrect because CERCLA liability applies to both past and current owners of property.

21. Marta inherited a commercial building from her husband 25 years ago. Both Marta and her husband leased space in the building to various retail stores or repair shops. Prior to the husband's 20-year ownership, the property had been the site of a paint manufacturer who disposed of chemicals in abandoned and leaky underground storage tanks. No chemicals were deposited during Marta's or her husband's ownership. The estimated liability to remove the tanks and clean the site is believed to be three times the current fair market value of the property. With respect to liability for cleanup and other response costs under CERCLA, which of the following statements is correct?

A. Marta is not a potentially responsible party for the costs because she has done nothing more than own property where someone else dumped hazardous waste.

B. Marta is not potentially liable for cleanup and other costs because the statute of limitations has expired.

C. Nonowners such as tenants are excluded from potential responsibility under the act.

D. When more than one party is liable for assessment costs or cleanup damages at a hazardous waste site, the responsible parties have joint and several liability making each liable for the entire cost.

The correct answer is (D). *(Publisher)*
REQUIRED: The correct statement concerning liability for site cleanup under the Superfund (CERCLA).
DISCUSSION: Under CERCLA, anyone who owns or has ever owned or operated a site on which hazardous waste is found, has transported waste to the site, or has owned waste that was deposited at the site is a potentially responsible party (PRP). PRPs are liable for the cost of cleaning up the site, the damage done to natural resources, and any required health assessments. The liability under CERCLA is joint and several, rendering each party fully liable for the entire cost. A party that has paid may bring an action for contribution against others that are or may be liable.
    Answer (A) is incorrect because Marta is potentially liable under the act as the current owner of a hazardous site. Answer (B) is incorrect because the act includes no statute of limitations. Answer (C) is incorrect because there is no express exclusion under the act for nonowners such as tenants. Tenants may be viewed as owners or site operators if by the terms of their leases they obtain authority to exercise control over the underground tanks or other sources of continuing pollution.

OOF QUESTION *(Publisher)* 15-20 minutes

Your client, McLean Corp., and a group of joint venture investors are considering buying Chizism Chemical Co., presently in reorganization under Chapter 11 of the Bankruptcy Reform Act of 1978. Chizism Co. has produced chemical cleaners and pesticides at several plant sites for many years. Several of the product patents are quite valuable. Unfortunately, hazardous waste has been disposed of by burial on the plant sites. Other waste disposal was contracted out and dumped at other sites. If McLean Group buys Chizism, the intent is to resume production of the potentially profitable items and develop a compatible product line. Mammoth Bank has agreed to extend a line of credit to the successor company but insists on some controls to protect its interests.

Required

For Questions 1 through 13, select answer A if the statement is correct; select B if it is incorrect.

1. If McLean Group forms a successor corporation to Chizism, there is little risk of liability for past environmental violations.

2. Manufacturers of pesticides are subject to regulation under the Toxic Substances Control Act (TOSCA), the Resource Conservation and Recovery Act (RCRA), and the Federal Insecticide, Fungicide, and Rodenticide Act (FIFRA).

3. Mammoth Bank has no potential liability for environmental violations by McLean Group.

4. The EPA or the Justice Department has exclusive jurisdiction to sue a business firm that violates environmental laws.

5. To reenter the manufacture and distribution of pesticides, McLean Corp. will be required to prepare an environmental impact statement (EIS).

6. A successor corporation should not be concerned with the Clean Air Act if it restarts the manufacture of pesticides.

7. The previous disposal sites could possibly involve violation of the Clean Water Act of 1948 as amended.

8. Any business firm that has contributed hazardous waste to a disposal site is potentially liable for cleanup costs.

9. Liability under most of the environmental laws is joint and several.

10. A successor corporation will be required to deal exclusively with federal regulations.

11. A successor corporation may incur liability for mere ownership of land containing hazardous waste disposal sites even if it never deposits any hazardous waste at the site.

12. The EPA is required to determine which by-products of manufacturers are hazardous and subject to regulation.

13. If McLean Group purchases Chizism Co., Chizism, its officers, directors, consultants, and shareholders have no further liability for environmental matters if the agreement between McLean Group and Chizism so provides.

Knowledge Tested

1. Requirements of various environmental protection laws and regulations

2. Liability under various environmental protection laws and regulations

3. Enforcement under various environmental protection laws and regulations

Authors' Comments

This question provides a comprehensive look at environmental regulation. Many of the details discussed in the outline are included to help solidify what you have learned.

1. The correct answer is (B).

DISCUSSION: The Comprehensive Environmental Response, Compensation, and Liability Act of 1980 (CERCLA) (Superfund), as amended, authorizes the federal government through the EPA to take remedial action in response to a release or threatened release of hazardous substances into the environment. The EPA may undertake remediation or require cleanup by the responsible persons. If the EPA performs, it can recover costs from responsible third parties. The federal courts have determined that Congress intended present owners including successor business organizations to be responsible parties under the act. The successor company has potential liability as an owner for the hazardous waste sites on its property and liability as a generator of hazardous waste transported to other sites.

2. The correct answer is (A).

DISCUSSION: Manufacturers of pesticides are subject to all three acts. The Toxic Substances Control Act (1976) regulates chemicals that are known to be toxic and requires manufacturers and processors to determine their effect on health and the environment. The EPA may require special labeling, limit the use of a substance, set production quotas, or prohibit the use of a substance. The Resource Conservation and Recovery Act (1976) requires the EPA to establish regulations to monitor and control hazardous waste disposal. Producers must label and package any hazardous waste to be transported. Under the Federal Insecticide, Fungicide, and Rodenticide Act (1947), pesticides and herbicides must be (1) registered before sale, (2) certified only for approved applications, and (3) used in limited quantities when applied to food crops. Stringent labeling requirements are imposed. If a pesticide or herbicide is identified as harmful, the EPA can suspend or cancel its registration after a hearing. The agency can also inspect facilities and records where pesticides and herbicides are manufactured.

3. The correct answer is (B).

DISCUSSION: Lenders have potential liability under environmental laws. Under CERCLA, creditors who participate in the day-to-day operational management in production or waste-disposal activities are considered owners or operators of a hazardous waste facility. Some decisions have held lenders that foreclose to be responsible parties under CERCLA. However, the current view is to exempt lenders from liability if they act solely to protect their security interests and divest themselves of any interest in a timely and reasonable manner.

4. The correct answer is (B).

DISCUSSION: The major enforcement efforts of environmental laws are by the U.S. Justice Department at the request of the EPA. However, states enforce federal environmental programs, as well as their own laws, within their boundaries. Most environmental statutes permit suits by private citizens who contend that laws are not being enforced by the EPA. A private citizen may also bring an action for damages allegedly caused by violation of environmental statutes.

5. The correct answer is (B).

DISCUSSION: An environmental impact statement (EIS) is a document prepared by a federal agency analyzing the overall environmental impact of a proposed project. Nongovernmental entities do not generate EISs. However, they may provide suggestions or assistance to the government agency.

6. The correct answer is (B).

DISCUSSION: The Clean Air Act authorizes the EPA to establish air quality standards for stationary sources such as manufacturing plants. These standards are primarily enforced through state implementation plans (SIPs). To the extent that the successor manufacturer emits pollutants into the air that are potentially harmful to human health or the environment, it must be concerned with the Clean Air Act. Should the company employ 100 or more people, it must have a plan to reduce air pollution through trip-reducing programs such as carpooling or mass transit. Finally, a manufacturer who produces odors or releases toxics into the air is subject to a private tort action.

7. The correct answer is (A).

DISCUSSION: Jurisdiction of the Clean Water Act (CWA) is based on the authority of the federal government to regulate interstate commerce. The CWA has been liberally interpreted and includes coastal and freshwater lakes, rivers, swamps and wetlands, thermal pollution, ocean dumping, and oil spills. States regularly enforce the CWA. It is possible that Chizism's illegal dump sites of toxic materials could contaminate groundwater flowing into a navigable waterway. Provisions of the CWA may be enforced by EPA under CERCLA. CERCLA applies to air, surface water, groundwater, and soil.

8. The correct answer is (A).

DISCUSSION: Waste generators (and successors) and transporters, as well as site owners and operators, are potentially liable for cleanup costs under CERCLA (Superfund).

9. The correct answer is (A).

DISCUSSION: Liability under CERCLA and most environmental laws is joint and several. This means that only one or several of a number of responsible parties can be held liable for the entire costs of investigation, testing, and cleanup. A party that has paid cleanup costs can seek contribution from other responsible parties.

10. The correct answer is (B).

DISCUSSION: The environmental laws illustrate shared authority. Congress has not preempted the field and specifically incorporates state regulations and enforcement actions into national environmental policy. In fact, states may adopt environmental standards that exceed the federal laws.

11. The correct answer is (A).

DISCUSSION: A successor organization may incur liability for hazardous waste disposal sites on several theories. First, interpretations of CERCLA have determined that Congress intended to impose liability on current owners of land containing hazardous waste, including successor organizations. Secondly, successor organizations, as in mergers or consolidations, assume all liabilities of defunct organizations. On either basis, a successor organization would be a responsible party despite never having deposited any of the hazardous waste at the site.

12. The correct answer is (A).

DISCUSSION: RCRA imposes this duty on EPA. RCRA oversees hazardous waste from cradle to grave. Producers of a hazardous waste product are required to report, properly package, label, and transport any hazardous waste under a Uniform Hazardous Waste Manifest, which identifies and accompanies the waste at all times. The manifest must be retained for 3 years.

13. The correct answer is (B).

DISCUSSION: Violators cannot contract away environmental law violations. Any attempt would be ineffective. Chizism has clearly incurred liability. Under recent interpretations of the environmental statutes, officers, directors, and consultants who exercise decision-making authority are civilly and criminally liable for noncompliance. A shareholder is not liable, but a shareholder that participates in policy decisions on environmental matters could be liable.

ESSAY QUESTION *(Publisher)* 15-25 minutes

This essay question is based on the fact statement of the OOF question on page 450. The investor group has formed Newcorp, a successor to Chizism Chemical, and is producing chemical cleaners and pesticides. Toxic substances are stored on the premises. As a result of accidental spills, deteriorating storage containers, and the previous unauthorized dump sites, toxins have saturated a large quantity of soil and seeped into the aquifer, contaminating the water supply over a large area. Several local water systems draw from this aquifer. A number of local residents have been treated for various symptoms allegedly caused from drinking the water. Several others have been hospitalized with a general diagnosis of toxic poisoning specifically affecting the central nervous system, liver, bladder, and kidneys. A group of residents advocate filing a tort action against Newcorp. Other residents advocate filing a complaint seeking relief under the various environmental statutes. Still others believe the residents should notify the EPA and rely on its recommendations for other actions to be pursued.

Required

1. What remedies may be available in a tort action?

2. What relief can be obtained under the environmental statutes?

Knowledge Tested

1. Torts of nuisance, negligence, and strict liability
2. Injunctions
3. Application of environmental laws
4. Relief from environmental violations

Authors' Comments

It appears that future questions on the exam will require an overall understanding of national environmental policy and general familiarity with specific environmental statutes. The focus should be on the ability to recognize potential liability under future interpretations of the laws and to assess the resulting financial impact on responsible parties. Due diligence is required in managing the risk of environmental liability. This is particularly true in mergers, buying or selling plant sites or other real property, leases, investing in capital equipment, and importantly, disclosure and reporting under SEC laws. Outside experts are frequently required.

Suggested Answer

1. **TORT ACTION.** Tort action for environmental activities may be based on the legal theories of nuisance, negligence, strict liability, and statutory violations. Newcorp is subject to an injunction and liability for money damages (compensatory and punitive) on each of these theories.

    Nuisance occurs when a defendant uses its property in a way that unreasonably interferes with the plaintiff's right to the use and enjoyment of his/her property. A nuisance may be public or private depending on the interest harmed. A private nuisance is a cause of action permitted when a citizen has experienced an injury that is personal and distinct from the public harm. The residents whose health has been affected by the pollutants injected into their water supply may obtain relief under nuisance theory. Since the offense is continuing, an injunction should be issued until abatement. Clearly the actions of Newcorp are unreasonable, and the interests of the citizens outweigh those of Newcorp. In addition, an award of monetary damages is warranted.

    Negligence is a defendant's failure to exercise reasonable care to avoid foreseeable injury to others. The violation of statutes designed to protect human health and the environment is negligence *per se* (on its face). The introduction of toxins into the aquifer resulted from improper storing and handling of these substances and a failure to adhere to environmental laws and regulations. These facts fully support a claim of negligence and entitle the citizens to compensatory damages and, very likely, punitive damages.

Because the nature of the toxic materials made them inherently and imminently dangerous, the citizens should be allowed to use **strict liability**. Under this theory, those that engage in ultrahazardous activities are liable for resulting harm without regard to reasonable care. Application of this doctrine would reduce the plaintiff's burden of proof and increase the likelihood of recovery of punitive and compensatory damages.

2. **STATUTORY VIOLATIONS.** Newcorp appears to be in serious violation of several federal environmental statutes (and, very likely, state statutes). The most direct and relevant to this case is the Clean Water Act (CWA). The CWA has both civil and criminal sanctions and allows private citizens or the EPA to bring actions to enjoin and/or recover damages from parties that violate the provisions of the act. The EPA seeks to protect the public interest in a clean and healthy environment and does not recover damages for private citizens. However, private enforcement actions for violation of environmental statutes are common. Private citizens may use environmental violations as a basis to recover damages for personal injury by proving the following:

    a. They are a party intended to be protected by the requirements of the statute.

    b. The provisions of the statute have been violated.

    c. Injury to the plaintiff has resulted from the violations of the defendant.

If the violations are intentional or grossly negligent, punitive damages may be awarded.

CHAPTER VI
UNIFORM COMMERCIAL CODE

These four study units will constitute approximately 20% of the Business Law section.

STUDY UNIT 15: NEGOTIABLE INSTRUMENTS AND BANK TRANSACTIONS

23 pages of outline
49 multiple-choice questions
1 OOF and 1 essay

A. Types of Negotiable Instruments
B. Requisites of Negotiability
C. Transfer and Negotiation
D. Holders and Holders in Due Course
E. Liabilities, Defenses, and Rights
F. Discharge
G. Bank Transactions

This chapter is based on Article 3 of the Uniform Commercial Code, "Negotiable Instruments," which was formerly titled "Commercial Paper." Negotiable instruments are formal written contracts used extensively in business transactions as a substitute for money and to extend credit. The important forms are notes and drafts. Success with questions on this topic requires recognition of the distinction between the transfer of an instrument by assignment and by negotiation, the ability to verify the requirements of negotiability, the ability to identify the parties to a note and a draft, recognition of the types of endorsement, and knowledge of the contract and the warranty liability of primary and secondary parties. Central to negotiable instruments is the holder in due course (HDC) concept. Questions frequently test the ability to identify an HDC and the distinction between real and personal defenses.

A. **Types of Negotiable Instruments.** Negotiation of instruments facilitates commerce by enabling the instruments to act as substitutes for money or as credit devices.

   1. Other instruments include documents of title and letters of credit.

   2. Negotiable instruments are formal written contracts and a form of property.

      a. Thus, negotiable instruments require mutual assent, consideration, capacity, and legality.

      b. A negotiable instrument, however, is presumed to have been issued for consideration.

   3. Negotiable instruments law is codified primarily in Article 3 of the Uniform Commercial Code (UCC) as revised in 1990.

   4. If a negotiable instrument is negotiated to a holder in due course, (s)he takes it free of all personal defenses and subject only to the real defenses. Defenses by type are discussed on pages 469 and 470.

      a. If the transferee does not qualify as a holder in due course, the law of assignments, not UCC Article 3, controls. Any real or personal defense good against the transferor will be good against the transferee.

5. Although all negotiable instruments may be classified as either drafts or notes, the UCC lists four forms of negotiable instruments: notes, certificates of deposit, drafts, and checks.

6. The **promissory note** is a written promise between two parties. It is an unconditional signed promise by one party, the maker, to pay a certain sum of money to a second party, the payee.

$500.00   Dayton, Ohio   May 2, 1999

Sixty days after date I promise to pay to the order of

_____Cash_____

_____Five hundred_____ Dollars

at   _____Miami, Florida_____

Value received with interest at the rate of nine percent per annum.

This instrument is secured by a conditional sales contract.

No. 11   Due July 1, 1999   *Mark Maker*
                                            Mark Maker

---

   a. The maker is the person who issues a promissory note to a payee.

   b. A note payable to the order of a named payee is called order paper. The named payee must endorse the note (by signing the back) to negotiate it (transfer it).

   c. A note payable to bearer (any person can present it for payment) may be negotiated without endorsement.

7. A **certificate of deposit** (CD) is an instrument containing acknowledgment by a bank of receipt of money with an engagement (promise) by the bank to repay it. It typically bears interest.

   a. A CD is a form of promissory note. It evidences the fact that funds have been deposited, but it contains an unconditional promise to repay the amount.

   b. CDs in small denominations are often sold by savings and loan associations.

   c. The bank is the maker, and the payee is generally an individual or a business.

   d. There are two classes of CDs:

      1) Demand certificates (payable on demand)
      2) Time certificates (payable at a definite time after issue)

8. A **draft** is an unconditional written order by one person, the drawer, to another person, the drawee, to pay a sum of money to a third person, either to a named payee or to bearer.

To: Home Commerce Bank
     Newtown, FL
                                May 15, 1999

Pay to the order of   Paul Payee $2,000.00
      Two Thousand and xx/100   Dollars
 on November 1, 1999

                        David Drawer
                        David Drawer

---

a. The drawee must be obligated to the drawer either by agreement or through a debtor-creditor relationship before the drawee is obligated to the drawer to honor the order.

b. Drafts are usually classified as one of the following:

　　1) A **time draft**: payable at a definite time in the future
　　2) A **sight draft**: payable on demand (i.e., upon presentation to the drawee)

c. A drawee is not liable for the draft until (s)he has accepted the instrument.

　　1) **Acceptance** is the drawee's signed agreement to pay a draft as presented (UCC 3-409).

d. For a sight draft, the drawee accepts the draft on demand of the payee (i.e., upon the payee's presentation of the draft) simply by paying the instrument.

e. For a time draft, the payee usually presents it to the drawee for acceptance before the instrument's due date.

　　1) The drawee accepts the draft by writing his/her acceptance on the instrument.

　　2) The acceptance may consist of the acceptor's signature alone.

　　3) It is usually written vertically across the face of the instrument.

　　4) Once accepted, the time draft is returned by the drawee-acceptor to the payee who holds it until its due date (at which time the payee presents it again for payment).

9. A **check** is a form of draft. It is always drawn on a bank, and it is always a sight draft that is payable on demand.

a. The drawer is a customer who has an account at a drawee bank.

b. The payee may be an individual, firm, or organization designated on the face of the check to receive payment.

c. Checks usually enable the drawer to make distributions from a single fund (the drawer's bank account).

d. The drawer obtains a record of expenditures: checks issued by the drawer eventually clear the bank collection process and are returned to the drawer and/or the drawer receives a bank statement (periodically).

e. Checks are generally issued as payment for goods or services and thus are issued as part of an underlying contract.

f. A postdated check bears a date later than the date on which the check is drawn.

　　1) A postdated check is valid and is payable on or after the indicated date.

　　2) Postdating a check is not illegal (unless to defraud a party to the check).

　　3) To facilitate the automated check collection system, a bank may pay a postdated check when presented and before the stated date unless the drawer gives notice to the bank.

10. A **certified check** is one that the drawee bank has accepted, or agreed in advance to pay, even if the funds in the drawer's account are insufficient. Certification is a specific type of acceptance.

a. The check is presented to the payor bank by either the drawer or the payee.

b. The objective of having a check certified is to make the check more equivalent to money and thus more readily acceptable.

11. A **cashier's check** is a check drawn by a bank on itself.

    a.   The cashier's check represents the obligation of the bank itself.

12. When a bank draws a check on another bank in which the first bank has money on deposit, the check is referred to as a **bank draft**.

13. A **trade acceptance** is a special form of time draft. It is used by sellers as a means to extend credit to buyers of their goods.

    a.   The seller draws a draft ordering the buyer to pay the seller (or a third party) at some time in the future.

    b.   The seller presents the draft to the buyer, and the buyer accepts it, thereby becoming liable on the instrument.

    c.   The seller can be both drawer and payee of the draft.

14. A **traveler's check** is a three-party instrument. The traveler is the drawer, and the bank or issuing firm is the drawee.

    a.   For purposes of identification, the traveler must sign the traveler's check twice, once when the seller issues it and a second time when the traveler cashes it.

    b.   When the drawee is a nonbanking organization such as American Express, the so-called traveler's check is not technically a check but is a draft.

15. Stop and review! You have completed the outline for this subunit. Study multiple-choice questions 1 through 6 beginning on page 476.

B. Requisites of Negotiability. If an instrument is negotiable, the holder may qualify for the special status of holder in due course.

1. Negotiability is strictly a matter of form. If an instrument is drafted and issued in a specified manner, it is negotiable; if not, it is not negotiable and is not subject to UCC Article 3 but may be enforceable as an ordinary contract.

    a.   Negotiability does not depend on the parties' intent, agreement, or understanding; it is dependent solely on form.

2. To be negotiable, an instrument must

    a.   Be written
    b.   Be signed by the maker or drawer
    c.   Contain an unconditional promise or order to pay a fixed amount of money

        1)   Payable on demand or at a definite time
        2)   Payable to order or bearer

3. A negotiable instrument must be in writing.

    a.   Writing includes printing, typewriting, or any other intentional reduction to tangible form.

    b.   The writing must be on material that has a degree of permanence and that is freely transferable in the ordinary course of business.

        1)   EXAMPLE: A writing in beach sand or on the back of a boat is not negotiable.

4. To be negotiable, an instrument must be signed by the maker (a note or CD) or the drawer (a draft or a check).

    a.   The signature may be in any form. It may be any symbol executed or adopted with intent to authenticate the writing.

      b.   Initials, an X, a thumbprint, or even a trade name imprinted by a machine will suffice.

      c.   The signature can be anywhere on the instrument. It is usually placed on the face of the instrument in the lower right-hand corner.

      d.   A signature may also be made by an agent or other authorized representative.

5.   A negotiable instrument must contain an unconditional promise or order to pay.

      a.   The terms of the instrument must not be conditioned upon the occurrence or nonoccurrence of some other event or agreement.

          1)   Payment may not be subject to or governed by another agreement.

          2)   The right to payment must be determined within the four corners of the instrument.

          3)   Mere reference to another agreement does not destroy negotiability.

      b.   A **promise** is a signed written undertaking to pay an obligation.

          1)   "I promise" evidences a promise. But, the word "promise" does not have to be used.

          2)   Mere acknowledgment of a debt is not a promise, e.g., an IOU.

      c.   An **order** is a direction to pay, e.g., "Pay."

          1)   A mere authorization or request is not an order.

      d.   Words of courtesy, such as "please" or "thank you," do not destroy negotiability as long as the proper terms are included.

          1)   EXAMPLE: I promise to pay $10,000 to the order of Hannah for the purchase of rings. Thank you.

      e.   Payment may be limited to a particular fund or source without affecting negotiability.

6.   A negotiable instrument must state the amount to be paid as a fixed amount of money.

      a.   It must be possible to compute the amount from the instrument itself.

      b.   The amount may vary depending on a simple formula and still be considered certain.

      c.   Typical provisions regarding installment payments and discounts or penalties for early retirement require only basic mathematics to determine the sum due. Thus, such provisions are enforceable. For example, clauses allowing attorney's fees to be paid upon default will not impair negotiability.

      d.   Interest on a negotiable instrument is as follows:

          1)   Any payment of interest must be provided for in the instrument.

          2)   If interest is payable, it accrues from the date of the instrument.

          3)   If an instrument does not provide for interest, it nevertheless will accrue after maturity until paid.

          4)   Interest may be stated in money or as a fixed or variable rate.

          5)   Calculation of interest may require reference to a source not within the four corners of the instrument, e.g., prime rate, banking rate, legal rate, or judgment rate.

7. The sum certain is to be payable in money.

   a. The instrument may contain no other promise or obligation.
   b. No goods or services may be promised or ordered.
   c. An option to pay in money or something else is not permitted.
   d. An instrument that states the sum is to be paid in a foreign currency is negotiable.

      1) The UCC defines money as a medium of exchange authorized or adopted by a domestic or foreign government as part of its currency.

8. The negotiable instrument must be payable on demand or at a definite time.

   a. A promise or order that does not state any time of payment is payable on demand.

   b. Instruments that are payable on demand include those that contain the words "payable on demand," "payable at sight," or "payable at presentation."

   c. By definition, a check is payable on demand.

   d. If an instrument is not payable on demand, it must be payable at a definite time specified on the face of the instrument.

   e. A promise or an order is payable at a definite time if it is payable

      1) On lapse of a definite period of time after sight or acceptance, or

      2) At a fixed date or dates (or at a time or times) readily ascertainable at the time the promise or order is issued,

      3) Subject to rights of

         a) Prepayment

         b) Acceleration

         c) Extension at the option of the holder

         d) Extension to a further definite time at the option of the maker or acceptor or automatically upon or after a specified act or event

   f. An instrument payable on or before a stated date is payable

      1) On demand until that date, and
      2) At a fixed date thereafter (if not yet paid).

   g. An **acceleration clause** may appear on the face of the instrument.

      1) An acceleration clause allows a payee or other holder of a time instrument to demand payment of the entire amount, with interest, before the stated due date if a triggering event occurs.

      2) A right to accelerate must be exercised in good faith.

   h. An **extension clause** permits the date of maturity to be extended beyond the time specified in the instrument.

      1) To maintain negotiable status, the period of extension must be specified if the right to extend is given to the maker or acceptor.

      2) If the holder of the instrument can extend it, the maturity does not have to be specified.

9. The words of negotiability, "payable to order" or "to bearer," are required for negotiability.

   a. These words clearly indicate that the parties intend that the instrument be capable of circulating in commerce as a money substitute.

    b.   Unless an instrument, other than a check, bears one of these phrases, either "payable to order" or "to bearer," the instrument is not negotiable and is merely assignable and thus governed by the law of contracts. A check that meets all requirements of negotiability except that it is not payable to order or bearer is nevertheless negotiable.

10.   **Order paper** enables a person identified on the instrument to designate the payee. The intended payee should be designated with reasonable certainty.

    a.   An order instrument is a promise or order not payable to bearer if it is payable

       1)   To the order of an identified person, or
       2)   To an identified person or order.

    b.   An instrument payable to bearer may become payable to an identified person if it is endorsed to be paid to the order of a person (bearer paper becomes an order instrument by special endorsement).

    c.   A promise or order that is payable to order is payable to the identified person.

    d.   Order paper allows the maker or drawer to transfer it to a specific person.

       1)   That person can transfer the instrument to whomever (s)he wishes.

    e.   Examples of acceptable language for an order instrument are

       1)   "Payable to the order of M. Cruz"
       2)   "Pay to M. Cruz or order."

    f.   The following language would denote the instrument as nonnegotiable:

       1)   "Payable to M. Cruz"
       2)   "Pay to M. Cruz only."

11.   **Bearer paper** is an instrument that does not designate a specific payee; the maker or drawer agrees to pay anyone who presents the instrument for payment.

    a.   A promise or order is payable to bearer if it

       1)   Does not state a payee
       2)   Indicates that it is not payable to an identified person

          a)   Or it is payable to cash or to the order of cash.

       3)   States that it is payable to bearer or to the order of bearer
       4)   Indicates that the person in possession is entitled to payment

    b.   An instrument payable to an identified person will become payable to bearer if it is endorsed in blank.

    c.   To illustrate, an instrument made payable as any of the following is bearer paper:

       1)   Pay bearer

       2)   Pay to the order of bearer

       3)   Pay to the order of M. Cruz or bearer

       4)   Pay any person presenting

       5)   Pay $500

       6)   Pay cash

       7)   Pay to the order of cash

       8)   Pay to the order of a barrel of tar

       9)   Pay one computer monitor (not negotiable because not a sum certain in money)

    d.   If an instrument is not order paper, it is bearer paper.

12. **Factors Not Affecting Negotiability**

    a.   The drawer of a draft or a check may include a provision that the payee acknowledge full satisfaction of an obligation by signing.

    b.   Inclusion or omission of words stating the consideration for which the instrument was issued will not preclude negotiability.

        1)   EXAMPLE: Phrases such as "for value received," "in payment for services rendered."

    c.   Failure to state the issue date does not affect negotiability, unless the date of an instrument is necessary to determine a definite time for payment.

        1)   An instrument with no date reference is treated as payable on demand.

        2)   The UCC allows for the issue date to be inserted if the maker or drawer intended the instrument to be complete; e.g., a phrase such as "payable 90 days after date" appears.

    d.   Any date that does appear on the instrument is presumed correct. Evidence may establish a contrary date.

    e.   Postdating or antedating an instrument does not affect negotiability.

    f.   It does not destroy negotiability to go off the face of the instrument to determine the rate of interest.

    g.   Omission of a statement describing where the instrument is drawn or payable does not impair negotiability.

    h.   Handwritten terms are appropriate and outweigh typewritten and printed terms.

    i.   Words outweigh figures.

13. Stop and review! You have completed the outline for this subunit. Study multiple-choice questions 7 through 15 beginning on page 477.

C. **Transfer and Negotiation**. Mere **transfer** of an instrument constitutes an assignment. Negotiation may allow the transferee to take free of personal defenses.

   1.   **Negotiation** is the transfer of an instrument in such form that the transferee qualifies as a holder.

     a.   There can never be negotiation unless the document is in negotiable form.

   2.   A **holder** is a person in possession of bearer paper or in possession of order paper that has been issued to him/her or transferred to him/her and properly endorsed.

     a.   Negotiation is effected, for

        1)   Bearer paper, by mere delivery and possession
        2)   Order paper, by delivery with the required endorsement

     b.   If a holder does not endorse, a mere transfer of the instrument occurs.

        1)   The transfer constitutes an assignment of the transferor's rights.

        2)   The transferee is merely an assignee and is subject to both real and personal defenses.

        3)   A transfer of an order instrument for value gives the transferee the right to the unqualified endorsement of the transferor unless it is specifically agreed that the transaction is an assignment.

    c.   Any holder of commercial paper or person acting on behalf of the holder can negotiate the commercial paper.

        1)   A transfer by a nonholder is merely an assignment of whatever rights, if any, the nonholder may have had.

        2)   But, if the transferor is a holder, that person has the power to negotiate the instrument even though the negotiation may be wrongful.

3.   An **endorsement** is the signature of a payee, a drawee, an accommodation endorser, or a holder of an instrument.

    a.   Endorsement is required on order instruments being negotiated.

        1)   A transferee of bearer paper may require endorsement, e.g., for identification purposes, but the UCC does not require endorsement of bearer paper.

    b.   Endorsements are written on the back of the instrument itself.

        1)   If there is no room on the instrument, endorsement can be written on another piece of paper (called an allonge) affixed to the instrument. It must be firmly attached to the instrument so as to become a part thereof (pins or paper clips will not suffice. Some courts hold that staples are sufficient).

    c.   The placement of any endorsement and the relative liability of endorsers, unless otherwise agreed, are presumed to be according to the order in which their signatures appear.

    d.   Endorsements are categorized as blank, special, restrictive, qualified, or anomalous.

4.   A **blank endorsement** specifies no particular person. It may consist of merely the signature of the endorser or his/her authorized agent.

    a.   A check payable to the order of Paul Payee can be endorsed in blank by his signing the back of the check.

    b.   An instrument payable to order and endorsed in blank becomes payable to bearer and is negotiable by delivery alone.

        1)   EXAMPLE: Slip endorses a check payable to him in blank and then loses it. Slick finds it and sells it to Happy for value without endorsing it. This constitutes a negotiation because Slick has made delivery of a bearer instrument.

5.   A **special endorsement** specifically designates the person to whom or to whose order the instrument is payable.

    a.   Thus, an endorsement "Pay to Grace Smith" or "Pay to the order of Grace Smith" is a special endorsement.

> Pay to Grace Smith
> *Grace Smith*

    b.   An instrument specially endorsed becomes payable to the order of the special endorsee and requires his/her endorsement for further negotiation.

    c.   This is so if the instrument was originally bearer paper or if it became bearer paper as a result of a blank endorsement.

    d.   Words of negotiability -- payable to order or bearer -- are not required in an endorsement.

e.   A holder with a blank endorsement may convert the blank endorsement into a special endorsement by writing over the signature of the endorser any contract consistent with the character of the endorsement.

f.   The last endorsement determines whether the instrument is order paper or bearer paper.

6.   A **restrictive endorsement** attempts to restrict or further limit the negotiation of the instrument.

a.   The negotiability of an instrument may be limited by a restrictive endorsement but is not destroyed.

b.   The UCC identifies the following four types of restrictive endorsements:

1)   Conditional endorsements
2)   Endorsements prohibiting further transfer
3)   Endorsements for deposit or collection
4)   Endorsements in trust

7.   A **conditional endorsement** is one by which the endorser purports to make the rights of the endorsee subject to the happening or non-happening of a specified event.

```
+---------------------------------------+
|         Pay to Paul Payee, provided   |
|      that he complete painting my house|
|        at 100 Safe Street by July 1999|
|                                       |
|              Lola Endorser            |
+---------------------------------------+
```

a.   A conditional endorsement is ineffective to condition payment.

b.   The maker, drawee, or subsequent endorser is obligated to pay the instrument when due without regard to whether or not the condition has been satisfied.

c.   The qualified endorsee may be liable in damages to the endorser on the underlying contract (i.e., behind the condition) for obtaining payment without performance.

8.   An **endorsement prohibiting further transfer** does not prevent negotiability.

```
+---------------------------------------+
|          Pay Paul Payee ONLY          |
+---------------------------------------+
```

9.   An **endorsement for deposit or collection** locks the instrument into the banking system for deposit or collection.

```
+---------------------------------------+
|            For Deposit Only           |
+---------------------------------------+
```

```
+---------------------------------------+
|             For Collection            |
+---------------------------------------+
```

```
+---------------------------------------+
|              Pay Any Bank             |
+---------------------------------------+
```

a.   Such endorsements limit negotiation consistent with its limitation and put all nonbanking persons on notice as to who has a valid interest in the instrument.

10. A **qualified endorsement** is used by an endorser to disclaim or limit contractual liability on the instrument.

    a. The notation "without recourse" is commonly used.

> Pay to Paul Payee without recourse,   *Mark Maker*

    b. An unqualified endorsement usually guarantees payment of the instrument.

    c. A person who endorses the instrument without recourse does not undertake to pay the instrument if not paid by the primary party.

        1) The qualified endorser does not undertake secondary liability.
        2) A qualified endorser may incur warranty liability.

    d. Qualified endorsement does not destroy negotiability or prevent further negotiation of the instrument but may lessen marketability of the instrument.

    e. A qualified endorsement is often used by persons acting in a representative capacity. The representative is merely endorsing payment through to the principal and should not be required to make good on the check if it is later dishonored.

    f. If the instrument is later dishonored, the holder cannot obtain recovery from the representative who endorsed without recourse.

    g. A qualified endorsement may reduce marketability of the instrument.

11. An **anomalous endorsement** is made by a person who is not the holder. It has no effect on negotiability, but it makes the signer liable as an endorser.

12. Sometimes an endorser signs in order to add his/her liability and thereby assist or accommodate another party who might otherwise be unable to obtain funds. Such party is a surety known as an **accommodation endorser**.

13. Stop and review! You have completed the outline for this subunit. Study multiple-choice questions 16 through 21 beginning on page 481.

D. **Holders and Holders in Due Course.** Generally, a mere holder acquires a negotiable instrument subject to all claims and defenses to the instrument, but a holder in due course (except in consumer credit transactions) takes the instrument free of all personal defenses but subject to real defenses.

1. The **holder** is the person who, by the terms of the instrument, is legally entitled to payment.

    a. The holder of a negotiable instrument may transfer it, negotiate it, discharge it, or enforce payment of it in his/her own name.

    b. A holder enjoys the same status as an assignee of a contractual right. The assignee generally steps into the shoes of the assignor(s) and (s)he obtains only those rights that the predecessor-transferor had in the instrument.

2. A holder (a possessor of bearer paper or of duly endorsed order paper) may become a **holder in due course** by meeting three requirements:

    a. Taking it in good faith
    b. Giving value for the instrument
    c. Taking it without notice of

        1) Defenses to payment
        2) Rival claims of ownership
        3) The instrument's being overdue or dishonored

3.   The first requirement for due course status is that a person be a holder.

4.   A holder in due course (HDC) must have given value for the instrument.

    a.   A person who receives an instrument as a gift or an inheritance is not an HDC.

    b.   A holder who fails to meet the value requirement can have the rights of an HDC by meeting the special requirements of the shelter principle. See page 465.

    c.   **Value** does not have the same meaning as **consideration** in the law of contracts. A promise is consideration, but it is not value.

    d.   UCC 3-303 provides that a holder takes the instrument for value in one of the following ways:

        1)   To the extent that the agreed-upon consideration has been paid or a security interest or lien is acquired

        2)   By taking an instrument in payment of or as security for an antecedent debt

        3)   By giving a negotiable instrument or irrevocable commitment as payment

5.   A holder must take the instrument in **good faith** to qualify as HDC.

    a.   Good faith means "honesty in fact and the observance of reasonable commercial standards of fair dealing."

    b.   The good-faith requirement applies only to the holder.

        1)   A person who takes from a thief can be an HDC.

    c.   Good faith is a subjective (honesty in fact) and an objective (reasonable commercial standards) determination.

    d.   But if a person takes an instrument under circumstances that clearly establish that there is a defense to the instrument, (s)he does not take it in good faith.

        1)   EXAMPLE: Slick purchases a $100,000 note for $1,000 from a stranger on a street corner. The issue of good faith will almost certainly arise.

6.   A person cannot be an HDC if (s)he acquires an instrument that (s)he knows, or that a person of ordinary intelligence would have known, is defective.

    a.   The most obvious signs of a defective instrument are

        1)   It is overdue.
        2)   It has been dishonored.
        3)   There is a defense against it.
        4)   There is another claim to it.

    b.   If there is sufficient visible evidence of alteration or forgery on the instrument, or if the instrument is otherwise sufficiently irregular or incomplete when it is issued or negotiated, a purchaser cannot be a holder in due course.

    c.   What constitutes notice of an overdue instrument depends on whether a person takes a time instrument or a demand instrument.

        1)   The holder of an instrument payable at a definite time who takes such paper the day after the due date is deemed to be on actual notice that it is overdue.

        2)   The purchaser of a demand instrument other than a check, e.g., a demand note, is deemed to be on notice that it is overdue (and thus cannot be an HDC) if at the time of purchase (s)he has reason to know that demand has already been made or that the purchaser is taking the instrument more than a reasonable time after its issue, e.g., 60 days.

a)   For a check drawn and payable in the United States, a reasonable time is presumed to be 30 days after issue.

d.   In certain circumstances, an original payee may qualify as an HDC. This is extraordinary because, under normal circumstances, if there are defenses, the payee will usually be aware of them since the payee normally deals directly with the maker or drawer.

1)   EXAMPLE: Dr. Care performed surgery on Mike. Mike owes Dr. Care $10,000 for the surgery. Mike, an attorney, had agreed to draft a lease agreement for Paula on condition that Paula issue a check payable to Dr. Care for $10,000. Paula sends the check to Dr. Care with a note, "In payment of medical services rendered to Mike." Mike leaves town and never performs the legal service for Paula. Paula stops payment on the check. Dr. Care is an HDC and can enforce payment.

7.   When an incomplete instrument has been improperly completed, a subsequent HDC may enforce it as completed.

a.   Mere knowledge that an incomplete instrument has been completed is not notice of a defense.

8.   **The Shelter Principle**. A person who does not qualify as an HDC but who derives his/her title through an HDC can acquire the rights and privileges of an HDC.

a.   Transfer of an instrument vests in the transferee any rights the transferor had in it.

1)   Transfer is delivery by a nonissuer for the purpose of giving the transferee the right to enforce the instrument.

b.   This shelter principle permits one who is not an HDC to share the shelter from claims and defenses enjoyed by the HDC from whom (s)he received the instrument.

c.   The shelter rule greatly expands the HDC doctrine by providing that a transferee (whether or not a holder) of a negotiable instrument from or after an HDC usually acquires the position of an HDC and may enforce the instrument free of claims and personal defenses.

1)   EXAMPLE: Slick fraudulently induces Mary to execute and deliver a note to him. Slick then negotiates the note to Bill, and Bill qualifies as an HDC. Bill makes a gift of the note to Bruce, who sells it to Ken, a friend of Slick's who knew of Slick's fraud. Ken sells it to Mike after maturity. Bruce, Ken, and Mike were not HDCs, but they have Bill's rights and are free of Mary's personal defenses.

d.   A transferee who was a party to fraud or illegality affecting the instrument cannot improve his/her position by later reacquiring the instrument from an HDC (UCC 3-203).

9.   **The FTC Rule**. Consumer groups objected to the idea that a maker or a drawer of an instrument is not permitted to assert a legitimate defense after the payee transfers a negotiable instrument for value to a third person.

a. The FTC protects consumers by requiring a seller or a lessor of consumer goods or services to include in a consumer credit contract the following prominently printed notice:

**NOTICE
ANY HOLDER OF THIS CONSUMER CREDIT
CONTRACT
IS SUBJECT TO ALL CLAIMS AND DEFENSES
WHICH THE DEBTOR COULD ASSERT AGAINST
THE SELLER OF GOODS OR SERVICES OBTAINED
PURSUANT HERETO
OR WITH THE PROCEEDS HEREOF**

b. The notice requirement applies to all consumer credit contracts affecting interstate commerce, especially

   1) A negotiable promissory note signed by the consumer

   2) An ordinary (nonnegotiable) consumer credit contract containing a waiver-of-defense clause

   3) A consumer credit loan arranged by the seller for the consumer buyer

c. The presence of this notice preserves all claims and defenses that a consumer may have, even against a good-faith purchaser for value without notice of any defenses and effectively cancels HDC status.

d. Failure of the seller to provide the required notice constitutes an unfair and deceptive practice under the FTC Act.

10. Stop and review! You have completed the outline for this subunit. Study multiple-choice questions 22 through 34 beginning on page 484.

E. **Liabilities, Defenses, and Rights**. Once it has been ascertained that an instrument is negotiable and in the hands of a holder, the person liable on it and the nature and amount of liability must be determined.

1. **Nature of Liability**. Liability may arise both from the contractual promise which a party has made by signing the instrument and from that party's transfer of the instrument as property.

   a. Distinguish this from liability on any underlying contract for which the instrument constituted consideration, e.g., a sale of goods.

2. **Contractual Liability**. The UCC imposes contractual liability on most signers of commercial paper for the face amount of the instrument (including interest).

   a. A person who issues a check, accepts a draft in which (s)he is named as drawee, or signs a promissory note is contractually liable on the instrument for the face amount.

      1) Similarly, when you endorse your paycheck to cash it, your endorsement, if unqualified, makes you contractually liable to the endorsee (bank, grocery store, check cashing service, university) and to any other transferee for the face amount if the drawee (your employer's bank) does not pay.

   b. Any person who signs a negotiable instrument is liable on it.

   c. **Agents**. The authorized signature of an agent acts as the signature of the principal and operates to bind the principal on the instrument.

1) The principal is liable if the agent is authorized whether or not the principal's name is on the instrument.

   a) Thus, an undisclosed principal incurs liability on a negotiable instrument in the same way as under a simple contract.

   b) The agent may or may not add his/her own name.

   c) If the agent signs the principal's name, the signature is presumed to be authorized and genuine.

   d) The agent's authority and the principal's liability is determined by agency law.

2) When a negotiable instrument is signed in the name of an organization, and the organization's name is preceded or followed by the name and office of an authorized individual, the organization is bound. The individual who signed the instrument in the agent's capacity is not bound.

   a) EXAMPLE: Primeco.
      Angie, President.

d. A person is not liable on an instrument unless the person signed it. There are two important exceptions:

   1) An unauthorized signature may be ratified by a principal.

   2) An unauthorized signature operates as the signature of the unauthorized signer in favor of a holder in due course.

      a) This means that a person who forges a check can be held personally liable by an HDC.

e. A party to the instrument may have either primary or secondary liability.

   1) A party is **primarily liable** if (s)he is required to pay by the terms of the instrument itself.

      a) The maker of a note and the acceptor of a draft are primary parties.

   2) A party is **secondarily liable** when an obligation to pay arises only if the party with primary liability fails to pay the instrument, i.e.,

      a) Drawers and endorsers

      NOTE: Unqualified endorsers are liable to all subsequent endorsers.

   3) Primary liability is unconditional. The primary party is liable to the holder of the instrument for the face amount and can be sued for it immediately when the instrument comes due.

   4) The maker of a note promises to pay the note. The words "I promise to pay" illustrate the maker's obligation to pay the instrument according to the terms as written at the time of the signing.

   5) The drawee/acceptor of a draft is in virtually the same position as the maker of a note.

      a) A drawee who does not accept owes a contractual duty to the drawer to pay in accordance with the drawer's orders but owes no duty to either the payee or any holder.

      b) A draft has no primarily liable party until acceptance by the drawee.

         i) EXAMPLE: Buyer purchases goods from Seller for $5,000. The goods are to be shipped October 15. Instead of giving Seller cash, Buyer draws a draft on a finance company for $2,000 payable to Seller on October 15. The finance company is not liable on the draft. It will not become liable on the draft until it accepts it.

f.   An **accommodation party** is a surety who signs an instrument for the purpose of lending his/her name (credit) to another party to the instrument.

  1)   An accommodation party signing on behalf of the maker, drawer, or acceptor is an accommodation maker and is primarily liable on the instrument.

  2)   An accommodation party signing on behalf of a payee or other holder is an accommodation endorser and is secondarily liable.

g.   A **guarantor** is a signer of commercial paper who adds "payment guaranteed" or equivalent words to the signature.

  1)   A guarantor promises that if the instrument is not paid when due, (s)he will pay it without the holder's being required to resort to (make demand on) any other party.

NOTE: Accommodation parties and guarantors are sureties.

3.   **Warranty Liability**. Because commercial paper is a type of property, the UCC imposes warranties on sellers and other transferors. This is in addition to the signature liability and applies both to endorsers and nonendorsers. Transfer warranties arise whenever an instrument is transferred for consideration or acceptance. Breach of warranty may occur whenever a person transfers or presents for payment an instrument (the property) which is defective in some respect, e.g., by a forged signature.

a.   Sellers of commercial paper make **transfer warranties**.

b.   Persons who present commercial paper for payment or acceptance make **presentment warranties**.

c.   Warranty liability often exists when contractual liability does not.

  1)   EXAMPLE: (1) A qualified endorser, (2) a person who negotiates an instrument without endorsing it, and (3) an endorser who has been discharged because of the holder's unexcused delay in making presentment have no contractual liability on the instrument. Warranty liability may be the only avenue of relief for a wronged party.

d.   Claims of breach of warranty usually arise in cases involving forged, altered, or stolen instruments.

e.   Warranty rules serve to allocate loss to the person in the best position to avoid it.

4.   **Transfer Warranties**

a.   Any person who transfers an instrument and receives consideration warrants, to the transferee, the following:

  1)   Transferor is entitled to enforce the instrument.

  2)   All signatures are genuine and authorized.

  3)   The instrument has not been altered.

  4)   No defense of any party is good against transferor.

  5)   Transferor has no knowledge of insolvency proceedings against the maker, drawer of an unaccepted instrument, or acceptor.

    a)   EXAMPLE: Suppose the maker issues a note for $3,000. The payee, without authority, materially alters the note to read $30,000 and negotiates the instrument to Jim for $29,400. Jim knows nothing of the alteration. Jim endorses "without recourse" and negotiates the note to Kight for $28,900. Kight presents the note to the maker who refuses to pay more than $3,000. Kight can collect the difference from Jim for breach of the implied transfer warranty against material alteration. Notice that Jim avoids contract liability, but not his warranty liability, by his qualified endorsement.

b. If the transfer is by endorsement, the preceding warranties are to any subsequent transferee. In a transfer without endorsement, the warranties extend only to the transferor's immediate transferee.

c. For breach, a good-faith transferee may recover as damages an amount equal to the loss suffered but not more than the amount of the instrument plus expenses and loss of interest.

d. Unless notice of a claim for breach of warranty is given to the warrantor within 30 days after the claimant has reason to know of the breach and the identity of the warrantor, the liability is discharged to the extent of any loss caused by the delay in giving notice.

e. Transfer warranties can be disclaimed except with respect to checks.

5. **Presentment Warranties**. Presenters' warranties apply only to persons who pay on or accept an instrument, i.e., makers, drawees, or acceptors. UCC 3-417(a).

a. Any person who seeks payment or acceptance of a negotiable instrument impliedly warrants, to any other person who in good faith pays or accepts the instrument, the following:

1) The party presenting is entitled to enforce the instrument or is authorized to obtain payment or acceptance on behalf of a person who has good title.

2) The instrument has not been altered.

3) The party presenting has no knowledge that the signature of the drawer is unauthorized.

b. The presentment warranties are made by the person actually presenting the instrument for payment or acceptance and by all prior transferors (both sellers and nonsellers) of that instrument.

6. **Defenses to Liability**. Defenses can bar collection from persons who would otherwise be primarily or secondarily liable on the instrument.

a. HDC status eliminates most, but not all, defenses.

b. Real defenses can be used against anyone, including an HDC.

c. Personal defenses cannot be asserted against an HDC. They can be asserted against anyone who is not an HDC or a holder through an HDC.

7. **Real Defenses**

a. When an instrument is void because it has been executed in connection with illegal conduct, the defense of **illegality** is absolute against both an ordinary holder and an HDC.

b. An instrument signed under **extreme duress** as opposed to ordinary duress (a personal, not a real, defense) is void and unenforceable by any holder or HDC.

c. If a party is deceived into signing a negotiable instrument, **fraud in the execution** is committed against the signer.

d. If a party signs a second party's name on an instrument without permission (an unauthorized signature or forgery), the second party is not liable, not even to an HDC.

1) However, full liability on the instrument is imposed against the forger, in favor of someone who pays or takes the instrument in good faith.

e. **Material alteration** is any unauthorized change in an instrument that modifies the liability of a party.

f.   **Lack of legal capacity**. An instrument issued by a person adjudicated to be mentally incompetent is null and void. Mental incapacity renders an instrument void from the beginning and unenforceable by any holder or HDC.

g.   **Minority** or **infancy** is a real defense only to the extent that state law recognizes it as a defense to a simple contract.

h.   A **discharge in bankruptcy** is an absolute defense on any instrument regardless of the status of the holder because the purpose of bankruptcy is to settle an insolvent party's debts.

i.   A **discharge of any party**. If the holder of a negotiable instrument has notice of the discharge of any prior party when (s)he takes the instrument, the holder, even if an HDC, is barred from collecting on the instrument.

8. **Personal Defenses**. Traditional contract defenses are usually personal defenses.

   a.   Personal defenses include the following:

      1)   Payment
      2)   Theft by the holder
      3)   Theft by a person through whom the holder holds
      4)   Slight duress
      5)   Fraud in the inducement
      6)   Unauthorized completion
      7)   Violation of a restrictive endorsement
      8)   No consideration
      9)   Failure of consideration
      10) Condition precedent not performed
      11) Delivery incomplete, conditional, or for a special purpose

   b.   If a real defense arose because of the negligence of an HDC, it is treated as a personal defense of that HDC.

9. **Presentment**. Article 3 requires that the holder of an instrument proceed through a number of formal steps in order to collect on a negotiable instrument: presentment, dishonor, and notice of dishonor.

   a.   Presentment is the formal term for the holder's demand for **acceptance** (drawee's agreement to pay the draft) or payment of an instrument.

   b.   For presentment to occur, the following requirements must be met:

      1)   The instrument must be exhibited.

      2)   The person presenting the instrument must have reasonable identification.

      3)   Agents who present the instrument must have evidence of their authority.

      4)   The holder must be willing to sign a receipt on the instrument or surrender the instrument.

   c.   Presentment may be made by any commercially reasonable means, including in person, by mail, through a clearinghouse, or through a collecting bank.

      1)   A clearinghouse is an association typically formed by banks to exchange checks, drafts, or other forms of indebtedness held by one member and owed to another.

    d. Timely presentment is required.

        1) If the instrument is payable on a specific date, presentment is due on that date.

        2) A demand instrument must be presented for acceptance or payment within a reasonable time, but

            a) If an instrument is payable after sight, it must be either presented for acceptance or negotiated within a reasonable time after issue or the date of the instrument, whichever is later.

                i) A reasonable time is presumed to be 30 days after issue or the date of the instrument, whichever is later.

                ii) A reasonable time is presumed to be 30 days after endorsement in order to hold an endorser liable.

        3) Presentment should be made on a day which is a full business day. Otherwise, it is postponed to the next day which is a full business day for both the holder and the drawee.

        4) Presentment must be made at a reasonable hour.

    e. Failure to timely present an instrument results in discharge of secondarily liable endorsers.

    f. Drafts can be presented for acceptance, but all negotiable instruments must ultimately be presented for payment.

        1) The purpose of presenting a draft for acceptance is to obtain the drawee's agreement to pay the draft and thereby ensure his/her primary liability.

10. **Dishonor**. Dishonor of an instrument occurs when it is duly presented for acceptance and payment is refused.

    a. Dishonor occurs when the primary party states that the instrument will not be paid or accepted.

    b. The party to whom presentment is made has a very limited period in which to decide whether to pay or accept; e.g., in the case of a draft (other than a check), failure to pay or accept on the day of presentment is a dishonor.

    c. Dishonoring an instrument triggers secondary liability on the instrument. Parties who are secondarily liable on a negotiable instrument promise to pay on the instrument only if

        1) The instrument is properly and timely presented.
        2) The instrument is dishonored.
        3) Timely notice of dishonor is given to the secondarily liable party.

11. **Notice of Dishonor**. In order for the holder to make secondary parties liable for payment of the instrument, proper notice must be given to all potential secondary parties.

    a. Adequate notice must be given to all prior endorsers of the instrument or they are discharged from liability for payment.

    b. Notice of dishonor can be given in any commercially reasonable manner, including by telephone, by mail, or in person.

        1) Notice is effective on the date of mailing.

    c.   Timely notice of dishonor is required.

        1)   All non-bank parties must give notice

            a)   Within 30 days after dishonor, or

            b)   In the case of an instrument taken for collection by a collecting bank, within 30 days of receipt of notice of dishonor from another party.

        2)   If the holder or endorser is a bank, it must give notice of dishonor before midnight of the next banking day.

    d.   Notice of dishonor (and/or presentment) may be excused or waived, expressly or implicitly, either before or after it is due.

        1)   If notice is excused or waived, a party will not be discharged from liability on the instrument even if no notice is given.

        2)   Presentment and notice of dishonor are usually waived with respect to notes.

  12.   Stop and review! You have completed the outline for this subunit. Study multiple-choice questions 35 through 43 beginning on page 488.

F. **Discharge**. The UCC provides a variety of ways in which a party may be discharged from liability on an instrument.

  1.   A party may be discharged, in whole or in part, from liability on an instrument by

    a.   Acts or agreements with other parties which would discharge a simple contract for the payment of money, or

    b.   One or more of the following:

        1)   Payment or satisfaction
        2)   Tender of payment
        3)   Cancellation or renunciation
        4)   Reacquisition of the instrument by a prior party
        5)   Certification of a check
        6)   Acceptance of a draft after endorsement
        7)   Acceptance varying a draft
        8)   Impairment of right of recourse or of collateral
        9)   Fraudulent and material alteration

  2.   **Payment**. A party who pays the amount of the instrument to a holder is completely discharged from liability on it.

    a.   If a secondary party makes payment, (s)he is likewise discharged. Other parties who may be liable to the party making payment are not discharged.

    b.   Partial payment discharges only to the extent of the payment.

    c.   A party who pays an instrument in full may request that the instrument be returned to him/her.

        1)   A negotiable instrument retains its negotiable character even if all the parties have been discharged.

        2)   A discharge is not effective against a subsequent HDC who takes the instrument without notice of the discharge.

        3)   To prevent fraudulent renegotiation, one should take possession of the instrument when making payment on it.

3. **Tender**. If a party tenders (offers) full payment to the holder on or after the maturity date of the instrument, and if the holder improperly refuses the tender, the tendering party is discharged to the extent of all subsequent liability for interest costs and legal fees.

   a. But the tendering party is not discharged as to the principal or interest accrued up to the date of tender.

   b. An endorser or accommodation party having a right of recourse with respect to the obligation to which the tender relates is also discharged.

      1) The amount of the tender is the amount discharged.

4. **Cancellation**. The holder of a negotiable instrument may discharge liability by canceling. Consideration is not required.

   a. The holder may cancel the instrument in its entirety, thus discharging all parties from liability.

   b. The holder may discharge an individual party by canceling that party's liability or by giving the instrument to the party to be discharged.

   c. Cancellation may be accomplished in any manner that is apparent on the face of the instrument or in the instrument, e.g., destruction. An endorser is discharged if the holder strikes out the endorser's signature.

5. **Renunciation**. A holder may also renounce his/her rights in an instrument by signing and delivering a written renunciation.

   a. A cancellation appears on the instrument itself; a renunciation often appears in a separate document or letter.

   b. A renunciation is ineffective against an HDC without notice of it.

6. **Impairment of right of recourse** means that the extent to which a party can enforce an obligation (on an instrument) is compromised or reduced and that the amount a party is able to recover upon enforcement is reduced.

   a. An extension of time for payment may constitute impairment of a right of recourse.

7. An unjustifiable **impairment of collateral** has the same effect as impairment of recourse. It discharges the party whose rights against others are impaired.

   a. The extent of discharge is again, essentially, limited to the loss resulting to the party from the impairment.

   b. EXAMPLE: Able executed a promissory note to Baker and pledged a yacht as collateral. Baker transferred the note to Carr. Carr allowed Able to sell the yacht. Carr has impaired the security. Baker is discharged to the extent of the collateral.

8. A **material alteration** of the instrument by the holder discharges any party whose contract is thereby changed.

   a. A subsequent HDC, however, may still enforce the instrument against any party according to its original terms.

      1) EXAMPLE: Able executes a $10,000 note payable to order of Baker. Baker endorses it in blank and transfers it to Carr. Carr raises the amount to $100,000 and transfers it to Danny, a holder in due course. Baker is completely discharged in that a party to the instrument intentionally made a material alteration such as would change the legal effect of the contract on the instrument. However, Able will still be liable to the holder in due course for the original $10,000. UCC Section 3-407. The HDC, by definition, took it for value, in good faith, and without notice of the defense.

   b. Negligence by the maker or acceptor bars use of the defense; e.g., the alteration could be made easily.

9.   **Reacquisition**. When an instrument is reacquired by a primary party, the primary party may discharge any intervening party.

   a.   EXAMPLE: Able issues a note to Baker. Baker sells it to Carr who sells it to Danny who then sells it to Able. Able cancels Baker's endorsement. Baker, Carr, and Danny are all discharged.

10.   Stop and review! You have completed the outline for this subunit. Study multiple-choice questions 44 through 48 beginning on page 491.

G.   **Bank Transactions**. The CPA exam does not directly test Article 4 of the UCC, entitled *Bank Deposits and Collections*. Article 4 deals with the contractual relationship between a bank and its customers, particularly checking account customers. The following basic concepts are relevant to the AICPA's testing of negotiable instruments.

1.   A **check** is a type of draft; it is always drawn on a bank and always payable on demand of the payee or other holder (unless it is postdated).

   a.   A check is a depositor's order or instruction to the drawee bank to pay a specified amount from the drawer's account.

   b.   Generally, a check does not operate as an assignment of funds in the account.

2.   The check collection process is the means by which a check, deposited in one bank but drawn on another, is paid.

   a.   Usually, a holder initiates the check collection process by depositing a check with his/her bank, typically not the payor bank.

      1)   The deposited check is transferred to the payor bank.

   b.   Collection is accomplished by debiting and crediting accounts that banks maintain between themselves for collection purposes. Collection is based on a system of "provisional" (reversible) credits that the depositor and the collecting banks expect to become "final." When a provisional credit becomes final, the bank becomes accountable to its customer for the amount. UCC 4-215(d).

   c.   A bank may allow a depositor to withdraw funds against a provisional credit, and by doing so becomes a holder for value of the deposited item. If the provisional item never becomes final, the bank has the right to recover the credited amount from the depositor.

3.   The general rule is that, when a bank honors a check properly drawn on the customer's account, or certifies a customer's check, it charges (debits) the customer's account for the amount of the check, assuming there are sufficient funds in the account.

4.   Banks have a duty to act seasonally, which means they must take appropriate action (either pay or dishonor) the check before the midnight deadline.

   a.   Unless the payor bank dishonors the check or returns it by midnight on the next banking day following receipt, the payor bank is accountable for the face amount of the check.

5.   Generally, a bank must recredit the customer's account when it pays on a forged signature. A forged signature on a check has no legal effect as the signature of a drawer.

   a.   When the customer's negligence substantially contributes to a forgery, the bank will not be liable.

        1)   The named drawer is precluded by his/her negligence from asserting the forged signature as a defense to liability to one who took the instrument for value or collection (or paid it) in good faith.

6.   A bank is liable to its customer for loss if the bank pays a check that has been altered as to amount.

    a.   The loss is the difference between the original amount of the check and the amount actually paid.

    b.   A customer's/depositor's negligence can shift the risk of loss from the bank to the customer, for example, when a person carelessly writes a check, leaving large gaps or spaces around the numbers and words so that additional words can be inserted.

    c.   Likewise, a person who signs a check and leaves the dollar amount blank and allows someone else to fill in the amount is barred from protesting when the bank knowingly and in good faith pays whatever amount is written.

    d.   Moreover, if a bank can trace its loss on successive altered checks to the depositor's failure to discover the initial alteration, then the bank can alleviate its liability to reimburse the customer's account.

7.   Banks have a duty to furnish the customer with a bank statement. Customers have a duty to exercise reasonable care in examining the statement and promptly notifying the bank of any irregularities.

    a.   Customers are given 30 days to examine the statement and give notice to the bank.

    b.   If the bank proves that the customer breached the above duties, the customer is precluded from recovering from the bank for unauthorized signatures or alterations.

8.   **Stale Checks.** A bank is not obligated to pay an uncertified check presented more than 6 months from its date of issuance.

    a.   The typical banking practice is to consult the customer, but if the bank pays in good faith without consulting the customer, it has the right to charge the customer's account for the amount of the check.

9.   A bank is liable to its customer/depositor for damages caused by wrongful dishonor; it is not liable to a holder or other party for dishonor.

10.   **Stop-Payment Order.** A check is not an assignment of funds but merely an order to pay. The UCC recognizes the right of the customer to instruct the drawee bank not to pay a certain check by issuing a stop-payment order.

11.   Death or incompetence of a principal generally revokes an agency agreement.

    a.   However, under the UCC, neither the death nor the incompetency of a depositor revokes a bank's authority to pay or collect an item, or to account for the proceeds of the collection, until the bank knows of the death or of an adjudication of incompetence and has a reasonable opportunity to act on it.

    b.   Additionally, even if a bank knows of its depositor's death, it may pay or certify checks for a period of up to 10 days from the date of death.

12.   Stop and review! You have completed the outline for this subunit. Study multiple-choice question 49 on page 493.

MULTIPLE-CHOICE QUESTIONS

A. Types of Negotiable Instruments

1. Which of the following instruments is subject to the provisions of the UCC article on negotiable instruments?

- A. Corporate bearer bond with a maturity date of December 1, 2001.
- B. Bill of lading payable to order.
- C. Installment note payable on the first day of each month.
- D. Warehouse receipt.

The correct answer is (C). *(CPA, adapted)*
REQUIRED: The instrument subject to the UCC provisions on negotiable instruments.
DISCUSSION: Article 3 of the UCC regulates negotiable instruments. This article specifically lists four kinds of negotiable instruments: checks, drafts, promissory notes, and certificates of deposit. An installment note falls within Article 3 and is subject to its provisions.
Answers (A), (B), and (D) are incorrect because, while the instrument may be negotiable, it does not meet the statutory definition of negotiable instruments.

2. For which of the following negotiable instruments is a bank not an acceptor?

- A. Cashier's check.
- B. Certified check.
- C. Certificate of deposit.
- D. Bank acceptance.

The correct answer is (C). *(CPA, adapted)*
REQUIRED: The negotiable instrument for which a bank is not an acceptor.
DISCUSSION: A certificate of deposit is a type of note in which a bank acknowledges receipt of money and promises to repay the money with interest in the future. As a note, a certificate of deposit is only a two-party instrument and does not require acceptance by a drawee.
Answers (A), (B), and (D) are incorrect because each is a draft on which a drawee bank must act as acceptor.

3. Under the Negotiable Instruments Article of the UCC, which of the following documents would be considered an order to pay?

I. Draft
II. Certificate of deposit

- A. I only.
- B. II only.
- C. Both I and II.
- D. Neither I nor II.

The correct answer is (A). *(CPA, adapted)*
REQUIRED: The instrument(s) considered payable on order.
DISCUSSION: A draft is an unconditional written order by one person, the drawer, to another person, the drawee (the bank), to pay a third party on demand or at some definite time. Therefore, a draft is an order to pay instrument.
Answers (B), (C), and (D) are incorrect because a CD is not considered an order to pay because a CD is a promise to pay on demand or at a specified date in the future. It is a form of promissory note.

4. Gold is holding the following instrument:

> To: Sussex National Bank
>   Suffolk, N.Y.
>
>   October 15, 1999
>
> Pay to the order of __Tom Gold__ $2,000.00
> __Two Thousand and xx/100__ Dollars
> __on November 1, 1999__
>
>   *Lester Davis*
>   Lester Davis

The instrument is

- A. A postdated check.
- B. A promissory note.
- C. A draft.
- D. Payable on demand.

The correct answer is (C). *(CPA, adapted)*
REQUIRED: The term that identifies the example instrument.
DISCUSSION: A draft is a three-party instrument in which one person (the drawer) orders a second person (the drawee) to pay a third person (the payee). With this instrument, Lester Davis is ordering Sussex National Bank to pay Tom Gold.
Answer (A) is incorrect because a check is a type of draft in which a bank is ordered to make the payment on demand. This instrument is payable on November 1, 1999. Answer (B) is incorrect because a promissory note is a two-party instrument in which one person promises to pay another person. Answer (D) is incorrect because the draft is payable on November 1, 1999, not on demand.

5. A trade acceptance usually

- A. Is an order to deliver goods to a named person.
- B. Provides that the drawer is also the payee.
- C. Is not regarded as a negotiable instrument under the UCC.
- D. Must be made payable "to the order of" a named person.

The correct answer is (B). *(CPA, adapted)*
   REQUIRED: The true statement about trade acceptance.
   DISCUSSION: A trade acceptance is a special form of negotiable instrument known as a time draft used by sellers as a way to extend credit to buyers of their goods. The seller draws a draft ordering the buyer to pay the seller at some time in the future. The seller is thus both drawer and payee of a trade acceptance.
   Answer (A) is incorrect because a trade acceptance is a form of negotiable instrument and must be payable in money. Answer (C) is incorrect because trade acceptances are a type of draft and as such are recognized as negotiable instruments under the UCC. Answer (D) is incorrect because a trade acceptance may be payable to order or to bearer.

6. Pam Payee holds the following:

May 19, 1999

I promise to pay to the order of Pam Payee $1,000 (One thousand dollars) with interest thereon at the rate of 12% per annum.

Mike Maker
Mike Maker

Guaranty

I personally guaranty payment by Mike Maker.

N. A. Abner
N.A. Abner

The instrument is a

- A. Promissory note.
- B. Draft.
- C. Certificate of deposit.
- D. Check.

The correct answer is (A). *(CPA, adapted)*
   REQUIRED: The term identifying the instrument.
   DISCUSSION: The instrument is a promissory note because it is a two-party instrument in which the maker unconditionally promises to pay a sum certain in money to the payee.
   Answer (B) is incorrect because a draft is a three-party instrument in which one person orders a second person to pay a third person. Answer (C) is incorrect because a certificate of deposit is a written acknowledgment by a bank of receipt of money with a promise to repay. It is one form of note. Answer (D) is incorrect because a check is a type of draft by which a bank is ordered to make the payment on demand.

B. Requisites of Negotiability

7. There are several legally significant differences between a negotiable instrument and a contract right, and the transfer of each. Which of the following statements is correct?

- A. A negotiable instrument is deemed prima facie to have been issued for consideration, whereas a contract is not.
- B. The transferee of a negotiable instrument and the assignee of a contract right take free of most defenses.
- C. Neither can be transferred without a signed writing or by a delivery.
- D. The statute of frauds rules apply to both.

The correct answer is (A). *(CPA, adapted)*
   REQUIRED: The correct statement comparing negotiable instruments and contract rights.
   DISCUSSION: A negotiable instrument is presumed to have been issued for consideration, but no such assumption is made regarding a contract. One must prove consideration to enforce a contract right, but not a negotiable instrument.
   Answer (B) is incorrect because the transferee of a negotiable instrument (who is not a holder in due course or a holder through an HDC) and the assignee of a contract right both take subject to all defenses the third party has against the assignor. Answer (C) is incorrect because a contract right can be transferred orally and without delivery. A negotiable instrument requires an endorsement and delivery if it is order paper or delivery alone if it is bearer paper in order to remain negotiable. Answer (D) is incorrect because the statute of frauds applies only to certain contracts. But an instrument must be in writing to be negotiable.

8. A secured promissory note would be nonnegotiable if it provided that

A. Additional collateral must be tendered if there is a decline in market value of the original collateral.

B. Upon default, the maker waives a trial by jury.

C. The maker is entitled to a 5% discount if the note is prepaid.

D. It is subject to the terms of the mortgage given by the maker to the payee.

The correct answer is (D). *(CPA, adapted)*

REQUIRED: The provision which defeats negotiability of a promissory note.

DISCUSSION: A negotiable instrument must include an unconditional promise or order to pay. When a promise or order is subject to the provisions of another agreement, it is conditional. A conditional instrument is nonnegotiable because the rights of a holder cannot be ascertained with reasonable certainty from the face of it -- within its four corners. A note that is subject to the terms of a mortgage violates this requirement and is rendered nonnegotiable.

Answer (A) is incorrect because a negotiable instrument may include a promise to maintain or protect collateral. Answer (B) is incorrect because waiver of a benefit for the advantage or protection of the obligor does not affect negotiability. Answer (C) is incorrect because the requirement of a sum certain in money does not preclude a provision for specified prepayment discounts.

9. Under the Negotiable Instruments Article of the UCC, which of the following circumstances would prevent a promissory note from being negotiable?

A. An extension clause that allows the maker to elect to extend the time for payment to a date specified in the note.

B. An acceleration clause that allows the holder to move up the maturity date of the note in the event of default.

C. A person having a power of attorney signs the note on behalf of the maker.

D. A clause that allows the maker to satisfy the note by the performance of services or the payment of money.

The correct answer is (D). *(CPA, adapted)*

REQUIRED: The circumstance that would prevent a promissory note from being negotiable.

DISCUSSION: A promissory note is an unconditional written promise between two parties for one to pay the other a fixed amount of money. A clause in the note that allowed the maker to satisfy the note by the performance of services would prevent the note from being negotiable.

Answer (A) is incorrect because extending the time period to pay off the note would not affect its negotiability because the note, as extended, is payable at a definite time stated in the note. Answer (B) is incorrect because a negotiable instrument may be payable on demand or at a definite time. Accelerating the date a note is due in the event of a default is permitted. Answer (C) is incorrect because, for an instrument to be negotiable, it must be signed by the maker or drawer or his/her authorized agent or representative. A person who holds a power of attorney for another can sign on behalf of that person.

10. An instrument reads as follows:

$10,000   Ludlow, Vermont   February 1, 1999

I promise to pay to the order of Custer Corp. $10,000 within 10 days after the sale of my two-carat diamond ring. I pledge the sale proceeds to secure by obligation hereunder.

R. Harris
R. Harris

Which of the following statements correctly describes the above instrument?

A. The instrument is nonnegotiable because it is not payable at a definite time.

B. The instrument is nonnegotiable because it is secured by the proceeds of the sale of the ring.

C. The instrument is a negotiable promissory note.

D. The instrument is a negotiable sight draft payable on demand.

The correct answer is (A). *(CPA, adapted)*

REQUIRED: The statement that describes the instrument.

DISCUSSION: The instrument is a signed writing promising to pay a fixed amount of money to the order of a designated person. A fixed amount of money means it is possible to compute the amount from the face of the instrument. But the obligation to pay and its timing depend on an uncertain event. The promise is thus conditional, not unconditional as required for negotiability. A "definite time" is not limited to one particular date. An instrument payable on or before a stated date is payable on demand until that date and is payable at a fixed date thereafter (if not yet paid).

Answer (B) is incorrect because existence of security does not condition the obligation to pay, nor does it affect the note's negotiability. Answer (C) is incorrect because the promise is conditioned upon the sale of the ring. Answer (D) is incorrect because by a draft the drawer orders the drawee to pay a third person.

11. Which of the following on the face of an otherwise negotiable instrument will affect the instrument's negotiability?

   A. The instrument is postdated.

   B. The instrument is payable 6 months after the death of the maker.

   C. The instrument contains a promise to provide additional collateral if there is a decrease in value of the existing collateral.

   D. The instrument is payable at a definite time subject to an acceleration clause in the event of default.

The correct answer is (B). *(CPA, adapted)*
   REQUIRED: The condition that affects negotiability.
   DISCUSSION: The UCC requires that negotiable instruments be payable on demand or at a definite time. An instrument payable after an event with an uncertain date, such as the death of the maker, violates this requirement.
   Answer (A) is incorrect because an antedated or postdated instrument is valid and negotiable if it meets the requirements for negotiability. Answer (C) is incorrect because negotiability is not affected by promises in the instrument to ensure payment. Answer (D) is incorrect because an instrument may be subject to acceleration. Unrestricted acceleration is equivalent to demand. The amount due can be computed at any time.

12. Which of the following prevents an instrument from being negotiable?

   A. An endorsement on the back of the instrument reads: "Pay Smith only."

   B. An instrument is payable after completion of a contractual obligation that is certain to happen but uncertain as to the time of occurrence.

   C. Whether the instrument is intended to be a note or a draft is unclear.

   D. The capacity in which the party signed was unclear.

The correct answer is (B). *(CPA, adapted)*
   REQUIRED: The condition that defeats negotiability.
   DISCUSSION: A negotiable instrument must meet a requirement that the instrument be payable on demand or at a definite time. "Payable at a definite time" means payable at 1) a stated date or a fixed period after such a date; 2) a fixed period after sight; 3) a definite time subject to any acceleration; or 4) a definite time subject to extension by the holder, extension to a further definite time by the maker or acceptor, or automatic extension upon a specified act or event. Hence, no definite time is stated if payment is conditioned upon contractual performance the time of which is uncertain.
   Answer (A) is incorrect because a special endorsement does not defeat negotiation. It merely restricts further negotiation until the specially named party has also signed the instrument. Answer (C) is incorrect because uncertainty about whether an instrument is a note or a draft allows the holder to treat it as either. Answer (D) is incorrect because, when it is unclear in which capacity a party signs an instrument, the party is assumed to be an endorser, and the instrument remains negotiable.

13. Shark holds the following:

May 19, 1999

I promise to pay to the order of A.B. Shark $1,000 (One thousand and one hundred dollars) with interest thereon at the rate of 12% per annum.

T.T. Tile
T.T. Tile

Guaranty

I personally guaranty payment by T.T. Tile.

Abner Jones
Abner Jones

The instrument is

   A. Nonnegotiable even though it is payable on demand.

   B. Nonnegotiable because the numeric amount differs from the written amount.

   C. Negotiable even though a payment date is not specified.

   D. Negotiable because of Abner's guaranty.

The correct answer is (C). *(CPA, adapted)*
   REQUIRED: The negotiability of the promissory note.
   DISCUSSION: To be negotiable, an instrument must promise or order payment of money on demand or at a definite time. If a payment date is not specified, the UCC treats the instrument as payable on demand, and negotiable as such. Note that the issue date is not required to appear on the face of the instrument.
   Answer (A) is incorrect because the note is a writing signed by the maker and contains an unconditional promise to pay a fixed amount of money to order. It is treated as payable on demand. Answer (B) is incorrect because different numeric and written amounts do not defeat negotiability. Handwritten terms outweigh typewritten and printed terms. Words outweigh figures. Answer (D) is incorrect because, although an unconditional promise is prerequisite to negotiability of a note, providing a guaranty or security does not preclude otherwise negotiable status.

14. Under the Negotiable Instruments Article of the UCC, for an instrument to be negotiable it must

  A. Be payable to order or to bearer.

  B. Be signed by the payee.

  C. Contain references to all agreements between the parties.

  D. Contain necessary conditions of payment.

The correct answer is (A). *(CPA, adapted)*
  REQUIRED: The requirement for an instrument to be negotiable.
  DISCUSSION: Negotiability is strictly a matter of form. If an instrument is drafted in a specific form, it is a negotiable instrument. To be negotiable, an instrument must be a writing that is signed by the maker or drawer, containing an unconditional promise or order to pay a sum certain in money on demand or at a definite time in the future to the order of a specified person or to the bearer.
  Answer (B) is incorrect because the instrument must be signed by the maker or drawer, not the payee. Answer (C) is incorrect because the instrument need not contain any information regarding prior relations between the parties. References have no effect on negotiability. Answer (D) is incorrect because an instrument is negotiable only if it contains an unconditional promise to pay.

15. The following instrument is in the possession of Bill North:

On May 30, 2000, I promise to pay Bill North, the bearer of this document, $3,800.

Joseph Peppers
Joseph Peppers

Re: Auto Purchase Contract

This instrument is

  A. Nonnegotiable because it is undated.

  B. Nonnegotiable because it is not payable to order or bearer.

  C. Negotiable even though it refers to the contract out of which it arose.

  D. Negotiable because it is payable at a definite time.

The correct answer is (B). *(CPA, adapted)*
  REQUIRED: The negotiability of the instrument.
  DISCUSSION: The instrument is a nonnegotiable note because it is not payable to order or bearer (UCC 3-104). It is only payable to Bill North and refers to him specifically as bearer on its face.
  Answer (A) is incorrect because an issue date is not necessary for negotiability. Answer (C) is incorrect because the instrument is nonnegotiable because it is not payable to order or to bearer. Reference to a separate agreement would impair negotiability only if the obligation were made subject to the other agreement. Answer (D) is incorrect because more is required for negotiability than that an instrument be payable at a definite time or on demand.

C. Transfer and Negotiation

16. Fred Anchor is the holder of the following check:

```
Peter Mason
Champaign, Illinois                    4/30  19 99

Pay to the order of Mary Nix or bearer    $ 93.00
 Ninety-Three------------------------------------- Dollars

Second Bank 0453-0978

                                    Peter Mason
```

The check is endorsed on the back as follows:

```
        Mary Nix
      Pay to John Jacobs
        Mark Harris
        John Jacobs
      (without recourse)
```

Jacobs gave the check to his son as a gift, who transferred it to Anchor for $78.00. Which of the following statements is correct?

- A. The unqualified endorsement of Jacobs was necessary in order to negotiate the check to his son.

- D. Nix's endorsement was required to negotiate the check to any subsequent holder.

- C. Anchor does not qualify as a holder because less than full consideration was given for the check.

- D. The check is bearer paper in the hands of Jacobs's son.

The correct answer is (D). *(CPA, adapted)*

REQUIRED: The correct statement concerning negotiability and endorsements.

DISCUSSION: The check, payable to order or bearer, is negotiable. The instrument may therefore be negotiated. Endorsement in blank by Mary Nix means that it was bearer paper to Mark Harris. Mark's endorsement is special. It rendered the instrument order paper in John Jacobs's hands. John's endorsement in blank converted the check to bearer paper.

Answer (A) is incorrect because, since John added the notation "without recourse," his endorsement was qualified. Qualified endorsement does not preclude further negotiability; it limits the endorser's liability. Answer (B) is incorrect because an instrument payable to order of a person or to bearer is bearer paper. Bearer paper can be negotiated by delivery alone. Answer (C) is incorrect because consideration is not required for effective negotiation.

17. Under the Negotiable Instruments Article of the UCC, which of the following statements best describes the effect of a person endorsing a check "without recourse"?

- A. The person has no liability to prior endorsers.

- B. The person makes no promise or guarantee of payment on dishonor.

- C. The person gives no warranty protection to later transferees.

- D. The person converts the check into order paper.

The correct answer is (B). *(CPA, adapted)*

REQUIRED: The effect of a qualified endorsement.

DISCUSSION: An endorser may disclaim or limit contractual liability by using a qualified endorsement. The statement "without recourse" disclaims liability for payment of the instrument to all later transferees. The qualified endorser does not accept any liability if the instrument is not paid by the primary party. A qualified endorsement has no effect on the instrument's negotiability.

Answer (A) is incorrect because any endorser of a negotiable instrument has no liability to prior endorsers. Answer (C) is incorrect because a qualified endorser makes the usual transfer warranties. Answer (D) is incorrect because a qualified endorsement alone does not affect whether the check is order or bearer paper.

18. Jen Day received a check originally made payable to the order of one of his customers, Al Pine. The following endorsement was written on the back of the check:

Al Pine, without recourse, for collection only

The endorsement on this check would be classified as

A.   Blank, unqualified, and nonrestrictive.

B.   Blank, qualified, and restrictive.

C.   Special, unqualified, and restrictive.

D.   Special, qualified, and nonrestrictive.

The correct answer is (B). *(CPA, adapted)*

REQUIRED: The classification of an endorsement without recourse, for collection only.

DISCUSSION: A blank endorsement specifies no particular endorsee. A special endorsement would have specified the person to whom or to whose order the instrument was payable. An endorsement is restrictive if it is "conditional; purports to prohibit further transfer of the instrument; includes the words 'for collection,' 'for deposit,' 'pay any bank,' or like terms signifying a purpose of deposit or collection; or otherwise states that it is for the benefit or use of the endorser or of another person." The endorsement "without recourse" is qualified. It disclaims contract liability but does not eliminate warranty liability.

Answer (A) is incorrect because an endorsement bearing the notation "without recourse" is qualified. Answers (C) and (D) are incorrect because a blank endorsement specifies no particular endorsee.

19. The following note was executed by Elizabeth Quinton on April 17, 1999 and delivered to Ian Wolf:

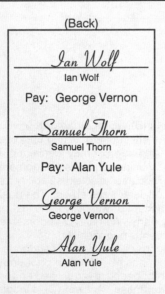

In sequence, beginning with Wolf's receipt of the note, this note is properly characterized as what type of negotiable instrument?

A.   Bearer, bearer, order, order, order.

B.   Order, bearer, order, order, bearer.

C.   Order, order, bearer, order, bearer.

D.   Bearer, order, order, order, bearer.

The correct answer is (B). *(CPA, adapted)*

REQUIRED: The status of a negotiable instrument as order and/or bearer paper.

DISCUSSION: To be negotiated, an instrument must be negotiable. The demand note payable to order of Ian Wolf required his endorsement for further negotiation. Endorsement in blank by Ian converted the instrument to bearer paper. It was negotiable by delivery alone. Sam, in possession of bearer paper, by adding a special endorsement, converted the paper back to order paper. Remember that, at any particular time, provided an instrument has been negotiated, the last endorsement determines the order or bearer status of the paper. The endorsement of the special endorsee George Vernon effected further negotiation of the paper. George's endorsement was special, so the paper is payable to Alan Yule on his order. The blank endorsement of Alan as special endorsee of the paper reconverted it to bearer paper.

Answers (A) and (D) are incorrect because the maker of the note expressly made it payable to order, not to bearer. Answer (C) is incorrect because the note was initially payable to order. Endorsement in blank by the designated payee converted it to bearer paper. Bearer paper, specially endorsed, becomes order paper.

20. The following endorsements appear on the back of a negotiable promissory note payable to Lake Corp.

> Pay to John Smith only
> *Frank Parker*, President of Lake Corp.
> *John Smith*
> Pay to the order of Sharp, Inc., without recourse, but only if Sharp delivers computers purchased by Mary Harris by December 15, 1999.
> *Mary Harris*
> *Sarah Sharp*, President of Sharp, Inc.

Which of the following statements is correct?

A. The note became nonnegotiable as a result of Parker's endorsement.

B. Harris's endorsement was a conditional promise to pay and caused the note to be nonnegotiable.

C. Smith's endorsement effectively prevented further negotiation of the note.

D. Harris's signature was not required to effectively negotiate the note to Sharp.

The correct answer is (D). *(CPA, adapted)*

REQUIRED: The correct statement concerning negotiability of the instrument.

DISCUSSION: The restrictive endorsement, "Pay to John Smith only," is an ineffective attempt to prohibit further negotiability. Endorsement by John Smith in blank converts this order instrument to bearer paper, which is negotiable by mere delivery. Therefore, Harris's signature was not necessary to negotiate the note.

Answer (A) is incorrect because restrictive endorsements are generally ineffective to limit negotiability. Answer (B) is incorrect because qualifying an endorsement "without recourse" does not hinder negotiability. Neither does a conditional endorsement. Answer (C) is incorrect because Smith's endorsement converted negotiable order paper to negotiable bearer paper.

21. Under the Negotiable Instruments Article of the UCC, when an instrument is endorsed "Pay to John Doe" and signed "Faye Smith," which of the following statements is (are) correct?

	Payment of the Instrument Is Guaranteed	The Instrument Can Be Further Negotiated
A.	Yes	Yes
B.	Yes	No
C.	No	Yes
D.	No	No

The correct answer is (A). *(CPA, adapted)*

REQUIRED: The correct statement(s) concerning the effect of an endorsement of a negotiable instrument.

DISCUSSION: When the holder of a negotiable instrument, Faye Smith, wrote the words "pay to John Doe" on the instrument, it constituted an unqualified special endorsement. The effect upon delivery to John is that John may further negotiate by endorsement and delivery. The unqualified endorsement by Faye results in contract liability on her part if the primary party defaults and proper notification is given.

Answers (B), (C), and (D) are incorrect because the form of the unqualified endorsement by Faye makes her secondarily liable if the primary party fails to pay. Further, John may negotiate the instrument by endorsement and delivery. The negotiability of an instrument is never altered by a subsequent endorsement following issuance. NOTE: Words of negotiability are not required on endorsements.

D. Holders and Holders in Due Course

Questions 22 through 25 are based on the following information. On February 15, 1999, P.D. Stone obtained the following instrument from Astor Co. for $1,000. Stone was aware that Helco, Inc. disputed liability under the instrument because of an alleged breach by Astor of the referenced computer purchase agreement. On March 1, 1999, Willard Bank obtained the instrument from Stone for $3,900. Willard had no knowledge that Helco disputed liability under the instrument.

February 12, 1999

Helco, Inc. promises to pay to Astor Co. or bearer the sum of $4,900 (four thousand four hundred and 00/100 dollars) on March 12, 1999 (maker may elect to extend due date to March 31, 1999) with interest thereon at the rate of 12% per annum.

        HELCO, INC.

By: _____A.J. Help_____
        A.J. Help, President
Reference: Computer purchase agreement
                dated February 12, 1999

The reverse side of the instrument is endorsed as follows:

Pay to the order of Willard Bank, without recourse

_____P.D. Stone_____
P.D. Stone

---

22. The instrument is a

A. Promissory note.

B. Sight draft.

C. Check.

D. Trade acceptance.

The correct answer is (A). *(CPA, adapted)*
   REQUIRED: The term identifying the instrument in the example.
   DISCUSSION: The instrument is a promissory note because it is a two-party instrument in which the maker (Helco) promises to pay a sum certain in money to the payee (Astor Co.).
   Answer (B) is incorrect because a draft is a three-party instrument in which one person orders a second person to pay a third person. A sight draft is payable on demand. Answer (C) is incorrect because a check is a type of draft payable on demand in which a bank is ordered to make the payment. Answer (D) is incorrect because a trade acceptance is a special form of negotiable instruments. It is a time draft used by sellers to extend credit to buyers of their goods.

---

23. The instrument is

A. Nonnegotiable, because of the reference to the computer purchase agreement.

B. Nonnegotiable, because the numerical amount differs from the written amount.

C. Negotiable, even though the maker has the right to extend the time for payment.

D. Negotiable when held by Astor, but nonnegotiable when held by Willard Bank.

The correct answer is (C). *(CPA, adapted)*
   REQUIRED: The negotiability of the instrument in the example.
   DISCUSSION: The instrument is a signed writing unconditionally promising to pay a fixed amount of money at a certain time to Astor or the bearer. It thus meets all of the requirements of negotiability. However, the note in this example contains an extension clause. An extension clause permits the date of maturity to be extended beyond the time specified in the instrument. To maintain negotiable status, the period of extension must be specified if the right to extend is given to the maker or acceptor. This is negotiable since the period of extension is specified as being until March 31.
   Answer (A) is incorrect because mere reference to an underlying contract does not impair negotiability. Answer (B) is incorrect because this does not preclude negotiability. Words outweigh figures on negotiable instruments.
Answer (D) is incorrect because negotiability is determined by the face of the instrument. Either Astor or Bank can negotiate it. Astor was a designated payee, as is Willard.

24. Which of the following statements is correct?

A. Willard Bank cannot be a holder in due course because Stone's endorsement was without recourse.

B. Willard Bank must endorse the instrument to negotiate it.

C. Neither Willard Bank nor Stone are holders in due course.

D. Stone's endorsement was required for Willard Bank to be a holder in due course.

The correct answer is (B). *(CPA, adapted)*
REQUIRED: The correct statement concerning the promissory note.
DISCUSSION: Stone, as holder, specially endorsed the note. This rendered it order paper. Thus, further negotiation requires Bank's signature.
Answer (A) is incorrect because an endorsement without recourse by a previous bearer does not of itself prevent the current bearer from being a holder in due course. Answer (C) is incorrect because, to be a holder in due course (HDC), a person must take an instrument for value, in good faith, and without notice that the instrument is overdue, that it has been dishonored, or that there exists any claim or defense to it. Stone is not an HDC, but Bank is. Answer (D) is incorrect because Stone, as a holder of bearer paper, did not have to sign it to negotiate it.

25. If Willard Bank demands payment from Helco and Helco refuses to pay the instrument because of Astor's breach of the computer purchase agreement, which of the following statements would be correct?

A. Willard Bank is not a holder in due course because Stone was not a holder in due course.

B. Helco will not be liable to Willard Bank because of Astor's breach.

C. Stone will be the only party liable to Willard Bank because he was aware of the dispute between Helco and Astor.

D. Helco will be liable to Willard Bank because Willard Bank is a holder in due course.

The correct answer is (D). *(CPA, adapted)*
REQUIRED: The correct statement concerning the status of a party as, and rights of, a holder in due course (HDC).
DISCUSSION: Bank gave value and took the negotiable instrument in good faith with no notice of any defense. As HDC, Bank is entitled to payment of the note, whether or not the maker has a valid personal defense.
Answer (A) is incorrect because, although Stone was a mere holder, a taker from a holder can be an HDC. Bank had no notice of the alleged breach and meets all other requirements for HDC status. Answer (B) is incorrect because personal defenses, such as traditional contract defenses, are ineffective against an HDC. Answer (C) is incorrect because each unqualified endorsee is liable to a subsequent HDC.

26. One of the requirements to qualify as a holder of a negotiable bearer check is that the transferee must

A. Receive the check that was originally made payable to bearer.

B. Take the check in good faith.

C. Give value for the check.

D. Have possession of the check.

The correct answer is (D). *(CPA, adapted)*
REQUIRED: The requirement to qualify as a holder of a negotiable bearer check.
DISCUSSION: A person who acquires a negotiable instrument absent negotiation is a mere transferee or possessor of the instrument. Negotiable bearer paper is negotiated by mere delivery. The current holder of the negotiable bearer paper must have it in legal possession.
Answer (A) is incorrect because a check could be negotiable bearer paper if it was originally made payable to order and subsequently endorsed in blank. Answers (B) and (C) are incorrect because these requirements for holder in due course status are not necessary to holder status.

27. Under the Negotiable Instruments Article of the UCC, which of the following requirements must be met for a transferee of order paper to become a holder?

I. Possession
II. Endorsement of transferor

A. I only.

B. II only.

C. Both I and II.

D. Neither I nor II.

The correct answer is (C). *(CPA, adapted)*
REQUIRED: The requirement(s) for a transferee of order paper to become a holder.
DISCUSSION: Mere transfer of an instrument constitutes an assignment. A transferee of order paper becomes a holder when the instrument is properly negotiated. Proper negotiation of order paper requires possession by the transferee and proper endorsement by the transferor.
Answers (A), (B), and (D) are incorrect because the transferee must have both possession of the instrument and the proper endorsement of the transferor in order to be a holder.

28. Under the Negotiable Instruments Article of the UCC, which of the following requirements must be met for a person to be a holder in due course of a promissory note?

- A. The note must be payable to bearer.

- B. The note must be negotiable.

- C. All prior holders must have been holders in due course.

- D. The holder must be the payee of the note.

The correct answer is (B). *(CPA, adapted)*
REQUIRED: The requirement to qualify as a holder in due course.
DISCUSSION: A holder, a person who is legally entitled to payment from the note, may become a holder in due course (HDC) if the note (s)he receives is a negotiable instrument. (S)he must take the instrument in good faith without notice of any defenses to payment, contested claim of ownership, or knowledge of the instrument being overdue or dishonored, and give value for it. If these elements are met, the holder takes the note free of all personal defenses as an HDC.
Answer (A) is incorrect because a negotiable note held by an HDC may be payable to either the bearer of the note or to the order of a specifically identified person. Answer (C) is incorrect because prior holders of the note are not required to have been HDCs in order for the transferee to become an HDC. Answer (D) is incorrect because the holder need not be the payee but must meet the requirements to become an HDC.

29. Under the Negotiable Instruments Article of the UCC, which of the following circumstances would prevent a person from becoming a holder in due course of an instrument?

- A. The person was notified that payment was refused.

- B. The person was notified that one of the prior endorsers was discharged.

- C. The note was collateral for a loan.

- D. The note was purchased at a discount.

The correct answer is (A). *(CPA, adapted)*
REQUIRED: The circumstance preventing a person from becoming a holder in due course.
DISCUSSION: A holder can become a holder in due course (HDC) only if the transferee takes the instrument in good faith and was unaware the instrument had been dishonored. Therefore, if the transferee has notice that payment was refused when the instrument was presented for payment, the holder cannot be an HDC.
Answer (B) is incorrect because the transferee may be an HDC regardless of notice of the discharge of a prior endorser if (s)he meets the requirements of good faith, no notice of claims, and payment of value. Answer (C) is incorrect because a transferee may be an HDC with respect to any negotiable instrument if the person had no notice of the claim. Therefore, if the transferee had no notice the note was collateral for a loan, as a good-faith purchaser, (s)he takes the note as an HDC. Answer (D) is incorrect because a transferee may become an HDC if (s)he gives value. The amount or adequacy of the consideration given is irrelevant.

30. A purchaser of a negotiable instrument would least likely be a holder in due course if, at the time of purchase, the instrument is

- A. Purchased at a discount.

- B. Collateral for a loan.

- C. Payable to bearer on demand.

- D. Overdue by 3 weeks.

The correct answer is (D). *(CPA, adapted)*
REQUIRED: The characteristic of a negotiable instrument most likely to preclude holder in due course (HDC) status.
DISCUSSION: A holder generally cannot qualify as an HDC if (s)he has notice that the instrument is overdue. The holder of a demand instrument (such as a check) has such notice if (s)he takes it more than a reasonable time after issue or after demand has been made. A reasonable time for a check drawn and payable in the United States is 30 days after issue. The holder of an instrument payable at a definite time who takes it the day after the due date is deemed to be on actual notice that it is overdue.
Answer (A) is incorrect because the amount of value given is only relevant if it is such that the purchaser took the instrument not in good faith or with notice of a defense or dishonor. Answer (B) is incorrect because an instrument can be collateral for a loan and be negotiable. Answer (C) is incorrect because both order and bearer paper can be negotiated to an HDC.

31. The value requirement in determining whether a person is a holder in due course with respect to a check will not be satisfied by the taking of the check

A. As security for an obligation to the extent of the obligation.

B. As payment for an antecedent debt.

C. In exchange for another negotiable instrument.

D. In exchange for a promise to perform services in the future.

The correct answer is (D). *(CPA, adapted)*

REQUIRED: The consideration not constituting value.

DISCUSSION: Under UCC 3-303, the value requirement is met (1) to the extent agreed consideration has been performed, (2) if the holder acquires a security interest in or a lien on the instrument, (3) if the holder takes in payment of or as security for an antecedent claim, (4) if the holder gives another negotiable instrument, or (5) if the holder makes an irrevocable commitment to a third person. Future consideration, such as a contractual promise, does not constitute value to qualify as a holder in due course.

Answers (A), (B), and (C) are incorrect because each constitutes a taking for value under UCC 3-303.

32. Silver Corp. sold 20 tons of steel to River Corp. with payment to be by River's check. The price of steel was fluctuating daily. Silver requested that the amount of River's check be left blank so that Silver could fill in the current market price. River complied with Silver's request. Within 2 days, Silver received River's check. Although the market price of 20 tons of steel at the time Silver received River's check was $80,000, Silver filled in the check for $100,000 and negotiated it to Hatch Corp. Hatch took the check in good faith, without notice of Silver's act or any other defense, and in payment of an antecedent debt. River will

A. Not be liable to Hatch, because the check was materially altered by Silver.

B. Not be liable to Hatch, because Hatch failed to give value when it acquired the check from Silver.

C. Be liable to Hatch for $100,000.

D. Be liable to Hatch, but only for $80,000.

The correct answer is (C). *(CPA, adapted)*

REQUIRED: The effect of an unauthorized completion of a check on the drawer's liability to a holder in due course.

DISCUSSION: Hatch took after proper negotiation, in good faith, without notice of the unauthorized completion, and for value (payment of an antecedent debt). UCC 3-304 expressly provides that mere knowledge that an incomplete instrument has been completed is not notice of a defense. Accordingly, Hatch is a holder in due course, and River is liable for the amount of the check as completed.

Answers (A) and (D) are incorrect because, when an incomplete instrument has been improperly completed, a subsequent holder in due course may enforce it as completed. Answer (B) is incorrect because a holder takes for value when (s)he takes in payment of an antecedent claim.

33. A $5,000 promissory note payable to the order of Neptune is discounted to Bane by blank endorsement for $4,000. King steals the note from Bane and sells it to Ott, who promises to pay King $4,500. After paying King $3,000, Ott learns that King stole the note. Ott makes no further payment to King. Ott is

A. A holder in due course to the extent of $5,000.

B. An ordinary holder to the extent of $4,500.

C. A holder in due course to the extent of $3,000.

D. An ordinary holder to the extent of $0.

The correct answer is (C). *(CPA, adapted)*

REQUIRED: The extent of holder or holder in due course (HDC) status after receiving notice of a defense prior to full payment.

DISCUSSION: To be an HDC, a holder must take for value, in good faith, and without notice that the instrument is overdue, dishonored, or subject to any defense or claim. An unsecured promise to pay is not considered giving value for a negotiable instrument (giving another promissory note or draft would be value). Prior to receiving notice of a defense against the instrument, Ott has given value to the extent of $3,000 and is an HDC only to that extent.

Answer (A) is incorrect because Ott is an HDC only with respect to the $3,000 value given prior to notice of a defense against the instrument. Answers (B) and (D) are incorrect because negotiability is determined by the face of the instrument. Blank endorsement rendered it bearer paper. Mere delivery to Ott constituted negotiation. Ott is an HDC to the extent of $3,000 because (s)he took it in good faith for $3,000 value given without notice of defenses, rival claims, or dishonor, and without knowledge that it was overdue.

34. Under the Negotiable Instruments Article of the UCC, which of the following parties will be a holder but not be entitled to the rights of a holder in due course?

- A. A party who, knowing of a real defense to payment, received an instrument from a holder in due course.

- B. A party who found an instrument payable to bearer.

- C. A party who received, as a gift, an instrument from a holder in due course.

- D. A party who, in good faith and without notice of any defect, gave value for a negotiable instrument.

The correct answer is (B). *(CPA, adapted)*
    REQUIRED: The party that will be a holder but will not be entitled to the rights of a holder in due course (HDC).
    DISCUSSION: A holder (a possessor of bearer paper or of duly endorsed order paper) may become an HDC by meeting three requirements: (a) taking an instrument in good faith, (b) giving value for it, and (c) taking it without notice of defenses to payment, rival claims of ownership, or that the instrument is overdue or dishonored. A party who found an instrument that is payable to bearer has not given value for the instrument and cannot be an HDC. Moreover, the shelter principle does not apply to give the finder the rights of an HDC because the finder has not taken by transfer from an HDC. Transfer is delivery by a nonissuer for the purpose of giving the transferee the right to enforce the instrument (UCC 3-203).
    Answer (A) is incorrect because a party who receives an instrument from an HDC will receive the rights of an HDC through the shelter principle even if there is a real defense to payment of the instrument. A real defense is effective against an HDC and one who takes from or through an HDC. Answer (C) is incorrect because a person who receives an instrument as a gift or an inheritance and not for value can receive the rights of an HDC through the shelter principle. Answer (D) is incorrect because a person who takes a negotiable instrument in good faith, for value, and without knowledge of any defect, is an HDC.

E. Liabilities, Defenses, and Rights

35. Price has in his possession an otherwise negotiable instrument that reads:

"I, Waldo, hereby promise to pay to the order of Mark or bearer...."

Which of the following is true with respect to the above instrument?

- A. Mark's signature is required to negotiate the instrument.

- B. The instrument is nonnegotiable.

- C. If Mark endorses the instrument, he assumes potentially greater liability to subsequent transferees than if he transfers it by mere delivery.

- D. Since the instrument is payable to Mark's order, it is a draft.

The correct answer is (C). *(CPA, adapted)*
    REQUIRED: The correct statement regarding negotiation of the given instrument.
    DISCUSSION: A person who transfers without endorsement only makes warranties to his/her transferee and the payor (maker or drawee), but not to subsequent holders. On the other hand, an endorser makes warranties to all subsequent holders of an instrument. Therefore, Mark would assume greater potential liability by endorsing the instrument.
    Answer (A) is incorrect because the instrument states that it is payable to "the order of Mark or bearer." It is therefore bearer paper. Only delivery is needed to negotiate it. Answer (B) is incorrect because the instrument is negotiable since it is stated to be otherwise negotiable and contains a promise to pay to "the order of Mark or bearer." Answer (D) is incorrect because the instrument is a note since it is a two-party instrument payable by the maker to the payee.

36. Blare bought a house and provided the required funds in the form of a certified check from a bank. Which of the following statements correctly describes the legal liability of Blare and the bank?

- A. The bank has accepted; therefore, Blare is without liability.

- B. The bank has not accepted; therefore, Blare has primary liability.

- C. The bank has accepted; therefore, Blare has secondary liability.

- D. The bank has not accepted; therefore, Blare is without liability.

The correct answer is (C). *(CPA, adapted)*
    REQUIRED: The correct statement about the liabilities involved in payment by certified check.
    DISCUSSION: A certified check is one that a bank has accepted. Acceptance is the drawee's signed engagement to honor the draft as presented. As acceptor, the bank bears primary liability for payment. As drawer, Blare is secondarily liable on the check and must pay the payee if the bank dishonors the certified check.
    Answer (A) is incorrect because Blare is secondarily liable. Answers (B) and (D) are incorrect because Blare is secondarily liable, and the bank is primarily liable as an acceptor.

37. Wilson drew a sight draft on Jimmy Foxx (a customer who owed Wilson money on an open account), payable to the order of Burton, one of Wilson's creditors. Burton presented it to Foxx. After examining the draft as to its authenticity and after checking the amount against outstanding debts to Wilson, Foxx wrote on its face "Accepted--payable in 10 days" and signed it. When Burton returned at the end of 10 days, Foxx told him he could not pay and was hard-pressed for cash. Burton did not notify Wilson of these facts. Two days later when Burton again presented the instrument for payment, Burton was told that Foxx's creditors had filed a petition in bankruptcy that morning. Which of the following statements is correct?

   A. The instrument in question is a type of demand promissory note.

   B. Wilson had primary liability on the draft at its inception.

   C. Foxx was secondarily liable on the draft at its inception.

   D. Foxx assumed primary liability at the time of acceptance.

The correct answer is (D). *(CPA, adapted)*
   REQUIRED: The correct statement regarding a sight draft that has been accepted and then dishonored by the drawee.
   DISCUSSION: A sight draft is essentially a demand draft payable on locating the drawee. A draft has no primarily liable party until acceptance by the drawee. Upon acceptance, Foxx assumed primary liability. However, the claim must be filed in the bankruptcy proceeding.
   Answer (A) is incorrect because the instrument is a type of draft (i.e., a three-party instrument), not a type of note. Answer (B) is incorrect because Wilson had only secondary liability as drawer. Answer (C) is incorrect because Foxx had no liability on the instrument until he accepted it.

38. Under the Negotiable Instruments Article of the UCC, in a nonconsumer transaction, which of the following are real defenses available against a holder in due course?

	Material Alteration	Discharge in Bankruptcy	Breach of Contract
A.	No	Yes	Yes
B.	Yes	Yes	No
C.	No	No	Yes
D.	Yes	No	No

The correct answer is (B). *(CPA, adapted)*
   REQUIRED: The real defenses available against a holder in due course.
   DISCUSSION: The holder in due course (HDC) status eliminates most, but not all, defenses to collection from persons who would otherwise be primarily or secondarily liable on the instrument. Real defenses can be used against anyone, including an HDC. These real defenses include material alterations of the instrument and discharge in bankruptcy. Breach of contract is a personal defense and cannot be asserted against an HDC.
   Answers (A), (C), and (D) are incorrect because an HDC is subject only to real defenses. A material alteration and discharge in bankruptcy are real defenses; therefore, an HDC would be subject to liability in these cases. However, breach of contract is a personal defense and may not be asserted against an HDC.

39. A maker of a note will have a real defense against a holder in due course as a result of any of the following conditions except

   A. Discharge in bankruptcy.

   B. Forgery.

   C. Fraud in the execution.

   D. Lack of consideration.

The correct answer is (D). *(CPA, adapted)*
   REQUIRED: The defense ineffective against a holder in due course.
   DISCUSSION: A holder in due course (HDC) takes an instrument free from all claims to it on the part of any person and all defenses of any party with whom the holder has not dealt except real defenses. Real defenses include infancy to the extent that it is a defense to a simple contract; incapacity, duress, or illegality that makes the obligation void; fraud in the execution; and discharge in insolvency proceedings. Material alteration and unauthorized signature may also be real defenses. Traditional contract defenses, such as lack of consideration, are usually personal defenses and thus not valid against an HDC. Fraud in the inducement and wrongful completion are other examples of personal defenses.
   Answers (A), (B), and (C) are incorrect because each is a real defense, effective against an HDC.

40. To the extent that a holder of a negotiable promissory note is a holder in due course, the holder takes the note free of which of the following defenses?

- A. Minority of the maker where it is a defense to enforcement of a contract.
- B. Forgery of the maker's signature.
- C. Discharge of the maker in bankruptcy.
- D. Nonperformance of a condition precedent.

The correct answer is (D). *(CPA, adapted)*
REQUIRED: The defense ineffective against a holder in due course.
DISCUSSION: A holder in due course (HDC) takes an instrument free from all claims to it on the part of any person and all defenses of any party with whom the holder has not dealt except real defenses. Real defenses include infancy to the extent that it is a defense to a simple contract; incapacity, duress, or illegality that makes the obligation void; fraud in the execution; and discharge in insolvency proceedings. Material alteration and unauthorized signature may also be real defenses. Traditional contract defenses, such as nonperformance of a condition precedent, are usually personal defenses and thus not valid against an HDC.
Answers (A), (B), and (C) are incorrect because each is a real defense, effective against an HDC.

41. Cobb gave Garson a signed check with the amount payable left blank. Garson was to fill in, as the amount, the price of fuel oil Garson was to deliver to Cobb at a later date. Garson estimated the amount at $700 but told Cobb it would be no more than $900. Garson did not deliver the fuel oil but filled in the amount of $1,000 on the check. Garson then negotiated the check to Josephs in satisfaction of a $500 debt with the $500 balance paid to Garson in cash. Cobb stopped payment, and Josephs is seeking to collect $1,000 from Cobb. Cobb's maximum liability to Josephs will be

- A. $0
- B. $500
- C. $900
- D. $1,000

The correct answer is (D). *(CPA, adapted)*
REQUIRED: The effect of unauthorized completion on the drawer's liability to a holder in due course.
DISCUSSION: Josephs took after proper negotiation, in good faith, without notice of the unauthorized completion, and for value (payment of an antecedent debt). UCC 3-304 expressly provides that mere knowledge that an incomplete instrument has been completed is not notice of a defense. Accordingly, Josephs is a holder in due course (HDC), and Cobb is liable for the amount of the check as completed.
Answers (A) and (C) are incorrect because, when an incomplete instrument has been improperly completed, a subsequent HDC may enforce it as completed. Answer (B) is incorrect because a holder takes for value when (s)he takes in payment of an antecedent claim.

42. Robb, a minor, executed a promissory note payable to bearer and delivered it to Dodsen in payment for a stereo system. Dodsen negotiated the note for value to Mellon by delivery alone and without endorsement. Mellon endorsed the note in blank and negotiated it to Bloom for value. Bloom's demand for payment was refused by Robb because the note was executed when Robb was a minor. Bloom gave prompt notice of Robb's default to Dodsen and Mellon. None of the holders of the note were aware of Robb's minority. Which of the following parties will be liable to Bloom?

	Dodsen	Mellon
A.	Yes	Yes
B.	Yes	No
C.	No	No
D.	No	Yes

The correct answer is (D). *(CPA, adapted)*
REQUIRED: The correct statement concerning liability of parties to a promissory note executed by a minor.
DISCUSSION: Any person who signs a negotiable instrument is liable on it. A party is primarily liable if (s)he is required to pay by the terms of the instrument itself. Unqualified endorsers are secondarily liable; they are liable only if the party with primary liability fails to honor the instrument and only if the holder gives timely notice of dishonor. A person who does not endorse an instrument is generally not liable on it. Note, however, that a person who transfers a negotiable instrument without endorsement, but for full consideration, does warrant to the immediate transferee that (s)he has good title.
Answers (A) and (B) are incorrect because Dodsen did not endorse the note. Answer (C) is incorrect because Mellon, as an HDC, can enforce the instrument against a holder who endorsed the instrument since timely notice of dishonor was provided.

43. Jim Bass is in possession of a negotiable promissory note made payable "to bearer." Bass acquired the note from Mary Frank for value. The maker of the note was Fred Jackson. The following endorsements appear on the back of the note:

```
Sam Peters
Pay Jim Bass
    Mary Frank
    Jim Bass
(without recourse)
```

Bass presented the note to Jackson, who refused to pay it because he was financially unable to do so. Which of the following statements is correct?

- A. Peters is not secondarily liable on the note because his endorsement was unnecessary for negotiation.

- B. Peters is not secondarily liable to Bass.

- C. Frank will probably not be liable to Bass unless Bass gives notice to Frank of Jackson's refusal to pay within a reasonable time.

- D. Bass would have a secondary liability to Peters and Frank if he had not qualified his endorsement.

F. Discharge

44. Vex Corp. executed a negotiable promissory note payable to Tamp, Inc. The note was collateralized by some of Vex's business assets. Tamp negotiated the note to Miller for value. Miller endorsed the note in blank and negotiated it to Bilco for value. Before the note became due, Bilco agreed to release Vex's collateral. Vex refused to pay Bilco when the note became due. Bilco promptly notified Miller and Tamp of Vex's default. Which of the following statements is correct?

- A. Bilco will be unable to collect from Miller because Miller's endorsement was in blank.

- B. Bilco will be able to collect from either Tamp or Miller because Bilco was a holder in due course.

- C. Bilco will be unable to collect from either Tamp or Miller because of Bilco's release of the collateral.

- D. Bilco will be able to collect from Tamp because Tamp was the original payee.

The correct answer is (C). *(CPA, adapted)*
REQUIRED: The correct statement about the liability of endorsers of a negotiable instrument.
DISCUSSION: Unqualified endorsers of an instrument are secondarily liable on the instrument and are obligated to pay if the primarily liable party fails to do so. But this liability is contingent on the holder's timely notice of dishonor. Bass must give Frank notice of Jackson's dishonor to hold Frank to her secondary liability as endorser of the instrument.
Answer (A) is incorrect because all unqualified endorsers, whether or not their endorsements were necessary for negotiation, are secondarily liable on an instrument. Answer (B) is incorrect because unqualified endorsers are liable to all subsequent endorsers, even if the instrument has multiple endorsers. Answer (D) is incorrect because a subsequent endorser is not secondarily liable to previous endorsers.

The correct answer is (C). *(CPA, adapted)*
REQUIRED: The liability of parties to a promissory note when a subsequent holder has impaired collateral.
DISCUSSION: The UCC provides many ways in which a party may be discharged from liability on an instrument. One way is the impairment of right of recourse or of collateral. The extent of discharge is limited to the loss resulting to the party from the impairment. Bilco's agreement to release the collateral effected discharge of Tamp.
Answer (A) is incorrect because each unqualified endorser is liable on the instrument. The blank endorsement, rather than limiting liability, operates to render the instrument payable to bearer. But Bilco's release of collateral discharged Miller from liability. Answer (B) is incorrect because a prior endorsee, HDC or otherwise, is discharged when a subsequent holder releases collateral. Answer (D) is incorrect because it is unqualified endorsement that renders a payee liable on the instrument. Also, the release discharged Tamp.

45. A subsequent holder of a negotiable instrument may cause the discharge of a prior holder of the instrument by any of the following actions except

    A.   Unexcused delay in presentment of a time draft.

    B.   Procuring certification of a check.

    C.   Giving notice of dishonor the day after dishonor.

    D.   Material alteration of a note.

The correct answer is (C). *(CPA, adapted)*
    REQUIRED: The action that would not cause the discharge of a prior holder.
    DISCUSSION: To the extent a person is discharged, (s)he is no longer liable on a negotiable instrument. Under the UCC, a person may be discharged by agreement or by one of several acts or omissions. Unexcused failure to timely present an instrument or provide notice of dishonor effects discharge of previous holders. (The failure impairs rights of recourse.) But giving notice of dishonor the day after dishonor is timely.
    Answer (A) is incorrect because, to hold secondary parties liable on a negotiable instrument with a specific payment date, presentment must be made on the due date. Answer (B) is incorrect because, once the drawee certifies a check, the drawer and all prior endorsers are discharged. Answer (D) is incorrect because a material alteration of the instrument by the holder discharges any party whose contract is changed thereby.

46. Which of the following actions does not discharge a prior party to a commercial instrument?

    A.   Good-faith payment or satisfaction of the instrument.

    B.   Cancellation of that prior party's endorsement.

    C.   The holder's oral renunciation of that prior party's liability.

    D.   The holder's intentional destruction of the instrument.

The correct answer is (C). *(CPA, adapted)*
    REQUIRED: The action that does not discharge a prior party to a commercial instrument.
    DISCUSSION: The holder of an instrument may discharge any party. No consideration is required. It may be done in any manner apparent on the face of the instrument or the endorsement, such as by intentionally canceling the instrument or the party's signature by destruction or mutilation or by striking out the party's signature. It may also be done by renouncing his/her rights by a writing signed and delivered or by surrender of the instrument to the party to be discharged.
    Answer (A) is incorrect because this discharges the prior party from liability on the instrument. Answer (B) is incorrect because a holder who cancels a prior party's endorsement discharges that party from liability on the instrument. Answer (D) is incorrect because the holder's destruction of the instrument, intending to cancel it, discharges all parties from liability on it.

47.

Pay to Ann Tyler

Paul Tyler

Ann Tyler

Mary Thomas

~~*Betty Ash*~~

Pay George Green Only

Susan Town

Susan Town, on receiving this instrument, struck Betty Ash's endorsement. Under the Negotiable Instruments Article of the UCC, which of the endorsers of this instrument will be completely discharged from secondary liability to later endorsers of the instrument?

    A.   Ann Tyler.

    B.   Mary Thomas.

    C.   Betty Ash.

    D.   Susan Town.

The correct answer is (C). *(CPA, adapted)*
    REQUIRED: The effect on liability after an endorsement is eliminated.
    DISCUSSION: Betty Ash is discharged from liability on the instrument. Susan Town, as the current holder, may discharge an individual by striking out that individual's signature. The holder's discharge of an endorser has the effect of discharging any endorsers subsequent to the relieved endorser. Here, there are no subsequent endorsers, so only Betty Ash is discharged.
    Answers (A), (B), and (D) are incorrect because the discharge of Betty Ash did not impair a right of recourse of Ann Tyler or Mary Thomas because neither had rights against Betty Ash, since she was a subsequent endorser. Susan Town is not discharged from liability as a result of her voluntary cancellation of Betty Ash's endorsement.

48. A check has the following endorsements on the back:

Paul Folk
without recourse

George Hopkins
payment guaranteed

Ann Quarry
collection guaranteed

Rachel Ott

Which of the following conditions occurring subsequent to the endorsements would discharge all of the endorsers?

- A. Lack of notice of dishonor.

- B. Late presentment.

- C. Insolvency of the maker.

- D. Certification of the check.

The correct answer is (D). *(CPA, adapted)*

REQUIRED: The condition that would discharge all the endorsers of a check.

DISCUSSION: Certification is an unconditional promise to pay or acceptance of primary liability. Prior to certification or acceptance, a drawee is not liable on a check. But once the drawee certifies a check, the drawer and all prior endorsers are discharged if certification is procured by the holder. Note that, by his qualified endorsement, Paul Folk is not liable on the instrument.

Answers (A) and (B) are incorrect because these impair a right of recourse and discharge secondarily liable endorsers. But the guarantors are primarily liable and are not discharged. Answer (C) is incorrect because it discharges nobody. A discharge in bankruptcy proceedings, however, effects discharge of only that person from liability on the instrument.

G. Bank Transactions

49. In general, which of the following statements is correct concerning the priority among checks drawn on a particular account and presented to the drawee bank on a particular day?

- A. The checks may be charged to the account in any order convenient to the bank.

- B. The checks may be charged to the account in any order provided no charge creates an overdraft.

- C. The checks must be charged to the account in the order in which the checks were dated.

- D. The checks must be charged to the account in the order of lowest amount to highest amount to minimize the number of dishonored checks.

The correct answer is (A). *(CPA, adapted)*

REQUIRED: The correct statement about the priority among checks presented to a bank for payment.

DISCUSSION: In general, the UCC provides that items may be accepted, paid, certified, or charged to the indicated account of its customer in any order convenient to the bank.

Answers (B), (C), and (D) are incorrect because a drawee bank has no obligation to pay the checks in any special order, even to minimize overdrafts.

OOF QUESTION *(CPA, adapted)* 10-15 minutes

During an audit of Trent Realty Corp.'s financial statements, Clark, CPA, reviewed the following instruments:

A.   Instrument 1.

$300,000   Belle, MD
                          September 15, 1999

For value received, ten years after date, I promise to pay to the order of Dart Finance Co. Three Hundred Thousand and 00/100 dollars with interest at 9% per annum compounded annually until fully paid. This instrument arises out of the sale of land located in MD.

It is further agreed that

1. Maker will pay all costs of collection including reasonable attorney fees.
2. Maker may prepay the amount outstanding on any anniversary date of this instrument.

G. Evans
G. Evans

The following transactions relate to Instrument 1:

- On March 15, 2000, Dart endorsed the instrument in blank and sold it to Morton for $275,000.
- On July 10, 2000, Evans informed Morton that Dart had fraudulently induced Evans into signing the instrument.
- On August 15, 2000, Trent, which knew of Evans's claim against Dart, purchased the instrument from Morton for $50,000.

Required

Items 1 through 5 relate to Instrument 1. For each item, select the correct answer from List I. An answer may be selected once, more than once, or not at all.

1. Instrument 1 is a (type of instrument).
2. Instrument 1 is (negotiability).
3. Morton is considered a (type of ownership).
4. Trent is considered a (type of ownership).
5. Trent could recover on the instrument from [liable party(ies)].

List I

A. Draft
B. Promissory note
C. Security agreement
D. Holder
E. Holder in due course
F. Holder with rights of a holder in due course under the shelter provision
G. Negotiable
H. Nonnegotiable
I. Evans, Morton, and Dart
J. Morton and Dart
K. Only Dart

B.   Instrument 2.

                 Front

To: Pure Bank
     Upton, VT

                 April 5, 1999

Pay to the order of M. West $1,500.00
One Thousand Five Hundred and 00/100 Dollars
on May 1, 1999.

       W. Fields
       W. Fields

                 Back

M. West
Pay to C. Larr
T. Keetin

C. Larr
without recourse

Required

Items 6 through 13 relate to Instrument 2. For each item, select the correct answer from List II. An answer may be selected once, more than once, or not at all.

6. Instrument 2 is a (type of instrument).
7. Instrument 2 is (negotiability).
8. West's endorsement makes the instrument (type of instrument).
9. Keetin's endorsement makes the instrument (type of instrument).
10. Larr's endorsement makes the instrument (type of instrument).
11. West's endorsement would be considered (type of endorsement).
12. Keetin's endorsement would be considered (type of endorsement).
13. Larr's endorsement would be considered (type of endorsement).

List II

A. Bearer paper
B. Blank
C. Check
D. Draft
E. Negotiable
F. Nonnegotiable
G. Note
H. Order paper
I. Qualified
J. Special

Knowledge Tested

Negotiable instruments

1. Types of instruments
2. Negotiability
3. Transfer and negotiation
4. Holder in due course

Authors' Comments

This question tests UCC Article 3, *Negotiable Instruments*. This article primarily concerns the requirements for negotiability of notes, CDs, drafts, and checks; their transfer in a manner that constitutes negotiation; the rights of holders; the liability of parties; and the discharge of obligations.

1. The correct answer is (B).

DISCUSSION: Instrument 1 is a promissory note. A promissory note is a written promise between two parties. It is an unconditional, signed promise from one party, the maker, to pay a fixed amount of money to a second party, the payee. In Instrument 1, G. Evans is the maker, and Dart is the payee.

2. The correct answer is (G).

DISCUSSION: Instrument 1 is negotiable. To be negotiable, a note must be in writing, be signed by the maker, contain an unconditional promise to pay a fixed amount of money, be payable on demand or at a definite time, and be payable to order or bearer. Since Instrument 1 meets each of these requirements, it is negotiable.

3. The correct answer is (E).

DISCUSSION: Morton is a holder in due course (HDC). An HDC has rights superior to those of prior parties and transferors. To be an HDC, one must be a holder of a negotiable instrument taken for value, in good faith, and without notice that it is overdue or has been dishonored or that any person has a defense or a claim to it. Since Morton met each requirement at the time of acquiring the instrument, he is an HDC.

4. The correct answer is (F).

DISCUSSION: Under the shelter provision of the UCC, a person who does not qualify as an HDC may have the same rights if such person acquired the instrument from a prior party who was an HDC. Trent, who knew of the claim against Dart, is entitled to the advantage of the shelter provision and effectively has the rights of Morton, who was an HDC.

5. The correct answer is (I).

DISCUSSION: Evans, the maker, along with Morton and Dart, the endorsers, is liable to Trent on the instrument assuming timely presentment for payment and timely notice to the endorsers after default. No real defenses exist, and personal defenses cannot be asserted against a holder through an HDC.

6. The correct answer is (D).

DISCUSSION: The instrument is a time draft. It is a three-party instrument containing an unconditional written order by one person, the drawer, to another person, the drawee, ordering him/her to pay a sum of money to a third party, either a named payee or bearer. Instrument 2 is not a check because it is not payable on demand.

7. The correct answer is (E).

DISCUSSION: Instrument 2 is negotiable. A negotiable draft is in writing, is signed by the drawer, contains an unconditional order to pay a fixed amount of money, is payable on demand or at a definite time, and is payable to order or bearer.

8. The correct answer is (A).

DISCUSSION: The endorsement by West on Instrument 2 changes the instrument from an order instrument to a bearer instrument. An instrument payable to an identified person will become payable to the bearer if it is endorsed in blank. West's endorsement was an endorsement in blank.

9. The correct answer is (H).

DISCUSSION: Following Keetin's endorsement, Instrument 2 becomes order paper. An order instrument is a promise or an order not payable to the bearer but payable to the order of an identified person. For further negotiation, Instrument 2 must be endorsed and delivered by C. Larr.

10. The correct answer is (A).

DISCUSSION: Instrument 2, following Larr's endorsement, is bearer paper. An instrument payable to an identified person becomes payable to bearer if it is endorsed in blank. A blank endorsement consists merely of the signature of the endorser or his/her authorized agent and specifies no particular person.

11. The correct answer is (B).

DISCUSSION: West's endorsement is a blank endorsement because it specifies no particular party and consists merely of the signature of West.

12. The correct answer is (J).

DISCUSSION: Keetin's endorsement specifies "Pay to C. Larr" and therefore is a special endorsement. A special endorsement specifically designates the person to whom or to whose order the instrument is payable.

13. The correct answer is (I).

DISCUSSION: Larr's endorsement of Instrument 2 is a qualified endorsement. A qualified endorsement is used by an endorser to disclaim or limit contractual liability. It does not affect negotiability but may affect marketability.

ESSAY QUESTION *(CPA, adapted)* 15-20 minutes

River Oaks is a wholesale distributor of automobile parts. River Oaks received the promissory note shown below from First Auto, Inc., as security for payment of a $4,400 auto parts shipment. When River Oaks accepted the note as collateral for the First Auto obligation, River Oaks was aware that the maker of the note, Hillcraft, Inc., was claiming that the note was unenforceable because Alexco Co. had breached the license agreement under which Hillcraft had given the note. First Auto had acquired the note from Smith in exchange for repairing several cars owned by Smith. At the time First Auto received the note, First Auto was unaware of the dispute between Hillcraft and Alexco. Also, Smith, who paid Alexco $3,500 for the note, was unaware of Hillcraft's allegations that Alexco had breached the license agreement.

PROMISSORY NOTE

Date: __1/14/99__

____Hillcraft, Inc.____ promises to pay to __Alexco Co. or bearer__ the sum of __$4,400__ ____Four Thousand and 00/100____ Dollars on or before __May 15, 2000 (maker may elect to extend due date by 30 days)__ with interest thereon at the rate of __9½%__ per annum.

Hillcraft, Inc.

By: *P.J. Hill*

P.J. Hill, President

Reference: __Alexco Licensing Agreement__

The reverse side of the note was endorsed as follows:

Pay to the order of First Auto without recourse

E. Smith

E. Smith

Pay to the order of River Oaks Co.

First Auto

By: *G. First*

G. First, President

First Auto is now insolvent and unable to satisfy its obligation to River Oaks. Therefore, River Oaks has demanded that Hillcraft pay $4,400, but Hillcraft has refused, asserting that

- The note is nonnegotiable because it references the license agreement and is not payable at a definite time or on demand.

- River Oaks is not a holder in due course of the note because it received the note as security for amounts owed by First Auto.

- River Oaks is not a holder in due course because it was aware of the dispute between Hillcraft and Alexco.

- Hillcraft can raise the alleged breach by Alexco as a defense to payment.

- River Oaks has no right to the note because it was not endorsed by Alexco.

- The maximum amount that Hillcraft would owe under the note is $4,000, plus accrued interest.

Required

State whether each of Hillcraft's assertions are correct, and give the reasons for your conclusions.

Knowledge Tested

1. Requirements for negotiability
2. Requirements for negotiation
3. Requirements for acquiring holder in due course (HDC) status
4. Liability on a negotiable instrument
5. Defenses to liability and the shelter principle

Authors' Comments

To answer this essay, you must identify the relevant requirements for negotiability of an instrument, for negotiating it, and for becoming an HDC. These determine rights to and liability on the instrument. Refresh your memory from the outline.

Requirements for negotiability are that the instrument be in writing, be signed by the maker or drawer, and contain an unconditional promise or order to pay a fixed amount of money, payable on demand or at a definite time and payable to order or to bearer. Mere reference to an underlying agreement is not a condition. A readily ascertainable date is a fixed time.

Negotiation is by transfer such that the transferee qualifies as a holder (the transferee's signature is not required).

A holder is a holder in due course if (s)he took the instrument in good faith, for value, and without notice of a defense to payment. "For value" is not identical to "consideration." Giving value includes taking the instrument in payment for, or as security for, an antecedent claim.

An endorser's liability on a negotiable instrument is independent of the contractual obligation on which the instrument is based. This is what enables negotiable instruments to substitute for money.

Read the outline material on the shelter principle carefully. Applying it can be tricky. Compare your conclusion to that in the unofficial answer.

Finally, an amount of money is "fixed" notwithstanding variation between words and letters on the instrument. Words take precedence over figures. The presumption is that a figure number is more easily indicated (or forged) than an unintended word.

This essay question shows that, if you have a good understanding of the study unit, you can quickly identify the issues and briefly apply the rules.

AICPA Unofficial Answer

Hillcraft's first assertion, that the note is nonnegotiable because it references the license agreement and is not payable at a definite time or on demand, is incorrect. The note is negotiable despite the reference to the license agreement because it does not make the note subject to the terms of the agreement; rather, the reference is regarded only as a recital of its existence.

Also, Hillcraft's right to extend the time for payment does not make the note nonnegotiable because the extension period is for a definite period of time.

Hillcraft's second assertion, that River Oaks is not a holder in due course (HDC) because it received the note as security for an existing debt and, therefore, did not give value for it, is incorrect. Under the UCC Negotiable Instruments Article, a holder does give value for an instrument when it is taken in payment of, or as security for, an antecedent claim.

Hillcraft's third assertion, that River Oaks is not an HDC because River Oaks was aware of Alexco's alleged breach of the license agreement, is correct. If a holder of a note is aware of a dispute when it acquires the note, that holder cannot be an HDC because the holder took with notice.

Hillcraft's fourth assertion, that it can raise the alleged breach by Alexco as a defense to payment of the note, is incorrect. Even though River Oaks is not an HDC under the UCC "shelter provision," it is entitled to the protection of an HDC because it took the instrument from First Auto, which was an HDC. Therefore, River Oaks did not take the note subject to Hillcraft's defense based on the alleged breach by Alexco. Hillcraft's defense is considered a personal defense and can be used only by Hillcraft against Alexco.

Hillcraft's fifth assertion, that River Oaks has no right to the note because it was not endorsed by Alexco, is incorrect. River Oaks acquired rights to the Hillcraft note without Alexco's endorsement because the note was a bearer instrument as a result of its being payable to "Alexco Company or bearer." A bearer instrument can be negotiated by delivery alone.

Hillcraft's final assertion, that the maximum amount Hillcraft would owe under the note is $4,000, plus accrued interest, is correct. If there is a conflict between a number written in numerals and also described by words, the words take precedence. Therefore, Hillcraft's maximum potential principal liability is $4,000 under the note.

STUDY UNIT 16: SALES

21 pages of outline
52 multiple-choice questions
2 OOFs and 1 essay

A. *Contracts Covering Goods*
B. *Warranties*
C. *Products Liability*
D. *Risk of Loss*
E. *Performance and Obligations*
F. *Remedies and Defenses*

The Uniform Commercial Code, Article 2, provides a set of rules to govern contracts for the sale of goods when the agreement of the parties fails to provide essential terms. Many of the rules of Article 2 were reviewed in Contracts, Study Units 7 and 8. The exam requires students to understand the philosophy of the sales article, which is to resolve disputes in favor of finding an enforceable contract when a reasonable basis for enforcement exists, to recognize contracts for the sale of goods rather than service or real property contracts, to identify the various warranties and other theories of recovery in products liabilities cases, to determine performance of sales contracts, to determine when the title and risk of loss is transferred from the seller to the buyer, and to delineate the defenses and remedies applied in suits for breach of sales contracts.

A. **Contracts Covering Goods**. Article 2 of the Uniform Commercial Code (UCC) deals specifically with contracts involving the sale of goods. Article 2 is referred to as the UCC Sales Article.

1. **Sale**. A contract for the sale of goods is to pass the ownership interest from the seller to the buyer for a consideration (price).

   a. A **gift** is a voluntary transfer of property without consideration.

   b. A **security interest** is an interest in either real or personal property which secures the payment of an obligation. In contrast, a sale transfers to the buyer all the ownership rights.

   c. By a **lease**, the owner transfers possession and the right to use property for a fixed or ascertainable period in exchange for rent.

      1) A lease does not involve a transfer of title.

   d. A **bailment** is a transfer of possession of personal property by the owner or rightful possessor (bailor) to another (bailee) for a determinable period without a transfer of title.

2. **Goods**. Article 2 deals only with goods. To be characterized as a good, the item of property must be tangible and movable.

   a. **Tangible property** has physical existence; it can be apprehended by the senses. It can be touched and seen.

   b. **Intangible property**, e.g., money, corporate stock, bonds, promissory notes, bank accounts, patents, and copyrights, is not within the scope of Article 2, even if it is evidenced by a tangible item and represents an interest in tangible property.

      1) EXAMPLE: Stock is evidenced by a stock certificate and is an equity interest in underlying assets of a corporation.

   c. **Movable property** can be carried from place to place.

   d. **Real property** is excluded from Article 2. Real property, essentially, refers to land, structures, and tangible items permanently attached thereto.

   e. Article 2 may apply to goods associated with real property.

f.   In sales contracts involving a combination of goods and services, courts resolve whether Article 2 applies by determining which is the predominant factor -- the goods or the services.

3.   **Merchants**. Article 2 applies to the sale of goods between all buyers and sellers. But special standards apply to transactions involving merchants.

   a.   A merchant is someone who

      1)   Deals in goods of the kind

      2)   Otherwise by his/her occupation holds him/herself out as having knowledge or skill peculiar to the practices or goods involved in the transaction

      3)   May be treated as having such knowledge or skill by his/her employment of an agent or broker or other intermediary who by his/her occupation holds him/herself out as having such knowledge or skill

   b.   Thus, a person is a merchant when (s)he, acting in a mercantile capacity, possesses or uses an expertise specifically related to the goods being sold.

4.   **Good Faith**. The obligation of good faith is imposed upon every UCC-governed contract.

   a.   The obligation may not be waived by either party. Thus, the parties may not contract to have no liability for failure to exercise good faith.

   b.   The UCC defines good faith as "honesty in fact." With respect to merchants, good faith also requires observance of reasonable commercial standards of fair dealing in the trade.

      1)   EXAMPLE: In a contract involving the sale of goods, Manuel and Jenny agree that Manuel (seller) will set the price. Manuel must establish the price in good faith. In most instances, good faith would require that the price be set at fair market value.

   c.   Good faith covers misrepresentation, failure to disclose material facts, and even failure to investigate material facts.

5.   **Unconscionability**. Any contract for the sale of goods may be scrutinized by a court to determine whether, in its purpose and effect, it is unconscionable (in its commercial setting).

   a.   The UCC does not define unconscionability; however, a court has described it as "monstrously extortionate, harsh, showing no regard for conscience."

6.   **Offer**. A sales contract requires an offer and acceptance, consideration, competent parties, and legal purpose. Good faith is required in formation and performance. No part of a contract found to be unconscionable will be enforceable.

   a.   At common law the terms of a contract are required to be definite and complete. The UCC has modified this strict approach by recognizing that a contract for the sale of goods may be made in any manner sufficient to show agreement.

   b.   That one or more terms are left open does not prevent the formation of a contract if it appears the parties intended to enter into a contract and there is a reasonably certain basis for granting a remedy.

      1)   If the quantity term is left open, the general rule is that a court may have no basis to grant a remedy; thus, a contract may not have been formed.

         a)   A contract does not fail for indefiniteness because it measures the quantity by the seller's output or the buyer's requirements that occur in good faith. However, the amount should not be unreasonably disproportionate to a stated estimate or, lacking such an estimate, to any normal or comparable prior amount.

2) If the parties have not agreed on price, the court will determine a reasonable price (generally market price) at the time of delivery.

3) If either the buyer or the seller is to determine price, it means a price fixed in good faith, which is generally the market price.

4) When parties do not specify payment or credit terms, payment is due at the time and place at which the buyer is to receive the goods.

5) When delivery terms are not specified, the buyer normally takes delivery at the seller's place of business.

6) If the time for shipment or delivery is not clearly specified in the sales contract, the court infers a reasonable time for performance.

c. An offer by a merchant, giving assurances that it will be held open, is irrevocable for the stated period of time up to a maximum of 90 days (Firm Offer Rule).

1) Consideration is not necessary to support this irrevocability.
2) The offer must be written and signed by the party making the offer.

d. A nonmerchant may revoke an offer. Irrevocability of an offer by a nonmerchant must be supported by consideration or promissory estoppel.

7. **Acceptance**. Unless otherwise indicated by language or circumstances, an offer is deemed to invite acceptance in any manner and by any medium reasonable under the circumstances.

a. If the offeror indicates that a particular medium of acceptance must be used, only the indicated medium is authorized.

b. Unless a particular medium is explicitly required by the terms of the agreement, any reasonable medium under the circumstances may be used.

1) EXAMPLE: The words "Please respond by letter" do not unambiguously make a letter the sole permitted medium of acceptance but merely indicate a preference.

c. If the offer does not require a particular manner or medium for acceptance, the UCC permits acceptance of an offer by either a prompt promise to ship or prompt shipment of the goods to the buyer.

1) The UCC provides that, if the seller does not ship conforming goods but instead ships nonconforming goods, the shipment constitutes both an acceptance and a breach.

2) If the seller notifies the buyer within a reasonable time that the nonconforming shipment is offered only as an accommodation, there is no breach.

a) The notice of accommodation must clearly indicate to the buyer that the shipment does not constitute an acceptance and that, therefore, no contract has been formed.

b) EXAMPLE: Dorothy orders 1,000 orange keyrings from Victor. Victor ships blue ones but does not notify Dorothy that the goods are offered only as accommodation. The shipment is both an acceptance of Dorothy's offer and a breach of the resulting contract.

d. Under the deposited acceptance, or mailbox rule, the acceptance is effective (an agreement is reached) at the moment of dispatch if the offeree has used an expressly or impliedly authorized medium of acceptance and the offer is still open.

      1)   The acceptance is effective even if it is never delivered provided it was properly dispatched.

      2)   An offeror may avoid the risk of a delayed or lost acceptance by specifying that any acceptance must be received by the offeror at his/her place of business on or before a specified date.

  e.   Commencement of performance by the offeree may be an appropriate method of acceptance.

      1)   But the offeree must notify the offeror within a reasonable time that performance has begun.

      2)   Otherwise, the offeror may treat the offer as having expired prior to acceptance.

8.   **Modified Acceptances**. Article 2 abandons the common-law mirror image rule that an offeree who departs from the terms of an offer, however slightly, has rejected the offer and presented a counteroffer.

  a.   The UCC position is that, if the offeree's response overall indicates a definite acceptance of the offer, a contract is formed, even if the acceptance includes terms in addition to or different from the original offer.

  b.   If the acceptance is expressly made conditional on assent to the different or additional term(s), there would be a counteroffer (and rejection) and no contract unless the original offeror agreed to the terms of the counteroffer.

  c.   If the seller or the buyer is a nonmerchant, different or additional terms in an acceptance are construed as mere proposals. The modifying terms do not become part of the contract unless the offeror agrees.

  d.   Between merchants, the additional proposed terms automatically become part of the contract unless one of the following applies:

      1)   The terms materially alter the original contract (e.g., price change or arbitration agreement).

      2)   The offer expressly limits acceptance to the terms of the offer.

      3)   The offeror timely objects to the modified terms.

9.   **Consideration** is required for contracts covered by Article 2, just as at common law, but there are two important exceptions:

  a.   Modifications, which can be binding
  b.   Firm offers, which are irrevocable offers made by merchants

10.   **Modifications**. The UCC varies the common-law rule that contract modification must be supported by new consideration.

  a.   An agreement modifying a contract needs no consideration to be binding.

  b.   If there is a written agreement signed by the parties excluding oral modification (or rescission), the contract can be modified (or rescinded) only by written agreement.

      1)   If a consumer (nonmerchant) is dealing with a merchant, and the merchant supplies the form that contains a prohibition against oral modification, the consumer must sign a separate acknowledgment of the clause for it to be enforceable.

  c.   Moreover, if any modification brings the contract within the statute of frauds, the modification must be in writing to be enforceable.

      1)   EXAMPLE: An oral contract for the sale of goods priced at $300 is modified so that the price for the goods is now $800. The modification must be in writing to be enforceable.

11. **Parol Evidence under Article 2**. The terms of a contract which are set forth in a writing intended by the parties to be a final expression of their agreement cannot be contradicted by evidence of any prior or contemporaneous oral or written agreement. However, such terms may be explained or supplemented.

   a. The UCC requires that the meaning of any agreement evidenced by the actions and language of the parties must be interpreted in light of commercial practices and other surrounding circumstances such as

      1) Course of dealing
      2) Usage of trade
      3) Course of performance
      4) Consistent additional terms

12. **Statute of Frauds**. Subject to the exceptions listed below, contracts for the sale of goods at a price of $500 or greater are not enforceable unless there is some writing signed by the party to be charged or by that party's agent.

   a. Unlike the common-law statute of frauds, the UCC provides that the writing need not contain all the essential terms of the contract.

      1) All that is required is some writing sufficient to indicate that a sales contract has been made.

      2) The writing must be signed by the party against whom enforcement of the contract is sought.

   b. A memorandum may be signed long after the parties have contracted orally.

   c. The signature may be located on any part of the document and may be made by any writing implement.

   d. The writing must indicate that a contract for sale of goods has been made between the parties, and the quantity of goods must be specified.

   e. In contracts for the sale of goods between merchants, if one party, within a reasonable time after an oral understanding has been reached, sends a written confirmation to the other party which binds the sender, it will satisfy the statute of frauds unless the recipient objects to the confirmation's content within 10 days of receipt.

   f. There are three fundamental situations in which contracts for the sale of goods for over $500 are enforceable without a sufficient writing.

      1) If the goods are to be specially made for the buyer and they are not suitable for sale to others in the ordinary course of the seller's business, and if the seller has made either a substantial beginning in their manufacture or commitments for their purchase before a notice of repudiation is received from the buyer, the contract is enforceable.

         a) This exception also applies to goods that are extensively modified at the buyer's request.

      2) If goods are actually received and accepted or payment has been made, the contract is enforceable (but not in excess of the quantity of goods so accepted or paid for).

      3) If a party admits in pleadings or in court that a contract for sale of goods exists, the contract is enforceable, but only for the quantity of goods admitted.

13. Stop and review! You have completed the outline for this subunit. Study multiple-choice questions 1 through 9 beginning on page 519.

B. Warranties. Three kinds of warranties addressed by the UCC are express warranties (e.g., stated orally or in writing), implied warranties, and the warranty of title (which is neither express nor implied).

1. A warranty is an assurance by one party to a sales contract of the existence of a fact upon which the other party may rely.

    a. A warranty gives rise to a duty on the part of the seller that the goods (s)he sells will conform to certain specific qualities, characteristics, or conditions.

2. **Express Warranties**. Any affirmation of fact or promise made by the seller to the buyer, including but not limited to any description of the goods, or any sample or model which becomes a basis of the bargain is an express warranty. The express warranty may be oral or written.

    a. In order to become the basis of the bargain, it is necessary that the communication was made at such a time that the buyer could have relied upon it when (s)he entered into the contract. This is so even if the buyer received the communication after the contract was formed, e.g., a pamphlet found in the box.

        1) It is not necessary for the buyer to prove that (s)he actually did rely.

        2) It is not necessary that the seller intended the affirmation of fact, description, or sample/model to make a warranty.

    b. A statement relating to the value of the goods or a statement purporting to be only the seller's opinion or commendation of the goods does not constitute an express warranty.

        1) Statements such as "the best in the world," "unsurpassable," "unbeatable quality," and "will sell like hotcakes," have been held to be mere sellers' talk or puffing and not warranties.

    c. An express warranty may arise from a description of the goods.

3. **Implied Warranty of Merchantability**. It is implied in every sale by a merchant who deals in goods of the kind sold. It does not apply to nonmerchants.

    a. The single most important test is "fit for the ordinary purposes for which such goods are used." A bottled drink with loose glass inside, a new automobile with defective brakes, or a racehorse with a broken leg would all fail.

    b. A seller is strictly liable for a breach of an implied warranty. Implied warranties are not based on principles of negligence.

        1) If the goods sold do not meet a standard of the warranty, the seller is liable even if (s)he exercised utmost care.

        2) It is irrelevant whether the seller knew of the defect or whether (s)he could not have discovered it, e.g., goods in a sealed container.

    c. In a suit for breach of implied warranty, it is necessary to show

        1) The implied warranty existed.
        2) The warranty was breached.
        3) The breach was the proximate cause of the damage sustained.

4. **Implied warranty of fitness for a particular purpose** arises whenever the seller has reason to know the particular purpose for which the goods are to be used and knows that the buyer is relying on the seller's skill and judgment to select suitable goods.

    a. A particular purpose of the buyer differs from the ordinary purpose for which goods are used. Goods can be merchantable but unfit for a buyer's particular purpose.

5. **Warranty of Title and against Infringement**. Unless agreed otherwise, sellers warrant that they have good and valid title to the goods sold and that transfer of title is good and rightful. Additionally, sellers generally represent that there are no liens or encumbrances against the title of which buyer is unaware at the time of contracting.

6. **Disclaimer of Warranties**. The UCC makes it difficult to disclaim warranties.

    a. For all practical purposes, it is impossible for a seller to disclaim an express warranty.

        1) An express warranty and a disclaimer are construed as consistent with each other, if it is reasonable to do so.

        2) If not, the disclaimer is ineffective.

    b. Implied warranties of both merchantability and fitness for a particular purpose may be disclaimed by the use of certain language, such as "as is," "with all faults" or other such commonly accepted expressions which call to the buyer's attention that there is risk associated with the purchase.

    c. Unless the goods were purchased as is or the like, the warranty of merchantability can be disclaimed or modified by specific mention of the word merchantability.

        1) One may orally disclaim the warranty of merchantability.

        2) However, if the disclaimer is part of a written contract, it must be stated conspicuously in the writing.

    d. Unless disclaimed by use of the words "as is," or very similar language, the warranty of fitness for a particular purpose cannot be excluded except in writing. Again, the disclaimer must be a conspicuous part of the writing.

        1) A written statement such as "There are no warranties which extend beyond the description on the face hereof" is sufficient to exclude implied warranties of fitness for a particular purpose.

    e. The warranty of title may only be disclaimed by specific language or by the buyer's knowledge of circumstances relating to title.

        1) It may be disclaimed orally or in writing.

    f. Even where all of the UCC requirements for language and form of disclaimer have been met, a court may refuse to enforce a disclaimer on the grounds that it is an unconscionable attempt to avoid the seller's fundamental obligations of "good faith, diligence, reasonableness and care."

        1) A court may even find that the enforcement of a disclaimer is unconscionable especially in a consumer transaction.

7. **Beneficiaries of a Warranty**. Some states allow third parties to a sales contract to recover for breach of express or implied warranties. Examples are

    a. Any natural person who is in the buyer's household or who is a guest in the buyer's home

    b. Any natural person who may reasonably be expected to use, consume, or be affected by the goods and who is injured in person by breach of the warranty

    c. A person described in b., except that it is sufficient that property damage occurs. (S)he need not have been injured physically.

8. Stop and review! You have completed the outline for this subunit. Study multiple-choice questions 10 through 17 beginning on page 522.

C. **Products liability** is a doctrine in the law of torts that holds a manufacturer or seller of a product liable if a defective product is placed into the market and causes injury. The liability may be based on negligence or on a warranty, or it may be strict liability.

1. The law of products liability allows users who are injured through no fault of their own and because of the fault with a product to recover from the manufacturer of the product or defective component, the wholesaler, or the retailer.

2. Products liability losses are direct and indirect (consequential).

3. **Negligence.** To recover under a negligence theory, one must prove duty, breach, causation, and harm.

   a. The standard of care applied to products liability claims is that the manufacturer, processor, or seller has a duty to use the care, skill, and diligence with respect to the product that a reasonably careful, skillful, and prudent manufacturer, etc., would use in the same or similar circumstances.

   b. The four principal ways in which a manufacturer/seller can be liable in products liability under a negligence theory are

      1) Negligent design
      2) Manufacturing flaw (a condition not intended)
      3) Failure to inspect
      4) Failure to warn

   c. Wholesalers and retailers have a responsibility to inspect for defects if they have reason to believe a product is likely to be defective, e.g., many complaints or a broken seal.

   d. Defenses to products liability claims include the following:

      1) Contributory negligence (unforeseeable misuse or substantial alteration of the product)

      2) Assumption of the risk

   e. Contributory negligence means the plaintiff did not act reasonably to protect him/herself from the loss.

      1) In some states it is an absolute defense.

      2) Other states apply comparative negligence rules; loss is borne in relationship to the relative fault of the parties.

   f. Remember, the manufacturer or distributor is liable under the theory of negligence only if it fails to exercise reasonable care under the circumstances. Absolute perfection is not required.

4. **Warranties** establish the characteristics of a product which the purchaser or other person is entitled to and relies on.

   a. Generally, a plaintiff is entitled to damages upon proof that

      1) An express or implied warranty exists.
      2) The product does not conform to the warranty.
      3) The plaintiff suffered harm as a result of the breach of warranty.

   NOTE: It is not necessary to prove that the manufacturer/seller was at fault.

b.   This cause of action in tort is in addition to any cause of action for breach of warranty under the UCC. Recovery for losses which result from a breach of warranty may be extended in a products liability suit to a party who would be denied recovery under the UCC. The types of damages recoverable may also vary.

   1)   A requirement for privity of contract generally does not restrict the right to sue.

      a)   Family, household, guests, and other persons who may reasonably be expected to use or consume the goods may have a cause of action.

   2)   Economic losses may be recovered, unless effectively disclaimed.

5.   **Strict Liability**. If negligence cannot be proven and the manufacturer/seller has not breached a warranty, an injured plaintiff may rely on a theory of strict liability to recover for injuries due to a defective product.

   a.   A **defective product** is one that does not meet reasonable expectations as to its safety.

   b.   There are two basic types of defects covered by strict liability: manufacturing defects and design defects.

   c.   No negligence or fraud need be proven.

   d.   A manufacturer is strictly liable in tort when an article he places on the market, knowing that it is to be used without inspection for defects, proves to have a defect that causes injury to a human being.

   e.   A seller is strictly liable in tort to a plaintiff who proves each of the following:

      1)   The seller was in the business of selling the product.

      2)   The product was defective.

      3)   The defect rendered it unreasonably dangerous.

      4)   The unreasonably dangerous condition caused physical harm or property damage.

      5)   The product reached the user or consumer without substantial change from the condition in which it was sold.

6.   Stop and review! You have completed the outline for this subunit. Study multiple-choice questions 18 through 21 beginning on page 525.

D.   **Risk of Loss**. The parties to a sales contract may agree between themselves which one is to bear the risk of loss or how it will be shared. Where the parties are silent as to risk, the UCC assigns it by means of practical rules that place the risk on the party most likely to control and insure the goods, or most able to prevent the loss.

1.   Generally, in the absence of breach of contract, if the seller is a merchant, risk of loss passes to buyer only upon his/her taking physical possession of the goods.

2.   If the seller is a nonmerchant, risk of loss passes to the buyer upon tender of delivery.

3.   Thus, which party bears the risk of loss is not determined by who has title to the goods.

4.   In **destination contracts**, the risk of loss passes to the buyer when the goods have reached the destination and are tendered to the buyer.

5. In **shipment contracts**, the risk of loss passes to the buyer when the seller delivers the goods to the carrier.

6. If goods are held by a warehouser or other bailee and are not to be shipped or moved as a part of the contract, risk passes to the buyer upon occurrence of any one of the following:

   a. The buyer's receipt of a negotiable document of title covering the goods

   b. An acknowledgment by the bailee of the buyer's right to the goods

   c. The lapse of a reasonable time for buyer to notify bailee of buyer's right in the goods after the buyer's receipt of a nonnegotiable document of title or other written direction requesting the bailee to deliver the goods

7. If goods are defective (nonconforming) to such an extent that the buyer has a right to reject them, the risk of loss does not pass to the buyer until

   a. The defects are cured, or
   b. The buyer accepts the goods despite the defects.

8. If the buyer rightfully revokes acceptance, the risk of loss is treated as having rested on the seller from the inception of the contract in an amount equal to the extent of any deficiency in buyer's insurance coverage.

   a. EXAMPLE: Boat Co. accepts delivery of a shipment of life vests from Suncrafters. Boat Co. discovers a hidden defect in the life vests and rightfully revokes acceptance. After notifying Suncrafters, and while awaiting instructions from them, and without any fault of Boat Co., the life vests were destroyed. Boat Co.'s insurance covers only 30% ($30,000) of the fair market value of the life vests ($100,000). Suncrafters bears the remaining loss of $70,000.

9. If the seller has identified conforming goods to the contract and the buyer repudiates or otherwise breaches the contract before the risk of loss has passed to the buyer, any loss occurring within a commercially reasonable time after seller learns of the breach falls on the buyer to the extent of any deficiency in the seller's insurance coverage.

   a. EXAMPLE: Buyer orders 5,000 small electric motors from Manufacturer under a destination contract. After manufacture and delivery to a carrier, Buyer repudiates before the goods have been tendered. Carrier delivers the goods to a warehouse per Manufacturer's instructions, where they are damaged by fire. Buyer is liable to the extent that Manufacturer's insurance is inadequate to cover the loss.

10. In a sale on approval, the risk of loss does not pass to the buyer until (s)he accepts.

    a. In a sale on approval, the buyer takes the goods to use and may return them even if they conform to the contract.

    b. Acceptance may occur by failure to return or failure to notify the seller of an intention to return the goods within the required time.

    c. If the buyer decides not to take the goods, return is at the seller's risk.

11. A sale or return contract is treated as an ordinary sale.

    a. The buyer is taking the goods to resell them but may return those which remain unsold.

    b. If the goods are returned, the buyer bears the risk of loss while they are in transit.

12. Stop and review! You have completed the outline for this subunit. Study multiple-choice questions 22 through 31 beginning on page 526.

E.   Performance and Obligations

1.   **Identification**. Before title to goods can pass from seller to buyer, the goods must exist and they must be identified to the contract.

   a.   Identification is designation of specific goods as the subject matter of the contract.

      1)   Usually, it is by specific designation.

   b.   The parties may agree upon the time and manner in which **existing goods** become identified to the contract. Absent explicit agreement, the time of identification is determined by the following rules:

      1)   Identification occurs at the time the contract is made if the contract is for specific, ascertainable, existing goods, e.g., a car.

      2)   If parties agree to buy and sell **growing crops**, identification occurs as soon as the crop is planted if it is to be harvested within the later of 12 months or the next normal harvest season after entering into the contract.

         a)   EXAMPLE: A field of wheat is planted in May 1998, and on July 28, 1998, Roger contracts to sell all the wheat harvested from the field this coming fall. Identification occurred when the contract was made.

      3)   **Unborn animals**. Identification takes place as soon as the young are conceived if birth will occur within 12 months after the contract is made.

      4)   When the contract is for **future goods**, identification occurs only when the goods are in some way designated or particularized by the seller or the buyer.

         a)   Future goods are goods that are not yet both existing and identified.

         b)   Designation may be by shipment, marking, or any other action sufficient to show the goods to which the contract refers.

         c)   Note that a purported present sale of future goods is treated not as a sale, but as a contract to sell.

      5)   **Fungible goods** are goods of which any one unit is the equivalent of any other unit by reason of their nature or commercial usage. Such goods are interchangeable or capable of substitution by nature or agreement.

         a)   Identification occurs as soon as the contract is made, unless the parties agree otherwise.

         b)   As long as the mass from which the goods are to be taken is identified at the time the contract is made, the contract is for specific rather than future goods even though the goods contracted for have not yet been segregated from the mass.

            i)   EXAMPLE: Harry contracts to sell 5,000 gallons of fuel to Gull Airways from his 1 million gallon storage tank. The exact quantity of fuel in the tank is unknown to both parties.

2.   **Insurable Interest**. A person has an insurable interest in the subject matter insured (such as goods) if (s)he will derive economic benefit or advantage from its preservation, or will suffer economic loss or damage from its destruction. A buyer has an insurable interest in identified goods even if (s)he neither has title nor bears the risk of loss. An insurable interest is a requirement for formation of an enforceable insurance contract.

   a.   The seller has an insurable interest in goods as long as (s)he retains either title to the goods or any security interest in the goods.

      b.   A buyer or seller or both may also have an insurable interest if it is recognized under any other statute or rule of law.

      c.   In property insurance, the insurable interest must exist at the time the property is damaged or destroyed.

3.   **Passage of Title**. Title to goods passes from the seller to the buyer in any manner and on any conditions explicitly agreed to by the parties.

      a.   Unless otherwise explicitly agreed to, title passes to the buyer at the time and place at which the seller completes performance of physical delivery of the goods as determined under the contract and the UCC, despite any reservation of a security Interest and even if a document of title is to be delivered at a different time or place.

      b.   If the contract requires the seller to deliver the goods to a certain destination, title passes when delivery is tendered at that specific destination.

      c.   Under a shipment contract, title passes when the goods are delivered to the carrier.

      d.   Unless the contract clearly indicates that it is a destination contract, a court will regard it as a shipment contract.

      e.   When delivery is to be made without moving the goods, e.g., when a bailee has possession, the following rules apply unless the parties explicitly agree otherwise:

          1)   If the seller is to deliver a document of title, title passes at the time when and the place where (s)he delivers such documents.

          2)   If the goods are already identified at the time of contracting and no documents are to be delivered, title passes at the time and place of contracting.

      f.   Conditional sales contracts often state that title shall remain in the seller until the buyer completes payment of all installments.

          1)   Reservation of a security interest has no effect on the passing of title.

      g.   A rejection or other refusal by the buyer to receive or retain the goods, whether or not justified, or a justified revocation of acceptance, revests title to the goods in the seller. Such revesting occurs by operation of law and is not a sale.

4.   **Bulk Transfers**. When a merchant sells all or a substantial portion of a business's assets in a single transaction not in the ordinary course of business, the buyer must satisfy certain requirements to acquire title to the goods and be free of all claims by the seller's creditors. If the requirements are not met,

      a.   The buyer is liable to the seller's creditors for monetary damages for 1 year.

      b.   Goods in the possession of the buyer continue to be subject to the claims of unpaid creditors of the seller for 6 months.

      c.   The goal is to prevent a merchant from defrauding creditors.

      d.   Among other requirements, the buyer must give notice of the proposed bulk transfer to each of the seller's creditors at least 10 days before the buyer takes possession of the goods or makes payment for them, whichever occurs first.

      e.   A subsequent purchaser for value who takes the goods from the buyer in good faith and without notice of noncompliance takes the goods free of title defect.

          1)   The buyer may remain personally liable for the value of the goods transferred subject to creditor claims even after disposition of the goods.

f.   The buyer's liability is limited to each creditor's claim reduced by any amount that creditor could not have collected even if the buyer had complied.

NOTE: Recently revised Article 6 includes the following changes:

1)   Limits applicability to sellers whose principal business is the sale of inventory from stock

2)   Excludes sales of less than $10,000 or greater than $25 million on the date of sale

3)   Provides that a sale in bulk constitutes more than half of the seller's inventory by value on the date of sale

4)   Increases the notice period to creditors of the seller from 10 to 45 days

5. **Sales by Nonowners**. Generally, a person cannot transfer better title than (s)he has.

a.   If the seller is a thief, the seller's title is void. Thus, the buyer acquires no title, and the real owner can reclaim the goods from the buyer.

b.   A seller has voidable title if the goods that (s)he is selling were obtained by fraud.

1)   A voidable title becomes valid when the goods are sold to a good-faith purchaser.

c.   Any entrusting of goods to a merchant who deals in goods of that kind gives the merchant power to transfer all rights of the entruster to a buyer in the ordinary course of business.

1)   Entrustment includes delivering the goods to the merchant or leaving purchased goods for later delivery.

6. **Seller's Obligations**. Once the parties have contracted, the seller is obligated to transfer and deliver the goods, and the buyer is obligated to accept and pay the price in accordance with the contract.

a.   A tender is an unconditional offer to perform coupled with a present ability to do so. If unjustifiably refused, the refusing party is in default, and the tendering party has remedies for breach of contract.

7. **The Perfect Tender Rule**. If the goods or the seller's tender of delivery fails in any respect to conform to the contract, the buyer may reject the goods or the tender.

a.   This rule is subject to the seller's rights, e.g., the right to cure.

b.   In noncarrier situations, the seller must put and hold conforming goods at the buyer's disposition for a time sufficient for the buyer to take possession.

1)   The tender must be at a reasonable hour.

2)   The seller must give notice to enable the buyer to take possession.

3)   Apart from agreement otherwise, the place of delivery is the seller's place of business or, if (s)he has none, his/her residence.

a)   If, at the time of contracting, the goods are known by both parties to be at some other place, that place is the place of delivery.

c.   If the parties intend for a carrier to move the goods, the seller is required to

1)   Place the goods into the care of the designated (or a reasonable) carrier and make a reasonable contract for their transportation to the buyer,

2)   Obtain and tender any documents required either under the terms of the contract or by usage of trade or otherwise necessary to enable the buyer to take possession, and

3) Promptly notify the buyer of the shipment.

d. **Shipment contract**. In a shipment contract, the seller is required to send the goods by carrier (but is not required to deliver to a particular destination). To fully perform, the seller must put the goods in the possession of the carrier, make a reasonable contract for their transportation, provide the buyer with any document necessary for the buyer to take possession of the goods from the carrier, and notify the buyer of the shipment.

e. **Destination contract**. In a destination contract, a seller has agreed to ensure that the goods are duly tendered to the buyer at a specified destination. The seller must, at the destination, put and hold conforming goods at the buyer's disposition. (S)he must give the buyer any reasonably necessary notice of tender and provide the buyer with any documents of title necessary to obtain delivery.

f. If the contract specifies that the goods, price, or delivery is **FOB** a particular point, the tender of delivery must be made at FOB point.

　1) The most common shipping term is FOB (free on board).

　　a) When a contract states, "delivery to be FOB the place of shipment," it is a shipment contract.

　　b) When a contract states, "delivery to be FOB the place of destination," it is a destination contract.

　2) Unless otherwise agreed, when a term of a contract is **FOB city of destination**, the seller must at his/her own risk and expense transport the goods to the named city and tender delivery there.

　3) Likewise, when a term of a contract is **FOB city of origin**, the seller must at his/her own risk and expense transport the goods merely to the carrier and not to the city of destination.

　4) **FAS vessel** (free alongside the vessel) denotes a shipment contract that requires the seller to deliver the goods alongside the vessel.

　5) **CIF** (cost-insurance-freight) indicates a shipment contract under which the seller must put goods in the carrier's possession, load the goods, and pay the cost of freight and insurance to the point of destination.

　　a) Risk of loss passes to the buyer on shipment.

　6) **C&F** or **CF** imposes like obligations, except that the seller need not purchase insurance.

　　a) Risk of loss passes on shipment.

　7) **Delivery ex-ship** (from the carrying vessel) means that risk of loss does not pass to the buyer until the goods leave the ship or are otherwise properly unloaded.

8. **Buyer's Duties**. When the seller has properly tendered conforming goods, the buyer is obliged to accept them and to pay the price. However, the buyer's obligations are conditional on the right to inspect the goods.

a. In the absence of an agreement to the contrary, the buyer must

　1) Furnish facilities reasonably suited for receipt of the goods.

　2) Make payment at the time and place the buyer receives the goods, even if the place of shipment is the place of delivery.

b. Acceptance of goods by the buyer precludes the buyer from exercising the right of rejection.

NOTE: Under proper circumstances, a buyer may revoke acceptance.

1) The buyer can manifest assent to the delivered goods in three ways, each of which constitutes acceptance.

a) The buyer can expressly accept the shipment by words or conduct.

b) Acceptance is presumed if the buyer has had a reasonable opportunity to inspect the goods and has failed to reject them within a reasonable period of time.

c) The buyer accepts the goods by performing any act inconsistent with the rights of the true owner (seller). Examples might include

i) Reselling of the goods (prior to rejection)
ii) Using them, other than for testing a sample or other inspection
iii) Commingling fungible goods with other goods
iv) Altering the goods
v) Incorporating them into another product

NOTE: Remember, rejection is available to the buyer for any defect, unless the perfect tender rule does not apply.

c. The legal effect of acceptance is that the buyer becomes obligated to pay the contract price.

NOTE: A buyer who accepts a defective tender is barred from receiving any remedy, unless the seller is notified of the defect within a reasonable time after it has been or should have been discovered.

d. Unless otherwise provided, in noncarrier cases, a sale is for cash and the price is due at tender.

e. In transactions in which there is no express provision as to payment or the contract specifies cash, and the contract is one for shipment by carrier, the seller may ship the goods under reservation. If so, the buyer will be unable to obtain the goods from the carrier unless and until (s)he pays.

f. Tender of payment by check is sufficient unless the seller demands legal tender (currency) and gives the buyer a reasonable amount of time to obtain the requested cash.

1) When a payment is made by check, payment is not final until the check is paid upon presentment to the proper bank (conditional payment).

2) If the check is not paid, the seller may recover the goods from the buyer if the seller makes effort to do so with reasonable diligence.

g. The buyer may make reasonable inspection of the goods unless the contract provides otherwise.

1) Unless otherwise agreed, the buyer's right to inspect the goods is absolute.

2) Generally, the right to inspect may be exercised prior to payment or acceptance.

3) However, if the contract between the parties provides for payment C.O.D. (collect on delivery) or against documents of title, or otherwise indicates that the buyer has promised to pay without inspecting the goods, there is no right of inspection prior to payment.

a) This is ordinarily the case with shipment contracts; e.g., the contract contains a CIF or C&F term.

4)   If payment is due before inspection, the fact that the goods are defective does not excuse nonpayment, unless the defect appears without inspection or there is fraud in the transaction.

   a)   EXAMPLE: Buyer in New Mexico and Seller in Florida contract for the sale of a supercomputer to be shipped to New Mexico. Nothing is said as to payment. Seller may ship the goods under reservation, but Buyer has a right to inspect the goods before payment. If the contract provides for payment against order bill of lading, Buyer must pay when the bank or other seller's agent in New Mexico notifies him that the bill of lading is ready. Buyer is required to pay first and inspect later.

9.   **Excused Nonperformance**. The UCC adopts commercial impracticability as the basis for excusing nonperformance. Performance must be rendered impracticable by an unforeseen supervening event not within the contemplation of the parties at the time of contracting. The tests for a finding of impracticability are

   a.   An unexpected circumstance must arise subsequent to formation of the contract.

   b.   The risk of the unexpected occurrence must not already have been allocated by the parties or by custom in the marketplace.

   c.   The consequence of this unexpected and unallocated contingency must have rendered performance commercially impracticable. Thus, hardship or increase in costs alone is not sufficient. Objectively, current circumstances must be such that no one could reasonably perform the contract.

      1)   EXAMPLE: An unforeseen international embargo cuts off Seller's supply. If an alternative supply is available at a cost which will merely render performance unprofitable, commercial impracticability will not excuse nonperformance.

   d.   If commercial impracticability partially impairs the seller's ability to perform, the seller must allocate production and deliveries among his/her customers in a fair and reasonable manner.

      1)   The seller must seasonally (within a reasonable time) notify the buyer that there will be a delay or nondelivery.

      2)   If there is merely partial impairment, the seller must inform the buyer of any quota to which the buyer is entitled.

      3)   In response, the buyer may inform the seller that (s)he will

         a)   Discharge any unperformed portion of the contract, or
         b)   Modify the contract by agreeing to take the available quota.

   e.   Courts are reluctant to discharge a contracting party on the basis of commercial impracticability unless the unforeseen circumstance is truly beyond the contemplation of the parties and the loss so great as to lie beyond the reasonable expectations of both parties.

10.   **Substitute Performance**. The UCC provides that, when neither party is at fault and the agreed-upon manner of delivery of the goods becomes commercially impracticable due to failure of loading or unloading facilities or the unavailability of an acceptable carrier, a substituted manner of performance must be tendered and accepted if commercially reasonable.

11.   Stop and review! You have completed the outline for this subunit. Study multiple-choice questions 32 through 41 beginning on page 530.

F.   Remedies and Defenses. The objective in awarding a remedy is neither to penalize the breaching party nor to enrich the nonbreaching party. Under the UCC, the law attempts to place the aggrieved party in approximately the same position (s)he would have been in had the breaching party properly performed under the contract.

1.   **Breach**. The seller breaches by any of the following:

    a.   Repudiating (renouncing) all or part of the contract
    b.   Failing to deliver
    c.   Failing to deliver conforming goods

2.   **Buyer**. The buyer's right is to inspect the goods at any reasonable time and place, and in any reasonable manner, either prior to or subsequent to delivery.

    a.   "Reasonableness" is determined by trade usage, past practices between the parties, and other circumstances of the transaction.

    b.   If the buyer fails to inspect the goods within a reasonable time after receipt, (s)he loses his/her right to inspect.

    c.   All expenses of inspection are borne by the buyer. But if the goods are rejected for nonconformance, the cost of inspection can be recovered from the seller.

3.   **Rejection of Nonconforming Goods**. When goods are tendered which do not conform exactly to the contract (not a perfect tender), the buyer may either keep them and sue for damages or reject them and either cancel the contract or sue for damages under the contract.

    a.   Rejection must be at a reasonable time after delivery or tender and before acceptance.

    b.   The buyer's right to reject nonconforming goods is subject to the seller's right to cure (remedy) the nonconformity.

4.   **Revocation of Acceptance**. A buyer who accepts goods and later discovers that they are nonconforming may revoke acceptance, but only if they are substantially nonconforming; i.e., the nonconformity substantially impairs the value of the goods to the buyer.

NOTE: Revocation of acceptance requires greater nonconformity than lack of a perfect tender.

5.   **Cover**. A buyer who rightfully rejects nonconforming goods or justifiably revokes acceptance has a right to cover.

    a.   To cover means to purchase substitute goods in the marketplace.

    b.   Cover is not mandatory. The buyer may choose between cover and damages.

    c.   Cover is not a remedy which is limited to merchants.

    d.   So long as the buyer acts reasonably and in good faith, the buyer may recover from the seller any excess of the cover price over the contract price, less any savings on expenses, as well as damages.

6.   **Damages**. Buyer's basic remedy when (s)he rejects or justifiably revokes acceptance or when the seller fails to deliver goods is the right to sue for monetary damages.

    a.   Typically, damages are any difference between contract price and market price.

        1)   Market price is the market price of the goods at the place of tender at the time the buyer learns of the breach.

    b.   The buyer may choose to measure damages by the difference between contract price and the amount (s)he actually must pay for replacement goods (cover).

    c.   The buyer is also entitled to incidental damages, e.g., expenses reasonably incurred in inspection, receipt, transportation, care, and custody of goods rightfully rejected and other such expenses reasonably related to the breach.

    d.   The buyer may be entitled to consequential damages (e.g., lost profits) if the seller knew or had reason to know, at the time of contracting, of the buyer's general or particular needs.

7.   **Recover Goods from Insolvent Seller**. A buyer may recover goods from an insolvent seller if

    a.   The goods have been identified to the contract,

    b.   The seller became insolvent within 10 days of receipt of the first installment of the price, and

    c.   Tender of any unpaid portion of the price is made and kept open.

8.   **Specific Performance**. If the goods are unique and monetary damages are not an adequate remedy, a court may order specific performance of the sales contract.

    a.   Under the UCC, specific performance is available whenever the subject matter of the sales contract is unique and "in other proper circumstances."

    b.   Thus, a buyer can seek specific performance of the sale of unique goods, such as antiques.

    c.   Specific performance is not available to a seller.

9.   **Seller**. The buyer's basic duty is to accept and pay for goods in accordance with the terms of the sales contract. When a buyer defaults, the seller has been deprived of that for which (s)he bargained. The UCC provides a variety of seller's remedies.

10. **Withhold Delivery of Goods**. A seller may withhold or discontinue performance when the buyer

    a.   Is insolvent
    b.   Fails to make a payment due on or before delivery
    c.   Wrongfully rejects goods
    d.   Wrongfully revokes acceptance
    e.   Repudiates the contract

NOTE: A seller who withholds goods or completes unfinished goods is entitled to damages whether or not (s)he resells.

11. **Identify and Resell Goods**. If a buyer breaches or repudiates a sales contract while the seller is still in possession of the goods, the seller can identify to the contract the conforming goods that are still in his/her possession or control. The seller can do so even if the goods were not identified at the time of the breach.

    a.   The seller can then resell the goods, holding the buyer liable for any loss.
    b.   When the goods contracted for are unfinished at the time of breach, the seller can

        1)   Cease manufacture of the goods at once and resell them for scrap or salvage value, or

        2)   Complete manufacture, identify the goods to the contract, and resell them, holding the buyer liable for any deficiency.

           a)   The seller must exercise reasonable commercial judgment in order to mitigate the loss and obtain maximum value for the unfinished goods. Thus, if finishing the goods would materially increase the seller's damages, finishing them would not be commercially reasonable.

12. **Recover Goods in Transit**. The seller may stop delivery of goods in the possession of a carrier or other bailee when (s)he discovers the buyer to be insolvent.

13. **Recover Goods from Insolvent Buyer**. When a seller discovers that the buyer has received goods on credit and is insolvent, (s)he may recover the goods upon demand made within 10 days after the buyer's receipt of the goods.

    a. The seller can demand and reclaim the goods at any time, i.e., without a 10-day limit, if a misrepresentation of solvency was made in writing to the seller within 3 months prior to the delivery of the goods.

    b. The seller's right to reclaim is subject to the rights of a good-faith purchaser for value or other buyer in the ordinary course of business who purchases the goods from the buyer before the seller demands recovery.

14. When a seller possesses or controls the goods at the time of the buyer's breach or duly reacquires the goods in transit, the seller has the right to resell the goods.

    a. The resale must be in good faith and in a commercially reasonable manner.

    b. The seller can recover any deficiency between sales price and the contract price, plus incidental damages, but less any savings.

        1) **Incidental damages** are those damages resulting to the seller from the breach.

    c. Perishable goods must be sold as rapidly as possible in order to mitigate damages.

    d. A good-faith purchaser in a resale takes the goods free of any rights of the original buyer.

15. **Recover Price plus Incidental Damages**. Under the UCC, an unpaid seller can bring an action to recover the purchase price plus incidental damages, but only under specific circumstances.

    a. The buyer has accepted the goods and has not revoked acceptance,

    b. Conforming goods have been lost or damaged after the risk of loss passed to the buyer, or

    c. The buyer has breached after the goods have been identified to the contract and the seller is unable to resell the goods.

        1) If a seller sues for the contract price of goods that (s)he has been unable to resell, the goods must be held for the buyer.

        2) The seller can resell at any time prior to collection, but the net proceeds from the sale must be credited to the buyer.

16. **Recover Damages for Buyer's Wrongful Repudiation**. When the buyer's breach consists of nonacceptance or repudiation, the seller may resell the goods but is not required to.

    a. The seller has the option to seek damages equal to the difference between the market price of the goods at the time and place of tender and the unpaid contract price.

        1) The seller may also recover any incidental damages.

    b. If the difference between the contract price and the market price is too small to place the seller in the same position (s)he would have been in had the buyer fully performed, the proper measure of damages is the seller's lost profits, including a reasonable allowance for overhead and other incidental expenses.

17. **Cancel Sales Contract**. A seller can cancel a contract if the buyer wrongfully rejects or revokes acceptance of conforming goods duly delivered, fails to make proper payment, or repudiates the contract in whole or in part.

   a. The buyer is not discharged. (S)he is considered to be in breach.

   b. If seller's cancellation is not justified, the seller is in breach of the contract, and buyer can sue for appropriate damages.

18. **Buyer or Seller**. Notwithstanding the specific buyer's remedies and seller's remedies discussed previously, Article 2 also sets forth remedies available to both buyer and seller.

19. **Right to Demand Assurances**. If a party has a reasonable basis for believing that performance will not be tendered, (s)he may in writing demand adequate assurance of performance. Until (s)he receives such assurance, (s)he may suspend further performance, if suspension is commercially reasonable.

   a. If the proper assurances are not provided within a reasonable period (not over 30 days), the party seeking assurance can treat the contract as repudiated.

   b. Just what constitutes an adequate assurance depends on the facts.

      1) EXAMPLE: Seller hears a rumor, in fact false, that Buyer is experiencing severe financial difficulty. Seller reasonably believes that the rumor is well founded. Seller is justified in making a demand for assurances and withholding any goods for which (s)he has not been paid. Buyer, within 1 week, sends a certified financial statement showing good financial condition. The certified financial statement is adequate assurance, and Seller must resume performance.

20. **Anticipatory Repudiation**

   a. When either party, through words, actions, or circumstances, repudiates the contract with respect to a performance not yet due, the aggrieved party may

      1) Await performance for a commercially reasonable time,

      2) Resort to any remedy for breach even though (s)he has also urged the other party to perform (e.g., the aggrieved party may sue at once), or

      3) Suspend his/her own performance.

   b. The repudiating party's words, actions, or conduct must make it unequivocally clear that (s)he is unwilling or unable to perform.

   c. A repudiating party may, at any time before his/her next performance is due, retract his/her repudiation unless the other party has

      1) Canceled
      2) Materially changed his/her position in reliance on the repudiation
      3) Otherwise indicated that (s)he considers the repudiation final

21. **Contractual Modifications**. The parties to a contract for the sale of goods may limit the remedies available to either buyer or seller, or may provide for an exclusive remedy for either or neither party.

   a. Substantial freedom of contract is permitted, but any remedy contracted for must not be unconscionable or fail to accomplish its essential purpose.

22. **Liquidated Damages**. The parties to a sales contract may stipulate an amount in the contract that the parties agree to be a reasonable estimation of the damages owing to one in the event of a breach by the other. The UCC permits such a clause provided it is reasonable in light of the anticipated losses, the difficulties of proof of loss, and the inconvenience of otherwise obtaining a remedy.

   a. To be enforceable, the liquidated damages amount must constitute a reasonable forecast of the damages likely to result from the breach.

      1) Usually, the liquidated damages provision establishes a ceiling on the defaulting party's liability.

   b. If the liquidated damages provision is an effort to deter breach as opposed to a good-faith effort to estimate probable damages, the provision will be deemed to be a penalty and will be declared void.

      1) If a liquidated damages clause has been deemed void, recovery will be limited to actual damages proved, if any.

   c. If a seller has properly withheld delivery of goods, the buyer may receive a refund of monies paid minus any liquidated damages agreed on. If no liquidated damages have been provided for, the seller may retain 20% of the value of the total contract price or $500, whichever is less (UCC 2-718).

   d. The buyer's right of restitution is subject to offset to the extent the seller establishes either a right to damages other than liquidated damages or an amount of benefits received by the buyer directly or indirectly under the contract.

23. **Statute of Limitations**. With the exception for breach of warranty, the UCC provides that one party to a contract for the sale of goods may sue another party for breach only if the legal action is started within 4 years after such breach.

   a. The parties may reduce the period, but not to less than 1 year.
   b. The parties may not extend the period.

24. **Rescission**. Fraud in the formation renders a contract voidable by the innocent party.

   a. A party who rescinds must return the consideration received from the other party.
   b. But rescission does not bar a claim for damages or any other remedy.
   c. The common-law elements of fraud must be present.

25. Stop and review! You have completed the outline for this subunit. Study multiple-choice questions 42 through 52 beginning on page 533.

MULTIPLE-CHOICE QUESTIONS

A. Contracts Covering Goods

1. Under the UCC Sales Article, which of the following statements is correct concerning a contract involving a merchant seller and a nonmerchant buyer?

A. Whether the UCC Sales Article is applicable does not depend on the price of the goods involved.

B. Only the seller is obligated to perform the contract in good faith.

C. The contract will be either a sale or return or a sale on approval contract.

D. The contract may not involve the sale of personal property with a price of more than $500.

The correct answer is (A). *(CPA, adapted)*
REQUIRED: The correct statement about a contract between a merchant seller and a nonmerchant buyer.
DISCUSSION: Article 2 of the UCC applies to transactions in goods. Goods are things movable other than the money in which the price is to be paid, investment securities, and things in action. Applicability of Article 2 does not depend on the dollar amount involved. Article 2 applies to both merchants and nonmerchants, but special rules are provided for certain aspects of transactions between or with merchants.
Answer (B) is incorrect because both seller and buyer must perform a contract under Article 2 in good faith. Answer (C) is incorrect because these are not the most common kinds of contracts by a merchant seller governed by the UCC. Answer (D) is incorrect because applicability of Article 2 does not depend on the dollar amount involved.

2. Under the Sales Article of the UCC, which of the following statements is correct?

A. The obligations of the parties to the contract must be performed in good faith.

B. Merchants and nonmerchants are treated alike.

C. The contract must involve the sale of goods for a price of more than $500.

D. None of the provisions of the UCC may be disclaimed by agreement.

The correct answer is (A). *(CPA, adapted)*
REQUIRED: The true statement about Article 2.
DISCUSSION: The obligations of good faith, diligence, reasonableness, and care provided by the UCC may not be disclaimed by agreement, but the parties may agree to determine the standards by which the performance of these obligations is measured if they are "not manifestly unreasonable" (UCC 1-102).
Answer (B) is incorrect because the UCC often sets different (and higher) standards for merchants. Answer (C) is incorrect because all contracts for the sale of goods are subject to the provisions of Article 2. Answer (D) is incorrect because provisions of the UCC may be disclaimed by agreement of the parties, except as otherwise provided by the UCC.

3. Which of the following statements would not apply to a written contract governed by the provisions of the UCC Sales Article?

A. The contract may involve the sale of personal property.

B. The obligations of a nonmerchant may be different from those of a merchant.

C. The obligations of the parties must be performed in good faith.

D. The contract must involve the sale of goods for a price of $500 or more.

The correct answer is (D). *(CPA, adapted)*
REQUIRED: The statement which does not apply to a contract governed by UCC Article 2.
DISCUSSION: Article 2 of the UCC applies to sales of goods. An oral contract for the sale of goods for more than $500 is unenforceable absent a writing. However, a dollar amount is not required to bring a sale of goods within Article 2.
Answer (A) is incorrect because Article 2 concerns sales of goods. Goods are things movable, and include many, but not all, types of personal property. Answer (B) is incorrect because special rules are provided for certain aspects of transactions between or with merchants. Answer (C) is incorrect because the UCC imposes an obligation of good faith in the formation and performance of every sales contract.

4. On May 2, Lace Corp., an appliance wholesaler, offered to sell appliances worth $3,000 to Parco, Inc., a household appliances retailer. The offer was signed by Lace's president and provided that it would not be withdrawn before June 1. On May 29, Parco mailed an acceptance of Lace's offer. Lace received the acceptance June 2. Which of the following statements is correct if Lace sent Parco a telegram revoking its offer, and Parco received the telegram on May 25?

- A. A contract was formed on May 2.

- B. Lace's revocation effectively terminated its offer on May 25.

- C. Lace's revocation was ineffective because the offer could not be revoked before June 1.

- D. No contract was formed because Lace received Parco's acceptance after June 1.

The correct answer is (C). *(CPA, adapted)*
   REQUIRED: The correct statement concerning an offer stating that it would not be withdrawn before a stated date.
   DISCUSSION: A firm offer is an assurance, in writing and signed by a merchant, that the offer will remain open. A firm offer remains open during the time stated, even if it is not supported by consideration. If no time is stated, the time is a reasonable time. But in no event may the period of irrevocability exceed 3 months.
   Answer (A) is incorrect because acceptance is prerequisite to contract formation. Answer (B) is incorrect because no consideration is necessary to support a firm offer irrevocable by the seller. Answer (D) is incorrect because acceptance is generally effective on dispatch.

5. Cookie Co. offered to sell Distrib Markets 20,000 pounds of cookies at $1.00 per pound, subject to certain specified terms for delivery. Distrib replied in writing as follows:

> "We accept your offer for 20,000 pounds of cookies at $1.00 per pound, weighing scale to have valid city certificate."

Under the UCC,

- A. A contract was formed between the parties.

- B. A contract will be formed only if Cookie agrees to the weighing scale requirement.

- C. No contract was formed because Distrib included the weighing scale requirement in its reply.

- D. No contract was formed because Distrib's reply was a counteroffer.

The correct answer is (A). *(CPA, adapted)*
   REQUIRED: The effect of a merchant adding a term in an unconditional acceptance.
   DISCUSSION: Additional or different terms in an unconditional, definite, and seasonable acceptance of an offer for a sale of goods are construed as proposals for addition to the contract. But between merchants such terms become part of the contract unless the offer expressly limits acceptance to its terms, the additional or different terms materially alter the offer, or the offeree objects within a reasonable time. Cookie and Distrib are most likely merchants, the acceptance was unconditional, and no exception applies. Hence, the weighing scale term becomes part of the agreement unless objected to in a reasonable time. (If the parties are not merchants, a contract is formed without the additional term.)
   Answers (B), (C), and (D) are incorrect because an additional term in an unconditional acceptance of an offer for a sale of goods does not constitute a rejection and counter-offer. Thus, a contract was formed regardless of whether either of the parties is a merchant.

6. Under the UCC Sales Article, which of the following conditions will prevent the formation of an enforceable sale of goods contract?

- A. Open price.

- B. Open delivery.

- C. Open quantity.

- D. Open acceptance.

The correct answer is (D). *(CPA, adapted)*
   REQUIRED: The condition that will prevent the formation of an enforceable sale of goods contract.
   DISCUSSION: The UCC favors open terms. One or more terms left open does not prevent the formation of a contract if it appears the parties intended to make a contract and there is a reasonably certain basis for granting a remedy. An offer is deemed to invite acceptance in any manner and by any medium reasonable under the circum-stances. However, the term "open acceptance" is not used by the UCC Sales Article. Also, prior to acceptance no contract can be formed.
   Answers (A) and (B) are incorrect because each is an example of open terms that do not prevent formation of a contract and for which the Code itself provides a gap filler. Answer (C) is incorrect because, if the quantity term is left open, a court may have no basis to grant a remedy, and thus a contract may not have been formed. However, circumstances may remedy this defect. For example, a requirement or output term in a contract may provide a reasonably certain basis for a remedy.

7. On May 2, Mason orally contracted with Acme Appliances to buy for $480 a washer and dryer for household use. Mason and the Acme salesperson agreed that delivery would be made on July 2. On May 5, Mason telephoned Acme and requested that the delivery date be moved to June 2. The Acme salesperson agreed to this request. On June 2, Acme failed to deliver the washer and dryer to Mason because of an inventory shortage. Acme advised Mason that it would deliver the appliances on July 2 as originally agreed. Mason believes that Acme has breached its agreement with Mason. Acme contends that its agreement to deliver on June 2 was not binding. Acme's contention is

A. Correct, because Mason is not a merchant and was buying the appliances for household use.

B. Correct, because the agreement to change the delivery date was not in writing.

C. Incorrect, because the agreement to change the delivery date was binding.

D. Incorrect, because Acme's agreement to change the delivery date is a firm offer that cannot be withdrawn by Acme.

The correct answer is (C). *(CPA, adapted)*
REQUIRED: The legal status of an oral modification without consideration.
DISCUSSION: An oral enforceable contract for the sale of goods was formed on May 2 because the price was not for $500 or more. An oral modification of a contract for the sale of goods does not require consideration to be binding. The modification need not be in writing provided that 1) the contract as modified is for less than $500, 2) the original contract did not require that modification be in writing, 3) the modification was sought in good faith, or 4) another exception does not apply.
Answer (A) is incorrect because status of one or both parties as a merchant does not affect whether a contract for the sale of goods or its modification must be in writing, provided the price is less than $500. Answer (B) is incorrect because an oral modification of a contract for the sale of goods is generally enforceable provided the price is less than $500. Answer (D) is incorrect because Acme's "agreement" was an acceptance of an offer to modify the contract formed on May 2.

8. Under the Sales Article of the UCC, a firm offer will be created only if the

A. Offer states the time period during which it will remain open.

B. Offer is made by a merchant in a signed writing.

C. Offeree gives some form of consideration.

D. Offeree is a merchant.

The correct answer is (B). *(CPA, adapted)*
REQUIRED: The condition for a firm offer under the UCC.
DISCUSSION: A firm offer is an assurance, in writing and signed by a merchant, that the offer will remain open. A firm offer remains open during the time stated, even if it is not supported by consideration. If no time is stated, the time is a reasonable time. But in no event may the period of irrevocability exceed 3 months.
Answer (A) is incorrect because a firm offer remains open for a reasonable time if no time is stated. Answer (C) is incorrect because no consideration is needed to support a firm offer. Answer (D) is incorrect because the offeror must be a merchant.

9. Under the Sales Article of the UCC, when a written offer has been made without specifying a means of acceptance but providing that the offer will remain open only for ten days, which of the following statements represent(s) a valid acceptance of the offer?

I. An acceptance sent by regular mail the day before the 10-day period expires that reaches the offeror on the eleventh day

II. An acceptance faxed the day before the 10-day period expires that reaches the offeror on the eleventh day, due to a malfunction of the offeror's printer

A. I only.

B. II only.

C. Both I and II.

D. Neither I nor II.

The correct answer is (C). *(CPA, adapted)*
REQUIRED: The statement(s), if any, representing a valid acceptance.
DISCUSSION: Under the UCC, an offer is deemed to invite acceptance in any manner and by any medium reasonable in the circumstances, unless otherwise indicated by language or circumstances. Assuming a mailed or faxed acceptance is reasonable in the circumstances, it is effective upon dispatch. Hence, each method resulted in a valid acceptance because dispatch occurred before expiration of the 10-day period.
Answers (A), (B), and (D) are incorrect because each statement describes a valid acceptance.

B. Warranties

10. Which of the following factors result(s) in an express warranty with respect to a sale of goods?

I. The seller's description of the goods as part of the basis of the bargain

II. The seller's selection of goods knowing the buyer's intended use

    A. I only.

    B. II only.

    C. Both I and II.

    D. Neither I nor II.

The correct answer is (A). *(CPA, adapted)*

REQUIRED: The factor which results in an express warranty.

DISCUSSION: An express warranty results if any affirmation of fact or promise made by the seller to the buyer that relates to the goods (by any description of the goods or by any sample or model) becomes part of the basis of the bargain (UCC 2-313). Note that reliance by the buyer need not be shown.

Answers (B) and (C) are incorrect because this may be relevant to an implied warranty of fitness for a particular purpose, but not to whether an express warranty was made. Answer (D) is incorrect because a seller's description is an affirmation of fact which, if it is part of the basis of the bargain, constitutes an express warranty.

11. Under the Sales Article of the UCC, most goods sold by merchants are covered by certain warranties. An example of an express warranty would be a warranty of

    A. Usage of trade.

    B. Fitness for a particular purpose.

    C. Merchantability.

    D. Conformity of goods to sample.

The correct answer is (D). *(CPA, adapted)*

REQUIRED: The example of an express warranty by a merchant in a sale of goods transaction.

DISCUSSION: Under UCC Article 2, any affirmation of fact or promise made by a seller to the buyer that 1) relates to the goods and 2) becomes part of the basis of the bargain creates an express warranty that the goods delivered will conform to the affirmation or promise. In addition to explicit verbal statements of fact or promises relating to the goods, express warranties may also be created by description, model, or sample. A sample that is made part of the basis of the bargain creates an express warranty that the goods will conform to the sample.

Answers (A), (B), and (C) are incorrect because each is an example of an implied warranty arising from operation of law rather than expressed contractual intent.

12. Under the Sales Article of the UCC, which of the following statements is correct regarding the warranty of merchantability arising when there has been a sale of goods by a merchant seller?

    A. The warranty must be in writing.

    B. The warranty arises when the buyer relies on the seller's skill in selecting the goods purchased.

    C. The warranty cannot be disclaimed.

    D. The warranty arises as a matter of law when the seller ordinarily sells the goods purchased.

The correct answer is (D). *(CPA, adapted)*

REQUIRED: The true statement about the warranty of merchantability.

DISCUSSION: In a sale of goods by a merchant who ordinarily sells goods of that kind, the UCC imposes an implied warranty of merchantability requiring that the goods be fit for the ordinary purposes for which they are used. The goods must also pass without objection in the trade under the contract description; be of fair average quality within the description (if fungible); run of even kind, quality, and quantity within and among the units involved; be adequately contained, packaged, and labeled; and conform to the promises of fact made on any container or label (UCC 2-314).

Answer (A) is incorrect because this warranty is implied. Answer (B) is incorrect because the warranty arising when the buyer relies on the seller's skill in selecting the goods is the implied warranty of fitness for a particular purpose. Answer (C) is incorrect because the warranty of merchantability may be excluded or modified by language that mentions merchantability.

13. Which of the following conditions must be met for an implied warranty of fitness for a particular purpose to arise in connection with a sale of goods?

I. The warranty must be in writing.

II. The seller must know that the buyer was relying on the seller in selecting the goods.

    A. I only.

    B. II only.

    C. Both I and II.

    D. Neither I nor II.

The correct answer is (B). *(CPA, adapted)*
    REQUIRED: The requirement for a warranty of fitness to be implied.
    DISCUSSION: Under UCC 2-315, a warranty of fitness for a particular purpose is implied (unless excluded or modified) when the seller has reason to know the particular purpose for which the goods will be used and that the buyer is relying on the seller's skill or judgment to choose the goods.
    Answers (A) and (C) are incorrect because no writing is necessary to a warranty implied by operation of law. Answer (D) is incorrect because the warranty of fitness is implied when the seller has reason to know the buyer's particular purpose for the goods and the buyer is relying on the seller's skill or judgment to choose the goods.

14. Under the Sales Article of the UCC, the warranty of title

    A. Provides that the seller cannot disclaim the warranty if the sale is made to a bona fide purchaser for value.

    B. Provides that the seller deliver the goods free from any lien of which the buyer lacked knowledge when the contract was made.

    C. Applies only if it is in writing and signed by the seller.

    D. Applies only if the seller is a merchant.

The correct answer is (B). *(CPA, adapted)*
    REQUIRED: The true statement about the warranty of title.
    DISCUSSION: Every contract for the sale of goods warrants that the title is good, its transfer is rightful, and the goods are free of encumbrances not known to the buyer. The warranty of title can be excluded or modified only by specific language or by circumstances giving the buyer reason to know that the transferor has no title or a limited title.
    Answer (A) is incorrect because the seller may disclaim the warranty by specific language to any buyer. Answer (C) is incorrect because a warranty of title can be made orally. Answer (D) is incorrect because a warranty of title is a part of every contract for the sale of goods and can be made by a nonmerchant.

15. Under the UCC Sales Article, the implied warranty of merchantability

    A. May be disclaimed by a seller's oral statement that mentions merchantability

    B. Arises only in contracts involving a merchant seller and a merchant buyer.

    C. Is breached if the goods are not fit for all purposes for which the buyer intends to use the goods.

    D. Must be part of the basis of the bargain to be binding on the seller.

The correct answer is (A). *(CPA, adapted)*
    REQUIRED: The correct statement about the implied warranty of merchantability.
    DISCUSSION: Unless the circumstances indicate otherwise, all implied warranties are excluded by expressions like "as is," "with all faults," or other language that in common understanding calls the buyer's attention to the exclusion of warranties and makes plain that there is no implied warranty. With certain exceptions, "to exclude or modify the implied warranty of merchantability or any part of it, the language must mention merchantability and in case of a writing must be conspicuous. To exclude or modify any implied warranty of fitness, the exclusion must be by a writing and conspicuous" (UCC 2-316). A disclaimer of the implied warranty of merchantability may be oral. Moreover, the UCC does not require a buyer to sign a disclosure.
    Answer (B) is incorrect because the buyer need not be a merchant. Answer (C) is incorrect because the standard is the ordinary purposes for which such goods are used. Answer (D) is incorrect because this is necessary to an express, but not an implied, warranty.

Questions 16 and 17 are based on the following information. On May 2, Handy Hardware sent Ram Industries a signed purchase order that stated, in part, as follows: "Ship for May 8 delivery 300 Model A-X socket sets at current dealer price. Terms 2/10/net 30." Ram received Handy's purchase order on May 4. On May 5, Ram discovered that it had only 200 Model A-X socket sets and 100 Model W-Z socket sets in stock. Ram shipped the Model A-X and Model W-Z sets to Handy without any explanation concerning the shipment. The socket sets were received by Handy on May 8.

16. Which of the following statements concerning the shipment is correct?

   A. Ram's shipment is an acceptance of Handy's offer.

   B. Ram's shipment is a counteroffer.

   C. Handy's order must be accepted by Ram in writing before Ram ships the socket sets.

   D. Handy's order can be accepted only by Ram's shipping conforming goods.

The correct answer is (A). *(CPA, adapted)*
REQUIRED: The correct statement concerning shipment under the signed purchase order.
DISCUSSION: Unless otherwise unambiguously indicated by the language or circumstances, an order to buy goods for prompt or current shipment invites acceptance either by a prompt promise to ship or by prompt shipment (UCC 2-206). If the offer clearly requires shipment as the method of acceptance (it does not here), a promise to ship is not a valid acceptance.
Answer (B) is incorrect because shipment of nonconforming goods is both an acceptance and a breach, unless the seller notifies the buyer within a reasonable time that the shipment is offered only as an accommodation. Answer (C) is incorrect because an order to buy goods for prompt or current shipment invites acceptance either by a prompt promise to ship or by prompt shipment. Answer (D) is incorrect because acceptance may also be by a prompt promise to ship.

17. Assuming a contract exists between Handy and Ram, which of the following implied warranties would result?

  I. Implied warranty of merchantability

  II. Implied warranty of fitness for a particular purpose

  III. Implied warranty of title

   A. I only.

   B. III only.

   C. I and III only.

   D. I, II, and III.

The correct answer is (C). *(CPA, adapted)*
REQUIRED: The warranty or warranties implied in a contract formed by shipment under a signed purchase order.
DISCUSSION: A warranty of title is implied in every contract for the sale of goods, unless the parties agree otherwise. The warranty of merchantability is implied only when the seller is a merchant. Ram is a merchant because it deals in goods of the kind sold. The implied warranty of fitness for a particular purpose arises only when a seller has reason to know the particular purpose for which the goods are to be used and that the buyer is relying on the seller's skill and judgment to select the goods.
Answer (A) is incorrect because, absent contrary agreement, the warranty of title is implied in every contract for the sale of goods. Answer (B) is incorrect because the seller is a merchant. Thus, a warranty of merchantability is also implied. Answer (D) is incorrect because the seller did not know the particular purpose for which the goods were to be used.

C. Products Liability

18. Which of the following factors is least important in determining whether a manufacturer is strictly liable in tort for a defective product?

- A. The negligence of the manufacturer.
- B. The contributory negligence of the plaintiff.
- C. Modifications to the product by the wholesaler.
- D. Injuries resulting from the defect of the product.

The correct answer is (A). *(CPA, adapted)*
REQUIRED: The least important factor in determining whether a manufacturer is strictly liable in tort.
DISCUSSION: In an action based on strict liability in tort for a defective product, the plaintiff need not prove that a breach of a legal duty to exercise reasonable care proximately caused the plaintiff's injury. Rather, in a strict liability suit against a seller of a product, a plaintiff who has suffered physical harm or property damage must prove that the product was defective, the defect rendered it unreasonably dangerous, the unreasonably dangerous condition of the product caused the harm or damage, the seller was in the business of selling the product, and the product reached the user or consumer without substantial change from the condition in which it was sold.
Answer (B) is incorrect because whether the plaintiff acted reasonably to protect him/herself may be a factor in the outcome of the suit. Thus, contributory negligence has been accepted as an absolute defense in at least a few states, and many states have adopted comparative fault or comparative negligence rules. Answer (C) is incorrect because substantial alteration of the product after its sale by the manufacturer may be a defense if the change caused the plaintiff's injury. Answer (D) is incorrect because plaintiff must prove that physical harm was caused to the ultimate user or consumer or to his/her property as a result of a defective condition of the product that made it unreasonably dangerous.

19. High sues the manufacturer, wholesaler, and retailer for bodily injuries caused by a power saw High had purchased. Which of the following statements is correct under strict liability theory?

- A. Contributory negligence on High's part will always be a bar to recovery.
- B. The manufacturer will avoid liability if it can show it followed the custom of the industry.
- C. Privity will be a bar to recovery insofar as the wholesaler is concerned if the wholesaler did not have a reasonable opportunity to inspect.
- D. High may recover even if (s)he cannot show any negligence was involved.

The correct answer is (D). *(CPA, adapted)*
REQUIRED: The true statement about strict liability.
DISCUSSION: In a strict liability suit against a seller of a product, a plaintiff who has suffered physical harm or property damage must prove the product was defective, the defect rendered it unreasonably dangerous, the dangerous condition caused the harm, the seller was engaged in the business of selling the product, and the product reached the user without substantial change from the condition in which it was sold. Negligence is not required to be proven by the plaintiff.
Answer (A) is incorrect because contributory negligence is not an absolute defense in most states. However, the plaintiff's negligence may reduce the recovery in comparative fault jurisdictions. Answer (B) is incorrect because custom of the industry is irrelevant to strict liability. Answer (C) is incorrect because privity is not required. Any reasonably foreseeable plaintiff may sue. Moreover, strict liability is imposed regardless of the degree of care that a defendant exercised or was able to exercise.

20. To establish a cause of action based on strict liability in tort for personal injuries that result from the use of a defective product, one of the elements the injured party must prove is that the seller

- A. Was aware of the defect in the product.
- B. Sold the product to the injured party.
- C. Failed to exercise due care.
- D. Sold the product in a defective condition.

The correct answer is (D). *(CPA, adapted)*
   REQUIRED: The element of an action based on strict liability in tort.
   DISCUSSION: In a strict liability suit against a seller of a product, a plaintiff who has suffered physical harm or property damage must prove the product was defective, the defect rendered it unreasonably dangerous, the dangerous condition caused the harm, the seller was engaged in the business of selling the product, and the product reached the user without substantial change from the condition in which it was sold. Negligence is not required to be proven by the plaintiff.
   Answers (A), (B), and (C) are incorrect because the seller need not have been aware of the defect, sold the product to the injured party (privity is not required), or failed to exercise due care.

21. Larch Corp. manufactured and sold Oak a stove. The sale documents included a disclaimer of warranty for personal injury. The stove was defective. It exploded, causing serious injuries to Oak's spouse. Larch was notified one week after the explosion. Under the UCC Sales Article, which of the following statements concerning Larch's liability for personal injury to Oak's spouse would be correct?

- A. Larch cannot be liable because of a lack of privity with Oak's spouse.
- B. Larch will not be liable because of a failure to give proper notice.
- C. Larch will be liable because the disclaimer was not a disclaimer of all liability.
- D. Larch will be liable because liability for personal injury cannot be disclaimed.

The correct answer is (D). *(CPA, adapted)*
   REQUIRED: The correct statement concerning liability for personal injury under the UCC Sales Article.
   DISCUSSION: The UCC warranty provisions were not intended to enlarge or restrict legal remedies for personal injuries (a developing area of the law). Strict liability for an unreasonably dangerous product may be viewed as the implied warranty of merchantability stripped of the contract defenses of notice of defect, privity, and disclaimer. Thus, strict liability for personal injury caused by a defective product cannot be disclaimed.
   Answer (A) is incorrect because the most restrictive option under the UCC allows a member of the purchaser's family to sue for physical injury. Answer (B) is incorrect because Oak gave reasonable notice by informing Larch of the injury within 1 week of its occurrence. Answer (C) is incorrect because, even if a disclaimer of the warranty of merchantability met all technical requirements, disclaimer of liability for personal injury is presumed unconscionable. Furthermore, as discussed above, strict liability for personal injury caused by a defective product cannot be disclaimed.

D. Risk of Loss

22. Under the Sales Article of the UCC, which of the following factors is most important in determining who bears the risk of loss in a sale of goods contract?

- A. The method of shipping the goods.
- B. The contract's shipping terms.
- C. Title to the goods.
- D. The manner in which the goods were lost.

The correct answer is (B). *(CPA, adapted)*
   REQUIRED: The most important factor in determining who has the risk of loss.
   DISCUSSION: The sale of goods agreement as to risk of loss may be express or implicit from trade usage, course of dealing, or course of performance. If the parties do not have an agreement about risk of loss but a carrier is involved, the shipping terms control. In a destination contract, risk of loss passes to the buyer when the goods have reached the destination and are tendered to the buyer. In a shipment contract, risk of loss passes to the buyer when the seller delivers the goods to the carrier.
   Answer (A) is incorrect because the type of carrier is irrelevant. Answer (C) is incorrect because the UCC never assigns risk of loss based on the location of the title. Answer (D) is incorrect because the manner in which the goods were lost by the carrier is irrelevant.

23. Under the Sales Article of the UCC, which of the following events will result in the risk of loss passing from a merchant seller to a buyer?

	Tender of the Goods at the Seller's Place of Business	Use of the Seller's Truck to Deliver the Goods
A.	Yes	Yes
B.	Yes	No
C.	No	Yes
D.	No	No

24. Bond purchased a painting from Wool, who is not in the business of selling art. Wool tendered delivery of the painting after receiving payment in full from Bond. Bond informed Wool that Bond would be unable to take possession of the painting until later that day. Thieves stole the painting before Bond returned. The risk of loss

- A. Passed to Bond on Wool's tender of delivery.
- B. Passed to Bond at the time the contract was formed and payment was made.
- C. Remained with Wool because the parties agreed on a later time of delivery.
- D. Remained with Wool because Bond had not yet received the painting.

25. Quick Corp. agreed to purchase 200 typewriters from Union Suppliers, Inc. Union is a wholesaler of appliances, and Quick is an appliance retailer. The contract required Union to ship the typewriters to Quick by common carrier, "F.O.B. Union Suppliers, Inc. Loading Dock." Which of the parties bears the risk of loss during shipment?

- A. Union, because the risk of loss passes only when Quick receives the typewriters.
- B. Union, because both parties are merchants.
- C. Quick, because title to the typewriters passed to Quick at the time of shipment.
- D. Quick, because the risk of loss passes when the typewriters are delivered to the carrier.

The correct answer is (D). *(CPA, adapted)*
REQUIRED: The time when risk of loss passes from a merchant seller to a buyer.
DISCUSSION: If the parties have no agreement about risk of loss, no carrier is involved, and the goods are not in the possession of a bailee, the risk of loss passes from a merchant seller to the buyer upon his/her receipt of the goods (UCC 2-509).
Answers (A), (B), and (C) are incorrect because tender of the goods at the seller's place of business or use of the seller's truck to deliver the goods does not pass the risk of loss to the buyer. Since the seller is a merchant, risk of loss passes when the buyer takes actual physical possession of the goods.

The correct answer is (A). *(CPA, adapted)*
REQUIRED: The correct statement about risk of loss given that the seller was not a merchant.
DISCUSSION: If the parties have no agreement as to risk of loss, no carrier is involved, and the goods are not in the possession of a bailee, the risk of loss passes to the buyer on his/her receipt of the goods if the seller is a merchant; otherwise, the risk passes to the buyer on tender of delivery. Because Wool is not a merchant (a person engaged in selling goods of the kind), risk passed to Bond on tender of delivery.
Answers (B) and (C) are incorrect because, generally, risk of loss passes to the buyer on his/her receipt of the goods if the seller is a merchant; otherwise, the risk passes to the buyer on tender of delivery. Answer (D) is incorrect because Wool is not a merchant.

The correct answer is (D). *(CPA, adapted)*
REQUIRED: The party who bears the risk of loss when goods are shipped F.O.B. the seller's loading dock.
DISCUSSION: F.O.B. means the seller bears both the risk and the expense of getting the goods to the point named. If the shipping term is F.O.B. place of shipment, the seller has the risk and expense of getting the goods to the carrier. Expenses and risk after delivery to the carrier are borne by the buyer in a shipment contract. Accordingly, absent a contrary agreement, the buyer bears the risk of loss during shipment. Thus, the risk of loss passed when the typewriters were delivered to the carrier.
Answer (A) is incorrect because the risk of loss passes under an F.O.B. shipping point contract when the goods are delivered to the carrier. Answer (B) is incorrect because, if the seller is a nonmerchant, risk of loss passes to the buyer of tender on delivery. However, if the seller is a merchant, risk of loss passes on delivery to the carrier under an F.O.B. contract. Answer (C) is incorrect because when title passes does not determine who bears the risk of loss.

26. Under the Sales Article of the UCC and the United Nations Convention for the International Sale of Goods (CISG), absent specific terms in an international sales shipment contract, when will risk of loss pass to the buyer?

- A. When the goods are delivered to the first carrier for transmission to the buyer.

- B. When the goods are tendered to the buyer.

- C. When the execution of the contract is concluded.

- D. When the goods are identified to the contract.

The correct answer is (A). *(CPA, adapted)*
   REQUIRED: The point at which risk of loss will pass to the buyer.
   DISCUSSION: The CISG is similar to Article 2 of the UCC. Under Article 2 and the CISG, title to goods passes from the seller to the buyer in any manner and on any conditions explicitly agreed to by the parties. Under a shipment contract, title passes when the goods are delivered to the carrier. Unless the contract clearly indicates that it is a destination contract, a court will regard it as a shipment contract (UCC 2-308).
   Answers (B), (C), and (D) are incorrect because, unless otherwise indicated, a sales contract is assumed to be a shipment contract under which title passes when the goods are delivered to the carrier.

27. On Monday, Wolfe paid Aston Co., a furniture retailer, $500 for a table. On Thursday, Aston notified Wolfe that the table was ready to be picked up. On Saturday, while Aston was still in possession of the table, it was destroyed in a fire. Who bears the loss of the table?

- A. Wolfe, because Wolfe had title to the table at the time of loss.

- B. Aston, unless Wolfe is a merchant.

- C. Wolfe, unless Aston breached the contract.

- D. Aston, because Wolfe had not yet taken possession of the table.

The correct answer is (D). *(CPA, adapted)*
   REQUIRED: The true statement about risk of loss given that the seller was a merchant.
   DISCUSSION: If the parties have no agreement as to risk of loss, no carrier is involved, and the goods are not in the possession of a bailee, "the risk of loss passes to the buyer on his/her receipt of the goods if the seller is a merchant; otherwise, the risk passes to the buyer on tender of delivery" (UCC 2-509). Because Aston is a merchant (a person engaged in selling goods of the kind), risk did not pass to Wolfe on tender of delivery.
   Answer (A) is incorrect because the UCC never assigns risk of loss to goods on the basis of title. Answer (B) is incorrect because it is the seller's status that is relevant. Answer (C) is incorrect because risk of loss would not have passed prior to receipt by Wolfe.

28. Lazur Corp. agreed to purchase 100 radios from Home Suppliers, Inc. Home is a wholesaler of small home appliances, and Lazur is an appliance retailer. The contract required Home to ship the radios to Lazur by common carrier, "F.O.B. Home Suppliers, Inc. Loading Dock." Risk of loss for the radios during shipment to Lazur would be on

- A. Lazur, because the risk of loss passes when the radios are delivered to the carrier.

- B. Home, because the risk of loss passes only when Lazur receives the radios.

- C. Home, because it is a shipment contract.

- D. Lazur, because title to the radios passes to Lazur at the time of shipment.

The correct answer is (A). *(CPA, adapted)*
   REQUIRED: The parties' rights under a shipment contract if goods are damaged in transit.
   DISCUSSION: FOB means the seller bears both the risk and the expense of getting the goods to the point named. If the shipping term is FOB place of shipment, the seller has the risk and expense of getting the goods to the carrier. Expenses and risk after delivery to the carrier are borne by the buyer in a shipment contract. Accordingly, absent a contrary agreement, Lazur (the buyer) bears the risk of loss, but it may be able to recover from the carrier or a third party.
   Answers (B) and (C) are incorrect because expenses and risk after delivery to the carrier are borne by the buyer in a shipment contract. Answer (D) is incorrect because, under the UCC, the location of title does not determine risk of loss.

29. If goods have been delivered to a buyer pursuant to a sale or return contract, the

- A. Buyer may use the goods but not resell them.

- B. Seller is liable for the expenses incurred by the buyer in returning the goods to the seller.

- C. Title to the goods remains with the seller.

- D. Risk of loss for the goods passed to the buyer.

The correct answer is (D). *(CPA, adapted)*
REQUIRED: The effect of delivery to a buyer under a sale or return contract.
DISCUSSION: If goods are delivered to a person for sale and that person keeps a place of business at which (s)he deals in goods of that kind, the goods will be deemed to be on "sale or return." Risk of loss in a sale or return passes at the same time and place as in any other sale of goods, i.e., in accordance with the shipping terms. Except for a sale on approval, delivery and receipt of the goods will customarily signify that risk of loss has passed to the buyer.
Answer (A) is incorrect because, under a sale or return arrangement, delivery is for resale. Answer (B) is incorrect because the return is at the buyer's risk and expense. Answer (C) is incorrect because, barring a contrary agreement, title passes when the seller completes performance regarding the physical delivery of the goods.

30. Which of the following statements applies to a sale on approval under the UCC Sales Article?

- A. Both the buyer and seller must be merchants.

- B. The buyer must be purchasing the goods for resale.

- C. Risk of loss for the goods passes to the buyer when the goods are accepted after the trial period.

- D. Title to the goods passes to the buyer on delivery of the goods to the buyer.

The correct answer is (C). *(CPA, adapted)*
REQUIRED: The correct statement about a sale on approval.
DISCUSSION: A sale is on approval if the goods are delivered to the buyer with an understanding that (s)he may test them for the purpose of determining if (s)he wishes to purchase them, and (s)he may return them without breaching the contract even though they conform to the contract. In a sale on approval, title and risk of loss do not pass to the buyer until acceptance. Acceptance may be express or implied, e.g., by not returning the goods in a reasonable period.
Answer (A) is incorrect because, in a normal sale on approval, the goods are primarily for the use of the buyer. If the goods are delivered primarily for resale, the transaction is a sale or return, and risk of loss and title pass to the buyer in accordance with the particular delivery situation. Answer (B) is incorrect because the buyer is normally acquiring the goods for his/her own use. Answer (D) is incorrect because, in a sale on approval, title and risk of loss do not pass to the buyer until acceptance.

31. Cey Corp. entered into a contract to sell parts to Deck, Ltd. The contract provided that the goods would be shipped "F.O.B. Cey's warehouse." Cey shipped parts different from those specified in the contract. Deck rejected the parts. A few hours after Deck informed Cey that the parts were rejected, they were destroyed by fire in Deck's warehouse. Cey believed that the parts were conforming to the contract. Which of the following statements is correct?

- A. Regardless of whether the parts were conforming, Deck will bear the loss because the contract was a shipment contract.

- B. If the parts were nonconforming, Deck had the right to reject them, but the risk of loss remains with Deck until Cey takes possession of the parts.

- C. If the parts were conforming, risk of loss does not pass to Deck until a reasonable period of time after they are delivered to Deck.

- D. If the parts were nonconforming, Cey will bear the risk of loss, even though the contract was a shipment contract.

The correct answer is (D). *(CPA, adapted)*
REQUIRED: The party bearing the risk of loss when nonconforming goods are shipped and then destroyed while in the buyer's possession.
DISCUSSION: If the contract does not cover risk, the most significant factor in determining who has the risk of loss is whether a breach has occurred. If a tender or delivery of goods is so nonconforming as to give a right of rejection, the risk of loss remains on the seller until cure or acceptance. The breaching party therefore has the risk of loss. Even if seller's shipment of nonconforming goods is an accommodation, it is a breach. The result is the same for either a shipment contract or a destination contract.
Answer (A) is incorrect because the result is the same for either a shipment contract or a destination contract. Answer (B) is incorrect because, if a tender or delivery of goods is so nonconforming as to give a right of rejection, the risk of loss remains on the seller until cure or acceptance. Answer (C) is incorrect because the buyer would have had the risk of loss in a shipment contract under which conforming goods had been delivered to the carrier.

E. Performance and Obligations

32. Under the Sales Article of the UCC, unless a contract provides otherwise, before title to goods can pass from a seller to a buyer, the goods must be

A. Tendered to the buyer.

B. Identified to the contract.

C. Accepted by the buyer.

D. Paid for.

The correct answer is (B). *(CPA, adapted)*
REQUIRED: The prerequisite for passage of title to goods.
DISCUSSION: In every contract for the sale of goods, a seller has a duty to pass title to the buyer in exchange for the price. UCC Article 2 provides that an express or explicit understanding between the buyer and the seller will determine when title passes. Before title can pass, two conditions must be satisfied: 1) The goods must be in existence, and 2) they must be identified to the contract. Identification is the method for designating the specific goods as the subject matter of the sales contract and, importantly, marks the point at which the buyer obtains an insurable interest. Goods not existing and identified are governed by Article 2 as a contract to sell future goods.
Answers (A), (C), and (D) are incorrect because the UCC has divorced the question of title from the various rights and obligations of the buyers and sellers such as tender of delivery, acceptance, or payment.

33. Webstar Corp. orally agreed to sell Northco, Inc. a computer for $20,000. Northco sent a signed purchase order to Webstar confirming the agreement. Webstar received the purchase order and did not respond. Webstar refused to deliver the computer to Northco, claiming that the purchase order did not satisfy the UCC Statute of Frauds because it was not signed by Webstar. Northco sells computers to the general public and Webstar is a computer wholesaler. Under the UCC Sales Article, Webstar's position is

A. Incorrect because it failed to object to Northco's purchase order.

B. Incorrect because only the buyer in a sale-of-goods transaction must sign the contract.

C. Correct because it was the party against whom enforcement of the contract is being sought.

D. Correct because the purchase price of the computer exceeded $500.

The correct answer is (A). *(CPA, adapted)*
REQUIRED: The enforceability of the oral contract when only the plaintiff signed a written confirmation.
DISCUSSION: In contracts for the sale of goods between merchants, if one party, within a reasonable time after an oral understanding has been reached, sends a written confirmation that binds the sender, it will satisfy the statute of frauds unless the recipient objects to the confirmation's content within 10 days of receipt.
Answer (B) is incorrect because the agreement was between merchants, and the written confirmation was signed by the party sending it. Answer (C) is incorrect because the writing must generally be signed by the party to be charged. Answer (D) is incorrect because, although a contract for the sale of goods in excess of $500 must generally be in writing, the written confirmation between merchants satisfies the statute of frauds.

34. Razor Corp. agreed to purchase 100 mixers from Home Suppliers, Inc. Home is a wholesaler of small home appliances, and Razor is an appliance retailer. The contract required Home to ship the mixers to Razor by common carrier, "F.O.B. Home Suppliers, Inc. Loading Dock." Under the UCC Sales Article

A. Title to the mixers passes to Razor at the time they are delivered to the carrier, even if the goods are nonconforming.

B. Razor must inspect the mixers at the time of delivery or waive any defects and the right to sue for breach of contract.

C. Home must pay the freight expense associated with the shipment of the mixers to Razor.

D. Razor would have the right to reject any shipment if Home fails to notify Razor that the goods have been shipped.

The correct answer is (A). *(CPA, adapted)*
REQUIRED: The correct statement concerning a contract for the sale of goods.
DISCUSSION: Unless otherwise explicitly agreed to, title passes to the buyer when the seller completes performance of physical delivery of the goods. An FOB place of shipment statement means the contract is a shipment contract. The seller's performance obligation is to physically deliver the goods to the place of shipment. If the buyer rejects, with or without justification, title reverts to the seller by operation of law.
Answer (B) is incorrect because a buyer who fails to inspect the goods within a reasonable time after delivery loses the right to inspect. Answer (C) is incorrect because FOB place of shipment indicates a shipment contract. The seller must, at his/her own risk and expense, transport the goods to the carrier. Answer (D) is incorrect because the buyer's right is to reject nonconforming goods, whether or not the seller provides notice of shipment.

35. On May 2, Lace Corp., an appliance wholesaler, offered to sell appliances worth $3,000 to Parco, Inc., a household appliances retailer. The offer was signed by Lace's president, and provided that it would not be withdrawn before June 1. It also included the shipping terms: "FOB -- Parco's warehouse." Parco accepted Lace's offer. If Lace inadvertently ships the wrong appliances to Parco and Parco rejects them 2 days after receipt, title to the goods will

A. Pass to Parco when they are identified to the contract.

B. Pass to Parco when they are shipped.

C. Remain with Parco until the goods are returned to Lace.

D. Revert to Lace when they are rejected by Parco.

The correct answer is (D). *(CPA, adapted)*
REQUIRED: The correct statement about passage of title when a seller ships nonconforming goods.
DISCUSSION: A rejection or other refusal by the buyer to receive or retain the goods, whether or not justified, or a justified revocation of acceptance, revests title to the goods in the seller. Such revesting occurs by operation of law.
Answers (A) and (B) are incorrect because title passes when the contract is formed if there are documents of title or, if there are none, when the seller completes its delivery obligation (in this case by putting and holding the goods at the warehouse). Answer (C) is incorrect because title did pass, but it reverted to the seller upon rejection.

36. Under the Sales Article of the UCC, which of the following events will release the buyer from all its obligations under a sales contract?

A. Destruction of the goods after risk of loss passed to the buyer.

B. Impracticability of delivery under the terms of the contract.

C. Anticipatory repudiation by the buyer that is retracted before the seller cancels the contract.

D. Refusal of the seller to give written assurance of performance when reasonably demanded by the buyer.

The correct answer is (D). *(CPA, adapted)*
REQUIRED: The event that releases the buyer from obligations under a sales contract.
DISCUSSION: If the buyer has reasonable grounds to believe performance may not occur, the buyer may in writing demand adequate assurance of performance. The seller's failure to provide adequate assurance within a reasonable time, not to exceed 30 days, is a repudiation of the contract that releases the buyer from its obligations.
Answer (A) is incorrect because, once the risk of loss passes to the buyer, destruction of the goods does not relieve the buyer of its responsibilities. Answer (B) is incorrect because delivery must be rendered commercially impracticable by unforeseen events in order for the seller or the buyer to be relieved from performing the contract. Courts are reluctant to release a party under this excuse unless the circumstances are extreme and unforeseeable. Answer (C) is incorrect because an anticipatory repudiation by the buyer, regardless of the seller's response, does not excuse the buyer's performance. The seller may still resort to remedies for breach of contract.

37. Smith contracted in writing to sell Peters a used personal computer for $600. The contract did not specifically address the time for payment, place of delivery, or Peters's right to inspect the computer. Which of the following statements is correct?

A. Smith is obligated to deliver the computer to Peters's home.

B. Peters is entitled to inspect the computer before paying for it.

C. Peters may not pay for the computer using a personal check unless Smith agrees.

D. Smith is not entitled to payment until 30 days after Peters receives the computer.

The correct answer is (B). *(CPA, adapted)*
REQUIRED: The correct statement about a contract with terms left open.
DISCUSSION: A contract for the sale of goods is enforceable if missing terms can be supplied. The buyer has a right to inspect the goods before payment unless contract terms waive the right, e.g., a C.O.D. or a documentary sale.
Answer (A) is incorrect because, unless otherwise agreed, tender is generally due at the seller's place of business. Answer (C) is incorrect because tender of payment by check is sufficient unless the seller demands legal tender (currency) and gives the buyer a reasonable amount of time to obtain it. Answer (D) is incorrect because, unless otherwise agreed, the price is due upon tender of delivery.

38. Rowe Corp. purchased goods from Stair Co. that were shipped C.O.D. Under the Sales Article of the UCC, which of the following rights does Rowe have?

- A. The right to inspect the goods before paying.
- B. The right to possession of the goods before paying.
- C. The right to reject nonconforming goods.
- D. The right to delay payment for a reasonable period of time.

The correct answer is (C). *(CPA, adapted)*
    REQUIRED: The right of a buyer of goods shipped COD.
    DISCUSSION: The seller has an obligation to deliver goods that conform to the contract. The perfect tender rule allows the buyer an absolute right to reject nonconforming goods. When goods are shipped C.O.D., payment is not considered to be an acceptance.
    Answers (A), (B), and (D) are incorrect because, when goods are shipped C.O.D., the buyer does not have the right to inspect the goods before payment, take possession before payment, or tender payment for the goods at a later time.

39. Mayker, Inc. and Oylco contracted for Oylco to be the exclusive provider of Mayker's fuel oil for 3 months. The stated price was subject to increases of up to a total of 10% if the market price increased. The market price rose 25%, and Mayker tripled its normal order. Oylco seeks to avoid performance. Oylco's best argument in support of its position is that

- A. There was no meeting of the minds.
- B. The contract was unconscionable.
- C. The quantity was not definite and certain enough.
- D. Mayker ordered amounts of oil unreasonably greater than its normal requirements.

The correct answer is (D). *(CPA, adapted)*
    REQUIRED: The best argument for avoiding performance on a requirements contract.
    DISCUSSION: Requirements and output contracts were often unenforceable under common law because they were too indefinite. They are permitted under UCC 2-306 provided that the parties act in good faith and demand or tender reasonable quantities. Absent stated estimates, normal or otherwise comparable prior requirements or output will provide the standard of reasonableness. No estimates were made, so if Mayker orders excessive amounts, it will have violated its duties, and Oylco may be able to avoid performance.
    Answer (A) is incorrect because, under the UCC, an agreement that one party will supply the other's requirements for a specified period within a given price range suggests a meeting of the minds (formation of a contract). Hence, Oylco's best argument is breach, not failure to reach an agreement. Answer (B) is incorrect because the difference between 10% and 25% above contract price is not so oppressive and unfair as to render the contract unconscionable. Answer (C) is incorrect because the contract does not fail for indefiniteness given that the parties must act in good faith and demand or tender reasonable quantities.

40. Yost Corp., a computer manufacturer, contracted to sell 15 computers to Ivor Corp., a computer retailer. The contract specified that delivery was to be made by truck to Ivor's warehouse. Instead, Yost shipped the computers by rail. When Ivor claimed that Yost did not comply with the contract, Yost told Ivor that there had been a trucker's strike when the goods were shipped. Ivor refused to pay for the computers. Under these circumstances, Ivor

- A. Is obligated to pay for the computers because Yost made a valid substituted performance.
- B. Is obligated to pay for the computers because title to them passed to Ivor when Ivor received them.
- C. May return the computers and avoid paying for them because of the way Yost delivered them.
- D. May return the computers and avoid paying for them because the contract was void under the theory of commercial impracticability.

The correct answer is (A). *(CPA, adapted)*
    REQUIRED: The effect of substituting for the agreed-to manner of delivery.
    DISCUSSION: If the goods or the seller's tender of delivery fails in any respect to the contract, the buyer may reject the goods or the tender (perfect tender rule). But when neither party is at fault and the agreed-upon manner of delivery of the goods becomes commercially impracticable due to failure of loading or unloading facilities or the unavailability of an acceptable carrier, a substituted manner of performance must be tendered and accepted if commercially reasonable.
    Answer (B) is incorrect because the payment obligation is not dependent on when title passes. Answers (C) and (D) are incorrect because, under these circumstances, the buyer must accept a substituted manner of performance when the agreed-upon manner of delivery of the goods becomes commercially impracticable.

41. Under the Sales Article of the UCC, and unless otherwise agreed to, the seller's obligation to the buyer is to

- A. Deliver the goods to the buyer's place of business.
- B. Hold conforming goods and give the buyer whatever notification is reasonably necessary to enable the buyer to take delivery.
- C. Deliver all goods called for In the contract to a common carrier.
- D. Set aside conforming goods for inspection by the buyer before delivery.

The correct answer is (B). *(CPA, adapted)*
REQUIRED: The seller's obligation to the buyer.
DISCUSSION: Once the parties have contracted, the seller is obligated to transfer and deliver the goods, and the buyer is obligated to accept and pay the price in accordance with the contract. If the goods or the seller's tender of delivery fail to conform to the contract in any respect, the buyer may reject the goods or the tender. In noncarrier situations, the seller must put and hold conforming goods at the buyer's disposition for a time sufficient for the buyer to take possession. The tender must be at a reasonable hour, and the seller must give notice to enable the buyer to take possession.

Answers (A) and (C) are incorrect because, unless otherwise agreed, the place of delivery is the seller's place of business. Answer (D) is incorrect because a right of inspection is part of answer (B); i.e., answer (B) is more complete.

F. Remedies and Defenses

42. Bush Hardware ordered 300 Ram hammers from Ajax Hardware. Ajax accepted the order in writing. On the final date allowed for delivery, Ajax discovered it did not have enough Ram hammers to fill the order. Instead, Ajax sent 300 Strong hammers. Ajax stated on the invoice that the shipment was sent only as an accommodation. Which of the following statements is correct?

- A. Ajax's note of accommodation cancels the contract between Bush and Ajax.
- B. Bush's order can be accepted only by Ajax's shipment of the goods ordered.
- C. Ajax's shipment of Strong hammers is a breach of contract.
- D. Ajax's shipment of Strong hammers is a counteroffer, and no contract exists between Bush and Ajax.

The correct answer is (C). *(CPA, adapted)*
REQUIRED: The correct statement about the shipment of goods solely as an accommodation.
DISCUSSION: Shipment of a brand different from that stipulated in the contract was a breach of the contract (UCC 2-601). Bush may accept the goods despite their nonconformity, rightfully reject them, or resort to any of the buyer's other remedies under the UCC. UCC 2-206 and 2-508, allowing accommodation shipments and the ability to cure, are not applicable because notice of acceptance was sent, and a cure must be made within the time for performance in most cases.

Answer (A) is incorrect because the breaching party cannot cancel the contract. Only a mutual rescission or the promised performance will discharge the seller's obligation unless the nonconforming goods are accepted. Answer (B) is incorrect because Bush's order constituted an offer to enter into either a bilateral or unilateral contract. It could be accepted either by a prompt promise to ship or by a prompt shipment, respectively. Answer (D) is incorrect because the shipment was not a counteroffer. The acceptance had already created a contract.

43. Under the Sales Article of the UCC, the remedies available to a seller when a buyer breaches a contract for the sale of goods may include

	The Right to Resell Goods Identified to the Contract	The Right to Stop a Carrier from Delivering the Goods
A.	Yes	Yes
B.	Yes	No
C.	No	Yes
D.	No	No

The correct answer is (A). *(CPA, adapted)*
REQUIRED: The remedies available to a seller when buyer breaches a contract for the sale of goods.
DISCUSSION: If a buyer breaches or repudiates a sales contract while the seller is still in possession of the goods, the seller can identify to the contract the conforming goods that are still in his/her possession or control. The seller can do so even if the goods were not identified at the time of the breach (UCC 2-704). The seller can then resell the goods, holding the buyer liable for any loss. The seller also may recover goods in transit. The seller may stop delivery of goods in the possession of a carrier or other bailee if a buyer breaches or repudiates a sales contract (UCC 2-705). The right to stop delivery can be exercised only for a truckload, planeload, carload, or larger freight shipment unless the buyer is insolvent.

Answers (B), (C), and (D) are incorrect because both remedies are available to a seller when a buyer breaches a sales contract.

44. On September 10, Bell Corp. entered into a contract to purchase 50 lamps from Glow Manufacturing. Bell prepaid 40% of the purchase price. Glow became insolvent on September 19 before segregating, in its inventory, the lamps to be delivered to Bell. Bell will not be able to recover the lamps because

- A. Bell is regarded as a merchant.
- B. The lamps were not identified to the contract.
- C. Glow became insolvent fewer than 10 days after receipt of Bell's prepayment.
- D. Bell did not pay the full price at the time of purchase.

The correct answer is (B). *(CPA, adapted)*
REQUIRED: The circumstances that will prevent the buyer from recovering goods from an insolvent seller.
DISCUSSION: A buyer may recover goods from an insolvent seller if the goods have been identified to the contract, the seller became insolvent within 10 days of receipt of the first installment of the price, and tender of any unpaid portion of the price is made and kept open (UCC 2-502). If the lamps have not been identified to the contract, Bell cannot obtain them.
Answer (A) is incorrect because the buyer's right to reach the goods is not dependent upon its status as a merchant. Answer (C) is incorrect because, to recover the goods, the seller must have become insolvent within 10 days of receipt of the first installment of the price. Answer (D) is incorrect because failure to pay the full price will not prevent Bell from obtaining the goods if it makes and keeps open a tender of the unpaid balance of the price.

45. Under the UCC Sales Article, which of the following legal remedies would a buyer not have when a seller fails to transfer and deliver goods identified to the contract?

- A. Sue for specific performance.
- B. Sue for punitive damages.
- C. Purchase substitute goods (cover).
- D. Recover the identified goods (capture).

The correct answer is (B). *(CPA, adapted)*
REQUIRED: The legal remedy not available to a buyer when the seller fails to deliver goods.
DISCUSSION: The buyer's basic remedy when the seller fails to deliver goods is the right to sue for monetary damages. The UCC, generally, allows only compensatory damages and does not provide for an aggrieved party to recover punitive damages.
Answer (A) is incorrect because, when the goods are unique and monetary damages are not an adequate remedy, a buyer might obtain specific performance. Answer (C) is incorrect because a buyer may generally cover, that is, purchase substitute goods in the marketplace. Answer (D) is incorrect because a buyer may recover goods from a seller that became insolvent within 10 days of receipt of the first installment of the price.

46. Under the Sales Article of the UCC, which of the following statements regarding liquidated damages is(are) correct?

I. The injured party may collect any amount of liquidated damages provided for in the contract.

II. The seller may retain a deposit of up to $500 when a buyer defaults even if there is no liquidated damages provision in the contract.

- A. I only.
- B. II only.
- C. Both I and II.
- D. Neither I nor II.

The correct answer is (B). *(CPA, adapted)*
REQUIRED: The true statement(s), if any, about liquidated damages.
DISCUSSION: A liquidated damages clause is a contractual clause specifying the damages to be paid in the event of breach. The UCC permits such a clause provided it is reasonable in light of the anticipated losses, the difficulties of proof of loss, and the inconvenience of otherwise obtaining a remedy. If excessive, it is a penalty and is unenforceable. If a seller has properly withheld delivery of goods, the buyer may receive a refund of monies paid minus any liquidated damages agreed on. If no liquidated damages have been provided for, the seller may retain 20% of the value of the total contract price or $500, whichever is less (UCC 2-718).
Answers (A), (C), and (D) are incorrect because the seller may retain a deposit of up to $500 when a buyer defaults even if there is no liquidated damages provision in the contract. Any liquidated damages provision must be reasonable.

47. Diana Corp. entered into a contract with Baker Suppliers, Inc. to purchase a used word processor from Baker. Diana is engaged in the business of selling new and used word processors to the general public. The contract required Baker to ship the goods to Diana by common carrier pursuant to the following provision in the contract: "FOB -- Baker Suppliers, Inc. loading dock." Assume that Diana refused to accept the word processor even though it was in all respects conforming to the contract and that the contract is otherwise silent. Under the UCC Sales Article,

- A. Baker can successfully sue for specific performance and make Diana accept and pay for the word processor.

- B. Baker may resell the word processor to another buyer.

- C. Baker must sue for the difference between the market value of the word processor and the contract price plus its incidental damages.

- D. Baker cannot successfully sue for consequential damages unless it attempts to resell the word processor.

The correct answer is (B). *(CPA, adapted)*
REQUIRED: The correct statement about a seller's remedies after wrongful rejection.
DISCUSSION: Resale of the goods and recovery of damages is a seller's remedy. After the buyer's breach, the resale in good faith and in a commercially reasonable manner permits the seller to recover the difference between the resale price and the contract price, plus any incidental damages allowed under UCC 2-710, minus expenses saved.
Answer (A) is incorrect because specific performance is a remedy that may be available to a buyer but not a seller of goods. Answer (C) is incorrect because an aggrieved seller has a variety of possible remedies, including but not limited to a suit for damages for nonacceptance or repudiation. In such an action, the measure of damages is the difference between the market price and the unpaid contract price, plus incidental damages, minus expenses saved. If this measure of damages is inadequate, the seller may recover the profit it would have made from full performance by the buyer, plus incidental damages, with due allowance for costs reasonably incurred and payments or proceeds of resale. Answer (D) is incorrect because the UCC expressly provides for an aggrieved buyer, not a seller, to recover consequential (special) damages. But the UCC does not prevent the seller from seeking this common-law remedy. Consequential damages are the losses resulting from the unique facts of the case, assuming the breaching party knew or had reason to know of these circumstances. Resale is not a prerequisite to their recovery.

48. Cara Fabricating Co. and Taso Corp. agreed orally that Taso would custom manufacture a compressor for Cara at a price of $120,000. After Taso completed the work at a cost of $90,000, Cara notified Taso that the compressor was no longer needed. Taso is holding the compressor and has requested payment from Cara. Taso has been unable to resell the compressor for any price. Taso incurred storage fees of $2,000. It Cara refused to pay Taso and Taso sues Cara, the most Taso will be entitled to recover is

- A. $92,000
- B. $105,000
- C. $120,000
- D. $122,000

The correct answer is (D). *(CPA, adapted)*
REQUIRED: The seller's recovery after a buyer's refusal to pay for specially made goods.
DISCUSSION: A seller may recover the contract price ($120,000) and any incidental damages ($2,000) if circumstances reasonably indicate that an effort at resale would be unsuccessful (UCC 2-709). Because the machine was made-to-order and not adaptable to others' use, Taso should be successful in recovering the price. After recovery of the price, seller would be holding the machine for buyer.
Answers (A), (B), and (C) are incorrect because a seller may recover the contract price ($120,000) and any incidental damages ($2,000) if circumstances reasonably indicate that an effort at resale would be unsuccessful.

49. Under the UCC Sales Article, a seller will be entitled to recover the full contract price from the buyer when the

- A. Goods are destroyed after title passed to the buyer.

- B. Goods are destroyed while risk of loss is with the buyer.

- C. Buyer revokes its acceptance of the goods.

- D. Buyer rejects some of the goods.

The correct answer is (B). *(CPA, adapted)*
REQUIRED: The circumstances under which a seller will be entitled to recover the full contract price.
DISCUSSION: A seller may be entitled to recover the full contract price for conforming goods lost or damaged after risk of their loss has passed to the buyer. UCC 2-709(1).
Answer (A) is incorrect because title passage does not govern who bears the risk of loss. Answers (C) and (D) are incorrect because, if rightful, the buyer's rejection or revocation triggers a seller's right to cure. Only if timely cure is effected will the seller be entitled to the full contract price.

50. On February 15, Mazur Corp. contracted to sell 1,000 bushels of wheat to Good Bread, Inc. at $6.00 per bushel with delivery to be made on June 23. On June 1, Good advised Mazur that it would not accept or pay for the wheat. On June 2, Mazur sold the wheat to another customer at the market price of $5.00 per bushel. Mazur had advised Good that it intended to resell the wheat. Which of the following statements is correct?

A. Mazur can successfully sue Good for the difference between the resale price and the contract price.

B. Mazur can resell the wheat only after June 23.

C. Good can retract its anticipatory breach at any time before June 23.

D. Good can successfully sue Mazur for specific performance.

The correct answer is (A). *(CPA, adapted)*
REQUIRED: The effect of a buyer's advance notice to the seller of an intent to breach.
DISCUSSION: Under UCC 2-610, when either party repudiates a future performance the loss of which will substantially impair the value of the contract to the other party, the possibilities are to (1) await performance for a commercially reasonable time, (2) resort to any remedies for breach available to a buyer (UCC 2-711) or a seller (UCC 2-703), and (3) suspend performance. Hence, an aggrieved seller may resell the goods and sue the buyer for the difference between the resale price and the contract price. (UCC 2-703 and 2-706).
Answer (B) is incorrect because, upon anticipatory repudiation, the buyer may immediately resort to any remedies available for breach. Answer (C) is incorrect because retraction is permitted only until the other party has canceled, materially changed his/her position in reliance on the repudiation, or otherwise indicated that (s)he considers the repudiation final. UCC 2-611. Answer (D) is incorrect because monetary damages would be an adequate remedy.

51. Under the Sales Article of the UCC, which of the following rights is(are) available to the buyer when a seller commits an anticipatory breach of contract?

	Demand Assurance of Performance	Cancel the Contract	Collect Punitive Damages
A.	Yes	Yes	Yes
B.	Yes	Yes	No
C.	Yes	No	Yes
D.	No	Yes	Yes

The correct answer is (B). *(CPA, adapted)*
REQUIRED: The rights available to the buyer after an anticipatory breach.
DISCUSSION: If a party has a reasonable basis for believing that performance will not be tendered, (s)he may in writing demand adequate assurance of performance. Until (s)he receives such assurance, (s)he may suspend further performance if suspension is commercially reasonable. When either party, through words, actions, or circumstances, repudiates the contract with respect to a performance not yet due, the aggrieved party may await performance for a commercially reasonable time, resort to any remedy for breach even though (s)he has also urged the other party to perform, or suspend his/her own performance. However, punitive damages are not ordinarily an appropriate remedy for breach of contract.
Answers (A), (C), and (D) are incorrect because the buyer may demand assurance of performance and cancel after an anticipatory breach but may not collect punitive damages.

52. Unless the parties have otherwise agreed, an action for the breach of a contract within the UCC Sales Article must be commenced within

A. Four years after the cause of action has accrued.

B. Six years after the cause of action has accrued.

C. Four years after the effective date of the contract.

D. Six years after the effective date of the contract.

The correct answer is (A). *(CPA, adapted)*
REQUIRED: The time within which an action for the breach of a contract within the UCC Sales Article must be commenced.
DISCUSSION: Under UCC 2-725, a 4-year statute of limitations applies to cases involving sales of goods. The parties, however, may reduce (but not extend) the period for suit, but not to less than 1 year. The limitations period generally begins to run when the cause of action has accrued.
Answer (B) is incorrect because the applicable period is 4 years. Answer (C) is incorrect because the limitations period begins when the cause of action has accrued (generally when the breach occurs). Answer (D) is incorrect because an action for the breach of a contract within the UCC Sales Article must be commenced within 4 years after the cause of action has accrued.

OOF QUESTION 1 *(CPA, adapted)* 15-20 minutes

On May 1, Starr Corp., a manufacturer and supplier of computers, mailed a proposed contract to Hac, Inc., offering to sell 20 items of specified computer equipment for $18,000. Hac was engaged in the business of selling computers to the public. Hac accepted Starr's offer by executing and returning the contract to Starr. Starr failed to sign the contract.

On May 15, Starr advised Hac by telephone that, due to certain market conditions, the price of computer parts had increased. Therefore, in order to avoid a loss on the sale to Hac, Starr requested an increase in the sales price to $20,000, which was orally agreed to by Hac. On May 17, Starr sent to Hac a signed letter acknowledging this agreement. Hac did not respond to the letter.

On September 15, Starr notified Hac that the equipment was ready for delivery. Due to substantial changes in computer technology subsequent to May 15, Hac indicated that it no longer wanted the equipment and that it would not pay for it. Starr was unable to resell the computer equipment for any price despite its reasonable efforts to do so. Therefore, Starr commenced a breach of contract action against Hac. Hac asserted the following defenses:

- The May 1 written contract between Starr and Hac is not enforceable because of the statute of frauds.

- Even if the May 1 contract is enforceable, the May 15 oral agreement to change the price of the equipment is not enforceable because the agreement lacked consideration and failed to satisfy the statute of frauds.

- In any event, Starr is not entitled to recover the full sales price because the equipment is still in Starr's possession.

Required

Each of items 1 through 15 is a conclusion from the facts above. For each item, indicate (A) if the conclusion is correct, or indicate (B) if it is incorrect. "UCC" will be used to abbreviate Uniform Commercial Code.

1. The transaction is subject to Article 2 of the UCC.

2. The May 1 agreement is not enforceable because Starr did not sign it.

3. Starr is a merchant with respect to these agreements.

4. Hac has a legal basis to assert as a defense to a breach of contract that the equipment was not fit for ordinary purposes for which such equipment is used.

5. Assuming Hac has a legal basis for a defense based on ordinary purposes for which such equipment is used, the defense would depend on Starr's negligence.

6. There was no warranty for a particular purpose in the May 1 agreement because such a warranty must be expressed.

7. Notwithstanding item 6., an oral disclaimer of a warranty of fitness is generally effective.

8. Hac and Starr's agreement to increase the price to $20,000 is unenforceable because it was not supported by consideration.

9. The agreement to increase the price to $20,000 is unenforceable because Starr did not propose it in good faith.

10. The agreement to increase the price to $20,000 would not have been enforceable without a writing.

11. Hac is a merchant with respect to these agreements.

12. Assuming Starr and Hac are merchants, the agreement to increase the price to $20,000 is still unenforceable against Hac because Hac signed no written memorandum of the agreement.

13. Under the UCC, the May 1 agreement obligated Starr to deliver the equipment to Hac's place of business or a warehouse designated by Hac.

14. Starr is entitled to recover the full sales price from Hac.

15. If Hac had accepted delivery of the equipment and subsequently notified Starr that a third party had sued Hac for patent infringement with respect to the equipment, Starr would be liable to Hac.

Knowledge Tested

1. Transactions subject to Article 2 of the UCC
2. UCC Statute of Frauds
3. Requirement to modify contracts
4. Special rules for merchants
5. Warranties in sales of goods
6. Performance obligations
7. Remedies upon breach

Authors' Comments

You should identify the point at which the UCC Sales Article applies and the $500 UCC Statute of Frauds amount without hesitating. Focus on differences between UCC and the common-law rules for contracts, on warranties and disclaimers, and on rules specific to merchants. Lack of familiarity with all the possible results of a breach can be picked up by a single question.

1. The correct answer is (A).

DISCUSSION: Article 2 of the UCC governs contracts for the sale of goods. By a sale, ownership of property passes from seller to buyer for consideration. Goods are tangible personal property. Personal property, generally, is movable. Thus, the sale of computer equipment is considered goods for Article 2 purposes.

2. The correct answer is (B).

DISCUSSION: A contract for the sale of goods for $500 or more is not enforceable unless there is some writing sufficient to indicate that a contract for sale has been made between the parties which is signed by the party against whom enforcement is sought. The contract is enforceable against Hac because he executed a sufficient writing.

3. The correct answer is (A).

DISCUSSION: Some special rules apply to merchants under Article 2 of the UCC. A merchant is one who deals in goods of the kind sold or otherwise, by his/her occupation, holds him/herself out as having knowledge or skill pertaining to the practices or goods involved in the transaction.

4. The correct answer is (A).

DISCUSSION: Unless excluded, a warranty of merchantability is implied in every sale by a merchant who deals in goods of the kind sold. The most important component of this warranty is that the goods be fit for the ordinary purposes for which such goods are used. There is, therefore, a legal basis for the defense. However, it is not clear whether there is a factual basis.

5. The correct answer is (B).

DISCUSSION: The seller is strictly liable for breach of an implied warranty. If the goods sold do not meet a standard of the warranty, the seller is liable even if (s)he exercised utmost care.

6. The correct answer is (B).

DISCUSSION: A warranty of fitness for a particular purpose is implied when the seller has reason to know the particular purpose for which the goods are to be used and that the buyer is relying on the seller's skill and judgment to select suitable goods.

7. The correct answer is (B).

DISCUSSION: To be effective, disclaimer of an implied warranty of fitness for a particular purpose must be in writing and conspicuous.

8. The correct answer is (B).

DISCUSSION: Under the UCC Sales Article, an agreement to modify a contract for the sale of goods needs no consideration to be binding.

9. The correct answer is (B).

DISCUSSION: The UCC imposes a duty of good faith in formation and performance of every contract for the sale of goods. Good faith is required for modification. Good faith is honesty in fact. A merchant must also observe reasonable commercial standards of fair dealing in the trade. The proposed price increase based on a shift in the market which would result in a loss to Starr was in good faith.

10. The correct answer is (A).

DISCUSSION: An agreement to modify a contract for the sale of goods must generally satisfy requirements of the UCC Statute of Frauds if the contract as modified is for more than $500.

11. The correct answer is (A).

DISCUSSION: Hac is a merchant because it deals in goods of the kind sold. Hac, acting in a mercantile capacity, possesses or uses an expertise specifically related to the goods sold.

12. The correct answer is (B).

DISCUSSION: Under the UCC, if both parties are merchants and a writing in confirmation of an oral agreement which is sufficient against the sender is received, the recipient receives the writing within a reasonable time, the recipient has reason to know of the contents of the writing, and the recipient does not give written notice of objection to the contents of the writing within 10 days after it is received, then the oral agreement is enforceable.

13. The correct answer is (B).

DISCUSSION: When delivery terms are not specified in a contract for the sale of goods, the buyer normally takes delivery at the seller's place of business.

14. The correct answer is (A).

DISCUSSION: The UCC provides that a seller may recover the price of goods identified to a contract and in possession of the seller if the seller is unable after reasonable effort to resell them at a reasonable price or the circumstances reasonably indicate that such effort will be unavailing. Thus, Starr may recover $20,000.

15. The correct answer is (A).

DISCUSSION: A merchant seller regularly dealing in goods of the type sold warrants that they are delivered free from any infringement on patent, trademark, copyright, or similar rights. Liability of the seller to the buyer is conditioned on the buyer notifying the seller of infringement litigation within a reasonable time (to enable the seller to defend the lawsuit).

OOF QUESTION 2 *(CPA, adapted)* 10-15 minutes

On February 1, 1999, Grand Corp., a manufacturer of custom cabinets, contracted in writing with Axle Co., a kitchen contractor, to sell Axle 100 unique, custom-designed kitchen cabinets for $250,000. Axle had contracted to install the cabinets in a luxury condominium complex. The contract provided that the cabinets were to be ready for delivery by April 15 and were to be shipped FOB sellers loading dock. On April 15, Grand had 85 cabinets complete and delivered them, together with 15 standard cabinets, to the trucking company for delivery to Axle. Grand faxed Axle a copy of the shipping invoice, listing the 15 standard cabinets. On May 1, before reaching Axle, the truck was involved in a collision, and all the cabinets were damaged beyond repair.

Required

For items 1 through 6, determine whether (A), (B), or (C) is correct.

1. A. The contract between Grand and Axle was a shipment contract.
   B. The contract between Grand and Axle was a destination contract.
   C. The contract between Grand and Axle was a consignment contract.

2. A. The risk of loss for the 85 custom cabinets passed to Axle on April 15.
   B. The risk of loss for the 100 cabinets passed to Axle on April 15.
   C. The risk of loss for the 100 cabinets remained with Grand.

3. A. The contract between Grand and Axle was invalid because no delivery date was stated.
   B. The contract between Grand and Axle was voidable because Grand shipped only 85 custom cabinets.
   C. The contract between Grand and Axle was void because the goods were destroyed.

4. A. Grand's shipment of the standard cabinets was a breach of the contract with Axle.
   B. Grand would not be considered to have breached the contract until Axle rejected the standard cabinets.
   C. Grand made a counteroffer by shipping the standard cabinets.

5. A. Had the cabinets been delivered, title would not transfer to Axle until Axle inspected them.
   B. Had the cabinets been delivered, title would have transferred on delivery to the carrier.
   C. Had the cabinets been delivered, title would not have transferred because the cabinets were nonconforming goods.

6. A. Axle is entitled to specific performance from Grand because of the unique nature of the goods.
   B. Axle is required to purchase substitute goods (cover) and is entitled to the difference in cost from Grand.
   C. Axle is entitled to punitive damages because of Grand's intentional shipment of nonconforming goods.

Knowledge Tested

1. Sale of goods transactions
2. Shipment and destination contracts
3. Passage of title and risk of loss
4. Effect of breach and choice of remedies
5. Attachment of security interest
6. Perfection
7. Priority of conflicting claims

Authors' Comments

Items 1 through 6 are a comprehensive group of basic questions that arise in a contract to sell future goods. The questions distinguish shipment, destination, and consignment contracts, and title and risk transfers. The effects of breach of contract and selection of remedies are presented.

This is probably a reliable pattern for future objective format test questions. The format lends itself to testing many of the important rules in each area of law tested on the exam.

1. The correct answer is (A).

DISCUSSION: Grand entered into a shipment contract because the terms agreed to were FOB seller's loading dock. This required Grand to send the goods to Axle by carrier but not to actually deliver them. A shipment contract is performed when a seller has placed goods in the possession of a carrier, contracted for their transportation, provided the buyer with the necessary documentation to take possession of the goods from the carrier, and notified the buyer of the shipment. A destination contract is performed when the goods are tendered at the destination specified in the contract. Unless a contract clearly indicates that it is a destination contract, it will be considered to be a shipment contract. A consignment contract is formed when the seller transfers goods to a buyer but retains title to the goods until they are actually sold.

2. The correct answer is (C).

DISCUSSION: In shipment contracts, the risk of loss for the goods passes to the buyer when the seller delivers the goods to the carrier. However, if the goods are nonconforming to such an extent that the buyer has the right to reject them, the risk of loss does not pass to the buyer until cure or acceptance. Even if the seller's shipment of nonconforming goods is an accommodation, it is still a breach, and the seller retains the risk of loss for the entire shipment.

3. The correct answer is (B).

DISCUSSION: When a merchant seller tenders nonconforming goods, the contract becomes voidable at the option of the buyer. A contract is not rendered invalid or void by a seller's breach or by destruction of identified goods. Rather, if the goods were delivered, the buyer would be able to accept or reject the nonconforming goods and pursue other remedies. The UCC allows a breaching party to cure the nonconformity if time permits. Another Code rule provides for delivery within a reasonable time if the contract is silent.

4. The correct answer is (A).

DISCUSSION: The seller is obligated to ship conforming goods in accordance with the terms of the contract. Failure to do so is a breach of contract unless completion of the goods is rendered commercially impracticable by an unforeseen event. The breach occurred upon shipping and is not dependent on the buyer's rejection. An accommodation shipment of nonconforming goods is a breach of contract by the seller and not a counteroffer.

5. The correct answer is (C).

DISCUSSION: In a shipment contract, unless agreed otherwise, the title to the goods passes when the seller completes the physical delivery of conforming goods to the carrier. However, since this was a shipment of nonconforming goods, title did not pass to the buyer when the seller delivered the goods to the carrier.

6. The correct answer is (A).

DISCUSSION: Specific performance is a remedy available to a buyer when the subject matter of the sales contract is unique, such as custom cabinets for a luxury condominium complex. Generally, specific performance occurs when the buyer relied on having the unique goods and cannot be adequately compensated with monetary damages. The remedy of cover is never mandatory, and punitive damage awards are rare in contract suits.

ESSAY QUESTION (CPA, adapted)

On June 1, Classic Corp., a manufacturer of desk chairs, orally agreed to sell 100 leather desk chairs to Rand Stores, a chain of retail furniture stores, for $50,000. The parties agreed that delivery would be completed by September 1, and the shipping terms were "F.O.B. seller's loading dock." On June 5, Classic sent Rand a signed memorandum of agreement containing the terms orally agreed to. Rand received the memorandum on June 7 and made no response.

On July 31, Classic identified the chairs to be shipped to Rand and placed them on its loading dock to be picked up by the common carrier the next day. That night, a fire on the loading dock destroyed 50 of the chairs. On August 1, the remaining 50 chairs were delivered to the common carrier together with 50 vinyl chairs. The truck carrying the chairs was involved in an accident, resulting in extensive damage to 10 of the leather chairs and 25 of the vinyl chairs.

On August 10, the chairs were delivered to Rand. On August 12, Rand notified Classic that Rand was accepting 40 of the leather chairs and 10 of the vinyl chairs, but the rest of the shipment was being rejected. Rand also informed Classic that, due to Classic's failure to perform under the terms of the contract, Rand would seek all remedies available under the Sales Article of the UCC.

Classic contended that it has no liability to Rand and that the shipment was strictly an accommodation to Rand because Rand failed to sign the memorandum of agreement, thus preventing a contract from being formed.

The above parties and transactions are governed by the provisions of the Sales Article of the UCC.

Required

a. Determine whether Classic's contention is correct and give the reasons for your conclusion.

b. Assuming that a valid contract exists between Classic and Rand, answer the following questions and give the reasons for your conclusions. Do not consider any possible liability owed by the common carrier.

1. Who bears the risk of loss for the 50 destroyed leather chairs?
2. Who bears the risk of loss for the 25 damaged vinyl chairs?
3. What is the earliest date that title to any of the chairs would pass to Rand?

c. With what UCC requirements must Rand comply to be entitled to recover damages from Classic?

d. Assuming that a valid contract exists between Classic and Rand, state the applicable remedies to which Rand would be entitled. Do not consider any possible liability owed by the common carrier.

Knowledge Tested

Article 2 of the UCC

1. Agreements between merchants
2. Risk of loss
3. FOB terms
4. Title
5. Remedies for breach

Authors' Comments

This question emphasizes that transactions in goods between merchants are governed by special rules. It also distinguishes between shipping and destination contracts with respect to passage of title and risk of loss. Furthermore, the UCC creates unique remedies and imposes substantial obligations on the party seeking relief.

Unofficial Answer

a. Classic's contention is incorrect. Under the provisions of the Sales Article of the UCC, a written memorandum stating an agreement between merchants does not have to be signed by both parties. The contract is enforceable against Classic because Classic signed the memorandum and against Rand because Rand did not object to the memorandum within 10 days of receiving it.

b. 1. Classic bears the risk of loss for the other 50 leather chairs destroyed by the fire. Even though the goods were identified to the contract and placed on the loading dock, the risk of loss remained with Classic. The shipping terms "F.O.B. seller's loading dock" provide that risk of loss remains with the seller until the goods are delivered to the common carrier. The 50 leather chairs destroyed in the fire had not yet been delivered to the carrier.

2. Classic bears the risk of loss for the damaged vinyl chairs. Even though these goods were delivered to the common carrier, the risk of loss did not pass to Rand because the vinyl chairs were nonconforming goods.

3. August 1 was the earliest date that title to any of the chairs passed to Rand. Title passed when goods identified to the contract were delivered to the carrier.

c. Under the Sales Article of the UCC, for Rand to be entitled to damages from Classic, Rand must comply with the following requirements:

- Rand has to notify Classic of the rejection of the goods within a reasonable time.

- Rand must act in good faith with respect to the rejected goods by following any reasonable instructions from Classic.

- Rand must give Classic the opportunity to cure until the contract time of performance expires.

d. Rand would be entitled to the following remedies:

- The right to cancel the contract

- The right of cover

- The right to recover monetary damages for nondelivery

STUDY UNIT 17: SECURED TRANSACTIONS

19 pages of outline
33 multiple-choice questions
2 OOFs and 1 essay

A. *Attachment of Security Interests*
B. *Perfection of Security Interests*
C. *Priorities*
D. *Rights of Debtors, Creditors, and Third Parties*

To protect against the risk of nonpayment of a debt, a promisee, seller, or lender may require the debtor to enter into a security agreement. A security agreement gives the creditor an interest in specific personal property owned by the debtor. A valid security interest allows the creditor, if the debtor defaults, to repossess the collateral, sell it at a reasonably conducted public or private sale, and apply the sale proceeds to the debt. The exam tests knowledge of the rules of Article 9, *Secured Transactions*, and the ability to apply these rules in various debtor-creditor transactions. The areas emphasized are the requirements of a security agreement; attachment of the security agreement to the collateral; the rules for determining priority among debtors, creditors, and third parties (including the exceptions to the general rules); and the remedies after default.

A. **Attachment of Security Interests**. Article 9 is the Secured Transactions Article of the Uniform Commercial Code (UCC). It covers any transaction that is intended to establish a security interest in personal property or fixtures, regardless of whether the security device is designated a pledge, chattel mortgage, etc.

1. A **security interest** is "an interest in personal property or fixtures which secures payment or performance of an obligation."

   a. A **purchase money security interest** (PMSI) is a security interest to the extent that it is taken or retained by a

      1) Seller of the collateral to secure the sales price, or
      2) Person who gives value to enable the debtor to acquire the collateral.

         a) The value given must be used to acquire the collateral or the security interest is not a PMSI.

         b) Value may be given by making advances or by incurring an obligation.

            i)   EXAMPLE 1: John purchases an office copier from We-R-Copies. One week later, John borrows $10,000 from Bank, Inc. and conveys to Bank a security interest in all his office equipment. Bank's security interest in the copier is not a PMSI.

            ii) EXAMPLE 2: Jane starts her own business. Jane borrows $10,000 from Bank, Inc. to purchase office equipment. She conveys to Bank a security interest in the equipment she intends to purchase. The next day, Jane purchases a desk. Bank's security interest in the desk is a PMSI.

2. **Secured Party**. A secured party is a lender, seller, or other person in whose favor a security interest exists, including a person to whom accounts or chattel paper have been sold.

   a. An **account** is any right to payment for goods sold or leased or for services rendered which is not evidenced by an instrument or chattel paper.

   b. **Chattel paper** is a writing or writings which evidence both a monetary obligation and a security interest in specific goods.

3. There are a variety of security devices, including

    a. **Pledge.** The secured party takes possession of the collateral pledged as security for an obligation. The secured party's possession of the collateral furnishes notice to the debtor's other creditors that the collateral is encumbered.

    b. **Chattel mortgage.** It is similar to a real property mortgage, but it attaches to personal property. Chattel mortgages are recorded in specified public offices, giving notice to the debtor's creditors that the property subject to the mortgage is encumbered.

    c. **Conditional sales.** Upon a conditional sale, the buyer receives possession and the right to use goods; transfer of legal title to buyer is deferred until performance of some condition, typically, full payment of the purchase price.

        1) At common law, conditional sales were not recorded in public records.

        2) Some states adopted statutes that require the recording of a conditional sale to validate the seller's rights in the property. The UCC embodies this requirement: A secured party generally must either have actual possession of the goods or file a financing statement.

    d. **Trust receipts.** Trust receipts are used in inventory financing. The creditor purchases and holds title to the inventory. The debtor is considered a trustee for purposes of selling the inventory and bears the risk of loss.

    e. **Field warehousing.** The creditor hires a field warehouseman to take possession of the inventory on the debtor's property. The field warehouseman rents space from the debtor. The inventory is released as needed for sale.

    f. **Factor's liens.** Factor's liens are principally liens held by a lender (the factor) on changing inventory stock held by the debtor. The lien secures the debt owed to the factor.

4. **Leases.** A lease may be a security interest if the parties objectively intend that the lease provide security. Under a lease agreement, the owner of property transfers the right to exclusive possession, use, and enjoyment for a limited period of time.

    a. Whether a transaction is to be treated as a true lease or as establishing a security interest is determined by the facts of the case.

        1) A transaction gives rise to a security interest if the lessee cannot terminate the obligation to pay the lessor and the obligation is for the term of the lease, and if one of the following applies:

            a) At inception, the lease term is greater than or equal to the remaining economic life of the leased property.

            b) At the end of the lease term, the lessee must renew the lease for the remaining economic life of the property or buy the property.

            c) The lessee can renew the lease at a nominal rate for the remaining economic life of the property.

            d) The lessee can buy the property for nominal consideration.

        2) UCC 1-201 states that a transaction does not grant a security interest merely because one of the following applies:

            a) The present value of the future lease payments is greater than or equal to the property's fair market value (FMV) at the inception of the lease.

        b)   The lessee assumes the risk of loss or agrees to pay insurance premiums, taxes, filing fees, or other costs.

        c)   The lessee has the option to renew or to buy the goods.

        d)   The lessee has the option to renew the lease at a fixed rent greater than or equal to the FMV of the renewed lease at the time the option is to be exercised.

        e)   The lessee has the option to buy the goods for a fixed price greater than or equal to FMV at the time the option is to be exercised.

    b.   New UCC Article 2A pertaining to leases does not require lessors to file a financing statement in connection with a true lease in order to protect their interests in leased property.

        1)   However, if it is apparent that the effect of a transaction which is framed as a lease is that the lessee will enjoy possession and use of the goods for their entire economic life, the transaction will be treated as a security interest and not a true lease.

5.   Article 9 does not apply to the following:

    a.   Security interests covered by federal statute, e.g., federal income tax liens

    b.   Landlord's liens

    c.   Statutory liens or liens arising by operation of law, e.g., mechanic's liens

    d.   Wage assignments

    e.   Transfers by a government

    f.   The sale of accounts or chattel paper as part of the sale of a business

    g.   An assignment of accounts or chattel paper for collection only

    h.   An assignment of a contractual right to payment when the assignee is to perform under the contract

    i.   A transfer of one account to an assignee in satisfaction of a preexisting debt

        1)   EXAMPLE: Ted, a lawyer, was owed $10,000 by a client. Ted owed Jack $5,000. Ted assigned the $10,000 receivable to Jack to secure the $5,000 debt. The assignment was not an Article 9 transaction.

    j.   Claims reduced to a judgment

    k.   Interests in or liens on real property

    l.   Tort claims

    m.   An interest in a deposit account

    n.   Sales of securities

6.   **Nature of Collateral**. The application of the rules and provisions of Article 9 often depends on the nature of collateral involved in a transaction. Article 9 applies to the following categories of personal property:

    a.   **Goods**, including fixtures and all things which are movable at the time a security interest attaches. Goods do

        1)   Not include accounts, general intangibles, documents, chattel paper, instruments, money, or unextracted minerals

        2)   Include the unborn young of animals, growing crops, and timber for which there is a contract for removal and sale

b.   There are four categories of tangible collateral (goods):

   1)   **Consumer goods** are used primarily for personal, family, or household purposes.

      a)   EXAMPLE: A refrigerator purchased for the home.

   2)   **Inventory** encompasses goods to be held for sale or lease, or to be furnished under a contract for service. Inventory includes raw materials, work in process, or supplies used or consumed in the business.

      a)   EXAMPLE: Don's Wholesale buys milk from farmers and sells it to restaurants. The milk is Don's inventory.

   3)   **Farm products** include crops, livestock, supplies used or produced in farming, and unprocessed products of crops or livestock.

      a)   The goods must be in the possession of a debtor engaged in farming operations.

      b)   EXAMPLE: Milk in the possession of a dairy farmer is a farm product. If it is for sale in a convenience store, it is inventory.

   4)   **Equipment** includes goods purchased for business purposes. Equipment is also a residual category for goods that do not meet the definitions of consumer goods, farm products, or inventory.

      a)   EXAMPLE: A refrigerator purchased for use in a convenience store is equipment.

c.   There are five types of intangible collateral:

   1)   **Instruments** -- any written evidence of the right to receive money, other than a lease or security agreement, which is transferred by delivery and endorsement in the ordinary course of business. Instruments include negotiable instruments and securities represented by a certificate, e.g., checks, bank drafts, promissory notes, bonds.

   2)   **Documents** -- documents of title and receipts, e.g., bills of lading, warehouse receipts

   3)   **Chattel paper** -- writing(s) evidencing both a monetary obligation and a security interest in or a lease of specific goods

   4)   **Accounts** -- rights not evidenced by an instrument or chattel paper

      a)   EXAMPLE: Jim sells meat to restaurants on credit. The restaurant managers routinely sign delivery tickets acknowledging receipt of the meat. Jim's rights to payment for the meat are accounts.

   5)   **General intangibles** -- any personal property other than goods, accounts, chattel paper, documents, instruments, and money, e.g., goodwill, a state-issued license to sell packaged liquor, or a patent

d.   **Proceeds**, i.e., all items received upon disposition of collateral. Proceeds constitute collateral that has changed in form.

   1)   Cash proceeds include money, checks, and deposit accounts.

   2)   Noncash proceeds include all other items.

   3)   EXAMPLE: A rancher obtains credit and grants the creditor a security interest in the wool from his sheep (a farm product type of tangible collateral). If the rancher exchanges the wool for a truck or cash, the truck or cash constitutes proceeds for the wool.

7. **Attachment** of a security interest is accomplished by meeting three requirements:

    a.   There must be a security agreement.

    b.   The secured party must give value for the security interest.

    c.   The debtor must have rights (i.e., ownership) in the collateral.

8. A **security agreement** is a contract between the debtor and the secured party by which the secured party is granted a security interest in the collateral.

    a.   The debtor and the creditor must intend that a security interest be conveyed.

9. The security agreement must be written, unless the secured party is in possession of the collateral pursuant to an agreement.

    a.   The debtor must sign the security agreement.

    b.   The security agreement must contain a description of the collateral.

        1)   If the collateral is growing crops or uncut timber, the land on which the collateral is located must be included in the description.

        2)   Some jurisdictions require a description of the land if the collateral is unextracted minerals, oil, or gas.

10. A security agreement may include the following optional items:

    a.   An **after-acquired property clause** conveys an interest in property to be acquired in the future. The clauses are important to lenders that finance inventory.

        1)   The clause provides for a floating lien that will attach to specified property that the debtor may acquire in the future.

        2)   The interest attaches to the property as soon as the debtor acquires an interest in it.

        3)   A security interest will attach to consumer goods under an after-acquired property clause only if the debtor acquires rights in the goods not more than 10 days after the secured party gives value.

    b.   A **future advance clause** provides that the security agreement extends to future liabilities of the debtor to the secured party.

        1)   EXAMPLE: Bank lends David $50,000 to purchase manufacturing equipment. David conveys to Bank a PM security interest in the equipment. A future advance clause would provide that repayment of any funds lent by Bank to David in the future will be secured by the original equipment.

    c.   A **waiver of defenses clause** provides that the debtor may not assert certain defenses against an assignee of chattel paper that might have been asserted against the secured party who is making the assignment.

    d.   An **acceleration of payment clause** provides for the full amount of the debt to mature immediately upon default or within a specified period of time if a default is not cured.

11. Stop and review! You have completed the outline for this subunit. Study multiple-choice questions 1 through 7 beginning on page 561.

B. Perfection of Security Interests. Perfection is the process by which the secured party gives notice of the security interest to third parties (the debtor's other creditors). Perfection provides the secured party priority over most third parties who may subsequently claim an interest in the collateral, e.g., other secured and unsecured creditors of the debtor.

1. Perfection cannot occur prior to attachment.

2. Security interests are perfected in one of three ways:

   a. Perfection by filing a financing statement
   b. Perfection by possession of the collateral
   c. Automatic perfection

3. **Perfection by Filing a Financing Statement**. This is the typical means of perfection.

   a. Usually, perfection can be achieved by filing a financing statement if the collateral is classified as

      1) Consumer goods
      2) Equipment
      3) Farm products
      4) Inventory
      5) Fixtures
      6) General intangibles (Filing is the only way to perfect.)
      7) Accounts (Generally, filing is the only way to perfect.)
      8) Chattel paper

      NOTE: Perfection of a security interest in a negotiable instrument requires that the secured party take possession of the instrument.

   b. The UCC requires that the financing statement

      1) Include the names of the debtor and secured party

      2) Be signed by the debtor

      3) Contain the parties' addresses

      4) Contain a statement identifying or listing the type of collateral

      5) Describe the pertinent real estate if the collateral is growing crops, uncut timber, or unextracted minerals

   c. A security agreement may also serve as a financing statement if it meets the requirements of a financing statement.

   d. The financing statement is filed under the debtor's name.

      1) It may not be filed under a trade name.

   e. A financing statement may be amended by filing a writing signed by both parties.

   f. The classification of collateral determines the public office where the financing statement is filed.

      1) Financing statements for land-related collateral generally are filed in the real property records of the county where the land is located. Land-related collateral includes

         a) Uncut timber
         b) Fixtures
         c) Goods that are to become fixtures
         d) Unextracted minerals
         e) Growing crops

       2)   Other collateral. Typically one of two statutory schemes is used.

          a)   Central filing. Some states require the financing statement be filed in a central state office, usually the office of the secretary of state.

          b)   Local filing. Some states require filing in the county of the debtor's residence. If the debtor is not a state resident, filing is required in the county in which the collateral is located.

g.   A duly filed financing statement is effective for 5 years. A continuation statement may be filed during the last 6 months of the 5-year period.

       1)   If it is not filed, the security interest becomes unperfected.
       2)   A continuation statement extends perfection for 5 years.
       3)   Only the secured party need sign a continuation statement.

h.   A debtor who has fulfilled its obligations is entitled to a termination statement. It states that the secured party no longer has a security interest under the financing statement.

       1)   If the collateral is consumer goods, the secured party must file a termination statement in each office in which a financing statement was filed within 1 month of the debtor fulfilling its obligations.

          a)   If the debtor makes written demand for a termination statement, the secured party must file within 10 days.

       2)   If the collateral is not consumer goods, the secured party must furnish the debtor with a termination statement pursuant to written request.

          a)   Filing is not required.

       3)   A secured party that fails to provide or file a termination statement as required is liable to the debtor for $100 and any loss caused by the noncompliance.

4.   **Perfection by Possession**. A security interest may be perfected by the secured party's taking possession of the collateral.

a.   A security interest may be perfected by possession of the following types of collateral:

       1)   Consumer goods
       2)   Farm products
       3)   Equipment
       4)   Inventory
       5)   Documents
       6)   Chattel paper
       7)   Instruments (Possession is the only way to perfect.)
       8)   Money (Possession is the only way to perfect.)

b.   If attachment occurs when the secured party takes possession of the collateral pursuant to agreement, perfection occurs simultaneously with attachment.

       1)   EXAMPLE: John owns a boat. John arranged to borrow $10,000 from Julie for 30 days and to provide Julie a security interest in the boat on June 1. On June 2, John surrendered possession of the boat to Julie, and Julie gave John $10,000. Attachment occurred on June 2 because on that date Julie had rights in the collateral, had given value, and was in possession of the collateral. Perfection occurred simultaneously with attachment because Julie had possession of the boat when attachment occurred.

       c.   Possession of the collateral by an agent of the secured party, e.g., a field warehouser, is sufficient to perfect the security interest.

       d.   Generally, if perfection is by possession, the security interest becomes unperfected when possession ceases unless the secured party files a financing statement while in possession of the collateral.

5.   **Automatic Perfection**. Neither filing nor possession is required to perfect a security interest in certain situations. In these situations, perfection is automatic upon attachment.

       a.   Purchase money security interests (PMSI) in consumer goods (other than motor vehicles) are automatically perfected.

           1)   A PMSI arises when a lender or a seller provides the purchase price of goods to the debtor and takes a security interest in the collateral purchased.

               a)   EXAMPLE 1: A store sells an appliance to a consumer on credit. The store has provided the purchase price and has a PMSI in the appliance.

               b)   EXAMPLE 2: Same as above except the debtor borrowed the purchase price from a bank and paid the store with the loan proceeds. The bank has a PMSI in the appliance.

           2)   Consumer goods are goods purchased by the debtor for personal, family, or household use.

           3)   PMSIs in consumer goods are automatically perfected upon attachment without the secured party filing or taking possession (other PMSIs must be perfected by filing or possession).

               a)   The automatic perfection by attachment gives the secured party priority over other creditors of the debtor.

               b)   However, to gain priority over a good-faith consumer who purchases the goods from the original debtor requires perfection.

                   i)   EXAMPLE 1: A store sells an appliance to a consumer on credit and reserves a security interest in the appliance. If the consumer sells the appliance to another consumer without notice of the lien, the store may not recover the appliance from the new owner.

                   ii)   EXAMPLE 2: If the debtor had sold the appliance to a nonconsumer (not for personal, family, or household use), the store could recover the collateral.

       b.   With respect to security interests in instruments or negotiable documents,

           1)   Perfection is automatic for the 21-day period after attachment.

           2)   There must be a written security agreement.

           3)   The security interest becomes unperfected at the end of 21 days unless the secured party

               a)   Takes possession if the collateral is an instrument

               b)   Files a financing statement or takes possession if the collateral is a document

    c.   Security interests in assigned accounts are automatically perfected.

        1)   The assignment, whether considered alone or with other assignments to the same assignee, may not transfer a significant part of the assignor's receivables.

6.   **Proceeds**. Typically, a security interest perfected as to collateral is perfected as to proceeds.

    a.   **Proceeds** are what is received upon disposition of the collateral.

        1)   Dispositions include sales, exchanges, collections, and other transfers.

        2)   Cash proceeds include money, checks, deposit accounts, and the like.

        3)   Noncash proceeds are any other proceeds, e.g.,

            a)   Accounts receivable

            b)   Other negotiable instruments

            c)   Barter, trade-in, and other exchanged property

    b.   **Cash proceeds**. The security interest in cash proceeds is automatically perfected, but only for 10 days.

        1)   The security interest in the cash proceeds is cut off if the cash proceeds are commingled with other cash or if the cash proceeds are transferred to a third party.

        2)   After 10 days, cash proceeds are perfected through possession.

    c.   **Second-generation proceeds**

        1)   A perfected security interest in inventory sold for cash continues in the cash proceeds as above.

        2)   When those proceeds are used to purchase more inventory, the security interest floats to (i.e., it is perfected in) the new inventory.

        3)   But if cash proceeds are used to buy property of a kind different from that described in the original filed financing statement, the security interest is not perfected in the second-generation proceeds, except for the first 10 days after the debtor receives them.

            a)   The creditor may extend the status of the security interest as perfected if (s)he again perfects it by possession or filing a financing statement within the 10 days.

    d.   **Noncash proceeds**. The general rule is that the creditor automatically has a perfected security interest in the proceeds for 10 days after the debtor receives them.

        1)   The creditor may continue that perfected status by acquiring possession of the proceeds or filing a financing statement covering it within the 10-day period.

            a)   The financing statement, to be effective, must be filed in the office required for collateral of the type of the proceeds.

7. **Removal of Collateral to New Jurisdiction**. Personal property can be moved out of the jurisdiction in which the security interest was perfected.

   a. A security interest in ordinary goods, documents, and instruments perfected in one state is treated under the UCC as perfected in a state to which the collateral has been removed until the earlier of

      1) The time perfection would lapse in the original jurisdiction, or
      2) Four months after the collateral is moved.

   b. A security interest in the collateral subsequently perfected in the new state will prevail after such a lapse.

      1) But if the earlier security interest is perfected in the new jurisdiction before lapse of perfection, it will prevail over a new security interest which attaches in the new jurisdiction, even if perfected.

   c. When the debtor granting a PMSI and the secured creditor agree that the collateral will be kept in another jurisdiction, perfection of the security interest is governed by the law of that other jurisdiction.

      1) The parties must understand that the collateral is to be kept in the other jurisdiction when the security interest attaches.

      2) Unless the goods remain in the jurisdiction in which the PMSI was granted for more than 30 days, the law of the other jurisdiction governs perfection during that 30-day period and its effect (that is, relative priority of the interest).

   d. A security agreement may provide that removal to a new jurisdiction without prior authorization of the secured party constitutes default for which repossession or foreclosure may be had.

   e. State vehicle licensing statutes frequently preempt these provisions, such that a buyer is not required to inquire into, and obtains title free of, perfected security interests not noted on the vehicle's certificate of title.

8. Stop and review! You have completed the outline for this subunit. Study multiple-choice questions 8 through 15 beginning on page 563.

C. **Priorities**. The degree of protection enjoyed by a secured party varies with the priority of the security interest relative to other claims. Generally, as between two unperfected security interests, the first to attach has priority; as between two perfected security interests, the first secured party to file a financing statement or take possession has priority.

   1. **Priority of Unperfected Security Interests**. An unperfected security interest is subordinate to the following:

      a. A perfected security interest in the same collateral

      b. A lien creditor. A lien creditor is one who acquires a lien either by attachment or judicial process.

         1) A trustee in bankruptcy has the same rights as a judicial lien creditor as of the date the debtor files a petition in bankruptcy.

            a) EXAMPLE: Bank has an unperfected security interest in Tom's equipment as of June 1. Tom files a petition in bankruptcy on August 1. The bankruptcy trustee has priority over Bank's security interest as of August 1. Knowledge of the unperfected claim by the trustee is not relevant to priority.

        b)   The bankruptcy trustee does not have priority over security interests perfected before that date.

   c.   Transferees in bulk and other buyers not in the ordinary course of business

      1)   A buyer of a substantial portion of a debtor's assets is a transferee in bulk.

      2)   The transferee or buyer need not be a secured party, but must, without knowledge of the unperfected security interest,

          a)   Give value
          b)   Take delivery of the collateral

      3)   The delivery requirement applies only if the collateral is goods, instruments, documents, or chattel paper.

          a)   If the collateral is accounts or general intangibles, physical delivery is impossible.

               i)   The transferee must give value without knowledge of the security interest.

   d.   An unperfected security interest has priority over claims of the debtor's general creditors.

      1)   EXAMPLE: Bank lends Tom $15,000 and takes a security interest in Tom's truck fleet. Bank fails to perfect the security interest by filing or taking possession of the collateral. John lends Tom $20,000 but does not take a security interest in collateral. In a priority contest between Bank and John, Bank will prevail.

2. Priority of Perfected Security Interests

   a.   Priority dates from the time of filing or perfection, whichever is first.

      1)   EXAMPLE 1: Bank agreed to lend Gran's Place, Inc. up to $50,000 as needed during the next year. Gran's executed a financing statement covering all owned or thereafter acquired kitchen equipment on January 2. Bank filed the financing statement on January 3, 1999. Finance, Inc. lent Gran's $10,000 on March 1. Gran's executed a financing statement covering all owned or thereafter-acquired kitchen equipment. Finance perfected its security interest by filing the financing statement on March 9. On July 1, Bank lent Gran's $30,000. On July 31, Gran's declared bankruptcy. Bank's security interest has priority over Finance's security interest because Bank filed before Finance filed or perfected.

      2)   EXAMPLE 2: Assume that Bank's first loan to Gran's was filed on July 1. On July 31, Finance's security interest has priority over Bank's security interest. Finance's priority dates from March 9. Bank's priority dates from July 1.

   b.   If a subsequent time period occurs when there is neither filing nor perfection, priority no longer dates from the time of filing or perfection.

      1)   EXAMPLE: In example 1 above, assuming there was no bankruptcy, Bank's filed financing statement will lapse on January 3, 2004 (see B.3.g. on page 548). On January 4, 2004, Finance has a perfected security interest and Bank has an unperfected security interest.

3. Exceptions.

Generally, a duly perfected security interest in goods is good against subsequent purchasers. However, there are situations in which certain third parties acquire the collateral (goods) free of the security interest, even though the interest has been perfected. See the following discussion.

4. **Buyers in the Ordinary Course of Business** (BIOC). (S)he takes free of a security interest conveyed by his/her seller to another.

    a. This includes perfected security interests.
    b. The BIOC's knowledge of the security interest is irrelevant.

        1) EXAMPLE: Family Grocery purchased frozen yogurt from Wholesaler. Wholesaler had conveyed a security interest in its inventory to Freezers, Inc. Freezers had properly perfected the security interest. The president of Wholesaler disclosed the security interest to Family's president before selling the yogurt. If Wholesaler defaults on its obligation to Freezers, Freezers cannot exercise its rights as a secured party against Family.

    c. This rule does not extend to buyers of farm products from farmers.

5. **Buyers of Consumer Goods outside the Ordinary Course of Business**

    a. A consumer buying consumer goods from another consumer takes free of a security interest If (s)he buys under the following conditions:

        1) Without knowledge of the security interest
        2) For value
        3) For consumer purposes
        4) Before the secured party files a financing statement

    b. This rule permits a qualifying buyer to take free of a purchase money security interest in consumer goods, unless the secured party filed a financing statement.

6. **Buyer of Instruments and Chattel Paper**

    a. (S)he has priority over a competing nonpossessory perfected security interest in proceeds of noninventory collateral, if (s)he satisfies the following requirements:

        1) Gives value

        2) Takes possession of the chattel paper or instrument in the ordinary course of his/her business

        3) Acts without knowledge of the competing security interest

            a) EXAMPLE: Bank A has a perfected security interest in Jake's equipment. Bank A's security interest was perfected by its filing a financing statement. Jake sold the equipment to Rose. Rose signed an installment sales contract which gave Jake a security interest in the equipment. The installment sales contract is chattel paper. It is also proceeds from the sale of collateral. The next day, Jake sold the installment sales contract to Bank B. Bank B took possession of the contract. Bank A has priority over Bank B because Bank B had knowledge of Bank A's security interest by virtue of Bank A's filed financing statement. Recall that Bank A's perfected security interest extends to the chattel paper as proceeds without further filing because the proper place for filing a financing statement is the same for equipment and chattel paper.

    b. (S)he also has priority over a competing nonpossessory perfected security interest in proceeds of inventory collateral if (s)he

        1) Gives value, and

        2) Takes possession of the chattel paper or instrument in the ordinary course of his/her business.

            a) The buyer's knowledge of the competing security interest is irrelevant.

b)   EXAMPLE: Bank A has filed a financing statement to perfect its security interest in Jake's new car inventory. Jake sold a car to Dawn. Dawn signed a promissory note for the price of the car. The next day Jake sold the promissory note to Bank B. Bank B took possession of the note. Bank B's president knew that Bank A had a perfected security interest in Jake's inventory. Bank B has priority in the promissory note, which is an instrument, even though Bank A's security interest was automatically perfected in the promissory note (as proceeds) for 10 days.

7.   **Purchase Money Security Interests**. A PMSI arises when a person obtains credit (borrows money) and applies it to acquire (purchase) property, and that property serves as the collateral which secures the obligation to satisfy the credit (repay the money borrowed).

a.   More than one generation of inventory may be financed with the same money (loan/credit). The security interest must be identifiable to the inventory and should be able to float to subsequent generations of the same class of inventory.

1)   Generally, a PMSI in inventory collateral has priority over a conflicting security interest in the same collateral if

a)   It is perfected when the debtor gets possession, and

b)   Written notice is given to all other secured parties before the debtor takes possession of the inventory.

i)   EXAMPLE: Bank is secured by Gavin's inventory. The security agreement contains an after-acquired property clause. Bank's security interest was perfected by filing. Subsequently, Expansion, Inc. began supplying Gavin with a new line of inventory. Expansion sold the inventory to Gavin on credit and retained a PMSI. Expansion filed a financing statement covering the collateral on June 1. Gavin took possession of the new products on June 23. On July 1, Expansion disclosed the PMSI in a letter to Bank. Expansion will not have priority over Bank with respect to the security interest in the new inventory in Gavin's possession because notice was given to Bank after Gavin took possession. If Expansion had notified Bank of the PMSI prior to June 23, however, Expansion's claim to the new inventory would have had priority over Bank's.

b.   A perfected PMSI in inventory extends to identifiable cash proceeds.

1)   EXAMPLE: Bank has a perfected PMSI in Mandy's car inventory. Sam buys a car from Mandy and pays with a check. Bank's perfected PMSI floats to the check as identifiable cash proceeds.

c.   A PMSI in noninventory collateral has priority over a conflicting security interest if the PMSI in noninventory collateral is perfected

1)   Before the debtor takes possession of the collateral, or
2)   Within 10 days of the debtor's taking possession of the collateral.

a)   EXAMPLE: On January 2, Bank lent Luke $50,000 and took a security interest in Luke's currently owned and after-acquired equipment. On June 2, Equip Corp. sold Luke equipment on credit and took a PMSI in the equipment. Luke immediately took possession of the equipment. On June 11, Equip Corp. perfected the PMSI. Equip Corp. has priority over Bank.

NOTE: Perfecting the PMSI in noninventory collateral within 10 days of the debtor's taking possession of the collateral protects the secured party against the rights of transferees in bulk and lien creditors to the extent the rights arise after the PMSI attaches and before it is perfected.

EXAMPLE: Equip Corp. sold a tractor to Luke for use in his lawn maintenance business. Equip Corp. took a PMSI in the tractor. Two days later, John purchased substantially all of Luke's equipment, including the tractor. The next day, Equip Corp. perfected the PMSI by filing a financing statement. Equip Corp. has priority over John because John's rights as a transferee in bulk arose after Equip Corp.'s PMSI attached and before it was perfected in the 10-day period.

8. **Liens Arising by Operation of Law**

    a.   UCC 9-310 provides priority for certain liens arising by operation of law over perfected security interests if the lienholder

        1)   Furnishes services or materials with respect to the goods in the ordinary course of his/her business, and

        2)   Is in possession of the goods.

            a)   If possession of the goods is relinquished, the lien becomes subordinate to a perfected security interest.

    b.   A state statute granting such a lien may expressly provide that it is subordinate to a perfected security interest.

    c.   Knowledge of a security interest by a lienholder has no effect on priority.

        1)   EXAMPLE: Wendy borrows $5,000 from Local Bank to purchase a car and conveys a security interest in the car to Local Bank. Bank perfects the security interest. A week later she takes the car to Best Body Shop for a new paint job. Best Body Shop knew of Local Bank's security interest. When Best Body finishes the job, Wendy has insufficient money to pay. Best retains possession of the car. Wendy defaults in paying the bank. Bank sues Best, demanding delivery of the car. Best alleges its lien, based upon common law, has priority over Bank's perfected security interest. Best's lien is not granted by statute. The court holds that, under UCC 9-310, Best's lien has priority. Best's awareness of Bank's interest is irrelevant.

9. **Security Interests in Fixtures vs. Real Estate Interests**. Occasionally, one party has a security interest in personal property that becomes a fixture, whereas another has a mortgage on the real property itself. Special rules under Article 9 of the UCC govern priorities in such a case.

    a.   In the case of non-PMSIs vs. real estate interests, the security interest has priority if a financing statement is fixture filed before the competing mortgage is recorded. The mortgage has priority if it is recorded first.

        1)   EXAMPLE: Finco lent Red's Barbeque $10,000 and took a security interest in Red's grill, a fixture. Subsequently, Bank lent Red $50,000 and took a mortgage on Red's land and building. Bank recorded the mortgage. Finco then filed on the grill. Bank has priority.

b.   In the case of PMSIs v. real estate interests, a PMSI perfected by fixture filing before goods become fixtures or within 10 days thereafter has priority over any earlier recorded real estate interest.

   1)   EXAMPLE: Appliances, Inc. sold an oven to Tony's Pizzeria and took a security interest in the oven. The oven was installed and became a fixture on October 1. Bank had a previously recorded mortgage on Tony's premises. Appliances perfected the PMSI by fixture filing on October 7. Appliances has priority over bank.

c.   With respect to security interests v. construction mortgages, a construction mortgage has priority over a security interest in fixtures if

   1)   The construction mortgage is recorded before the goods become fixtures, and

   2)   The goods become fixtures before construction is completed.

   NOTE: A mortgage given to refinance a construction mortgage has the priority of the construction mortgage.

10.   Stop and review! You have completed the outline for this subunit. Study multiple-choice questions 16 through 26 beginning on page 566.

D.   Rights of Debtors, Creditors, and Third Parties

1.   **Possession of Collateral**. The secured party in possession of collateral is a bailee and must use reasonable care at all times to preserve the collateral.

   a.   Unless the parties agree otherwise, the debtor bears the cost of reasonable expenses incurred for preservation, use, or custody of the collateral, e.g., costs of insurance and taxes, and of accidental loss or damage in excess of insurance coverage.

   b.   Unless the parties agree otherwise, the secured party

      1)   May keep any increase in the collateral, other than money, as additional security

         a)   EXAMPLE: Stock is pledged as security. A stock dividend is paid to the secured party. The secured party may keep the additional shares of stock. But if a cash dividend is paid to the secured party, it must be remitted to the debtor.

      2)   Must keep the collateral identifiable. However, fungible collateral may be commingled, e.g., grain.

      3)   May repledge the collateral upon terms which do not impair the debtor's right to redeem the collateral

      4)   May use or operate the collateral for the purpose of preserving it, providing it is

         a)   Pursuant to a valid court order, or
         b)   Only to the extent provided for in the security agreement

   c.   A secured party is liable for any loss caused by his/her failure to meet an obligation imposed by the above requirements. But the secured party does not lose his/her security interest by such failure.

2.   **Assignment**. Generally, the account debtor may not restrict the seller's ability to assign the installment contract and security interest.

   a.   Unless otherwise provided, the assignee's rights are subject to

      1)   The terms of the contract between the account debtor and the assignor

      2)   Claims or defenses arising from the sales contract

      3)   Other claims or defenses of the account debtor that accrue before the account debtor is notified of the assignment

   b.   An installment sales contract and security agreement may contain a waiver of defenses clause by which the buyer waives rights to sue or defend against an assignee.

      1)   The clause is generally enforceable if the assignee takes the assignment

         a)   In good faith
         b)   Without notice of a claim or defense
         c)   By giving value

      2)   The clause is generally not effective to waive real defenses. **Real defenses** are

         a)   Infancy of the account debtor

         b)   Incapacity of the account debtor

         c)   Duress

         d)   Misrepresentation which induced the account debtor to sign the contract

         e)   Any other defense which would be viable against a holder in due course of a negotiable instrument

      3)   A Federal Trade Commission rule has rendered ineffective waiver of defense clauses in contracts for consumer goods.

   c.   The seller of goods on installment credit who takes a security interest in the goods often assigns the security interest to a financing institution. The financing institution then lends the seller funds that are used in operations.

      1)   The seller is known as the assignor.
      2)   The financing institution is a secured party known as the assignee.
      3)   The purchaser of the goods is commonly known as an account debtor.

3.   **Default** occurs when the debtor fails to fulfill obligations under the security agreement. A security agreement may provide that an act or occurrence constitutes default. Typical events constituting default are

   a.   Lack of current payments
   b.   Failure to insure the collateral
   c.   Removal of the collateral
   d.   Bankruptcy or insolvency of the debtor
   e.   Failure by the debtor to pay debts to third parties when due

4.   The secured party has three options if the debtor defaults: sue the debtor for the amount due, repossess the collateral, or foreclose on the collateral.

5.   **Repossession**. Upon the debtor's default, the secured party may utilize self-help repossession or repossession by judicial action.

    a.   **Self-help repossession** is taking possession of the collateral without judicial action. Self-help repossession must be peaceable.

        1)   Peaceable means not constituting a breach of the peace. Acts probably peaceable are removal of the collateral

            a)   From a parking lot or street,
            b)   From the open premises of the debtor, or
            c)   With the debtor's consent.

        2)   Acts probably a breach of the peace are removal of the collateral

            a)   Despite the debtor's express objection,
            b)   By a threat of violence, or
            c)   By impersonating an officer of the law.

    b.   **Repossession by judicial action** generally requires obtaining a judicial order or judgment against the debtor.

6.   **Foreclosure**. After repossession, the secured party may dispose of the collateral by means of a foreclosure sale. Foreclosure sales may be either public or private.

    a.   A **public sale** is an auction open to the public.

    b.   A **private sale** is one which is arranged by the secured party through commercial channels.

        1)   EXAMPLE: A secured party contacts a dealer in used equipment and negotiates an agreement for the sale of repossessed power tools. The dealer purchases the tools for resale in the ordinary course of his/her business.

    c.   Foreclosure sales must meet three criteria:

        1)   Reasonable notice of the sale must be given to the debtor.

            a)   Notice is reasonable if it is given in time to allow the debtor to protect his/her interests. A lender who fails to give reasonable notice of a sale is not entitled to a deficiency judgment.

            b)   A debtor may waive his/her right to notice.

                i)   The waiver generally must be written.
                ii)   The waiver must be signed after default.

            c)   In the case of collateral other than consumer goods, notice must be sent to other secured parties from whom the secured party received written notice of an interest in the collateral.

            d)   Notice to the debtor is not required if the collateral is

                i)   Of a type normally sold on a recognized market, e.g., corporate securities

                ii)   Perishable, e.g., fresh vegetables

                iii) Likely to decline quickly in value, e.g., souvenir caps featuring the logo of a team competing in the Superbowl

        2)   The timing of the sale must be reasonable.

            a)   The secured party may not delay the sale without reason.

            b)   Consumer goods must be sold within 90 days of repossession if the debtor has paid more than 60% of the secured obligation.

3) The foreclosure sale must be commercially reasonable. Each aspect of the sale is considered, including the time, place, manner, method, and terms.

    a) A sale is not unreasonable simply because a better price might have been obtained at another time.

        i) However, a sale immediately followed by a similar sale at a substantially greater price is probably not reasonable.

    b) A sale is conclusively presumed to be commercially reasonable if it has been approved in any judicial proceeding or by any bona fide creditors' committee or representative of creditors.

    c) A sale is usually considered to be commercially reasonable if the collateral is sold

        i) In conformity with reasonable commercial practices among dealers in the same type of property,

        ii) In a normal manner in a recognized market, or

        iii) At a market price which is current in a recognized market.

d. A good-faith foreclosure sale buyer for value takes the collateral free of the security interest under which the sale took place and receives all the debtor's rights in the collateral.

    1) The buyer takes the goods free of all claims even if the secured party fails to comply with the rules of foreclosure and sale.

    2) The debtor or other party may recover any losses caused by the improper sale from the secured party.

    3) The buyer also takes free of inferior or junior security interests in the collateral.

e. The secured party may buy the collateral at any public sale. If the collateral is of a type customarily sold in a recognized market or is the subject of widely distributed price quotations, the secured party may buy it at private sale.

f. Foreclosure sale proceeds are applied in the following order:

    1) Expenses of the repossession and foreclosure sale
    2) The debt owed the secured party
    3) The debts owed inferior secured parties
    4) Remaining proceeds paid to the debtor

g. If the sale is commercially reasonable but the proceeds are insufficient to satisfy items 1) through 3) above, the debtor is liable for any deficiency.

h. If the underlying transaction was a sale of accounts or chattel paper, the debtor is entitled to any surplus (or liable for any deficiency) only if the security agreement so provides.

i. Strict foreclosure may be an alternative to a foreclosure sale.

    1) Secured party keeps the collateral in satisfaction of the debt.

    2) Secured party must send written notice of strict foreclosure to the debtor.

        a) After default, the debtor may waive his/her right to notice.

        b) If the collateral is other than consumer goods, written notice must also be sent to

            i) Any person who filed a financing statement covering the collateral

            ii) Any person who the secured party knows claims a security interest in the collateral

3) Strict foreclosure is not allowed if the collateral is consumer goods and 60% of the secured debt has been paid except

    a) The secured party must sell the collateral within 90 days of taking possession of it, unless the debtor, after default, approves of the secured party's retaining the collateral.

    b) No deficiency judgment is allowed when strict foreclosure has taken place.

4) Strict foreclosure is not allowed, and the collateral must be sold, if the debtor or any party to whom notice is required to be sent objects. The objection must be

    a) Written

    b) Received by the foreclosing secured party within 21 days of sending the notice of strict foreclosure

7. **The Debtor's Remedies**

  a. The debtor may redeem his/her interest in the collateral at any time before

    1) The debt is satisfied by strict foreclosure,
    2) The collateral is sold, or
    3) A binding contract for the sale of the collateral is entered into.

  b. Redemption requires the debtor to pay the full amount of secured debt and any expenses the secured party reasonably incurred in dealing with the collateral.

    1) The security agreement may provide for payment of legal expenses.

  c. Prior to disposition of the collateral, a court may order or restrain disposition if the secured party fails to comply with the UCC provisions governing default.

  d. After disposition, the secured party is liable for any loss resulting from his/her noncompliance with the default provisions.

    1) In the case of consumer goods, the debtor may recover the greater of

      a) 10% of the principal of the debt plus the credit service charge, or
      b) 10% of the cash price plus the time-price differential.

    2) EXAMPLE: The cash price of a chain saw is $800. If the chain saw is financed for 36 months, the payments total $1,200. The time-price differential is $1,200 − $800 = $400. Under b), the debtor could recover $400 plus 10% of $800, for a total of $480. Under a), the recovery would be only $80 plus any credit service charges.

  e. If the secured party does not comply with the mandatory sale provision relating to consumer goods, the debtor may recover

    1) Under the Code, or
    2) In conversion.

      a) Conversion is a tort.
      b) Monetary damages may be awarded.

8. Stop and review! You have completed the outline for this subunit. Study multiple-choice questions 27 through 33 beginning on page 570.

MULTIPLE-CHOICE QUESTIONS

A. Attachment of Security Interests

1. The scope of secured transactions under Article 9 of the Uniform Commercial Code does not include

- A. Pledges.
- B. Transactions in which title has not passed.
- C. After-acquired collateral.
- D. Sale of corporate debentures.

The correct answer is (D). *(CPA, adapted)*
REQUIRED: The transaction excluded from Article 9 of the UCC.
DISCUSSION: Article 9 applies to security interests in personal property and fixtures, and also to sales of accounts or chattel paper. It does not apply to a sale of corporate debentures. These are governed by Article 8 of the UCC, other state statutes, and possibly the federal securities laws.
Answers (A), (B), and (C) are incorrect because each is within the scope of Article 9 of the UCC.

2. Under the UCC Secured Transactions Article, for a security interest to attach, the

- A. Debtor must agree to the creation of the security interest.
- B. Creditor must properly file a financing statement.
- C. Debtor must have title to the collateral.
- D. Creditor must be in possession of part of the collateral.

The correct answer is (A). *(CPA, adapted)*
REQUIRED: The condition necessary for attachment of a security interest.
DISCUSSION: Article 9 of the UCC governs secured transactions and sales of accounts and chattel paper. UCC 9-203 states that attachment occurs when all of the following events have taken place unless the time is postponed by an explicit agreement: value has been given, the debtor has rights in the collateral, and the collateral is in the possession of the secured party pursuant to agreement, or the debtor has signed a security agreement containing a description of the collateral.
Answer (B) is incorrect because a financing statement is not mandatory for attachment, but it may be necessary to perfect a security interest. Answer (C) is incorrect because the debtor must have rights in, but not necessarily title to, the collateral. Answer (D) is incorrect because the secured party may, but is not required to, have possession of the collateral pursuant to the agreement.

3. On March 1, Green went to Easy Car Sales to buy a car. Green spoke to a salesperson and agreed to buy a car that Easy had in its showroom. On March 5, Green made a $500 down payment and signed a security agreement to secure the payment of the balance of the purchase price. On March 10, Green picked up the car. On March 15, Easy filed the security agreement. On what date did Easy's security interest attach?

- A. March 1.
- B. March 5.
- C. March 10.
- D. March 15.

The correct answer is (C). *(CPA, adapted)*
REQUIRED: The time a security interest attaches.
DISCUSSION: Attachment is the process by which a security interest becomes enforceable against a debtor by a secured party. Attachment occurs when the following three conditions are satisfied: the debtor has signed a security agreement describing the collateral (or collateral is in the hands of the secured party), value has been given, and the debtor has rights in the collateral. These three conditions were clearly satisfied by March 10.
Answer (A) is incorrect because, on March 1, Green had signed a security agreement. Answer (B) is incorrect because, although the debtor is not required to have possession, it is not clear on these facts that Green had rights in the collateral before (s)he took possession. Answer (D) is incorrect because filing is relevant to perfection. It is not necessary for attachment.

4. Winslow Co., which is in the business of selling furniture, borrowed $60,000 from Pine Bank. Winslow executed a promissory note for that amount and used all of its accounts receivable as collateral for the loan. Winslow executed a security agreement that described the collateral. Winslow did not file a financing statement. Which of the following statements best describes this transaction?

A. Perfection of the security interest occurred even though Winslow did not file a financing statement.

B. Perfection of the security interest occurred by Pine having an interest in accounts receivable.

C. Attachment of the security interest did not occur because Winslow failed to file a financing statement.

D. Attachment of the security interest occurred when the loan was made and Winslow executed the security agreement.

5. Under the Secured Transactions Article of the UCC, which of the following requirements is necessary to have a security interest attach?

	Debtor Has Rights in the Collateral	Proper Filing of a Security Agreement	Value Given by the Creditor
A.	Yes	Yes	Yes
B.	Yes	Yes	No
C.	Yes	No	Yes
D.	No	Yes	Yes

6. Under the UCC Secured Transactions Article, which of the following events will always prevent a security interest from attaching?

A. Failure to have a written security agreement.

B. Failure of the creditor to have possession of the collateral.

C. Failure of the debtor to have rights in the collateral.

D. Failure of the creditor to give present consideration for the security interest.

The correct answer is (D). *(CPA, adapted)*
REQUIRED: The correct statement about attachment and/or perfection of a security interest.
DISCUSSION: According to UCC 9-203, attachment of a security interest occurs upon the completion of all of the following requirements. The requirements include the debtor having rights in the collateral, the giving of value by the creditor, and the existence of a security agreement. Because Pine gave value of $60,000 and Winslow had rights in the accounts receivable, attachment occurred upon Winslow's execution of the security agreement.
Answer (A) is incorrect because, although most security interests are perfected through filing, one of the exceptions is for accounts. However, the exception applies only to an assignment that alone or in conjunction with others to the same assignee does not transfer a significant part of the assignor's accounts. Winslow used all the receivables. Answer (B) is incorrect because, although attachment is prerequisite to perfection, a prerequisite for attachment is that the debtor have an interest in the collateral. Answer (C) is incorrect because the filing of a financing statement is not required by Article 9 for attachment to occur.

The correct answer is (C). *(CPA, adapted)*
REQUIRED: The conditions for attachment.
DISCUSSION: UCC 9-203 states that attachment occurs when all of the following events have taken place unless the time is postponed by an explicit agreement: value has been given, the debtor has rights in the collateral, and the collateral is in the possession of the secured party pursuant to agreement, or the debtor has signed a security agreement containing a description of the collateral.
Answers (A), (B), and (D) are incorrect because attachment requires that the debtor have rights in the collateral and that value be given by the creditor, but not that a security agreement be filed.

The correct answer is (C). *(CPA, adapted)*
REQUIRED: The condition that will prevent a security interest from attaching.
DISCUSSION: UCC 9-203 states that attachment occurs when all of the following events have taken place, unless postponed by explicit agreement: value has been given by the secured party, the debtor has rights in the collateral, and the collateral is in the possession of the secured party pursuant to an agreement, or the debtor has signed a security agreement containing a description of the collateral.
Answer (A) is incorrect because the security agreement need not be written if the secured party is in possession of the collateral. Answer (B) is incorrect because the secured party may, but is not required to, have possession of the collateral pursuant to the written agreement. Answer (D) is incorrect because the secured party must give value (not mere consideration).

7. Under the UCC Secured Transactions Article, which of the following after-acquired property may be attached to a security agreement given to a secured lender?

	Inventory	Equipment
A.	Yes	Yes
B.	Yes	No
C.	No	Yes
D.	No	No

The correct answer is (A). *(CPA, adapted)*
REQUIRED: The scope of an after-acquired property clause.
DISCUSSION: Under UCC 9-204, a security agreement may include after-acquired property as collateral for the obligations secured. It does not apply to consumer goods given as additional security unless the debtor acquires them within 10 days after the secured party gives value. An after-acquired property clause can apply to both inventory and equipment.
Answers (B), (C), and (D) are incorrect because an after-acquired property clause covering either inventory or equipment may be enforced.

B. Perfection of Security Interests

8. Perfection of a security interest permits the secured party to protect its interest by

A. Avoiding the need to file a financing statement.

B. Preventing another creditor from obtaining a security interest in the same collateral.

C. Establishing priority over the claims of most subsequent secured creditors.

D. Denying the debtor the right to possess the collateral.

The correct answer is (C). *(CPA, adapted)*
REQUIRED: The correct statement about perfection of a security interest.
DISCUSSION: For a secured party to gain rights superior to the rights of a prior unperfected creditor or over a subsequent secured creditor, a secured party must give notice by perfecting its security interest through the filing of a financing statement, by taking possession of the collateral, or automatically, in some cases, by attachment. The secured party maximizes rights with respect to the collateral by establishing priority over prior unperfected security interests and subsequent secured parties.
Answer (A) is incorrect because filing a financing statement is required to perfect an interest in certain types of collateral, such as accounts receivable. Answer (B) is incorrect because perfection of a security interest does not bar other creditors from obtaining a security interest in collateral. Answer (D) is incorrect because possession is one means of perfecting a security interest, but the parties ordinarily contemplate that the debtor will have possession.

9. Under the UCC Secured Transactions Article, what is the effect of perfecting a security interest by filing a financing statement?

A. The secured party can enforce its security interest against the debtor.

B. The secured party has permanent priority in the collateral even if the collateral is removed to another state.

C. The debtor is protected against all other parties who acquire an interest in the collateral after the filing.

D. The secured party has priority in the collateral over most creditors who acquire a security interest in the same collateral after the filing.

The correct answer is (D). *(CPA, adapted)*
REQUIRED: The effect of perfecting a security interest by filing a financing statement.
DISCUSSION: Perfection of a security interest maximizes a secured party's rights with respect to the collateral. Although perfection by filing a financing statement will not give the secured party priority over all subsequent secured parties, it will give priority over all unperfected interests and over most subsequent secured interests.
Answer (A) is incorrect because perfection puts those not privy to the secured transaction on notice of the secured party's interest. However, it is not required to enforce the secured party's rights against the debtor. Answer (B) is incorrect because perfection will generally lapse 4 months after the collateral is removed to another state. Answer (C) is incorrect because perfection by filing a financing statement will give the secured party priority over all unperfected creditors and some, but not all, subsequent secured parties.

10. Which of the following transactions would illustrate a secured party perfecting its security interest by taking possession of the collateral?

- A.   A bank receiving a mortgage on real property.

- B.   A wholesaler borrowing to purchase inventory.

- C.   A consumer borrowing to buy a car.

- D.   A pawnbroker lending money.

The correct answer is (D). *(CPA, adapted)*

REQUIRED: The situation representing a secured party perfecting its security interest by possession.

DISCUSSION: A secured party may perfect a security interest by taking possession of the collateral. Pawnbrokers, to secure loans, would usually take possession of the collateral. UCC Section 9-305 provides in pertinent part: a security interest in goods, instruments, money, negotiable documents or chattel paper may be perfected by the secured party's taking possession of the collateral.

Answers (A), (B), and (C) are incorrect because, in such a transaction, perfection is usually by filing because possession would defeat the purpose of the loans.

11. A secured creditor wants to file a financing statement to perfect its security interest. Under the UCC Secured Transactions Article, which of the following must be included in the financing statement?

- A.   A listing or description of the collateral.

- B.   An after-acquired property provision.

- C.   The creditor's signature.

- D.   The collateral's location.

The correct answer is (A). *(CPA, adapted)*

REQUIRED: The item which must be included in the financing statement to perfect a security interest.

DISCUSSION: The financing statement must comply with the requirements of UCC 9-402. To be effective, it must (1) include the names of the debtor and third party, (2) be signed by the debtor, (3) contain the parties' addresses, and (4) contain a statement identifying or listing the type of collateral. If the collateral is growing crops, uncut timber, or unextracted minerals, the financing statement must also describe the pertinent real estate.

Answers (B), (C), and (D) are incorrect because their inclusion is not required for the financing statement to be effective.

12. The Town Bank makes collateralized loans to its customers at 1% above prime on securities owned by the customer, subject to existing margin requirements. In doing so, which of the following is correct?

- A.   Notification of the issuer is necessary in order to perfect a security interest.

- B.   Filing is a permissible method of perfecting a security interest in the securities if the circumstances dictate.

- C.   Any dividend or interest distributions during the term of the loan belong to the bank.

- D.   A perfected security interest in the securities can be obtained only by possession.

The correct answer is (D). *(CPA, adapted)*

REQUIRED: The correct statement concerning loans using securities as collateral.

DISCUSSION: The definition of instruments includes securities (UCC 9-105), and a security interest in instruments can be perfected only by the secured party's taking possession (UCC 9-304). Exceptions are automatic perfection for 21 days after attachment if new value is given and temporary surrender of the securities to the debtor for a period of 21 days. But even then a bona fide purchaser or a holder in due course will take priority.

Answer (A) is incorrect because notification of the issuer (e.g., a corporation) is not necessary for the perfection of a security interest in securities. Answer (B) is incorrect because filing is not a permissible method of perfecting a security interest in the securities due to their ease of transfer. Answer (C) is incorrect because cash distributions during the term of the loan belong to the debtor.

13. Under the UCC Secured Transactions Article, which of the following actions will best perfect a security interest in a negotiable instrument against any other party?

    A. Filing a security agreement.

    B. Taking possession of the instrument.

    C. Perfecting by attachment.

    D. Obtaining a duly executed financing statement.

The correct answer is (B). *(CPA, adapted)*
    REQUIRED: The action which will best perfect a security interest in a negotiable instrument.
    DISCUSSION: UCC 9-305 provides a security interest in goods, instruments, money, negotiable documents, or chattel paper may be perfected by the secured parties taking possession of the collateral. In the case of instruments, possession is the only way to perfect.
    Answers (A) and (D) are incorrect because, in the case of a negotiable instrument, perfection can only be by possession of the instrument. Answer (C) is incorrect because a security interest in an instrument can never be perfected by attachment alone.

14. Motor Sales, Inc. sells motor vehicles at retail. It borrowed money from Finance Company and gave a properly executed security agreement in its present and future inventory and in the proceeds therefrom to secure the loan. The security interest was duly perfected under the laws of the state where Motor does business and maintains its entire inventory. Thereafter, Motor sold a new pickup truck from its inventory to Archer and received a certified check in payment of the full price. Which of the following is correct?

    A. Finance must file an amendment to the financing statement every time Motor receives a substantial number of additional vehicles from the manufacturer if Finance is to obtain a valid security interest in subsequently delivered inventory.

    B. Finance's security interest in the certified check Motor received is perfected against Motor's other creditors.

    C. Unless Finance specifically included proceeds in the financing statement it filed, it has no rights to them.

    D. The term "proceeds" does not include used cars received by Motor since they will be resold.

The correct answer is (B). *(CPA, adapted)*
    REQUIRED: The correct statement concerning the sale of an item of inventory which was subject to a perfected security interest.
    DISCUSSION: The certified check received by the debtor constitutes proceeds from the sale of the inventory. At a minimum, the security interest in the proceeds remains perfected for 10 days after receipt by the debtor (UCC 9-306). However, in many circumstances, identifiable proceeds will remain perfected after 10 days without any action by the secured party.
    Answer (A) is incorrect because the after-acquired property (future inventory) clause in the perfected security agreement renders it unnecessary for Finance to file an amendment every time Motor receives additional vehicles from the manufacturer. Answer (C) is incorrect because a security interest continues in proceeds unless the security agreement provides otherwise, and the interest is perfected for a minimum of 10 days. Answer (D) is incorrect because the term "proceeds" includes whatever is received upon the sale, exchange, collection, or other disposition of collateral or proceeds. It includes cash, checks, notes, deposit accounts, exchanged property, insurance property, etc.

15. Grey Corp. sells computers to the public. Grey sold and delivered a computer to West on credit. West executed and delivered to Grey a promissory note for the purchase price and a security agreement covering the computer. West purchased the computer for personal use. Grey did not file a financing statement. Is Grey's security interest perfected?

    A. Yes, because Grey retained ownership of the computer.

    B. Yes, because it was perfected at the time of attachment.

    C. No, because the computer was a consumer good.

    D. No, because Grey failed to file a financing statement.

The correct answer is (B). *(CPA, adapted)*
    REQUIRED: The correct statement about perfection of a security interest.
    DISCUSSION: UCC 9-302 lists the circumstances in which filing is not required to perfect a security interest. Included in the exceptions to filing is a purchase money security interest in consumer goods other than motor vehicles. A purchase money security interest is any interest taken in collateral to secure payment of the purchase price of that collateral. Thus, perfection of the security interest is automatic upon attachment when the sale is made to consumers.
    Answer (A) is incorrect because retaining a security agreement does not prevent title from passing to the buyer. Answers (C) and (D) are incorrect because perfection of a purchase money security interest in goods is automatic upon attachment.

C. Priorities

16. Burn Manufacturing borrowed $500,000 from Howard Finance Co., secured by Burn's current and future inventory, accounts receivable, and the proceeds thereof. The parties signed a financing statement that described the collateral, and the statement was filed in the appropriate state office. Burn subsequently defaulted on the repayment of the loan, and Howard attempted to enforce its security interest. Burn contended that Howard's security interest was unenforceable. In addition, Green, who subsequently gave credit to Burn without knowledge of Howard's security interest, is also attempting to defeat Howard's alleged security interest. The security interest in question is valid with respect to

    A. Both Burn and Green.

    B. Neither Burn nor Green.

    C. Burn but not Green.

    D. Green but not Burn.

The correct answer is (A). *(CPA, adapted)*
    REQUIRED: The correct statement about the validity of a security interest.
    DISCUSSION: Before attachment of the security interest, Article 9 of the UCC requires the creditor to give value, the debtor to have rights in the collateral, and a security agreement to exist. In this case, Howard has given value ($500,000), Burn has rights in the inventory and accounts receivable, and a security agreement exists. Thus, attachment has occurred, and the security interest is enforceable between the debtor and the secured party. Because Howard's security interest was perfected by filing a financing statement, notice of Howard's security interest is imputed to Green, and Howard's claim has priority over Green's.
    Answers (B), (C), and (D) are incorrect because the security interest is enforceable against both Burn and Green.

17. Roth and Dixon both claim a security interest in the same collateral. Roth's security interest attached on January 1, 1999, and it was perfected by filing on March 1, 1999. Dixon's security interest attached on February 1, 1999, and it was perfected on April 1, 1999 by taking possession of the collateral. Which of the following statements is correct?

    A. Roth's security interest has priority because Roth perfected before Dixon perfected.

    B. Dixon's security interest has priority because Dixon's interest attached before Roth's interest was perfected.

    C. Roth's security interest has priority because Roth's security interest attached before Dixon's security interest attached.

    D. Dixon's security interest has priority because Dixon is in possession of the collateral.

The correct answer is (A). *(CPA, adapted)*
    REQUIRED: The correct statement about the priority of perfected security interests.
    DISCUSSION: UCC 9-312 states that conflicting security interests in the same collateral will rank in priority according to the time of filing. Perfection of a security interest can occur only after the attachment requirements have been met. Attachment has occurred for both parties, and the party whose security interest was perfected first will have priority. Roth's security interest was perfected 1 month prior to the perfection of Dixon's security interest, so Roth has priority.
    Answers (B) and (C) are incorrect because attachment is used to establish priority only when the conflicting security interests are unperfected. Answer (D) is incorrect because Dixon's security interest was perfected by possession only after Roth's was perfected.

18. Under the UCC Secured Transactions Article, what is the order of priority for the following security interests in store equipment?

    I. Security interest perfected by filing on April 15, 1999

    II. Security interest attached on April 1, 1999

    III. Purchase money security interest attached April 11, 1999 and perfected by filing on April 20, 1999

    A. I, III, II.

    B. II, I, III.

    C. III, I, II.

    D. III, II, I.

The correct answer is (C). *(CPA, adapted)*
    REQUIRED: The order of priority for the security interests in equipment.
    DISCUSSION: UCC 9-312 states that conflicting security interests in the same collateral will rank in priority according to the time of perfection. If a purchase money security interest (PMSI), in collateral other than inventory, is perfected before or within 10 days after the debtor receives possession of the collateral, the PMSI has priority over conflicting security interests. This is so even if the conflicting security interest was perfected first. Furthermore, a perfected security interest generally has priority over a security interest that is not perfected.
    Answer (A) is incorrect because the purchase money security interest was perfected before or within 10 days after the debtor received possession of the collateral. Answers (B) and (D) are incorrect because a perfected security interest generally has priority over an unperfected security interest.

19. Under the Secured Transactions Article of the UCC, what would be the order of priority for the following nonpurchased money security interests in consumer goods?

I. Financing agreement filed on April 1

II. Possession of the collateral by a creditor on April 10

III. Security interest perfected on April 15

    A. I, II, III.

    B. II, I, III.

    C. II, III, I.

    D. III, II, I.

The correct answer is (A). *(CPA, adapted)*
    REQUIRED: The priority of perfected security interests.
    DISCUSSION: Under the general priority rules of the UCC, a creditor perfects a security interest in consumer goods either by taking possession of the collateral or by filing a financing statement. A perfected security interest takes priority according to the date it was perfected (April 1, April 10, and April 15) unless it is a purchase money security interest. A PMSI in collateral other than inventory has priority if it is perfected when the debtor receives possession or within 10 days thereafter.
    Answers (B), (C), and (D) are incorrect because the security interest perfected by filing on April 1 has priority over that perfected by possession on April 10, which has priority over the security interest perfected on April 15.

20. A party who filed a security interest in inventory on April 1, 1999 would have a superior interest to which of the following parties?

    A. A holder of a mechanic's lien whose lien was filed on March 15, 1999.

    B. A holder of a purchase money security interest in after-acquired property filed on March 20, 1999.

    C. A purchaser in the ordinary course of business who purchased on April 10, 1999.

    D. A judgment lien creditor who filed its judgment on April 15, 1999.

The correct answer is (D). *(CPA, adapted)*
    REQUIRED: The party who will have a superior interest in inventory.
    DISCUSSION: When two perfected security interests conflict, the first secured party to file a financing statement or take possession of the collateral has priority. A secured party who filed on April 1, 1999 would have priority over a judgment lien creditor who filed on April 15, 1999. The judgment lien creditor's interest would be superior to an unperfected security interest or one perfected after attachment of the lien.
    Answer (A) is incorrect because a mechanic's lien filed before another secured party's interest was filed would have priority. Answer (B) is incorrect because a PMSI in inventory collateral has priority over a conflicting security interest in the same collateral if (1) it is perfected at the time the debtor gets possession and (2) written notice is given to all other secured parties before the debtor takes possession of the inventory. Answer (C) is incorrect because a buyer in the ordinary course of business takes the collateral free of perfected or unperfected security interests even if the secured party did not authorize the sale.

21. Noninventory goods were purchased and delivered on June 15, 1999. Several security interests exist in these goods. Which of the following security interests has priority over the others?

    A. Security interest in futu goods attached June 10, 1999.

    B. Security interest attached June 15, 1999.

    C. Security interest perfected June 20, 1999.

    D. Purchase money security interest perfected June 24, 1999.

The correct answer is (D). *(CPA, adapted)*
    REQUIRED: The security interest that has priority.
    DISCUSSION: If a purchase money security interest (PMSI), in collateral other than inventory, is perfected before or within 10 days after the debtor receives possession of the collateral, the PMSI has priority over conflicting security interests. This is so even if the conflicting security interest was perfected first.
    Answers (A) and (B) are incorrect because both are unperfected security interests and subordinate to a perfected security interest in the same collateral. Answer (C) is incorrect because the PMSI has priority in that it was not in inventory and it was perfected within 10 days after the debtor received possession.

22. On June 15, Harper purchased equipment for $100,000 from Imperial Corp. for use in its manufacturing process. Harper paid for the equipment with funds borrowed from Eastern Bank. Harper gave Eastern a security agreement and financing statement covering Harper's existing and after-acquired equipment. On June 21, Harper was petitioned involuntarily into bankruptcy under Chapter 7 of the Federal Bankruptcy Code. A bankruptcy trustee was appointed. On June 23, Eastern filed the financing statement. Which of the parties will have a superior security interest in the equipment?

    A. The trustee in bankruptcy, because the filing of the financing statement after the commencement of the bankruptcy case would be deemed a preferential transfer.

    B. The trustee in bankruptcy, because the trustee became a lien creditor before Eastern perfected its security interest.

    C. Eastern, because it had a perfected purchase money security interest without having to file a financing statement.

    D. Eastern, because it perfected its security interest within the permissible time limits.

The correct answer is (D). *(CPA, adapted)*
    REQUIRED: The party with a superior security interest in equipment after bankruptcy.
    DISCUSSION: A purchase money security interest (PMSI) is an interest taken in collateral to secure payment of the purchase price of that collateral. Because the loan proceeds were used to purchase the equipment, Eastern Bank has a PMSI. UCC 9-312 states that a PMSI in collateral other than inventory has priority over a conflicting security interest in the same collateral or its proceeds if it is perfected at the time the debtor receives possession of the collateral or within 10 days thereafter. Even in bankruptcy proceedings, a secured creditor with a perfected security interest may pursue its remedy against the particular property. Thus, Eastern Bank's perfected PMSI in the equipment is superior (it is not inventory). However, the trustee in bankruptcy has the status of a hypothetical lien creditor and can defeat a nonperfected security interest in personal property (UCC 9-301).
    Answer (A) is incorrect because filing is not a transfer. It perfects the PMSI. Answer (B) is incorrect because, even in bankruptcy proceedings, a secured creditor with a perfected security interest may pursue its remedy against the particular property. Answer (C) is incorrect because filing was required for perfection, even though it could be done up to 10 days after the debtor received possession of the collateral.

23. Under the UCC Secured Transactions Article, perfection of a security interest by a creditor provides added protection against other parties in the event the debtor does not pay its debts. Which of the following parties is not affected by perfection of a security interest?

    A. Other prospective creditors of the debtor.

    B. The trustee in a bankruptcy case.

    C. A buyer in the ordinary course of business.

    D. A subsequent personal injury judgment creditor.

The correct answer is (C). *(CPA, adapted)*
    REQUIRED: The party not affected by perfection of the security interest.
    DISCUSSION: A buyer in the ordinary course of business means a person who, in good faith and without knowledge that the sale to him/her is in violation of the ownership rights or security interest of a third party in the good, buys in the ordinary course of business from a person in the business of selling goods of that kind. Such a buyer takes free of a perfected security interest granted by the seller (even if the buyer knows of its existence).
    Answers (A) and (D) are incorrect because each subsequent creditor is affected. Answer (B) is incorrect because, although a trustee in bankruptcy is hypothetically a lien creditor, a secured party with a prior perfected security interest will prevail.

24. Under the Secured Transactions Article of the UCC, which of the following purchasers will own consumer goods free of a perfected security interest in the goods?

    A. A merchant who purchases the goods for resale.

    B. A merchant who purchases the goods for use in its business.

    C. A consumer who purchases the goods from a consumer purchaser who gave the security interest.

    D. A consumer who purchases the goods in the ordinary course of business.

The correct answer is (D). *(CPA, adapted)*
    REQUIRED: The purchaser that can acquire goods free of a perfected security interest.
    DISCUSSION: According to Article 1 and Article 9 of the UCC, a buyer in the ordinary course of business takes the goods free of any security interest if (s)he buys the goods from a seller of that kind of goods. The right is extended to the buyer regardless of whether the security interest is perfected or the buyer has knowledge of its existence.
    Answers (A) and (B) are incorrect because no exception to the general priority rules is provided for a merchant who purchases goods for resale or use in its business. Answer (C) is incorrect because, once a security interest has been perfected by filing, a consumer who purchases goods from another consumer is not protected.

25. On July 8, Ace, a refrigerator wholesaler, purchased 50 refrigerators. This comprised Ace's entire Inventory and was financed under an agreement with Rome Bank that gave Rome a security interest in all refrigerators on Ace's premises, all future acquired refrigerators, and the proceeds of sales. On July 12, Rome filed a financing statement that adequately identified the collateral. On August 15, Ace sold one refrigerator to Cray for personal use and four refrigerators to Zone Co. for its business. Which of the following statements is correct?

A. The refrigerators sold to Zone will be subject to Rome's security interest.

B. The refrigerator sold to Cray will not be subject to Rome's security interest.

C. The security interest does not include the proceeds from the sale of the refrigerators to Zone.

D. The security interest may not cover after-acquired property even if the parties agree.

The correct answer is (B). *(CPA, adapted)*

REQUIRED: The correct statement concerning the scope and priority of a security interest in inventory.

DISCUSSION: Automatic perfection upon attachment of a purchase money security interest (PMSI) is only possible when the PMSI is in consumer goods. Thus, Rome Bank's PMSI was perfected on July 12.

A buyer in the ordinary course of business takes the goods free of any security interest if (s)he buys the goods from a seller of that kind of goods. This right is extended to the buyer regardless of whether the security interest is perfected or the buyer has knowledge of its existence.

Answer (A) is incorrect because the purpose for which a good is purchased is irrelevant if the buyer purchases in the ordinary course of business. Answer (C) is incorrect because the security interest is perfected as to the proceeds for at least 10 days. But it still does not have priority over the claim of the buyer in the ordinary course of business. Answer (D) is incorrect because the parties may agree that a security interest extends to after-acquired property.

26. Larkin is a wholesaler of computers. Larkin sold 40 computers to Elk Appliance for $80,000. Elk paid $20,000 down and signed a promissory note for the balance. Elk also executed a security agreement giving Larkin a security interest in Elk's inventory, including the computers. Larkin perfected its security interest by properly filing a financing statement in the state of Whiteacre. Six months later, Elk moved its business to the state of Blackacre, taking the computers. On arriving in Blackacre, Elk secured a loan from Quarry Bank and signed a security agreement, putting up all inventory (including the computers) as collateral. Quarry perfected its security interest by properly filing a financing statement in the state of Blackacre. Two months after arriving in Blackacre, Elk went into default on both debts. Which of the following statements is correct?

A. Quarry's security interest is superior because Larkin's time to file a financing statement in Blackacre had expired prior to Quarry's filing.

B. Quarry's security interest is superior because Quarry had no actual notice of Larkin's security interest.

C. Larkin's security interest is superior even though at the time of Elk's default Larkin had not perfected its security interest in the state of Blackacre.

D. Larkin's security interest is superior provided it repossesses the computers before Quarry does.

The correct answer is (C). *(CPA, adapted)*

REQUIRED: The correct statement concerning priority of the security agreements.

DISCUSSION: The perfection of the security interest continues until the earlier of the perfection period in the original jurisdiction or 4 months after removal from the jurisdiction in which the perfection was obtained. Here, the security was perfected until the day of removal. It would have continued perfected until 4 months later without any action by Larkin. Thus, 2 months after arriving in Blackacre, Larkin's security interest had the status of being perfected prior to the subsequent security interest (UCC 9-103).

Answer (A) is incorrect because Larkin had 4 months to file a financing statement in Blackacre after the collateral had been moved there. Answer (B) is incorrect because Larkin's perfection of the security interest in the state of Whiteacre provided constructive notice and priority over subsequently perfected security interests. Answer (D) is incorrect because the status of Larkin's perfected security interest provided the priority over Quarry's security interest, not the date of repossession.

D. Rights of Debtors, Creditors, and Third Parties

27. Under the Secured Transactions Article of the UCC, which of the following remedies is available to a secured creditor when a debtor fails to make a payment when due?

	Proceed against the Collateral	Obtain a General Judgment against the Debtor
A.	Yes	Yes
B.	Yes	No
C.	No	Yes
D.	No	No

The correct answer is (A). *(CPA, adapted)*
REQUIRED: The remedies available to a secured creditor upon default by a debtor.
DISCUSSION: Part 5 of Article 9 of the UCC governs default by debtors and the remedies afforded to secured parties. Although default by a debtor does not require a secured creditor to take action, there are three options given to a secured party. The secured party can sue the debtor for the amount owed, foreclose on the collateral, or repossess the collateral privately through the self-help provision of Article 9.
Answers (B), (C), and (D) are incorrect because the creditor may sue on the debt, attempt self-help repossession, or foreclose on the collateral.

28. Under the UCC Secured Transactions Article, if a debtor is in default under a payment obligation secured by goods, the secured party has the right to

	Reduce the Claim to a Judgment	Sell the Goods and Apply the Proceeds toward the Debt	Peacefully Repossess the Goods without Judicial Process
A.	Yes	Yes	No
B.	Yes	No	Yes
C.	No	Yes	Yes
D.	Yes	Yes	Yes

The correct answer is (D). *(CPA, adapted)*
REQUIRED: The rights of a secured party when a debtor defaults under a payment obligation.
DISCUSSION: Part 5 of Article 9 of the UCC governs default by debtors and the remedies afforded to secured parties. Although default by a debtor does not require a secured creditor to take action, there are essentially three options given to a secured party. The secured party can sue the debtor for the amount owed, foreclose on the collateral, or repossess the collateral privately through the self-help provision of Article 9.
Answer (A) is incorrect because the secured party has the right to repossess the collateral either privately or with judicial assistance. Answer (B) is incorrect because the secured party has the right to foreclose on the collateral and have the proceeds of a judicial sale applied to repayment of the debt. Answer (C) is incorrect because the secured party has the right to sue the debtor for the amount paid.

29. In what order are the following obligations paid after a secured creditor rightfully sells the debtor's collateral after repossession?

I. Debt owed to any junior security holder
II. Secured party's reasonable sale expenses
III. Debt owed to the secured party

A. I, II, III.

B. II, I, III.

C. II, III, I.

D. III, II, I.

The correct answer is (C). *(CPA, adapted)*
REQUIRED: The order for paying obligations after a secured creditor rightfully sells the debtor's collateral.
DISCUSSION: Proceeds of disposition are applied in the following order: (1) reasonable sale expenses, (2) the secured debt, and (3) subordinate secured debts.
Answers (A) and (B) are incorrect because the debt secured by the security interest under which the disposition is made is satisfied before subordinate secured debts. Answer (D) is incorrect because proceeds are first applied to reasonable costs of disposing of the collateral.

30. Under the UCC Secured Transactions Article, which of the following statements is correct concerning the disposition of collateral by a secured creditor after a debtor's default?

  A. A good-faith purchaser for value and without knowledge of any defects in the sale takes free of any subordinate liens or security interests.

  B. The debtor may not redeem the collateral after the default.

  C. Secured creditors with subordinate claims retain the right to redeem the collateral after the collateral is sold to a third party.

  D. The collateral may only be disposed of at a public sale.

The correct answer is (A). *(CPA, adapted)*
REQUIRED: The correct statement under the UCC Secured Transactions Article concerning disposition of collateral.
DISCUSSION: UCC 9-504 states that, when a secured party disposes of collateral after default, the purchaser for value takes the property free of any subordinate security interests or liens and free of the security interest under which the sale was made. As long as the purchaser acts in good faith, the purchaser will receive the property free of any security interest even if the secured party does not comply with the requirements for the sale under Article 9.
Answer (B) is incorrect because the debtor may redeem his/her interest in the collateral after default as long as it is before disposition. Answer (C) is incorrect because a good-faith purchaser for value takes the property free of any subordinate security interests or liens. Answer (D) is incorrect because foreclosure sales may be either public or private.

31. Wine purchased a computer using the proceeds of a loan from MJC Finance Company. Wine gave MJC a security interest in the computer. Wine executed a security agreement and financing statement, which was filed by MJC. Wine used the computer to monitor Wine's personal investments. Later, Wine sold the computer to Jacobs, for Jacobs' family use. Jacobs was unaware of MJC's security interest. Wine now is in default under the MJC loan. May MJC repossess the computer from Jacobs?

  A. No, because Jacobs was unaware of the MJC security interest.

  B. No, because Jacobs intended to use the computer for family or household purposes.

  C. Yes, because MJC's security interest was perfected before Jacobs' purchase.

  D. Yes, because Jacobs' purchase of the computer made Jacobs personally liable to MJC.

The correct answer is (C). *(CPA, adapted)*
REQUIRED: The right of a secured party to repossess collateral sold by the debtor.
DISCUSSION: A buyer from the original purchaser of consumer goods (a buyer outside the ordinary course of business) will have priority over a secured party whose security interest is perfected by attachment if the buyer has no knowledge of the security interest; gives value; and buys for his/her personal, family, or household purposes. If a financing statement has been filed, constructive knowledge of the security interest is imputed to the buyer, and the secured party will prevail. Thus, MJC may repossess after Wine's default (UCC 9-307).
Answer (A) is incorrect because, in that a financing statement was filed, Jacobs had constructive knowledge of the security interest, and the secured party will prevail. Answer (B) is incorrect because a person who buys from the original purchaser is a casual purchaser, not a buyer in the ordinary course of business who would prevail even with actual knowledge of the security interest. Answer (D) is incorrect because there was neither an assignment nor a novation.

Questions 32 and 33 are based on the following information. Drew bought a computer for personal use from Hale Corp. for $3,000. Drew paid $2,000 in cash and signed a security agreement for the balance. Hale properly filed the security agreement. Drew defaulted in paying the balance of the purchase price. Hale asked Drew to pay the balance. When Drew refused, Hale peacefully repossessed the computer.

32. Under the UCC Secured Transactions Article, which of the following remedies will Hale have?

   A. Obtain a deficiency judgment against Drew for the amount owed.

   B. Sell the computer and retain any surplus over the amount owed.

   C. Retain the computer over Drew's objection.

   D. Sell the computer without notifying Drew.

The correct answer is (A). *(CPA, adapted)*
   REQUIRED: The secured party's remedy after default by the debtor.
   DISCUSSION: The secured party may dispose of collateral at a public or private sale provided the disposition is commercially reasonable. Proceeds are applied to reasonable sale expenses, the secured debt, and subordinate secured debt. If proceeds are insufficient, the creditor may seek a deficiency judgment against a debtor for the balance owed.
   Answer (B) is incorrect because the secured party must account to the debtor for any surplus on disposition of the collateral after default (UCC 9-504). Answer (C) is incorrect because the UCC provides for compulsory disposition if the debtor objects to strict foreclosure. Answer (D) is incorrect because the UCC requires that reasonable notice be given to the debtor unless the debtor has waived that right.

33. Under the UCC Secured Transactions Article, which of the following rights will Drew have?

   A. Redeem the computer after Hale sells it.

   B. Recover the sale price from Hale after Hale sells the computer.

   C. Force Hale to sell the computer.

   D. Prevent Hale from selling the computer.

The correct answer is (C). *(CPA, adapted)*
   REQUIRED: The debtor's rights after peaceful repossession of the collateral.
   DISCUSSION: If the debtor has paid at least 60% of the debt in the case of consumer goods, the secured party must dispose of the goods (UCC 9-505). However, a waiver or renunciation of rights may be made in writing by the debtor after default. Similarly, if the debtor objects to the creditor's retention of the goods (strict foreclosure), then the creditor is required to sell the goods in a commercially reasonable manner.
   Answer (A) is incorrect because the debtor has a right of redemption, which cannot be waived or varied, but this right does not continue after the collateral has been sold by the secured party. Answer (B) is incorrect because proceeds of this sale are allocated to the costs of the sale, to the debt that was secured, and to other secured debts. Answer (D) is incorrect because the debtor's right is not to prevent the creditor from selling the collateral but to prevent strict foreclosure (the debtor retaining the goods).

OOF QUESTION 1 *(CPA, adapted)* 10-15 minutes

On January 2, 1999, Gray Interiors Corp., a retailer of sofas, contracted with Shore Furniture Co. to purchase 150 sofas for its inventory. The purchase price was $250,000. Gray paid $50,000 cash and gave Shore a note and security agreement for the balance. On March 1, 1999, the sofas were delivered. On March 10, 1999, Shore filed a financing statement.

On February 1, 1999, Gray negotiated a $1 million line of credit with Float Bank, pledged its present and future inventory as security, and gave Float a security agreement. On February 20, 1999, Gray borrowed $100,000 from the line of credit. On March 5, 1999, Float filed a financing statement.

On April 1, 1999, Dove, a consumer purchaser in the ordinary course of business, purchased a sofa from Gray. Dove was aware of both security interests.

Required

For each item, determine whether (A), (B), or (C) is correct.

1. Shore's security interest in the sofas attached on

   A. January 2, 1999.
   B. March 1, 1999.
   C. March 10, 1999.

2. Shore's security interest in the sofas was perfected on

   A. January 2, 1999.
   B. March 1, 1999.
   C. March 10, 1999.

3. Float's security interest in Gray's inventory attached on

   A. February 1, 1999.
   B. March 1, 1999.
   C. March 5, 1999.

4. Float's security interest in Gray's inventory was perfected on

   A. February 1, 1999.
   B. February 20, 1999.
   C. March 5, 1999.

5. A. Shore's security interest has priority because it was a purchase money security interest.
   B. Float's security interest has priority because Float's financing statement was filed before Shore's.
   C. Float's security interest has priority because Float's interest attached before Shore's.

6. A. Dove purchased the sofa subject to Shore's security interest.
   B. Dove purchased the sofa subject to both the Shore and Float security interests.
   C. Dove purchased the sofa free of either the Shore or Float security interests.

Knowledge Tested

1. Attachment of security interest
2. Perfection
3. Priority of conflicting claims

Authors' Comments

This question tests the requirements of attachment, the distinction between attachment and perfection, and the critical issue of priority. The format lends itself to testing many of the important rules in each area of law tested on the exam.

1. The correct answer is (B).
   DISCUSSION: The attachment of a security interest occurs when the following three conditions are satisfied: The debtor signs a security agreement describing the collateral (unless the secured party has possession of the collateral), the secured party gives value in exchange for the security interest, and the debtor has rights in the collateral. Although the first two criteria were satisfied on January 2, 1999, Gray did not have rights to the sofas until they were identified. Therefore, Shore's security interest attached on March 1, 1999, the date of delivery.

2. The correct answer is (C).
   DISCUSSION: The typical method used to perfect a security interest in inventory is by filing a financing statement. Shore filed the financing statement on March 10, 1999 and thus perfected its security interest in the sofas on that date.

3. The correct answer is (A).
   DISCUSSION: The attachment of a security interest occurs when the following three conditions are satisfied: The debtor signs a security agreement describing the collateral (unless the secured party has possession of the collateral), the secured party gives value in exchange for the security interest, and the debtor has rights in the collateral. The security interest attached on February 1, 1999 because all three conditions were satisfied. Gray has rights in the present inventory that it pledged to Float, although Gray does not yet have rights in the future inventory that it also pledged.

4. The correct answer is (C).
   DISCUSSION: The typical method used to perfect a security interest is by filing a financing statement. Float filed the financing statement on March 5, 1999 and thus perfected its security interest in the sofas on that date.

5. The correct answer is (B).
   DISCUSSION: Generally, between two perfected security interests, the first secured party to file or perfect has priority. Since Float perfected by filing its financing statement before Shore, Float's security interest has priority. While Shore's security interest was a purchase money security interest (PMSI) in inventory, a PMSI in inventory has priority over a conflicting security interest in the same collateral only if it is filed before the debtor gets possession of the inventory and if written notice is given to all other secured parties before the debtor takes possession. Gray took possession of the goods on March 1, but Shore did not perfect until March 10. The 10-day grace period applies only to a PMSI in noninventory. Note that the date a security interest attaches is irrelevant to the priorities of secured parties.

6. The correct answer is (C).
   DISCUSSION: A purchaser in the ordinary course of business takes the goods free of any perfected and unperfected security interests conveyed from one seller to another secured party. Even if the purchaser has knowledge of the prior security interests, (s)he still takes the goods free of these security interests.

OOF QUESTION 2 *(CPA, adapted)* 15-20 minutes

Newco sells computers to the general public. On April 30, Newco financed the purchase of its computer inventory with National Bank. Newco executed and delivered a promissory note and a security agreement covering the inventory. National filed a financing statement on the same day.

On May 1, Newco sold a computer out of its inventory to Kast, who intended to use it to do some household budgeting. Kast made a 50% cash down payment toward the purchase price. Kast executed and delivered to Newco a promissory note for the balance and a security agreement covering the computer. Kast was aware that Newco financed its inventory with National. Newco did not file a financing statement.

On May 6, Kast, who was dissatisfied with the computer, sold it on credit to Marc, who intended to use it to assist in family budgeting. Marc, who was unaware that Kast had purchased the computer on credit, paid 25% of the purchase price and executed and delivered to Kast a promissory note for the balance and a security agreement covering the computer. Kast did not file a financing statement.

On May 12, Marc borrowed $6,000 from Alcor Finance. Marc gave Alcor a promissory note for the loan amount and a security agreement covering the computer and other household appliances owned by Marc. Alcor did not file a financing statement.

Marc failed to pay Alcor or Kast. In turn, Kast has been unable to pay Newco. On June 2, Newco defaulted on its obligation to pay National.

Required

Each of items 1 through 6 to the right contains a statement related to one or more aspects of secured transactions. Select the term or phrase associated with (A) through (F) from the list below which is best matched to the statement in each of items 1 through 6. Each answer may be used only once.

(A) Artisan's lien
(B) Trustee in bankruptcy
(C) Security interest in an instrument
(D) Statutory lien
(E) Future advances clause
(F) Perfected security interest

1. Security interest initially can be perfected only by possession.

2. The security interest has priority over an unperfected one which attached earlier.

3. Assures secured party that loans subsequently made to debtor will be paid.

4. A security interest which has priority over and arose after one which was already perfected.

5. Does not have priority over security interests perfected before petition was filed.

6. Article 9 does not apply to this lien.

Items 7 through 15 contain statements or conclusions from the facts to the left. If the statement or conclusion is correct, indicate it by an (A); if it is incorrect, mark (B) as your answer. "UCC" is used to abbreviate Uniform Commercial Code.

7. Kast had no security interest in the computer because no financing statement was filed.

8. Newco's security interest was a purchase money security interest.

9. National Bank's security interest in the computers was perfected before it filed the financing statement.

10. Kast acquired the computer subject to National Bank's security interest.

11. National Bank acquired a security interest in the cash paid and the promissory note given by Kast, and the security interest was perfected without any further action by National or Newco.

12. If Newco purchased new inventory with the cash paid by Kast more than a week after the sale, National has no interest in that inventory.

13. Marc acquired the computer subject to Newco's security interest.

14. Alcor cannot enforce its security interest against Marc because Alcor did not file a financing statement.

15. Alcor's security interest was nevertheless automatically perfected because the collateral constituted consumer goods.

Knowledge Tested

1. Applicability of Article 9 of the UCC
2. Attachment of security interests
3. Perfection of security interests
4. Identify purchase money security interest
5. Priority among security interests
6. Security interests in proceeds
7. Interests when collateral is transferred

Authors' Comments

General applicability of Article 9 is easy to recognize. Watch for the exceptions. Rules for attachment and perfection are straightforward. The material becomes challenging when priority among competing security interests must be determined. Read the outline several times for understanding the relationships. A set such as this is less demanding when the easy questions are answered first.

1. The correct answer is (C).

DISCUSSION: The method by which a security interest is perfected depends on the nature of the collateral. Security interests in instruments, including negotiable instruments and securities represented by a certificate, can be perfected initially only by possession.

2. The correct answer is (F).

DISCUSSION: A perfected security interest generally has priority over an unperfected security interest in the same collateral.

3. The correct answer is (E).

DISCUSSION: A future advance clause provides that repayment of funds lent to the debtor by the secured party in the future will be secured by the original collateral. Distinguish an after-acquired clause, which conveys an interest in property acquired in the future.

4. The correct answer is (A).

DISCUSSION: UCC 9-310 provides priority for certain liens arising by operation of law over perfected security interests. If the lienholder furnishes services or materials with respect to the goods in the ordinary course of his/her business, and is in possession of such goods, the lienholder has priority. The common-law artisan's lien is such a lien.

5. The correct answer is (B).

DISCUSSION: A trustee in bankruptcy has the same rights as a judicial lien creditor as of the date the debtor files a petition in bankruptcy. However, the trustee does not have priority over security interests perfected before that date.

6. The correct answer is (D).

DISCUSSION: There are a number of interests in property related to payment of debt which Article 9 does not govern; e.g., Article 9 does not apply to liens on real property or statutory liens.

7. The correct answer is (B).

DISCUSSION: A security interest under Article 9 of the UCC is an interest in personal property or fixtures which secures payment of an obligation. Perfection of security interests affects their priority but is not necessary to their existence. Filing a financing statement is necessary to perfect some, but not all, security interests.

8. The correct answer is (A).

DISCUSSION: A purchase money security interest (PMSI) arises when a person applies credit (including money) to acquire property, and that property serves as the collateral which secures the obligation to satisfy the credit.

9. The correct answer is (B).

DISCUSSION: A creditor perfects a security interest by filing a financing statement (at a location designated under Article 9) if the collateral is classified as consumer goods, inventory, fixtures, etc. The computer was part of Kast's inventory.

10. The correct answer is (B).

DISCUSSION: Since Kast purchased the computer in the ordinary course of business, Kast acquired it free of any security interest given by Newco. The BIOC is free of the security interest to National even though (s)he knew of it.

11. The correct answer is (A).

DISCUSSION: A security interest perfected as to collateral is perfected as to proceeds. Proceeds include both cash proceeds and noncash proceeds such as accounts receivable and negotiable instruments. Checks are considered cash proceeds. The security interest is automatically perfected for no more than 10 days.

12. The correct answer is (B).

DISCUSSION: A perfected security interest in collateral proceeds continues in the cash proceeds. When those proceeds are used to purchase more inventory, the security interest "floats" to and is perfected in the new inventory.

13. The correct answer is (B).

DISCUSSION: Marc was a consumer buying consumer goods from another consumer. As a buyer of consumer goods outside of the ordinary course of business, Marc acquired the goods free of Newco's interest because Marc bought (1) for value, (2) for consumer purposes, (3) before Newco filed a financing statement, and (4) without knowledge of Newco's security interest.

14. The correct answer is (B).

DISCUSSION: Alcor's security interest attached because value was given, the debtor (Marc) had rights in the collateral, and the debtor (Marc) executed and delivered a security agreement covering the collateral to the debtor (Alcor). Perfection affects priority between creditors. A creditor can enforce a security interest which has attached against the debtor, whether it is perfected or not.

15. The correct answer is (B).

DISCUSSION: Purchase money security interests in consumer goods are automatically perfected, that is, without filing. However, Alcor does not have a PMSI since Marc's credit (money lent) from Alcor was not used to purchase the collateral.

ESSAY QUESTION *(CPA, adapted)* 15-20 minutes

Mead, a junior member of a CPA firm's audit staff, was assigned to assist in auditing Abco Electronics, Inc.'s financial statements. Abco sells various brands of computer equipment to the general public and to distributors who sell the equipment to retail customers for personal and business use. One of Mead's assignments was to evaluate the following transactions:

* On September 1, Abco sold a CDM computer out of its inventory to Rice, who intended to use it for business purposes. Rice paid 25% of the purchase price and executed and delivered to Abco a promissory note for the balance. A security agreement was signed only by the Abco sales representative. Abco failed to file a financing statement. Rice is in default under the promissory note. Rice claims that Abco does not have an effective security interest in the computer because Rice did not sign the security agreement and because Abco did not file a financing statement.

* On August 18, Abco sold a computer to Baker, who intended to use it for business inventory and accounts payable control and payroll processing. Baker paid 20% of the purchase price and executed and delivered to Abco a promissory note for the balance and a security agreement covering the computer. Abco filed a financing statement on August 27. On August 25, Baker borrowed $5,000 from Condor Finance Co., giving Condor a promissory note for the loan amount and a security agreement covering the computer. Condor filed a financing statement on August 26. Baker defaulted on the promissory note given to Abco and its obligation to Condor. Condor has asserted that its security interest in the computer is superior to Abco's.

Required

State whether the claims of Rice and Condor are correct, and give the reasons for your conclusions.

Knowledge Tested

1. Requirements for attachment of security interest
2. Identifying purchase money security interest (PMSI)
3. Perfecting security interests
4. Priority among security interests

Authors' Comments

The AICPA unofficial answer identifies the requirements for attachment and then points out which one was not satisfied. Another approach is to identify each requirement by indicating how it is or is not satisfied by the facts.

Attachment is required for perfection, which affects priority. Failure to memorize the basic types of perfection (e.g., automatic) and the requirements for each costs exam points. These types of knowledge lend themselves to testing by objective or essay questions. The same applies to recognizing a purchase money security interest and priority between security interests. They are all clearly presented in the outline.

AICPA Unofficial Answer

Rice's assertion that Abco does not have an effective security interest in the CDM computer purchased by Rice is correct. For Abco to have an enforceable security interest in the collateral, the security interest claimed must have attached. Attachment requires that

* The secured party (Abco) has given value,
* The debtor (Rice) has rights in the collateral, and
* The debtor (Rice) has executed and delivered to the creditor (Abco) a security agreement covering the collateral.

In this case, all but one of the requirements are met. The security agreement is ineffective because it was not signed by the debtor (Rice). Abco's failure to perfect its security interest by filing a financing statement would have no effect on the enforceability of the security interest against Rice.

Condor's assertion that its security interest in the computer is superior to Abco's is incorrect. Both Condor's and Abco's security interests are perfected. Condor's security interest was perfected when it filed its financing statement on August 26. Because Abco's security interest was a purchase money security interest in collateral other than inventory, its security interest was perfected at the time of the sale to Baker (August 18), provided it filed a financing statement at the time Baker took possession of the computer or within the UCC time period for perfection. Abco's security interest was perfected on August 18 before Condor's was perfected (on August 26) because Abco filed a financing statement within the applicable UCC time period. Therefore, Abco's security interest is superior to Condor's.

STUDY UNIT 18: DOCUMENTS OF TITLE   *A. Documents of Title*

3 pages of outline
11 multiple-choice questions

The transfer of ownership of goods in transit or storage is often accomplished by written instruments called documents of title. Article 7 of the UCC governs these documents, in particular bills of lading and warehouse receipts. The topics likely to be tested are recognition of documents of title in various forms, determination of whether a document is negotiable or nonnegotiable, determination of whether a particular document is an order or a bearer instrument, the negotiation or transfer of a document, the rights of a holder, and the duties of the carrier or warehouse in regard to care and surrender of the goods.

A. Documents of Title

  1. **Definition, Functions, Types.** Documents of title are written instruments that permit transfer of the ownership of goods that are in storage or transit. A document of title is any writing that in the regular course of business or financing is treated as adequate evidence that the person in possession is entitled to receive, hold, and sell or otherwise dispose of the document and the goods it covers. UCC 1-201(15)

      a. Documents of title are governed by Article 7 of the UCC. Article 3 of the UCC, which concerns negotiable instruments, does not apply even if the documents of title are negotiable (UCC 3-103). However, negotiable instruments and documents of title share many similarities.

      b. A document of title has three practical functions:

          1) It is a written receipt for goods.

          2) It is a contract between bailor and bailee for the storage or transport of the goods (a bailment, e.g., the delivery of personal property to a warehouser or carrier).

          3) It is evidence of title to the goods.

      c. The two fundamental types of documents of title are

          1) Warehouse receipts
          2) Bills of lading

      d. These documents are generally issued by professional bailees who are in the business of either storing or delivering goods, e.g., warehousers and common carriers.

      e. Documents of title may be either negotiable or nonnegotiable.

          1) Nonnegotiable documents of title are frequently referred to as "straight."

  2. **Negotiable vs. Nonnegotiable.** A document of title is a negotiable document if it states that the goods are to be delivered either to bearer (a person in possession of the document) or to the order of someone. If neither of these statements is in the writing, the document is not negotiable.

      a. Negotiable documents of title are negotiated in much the same manner as negotiable notes, drafts, and checks under UCC, Article 3.

          1) "Order" documents of title are negotiated by endorsement and delivery.

          2) "Bearer" documents are negotiated by delivery alone.

          3) A blank endorsement (signature only) of an order document converts it to bearer paper.

4) A special endorsement, e.g., endorsement to a specified person, of a bearer document converts it to order paper.

     a) Conditional or qualified endorsements do not apply to documents of title.

5) A forged endorsement does not result in negotiation because the transferee is not a holder. It represents a real defense to enforcement.

   b. The distinction between negotiable and nonnegotiable documents is important in determining the seller's obligation to deliver, the risk of loss, and the passage of title when goods covered by a document of title are sold. These topics are covered in Study Unit 16, Sales.

   c. If the document is negotiable, the goods must be delivered to the holder of the document.

1) If the document is nonnegotiable, the goods usually must be delivered to the person named in the document.

     a) The person requesting the goods is not required to present the document itself to obtain the goods if (s)he can prove that (s)he is the bailor or an assignee of the rights of the bailor.

     b) Consistent with the law of bailments, Article 7 imposes absolute liability on carriers and warehousers for misdelivery.

   d. If there has been due negotiation, the holder takes the document and the goods free of claims and defenses raised by either the bailee or third parties. There are, however, two exceptions:

1) The bailee is entitled to compensation for transportation or storage charges, which are usually specified on the document.

2) The holder will not be entitled to the goods in cases in which the bailor had no authority to deliver the goods to the bailee carrier or warehouser.

     a) A document of title issued to a bailor who was a thief of the goods does not represent title to the goods.

3) The due negotiation doctrine in Article 7 provides a holder of a document of title the same protection as the holder-in-due-course doctrine affords a holder of a negotiable instrument.

3. **Warehouse Receipts.** A warehouse receipt is a writing issued by a warehouser to the firm or other person that deposits goods at the warehouse for storage. The depositor is the bailor and the warehouser is the bailee.

   a. A warehouse receipt need not be in any special form, but it must contain the following information:

1) The location of the warehouse

2) The date of issue of the receipt

3) The one to whom the goods are to be delivered

4) The storage or handling charges

5) A description of the goods or their container

6) A statement that advances have been made or liabilities incurred for which the warehouser claims a lien or security interest

b.   For a warehouse receipt to be negotiable, the document must contain order or bearer language. A document that lacks order or bearer language is not negotiable.

   1)   A bailee who issues a negotiable warehouse receipt must deliver the goods described in the document to any holder who surrenders it to the bailee.

      a)   A holder is any person who appears to be in rightful possession of a negotiable warehouse receipt that has been properly endorsed.

   2)   A bailee who issues a nonnegotiable warehouse receipt must deliver the goods only to the person specifically named in the document, or in accordance with that person's written instructions.

c.   With respect to the goods, a warehouser must exercise the same amount of care that a reasonable person would under like circumstances.

   1)   The warehouser, like most other bailees, is liable for only those damages caused by negligence or lack of due care.

d.   A warehouser must keep goods covered by each receipt separate.

   1)   However, different lots of fungible goods may be commingled.

4.   **Bills of Lading.** A carrier is the issuer of a written bill of lading evidencing the carrier's receipt of goods for shipment. The carrier is a bailee of the goods. The person delivering the goods to the carrier for shipment is the shipper and also the bailor.

a.   The shipper/bailor's act of delivering the goods to a carrier for transport is called a **consignment**.

   1)   The shipper/bailor is the **consignor**.

   2)   The person to whom the carrier is to deliver the goods at their destination is the **consignee**.

b.   UCC Section 1-201(6) defines bill of lading as follows:

   "Bill of lading" means a document evidencing the receipt of goods for shipment issued by a person engaged in the business of transporting or forwarding goods, and includes an airbill.

   1)   A destination bill is a bill of lading that is issued by a carrier at the place of destination to the sender's agent.

c.   For a bill of lading to be negotiable, the document must contain order or bearer language.

d.   A bill of lading is both a contract and a receipt.

5.   An endorser or transferor of a document of title warrants to the transferee that

a.   The document is genuine and not a forgery.

b.   (S)he has no knowledge of any fact that impairs the document's worth or validity.

c.   His/her transfer or negotiation is rightful and fully effective with respect to the title to the document and the goods it represents.

6.   Stop and review! You have completed the outline for this study unit. Study multiple-choice questions 1 through 11 beginning on page 580.

MULTIPLE-CHOICE QUESTIONS

A. Documents of Title

1. Documents of title do not perform which of the following functions?

- A. Obligation of repayment.
- B. Receipt for a bailment.
- C. Contract for storage or shipment.
- D. Symbol evidencing ownership of goods.

The correct answer is (A). *(Publisher)*
REQUIRED: The function that documents of title do not perform.
DISCUSSION: Documents of title function as receipts for bailments, contracts for storage or shipment, and symbols evidencing ownership of goods. However, a document of title does not encompass an obligation of repayment. An obligation of repayment is generally represented by a note, draft, certificate of deposit, etc.
Answers (B), (C), and (D) are incorrect because each is a function of a document of title.

2. The procedure necessary to negotiate a document of title depends principally on whether the document is

- A. An order document or a bearer document.
- B. A document issued by a bailee or a consignee.
- C. A receipt for goods stored or goods already shipped.
- D. A bill of lading or a warehouse receipt.

The correct answer is (A). *(CPA, adapted)*
REQUIRED: The factor most affecting the negotiation of a document of title.
DISCUSSION: The negotiation of a document of title principally depends on whether the document is an order document or a bearer document. An order document must be endorsed and delivered to be properly negotiated. But delivery suffices to complete the negotiation of a bearer document.
Answers (B) and (C) are incorrect because they are irrelevant to the negotiation of a document of title. Answer (D) is incorrect because bills of lading and warehouse receipts are both documents of title, and negotiation requires the same procedures for both.

3. Under the UCC, a warehouse receipt

- A. Will not be negotiable if it contains a contractual limitation on the warehouser's liability.
- B. May qualify as both a negotiable warehouse receipt and a negotiable instrument if the instrument is payable either in cash or by the delivery of goods.
- C. May be issued only by a bonded and licensed warehouser.
- D. Is negotiable if by its terms the goods are to be delivered to bearer or the order of a named person.

The correct answer is (D). *(CPA, adapted)*
REQUIRED: The correct statement about a warehouse receipt.
DISCUSSION: Article 7 of the UCC controls documents of title. A document of title known as a warehouse receipt is issued by a person storing goods for hire as a receipt for goods and to represent these goods. A document of title may be negotiable if by its terms the goods are to be delivered to the order of a named person or to bearer (UCC 7-104).
Answer (A) is incorrect because limits on a warehouser's liability do not affect negotiability of a warehouse receipt. Answer (B) is incorrect because negotiable instruments must be payable only in money. Answer (C) is incorrect because the UCC does not require that warehousers be bonded and licensed before they can issue warehouse receipts.

4. Under the Documents of Title Article of the UCC, which of the following terms must be contained in a warehouse receipt?

I. A statement indicating whether the goods received will be delivered to the bearer, to a specified person, or to a specified person or his/her order

II. The location of the warehouse where the goods are stored

    A. I only.

    B. II only.

    C. Both I and II.

    D. Neither I nor II.

The correct answer is (C). *(CPA, adapted)*
    REQUIRED: The term(s), if any, that must be included in a warehouse receipt.
    DISCUSSION: A warehouse receipt is a written document issued by a warehouser to a person or persons who deposit goods at the warehouse for storage. Warehouse receipts are governed by UCC Article 7. No special form is required, but a receipt must include the location of the warehouse; the date of issue; a description of the goods; a statement as to whether the goods will be delivered to bearer, to a specified person, or to a specified person or his/her order; the storage charges; etc. Warehouse receipts may be negotiable or nonnegotiable. A negotiable document always contains order or bearer language. If issued to the order of a named person, the document must be endorsed to negotiate the receipt to a subsequent holder.
    Answers (A), (B), and (D) are incorrect because Article 7 requires a warehouse receipt to include the delivery obligation and the location of the warehouse.

5. Under the Documents of Title Article of the UCC, a negotiable document of title is "duly negotiated" when it is negotiated to

    A. Any holder by endorsement.

    B. Any holder by delivery.

    C. A holder who takes the document in payment of a money obligation.

    D. A holder who takes the document for value, in good faith, and without notice of any defense or claim to it.

The correct answer is (D). *(CPA, adapted)*
    REQUIRED: The requirements to be a holder of a duly negotiated document of title.
    DISCUSSION: Due negotiation is a term peculiar to UCC Article 7 that requires the purchaser of a negotiable document of title to take it in good faith, pay value, be without notice of any adverse claim or defense, and take it in the regular course of business or financing and not in settlement or payment of a money obligation. Due negotiation establishes rights in holders of negotiable documents of title similar to a holder in due course in negotiable instruments and avoids treatment as a mere transferee or assignee. However, the due negotiations doctrine does not cut off claims of theft of the underlying goods or forgery of an endorsement.
    Answers (A), (B), and (C) are incorrect because these holders do not meet the special requirements of due negotiation set out in Article 7.

6. Klep stole several negotiable warehouse receipts, which were deliverable to the order of Apple from the premises of Store Co. Klep endorsed Store's name on the instruments and transferred them to Margo Wholesalers, a bona fide purchaser for value. As between Store and Margo,

    A. Store will prevail because the warehouser must be notified before negotiation is effective.

    B. Store will prevail because Klep's endorsement prevents negotiation.

    C. Margo will prevail because it has taken a negotiable warehouse receipt as a bona fide purchaser for value.

    D. Margo will prevail because the warehouse receipt was converted to a bearer instrument by Klep's endorsement.

The correct answer is (B). *(CPA, adapted)*
    REQUIRED: The effect of a forged endorsement on a document of title.
    DISCUSSION: A holder to whom a negotiable document of title has been "duly negotiated" acquires title to the document (UCC 7-502). However, negotiation requires an endorsement as well as delivery if the document runs to the order of a named person (UCC 7-501). In addition, the holder must have purchased in good faith, for value, and in the ordinary course of business. Klep's forgery of Store's endorsement does not constitute negotiation and provides Store a real defense against Margo, even though Margo was a bona fide purchaser for value.
    Answer (A) is incorrect because negotiation does not require notification of the warehouser. Answer (C) is incorrect because the warehouse receipt was not duly negotiated. Answer (D) is incorrect because a forged endorsement does not convert a warehouse receipt into a bearer instrument.

7. Field Corp. issued a negotiable warehouse receipt to Hall for goods stored in Field's warehouse. Hall's goods were lost due to Field's failure to exercise such care as a reasonably careful person would under like circumstances. The state in which this transaction occurred follows the UCC rule with respect to a warehouser's liability for lost goods. The warehouse receipt is silent on this point. Under the circumstances, Field is

- A. Liable because it is strictly liable for any loss.
- B. Liable because it was negligent.
- C. Not liable because the warehouse receipt was negotiable.
- D. Not liable unless Hall can establish that Field was grossly negligent.

The correct answer is (B). *(CPA, adapted)*
REQUIRED: The liability of a warehouser that failed to exercise reasonable care.
DISCUSSION: A warehouser is liable for damages for loss of, or injury to, goods caused by its failure to exercise reasonable care (UCC 7-204). Bond's negligence in failing to exercise the care of a reasonable person makes Bond liable for the lost goods.
Answer (A) is incorrect because warehousers are not liable for losses caused by events beyond their control, provided that due care was exercised. Answer (C) is incorrect because negotiability of the warehouse receipt is irrelevant to the warehouser's liability. Answer (D) is incorrect because Hall need not prove gross negligence, only simple negligence.

8. Which of the following is not a warranty made by the seller of a negotiable warehouse receipt to the purchaser of the document?

- A. The document transfer is fully effective with respect to the goods it represents.
- B. The warehouser will honor the document.
- C. The seller has no knowledge of any facts that would impair the document's validity.
- D. The document is genuine.

The correct answer is (B). *(CPA, adapted)*
REQUIRED: The warranty not made by the seller of a negotiable warehouse receipt.
DISCUSSION: The seller of a negotiable warehouse receipt does not guarantee that the warehouser will honor the document.
Answers (A), (C), and (D) are incorrect because UCC 7-507 provides that a transferor for value makes these specific warranties to his/her immediate purchaser.

9. A carrier who has issued a bill of lading may release the goods to

- A. The bailor without surrender of a nonnegotiable document of title.
- B. The bailor without surrender of a negotiable document of title.
- C. The holder of a document of title as against the previous holder whose endorsement was forged.
- D. The bailor as against a holder who took by due negotiation from a thief.

The correct answer is (A). *(Publisher)*
REQUIRED: The party to whom a carrier may release goods subject to a bill of lading.
DISCUSSION: In the case of a nonnegotiable document of title, the document itself is not required in order to obtain the goods so long as the person requesting release can prove (s)he is either the bailor or an assignee of the rights of the bailor.
Answer (B) is incorrect because goods subject to a negotiable document of title may be released only upon presentment of that document. Answer (C) is incorrect because a holder claiming under a forged endorsement cannot acquire rights paramount to the previous owner's since the forged endorsement precludes a due negotiation. Answer (D) is incorrect because a thief can negotiate a bearer instrument or an order instrument which was endorsed in blank. A subsequent holder could have taken by due negotiation and acquired rights paramount to the original bailor's.

10. Which of the following statements is correct concerning a bill of lading in the possession of Major Corp. that was issued by a common carrier and provides that the goods are to be delivered "to bearer"?

- A. The carrier's lien for any unpaid shipping charges does not entitle it to sell the goods to enforce the lien.

- B. The carrier will not be liable for delivering the goods to a person other than Major.

- C. The carrier may require Major to endorse the bill of lading prior to delivering the goods.

- D. The bill of lading can be negotiated by Major by delivery alone and without endorsement.

The correct answer is (D). *(CPA, adapted)*
REQUIRED: The correct statement about a bearer bill of lading.
DISCUSSION: A bill of lading is negotiable only if the written document contains order or bearer language. If the document provides that the bailed goods are to be delivered to bearer, the document is negotiated by delivery alone, and the carrier must deliver the goods to the holder.

Answer (A) is incorrect because a carrier has a lien on the goods that may be enforced by public or private sale (UCC 7-307 and 7-308). Answer (B) is incorrect because Major is the holder of the bearer bill of lading. Answer (C) is incorrect because the holder of a bearer bill of lading is entitled to delivery of the goods without endorsing the document.

11. Under the Documents of Title Article of the UCC, which of the following statements is(are) correct regarding a common carrier's duty to deliver goods subject to a negotiable bearer bill of lading?

I. The carrier may deliver the goods to any party designated by the holder of the bill of lading.

II. A carrier who, without court order, delivers goods to a party claiming the goods under a missing negotiable bill of lading is liable to any person injured by the misdelivery.

- A. I only.

- B. II only.

- C. Both I and II.

- D. Neither I nor II.

The correct answer is (C). *(CPA, adapted)*
REQUIRED: The true statement(s), if any, about the delivery of goods by a common carrier.
DISCUSSION: A bill of lading is a document issued by a carrier evidencing the receipt of goods for shipment. It may be in negotiable or nonnegotiable form. If negotiable, the bill may be an order or a bearer instrument. UCC Article 7 requires the carrier under a negotiable bearer instrument to deliver the goods to the holder of the document or his/her agent or assignee. A negotiable bearer bill of lading may be negotiated by delivery without endorsement. To receive the goods, the consignee must tender the document. A carrier who delivers goods without surrender of the negotiable bill of lading is strictly liable to any person rightfully entitled to the goods.

Answers (A), (B), and (D) are incorrect because a common carrier must deliver the goods to the holder of the bill of lading (or designate) and is liable to any injured party for misdelivery.

CHAPTER VII
PROPERTY

STUDY UNIT 19: REAL PROPERTY AND INSURANCE

21 pages of outline
57 multiple-choice questions
 4 OOFs and 2 essays

A. Types of Ownership
B. Lessor-Lessee
C. Deeds, Recording, Title Defects, and Title Insurance
D. Mortgages and Other Liens
E. Fixtures
F. General Insurance Concepts
G. Multiple Insurance Coverage
H. Insurable Interest

Transactions involving the transfer of legal interests in real property are common occurrences and take many forms. This study unit reviews the various forms of ownership of real property, leases, real estate contracts, instruments used in transferring real property, mortgages and liens, and fixtures. Past exams have focused on the following areas of real property law:

1. Recognition of, and distinctions between, fee simple estates and life estates

2. Identification of concurrent forms of ownership, such as tenancies in common, joint tenancies, and tenancies by the entirety

3. The types and forms of leases; the rights and duties of the lessor and the lessee; and the right to, and effect of, assignment or subletting an existing lease

4. The legal effects of the several types of recording acts, deeds, and title insurance

5. Mortgages, with an emphasis on priorities among mortgages, foreclosures, and the distinction between a purchaser's assuming or taking subject to a mortgage.

Insurance is a two-party contract, called an insurance policy, that shifts the risk of financial loss caused by certain specified perils from the insured party to the insurer. Insurance encompasses all the contract problems of valid formation, enforceability, performance, and the rights of third parties. A special requirement of insurance contracts is that the insured must have an insurable interest in the property or life insured. The purpose of this provision is to assure that insurance proceeds indemnify the insured against an economic loss and that the motive for entering into an insurance contract is not profit.

This study unit reviews the main principles of fire and casualty insurance. The exam has emphasized property insurance. The likely areas of testing are insurable interest, the effect of misrepresentations in insurance applications, the ability to apply various standard provisions of insurance (e.g., pro rata and coinsurance clauses), the subrogation rights of an insurer, and assignment of policies.

A. **Types of Ownership**. Property refers to the set of legally recognized and enforceable rights in one or more items. Personal property, generally, encompasses rights in movable tangible (physical) and intangible items. Real property encompasses rights with respect to land.

    1. **Real property** generally consists of rights with respect to

        a. The surface of the land

        b. Items attached to the land, e.g., trees, structures, fixtures (otherwise personal property annexed to the land and structures)

        c. Materials below the surface, e.g., minerals, oil, water

        d. Airspace (generally limited to that part necessary for use and enjoyment of the surface)

    2. An **estate in land** is an interest that is presently possessory or may become possessory.

        a. A possessory interest is a right to exert control over certain land to the exclusion of others, coupled with an intent to exercise that right.

        b. Interests that may become possessory at some future time are called future interests.

        c. **Freehold estates** give possession through legal title and have a duration of life or longer.

        d. Nonfreehold estates give mere possession.

    3. A **fee simple absolute** is the most extensive interest in land. It has potentially infinite duration. "Fee" indicates an estate of inheritance. "Simple" indicates no restrictions with respect to inheritance.

        a. The modern trend is for every estate in land to be considered a fee simple absolute unless a lesser estate, e.g., a life estate, is clearly indicated by the transferor.

    4. A **fee simple determinable** is a fee simple estate that continues until some specified event occurs.

        a. EXAMPLE: "O to A so long as the property is used as a school of accounting."

        b. The fee simple determinable is recognized in nearly every jurisdiction, and it terminates automatically if and when the event occurs.

    5. A **fee simple subject to a condition subsequent** is a fee simple estate that may be terminated (but not automatically) by the transferor or his/her successors in interest upon the happening of a named event.

        a. EXAMPLE: "O to A and his heirs, on condition that use of the property as an accounting school is commenced within 7 years; otherwise O may reenter the land."

        b. The term **fee simple defeasible** (also qualified fee, base fee, conditional fee, etc.) is now often used for any fee simple estate that may end, whether or not automatically, upon the occurrence of some limiting event.

6. A **life estate** is a freehold estate the duration of which is fixed by reference to the life or lives of one or more human beings.

   a. EXAMPLE 1: "O to A for life."

   b. EXAMPLE 2: "O to A for life and then to B."

   c. A life estate *pur autre vie* is a life estate measured by the life of someone other than the life tenant.

      1) EXAMPLE: "O to A for the life of C."

   d. The life tenant is entitled to all ordinary uses of and profits from the land. However, (s)he may not impair the value of the land (waste).

7. A **future interest** is an estate in land which is presently owned but will not become possessory until a future date. Because the interest is presently owned, it may be presently sold or otherwise transferred.

   a. EXAMPLE: "O to A for life and then to B." A is a life tenant. B owns a future interest.

8. A **reversion** is the estate which remains in a grantor/transferor who conveys a lesser estate (with respect to duration) than (s)he holds.

   a. A reversion is a future interest; it becomes possessory only after the lesser estate has come to an end.

      1) EXAMPLE: Owen, the owner of a fee simple absolute, conveys an estate to "Able for life." Owen has retained a reversion in fee simple that will become possessory (returned to the grantor, Owen) only upon Able's death.

   b. An owner of a freehold estate who grants a lease usually has a reversion.

9. A **remainder** is a future interest, conveyed to a third party, that is capable of present possession only upon the natural termination of the prior possessory estate.

   a. EXAMPLE: "O to A for life, and on A's death to B and her heirs."

10. **Concurrent Estates.** Any interest in real property which can be owned by one party can also be owned jointly by two or more parties. The major forms of concurrent ownership are joint tenancy, tenancy by the entirety, and tenancy in common.

11. The **tenancy in common** is a concurrent estate with no rights of survivorship; that is, upon the death of a tenant in common, the decedent's interest does not automatically pass to the surviving co-tenants. Instead, it passes to his/her estate or heirs.

    a. Transfer of an estate to two or more persons jointly (who are not spouses) is presumed to convey to each a tenancy in common.

    b. The tenant in common owns an undivided separate and distinct share of the underlying property.

       1) A tenant in common does not own the whole property as in a joint tenancy.
       2) The only unity involved is the unity of possession.

    c. Each tenant in common can dispose of his/her interest by an *inter vivos* or testamentary transfer.

12. **Joint tenancy** is a form of co-ownership whereby each tenant owns an undivided interest in the entire estate.

    a.   The distinctive characteristic of a joint tenancy is the right of survivorship; upon the death of one joint tenant, the surviving co-tenant(s) automatically own(s) the entire property. No interest in the property passes to the heirs of the decedent. A decedent's will has no effect on the property.

    b.   At common law, four unities are required to acquire a joint tenancy.

        1)   **Time**. Interests vest at the same time.
        2)   **Title**. Interests are acquired under the same instrument.
        3)   **Interest**. Interests are of the same type and duration.
        4)   **Possession**. Interests represent identical rights of enjoyment.

    c.   The modern view is that the conveyance to two or more parties must specifically express a clear intention to form a joint tenancy. Otherwise, a tenancy in common will be presumed.

        1)   In some states, the deed must include the words "with right of survivorship and not as tenants in common (or by the entirety)," or must otherwise expressly mention the right.

        2)   EXAMPLE: "O to A and B and their heirs." At common law, a joint tenancy was typically recognized. Today, a tenancy in common would usually be presumed.

    d.   A conveyance *inter vivos* (between the living) severs the joint tenancy; i.e., the new tenant holds as tenant in common with any remaining joint tenants (the new tenant has no right of survivorship).

        1)   EXAMPLE: A, B, and C hold Whiteacre as joint tenants. A conveys her undivided one-third interest to Z. Thereafter, B and C hold their undivided two-thirds as joint tenants. Z holds a one-third interest as a tenant in common with B and C.

    e.   A contract for sale terminates the joint tenancy (even without transfer of legal title) in most states.

13. A **tenancy by the entirety** is an estate held by spouses with a right of survivorship.

    a.   Five unities are necessary for a valid tenancy by the entirety: time, title, interest, possession, and person (the unity of husband and wife).

    b.   In most states, formation of a tenancy by the entirety is presumed from a joint conveyance to the spouses. For example, if a deed transfers title to "Adam and Eve, his wife," they acquire the property as tenants by the entirety. If Adam dies, Eve will automatically own the whole property.

    c.   A tenancy by the entirety is terminated by death of either spouse, mutual agreement of the spouses, or divorce.

        1)   Conveyance also terminates this tenancy. In most states, neither spouse can independently dispose of any interest in the estate; both spouses must join in the transfer.

        2)   Furthermore, execution proceedings in favor of a joint creditor of both husband and wife terminate a tenancy by the entireties. A creditor of one spouse cannot levy upon the tenancy.

d.   **Community property** is recognized by some western and southern states. It is property acquired during marriage and is equally owned by the spouses, regardless of which person's labor or skills produced the property. However, separate property, that is, property acquired before marriage or by gift or inheritance, is not community property. Moreover, property acquired in exchange for separate property is separately owned.

14. **Adverse possession** is a means to acquiring title to property. The doctrine permits a person in possession of land for a statutorily determined time period, e.g., 20 years, to have possession ripen into title.

   a.   To acquire title by adverse possession, the possession must be

   1)   Open and notorious, not secret or clandestine
   2)   Continuous, without interruption for the statutory period
   3)   Adverse to the true owner, not permissive
   4)   Exclusive, not shared with the true owner
   5)   Peaceable, without physical or judicial eviction

   b.   Periods of adverse possession can be joined. Adverse possession by two or more possessors can also be joined if they are in privity, e.g., by inheritance or contract.

15. **Easements and profits** are interests in land which are not possessory.

   a.   An **easement** is the right of one person to legally enter onto the land of another and make limited use of it. The holder of a **profit** (a *profit-à-prendre*) is entitled to enter land in possession of another and take some part of the land itself or some product of the land, e.g., oil, gravel, sand, grass, trees.

   b.   An easement or profit may arise from an **express grant** or **express reservation** of the interest. The grant must meet the formal requirements of a deed.

   1)   A writing is generally required to satisfy the statute of frauds.

   c.   **Prescription**. An easement can be acquired by meeting the requirements for adverse possession, except that the use need not be exclusive of the true owner. This is referred to as prescription.

   d.   **Implication**. Easements may be implied by operation of law, in the absence of an express grant and without regard to the statute of frauds.

   1)   **Necessity**. An easement by necessity is implied when the owner of land conveys part of it that has no access to a public road other than over the part retained by the seller.

   a)   It terminates automatically when the necessity terminates.

   2)   **Existing use**. When on the part of a tract of land conveyed there was apparent and continuous use reasonably necessary to the use and enjoyment of the part retained, an easement is implied.

16. Land which abuts a lake or stream is riparian. To be a riparian, one must own riparian land. A riparian has certain rights called **riparian rights** or water rights.

   a.   Under the **reasonable use theory**, each riparian has the right to make the maximum reasonable use of the water as long as it does not interfere with use by other riparians.

17. Stop and review! You have completed the outline for this subunit. Study multiple-choice questions 1 through 6 beginning on page 606.

B.   Lessor-Lessee. The renting of real property is based on a lease (rental agreement). The lessor-lessee (landlord-tenant) relationship is formed by the lease. A person who owns real property conveys the use and possession of the property (not title) to another for consideration called rent.

1.   By a lease, a tenant acquires an **estate in land** which is an interest in real property called a leasehold.

   a.   The landlord retains title to the property during the term of the lease and possesses a reversionary interest. The right of possession reverts upon termination of the lease.

   NOTE: Sale of the leased property does not, of itself, affect the lease. But if it is purchased by the lessee, the lease is merged into the fee simple interest (and is thereby terminated).

2.   The lease is also a contract. There must be an offer, acceptance, consideration, capacity to contract, and lawful purpose.

3.   A lessor-lessee relationship can result from one of the following four types of leaseholds: tenancy for years, periodic tenancy, tenancy at will, tenancy at sufferance.

4.   The **tenancy for years** (also known as a term of years or a tenancy for a term) is an estate with the beginning and the ending dates fixed in advance. The estate lasts for a fixed period of time.

   a.   Its duration may be measured in days, weeks, months, or years.

   b.   A tenancy for years terminates automatically without either party giving notice because the parties agreed when the tenancy would end.

   c.   Death of a landlord or tenant does not terminate the tenancy. The rights and duties flow to the heirs or beneficiaries.

5.   The **periodic tenancy** (also known as a tenancy from period to period) is a tenancy for successive periods of equal duration, e.g., year to year, month to month, or other successive fractions of a year.

   a.   Although the beginning date and duration of the periods are known, the lease does not specify how long the leasehold will last.

   b.   The parties may expressly contract for periodic tenancy or one may be implied from provision for periodic rental payments.

      1)   EXAMPLE: Larry and Ted enter into a lease. It states that Ted has the exclusive right to possess the premises for $50 per week. A periodic tenancy for successive periods of 1 week will be implied from the weekly rental provision.

   c.   In some states, a holdover by a tenant after the expiration of a tenancy for years with the landlord's approval creates a periodic tenancy. In other jurisdictions, a holdover creates a tenancy at will.

   d.   A periodic tenancy does not automatically terminate at the end of any period but renews for the next successive period, e.g., week, month, year.

   e.   Notice as per agreement or statute must be given by either the landlord or the tenant to terminate a periodic tenancy.

6. The **tenancy at will** exists for an indefinite period. It is terminable at the will of either landlord or tenant.

   a. A tenancy at will can arise by any of the following:

   1) Express agreement between landlord and tenant (that either may terminate at will)

   2) Landlord's permission to the tenant to possess the premises without agreement on a specific period (single or renewable) of occupancy

7. A **tenancy at sufferance** arises when a tenant in lawful possession of property under one of the three leasehold estates remains in possession after expiration of the lease term without consent of the landlord (the tenant holds over). It results from unlawful possession by the tenant, not from agreement.

8. **Statute of Frauds**. A lease involves conveyance of an estate in land (a leasehold).

   a. Most states require a lease for longer than 1 year to be in writing.

9. **Lessor's Rights**. The landlord's foremost right is to collect rent.

   a. Absent a specific covenant providing for payment of rent, courts infer a reasonable amount of rent payable at the end of the term.

   1) In many states, the lessor has a lien on personal property of the tenant which is physically located on the premises.

   a) This lien is exercised in a proceeding known as a distress for rent. The landlord is entitled to physically distrain (hold) personalty until the rent is paid. Otherwise, the property may be sold pursuant to court order.

   2) If a tenant vacates the premises early and refuses to pay any further rent, in some states the lessor

   a) Must seek a new tenant to mitigate damages or the tenant's liability is reduced, or

   b) May treat the tenant's actions as a surrender of the premises and reenter and take possession, thereby terminating the tenancy.

   b. The landlord has a right to inspect the premises. This right must be exercised in a reasonable manner so that the tenant's right to quiet enjoyment is not violated.

10. **Lessor's Duties**. The essence of the landlord-tenant relationship is that the tenant enjoys exclusive possession against all the world as though (s)he is the actual (title) owner.

    a. The duty of a landlord to deliver possession of the premises varies.

    1) The modern trend is to require the landlord to deliver actual possession to the tenant unless there is a contrary provision in the lease.

    b. Under the covenant of quiet enjoyment, the landlord may not interfere with the tenant's right to physical possession, use, and enjoyment of the premises.

1)   The tenant may be constructively evicted: The landlord fails to fulfill a promise in the lease, and the result of that failure substantially interferes with the tenant's enjoyment of the premises.

    a)   EXAMPLE: Lil Landlord promised to make repairs. A tornado damaged the roof. When it rained, the den flooded. Lil refused to repair the damage. A flooded den would be viewed as constructive eviction in that it substantially interferes with the tenant's enjoyment of the premises. Lil breached the covenant of quiet enjoyment.

c.   Most courts have implied a warranty of habitability in a lease of residential property.

    1)   The common-law rule was *caveat lessee*, let the lessee beware. Absent an express provision in the lease, the landlord was under no obligation to maintain the premises in a reasonable state of repair.

    2)   The modern trend imposes affirmative duties on landlords to furnish habitable premises during the period of the lease.

        a)   Courts have held that the tenant's covenant to pay rent is dependent on the implied warranty of habitability. If a landlord breaches the implied warranty of habitability, a tenant can

            i)   Vacate the premises
            ii)   Rescind the lease
            iii) Offset repair costs against rent due
            iv)   Seek monetary damages

d.   **Tort liability**. As a general rule, a landlord makes no warranty that the premises are safe for the use intended by the tenant.

    1)   However, a landlord must give notice of latent defects (defects that are concealed, not readily apparent) which exist at the commencement of the lease if the landlord knew or should have known of such dangerous conditions.

    2)   Certain duties imposed under housing codes and local ordinances may not be delegated to tenants. That is, without regard to the lease agreement, a lessor may be held liable for injury/loss caused by failure to comply with the code/ordinance.

    3)   Crime. A landlord may be liable for a crime which is reasonably foreseeable from a lessor's breach of duty, e.g., theft after the tenant notifies the landlord that the dead bolt lock is broken.

        a)   Lessors have been held liable for failure to warn of or protect against crime after the lessor knew of repeated criminal acts against tenants.

11. **Tenant's Rights**. Generally, the tenant is entitled to exclusive possession and control of the premises. The landlord has no right to go upon the premises except to collect rent and inspect for damage.

a.   A tenant has the right to quiet enjoyment; the tenant generally has the right to use the premises as if (s)he owns them. The key concept is reasonable use.

b.   The tenant may have a right to expect repair of the premises.

    c.   A number of states have adopted some form of provisions of the Uniform Residential Landlord and Tenant Act. Tenants are provided statutory protection against retaliatory eviction, i.e., for exercising rights such as a right to repair.

    d.   A tenant generally has the right to assign or sublease the premises without the consent of the landlord. The right may be restricted by the lease agreement. Refer to 13 and 15 below.

    e.   In many commercial leases, the tenant has the right to remove trade fixtures (s)he installed.

12. **Tenant's Duties**. Absent express lease provision, the tenant has a duty to pay a reasonable amount of rent on the last day of the lease term.

    a.   Unless the landlord has a duty to repair, the tenant has a duty to make ordinary repairs to maintain the property in the same condition as at the inception of the lease.

        1)   This duty does not include repairs for ordinary wear and tear.

        2)   EXAMPLE: A tenant is not obligated to replace a leaking roof or a worn-out heating or air-conditioning system. However, a tenant is obligated to make minor repairs such as replacing a broken window.

    b.   The tenant has a duty not to commit affirmative waste.

        1)   Failure to make minor repairs may result in affirmative waste.

    c.   A tenant is responsible to use the property only for legal purposes.

    d.   **Tort liability**. If the tenant has a duty to repair, (s)he may be liable for injuries suffered as a result of negligent failure to repair.

        1)   A tenant, as occupier of the premises, may be liable in tort to third parties, e.g., licensees, invitees, for dangerous conditions or activities on the leased property.

13. An **assignment** of a lease is the lessee's transfer of his/her interest in the leased premises for the entire unexpired term of the original lease. The assignee stands in the shoes of the original tenant (assignor).

    a.   Unless prohibited by the terms of the lease, a tenant may assign the lease without the consent of the landlord.

    b.   The assignee (new tenant) is primarily liable to the landlord for rent.

    c.   The assignor remains secondarily liable to the landlord.

14. The landlord's reversionary interest is also assignable, e.g., on the sale of an apartment building. Recognition of the new landlord by the tenants is called **attornment**.

15. **Subleases** involve a partial transfer of the original tenant's rights under the lease.

    a.   Unless prohibited by the terms of the lease, a lessee may sublet the rented premises without the consent of the lessor.

    b.   A sublease is an agreement by which the tenant (sublessor) transfers part of his/her rights and interest in the leasehold to a sublessee.

       c.   Unlike an assignor, the sublessor retains an interest in the leasehold. (S)he remains both in privity of estate and in privity of contract with the landlord.

           1)   Thus, the sublessor remains primarily liable to the landlord.

           2)   The sublessee is not liable to the landlord, but to the sublessor, for rent accruing during the term of the sublease.

       d.   A lease term which prohibits assignment alone does not operate to prohibit subleasing, and vice versa.

16.   Stop and review! You have completed the outline for this subunit. Study multiple-choice questions 7 through 15 beginning on page 607.

C.   Deeds, Recording, Title Defects, and Title Insurance. The purchase and sale of real property involves a real estate contract between two parties, the seller (vendor) and the buyer (vendee or purchaser). Under a typical contract, the seller agrees to transfer ownership of property to the buyer in exchange for the payment or a promise to make payment of a specified price.

    1.   **Statute of Frauds**. A real estate contract must be in writing.

    2.   **Marketable Title**. Absent agreement to the contrary, implied in every contract for the sale of land is the seller's promise that (s)he will deliver marketable title at the time of closing.

       a.   Title is marketable if a reasonably prudent buyer, ready, willing, and able to purchase, will conclude, after conducting a search of the public records, that the seller's title is valid and will accept it. Perfect title is not required.

    3.   **Time**. A party can enforce the contract even if late in tendering his/her performance if (s)he tenders within a reasonable time after the time set in the contract.

       a.   If time is of the essence, a party who fails to tender performance on or before the closing date is in breach and loses his/her right to enforce the contract. Time will be considered of the essence if one of the following conditions applies:

           1)   The contract so states.

           2)   Circumstances indicate that was the parties' intention; e.g., the real property value is fluctuating rapidly.

           3)   One party gives the other party reasonable notice that (s)he desires to make time of the essence.

       b.   If the buyer claims that the seller's title is not marketable, (s)he must notify the seller and give reasonable time to cure the defects. This may require delay of the closing date.

    4.   **Remedies** for breach of a real estate sales contract are damages or specific performance.

       a.   Damages are typically any difference between the contract price and the market value on the date of breach.

       b.   A court may order specific performance when the remedy at law is inadequate.

           1)   Because each parcel of land is deemed unique, monetary damages are rarely adequate.

5. **Risk of Loss**. Absent a contractual provision to the contrary, the majority rule is that risk of loss is on the buyer after a contract has been signed.

   a. Under the doctrine of equitable conversion, the buyer is regarded as the equitable owner of the land, and the seller, although (s)he still holds legal title to the land, is regarded as the beneficial (equitable) owner of personal property, i.e., the right to the purchase price.

   b. Some states have adopted the Uniform Vendor and Purchasers Risk Act. It provides that loss is on the buyer only if (s)he has either legal title to, or possession of, the property.

   c. If a seller dies, the beneficial interest passes as personal property.

   d. If a buyer dies, the right to receive the property generally passes as real property.

6. **Real Estate Brokers**. A **listing agreement** is a contract in which a real estate broker undertakes to act as the agent of a property owner.

7. **Deeds**. Execution and delivery of a deed is the traditional method of transferring title to real property.

   a. A **deed** is a written instrument expressing a grantor's intent to convey or pass an interest in real property to a grantee. Typically the deed must contain

      1) The name of the grantor
      2) The name of the grantee
      3) Operative words of conveyance
      4) A description (preferably legal) of the land
      5) The signature of the grantor

   b. A writing which evidences an intention to convey an interest in land will be sustained as a conveyance despite informal language.

8. **Delivery**. The grantor must deliver the deed to the grantee to complete the transfer of real property. Absent delivery, the grantor retains legal title.

9. Generally, one of the following four types of deeds is used:

   a. A **quitclaim deed**. It conveys only the interest (not the land itself), if any, that the grantor has in a specified piece of property. If the grantor holds no interest, nothing will pass.

   b. A **bargain and sale deed**. The grantor purports to convey the land itself. The grantor makes no promise, express or implied, that (s)he has good title.

      1) The grantee is in no better position than the grantee of a quitclaim deed.

   c. A **general warranty deed** not only purports to transfer the land itself, but it also contains warranties (assurances by the grantor of facts upon which the grantee may rely) that the grantor has good title to the property and that (s)he will protect the grantee from any and all claims that might arise from a defect in the grantor's purported ownership interest.

   d. A **special warranty deed**. It contains all covenants of the general warranty deed, but the grantor promises only that (s)he has not him/herself caused any defects in title. By the general warranty deed, the grantor warrants that no one else (previous titleholder, etc.) has caused any defects in title.

10. **Notice**. A bona fide purchaser (BFP) without notice of liens or other claims may take title free of them. Record notice is one type of notice that may bar BFP status.

    a. A **bona fide purchaser** is one who pays value, in good faith, and is without notice of an earlier interest in the property.

b. **Actual notice**. If a purchaser has actual notice of an encumbrance on the property, (s)he does not take free of the encumbrance merely because (s)he is otherwise protected under the recording/notice statutes. See below.

c. **Constructive notice**. Although a transferee of title may in fact have no notice of legal claims to property, the law may imply such notice (knowledge).

   1) **Record notice**. A purchaser is presumed to have knowledge of interests recorded in the chain of title under the state recording statutes.

   2) **Inspection notice**. The law presumes the purchaser has inspected the property. Thus the purchaser is deemed to know what inspection of the property would have disclosed (e.g., possession).

11. **Recording**. Recording statutes are in effect in all 50 states. While recording is not essential to making a deed or other instrument valid, it does give constructive notice of a transaction, e.g., sale, mortgage. Thus, recording generally affords protection to a grantee against claims of all subsequent transferees of the same property.

   a. Although between the grantor and the grantee an otherwise valid deed is good even if it is not recorded, it is void with respect to any subsequent bona fide purchaser (takes in good faith, for value, without notice).

12. **Types of Recording Statutes**. There are three types.

   a. A **notice recording statute** protects a subsequent BFP, regardless of who was the first to record. This is the most common type of recording statute.

   1) Priority is given to the purchaser qualifying as a BFP at the time the deed, mortgage, or other interest is acquired.

   b. A **race-notice recording statute** protects a subsequent BFP if and only if (s)he is the first to record.

   1) Priority is determined by the BFP who records first.
   2) CPA exam questions use race-notice and notice-race interchangeably.

   c. A **race recording statute** protects a subsequent purchaser if and only if (s)he is the first to record.

   1) Priority is determined by who wins the race to the recording office.
   2) The subsequent purchaser need not be a BFP.

13. The **title search** is a search of public land records for all recorded interests in a particular piece of real property.

14. **Title insurance** repays the insured for a loss arising from defects in the title to real property.

   a. A title policy, like other insurance, is a contract of indemnification.
   b. The title insurer conducts a title search prior to issuing the policy.
   c. The policy usually protects against loss if

   1) Title is nonmarketable.
   2) Title is actually in another person.
   3) Title is subject to an encumbrance.

15. Stop and review! You have completed the outline for this subunit. Study multiple-choice questions 16 through 28 beginning on page 610.

D. Mortgages and Other Liens. A typical mortgage is a voluntary lien on real property arising from a contract; it is a security interest in real property, typically conveyed by a written instrument to assure payment of a debt. The mortgagor (landowner/borrower) grants the mortgage to the mortgagee (the creditor/lender). Because of the disparity of bargaining power between mortgagors and mortgagees, statutes reduce freedom of contract in favor of greater legislative and judicial oversight of mortgage formation and foreclosure.

1. The underlying debt is usually evidenced by a promissory note. The lender has alternative remedies in the event of default (failure to make payments when due). Suit may be brought on the note and a personal judgment obtained against the debtor, or the real property may be sold under court supervision and the proceeds applied against the debt (foreclosure).

2. Under the title theory, a mortgage is viewed as a conveyance (transfer) of property, albeit only for security purposes. The mortgagee (lender) acquires title but does not have the right of possession until after the mortgagor defaults.

3. Under the lien theory, the mortgage is not a conveyance of legal title but is merely a lien on the property to secure payment of the debt.

    a. The mortgagor retains title until foreclosure and ordinarily is entitled to exclusive possession and use of the mortgaged premises.

    b. The lien theory is the more commonly followed policy.

4. The mortgagor ordinarily has the right to possess, use, and dispose of the property.

    a. The mortgagor can generally lease the property to another and collect rent.

5. The mortgagor is under an affirmative duty not to commit waste. (S)he must preserve the property at least to the amount of the debt.

    a. The mortgagor customarily pays taxes and assessments levied on the underlying property.

6. The mortgagee has the right to protect his/her interest in the real property.

    a. The mortgagee may obtain insurance or pay off liens that affect his/her interest.

    b. If the mortgagee elects to defer foreclosure and pays delinquent taxes or assessments to protect his/her interest, (s)he is entitled to be reimbursed by the mortgagor. These payments are also secured by the mortgage.

7. A mortgagee can assign (transfer) the mortgage and underlying debt to a third person.

    a. If the mortgagee dies, the mortgage passes to his/her heirs or beneficiaries as personal property.

8. A **purchase money mortgage** (PMM) is a mortgage granted by a purchaser to secure payment of the purchase price. The money or credit is provided to purchase the property. The mortgage must be granted at the same time that the deed is delivered.

    a. PMM mortgagees are usually entitled to preference over other claims or liens.

9. An owner of property subject to a mortgage can grant a **second mortgage** (and others) on the same property to secure a debt.

    a. After default and foreclosure, the first mortgage has priority and is first satisfied (in full) out of sale proceeds.

10. An **open-end mortgage** is one that is granted to secure not only present debt but future advances of money.

   a. The lender retains the right to disburse loan installments as the value of the mortgaged property increases.

   b. Note that, in many states, a future advance clause permits a mortgagee to retain the same priority for a future advance as for the original mortgage.

      1) Theoretically, persons with subsequent liens have the same notice of the mortgage and the future advance clause.

11. A **wraparound mortgage** is a form of second mortgage. The face amount of the note is the sum of the existing first mortgage liability plus the amount of credit extended by the second mortgagee.

   a. The wraparound mortgagor makes payments on the wraparound mortgage debt to the wraparound lender. The wraparound lender then makes payments on the first mortgage debt to the first mortgagee.

   b. The wraparound mortgagee receives interest on the full amount of the wraparound note, not only on the additional funds lent or credit extended.

12. By a **trust deed**, a debtor transfers title to a disinterested third party (the trustee) to be held in trust (property held by one party for the benefit of another) as security for the performance of an obligation, usually the payment of a debt.

   a. The trustee is typically given the power to sell the property if the debtor (mortgagor) defaults.

   b. The proceeds of the sale are then applied toward payment of the debt.

   c. There are only two parties to a mortgage (mortgagee and mortgagor), but there are three parties to a trust deed: trustor (debtor); beneficiary (creditor); and trustee.

   d. The trustee holds bare legal title, not a true ownership interest.

   e. The trust deed is generally treated as a lien (mortgage) on the real property.

   f. When the obligation is satisfied, the trustee reconveys legal title to the trustor/debtor.

13. A **land sale contract** is an agreement between a purchaser and a seller for the conditional sale of land, subject to payment of the entire purchase price by the purchaser.

   a. During the term of the land sale contract, the purchaser has the right to control, possess, use, and enjoy the land and improvements but may not materially change the real property without permission of the seller.

   b. The seller retains ownership (legal title) of the property until final payment is made. The purchaser is the equitable title holder; (s)he does not actually own the real property itself, but his/her rights can be enforced in equity. The purchaser acquires legal title to the land when the entire contract price has been paid.

   c. In some states, when the purchaser in a land sale contract defaults, the seller (lender) must follow the state statutory procedure used for foreclosing a mortgage.

14. An **equitable mortgage** does not meet the technical requirements of a mortgage. Courts may recognize and enforce an equitable mortgage when, by written agreement, one party clearly expresses intent to make particular property security for a debt, if rights of third parties are not compromised.

15. **Formal Requirements**. Some fundamental elements must be contained in every mortgage.

    a. A mortgage relates to an interest in land and thus must be in writing (statute of frauds).

    b. The mortgage must be delivered to the mortgagee.

16. **Recording**. Mortgages, like deeds to real property, can be and usually are recorded.

    a. In a majority of states, the mortgage attaches when executed (signed) and delivered.

    b. Once executed and delivered, the mortgage instrument sets forth the rights and duties enforceable between the mortgagor and the mortgagee, whether the mortgage is recorded or not.

    c. By recording a mortgage, the public is given constructive notice (as opposed to actual notice) that a specific party is claiming a security interest in the real property.

        1) Failure to record may invalidate the mortgage if the property is sold to a bona fide purchaser or subordinate it to a subsequent mortgage or other lien.

17. **Satisfaction**. Upon full payment of the debt, the mortgagee's security interest in the real property terminates automatically. The mortgagee's interest in land immediately reverts to the mortgagor, by operation of law.

18. **Default**. A mortgagor who fails to satisfy the obligation when it matures is in default.

    a. Default by nonperformance occurs when there is failure to perform any obligation in the contract, e.g., to make a payment, to pay real property taxes, to maintain the property in reasonable repair, to maintain fire and casualty insurance.

    b. An acceleration clause states that, upon failure of the mortgagor to pay any installment when due, the entire debt shall become due and payable immediately. It permits foreclosure of the entire debt.

    c. A due-on-sale clause is an acceleration clause that authorizes a mortgagee to accelerate the entire loan balance if the mortgagor sells or otherwise conveys the property without permission of the mortgagee.

19. **Foreclosure**. The right to foreclose usually arises upon default. Foreclosure is an action by the mortgagee (or assignee) to take the property away from the mortgagor, sell it to pay the debt, and end the mortgagor's rights in the property.

    a. In the event of foreclosure, the mortgagee usually must initiate a judicial proceeding to secure an order of sale. The sheriff or other officer of the court then conducts a sale by auction as specified by state statute.

    b. Generally, the sale is confirmed by court order following a hearing.

    c.   The debt is then satisfied with proceeds of the sale.

        1)   If the sale proceeds are insufficient to cover the debt (plus costs and interest), the mortgagee may generally obtain a judgment against the mortgagor for the deficiency. Some jurisdictions do not allow deficiency judgments when property is over-mortgaged.

        2)   If the sale produces surplus proceeds (over mortgage debt and related costs), the surplus belongs to the mortgagor.

20. The mortgagor has an equitable right of redemption; prior to the foreclosure sale, (s)he may regain rights by paying the full amount of the mortgage debt plus interest.

    a.   The equity of redemption cannot be waived or relinquished by agreement. Any such attempt is considered void as against public policy.

21. The mortgagor may have a statutory right of redemption. It provides the mortgagor with the opportunity to repurchase the property after the foreclosure sale, for a certain statutorily specified period generally not exceeding 1 year, by payment of the auction sale price.

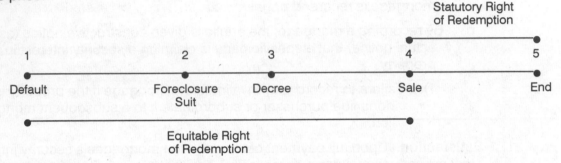

22. **Strict foreclosure** is foreclosure without sale; the mortgagee automatically succeeds to the real property if the mortgagor defaults.

    a.   Strict foreclosure is permitted in only a few states.

    b.   The mortgagee obtains the real property with no duty to account for a surplus (the difference between the value of the real estate and the amount of debt plus interests and costs) and with no right to seek payment from the mortgagor for a deficiency.

23. **Foreclosure by judicial decree** begins with a suit brought against the mortgagor.

    a.   At the proceeding, the mortgagor may raise defenses; e.g., payment was made.

    b.   If the court finds a default, it rules that the mortgagee has a right to foreclose and orders sale of the property under court supervision.

24. **Transfer and Assignment**. Generally, the mortgagor may sell or otherwise transfer the property. However, apart from agreement to the contrary, the mortgagor may not delegate his/her duties or performance under the mortgage unless specifically released by the mortgagee (novation).

25. A transfer of real property is subject to the mortgage when the purchaser pays the seller the (agreed to) value of the land.

    a.   The purchaser is not personally liable on the existing mortgage to either the mortgagor or mortgagee. The original mortgagor is still bound. The mortgagee looks to the original mortgagor for payment.

    b.   The land still serves as security for the debt.

    c.   A due-on-sale or other acceleration clause may prevent the sale of property with an existing mortgage.

26. In contrast, if a purchaser assumes the mortgage, the purchaser pays the mortgagor the value of the land less the amount of the debt secured by the mortgage and also promises the mortgagor that (s)he will pay the balance of the original debt.

    a. The mortgagee can hold either party liable for payment.

    b. If the mortgagee collects from the mortgagor, the mortgagor has a right to reimbursement from the purchaser.

27. The mortgagee can assign a mortgage.

28. **Mechanic's and materialman's liens** are statutory liens against real property. The liens secure unpaid debts that arise from contracts for labor, materials, or services to improve real property. These liens prevent transferring real property with a clear title.

    a. Preliminary notice to the property owner of intent to file the lien is generally required. It must identify the kind of labor or materials furnished, the value of the labor or materials, and the person to whom the labor or materials were furnished.

    b. Recording the claim in the public records is typically required within 60 to 180 days of completing the work or furnishing the materials.

    c. When the mechanic's and materialman's liens have arisen and are perfected, they attach as of the date the work was first performed or materials were supplied.

    d. Mechanic's and materialman's liens may be enforced by foreclosure and sale of the property.

        1) State statutes provide a specific, limited period, typically 1 year, within which suit may be filed to enforce the lien.

29. Stop and review! You have completed the outline for this subunit. Study multiple-choice questions 29 through 40 beginning on page 614.

E. **Fixtures**. A fixture is an article which was personal property (a tangible, movable thing) but has become so closely connected to real property that it has become part of the real property.

    1. Whether a particular article is a fixture is determined primarily by the intention of the annexor at the time of annexation.

    2. Intent is objectively tested. It may be inferred from facts such as the following:

        a. Nature of the item being attached
        b. Manner of annexation
        c. Integration of the item into the land
        d. The use to which it is being put
        e. Relationship of the annexor to the land, e.g., trespasser
        f. Relationship of the annexor to the chattel, e.g., owner
        g. Injury to the land, if any, by its removal

    3. Unless agreed otherwise, fixtures are included in any sale or transfer of real property.

    4. A mortgage granted on real property typically covers fixtures, including those subsequently affixed.

    5. A trade fixture is placed on the premises by a lessee for the purpose of carrying on a trade or business, e.g., racks, showcases.

        a. The trade tenant is permitted to remove trade fixtures within a reasonable time after expiration of a lease. Removal must be accompanied by payment of any damage to the realty.

6. Real property taken in eminent domain or condemnation proceedings includes fixtures. The government must reimburse for the reasonable value of the property. Personal property need not be paid for; it should be removed.

7. Many of the rules governing fixtures and other real property differ from those dealing with personal property.

    a. A will may provide for distribution of real property to one beneficiary and personal property to another.

    b. At common law, if a decedent died intestate (without a valid will), realty descended to the heir whereas personalty passed to the next of kin.

    c. State property tax rates may vary between real and personal property.

8. Stop and review! You have completed the outline for this subunit. Study multiple-choice questions 41 through 43 beginning on page 618.

F. **General Insurance Concepts**. Property insurance protects a person with an insurable interest in real or personal property against loss resulting from damage to or destruction of the property by certain perils. An **insurance policy** is a contract to shift the risk of financial loss from certain specified occurrences from the insured to the insurer. Because the insurance relationship is a contractual one, the concepts of offer and acceptance, consideration, capacity, and legality of purpose are highly relevant.

1. A **loss** is an unexpected destruction, reduction, or disappearance of economic value.

2. A **peril** is the cause of a loss. A single peril can cause more than one type of loss. Commonly insured-against perils include fire, theft, explosion, and illness.

3. A **hazard** is a certain condition that increases the likelihood of loss due to a particular peril, e.g., storing explosives.

4. Under a **specified perils contract**, the insurer covers only those losses resulting from one or more perils specifically included by the contract.

5. An **all risk contract** covers loss resulting from any perils, except those specifically excluded by the contract.

6. Coverage is limited to the face amount of the policy.

7. **Indemnity** applies. Coverage is limited to the amount of loss, unless agreed otherwise.

8. Insured losses are unintended; they do not include the wearing out or normal depreciation of property used in a trade or business, nor do they include damage which is intentionally inflicted to property by the insured.

    a. But negligence or intentional acts of third parties do not preclude indemnification.

9. **Representations and Warranties**. Both representations and warranties in a property insurance contract are enforceable. A **representation** is an oral or written statement given by the insured before the contract is made and is not necessarily incorporated into the policy itself. It is considered to be an inducement to form the contract. A **warranty** is a statement, a description, or an undertaking by an insured that appears in the insurance policy and relates to the risk insured against. A warranty is part of the completed contract and is presumed to be material.

    a. Concealment by the applicant of matters that are material to the risk invalidate the policy. The test of materiality is whether a fact, if stated, might reasonably have influenced the insurer either to reject the risk or to accept it and charge a higher premium.

1)   EXAMPLE: Owner states, as a condition of coverage, that (s)he will not store petrochemicals on the property. The store is shown to have been damaged more by a fire than it would have been had gasoline not been stored on the premises. Recovery under the policy might be precluded because the owner's statement was material and relied on by the insurer.

b.   Modern insurance codes have eliminated the distinction between warranties and representations and treat all statements by the insured under the materiality standard even though the policy may specify rescission.

10.   **Fire insurance** is the most common type of **property insurance**. By a contract, the insurer agrees to pay the insured a specified amount for property loss or property damage due to fire.

a.   Most states recognize the standard fire policy: a standard contract of insurance prescribed by statute or administrative rule or regulation.

b.   Frequently, fire insurance policies also insure against damage from wind, hail, and other forces of nature, as well as faulty plumbing or smoke damage.

c.   Fire insurance does not indemnify for lost profits, business interruption, or other special matters unless there is a special endorsement or rider attached to the policy.

d.   Fire insurance policies usually limit coverage to loss from hostile fires, not friendly fires.

1)   A **friendly fire** is one that is contained where it is intended to be, e.g., a fire in a fireplace, furnace, or stove.

2)   A **hostile fire** is any other fire that is unintended or not in its usual place.

11.   Property or fire insurance is distinct from casualty insurance.

a.   **Casualty insurance** typically covers loss due to damage or destruction of personal property by various causes other than fire or the elements.

12.   A **coinsurance clause** is used by many property and casualty insurers to encourage policyholders to insure property, especially commercial property, for an amount that is near to its full replacement cost.

a.   A coinsurance clause typically provides that, if the property is insured for at least a stated percentage (usually 80%) of its actual cash value, any loss will be paid in full up to the face amount of the policy.

b.   The coinsurance requirement is the stated percentage times the fair market value of the insured property at the time of the loss.

Coinsurance requirement = Stated % × FMV at time of loss

c.   If the amount of insurance coverage is less than the required coinsurance amount, the insurance company pays only a fraction of the repair or replacement cost:

$$\frac{Amount\ of\ insurance}{Coinsurance\ requirement} \times Loss = Recovery\ amount$$

d.   The coinsurance requirement applies only to partial losses. Total losses result in recovery of the face amount of the policy.

NOTE: The insurer is liable to pay no more than the face amount of the policy, even if the coinsurance formula applies and yields a recovery amount greater than the face amount of the policy.

13. Formation and interpretation of insurance contracts are essentially the same as for other contracts. It is worth noting the following:

    a. The parties must agree on the property to be insured, the amount of coverage, the perils insured against, the starting and ending dates, and the amount of the premium.

    b. State insurance codes detail the standard provisions which must be included in each type of policy sold. If the insurance company violates state law by failing to include a required provision (intended to protect policyholders) in a policy, a policyholder may still enforce the policy as if it contained the provision.

    c. The statute of frauds does not require an insurance contract to be in writing to be enforceable (state insurance codes usually require the insurer to provide the insured with a written policy). Neither delivery of an insurance policy nor prepayment of the premium is a prerequisite for a valid and binding insurance contract.

    d. Courts interpret ambiguous clauses in insurance policies in accordance with the reasonable expectations of the insured party and against the insurance company that drafted the contract.

14. **Nonassignability**. Absent express consent of the insurer, the insured may not assign or otherwise transfer property insurance rights.

    a. Property and casualty insurance is treated as personal in nature.
    b. Transfer might materially increase the insurer's risk.

    NOTE: But the policy cannot preclude an assignment of the right to receive proceeds after an insured-against loss has occurred. Consent of the insurer is not required.

15. **Subrogation** entitles the insurer, to the extent it has paid for a loss, to any rights of its policyholder to recover from any third party. Subrogation reduces the cost of insurance coverage for the insured.

    a. If loss is caused by the insured's own negligence, subrogation does not apply.

    b. Subrogation is never applicable to life insurance and rarely to health insurance.

    c. Subrogation precludes double recovery for the same loss.

    d. Subrogation, as an equitable remedy, arises without need for a clause in the insurance policy.

16. **Cancellation** is commonly defined as the exercise of a right to rescind, abandon, or abrogate a contract of insurance.

    a. The form and the notice of proper cancellation are determined by provisions in the policy.

    b. Both the insurer and the insured can cancel or rescind an insurance policy.

    c. Restrictions on cancellation of a policy may apply. Statutes and administrative rules or regulations restrict cancellation in many states, e.g., by requiring that insurers give reasons for cancellation or nonrenewal.

17. Stop and review! You have completed the outline for this subunit. Study multiple-choice questions 44 through 48 beginning on page 619.

G. **Multiple Insurance Coverage**. A risk of loss may be covered under more than one policy. An "other insurance" or "pro rata" clause is common.

1. A typical **pro rata clause** specifies that, if an insured obtains insurance on the same property from multiple insurance companies, each company is responsible for only a proportionate share of the loss.

    a. EXAMPLE: Store, Inc. has two fire insurance policies on its building: with X Insurance Co. for $40,000 and with Y Insurance Co. for $20,000. Each policy includes an 80% coinsurance clause and a pro rata clause. A fire caused $80,000 damage when the building was worth $100,000. The coinsurance requirement was .8 x $100,000. The liability of both insurance companies was 75% of the actual loss, or $60,000. X's liability was ⅔ of that loss ($40,000 ÷ $60,000). Y's was ⅓.

2. Stop and review! You have completed the outline for this subunit. Study multiple-choice questions 49 through 51 beginning on page 621.

H. **Insurable Interest**. In the context of property and liability insurance, the insured is any person who is protected by a policy from risk of loss. (Contrast these types of insurance with life insurance, in which the insured is the person whose life is the subject of the insurance contract.)

1. The general requirement that a person who procures insurance must have an insurable interest applies to property insurance.

2. For property, the insured must have an insurable interest at the time of the loss.

    a. For life insurance, the purchaser must have an insurable interest when the policy is issued.

3. A person has an insurable interest in the subject matter insured if (s)he will derive economic benefit or advantage from its preservation, or will suffer economic loss or damage from its destruction.

4. In addition to the owner, examples of persons with an insurable interest in property include the following:

    a. A lessee in leased premises
    b. A partner in partnership property
    c. A person with contract rights in the subject matter of the contract
    d. A secured creditor in the collateral
    e. A bailee
    f. A grantor liable for a mortgage

5. The buyer of goods under the UCC acquires an insurable interest when goods are identified to the contract, i.e., generally, when goods are designated as those being sold.

6. Stop and review! You have completed the outline for this subunit. Study multiple-choice questions 52 through 57 beginning on page 622.

MULTIPLE-CHOICE QUESTIONS

A. Types of Ownership

1. A person may own property as a joint tenant with the right of survivorship with any of the following except a(n)

- A. Divorced spouse.
- B. Related minor child.
- C. Unaffiliated corporation.
- D. Unrelated adult.

The correct answer is (C). *(CPA, adapted)*
REQUIRED: The person who may not own property as a joint tenant with the right of survivorship.
DISCUSSION: Because a corporation is granted perpetual existence at law, it usually may not be a joint tenant of property. If a corporation were a joint tenant, the right of survivorship would be meaningless to the other joint tenants.
Answers (A), (B), and (D) are incorrect because each may hold property with a right of survivorship.

2. Which of the following unities (elements) are required to establish a joint tenancy?

	Time	Title	Interest	Possession
A.	Yes	Yes	Yes	Yes
B.	Yes	Yes	No	No
C.	No	No	Yes	Yes
D.	Yes	No	Yes	No

The correct answer is (A). *(CPA, adapted)*
REQUIRED: The unities required to establish a joint tenancy.
DISCUSSION: At common law, four unities are required to acquire a joint tenancy: (1) time (the interests must vest at the same time); (2) title (the interests must be acquired under the same instrument); (3) interest (the interests of the same type and duration); and (4) possession (the interests must represent identical rights of enjoyment).
Answers (B), (C), and (D) are incorrect because, under common law, each of the four elements is required to form a joint tenancy.

3. Tower, Nolan, and Oak were deeded a piece of land as tenants in common. The deed provided that Tower owned half the property and Nolan and Oak owned one-quarter each. If Oak dies, the property will be owned as follows:

- A. Tower 1/2, Nolan 1/4, Oak's heirs 1/4.
- B. Tower 1/3, Nolan 1/3, Oak's heirs 1/3.
- C. Tower 5/8, Nolan 3/8.
- D. Tower 1/2, Nolan 1/2.

The correct answer is (A). *(CPA, adapted)*
REQUIRED: The effect on property ownership following the death of a tenant in common.
DISCUSSION: A tenancy in common is a type of concurrent estate with no rights of survivorship. Upon the death of one of the owners in common, that person's share passes to his/her estate or heirs. Upon Oak's death, her one-fourth share of the land would pass to her heirs. Tower's and Nolan's shares are unaffected by Oak's death.
Answers (B), (C), and (D) are incorrect because there are no rights of survivorship for tenants in common. Therefore, the ownership percentages are unchanged. Oak's ownership would transfer to her estate or heirs.

4. Long, Fall, and Pear owned a building as joint tenants with the right of survivorship. Long gave Long's interest in the building to Green by executing and delivering a deed to Green. Neither Fall nor Pear consented to this transfer. Fall and Pear subsequently died. After their deaths, Green's interest in the building would consist of

- A. A one-third interest as a joint tenant.
- B. A one-third interest as a tenant in common.
- C. No interest because Fall and Pear did not consent to the transfer.
- D. Total ownership due to the deaths of Fall and Pear.

The correct answer is (B). *(CPA, adapted)*
REQUIRED: The effect of a conveyance by deed of a joint tenant's interest prior to the death of the other joint tenants.
DISCUSSION: The conveyance by deed of the joint tenant's interest made during life severed the joint tenancy with respect to the interest transferred. It gave rise to a tenancy in common with a ⅓ interest held by the donee (Green) and a ⅔ interest held by Fall and Pear. The latter parties held their interest as joint tenants with rights of survivorship; that is, the gift did not sever the portion of the joint tenancy not transferred. Consequently, Fall's and Pear's deaths resulted in the passage to the heirs of the later to die of full ownership of the ⅔ interest.
Answer (A) is incorrect because the conveyance severed the joint tenancy with respect to the donor's interest. Answer (C) is incorrect because their consent was unnecessary. Answer (D) is incorrect because Long's gift during life transferred a ⅓ interest to Green. The deaths of Fall and Pear had no effect on that interest.

5. Jane and John, each of whom owns a one-half interest in certain real property, are tenants in common. Jane's interest

- A. Will pass by operation of law to John on Jane's death.

- B. Will pass on Jane's death to her heirs.

- C. May not be transferred during Jane's lifetime without John's consent.

- D. Is considered a life estate.

The correct answer is (B). *(CPA, adapted)*
    REQUIRED: The characteristic of the interest of a tenant in common.
    DISCUSSION: The two tenants in common are each entitled to possession and an undivided interest in the whole property. The interest of a tenant in common may be transferred by deed or by will. Absent a will, it would pass to the tenant's heirs under state intestacy laws. In contrast, a joint tenant's interest contains a right of survivorship and cannot be transferred by will.
    Answer (A) is incorrect because, if it is not conveyed during Jane's lifetime, Jane's interest will pass under a will or state intestacy law. Answer (C) is incorrect because Jane's interest may be transferred by sale, gift, assignment, or will. Answer (D) is incorrect because a tenant in common is entitled to possession and an undivided interest in the whole property. The holder of a life estate is entitled to possession and beneficial use of the property only during his/her life. Absent an agreement to the contrary, the approval of other co-tenants is not required.

6. Abe, Bo, and Cy own a building as joint tenants with the right of survivorship. Abe gave his interest in the building to Zeb by executing and delivering a deed to Zeb. Neither Bo nor Cy consented to this transfer. Bo and Cy subsequently died. After their deaths, Zeb's interest in the building would consist of

- A. A 1/3 interest as a tenant in common.

- B. A 1/3 interest as a joint tenant.

- C. Total ownership due to the deaths of Bo and Cy.

- D. No interest because Bo and Cy did not consent to the transfer.

The correct answer is (A). *(CPA, adapted)*
    REQUIRED: The effect of a gift of a joint tenant's interest prior to the death of the other joint tenants.
    DISCUSSION: The gift of the joint tenant's interest made during life severed the joint tenancy with respect to the interest transferred. It gave rise to a tenancy in common with a 1/3 interest held by the donee (Zeb) and a 2/3 interest held by Bo and Cy. The latter parties held their interest as joint tenants with rights of survivorship; that is, the gift did not sever the portion of the joint tenancy not transferred. Consequently, Bo's and Cy's deaths resulted in the passage to the heirs of the last to die of full ownership of the 2/3 interest.
    Answer (B) is incorrect because the gift severed the joint tenancy with respect to the donor's interest. Answer (C) is incorrect because Abe's gift during life transferred a 1/3 interest to Zeb. The deaths of Bo and Cy had no effect on that interest. Answer (D) is incorrect because their consent was unnecessary.

B. Lessor-Lessee

7. Which of the following forms of tenancy will be created if a tenant stays in possession of the leased premises without the landlord's consent, after the tenant's 1-year written lease expires?

- A. Tenancy at will.

- B. Tenancy for years.

- C. Tenancy from period to period.

- D. Tenancy at sufferance.

The correct answer is (D). *(CPA, adapted)*
    REQUIRED: The type of leasehold tenancy.
    DISCUSSION: When a lessee holds over after a tenancy for years has expired and the lessor continues to treat the lessee as a tenant (for example, by accepting rent), a periodic tenancy is formed. A tenancy at sufferance arises when a lessee holds over without consent.
    Answer (A) is incorrect because a tenancy at will is for an indefinite time and is terminable by either party. It is usually granted expressly. It often involves either no rent payments or payment at irregular intervals. Answer (B) is incorrect because an estate for years is a lease for any definite time. It arises only by consent of the parties. Answer (C) is incorrect because a periodic tenancy continues from period to period until terminated. It arises by expressed or implied consent (agreement) of the parties. Note that, when a lessee holds over after a tenancy for years has expired and the lessor continues to treat the lessee as a tenant (for example, by accepting rent), a periodic tenancy is formed.

8. Which of the following rights is(are) generally given to a lessee of residential property?

I. A covenant of quiet enjoyment
II. An implied warranty of habitability

   A. I only.

   B. II only.

   C. Both I and II.

   D. Neither I nor II.

The correct answer is (C). *(CPA, adapted)*
   REQUIRED: The right(s), if any, enjoyed by a residential lessee.
   DISCUSSION: Under the covenant of quiet enjoyment, the landlord may not interfere with the tenant's right to physical possession, use, and enjoyment of the premises. Wrongful eviction and eviction by a party having better title than the landlord are breaches of this covenant. Furthermore, most courts have implied a warranty of habitability in a lease of residential property. The common-law rule was *caveat lessee*, let the lessee beware. Absent an express provision in the lease, the landlord was under no obligation to maintain the premises in a reasonable state of repair. However, the modern trend imposes affirmative duties on landlords to furnish habitable premises during the period of the lease. Courts have held that the tenant's covenant to pay rent is dependent on the implied warranty of habitability. If a landlord breaches the implied warranty of habitability, a tenant can vacate the premises, rescind the lease, offset repair costs against rent due, or seek damages.
   Answers (A), (B), and (D) are incorrect because the landlord has a duty to provide habitable premises and not to interfere with the tenant's quiet enjoyment of the property.

9. To be enforceable, a residential real estate lease must

   A. Require the tenant to obtain liability insurance.

   B. Entitle the tenant to exclusive possession of the leased property.

   C. Specify a due date for rent.

   D. Be in writing.

The correct answer is (B). *(CPA, adapted)*
   REQUIRED: The requirement for a residential lease to be enforceable.
   DISCUSSION: A lease is a contract and conveys rights to use real property. A tenant also has an estate in land (through the lease) characterized by the right to possession. Thus, a lease can be described as a grant of an exclusive possessory right of finite duration.
   Answer (A) is incorrect because, although the parties may make such a condition or covenant, it is not essential to a lease. Answer (C) is incorrect because, absent an express lease provision, the tenant generally has a duty to pay a reasonable amount of rent on the last day of the lease term. Answer (D) is incorrect because only in the minority of states that treat a lease as the sale of an interest in land must all leases be written. But a lease for longer than 1 year must generally be in writing.

10. A tenant renting an apartment under a 3-year written lease that does not contain any specific restrictions may be evicted for

   A. Counterfeiting money in the apartment.

   B. Keeping a dog in the apartment.

   C. Failing to maintain a liability insurance policy on the apartment.

   D. Making structural repairs to the apartment.

The correct answer is (A). *(CPA, adapted)*
   REQUIRED: The circumstances under which the tenant may be evicted.
   DISCUSSION: A tenant's basic responsibilities are to pay rent, avoid waste, return possession of the premises, perform the obligations agreed to in the lease, and not to make illegal use of the property. A use of the property that constituted a nuisance (for example, raising hogs in a residential area) or a criminal activity (operating an illegal gambling establishment) would breach the obligation to make lawful use of the premises.
   Answer (B) is incorrect because eviction should not result unless keeping the dog breached an expressed dependent covenant or condition, resulted in waste, or constituted a nuisance. Answer (C) is incorrect because eviction should not result unless maintaining the insurance was an express dependent covenant or a condition of the lease. Answer (D) is incorrect because, under common law, the landlord had no duty to repair and maintain the premises. Some state statutes require the landlord to maintain residential premises in a habitable condition. But a tenant who does not thereby cause waste to the premises does not generally breach a duty, condition, or dependant covenant by making structural repairs.

11. Bronson is a residential tenant with a 10-year written lease. In the absence of specific provisions in the lease to the contrary, which of the following statements is correct?

    A. The premises may not be sublet for less than the full remaining lease term.

    B. Bronson may not assign the lease.

    C. The landlord's death will automatically terminate the lease.

    D. Bronson's purchase of the property will terminate the lease.

The correct answer is (D). *(CPA, adapted)*
    REQUIRED: The correct statement concerning a 10-year written residential lease.
    DISCUSSION: A leasehold estate is an interest in real property that, unless expressly prohibited by the lease, may be assigned, sublet, donated, or devised. If the lessee purchases the property, the lease is merged in the fee simple estate.
    Answer (A) is incorrect because subleases are permitted unless expressly prohibited. Answer (B) is incorrect because both assignments and subleases are permitted unless expressly prohibited by the lease. Answer (C) is incorrect because neither freehold (generally outright ownership) nor nonfreehold (generally leaseholds) estates would terminate on the death of the grantor.

12. Delta Corp. leased 60,000 square feet in an office building from Tanner under a written 25-year lease. Which of the following statements is correct?

    A. Tanner's death will terminate the lease and Delta will be able to recover any resulting damages from Tanner's estate.

    B. Tanner's sale of the office building will terminate the lease unless both Delta and the buyer consented to the assumption of the lease by the buyer.

    C. In the absence of a provision in the lease to the contrary, Delta does not need Tanner's consent to assign the lease to another party.

    D. In the absence of a provision in the lease to the contrary, Delta would need Tanner's consent to enter into a sublease with another party.

The correct answer is (C). *(CPA, adapted)*
    REQUIRED: The correct statement concerning a long-term leasehold interest.
    DISCUSSION: The 25-year leasehold interest is a tenancy for years because it is a leasehold interest for a fixed period of time. Both assignments and subleases are permitted unless expressly prohibited by the lease. Public policy favors transferability of property.
    Answer (A) is incorrect because a tenancy for years does not automatically terminate upon the death of the lessor. It is assignable and inheritable. A lease is more than a personal contract. Answer (B) is incorrect because a lessor may also transfer his/her interest in the property without terminating the leasehold. The transferee would take subject to Delta's interest. Answer (D) is incorrect because, absent an express lease term to the contrary, landlord consent is not prerequisite to a sublease.

13. Sisk is a tenant of Met Co. and has 2 years remaining on a 6-year lease executed by Sisk and Met. The lease prohibits subletting but is silent as to Sisk's right to assign the lease. Sisk assigned the lease to Kern Corp., which assumed all of Sisk's obligations under the lease. Met objects to the assignment. Which of the following statements is correct?

    A. The assignment to Kern is voidable at Met's option.

    B. Sisk would have been relieved from liability on the lease with Met if Sisk obtained Met's consent to the assignment.

    C. Sisk will remain liable to Met for the rent provided for in the lease.

    D. With respect to the rent provided for in the lease, Kern is liable to Sisk but not to Met.

The correct answer is (C). *(CPA, adapted)*
    REQUIRED: The rights and duties of a lessor and lessee under a lease prohibiting subletting but not assignments.
    DISCUSSION: Absent a restriction against assignments in the lease, the lessee will retain the right to assign his/her interest. The prohibition against subletting does not prohibit assignments. Sisk will remain liable to Met for the rent until such time as Met agrees to a novation or a release and allows Kern to assume all of Sisk's legal obligations to Met.
    Answer (A) is incorrect because the lease does not specifically limit Sisk's right of assignment. Thus, Met does not have the option to void the assignment. Answer (B) is incorrect because only a novation would relieve Sisk from his/her lease liability. Met's consent to the assignment would not be equivalent to a novation. Answer (D) is incorrect because after an assignment, the assignee is in privity of estate with the original landlord. Thus, Kern is liable to Met for the rent provided for in the original lease. If Kern does not pay and Met recovers the rent from Sisk, Sisk will be able to seek reimbursement from Kern.

14. Drake Corp. entered into a 5-year lease with Deb Samon that provided for Drake's occupancy of three floors of a high-rise office building at a monthly rent of $16,000. The lease stated, "The lessee may sublease the premises but only with the landlord's (Samon's) prior written consent." The lease was silent as to whether Drake could assign the lease. Which of the following statements is correct?

- A. Subleasing of the premises with Samon's consent will relieve Drake from its obligation to pay rent.

- B. Assignment of the lease with Samon's consent will relieve Drake from its obligation to pay rent.

- C. Samon may refuse to consent to a subsequent sublease even if she has consented to a prior sublease.

- D. Subleasing of the premises without Samon's consent is void.

The correct answer is (C). *(CPA, adapted)*
REQUIRED: The correct statement about a lease that required prior written consent to a sublease.
DISCUSSION: The landlord (Samon) retains all rights reserved to her in the terms of the lease. This lease provides that the lessee (Drake) may sublease the property only after obtaining Samon's prior written consent. Thus, Samon retains the right to refuse consent to a sublease, even after approving a prior sublease.
Answers (A) and (B) are incorrect because neither a sublease nor an assignment of a lease relieves Drake of its obligations under the lease, unless Samon agrees to a novation. Answer (D) is incorrect because a sublease made in violation of the lease would be voidable, not void.

15. Tell, Inc. leased a building from Lott Corp. Tell paid monthly rent of $500 and was also responsible for paying the building's real estate taxes. On January 1, Vorn Co. and Tell entered into an agreement by which Vorn was entitled to occupy the building for the remainder of the term of Tell's lease in exchange for monthly payments of $600 to Tell. For the year, neither Tell nor Vorn paid the building's real estate taxes, and the taxes are delinquent. Learning this, Lott demanded that either Tell or Vorn pay the delinquent taxes. Both refused, and Lott has commenced an action against them. Lott will most likely prevail against

- A. Vorn but not Tell because the lease was assigned to it.

- B. Tell and Vorn because they are jointly and severally liable for the delinquent taxes.

- C. Tell without Vorn because their January 1 agreement constituted a sublease.

- D. Vorn but only to the extent of $100 for each month that it occupied the building during the year.

The correct answer is (B). *(CPA, adapted)*
REQUIRED: The obligations of a lessee and its transferee to the original lessor.
DISCUSSION: The legal relationship between an original lessee and lessor is not altered by an assignment or a sublease. An assignment is a transfer of all of the lessee's rights, whereas a sublease is characterized by a retention of some right(s) by the lessee. If this agreement had constituted a sublease, Tell would remain liable to Lott for any breach of the terms of the original lease. But as sublessee, Vorn would not be in privity of contract or estate with Lott and could not be successfully sued by it for the delinquent taxes. However, the Tell-Vorn agreement apparently conveyed Tell's entire interest. Tell did not have a reversionary interest in possession, even for a few hours, and no mention is made of other rights retained by the lessee. Thus, the agreement is an assignment. Vorn is an assignee who stands in privity of estate with Lott, and both Tell and Vorn will be liable for the full amount of the taxes.
Answers (A) and (D) are incorrect because, whether the agreement constituted a sublease or an assignment, Tell remains liable. Answer (C) is incorrect because Vorn is liable as an assignee.

C. Deeds, Recording, Title Defects, and Title Insurance

16. A method of transferring ownership of real property that most likely would be considered an arm's-length transaction is transfer by

- A. Inheritance.

- B. Eminent domain.

- C. Adverse possession.

- D. Sale.

The correct answer is (D). *(CPA, adapted)*
REQUIRED: The method of transferring realty most likely considered to be an arm's-length transaction.
DISCUSSION: A transaction is at arm's length when the parties are independent and on an equal footing. Thus, a sale between a willing buyer and a willing seller is most likely to be at arm's length, that is, between independent, equal parties representing their own interests.
Answer (A) is incorrect because the transfer of realty to the heirs of the owner is ordinarily not between independent parties. Answer (B) is incorrect because eminent domain is the power of government to condemn realty for a public purpose if just compensation is given. Answer (C) is incorrect because transfer by adverse possession is not a consensual process.

17. Which of the following is a defect in marketable title to real property?

A. Recorded zoning restrictions.

B. Recorded easements referred to in the contract of sale.

C. Unrecorded lawsuit for negligence against the seller.

D. Unrecorded easement.

The correct answer is (D). *(CPA, adapted)*
REQUIRED: The item that is a defect in marketable title to real property.
DISCUSSION: Unless a contract for the sale of real property specifically states otherwise, the seller must deliver marketable title. A marketable title is clear of restrictions. Easements or restrictive covenants make a title unmarketable.
Answers (A) and (B) are incorrect because recording provides constructive notice of the item recorded. Title is marketable notwithstanding restrictions which had been recorded. Answer (C) is incorrect because an unrecorded lawsuit for negligence is not a defect in marketable title to real property.

18. Which of the following elements must be contained in a valid deed?

	Purchase Price	Description of the Land
A.	Yes	Yes
B.	Yes	No
C.	No	Yes
D.	No	No

The correct answer is (C). *(CPA, adapted)*
REQUIRED: The element(s), if any, of a valid deed.
DISCUSSION: A deed is a written instrument expressing a grantor's intent to convey or pass an interest in real property to a grantee. Typically the deed must contain the name of the grantor, the name of the grantee, operative words of conveyance, a description (preferably legal) of the land, and the signature of the grantor.
Answers (A), (B), and (D) are incorrect because a valid deed need not recite the price.

19. For a deed to be effective between a purchaser and a seller of real estate, one of the conditions is that the deed must

A. Be recorded within the permissible statutory time limits.

B. Be delivered by the seller with an intent to transfer title.

C. Contain the actual sales price.

D. Contain the signatures of the seller and purchaser.

The correct answer is (B). *(CPA, adapted)*
REQUIRED: The requirement for a deed to convey property effectively.
DISCUSSION: For a conveyance of property by deed to be effective, the seller must deliver the deed to the buyer with the objective intent to transfer the title. Legal title to the real property does not pass to the buyer until (s)he accepts the deed. Equitable title may pass upon the signing of a contract to purchase and sell the property.
Answer (A) is incorrect because a deed need not be recorded for the title to the property to be transferred effectively. Recording gives constructive notice of the transaction and protects the buyer (grantee) against claims of subsequent parties. Answer (C) is incorrect because the deed must contain a recital of consideration but not the actual price. Answer (D) is incorrect because only the seller (grantor) must sign the deed.

20. Which of the following warranties is (are) contained in a general warranty deed?

I. The grantor has the right to convey the property.

II. The grantee will not be disturbed in possession of the property by the grantor or some third party's lawful claim of ownership.

A. I only.

B. II only.

C. I and II.

D. Neither I nor II.

The correct answer is (C). *(CPA, adapted)*
REQUIRED: The warranty coverage given by a general warranty deed.
DISCUSSION: Of the deeds customarily used in modern conveyances, the warranty deed with full covenants (general warranty deed) provides the greatest protection for the buyer. The seller who gives such a deed warrants that (s)he has the authority to convey the property, that there are no undisclosed encumbrances, and that (s)he will defend the rights of the buyer against the claims of any other person.
Answers (A), (B), and (D) are incorrect because both of the warranties are included by a general warranty deed.

21. Which of the following deeds gives the grantee the least amount of protection?

    A. Bargain and sale deed.

    B. Grant deed.

    C. Quitclaim deed.

    D. Warranty deed.

The correct answer is (C). *(CPA, adapted)*

    REQUIRED: The deed that gives the grantee the least amount of protection.

    DISCUSSION: A quitclaim deed merely relinquishes to the grantee whatever interest the grantor may have. Such a deed contains no covenants (warranties). Thus, it does not warrant that the grantor has a clear title or any title at all. If an adverse claimant prevails, the grantee will have no recourse against the grantor.

    Answer (A) is incorrect because a bargain and sale deed is essentially a contract, and the seller is considered to imply that (s)he has a right to convey the property. It may also contain a covenant that the seller has not impaired the title. Answer (B) is incorrect because a grant (special warranty) deed provides warranty protection, but only with respect to events occurring after the grantor acquired the property. Answer (D) is incorrect because a general warranty provides the fullest possible protection.

22. To be enforceable against the mortgagor, a mortgage must meet all the following requirements except

    A. Be delivered to the mortgagee.

    B. Be in writing and signed by the mortgagor.

    C. Be recorded by the mortgagee.

    D. Include a description of the debt and land involved.

The correct answer is (C). *(CPA, adapted)*

    REQUIRED: The incorrect statement about a mortgage on a building.

    DISCUSSION: Recording the transfer of an interest in realty (whether a deed, mortgage, contract to sell, lien, or judgment) does not affect the rights of the parties to the transaction. Instead, it operates to give constructive notice of the interest to third parties. Thus, recording protects the rights of the mortgagee against third parties who do not have actual notice of the mortgage.

    Answer (A) is incorrect because, in the majority of states, the mortgagor is regarded as transferring a security interest to the mortgagee. The mortgage must be delivered to the mortgagee. Answer (B) is incorrect because a mortgage is an interest in real property and is therefore within the statute of frauds. The mortgage must be in writing and signed by the party to be bound (the mortgagor). Answer (D) is incorrect because the mortgage must be executed with the same formalities as a deed. Hence, it must contain a legally sufficient description of the debt and of the property.

23. On February 2, Mazo deeded a warehouse to Parko for $450,000. Parko did not record the deed. On February 12, Mazo deeded the same warehouse to Nexis for $430,000. Nexis was aware of the prior conveyance to Parko. Nexis recorded its deed before Parko recorded. Who would prevail under the following recording statutes?

	Notice Statute	Race Statute	Race-Notice Statute
A.	Nexis	Parko	Parko
B.	Parko	Nexis	Parko
C.	Parko	Nexis	Nexis
D.	Parko	Parko	Nexis

The correct answer is (B). *(CPA, adapted)*

    REQUIRED: The interests having priority under different types of recording statutes.

    DISCUSSION: Under a notice statute, an unrecorded deed is ineffective against a subsequent bona fide purchaser (for value and without notice). Under a race-notice statute, the subsequent bona fide purchaser must record before the prior grantee. In two states, a race is in effect: regardless of notice, the first to record prevails. Nexis, not a bona fide purchaser (Nexis had notice), has no priority over Parko under a notice or race-notice statute. Being first to record, Nexis has priority over Parko in the race statute jurisdiction, without regard to actual notice.

    Answers (A) and (C) are incorrect because Nexis was not a bona fide purchaser. Answer (D) is incorrect because, under a race statute, the first to record prevails without regard to notice.

24. Fern purchased property from Nix for $150,000. Fern obtained a $90,000 loan from Bank to finance the purchase, executing a promissory note and mortgage. By recording the mortgage, Bank protects its

- A. Priority against a previously filed real estate tax lien on the property.
- B. Priority against all parties having earlier claims to the property.
- C. Rights against the claims of subsequent bona fide purchasers for value.
- D. Rights against Fern under the promissory note.

The correct answer is (C). *(CPA, adapted)*
   REQUIRED: The effect of the mortgagee's recording the mortgage.
   DISCUSSION: If the mortgagee's interest is recorded, a subsequent purchaser has notice of the mortgage and will take subject to it. Recording will also give Bank priority over a subsequent mortgagee.
   Answer (A) is incorrect because a previously filed tax lien has priority since it was recorded first. Recording the mortgage establishes priority over subsequent transferees and mortgages. Answer (B) is incorrect because earlier claims, if recorded, have priority. Answer (D) is incorrect because the contract between Bank and Fern is sufficient to establish their rights against each other.

25. If a mortgagee fails to record its mortgage in a jurisdiction with a notice-race recording statute,

- A. A subsequent recording mortgagee who has no knowledge of the prior mortgage will have a superior security interest.
- B. A subsequent recording mortgagee who has knowledge of the prior mortgage will have a superior security interest.
- C. A subsequent purchaser for value who has no knowledge of the mortgage will take the property subject to the mortgage.
- D. A subsequent purchaser for value who has knowledge of the mortgage will take the property free of the prior security interest.

The correct answer is (A). *(CPA, adapted)*
   REQUIRED: The effect of failure to record given a notice-race statute.
   DISCUSSION: Under a notice-race statute, an unrecorded interest in real property is ineffective against a subsequent bona fide purchaser (for value and without notice) if (s)he records before the prior interest is recorded.
   Answers (B) and (D) are incorrect because the mortgagee's unrecorded interest is superior to that of any subsequent party with knowledge of the existing mortgage. Answer (C) is incorrect because the subsequent bona fide purchaser (for value and without notice) takes free of the unrecorded mortgage.

26. On May 1, 1998, Chance bought a piece of property by taking subject to an existing unrecorded mortgage held by Hay Bank. On April 1, 1999, Chance borrowed money from Link Finance and gave Link a mortgage on the property. Link did not know about the Hay mortgage and did not record its mortgage until July 1, 1999. On June 1, 1999, Chance borrowed money from Zone Bank and gave Zone a mortgage on the same property. Zone knew about the Link mortgage but did not know about the Hay mortgage. Zone recorded its mortgage on June 15, 1999. Which mortgage would have priority if these transactions took place in a notice-race jurisdiction?

- A. The Hay mortgage because it was first in time.
- B. The Link mortgage because Zone had notice of the Link mortgage.
- C. The Zone mortgage because it was the first recorded mortgage.
- D. The Zone and Link mortgages share priority because neither had notice of the Hay mortgage.

The correct answer is (B). *(CPA, adapted)*
   REQUIRED: The mortgagee with priority in a notice-race state.
   DISCUSSION: A notice-race statute gives priority to the first party to record unless (s)he had actual notice of a preexisting interest. Zone had actual notice of the Link mortgage when it recorded, so its interest would be subordinate to Link's.
   Answer (A) is incorrect because Link would have priority since it was the first to record without actual notice of Hay's prior claim. Answers (C) and (D) are incorrect because only in one of the few states with a pure race statute (one that ignores a party's actual notice of an existing, unrecorded interest if (s)he is the first to record) would Zone have priority.

27. Unless an exception to title is noted in the title insurance policy, a title insurance company will be liable to a land purchaser for

- A. Closing costs.
- B. Recorded easements.
- C. Unrecorded assessments.
- D. Zoning violations.

The correct answer is (B). *(CPA, adapted)*
REQUIRED: The item for which the title insurance company will usually be liable.
DISCUSSION: The title insurer searches the public records. A title policy, like other insurance, is a contract of indemnification. The policy gives protection if title is actually in another person, if title is subject to an encumbrance or other kind of defect, if the insured has no access to his/her land, and possibly if (s)he suffers loss from nonmarketability of the title. A title insurer may be liable, even without having been negligent, for an unexcepted recorded easement.

Answer (A) is incorrect because closing costs include such items as title insurance and are not covered by title insurance. Answer (C) is incorrect because, although other risks may be insured, the policy usually applies only to recorded items. Answer (D) is incorrect because the title insurance company usually does not insure that the property has not been used in violation of a zoning ordinance.

28. A standard title insurance policy will generally insure that

- A. There are no other deeds to the property.
- B. The purchaser has good record title as of the policy's date.
- C. All taxes and assessments are paid.
- D. The insurance protection will be transferable to a subsequent purchaser.

The correct answer is (B). *(CPA, adapted)*
REQUIRED: The correct statement about a title insurance policy.
DISCUSSION: A standard title insurance policy insures the holder has good record title at the policy's date. If the title turns out to be defective, subject to exceptions listed in the policy, the title insurer will reimburse the insured for loss.

Answer (A) is incorrect because title insurance does not change the fact of previously executed deeds. Neither does it completely clear title. It does represent a promise to reimburse the insured for covered losses. Answer (C) is incorrect because unpaid taxes are commonly listed as an exception in a title insurance policy. Answer (D) is incorrect because the insurance protection is not generally transferable to a subsequent purchaser. That purchaser must obtain his/her own title insurance.

D. Mortgages and Other Liens

29. Which of the following conditions must be met to have an enforceable mortgage?

- A. An accurate description of the property must be included in the mortgage.
- B. A negotiable promissory note must accompany the mortgage.
- C. Present consideration must be given in exchange for the mortgage.
- D. The amount of the debt and the interest rate must be stated in the mortgage.

The correct answer is (A). *(CPA, adapted)*
REQUIRED: The condition that must be met to have an enforceable mortgage.
DISCUSSION: A mortgage relates to an interest in land and is within the statute of frauds. The mortgage must be executed with the same formalities as a deed. It must contain a legally sufficient description of the property, that is, one precise enough to accurately determine the location of the land.

Answer (B) is incorrect because, although a mortgage secures an underlying obligation, enforceability of the mortgage does not depend on its being accompanied by a negotiable instrument. Answer (C) is incorrect because a mortgage represents the security interest for which value must be given. However, a mortgage may provide security for payment of an antecedent obligation. Answer (D) is incorrect because, although contained in most mortgages, the amount of debt and the interest rate are not required.

30. In general, which of the following statements is correct with respect to a real estate mortgage?

- A. The mortgage may not be given to secure an antecedent debt.

- B. The mortgage must contain the actual amount of the underlying debt.

- C. The mortgage must be signed by both the mortgagor (borrower) and mortgagee (lender).

- D. The mortgagee may assign the mortgage to a third party without the mortgagor's consent.

The correct answer is (D). *(CPA, adapted)*
REQUIRED: The correct statement with respect to a real estate mortgage.
DISCUSSION: In a lien theory state, the mortgage is merely a security interest in the real property. Thus, it can be transferred by an assignment without the mortgagor's consent, rather than by deed (which would be required in a title theory state). The majority of states adhere to the lien theory. The note and mortgage are assignable in most states because they represent only a right to payment and security therefor.
Answer (A) is incorrect because a mortgage may provide security for payment of a debt which may be antecedent to the grant of the mortgage, concurrent with the grant of the mortgage, or arising after the grant of the mortgage. Answer (B) is incorrect because, even though the amount of indebtedness and the rate of interest are usually included on most mortgages, they are not legally required. Answer (C) is incorrect because the mortgage must be in writing and signed by the party to be bound (the mortgagor). It does not have to be signed by the mortgagee.

31. Gilmore borrowed $60,000 from Dix Bank. The loan was used to remodel a building owned by Gilmore as investment property and was secured by a second mortgage that Dix did not record. FCA Loan Company has a recorded first mortgage on the building. If Gilmore defaults on both mortgages, Dix

- A. Will not be entitled to any mortgage foreclosure sale proceeds, even if such proceeds are in excess of the amount owed to FCA.

- B. Will be unable successfully to claim any security interest in the building.

- C. Will be entitled to share in any foreclosure sale proceeds pro rata with FCA.

- D. Will be able to successfully claim a security interest that is subordinate to FCA's security interest.

The correct answer is (D). *(CPA, adapted)*
REQUIRED: The right of an unrecorded second mortgagee when there is a recorded first mortgage.
DISCUSSION: Recording is not essential to an enforceable mortgage. Recording gives constructive notice of the mortgagee's interest to third parties. The loan contract and mortgage is effective between the mortgagor and mortgagee without reference to recording. Dix Bank had constructive notice of FCA's mortgage. Dix's security interest is therefore subordinate to FCA's.
Answer (A) is incorrect because proceeds in excess of the full amount due on a superior interest are payable in satisfaction of a subordinate interest. Answer (B) is incorrect because recording is not essential to render a mortgage valid. Answer (C) is incorrect because a superior interest is satisfied in full before proceeds are applied to a subordinate one.

32. Sussex, Inc. had given a first mortgage when it purchased its plant and warehouse. Sussex needed additional working capital. It decided to obtain financing by giving a second mortgage on the plant and warehouse. Which of the following statements is true with respect to the mortgages?

- A. Default on payment of the second mortgage will constitute default on the first mortgage.

- B. The second mortgage may not be prepaid without the consent of the first mortgagee.

- C. The second mortgagee may not pay off the first mortgage to protect its security.

- D. If both mortgages are foreclosed, the first mortgage must be fully paid before paying the second mortgage.

The correct answer is (D). *(CPA, adapted)*
REQUIRED: The correct statement concerning the legal status of first and second mortgages.
DISCUSSION: The nature of the second mortgage is that it represents a claim that is subordinate to the first mortgage. Upon foreclosure and judicial sale of the property, the proceeds would be distributed to all senior liens (the first mortgage) and to expenses of sale before the second mortgagee received anything. In some jurisdictions, foreclosure of a second mortgage leaves the first mortgage intact and unaffected by the foreclosure sale.
Answer (A) is incorrect because default on one mortgage is not default on the other mortgage. They are separate contractual undertakings. However, a provision can be placed in a mortgage agreeing that a breach of one mortgage is also breach of another. Answer (B) is incorrect because prepayment does not require consent of the first mortgagee. Answer (C) is incorrect because the second mortgagee may pay off the first mortgage to protect its security.

33. Sklar Corp. owns a factory that has a fair market value of $90,000. Dall Bank holds an $80,000 first mortgage, and Rice Finance holds a $20,000 second mortgage on the factory. Sklar has discontinued payments to Dall and Rice, who have foreclosed on their mortgages. If the factory is properly sold to Bond at a judicial sale for $90,000, after expenses,

A. Rice will receive $10,000 out of the proceeds.

B. Dall will receive $77,500 out of the proceeds.

C. Bond will take the factory subject to the unsatisfied portion of any mortgage.

D. Rice has a right of redemption after the judicial sale.

The correct answer is (A). *(CPA, adapted)*
REQUIRED: The correct statement about the effects of a judicial sale.
DISCUSSION: A first mortgage holder has priority upon foreclosure and must be paid in full prior to payment of subsequent mortgage holder. Thus, Dall Bank will receive the first $80,000 of the proceeds, and Rice will receive the remaining $10,000. Rice will be an unsecured creditor for the remaining $10,000 of its debt.
Answer (B) is incorrect because Dall will receive payment in full before the second mortgage holder is paid anything. The proceeds are not prorated. Answer (C) is incorrect because the purchaser at the judicial sale will take the property free of any claim. Answer (D) is incorrect because the mortgagor (Sklar), not a mortgagee, has the right of redemption after the sale.

34. In 1992, Smith gave a mortgage to State Bank to secure a $100,000 loan. The mortgage was silent as to whether it would secure any other loans made by State to Smith. In 1994, Smith gave a second mortgage to Penn Bank to secure an $80,000 loan. Both mortgages described the same land and were properly recorded shortly after being executed by Smith. By 1998, Smith had repaid State Bank $40,000 of the $100,000 debt. State Bank then lent Smith an additional $20,000 without taking any new security. Within a few days, Smith defaulted on the loans from both banks, and the first and second mortgages were foreclosed. The balance on the Penn loan was $20,000. The net proceeds of the foreclosure sale were $70,000. State is entitled to receive from the proceeds a maximum of

A. $52,500

B. $56,000

C. $60,000

D. $70,000

The correct answer is (C). *(CPA, adapted)*
REQUIRED: The maximum proceeds to which the first mortgagor is entitled if it made a subsequent loan without new security.
DISCUSSION: When all mortgages on the same property are properly executed and recorded, the first mortgage will have priority over subsequent mortgages. Upon foreclosure, the mortgages must be fully satisfied in order of their priority. In this situation, State Bank holds a first mortgage for $60,000, and Penn Bank holds a second mortgage for $20,000. State Bank is an unsecured creditor for the additional $20,000 loan. Thus, State Bank will receive the first $60,000 from the foreclosure proceeds, and Penn Bank will receive the remaining $10,000. State Bank's unsecured loan will not be considered in the distribution of proceeds.
Answers (A) and (B) are incorrect because the first mortgage balance is satisfied in full first. State Bank's second loan was not secured. Proceeds are not prorated. Answer (D) is incorrect because State Bank's unsecured loan is not satisfied by proceeds from sale of the property. A future advance clause would have secured the loan.

35. If a mortgagor defaults in the payment of a purchase money mortgage and the mortgagee forecloses, the mortgagor may do any of the following except

A. Obtain any excess monies resulting from a judicial sale after payment of the mortgagee.

B. Remain in possession of the property after a foreclosure sale if the equity in the property exceeds the balance due on the mortgage.

C. Refinance the mortgage with another lender and repay the original mortgage.

D. Assert the equitable right of redemption by paying the mortgage.

The correct answer is (B). *(CPA, adapted)*
REQUIRED: The right not held by a defaulting mortgagor.
DISCUSSION: Most states recognize the mortgage as a security interest. The mortgagor-debtor signs a promissory note for the sum borrowed from the mortgagee-creditor. (S)he also signs a mortgage document representing the right of the mortgagee to seek judicial foreclosure of the mortgage and sale of the property upon default. The purchaser will receive a right to possession after the sale (or in some states after the redemption period elapses).
Answer (A) is incorrect because the mortgagor has an equity in the process equal to any amount left after payment of the debt, interest, and costs. Answer (C) is incorrect because redemption might be accomplished by refinancing. Answer (D) is incorrect because a defaulting mortgagor has an equitable right to redeem the property before the foreclosure proceedings are complete by payment of the debt, interest, and costs. In many states, the mortgagor also has a statutory right of redemption after foreclosure.

36. A mortgagor's right of redemption will be terminated by a judicial foreclosure sale unless

A. The proceeds from the sale are not sufficient to satisfy the mortgage debt fully.

B. The mortgage instrument does not provide for a default sale.

C. The mortgagee purchases the property for market value.

D. The jurisdiction has enacted a statutory right of redemption.

The correct answer is (D). *(CPA, adapted)*
REQUIRED: The correct statement concerning a mortgagor's right of redemption.
DISCUSSION: A foreclosure sale occurs when a mortgage is in default and the mortgagee elects to satisfy its debt by sale of the property rather than by obtaining a personal judgment against the mortgagor. It generally terminates the mortgagor's equitable right of redemption. A statutory right of redemption provides the mortgagor with the opportunity to repurchase the property after the foreclosure sale, for a certain statutorily specified period generally not exceeding 1 year, by payment of the auction sale price.
Answer (A) is incorrect because proceeds insufficient to satisfy the mortgage debt does not operate to limit the statutory right of redemption. The mortgagee is entitled to the proceeds. Answer (B) is incorrect because, unless the statute so provides, failure to provide for a default sale in the mortgage instrument does not preclude the statutory right of redemption. Answer (C) is incorrect because the mortgagee is generally permitted to bid on and buy the property at a foreclosure sale. This alone does not terminate a statutory right of redemption.

37. Wilk bought an apartment building from Dix Corp. There was a mortgage on the building securing Dix's promissory note to Xeon Finance Co. Wilk took title subject to Xeon's mortgage. Wilk did not make the payments on the note due Xeon and the building was sold at a foreclosure sale. If the proceeds of the foreclosure sale are less than the balance due on the note, which of the following statements is correct regarding the deficiency?

A. Xeon must attempt to collect the deficiency from Wilk before suing Dix.

B. Dix will not be liable for any of the deficiency because Wilk assumed the note and mortgage.

C. Xeon may collect the deficiency from either Dix or Wilk.

D. Dix will be liable for the entire deficiency.

The correct answer is (D). *(CPA, adapted)*
REQUIRED: The result when the proceeds of a foreclosure sale on a mortgage which had been taken "subject to" are less than the balance due on the note.
DISCUSSION: By taking "subject to" a mortgage, Wilk avoided personal liability either to Dix or to the mortgagee. If Wilk had "assumed" the mortgage, Wilk would have been personally liable both to Dix and to the mortgagee. In either case, Dix could not avoid liability on his contractual duty to perform. Only if the mortgagee had released Dix (e.g., by a novation) could it have escaped liability.
Answers (A) and (C) are incorrect because Wilk took encumbered property but without personal liability. Wilk merely took "subject to" the mortgage. Answer (B) is incorrect because Wilk did not assume it. If Wilk had, Dix would still have been liable as a surety.

38. Generally, which of the following federal acts regulate(s) mortgage lenders?

	Real Estate Settlement Procedures Act (RESPA)	Federal Trade Commission Act
A.	Yes	Yes
B.	Yes	No
C.	No	Yes
D.	No	No

The correct answer is (B). *(CPA, adapted)*
REQUIRED: The act(s) that regulate(s) mortgage lenders.
DISCUSSION: The Real Estate Settlement Procedures Act (RESPA) was enacted to regulate the conduct of and practices and procedures of mortgage lenders. The primary purpose of the act is the disclosure of information needed by consumers. The Federal Trade Commission (FTC) does not specifically regulate the conduct of mortgage lenders. The FTC regulates interstate commerce to promote free and fair competition.
Answers (A), (C), and (D) are incorrect because RESPA regulates the conduct and practices of mortgage lenders, but the Federal Trade Commission Act does not.

39. Ritz owned a building on which there was a duly recorded first mortgage held by Lyn and a recorded second mortgage held by Jay. Ritz sold the building to Nunn. Nunn assumed the Jay mortgage and had no actual knowledge of the Lyn mortgage. Nunn defaulted on the payments to Jay. If both Lyn and Jay foreclosed, and the proceeds of the sale were insufficient to pay both Lyn and Jay,

A. Jay would be paid after Lyn was fully paid.

B. Jay and Lyn would be paid proportionately.

C. Nunn would be personally liable to Lyn but not to Jay.

D. Nunn would be personally liable to Lyn and Jay.

The correct answer is (A). *(CPA, adapted)*
REQUIRED: The result on foreclosure when the proceeds were insufficient to satisfy both mortgages.
DISCUSSION: When a buyer of real estate assumes an existing mortgage, the seller remains liable if there has been no novation. Between the seller and buyer, the buyer has become the primary debtor, and the seller is a surety. Because Nunn had constructive notice of both security interests, the interests in the property are superior to Nunn's. Thus, both Lyn and Jay have a right to foreclose. When all mortgages on the same property are recorded, a first mortgage holder has priority upon foreclosure and must be paid in full prior to payment of a second mortgage holder.
Answer (B) is incorrect because the holder of a second mortgage is paid only any excess over a first mortgage holder's claim. Answer (C) is incorrect because Nunn agreed to assume personal liability to Jay, but not to Lyn. Answer (D) is incorrect because Nunn did not agree to assume personal liability to Lyn.

40. Builder, Inc. contracts to sell Buyer a new house, with all work to be completed by June 1, the closing date. On June 1, the title search indicates no adverse interests of record; Buyer pays the $45,000 price and moves in. On June 25, Buyer receives a notice from Subcontractor that she claims a mechanic's lien in the amount of $30,000 on the house for work completed on May 25. Subcontractor has a valid direct lien pursuant to a state statute. Which of the following is false?

A. If Buyer does nothing and Subcontractor is not paid, Subcontractor can foreclose the lien, force the sale of Buyer's house, and receive the first $30,000 of proceeds.

B. The lawyer who prepared the title report is not liable for malpractice because the mechanic's lien was not of record on June 1.

C. If no recovery can be had from Builder and Buyer desires to keep the house, Buyer may have to pay an additional $30,000.

D. If Subcontractor does not file a foreclosure action within the specified statutory period, she will lose all of her rights.

The correct answer is (D). *(Publisher)*
REQUIRED: The effect of a mechanic's lien as a hidden interest in property.
DISCUSSION: A mechanic's lien is statutory, and the specific rules vary from state to state. The notice periods under the various statutes range from 30 to 90 days after the last work is performed. A mechanic's lien filed within the allotted period attaches as of the time the first work is done. Consequently, the record may not reveal existence of the lien to third parties (in this case Buyer). Moreover, the foreclosure action must be filed within a limited period. But failure to do so will not impair the lienholder's private contract rights against the party with whom (s)he contracted.
Answers (A) and (C) are incorrect because such is the plight of the buyer who fails to protect against a hidden lien by getting waivers or having funds retained in escrow. Subcontractor, as an unsatisfied lienholder, has typical foreclosure rights. Answer (B) is incorrect because the lawyer has performed his/her contract competently by reporting the absence of any liens of record.

E. Fixtures

41. A tenant's personal property will become a fixture and belong to the landlord if its removal would

A. Increase the value of the personal property.

B. Cause a material change to the personal property.

C. Result in substantial harm to the landlord's property.

D. Change the use of the landlord's property back to its prior use.

The correct answer is (C). *(CPA, adapted)*
REQUIRED: The consideration in determining whether a tenant's personal property will become a fixture and belong to the landlord.
DISCUSSION: The intent of the parties controls whether a tenant's personal property will become a fixture and belong to the landlord. However, other factors may be considered to determine that intent in the absence of an explicit statement. The most important are the mode of annexation, the amount of damage to the realty and to the item if it is removed, and the degree to which the item is specifically adapted to the realty.
Answers (A), (B) and (D) are incorrect because each is relatively insignificant.

42. Which of the following factors help(s) determine whether an item of personal property has become a fixture?

	Manner of Affixation	Value of the Item	Intent of the Annexor
A.	Yes	Yes	Yes
B.	Yes	Yes	No
C.	Yes	No	Yes
D.	No	Yes	Yes

The correct answer is (C). *(CPA, adapted)*
   REQUIRED: The factor(s) considered when determining whether personal property has become a fixture.
   DISCUSSION: An item of personal property becomes a fixture if it is so closely connected to real property that it becomes part of the real property. Whether an item of personal property becomes a fixture is dependent upon the intention of the annexor. To determine the objective intent of the annexor, it is necessary to consider the manner in which the item is affixed to the real property.
   Answers (A), (B), and (D) are incorrect because the objective intent of the annexor and the manner in which the item is affixed to the real property are pertinent to the determination of whether the item of personal property has become a fixture. However, the value of the item affixed is relatively unimportant.

43. Which of the following factors help(s) determine whether an item of personal property is a fixture?

I. Degree of the item's attachment to the property
II. Intent of the person who had the item installed

   A. I only.

   B. II only.

   C. Both I and II.

   D. Neither I nor II.

The correct answer is (C). *(CPA, adapted)*
   REQUIRED: The consideration(s), if any, in determining whether personal property is a fixture.
   DISCUSSION: The intent of the party who attached the personal property controls whether personal property is a fixture. However, other factors may be considered to determine that intent in the absence of an explicit statement. The most important are the mode of annexation, the amount of damage to the realty and to the item if it is removed, and the degree to which the item is specifically adapted to the realty.
   Answers (A), (B), and (D) are incorrect because the intent of the party who attached the personal property and the degree of attachment should be considered.

F. General Insurance Concepts

44. One of the primary purposes of including a coinsurance clause in a property insurance policy is to

   A. Encourage the policyholder to insure the property for an amount close to its full value.

   B. Make the policyholder responsible for the entire loss caused by some covered perils.

   C. Cause the policyholder to maintain a minimum amount of liability insurance that will increase with inflation.

   D. Require the policyholder to insure the property with only one insurance company.

The correct answer is (A). *(CPA, adapted)*
   REQUIRED: The true statement about the coinsurance clause.
   DISCUSSION: Coinsurance is a provision in which the owner agrees to insure the property up to a given percentage (usually 80%) of its value. A policyholder who complies with the coinsurance agreement will recover any loss in full up to the face amount of the policy. If the policyholder insures for less than the agreed percentage, (s)he becomes a coinsurer and must bear any partial loss proportionately with the insurance company. The purpose is to prevent the insured from insuring for a minimal amount (and minimal premium) and recovering in full for a partial loss.
   Answer (B) is incorrect because this is addressed by an exclusion clause. Answer (C) is incorrect because liability insurance protects against tort liability. Answer (D) is incorrect because a coinsurance clause is intended to prevent underinsuring, not multiple insurance.

45. Hart owned a building with a fair market value of $400,000. The building was covered by a $300,000 fire insurance policy containing an 80% coinsurance clause. What amount would Hart recover if a fire totally destroyed the building?

A. $0

B. $240,000

C. $300,000

D. $400,000

The correct answer is (C). *(CPA, adapted)*

REQUIRED: The amount recoverable under an 80% coinsurance clause.

DISCUSSION: A coinsurance clause requires the insured to maintain insurance equal to or greater than a specified percentage (usually 80%) of the value of the insured property. If the insured has not carried the specified percentage and a partial loss occurs, the insurance company is liable for only a proportionate part of the loss. This is to deter people from paying for insurance on only a small part of the property's value. However, the coinsurance clause has no application when an insured building is totally destroyed. Thus, Hart can recover the $300,000 face value of the policy.

Answer (A) is incorrect because partial recovery is available when a coinsurance requirement is not complied with. Answer (B) is incorrect because a coinsurance clause does not limit recovery when the insured property is a total loss. Answer (D) is incorrect because an insured cannot collect more from an insurance company than the face value of the policy.

46. Which of the following losses, resulting from a fire, generally may be recovered under a standard fire insurance policy?

	Water Damage Resulting from Extinguishing the Fire	Loss of Income Due to Business Interruption
A.	Yes	Yes
B.	Yes	No
C.	No	Yes
D.	No	No

The correct answer is (B). *(CPA, adapted)*

REQUIRED: The loss(es) covered under standard insurance policies.

DISCUSSION: The standard fire insurance policy protects the homeowner against damage caused by the fire as well as smoke and water damage. It does not provide for recovery for business interruption, lost profits, or other special matters unless there is a special endorsement or rider attached to the policy.

Answers (A) and (C) are incorrect because loss of income due to business interruption is not covered. Answer (D) is incorrect because water damage is usually covered.

47. On April 2, 1997, Ritz Corp. purchased a warehouse that it insured for $500,000. The policy contained a 75% coinsurance clause. On April 25, 1998, a fire caused $900,000 damage to the warehouse. The fair market value of the warehouse was $800,000 on April 2, 1997 and $1 million on April 25, 1998. Ritz is entitled to receive insurance proceeds of, at most,

A. $375,000

B. $500,000

C. $600,000

D. $750,000

The correct answer is (B). *(CPA, adapted)*

REQUIRED: The amount of recovery under a policy containing a coinsurance clause.

DISCUSSION: Under a standard coinsurance clause, the insured agrees to maintain insurance equal to a specified percentage of the value of the property. If the insured has not carried the specified percentage and a loss occurs, the insurance company pays only part of the loss. The coinsurance requirement is $750,000 (75% x $1,000,000 FMV at the time of the loss). Under the formula below, Ritz might recover $600,000 of the $900,000 loss.

$$\frac{\text{Amount of insurance}}{\text{Coinsurance requirement}} \times \text{Loss} = \text{Recovery}$$

$$\frac{\$500,000}{\$750,000} \times \$900,000 = \$600,000$$

But Ritz may recover no more than the face amount of the policy.

Answer (A) is incorrect because the coinsurance percentage is applied to compute the coinsurance requirement, which in turn is the denominator of the fraction multiplied by the loss. Answers (C) and (D) are incorrect because under no circumstances would the insurance company pay more than the face value of the policy.

48. Jewelry, Inc. took out an insurance policy with Insurance Company which covered the stock of jewelry. Insurance agreed to indemnify for losses due to theft of the jewels displayed. The application contained the following provision: "It is hereby warranted that the maximum value of the jewelry displayed shall not exceed $10,000." The insurance policy's coverage was for $8,000. Subsequently, thieves smashed the store window and stole $4,000 worth of jewels when the total value of the display was $12,000. Which of the following is correct?

A. Jewelry, Inc. will recover nothing.

B. Jewelry, Inc. will recover $2,000, the loss less the amount in excess of the $10,000 display limitation.

C. Jewelry, Inc. will recover the full $4,000 since the warranty will be construed as a mere representation.

D. Jewelry, Inc. will recover the full $4,000 since attaching the application to the policy is insufficient to make it a part thereof.

The correct answer is (A). *(CPA, adapted)*
REQUIRED: The amount an insured will recover when a warranty is breached.
DISCUSSION: Conditions precedent, called warranties, are part of the property insurance policy. Breach of a warranty precludes recovery and results in a forfeiture. Since the law disfavors forfeitures, courts construe questions of interpretation favorably to the insured and against the insurer that drafted the policy. However, if the parties expressly agree that certain statements are warranties, then a court would recognize them as warranties. Since Jewelry warranted never to display more than $10,000 of jewelry, the breach of warranty prevents recovery.
Answer (B) is incorrect because Jewelry will recover nothing; it is not entitled to $2,000. Answer (C) is incorrect because the warranty will not be construed as a mere representation; the intention of the parties clearly was to make it a warranty. Answer (D) is incorrect because attachment of the application to the policy is usually sufficient to make it a part thereof. It may also be incorporated into the policy by reference to it.

G. Multiple Insurance Coverage

49. Mason Co. maintained two standard fire insurance policies on one of its warehouses. Both policies included an 80% coinsurance clause and a typical "other insurance" clause. One policy was with Ace Fire Insurance, Inc., for $24,000, and the other was with Thrifty Casualty Insurance Co., for $16,000. At a time when the warehouse was worth $100,000, a fire in the warehouse caused a $40,000 loss. What amounts can Mason recover from Ace and Thrifty, respectively?

A. $0 and $0.

B. $10,000 and $10,000.

C. $12,000 and $8,000.

D. $24,000 and $16,000.

The correct answer is (C). *(CPA, adapted)*
REQUIRED: The amount collectible under two fire insurance policies with coinsurance clauses.
DISCUSSION: Under a coinsurance clause, the insured agrees to maintain the insurance equal to a specified percentage of the value of his/her property. If a loss occurs, the insurer pays only a proportionate share if the insured has not carried the specified percentage. In this case, the insured agreed to carry 80%, but in fact carried only 40%; thus, it became a 50% insurer, and the insurance companies' liability was reduced to 50% of any loss. The total combined liability of the fire insurance companies in the problem is $20,000.
Under the standard pro rata clause, a person who is insured with multiple policies can collect from each insurance company only a proportionate amount of the loss. Even though Ace issued a policy for $24,000, it is liable for only three-fifths (24,000/40,000) of the recoverable loss after applying the coinsurance formula (3/5 x $20,000 = $12,000). Likewise, Thrifty is liable for 2/5 of $20,000.
Answer (A) is incorrect because part of the loss is recovered when a coinsurance clause is not complied with. Answer (B) is incorrect because each pays the amount recoverable times the percentage of the total insurance it agreed to provide. Answer (D) is incorrect because the insurer pays only a proportionate share if the insured has not carried the specified percentage.

Questions 50 and 51 are based on the following information. Pod bought a building in 1995 for $220,000. At that time, Pod purchased a $150,000 fire insurance policy with Owners Insurance Co. and a $50,000 fire insurance policy with Group Insurance Corp. Each policy contained a standard 80% coinsurance clause. In 1999, when the building had a fair market value of $250,000, it was damaged in a fire.

50. How much would Pod recover from Owners if the fire caused $180,000 in damage?

- A. $90,000
- B. $120,000
- C. $135,000
- D. $150,000

The correct answer is (C). *(CPA, adapted)*
REQUIRED: The amount collectible under two fire insurance policies with coinsurance clauses.
DISCUSSION: A coinsurance clause requires the insured to maintain insurance equal to or greater than a specified percentage (usually 80%) of the value of the insured property. If the insured has not carried the specified percentage and a partial loss occurs, the insurance company is liable for only a proportionate part of the loss. A pro rata clause generally provides that a person who is insured with multiple policies can collect from each insurance company only a proportionate amount of the loss based on the amount of insurance carried with each insurer. Pod was in compliance with the coinsurance clause (80% x $250,000 = $200,000). Pod would recover in full. The pro rata portion Pod would recover from Owners is $135,000 [($150,000 ÷ $200,000) x $180,000].
Answers (A), (B), and (D) are incorrect because, since Pod was in compliance with the coinsurance requirement, Owners will pay a proportionate amount of the loss based on the amount of insurance carried with each insurer.

51. How much would Pod recover from Owners and Group if the fire totally destroyed the building?

- A. $160,000
- B. $200,000
- C. $220,000
- D. $250,000

The correct answer is (B). *(CPA, adapted)*
REQUIRED: The effect of a coinsurance clause when property is totally destroyed.
DISCUSSION: A coinsurance clause does not apply when the property insured is totally destroyed. Pod would recover the face amount of the policies.
Answer (A) is incorrect because a coinsurance clause does not apply when the property insured is totally destroyed. Answers (C) and (D) are incorrect because recovery is limited to the face amount of the policies.

H. Insurable Interest

52. Which of the following statements correctly describes the requirement of insurable interest relating to property insurance? An insurable interest

- A. Must exist when any loss occurs.
- B. Must exist when the policy is issued and when any loss occurs.
- C. Is created only when the property is owned in fee simple.
- D. Is created only when the property is owned by an individual.

The correct answer is (A). *(CPA, adapted)*
REQUIRED: The true statement about an insurable interest in property.
DISCUSSION: The insurable interest in property must be present when the loss occurs but not when the policy is issued. The rule permits the insured to obtain insurance in advance so that coverage will begin immediately upon acquisition of an interest in property. When a loss occurs, the insured party may recover only up to the amount of his/her interest in the property at that time.
Answer (B) is incorrect because the insurable interest need not exist when the policy is issued. Answer (C) is incorrect because the insured need not be an owner. However, the insured must be in a position to suffer economic loss or damage from destruction of the property. Answer (D) is incorrect because the insured may be a party other than an individual, e.g., a corporation.

53. Which of the following parties has an insurable interest?

I. A corporate retailer in its inventory
II. A partner in the partnership property

  A. I only.

  B. II only.

  C. Both I and II.

  D. Neither I nor II.

The correct answer is (C). *(CPA, adapted)*
  REQUIRED: The conditions to test for insurable interest.
  DISCUSSION: The parties have an insurable interest because, in both cases, they would suffer economic loss from the destruction of the item or derive monetary benefit from the preservation of the property. A corporate retailer will sustain an economic loss if the inventory is destroyed and will derive economic benefit from the inventory's existence because it sells the inventory items to obtain a profit. A partner may also sustain an economic loss and derive economic benefit from partnership property because the partner has an interest in the partnership.
  Answers (A), (B), and (D) are incorrect because both a corporate retailer and a partner have an insurable interest in their respective assets because each has a substantial interest in specific property and each would suffer an economic loss if their respective assets were destroyed.

54. Beal occupies an office building as a tenant under a 25-year lease. Beal also has a mortgagee's (lender's) interest in an office building owned by Hill Corp. In which capacity does Beal have an insurable interest?

	Tenant	Mortgagee
A.	Yes	Yes
B.	Yes	No
C.	No	Yes
D.	No	No

The correct answer is (A). *(CPA, adapted)*
  REQUIRED: The correct statement as to whether tenants and mortgagees have an insurable interest.
  DISCUSSION: Both a tenant and a mortgagee could suffer monetary loss if the office building were damaged or destroyed, and both also have a valid legal interest in the building. Thus, Beal has an insurable interest in both capacities.
  Answers (B) and (D) are incorrect because a mortgagee can have an insurable interest. The destruction of the security for the loan may cause loss to the lender. Answers (C) and (D) are incorrect because a tenant has a risk of monetary loss.

55. Daly tried to collect on a property insurance policy covering a house that was damaged by fire. The insurer denied recovery, alleging that Daly had no insurable interest in the house. In which of the following situations will the insurer prevail?

  A. The house belongs to a corporation of which Daly is a 50% shareholder.

  B. Daly is not the owner of the house but a long-term lessee.

  C. The house is held in trust for Daly's mother and, on her death, will pass to Daly.

  D. Daly gave an unsecured loan to the owner of the house to improve the house.

The correct answer is (D). *(CPA, adapted)*
  REQUIRED: The condition under which a person may not enforce an insurance policy.
  DISCUSSION: For an insurance policy to be valid, the insured must satisfy the insurable interest requirement. The insured may, but need not, have a legally or equitably recognized present or vested future interest. The insured must have a potential for economic loss if the property is damaged or destroyed. This potential for loss must exist at the time of the loss. An unsecured creditor has an insurable interest in the life of the debtor to the extent of the debt. Only a secured creditor has an insurable interest in property owned by the debtor because (s)he has a direct legal interest in that property and could suffer a pecuniary loss if it were destroyed.
  Answers (A), (B), and (C) are incorrect because, under these circumstances, damage to the property might represent economic loss to Daly.

56. Orr is an employee of Vick Corp. Vick relies heavily on Orr's ability to market Vick's products and, for that reason, has acquired a $50,000 insurance policy on Orr's life. Half of the face value of the policy is payable to Vick and the other half is payable to Orr's spouse. Orr dies shortly after the policy is taken out but after leaving Vick's employ. Which of the following statements is correct?

- A. Orr's spouse does not have an insurable interest because the policy is owned by Vick.

- B. Orr's spouse will be entitled to all of the proceeds of the policy.

- C. Vick will not be entitled to any of the proceeds of the policy because Vick is not a creditor or relative of Orr.

- D. Vick will be entitled to its share of the proceeds of the policy regardless of whether Orr is employed by Vick at the time of death.

The correct answer is (D). *(CPA, adapted)*

REQUIRED: The correct statement regarding effectiveness of a life insurance policy.

DISCUSSION: For an insurance policy to be valid, the insured must satisfy the insurable interest requirement. An insurable interest is found when the insured has a legally or equitably recognized present or vested future interest. In the case of life insurance, the potential for loss must exist only at the time the policy is issued. This type of policy is called key employee insurance.

Answer (A) is incorrect because having an insurable interest is independent of policy ownership; it relates to who may receive proceeds. Answer (B) is incorrect because, in that Vick has an insurable interest, Vick is entitled to half the proceeds. Answer (C) is incorrect because other parties may have an insurable interest in another's life if, at the time of issuance, the party may suffer economic loss if the insured dies.

57. The earliest time a purchaser of existing goods will acquire an insurable interest in those goods is when

- A. The purchaser obtains possession.

- B. Title passes to the purchaser.

- C. Performance of the contract has been completed or substantially completed.

- D. The goods are identified to the contract.

The correct answer is (D). *(CPA, adapted)*

REQUIRED: The earliest time a purchaser will have an insurable interest in the goods.

DISCUSSION: Under UCC 2-501, a buyer of goods has an insurable interest in them when they are identified to the contract. This identification can occur when the seller selects goods that correspond to the description in the contract and marks or otherwise designates them as belonging to the contract.

Answer (A) is incorrect because a purchaser can acquire an insurable interest as soon as the goods are identified and need not wait until delivery. Answers (B) and (C) are incorrect because passage of title and contract performance are irrelevant to acquiring an insurable interest.

Use Gleim's ***CPA Test Prep*** for interactive testing with over 2,000 additional multiple-choice questions!

OOF QUESTION 1 *(CPA, adapted)* 10-15 minutes

This OOF question consists of six items. Select the best answer for each item.

Items 1 through 6 are based on the following information. On January 12, 1999, Frank, Inc. contracted in writing to purchase a factory building from Henderson for $250,000 cash. Closing took place on March 15, 1999. Henderson had purchased the building in 1995 for $225,000 and had, at that time, taken out a $180,000 fire insurance policy with Summit Insurance Co.

On January 15, 1999, Frank took out a $140,000 fire insurance policy with Unity Insurance Co. and a $70,000 fire insurance policy with Imperial Insurance, Inc.

On March 16, 1999, a fire caused $150,000 damage to the building. At that time, the building had a market value of $250,000. All fire insurance policies contain a standard 80% coinsurance clause. The insurance carriers have refused any payment to Frank or Henderson alleging lack of insurable interest and insufficient coverage. Frank and Henderson have sued to collect on the policies.

Required

Items 1 through 6 relate to the suits by Frank and Henderson. For each item, determine whether the statement is true (T) or false (F).

1. Frank had an insurable interest at the time the Unity and Imperial policies were taken out.

2. Henderson had an insurable interest at the time of the fire.

3. Assuming Frank had an insurable interest, Frank's coverage would be insufficient under the Unity and Imperial coinsurance clauses.

4. Assuming Henderson had an insurable interest, Henderson's coverage would be insufficient under the Summit coinsurance clause.

5. Assuming only Frank had an insurable interest, Frank will recover $100,000 from Unity and $50,000 from Imperial.

6. Assuming only Henderson had an insurable interest, Henderson will recover $135,000 from Summit.

Knowledge Tested

Insurance: insurable interest; coinsurance

Authors' Comments

This question involves distinguishing between when the insurable interest exists and when it must exist to be able to recover for a particular loss. Note that the coinsurance requirement is tested using the combined coverage of the two insurers.

1. The correct answer is (T).
DISCUSSION: For property, the insured must have an insurable interest at the time of the loss. A person has an insurable interest in the subject matter insured if (s)he will derive economic benefit or advantage from its preservation or will suffer economic loss or damage from its destruction. In that Frank had contract rights on January 15, he had an insurable interest in the property.

2. The correct answer is (F).
DISCUSSION: The sale closed on March 15, before the fire on March 16. Thus, when the loss occurred, Henderson had no potential for economic loss or advantage from preservation or destruction of the property, respectively. Thus, Henderson had no insurable interest in the property at the time of the fire.

3. The correct answer is (F).
DISCUSSION: Under a coinsurance clause, the insurer agrees to insure the property up to the given percentage of its value (80%). The coverage under the Unity and Imperial policies was $210,000 ($140,000 + $70,000). This is more than $200,000, which is 80% of the $250,000 fair market value of the building on the date of the fire. Thus, Frank's coverage was sufficient under the Unity and Imperial coinsurance clauses.

4. The correct answer is (T).
DISCUSSION: Assuming Henderson had an insurable interest, Henderson's $180,000 coverage under the policy with Summit was less than 80% of the $250,000 fair market value of the building on the date of the fire. Thus, Henderson's coverage would be insufficient under the Summit coinsurance clause.

5. The correct answer is (T).
DISCUSSION: In that Frank met the coinsurance requirement, Frank is entitled to recover the full amount of the $150,000 loss (since the loss was less than the face amount of the policy). Under the standard pro rata clause, a person who is insured with multiple policies can collect from each insurance company only a proportionate amount of the loss. Each insurer pays the amount recoverable times the percentage of the total insurance it agreed to provide. Thus, Unity is responsible to pay two-thirds of the loss ($140,000 ÷ $210,000), or $100,000 (2/3 x $150,000), and Unity is responsible to pay one-third, or $50,000, of the $150,000 loss.

6. The correct answer is (T).
DISCUSSION: Assuming only Henderson had an insurable interest, and given that Henderson did not meet the coinsurance requirement under the Summit policy, the insurer pays only a proportionate share. In this case, the insured agreed to carry 80% but in fact carried only 72% ($180,000 ÷ $250,000). This 72% is 90% of the percentage which Henderson, by the coinsurance clause, agreed to carry. Thus, the insurer's liability was reduced to 90% of any loss. 90% of $150,000 is $135,000.

OOF QUESTION 2 *(CPA, adapted)* 15-20 minutes

Dunn & Co., CPAs, while performing the 1999 year-end audit of Starr Corp.'s financial statements discovered that certain events had resulted in litigation with certain insurance companies.

Starr had purchased a warehouse on March 1, 1993 from Investment Corp. for its fair market value of $150,000. Starr paid $50,000 in cash and executed and delivered to Investment a promissory note and mortgage for the balance. The note was paid in full on December 31, 1996, and the security interest was released.

On October 30, 1999, a fire caused $80,000 damage to the warehouse at a time when its fair market value was $200,000. Starr had obtained a $160,000 fire insurance policy on February 15, 1993, from Pica Casualty Co., covering the warehouse. On April 11, 1998, Starr obtained another fire insurance policy from Drake Insurance Co. covering the warehouse for $40,000. Each policy contained an 80% coinsurance clause and a provision limiting each company's liability to its proportion of all insurance covering the loss. Pica has refused to pay any amount on its policy. On March 2, 1993, Investment obtained a $100,000 fire insurance policy from General Insurance Co. which also contained the standard clauses. Investment prepaid premiums for 10 years, the original term of the note.

Required

Items 1 through 15 to the right are statements based on the above facts. If the statement is correct, select (A) as your choice. Select (B) if the statement is incorrect.

1. Starr has an insurable interest in the warehouse with respect to the policy issued by Drake.

2. Starr has an insurable interest in the warehouse with respect to the policy issued by Pica.

3. Investment has an insurable interest in the warehouse with respect to the policy issued by General.

4. The fire is classified as friendly if an insurance policy was in effect and proceeds enabled replacement of a hazardous structure destroyed in the fire.

5. Starr's coinsurance requirement under Pica's policy is $100,000.

6. Starr's coinsurance requirement under Drake's policy is $160,000.

7. Assuming Starr failed to meet the coinsurance requirement of an insurer, Starr may recover only 80% of the loss.

8. Assuming Starr met the coinsurance requirement of both insurers, the total Starr may recover from both is the building's $200,000 fair market value.

9. If Starr did not have the policy with Drake, Starr would recover $80,000 from Pica.

10. If Starr did not have the policy with Pica, Starr would recover $40,000 from Drake.

11. Starr is entitled to recover no less than $80,000 from Pica even though it has a policy with Drake.

12. The amount, if any, that Starr is entitled to recover from Pica is $128,000.

13. The amount, if any, that Starr is entitled to recover from Drake is $16,000.

14. The amount, if any, that Starr is entitled to recover from General is $26,667.

15. If the Drake policy provided for $15,000 of coverage, Starr would be entitled to recover the full $15,000 from Drake.

Knowledge Tested

1. Insurable interest
2. Coinsurance requirement
3. Multiple insurance
4. Assignability of insurance
5. Limits on recovery

Authors' Comments

Be clear on when an insurable interest must exist. This question set provides practice computing a coinsurance requirement and portion of recovery payable by multiple insurers. Recovery is generally limited to indemnification and by the face amount of the policy. Avoid applying a coinsurance requirement if a fire totally destroys a property.

1. The correct answer is (A).

DISCUSSION: A person has an insurable interest if (s)he will derive an economic benefit from preservation of the subject matter or will suffer economic loss or damage from its destruction. Starr was the owner of the insured structure on the date of the fire and has an insurable interest.

2. The correct answer is (A).

DISCUSSION: Starr would incur financial or economic loss from damage to or destruction of the warehouse. For property insurance, the insured must have an insurable interest at the time of the loss, but not necessarily when the policy was issued.

3. The correct answer is (B).

DISCUSSION: The note secured by the mortgage had been fully paid at the time of the fire. Thus, Investment would incur neither economic advantage nor economic loss from the warehouse's preservation or destruction.

4. The correct answer is (B).

DISCUSSION: A friendly fire is one that is contained where it is intended to be, e.g., in a fireplace.

5. The correct answer is (B).

DISCUSSION: Coinsurance is a provision under which the insured agrees to insure the property for a stated percentage of its value. Starr's coinsurance amount was $160,000 (80% x $200,000 FMV at the time of the loss).

6. The correct answer is (A).

DISCUSSION: The purpose of a coinsurance clause is to prevent the insured from insuring for a minimal amount (and minimal premium) and recovering in full for a partial loss (the most common). Starr's coinsurance requirement is the stated percentage of the property's value, or $160,000 (80% x $200,000 FMV at the time of the loss).

7. The correct answer is (B).

DISCUSSION: A policyholder who insures for less than the coinsurance requirement is a coinsurer who bears any partial loss proportionately with the insurance company. The percentage Starr may recover is the amount of insurance divided by the coinsurance requirement, expressed as a percentage, or 100% [($160,000 + $40,000) ÷ $160,000].

8. The correct answer is (B).

DISCUSSION: The principle of indemnity applies to property insurance. The amount the insured may recover upon the occurrence of a loss is limited to the amount of the loss, i.e., $80,000 on these facts.

9. The correct answer is (A).

DISCUSSION: Starr satisfied the $160,000 coinsurance requirement even without the Drake policy. Thus, without multiple insurance, Starr could recover up to the full amount of the $80,000 loss.

10. The correct answer is (B).

DISCUSSION: Without the Pica policy, Starr did not meet the $160,000 coinsurance requirement of the Drake policy. Drake is liable for no more than a proportionate part of the loss. Starr's recovery would be limited to $20,000, that is, the loss ($80,000) multiplied by the ratio of the amount of insurance ($40,000) to the coinsurance requirement ($160,000).

11. The correct answer is (B).

DISCUSSION: Since the coinsurance requirement was met, Starr is entitled to recover the full amount of the loss. However, under the pro rata clause, Pica is liable for only a proportionate part of the loss.

12. The correct answer is (B).

DISCUSSION: Since Starr met the coinsurance requirement, Pica is liable under the pro rata clause for a portion of the full $80,000 loss. Pica issued a policy for $160,000. Drake issued a policy for $40,000. Pica is liable for $64,000, that is, for 4/5 of the $80,000 loss [$160,000 ÷ ($160,000 + $40,000) = 4/5].

13. The correct answer is (A).

DISCUSSION: Under the pro rata clause, Drake is liable for 1/5 of the $80,000 loss, i.e., for $16,000. [$40,000 ÷ ($40,000 + $160,000) = 1/5].

14. The correct answer is (B).

DISCUSSION: Starr was neither a party to the insurance contract between Investment and General, nor the insured (i.e., the person protected from risk of loss by property insurance). Absent express consent of the insurer, the insured may not assign property insurance rights. No indication that the policy was assigned appears in the facts.

15. The correct answer is (B).

DISCUSSION: The $160,000 coinsurance requirement was met. Drake's share of the loss under the pro rata clause was $6,857 {[$15,000 ÷ ($15,000 + $160,000)] × $80,000}.

OOF QUESTION 3 *(CPA, adapted)* 15-20 minutes

On June 10, 1998, Bond sold real property to Edwards for $100,000. Edwards assumed the $80,000 recorded mortgage Bond had previously given to Fair Bank and gave a $20,000 purchase money mortgage to Heath Finance. Heath did not record this mortgage. On December 15, 1999, Edwards sold the property to Ivor for $115,000. Ivor bought the property subject to the Fair mortgage but did not know about the Heath mortgage. Ivor borrowed $50,000 from Knox Bank and gave Knox a mortgage on the property. Knox knew of the unrecorded Heath mortgage when its mortgage was recorded. Ivor, Edwards, and Bond defaulted on the mortgages. Fair, Heath, and Knox foreclosed, and the property was sold at a judicial foreclosure sale for $60,000. At the time of the sale, the outstanding balance of principal and accrued interest on the Fair mortgage was $75,000. The Heath mortgage balance was $18,000, and the Knox mortgage was $47,500.

Fair, Heath, and Knox all claim that their mortgages have priority and should be satisfied first from the sale proceeds. Bond, Edwards, and Ivor all claim that they are not liable for any deficiency resulting from the sale.

The above transactions took place in a jurisdiction that has a notice-race recording statute and allows foreclosure deficiency judgments.

Required

a. For items 1 through 3, select from List A below the priority (A-C) of the mortgage. Each answer may be used only once.

List A

1.	Knox Bank	A.	First priority
2.	Heath Finance	B.	Second priority
3.	Fair Bank	C.	Third priority

b. For items 4 through 6, select from List B (A-E) below the reason for each mortgage's priority. Each answer may be used once, more than once, or not at all.

List B

4. Knox Bank
5. Heath Finance
6. Fair Bank

A. An unrecorded mortgage has priority over any subsequently recorded mortgage.
B. A recorded mortgage has priority over any unrecorded mortgage.
C. The first recorded mortgage has priority over all subsequent mortgages.
D. An unrecorded mortgage has priority over a subsequently recorded mortgage if the subsequent mortgagee knew of the unrecorded mortgage.
E. A purchase money mortgage has priority over a previously recorded mortgage.

c. For items 7 through 9, select from List C (A-G) the amount of the sale proceeds that each mortgagee is entitled to receive. An amount may be selected once, more than once, or not at all.

List C

7.	Knox Bank	A.	$0
8.	Heath Finance	B.	$12,500
9.	Fair Bank	C.	$18,000
		D.	$20,000
		E.	$42,000
		F.	$47,500
		G.	$60,000

d. For items 10 through 12, determine which party(ies) is(are) liable, if anyone, to pay a mortgage foreclosure deficiency judgment on the Fair Bank mortgage. Select from List D below the reason for the party's liability and enter (A), (B), or (C) as your answer. If you determine there is no liability, enter (D) as your answer. A reason may be selected once, more than once, or not at all.

List D

10.	Edwards	A.	Original mortgagor
11.	Bond	B.	Assumed the mortgage
12.	Ivor	C.	Took subject to the mortgage
		D.	Not liable

e. For items 13 through 15, determine which party(ies) is(are) liable to pay a mortgage foreclosure deficiency judgment on the Heath Finance mortgage. If the party can be held liable, select from List E the reason for that party's liability and enter (A), (B), or (C) as your answer. If you determine there is no liability, mark (D) as your answer. A reason may be selected once, more than once, or not at all.

List E

13.	Edwards	A.	Original mortgagor
14.	Bond	B.	Assumed the mortgage
15.	Ivor	C.	Took subject to the mortgage
		D.	Not liable

f. For items 16 through 18, determine which party(ies) is(are) liable to pay a mortgage foreclosure deficiency judgment on the Knox Bank mortgage. If the party can be held liable, select from List F the reason for that party's liability and enter (A), (B), or (C) as your answer. If you determine there is no liability, mark (D) as your answer. A reason may be selected once, more than once, or not at all.

List F

16.	Edwards	A.	Original mortgagor
17.	Bond	B.	Assumed the mortgage
18.	Ivor	C.	Took subject to the mortgage
		D.	Not liable

Knowledge Tested

1. Personal liability under a mortgage
2. Priority between mortgagees
3. Effect of notice-race recording statute
4. Rights to foreclosure sale proceeds
5. Liability for mortgage deficiency judgment

Authors' Comments

The CPA exam has twice tested this subject matter in other objective format. The subject matter is not difficult. The notice-race statute establishes priority between mortgagees when the subsequent mortgagee records without actual knowledge of the former. Higher-priority mortgages are satisfied in full out of foreclosure sale proceeds before a lower-priority mortgagee receives anything. Only a contracting party or one who assumes a mortgage has personal liability for a mortgage deficiency judgment.

1. The correct answer is (C).
DISCUSSION: Knox Bank had constructive notice of Fair Bank's mortgage and actual notice of Heath Finance's mortgage. Under a notice-race statute, Knox's recording would have given priority over Heath only if Knox had no notice of Heath's mortgage.

2. The correct answer is (B).
DISCUSSION: Heath Finance had constructive notice of Fair Bank's (recorded) mortgage. Since Knox knew of Heath's mortgage when Knox recorded, Knox was not protected against the Heath mortgage by recording.

3. The correct answer is (A).
DISCUSSION: Since Fair Bank's mortgage was recorded before Knox and Heath acquired their mortgages, Knox and Heath had constructive notice of it, and would not gain priority under a notice-race recording statute.

4. The correct answer is (D).
DISCUSSION: Under a notice-race recording statute, priority is determined by the bona fide purchaser (BFP) who records first. A BFP is one without notice of the preexisting mortgage.

5. The correct answer is (D).
DISCUSSION: Under a notice-race recording statute, priority is determined by the bona fide purchaser (BFP) who records first. A BFP is one without notice of the preexisting mortgage.

6. The correct answer is (C).
DISCUSSION: All subsequent mortgagees have constructive notice of a previously recorded mortgage.

7. The correct answer is (A).
DISCUSSION: A mortgage with higher priority is paid in full from proceeds of a foreclosure sale before a subordinate mortgagee receives anything. There were no excess proceeds over the balance of Fair Bank's mortgage.

8. The correct answer is (A).
DISCUSSION: A mortgage with higher priority is paid in full from proceeds of a foreclosure sale before a subordinate mortgagee receives anything. There were no excess proceeds over the balance of Fair Bank's mortgage.

9. The correct answer is (G).
DISCUSSION: A mortgage with higher priority is paid in full from proceeds of a foreclosure sale before a subordinate mortgagee receives anything.

10. The correct answer is (B).
DISCUSSION: A person who assumes a liability is personally liable for its payment. The liability was only partially discharged by the foreclosure sale proceeds.

11. The correct answer is (A).
DISCUSSION: There was no release or novation. Thus, Bond remained primarily liable for the obligation under the original mortgage, even though there was an assignment.

12. The correct answer is (D).
DISCUSSION: A purchaser who acquires the property subject to a mortgage is not personally liable on the mortgage to either mortgagor or mortgagee. The mortgagee looks to the original mortgagor for payment of excess over foreclosure sale proceeds.

13. The correct answer is (A).
DISCUSSION: The original mortgagor may not delegate his/her duties under the mortgage unless the mortgagee releases the mortgagor or there is a novation. The original mortgagor remains primarily liable even if another assumes or acquires the property subject to the mortgage.

14. The correct answer is (D).
DISCUSSION: Bond was not a party to the mortgage agreement and (s)he did not assume any duties under it.

15. The correct answer is (D).

   DISCUSSION: A purchaser who acquires the property subject to a mortgage is not personally liable on the mortgage to either the mortgagee or the mortgagor.

16. The correct answer is (D).

   DISCUSSION: Edwards was not a party to the mortgage agreement, and (s)he did not assume any duties under it.

17. The correct answer is (D).

   DISCUSSION: Bond was not a party to the mortgage agreement, and (s)he did not assume any duties under it.

18. The correct answer is (A).

   DISCUSSION: The original mortgagor may not delegate his/her duties under the mortgage unless the mortgagee releases the mortgagor or there is a novation. The original mortgagor remains primarily liable even if another assumes or takes the property subject to the mortgage.

OOF QUESTION 4 (CPA, adapted) 10-15 minutes

Wolf purchased a factory building for $800,000. At the time of the purchase, Wolf obtained a fire insurance policy with a face value of $400,000 from Acme Fire Insurance Co. At the same time, Wolf obtained another fire insurance policy with a face value of $200,000 from Prevent Fire Insurance Corp. Each policy contained a standard 80% coinsurance clause and a pro rata clause. Two years later, when the building had a fair market value of $1 million, a fire caused $600,000 damage.

Required

For Items 1 through 5, select the correct answer from List I. An answer may be selected once, more than once, or not at all.

1. What dollar amount of fire insurance coverage should Wolf have obtained when purchasing the building to avoid being considered a coinsurer?

2. What dollar amount of fire insurance coverage should Wolf have at the time of the fire to avoid being considered a coinsurer?

3. What dollar amount should Wolf recover from Acme and Prevent under the fire insurance policies.

4. What dollar amount should Wolf recover under the Acme fire insurance policy?

5. What dollar amount should Wolf recover under the Prevent fire insurance policy?

LIST I

A. $0
B. $150,000
C. $160,000
D. $200,000
E. $300,000
F. $360,000
G. $400,000
H. $450,000
I. $480,000
J. $600,000
K. $640,000
L. $750,000
M. $800,000

Knowledge Tested

1. Standard clauses in fire insurance policies

2. Calculation of required coverage under coinsurance clauses

3. Application of coinsurance formula to determine recovery

4. Allocation of recovery between multiple insurers

Authors' Comments

Dealing successfully with fire insurance questions usually requires understanding the requirements of insurable interest, applying the formula for coinsurance, and allocating recovery among multiple insurers. The best preparation is to commit the formulas and rules of these topics to memory and practice making the calculations illustrated in this study unit.

1. The correct answer is (K).
DISCUSSION: A coinsurance clause in a fire insurance policy requires that the insured maintain coverage for a stated percentage of the full value of the insured property to avoid bearing any partial loss proportionately with the insurance carrier(s). Wolf's policies required coverage of 80%, or $640,000, based on the purchase price of $800,000 ($800,000 × .8 = $640,000). Wolf's total coverage of $600,000 did not meet the coinsurance requirement at the time of purchase. As a result, Wolf was a coinsurer.

2. The correct answer is (M).
DISCUSSION: The coinsurance percentage must be satisfied at the time of a partial loss. To avoid being a coinsurer, Wolf was contractually required to have coverage of $800,000 or more at the time of the loss: FMV of property × coinsurance % ($1,000,000 × .8 = $800,000). Wolf's coverage totaled $600,000 at the time of the loss and did not meet the coinsurance requirement. Wolf as a coinsurer will bear a portion of the loss.

3. The correct answer is (H).
DISCUSSION: When the insured is a coinsurer, the portion of the loss payable by the insurance company is as follows: Total insurance ÷ (FMV of property at time of loss × coinsurance percentage) × amount of loss = recovery. ($600,000 ÷ $800,000 × $600,000 = $450,000). Wolf is self-insured for the remaining loss.

4. The correct answer is (E).
DISCUSSION: In situations when property is insured under multiple policies, a pro rata clause determines what portion of the recovery is the responsibility of each insurer. The calculation is as follows: Acme's policy of $400,000 = 2/3 of the total insurance ($400,000 ÷ $600,000 = 67% or 2/3). Acme must pay $300,000 of the $450,000 recovery.

5. The correct answer is (B).
DISCUSSION: Under the pro rata clause, Wolf can recover $150,000 under the Prevent policy. Prevent is liable for 33%, or 1/3, of the $450,000 loss, or $150,000 ($200,000 ÷ $600,000 = 33%, or 1/3).

ESSAY QUESTION 1 *(CPA, adapted)* 15-25 minutes

On May 15, 1998, Strong bought a factory building from Front for $500,000. Strong assumed Front's $300,000 mortgage with Ace Bank, gave a $150,000 mortgage to Lane Finance Co., and paid $50,000 cash.

The Ace mortgage had never been recorded. Lane knew of the Ace mortgage and recorded its mortgage on May 20, 1998.

Strong bought the factory for investment purposes and, on June 1, 1998, entered into a written lease with Apex Mfg. for 7 years. On December 1, 1998, Apex subleased the factory to Egan Corp. without Strong's permission. Strong's lease with Apex was silent concerning the right to sublease.

On May 15, 1998, Strong had obtained a fire insurance policy from Range Insurance Co. The policy had a face value of $400,000. Apex and Egan obtained fire insurance policies from Zone Insurance Co. Each policy contained a standard 80% coinsurance clause. On May 1, 1999, when the factory had a fair market value of $600,000, a fire caused $180,000 damage.

Strong made no mortgage payments after the fire and, on September 1, 1999, after the factory had been repaired, the mortgages were foreclosed. The balances due for principal and accrued interest were Ace, $275,000, and Lane, $140,000. At a foreclosure sale, the factory and land were sold. After payment of all expenses, $400,000 of the proceeds remained for distribution.

As a result of the above events, the following actions took place:

- Strong sued Apex for subleasing the factory to Egan without Strong's permission.
- Zone refused to honor the Apex and Egan fire insurance policies claiming neither Apex nor Egan had an insurable interest in the factory.
- Strong sued Range to have Range pay Strong's $180,000 loss. Range refused, claiming Strong had insufficient coverage under the coinsurance clause.
- Ace and Lane both demanded full payment of their mortgages from the proceeds of the foreclosure sale.

The preceding took place in a "notice-race" jurisdiction.

Required

Answer the following questions, and give the reasons for your conclusions.

a. Would Strong succeed in the suit against Apex for subletting the factory to Egan without Strong's permission?

b. Is Zone correct in claiming that neither Apex nor Egan had an insurable interest in the factory at the time of the fire?

c. What amount will Strong be able to recover from Range?

d. What amount of the foreclosure proceeds will Lane recover?

Knowledge Tested

1. The right of a lessee to sublease
2. Insurable interest of a lessee and a sublessee
3. Amount recoverable under a coinsurance clause
4. The distribution of proceeds in a foreclosure sale

Authors' Comments

This essay appropriately combines insurance law with issues arising from the leasing and financing of property. The right of a tenant to sublet, the determination of the presence of an insurable interest, and the calculation of the effect of a coinsurance clause are typical issues on the exam.

AICPA Unofficial Answer

a. Strong will lose its suit against Apex for subletting the factory to Egan without Strong's permission. Unless a lease provides otherwise, a tenant may sublet the premises without the landlord's consent.

b. Zone is incorrect in claiming that neither Apex nor Egan had an insurable interest in the factory. Apex has an insurable interest because it was the original lessee of the factory. Apex has a financial interest in both receiving rent from Egan and it's liability to Strong under the original lease. Egan has an insurable interest and a financial interest as tenant in possession.

c. Strong will recover only $150,000 from Range. Strong's recovery is based on the coinsurance formula:

$$\frac{\text{Insurance carried (Policy amount)}}{\text{Insurance required (Coinsurance \% } \times \text{ Fair market value of the property at the time of the loss)}} \times \text{The amount of loss} = \text{Recovery}$$

$$\frac{400,000}{.80 \times 600,000} \times 180,000 = \$150,000$$

Strong will be able to recover $150,000 from Range, despite having insufficient coverage.

d. Lane will recover $125,000 of the foreclosure proceeds. Lane's recovery is limited to the amount left after the satisfaction of the Ace mortgage. In a notice-race jurisdiction, Lane's recorded mortgage will not have priority over Ace's earlier unrecorded mortgage because Lane knew of the Ace mortgage.

ESSAY QUESTION 2 *(CPA, adapted)* 15-20 minutes

On February 1, 1997, Tower and Perry, as tenants in common, purchased a two-unit apartment building for $250,000. They made a down payment of $100,000 and gave a $100,000 first mortgage to Midway Bank and a $50,000 second mortgage to New Bank.

New was aware of Midway's mortgage but, as a result of a clerical error, Midway did not record its mortgage until after New's mortgage was recorded.

At the time of purchase, a $200,000 fire insurance policy was issued by Acme Insurance Co. to Tower and Perry. The policy contained an 80% coinsurance clause and a standard mortgagee provision.

Tower and Perry rented an apartment to Young under a month-to-month oral lease. They rented the other apartment to Zimmer under a 3-year written lease.

On December 8, 1998, Perry died leaving a will naming the Dodd Foundation as the sole beneficiary of Perry's estate. The estate was distributed on January 15, 1999. That same date, the ownership of the fire insurance policy was assigned to Tower and Dodd with Acme's consent. On January 21, 1999, a fire caused $180,000 in structural damage to the building. At that time, its market value was $300,000, and the Midway mortgage balance was $80,000 including accrued interest. The balance on the mortgage to New was $40,000 including accrued interest.

The fire made Young's apartment uninhabitable and caused extensive damage to the kitchen, bathrooms, and one bedroom of Zimmer's apartment. On February 1, 1999, Young and Zimmer moved out. The resulting loss of income caused a default on both mortgages.

On April 1, 1999, Acme refused to pay the fire loss claiming that the required insurable interest did not exist at the time of the loss and that the amount of the insurance was insufficient to provide full coverage for the loss. Tower and Dodd are involved in a lawsuit contesting the ownership of the building and the claims both of them made for any fire insurance proceeds.

On June 1, 1999, Midway and New foreclosed their mortgages and are also claiming any fire insurance proceeds that may be paid by Acme.

On July 1, 1999, Tower sued Zimmer for breach of the lease and is seeking to collect the balance of the lease term rent.

The above events took place in a notice-race statute jurisdiction.

Required

Answer the following questions and give the reasons for your conclusions.

a. Who had title to the building on January 21, 1999?

b. Did Tower and/or Dodd have an insurable interest in the building when the fire occurred? If so, when would such an interest have arisen?

c. Does Acme have to pay under the terms of the fire insurance policy? If so, how much?

d. Assuming the fire insurance proceeds will be paid, what would be the order of payment to the various parties and in what amounts?

e. Would Tower succeed in the suit against Zimmer?

Knowledge Tested

1. Insurable interest
2. Assignment of property insurance
3. Coinsurance clause
4. Mortgagee's clause
5. Other recovery limits

Authors' Note

This essay question is a challenging one. Concepts of property ownership rights and priorities among mortgages are interwoven with one regarding insurance. Our focus here is property insurance. Nevertheless, use this essay to evaluate your competence in coordinating and applying different sets of rules and in preparing an organized, well-written responsive essay.

Authors' Comments

An insurable interest is a fundamental requirement for recovery. Define it. Apply it. Explain when it must be present.

Next, you must distinguish an insurance contract from others under which assignment is generally effective without consent of the parties.

Third, you must compute the coinsurance requirement and explain the result when it is not met. (Refer to the outline.) Note also that recovery will not exceed the amount of coverage purchased.

Finally, you should note that the mortgagee has an insurable interest and that the clause designating a mortgagee as a beneficiary is effective.

AICPA Unofficial Answer

a. Tower and Perry owned the property as tenants in common. This form of ownership allows either party to dispose of his/her undivided interest by sale or on death. Any person purchasing or inheriting Perry's interest would become a tenant in common with Tower. Thus, on January 21, 1999, Tower and Dodd are tenants in common, each owning a one-half undivided interest in the house.

b. Both Tower and Dodd have an insurable interest in the house. Tower's interest arose when the property was purchased, continued when the insurance policy was purchased, and still existed at the time of the fire loss.

Dodd's interest arose when Dodd inherited Perry's interest in the house. Acme's consent to the assignment of the policy to Tower and Dodd entitles Dodd to a share of the proceeds of the policy.

c. Acme must honor the insurance contract and pay part of the loss. Even though Tower and Perry did not maintain insurance coverage of 80% of the property's market value, the coinsurance clause allows for a percentage of recovery. The formula is as follows:

$$\frac{Amount\ of\ coverage}{Actual\ market\ value \times Coinsurance\ \%} \times Amount\ of\ loss$$

This would allow a recovery as follows:

$$\frac{\$200,000}{\$300,000 \times .8} \times \$180,000 = \$150,000$$

d. The conflict between Midway and New would be resolved in favor of Midway. In a notice-race statute jurisdiction, New's knowledge of Midway's first mortgage would give Midway priority despite New's earlier filing. The insurance proceeds would be distributed as follows:

- $80,000 to Midway representing the balance due on the mortgage including accrued interest. This is due because Midway as a mortgagee is included as a contingent beneficiary in the policy.

- $40,000 to New for the same reasons as above but not paid unless and until Midway is fully paid

- $30,000 to be divided equally between Tower and Dodd as tenants in common

e. Tower would not be able to collect rent from Zimmer for the balance of the term of the lease because Zimmer moved as a result of the extensive fire damage to the apartment. The implied warranty of habitability would be considered breached by the landlord and a constructive eviction of Zimmer would be deemed to have taken place because the premises could no longer be used for their intended purpose. Constructive eviction releases both the landlord and the tenant from their obligations under the lease.

STUDY UNIT 20: PERSONAL PROPERTY, BAILMENTS, AND COMPUTERS

16 pages of outline
37 multiple-choice questions
2 essays

A. Ownership of Personal Property
B. Bailments
C. Special Bailments
D. Computer Technology Rights

Property is created by the legal system of an organized society. Property is the bundle of legal rights which allows an owner to possess, use, enjoy, exclude, and dispose of something. The two major classifications are real and personal property. Personal property is any property which is not real property. This study unit reviews the types of personal property and the methods of acquiring title. This study unit also covers bailments (the transfer of possession, but not title, of personal property) and computer technology rights (a new item in the AICPA content specification outlines).

A. **Ownership of Personal Property.** Property refers not to a thing but to a bundle of rights in the thing, i.e., to its possession, use, enjoyment, and disposal.

1. **Tangible property** has perceptible physical existence, e.g., banjo.

2. **Intangible property** has no physical existence, e.g., contract rights.

3. **Real property** consists of land, whatever is attached to it, whatever is beneath it, and to a limited degree, the area above it.

4. **Personal property** consists of all things movable, as distinguished from real property.

5. Real property can become personal property if it is detached from the land. Similarly, personal property can be attached to land and become real property. When personal property is attached to the land in such a way as to be treated as part of the real property, it is known as a **fixture**.

6. The term chattel is sometimes used to describe personal property generally, but chattels may also be classified as chattels real and chattels personal.

   a. A **chattel real** describes an interest in land, such as a leasehold.

   b. A **chattel personal** is used to describe movable personal property.

   c. When the phrase chattel is used in connection with intangible personal property, the property is referred to as **chattels personal in action**, or a chose in action.

      1) A **chose in action** is something to which one has a right of possession; however, one may be required to bring some legal action in order to enjoy such possession. Examples of choses in action include corporate stock, negotiable instruments, contract rights, copyrights, and patents.

7. **Intellectual property** is intangible personal property formed by intellectual, as opposed to physical, efforts. Types include the following:

   a. **Patents** are exclusive legal rights to use or sell inventions and discoveries.

   b. **Copyrights** are legal protection for tangible expressions of ideas, e.g., songs.

   c. **Trademarks** are words, names, symbols, or devices used by manufacturers to identify and distinguish goods.

   d. **Trade secrets** are information protected by a business because it provides economic advantage.

   NOTE: The first three types are granted limited protection under federal law; the fourth, under state law.

8. **Title** is a legal concept indicating ownership, not merely possession. Title confers upon the owner of property the exclusive right to possess, use, enjoy, and dispose of it.

9. **Possession**. A person who possesses property usually prevails against all claimants except the true (title) owner.

   a. **Legal possession** refers to rightful possession, actual or constructive.

   b. **Actual possession** refers to immediate physical control over property.

   c. A person is said to be in **constructive possession** when (s)he has conscious power and intent to exercise dominion and control over property but does not have immediate direct control over it.

10. **Acquisition** of personal property may be by purchase, gift, will, descent, finding, development, confusion, or accession.

11. **Purchase**. The rights of an owner of the property are transferred for consideration (in exchange for something of value) to another.

12. A **gift** is a voluntary transfer of property, not for consideration. The person making the gift is the donor, and the person receiving the gift is the donee.

    a. A legally effective gift meets each of the following requirements:

       1) The intent to make a voluntary transfer of property
       2) Present delivery of the property to the donee or agent
       3) Unconditional transfer
       4) Title vested in the donee by the donor
       5) Acceptance of the gift by the donee

    b. If it is impractical to make physical delivery of an item, the law permits a constructive or symbolic delivery, e.g., by giving the key to a storage locker and stating to the donee, "You may have the contents of my locker."

    c. There must be a present intention to make a gift.

    d. An *inter vivos* gift is one made between living persons. The transfer takes place during the lifetime of the donor and donee.

    e. A testamentary gift is intended to be effective at the death of the donor and must be made by a will.

    f. A gift *causa mortis* is a conditional transfer of only personal property by a donor in the belief that (s)he will die imminently.

       1) If the donor recovers and lives, the gift is automatically revoked.
       2) If the donee dies before the donor, the gift is automatically revoked.

    g. In every state, an adult can make a gift of money to a minor by depositing it with a broker or a bank under the Uniform Gifts to Minors Act.

       1) The donor deposits money in the donor's name as custodian for the donee.

13. **By Will or Descent**. When a person dies, the decedent's property passes to others, called beneficiaries (under a will) or heirs (under descent and distribution statutes). State laws that determine the inheritance of an intestate's (without a will) property are called statutes of descent and distribution or intestacy statutes. Descent, in its broadest sense, applies to the transmission or inheritance of real or personal property by operation of law upon the death of the decedent.

14. **Finding**. A finder of lost property is entitled to possession of the property against everyone in the entire world except the true owner.

   a. Finder's rights permit a finder to bring an action against any third person who interferes with his/her possession of the property.

   b. One may acquire ownership of abandoned property by taking possession of it with the intent to exclude others.

      1) Abandonment is the intentional relinquishment of all rights in an object without transferring ownership to another person.

      2) The distinction between lost and abandoned property is in the intent of the owner. Contrast unintentionally giving up possession with consciously relinquishing possession with the intent to give up ownership permanently.

      3) Courts consider three factors in determining the intent of the owner: location, value, and utility.

   c. Mislaid property is property that the owner has voluntarily and intentionally placed in a particular location. Subsequently, (s)he forgets where (s)he has placed the property.

      1) Mislaid property is presumed to be left in custody of the owner or occupant of the premises upon which it is found. (S)he is generally entitled to possession against all except the owner thereof.

      2) The finder of lost property or the owner/occupier of premises wherein property is mislaid may be an involuntary bailee of the property with duties and liability imposed by law with respect to the care and disposition of the property.

15. **Development**. The value added is the property of the person who developed the value.

16. **Confusion**. The condition in which property belonging to two or more persons becomes commingled to the extent that it is impossible to separate the parts belonging to each is known as confusion.

   a. If the confusion is rightful, e.g., according to agreement, or innocent, each owner shares in the resulting property, or any losses, either according to their agreement or in proportion to their relative contributions to the whole.

   b. If the confusion is the result of one owner's negligence, the innocent owner is entitled to the return of his/her property, if possible, and the negligent party is liable in damages for any injury (loss) to the innocent owner.

   c. If the confusion results from intentional wrongdoing of one of the parties and the innocent party's property cannot be separated, the entire result (all commingled property) belongs to the innocent party until or unless the wrongdoer proves his/her contribution to the value of the resulting mass.

17. **Accession** is a means of acquiring ownership of personal property created by additions to property already in existence. It occurs when a person's property is changed into a new item by the addition of another's labor or property. It may occur by agreement or it may be unauthorized.

   a. The law must determine the rights of the parties in the new article.

      1) When the article is created by the combination of goods of both parties, title is usually awarded to the owner of the principal good/chattel even if the owner willfully authorizes changes.

2)   When the increase in value is caused by labor of an innocent trespasser, title is determined by evaluation of the relative contribution of the labor to the value of the finished product.

3)   Decisions conflict concerning the willful trespasser. The general rule is that a willful trespasser cannot acquire title by accession even when there is a change of form or a substantial increase in value.

4)   A good-faith owner of the original property is entitled to recover damages equal to the fair market value at the time the accession occurred.

18.   Stop and review! You have completed the outline for this subunit. Study multiple-choice questions 1 through 8 beginning on page 651.

B.   Bailments

1.   **Defining a Bailment**. A bailment is the legal relationship that results whenever one person (bailor) transfers possession (but not title) of his/her personal property to another person (bailee) to return it or otherwise dispose of it, according to his/her instructions.

a.   To form a bailment, the owner of any interest in personal property must make delivery of possession and control of the property to the bailee, who must accept it. A bailment can exist only with respect to personal property.

b.   Whether or not a bailment exists is determined from all the facts and circumstances of a particular situation.

1)   EXAMPLE: A patron in a restaurant hung her raincoat on an unattended coatrack. It is unlikely that a bailment was formed. The restaurant never assumed control over the coat. No agreement was reached between the parties. However, if there is a coat checkroom and the coat is checked with an attendant, a bailment will arise.

c.   Possession can be constructive or symbolic rather than actual by the bailee's receipt of something closely related to the property, such as keys to a car.

d.   The bailee's possession must be rightful. A party in wrongful possession of stolen property is not a bailee.

e.   Custody is insufficient to constitute a bailment. A person who exercises physical control over personal property without intending to possess it has mere custody and not possession.

1)   Thus, physical delivery of property by one person to another does not give rise to a bailment unless the recipient knowingly and intentionally accepts possession of the property.

2)   In deciding whether a parking lot transaction is a bailment or a lease of space, courts have determined that the most important factor is whether the keys are retained by the owner.

a)   Giving the keys to a parking attendant or leaving them in the car at the parking attendant's direction is a constructive delivery of possession and acceptance.

b)   However, a bailment of a parked vehicle can occur other than through delivery of keys (e.g., premises locked up).

          c) A bailee is responsible for the automobile and other items of personal property that (s)he knows are in the automobile or that (s)he can reasonably anticipate, e.g., a spare tire, jack, and tools.

              i) EXAMPLE: Mike leaves his car in a parking lot under circumstances in which a bailment exists as to the car. Mike has a package in the trunk of the car. There is no bailment of the package unless Mike notifies the parking lot attendant of its presence, and the attendant knowingly and intentionally accepts possession.

    f. A bailment is distinguished from a sale or gift in that the bailee does not receive title and, at the end of the term of bailment, the bailee must return or account for the property.

        1) The bailee has a duty to restore possession of the property to the bailor.

        2) Generally, the bailee is required to return the specific property unless the property is fungible.

          a) In the case of fungible goods (e.g., grain), the bailee need only return goods of the same quality and quantity.

2. **Classification of Bailments.** The legal rights and duties of bailor and bailee vary according to whether the bailment is voluntary, gratuitous, or ordinary, and according to whom it benefits.

    a. **Involuntary bailments.** A bailee can come into possession of property without the affirmative consent of its true owner.

        1) In certain such situations, the law implies a bailment.

          a) It is called a constructive bailment.

        2) Taking or having possession of lost or mislaid property may result in an involuntary bailment.

        3) The involuntary bailee owes the owner a slight duty of care and is only liable for gross negligence.

    b. **Gratuitous bailments.** A bailment for which neither the bailor nor the bailee receives compensation is classified as gratuitous.

        1) Compensation refers to economic value. It includes

          a) Money
          b) Advancement of the bailor's business interests

              i) EXAMPLE: Auto, Inc. lends, without charge, a car to Mary while it repairs her station wagon, as it advertised it would. The bailment to Mary is not gratuitous.

    c. **Contract bailments** are those which are not gratuitous.

    d. **Extraordinary bailments.** When the law imposes unusual duties or liability on a bailee, the bailment is referred to as extraordinary or special.

        1) Bailments to common carriers and innkeepers are extraordinary.
        2) Ordinary bailments are those which are not extraordinary.

    e. **Benefit.** Bailments are also classified according to which of the parties derives benefit therefrom. These classifications are discussed on the next page.

1) **Bailments for the sole benefit of the bailee**. A bailment for the sole benefit of the bailee exists when the owner of personal property permits another to use it without compensation or any other benefit; e.g., Fred lends his car to Barney.

   a) A bailment that is solely for the benefit of the bailee is often referred to as a gratuitous bailment.

   b) The bailee in a gratuitous bailment must return the property in substantially the same condition as it was when received.

      i) A gratuitous bailee is liable for damage caused to bailed property by his/her slight negligence. The gratuitous bailee has a duty, therefore, to exercise extraordinary (or great) care with respect to the property.

2) **Bailments for the sole benefit of the bailor**. A bailment for the sole benefit of the bailor exists when a person stores or takes possession of personal property solely as an accommodation to the bailor; e.g., Nancy permits Steven to store his furniture in her garage while he is away for the summer, with no benefit to Nancy.

   a) The bailee must exercise slight care and is not liable to the bailor in this situation unless it can be shown that loss or injury occurred due to gross negligence or intentional misconduct.

3) **Mutual benefit bailments**. Most mutual benefit bailments involve a bailor and a bailee who receives direct compensation, e.g., equipment repair contract.

   a) It is possible for the benefit to be an indirect one, e.g., an employer who maintains a separate coatroom with no charge.

   b) The duty of care owed in a mutual benefit bailment is substantial, although somewhat less than a gratuitous bailment.

      i) The bailee is liable only if the value of the personal property is reduced as a result of his/her fault. His/her liability encompasses loss or injury caused by ordinary negligence.

3. **Rights of the Bailee**. The bailee's rights under a bailment depend almost entirely on the express or implied terms of the parties' contract.

   a. If the contract provides that the bailee is to have possession for a specified period of time and the bailor is to receive compensation, the bailee will generally have a property interest and the right to retain possession for the entire time.

   b. Whether the bailee has the right to use the bailed property depends on the express terms of the contract.

     1) When the purpose of the bailment is the use of the bailed article, the bailee has the right to use the article in a fair and reasonable manner.

     2) If the purpose of the bailment contract is storage, shipment, or repair, the bailor does not expect any use of his/her property. The bailee has no right to use the property while it is in his/her possession. Thus, the bailee would be strictly liable for any use made of the property.

       a) EXAMPLE: Jacqui stores her fur coat at XYZ Fur Storage, Inc. Charles, who works there, borrows the coat and allows his girlfriend to wear it. Jacqui would have a cause of action against XYZ and Charles.

c. Except when there is a clear understanding that the bailee is not to receive any payment, the bailee normally has the right to reasonable compensation for services.

     1) If the amount of compensation is not expressly agreed to, the bailee is entitled to the reasonable value of his/her services.

     2) To secure payment, the bailee is ordinarily entitled to a possessory lien.

         a) Many states allow a bailee to foreclose the lien and sell the property at a public sale if the bailor does not pay.

     3) The bailee is generally entitled to reimbursement for extraordinary expenses of the bailment but not for ordinary expenses.

         a) EXAMPLE: Professor Biggs delivers personal property to Relo Corp. for storage. Biggs leaves for the airport before the Relo clerk finalizes details. Relo is entitled to reasonable compensation for storing Biggs' property. If Relo incurs extraordinary expenses to maintain Biggs' tropical birds, Relo is also entitled to reimbursement.

d. The bailor and bailee each have a right of action against a third party who wrongfully interferes with the bailed property. The bailor and bailee both have a property interest in the bailed goods.

4. **Duties of the Bailee**. A bailee has the fundamental duties of using and returning the bailed property in accordance with the bailment contract and exercising reasonable care in handling the property.

a. The bailee must use the personal property for bailment purposes only. If the bailee uses the property in any manner inconsistent with the bailor's rights, the bailee will be liable to the bailor for misuse of the bailed property.

     1) If property is lost or damaged while in the bailee's possession, most courts hold that the bailee is presumed to be negligent.

         a) Thus, the burden rests on the bailee to prove that (s)he acted with due care under the circumstances.

         b) EXAMPLE: Jeff leaves his LORAN navigation system for his aircraft in storage at a private hangar. The navigation system is stolen. The owner of the private hangar is presumed negligent in failing to prevent the theft. If the bailee can prove that the navigation system was stored safely, that a night watchman patrolled regularly, and that closed-circuit television monitored out-of-the-way entrances to the hangar, a court may conclude that the bailee exercised the degree of care expected of a reasonable aircraft storage company and is not liable to the bailor.

b. The bailee is strictly liable for unauthorized use or misdelivery of the bailed property. A bailee that departs from the terms of the bailment effectively becomes an insurer of the property.

     1) Misdelivery refers to transfer of possession to anyone other than the bailor or a person designated in the bailor's express instructions.

         a) The bailee must be positive that the person to whom the property is delivered is the owner or has authority from the owner to take possession of the goods.

b)   EXAMPLE: Salisha attended a social event. Upon checking her silk cape, she was handed a numbered ticket. Reaching for hors d'oeuvres, she deposited her ticket on a lamp stand. After greeting a friend, she forgot to recover the ticket. When she decided to leave, she explained to the cloakroom steward that she had misplaced her ticket. She described the cape to the steward and asked him to retrieve it. The steward had delivered Salisha's cape to Augustine, who presented her ticket when gathering his group's items. Courts usually declare the bailee is holding the property for the person with the receipt unless the bailee knows the claimant is not the bailor. Thus, no misdelivery occurred. Had he delivered possession of the cape to a uniformed person delivering a bouquet, however, he might be held responsible for being aware of another's claim to the cape. Note that, except for claim check cases, courts impose strict liability for any misdelivery by a bailee without regard to fault.

  i)   A bailee can institute an **interpleader** action, whereby the property is delivered to the jurisdiction of a court, which resolves adverse claims to it.

  ii)   Bailee's wrongful refusal to return the goods to the rightful owner is an act of conversion.

  iii)   The tort of conversion is an intentional interference with the plaintiff's right to possess his/her property.

  iv)   Theft, destruction, and wrongful detention of property are also acts of conversion.

  v)   The owner may seek compensatory damages or attempt to reacquire the property by means of **replevin** (a civil action brought to regain possession of wrongfully detained property).

  vi)   Damages are usually compensatory but may also be punitive.

c.   The ordinary bailee may expand or limit his/her liability for negligence or breach of contract by a separate agreement or in the bailment contract.

  1)   Liability for willful misconduct may not be limited.

  2)   The ability to modify liability may be restricted by statute.

  3)   Exculpatory clauses or other attempts to contractually limit liability might not be enforced if they are not brought to the attention of the bailor, or if they are against public policy.

  a)   Thus, a court may disregard a bailor's or bailee's disclaimer of liability for his/her own negligence.

  i)   EXAMPLE: Miles rents a car from ExecuRent at City airport. He is given a form to sign, entitled Key Receipt and Car Agreement. A clause on the reverse, in small print, states that ExecuRent is not liable for any damages that might arise under the contract. All the auto rental companies providing service at City airport have the same clause on their forms. A court may not enforce the clause if brake failure results in injury to Miles. Furthermore, the bailor may be strictly liable under the implied warranty that the subject of the bailment was reasonably fit (suitable) for its intended use or purpose.

        b)   Disclaimers or exculpatory clauses offered on a take-it-or-leave-it basis and not the subject of arm's-length bargaining are not likely to be enforced.

   d.   Each category of bailments may require a different degree of care. Liability is imposed for varying degrees of negligence.

      1)   The bailee in a mutual benefit bailment is required to exercise ordinary care and is liable for ordinary negligence.

      2)   The bailee in a bailment for the sole benefit of the bailee is required to exercise extraordinary or great care and is liable for slight negligence.

      3)   The bailee in a bailment for the sole benefit of the bailor must exercise only slight care and is liable only for gross negligence.

      4)   Modern view. A recent trend is for courts not to impose liability based upon different standards of care according to various categories of ordinary bailments. Rather, liability depends on whether the bailee exercised ordinary care under all the circumstances, e.g., type and value of goods, type of bailment, type of business, etc.

         a)   Thus, without regard to the type of bailment or bailee, a party is liable for unexcused failure to meet a standard of reasonable care under all the circumstances.

5.   **Rights of the Bailor**. The bailor has the right to have bailed property returned at the end of the bailment period, to have the bailee use reasonable care in protecting the property, and to have the bailee use the property (if at all) in conformity with the terms of the bailment contract.

   a.   If the purpose of the bailment is use of the property by the bailee, the bailor has the right to receive compensation under the express or implied terms of the contract.

6.   **Duties of the Bailor**. The bailor must not knowingly deliver property containing a hidden defect that is likely to cause injury.

   a.   EXAMPLE: If Rob lends a snowblower to his neighbor, and Rob knows that the snowblower has a loose belt, Rob must inform his neighbor of that fact.

   b.   In either a mutual benefit bailment or one for the sole benefit of the bailee, the bailor must notify the bailee of any dangerous defect about which the bailor has actual knowledge.

      1)   In a mutual benefit bailment, the bailor may be liable for injury caused by hidden defects about which the bailor either knew or should have known.

   c.   A bailor may also be exposed to strict products liability, e.g., for injury caused by a defective leased product.

7.   **Termination**. Ordinary bailments are terminated in the following ways:

   a.   Expiration of specified term
   b.   Purpose of bailment accomplished
   c.   Mutual agreement of bailor and bailee
   d.   Serious misuse of bailed property by bailee
   e.   Decision by either party if bailment is at will

8.   Stop and review! You have completed the outline for this subunit. Study multiple-choice questions 9 through 18 beginning on page 653.

C.   Special Bailments

1.   **Special Rules**. Special bailments involve professional bailees such as innkeepers, common carriers, and warehouse companies. Special bailments are subject to the same rules as ordinary bailments and also additional special rules and regulations.

2.   **Innkeepers**. An innkeeper (hotelkeeper) is a person who operates an inn, hotel, motel, or the like.

    a.   At common law, property placed in guestrooms is constructively in the possession of the innkeeper, and an innkeeper is absolutely liable for loss of, or damage to, the personal property of his/her guests.

    b.   This rule applies only to those who furnish lodging to the transient public for compensation as a regular business. (Owners of apartment complexes are not innkeepers.)

        1)   Liability extends only to the belongings of registered guests.

    c.   The common-law rule has been significantly modified by statute in most states, permitting the innkeeper to avoid strict liability for the loss of personal property by guests.

        1)   Liability for loss of, or damage to, a guest's property not kept in the hotel safe is subject to a statutory ceiling, e.g., $1,000.

        2)   However, if the innkeeper is at fault for the loss, (s)he is liable for the entire value of the lost property.

    d.   The innkeeper is not responsible for a guest's automobile unless the innkeeper provides parking facilities and a separate bailment situation arises.

    e.   The innkeeper's duty to a guest terminates when the guest ceases to be a registered guest.

    f.   An innkeeper is given a lien on all goods brought onto the premises by guests to secure charges for the accommodations and services.

        1)   At common law, this lien was only possessory, but under modern statutes, the innkeeper may ultimately sell such goods to enforce the lien.

3.   **Common Carriers**. A common carrier is a person or organization engaged in the business of transporting goods for others for a fee. A company doing business as a common carrier must make services available to the public on a nondiscriminatory basis.

    a.   The common carrier is strictly liable without fault for damage to, or loss of, the goods being transported.

        1)   The contract for carriage of property constitutes a mutual benefit bailment.

            a)   The bailee in a mutual benefit bailment is usually liable for damage or loss of the bailed property caused by his/her ordinary negligence.

            b)   The bailment of the common carrier is extraordinary. (S)he has liability even if (s)he is not at all negligent and exercises the utmost care.

            c)   The common carrier is in effect an insurer of the bailed property.

b. There are five exceptions. Loss falls on the bailor (not the carrier) if it is caused by

    1) A *force majeure*, e.g., tornado

        a) *Force majeure* refers to operation of forces of nature that could not have been prevented or avoided by foresight or prudence.

    2) Action by an alien enemy, e.g., war
    3) Order of public authority, e.g., public health agency
    4) The inherent nature of the property, e.g., goods subject to spoilage
    5) The bailor's negligence in packaging

c. Actual proof that the goods were in good condition when the bailor delivered them is required.

d. Common carriers are permitted, statutorily, to limit their dollar amount of liability by use of a shipping contract.

e. Moreover, a common carrier is not bound to accept and carry goods which are

    1) Beyond the carrier's capacity to carry
    2) Of a kind not normally transported by carrier
    3) Dangerous
    4) Defectively packaged
    5) High-risk, e.g., economically

f. The common carrier is under an absolute duty to deliver the goods to the correct person. A carrier that misdelivers goods is strictly liable for any loss or damage that results.

4. **Warehouse Companies**. A warehouse company is in the business of storing other parties' property for compensation.

a. A warehouse company is deemed to be an ordinary mutual benefit bailee and must exercise only ordinary care and is liable for only ordinary negligence.

b. Thus, for most purposes, a warehouse company is an ordinary mutual benefit bailee. However, like a common carrier, a warehouse company may

    1) Limit monetary liability by contractual agreement
    2) Issue documents of title, i.e., warehouse receipts, for the goods it receives

c. However, when a bailee deviates from the terms of the contract, the law imposes strict liability for any harm to the bailor's goods instead of the usual standard of reasonable care. In effect, the bailee becomes an insurer of the goods.

d. Moreover, a warehouse company is subject to more extensive state regulation than most ordinary bailees, e.g., special building standards and fire prevention methods.

5. Stop and review! You have completed the outline for this subunit. Study multiple-choice questions 19 through 22 beginning on page 656.

D. Computer Technology Rights

1. **Existing and New Law**. Computer development and use have resulted in extension of existing legal principles by both statutory modification and judicial interpretation. New laws have also been enacted to address issues unique to a computerized society.

2. **Purchasing a Computer System**. Whether the common law or UCC applies to the purchase of a computer system must be determined. Generally, contracts for services are governed by common law, and the UCC applies to contracts that involve goods.

   a. The UCC typically applies to sales of hardware, leases of hardware, and sales or licensing of mass-produced software.

   b. In contrast, the common law typically applies to sales of custom-designed, as opposed to mass-produced, software. Custom-designed software usually refers to a customized program that results from a consultant's services. The critical issue is whether the buyer bargained for goods or a consultant's services.

   c. Generally, a contract involving the purchase of both hardware and custom-designed software is classified as a contract for goods, and the UCC is the governing law. If the hardware acquisition is the primary purpose for the contract and the custom-designed software is merely incidental to the sale of the hardware (goods), the UCC applies; common law applies if the custom-designed software is the primary purpose for the contract. Comparing the relative costs of the software and hardware may help to determine whether one purchase is incidental to the other and, if so, which one is the primary purchase.

3. **Computer Product Liability**. If the UCC applies to a transaction involving computer equipment (i.e., it is a sale of goods), certain specific warranties arise pursuant to Article 2. Sellers of computer products may attempt to contractually limit their warranty liability by use of disclaimer clauses, by placing limits on remedies, and by availing themselves of integration clauses. These protective yet one-sided measures are counterbalanced by the buyer's right to seek remedies in tort, e.g., for fraud, negligence, and strict liability.

   a. **Warranty liability**. A warranty is an assurance or a guarantee that goods will conform to certain standards. If these standards are not met, the buyer may be able to recover from the seller based on the theory of breach of warranty.

      1) **Express warranties** arise from words or conduct of the seller.

         a) To make an express warranty, the seller merely does one of the following:

            i) Affirms a fact or promise relating to the goods; e.g., "This computer has 32 MB of RAM."

            ii) Affirms a fact or promise by describing the goods; e.g., "This particular computer will outperform all other 486SX computers."

            iii) Provides a sample or model of the goods, e.g., a computer set up in a retail store for display

         b) A seller's expression of opinion or sales talk does not constitute an express warranty; e.g., "This computer is a first-class machine with five of the very best features offered."

            i) An express warranty is likely to be found if the statement is objectively verifiable; e.g., "The machine is brand new."

         c) Disclaimers of express warranties are usually ineffective.

2) A warranty of merchantability and/or fitness for a particular purpose may be implied into a contract for the sale of a computer (system).

    a) **Warranty of merchantability.** If the seller is a merchant with respect to the type of goods being sold, the seller warrants that the goods are fit for the ordinary purpose for which the goods are to be used.

        i) The warranty of merchantability requires that the goods be adequately packaged and labeled, and of at least average or fair quality.

        ii) Under the UCC a merchant is a person who deals in goods of the kind or otherwise by occupation holds him/herself out as having special knowledge or skill peculiar to the practice or goods involved in the transaction. Thus, a one-time seller not dealing in goods of the type in question is not a merchant.

    b) **Warranty of fitness for a particular purpose.** If the seller has reason to know the particular purpose for which goods are required and the buyer relies on the seller's skill and judgment to furnish suitable goods, an implied warranty exists that the goods will be fit for the particular purpose (and not merely merchantable).

        i) The seller is not required to be a merchant.

3) There are two fundamental types of **warranty of title**.

    a) The first warrants that the title conveyed is good and its transfer rightful; e.g., the goods are not stolen or do not infringe on another's (intellectual) property rights, such as a patent.

    b) The second warrants that the goods are delivered free from any security interest or other lien or encumbrance of which the buyer at the time of contracting has no knowledge.

4) Sellers may in some instances disavow the existence of (disclaim) an implied warranty by conspicuously including a disclaimer in the sales documentation, e.g., by language such as "as is" or "with all faults."

    a) An implied warranty of fitness for a particular purpose must be in writing to be disclaimed.

5) Sellers attempt to limit available remedies by including a clause in the sales documentation that provides that repair or replacement, but neither refunds nor consequential damages, is permitted.

6) An integration clause states that the entire agreement is contained in the written contract. No oral discussions provide a warranty.

b. **Tort liability.** The seller of a computer may be liable in tort for fraud or negligence, or may have strict liability.

1) A buyer who is fraudulently induced to purchase the computer may bring suit if (s)he can establish fraud on the part of the seller. A necessary element of fraud is a specific intent of the seller to misrepresent a material fact about the product. That is, the buyer is injured as a result of fraudulent information supplied (or essential information not supplied) by the seller in the course of the sale, and the buyer detrimentally relied on the information.

2) An injured buyer may have a cause of action in negligence against the seller of a defective computer.

3)   An injured buyer may have a cause of action based on strict liability concerning a defective computer. Currently, most actions against computer manufacturers are for economic injuries as opposed to personal injury or property damage.

4.   **Intellectual Property**. Computer software is treated as intellectual property. Protection of intellectual property is provided for by copyright, patent, and trade secret laws.

   a.   Copyright law and software. Copyright law protects the expression of an idea. The Copyright Act was amended in 1980 to cover computer software.

      1)   Courts disagree as to whether the structure, sequence, and organization of a computer program is protected under the copyright laws. Some courts hold that all three components of a program are the expression of an idea and therefore are protected under copyright law.

      2)   Amendments to the Copyright Act of 1980 permit a customer who purchases software to duplicate it solely for his/her own use.

         a)   To avoid application of this amendment, software has been distributed under licenses, as opposed to by direct sales.

         b)   Under the 1980 amendment, only the purchaser of a program, as opposed to a licensee, may copy the program for his/her own use.

   b.   Trade secret law and software. Trade secret law protects commercially valuable information not generally known in the industry. Trade secret law protects ideas, not just the expression of ideas. Consequently, the conceptual basis of a computer program may be protected by trade secret law.

      1)   Unlike patent and copyright protection, trade secret protection is not predicated on registering the secret with the government.

      2)   Generally, software will no longer be extended protection as a trade secret if a competitor acquires (knowledge of) the idea by legal means. Therefore, software manufacturers use various means to prevent discovery.

         a)   Licensing agreements may include terms that prohibit disclosure and restrict program use to a single computer, e.g., by way of a site restriction.

         b)   Employees may be required to sign secrecy agreements.

         c)   Access to software may be restricted to certain employees.

   c.   Semiconductor chip and mask work protection. A **mask work** is a form of expression used on a chip design. It includes stencils used in the manufacturing of chips. Semiconductor chip products include analog chips, microprocessors, and RAM or ROM memory chips.

      1)   The Semiconductor Chip Protection Act (SCPA) of 1984 protects, for a 10-year period, mask works and the semiconductor chip products where they are found.

         a)   The act requires mask work owners to register within 2 years of a work's first commercial exploitation.

         b)   Unlike copyrighted works, the SCPA does not grant the mask owner the right to prevent others from copying its product. Instead, some copying is permitted. For instance, the mask work can be reverse-engineered and used in other semiconductor chip products if the newly created products are the result of substantial study and not mere copying.

c) Infringement of this protection can result in actual damages and loss of profits or statutory damages up to $250,000.

d. Patent law and software. Federal patent law will protect software included in an invention. While copyright protection only protects expression, a patent protects the underlying idea behind the software.

1) In defining the nature of a patentable process, the Supreme Court has stated

> *A process is a mode of treatment of certain materials to produce a given result. It is an act, or a series of acts, performed upon the subject matter to be transferred and reduced to a different state or thing. If new and useful, it is just as patentable as is a piece of machinery. The machinery pointed out as suitable to perform the process may or may not be patentable; whilst the process itself may be altogether new and produce an entirely new result.*

a) Typically, the invention must meet the criteria listed below:

i) Be a process, machine, or composition of matter
ii) Have utility
iii) Be novel
iv) Not be obvious
v) Be adequately disclosed

b) Patent protection grants the software developer the exclusive right to use, make, and market the patented product for 20 years from the date of filing.

5. **Invasion of Privacy**. The computerized accumulation of information concerning private individuals poses a potential threat to an individual's right of privacy. Protection of the individual's right of privacy is provided by both common-law doctrines and statutes.

a. Statutory protection. Both federal and state governments have enacted statutes to protect privacy rights. Federal statutes particularly relevant to computer use include

1) The Family Educational Rights and Privacy Act of 1974. It gives students over the age of 18 and parents of dependent students rights of inspection, correction, and disclosure of educational records at institutions of higher education.

2) The Right to Financial Privacy Act of 1978. It restricts government access to customer records at financial institutions unless the customer authorizes disclosure or the government properly requests the records.

3) The Fair Credit Reporting Act. It requires consumer credit reporting agencies to implement safeguards to ensure that only accurate information is included in consumer credit reports.

4) The Counterfeit Access Device and Computer Fraud Abuse Act of 1984. It forbids the removal or destruction of federal records, and it protects bank and credit reports by prohibiting computer access to such information.

5) The Computer Matching and Privacy Act of 1988. It regulates computer programs that compare two or more automated systems of records. These types of matches are used to determine eligibility for, and compliance with, federal benefit programs such as Social Security or student financial aid.

b. Common-law protection. The widespread ability of individuals and businesses to use computers has a significant potential impact on interests in, and rights to, the privacy of persons acting in either a personal or business context. The role of common law in recognizing and protecting privacy interests and rights may have become more crucial because of enhanced information-related capabilities.

   1) The conduct required to meet, and the standard of, a common-law duty of care affecting privacy interests and rights may need to be effectively modified with respect to computerized environments.

      a) A professional, for example, might develop a computerized information file on a client that contains some confidential information. The professional may be subject to common-law liability for failure to adequately protect that information from unauthorized access by, or disclosure to, third parties.

      b) The steps a reasonable person or a reasonable professional person would be required to take to avoid liability to meet the required standard of care may be affected by the computer media in which the information is stored.

6. **Computer Crime**. Computer crime is any illegal act that uses, involves, or is directed against computers. Computer crimes can be grouped into four general categories: theft, damaging and destructive programming, software piracy, and financial crimes. Traditional criminal, tort, patent, copyright, and trade secret laws plus new legislation are used to combat and prevent computer crime.

   a. Types of computer crime. Computer-assisted crime arises in a variety of situations and comes in a variety of types. The following are more common types:

      1) Theft includes stealing computer equipment (hardware) and unauthorized use, for personal gain, of data stored in a computer system.

      2) Financial crimes include embezzlement, fraud, and any other illegal act involving financial resources or transactions.

      3) Damaging and destructive programming includes physical abuse of hardware and computer programming that alters or automatically destroys data.

      4) Software piracy involves unauthorized reproduction of software. Patent, copyright, and trade secret laws have recently been expanded to protect software against piracy.

   b. Federal legislation forbids specific acts related to the use of computers.

      1) The Counterfeit Access Device and Computer Fraud and Abuse Act prohibits unauthorized use of a computer to obtain, alter, etc., restricted government information, information contained in the financial records of a financial institution, and information contained in a consumer reporting agency's files concerning a consumer.

      2) The Electronic Funds Transfer Act (EFT Act) prohibits the sale, use, or interstate transportation of any lost, stolen, forged, counterfeit, altered, or fraudulently obtained device used to execute an electronic funds transfer.

7. Stop and review! You have completed the outline for this subunit. Study multiple-choice questions 23 through 37 beginning on page 658.

MULTIPLE-CHOICE QUESTIONS

A. Ownership of Personal Property

1. Which of the following would change if an asset is treated as personal property rather than as real property?

	Requirements for Transfer	Creditor's Rights
A.	Yes	No
B.	No	Yes
C.	Yes	Yes
D.	No	No

The correct answer is (C). *(CPA, adapted)*
   REQUIRED: The effect(s) of classification as personal property rather than as real property.
   DISCUSSION: Classification of property as real or personal has significant legal effect. Generally, personal property is movable and real property is land and things attached to it. Delivery of a deed is an example of a requirement to transfer real but not personal property. Creditor's rights might also vary depending on property classification. For example, perfection affects the priority of creditor's rights in personal property, whereas recording provides constructive notice of interests in real property.
   Answers (A), (B), and (D) are incorrect because both may vary with the asset's classification.

2. Personal property is

A. Minerals to be mined by the buyer.

B. Immovable.

C. Something that is not real property but is firmly attached to land.

D. Something capable of being owned, but not real property.

The correct answer is (D). *(Publisher)*
   REQUIRED: The correct statement which describes personal property.
   DISCUSSION: The legal definition of personal property is negative. Personal property is classified as anything capable of being owned that is not real property.
   Answer (A) is incorrect because a mineral which is to be mined and removed from the ground by the buyer is part of the soil and therefore real property. It would not become personal property until actually severed from the land. Answer (B) is incorrect because personal property is characterized by mobility while real property is immovable. Answer (C) is incorrect because something which is not real property but is firmly attached to land is generally classified as a fixture and considered to be real property.

3. Which of the following items is tangible personal property?

A. Share of stock.

B. Trademark.

C. Promissory note.

D. Oil painting.

The correct answer is (D). *(CPA, adapted)*
   REQUIRED: The item of tangible personal property.
   DISCUSSION: Tangible personal property has a perceptible physical existence and consists of items that are movable, as distinguished from intangible property, which is not movable. An oil painting is an item of personal property.
   Answers (A), (B), and (C) are incorrect because each is an example of intangible personal property. Intangible property represents some set of rights and interests but has no real physical existence and is not movable.

4. Which of the following methods of obtaining personal property will give the recipient ownership of the property?

	Lease	Finding Abandoned Property
A.	Yes	Yes
B.	Yes	No
C.	No	Yes
D.	No	No

The correct answer is (C). *(CPA, adapted)*
   REQUIRED: The method(s) of obtaining personalty, if any, that confers ownership.
   DISCUSSION: Property that has been discarded by the owner, with no intent of asserting title, is abandoned. Accordingly, the party who finds abandoned property acquires good title to it, even against the original owner. A lease, however, gives possession but not ownership.
   Answers (A), (B), and (D) are incorrect because finding abandoned property but not a lease confers ownership.

5. Donor was in a hospital suffering from a serious illness. The doctor and a friend, Donee, were nearby when Donor told them she wanted to give her bank account to Donee. She wanted the doctor to give her savings bank book to Donee. The doctor, a member of the hospital staff and agent of the hospital, said the bank book and other personal effects were locked in the cashier's office, which would not be open until 8:00 a.m. the next morning. However, the doctor informed Donor and Donee that, if Donee came by the next morning, the doctor would see that the bank book was given to him. Donee said that would be fine. Donor did not live through the night. When Donee appeared the next morning, the doctor went with him to the cashier's office and gave him the bank book.

A. If Donor died intestate, the money in the savings account will go to her heirs.

B. The delivery of a deposit book of a savings account is not sufficient to effect a gift of the funds on deposit because there has been no delivery.

C. A gift *causa mortis* is irrevocable once it is made.

D. All the elements of a valid gift were present, so the attempted gift is valid.

The correct answer is (D). *(Publisher)*
REQUIRED: The correct statement regarding the validity of an attempted gift.
DISCUSSION: A valid gift requires intent of the donor, acceptance by the donee, and delivery. These requirements must occur during the lifetime of the donor. Here, the elements of intent and acceptance are clearly present. The depositing of the bank book with the hospital created a bailment. Delivery of personal property in the possession of a bailee becomes effective as soon as the bailee agrees to hold it for a donee or a purchaser. Since the doctor is an agent for the hospital (bailee), his agreement to hold the bank book for Donee constituted a delivery during the lifetime of the decedent. A delivery of a deposit book of a savings account is considered a constructive delivery of the balance of the funds in the account.
Answer (A) is incorrect because the gift *causa mortis* was valid, and the money in the savings account will not go to Donor's heirs. Answer (B) is incorrect because the delivery of a deposit book of a savings account is considered a constructive delivery of the funds in the account, although the delivery of a book for a checking account would not have the same effect. Answer (C) is incorrect because a gift *causa mortis* is revocable, but an *inter vivos* gift is not.

6. Ada was hospitalized in critical condition. Just before going into surgery, she gave Bea, her sister, a check for $20,000, remarking that her chances of survival were not good and she wanted Bea to have the money in the event of her death. Ada survived the operation but died a month later from a cause unrelated to her original injury. She did not specifically revoke the gift.

A. Ada made a valid *inter vivos* gift.

B. The donee has no right to the money since the donor did not die from the contemplated cause.

C. A valid gift *causa mortis* was made since the gift was not revoked.

D. A valid gift *causa mortis* was not made since the gift was not properly delivered.

The correct answer is (B). *(Publisher)*
REQUIRED: The requirements of gifts *inter vivos* and *causa mortis*.
DISCUSSION: A gift *causa mortis* (in contemplation of death) is a conditional gift. It must be made in view of impending death from some specific illness or peril, the donor must die from the illness or peril without having revoked the gift, the donee must survive the donor, and the subject matter must have been delivered to the donee. Since Ada died from an unrelated cause, the gift was ineffective (automatically revoked) despite the lack of an express revocation.
Answer (A) is incorrect because a gift *inter vivos* is between the living and not conditional upon death. Answers (C) and (D) are incorrect because failure to die from the specific cause automatically revoked the gift. The money must be returned to the estate.

7. Which of the following rights is(are) considered intangible personal property?

	An Easement	A Contract Right
A.	Yes	Yes
B.	Yes	No
C.	No	Yes
D.	No	No

The correct answer is (C). *(CPA, adapted)*
REQUIRED: The right(s) classified as personal property.
DISCUSSION: Personal property is classified as anything capable of being owned that is not real property. Intangible property lacks a physical existence. A primary example of intangible personal property is a contract right. An easement grants a person the right to use another person's real property. It is not considered intangible personal property.
Answers (A) and (B) are incorrect because an easement is attached to real property. Answer (D) is incorrect because a contract right is considered intangible personal property.

8. Ann cut 1,000 logs belonging to Bob. Upon discovery that she had trespassed, Ann marked the logs as hers, mixed them with 100 of her own, and started them down river to market. The logs of Ann and Bob cannot be distinguished.

- A. If Bob seizes the logs and sells them to Carol, Ann will be unable to recover any logs if Carol is a bona fide purchaser.

- B. Ann and Bob are owners in common of the mass of logs.

- C. Accession of personal property has occurred.

- D. Ann should be entitled to half the logs since the trespass was not intended.

The correct answer is (A). *(Publisher)*
   REQUIRED: The correct statement concerning the confusion of logs by a trespasser.
   DISCUSSION: Confusion is a legal term describing the intermingling of property of different owners. If confusion of personal property results from an innocent act or accident and the goods are of the same kind, each person is an owner of a proportionate share of the confused mass. However, where the confusion results from wrongdoing or intentional trespass, most courts vest title to the entire mass in the innocent party until the wrongdoer proves a portion is his/hers. Thus, title is vested in Bob, and Carol has title free of any claim of Ann if Carol is a bona fide purchaser.
   Answer (B) is incorrect because Ann and Bob are not owners in common of the mass since Ann was a willful confuser and title vested in Bob. Answer (C) is incorrect because the problem concerns confusion, not accession. Answer (D) is incorrect because the confusion was intended.

B. Bailments

9. Which of the following requirements must be met to create a bailment?

I. Delivery of personal property to the intended bailee

II. Possession by the intended bailee

III. An absolute duty on the intended bailee to return or dispose of the property according to the bailor's directions

- A. I and II only.

- B. I and III only.

- C. II and III only.

- D. I, II, and III.

The correct answer is (D). *(CPA, adapted)*
   REQUIRED: The requirement(s) to form a bailment.
   DISCUSSION: A bailment is the legal relationship resulting from the transfer of possession of personal property from one person (the bailor) to another person (the bailee) under such circumstances that the bailee is under a duty to return the item to the bailor or dispose of it as directed by the bailor.
   Answer (A) is incorrect because a bailment is distinguished from transfer of title by the absolute duty of the intended bailee to return or dispose of the property according to the bailor's directions. Answer (B) is incorrect because possession of the bailed property by the intended bailee is a definitional requirement of bailment. Answer (C) is incorrect because a bailment relationship does not arise until the personal property has been delivered to the intended bailee.

10. Tom had a dairy products factory. He contracted with many dairymen to accept their surplus milk which he agreed to manufacture into dairy products such as butter, cottage cheese, sour cream, etc.; market the products; deduct his commissions; and divide the remaining proceeds among the dairymen in proportion to the amount of milk each contributed. Tom's factory and its contents burned. Which of the following is correct?

- A. The transaction is not a sale but a bailment with a power of sale granted to the bailee.

- B. The transaction is a sale because the same item of property is not to be returned.

- C. Until Tom sold the dairy products, title and risk of loss was on Tom.

- D. Tom, as the party in possession of goods owned by another, is an insurer of the safety of the goods.

The correct answer is (A). *(Publisher)*
   REQUIRED: The correct statement as to whether a bailment contract has been formed.
   DISCUSSION: Title does not pass in a bailment. Here, there is a bailment because the fungible property is to be returned, even though in a changed form as proceeds. The proceeds of sale were being divided among the milk suppliers in proportion to milk supplied. Tom was only providing services and receiving compensation for them. The transaction should thus be classified as a bailment (not a sale) with a power of sale granted to the bailee.
   Answer (B) is incorrect because Tom was merely authorized to sell the property after processing it and was responsible to strictly account for the proceeds received from the sale. Answer (C) is incorrect because Tom never acquired title. The risk of loss remained on the dairymen at all times. A bailee has neither title nor risk of loss (provided (s)he acts in a nonnegligent manner). Answer (D) is incorrect because a bailee is not an insurer, but must only exercise reasonable care for their safety.

11. Gal lends Guy her car so that he may run errands for her. Subsequently, Gal lends Guy her lawn mower so that he may mow his own yard. Which is the correct statement concerning the traditional duties of care owed by the parties?

    A.   Guy is required to exercise ordinary care with respect to his use of the lawn mower.

    B.   If Gal had rented the lawn mower to Guy, she would have owed a duty to him to inform regarding defects which would have been discovered by the exercise of reasonable care.

    C.   Guy must exercise great care in the use of the car.

    D.   If Guy had been compensated by Gal for running the errands, he would have been required to exercise great care in the use of the automobile.

The correct answer is (B). *(Publisher)*

    REQUIRED: The duties of care traditionally imposed in bailments.

    DISCUSSION: Under traditional tort principles, the duty of care owed by a party to a bailment depends upon the party benefited. When a bailment is for the mutual benefit of the bailor and the bailee, the duty owed by the bailor (Gal) is that of ordinary care. Exercise of ordinary or due care includes an affirmative obligation to use reasonable care to discover dangerous defects in the goods. These duties have generally been replaced with the standard of reasonable care.

    Answer (A) is incorrect because, in a bailment for the bailee's sole benefit, (s)he is required to use great care. Answer (C) is incorrect because, if the bailment is for the sole benefit of the bailor and the bailee is uncompensated, the bailee is required to exercise only slight care. Answer (D) is incorrect because, if Guy had been compensated by Gal for running the errands, the bailment would have been mutually beneficial, and he would have been required to use only ordinary care.

12. To recover when bailed property is damaged or lost while in the possession of the bailee, the plaintiff-bailor

    A.   Must prove fault.

    B.   Need not prove fault because the bailee is presumed to have been negligent.

    C.   Need not prove fault because the bailee is presumed to have been an insurer.

    D.   Must prove fault if the bailee explains the exact cause of the damage or loss.

The correct answer is (B). *(Publisher)*

    REQUIRED: The proof required in an action by a bailor against a bailee.

    DISCUSSION: When the bailed item is damaged or lost, the presumption is that the bailee was at fault. Accordingly, (s)he has the burden of proving that (s)he exercised due care and of providing an explanation of the exact cause of the damage or loss. The burden is placed on the bailee because the item was in his/her possession and the bailor would have more difficulty obtaining proof of negligence. The legal principle involved is *res ipsa loquitur* (the thing speaks for itself).

    Answer (A) is incorrect because the bailee's fault is rebuttably presumed. Answer (C) is incorrect because, absent an explicit agreement, the bailee is liable only for not acting with the care required in the circumstances. Answer (D) is incorrect because the bailee also has the burden of proving that (s)he was not negligent.

13. Jon Hailey deposited his suitcase (and contents) valued at $300 with the clerk of the New York Middle Railroad after being informed that the price was only $1. He received a check stub or claim receipt upon which was printed a limitation for loss of $25. Which statement is correct?

    A.   The claim check is part of the agreement whether Hailey read the limitation or not.

    B.   The parties to a bailment may by contract limit the liability of the bailee, but that rule is not applicable here because Hailey never agreed to the limitation.

    C.   Railroads, as common carriers, are not permitted to limit their liability.

    D.   The railroad was merely a custodian and not a bailee of Hailey's suitcase.

The correct answer is (B). *(Publisher)*

    REQUIRED: The correct statement concerning an attempt to limit liability of the bailee.

    DISCUSSION: Parties to a bailment may agree to limit their liability. Hailey never agreed to the limitation; it was merely printed on a receipt delivered to him after the contract was entered into. The courts are strict in their interpretation of modification of liability and require that the limitation be called to the attention of the bailee prior to the contract being formed. This could be done by specific mention, with a sign, or by the limitation being conspicuously printed in a place where it is seen and agreed to before the contract is formed.

    Answer (A) is incorrect because a claim check is generally not considered by the courts to be part of the agreement; it is merely a receipt or form of identification for return of the bailed property. Answer (C) is incorrect because, even though railroads are common carriers, and in many instances in their capacity as carriers are held to strict liability, they are permitted to limit their liability by contract unless unconscionable. Answer (D) is incorrect because the railroad was a bailee since it had received and accepted physical possession and legal control.

14. Marrieo and Dreddy built a custom roadster. They drove it through an automatic gate into a parking lot, received a ticket from a machine, parked, and took their keys with them. To leave they are required to drive to the exit and present the ticket to an attendant who collects the parking fee. Which of the following statements is incorrect?

    A. If this arrangement were a bailment, the parking lot would be responsible for a spare tire, jack, and tools locked in the trunk.

    B. Marrieo and Dreddy have rented a parking space since they retained control of their car.

    C. The most important factor in deciding whether this is a bailment is the fact that Marrieo and Dreddy received the ticket from a machine and not an attendant.

    D. If a third person wrongfully damages personal property in the possession and control of a bailee, the bailee may bring suit for him/herself and for the bailor.

The correct answer is (C). *(Publisher)*
    REQUIRED: The incorrect statement concerning parking a car in an automated lot.
    DISCUSSION: In deciding whether a parking lot transaction is a bailment or lease of space, courts have determined that the most important factor is whether the keys are retained by the owner. Giving the keys to a parking attendant or leaving them in the car at the parking attendant's direction is a constructive delivery of possession and acceptance. However, a bailment of a parked vehicle can occur other than through delivery of keys (e.g., premises locked up).
    Answer (A) is incorrect because a bailee would be responsible for reasonable care of the automobile and other items of personal property which (s)he knew were in the automobile or which (s)he could have reasonably anticipated, e.g., a spare tire, jack, and tools. Answer (B) is incorrect because courts interpret retention of keys as retention of control of the car, resulting in a rental or lease of a parking space. Answer (D) is incorrect because the bailee's rights are generally held broad enough to permit him/her to bring an action against the third party for damages to the bailor's reversionary interest in the bailed property in addition to the bailee's interest.

15. Molly Tiff visited Happy Landing Riding Stables and rented a horse. The stable was busy and Tiff was mistakenly given a spirited horse suitable only for excellent riders, which Tiff was not. Hondo, an employee of Riding Stables, in saddling the horse failed to tighten the saddle. Tiff fell when the saddle slipped.

    A. Tiff cannot recover unless she clearly told the riding stable of her limited riding skills.

    B. Tiff assumed those risks that are the natural dangers inherent in a particular activity and, since falling off a horse was the obvious danger, Tiff cannot collect.

    C. Riding stables such as Happy Landing impliedly warrant their horse's suitability and its tack.

    D. If Tiff ever returns to Happy Landing Stables, Happy Landing could avoid all liability by requiring Tiff to sign a disclaimer of liability.

The correct answer is (C). *(Publisher)*
    REQUIRED: The relationship between a riding stable and its customer.
    DISCUSSION: The rental of the horse was a bailment. A bailor, unless agreed otherwise, impliedly warrants that the subject of the bailment is reasonably fit for its intended use or purpose. A spirited horse suitable only for an excellent rider is not reasonably fit for rental to the general public. The riding stable also impliedly warranted that the saddle and other equipment were in proper repair and correctly adjusted.
    Answer (A) is incorrect because the burden is on the riding stable to furnish a horse that is suitable to the skills of the rider-customer. Answer (B) is incorrect because a customer of a riding stable does not assume the risk of being assigned a highly spirited horse, nor one whose saddle has not been properly attached. A rider only assumes the risks of natural dangers inherent in horseback riding. Answer (D) is incorrect because such a disclaimer of liability is probably against public policy and would not be upheld by the courts when the horse was known to be spirited and it was improperly saddled.

16. Hurts Corporation leases a car to Benny for 30 days. The lease can be terminated except by

    A. Performance or the expiration of 30 days.

    B. Mutual rescission of the parties.

    C. The will of either party who gives notice of termination and agrees to pay damages to the other party.

    D. Notification by Hurts to Benny that the lease is canceled because Benny has engaged in an unauthorized use (and abuse) of the vehicle.

The correct answer is (C). *(Publisher)*
    REQUIRED: The correct statement concerning proper termination of a bailment.
    DISCUSSION: A bailment for a definite time or purpose cannot, as a general rule, be terminated at the will of either party since a bailment of specific property gives the bailee a property interest that will be protected against everyone including the bailor. The bailment contract may be terminated at the will of the bailee if the bailee voluntarily surrenders his/her property interest in the bailed property.
    Answer (A) is incorrect because it contains two proper methods of termination of a bailment. Answer (B) is incorrect because a bailment (like any other contract) may be terminated by mutual rescission. Answer (D) is incorrect because the bailor can notify the bailee that the bailment is canceled if the bailee has misused or abused the bailed property.

17. A bailee was instructed by the bailor to return the bailed property by means of Quickie Express. A man dressed similarly to the usual Quickie Express employee came into the bailee's office and called out, "Quickie Express." Bailee delivered the bailed property to him and had him sign an official Quickie Express receipt. Despite the reasonable care of bailee and the good-faith belief that he was dealing with a Quickie Express agent, the person taking the bailed property was an impostor. Which of the following is correct?

    A. Quickie Express is liable because the bailee acted in good faith in delivering to the imposter.

    B. The bailee is liable, good faith or not.

    C. The bailor must bear the loss because (s)he owns the property and the bailee acted with reasonable care.

    D. The bailee would have less liability if this were a bailment for the sole benefit of the bailor.

The correct answer is (B). *(Publisher)*
    REQUIRED: The correct legal conclusion regarding misdelivery of bailed property.
    DISCUSSION: The usual standard of care imposed on bailees is reasonable care. However, the bailee owes a strict duty to return the bailed property to the bailor. Misdelivery of the bailed property to a third party who is not legally entitled to it results in strict liability to the bailee and cannot be justified by reasonable care and good faith.
    Answer (A) is incorrect because Quickie Express is not liable for the actions of impostors unless it has been negligent in permitting uniforms to remain in the hands of ex-employees. The courts ask whom the impostor intended to deceive. The answer is the victim of the fraud. Answer (C) is incorrect because, even though the bailor owns the property and the bailee may have acted with reasonable care, a bailee is strictly liable to the bailor for misdelivery. Answer (D) is incorrect because strict liability for misdelivery applies to a gratuitous bailee also.

18. With respect to involuntary bailments, which of the following is correct?

    A. An involuntary bailee has no liability to the bailor-owner because (s)he is only a custodian.

    B. The liability of an involuntary bailee will be the same as the liability of an ordinary bailee.

    C. Common examples of involuntary bailment would be finding a lost wallet, a horse straying onto your property, or a storm depositing property on your land.

    D. An involuntary bailee should not be entitled to recover for the value of his/her services in quantum meruit.

The correct answer is (C). *(Publisher)*
    REQUIRED: The correct statement regarding an involuntary bailment.
    DISCUSSION: Finding a lost wallet, having an animal stray onto your property, or having property of another deposited on your property may result in an involuntary bailment. The bailee has taken legal possession and control of the property of another due to the circumstances.
    Answer (A) is incorrect because an involuntary bailee has a legal responsibility to the owner to exercise reasonable care under the circumstances. Answer (B) is incorrect because the courts do not impose the same liability on an involuntary bailee as on an ordinary one. Answer (D) is incorrect because an involuntary bailee is entitled to recover the value of his/her services. This equitable remedy is called quantum meruit.

C. Special Bailments

19. Which of the following standards of liability best characterizes the obligation of a common carrier in a bailment relationship?

    A. Reasonable care.

    B. Gross negligence.

    C. Shared liability.

    D. Strict liability.

The correct answer is (D). *(CPA, adapted)*
    REQUIRED: The proper characterization of a common carrier's liability in a bailment relationship.
    DISCUSSION: A common carrier is a type of special bailee whose business is to transport goods for the public on a nondiscriminatory basis. A higher standard of care is required of common carriers than ordinary bailees. The common carrier generally is held strictly liable for damages to, or losses of, any goods.
    Answer (A) is incorrect because a reasonable care standard is imposed when the parties enter into a standard bailment relationship. Answer (B) is incorrect because a gross negligence or reckless disregard of the consequences standard is not the appropriate measure in determining common carrier liability. Answer (C) is incorrect because a shared negligence standard is not appropriate under a common carrier bailment because of the nature of the relationship between the parties.

20. With respect to a carrier, which of the following is incorrect?

   A.   Common carriers are required to use ordinary care as the bailee in a mutual benefit bailment.

   B.   Common law provides that a common carrier is an insurer of the goods entrusted to it as a carrier without exception.

   C.   The liability of a carrier frequently changes to that of a warehouseman.

   D.   A common carrier acquires a possessory lien on the goods to secure the shipping and storage charges.

The correct answer is (B). *(Publisher)*
   REQUIRED: The false statement regarding a carrier.
   DISCUSSION: The common law does impose strict liability on a common carrier. A *force majeure*, acts of public enemy, acts of public authority, acts of the shipper, and damage due to the inherent nature of the goods themselves are excepted matters for which the common carrier is not liable. The carrier can also reduce its liability by contract.
   Answer (A) is incorrect because a common carrier is subject to strict liability. Answer (C) is incorrect because the liability of a common carrier changes to that of a warehouseman after the carrier has fulfilled the carriage contract and is holding the goods for the consignee. Answer (D) is incorrect because common carriers acquire a possessory lien on the goods they handle to secure shipping and storage charges.

21. A common carrier bailee generally would avoid liability for loss of goods entrusted to its care if the goods are

   A.   Stolen by an unknown person.

   B.   Negligently destroyed by an employee.

   C.   Destroyed by the derailment of the train carrying them due to railroad employee negligence.

   D.   Improperly packed by the party shipping them.

The correct answer is (D). *(CPA, adapted)*
   REQUIRED: The basis for a common carrier's avoidance of liability.
   DISCUSSION: A common carrier is a person or organization engaged in the business of transporting goods for others for a fee. The common carrier is strictly liable for damage to or loss of the goods being transported. However, loss falls on the bailor if it is caused by one of the following: a *force majeure*, action by an alien enemy, order of a public authority, the inherent nature of the property, or the bailor's negligence in packaging.
   Answers (A), (B), and (C) are incorrect because the common carrier is strictly liable.

22. Brenda McOwns took her property to Security Storage and Warehouse to be kept at 1220 South Main Street for storage. She paid a fee and was given a warehouse receipt in usual form. Later the warehouser moved the goods from the original storage place to a different but equally safe building. The goods were destroyed by a fire set by an unknown arsonist. With respect to liability,

   A.   The warehouse has no liability to McOwns because title and risk of loss remained with the bailor.

   B.   The standard of care imposed on the warehouse is ordinary care under the circumstances.

   C.   A bailee cannot move goods from the agreed place of storage for any reason.

   D.   The warehouse is strictly liable for any harm to McOwns's goods.

The correct answer is (D). *(Publisher)*
   REQUIRED: The correct statement concerning the liability of a warehouse.
   DISCUSSION: A warehouser is subject to the general rules of bailment. When a bailee deviates from the terms of the contract, the law imposes strict liability for any harm to the bailor's goods instead of the usual standard of reasonable care. It appears a contract was made to store the goods at a particular location and the bailee, without the bailor's consent, moved them to a different, although equally safe, place. Even though the goods were destroyed through no fault of the bailee, the bailee is liable for the value of the goods under the strict liability rule.
   Answer (A) is incorrect because the warehouse is under an obligation to adhere to the contract and exercise reasonable care. Since the warehouse did not adhere to the terms of the contract, it is liable. Answer (B) is incorrect because the warehouse deviated from the terms of the contract, which results in strict liability. Answer (C) is incorrect because a bailee may move goods from the agreed place of storage, despite the contract, but only for reasons of safety.

D. Computer Technology Rights

23. Which of the following is a correct statement about the scope and origin of computer law?

   A. Computer law developed as a distinct body of law solely from court cases involving computers.

   B. Invasion of privacy involving computers is a constitutional issue rather than a computer law issue.

   C. Copying of micro-computer software is not a crime.

   D. Computer law uses principles and precedents from other areas of law as well as court cases involving computers.

The correct answer is (D). *(Publisher)*
   REQUIRED: The correct statement about computer law.
   DISCUSSION: Computer law began to evolve with court cases involving the earliest computers, but the courts have usually relied on principles from other areas of law, such as contracts, warranty, torts, intellectual property, and statutory protection of privacy, in rendering decisions in cases involving computers.
   Answer (A) is incorrect because computer law is not a distinct body of law but instead relies on principles and precedents from other areas of law. Answer (B) is incorrect because invasion of privacy using a computer is both a constitutional and computer law issue. Answer (C) is incorrect because introducing fraudulent data into a computer system and unauthorized duplication of copyrighted material could be criminal acts.

24. Hightech, Inc. sells several lines of computer-related products. Its product line includes a bundled package of hardware and software, mass-produced application software, and specialized, custom accounting software. With regard to these products, Hightech will be liable under Article 2 of the UCC or common law based on whether the products sold are considered goods or services. If the hardware is relatively more expensive than the software, are Hightech's products goods or services?

	Bundled Package	Mass-produced Application Software	Specialized Custom Software
A.	Goods	Goods	Goods
B.	Both goods and services	Services	Goods
C.	Goods	Services	Goods
D.	Goods	Goods	Services

The correct answer is (D). *(Publisher)*
   REQUIRED: The proper classification of computer products as goods or services.
   DISCUSSION: When computer products are bundled and sold, courts have held that those transactions involve goods, not services. In making that decision, some courts have considered the relative costs of the hardware and software in determining the parties' intentions. Also, mass-produced software is most likely to be considered goods, but specialized custom software is usually considered a service.
   Answer (A) is incorrect because, whereas a bundled package and mass-produced software are considered goods, specialized software is considered a service because it is usually the result of services provided by a consultant. Answers (B) and (C) are incorrect because bundled software is not a service. Mass-produced software is usually considered a good, and specialized software is considered a service.

25. Hacker Corporation sold Micro International its Hacker Operating System (HOS). Micro sold HOS bundled with its new computers to several thousand customers. On April 1, a Trojan horse program embedded in HOS's code was executed on all computers running HOS. The program rendered all of the programs, data, and files on these computers' hard disks unusable. If the transactions were transactions in goods, what is Hacker's potential liability to Micro and third parties?

	Economic Losses	Personal Injury	Punitive Damages
A.	Yes	Yes	Yes
B.	Yes	No	No
C.	No	Yes	No
D.	No	No	No

The correct answer is (A). *(Publisher)*
   REQUIRED: The liability by a software developer for damages resulting from the use of the software.
   DISCUSSION: Hacker would be liable under the UCC for economic losses for breach of implied warranty of merchantability because the destruction of customers' data implies HOS was not fit for the ordinary purpose for which it was intended. If HOS were the proximate cause of the malfunction of computer-operated equipment that injured employees, customers, or innocent bystanders, Hacker would be liable in tort for those personal injuries as well as any economic losses. If the Trojan horse program were intentionally embedded in HOS by Hacker's personnel, Hacker would be liable for punitive damages as well as economic loss and personal injury.
   Answers (B), (C), and (D) are incorrect because Hacker could be liable for economic losses, personal injury, and punitive damages.

26. CPA Firm contracted to purchase 100 ISM Lap 10 microcomputers. ISM's sales representative, Skip, claimed the computers would run an advanced operating system that ISM planned to market. The contract included a standard integration clause but was silent as to the advanced operating system. After the computers were delivered and paid for, ISM introduced the new system, which CPA Firm learned was incompatible with its Lap 10s. Is ISM liable to CPA Firm?

  A. ISM is liable because the integration clause made Skip's claims part of the contract.

  B. ISM is liable because Skip's action was fraudulent.

  C. ISM is not liable because a salesperson's representations are excluded from sales contracts unless expressly included.

  D. ISM is not liable because the parol evidence rule excludes the prior statements.

The correct answer is (D). *(Publisher)*
REQUIRED: The liability of the seller of computer products for prior representations by its agent.
DISCUSSION: The integration clause indicates that the contract is meant to be complete, that is, to embody the entire understanding of the parties. Thus, the parol evidence rule will apply. It bars evidence of prior agreements or of contemporaneous oral agreements that would vary, alter, or contradict the terms of a written contract intended to be entire. Consequently, ISM will not be liable because evidence of Jones's representations is inadmissible.
Answer (A) is incorrect because an integration clause excludes rather than includes prior agreements. Answer (B) is incorrect because no evidence is given that the elements of fraud are present. Answer (C) is incorrect because, in the absence of an integration clause, these representations may be included in sales contracts unless expressly excluded.

27. If a transaction involving computer products is considered a sale of goods, the UCC applies and

  A. The seller may be liable for consequential damages even if the contract had an express exclusion of such damages.

  B. The agreement of the parties to limit the buyer's remedies will be ineffective.

  C. The seller is more likely to prevail because the UCC favors sellers rather than buyers.

  D. The implied warranty of fitness for a particular purpose will protect the seller.

The correct answer is (A). *(Publisher)*
REQUIRED: The seller's liability under the UCC for a transaction in computer products.
DISCUSSION: Under the UCC, a seller of goods is liable for economic losses resulting from breach of express and implied warranties. However, an exclusion of the seller's liability for consequential damages may be rendered invalid if it is unconscionable (UCC 2-719). Thus, a seller may be liable for consequential damages despite the terms of the contract.
Answer (B) is incorrect because a contractual modification or limitation of remedies is effective unless the circumstances cause an exclusive or limited remedy to fail of its essential purpose. Answer (C) is incorrect because buyers are favored under the UCC, not sellers. Answer (D) is incorrect because an implied warranty of fitness for a particular purpose protects buyers, not sellers.

28. Intellectual property embodied in computer hardware and/or software may be protected via

	Patent Law	Copyright Law	Trade Secret Protection
A.	No	No	No
B.	Yes	No	Yes
C.	Yes	Yes	Yes
D.	No	No	Yes

The correct answer is (C). *(Publisher)*
REQUIRED: The area(s) of law applicable to intellectual property embodied in computer hardware and/or software.
DISCUSSION: To be patentable, the subject matter must be a process, a machine, or a composition of matter. Additionally, the subject matter of the patent must have utility, be a novelty, be nonobvious, and be adequately disclosed. Clearly, computer hardware is patentable. However, the courts have given protection to software under the copyright laws as the expression of an idea, not the idea itself. Finally, hardware or software not patentable or copyrightable may be protected as a trade secret.
Answers (A), (B), and (D) are all incorrect because computer hardware is patentable, computer software is copyrightable, and both may be protected as trade secrets.

29. Which of the following is a correct statement about the protection offered by the law of patents, copyrights, or trade secrets?

    A.   Once granted, the patent is good for the life of the inventor plus 50 years.

    B.   Copyright law permits ideas to be protected, not expressions of those ideas.

    C.   Trade secrets must be registered as either a patent or a copyright.

    D.   Trade secrets have perpetual life until honestly discovered by others, and they require no public filings or disclosure.

The correct answer is (D). *(Publisher)*

REQUIRED: The correct statement about the protection of intellectual property.

DISCUSSION: Information is a trade secret if the information gives its owner an advantage, is a protected secret, has value, and is not easily discovered by others. A trade secret has a longer potential life than patents or copyrights, which are limited to 20 years from date of application or 50 years plus the author's life, respectively. A trade secret will be protected until honest discovery by another. Moreover, no public filings or disclosures are required for trade secrets.

Answer (A) is incorrect because a patent is good for 17 years. Answer (B) is incorrect because copyrights protect the expression of ideas, not the ideas themselves. Answer (C) is incorrect because trade secrets do not have to be registered.

---

30. Which federal act gives a student rights with respect to his/her academic records stored on the university's computer?

    A.   The Family Educational Rights and Privacy Act of 1974.

    B.   The Freedom of Information Act.

    C.   The Privacy Act of 1974.

    D.   The Securities Act of 1933.

The correct answer is (A). *(Publisher)*

REQUIRED: The federal act that protects the privacy of a student's academic records.

DISCUSSION: The Family Educational Rights and Privacy Act of 1974 gives students over 18 and parents of dependent students certain rights of inspection, correction, and disclosure of that information.

Answer (B) is incorrect because the Freedom of Information Act grants citizens access to federal government records. Answer (C) is incorrect because the Privacy Act of 1974 safeguards computerized data in federal agencies and the Federal Reserve Banks. Answer (D) is incorrect because the Securities Act of 1933 concerns the initial registration of publicly traded securities.

---

31. Hill frequently cashed checks of more than $10,000 (interest on municipal bonds) at First Bank. Hill deposited the money in her account at Second Bank. The teller notified the IRS of Hill's banking activity. Second Bank allowed an IRS agent to search the bank's computer files for any information on Hill. Which of the following statements is correct?

    A.   The bank had no authority to report the cash transactions to the IRS.

    B.   The Freedom of Information Act specifically gives the IRS the right to examine banks' computer databases.

    C.   The Right to Financial Privacy Act of 1978 protects Hill's right to privacy from governmental intrusion.

    D.   The Privacy Act of 1974 protects Hill against governmental intrusion into her private banking records.

The correct answer is (C). *(Publisher)*

REQUIRED: The correct statement about computerized banking records.

DISCUSSION: For the IRS to escape liability, it will have to prove that it followed the specific procedures outlined in the Right to Financial Privacy Act of 1978 when it accessed Hill's banking records.

Answer (A) is incorrect because the bank is required to report large cash deposits to federal banking authorities, not the IRS. Answer (B) is incorrect because the Freedom of Information Act concerns the public's right to access government records. Answer (D) is incorrect because the Privacy Act of 1974 relates to the privacy of government-held computerized databases.

32. Herman used his modem and personal computer to breach the security of Ann's computer. Herman wrote a program that determined which of Ann's customers were the best traders by instantaneously calculating their returns. The program produced a list of securities to buy and sell. Herman gave the list to his neighbor, Mike, who used it to make large profits. Mike was bragging at the country club when one of Ann's successful traders learned that Mike was buying and selling exactly the same basket of stocks. Who is liable and for what?

    A. Mike is liable under the Securities Exchange Act of 1934 for insider trading.

    B. Ann cannot be liable for negligence for allowing Herman to breach her computer system.

    C. Herman is liable under the Right to Financial Privacy Act of 1978.

    D. Herman is liable for the tort of invasion of privacy.

The correct answer is (D). *(Publisher)*
    REQUIRED: The extent of liability for unauthorized access to private computerized data.
    DISCUSSION: Under the tort theory of intrusion, a person is deemed to suffer damage from an invasion of his/her seclusion or solitude that a reasonable person would regard as offensive. Thus, one has a reasonable expectation of privacy for private records. Trading activities not required to be reported to the SEC are private information. Those who examine another's private records without authorization are liable in tort for invasion of privacy.
    Answer (A) is incorrect because Mike is not an insider. Answer (B) is incorrect because Ann could be liable for negligence if her hardware or software did not reasonably control access to confidential customer data. Answer (C) is incorrect because the Right to Financial Privacy Act of 1978 addresses government access to private information held by financial institutions. Such access is permitted only if authorized by the customer or the government follows appropriate procedures.

33. Bill Galant purchased a car from Smith Motors that was financed by Smith's bank. Six months later, the bank contacted Galant by mail to give notice of default. Galant replied in writing that he had made the first six payments on time and had the check stubs to prove it. A week later the bank physically repossessed the car. The bank later admitted that the repossession was a computer error made by an outside computer service bureau. The bank relied solely on the representations of the service bureau. The bank is potentially liable for

	Compensatory Damages	Punitive Damages
A.	No	Yes
B.	Yes	Yes
C.	Yes	No
D.	No	No

The correct answer is (B). *(Publisher)*
    REQUIRED: The creditor's liability for a computer error made by an outside computer service bureau.
    DISCUSSION: The bank is certainly liable for compensatory damages because it was negligent for not ascertaining for itself whether Galant had made his payments according to the financing agreement. Because the bank relied solely on the report of the outside service bureau, it is probably liable for gross negligence, which would subject it to liability for punitive damages as well. Computer errors beyond the control of users do not excuse the users from liability for the damages caused.
    Answers (A), (C), and (D) are incorrect because the bank is potentially liable for both compensatory and punitive damages.

34. Criminal liability for the theft of computer time requires

    A. A narrow interpretation of state and federal statutes.

    B. The intent of the perpetrator to deprive the true owner of computer time.

    C. Prosecution under the provisions of federal computer acts.

    D. The true owners of the computer time to prove they were deprived by the perpetrator.

The correct answer is (B). *(Publisher)*
    REQUIRED: The requirement for criminal liability for theft of computer time.
    DISCUSSION: Absent a specific statute, criminal liability for theft of computer time will often require a broad interpretation of traditional state or federal statutes that concern theft or larceny because not all courts regard computer time or data stored in a computer to be property. Also, intent by the perpetrator to deprive, and actual deprivation of, the true owner of his/her rights are necessary elements.
    Answer (A) is incorrect because a broad interpretation of statutes is typically required in cases involving criminal liability for the theft of computer time. Answer (C) is incorrect because criminal liability for theft of computer time may be prosecuted under state statutes as well as federal.
Answer (D) is incorrect because the burden of proof in criminal cases rests on state or federal prosecutors, not victims.

35. Without the authorization or knowledge of their employer, Robb and Conn used the company computer to develop a set of programs to be marketed commercially for their personal gain. In furtherance of this scheme, they mailed promotional letters to potential clients. A state computer crime statute was enacted 6 months after these events. Robb and Conn are

A. Liable under the computer crime statute.

B. Liable under the federal mail fraud statute.

C. Not liable unless they appropriated property or money of the employer.

D. Not liable even if they appropriated computer programs and electronically stored information.

The correct answer is (B). *(Publisher)*
REQUIRED: The liability of persons making unauthorized use of computer facilities.
DISCUSSION: In many cases courts have had to extend existing law to apply to computers. In this case, the court found a scheme using the U.S. mails to defraud an employer for illicit personal gain. An activity otherwise fraudulent under state law becomes a federal crime when the mails are used to convey a writing furthering a scheme to solicit money under false pretenses.
Answer (A) is incorrect because imposition of criminal sanctions retroactively (on actions before the statute existed) is unconstitutional. Answers (C) and (D) are incorrect because various kinds of computer usage are illegal. For example, computers have been used to assist embezzlement or to steal intangibles such as computer programs and electronically stored data.

36. Chuck Choppy was dismissed from his position as a management consultant for SNL, CPAs, when he failed to be promoted to partner. Choppy had advised SNL's financial institution clients about computer security of depositor records. After he was dismissed, he used his home computer to breach the security of several of SNL's clients' computers and transfer minuscule amounts from each depositor's account to his own account. Choppy is

A. Not criminally liable under state statutes because the amounts were immaterial.

B. Not criminally liable under the Counterfeit Access Device and Computer Fraud and Abuse Act of 1984 as amended in 1986.

C. Criminally liable under both the Counterfeit Access Device and Computer Fraud and Abuse Act of 1984 as amended in 1986 and the Electronic Funds Act of 1978.

D. Criminally liable under a narrow interpretation of state and federal theft statutes.

The correct answer is (C). *(Publisher)*
REQUIRED: The liability for theft of depositor funds using a computer.
DISCUSSION: The Counterfeit Access Device and Computer Fraud and Abuse Act of 1984 as amended in 1986 prohibits unauthorized access to financial institution computers. The Electronic Funds Transfer Act of 1978 prohibits unauthorized alteration of data in financial institution computers. Hence, Choppy is criminally liable under both acts.
Answers (A) and (B) are incorrect because Choppy is criminally liable regardless of materiality. Answer (D) is incorrect because computer crimes ordinarily require a broad interpretation of state and federal theft statutes to subject an individual to criminal liability.

37. Jon hacks into Victim Company's computer system and infects it with a virus that causes loss of data. Jon has committed a

A. Violation of the RICO Act.

B. Tort but not a crime.

C. Crime under the Electronic Funds Transfer Act.

D. Computer crime by damaging and destructive programming.

The correct answer is (D). *(Publisher)*
REQUIRED: The violation resulting from infecting a system with a virus that causes loss of data.
DISCUSSION: Computer crime is any illegal act that uses, involves, or is directed against computers. Computer crimes can be grouped into four general categories: theft, damaging and destructive programming, software piracy, and financial crimes. Damaging and destructive programming includes physical abuse of hardware and computer programming that alters or automatically destroys data. Thus, infecting a system with a virus that destroys data is a crime.
Answer (A) is incorrect because the RICO Act (Racketeer Influenced and Corrupt Organizations Act) applies to the use of computers for illegal funds transfer, wire fraud, securities fraud, and money laundering. Answer (B) is incorrect because shutting down an organization's computerized system is considered damaging and destructive programming and is therefore a computer crime. Answer (C) is incorrect because the EFT Act prohibits the sale, use, or interstate transportation of any lost, stolen, forged, counterfeit, altered, or fraudulently obtained device used to execute an electronic funds transfer.

ESSAY QUESTION 1 *(Publisher)* 15-20 minutes

During the annual audit of Starr Company, you reviewed the real property tax assessment. Your investigation revealed that Starr recently renovated its office building and that subsequently the county tax assessor increased the appraised value of the office building by the cost of a new heating and air-conditioning system, including new ducting, a vault door, and landscape office furniture throughout the building. Starr intends to appeal to the Tax Adjustment Board claiming that each of these items of property is personalty and not realty. In anticipation of the appeal, the following issues are being reviewed:

Required

a. What are the criteria for distinguishing real and personal property?

b. Do the air-conditioning, heating, ductwork, vault door, and landscape furniture meet the criteria for personal or real property?

c. In what other situation might a dispute arise with respect to the proper classification of property?

Knowledge Tested

1. Criteria to distinguish between real and personal property
2. Importance of proper classification of property

Authors' Comments

It is important in many situations to properly classify property as real or personal. Taxation, priorities among competing interests in the same property, and methods of transferring title are some of the differences in treatment of real and personal property.

Suggested Answer

a. Real property consists of land, whatever is attached to it, whatever is beneath it, and to a limited extent, the area above it. Personal property consists of rights in tangible and intangible things that are not real property. Tangible personal property is rights in things that are movable, as distinguished from immovable real property. Intangible personal property has no physical existence but consists of rights to something of value that is not real property. A fixture is an article that was personal property but has become so associated with real property to which it is attached that the law considers it real property. The principal criterion of whether property is personal or a fixture is the intention of the annexor at the time of annexation.

Intent may be inferred from the following:

1. Nature of the item being attached
2. Manner of annexation
3. Integration or adaptation of the item into the land
4. The use to which it is being put
5. Relationship of the annexor to the land, e.g., trespasser
6. Relationship of the annexor to the chattel, e.g., owner
7. Injury to the land, if any, by its removal

Unless agreed otherwise, fixtures are included in any mortgage, sale, or transfer of real property.

b. Applying the legal criteria to these facts, it seems clear that air-conditioning and heating equipment and ductwork are property that has been converted from personal to real when installed in the office building. Heating and air-conditioning equipment and its associated ductwork together constitute a system that is usually annexed to a building by permanent means, becomes an integral part of the building, and seriously affects the utility and value of the real property by removal. Therefore, the objective intent of Starr was that the air quality system would be real property.

Landscape furniture is a trade term to describe commercial office furniture consisting of portable walls with desks and shelves attached which provide a semi-private work cubicle. Permanent attachment to the walls, floors, or ceilings of an office building is avoided. The nature of landscape furniture is that it is designed and marketed as movable furnishings or equipment that is basically not annexed to the office building, and its removal would cause little or no damage. These criteria indicate that the objective intent of Starr Company was for the furniture to remain personalty and not be converted to real property.

While the vault door is undoubtedly removable, the method and degree of annexation, its adaptation to the use of a built-in vault, and the loss of utility by removal indicate the objective intent of the owner as annexor was to make it a permanent improvement to the office building, leading to the conclusion that the vault door has become real property.

c. Listed below are other situations in which disputes arise with respect to proper classification of property:

1. Mortgagor versus mortgagee regarding the property included in a real property mortgage
2. Mortgagee versus various creditors of the mortgagor that have a security interest in property of the mortgagor
3. Seller versus buyer of real property concerning property included in the contract
4. Lessor versus lessee concerning property that may be removed upon expiration of a lease
5. Executors versus separate takers under a will of real property and personal property.

ESSAY QUESTION 2 *(Publisher)* 10-15 minutes

Sam Success, CPA, hosted a party at his home for his accounting firm's partners. The following morning, he saw a gold watch with an airplane design on its face on a lamp stand. He placed it in a desk drawer. His house was burglarized the next day.

That weekend Sam went to Keytona Beach. He recognized the watch on display at Shady's Recyclables Store. Shady said he bought it from a transient. Shady allowed Sam to take the watch after Sam provided a $1,000 security deposit for its return if Sam did not establish that someone else's right to the watch was superior to Shady's right.

Back at Jen's Motel, Sam asked the clerk to put the watch in the motel safe. Sam checked out Sunday. Upon remembering the watch later, Sam returned to the motel, and Jen, the proprietor, told him the watch appeared to be lost.

When Sam told the story at the office, Reni, a partner, said she owned the watch.

During a lawsuit to determine the parties' rights and liabilities, evidence showed that Shady knew he was purchasing the watch from the person who stole it. It was stipulated that Reni owned the watch prior to the party.

- Sam argued that Reni abandoned the watch, that he became the rightful owner, and that he was entitled to the return of his security deposit and Jen was liable to him for its value.

- Reni argued that she mislaid her watch, that Sam was a bailee, and that he was liable to pay her its value or return it.

- Shady argued that he was the true owner because he purchased the watch.

- Jen argued that, because the motel had followed established procedures, it was not even slightly negligent and therefore was not liable for damages.

Required

Discuss each of the above arguments.

Knowledge Tested

1. Methods of acquiring personal property
2. Types of bailments
   a. Standards of care
   b. Rights and liabilities of bailors and bailees
3. Rights of purchasers
4. Extraordinary bailments

Authors' Comments

Although the facts could be discussed for hours, develop an answer that can be written in less than 10 minutes by focusing on the parties' arguments. Categorize the effect of each event. Note that the conclusion is not absolute.

Suggested Answer

It is improbable that Reni intended to relinquish ownership of the watch at the party. She mislaid it if she intentionally placed it in a location and then forgot she had done so. Sam obtained custody (control) of it. Even if the court implies a constructive bailment, it was involuntary, and placing the watch in the desk drawer probably satisfied the correlative duty of slight care.

Even if the transient found the watch, his/her rights would not have been superior to those of its owner. Shady acquired no better title than the thief, who had no title.

The bailment to the innkeeper is extraordinary. The innkeeper is absolutely liable at common law for loss or damage to the personal property of its guests. The bailment terminates when the guest checks out. The law presumes that the bailee is liable for loss of the property. The innkeeper at least has the burden to prove that the watch was not lost while Sam was a guest.

REVIEW CHECKLIST
BUSINESS LAW AND
PROFESSIONAL RESPONSIBILITIES

Your objective is to prepare to pass this section of the CPA exam. It is **not** to do a certain amount of work or spend a certain amount of time with this book or other CPA review material/courses. Rather, you **must**

1. Understand the CPA exam thoroughly -- study *CPA Review: A System for Success* and the Introduction in this book.

2. Understand the subject matter in the 20 study units in this book. The list of subunits in each of the 20 study units (presented below) should bring to mind core concepts, basic rules, principles, etc.

3. If you have not already done so, prepare a 1- to 2-page summary of each study unit for your final review just before you go to the exam (do not bring notes into the examination room).

Study Unit 1: AICPA Ethics

A. Code of Professional Conduct
B. Interpretations and Rulings
C. Consulting Services
D. Personal Financial Planning
E. Disciplinary Systems within the Profession

Study Unit 2: CPAs and the Law

A. Common-Law Liability to Clients and Third Parties
B. Federal Statutory Liability
C. Privileged Communication and Confidentiality

Study Unit 3: Agency

A. Formation and Termination
B. Principal's Liabilities
C. Disclosed and Nondisclosed Principals
D. Agent's Authority and Liabilities

Study Unit 4: Partnerships

A. Formation and Existence
B. Authority and Liabilities
C. Allocation of Profit or Loss
D. Transfer of Interest
E. Dissolution and Termination

Study Unit 5: Corporations

A. Formation, Purposes, and Powers
B. Shareholders, Directors, and Officers
C. Financial Structure, Capital, and Distributions
D. Merger, Consolidation, and Dissolution

Study Unit 6: Estates and Trusts

A. Formation and Purposes
B. Allocation between Principal and Income
C. Fiduciary Responsibilities
D. Distributions and Termination

Study Unit 7: Contract Formation

A. Offer and Acceptance
B. Consideration
C. Statute of Frauds
D. Capacity and Legality
E. Mutual Assent
F. Interpreting a Contract

Study Unit 8: Contract Performance

A. Duties of Parties to Contract
B. Contract Beneficiaries and Assignees
C. Types of Discharges and Contract Remedies

Gleim's *CPA Review* Support via FAX

If you FAX us inquiries about errors, omissions, etc., before 1:00 p.m. eastern time, we will respond by FAX the following business day. If we have trouble FAXing our response, it will be mailed. Technical support is also available via e-mail (support@gleim.com). Please include your e-mail address on the fax form below if you wish to receive a response to your request by e-mail (required if you are outside the United States).

Please photocopy this *CPA Review* FAX Support Request form. It must be completed as requested so we can address the issues and questions you have. All items should refer to a specific page number and outline letter/number or question number.

Wait until after you take the CPA exam to send us the separate evaluation form provided on pages 681 and 682. Please DO NOT duplicate items via FAX that you will be sending to us on the evaluation form.

Gleim Publications, Inc. FAX (352) 375-6940
CPA REVIEW SUPPORT REQUEST

Complete this form and attach additional pages as necessary.

Title: *CPA Review:*

___ *Business Law*   ___ *Financial*   ___ *Auditing*   ___ *TAX-MAN-GOV*   ___ *System for Success*

Your name _____   Your Fax # (____) _____-_____

Address: _____

_____

City: _____   State: _____   Zip: _____

E-mail: _____

Inquiry: _____

_____

_____

_____

_____

_____

_____

_____

Gleim Publications, Inc.
P.O. Box 12848
Gainesville, FL 32604

TOLL FREE:	(800) 87-GLEIM/(800) 874-5346	Customer service is available:
LOCAL:	(352) 375-0772	8:00 a.m. - 7:00 p.m., Mon. - Fri.
FAX:	(888) 375-6940 (toll free)	9:00 a.m. - 2:00 p.m., Saturday
INTERNET:	http://www.gleim.com	Please have your credit card ready or
E-MAIL:	sales@gleim.com	save time by ordering online!

CPA REVIEW *(99-00 Ed.)*

	Books	Audiotapes	CPA Test Prep Software	
Auditing	☐ @ $29.95	☐ @ $79.95	☐ @ $39.95	$_____
Business Law	☐ @ $29.95	☐ @ $79.95	☐ @ $39.95	_____
TAX-MAN-GOV	☐ @ $29.95	☐ @ $79.95	☐ @ $39.95	_____
Financial	☐ @ $29.95	☐ @ $79.95	☐ @ $39.95	_____

☐ A System for Success (112 pp.) (FREE with any Gleim CPA Review book)

Save 16% on the Complete Gleim CPA System (add $18 S&H below) . . . . $500.00 _____
[5 books, 4 audiocassette albums (41 tapes), 4 CPA Test Prep diskettes, bonus calculator and book bag]

CIA REVIEW

	Books	CIATP Software	CPE (book required)	
Part I, Internal Audit Process	☐ @ $22.95	☐ @ $35.00	☐ @ $25.00	$_____
Part II, Internal Audit Skills	☐ @ $22.95	☐ @ $35.00	☐ @ $25.00	_____
Part III, Management Control and Information Technology	☐ @ $22.95	☐ @ $35.00	☐ @ $25.00	_____
Part IV, The Audit Environment	☐ @ $22.95	☐ @ $35.00	☐ @ $25.00	_____

EA REVIEW

	Books	EATP Software	CPE (book required)	
Part 1	☐ @ $22.95	☐ @ $35.00	Over 80 hours available -- call for details!	$_____
Part 2	☐ @ $22.95	☐ @ $35.00		_____
Part 3	☐ @ $22.95	☐ @ $35.00		_____
Part 4	☐ @ $22.95	☐ @ $35.00		_____

CMA/CFM REVIEW

	Books	Audiotapes	CMA/CFMTP Software	CPE (book required)	
Part 1	☐ @ $22.95	☐ @ $60.00	☐ @ $35.00	☐ @ $25.00	$_____
Part 2CMA	☐ @ $22.95	☐ @ $60.00	☐ @ $35.00	☐ @ $25.00	_____
Part 2CFM	☐ @ $22.95	☐ @ $60.00	☐ @ $35.00	☐ @ $25.00	_____
Part 3	☐ @ $22.95	☐ @ $60.00	☐ @ $35.00	☐ @ $25.00	_____
Part 4	☐ @ $22.95	☐ @ $60.00	☐ @ $35.00	☐ @ $25.00	_____

"THE GLEIM SERIES" EXAM QUESTION AND EXPLANATION BOOKS & CPE

	Book Only	Software	Book & Software	Book & CPE	
Auditing & Systems	☐ $19.95	☐ $20.00	☐ $29.95	☐ $125.00	$_____
Business Law/Legal Studies	☐ $19.95	☐ $20.00	☐ $29.95	☐ $125.00	_____
Federal Tax	☐ $19.95	☐ $20.00	☐ $29.95	☐ $125.00	_____
Financial Accounting	☐ $19.95	☐ $20.00	☐ $29.95	☐ $125.00	_____
Cost/Managerial Accounting	☐ $19.95	☐ $20.00	☐ $29.95	☐ $125.00	_____

Shipping (nonrefundable): **First item = $5; each additional item = $1.**. . . . . _____

Add applicable sales tax for shipments within Florida. . . . . _____

Fax or write for prices/instructions for shipments outside the 48 contiguous states.   **TOTAL** $_____

1. We process and ship orders daily, within one business day over 98.8% of the time. Call by noon for same-day service!

2. Please PHOTOCOPY this order form for others.

3. No CODs. Orders from individuals must be prepaid. Library and company orders may be purchased on account.

4. Gleim Publications, Inc. guarantees the immediate refund of all resalable texts and unopened softwware and audiotapes if returned within 30 days. Applies only to items purchased direct from Gleim Publications, Inc. Our shipping charge is nonrefundable.

5. Components of specially priced package deals are nonreturnable.

Printed 06/99. Prices subject to change without notice.

NAME (please print) _____

ADDRESS _____ Apt. _____
(street address required for UPS)

_____

CITY _____ STATE ____ ZIP _____

____ MC/VISA/DISC ____ Check/M.O.   Daytime Telephone (____)_____

Credit Card No. _____ - _____ - _____ - _____

Exp. ___/___   Signature _____
    Mo. / Yr.

SUCCESSFUL
CAREERS IN
ACCOUNTING
BEGIN WITH
THE GLEIM SERIES OF EXAM
QUESTIONS AND EXPLANATIONS . . .

*...AND ARE
ACCELERATED
WITH*

The Gleim
CPA Review Series

- **AUDITING & SYSTEMS**
- **BUSINESS LAW/LEGAL STUDIES**
- **COST/MANAGERIAL ACCOUNTING**
- **FEDERAL TAX**
- **FINANCIAL ACCOUNTING**

CONTENT:

- Each book contains about 2,000 multiple-choice questions, and can be used in two or more classes.
  - The questions are organized into *modules* (study units) with learning concepts progressing from basic to complex.
  - Each question has an explanation of the correct answer **PLUS** explanations of why each incorrect answer is wrong.
- Exhaustive **cross-references** are presented for all related textbooks so that you can easily determine which group of questions pertains to a given chapter in your textbook.

PURPOSE:

- To provide *programmed learning* so that you absorb important information more efficiently, more quickly, and more permanently.
- To support other accounting texts by providing questions and answer explanations so that you can test your knowledge before taking exams.
- To give you practice for CIA, CMA, and CPA exams.
- To demonstrate to you the **standards** to which you will be held as a professional accountant.
- To provide complete coverage of all topics, enabling you to improve your college test scores and prepare for certification exams later.

CPA Review (illustrated above), *CIA Review*, and *CMA/CFM Review* are each multi-volume, comprehensive study programs designed to prepare you to pass the CPA (Certified Public Accountant), CIA (Certified Internal Auditor), and CMA/CFM (Certified Management Accountant/Corporate Financial Management) exams.

Each set of books contains structured, point-by-point outlines of all material tested, and clear and concise phraseology to help you understand and remember the concepts. They also explain the respective certification programs, introduce you to examination preparation and grading procedures, and help you organize your examination strategy. Thousands of past exam questions (with our answer explanations) complement the outlines to provide you with a complete and effective study package.

NEXT: PASS THE CIA AND CMA/CFM EXAMS!

CIA - Certified Internal Auditor, offered by the Institute of Internal Auditors, consists of four 3½-hour exam parts, each consisting of 80 multiple-choice questions. The exam is given on a Wednesday and a Thursday in the middle of May and November and will be converted to an on-demand, computer-administered exam by the year 2000. Part IV is waived for CPAs.

CMA - Certified Management Accountant and **CFM - Certified in Financial Management**, offered by the Institute of Management Accountants, are on-demand, computer-administered exams. Each exam consists of four 3-hour, 120 multiple-choice-question tests. Parts 1, 3, and 4 are the same for both tests. Thus both designations are available by passing all five parts. Part 2 of the CMA is waived for CPAs.

An additional professional designation(s) will help you in many ways, including

1. Additional professional skills obtained while studying for the exam
2. Employer, peer, and other recognition of additional professional expertise
3. Personal pride in "another" impressive accomplishment
4. Broadened career and employment opportunities
5. More income

What does multiple certification require?

1. Cost

   CIA: $70 per part after one-time $60 registration fee
   CMA/CFM: $80 per part after one-time $50 credentialling fee plus IMA membership

   Gleim books and software: less than $60 per part

2. Time

   Exam: 3 - 4 hours per part
   Study: 20 - 50 hours per part

3. Number of parts

   CIA: three (CPAs get credit for Part IV)
   CMA: three (CPAs get credit for Part 2)
   CFM: one (CMAs get credit for Parts 1,3, and 4)

4. Application forms. We can send them to you with your books and software or you can call or e-mail:

   CIA (407) 830-7600, ext. 1 e-mail: custserv@theiia.org
   CMA/CFM (800) 638-4427, ext. 510 e-mail: certification@imanet.org

5. Action items

   a. Obtain, complete, and submit application forms.
   b. Order Gleim books/software.
   c. Study the "Introduction" to become an expert on that exam. Your recent preparation for and completion of the CPA exam will be very helpful.
   d. Study each of the 10 Gleim study units for each exam part.
   e. Take and pass each exam part.

Index

Our comprehensive **CPA Review** Texts (outlines, questions, answer explanations, etc.) are designed to prepare you for the CPA exam. We need your feedback to help us improve our study materials to better prepare CPA candidates to pass the CPA exam. The CPA exam is nondisclosed and you have signed an attestation which included, "I hereby attest that I will not divulge the nature or content of any question or answer to any individual or entity...." The information requested on these pages is in full compliance with the AICPA's policy on candidate disclosure of exam information.

PLEASE DO NOT PROVIDE INFORMATION ABOUT SPECIFIC CPA EXAM QUESTIONS. Note that this feedback form concerns our **CPA Review** books and **not** "the nature or content of any question or answer" on the CPA exam.

Please write down suggestions, criticisms, corrections, and comments including typographical errors, etc., as you use this book. Please add more comments after you take the exam. Forward to **Irvin N. Gleim • c/o Gleim Publications, Inc. • P.O. Box 12848 • University Station • Gainesville, Florida • 32604** or FAX to **(352) 375-6940** so he can personally review your feedback and correspond with you. Allow 3 weeks for him to respond.

Date: _____   Have you taken the CPA Exam? Yes___ No___   If yes, please indicate month/year: ____/___

Sections taken: LPR _____   AUD _____   ARE _____   FARE _____

How can this book be improved for CPA candidates? _____

_____

_____

Which topics need to be strengthened? _____

_____

_____

Use the opposite side for additional comments and attach extra sheets if needed.

Please score each section of this book by circling the appropriate number. We solicit your comments on each and every aspect of this book, **especially** topics not currently covered.

	Excellent	Good	Adequate	Poor	Totally Inadequate
Optimizing Your Business Law Score	5	4	3	2	1
Chapter I: Professional Responsibilities					
Study Unit 1: AICPA Ethics	5	4	3	2	1
Study Unit 2: CPAs and the Law	5	4	3	2	1
Chapter II: Business Organizations					
Study Unit 3: Agency	5	4	3	2	1
Study Unit 4: Partnerships	5	4	3	2	1
Study Unit 5: Corporations	5	4	3	2	1
Study Unit 6: Estates and Trusts	5	4	3	2	1
Chapter III: Contracts					
Study Unit 7: Contract Formation	5	4	3	2	1
Study Unit 8: Contract Performance	5	4	3	2	1
Chapter IV: Debtor-Creditor Relationships					
Study Unit 9: Rights and Duties	5	4	3	2	1
Study Unit 10: Guarantors	5	4	3	2	1
Study Unit 11: Bankruptcy	5	4	3	2	1
Chapter V: Government Regulation of Business					
Study Unit 12: Securities	5	4	3	2	1
Study Unit 13: Employment	5	4	3	2	1
Study Unit 14: Environmental Regulation	5	4	3	2	1
Chapter VI: Uniform Commercial Code					
Study Unit 15: Negotiable Instruments and Bank Transactions	5	4	3	2	1
Study Unit 16: Sales	5	4	3	2	1
Study Unit 17: Secured Transactions	5	4	3	2	1
Study Unit 18: Documents of Title	5	4	3	2	1
Chapter VII: Property					
Study Unit 19: Real Property and Insurance	5	4	3	2	1
Study Unit 20: Personal Property, Bailments, and Computers	5	4	3	2	1
Overall Evaluation	5	4	3	2	1

Please use page 682 for additional comments. Attach additional sheets as needed.

_____

_____

_____

_____

_____

_____

_____

_____

_____

_____

Remember for superior service: Mail, e-mail, or fax questions about our books or software. Telephone questions about orders, prices, shipments, or payments.

Optional: Please include your name and address so we can properly thank you for your help and respond to any questions. If you leave this blank and include your name and address on your envelope, we will add your name and address to our mailing list and dispose of the envelope (i.e., your response will be confidential).

Name: _____

Company: _____

Address: _____

City/State/Zip: _____

Phone: Home: _____   Work: _____   Fax: _____

E-mail: _____

GLEIM BOOKMARK

Dr. Gleim's Recommendation: Cover the answers and explanations in our book with this bookmark to make sure you do NOT cheat yourself. Answers will not be alongside questions when you take your exam. Use our software and audiotapes to complete your study program.

Exam Questions and Explanations

Certified Public Accountant

Certified Management Accountant
Certified in Financial Management + CPE

Certified Internal Auditor + CPE

Enrolled Agent Review

(800) 87-GLEIM
www.gleim.com